A
COMPLETE
COURSE IN
FRESHMAN
ENGLISH

A COMPLETE COURSE IN FRESHMAN ENGLISH

HARRY SHAW

FORMERLY DIRECTOR, WORKSHOPS IN COMPOSITION

NEW YORK UNIVERSITY

&

LECTURER IN ENGLISH, COLUMBIA UNIVERSITY

SIXTH EDITION

Harper & Row

PUBLISHERS

NEW YORK, EVANSTON, AND LONDON

A Complete Course in Freshman English, SIXTH EDITION
Copyright © 1940, 1945, 1949, 1951, 1955 BY HARPER & ROW, PUBLISHERS.
Copyright © 1959, 1967 BY HARRY SHAW.
A portion of this book has been published under the title, *The Shorter
Handbook of College Composition,* copyright © 1965 BY HARRY SHAW AND
RICHARD H. DODGE.

LIBRARY OF CONGRESS CATALOG CARD NUMBER: 67–10803

Contents

Forms, Methods, & Types

BOOK TWO: REWRITING

A HANDBOOK OF REVISION

Part I: The Shorter Handbook

Contains entries in alphabetical arrangement which fall into six somewhat overlapping categories:

1   *Entries on particular words and expressions, such as* ability, capacity; party, person, individual; principal, principle; their, there, they're; *etc.*

BOOK THREE: READING

A COLLECTION OF READINGS FOR WRITERS

Thinking & Propaganda

Problems & Points of View

Reading, Writing, & Education

Informal Essays

Criticism

Autobiography, Profile, & Portrait

Short Stories

Plays

Poetry

Narrative Poems

Lyric Poems

Foreword

The first edition of *A Complete Course in Freshman English* appeared in 1940. It made no radical departure from traditional aims of first-year English: I believed then, as I believe now, that the fundamental objective of the course should be training in clear thinking, intelligent and creative reading, and—that optimum without which nothing else really matters—correct, clear, effective, and appropriate writing and rewriting. Although traditional in aims, *A Complete Course* did, however, mark an innovation in both scope and materials. Hitherto, in most freshman English classes, the use of a handbook or rhetoric or both had been combined with that of a separate book of readings. This new volume consisted of a carefully inter-related rhetoric, handbook, and collection of readings in which writing, rewriting, and reading were linked as stages of a dynamic and ongoing process.

The economy, common sense, and convenience of this articulation are still apparent after five major revisions. The present sixth edition offers a thorough reworking of the elements of that plan—emendation, addition, deletion, expansion—but no really basic changes in scope or purpose.

During nearly three decades, emphasis in first-year English has shifted, now here, now there: semantics, communication, introduction to literature, speed and skill in reading, *explication de texte*, linguistics, grammar by rote, aesthetics, together with an influx of paperbacks and a revived interest in rhetoric. Each of these approaches has made a contribution; some continue to do so. In the present edition, I have tried to retain what has proved most helpful from each and have emphasized certain current trends in the study of rhetoric and language which seem most helpful at this stage of the long evolution of freshman English.

But this edition rides no hobby horse. Instead, it offers a full year's work in English of such variety and richness that the individual instructor can evolve any of several courses in accordance with his own predilections, tastes, interests, and teaching methods as they are related to departmental objectives and the needs of a particular section or class. You may ride your own horse.

It would be an unusual group which could assimilate every approach presented and could utilize every device afforded in this purposefully *complete*, many-sided volume. Freshman English is not a cut-and-dried course, nor should it ever be. The thousands who teach it have varied methods and aims; students have diverse needs; the shared experiences of teachers and the findings of contemporary researchers demand that flexibility, not rigidity, be a hallmark of the strong and unwavering discipline underlying any English course worthy of its name. A full year's work in freshman English is offered here, plenty and to spare, but the individual teacher is urged to use this volume in accordance with his own judgments and professional experience.

THE THREE PARTS

Book One (the rhetoric) is more succinct than most rhetorics. And yet its comparative brevity permits an intensive and vigorous survey of those principles—and only those—which seem genuinely important. I am fully aware that the study of rhetoric is considered more significant and useful now than it has been in fairly recent years, and therefore I have attempted in this edition to revise and expand discussion of rhetorical matters where it was within my ability to do so. For example, one weakness of the previous edition was lack of a chapter on style which, in students' terms, discussed what basic style is and which suggested concrete and easily attained goals in writing. Such a chapter has been supplied.

I believe that rhetoric is well worth teaching but that students are indifferently served when forced to wade through thousands of words devoted to topics of obscure interest and rare application. Emphasis in Book One is placed upon contemporary methods and practices, with enough direct mention of earlier writers to prevent anyone's thinking that no one wrote well before the twentieth century. Important though it is, rhetoric is no cure-all. It should be stressed—but not overstressed—along with composition, the study of language, and the reading of literature. The eight chapters comprising Book One are designed to present in as cogent and understandable terms as possible the basic ingredients of rhetorical study and analysis. What has been omitted may well be left to the advanced student or to the specialist.

The seeming brevity of Book One, however, is deceptive. Because of frequent cross references to Book Three (readings), principles and rhetorical precepts are driven home without need for the elaborate quotations which comprise the bulk of most rhetorics. Clear and precise examples, offered in full, are immediately available and yet do not occupy space that is used for direct and hopefully lucid exposition of rhetorical matters.

Book Two (the Handbook) is completely new in this edition. It consists of *The Shorter Handbook of College Composition* by the undersigned and Professor Richard H. Dodge, who has graciously consented to this use. Portions of *The Shorter Handbook* have been amended for appearance here; most notably, several items in Part II have been expanded: *linguistics*, the *paraphrase*, the *précis*, *rhetoric*, *semantics*, and *tone*, among others. Items in Part II of the Handbook that are new in this edition include *conversation*, *group discussion*, *lecture notes*, *listening*, and *oral communication*.

The most distinctive addition to the Handbook is the copious and imaginative exercise material prepared largely by Professor Macklin Thomas of Illinois Teachers College, Chicago, South. Dr. Thomas, a widely experienced college teacher of English and an expert in test-making, has added much to the effectiveness of the Handbook in an area not previously covered at all.

Book Two is intended for actual use in the classroom, although it is likely that Part I will prove more helpful in this function than will Part II, which is designed primarily for reference work and as a supplement to Part I. Like the rhetoric, the Handbook in *A Complete Course* is comparatively brief: I feel strongly that emphasis upon relatively few basic essentials of good writing will help most students more than will discussion of minor errors and less dominant aims of effective communication. Such concentration may also assist the instructor in selecting from a bewildering mass of material available elsewhere only those items of true significance and immediate need. Every part of the Handbook can be used for study, for reference, and for correcting themes.

Another guiding principle of the Handbook should be mentioned: it adopts a "middle-of-the-road" approach which may seem too reactionary to some and too liberal to others. Staying in the middle of the road can be fatal on a highway, but perhaps not on the highway to better composition. This approach is based on many years of teaching experience and hundreds of talks with teachers throughout the country over more than three decades. Obviously, added attention is given in this book to the findings and recommendations of modern linguists, but the present edition does not claim to be in the avant-garde of linguistic theory, nor does it try to stretch its purpose beyond those firmly established ones already mentioned in this Foreword.

The writing of college-trained people is expected to be somewhat different, on occasion, from informal speech. This is a normal, justified expectation. No matter what some lexicographers and linguists heatedly maintain, a laissez-faire attitude of "anything goes" can be, and repeatedly is, costly to students in business and social affairs. The late Will Rogers was genuinely humorous when he remarked: "A lot of people who don't say *ain't*, ain't eatin'." And yet, in certain clearly defined circumstances, using *ain't*, misspelling a word, employing an unidiomatic expression, or saying *went* when *gone* is indicated can cost a job, advancement, a social opportunity, or even a potential friend. English composition has many values, one of which is practicality.

In short, the credo in *The Shorter Handbook* is that expressed by Theodore M. Bernstein, brilliant staff editor for *The New York Times*, in *Watch Your Language:*

> To be sure, the English language is a changing and growing thing. All its users have, of course, a perceptible effect upon it. But in changing and growing it needs no contrived help from chitchat columnists or advertising writers or comic strip artists or television speakers. It will evolve nicely by itself. If anything, it requires protection from influences that try to push it too

fast. There is need, not for those who would halt its progress altogether, but for those who can keep a gentle foot on the brake and a guiding hand on the steering wheel. . . .

Book Three contains a diversified, representative, and interesting collection of readings. Obviously, more material is included than most classes can possibly absorb, but overabundance will provide opportunity for the individual instructor to assign only those selections especially useful to a particular class. The editor's original aim was to make selections which represent good writing, which would appeal to students, and which would stimulate class discussion and foster imitation of writing techniques. At times, selections were made as much on the basis of interest and provocativeness as of purely literary qualities. Also, in addition to much material that is recent, the editor chose several selections which through the years have proved their value in the classroom. Still another purpose of the editor was to represent major types of writing and thus provide an adequate introduction to literature itself. The attainment of these identical aims is the editor's goal in this sixth edition.

In successive editions, selections which have become "dated" or have not proved sufficiently stimulating have been removed and new ones have been added. In this sixth edition appear new essays, critical articles, biographical sketches, short stories, plays, and poems.

Book Three is preceded by "A Note on Reading" which attempts to offer helpful suggestions to students and which contains devices by which an instructor can learn something about the reading speed and comprehension of students. New in this edition are separate brief essays, preceding the selections, on (1) autobiography, profile, and portrait, (2) short stories, (3) plays, and (4) poetry. Each such introductory note on reading comments directly on the genre being taken up and provides specific topics for study, discussion, and writing.

The four traditional forms of discourse are amply represented. The presence of *exposition* and *narration* is readily apparent in essay and narrative selections. Examples of *argument* are to be found in many of the essays, especially those by T. H. Huxley, Bronowski, Davis, Thouless, Highet, Rabi, Krutch, Clarke, Cluett, Stoke, Seldes, Bennett, Brown, Fuess, and Smith. A number of these present contrasting points of view, and the questions call attention to opposing ideas which virtually constitute a debate.

Similarly, *description* will be found and may be studied in many of the selections. Descriptive passages dealing with people or places are particularly notable in the selections by Thoreau, Muir, Aldous Huxley, Stevenson, Stoke, Morley, Lukacs, Kennedy, Orwell, Steffens, Atkinson, Keller, Brooks, Angle, and, of course, in all the short stories and plays and the majority of the poems.

Questions and theme suggestions following most of the selections are resigned to determine the student's familiarity with the item being studied and to call attention to matters of form, technique, and style. Such questions and assignments are designedly brief and only suggestive. Increased emphasis is placed in this edition on questions which deal searchingly with matters of technique, form, and tonal quality.

ACKNOWLEDGMENTS

In short, this edition of *A Complete Course in Freshman English* has been thoroughly revised and updated while retaining its original plan, scope, and purpose. But this sixth edition would be far less helpful than hopefully it is had not scores of former colleagues at New York University and Columbia University, present associates, former students, and many others contributed their thoughts and suggestions. Some contributors must remain unnamed because my memory is sometimes faulty and because their number is so great. But I can and do acknowledge indebtedness to Professors Macklin Thomas and Richard H. Dodge, who have already been mentioned in this Foreword. Dr. Thomas has not only contributed many excellently realistic and challenging exercises but has also reviewed the entire fifth edition and made many cogent suggestions for the present volume. Similarly, I have had the benefit of thorough analyses made by Professor Nils T. Peterson of San Jose State College and Professor Blaine D. Moody of Auburn Community College, New York. These gifted teachers, intimately familiar with *A Complete Course* through classroom use, have helped in strengthening this edition in many areas.

For contributions to Book Two, I acknowledge my indebtedness to Professors George S. Wykoff of Purdue University, the late Cecil B. Williams of Texas Christian University, and Alan H. Casty of Santa Monica City College. This portion of my work has also been aided by many conversations over the years with Dr. Paul Roberts, peripatetic scholar and my longtime friend, who has educated himself and tried to educate me in the field of linguistics. I am also grateful to the late J. Wilson McCutchan of the University of Waterloo, Canada. Dr. McCutchan provided recommendations based on his varied teaching experience in both the United States and Canada and, notably, contributed many of the glosses which accompany *Macbeth* in Book Three. Professor William H. Davenport, formerly of the University of Southern California and now of Harvey Mudd College, and the late Professor Lowry C. Wimberly of the University of Nebraska have made oblique but important contributions to the selections of essays, plays, and poems in Book Three. Drs. Wimberly and Davenport joined with me in editing *Dominant Types in British and American Literature* (New York, 1949). As a result of many conferences and vast correspondence while this editorial chore was progressing, my ideas about these major types were altered and strengthened; furthermore, a few of the notes concerning essays, poems, and plays in Book Three of *A Complete Course* stem directly from material which they wrote for the volume mentioned. Miss Anne L. Corbitt, formerly reference librarian at New York University; Professor S. I. Hayakawa of San Francisco State College; Leonard A. Stevens, and Professor Ralph G. Nichols, University of Minnesota; and Miss Lousene Rousseau, formerly of

Harper & Row, each made important contributions to an earlier edition of this work. Their influence and a few of their actual phrases appear at various places in the present edition.

A Complete Course, widely used annually in hundreds of colleges and universities for nearly three decades, has not "just happened." The first edition, which required ten years for preparation, has steadily evolved into the volume you now hold. But the hands which have guided this growth are not alone those of the undersigned. I am fully aware that through the years scores of dedicated teachers and loyal friends have given invaluable aid. The very first edition was helped into shape by the late Douglas Bement, then professor at George Washington University and later of the University of Washington, and by the late A. J. Bryan of Louisiana State University. As these two estimable scholars and friends look over the ramparts, my hope is that they will not disapprove the evolution of their work and will know how grateful I remain to them. In later editions, somewhat similar assistance was given by the late William H. Hildreth of Ohio State University and by Philip Burnham, then of Harvard University and now of St. Paul's School, Concord, New Hampshire.

The roll call of those who have helped all along the line is indeed lengthy. But I should be remiss in duty and lacking in gratitude if I failed to mention a number of gifted teachers—some now departed, some increasingly valorous in classroom and library—who have been my friends, hand-holders, and counselors during the years of constant study and planning which have gone into *A Complete Course*. Their names (those of some of the women perhaps now changed) and their affiliations (some of these also now changed) at the time they offered help are as follows:

C. Merton Babcock, Michigan State University; Havilah Babcock, University of South Carolina; Kingsbury Badger, Boston University; Warren Bower, New York University; Woodrow W. Boyett, University of Alabama; Arthur W. Brown, Utica College; Jack R. Brown, Marshall College; E. F. Bunge, Washburn University; J. H. Chamberlin, Columbia University; Donald C. Clarke, Columbia University; Mrs. Donald Cornu, University of Washington; Troy C. Crenshaw, Texas Christian University; William A. Darden, United States Naval Academy; Neal Frank Doubleday, James Millikin University; Lois Smith Douglas, Baylor University; Robert Bruce Dow, New York University; Howard Dunbar, New York University; Louis C. Grafious, Eastern Washington College of Education; Earl Harlan, State University Teachers College, Plattsburgh; Clifton E. Hazard, University of Cincinnati; Elinor W. Hiatt, Long Beach City College; Lee E. Holt, American International College; Lillian Hornstein, New York University; Lucille M. Johnson, Pacific Lutheran College; Wendell Johnson, University of Iowa; Herbert C. Kalk, Wilson Junior College; Donald C. McCoy, University of Minnesota; Paul Ansley McGhee, New York University; Mildred Marcett, New York University; Lucy Anna Nielsen, Reedley College; Gustav H. Offerman, Sacramento Junior College; J. D. A. Ogilvy, University of Colorado; Brother Cormac Philip, Manhattan College; Mary Alice Polk, Modesto Junior College; Robert Price, Otterbein College; David M. Rein, Case Institute of Technology; Joseph H. Schick, Indiana State Teachers College; Samuel E. Small, West Virginia Wesleyan College; Eugene B. Vest, University of Illinois; Eugene M. Waffle, Eastern Illinois University; Kathryn Painter Ward, University of Maryland; Homer A. Watt, New York University; Eloise Wilson, Rider College.

The affiliations mentioned may have changed; the minds and interests of individuals may also have changed. But everyone here recorded has made a contribution at one time or another, and the present volume mirrors to some degree the help each has extended along the way.

My children (Harry, Ned, Stephen, Jill, and Gray), to whom the previous edition was dedicated, have suffered with me during the years I have been working on this edition. My understanding wife, Joy, has contributed tolerance, forbearance, and editorial acumen. And I am especially grateful to Eleanor Bouvier Curtis, who has loyally performed many and varied research and secretarial chores with unfailing good humor and intelligence.

H.S.

BOOK ONE
WRITING

A Manual of Rhetorical Principles

To the man with an ear for verbal delicacies—the man who searches painfully for the perfect word and puts the way of saying a thing above the thing said—there is in writing the constant joy of sudden discovery, of happy accident.

> —HENRY LOUIS MENCKEN, *A Book of Prefaces*

It is my ambition to say in ten sentences what everyone else says in a whole book—what everyone else does *not* say in a whole book.

> —FRIEDRICH NIETZSCHE, *Skirmishes in a War with the Age*

By being so long in the lowest form . . . I gained an immense advantage over the cleverer boys. . . . I got into my bones the essential structure of the ordinary British sentence—which is a noble thing.

> —SIR WINSTON CHURCHILL, *Roving Commission: My Early Life*

CHAPTER 1

GETTING UNDER WAY

Freshman English is a course that makes no demands beyond the ability of the average student. In no sense is it a course designed for the training of professional writers or speakers.

Its primary aim is to give you practice in the correct, clear, and effective expression of *your own* ideas, emotions, and reactions. You will have some reading to do, not for the purpose of providing models for slavish imitation but to stock your mind with ideas that may be assimilated, to give you experiences quite as real and quite as important as any job or position or physical activity. In addition, the course will teach you much about both listening and speaking. But its primary purpose is to help you establish and confirm good habits in writing.

Actually, you may have had little genuine experience in formal writing, although you have been speaking (that is, uttering sounds or real words) since infancy. What you say and how you say it may sometimes be neither clear nor effective, yet such shortcomings rarely result from lack of practice in speaking. But few students entering college have made more than isolated or sporadic writing efforts in the past, no matter how much they may have soundlessly composed in their minds. The slim total may well consist of an occasional theme or book report or "research" paper, a few letters, a job application or two, answers on school examinations, and the like. Freshman English is specifically designed to provide writing experiences that are considered an integral part of every educated person's basic equipment.

Through practice, and only through practice, can we effectively learn any really necessary or worthwhile activity: talking, walking, dressing, playing games, dancing, thinking—and writing. Even such automatic activities as breathing, eating, and sleeping can be modified and improved through practice and training, as hosts of singers, athletes, and counselors on etiquette can testify.

Speaking and writing are important forms of behavior, and the different ways we perform these acts reveal much about us: our standards of taste, our judgment, our goals, even our potential or actual position in life. When George Bernard Shaw wrote *Pygmalion* (see p. 1066), he insisted that it was Eliza's Cockney speech which "kept her in her place." The thesis of the play is that proper training in speaking could change Eliza's entire existence. Proper training in writing, such as you will receive in this course, is not likely to alter so radically *your* entire existence, but it will aid your intellectual growth and may well make you vastly more interesting to yourself and to others.

Writing has at least two dimensions worthy of comment here. The first is *literacy:* the ability to spell, to punctuate, to follow acceptable conventions of word choice and usage, to employ words in their everyday meanings. Nearly everyone recognizes that such ability is important, that writing which lacks these essential qualities is slovenly, irritating, and incomprehensible. Although *literate* English is largely negative—the capacity *not* to make mistakes—it is no minor achievement. In fact, attaining just this goal is worthy of praise, the kind of praise often resulting in at least a passing grade in freshman English. But it is hardly enough. Some rebels and beatniks excluded, do not all of us wish to "write acceptably" just as we desire to "make a good appearance," dress suitably, and not be thought dull, boring, and lacking a sense of humor?

Another dimension of writing is *competence*. By contrast with literacy, competence involves the ability to conceive, arrange in order, and clearly express ideas; to handle and control language as a means of expressing thought and feeling; to define a quality; to support an idea; to express differences of mood and emotion and meaning. Literacy should be the minimum achievement of every student in freshman English. Those who enter the course already possessing it can seek to achieve varying and greater degrees of competence.

In short, this course should help you (1) to free your writing of "grammatical" and mechanical errors, (2) to present ideas in clearly constructed sentences, (3) to develop and expand these ideas into organized units of paragraphs and compositions, (4) to gain confidence that these ideas will be understood, respected, and fairly evaluated. As the course proceeds, your instructor will aid this growth and development by leading you into more difficult and more mature assignments and subjects.

At no time during this period of training should you lose heart. Writing is difficult, difficult for everyone regardless of his training and experience. Voltaire, one of the world's all-time literary masters, wrote:

> The necessity of saying something, the embarrassment produced by the consciousness of having nothing to say, and the desire to exhibit ability, are three things sufficient to render even a great man ridiculous.

Disappointments may come as often as triumphs during freshman English. For some, they will come more often. Try to accept both as a part of the effort, excitement and, yes, fun, involved in mastering a worthwhile skill.

Also, try to form a suitable attitude toward writing. Despite the numerous corrections on papers returned to you, don't think of writing as a complicated series of *do's* and *don't's*, a long list of prohibitions and *thou-shalt-not's*. Try to approach it as what it is: a flexible medium which will help you to communicate clearly and interestingly to and with others. What possible activity could be more important to you or to anyone?

SELF-EVALUATION

The first common-sense approach to writing is *self-evaluation*. Some of us go for years at a time without doing what a good storekeeper does periodically—take stock. The whole process of writing consists of two steps: first, finding out what we think and feel about people, places, happenings, and ideas, and, second, communicating our thoughts and feelings to our readers. The first step is thinking and the second is writing; the two are inseparably linked. A good starting place is to think about what the members of your family mean and have meant to you, what friends you have and what kind of people they are, what you have obtained from your schooling thus far, your ideas (or lack of them) about religion, politics, love and marriage, sports, hobbies. The ideas you have now may change in a few months or even a few days, but that is not significant. What is important is that you take the first step in becoming a writer, the first step in learning to communicate your thoughts and feelings effectively—find out some things about yourself which, perhaps, you have never realized before.

Answer as thoroughly and accurately as you can one or more (or all) of the following questions:

What are my *social* beliefs? (Do I like people in general? What kinds of people? What are the qualifications necessary to gain my friendship? Do I like men better than women? Do I like children, as a general rule, occasionally, never? Have I any real concern for underprivileged people? *Why* do I hold these attitudes?)

What are my *religious* beliefs? (Do I believe in God? If so, under what aspect—as a transcendentalist, a Baptist, as Hardy's "President of the Immortals"? If not, am I agnostic or atheistic? *Why* do I hold these beliefs?)

What are my *political* beliefs? (Am I interested in national and international politics? Am I a reactionary in politics, a conservative, a radical, an extremist? What do I mean by these terms? *Why* do I hold these attitudes?)

What are my *moral* beliefs? (Do I subscribe to, and practice, the "Golden Rule"? Do I believe that "Honesty is the best policy"? What do I really think of the Ten Commandments as a guide for human conduct? Do I believe in the single or double standard? Do I believe in the sanctity of marriage? romantic love? free love? *Why* do I hold these attitudes?)

What do I want to be, and to be doing, five (ten) years from now? *Why?*

What do I expect to be, and to be doing, five (ten) years from now? *Why?*

What, for me, is the single major problem facing the world today? Why have I selected this from scores of possible choices?

What would constitute, for me, the greatest happiness I can imagine? The greatest disaster? *Why?*

Am I an observing person, alert to what is going on about me? Am I capable of self-analysis and criticism? Am I open-minded—tolerant of other people and their ideas? Am I capable of reflection and meditation? Am I aware of my limitations?

How did I get to be the way I am? What were (or are) the principal events, persons, and places that have molded my life thus far?

PURPOSE

When you write about something which really means something to you, something which is or was really important, your writing is interesting, even though you may think it will sound flat to others. If you have a genuine purpose when you write, you need never fear that your compositions will lack interest. As a matter of fact, *purpose* is a second practical approach to this problem of writing. After you have made a preliminary study of yourself—that is, your experiences, observations, and ideas—you then have to consider to what purpose you are going to write about them. Writing of all kinds should have as a central purpose the communication of ideas or feelings. Writing which doesn't correctly and clearly convey ideas or feelings from you to your reader isn't really writing at all.

Each of the reading selections in this volume is controlled by the author's central purpose. A good writer may seem to digress for a sentence, a paragraph, even a page, but when you have finished reading the entire selection you can always state the author's *central* purpose in a thesis sentence.

For example, Thomas Henry Huxley in "The Method of Scientific Investigation," p. 470, writes about ways of thinking that are familiar to us all. His central purpose is to show us that scientists use these identical processes of reasoning but exert unusual care and caution in doing so. Through rigorous selection of details, clear structure, and appealing narrative examples he achieves his purpose.

For another example, turn to "Lucinda Matlock," p. 1163. Edgar Lee Masters' purpose is to show us that "it takes life to love Life," that living is difficult, strenuous, often sorrowful, and frequently beautiful. No other purpose is allowed to intrude.

Turn to Section 37, p. 251, for further study of this all-important matter of purpose. Better still, discover and write for each selection you study in Book Three a "thesis sentence." Doing this will conclusively prove to you that all worthwhile writing, at least all that appears in Book Three, is controlled by the central aim, the primary intent, of the author.

MATERIALS

When we come to consider what *materials,* what substance to use in writing —a third common-sense approach to the problem of composition—we always find that we have to write from our own experience, observation, curiosity, imagination, and reflection. Naturally, we get much of our material from others in discussions or conversations, in interviews or lectures, or in reading. But we must assimilate all this material and make it our own. Otherwise, what we write will be not ours but someone else's. True originality is not so much a matter of substance as of individualized treatment. The most interesting and effective subjects for themes are those about which we either have some knowledge or genuinely want to learn something. Writing is made out of the ideas and impressions which we have obtained from various sources and made a part of ourselves.

You cannot avoid writing about yourself or revealing yourself in many ways. When you write a paper which, for example, explains or defines something, you can write somewhat more objectively, but even then you will be giving your personal explanation, telling what that something means to you. Anatole France once wrote that, to be frank, even the critic ought to say: "Gentlemen, I am going to speak of myself apropos of Shakespeare, apropos of Racine, or of Goethe."

Here is the first half of a theme written by a freshman who had done some self-evaluating and had settled on a definite purpose to be achieved with unified material:

> When I began to take stock of all the friends whom I have had, I quickly came to the conclusion that Jerry was the most important and had exerted the greatest influence upon my life. His family moved to my block when I was only 10. Jerry was 15 at the time, but the fact that he was so much older than I seemed to make no difference to him. I was highly flattered that he seemed to like me, and I haunted his house day after day. We took long walks together, on which he would tell me stories from Cooper's *Leather-Stocking Tales.* They were Jerry's improvisations, of course, and it was years later that I realized Jerry was paraphrasing. Doubtless, Cooper would have been annoyed had he known what twists Jerry gave to his stories, but then again, he might not have been, for Jerry had a quick imagination and an excellent sense of what parts of the stories would especially appeal to a 10-year-old whose mind was full of Indians, pioneer forts, and even pirates and buried gold.
>
> Jerry never seemed to mind giving me so much of his time and, although he had many other friends, he always made me feel that I was his special crony. He taught me all I still know about birds and flowers; he came over to read to me every day when I broke my leg and had to stay in the house for weeks. His ideas about people and moving pictures and even food and clothes were my ideas. I gradually came to feel that Jerry meant more to me than either my father or mother did. During that whole first year of our

acquaintance he never said or did an unkind thing to me and I began to look up to him as I would have to a god.

The idyllic friendship recounted here did not continue. And the story of its dissolution is the meat of the theme. The writer traced that one year's beautiful friendship and then described a change that began to come over Jerry. When Jerry became 16, his interests and tastes shifted; he grew concerned with girls and dances and things which to an 11-year-old were wholly unimportant. Annoyed at attempts to keep the friendship going, he finally had to hurt the younger boy's feelings before the latter could understand that they had to come to a real parting of the ways. The theme is a nostalgic account of a long-dead friendship such as you and I and millions of other people have experienced. And it is because we have all had such an experience that we are interested in this account. Probably you have not had many unusual experiences. But each of you is an individual, and things seem different to you. Part of the training of freshman English is to enable you to see how your mind works, how your thoughts are at least slightly different from those of everyone else. It is in precisely this area that you will find materials for writing.

It is difficult to get at the truth about oneself. Unearthing the facts requires digging, hard thinking, careful reflecting. And when you have arrived at some truth about yourself, or what you believe is the truth, when you have evaluated what some experience or person has done to shape your thought and life, it takes courage to put on paper what you have found. All of us keep a curtain between ourselves and others, we hide behind masks, we keep to ourselves some secret and inviolate part of self. Such reticence (or self-preservation) is normal; in some areas of thought and experience it may be as wise as it is necessary. But how refreshing to writer and reader to discover an honest revelation rather than a set of standard pretenses! Many analyses of character and attitudes are predictable because they result from a search for what is considered expected and recognizable rather than from what is truly individual and distinctive. One experienced teacher of freshman English has remarked that if you remove the pronouns in most themes of character analysis and self-revelation, it is impossible to tell whether the writer is a boy or a girl. Even if some of your innermost thoughts and feelings must be kept sacred, others you should be able honestly to reveal without hopelessly incriminating yourself.

Perhaps each of us has bought some machine-made article which soon proved faulty or worthless: a ball-point pen, a tennis racket, a shirt. Feeling cheated, we may have reflected on today's standards of workmanship. Such an experience and such a reaction are material for writing. Turn to p. 873 to see what John Galsworthy made of a somewhat similar situation.

Have you ever thought that the things you have learned which seem really valuable were derived more from daily living than from formal education? That sometimes you seem to be most profoundly thoughtful when you are apparently least active? That life is so crowded, so frantic, that you have little or no time to relax, to absorb, to enjoy life as it rushes by? If any of these thoughts come to you—and they have occurred and will come again—turn to "An Apology for Idlers," p. 739, and "The World Is Too Much with Us," p. 1154, to see what Stevenson and Wordsworth wrote about such ideas. What you write may be far less effective than either the essay or the poem, but what you write can and should be your own material and no one else's.

YOUR READERS

To be certain that what you write will be communicable and interesting, always *consider your readers*. Their interests and capacities for understanding are important. Every theme should be written for a particular reader or group of readers, with full account taken in advance of such matters as age, educational level, sex, tastes, experience, and interests. The pages of this volume contain numerous suggestions designed to enable you to vary your writing style according to the needs and interests of your readers.

It is short-sighted to maintain that what seems clear and interesting to you, as a writer, will necessarily appeal to your readers. Professional writers sometimes say that the best test of something they have written is whether or not it pleases them. But the difficulty with our using any such standard is that in writing to please only ourselves we frequently are too easily pleased. Most professional writers and editors have undergone an apprenticeship which has made them reasonably certain that their tastes accurately reflect those of their readers—but they always do keep their readers in mind. You will find that this is really a necessary approach to writing.

Applied to language, communication consists of two major divisions, each containing two closely related parts: (1) writing and reading, (2) speaking and listening.

Achieving communication can be likened to the successful use of the telephone and radio because a sender and a recipient are always involved. The writer writes for, or sends to, a reader; the reader reads or receives what the writer has sent. The speaker speaks for a listener; the listener receives what the speaker has transmitted. Between the sender and the receiver is, of course, the subject, the material being transmitted. When the recipient understands what the sender has wanted to convey, communication is completed. The more clearly and effectively the reader or listener understands the subject presented, the more successful the communication is.

The process is illustrated by the following diagram:

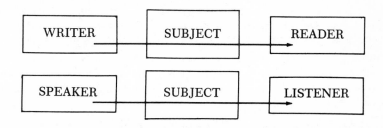

As a writer, you will never be judged by your private vision, only by that part of it which shows on paper. It is a mistake for a writer to sit around admiring his mental processes, his extraordinary insights, his captivating ideas. A reader is not sitting around in any such admiring state. His demand is "Show me," and he is quite justified in his insistence.

SUMMARY

Although there is no one set procedure for learning to write, there are some basic principles which can be applied. Choosing material which has interest for you and really trying to convey what you have in mind are essential. Also, remember that your writing must have a clear purpose, a definite direction. It shouldn't wander off into bypaths, no matter how interesting they may be. Even if a theme you write is on so prosaic a subject as how to clean a room, it should stick to its definite purpose. And, too, it should be clear to the reader in every particular. Such a theme may be difficult to make interesting, but if you furnish enough concrete detail, your reader is not likely to be bored. Someone has remarked that nine-tenths of good writing consists of furnishing concrete, specific details and that the other tenth doesn't really matter. In other words, everything you write should have a *clear purpose, definite direction,* and *plentiful substance.* If it has these elements and is written without grammatical and other errors, it will adhere to the major principles of good writing.

If you will sit down *to write what you have thought* and *not* sit down *to think what you will write,* you are going to find the ideas coming. They may develop slowly on paper, and you may have to revise your sentences and paragraphs again and again, but if you try hard enough and take enough time, you can write without inspiration. As Lord Dunsany once said: "When you can with difficulty say anything clearly, simply, and emphatically, then, provided that the difficulty is not apparent to the reader, that is style. When you can do it easily, that is genius."

Has it ever occurred to you that in a sense you have been engaged in a form of writing for many years, just as you have always been "speaking prose"? Haven't you "thought through" some letters before putting them on paper? Haven't you uttered many remarks to yourself before saying them aloud? The late Somerset Maugham had this to say of writers, all writers, including students in first-year English:

> The author does not only write when he's at his desk, he writes all day long, when he is thinking, when he is reading, when he is experiencing: everything he sees and feels is significant to his purpose and, consciously or unconsciously, he is forever storing and making over his impressions.

Just one final word: Your success in freshman English and, indeed, in all your college work will depend upon constant, earnest application and not upon so-called "flashes of inspiration" and sudden bursts of effort. Robert Littell once wrote:

> Inspiration? A question that is sure to be raised. It's not a visitation, of course, but is inside you all the time. Don't wait for it—that is an old saw— keep on writing and writing and ever so often it will come roaring up out of your insides and take the pencil from your hands. Nobody knows how to

coax it up. Don't press, as the golfers say; learn to lie fallow and soak up the sun; the shy beast will come up or not, as he chooses.

On this aspect of the subject, another successful author has said:

> Too many people let time pass while they wait for an idea. If they'd simply start to write about a fellow named Joe Jones in the lumber business, ideas on Joe and his job would come fast. It is work, and that is, of course, harder than just waiting. But it is effective.

Good luck in your engrossing task of learning to write by writing, rewriting, and reading! Winning your bachelor's degree, getting married, having your first baby or earning your first million dollars, getting a Pulitzer or Nobel Prize—these may seem more exciting and dramatic than learning to write with literacy and competence. And yet, this year of work can be filled with fun, with excitement, with the everlasting rewards that come with attaining any really worthwhile goal.

CHAPTER 2

WRITING THE THEME

Laboratory work is the method a physical scientist employs to turn theory into fact. Field work is one important means by which a social scientist translates theories and formulas into helpful techniques and tools. Chemists and biologists and sociologists and engineers and home economists use retorts, microscopes, case studies, testing machines, and demonstration homes to relate theory to actuality. For those who wish to use English correctly, clearly, and effectively the prescribed laboratory work is theme-writing.

When writing is done well it becomes an art; even when done poorly or only adequately it reflects personal characteristics and is subject to numerous variations. But mere knowledge of words and their ways is worthless unless it can be applied. The word, the sentence, and the paragraph are only means to an end, the bricks which make up a house. You can never be said to write well until you can achieve a completed whole, an entire composition.

Many a beginning student of biology or physics has been appalled at how rapidly his instructor set him to performing actual laboratory work. Such a student, feeling inadequate in both knowledge and technique, might wonder how he could ever get in mind, or remember, hundreds and hundreds of applicable and immediately needed facts. Similarly, some beginning composition students are unprepared to write themes because they have many facts about grammar or diction or spelling or structure to learn or relearn, many particulars and details to keep in mind. And yet the only way to learn to write is to write; and the sooner the process is started, the quicker the whole design of theme-writing becomes clear. When this process begins, you are well on the way to becoming a soundly practical and effective handler of language.

To learn to write correctly, clearly, and effectively you may require a semester of theme-writing, or a year or two, or eternity, but everyone can improve his ability to write if he will conscientiously try. This chapter deals with several specific approaches to writing themes, but before examining them, ask yourself these questions about any composition you write:

1. Does my theme have a *central purpose*? (Have I carefully analyzed the subject?) See p. 6 and Section 37a.
2. Does my theme have *ample substance*? See p. 7 and 38.
3. Is this substance *arranged* logically and effectively? See 39.
4. Is my theme *unified*? See 43.
5. Is my theme *clear*? (Will it mean to any reasonably intelligent reader exactly or approximately what it means to me?) See 41.
6. Is the substance presented so interestingly and emphatically that it will make a *definite appeal* to the reader? See p. 9.
7. Is my theme *correct* in all mechanical and grammatical details? See 36.

If you can truthfully and correctly answer "yes" to these seven questions, your task is completed and your instructor will probably exempt you from all further required assignments. But as is pointed out on p. 3, none of these requirements is beyond the ability of the ordinary student. That is, none is too much for the ordinary student who will work intelligently and industriously.

WHAT TO WRITE ABOUT

Every writer has had the discouraging experience of writing something with great care, something which pleased him and seemed to be correct and clear, only to find that others did not enjoy reading it, that it did not "get across." There is truth in the statement that "everything has interest for somebody," but it is equally true that some subjects are inherently more interesting than others and can be presented more effectively.

Students manage to turn in themes of a sort when definite topics are assigned by their instructors, but they are often puzzled when required to write compositions on topics of their own choosing. After some thought, they select topics that frequently are neither original nor easily capable of effective treatment. But there are three simple rules which will enable you to choose subjects that you can handle effectively.

1. *Choose an interesting topic.* This seems to be a vague suggestion, but it can be given specific application.

First, does the topic interest you yourself? It is difficult to write effectively unless you are actually interested in the material. Vagueness, aimlessness, dullness, and sketchiness are the hallmarks of uninterested writing; force and vigor are usually present when you are "wrapped up in your subject" and "let yourself go." You may not be interested in labor unions, for example, but if you have a friend who has lost his job because of joining or not joining a union, you are likely to write with genuine interest.

You may have no special interest in economics, but if you find that the money at your disposal is buying less and less, you may well become really concerned about inflation and the rising cost of living. Your interest in South America may be nonexistent, but if you become friends with a Brazilian in your dormitory, you may discover that that continent and his country have a new interest, meaning, and appeal for you.

You necessarily will write several themes on topics in which you are not really interested; but when you are *choosing* an effective topic, select one which has definite appeal for yourself in general, or in some particular aspect.

Second, will the topic interest your readers, that is, classmates and instructor? A writer is a salesman: he has to "sell" his ideas to his readers. He will quite profitably spend considerable time in analyzing his reader's likes and dislikes, in planning ways to overcome their "sales resistance" by interesting them in his material, or presenting material in which they are already interested.

Experts agree that man is first of all interested in himself. This belief is not cynical so much as it is a sort of corollary to the law of self-preservation. Your reader, any reader, is constantly looking for information which will benefit him in some way. He is also constantly looking for, and interested in, material to which he can relate and by which he can measure himself. Nearly everything that we see and hear we identify with ourselves if we possibly can. What, for example, does anyone first look for in a photograph of a meeting he has attended? What does one think about on seeing an advertisement for a dress or suit other than "How will that look on me?" or "Can I afford it?" or "Will I like it?"

In addition to oneself, what are some other compelling interests, matters to which your readers are nearly always attuned and to which their responses will usually be quick and strong? The late Joseph Pulitzer, famed newspaper publisher and editor, once stated that the most effective topics for front-page treatment are murders, sex, wills, and how the rich spend their money. The newspaper with the largest circulation in the United States, *The New York Daily News,* adheres fairly closely to this somewhat sensational formula, although many responsible papers are more sedate. In freshman English, you and your instructor would probably be wise to settle on more prosaic topics, too. But the following list may suggest ideas for selecting topics and may provide tests for measuring the appeal to others of what you have already chosen to write about:

a *Timely topics:* either new ideas or late facts, or the development of some old idea by emphasis upon its contact with recent developments.

b *People:* unique, prominent, or familiar.

c *Important matters:* those which involve the life and property of others and which have a relation to the reader's own welfare.

d *Conflict:* contests between people, between man and nature, and internal conflicts (within the person).

e *Amusements and hobbies.*

An analysis of currently popular magazines will provide still further evidence of what apparently interests people in general. Many topics constantly treated in periodicals are unsuitable for college theme purposes, but they do provide fascinating insights into people's tastes and concerns: health (how to get and keep it); catastrophes (everything from accidents to obituary columns—"There but for the grace of God . . ."); self-improvement; religion and religious or ethical experiences; relationships between the sexes; money (who has it, how he got it, what he does with it); and scores of other subjects. With such clues to readers' interests, it should not be overwhelmingly difficult to select topics appealing to others or to remember that certain topics, not intrinsically so appealing, will require added effort to make them come alive for readers.

2. *Choose a topic about which you know something.* Material from personal experience and observation can not only be effectively incorporated in themes; an entire composition may be suggested by, and written from, such material. If you write about something you actually know, something you have thought or seen or heard, you have a more than even chance of presenting your material effectively.

Just as one cannot expect to handle a tool or machine efficiently and expertly without some previous experience, some first-hand acquaintance, so one cannot expect to write effectively without some experience and first-hand acquaintance with the topic of the composition. John R. Tunis' books and articles on sport are based on many years of direct observation and study; the late Kenneth Roberts' stories of Arundel—*The Lively Lady, Arundel, Captain Caution,* etc.—came out of Roberts' personal familiarity with the Kennebunk, Maine, area, his considerable study and research, and careful observation of people. Herman Melville shipped as a sailor in 1839. Two years later he sailed around Cape Horn in the whaler *Acushnet,* and the following year was "captured" by cannibals in the South Seas. These experiences—and his keen observation of men and the sea—he used in *Typee, Redburn,* his great novel *Moby Dick,* and other writings.

Every good writer goes to his own experience—to those things he knows or has thought or seen or heard. Remember, however, that your own special experiences (hobbies, jobs, dates, parties, travels, and the like) are quickly exhausted as writing materials unless you can develop from them some new aspects of thought, new insights, and novel conclusions and judgments. Almost any of your particular experiences will quickly become wearisome even to you unless, through thought, which is the only ever-reliable source of interest, you can develop some new relationship, some fresh insight which has meaning above and beyond the incident itself.

3. *Choose a topic you can handle adequately.* It is impossible to write an effective 500-word theme on a subject which requires 5000 words. If you choose a "big" subject and fail to limit it, you are likely to become discouraged and to write sketchily and illogically. You may select a topic which is interesting to both yourself and your reader, and which you know something about; yet it may not be a good one simply because you cannot handle it adequately in the prescribed limits of the paper. "College Fraternities," "Professional Football," "The History of My University" are examples of such topics. They cannot be treated in a short paper; and even if the paper is to be lengthy, they will require more extended research than you can or will undertake.

The very word *theme* implies a single, well-defined *phase* of a subject. Be careful not to select a subject so large and inclusive that it cannot possibly be treated in a short theme. Such subjects as "Aviation," "The United States Constitution," "Missile Warfare," "Sex and Censorship" are obviously too broad to permit adequate treatment in a 500-word composition. "Aviation," for example, is a hopelessly broad subject; limited to "Aviation in America," it is still too large, perhaps even for a book; "The Career of Wilbur Wright" might be developed in a very long paper; "That Last Flight of ——" would be more suitable for ordinary theme treatment.

You must rigorously limit a subject to some phase which you can develop with reasonable thoroughness and unity in the space at your command. A small composition on a large subject is necessarily a fragmentary, disconnected, ineffective treatment.

GETTING MATERIAL FOR WRITING

After you have selected a topic, or have had one assigned, the first logical step is to decide what it involves and what you intend to do with it. The second step is to secure material for its development.

There must be an objective for the theme other than the completion of a required assignment, for there can be no such thing as good *purposeless* writing. How you decide your purpose will control and direct your selection of developing material. Every theme is a project for communicating to some clearly defined person, or group of persons, a series of thoughts, facts, or emotions. Thus, writing is either a search for means to accomplish a central aim or, as it all too often is, a mere setting down of words according to mechanical requirements.

Before you begin to write, state in a single sentence—which may or may not be included in the theme later—your central purpose, your controlling idea. To play on words, what is the *theme* of your theme? Write a *thesis* statement, a *topic sentence* for the paper, a sentence that summarizes your entire material. Until you have done this, you have not fully or clearly defined your purpose. See 37, p. 251.

Ordinarily, a theme about *camping* is likely to be dull, repetitious, and utterly without appeal to readers and even to the writer. (Some critics feel that even so talented a writer as Hemingway was never more dull or long-winded than in his account of Nick's fishing trip, "Big Two-Hearted River.") Like several other well-worn topics, camping is intrinsically dull and ordinarily should be avoided. But if you do select so potentially uninteresting a subject as this, clarifying your purpose and giving real thought to its handling and development may provide a spark of interest. For example, consider this framework for a theme on the general subject of "A Camping Trip":

Limited subject:	"Advice to a Beginning Recreational Director"
Possible title:	"Let's Take the Boys Camping"
Reader:	A recreational director or assistant director who is starting his first summer of service
Length:	1,000 words

Thesis sentence (general): Boys between 12 and 15 enjoy most those group
               or   activities—especially outdoors—which call for vig-
                            orous exertion.

Thesis sentence (specific): The kinds of recreational activities that appeal to
                            boys between 12 and 15 are (1) athletic and com-
petitive (softball, baseball, tennis, swimming, horse-
shoes); (2) athletic and social (rowing, canoeing,
hiking, woodcraft); (3) handicrafts; (4) mental
(reading appropriate books, group discussions).

In determining your central purpose, make a list of 15 or 20 details
that might be used. For example, in a theme, "The High School I Attended,"
your list might include, among other items:

1. Size	11. Commercial courses
2. Building	12. Vocational courses
3. Location	13. Athletic program
4. History and name	14. Basketball championships
5. Number of students	15. Publications
6. Kinds of students	16. Social activities
7. Number of teachers	17. Class trips
8. Kinds of teachers	18. Dramatic presentations
9. Courses of study	19. Musical activities
10. College prep courses	20. English courses

Naturally you would not include all such details in your theme nor in
this first-draft order. But such a listing gives you an "overview" and can
suggest direction and what details to include or exclude.

Even when you have sharply limited your subject, you must still do
more. You must choose some method of development which will most clearly
accomplish your purpose. Naturally, not all subjects can be developed in
the same way. Some require a definition of terms and a serious, critical
approach. For example, in discussing the aims of education, Alfred North
Whitehead wrote this paragraph:

> Style, in its finest sense, is the last acquirement of the educated mind;
> it is also the most useful. It pervades the whole being. The administrator
> with a sense of style hates waste; the engineer with a sense of style econo-
> mizes his material; the artisan with a sense of style prefers good work.
> Style is the ultimate morality of mind.

Had Whitehead been writing with less formality, been addressing a less
cultivated audience, or dealing with a different subject, he might have
supplied narrative or descriptive details instead of direct exposition. The
subject of democracy is at least as important and abstract as that of style,
yet E. B. White used a narrative, humorous approach:

> We received a letter from the Writers' War Board the other day asking
> for a statement on "The Meaning of Democracy." It presumably is our duty
> to comply with such a request, and it is certainly our pleasure.
> Surely the Board knows what democracy is. It is the line that forms on
> the right. It is the *don't* in don't shove. It is the hole in the stuffed shirt
> through which the sawdust slowly trickles; it is the dent in the high hat.
> Democracy is the recurrent suspicion that more than half of the people are
> right more than half of the time.

It is the feeling of privacy in the voting booths, the feeling of communion in the libraries, the feeling of vitality everywhere. Democracy is a letter to the editor. Democracy is the score at the beginning of the ninth. It is an idea which hasn't been disproved yet, a song the words of which have not gone bad. It's the mustard on the hot dog and the cream in the rationed coffee. Democracy is a request from a War Board, in the middle of the morning in the middle of a war, wanting to know what democracy is.

Some subjects can best be developed ironically, some humorously. Others require narrative and descriptive details, still others analogy, or comparison, or contrast.

Having limited and sharply focused your theme topic and chosen a method of development, you now face the always challenging problem of securing ample substance for its development. You must have something to say, perhaps more than you really need or can use, before you can write effectively. Lack of purpose, vagueness, and lack of interest inevitably result from lack of ample substance, full detail. But unless you have a special knowledge of your subject, you will find that securing ample substance requires considerable time and effort. The successful theme-writer will exert genuine effort in collecting material for his theme *before* he actually begins to write.

Many students feel that their own ideas and experiences are not significant or interesting. Others have a false modesty, and so refuse to consider subjects in terms of their own experience. Actually, personal experience has a freshness and interest for the writer which are likely to be most effectively conveyed to the reader. One does not necessarily have an inflated ego when he uses experiences of his own as illustrative material. Significant and interesting material can and should be drawn from the writer's own *observation, curiosity, imagination,* and *reflection.*

Indeed, it is impossible for one to write wholly objectively; the writer necessarily puts something of himself into everything he writes. The more of himself he puts into his writing—that is, his own ideas, reactions, and observations—the more likely he is to write with full, interesting, concrete detail. There is no better source of substance than one's own self.

Although a writer necessarily gathers substance from himself, he should not neglect the material he may derive from others, unless he is an acknowledged authority on the particular subject being treated.

The easiest and perhaps most pleasant way of getting material for themes from other people is *discussion*. This may take the form of an *interview* in which the ideas of the interviewed person may constitute almost the whole of the theme. (See pp. 157–159.) Or it may be merely a *conversation* with a member of your family, an acquaintance, or an instructor, in which there is an interchange of ideas, a give-and-take which results in clarified and expanded thought. Classroom discussions are often an excellent source of material for compositions.

The other important way of getting substance from people is reading. Magazines, newspapers, and books are almost inexhaustible sources of material which may be utilized. Half-formed ideas of your own may be intensified and expanded by reading. Entirely new phases of thought may be suggested, which, when put through the hopper of your mind, may legitimately be used as your own. Likewise, you may obtain material for themes from television programs, motion pictures, and plays. Although these are not usually read, they do constitute the experiences and thoughts of other people, and as such are a fruitful source of substance.

In drawing upon the experiences and impressions of others, be careful to make them your own. That is, strive to assimilate the ideas and then express them in your own words, unless you quote directly and mention sources. When you make use of an idea new to you, acknowledge your indebtedness courteously and fully. Sometimes a phrase is sufficient: "As Thomas Carlyle points out in *The French Revolution, . . .*" or "These novelists, Joseph Warren Beach says in *American Fiction, 1920–1940,* were profoundly affected by the social conditions. . . ." Sometimes—in a research paper, for example—fuller acknowledgment is necessary; for the proper method and forms of documentation in research papers, see pp. 265–271. The charge of plagiarism must be avoided; taking the ideas and words of another and passing them off as your own is plagiarism. See 38b.

After you have gathered material suitable for your predetermined purpose, you must outline what you have collected and correctly proportion it. These two important concerns are discussed in 39 and 40, pp. 253–257. They need not be treated here, but the importance of outlining and proportion require that you study carefully both sections referred to.

BEGINNING THE THEME

After you have gathered material and correctly outlined and proportioned this substance, you are faced with the problem of *beginning* the composition.

A theme *does* have a beginning, a middle, and an end. Do not make the mistake of thinking that the body of a theme is the only important element and that beginnings and endings are merely tacked on as appendages. Prefixes and suffixes are very real parts of words; likewise, the introduction and conclusion of a theme are of genuine importance to the whole theme.

Do not, however, write an introduction unless your theme requires one. Avoid writing a formal beginning for every theme, because, usually, only long papers require extended definition of terms, or a history of the subject, or a long statement of its significance. Be careful not to make a formal series of general statements or to give needless explanations and details. Of course, you must not bewilder your reader by beginning so abruptly that he is unable to understand what follows. If antecedent details are needed, you must give them.

At the end of the first paragraph, will your reader have his bearings? Will he know where he is and in what direction he is moving? If not, make another start.

Some experienced teachers encourage students to jot down memoranda when starting a theme. Such jottings help to get more specific and concrete data which can be organized more effectively.

To begin at the beginning, directly and clearly, is not easy. Many writers ramble for some time before they warm to their subject and really come to grips with it. But if you will think through what you have to say, you can make the important opening position really count by attacking the heart of the subject, thus avoiding false starts and loose generalities. Note the directness of the following beginnings of themes on the subject "Television Advertising":

1. Of all forms of advertising, television commercials are the most blatant and least effective.
2. Although some of my fellow students think that such telecasting is an unalloyed blessing, it should be pointed out to them that advertisers have usurped the supposedly free air for personal gain.
3. Everyone is familiar with television, but not everyone realizes that programs are used not only to give information and entertainment, but also to enrich those who prepare, present, and pay for them.

A good beginning gains the reader's attention and so interests him that he wishes to continue reading. Perhaps the most commonly used opening is either a combination of narrative and descriptive details or a summary of the ideas to follow. The former method is illustrated in this paragraph from the late Frederick Lewis Allen's biography of J. P. Morgan:

> During the summer and autumn of 1897 there came a change in the economic weather. It was something like the change which comes when, after many a day of rain and wind and fitful sunshine and renewed storm, suddenly the wind veers into another quarter, the clouds begin to break and scatter, patches of deep blue sky appear, and men and women walk with a fresh briskness. For more than four years following the Panic of 1893 America had been beset with depression, unemployment, unrest, and uncertainty; brief recoveries had been followed by renewed distress; now, all at once, men began to look ahead with lively hope. On this new tide of confidence J. Pierpont Morgan, the mightiest banker in America, was to rise to the crest of his power and prestige.

The use of a summary paragraph involving both narrative and descriptive details is exemplified by the following opening for an article on skiing by Eric Swenson:

> Late last autumn, when the first snow flurries dusted across the northern half of the United States, an estimated three million pairs of knees began to twitch. This mass flexing was the first symptom of a seasonal phenomenon that has progressed in twenty years from the status of a foreign foolishness to that of a national mania. Although still in early stages of development, this phenomenon has reversed migratory instincts, cut scars in the faces of ancient mountains, created an economic revolution in rural areas, upped the income of the medical profession, and released several million inmates of modern society into flights of ecstatic freedom.

A direct beginning is usually effective, but there are several other specific ways in which emphasis may be gained.

1. An illustrative *incident* is always effective because people are interested in narrative. A well-chosen *anecdote* will gain the reader's interest and at the same time illustrate the theme itself. Many of the best writers begin articles in this way; an issue of a magazine such as *Harper's, The New Yorker,* or the *Atlantic Monthly* will contain several articles which have narrative leads. The selections in this volume by Feibleman, p. 658,

Stoke, p. 669, Smith, p. 678, Thoreau, p. 684, White, p. 690, Baker, p. 705, Muir, p. 696, Reston, p. 715, Bishop, p. 720, and Kennedy, p. 814, have different forms of narrative beginnings. Study them.

2. A *startling or paradoxical statement* is usually an effective beginning. It secures attention and arouses interest. But such statements should not be used only to gain interest; they should have some connection with what is to follow. In varying forms, the following selections in this volume have startling or paradoxical beginnings: "Snapshot of America," p. 532, "Why a Classic Is a Classic," p. 611, and "The Case for Greater Clarity in Writing," p. 654.

3. A direct *personal appeal* is effective because people are always interested in themselves. The selections by McGuire, Osler, and Shores, beginning respectively on pp. 554, 601, and 615, have leads that are directly or indirectly personal.

4. *The report of a conversation,* or *quoted material* of some kind, such as an apt, familiar quotation, or an exclamation, is often effective. Selections in this volume which begin with quoted material of one sort or another may be found on pp. 633 and 779; the authors responsible are Robert Cluett and Mary McCarthy.

ENDING THE THEME

The important thing to remember in ending themes is this: When you have said all you intended to say, stop. Do not write a conclusion simply for the sake of the conclusion. A short composition usually requires no formal conclusion; a summarizing sentence will suffice. A rambling and wordy ending will destroy the effect of what has been said. Except in argumentative writing, there can be little excuse for such phrases as "thus we see" or "in conclusion, let me state." Do you remember the story of the guest who lingered at the door mumbling, "There was something else I wanted to say"? To this the hostess made the apt response, "Perhaps it was *good-by.*"

Do not make the ending too abrupt, however; that is, leave an impression of completeness, of having rounded out a discussion and reached a goal.

In other words, although short compositions do not usually require formal conclusions, they should end effectively. This means not only that they should not end too abruptly but also that the ending, because of its very position, should contain a thought of such importance that it is a real contribution to the theme. For example, the closing statement generally should deal with the main thought of the composition, not with some minor detail of the discussion. In well-planned themes, afterthoughts are never so important as main thoughts.

Effective endings may be attained by sentences which summarize or clinch the *theme* of the composition, by sentences which show that the subject has some new or practical application, or by sentences which link the subject with some matter of current interest. Actually, the beginning and ending of a well-planned theme can be interchangeable.

Every selection in the latter part of this volume has a strong and effective ending, although understandably some are more effective than others. To discover the extraordinary variety of endings available to you, study the conclusions of pieces by Bronowski, p. 477, Huff, p. 504, Highet, p. 510, Krutch, p. 557, Clarke, p. 564, Sherwood, p. 618, Fadiman, p. 747, Kennedy, p. 814, and Orwell, p. 840.

Keep in mind that endings, like beginnings, are genuinely important parts of themes if for no other reason than that they are analogous to first and last impressions. Do not all of us remember best about other people either our first or last glimpses of them, or both? Introductions and conclusions of all short themes should be direct, clear, and unobtrusive. They should be neither abrupt nor diffuse. In a 500-word theme, every sentence should count; there is no room for waste motion. But a concise and emphatic beginning and an equally effective ending to a theme can cover up loose and ineffective material that is tucked in between them.

EFFECTIVENESS

If a composition is correctly, clearly, and fully expressed and coherently arranged, it will usually be decisive and striking. Ample substance expressed with correctness and clearness is not always effective, however; you must never forget that in order to communicate ideas you must *interest* your readers. Many students, with the aid of textbooks and instructors, learn to write correctly and clearly; comparatively few achieve the ability to express their ideas in such a manner as to gain and hold the attention of their readers.

The title of an opera by Verdi, *Aïda,* contains the letters of a mnemonic device which you should remember: A—Attention; I—Interest; D—Desire; A—Action. That is, a theme should first command the *attention* of the reader, then attract his *interest* so that he will actually *desire* to read it and perhaps be led to agree or disagree with what is said, or wish to take *action* suggested by the theme, or fall in with whatever your purpose is.

Such effectiveness in writing is dependent upon correctness and clarity, but their presence does not insure force; this can be achieved, however, by the proper position and proportion of ideas, and by statements which are expressed definitely and with animation.

Many papers which are reasonably correct and clear are not genuinely effective because of abstractness, indefiniteness. Good writing is definite, concrete; it contains specific details which arouse interest. In other words, it either contains facts or conveys a sense of fact. A composition on taxation will hardly be effective so long as you abstractly discuss the theory of taxation; but when you make a statement such as this you make your work come alive: "Whether or not you own real property, you pay taxes. According to a recent estimate, the citizens of our town paid an average tax of $850 this past year."

Specific answers to the questions Who? What? Where? When? Why? How? always achieve effectiveness. They furnish realistic touches and clear imagery, which the reader has a right to expect. Note the difference in effectiveness between these two excerpts taken from student themes:

1. My roommate was selfish. He cared nothing for me or anyone else and was completely absorbed in looking out for his own interests.
2. John was selfish. He borrowed my neckties and razor blades, sometimes without asking permission, but he hated for me to borrow even a sheet of paper from him. When he had to get up for an early class, he walked around noisily and made no effort to keep from waking me. But he grumbled for ten minutes one morning when I accidentally dropped my history book and waked him.

These suggestions can help you convey an actual sense of fact: (1) enumerate specific details; (2) narrate specific incidents; (3) use comparison and contrast; (4) show definite relationships of causes and effects.

Writing which is studded with facts may be very dull and lifeless. History books are commonly considered dull, for example, but they are certainly not thin in facts. Neither are stock market statistics, or insurance reports, or legal briefs. But none of these is interesting, effective, *alive*. They have little dramatic effect, human interest, movement, humor, satire, or any of the other qualities which make writing more than merely readable. Not every writer can be humorous or satirical or urbane, but everyone can make occasional use of dialogue, or of a series of questions or exclamations, and everyone can get *movement* of some kind into his narrative and descriptive writing. Study the following:

1. She was not certain that she should have stopped payment on the check. She thought she might be sued for nonpayment.

Should she have stopped the check? What could Mr. Jones do to her? What would he do? Oh, if only she could get her father's advice!

2. The house had been freshly painted and shone in the afternoon sun.

"I see you have had your house painted, Mr. Dodge."
"Yes, Lem and I decided a fresh coat of green and white would help, so we bought paint and brushes and did the job ourselves."
"Did you, indeed? Well, the house certainly does look lovely in the afternoon sun."

3. A friend of mine was talking to a theatrical agent who was not particularly distinguished for the range or choice of his vocabulary. He was therefore a little startled to hear the word *eclectic* suddenly pop out.
"Joe! Where did you get hold of that elegant word?"
"*Eclectic?* Oh, I just happened to come across it in the dictionary."
"What do you mean you *just* happened to come across it in the dictionary?"
"Well, you see, I was looking up the word *egregious* and on my way to *egregious* my eye caught the word *eclectic* and I liked it."
"O.K. But how did you *happen* to be looking up the word *egregious?*"
"I always look up the word *egregious!*"

—*Pleasures in Learning,*
a publication of New York University

4. Startled by a cop, this same comedian might grab his hatbrim with both hands and yank it down over his ears, jump high in the air, come to earth in a split violent enough to telescope his spine, spring thence into a

coattail-flattening sprint and dwindle at rocket speed to the size of a gnat along the grand, forlorn perspective of some lazy back boulevard.

—JAMES AGEE, *Agee on Film*

Parallel structure is also a valuable aid in gaining effectiveness because of the obvious similarity it gives to related ideas.

Note the repetition of words and structure in the following:

Verse is patterned language. That is, verse is composition in which words are arranged according to a pattern, a form which is metrical, rhythmical. Verse may be mere doggerel, such as

"Here lies the body of Samuel Blank;
He dropped a match in a gasoline tank."

These lines are verse because they consist of words arranged according to a pattern.

Poetry is patterned language, plus. That is, poetry is composition arranged in a pattern. But poetry is more than verse. It signifies high thought, imagination, or emotion.

"Heard melodies are sweet, but those unheard
Are sweeter; therefore, ye soft pipes, play on."

These lines are poetry because they are patterned language which contains genuine thought and imagination. All poetry is verse, but not all verse can be called poetry.

Avoid a long series of paragraphs which are similar in structure, however. Variety in paragraph structure is fully as desirable as variety in sentence structure. Just as a reader will tire of pages with no paragraph breaks at all, he will lose interest in a group of paragraphs which are monotonously similar in construction.

Avoid excessive use of the passive voice (see p. 331). To say "A trip was made" when you mean "I made a trip" is to commit a structural fault which is simple and easy to correct. Students overuse the passive voice and the verbs *to be, to make, to have, to do,* and *to cause.* Use verbs in the active voice whenever you want to imply action, mental or physical, unless the point of the sentence is to represent the subject as being acted upon. A needless shift from active to passive voice confounds the sense: "I started up and a scream was heard." No reader can tell who screamed, who heard, whether the scream was involuntary or took the speaker by surprise. When encountering such a sentence, the reader could hardly care less.

Several suggestions for increasing the effectiveness of your style are given in Chapter 6. You are here and now urged to consider them carefully as you evaluate the appeal of any composition you are planning to write or have written. Also, Sections 40–44 of the Handbook contain recommendations designed to help you add vigor and appeal to your style. Study them, too.

THE TITLE

Just as a topic sentence is frequently helpful in keeping you on the track within the paragraph, a well-chosen title may help you stick to your subject throughout a theme.

But the title has another important function. A well-chosen title is a most effective means of gaining the attention of the reader. Who has not been led to read a certain book, magazine article, or story because of its attractive title? Motion-picture and television producers frequently have paid large sums of money merely for the use of an effective title. Give your theme a good title, not a mere tag, and you have already taken an important step in making the whole composition more effective.

The term *subject* is broader and more inclusive than the word *title*. If the instructor asks for a composition on "My Reading Habits," he has assigned a *subject,* not a *title,* and you should sharpen this subject to a more specific and more interesting title. Conversely, if the actual title of a theme is assigned, you must discover precisely what subject it covers. Do not assume that the title of a specific theme should be the same as a general subject which has been assigned. The best titles indicate not a general subject but the actual theme of the composition.

It is impossible, of course, for a title to mention everything which the theme contains. But a title should not be misleading; it should give at least a hint of the contents of the theme. Do not announce a title and then develop ideas which have no relation whatever to that title. Motion pictures and novels are often misleadingly titled in an effort to attract attention, but you can usually phrase an effective title without any such subterfuge.

As has been pointed out, a good title is a most effective aid in interesting the reader. Occasionally, writers neglect to employ this aid to interest by using titles which are too *long:* "How To While Away an Afternoon Among the Stacks of the Belton Library" is certainly less effective than "Browsing in the Belton Library." Other writers may use titles which are too *vague* and *commonplace:* "College Athletics Are Overemphasized," "A Camping Trip," "The Federal Constitution," "Contemporary Morals."

To be effective, a title must usually be short and fresh and definite. Note these titles:

1. "Socrates Crosses the Delaware." (An article about the "great books" program at St. John's College, Maryland.)
2. *Rich Land, Poor Land.* (A study of America's natural resources.)
3. "The Great Sports Myth." (A criticism of the American system of sports.)
4. "That Burrowing Bean." (An article about peanuts.)
5. *Only Yesterday.* (An informal history of the 1920's.)
6. "I Love Him!" (A profile of a popular religious leader.)

The title is independent of the composition. In a theme called "My European Journey," do not begin, "This trip was the most . . ." The first sentence should be complete in itself: "My trip to Europe was the most . . ." Center the title on the page and leave a space between it and the first line of the theme. Capitalize important words, but do not italicize the title or enclose it in quotation marks (unless it is itself a quotation) except when you refer to it in the theme. Do not place a period after the title; a question mark or exclamation point may be used if needed. See Section 36a.

REVISION

"There is no such thing as good writing; there is only good *rewriting*."
Many students are likely to object to such a statement; they will recall a
time when they really "got going" and turned out a first and only draft
which was superior to anything they had laboriously revised, or they will
recall having heard that Scott or O. Henry or this or that writer never
rewrote. But the statement is sound and capable of proof.

A. E. Housman told this interesting story about one of his poems:
"I happen to remember distinctly the genesis of the piece which stands last
in my first volume. Two of the stanzas, I do not say which, came into my
head, just as they are printed, while I was crossing the corner of Hampstead
Heath between the Spaniard's Inn and the footpath to Temple Fortune. A
third stanza came with a little coaxing after tea. One more was needed, but
it did not come: I had to turn to and compose it myself, and that was a
laborious business. I wrote it thirteen times, and it was more than a twelvemonth before I got it right."

Frequently a student will say: "I wrote this theme in an hour and got
a C grade on it; my last week's theme took me three hours and yet was
marked D." Such an instance is offered as proof that revision does not pay,
is not worth the effort it requires. But, nine times out of ten, the writer of
a good "hour" theme has composed his theme before actually writing it.
He has thought it through many times; he has, as Charles A. Brooks puts
it, composed "on the hoof." He has collected something to say, perhaps
unconsciously, and has secured some real interest in saying that something.
His "quickly written" theme is thus not quickly written at all.

No one, not even an accomplished professional writer, can plan, write,
and proofread a theme all at one time. Perhaps the best plan to follow
is this: First, gather material for your theme and then plan and arrange
it. Next, without paying special attention to grammatical, rhetorical, or
mechanical details, write the theme with all the vigor and interest you can.
After that, and preferably some time later, revise the theme carefully. "Easy
writing makes hard reading; hard writing makes easy reading."

As is stated many times in this book, writing *is* hard work. A naive
and inexperienced person tends to think that a writer just writes and that
something is wrong with him if his words do not pour out on paper. And
yet most writers, and certainly most skilled professional writers, have testified that writing is painful, laborious, time-consuming labor. If an experienced professional writer can get on paper only a few hundred words during
a full working day, he feels encouraged and even elated. Consider this
comment from a Nobel-Prize winner, John Steinbeck:

> Many years of preparation preceded the writing of *Grapes of Wrath*.
> I wrote it in one hundred days, but the preparation, false starts, and wasted
> motion took two and a half years. The actual writing is the last process.

Only three kinds of alterations are possible when you revise a theme.
You can *substitute*, you can *delete*, and you can *insert*. But when your
reasons for making such changes are taken into account, subdivisions

appear. One such subdivision consists of the "mopping up" operations mentioned on pp. 246–247. Another group of alterations consists of efforts to achieve greater accuracy of expression, or more clarity, or to drive home to your reader more forcefully a particular point or impression. In this kind of revision, you check and recheck your choice of words; you revise the structure and word order of a sentence or group of sentences; you alter a figure of speech to make an image clearer or sharper; you add an incident or anecdote to illustrate or reinforce an idea or remove one which seems stale and ineffective; you alter the position of sentences within paragraphs or the order of paragraphs in the theme.

Rewriting is often a grueling process, especially when it causes you to destroy entire sentences or paragraphs. Such drastic treatment may be more than you can bring yourself to accept at this stage of your writing development. If your writing aims are not high now, perhaps they will become so later. Until then, you can settle for no less than minimum standards.

Any student who uses a reference book and a dictionary should be able to write at least *correctly*. But in the haste of composing a first draft, the writer frequently makes careless slips which are not due to ignorance. Careless errors should be corrected *before* the theme is submitted. Go through the theme once for the sole purpose of making sure that all the words are *spelled correctly*. Read it through again to insure correct *punctuation* and *mechanics*. Pay special attention to commas.

Read the theme again to improve the sentences, their diction and structure. Make sure that all the sentences are unified and complete; that there are no "period-fault," "comma-fault," or "fused" sentences; and that the sentences are clearly and effectively phrased.

Read the theme for the fourth time in order to make sure that it is unified, coherent, and effective as a whole. Delete the extraneous material; rephrase all vague or rambling thoughts; substitute specific details for vague generalities.

Finally, read the theme aloud to yourself. The ear is often more sensitive to unreadable or faulty sentences than is the eye.

If you are a person who, in reading your theme aloud, is likely to give it a satisfactory interpretation regardless of how poorly it may be written, different advice might help. Try having a friend read your theme to you; you can judge from the reader's interpretation whether the communication is registering correctly and effectively.

Allow as much time as possible to elapse between writing the theme and revising it. If there is sufficient time between the two steps (the actual composition and the suggested rereadings), you will see errors which were not apparent to you when you had just completed writing it. You can approach your theme more objectively; errors not seen before will be prominent. Every writer has noted that he can detect errors in another's work more easily than he can in his own. If you will allow your work to "jell," you can see it almost as objectively as you can the compositions of someone else.

The following statistics should effectively illustrate the need for revision. Sixty-six freshman themes, chosen at random and graded from A to F, revealed the following errors in correctness alone:

1. Misspelled words: average per theme, 3.
2. Errors in use of comma, 8.
3. Errors in use of terminal marks of punctuation, 3.
4. All other errors in punctuation and mechanics, 3.
5. Grammatical errors, 6.

An average of 23 errors per theme in spelling, punctuation, mechanics, and grammar! Ten of the 66 themes contained three or fewer such errors; five of them contained more than 50!

Twenty-three seems a large number of errors. But there is a significant explanation; each of the 66 themes was written impromptu, in less than one hour. And an even more revealing fact is that the same 66 students averaged approximately one-half fewer errors in correctness on themes prepared formally as homework assignments.

As a short cut to more rapid improvement in writing, concentrate on the 12 items mentioned on p. 246. You should check every theme against this list before handing it in. Such planned revision, small though it is, will have a tonic effect on your writing—and on the grades which it receives.

If you will further check your writing against the suggestions given in Sections 36–44 of the Handbook and against comments on style in Chapter 6, you will be taking added steps on the way to becoming a really efficient writer. Your own satisfaction, your instructor's pleasure, and your grades should grow proportionately and happily.

Do not underestimate the value of a conference with your instructor in which one or more of your themes receives careful, pinpointed consideration. Your teacher's reactions to what you have written and his comments about it can be invaluable aids in your rewriting of a completed theme and also in revision of future work before it is submitted. If, for example, your instructor suggests that your theme really begins on page 3 and that all that goes before is largely verbiage, go ahead, groan—but don't argue. He really does know more about writing than you do and, in addition, is trying to help you, not hurt you. In a conference it is quite all right to insist "That's not what I meant at all; this is what I intended to say." Your teacher will encourage you to discover and comment on differences between your intention and accomplishment. But if you argue with your instructor, trying to justify or rationalize errors and mistakes, you will waste his time and your own, losing the benefits of a potentially valuable learning opportunity.

Another friendly suggestion is this: never say to your instructor "I spent four [or six, or whatever] hours on this theme and still I got a low mark." What might be forgiven as the result of a careless hour is damning when considered as the product of a day's work.

Ordinarily, however, your English teacher and your English class will allow you more freedom of thought than you are likely to find in any other formal learning situation on campus. More often with your English instructor than with any other college official can you "open up" in a conference, because he is interested in your life of thought and wants you honestly to reveal at least some part of it. Never overlook or downgrade the opportunity for improvement which candid interchange can provide. One reason so many students find the English classroom a rewarding spot during their first college year is that there, more than in many other college learning situations, they can escape the penalties and cautions which our competitive culture enforces. The opportunity to reshape and revise your work in conference should be looked upon not as a wearisome task but as a bright and helpful experience.

· EXERCISES ·

The exercises given here and elsewhere throughout this volume are purposely numerous and varied. Their number and variety permit selecting only those most needed at a particular time.

WHAT TO WRITE ABOUT

A. Make a list of five incidents in your life which you think might be interesting to your readers: your instructor and the members of your class.

B. List five subjects about which you think you know details not known to your classmates.

C. Make a list of conventional theme topics which you think are trite and uninteresting ("My Summer in Camp," "A Fishing Trip," "A Dream I Had," etc.).

D. Apply the three tests for topics to the following suggestions for themes and suggest what readers you have in mind:

1. An interview with a well-known campus personality.
2. An account of a visit to a law court during a criminal trial.
3. The history, including a description, of one of the buildings of the college.
4. A description and character sketch of one of the best-known employees of the college.
5. A description of the college cafeteria during the luncheon hour.
6. A description of college "types": the athlete, the aesthete, the iconoclast, the bluffer, the beatnik.
7. A description of, and commentary upon, a popular television program.
8. A criticism of a motion picture currently being shown.
9. An account of the conversation among a group of friends after a college dance.
10. A commentary upon the "easiest" and the "most difficult" courses and professors in the college.
11. My Favorite Magazine, and Why.
12. Why I Am a Liberal (a Reactionary, a Radical).
13. My Pet Aversion (radio crooners, tabloid newspapers, practical jokes, eight-o'clock classes, tourist camps, etc.).
14. An account of how you budget your time for a day, a week, a month of college life.
15. What I want to be, and to be doing, 10 years from now.
16. What I expect to be, and to be doing, 10 years from now.
17. The greatest personal disaster I can imagine.
18. A list of five books (with reasons for their choice) which I should like to take with me if I were to be marooned on a desert island for the rest of my life.
19. The qualities I shall want my wife (husband) to have.
20. The Ideal English Composition Course.

E. Using the following official or unofficial American holidays as general subjects, for each write three to five limited topics which you think will interest specific readers whom you designate: New Year's Eve, New Year's Day, Lincoln's Birthday, Washington's Birthday, St. Patrick's Day, Good Friday, Easter, April

Fool's Day, May Day, Memorial Day, Fourth of July, August Vacation Days, Labor Day, Columbus Day, Homecoming, Halloween, Armed Services Day, Thanksgiving, Christmas Eve, Christmas Day.

F. Prepare a list of 10 limited theme topics designed to be developed by telling a story (narrative); 10 designed to be developed by giving a picture in words (description); 10 to be developed by explaining (exposition); 10 to be developed by convincing (argument).

G. Using the following as general subjects, for each write three to five limited topics which you think will interest specific readers whom you designate: Animals, Athletics, Atoms, Bravery, Business, Campus Activities, Childhood, Contests, Education, Food, Friends, Health, Heroes, Illness, Medicine, Memories, Missiles, Moon Shots, Music, Nature, Night, One Week, Personal Experience, Recreation, Relatives, Soil Conservation, Sorrow, Success, Superstition, Tall Stories, Vacations, Weather.

GETTING MATERIAL FOR WRITING

A. Comment on the following as the readers for whom papers in the past have been written, according to students in freshman English classes. Which seem appropriate or inappropriate, which too general, and which properly specific? (1) Anyone who has an older sister. (2) Anyone who has a young brother. (3) Anyone with patience. (4) People who have not lived on a farm. (5) Any unmarried person. (6) Basketball lovers. (7) Anyone interested in traveling to Mexico. (8) A boy or girl, 14 to 17 years old. (9) A pen pal in England. (10) Anyone not from New York City.

B. Restrict the following broad subjects to some phase which can be treated within the limits of a theme-length paper:
1. Communism in America—Past and Present.
2. The Cosmetics Industry.
3. How People Lived in the Depression '30's.
4. My College Career.
5. Games of Chance.
6. Campus Politics.
7. Campus Activities.
8. Academic Activities.
9. Misunderstandings Between Americans and Europeans.
10. TV Advertising.
11. The Motion Picture Industry.
12. Atomic Energy.
13. Atomic Weapons.
14. Weekend Recreations.
15. National and State Parks.

C. Using one of the limited subjects you have prepared for Exercise B, discuss various methods of development to suit different purposes and different kinds of readers.

D. Make a list of 10 subjects which are likely to be uninteresting to your fellow students. Mention methods of analysis and treatment which might make these subjects interesting.

E. Mention some personal experience or incident you have witnessed that could be used in developing a theme based on one of the following topics:
Social Fraternities Should (Should Not) Be Abolished.
Few Athletes Are Good Students.
Buying Secondhand Furniture.

The Care and Feeding of Co-eds.
The Value of a Time Budget.
My First Afternoon in Chemistry Lab.

F. Name a book, magazine article, motion picture, or play from which ideas might be drawn for a theme dealing with:

Underprivileged Children.
Social Injustice.
Man's Greed.
The Horror of Dictatorships.
Safe Automobile Driving.

G. What is the most successful theme you have written? How much of its material was based upon personal thought and experience? How much was derived from other people?

H. "The process of writing is more a rejection than a selection of detail." Discuss this statement.

Beginning and Ending the Theme

A. Select from the readings in this volume three essays or articles which seem to you to have effective beginnings.

B. Select, as in Exercise A, three effective endings.

C. Analyze the beginning and ending of one of your recent themes. If necessary, rewrite both introduction and conclusion, making them more direct, clear, and effective.

Effectiveness

A. From the readings in this volume select the three most effective articles; three informal essays; three short stories; three poems.

B. What are the psychological bases for the effectiveness in themes of dialogue, of movement or an effect of movement, of narrative detail?

C. Does the discussion in this chapter help to account for the difference in people's interest in the news columns of a daily paper as contrasted with their interest in editorials?

D. Analyze one issue of *Time* ("the weekly newsmagazine") in order to determine the reasons for its frequently effective style.

The Title

A. Make a list of several television programs and motion pictures which you think have good titles.

B. Make the following titles more interesting and effective:

1. A Day in New York City.	11. A Theme About Myself.
2. Spring Sports.	12. Thoughtfulness.
3. A Canoeing Trip.	13. Autumn Activities on the Farm.
4. Flying.	14. Aboard Ship.
5. Why I Came to College.	15. My Budget.
6. Cold Weather.	16. Campus Clothes.
7. My Religion.	17. A Rainy Day.
8. Spending Money.	18. Study Habits.
9. TV Programs I Dislike.	19. Blind Dates.
10. Table Manners.	20. College Vacations.

C. Select from among the titles of articles in this volume the 10 which seem most descriptive and arresting.

D. In the same way, select 10 titles of poems.

Revision

A. Find out what you can about the amount of revision done by Robert Louis Stevenson, Benvenuto Cellini (see his *Autobiography*), John Galsworthy, Thomas Hardy, Samuel Butler, George Eliot, Henry James, or any modern essayist or short-story writer.

B. Make an honest analysis of the time spent on various themes of yours. Estimate the amount of time spent on "thinking before writing," the actual time spent in writing and in revising.

C. "Technical errors hinder communication in writing as much as stammering does in conversation." Discuss the meaning and application of this statement.

CHAPTER 3

WRITING THE PARAGRAPH

Good paragraphing is essential for clarity and effectiveness. Properly separated groups of sentences enable the writer to plot his course and see the progress he is making. They serve the reader by making the structure and development of ideas easily apparent. Paragraphing involves some of the principles of punctuation in that it separates certain ideas from others because of their structural relationships, thus furnishing the reader signposts or road markers to guide him along the paths of thought which the writer is developing. A series of carefully constructed paragraphs aids clarity just as does a series of correctly punctuated sentences: by developing ideas so that the reader, following the signs laid out for him, can obtain, quickly and clearly, a grasp of the parts and of the whole which they constitute.

THE PARAGRAPH DEFINED

Thus, a paragraph may be called both a visual unit—a group, or bundle, of sentences tied together for the convenience of the reader—*and* a sequence of structurally related sentences, a logical entity developing one thought or a part of one thought. The structural unit of the paragraph is the sentence; the structural unit of a theme is the paragraph. Inasmuch as a theme has, or should have, a central dominant aim, one particular point to make or idea to reveal, it follows that each paragraph within a theme is likely to develop only one phase of this central thought rather than a concept considered complete and final in itself. For this reason, training in writing paragraphs is often begun with assignments requiring the development of a single idea, with building one paragraph which can stand alone but may be one of a group if complete treatment of the subject permits or demands such expansion.

The sentence is the unit of writing, but the paragraph is the unit of thought. In fact, the very heart of learning to write effectively is found in paragraph development. The secret of the effective writer—if he may be said to have a secret—is his ability to form a thought, however fragmentary or vague, and then develop it so that it is clear and both helpful and interesting to his readers. Hasn't everyone had the experience of making a statement or writing a sentence and then halting, aware that it needs expansion, certain that the one idea standing alone seems bare and incomplete but not knowing what to say or write to "flesh it out"? This problem, and only this problem, may be called the core of the writing process. In truth, it's what freshman English is all about. It's what any course in writing and most courses in speaking and all the reading you do are all about.

Suppose, for example, the thought occurs to you, as well it might, "The calendar is a foolish invention." But if you express this idea to yourself or say it aloud to someone, it stands naked and forlorn, obviously needing further comment. Can you explain what you mean? Add a thought or two to it? Build it into a paragraph? After some thought, you may at least be able to write this much:

> The calendar is a foolish invention. It tells us that the new year begins in winter. But everyone knows that school and business start afresh in the autumn, and nature has its renaissance in spring.

This is still a weak and only partly clothed idea, but it does have a little something to wear.

Again, suppose that you have just finished reading MacLeish's "Loyalty and Freedom," p. 543. Musing over the types of freedom envisioned by the Founding Fathers of our nation, you may think that your own freedom today seems sharply limited. This is certainly a tenable idea. What can you say or write to make clear and emphatic what you have in mind? Here is what a capable writer, John Ciardi, has said on this subject:

> Americans are still born free, but their freedom neither lasts as long nor goes as far as it used to. Once the infant is smacked on the bottom and lets out his first taxable howl, he is immediately tagged, footprinted, blood-tested, classified, certificated, and generally taken in census. By the time that squawler has drawn the breath of adulthood he must have some clerk's permission to go to school or stay away, ride a bike, drive a car, collect his salary, carry a gun, fish, get married, go into the army or stay out, leave or re-enter the country, fly a plane, operate a power boat or a ham radio, buy a piece of land, build a house or knock one down, add a room to the house he has bought, burn his trash, park his car, keep a dog, run his business, go bankrupt, practice a profession, pick the wildflowers, bury the garbage, beg in the streets, sell whiskey in his store, peddle magazines from house to house, walk across a turnpike from one of his fields to another now that

the state has divided him—the list is endless. Even in death his corpse must be certificated and licensed before the earth may swallow him legally. Freedom is no longer free but licensed.

Perhaps after reading Huxley's "The Method of Scientific Investigation," p. 470, or "The Nature of Science," p. 520, you may reflect that you never have been able to understand why Nature is usually considered benevolent when you have often found her quite the opposite. This is a legitimate concept; can you explain what you mean? Perhaps so, perhaps not. This is a paragraph from what Eric Hoffer said in an article about his war with nature:

All through adult life I have had a feeling of revulsion when told how nature aids and guides us, how like a stern mother she nudges and pushes man to fulfil her wise designs. As a migratory worker from the age of eighteen I knew nature as ill-disposed and inhospitable. If I stretched on the ground to rest, nature pushed its hard knuckles into my sides, and sent bugs, burrs, and foxtails to make me get up and be gone. As a placer miner I had to run the gantlet of buckbrush, manzanita, and poison oak when I left the road to find my way to a creek. Direct contact with nature almost always meant scratches, bites, torn clothes, and grime that ate its way into every pore of the body. To make life bearable I had to interpose a protective layer between myself and nature. On the paved road, even when miles from anywhere, I felt at home. I had a sense of kinship with the winding, endless road that cares not where it goes or what its load.

Or choose another illustration from Book Three. After reading Beard's "The Idea of Progress," p. 525, you may decide that although the idea of progress is indeed a "profound and germinal" one, you, for one, feel uneasy about the rapid changes evident everywhere. Can you express your fears in a sentence and develop them in a paragraph? Here is what a noted writer, E. B. White, managed to do with this concept:

We were encouraged at reading the prediction that this country would be out of gas in about ten years. There is probably nothing in the report. Still, it bucks a man up. We can now dismiss the revolting picture of the postwar world which has been painted for us—a world agitated by an unlimited supply of petrol and by the spirit of total motion. The automobile, the helicopter, the family plane, the stratoliner, and the folding house which flaps together and jumps around from place to place have been woven into a dream in Technicolor by the excitable prophets of industry. They push this dream down our throats at every turn of the page. Unless a man believes that the highest form of life is that which darts about, he can face the future only with an effort of will. As for us, we are an exponent of the sit-still, or stay-where-you-are, theory of life and have always had more respect for the horned toad than for the black ant. The bicycle is our idea of a decent acceleration of the normal body movements and the Model T Ford is the highest point to which we deem it advisable to develop the gas engine. We therefore hail with cries of unprincipled joy the news of the drying up of the wells. Ah, lovely wilderness, if only it were true!

By now, it should be clear that writing a good paragraph depends upon *effective thinking*. We must train our minds to deal fully and logically with an idea, or series of ideas, to develop concepts and relate them to each other.

Such thinking is not easy now and never was. And yet learning to write consists in large part of learning to think. One must use his mind. Poor though it may be, a mind is all any of us has for thinking.

Suppose, for example, that you have decided to write a character sketch of your friend George. Having made your decision, you then must ask, "What can I say about him?" After considerable mental anguish, you might come up with five statements about George, each of them indicating one phase of the subject. You phrase these thoughts:

1. He is tall, handsome, athletic.
2. He has always been interested in how things work and is now studying mechanical engineering at college.
3. He is generous and fun-loving but lacks will power.
4. The outstanding influence upon his life has been his mother, who has always pampered him and restrained his normal development.
5. He is completely sincere in his belief that success can be measured only in terms of money and consequently he cares little for so-called culture.

The five sentences about George will mean little to the reader until they are expanded into paragraphs. Their shaping and expansion require thought, more thought than is ordinarily used in conversation. Good paragraphs, which are fundamental to all good writing, are predicated upon clear thinking. These five ideas indicate different and interesting characteristics and will, perhaps, serve as the nucleus of an effective description. Your writing problem is to arrange and develop these statements and combine them into a whole. Your "developed" statements will be the paragraphs of your theme. Your theme will be as effective, and only as effective, as the individual paragraphs. It is as simple, and as difficult, as that.

A well-constructed paragraph, like good diction or a good sentence, should be *correct, clear,* and *effective*—characteristics dependent upon careful thinking. Such a statement may seem vague, but it has specific meaning if you thoroughly understand the elements which give paragraphs correctness, clearness, and effectiveness.

For convenience and ready reference, eight desirable paragraph characteristics are listed on p. 236 and developed in Sections 31–35. Each of these eight matters necessitates using your mind. If your paragraphs possess these eight qualities, they evidence careful thinking and resultant correctness, clarity, and effectiveness. If they do not, they reveal that you have been guilty of careless, insufficient thought, or ignorance, or laziness. In the remaining pages of this chapter and in Sections 31–35 you will find concrete suggestions for improving your handling of paragraphs. They are worth study solely because the paragraph is the central link between a sentence, the unit of writing, and the whole theme, the capstone of the entire process of writing in freshman English.

TOPIC SENTENCES

A topic sentence is a statement of the gist of the paragraph; it contains the heart of the idea which is to be, is being, or has been, developed. It does not mention everything that the paragraph contains, nor does it summarize the full contents of the paragraph. A topic sentence indicates the unity of the paragraph by pointing out the topic, the central thought with which the group of sentences is concerned.

Not every well-constructed paragraph contains an expressed topic sentence, but every good paragraph is so well knit that it at least *implies* one; the reader, reflecting, can sum up the central thought of the paragraph in his own "topic sentence." Topic sentences are also guides by which you keep on the subject and avoid introducing irrelevant material.

The topic sentence nearly always comes first in a paragraph, premier in a sequence of related sentences dealing with the central idea to be developed. Occasionally, the topic of a paragraph will be embedded in the final sentence; very rarely will it be found at some other position. Some teachers and other students of writing have assumed that because logic is both deductive and inductive, both analytic and synthetic, topic sentences appear anywhere within a paragraph. Theoretically, this view is correct, but actually it is not easy to find topic sentences anywhere other than at the beginnings of paragraphs. (This fact should be helpful to you when studying: master the thought of the initial sentence of every paragraph of exposition you read and normally you will get at least the central thread of the thought.) Sometimes, too, you will find that the topic sentence, appearing first, is repeated, usually in different words, in the final sentence. The last sentence of the paragraph by John Ciardi, p. 34, is a repetition and reinforcement of the first.

Some instructors urge students to place topic sentences at different places within paragraphs to avoid monotony. This is sound advice so long as the topic sentence does not seem artificially added when it does appear and does not destroy the train of thought or the rhythm of sentence structure. However, although no teacher will object to the constant initial appearance of topic sentences, one might correctly point out that their form and structure can be varied from time to time. For example, a topic sentence can ask a question as well as make a statement. It may generalize or summarize. It may be long or short; it may be simple, compound, complex, or compound-complex.

In the vast majority of well-constructed paragraphs, the first sentence states the topic and all succeeding sentences are related to it by coordination or, more often, by subordination. That is, the second sentence is quite likely to be a comment upon the first or an example or illustration of what it says. Notice that in the Hoffer paragraph quoted on p. 35, the second, third, fourth, and fifth sentences illustrate the thought of the first (topic) sentence. In the last two sentences, the author cites an example of how he resisted the problems mentioned in preceding sentences. All of the sentences are related structurally and deal with the identical subject. But the sentences may be said to move up and down the ladder of generality. Mr. Hoffer's general opening statement is followed by specific examples which, in turn, are followed by a new generalized statement—all of them closely, organically related. One experienced teacher has referred to such units of writing as "escalator sentences," moving up and down from generality to details to generality. Good writing is specific, but sometimes specific details lose their effectiveness unless they are carefully woven into the central thought of the paragraph.

In order to understand fully what a topic sentence is and how it may be used, refer to the readings in Book Three. For example, notice that in the second paragraph of Bennett's "Why a Classic Is a Classic," p. 611, the topic is stated in the second sentence and is repeated in the fourth. Study the first paragraph of Huxley's "Comfort," p. 707; probably most students would select the second as the topic sentence, but a good case can also be made for the first and third because each of the first three sentences actually makes the same point in different ways. And yet the material is not repetitious because of the different words used and the varying structure of the sentences. The fourth sentence is not sufficiently inclusive to be considered, but the fifth is as close to the topic of the paragraph as are any others. It is rare to find a paragraph with a topic sentence stated in four different ways, yet analysis such as this of still other paragraphs will teach you more about topic sentences than any other form of instruction.

As an easy check on the presence or absence of a paragraph topic and its effective phrasing, reread carefully each paragraph that you write. Put in the margin the one or two words that are the subject of the paragraph. Or apply the methods of some textbooks which print in boldface type the paragraph topic at the beginning of the paragraph. (If you follow any of these suggestions, be sure to eliminate all mechanical indications of the paragraph topic from your final draft—that is, marginal notations, underlining, etc.)

One criterion of the good paragraph is that it must be so unified that its gist, or pith, *can* be expressed in a topic sentence, even though this sentence is not expressed. Only thus can you be certain that you have kept to the subject; only thus can the reader follow clearly the development of your idea. But keep in mind that a topic sentence contains merely the main point, or points, of a paragraph, not every idea mentioned.

SUBSTANCE

After you have determined the thought to be expressed in the paragraph and put it in a topic sentence, expressed or implied, you then encounter the problem of developing the thought. Many students have no difficulty in expressing a main idea or a group of ideas, but all writers are vexed with the ever-present problems of expanding, shaping, and explaining thoughts so that they will be clear and effective.

Topic sentences are but the trunk of a tree; they must be developed in such a way that the reader will see a tree with branches and leaves. Readers will not fully understand a series of topic sentences because only the skeleton, the bare outline, of the thought is presented. Completely developed paragraphs contain an abundance of vital, pertinent detail. Everyone who has read the closely woven essays of Emerson or Bacon has sighed, "Each sentence is a paragraph, or a whole paper, in embryo. If only the author had expanded the main ideas, I could understand so much better."

If you know something about the subject upon which you are writing, and have some real interest in expressing your ideas, you can always avoid weak, incomplete paragraphs by making enough mental effort, and taking enough time, to fulfill the statement of a topic sentence. The five topic sentences listed (p. 36) for a theme about George may be quite satisfactory; the effectiveness of the theme will depend upon how those bare ideas are developed.

One student chose to write a theme with the title "I Enjoyed Summer Camp." He jotted down the following items as a guide to development:

Camp property	Badminton
Equipment	Friends
Entertainment	Craft work
Carefully selected location	Sailing
Staff and director	Volley ball
Dramatics and movies	Library
Baseball	Nature study and nature room
Swimming	Canoe trips
Tennis	Horseback riding
Cabins	Overnight camping
Archery	Cook-outs

These items overlapped and were in no particular order. He grouped them into larger heads, each designed to form a part of his theme:

Camp activities, physical	Camp property
Camp activities, mental and social	Camp equipment
Management	Sportsmanship and friends

For the paragraph dealing with *camp equipment* he jotted down the following:

Buildings	Shops
Baseball fields	Club rooms
Tennis courts	Archery range
Eating facilities	Rifle range
Cabins	Badminton and volley ball
Lake	Theater
Craft rooms	Library
Riding	Service buildings
Living quarters	Outdoor chapel
Infirmary	Water supply

These items enabled the writer to produce this paragraph:

Within the limits of the campus area are 40 buildings, several playing fields, and many facilities for riding, shooting, and outdoor camping. The largest building contains the dining room and kitchens with facilities for storage and refrigeration. In another building is the theater, with stage and props for music, dramatics, and movies. On rainy days the theater provides space for indoor activities, including story-telling and lie-swapping. A shop is well-equipped with power and hand tools. In the Junior Club House are a leathercraft shop and a crafts room. (Each section has its own club house where activities and games of interest to boys of its age group may be enjoyed.) A library with a collection of boys' books and a fireplace, a reading table, and a porch provides space for quiet reading. At convenient locations are the nature room, counselors' lounge, infirmary, camp offices, laundry, garages, wash houses, campfire areas, and outdoor assembly places. At the waterfront are the boat house and dressing quarters. The sleeping cabins, screened and fully equipped, each provide quarters for five boys and a counselor.

This is not a lively paragraph, and the order of sentences is not perfect, but no one can deny that it contains a topic sentence (the first) and plentiful detail.

In your study of history or science, it may have occurred to you that, in the past, some daring thinker or some new discovery or invention has been ridiculed. Such shortsightedness and contempt now seem savage and unbelievable, just as students in the twenty-first century may regard some of our oversights and intolerances of the twentieth century. Not long ago, a freshman seized upon the idea that some great thinkers and innovators have been laughed at or scorned by their contemporaries. He did some reading and jotted down some of his findings about

de Forest	the vacuum tube
the locomotive	Murdoch
the automobile	coal gas
Daguerre	Socrates

These jottings and, above all, some hard thinking and rewriting enabled him to produce this paragraph filled with solid, informative, arresting substance:

History follows a disturbing pattern of first viciously denouncing great discoveries, only to honor them after the discoverers themselves are destroyed or ridiculed by their detractors. For centuries, men have honored the teachings of Socrates as preserved in the *Dialogues* of Plato, but the man himself was condemned to death for corrupting youth with his novel ideas. Lee de Forest was prosecuted for using the mails to defraud because he wrote that his vacuum tube "would transmit the human voice across the Atlantic." And this was as recent as 1913! Daguerre, the creator of photography, was committed to an insane asylum for insisting that he could transfer a likeness to a tin plate. The automobile was opposed because agriculture was felt to be doomed by a vehicle that ate neither oats nor hay. Stephenson's locomotive was denounced on the grounds that its speed would shatter men's minds and bodies. The eminent Sir Walter Scott called William Murdoch a madman for proposing to light the streets of London with coal gas, and the great Emperor Napoleon laughed off the idea as a "crazy notion." Some churchmen argued against the plan as being blasphemous, since God had divided the light from darkness. And some physicians insisted coal-gas lights would induce people to stay out late and catch cold. Who are the heretics and madmen of the 1960's who will be honored and acclaimed a decade or century from now?

There are various methods of developing topic sentences, involving the use of different kinds of material which may be employed individually or in combination. All methods of paragraph development have essentially the same purpose, however, and the different technical names to label material are of little importance and less help. The primary aim in writing paragraphs is to make the reader see exactly and fully the ideas contained in the expressed or implied topic sentences. The only test of the substance of a paragraph is that of communication. *Define,* if the terms are not clear; *explain in detail* if the idea is difficult or abstruse; *give instances and examples* of the concept which will relate to the reader's experience and understanding; *compare* or *contrast* the idea with something which the reader already comprehends.

Experienced writers do not say to themselves: "Now I shall give an illustration and example to develop the thought of this paragraph." Many writers would be hard put to it to define and explain the kinds of substance which they do use. Nevertheless, a good writer does flesh out the bare bones of a topic sentence with plentiful substance.

Analysis may help in showing you how to develop paragraphs, despite the fact that the analysis is somewhat artificial and even forced. For example, one of the methods of developing a paragraph is *definition.* Development by this method involves the use of details which answer the implied question of the reader, "What do you mean by this?" In the last paragraph of "Why a Classic Is a Classic," p. 614, Arnold Bennett defines his meaning. The final three paragraphs of Smith's "Lo, the Old College Spirit," p. 683, are an extended definition which summarizes, by implication, the entire thesis of the article, a definition which makes unmistakably clear precisely what the author has in mind.

Paragraphs developed by *illustration* and *example* involving narrative and descriptive details may easily be found in Book Three. For only one example, note the first paragraph in "College Athletics: Education or Show Business?", p. 669. The narrative and descriptive materials used clarify the meaning of the topic sentence, which comes last in the paragraph.

As previously pointed out, many paragraphs are developed by the use of several methods in combination. In the paragraph from Huxley's "Comfort" beginning "Another essential component . . . ," p. 711, illustration, example, comparison, contrast, and definition all appear. Varied methods in combination are also well illustrated in the first paragraph of Wecter's "How Americans Choose Their Heroes," p. 548.

All methods of paragraph development are genuine and sensible; they actually represent the varied ways in which our minds work when we are composing a sentence, writing a paragraph, or planning a theme. The effective paragraph which does not employ a combination of methods is rare, for the perfectly sound reason that our minds attack problems of whatever kind in several ways. The search for interest and significance in a subject calls for more than one kind of approach.

Analysis of other paragraphs from your book of readings may enable you to find ways of acquiring adequate substance. Such analysis, however, is primarily a set of finger exercises. Remember: a good paragraph consists of a tightly knit series of thoughts woven around the core of an expressed or implied topic sentence. The specific type of development is not important in itself; the *presence* of thought is all-important.

Adequate substance consists of definite, concrete ideas, impressions, and observations. Generalizations are frequently trite, vague, and ineffective. Note the lack of worthwhile substance in this student paragraph:

Cheating never pays. After all, "honesty is the best policy"; also when one gets something for nothing he does not appreciate it. I think that every student should be on his own, even if his "own" is not good enough for him to pass his courses. One should be honest, no matter what the cost. The student who thinks cheating is a sin only when it is detected is fooling nobody but himself. Sooner or later, his sins will find him out, and he will have nobody but himself to blame.

The student rewrote this paragraph with greater effectiveness because he used a specific illustration:

Cheating never pays. A friend of mine, whom we shall call John, thought that it did. He once said to me: "Why should I study when it is so easy to get the desired results without work? The only sin in cheating is being caught." And so John was dishonest all through his four years at school. But when he took the college board examinations, he could not cheat because the proctors were efficient. He failed and was bitterly disappointed, because he wanted very badly to enter ―― College. Now he believes, as I do, that cheating never pays.

UNITY

As it is important that every sentence should be unified, should contain only facts and ideas that belong together and present a clear and consistent point of view, so is it important that the related sentences forming a paragraph should develop consistently a larger idea which presides over the whole group. If a paragraph contains substance, no matter how excellent, which is irrelevant to the central theme, it is not unified. A lack of unity causes a lack of effectiveness because the reader, prepared for a discussion of topic A, is confused by the introduction of detail about topic B; he shifts his attention from both A and B in an attempt to see how they are related.

Any idea which is not related to the main thought of the paragraph should be omitted or placed in another paragraph where it does belong. The only test for unity is this: Does this statement refer to the thought contained in the expressed or implied topic sentence? Style has been defined as that element which makes writing more than merely comprehensible; if you introduce irrelevant details into your paragraphs, you will both confuse and irritate your reader. Let each paragraph develop and convey its own idea—and no other.

The following paragraphs do not possess unity:

She loved the wild flowers which grew near our home. Nearly every day she would wander into the fields and return with an armful of daisies or Queen Anne's lace which she would carefully arrange in bowls of water. *These bowls were of all kinds: pewter, silver, and copper. We had bought them at Woodward & Lothrop's, many years ago.* She would put the flowers in every room in the house and walk from room to room admiring their texture and color.

It was a lovely summer day. The green of the trees and grass was brilliant; the sun shone brightly from a blue sky which was filled with fleecy, white clouds. Hardly a sound could be heard save for the birds which were happily singing in the trees and the distant shouts of a group of tennis players. *Two of these players were students from a nearby college, where they were attending summer school.* Such days as this were rare, even in June.

ORDER

The first great problem in writing a paragraph is securing full, interesting, unified material. The second great problem is *arranging* the material which has been collected. Even excellent substance will lose much of its effectiveness if it is incorrectly and illogically arranged. The excellent student paragraph quoted on p. 40 would be even better if the writer had used any one of a fairly definite series of orders available to him. A few of these kinds of order are listed in Section 33, to which you should refer. Probably a *chronological* order, the most common method employed in expository paragraphs involving narrative details, would have been best for the quoted paragraph. Restudy the paragraph and decide in what order you think the sentences should appear.

Far more important than any one specific kind of order used is the necessity for planned order of some kind which is adhered to throughout a paragraph. If you begin a paragraph with a particular order in mind, do not shift to some other arrangement. However, the arrangement of sentences within *separate* paragraphs should vary so as to avoid monotony and increase reader interest. A disordered string of jumbled sentences has little effectiveness because a reader must concentrate on searching for a plan which has tumbled into chaos.

The following paragraph is developed in what is known as *logical* order. As you will note in Section 33, this means only that the author has made a general statement and then followed with details:

> From time immemorial work has been glorified. Song and story yield their homage to the solid merits of work, however romantically they may extol the delights of indolence, while essay and biography axiomatically acclaim work as the sure means to personal success and social esteem. The more prosaic and academic discussions of contemporary life, in their exaltation of work as the great social panacea, do but reecho the words of Carlyle, who describes it as "the grand cure of all the maladies and miseries that ever beset mankind." The Rotarian mind makes work co-equal, if not identical, with service. Nowhere has this doctrine been better summed up than in the words of that past master of pious platitudes, Calvin Coolidge: "To provide for the economic well-being of our inhabitants, only three attributes, which are not beyond the reach of the average person, are necessary— honesty, industry, and thrift." (Oh, if it were only so simple!)
> —HENRY PRATT FAIRCHILD in *Harper's Magazine*

In the following paragraph from J. B. Priestley's "Delight" the point of view is that of a fixed observer at a window looking at scenes in a physical order clearly indicated:

> The view is very special. I might have put it together myself, like the scenery of our dreams. There is in this view nearly everything I love in the English scene. Down below on the right are downlands and heath, green

slopes and gorse in bloom. Lower and nearer the center are cultivated fields; then, toward the left, some woods; and beyond, just in the picture, a glimpse of a tiny church, some cottages, and the ruin of a large manor house. Farther off, but dominating the scene, is the long chalk cliff that ends in the Needles, which have been to so many travelers the first sign of England. And full in the middle panes of my window is that flashing mirror, that blue diamond or that infinite haze, that window for the mind, which is the sea. I hold this tenure of the delighted eye in the most precarious world since the Ice Age. My security is as brittle as the teeth I am fast losing. But I have arrived at my high window; I have already lolled at the broad seat; I have looked down by the hour upon the gorse, the woods, the cliffs, the sea; and the glory my eyes have seen—praise the Lord! cannot be robbed of its yesterdays. . . .

Note the disorder of the following:

Viewed from the outside, the house seemed large and rambling. It was enclosed by a picket fence which needed a coat of paint. The agent who was accompanying me said that the house had only nine rooms, but that they were large. The dining room was covered with wallpaper which was faded and torn. The lawn needed mowing, and ugly weeds were growing in the cracks between the front steps. The bedrooms badly needed repairing. I reached the property early in the afternoon. After going over the house thoroughly, I decided not to lease it. The agent was from St. Louis; his name was Brown.

Order in the paragraph involves not only logic but effectiveness. The effectiveness of any paragraph can be improved by a careful arrangement of thoughts. Ordinarily, the sentences developing the most important phase of the idea of the paragraph should be placed at the beginning or the end. It is not always advisable to place significant detail in these positions; consistently doing so will cause monotony of structure. The most trenchant statement of the paragraph, however, should usually not be embedded somewhere within the paragraph. First and last impressions of paragraphs, as of people, are genuinely important.

A somewhat similar method of achieving stylistic effectiveness in the paragraph is to arrange the thoughts in climactic order. If the most dramatic idea is saved for the end, the reader will eagerly read on, lured by the prospect of a climactic statement. Notice how Norman Thomas builds up to a trenchant statement in this paragraph from "Is Decline of the Profit Motive Desirable?":

Economic experts tell us that we in America have the capacity for a minimum income of $2,000 or $2,500 a year. Why, then, our bitter poverty? If the profit system isn't to blame, what is? You can't laugh off the desire of the masses for abundance. But you will never conquer the movement to abolish the profit system, unless temporarily by the despicable means of force, unless you can dispose of the Great Agitator, poverty in the midst of potential plenty.

If you consistently fail to "keep something in reserve," if you always fully inform your reader in advance of what your statement implies, you will lose the effectiveness which climactic arrangement affords.

PROPORTION

Paragraphs should have not only adequate substance, unity, and correct order of sentences, but also right proportion. This term implies *symmetry;* a paragraph should be developed according to its relative idea value. If a paragraph contains discussion of a proportionately important idea, its length should be greater than that of a paragraph which develops a comparatively minor topic. Readers are likely to attribute importance to ideas on the basis of the length of the paragraphs in which they are discussed. Often such emphasis is undue; it causes distorted, out-of-proportion understanding.

In writing a theme of 500 words, a student may compose a long introductory paragraph, follow it with a transitional paragraph, and have left only 100 or so words for the final paragraph which contains the actual *theme,* the central idea of the entire paper. Such a composition is badly proportioned. Do not expand ideas that are relatively subordinate or treat sketchily ideas that are of fundamental importance.

Correct proportion necessitates careful planning. The writer who dwells at length upon some phase of the theme because he is interested in that phase or knows it thoroughly may not be taking into account its importance in relation *to the reader.* The thoughtless writer will consider only his own interest or knowledge; to achieve correct paragraph proportion, he must consider the relation of the paragraph to the whole subject, and also his reader's reaction.

A study of the comparative length of paragraphs in selections from Book Three will be helpful and instructive. Also, examine and apply to your own themes the five specific suggestions for attaining proportion given in Section 34.

LENGTH

The principle governing proportion is that the length must be determined by the relative importance of the thought unit the paragraph embraces. But the problem of paragraph length not considered proportionately is also troublesome. No specific rule for paragraph length can be laid down, save the principle mentioned above.

In general, however, you should avoid a series of short, choppy paragraphs. Such a series usually implies that you have not developed fully and coherently the central idea of each paragraph or that you have failed to see the relationship of ideas and have thus violated the principle of unity. Note the choppy effect of the following paragraphs:

> Each day he arises at an early hour and sets out for the city with his vegetables.
>
> He arrives there before most people are awake and has his produce neatly arranged before the housewives start out to market.
>
> Because his vegetables are fresh, and attractively displayed, he usually has little difficulty in selling them. Besides, he is a good salesman.
>
> By noon each day he has completed his sales and returns to his farm to work in the fields until sunset.

Short paragraphs may be used correctly to gain emphasis. For example, in description or narration, short paragraphs are often used to achieve a vigorous, emphatic style. Frequently they are necessary in dialogue to indicate changes of speakers. But remember: very short paragraphs should not be written except for a definite stylistic effect. The short paragraphs in some newspapers and advertisements are used for effect, not thoughtlessly.

Often it is possible to break a long paragraph into two or more shorter ones without violation of unity, provided that transitional words or phrases are used to insure coherence. See Section 44b.

Do not awkwardly and artificially avoid either long or short paragraphs. Use them according to the proportionate value of the thought units they express. It is only a *series* of either that is usually ineffective. Many excellent writers now tend to write shorter paragraphs than formerly were used, but in scholarly or technical papers the paragraphs still run to considerable length.

As a general rule, avoid paragraphs of less than 20 words and more than 100. Paragraphs shorter than the former usually (but not always) require added detail; those longer than the latter may well be difficult to keep unified. If the subject you are treating requires point development in varying degrees of importance, then the length of your paragraphs should reflect this variance.

TRANSITION

When we say that paragraphs should be coherent, what we really mean is that they should be properly tied together. That is, each paragraph should contain sentences which are logically related, and separate paragraphs within the same theme should be unmistakably connected. Coherence depends upon clarity of thought, but the secret of coherence lies in the use of connectives, *transitional expressions*. Even though a paragraph contains ample substance, with its sentences logically and clearly arranged, it will not seem coherent if the sentences appear to the reader to be loosely joined. A series of paragraphs will be coherent to him only if the connections between them are unmistakably clear. We carelessly assume that our readers, without the assistance of connectives, can readily understand our shifts in thought. We fail to write the hidden, unspoken connectives which we use in thinking; unless some of these connectives are employed, the reader will become confused.

Even if the train of our thought is coherent and without gaps or omissions, the relationship of one thought to a succeeding one often requires indication through the use of transitional words. Haven't you noticed that some teacher or lecturer is particularly easy to follow because he constantly *relates* one thought to another by using such standard transitional words as *for example, however, but, on the other hand, similarly,* and the like? (A fuller list of transitional expressions is given in Section 44b. Study them.) On occasion, however, you may wish or need to go beyond these standard expressions and use one specifically tailored for the situation at hand, an *ad hoc* expression designed to indicate the precise relationship between two of your passages. Such handling of transitions is one accurate measure of maturity in style. One can become tiresome if he overuses such transitional devices as *even more to the point, true, but again, however that may be,* and *oddly enough,* but now and again you should go beyond the everyday expressions which grow wearisome through repetition.

An entire sentence may also be used transitionally. Likewise, coherence may be gained by the repetition of words at the close of one paragraph and the beginning of another. Note the following italicized expressions:

   . . . This concludes the author's comments on taxation.
    But taxation is not the only problem which he discusses . . .

   . . . Thus we may say that he is a splendid specimen, physically.
    On the other hand, his mentality is of a low order . . .

   . . . The valence of certain elements varies in different compounds.
    But let us first discuss the valence of two common elements, oxygen and hydrogen . . .

Sometimes the shift in thought between two paragraphs, or two groups of paragraphs, is so marked that a word or phrase is not sufficient fully to indicate the transition. In such a situation a short transitional paragraph may be used to give a summary of what has been said and to suggest what is to follow. Note the following italicized paragraph:

   There are three primary essentials to the good theme: correctness, clearness, and effectiveness. If a theme lacks any one of these elements, it is not a good theme; if it lacks more than one, or lacks any one to an unusual degree, it is a very poor theme.
   These elements, then, are the sine qua non *of the good theme. It now remains for us to define each of these terms and apply them to such matters as diction, punctuation, and sentence structure.*
   A good theme must be correct in its diction. Correct diction implies . . .

Frequently paragraph connection is faulty because the writer fails to give all pertinent details of relation. For example, in a descriptive theme, one paragraph may end with a description of the exterior of a house, and the next begin with a discussion of the view from an upstairs room. Or one paragraph may discuss the industry of the Belgians, and the next begin: "Thus we see that they are a warlike nation of people." The reader properly asks why. Does industry cause a martial spirit? A gap has been left in the thought and must be filled in with, perhaps, a statement that industry has resulted in a need for raw materials, and this need has fostered a desire for acquisition of territory which contains these materials.

Good writing is always characterized by skill in the revelation of thought relationships. Transitional aids are indispensable to the writer who wishes *fully* to *communicate* his thoughts, and the exact shadings of his thought, to the reader.

MECHANICS

Mechanical correctness in the handling of paragraphs is simple to attain. The rules pertaining to indentation, the paragraphing of dialogue, etc., are few and easily learned. But they must be mastered. The absence of errors is a mechanical and negative aspect of style, but is an element without which style loses much of its effectiveness.

1. Every paragraph should be indented a uniform distance, perhaps one inch. In typing, a common practice is to indent five spaces. The break of distinct paragraph indentation is a real aid to both writer and reader in recognizing the divisions of thought within the whole theme. Further, paragraph indentation aids in reading; the break serves as a signal that a clear distinction between separate parts of the whole composition is about to be made.

2. Part of a line should not be left blank unless a new paragraph begins on the next line. Blanks in lines which are not last lines of paragraphs not only cause a jagged appearance but also make less efficient the mechanical process of reading—the eye, in sweeping over the line, has to make several extra movements in order to adjust itself and to transfer meaning to the brain. Margins at the left of the page should, of course, always be uniform, for the same reasons.

3. Dialogue and quoted conversations require separate paragraphs for each speech. Notice the mechanical forms in the following excerpt from Mary Porter Russell's short story, "Arrival." Three particulars may be observed: correct paragraphing of conversation, correct paragraphing of explanatory material, and correct form for introductory and explanatory words within paragraphs which contain dialogue.

> "Are we *here*?" she called to the driver, and something inside her seemed trying to burst.
> "You bet," he answered. "See that building? That's the church. And d'yer see that one? That's the school."
> Such funny little houses they were. Not at all like a church and a school.
> "And here's the post office," said the driver, drawing up before a building that was really a grocery store.
> Mother hadn't said anything for a long time, but she had reached over for Joan's hand and was squeezing it very hard. "I see Father," she cried out all at once, in a choky sort of voice.
> "Yeah, that's him," said the driver.

The mechanics of writing paragraphs and themes are further discussed in Section 36, p. 247. Study this section for additional comment on the somewhat prosaic but highly important subject of the machinery involved in writing.

SUMMARY

Good themes are the result of good paragraphs. Good paragraphs are difficult to compose, but anyone can create them who has two ideas to rub together and who will write and rewrite thoughtfully. Never lose sight of these three basic steps in paragraph development: (1) Phrase your topic sentences so that each develops some clearly defined phase of the whole subject. (2) Clearly and fully expand the ideas contained in your topic sentences by means of definition, illustration, comparison and contrast, or combinations of these and other types of material. (3) Make each paragraph as stylistically effective as possible by means of mechanical correctness, unity, proper order and arrangement of thought, sound proportion and varied length, and by making each paragraph develop out of its predecessor. These three steps may appear involved, and you may argue that good writers hardly follow any such mechanical methods of shaping paragraphs. Your argument will have some merit, but the fact remains that good professional writers do achieve the results brought about by these three steps, whether or not they consciously use the methods involved. Until you master the technique of paragraph-writing, follow these three suggestions carefully and deliberately.

· EXERCISES ·

TOPIC SENTENCES

A. Pick out the topic sentences of a number of paragraphs in one of your textbooks.

B. From your reading, select a well-constructed paragraph which has no topic sentence. State the implied topic sentence.

C. Write a paragraph based on this topic sentence: "Not all men and women should marry."

D. Use this topic sentence (Exercise C) in various forms and at different positions within other paragraphs constructed by you.

E. By means of topic sentences make an outline of some essay in Book Three.

F. List a half-dozen or more topic sentences to be used in developing each of the following theme subjects:

1. Why I Am Attending —— College.
2. The Problem of Cheating.
3. The Best Way To Sell Used Cars.
4. How To Be Happy Though Unhappy—A Commentary on "Success" Books.
5. How To Spend a Rainy Day.

SUBSTANCE

A. Write a paragraph which is developed by the use of *instances* that prove the statement contained in the topic sentence.

B. Write a paragraph that is developed by effective *repetition* of the thought contained in the topic sentence.

C. Develop one of the following topic sentences by using any of the kinds of material mentioned in this chapter:

1. Of course, Henry is no Einstein.
2. Most lectures are forgotten in a day.
3. Is it true that girls are usually more conscientious students than boys?
4. Motion pictures are constantly becoming more intelligent.
5. Food, shelter, and sex: these are man's dominant urges.

D. From your reading, select paragraphs which are developed by use of the various kinds of substance mentioned in this chapter.

E. Use different kinds of material (definition, illustration, explication, comparison or contrast) in developing each of the following topic sentences:

1. Hazing may be beneficial, but it is always cruel.
2. A sound use of connectives reveals more clearly than anything else a writer's mastery of his material.
3. Lucy was the stingiest girl whom I have ever known.
4. I believe that —— is the most interesting magazine published in America today.
5. There are more disadvantages than advantages in living in a big city.
6. College football is no place for amateurs.
7. College athletics should not be carried on for profit.
8. We all talk about sex, but few of us know much about it.
9. A man's best friend is his ——.
10. College is a poor place in which to get an education.

UNITY

Show why the following paragraphs do not possess unity.

A. The year Robert, my brother, first entered college, the college population explosion was just beginning to show its effects but not to any great extent. When he first started, he commuted for a while and had a locker at Craven Hall where he threw his coat and books along with perhaps three or four hundred other boys. He sometimes ate lunch there and once in a while at the Union, where the freshmen who lived on the campus ate. At that time there were no graduate students living on the campus.

B. Henry Adams embarked on an intellectual career. He toured all of Europe and gained the friendship of many great men of his time such as John Hay and St. Gaudens. All the time he was seeking reasons and rules for the actions of life. He was influenced by Darwin and Marx, but he was constantly being disappointed by seeing one of his theories disproved. Adams was sincere in all the inquiry he made into the meaning and culture of humanity. His philosophy is simple and understandable although it is often untrue. His dynamic theory of history and his belief regarding the dynamo are well known to all those who read *The Education of Henry Adams.* Without a doubt, Henry Adams was a great intellect, yet he did not continue in the lines of his forefathers. To be a statesman at the time of the capitalistic era was not typical of the Adams style.

C. Malta lies almost in the middle of the Mediterranean—55 miles from Sicily and about 150 miles from Africa. Its area is less than 100 square miles. The island was originally all rock, no soil whatever. Legend has it that all the soil was shipped in from Sicily years ago. The highest point on the island is the small town of Rabat, 700 feet above sea level. Malta's strategic location made possible raids on Italian and German shipping to Africa, when Rommel was in Egypt and Tunisia.

D. During the greater part of the last century, Cuba was ruled by a captain-general, later called governor-general. The population of Cuba was divided into four classes: (1) the Spaniards, who occupied the offices and positions of power; (2) the Creoles, who were the planters, businessmen, and lawyers of the island; (3) the free mulattoes and Negroes, making up one-sixth of the population; and (4) the slaves, estimated at one-third the total population. The third class was excluded by law from holding any civil office; the fourth class were mere chattels. Although the native Cubans had little civil, political, or religious freedom, they were heavily taxed to maintain Spanish military forces on the island and a large number of Spanish officials.

ORDER

A. Rewrite the paragraph below, previously given on p. 44. Follow a correct *point-of-view* order. Supply any transitional aids which will insure greater coherence.

Viewed from the outside, the house seemed large and rambling. It was enclosed by a picket fence which needed a coat of paint. The agent who was accompanying me said that the house had only nine rooms, but that they were large. The dining room was covered with wallpaper which was faded and torn. The lawn needed mowing, and ugly weeds were growing in the cracks between the front steps. The bedrooms badly needed repairing. I reached the property early in the afternoon. After going over the house thoroughly, I decided not to lease it. The agent was from St. Louis; his name was Brown.

B. Write a paragraph which involves *chronological* order, from *earlier* to *later* time, or vice versa.

C. "He became desperately ill." Consider this as a topic sentence which states an effect, and write a paragraph in which the sentences are logically ordered as *causes* for illness.

D. Rewrite the following poorly ordered paragraph:

1. He was a good athlete. 2. At first, his freshman coach thought that John would never make his letter. 3. At the end of his junior year, John almost made the trip abroad with the Olympic team. 4. His high school coach knew he had ability, and when John left for college, the coach wrote the athletic director not to overlook him. 5. John did not make the freshman team, but he worked diligently and showed great improvement. 6. Although he did not make the Olympic team, he went as a spectator. 7. This year he won a first place at the Western Conference Meet.

E. Rewrite a paragraph from a theme so as to place the most important idea at the beginning or the end.

PROPORTION

A. Study one of the essays in your book of readings. Comment upon the paragraph proportion. Are the paragraphs symmetrical?

B. Comment upon the apportioning of space (time) in some lecture or debate you have recently heard. Did some phases (paragraphs) seem *unduly* long, or sketchy?

C. Choose a few topics for 500-word themes and estimate the proportionate importance of the several developing paragraphs.

D. Indicate the number of words proportionately correct for each paragraph of a 500-word theme based on the following plan:

LEARNING TO BOWL
1. Correct mental attitude for the beginner.
2. Correct body position.
3. How to handle the arms and hands.
4. How to handle the feet.
5. Errors to be avoided.
6. Summary.

LENGTH

A. Compare the average length of the paragraphs in an article in the *Atlantic Monthly* with the length of those in an article in *Time*.

B. Ascertain the average length of the paragraphs in a newspaper story and in a full-page advertisement printed in a popular magazine. What effects are achieved, in your opinion, by the brief paragraphs?

C. Count the number of words in several consecutive paragraphs of some essay in Book Three.

D. Compare the number of words in the opening three or four paragraphs of any two of the essays in your book of readings.

E. Place in larger units these choppy paragraphs:

Every year, many thousands of people buy new television sets for the first time. Other thousands replace their old sets with new ones.

Why?

All these people want entertainment. Buying a television set is buying a seat for the big show.

Who gives the show?

The advertisers give the show. They want the attention of the public, and they are willing to pay heavily to get it.

But some advertisers seem to forget that the entertainment value of the programs they provide is, for the public, of paramount importance. The advertising message is accepted only if it is not too insistent and blatant.

If advertisers wish to be repaid for the show, if they wish to win good will, they must avoid antagonizing the public with too obvious intrusion of the advertising message into the entertainment of the program.

TRANSITION

A. Underline all the transitional words and phrases which occur in one of your recent themes. Compare them with the list given in Section 44b.

B. Underline all the reference words and transitional expressions to be found on one page of a selection in your book of readings. Note especially the transitional devices which occur at the *beginnings* of paragraphs.

C. Expand into a short transitional paragraph some linking phrase or sentence which you have used in a recent theme.

D. From your book of readings select three paragraphs which seem to you particularly skillful in the use of connectives.

E. Underline all the transitional expressions in the following paragraph:

The snow began to fall in tiny, hard flakes that nestled on the roof of the car. At first we paid little attention; however, we realized before long that we were in for trouble. In the first place, my worn rear tires began to lose traction. Of course, this was not serious yet, but it would be in time. The snow, as I said, was hard and made sand-like drifts on the road, which we began to slide in. Moreover, the fall was so heavy that my headlights seemed to be shining against a dazzling white wall. This blindness, fortunately, was not as serious as it would have been were the road not deserted. We would, as a matter of fact, have been glad to risk hitting an occasional car just to have some company. As a result of our loneliness and increasing nervousness, Jim and I chatted away like a couple of old gossips. But we were not fooling each other one little bit. Just the same, the idle conversation was better than plowing along in tense silence. Perhaps it made me drive better. Fortunately, the lights of the Greenville gas station suddenly glowed through the whiteness. We were, in short, safe again.

GENERAL EXERCISES

A. Comment on the following statements:

1. Short paragraphs are more emphatic than long paragraphs because they more effectively catch and hold the reader's attention.
2. Parallel structure should be used almost entirely when one is writing in an oratorical style.
3. If a paragraph contains ample substance and is unified and coherent, the effectiveness to be gained by *position* or *repetition* of words is relatively unimportant.

B. The following selection lacks unity, order, and proper transitional aids. Make all necessary changes for correct paragraphing.

Several hundred years ago, it was customary for European towns to hold annual fairs in their market places. To these fairs came farmers who wished to sell their products and peddlers who wished to sell their wares. Only small businessmen went to customers' homes to make sales. Large business houses hire men and women to sell wares from door to door. One day a young man came to my home. When the lady of the house appeared, he began to talk rapidly. I answered the doorbell and let him into the house. "How do you do, Mrs. Johnson? Any of the articles I have may be bought for one dollar. Each is worth more. Which would you prefer?" And he kept on and on. Finally my mother had a chance to say, "I am very busy and, furthermore, do not wish to buy anything. Please go at once." But the sale was eventually made, and the canvasser left for the next house. This type of canvasser can never amount to much, for he relies more upon the appeal of sympathy than upon salesmanship. I was sitting in a friend's home one afternoon when one of these dynamic salesmen appeared. It was a very cold day, and I had gone to see my friend in preference to playing football. He carried a small vacuum cleaner in one hand and a valise in the other. He rang the doorbell and made himself at home. He demonstrated the machine, explaining its mechanism clearly. He was close to 60 years of age, and his hair was graying around the temples. Then he compared his prospect's machine with his new one and made a trade-in offer. The gentleman's sales argument was perfect. He departed as soon as the sale was made. She accepted the offer and bought a new vacuum cleaner. He did not give the customer time to regret the purchase. Modern canvassers are indeed different from the peddlers who sold their wares in medieval times. Today in all parts of the world, especially in thickly populated districts, these modern peddlers can be found.

C. The following paragraphs are choppy and ineffective. Revise them.

He is now a physician, but it took him many years to become one.

He was a poor boy and had to work his way through high school, college, and medical school.

He worked in a department store in St. Louis for four years while he was going to college. He made good grades while he was in college and had no difficulty in gaining entrance to a medical school.

He made his tuition money at medical college by tutoring some high-school students who lived near his room.

He is now a successful practitioner of medicine. He says that his own son wants to become a doctor and he is willing for him to do so, provided money is plentiful enough. His own experience was rather bitter, and he has no desire for his son to have to earn money while attending school.

D. Comment upon the lack of unity and the ineffectiveness of the following paragraph:

Henry Adams wrote as a person who knew the answers to nearly every question—as a man who had the final word. Since Mr. Adams had found no order or pattern in the universe, he claimed there was none. True, he was not satisfied with the conclusions he drew, but he felt that they were the only answers. I don't think Adams had any right to criticize life because he had never really lived. He tended to float through things and thus never got as much out of the world as most people do. I think everyone gets out of a thing what he puts into it. Adams had potentially great talents to give but he never gave them. Instead, he remained inactive, studying and drawing his almost useless conclusions. I am not condemning Adams for living the life of a student and a philosopher. Many philosophers have greatly helped the world. However, Adams drew conclusions based on what life had been to him and attempted to apply those conclusions to people in general. They were, however, invalid to ordinary people because Adams had disassociated himself too far from the life that the average person led.

E. What advice, in writing, would you give concerning paragraphing to students who write themes like this:

THIS IS MY SISTER

Her name is Charlotte Ann and she is a junior at Millvale State Teachers College. She has light brown hair and brown eyes, and is an attractive young lady.

She has a quick smile and a word of greeting for everyone. Everyone who knows her thinks very highly of her. She has many friends.

She is going to college on a scholarship. She has a part-time job during the school year and a full-time job during the summer. The scholarship does not pay for everything.

She has been a success in college, both at making good grades and at making good friends. She has to keep her grades up to a certain level to keep her scholarship. She is also vice-president of the Women's Residence Hall Student Council.

She wants to learn to drive an automobile. Almost every time I see her during the summer, she wants me to give her a driving lesson. I usually do give her one, but since I am seldom home it doesn't help her too much.

To sum everything up, I am proud of my sister and I hope she thinks the same of me.

CHAPTER 4

WRITING THE SENTENCE

You cannot shingle a house or paint a roof before you have laid a foundation and built the framework. Your sentences must be effective if your paragraphs and resultant themes are to be clear, correct, and appropriate. Thoreau once wrote: "A sentence should read as if its author, had he held a plough instead of a pen, could have drawn a furrow deep and straight to the end."

"We think in terms of words, speak in terms of sentences, and write in terms of paragraphs." Such a statement is not wholly true, but it at least implies that by the use of concepts (words) we phrase sentences which we tie together into complete paragraphs. A sentence is the link between a thought and the full development of that thought, and, like all links, it is of great importance. Good sentences derive from good diction, good paragraphs from good sentences, and good themes from good paragraphs. The paragraph can be only so good as its component parts, its sentences, the units of expression.

The most important objectives in writing are having something to say and having some interest and purpose in expressing that something. But it is hardly less important that the writer pay attention to the details which will insure the correct, clear, and effective communication of his ideas to the reader.

If your sentences are awkward, or faulty, or vague, the primary purpose of your writing at all has been defeated. You must learn how to avoid writing cumbersome, faulty, or cloudy sentences; you must know how to give your sentences unity, completeness, clearness, and effectiveness. Understanding how to obtain such characteristics in sentence structure depends upon a solid foundation, a substantial framework. You must first know what a sentence *is;* you must understand certain grammatical functions and structures. Upon such a foundation of knowledge you can construct sentences that are direct, clear, and complete.

THE GRAMMAR OF SENTENCES

A usable definition of a sentence is that it is "one or more words conveying to the reader a sense of complete meaning." The word (or group of words) normally, but not always, has a subject and predicate; the subject may be expressed or it may be understood and not expressed; either subject or predicate may be understood from the context.

Remember that the foregoing statements refer to *grammatical* completeness. In one sense we do not have a complete thought until we have read or written a series of sentences. A pronoun in one sentence may take its meaning from an antecedent in another. Such words as *thus, these, another,* and *again,* and such phrases as *for example* and *on the other hand* frequently show that the thought about to be presented in a new sentence is related to the thought in a preceding sentence or paragraph.

When we say, then, that a sentence conveys a "sense of complete meaning" to the reader, we do not imply that we can dispense with its context (the statements which precede or follow it). We mean only that we have a group of words so ordered as to be *grammatically* self-sufficient. For example, the statement, "He took command on July 3, 1775," is grammatically complete. It has a subject, the pronoun *he,* and it has a verb, *took* (took command). In this sense the entire statement is complete and must be begun with a capital letter and be followed by a period. So far as total meaning is concerned, however, we need other sentences to tell us that *he* refers to George Washington and that the command which he assumed was that of Continental Forces in the War of the American Revolution.

The study of grammar may be of little value in itself. To be able to say by rote "A sentence is a group of words containing a single, complete thought, or a group of very closely related thoughts" is valueless in writing or speaking grammatically correct sentences unless the terms of the definition are understood, unless comprehension of the functions of parts of speech, of various kinds of sentences, gives meaning to that definition. To learn the parts of speech, to distinguish simple, complex, and compound sentences—such additions to our knowledge represent wasted effort until we see such knowledge operating upon the sentences which we write or speak. We will then see why the study of grammar is of little value in itself, but we will see more than that—we will find ourselves writing sentences grammatically correct and will know *why* and *how* we do so.

To learn to phrase good sentences, basic units of thought, is a worthwhile achievement. It has been said, in fact, that the simple declarative sentence is the greatest invention of the human intellect.

Unless your mastery of grammar is so thorough that you rarely, if ever, make "mechanical" errors in writing, you should review Sections **61–70** of the Handbook. Correctness and clarity may be called the negative or neutral qualities of good sentences, but without them sentences are usually ineffective. The most common and most serious faults occurring in sentence structure are discussed in Sections **1–15.** Refer to these sections, too, as you study the sentence.

In studying the paragraph you can learn something about substance through analysis of well-constructed examples. Similarly, some students learn sentence structure by analyzing and diagraming examples of effective sentences. Analysis and diagraming are rather involved and largely mechanical processes which do not appeal to all teachers or prove helpful to all students. If your instructor suggests that you do so, study the entries for *Analysis of a sentence* and *Diagraming* on pp. 352 and 369. In this same section of the Handbook, you may wish to consider these entries: *Sentence, arrangement of content; Sentence, grammatical structure of;* and *Sentence, meaning and purpose of.*

With this review of basic principles out of the way, we can now enter upon the important and difficult task of learning to make sentences more than merely correct and clear. That is, we may consider for the remainder of this chapter what can be called the *rhetoric* of the sentence, the phrasing of sentences which are pleasing and forceful.

EFFECTIVENESS

Effectiveness in sentence structure is complex, for it depends upon synthesis of a wide variety of sentence elements and characteristics. Jonathan Swift's celebrated remark, "Proper words in proper places make the true definition of a style," by its generality indicates that one must first comprehend the concrete details which make up the "proper" words and put them in the "proper" places.

Most persons would agree that the following sentences are effective, although knowledgeable students of writing might disagree on names for the qualities which make them so. Several of them were collected in stores or shops where they had been prominently displayed to gain attention and interest:

> An educated man is one who can entertain others, entertain himself, and entertain an idea.
> If you want to rest in a bed of roses, you have to do more than read seed catalogs.
> Books are the memory of mankind.
> Have you ever noticed that most knocking is done by people who can't ring the bell?
> If you are dog tired at night, maybe you have been growling too much during the day.
> Big shots are only little shots who kept shooting.

Some men wonder how they could live without women; the answer is: cheaper.

If ignorance is bliss, why are there not more happy people?

If there's a destiny that shapes our ends, some people waddling down the street should sue destiny.

A democratic country is a place where people say what they think without thinking.

The diction, wisdom, and humor of some of these sentences may not appeal to you, but each sentence undeniably contains a thought. This, then, is the first criterion of an effective sentence: it *may* contain several ideas but it *must* possess at least one. Not only that: this thought must be shaped so that, with proper words in proper places, it correctly, clearly, and emphatically "gets across" to a reader. We may argue about the specific qualities of sentence effectiveness, but most of us would agree when we come across that rarity, a perfectly phrased thought.

In a preceding paragraph, correctness and clarity were called negative or neutral qualities. Yet they do possess positive values as well. The kind of *balance* which one may obtain through the use of parallelism (see p. 411), for example, adds more to a sentence than grammatical correctness or appropriateness of idiom. One may correctly and clearly write, "He was clever, ambitious, and had a sense of responsibility," but to do so is to overlook the force which parallelism adds to communication of meaning: "He was clever, ambitious, and responsible." Consider the difference in force of these sentences:

> Severity breeds fear, but hate is bred by roughness.
> Severity breeds fear, but roughness breeds hate.

The second sentence is more effective for several reasons: It is shorter (Section 15); it employs the active voice in both clauses (Section 68b); the two clauses are identical in structure, even to the repetition of *breeds,* and the important word *hate* comes at the end of the sentence. Similarly, positive values contributing to sentence effectiveness are contained in other suggestions designed primarily to make sentences correct and clear.

Sentence effectiveness is so complex and many-faceted a subject, however, that it may be wise to concentrate on only a few relatively simple methods for achieving it.

Four specific ways to achieve effective sentences and sentence patterns are to make them *concise,* to provide *varied word order,* to vary their *length and structure,* and to make them *pleasing* in sound.

Conciseness

Using too many words is the besetting sin of most inexperienced writers. Indeed, is it prevalent among even professional writers; the editor of one of America's leading "quality" magazines recently stated that wordiness was the greatest stylistic fault in the manuscripts submitted for publication. It is a vague and pervasive flaw, sometimes hard to detect. Of its several causes, perhaps the most common among inexperienced writers is this: In an effort to make sentences unmistakably clear they add all the words they possibly can so that nothing will be omitted. English instructors, commenting on the fact that their students' themes often contain twice as many words as are necessary, scornfully refer to "kitchen stove style"—everything in "including the kitchen stove." See Section 15.

Another cause results from an effort to avoid incompleteness of structure: telegraphic style, the period fault, etc. Making sentences complete in both structure and idea content is laudable; making them wordy is a vice which defeats their potential effectiveness. Even though your instructor assigns a theme of 500 words, he would prefer a 300-word theme which is compact and effective to one of 500 words which is padded. The student who has labored to "get" his 500 words finds it difficult to delete, condense. But it is certainly true that most first drafts of themes are overwritten and need trimming badly. You may find that in the first writing of a theme you have piled up prepositions. Or, because of the inadequacy of your vocabulary, you may have used a phrase, clause, or even an entire sentence to express the idea contained in one exact, emphatic word.

All wordiness is attributable to lack of thought, to laziness. The author who wrote "Please forgive this long letter; I haven't had time to be brief" put his finger squarely on the fundamental cause of wordiness. One may see effective revision in sentences which writers have put down in journals or notebooks and revised for use in later writings. In his journal Emerson wrote the first sentence quoted below. When revising, seven years later, he did not materially shorten the sentence but he twice removed an unnecessary *very* and changed "by the opinion of the world" to "after the world's opinion."

> It is very easy in the world to live by the opinion of the world. It is very easy in solitude to be self-centered. But the finished man is he who in the midst of the crowd keeps with perfect sweetness the independence of solitude. (1834)
>
> It is easy in the world to live after the world's opinion; it is easy in solitude to live after our own; but the great man is he who in the midst of the crowd keeps with perfect sweetness the independence of solitude. (1841)

In all forceful writing the ratio of ideas to words is high. No sentence can be striking if it rambles. Verbose sentences are always unemphatic. If, for no purpose, you repeat an idea in different words, if you pile up details, you write fuzzily, confusedly. Note these flabby and ineffective sentences from students' themes:

> There is nothing that I enjoy more on a hot day than taking a cooling swim in the refreshing surf.
>
> It is my opinion that more and more people are becoming disgusted with romantic motion pictures and are eagerly looking for those which have at least some slight degree of social significance.
>
> In learning to dive, the first and most important thing is to remember to keep your feet together.
>
> No one was more surprised and bewildered than I to find that I had been elected unanimously, without a single dissenting vote.
>
> The next day found me boarding a train for college after many hurried preparations on my part that night and after considerable expenditure of time and effort on the part of my mother in packing my clothes and other possessions.

These sentences are wordy because their writers did not think carefully what they were trying to convey, did not take time to revise, entirely disregarded the effect of the sentences upon the reader. Sometimes you have to delete whole ideas in order to gain conciseness; at other times you can merely reduce predication—make phrases of clauses and single words of phrases. Note the vigorous effect of these lean, trim sentences:

> The Saturday crowd kept coming. Soon all grandstand seats were gone. A row of standees pushed in behind us. Boxes like ours were valuable as more persons lined up. Someone poked my brother in the ribs and offered us a dollar for our perch. One dollar! We gasped. Then we looked back to the street where we'd seen the matches of the first afternoon. The club had erected a high green curtain to shut off the view of the courts. We declined the offer.
>
> —JOHN R. TUNIS

(Of course, if such brief sentences were used in a more extended series, they would become monotonous. Here they are terse, without padding, to convey the ideas of excitement and activity.)

Terse sentences have another value; in addition to being effective, the best of them are memorable. Most quotable sentences are brief. They contain *multum in parvo;* their content is succinctly expressed, is never verbose. One kind of terse sentence, the *epigram,* has been defined by Arlo Bates as "a notion rounded like a snowball for throwing." His definition is, of course, itself an epigram, more memorable than the dictionary definition: An epigram is "any witty, ingenious, or pointed saying tersely expressed."

The *proverb* is another kind of short, pithy saying. Popular and long current, it embodies some familiar truth or useful thought in effective language ("A stitch in time saves nine"). You should avoid frequent use of proverbs, however, because they are as trite as they are expressive (see Section 22, p. 219). So with the *maxim,* a brief statement of a general, practical truth or rule of conduct ("It is wise to risk no more than one can afford to lose"). Sometimes you can cleverly and effectively rephrase a proverb or maxim or give it a new and unexpected application; when this is done, you avoid triteness.

Another kind of terse sentence is the *bon mot.* The bon mot—from the French, meaning "good word"—is a clever saying or witticism such as abounds in the works of Oscar Wilde and in the pages of *The Reader's Digest.*

Proverbs and maxims are easily recognizable, and for practical purposes you need not attempt to distinguish between epigrams and bons mots. Examples are given below.

Remember that it is always the concise (and nearly always brief) sentence which possesses pungency and pithiness. Such a sentence is so effective that it will make a whole page "come alive." Naturally, if you write only in an epigrammatic style, your writing will be fearfully awkward and strained. A few such sentences as these will go a long way:

> If the nose of Cleopatra had been shorter, the whole face of the earth would have been changed.
>
> —BLAISE PASCAL

An undevout astronomer is mad.

—EDWARD YOUNG

Everything suffers by translation, except a bishop.

—LORD CHESTERFIELD

Nothing except a battle lost can be half so melancholy as a battle won.

—DUKE OF WELLINGTON

Poetry teaches the enormous force of a few words, and, in proportion to the inspiration, checks loquacity.

—RALPH WALDO EMERSON

One thought fills immensity.

—WILLIAM BLAKE

The vanity of teaching often tempteth a Man to forget that he is a Blockhead.

—LORD HALIFAX

Nothing is so firmly believed as what we least know.

—MONTAIGNE

You can't tell whether an author is alive until he is dead.

—WALTER RALEIGH

A sword, a spade, and a thought should never be allowed to rust.

—JAMES STEPHENS

A cynic is one who never sees a good quality in a man and never fails to see a bad one.

—HENRY WARD BEECHER

There are not many works extant . . . which are worth the price of a pound of tobacco to a man of limited means.

Atlas was just a gentleman with a protracted nightmare!

—ROBERT LOUIS STEVENSON

There are some people who so arrange their lives that they feed themselves only on side dishes.

—JOSÉ ORTEGA Y GASSET

Those who make peaceful evolution impossible make violent revolution inevitable.

—JOHN F. KENNEDY

Wicked women bother one; good women bore one. That is the only difference between them.

Scandal is gossip made tedious by morality.

—OSCAR WILDE

VARIED WORD ORDER

The established order of words in a sentence is Subject-Verb-Complement. Sentences built on this pattern predominate in our speech and writing. In fact, we are so accustomed to speaking and writing and reading sentences based on this word plan that any departure from it attracts our attention. For this reason, a definite method of securing attention for a word or phrase is to remove it from its accustomed place and put it elsewhere.

The inverted sentence is an unusual way of gaining effectiveness, and you are warned not to use the method too frequently. But never to compose a sentence which varies the pattern of Subject-Verb-Complement is to overlook one method of gaining emphasis in your writing.

The most conspicuous parts of a sentence are the beginning and the end. Hence, sentences which begin or end with important, "pivotal" words are most effective. Phrase your sentences so that they will not invariably begin or end with weak, colorless words and qualifying phrases (*however, I think, in my opinion, it is my belief*). The end of a sentence is even more important than the beginning; sentences may begin weakly and yet end effectively, but they cannot be effective if their endings are lame. Sentences should not "sag" at the end; each succeeding idea should have greater force than its predecessor. It is sound advice, then, to arrange ideas in the order of their importance, so as to gain *climax*. This, too, is a counsel of perfection and can only rarely be obtained. But try to write at least an occasional sentence which builds up to a climax. For example: "Mankind has many hopes, aims, and desires, but they are all obscured by an overwhelming lust for just one thing—peace." Note that in these sentences the pivotal expression comes at the end:

> But now abideth faith, hope, love, these three; and the greatest of these is love.
>
> —THE BIBLE (REVISED VERSION)
>
> A steadfast concert for peace can never be maintained except by a partnership of democratic nations.
>
> —WOODROW WILSON
>
> Hence it is that it is almost a definition of a gentleman to say that he is one who never inflicts pain.
>
> —JOHN HENRY NEWMAN

Closely allied to the principle of climax is that of *suspense*. Because the end of the sentence is its most emphatic part, you can increase emphasis by suspending the thought, maintaining the secret to the end. Such a sentence should be sparingly used, however, for it is likely to seem either strained or artificial. These sentences illustrate what is meant by suspense in sentence structure:

> Nowhere has the competitive impulse of Americans been better illustrated than in its attitude toward women.
>
> And my heart from out that shadow that lies
>   floating on the floor
> Shall be lifted—nevermore.
>
> —EDGAR ALLAN POE
>
> Gone are the days when my heart was young and gay.

Both climax and suspense in sentence structure may be obtained, as will have been noted, without departing from the usual order of Subject-Verb-Complement. Actual transposition or inversion of sentence elements is involved in the *periodic* sentence, one so constructed that its full meaning is not apparent until the end, or nearly the end, of the sentence is reached. That is, it "depends upon the period," does not make complete sense before the terminal mark of punctuation is reached. The periodic sentence may be climactic, but not necessarily. Its effect does depend upon suspense, but not necessarily suspense derived from a pivotal word or expression. The simplest means of writing a periodic sentence is to "put something before the subject."

Most of the sentences which we speak and write are *loose;* phrased in the normal pattern of Subject-Verb-Complement, they make sense if stopped at one or more places before the period is reached. Loose sentences are natural and easy and they rightly predominate in our speech and writing. But periodic sentences, sparingly used, are effective departures from usual word order. Note the effectiveness of the following:

> From the bed on which he was reclining, he slowly, laboriously, and painfully arose.

> From the hour of his dreadful death, cloven to the brainpan before the high altar of Canterbury Cathedral, Thomas à Becket has fascinated mankind.

> The great question that has never been answered, and which I have not yet been able to answer despite my thirty years of research into the feminine soul, is this, "What does a woman want?"
> —SIGMUND FREUD

> And pulseless and cold, with a Derringer by his side and a bullet in his heart, though still calm as in life, beneath the snow lay he who was at once the strongest and yet the weakest of the outcasts of Poker Flat.
> —BRET HARTE

> To transfer admiration from the thing possessed to its possessor; to conceive that the mere possession of material wealth makes of its possessor a proper object of worship; to feel abject before another who is wealthier—such emotions do not so much as enter the American mind.
> —HILAIRE BELLOC

Another device, already mentioned in this chapter, which contributes to sentence effectiveness is arranging words so that similar or contrasted ideas are placed against one another in phrases and clauses of parallel structure. A sentence such as "Honesty recommends that I speak; self-interest demands that I remain silent" is called *balanced*. Another example of the occasionally effective balanced sentence: "We have the right to disagree; we do not have the right to be disagreeable." Good balanced sentences are hard to write and, if too frequently employed, become monotonous. Their matching word structure does, however, give genuine emphasis to parallel thoughts. See *Parallelism*, p. 411. The following sentences are effective:

> The notice which you have taken of my labours, had it been early, had been kind; but it has been delayed till I am indifferent, and cannot enjoy it; till I am solitary, and cannot impart it; till I am known, and do not want it.
> —SAMUEL JOHNSON

> This man I thought had been a Lord among wits; but, I find, he is only a wit among Lords!
> —SAMUEL JOHNSON as quoted by James Boswell

> Crafty men condemn studies, simple men admire them, and wise men use them.

> Some books are to be tasted, others to be swallowed, and some few to be chewed and digested.
> —FRANCIS BACON

> He [the American] sits secure in the possession of his vast domain, rich beyond all experience in resources; sees its inevitable force unlocking itself in elemental order day by day, year by year; looks from his coal-fields, his wheat-bearing prairie, his gold-mines, to his two oceans on either side, and feels the security that there can be no famine in a country reaching through

so many latitudes, no want that cannot be supplied, no danger from any excess of importation of art or learning into a country of such native strength, such immense digestive power.

—RALPH WALDO EMERSON

In every free country, great or small, the spirit of patriotism and nationality grew steadily; and in every country, bond or free, the organisation and structure into which men were fitted by the laws, gathered and armed this sentiment.

—WINSTON CHURCHILL

Swift pictures of himself, apart, yet in himself, came to him—a blue, desperate figure leading lurid charges with one knee forward and a broken blade high—a blue, determined figure standing before a crimson and steel assault, getting calmly killed on a high place before the eyes of all.

—STEPHEN CRANE

This celebrated paragraph from Lincoln's *Gettysburg Address* reveals parallelism between and within sentences:

But, in a larger sense, we cannot dedicate—we cannot consecrate—we cannot hallow—this ground. The brave men, living and dead, who struggled here, have consecrated it far above our poor power to add or detract. The world will little note nor long remember what we say here, but it can never forget what they did here. It is for us, the living, rather, to be dedicated here to the unfinished work which they who fought here have thus far so nobly advanced. It is rather for us to be here dedicated to the great task remaining before us—that from these honored dead we take increased devotion to that cause for which they gave the last full measure of devotion; that we here highly resolve that these dead shall not have died in vain; that this nation, under God, shall have a new birth of freedom; and that government of the people, by the people, for the people, shall not perish from the earth.

Summary: Varied Word Order

The arrangement and thought content of the whole sentence, not the position of any single word or idea, make that sentence effective or ineffective. You cannot attain emphasis by an artificial, thoughtless use of inversion. A periodic sentence is not necessarily more effective than a loose sentence. Varied word order will be effective only if its employment does not destroy correctness, clarity, naturalness. Through lack of thought, however, most of us write sentences based on the usual pattern; occasional, not habitual, rearrangement of words will aid in making our sentences more effective.

A naive or inexperienced writer is likely to set down his main thought first in a sentence and then follow with qualifications as they occur to him, thus producing either false emphasis or weak structure, or both. An experienced writer may be said to have a tendency toward inversion of some sort; that is, he is likely to get subordinate material partly out of the way by putting it at the beginning or within the sentence rather than at the end. Thus when he does employ some sort of inversion by placing such material toward the end he secures special emphasis. A tendency toward periodic sentence construction is one form of stylistic maturity; but varied word order, like any other stylistic effect or mannerism, should be used sparingly and carefully.

The following sentences are unusually effective. Is the effectiveness of each due to its conciseness? its arrangement in climactic order? its periodic form? inversion?

Once by chance—the kind of simple human chance that seems to come very rarely to seekers after universal truths—I heard a woman say to her husband, with tears in her eyes and anguish in her voice, "Oh God, I wish I had been born in America."

—GRACE ADAMS

Whether they succeeded is not yet known. But it can be said of them that in their own minds they continued to be reasonably secure. For never would there be written a book which they could not understand simply by reading it from the first word to the last. They might not save the world. They might not change it. But they would comprehend it.

—MARK VAN DOREN

If, however, the democracy to be defended is a future democracy, a true democracy which will admit the failures of this democracy and set them straight—if the democracy to be defended is a free man's way of dealing with a free man's evils in order to create a free man's world, then the will to defend and protect that democracy will be strong enough to sweep over any challenge.

—ARCHIBALD MACLEISH

Indeed, one may say that even today, in the midst of the greatest of all persecutions, their mission stands out clearly: to awaken us from the stupor in which we dreamed that a civilized society might rest on some other basis than that which has been tested by time—good will to men.

—ALVIN JOHNSON

One art alone has made indisputable progress in history, and that is the art of war. . . .

Our inveterate habit of eating is the oldest and deepest cause of war. . . .

History, like nature, makes no leaps. . . .

But a fresh generation grows up, pacifism subsides; aged reminiscence idealizes the past, and the young are ready to believe that war is 99 percent glory, and only 1 percent diarrhea.

—WILL DURANT

To understand any period of history—to say nothing of writing about it—is like trying to design a house to be made of blocks every one of which varies in size and weight and color with the temperament and experience of the builder, the place where he happens to be standing at the moment, and the passage of time.

—FREDERICK LEWIS ALLEN

Modern America is the first country since Athens which believes that Socrates actually died when he took the hemlock. . . .

There is no magic in books; no guarantee goes with them. Men have read them and still turned out bad. But we want our children to learn how to think; the men who wrote these books thought well. We want our children to think about important things; the men who wrote immortally did that.

—MILTON S. MAYER

VARIETY IN LENGTH AND STRUCTURE

A long series of sentences identical in structure cannot be forceful. You should, for example, compose periodic sentences because of the effectiveness of their suspense. But you should not write a long series of periodic sentences because, no matter how effective each sentence is individually, your reader will tire of the monotonous structure. See to it that the sentences within a paragraph or composition evidence variety as well as individual effectiveness.

Sentences may be divided according to the number of words which they contain, according to the order of the words, and according to grammar (function and type). That is, sentences may be long or short; loose or periodic or balanced; or simple, compound, complex; or declarative, interrogative, imperative, exclamatory. Analyze your own sentence structure to find out what kinds of sentences you use. You may find that you compose several times as many simple and compound sentences as complex. You may find that in an entire theme you have not written a single periodic sentence. You may find that your sentences are monotonously similar in length. You may find that every sentence in a given composition is declarative. (Have you noticed that the four preceding sentences are monotonously similar in structure?)

No definite rule can be set down about how much variety you should have in your sentences. But there must be some variety. If all the sentences on a page of one of your themes are declarative, try making at least one of them interrogative; if all the sentences in a paragraph are simple or compound, try to combine or relate them so as to secure a complex sentence or two; if all your sentences are from 10 to 15 words long, try to phrase an occasional five-word sentence, an occasional 25-word sentence.

You should guard particularly against a series of short, jerky sentences and a series of stringy, "run-on" sentences which monotonously reflect improper coordination and subordination. The former gives undue emphasis to relatively unimportant ideas; the latter tends to bury salient detail within a mass of less important thoughts.

We smile when we hear a little child say, "That's my train. That's a blue car. This is a yellow one. That one is the engine. It's red." In such an exaggerated series of choppy sentences, the weakness of the structure is readily apparent. Although you are not likely to write a patently childish series like the above, you must remember that a good writer is notable for his frequent and efficient use of subordination (and coordination). It is not brevity which is ineffective—quite the contrary; choppiness, jerkiness, and lack of understanding of thought relationships are the errors to be overcome. As you revise themes, make certain that you have not written a series of choppy sentences and that you have linked your thoughts with the proper connectives. See Section 13.

Stringy or "run-on" sentences—almost as childish as choppy ones—are caused by faulty coordination or subordination. In particular, avoid the *and* habit, the *but* habit, and the *so* habit. These sentences will illustrate:

> The workman placed the tools in the box, and he climbed up the ladder; he took the tools from the box and placed them on the roof.
> I asked him to go, but he said that he didn't want to, but when I insisted, he said he would.
> It is getting late so we will have to leave now so as to be on time.

The remedy for "run-on" sentences is to reduce predication, that is, condense. *And, but,* and *so* are perfectly proper words which we cannot get along without, but we must not overwork them. Use them sparingly in close proximity.

Closely related and fully as ineffective is the so-called "accordion" sentence, one containing a series of overlapping subordinate clauses introduced by *who, which, that.* Example: "The kind of dessert which he likes is one which has plenty of whipped cream and that contains chopped nuts." The remedy? Reduce predication: "He likes desserts which have plenty of whipped cream and chopped nuts." See Sections 8, 15a.

As important to sentence effectiveness as varied structure is varied length. The length of an individual sentence depends upon the amount of material needed to round out the thought in the writer's intended manner for his intended readers. Sentences are inclining toward brevity these days, possibly influenced by dialogue in radio, motion pictures, and television plus the practice of newspapers and magazines. Furthermore, long sentences do tend to become cluttered. You are urged to follow the advice of Anatole France: "Whenever you can shorten a sentence, do." But far more important than writing short, clear sentences is writing series of them which by their very patterns are not only clear but varied and refreshing. Depending upon the thoughts to be expressed, vary the length of your sentences; but when you venture into a lengthy one, be certain that all details are closely related to the main idea, as in this sentence of almost 100 words from James Harvey Robinson:

> But should the dynamos and motors which have come into being as the outcome of Faraday's experiment be stopped this evening, the businessman of today, agitated over labor troubles, might, as he trudged home past lines of "dead" cars, through dark streets to an unlighted house, engage in a little creative thought of his own and perceive that he and his laborers would have no modern factories and mines to quarrel about if it had not been for the strange, practical effects of the idle curiosity of scientists, inventors, and engineers.

Richard Hughes clearly illustrates sentence variety in the short passage which follows. Note that although the first and third sentences are approximately the same length, the first is complex, the other compound. Also, they are separated by a brief sentence fragment which accentuates the importance of the fact presented:

> Now, when the water in air condenses, it releases the energy that held it there, just as truly as the explosion of petrol releases energy. *Millions of horse power up there loose.* As in a petrol-motor, that energy is translated into motion: up rises the boundless balloon still higher, faster spins the vortex.

There are many different kinds of sentences, each of which is good in itself. No kind is effective if used too much. Good professional writers neither count the number of words in their sentences nor consciously intersperse simple and compound sentences with complex. But they do achieve variety in sentence structure. Analyze, for example, the sentences in the next-to-last paragraph of "How Americans Choose Their Heroes," p. 552.

Notice the variety in length, word order, and grammatical structure and function.

PLEASING SENTENCES

Beauty in sentences is as elusive and as difficult to define as it is everywhere else. But we do recognize that some sentences please more than others because of their grace or charm, just as some people or sights do. Sentences may be pleasing because they possess qualities already discussed in this chapter: variety, balance, climax, suspense, etc. A few additional methods of making sentences beautiful or pleasing, of giving them an air of perfection, of completeness, of being just right, may be briefly discussed: *euphony,* effective *repetition,* and *rhythm.*

Euphony comes from a Greek word meaning "well sounding." Prose is ordinarily not intended to "sound well" in the manner of poetry, but neither should it contain markedly harsh sounds. When books were few and reading aloud was more customary than it is now, appeals to the ear were important and many authors consciously employed devices to achieve euphony. Such attempts now seem artificial; but as we become more and more ear-minded because of the radio, sound pictures, and television, euphony is acquiring renewed significance. Speakers on radio and television, for example, frequently go through their scripts removing or revising groups of words either difficult to pronounce or easily confused.

As is pointed out on p. 377, certain groups of vowels and consonants are agreeable and harmonious to the ear; others are harsh, cacophonous. Some consonants (g, s, sh, k) are often less pleasing than others (l, m, n). You should not make your sentences artificially contain only these pleasant-sounding consonants but you should read your work aloud so that your ear will detect markedly harsh sounds. Occasionally, an otherwise effective sentence can be improved by removing cacophony.

You should not be overly conscious of euphony in your writing because artificiality and weakness may result. But you should keep in mind that certain words have pleasing sounds because of a correspondence between idea and sound. *Home, love, honor,* and *holy* are pleasing in sound not only because they contain an agreeable accented vowel but because they are associated with cherished ideas and concepts.

Again, the *repetition* of same or similar sounds provides pleasure in reading. Rhyme is out of place in prose, but occasional use of *alliteration* is not. Alliteration is the commencement of two or more words of a word group with an identical sound. It is illustrated in the first sentence of this paragraph: *same, similar, sounds; provides, pleasure; repetition, reading.* Alliteration is perhaps all too prevalent in the titles of current books, motion pictures, and plays, and in advertising, but it is an effective device if employed sparingly. No prose sentence should contain as much alliteration as these lines from Masefield's "Sea-Fever," but they illustrate the pleasing quality it provides:

> I must go down to the seas again, to the lonely sea and the sky,
> And all I ask is a tall ship and a star to steer her by.

Assonance is another device which, if employed thoughtfully and sparingly, will help to make sentences sound attractive. Assonance, the repetition of accented vowels, is more common in prose than is alliteration, but it, too, should be deliberately employed and with caution. No prose sentence will intentionally use as much assonance as Poe's "Once upon a midnight dreary, while I pondered, weak and weary," but restrained modification of this device will occasionally be effective in making sentences pleasing.

The poetic device of rhyme is not effective in prose, and such sentences as "When it became day we sailed into the bay" or "He will be late for his date" should be revised.

The following are euphonious passages. Read them aloud.

> Ideals are like stars; you will not succeed in touching them with your hands. But like the seafaring man on the desert of waters, you choose them as your guides, and following them you will reach your destiny.
>
> —CARL SCHURZ
>
> Those who compare the age in which their lot has fallen with a golden age which exists only in imagination, may talk of degeneracy and decay; but no man who is correctly informed as to the past will be disposed to take a morose or desponding view of the present.
>
> —MACAULAY

The following passage from Simeon Strunksy's *Night Life* provides a different effect. Read it aloud, too.

> A cartload of pasteurized milk for nurslings at four o'clock in the morning represents more service to civilization than a cartful of bullion on its way from the subtreasury to the vaults of a national bank five hours later.

Effective *repetition* of entire words and phrases may be as pleasing as repetition of the same or similar sounds within a sentence. We frequently delight in discovering the familiar; in some music, much of our pleasure derives from a reiterated theme. But repetition, like euphony, should not be your conscious and ever-present concern; employ it only when you can shape and present a particular thought more effectively.

The following sentences illustrate repetition. Do you find the repetition effective and pleasing or does it seem monotonous and artificial? Is the effectiveness of these sentences traceable in part to devices other than repetition?

> There is tolerable traveling on the beaten road, run how it may; only on the new road not yet leveled and paved and on the old road all broken into ruts and quagmires is the traveling bad or impracticable.
>
> —CARLYLE
>
> A sense of duty pursues us ever. It is omnipresent, like the Deity. If we take to ourselves the wings of the morning, and dwell in the uttermost parts of the sea, duty performed or duty violated is still with us, for our happiness or our misery.
>
> —DANIEL WEBSTER
>
> Raphael paints wisdom; Handel sings it, Phidias carves it, Shakespeare writes it, Wren builds it, Columbus discovers it, Luther preaches it, Washington arms it, Watt mechanizes it.
>
> —EMERSON

Effective repetition of both sound and word is illustrated in the follow-ing passage from the Bible. This, one of the most beautiful and pleasing passages in literature, would lose much of its effectiveness without allitera-tion, assonance, and repetition of words:

Vanity of vanities, saith the Preacher; vanity of vanities; all is vanity. What profit hath man of all his labor wherein he laboreth under the sun? One generation goeth, and another generation cometh; but the earth abideth forever. The sun also ariseth, and the sun goeth down, and hasteth to its place where it ariseth. The wind goeth toward the south and turneth about unto the north; it turneth about continually in its course, and the wind returneth again to its circuits. All the rivers run into the sea, yet the sea is not full; unto the place whither the rivers go, thither they go again. All things are full of weariness; man cannot utter it; the eye is not satisfied with seeing, nor the ear filled with hearing. That which hath been is that which shall be; and that which hath been done is that which shall be done: and there is no new thing under the sun.

—*Ecclesiastes*, 1:2–9

This passage also reminds us that prose has a varied but quite definite *rhythm*. In ordinary reading we rarely detect rhythm, but if sentences possess faulty rhythm or lack of balance, our ear quickly notes this. Robert Louis Stevenson, whose own prose is remarkably rhythmic, reminds us: "Literature is written by and for two senses: a sort of internal ear, quick to perceive 'unheard melodies,' and the eye, which directs the pen and deciphers the printed phrase."

A simple movement, such as characterizes the rhythm of conversation, is quite different from the elaborate and varied kinds to be found in poetry and "literary" prose. These latter types are more closely allied to music than are casual conversation and even most carefully written prose. You should remember to read aloud what you have written so as to remove obviously unrhythmical or harsh combinations of sounds.

Rhythm, euphony, and effective repetition of words are illustrated in the paragraph from "The Devil and Daniel Webster" beginning "And he began with the simple . . . ," p. 977. Analysis of such a superb paragraph should reveal much about sentence effectiveness in its many phases. So, too, will study of this paragraph from p. 897:

And this is how I see the East. I have seen its secret places and have looked into its very soul; but now I see it always from a small boat, a high outline of mountains, blue and afar in the morning; like faint mist at noon; a jagged wall of purple at sunset. I have the feel of the oar in my hand, the vision of a scorching blue sea in my eyes. And I see a bay, a wide bay, smooth as glass and polished like ice, shimmering in the dark. A red light burns far off upon the gloom of the land, and the night is soft and warm. We drag at the oars with aching arms, and suddenly a puff of wind, a puff faint and tepid and laden with strange odors of blossoms, of aromatic wood, comes out of the still night—the first sigh of the East on my face. That I can never forget. It was impalpable and enslaving, like a charm, like a whis-pered promise of mysterious delight.

—JOSEPH CONRAD, *Youth*

GENERAL SUMMARY — THE SENTENCE

Good sentences depend upon good diction. Even more fundamentally, however, they depend upon clear thinking. Our concepts may be sound, but they must be closely related before they can be put into unified sentences; they must be completely and clearly phrased—fuzzy, inaccurate thinking causes incompleteness and obscurity; they must be so arranged as to communicate an idea with maximum effectiveness to the reader. There is no short cut to good sentences; they depend upon careful thinking. Sentences are, however, comparatively short. Because they are, they are the primary units for revision. Words are not usually considered alone—their clarity and effectiveness depend upon their use in a specific sentence. When you speak of the need for rewriting a theme or revising a paragraph, what you mean is that the component sentences require attention. The sentence, then, is *the* unit of revision. Make your sentences correct, clear, and emphatic, and the whole theme will largely take care of itself.

Despite all the rhetorical advice provided in this chapter, first make certain that your sentences are *correct* in structure and *clear* in meaning. To this end, pay constant attention to Sections 1–15 of the Handbook. When you have mastered the basics of sentence writing, then, and only then, should you strive for genuine sentence effectiveness. But do not forsake this final effort; merely postpone it until you have demonstrated your mastery of sentence essentials.

· EXERCISES ·

CONCISENESS

A. The following paragraph lacks conciseness. Rewrite it, removing unnecessary words and extraneous ideas.

Without a single opposing opinion Ernest Hemingway was declared to be the author most liked and enjoyed by our class. We read several of his far-famed and world-renowned stories and narratives during the course and were constantly impressed and moved by the author's wonderful choice of words; he is unsurpassed in his beautiful selection of diction. But the main and principal reason for our admiration is that he always and unfailingly chooses real human beings as his characters and puts them in situations which are lifelike and real.

B. Analyze a paragraph you have recently written. Does it contain any unnecessary words? Does it have a whole idea which could be dropped without loss?

C. The following two paragraphs contain remarkably concise sentences. Do they form effective sentence patterns or tend to become monotonous? Are these sentences so deliberately impressionistic that their very conciseness adds to effectiveness? fails to communicate?

Searched long for the word. How to describe one's life without dragging in irrelevancies. Syncopated. Ordered here and there. Moving. No rest. A fabled flicker-show with murmur of mechanism as an undertone and accompaniment. Ordered away—to Philadelphia. Strap-hanging and studying time-tables simultaneously. Sudden thought—car battery needs recharging. Thought unfolds without pause. Use car to get baggage to terminal. Excellent. Thought goes on relentlessly. Use car for journey. What is life without adventure? No more than a dead battery—a malodorous inconvenience.

Fresh battery installed—$10 deposit—engine humming amiably, and ahead the asphalted felicity of Riverside Drive—mist pearling the fleet in the river. Set meter at zero for the trip. Uptown, farewell! We syncopate.

—WILLIAM MCFEE

D. From your reading or from a book of quotations select a half-dozen *epigrams* which appeal to you. Show how each could be used (with proper credit to the author) to make emphatic some paragraph or theme topic of your selection.

E. From memory, write down a half-dozen *proverbs*. (Doesn't the fact that you can do so prove their triteness?) Can you rephrase one of these or give it a new application?

F. From a book of quotations select three *maxims*. Try to rephrase one of them or give it an unexpected application.

G. Some people object to the epigrammatic style of authors such as Francis Bacon and Ralph Waldo Emerson. Do you? Can you demonstrate that thoughtless and too frequent use of epigrams results in awkwardness?

VARIED WORD ORDER

A. Write a half-dozen sentences in which you put something before the subject. (They may be revisions of sentences taken from one of your recent themes.)

B. Make the following loose sentences periodic:

1. Most athletes require conditioning after a lengthy period of inactivity.
2. I lost my best friend on a cold winter morning over the city of Brooklyn, New York.
3. A group of students banded themselves together for the purpose of encouraging better concerts on the campus.
4. Dick watched the procession day after day and became more and more bewildered.
5. The air is sweet with the smell of flowers, of grass wet with dew, and of frying bacon.

C. Change five loose sentences from one of your recent themes into periodic sentences. Do these sentences gain or lose effectiveness by the change?

D. Compose five sentences which are arranged in climactic order. (These may or may not be periodic.)

E. Write five sentences which reveal balanced structure.

VARIETY IN LENGTH AND STRUCTURE

A. Analyze for sentence length any two opening paragraphs of selections in Book Three. Do the sentence lengths have relationship to the writers' purposes?

B. Analyze for sentence length the best and worst of your corrected themes. Do you find any noticeable difference in average sentence length? If you do, is there any relation between sentence length and the grade which the theme received?

C. Of the first 10 sentences of one of your recent themes, how many are simple? how many compound? complex? compound-complex?

D. Of these 10 sentences (Exercise C) how many are loose? periodic? balanced?

E. Of these 10 sentences (Exercise C) how many are declarative? interrogative? imperative? exclamatory?

F. What conclusions do you reach as a result of Exercises C, D, E?

G. Analyze a paragraph composed of choppy sentences. Then carefully combine as many of these sentences as possible into longer sentences which reflect correct relationships of thought.

H. Analyze a recent theme which you have written. How many "run-on" sentences can you find? Do you have the *and* habit, the *but* habit, the *so* habit?

PLEASING SENTENCES

A. Write five sentences which contain sounds not pleasing to the ear. Point out how these sentences can be made euphonious.

B. Distinguish among *euphony, euphemism, euphuism*. Consult your dictionary, if necessary.

C. From your reading or from a book of quotations select five lines of poetry or prose which contain alliteration.

D. From the same source (Exercise C) select five lines which exhibit assonance.

E. From the same source (Exercise C) select five lines or passages which contain repetition of words or phrases.

F. From your reading select two paragraphs in which the sentences have pronounced rhythm. Perhaps you will be able to scan a few lines of each.

G. Study the titles of a half-dozen essays or stories in your book of readings. (Select only those containing at least three words.) Do they *sound* all right? Is the rhythm of word arrangement unmistakable?

H. In Act I of *Pygmalion*, p. 1066, how do the sound and rhythm of Eliza's remarks contribute to the playwright's characterization of her?

GENERAL EXERCISES

A. Look before you leap.

He who hesitates is lost.

Using one or both of these proverbs sharply contrasting in advice, compose the following:

1. A compound sentence.
2. A compound-complex sentence.
3. A balanced sentence.
4. A periodic sentence.
5. A sentence containing "nevertheless."
6. A sentence beginning with "Leap" and ending with "hesitates."
7. A sentence beginning "It is odd that."
8. A sentence providing the same contrary advice in different words.
9. A sentence on another subject providing equally contrary advice.
10. A brief, memorable sentence rebutting either or both of these proverbs.

B. Analyze the following paragraphs as to sentence effectiveness—conciseness, varied word order, variety in length and structure, beauty:

1. The first paragraph of "How To Look at a Statistic," p. 504.
2. The second paragraph of "The Human Community," p. 554.
3. The first paragraph of "The Uses of the Moon," p. 564.

4. The second paragraph of "Language Inflation," p. 633.
5. The final paragraph of "The Case for Greater Clarity in Writing," p. 657.
6. The first paragraph of "Where I Lived and What I Lived For," p. 684.
7. The final paragraph of "Herman Melville," p. 752.
8. The first paragraph of "Daniel Webster, American," p. 814.
9. The final paragraph of "Gettysburg," p. 857.
10. The third paragraph of "The Devil and Daniel Webster," p. 969.

CHAPTER 5

BUILDING AND USING A VOCABULARY

"Don't you see what I mean?" "Why can't I explain this to you?" "It was the most—, er, well—" "If I could only say what I think . . ." "I know it but I can't say it."

Familiar phrases to all of us, aren't they? Never a day, hardly an hour, passes but we have occasion to express some thought which seems difficult to put into words. The reason is obvious: all our thinking is done in terms of concepts, words; and since we can't "keep our minds still" for long at a time, we are constantly using words in our thinking and in our attempts to communicate our thoughts to others. Thinking and diction, which is the choice and use of words, are inseparable. In a very real sense, a person's thinking can be no more effective than his word supply.

When you write a letter or a theme, or enter into conversation, you *have* to have something to say and you *should* have some interest and purpose in expressing that something, whatever it is. Therefore, you "unlock your word-hoard," to use the picturesque phrase of the Anglo-Saxons, and select those words at your command which will most accurately convey your meaning to others. But nearly everyone feels the inadequacy of his vocabulary at times. All of us have had the experience of not being able to find the right words to express our thoughts, of being misunderstood, of not being able to make ourselves clear. Since there is an almost complete interdependence of thought and language—Oliver Wendell Holmes once said,

"A word is the skin of a living thought"—it follows that by using the most effective words we possibly can we not only communicate our ideas more clearly to other people but also strengthen and clarify our own thinking.

BUILDING A VOCABULARY

Because it is difficult to think clearly and exactly, it is difficult to achieve good diction. Each of us makes vows, perhaps sporadically, to "recruit the vigor" of his vocabulary. We are aware that our lack of mastery of words prevents our full possession of hundreds of impressions, thoughts, and feelings which come to us as results of our observation and thinking. But although intelligent people wish to increase and strengthen their vocabularies, few are willing to make a real effort to do so. Do not be misled; there are no easy methods of acquiring and mastering a good vocabulary. Occasionally looking up a word in the dictionary will help very little. Sitting down in a burst of enthusiasm to memorize, at random, scores of words from it is also valueless. Perhaps the most direct attack upon the problem is to learn to utilize words which we already have in our potential vocabularies.

Each of us has three vocabularies. First, there is our *active*, or *speaking*, vocabulary. This is our productive word stock, the words which we use daily in our speaking. Second, there is our *writing* vocabulary. This also is active in that we have frequent occasion to use its word supply in our writing; it contains some words which we do not habitually use in speech. In addition to these two active, or productive, vocabularies, each of us has a *potential*, or *recognition*, vocabulary. By means of this potential vocabulary, the largest of the three, we can understand speakers and can read and understand books, magazines, and newspapers. But in our reading and listening we encounter many words which we recognize and of which we have some understanding, possibly from the context, but which we would be unable to use in our own speaking and writing. Until we use such words, however —put them into circulation, that is—they are not really ours.

To get words from our potential into our active vocabularies requires systematic effort, but it is the logical way to begin vocabulary improvement. Why? Because words in a recognition vocabulary already have made some impression on our consciousness; they are already partly ours. Their values, although still vague to us, can be made exact and accurate. Furthermore, quite likely they are words which we shall want in our vocabularies. Probably we have come across them time and again; they are not unusual and high-sounding words. They are words that have *use* value. Mastering them will help us to avoid the pitfall of "swallowing the dictionary," a useless task which fails because it has no direct connection with our needs.

We have both to learn, and to learn how to use, words before they can become parts of our active vocabularies. A college English teacher once told one of his students that he felt the student was using words which he did not really understand. The student protested that he did know the meanings of the words, that many of them were words which he had noted in his regular reading of a well-known weekly magazine. The instructor commended the student for his enterprise, and then asked him to read the current issue of the magazine over the weekend and bring his copy to class on the following Monday. The teacher also got the issue and read it carefully. He marked 102 words, a few of which he had to look up in a dictionary himself, but most of which he felt certain the student did not know. On Monday, the instructor underlined the 102 words in the student's copy and requested the student to give a "working" definition of each and to use it in a sentence. Half an hour later, the student announced that he could define and use only about half of them. He was told to define as many as he could. After cutting down the number several times, he finally managed to define roughly and use correctly only eight of the words! He was an intelligent student, the magazine was widely circulated and was written for popular consumption, the great majority of the words were not unusual—he had simply assumed that he knew words which he did not know. They had some recognition value for him, but no *use* value. After being cautioned by the instructor not to learn all the 102 words (a few were esoteric), he set out to master the others, thus moving them from his potential to his active vocabulary.

Actually, acquiring an active vocabularly of considerable range is not so formidable a task as it may seem at a despairing moment when you are looking at a huge, unabridged dictionary. A reliable scholar has revealed that even Shakespeare, that master of diction, used fewer than 17,000 words in all his plays. And yet, as the late S. Stephenson Smith[1] pointed out, the "average" American knows about 10,000 words—the words most common in newspapers, general magazines, and daily speaking.

Mr. Smith reported that certain quality magazines—*Saturday Review*, the *Atlantic Monthly, Harper's Magazine*—assume that their readers command the vocabulary of the "average" college graduate: 20,000–25,000 words. Naturally, these are not always the same words; an English major and a premedical student are quite likely to possess somewhat different vocabularies upon graduation from college.

However, a number of careful studies have revealed that certain basic words are used most freqeuntly in writing and speaking. One such study, Thorndike and Lorge's *The Teacher's Word Book of 30,000 Words*, contains from 10,000 to 15,000 words that are known to nearly every adult and are commonly used. It is reasonable to assume, therefore, that you have a vocabulary of at least this size. With this number as a starter, you can begin to build. College courses will provide many opportunities for you to double the size of your vocabulary. Words new to you appear on every page of the daily newspaper. Conversations and lectures will be full of them. Television and radio programs fill the air with them. Try to master them not only because doing so will enrich your reading, writing, and speaking but because a good vocabulary will be important to you in later life. A scientific investigator, Johnson O'Connor, has written:

> An extensive knowledge of the exact meanings of English words accompanies outstanding success in this country more often than any other single

---

[1] S. Stephenson Smith, *The Command of Words*, Thomas Y. Crowell Company, 2nd ed., 1949.

characteristic which the Human Engineering Laboratory has been able to isolate and measure.

In order to see what your task is, try these two tests:

1. Define and use in sentences each of these words:

essence	pancreas
inimitable	inevitably
quintessence	copiously
tinctures	anthropologists
incessantly	contrived
equation	caste
articulate	transmit
symbols	fertility
primitive	republican
intricate	Renaissance

After you have given yourself this test, turn to Highet's "The Necessity for Reason," p. 510, from which the words were selected. Do you agree that the test is fair?

2. Select in each series the word or word group which is closest in meaning to the word italicized in the phrase. Put your list on a separate sheet. Check it with a dictionary.

1. *propriety* of actions — property/properness/standard/principle/behavior
2. I replied *glibly* — fast/profoundly/slowly/loudly/fluently
3. your reasoning is *erroneous* — incorrect/convincing/right/pleasing/learned
4. *edified* by the sermon — pleased/disgusted/saddened/amused/uplifted
5. these fruits are *indigenous* — common/expensive/sweet/native/nonexistent
6. *harassed* by upperclassmen — praised/ignored/loved/guided/tormented
7. completely *exasperated* — thoughtful/exalted/pleased/worn out/angered
8. a *sagacious* decision — shrewd/foolish/unanimous/necessary/overdue
9. to eat *voraciously* — rapidly/slowly/politely/indifferently/greedily
10. with much *vehemence* — pettiness/violence/venom/expression/ease
11. religious *intolerance* — unwillingness/uneasiness/narrow-mindedness/faith/sincerity
12. *ostensibly* confused — much/unexpectedly/professedly/possibly/stupidly
13. an *antiquated* building — rustic/outdated/magnificent/modern/haunted
14. to *dominate* a conversation — improve/interrupt/participate in/rule/object to
15. a *boon* to mankind — legacy/blessing/boost/friend/curse
16. a *lucrative* occupation — dull/interesting/overcrowded/lucky/profitable

17. we *subjugated* the natives — educated/clothed/conquered/harassed/victimized
18. the action was *deplorable* — useless/desirable/regrettable/necessary/decisive
19. the child wept *copiously* — little/abundantly/often/secretly/openly
20. complete *annihilation* — destruction/praise/anger/despair/victory
21. a *peculiarity* of manners — politeness/quality/genuineness/change/oddity
22. acting *flippantly* — pertly/half-scared/half-apologetically/flinchingly/stupidly
23. a *beatific* smile — silly/flashing/beaming/blissful/sincere
24. to *succumb* to a disease — overcome/yield to/ignore/be immune to/be cured of
25. a *colossal* undertaking — approved/amazing/huge/impossible/secret

Your scores on these two tests may suggest that you should make friends immediately with a good dictionary. There is no better place to start. But you should learn to use your dictionary intelligently and fully. You should read carefully the entire entry and thus make the word a part of your own vocabulary. A dictionary is much more than a guide to spelling, as the exhibit on pp. 82–83 indicates. This chart was prepared specifically for *Webster's Seventh New Collegiate Dictionary*, but any good desk dictionary will reveal similar rich resources. Becoming thoroughly acquainted with your dictionary and your college library may mean more to you over the years than any particular friends you make or courses you take during your entire college career.

Some instructors recommend that you record on 3-by-5 cards information about words you are adding to your vocabulary. Both sides of the card may be used:

WORD	PRONUNCIATION
OTHER FORMS	
SOURCE	DATE

Front of card

```
┌─────────────────────────────────────────────────────────────┐
│                                                             │
│   CONTEXT                                                    │
│                                                             │
│                                                             │
│   DEFINITION                                                │
│                                                             │
│                                                             │
│   ETYMOLOGY                                                 │
│                                                             │
│                                                             │
│   ORIGINAL SENTENCE                                         │
│                                                             │
│                                                             │
└─────────────────────────────────────────────────────────────┘
```

Back of card

In addition to careful and judicious use of your dictionary, there are several other methods of stimulating and advancing this process of acquiring new words. *Précis-writing* will prove helpful (see p. 419). The careful attention to subject matter which this demands calls for weighing each word and its value.

Similarly, the making of *paraphrases* will prove a stimulus to increasing your vocabulary (see p. 412). In a sense, paraphrasing is a form of translation which requires an almost painfully exact use of words. *Translation from a foreign language* to English is also helpful. In translating, one has to grope for and find those words which will catch and convey the complete thought of a passage.

Collecting lists of *synonyms* and distinguishing their meanings is an effective, often stimulating, way to enlarge your vocabulary. Those words which have the same or a similar meaning are synonyms for one another, but remember that one or more of their other meanings may differ. Becoming aware of distinctions between similar words adds to your understanding as well as your vocabulary. A study of the word *old* may add to your vocabulary such other words as *aboriginal, aged, ancient, antediluvian, antiquated, antique, decrepit, elderly, hoary, passé, patriarchal, venerable,* and several more.

Your dictionary includes listings and often brief discussions of hundreds of synonyms, showing the differences in meaning of apparently similar words. When looking up a word, be certain to study the treatment of synonymous words, if included; you may be able to choose a more exact and emphatic word for your meaning and also add new words to your vocabulary. With the aid of a dictionary such as one of those listed on p. 371, a thesaurus (*Roget's International Thesaurus*, third edition, is excellent), or a dictionary of synonyms (recommended are *Webster's Dictionary* of *Synonyms* and the *Standard Book of Synonyms, Antonyms, and Prepositions*), try to find synonyms for these words:

answer (noun)	effort
blemish	frank
blunt	growth
colloquial	idea
defame	wise

Now that you have made a preliminary study of synonyms, will you necessarily have to write that the boy is *cute,* the dress *glamorous,* the idea *interesting,* the game *thrilling,* or the movie *exciting?* In short, a word that is apt on many occasions is rarely suitable for all. Enrich your writing and speaking by a systematic search for accurate synonyms.

Similarly, studying *antonyms* will improve your understanding of words and will help to build your vocabulary. Learning the opposite, or negative, of one or more of the meanings of another word will not be so valuable as studying synonyms, but the effort is worthwhile. Seeking antonyms for the verb *praise* may add, among others, these words to your vocabulary: *abuse, blame, censure, condemn, deprecate, disparage, impugn, inveigh against, lampoon, stigmatize, vilify.* The word *join,* for example, has such opposites, or approximate opposites, as *cleave, disconnect, dissever, separate,* and *sunder.*

These opposite meanings are not all-inclusive: a word may be an antonym of another only in a limited meaning. For example, one antonym of *man* concerns sex; another, age; another, biology; another, religion. Like synonyms, antonyms must be selected carefully and used with exactness.

Another method of adding to your vocabulary is to make a study of *prefixes and suffixes.* A prefix is an element placed *before* a word or root to make another word of different function or meaning. (The prefix *pre* means *before:* pre-American, preeminent, prearrange.) A suffix is an element that is placed *after* a word to make a word of different meaning or function: play*ful,* speedo*meter.* You can add considerably to your vocabulary by learning the meanings of several prefixes and suffixes. Here is a brief list of them:

ante- (before)	antedate anteroom	*poly-* (many)	polygon polysyllable
anti- (against, opposite)	antisocial antiwar	*post-* (after)	postwar postseason
auto- (self)	automobile autograph	*syn-* (with)	synthesis synonym
eu- (well)	eulogy euphony	*-graph* (writing)	geography orthography
hyper- (beyond the ordinary)	hypercritical hypersensitive	*-logos* (study)	biology geology
im-, in- (not)	impossible immature inaccurate indefinite	*-meter* (measure) *-phone* (sound)	speedometer thermometer dictaphone homophone
peri- (all round)	perimeter periphery		

angle bracket **12.1**	
author quoted **12.2.1**	
binomial **13.1**	
boldface type **1.1, 19.1**	
capitalization label **5.1**	
centered period **1.6**	
cognate cross-reference **1.7.3**	
comb form **3.3, 18.**	
definition	
directional cross-reference **15.1**	
double hyphen **1.6.1**	
equal variant **1.7.1**	
etymology **7.**	
functional label **3.1**	
homographs **1.4.1**	
hyphened compound **1.1**	
inflectional forms **4.1, 4.2**	
lightface type **1.1**	
lowercase **5.1**	
main entry **1.1, 19.1**	
often attrib **6.**	
open compound **1.1, 2.6**	
pl but sing in constr **4.3**	
prefix **3.3, 18.1**	

⁴save \(ₜ)sāv\ *conj* **1 :** were it not : ONLY — used with *that* **2 :** BUT, EXCEPT — used before a word often taken to be the subject of a clause 〈no one knows about it ~ shé〉 **3 :** UNLESS 〈~ they could be plucked asunder, all my quest were but in vain —Alfred Tenny-son〉

scar·a·bae·us \ₜskar-ə-'bē-əs\ *n* [L] **1** *pl* **scar·a·bae·us·es** *or* **scar·a·baei** \-'bē-ₜī\ **:** a large black or nearly black dung beetle (*Scarabaeus sacer*) **2 :** a stone or faience beetle used in ancient Egypt as a talisman, ornament, and a symbol of the resurrection

scar·a·mouch *or* **scar·a·mouche** \'skar-ə-ₜmüsh, -ₜmüch, -ₜmaúch\ *n* [F *Scaramouche*, fr. It *Scaramuccia*] **1** (*cap*)**:** a stock character in the Italian commedia dell' arte drawn to burlesque the Spanish don and characterized by boastfulness and poltroonery **2 a :** a cowardly buffoon **b :** RASCAL. SCAMP

sce·nog·ra·phy \sē-'näg-rə-fē\ *n* [Gk *skēnographia* painting of scenery, fr. *skēnē* + *-graphia* -graphy] **:** the art of perspective representation applied to the painting of stage scenery (as by the Greeks)

sceptic *var of* SKEPTIC

schiz- *or* **schizo-** (*comb form*) [NL, fr. Gk *schizo-*, fr. *schizein* to split] **1 :** split : cleft 〈*schizo*carp〉 **2 :** characterized by or involving cleavage 〈*schizo*genesis〉 **3 :** schizophrenia 〈*schizo*thymia〉

scho·las·ti·cism \skə-'las-tə-ₜsiz-əm\ *n* **1** *cap* **a :** a philosophical movement dominant in western Christian civilization from the 9th until the 17th century and combining a fixed religious dogma with the mystical and intuitional tradition of patristic philosophy esp. of St. Augustine and later with Aristotelianism **b :** NEO-SCHOLASTICISM **2 :** close adherence to the traditional teachings or methods of a school or sect

¹scru·ple \'skrü-pəl\ *n* [ME *scriple*, fr. L *scrupulus* a unit of weight, fr. *scrupulus* small sharp stone] **1** (— see MEASURE table) **2 :** a minute part or quantity : IOTA

²sculpture *vb* **sculp·tur·ing** \'skəlp-chə-riŋ, 'skəlp-shriŋ\ *vt* **1 a :** to form an image or representation from solid material (as wood or stone) **b :** to carve or otherwise form into a three-dimensional work of art **2 :** to change (the form of the earth's surface) by erosion ~ *vi* : to work as a sculptor

sea-maid \'sē-ₜmād\ (*or* **sea-maid·en** \-ₜmād-²n\ *n* **:** MERMAID; *also* **:** a goddess or nymph of the sea

se·clude \si-'klüd\ *vt* [ME *secluden* to keep away, fr. L *secludere* to separate, seclude, fr. *se-* apart + *claudere* to close — more at SECEDE, CLOSE]) **1 a :** to confine in a retired or inaccessible place **b :** to remove or separate from intercourse or outside influence : ISOLATE **2** *obs* **:** to exclude or expel from a privilege, rank, or dignity : DEBAR **3 :** to shut off : SCREEN

¹sec·ond·hand \ₜsek-ən-'\ (*adj*) **1 :** received from or through an intermediary : BORROWED **2 a :** acquired after being used by another : not new 〈~ books〉 **b :** dealing in secondhand merchandise 〈a ~ bookstore〉

²secondhand \ₜsek-ən-'\ *adv* : at second hand : INDIRECTLY

secretary-general *n, pl* **secretaries-general :** a principal administrative officer

²seer \'si(ə)r\ *n, pl* (**seers** *or* **seer**) [Hindi *ser*] **1 :** any of various Indian units of weight; *esp* : a unit equal to 2.057 pounds **2 :** (an Afghan unit of weight equal to 15.6 pounds)

²seethe *n* : a state of seething : EBULLITION

¹seg·ment \'seg-mənt\ *n,* (*often attrib*) [L *segmentum*, fr. *secare* to cut — more at SAW] **1 a :** a piece or separate fragment of something : PORTION **b** (1) **:** a portion cut off from a geometrical figure by a line or plane; *esp* : the part of a circular area bounded by a chord and an arc of that circle or so much of the area as is cut off by the chord (2) **:** the part of a sphere cut off by a plane or included between two parallel planes (3) **:** the finite part of a line between two points in the line **2 :** one of the constituent parts into which a body, entity, or quantity naturally divides : DIVISION **syn** see PART — **seg·men·tary** \'seg-mən-ₜter-ē\ *adj*

selling race *n* : a claiming race in which the winning horse is put up for auction

se·man·tics \si-'mant-iks\ (*n pl but sing or pl in constr*) **1 :** the study of meanings : **a :** the historical and psychological study and the classification of changes in the signification of words or forms viewed as factors in linguistic development **b** (1) **:** SEMIOTIC (2) **:** a branch of semiotic dealing with the relations between signs and what they refer to and including theories of denotation, extension, naming, and truth **2 :** GENERAL SEMANTICS **3 a :** the meaning or relationship of meanings of a sign or set of signs; *esp* : connotative meaning **b :** the exploitation of connotation and ambiguity (as in propaganda)

semi- \ₜsem-i, 'sem-, -ₜī\ (*prefix*) [ME, fr. L; akin to OHG *sāmi-* half, Gk *hēmi-*] **1 a :** precisely half of: (1) **:** forming a bisection of 〈*semi*ellipse〉 〈*semi*oval〉 (2) **:** being a usu. vertically bisected form of 〈a specified architectural feature〉 〈*semi*arch〉 〈*semi*dome〉 **b :** half in quantity or value : half of or occurring halfway through a specified period of time 〈*semi*annual〉 〈*semi*centenary〉 — compare BI- **2 :** to some extent : pa . incompletely 〈*semi*civilized〉 〈*semi*-independent〉 〈*semi*dry〉 — npare DEMI-, HEMI- **3 a :** partial : incomplete 〈*semi*consciousne.s〉 〈*semi*darkness〉 **b :** having some of the characteristics of 〈*semi*porcelain〉 **c :** quasi 〈*semi*governmental〉 〈*semi*monastic〉

By permission. From *A New Outline for Dictionary Study*, copyright 1965 by

CHART

stato·blast \'stat-ə-,blast\ *n* [ISV] **1 :** a bud in a freshwater bryozoan that overwinters in a chitinous envelope and develops into a new individual in spring **2 :** GEMMULE

primary stress
2.2

stat·ol·a·try \stāt-'äl-ə-trē\ *n* **:** advocacy of a highly centralized and all-powerful national government

pronunciation
2.

stead·ing \'sted-ᵊn, 'stēd-, -iŋ\ *n* [ME steding, fr. stede place, farm] **1 :** a small farm **2** *chiefly Scot* **:** the service buildings or area of a farm

regional label
8.3.4

²steer *vb* [ME steren, fr. OE stīeran; akin to OE stēor- steering oar, Gk stauros stake, cross, stylos pillar, Skt sthavira, sthūra stout, thick, L stare to stand — more at STAND] *vt* **1 :** to direct the course of; *specif* **:** to guide by mechanical means (as a rudder) **2 :** to set and hold to (a course) ~ *vi* **1 :** to direct the course (as of a ship or automobile) **2 :** to pursue a course of action **3 :** to be subject to guidance or direction ⟨an automobile ~s well⟩ **syn** see GUIDE — **steer·able** \'stir-ə-bəl\ *adj* — **steer·er** *n* — **steer clear** ⟨: to keep entirely away — often used with *of*⟩

run-on entry (derivative)
16.1

run-on entry (phrasal)
16.2

stel·late \'stel-,āt\ *adj* **:** resembling a star (as in shape) **:** RADIATED ⟨a ~ leaf⟩ — **stel·late·ly** *adv*

secondary stress
2.2

³stint *n, pl* **stints** also **stint** [ME stynte] **:** any of several small sandpipers

secondary variant
1.7.2

²stipple *n* **:** production of gradation of light and shade in graphic art by stippling small points, larger dots, or longer strokes; also **:** an effect produced by or as if by stippling

sense divider
11.4.2

¹stom·ach \'stəm-ək, -ik\ *n, often attrib* [ME stomak, fr. MF estomac, fr. L stomachus gullet, esophagus, stomach, fr. Gk stomachos, fr. stoma mouth; akin to MBret staffu mouth, Av staman-] **1 a :** a dilatation of the alimentary canal of a vertebrate communicating anteriorly with the esophagus and posteriorly with the duodenum **b :** an analogous cavity in an invertebrate animal **c :** the part of the body that contains the stomach **:** BELLY, ABDOMEN **2 a :** desire for food caused by hunger **:** APPETITE **b :** INCLINATION, DESIRE **3** *obs* **a :** SPIRIT, VALOR **b :** PRIDE **c :** SPLEEN, RESENTMENT

sense letter
11.2

sense number
11.1

¹strike \'strīk\ *vb* **struck** *also* **strak\ struck** *also* **strick·en** \'strik-ən\ **strik·ing** \'strī-kiŋ\ [ME striken, fr. OE strican to stroke, go; akin to OHG strīhhan to stroke, L stringere to touch lightly, striga, stria furrow] *vi* **1 :** to take a course **:** GO **2 :** to deliver or aim a blow or thrust **:** HIT **3 :** CONTACT, COLLIDE **4 :** DELETE, CANCEL **5 :** to lower a flag usu. in surrender **6 a :** to be indicated by a clock, bell, or chime **b :** to make known the time by sounding **7 :** PIERCE, PENETRATE **8 a :** to engage in battle **b :** to make a military attack **9 :** to become ignited **10 :** to discover something **11 a :** to pull on a fishing rod in order to set the hook **b** *of a fish* **:** to seize the bait **12 :** DART, SHOOT **13 a** *of a plant cutting* **:** to take root **b** *of a seed* **:** GERMINATE **14 :** to make an impression **15 :** to stop work in order to force an employer to comply with demands **16 :** to make a beginning **17 :** to thrust oneself forward **18 :** to work diligently **:** STRIVE ~ *vt* **1 a :** to strike at **:** HIT **b :** to drive or remove by or as if by a blow **c :** to attack or seize with a sharp blow (as of fangs or claws) ⟨struck by a snake⟩ **d :** INFLICT **e :** to produce by or as if by a blow or stroke **f :** to separate by a sharp blow ⟨~ off flints⟩ **2 a :** to haul down **:** LOWER **b :** to dismantle and take away

small capitals
15.0, 15.2

status label
8.

subject label
9.1

swung dash (boldface)
3.2

swung dash (lightface)
12.1

strin·gent \'strin-jənt\ *adj* [L stringent-, stringens, prp. of stringere to bind tight] **1 :** TIGHT, CONSTRICTED **2 :** marked by rigor, strictness, or severity esp. with regard to rule or standard **3 :** marked by money scarcity and credit strictness **syn** see RIGID — **strin·gent·ly** *adv*

symbolic colon
10.

strong \'stròŋ\ *adj* **stron·ger** \'stròŋ-gər\ **stron·gest** \'stròŋ-gəst\ [ME, fr. OE strang; akin to OHG strengi strong, L stringere to bind tight — more at STRAIN] **1 :** having or marked by great physical power **:** ROBUST **2 :** having moral or intellectual power **3 :** having great resources (as of wealth) **4 :** of a specified number ⟨an army ten thousand ~⟩ **5 :** effective or efficient esp. in a specified direction **6 :** FORCEFUL, COGENT **7 :** not mild or weak **:** INTENSE: as **a :** rich in some active agent (as a flavor or extract) ⟨~ beer⟩ **b** *of a color* **:** high in chroma

synonymous cross-reference
15.2

synonymy cross-reference
17.2

syn STRONG, STOUT, STURDY, STALWART, TOUGH, TENACIOUS mean showing power to resist or to endure. STRONG may imply power derived from muscular vigor, large size, structural soundness, intellectual or spiritual resources; STOUT suggests an ability to endure stress, pain, or hard use without giving way; STURDY implies strength derived from vigorous growth, determination of spirit, solidity of construction; STALWART suggests an unshakable dependability and connotes great physical strength; TOUGH implies great firmness and resiliency; TENACIOUS suggests strength in seizing, retaining, clinging to, or holding together

synonymy paragraph
17.1

uppercase

stron·tia \'strän-ch(ē-)ə, 'strünt-ē-ə\ *n* [NL] fr. obs. E strontian, fr. Strontian, village in Scotland] **1 :** a white solid monoxide SrO of strontium resembling lime and baryta **2 :** strontium hydroxide $Sr(OH)_2$

usage note
14.

sty·loid \'stī(ə)l-,òid\ *adj* **:** resembling a style **:** STYLIFORM — used esp. of slender pointed skeletal processes (as on the temporal bone or ulna)

verbal illustration
12.1

sub·ac·id \-'as-əd\ *adj* [L subacidus, fr. sub- + acidus acid] **1 :** moderately acid ⟨~ fruit juices⟩ **2 :** rather tart ⟨~ prose⟩ — **sub·ac·id·ly** *adv* — **sub·ac·id·ness** *n*

²sun *vb* **sunned; sun·ning** *vt* **:** to expose to or as if to the rays of the sun ~ *vi* **:** to sun oneself

verb principal parts
4.5, 4.6

G. & C. Merriam Company, Publishers of the Merriam-Webster Dictionaries.

For other examples, see the headings *Prefix* and *Suffix* in the Handbook. Also in the Handbook, read the study of prefixes and suffixes under their generic name, *Affixes*. And do you really know, and know how to use, that useful word *generic*?

The single most important factor in improving the vocabulary is the *will* to learn, and to learn how to use, new words. Wide reading and intelligent listening should lead straight to a use of the dictionary. In précis-writing, in paraphrasing, translating, verse-writing, studying synonyms, antonyms, and prefixes and suffixes, the dictionary is directly useful, always indispensable. If in reading, for example, you dislike to "break the chain of thought" by looking up words in a dictionary (although the chain has already been broken by the very necessity for using a dictionary!), jot down unfamiliar words and look them up as soon as possible. It is a good idea to have a notebook with you when you read. There are on the market word-books, small enough to be carried around in your pocket or handbag, which contain headings such as "origin," "meaning," etc. Set down in such a book the unfamiliar words you come across and look them up later, filling out the entries completely. Failure to master words because of your assumption that you "know the meanings well enough" will continue to prove the greatest single hindrance to your vocabulary improvement. And remember, after you have thoroughly studied a new word, use it in speech and writing until it is yours. Adding words to one's stock can be fascinating, but there must be a constant and systematic use of your *will* to study and employ these acquisitions.

LOSING A VOCABULARY

Although it is a first and indispensable step, enlarging your vocabulary is only one part of the problem of diction. This problem is somewhat similar to that of managing a store. The storekeeper has to keep replenishing his stock, but he also has to get rid of certain items which have proved unsatisfactory. He has to know what stock will be salable to what customers at what seasons of the year. He tries to keep in stock all the items for which there will be a demand, but frequently he has to place a "rush" order with a wholesaler for something not on his shelves.

So it is with our diction. We stock our word supplies as well as we can; we constantly replenish our stock; we cease using certain words as we find others that are more effective; we realize that certain words will "do" on one occasion and not on another; and we frequently find that, no matter how large our vocabularies, we have to put in "rush" orders to wordbooks and dictionaries.

The problem of diction is threefold: first, acquiring a good stock of words; second, eliminating from our use certain words and expressions which do not come up to acceptable standards; third, choosing from our own stock or from dictionaries and similar books those words which will most correctly, clearly, and forcefully express our meaning.

No standards of diction can be absolute, but it is safe to say that good English is that which is used by reputable speakers and writers. Such usage is never fixed but changes constantly as the product of custom or of appropriateness of words to context (see *Levels of usage*, p. 398). For a writer's vocabulary is the *number* of words he can command; a writer's diction is the *kind* of words he uses. Words once considered not acceptable are now sanctioned, and vice versa. Diction ranges from philosophical abstractness to racy slang, from lofty Shakespearean utterances to the dialect of *Huckleberry Finn*. No single kind, in itself, is "good" or "bad," for a word perfect in one context may be inappropriate in another. But there are three general principles that apply to correct usage which have remained constant and may serve as guides: Words should be in *present* use, in *national* use, and in *reputable* use. It is quite possible that you habitually use words which violate one or more of these principles. If so, weed out such words and expressions; at least, be on guard when you want to use them.

Present Use

We should use only words that are currently accepted and sanctioned. Detailed comments on archaic and obsolete words will be found in Section 17, p. 216. Look there for mention of these violations of the principle of present use. But we can also err by using neologisms, newly coined words which have not yet been sanctioned and which may not be understandable. Many neologisms are not incorrect. New discoveries and new inventions give rise to new words which gradually filter into people's general understanding. Such words are necessarily used, of course, but there are other types of neologisms to be avoided.

Several well-known columnists and broadcasters repeatedly contrive neologisms. So do many advertising writers and some commentators on sports. Their products are occasionally colorful and nearly always attention-getting because of their picturesqueness, but probably few will prove permanently valuable. In recent years many such neologisms have had brief lives: *aristobrat* (a son or daughter of the "idle rich"), *glamorize, aquabelle* (a girl swimmer), *scientifiction* (science fiction), *picturize* (to draw a picture or to make a motion picture from a book or play), *tubbable* (washable), *radioration* (radio talk), *publicator* (press agent), and *tube steak* (frankfurter, or the lowly hot dog). A reduction to absurdity of such artificial coinages is illustrated in this comment from an anonymous writer several years ago:

> One of the early *Time*words, if you recall, was *cinemaddict*, accent on any syllable you pleased. *Time* has marched on with the word cinema and now has a stable of a dozen or more *cinemacombinations*, all of them *Time*-worthy, all fascinating, all as treacherous as a fishbone in the upper or lower larynx. *Cinemactor, cinemactress, cinematrocity, cinemaudience, cinegogue, cinemilestone*—these have arrived, not exactly in the English language, but in the shadow world where *GOPoliticians* dip and whirl. The world is a weird place these days, and getting weirder, but we have found one easy temporary escape. Whenever we are working at high pitch and feel the need of something to relieve the tension, we drop what we're doing and construct a new *cinemaword*, or *cinemanodyne*. Nothing soothes us more quickly. Today, in our restlessness, we produced *cinemalformed* (a badly shaped plot or actor), *Missiscinemaddict* (a person living in the Mississippi Valley who is fond of the screen), *cinenymph* (a Hollywood girl), and *mis-*

cinemagenation (white person and colored person attending the movies together).

These lines from Alexander Pope are sound advice:

> In words, as fashions, the same rule will hold,
> Alike fantastic if too new or old:
> Be not the first by whom the new are tried,
> Nor yet the last to lay the old aside.

National Use

It is also important that we use words which are generally understandable throughout the entire country. Many of us do not realize that words and expressions thoroughly understandable to us may, to others, be localisms, technical terms, or Anglicisms. Also, idiomatic expressions acceptable in one part of the country may not be understandable elsewhere. If you habitually use such expressions as the following in your speech and writing, it will perhaps be wise to "lose" them from your vocabulary, unless they are needed for some definite stylistic effect: the Anglicisms *navvy* (for laborer), *bowler* (for derby), *lorry* (for truck), *lift* (for elevator); the localisms *calculate, reckon,* and *guess* (for think or suppose); such semitechnical words as *half-volley, eagle, double steal, full gainer* (unless these terms are used in direct reference to various sports).

Actually, if English is to remain a world language, it is important that words have not only national, but international, acceptance. Some observers have mentioned that perhaps unavoidably we have, among many varieties, what might be called "Oxford English," "Australian English," and "New York English." When Confucius was asked what his first deed would be if he were to be made Emperor of China, he replied, "I would reestablish the precise meaning of words." Such an aim was impossible then and is impossible now in both the Chinese and English languages. The difficulty of worldwide acceptance of word meanings is illustrated by this remark: "I was mad about my flat." In England it means "I really liked my apartment." In the United States it would usually mean "I was angry because I had a punctured tire." An Americanism such as *lickety-split* is more vivid and picturesque than "fast" or "rapid," but its meaning might be unclear in Wales, South Africa, or New Zealand. *Jim-dandy* is more expressive than "excellent," but can we be sure that it would be understood in Liverpool, Montreal, and Sydney, Australia? Even in our own country, the problem is not always simple. Will everyone understand this sign posted in a North Carolina country store: "Kwittin credit till I get my outins in"? To those who can translate, however, the sentence is more quaint and expressive than "I shall extend no further credit to anyone who has not made full payment for goods already received." Not all localisms, Anglicisms, nationalisms, and semitechnical words should be avoided, but only those which will not communicate clearly what we have in mind.

For additional comment on matters of national usage, see Sections 18 (localisms and nationalisms), 27 (colloquialisms), and 28 (idiom). Also see *Levels of usage*, p. 398.

Reputable Use

The first, most important, and fairest test of a word is usage. That great body of accomplished speakers and writers, those who we have reason to believe know the language best, set the standards for others to follow. These standards rule out a number of words which most of us have in our vocabularies. We may object to following the dictates of others in our own speech and writing, but our protests will be no more fruitful than they are against the arbitrary setting of fashions in clothes, food, or social customs. Some of the dictates may seem unwise, but we have to "follow the leader" here as well as in many other activities. The various kinds and groups of words which violate the principle of reputable usage are discussed in Sections 17–28.

In our endeavor to use words as richly and vigorously as possible, we must keep several other points in mind so as not to undo the good effects we have achieved. For example, you may heedlessly have learned that the power of a vocabulary is always in direct proportion to its size. This notion is not necessarily correct. It has been estimated that the active vocabulary of some effective speakers and writers is less than 10,000 words. You may also have the incorrect idea that using big words, polysyllabic words, is a sign of word power. On the contrary, words of many syllables usually give an effect of pomposity, affectation. If the exact and emphatic word is long, do not hesitate to use it. But do not use a word just because it is long. The best writing ordinarily consists of direct and simple words.

Another somewhat generally held idea is that a "pleasant" word should always be preferred to an "unpleasant" one. Such use constitutes a euphemism, which is a softened, inoffensive expression for another which may suggest something unpleasant. The best writers today condemn a circumlocutory, roundabout way of skirting a supposedly uncouth idea. If a subject can be discussed at all, it should be treated directly. The euphemism, as a figure of speech, is still widely used, but not by the best speakers and writers. These are examples of euphemisms the value of which is doubtful: *obsequies* (for funeral); *expectorate* (for spit); *mortician* (for undertaker).

Further discussion of euphemisms, jargon, and gobbledygook will be found in Sections 23–25. Study them carefully. Such expressions are most in need of being lost from our vocabularies. Diffidence and pretense are greater sinners against expressive English than are colloquialisms and even "bad grammar." A recent magazine article contained this paragraph:

> The opportunity for options in life distinguishes the rich from the poor. Perhaps through better motivation, the upper levels of the poor could be tempted onto the option track. It is important to motivate such people close to the breakthrough level in income because they are closest to getting a foot on the option ladder.

One critic has noted that what the writer meant was "The more money you have, the more choices you have."

Be on the lookout for examples of "overly refined" English which you may encounter in your reading and listening. Here is a brief list of expressions recently noted in magazine and newspaper articles and stories, together with possible translations into useful English:

> archivist—library worker
> cardiovascular accident—stroke
> mortical surgeon—undertaker
> collection correspondent—bill collector
> finalize—end
> custodial engineer—janitor
> public works combustible fieldman—garbageman
> park under construction—town dump
> problem skin—acne
> preowned car—secondhand car
> senior citizens—old people
> motion discomfort—nausea
> extrapolation—educated guess
> creative conflict—civil rights demonstration
> crowd engineers—police dogs
> experienced tires—retreads or recaps
> amenity center—village green or public toilet
> exceptional child—moron
> less-privileged, less-developed, emerging, developing,
>   low-income—backward

"Losing a vocabulary" consists of becoming aware of certain words and expressions which violate the standards and principles of present, national, and reputable usage. As we become aware of them, we find that many should be completely removed from our vocabularies and that others should be used with caution and on particular occasions only. But this is largely a negative aspect of word study and is more directly concerned with matters of correctness and revision than with the larger and, in many ways, more important aspects of clarity and effectiveness.

USING A VOCABULARY

How to use words exactly and emphatically is the third and most important phase of the problem of diction. It is indeed necessary to increase our vocabularies and not to use words incorrectly. But as has been mentioned, the mere size of one's vocabulary is not always a criterion of his speaking or writing ability, nor does it follow that if one adheres to the principles of merely correct usage he will write effectively. Much dull and feeble writing is correct, but correctness alone is a negative virtue. Using words clearly, exactly, strongly—that is what is most important and most difficult to do.

Who is the best conversationalist you know? What are the characteristics of his or her language? If you reply honestly, you will probably select a person whose speech seems *forceful* or *vivid* to you, someone who talks *clearly*, someone whose conversation is *smooth* or even *logical* or *precise* or *animated*. Few will select a person whose talk is notably *correct;* rarely will any comment be made on the niceties of conventional grammar, on violations of established usage, on subject-verb agreement or the right case of pronouns. True, the person whom you choose may be a user of correct

English—more often than not he will be—but your remarks will not be "He uses correct English" nearly so often as "He's interesting to listen to" or "He knows how to get his ideas across." "Bad grammar" affects most of us far less than do pompous language, longwindedness, affectation, and insincerity. None of these comments is designed to minimize the importance of correctness but, rather, to suggest that correctness alone is a limited goal in diction. The best speakers—and best writers—are those who in addition to using words correctly also use them clearly, vividly, and forcefully.

Can you use words which are so emphatic and so exact that your reader will be forced to see precisely what you are describing? In the following paragraphs from George Milburn's "A Student in Economics,"[2] observe the word choices:

> All of the boys on the third floor of Mrs. Gooch's approved rooms for men had been posted to get Charlie Wingate up that afternoon. He had to go to see the Dean. Two or three of them forgot about it and two or three of them had other things to do, but Eddie Barbour liked waking people up. Eddie stuck his weasel face in at Charlie's door just as the alarm clock was giving one last feeble tap. The clock stood on the bottom of a tin washpan that was set upside-down on a wooden chair beside the bed. The alarm had made a terrific din. Eddie had heard it far down the hall. The hands showed two o'clock. Pale needles from a December sun were piercing the limp green window shade in a hundred places.
>
> Eddie Barbour yelled, "Aw right, Charlie! Snap out of it!" He came into the chilly room and stood for a moment staring vaguely at the ridge of quilts on the sagged iron bed. The only sound was the long, regular sough of Charlie Wingate's breathing. He hadn't heard a thing. Eddie made a sudden grab for the top of the covers, stripped them back and began jouncing the sleeper by the shoulders. Charlie grunted every time the bed springs creaked, but he nuzzled his pillow and went on sleeping. Eddie went over to the study table where a large, white-enameled water pitcher stood and he came back to the bed with the water, breathing giggles. He tipped the water pitcher a little and a few drops fell on the back of Charlie's neck without waking him. Eddie sloshed the icy water up over the pitcher's mouth. A whole cupful splashed on Charlie's head. Charlie sat up quickly, batting his arms about, and Eddie Barbour whinnied with laughter.
>
> "Arise, my lord, for the day is here," he said, going across and ceremoniously raising the crooked window shade. Charlie sat straight up among the rumpled quilts with his head cocked on one side, staring dully. He had slept with his clothes on. He sat up in bed all dressed, in a soldier's brown uniform, all but his shoes and roll puttees.
>
> "You got army today?" Eddie asked, putting the pitcher down.
>
> Charlie looked at him for a moment and blinked. Then he said in a voice stuffy with sleep. "Naw. I had army yesterday. I got army make-up today." He worked his mouth, making clopping noises.

Note the following expressions: "weasel face," l. 5; "one last feeble tap," l. 6; "pale needles . . . were piercing," l. 9; "ridge of quilts," l. 12; "long, regular sough," l. 13; "jouncing," l. 15; "nuzzled," l. 17; "breathing giggles," l. 19; "sloshed," l. 21; "batting," l. 22; "whinnied with laughter," l. 23; "clopping

---

[2] From *No More Trumpets* by George Milburn. Copyright 1933 by Harcourt, Brace & Company, Inc.

noises," l. 32. Mr. Milburn, by effective use of exact, vigorous words, has achieved real success in this piece of narrative and descriptive writing. His words seem to fit the thought perfectly; they paint a communicable picture for us. Now Milburn may be presumed to have a large vocabulary, and obviously he knows how to avoid an incorrect use of words. The success of the passage is not dependent upon these considerations, however; it results from his ability to find exactly the right word to convey the meaning. Many of us would have been content with the first words which came to mind, say "giggling" or "laughing softly" or "smiling." Mr. Milburn may have thought of those words and many others, but he finally wrote the exact and delicious phrase, "breathing giggles." And by doing so, probably as the result of considerable thought, he created an idea that is "picture clear." Analyze the other words and phrases just mentioned and suggest possible synonyms. Does not each of those used seem to have a personality, an individuality which no other word could supply?

Consider the opening three paragraphs of Katharine Brush's "Night Club":

> Promptly at quarter of ten P.M. Mrs. Brady descended the steps of the Elevated. She purchased from the newsdealer in the cubbyhole beneath them a next month's magazine and a tomorrow morning's paper and, with these tucked under one plump arm, she walked. She walked two blocks north on Sixth Avenue; turned and went west. But not far west. Westward half a block only, to the place where the gay green awning marked Club Français paints a stripe of shade across the glimmering sidewalk. Under this awning Mrs. Brady halted briefly, to remark to the six-foot doorman that it looked like rain and to await his performance of his professional duty. When the small green door yawned open she sighed deeply and plodded in.
>
> The foyer was a blackness, an airless velvet blackness like the inside of a jeweler's box. Four drum-shaped lamps of golden silk suspended from the ceiling gave it light (a very little) and formed the jewels; gold signets, those, or cuff-links for a giant. At the far end of the foyer there were black stairs, faintly dusty, rippling upward toward an amber radiance. Mrs. Brady approached and ponderously mounted the stairs, clinging with one fist to the mangy velvet rope that railed their edge.
>
> From the top, Miss Lena Levin observed the ascent. Miss Levin was the check-room girl. She had dark-at-the-roots blonde hair and slender hips upon which, in moments of leisure, she wore her hands, like buckles of ivory loosely attached. This was a moment of leisure. Miss Levin waited behind her counter. Row upon row of hooks, empty as yet, and seeming to beckon—wee curved fingers of iron—waited behind her.

Study the following: "paints a stripe of shade," l. 6; "door yawned open," l. 10; "airless velvet blackness like the inside of a jeweler's box," l. 11; "cuff-links for a giant," l. 14; "black stairs, faintly dusty, rippling upward toward an amber radiance," l. 14; "mangy velvet rope," l. 17; "dark-at-the-roots blonde hair," l. 19; "hips upon which . . . she wore her hands, like buckles of ivory loosely attached," l. 19. Neither Miss Brush's large vocabulary nor her knowledge of correct usage enabled her to make the effects which those words have. Milburn and Brush and all other good writers search diligently for the exact word, the emphatic, vigorous word; they use figurative language and avoid triteness. They are not content with "any old word"; they recognize the power of language and utilize it to achieve positive effects. Our aim must be to do likewise, so far as we can.

To communicate clearly and forcefully all that he had observed, Henry Thoreau used exact, vigorous words in the following narrative and descriptive account of a battle:

One day when I went out to my wood-pile, or rather my pile of stumps, I observed two large ants, one red, the other much larger, nearly half an inch long, and black, fiercely contending with one another. Having once got hold they never let go, but struggled and wrestled and rolled on the chips incessantly. Looking farther, I was surprised to find that the chips were covered with such combatants, that it was not a *duellum*, but a *bellum*, a war between two races of ants, the red always pitted against the black, and frequently two red ones to one black. The legions of these Myrmidons covered all the hills and vales in my wood-yard, and the ground was already strewn with dead and dying, both red and black. It was the only battle which I have ever witnessed, the only battle-field I ever trod while the battle was raging; internecine war; the red republicans on the one hand, and the black imperialists on the other. On every side they were engaged in deadly combat, yet without any noise that I could hear, and human soldiers never fought so resolutely. I watched a couple that were fast locked in each other's embraces, in a little sunny valley amid the chips, now at noonday prepared to fight till the sun went down, or life went out. The smaller red champion had fastened himself like a vice to his adversary's front, and through all the tumblings on that field never for an instant ceased to gnaw at one of his feelers near the root, having already caused the other to go by the board; while the stronger black one dashed him from side to side, and, as I saw on looking nearer, had already divested him of several of his members. They fought with more pertinacity than bulldogs. Neither manifested the least disposition to retreat. It was evident that their battle-cry was "Conquer or die." In the meanwhile there came along a single red ant on the hillside of this valley, evidently full of excitement, who either had despatched his foe, or had not yet taken part in the battle; probably the latter, for he had lost none of his limbs; whose mother had charged him to return with his shield or upon it. Or perchance he was some Achilles, who had nourished his wrath apart, and had now come to avenge or rescue his Patroclus. He saw this unequal combat from afar,—for the blacks were nearly twice the size of the red,—he drew near with rapid pace till he stood on his guard within half an inch of the combatants; then, watching his opportunity, he sprang upon the black warrior, and commenced his operations near the root of his right fore leg, leaving the foe to select among his own members; and so there were three united for life, as if a new kind of attraction had been invented which put all other locks and cements to shame. I should not have wondered by this time to find that they had their respective musical bands stationed on some eminent chip, and playing their national airs the while, to excite the slow and cheer the dying combatants. I was myself excited somewhat even as if they had been men. The more you think of it, the less the difference. And certainly there is not the fight recorded in Concord history, at least, if in the history of America, that will bear a moment's comparison with this, whether for the numbers engaged in it, or for the patriotism and heroism displayed. For numbers and for carnage it was an Austerlitz or Dresden. Concord Fight! Two killed on the patriots' side, and Luther Blanchard wounded! Why here every ant was a Buttrick,—"Fire! for God's sake fire!"

—and thousands shared the fate of Davis and Hosmer. There was not one hireling there. I have no doubt that it was a principle they fought for, as much as our ancestors, and not to avoid a three-penny tax on their tea; and the results of this battle will be as important and memorable to those whom it concerns as those of the battle of Bunker Hill, at least.

The success of the passage is not dependent upon *size of vocabulary* and *avoidance of incorrect words* alone; it results from Thoreau's ability to find exactly the right words to convey most accurately and vividly the meaning. How much sharper is the picture one gets from "struggled and wrestled and rolled," l. 4, than from merely "struggled" or than from, say, "fought" used in place of the three verbs. See how much more vivid is "fast locked in each other's embraces" than would be "fighting together." Similarly, note the effectiveness of "all the tumblings on that field," l. 18; "dashed him from side to side," l. 21; "who had nourished his wrath apart," l. 29; "as if a new kind of attraction had been invented which put all other locks and cements to shame," l. 36; "some eminent chip," l. 39; "carnage," l. 45. Thoreau did not simply record that "many showed bravery in battle and many were killed"; rather: "Why here every ant was a Buttrick,—'Fire! for God's sake fire!'—and thousands shared the fate of Davis and Hosmer." Even though we may not know exactly who these men were, we understand from the context the quality of their deeds; Thoreau's description is considerably heightened.

Effectiveness in diction is a complex quality. It depends upon many factors: careful thinking, close observation, painstaking search for the right word, the inevitable word, the *mot juste*. Power in language results from using exact words, from being specific and concrete, from recognizing the suggestive power of words, from using figures of speech, and from avoiding hackneyed language, wordiness, jargon, "fine" writing, and mixed figures of speech.

Using Exact Words

The exact use of words depends upon *clear thinking*. If we have only a vague idea, we are prone to choose for its expression the first words that come to mind. But if we know *exactly* what we have in mind, we will search for the word or words which will most completely and accurately express what we mean to say. For example, let us consider one of the most overworked words in the language, *pretty*. We speak of a pretty girl, a pretty flower, a pretty day, and so on. The word *pretty* carries a somewhat general meaning and cannot be called incorrect. But does it express exactly what we mean to convey? Perhaps it would be more accurate to say that a certain girl is *comely*, or *well-favored*, or *attractive*, or *beautiful*, or *personable*, or *charming*, or *exquisite*, or *fair*, or *sensuous*, or *sightly*, or *dainty*, or *engaging*. These words are not all synonyms for *pretty*, but perhaps one of them would more exactly express our impression than the now somewhat dull and ineffective *pretty*. If we will think carefully, call on the resources of our own vocabularies, and use a dictionary or a thesaurus, we will have no insuperable difficulty in finding the right word for the thought.

In the preface to *Pierre et Jean*, Guy de Maupassant wrote:

Whatever one wishes to say, there is one noun only by which to express it, one verb only to give it life, one adjective only which will describe it. One must search until one has found them, this noun, this verb, this adjective, and never rest content with approximations, never resort to trickery, however happy, or to illiteracies, so as to dodge the difficulty.

Since words stand for ideas in our minds and do not stand *directly* for objects or actions, carefully distinguish the basic elements in words in order to use them exactly. These elements are: (a) the word itself, which is merely a sign or symbol; (b) the idea in the mind which the word suggests or for which it stands; (c) the real objects which the idea concerns. Sometimes confusion or misunderstanding results because these distinctions are not recognized; the word as a sign or symbol is mistaken for the idea or for the real thing, or the idea is mistaken for the real object. Not always are these three elements present, and we must be on our guard in writing —and in listening and in reading—that both the transmitter and the receiver of the communication understand exactly the sense in which a word is used and the meaning which it has. For example, one of the great objects of alchemy (medieval chemical science) was to find the "philosopher's stone" by which alchemists thought they could transmute base metals into gold. The words "philosopher's stone," then, stood for an *idea;* no such *real* stone was ever found to exist. The trite expression to indicate disapproval of an action, "That's not my idea of fun," illustrates the separation of the second and third elements mentioned above; the person speaking would, perhaps, call the action "a bore" or "hard work" or something similar. See the Sherwood article, p. 618, and *Semantics*, p. 430.

To determine the exact word for the context, you must become aware of shades of meaning, of distinctions which clarify the idea for which you wish to use the word as symbol. When you wish to describe a surface which, from every point of view, lies on a line corresponding to or parallel with the horizon, will you use *flat, plane, level, even, flush, smooth?* Choose always the word which shows most exactly the meaning you intend. Which is most appropriate and exact for your context: *face, countenance, physiognomy, visage, puss, mug?* See the Thouless article, p. 495.

In *Giants in the Earth*, O. E. Rölvaag wrote: "Foggy weather had now been hanging over the prairie for three whole days; a warm mist of rain mizzled continuously out of the low sky." By their appropriateness and exactness both "hanging" and "mizzled" make sharper and clearer for the reader the picture which Rölvaag wanted to create. Later in the same paragraph Rölvaag speaks of "a lonely wagon." He could have said "one wagon" or "a single wagon," but the phrase would lack its present exactness and emphasis.

Undoubtedly the author of this same novel thought carefully and searched diligently for the exact words to create the mood and impression of this passage:

The afternoon breeze lulled, and finally dropped off altogether. The sun, whose golden lustre had faded imperceptibly into a reddish hue, shone now with a dull light, yet strong and clear; in a short while, deeper tones of violet began to creep across the red. The great ball grew enormous; it retreated farther and farther into the empty reaches of the western sky; then it sank suddenly. . . . The spell of evening quickly crowded in and laid hold of them all; the oxen wagged their ears; Rosie lifted her voice in a long moo, which died out slowly in the great stillness. At the moment when the sun closed his eye, the vastness of the plain seemed to rise up on every hand— and suddenly the landscape had grown desolate; something bleak and cold had come into the silence, filling it with terror. . . . Behind them, along the way they had come, the plain lay dark green and lifeless, under the gathering shadow of the dim, purple sky.

For further discussions of exactness in diction, see Section 29.

B E I N G   S P E C I F I C   A N D   C O N C R E T E

In order to write vividly, to cause our readers to sense and feel what we have in mind, we must use concrete, specific words rather than vague, general terms. Many inexpert writers (and many who could be more expert were they less lazy!) blunt the edge of their ideas with general words which have no trenchant meaning. If you tell a reader that "a man entered the store," you give a general picture. But if you say that "a swarthy man slouched into the store," the picture is more concrete. Perhaps his entrance into the store was violent: "rushed" or "slammed" or "stormed" gives a specific meaning not secured with "entered."

Your readers will never know what you mean unless you use specific words. "If you have committed a crime, escape to the woods with ammunition and clothing. The people there will give you food and you need worry about nothing." These two sentences are correct in form and reasonably clear in meaning; but notice the greater power and effectiveness of these sentences from Mérimée's "Mateo Falcone": "If you have killed a man, go into the *mâquis* of Porto-Vecchio with a good gun and powder and shot. You will live there quite safely, but don't forget to bring along a brown cloak and hood for your blanket and mattress. The shepherds will give you milk, cheese, and chestnuts, and you need not trouble your head about the law or the dead man's relatives, except when you are compelled to go down into the town to renew your ammunition."

One of the secrets of all good writing is the use of concrete, specific words. The meanings a writer has in mind for such abstract words as *beauty, ambition, power,* for example, must be thoroughly understood by a reader—must be the same in the reader's mind as in the writer's—if communication of ideas is to succeed. By using specific detail, make clear what you mean. What specifically is the *gallantry,* the *grandeur,* the *glory* of which you write? Again, you can create a more specific picture in a reader's mind with *birch* or *oak* or *maple* than with the general word *tree.* You have occasion to mention someone's dwelling place. *House* is more specific than *dwelling,* but notice how the word can be made still more specific: *house; bungalow; white bungalow; white frame bungalow; new white frame bungalow; new white frame bungalow with a wide veranda.* If any more modifiers were added, top-heaviness would result; but how much clearer and more vivid for the reader is the last descriptive phrase than the general word *dwelling!* Not always will you need to tell the kind of tree, the kind of dwelling; but examine the context in which you use words to determine where you need to be exact, to be concrete, in order to present facts or ideas forcefully and effectively. (For further discussion of specific words, see Section 30.)

Being exact and being emphatic in your diction are twin problems. Usually your success in finding the exact word you need to convey meaning will also solve your problem of being emphatic, concrete, and specific. Most skilled writers who employ exact and emphatic diction are probably not aware of the separate difficulties discussed here. With careful thought and intelligent use of a dictionary or thesaurus you should be able to approximate the exactness and concreteness of such a passage as the first paragraph of Eudora Welty's "A Worn Path," p. 962. This excerpt alone should convince anyone that exact and specific diction can convey a powerful image and meaning.

RECOGNIZING THE SUGGESTIVE POWER OF WORDS

Nearly all words mean more than they seem to mean; they possess associated meanings, a sort of periphery of suggestive, or connotative, values. The bare, literal meaning of a word is its *denotation*. The *connotation* of a word is the suggestions and associations which have surrounded it. For example, a dictionary definition of the word *gold* is "A precious yellow metal, highly malleable and ductile, and free from liability to rust." This is its denotation. But with *gold* have long been associated color, riches, power, happiness, evil, unhappiness. Beyond the core of meaning which the dictionary definition gives are suggestions, associations, implications. Not always are these connotations present, but you must be aware of this suggestive power in words.

All good writers avail themselves of the latent magic in words, but as Robert Thouless points out in his essay, "Emotional Meanings," p. 495, connotative values are intricate and must be watched. Indeed, in order to discuss emotional meanings of words, Thouless carefully distinguishes between denotation and connotation in his first paragraphs.

Later in the essay Thouless quotes these beautiful lines from Keats' "The Eve of St. Agnes":

> Full on this casement shone the wintry moon,
> And threw warm gules on Madeline's fair breast.

He then shows how all the connotative values of the lines, all their beauty and richness can be destroyed by substituting "neutral," or denotative, words:

> Full on this window shone the wintry moon,
> Making red marks on Jane's uncolored chest.

If you do not employ connotation, your writing will be flatter, more insipid, than it should be. But the power lurking in connotative meanings of words must be handled carefully. Misinterpretation or misunderstanding can result from failure to consider the values of words. The late Alben W. Barkley commented on this problem when discussing the language in a veto message:

I realized that sometimes language in a written document carries with it connotations not intended by the writer. Sometimes the expressions on one's countenance or the intonations in one's voice indicate a meaning not always carried in the written word. But I feel that upon reflection you will agree that some of the language contained in your veto message was abundantly susceptible of the interpretations which I put upon it in my address to the Senate and which many others put upon it throughout the country.

John Marshall, an early Chief Justice of the Supreme Court, based an opinion in the important case of McCulloch *v.* Maryland on a careful analysis of this suggestive power of words, especially of the word "necessary":

Such is the character of human language that no word conveys to the mind, in all situations, one single definite idea; and nothing is more common than to use words in a figurative sense. Almost all compositions contain words which, taken in their rigorous sense, would convey a meaning different from that which is obviously intended. It is essential to just construction that many words which import something excessive should be understood in a more mitigated sense,—in that sense which common usage justifies. The word "necessary" is of this description. It has not a fixed character peculiar to itself. It admits of all degrees of comparison; and is often connected with other words which increase or diminish the impression the mind receives of the urgency it imports. A thing may be necessary, very necessary, absolutely or indispensably necessary. To no mind would the same idea be conveyed by these several phrases. . . . This word, then, like others, is used in various senses; and in its construction, the subject, the context, the intention of the person using them, are all to be taken into view.

Skilled writers on occasion use words with different connotative values to achieve different effects. For example, the striking contrast in the following lines is achieved largely through the use of words with dissimilar connotations:

CARGOES [3]

Quinquireme of Nineveh from distant Ophir,
Rowing home to haven in sunny Palestine,
With a cargo of ivory,
And apes and peacocks,
Sandlewood, cedarwood, and sweet white wine.

Stately Spanish galleon coming from the Isthmus,
Dipping through the Tropics by the palm-green shores,
With a cargo of diamonds,
Emeralds, amethysts,
Topazes, and cinnamon, and gold moidores.

Dirty British coaster with a salt-caked smoke stack,
Butting through the Channel in the mad March days,
With a cargo of Tyne coal,
Road-rails, pig-lead,
Firewood, iron-ware, and cheap tin trays.

---

[3] From John Masefield, *The Story of a Round House*. Copyright 1912 by The Macmillan Company and used with permission.

We sometimes fail to create with words a feeling which transcends the power of accepted, denotative meanings; we fail to suggest meanings and associations which will appeal to the experience of our readers. To use words both accurately and effectively, it is necessary to understand their connotations as well as their denotations. Despite necessary caution in their use, you are urged to avail yourself of the suggestive powers which nearly all words have. Only when we wish to express something with literal accuracy do we rely wholly upon the standards set by dictionary definitions.

To increase your awareness of the suggestive powers of words, turn to one of the poems reprinted in this volume, say, Mrs. Browning's "How Do I Love Thee?" (p. 1156). Study the words which have connotative values; it would be instructive to try to substitute for such words others which are neutral and colorless, as Thouless did in the lines from Keats' poem. You would "butcher" a great sonnet, but never again would you doubt that words have powerful associated values.

Also, notice the difference in meanings which the following words have:

car, automobile, limousine	dishonor, disgrace, ignominy
galluses, suspenders, braces	disloyalty, treachery, treason
smell, smell bad, stink	salacious, licentious, lecherous
inebriated, intoxicated, drunk	complaisance, affability, courteousness
portly, stout, obese	sorrow, lament, moan
slow, lazy, sluggish	wealthy, affluent, opulent

(For further discussion of connotation, see Section 30c.)

USING FIGURES OF SPEECH

Figures of speech are referred to as the ornaments of prose. And yet they are ornaments which we constantly use. Frequently we are unaware that we use figurative language when, for example, we speak of a *heavy* heart, a *heavy* silence, *heavy* grief, *heavy* style, *heavy* rain, a *heavy* sky, a *heavy* sound, a *heavy* grade, *heavy* food, a *heavy* villain, *heavy* features, or *heavy* humor. The literal meaning of the word *heavy* is "weighty, of high specific gravity," a meaning only remotely connected with some of the above-mentioned uses of the word. Much of our use of language is consciously or unconsciously figurative.

By using words in a figurative rather than a literal sense, we augment their power and suggestiveness. Figurative language is vivid, and it also enables us to say in a phrase or a sentence that which would require sentences or a paragraph of straight exposition. You should avail yourself of the vividness and conciseness which figures of speech supply, but you should also avoid using too many of them (see Section 30c), and mixing them (see Section 26).

There are a large number of figures of speech, but these are most important: simile, metaphor, personification, hyperbole, and metonymy.

Simile is a comparison of two images which are essentially different but are alike, or thought to be alike, in at least one respect. The point of resemblance is stated by means of *as, as if,* or *like.* "She is as beautiful as a flower" and "He eats like a wolf" are examples. Most similes are trite, however, and should be used sparingly for that reason. The following similes are probably too worn out to be really effective, but variations or adaptations of them may occasionally be emphatic: "a grin like a Cheshire cat," "eyes as big as saucers," "like the wolf on the fold," "as flat as a pancake," "like the last rose of summer."

A good simile is vividly effective, as in the following:

> Life, like a dome of many-colored glass,
> Stains the white radiance of eternity.
> > —PERCY B. SHELLEY
>
> Eager as a cry for life.
> > —GEORGE MEREDITH
>
> She was as immutable as the hills, but not quite so green.
> > —RUDYARD KIPLING

Metaphor is identical with simile except that the words *as, as if,* and *like* are not used. That is, a simile is a *stated* comparison whereas a metaphor is an *implied* comparison. Likeness is felt so vividly that the writer can call one thing by the name of another: "She is a perfect lamb." Metaphors, like similes, however, should be used cautiously and sparingly because the best of them are trite. "He is in the winter of his life" is a vivid, image-producing sentence, but by now it has lost much of its original force because of overuse. The following passages further illustrate metaphor:

> That time of year thou may'st in me behold,
> When yellow leaves, or none, or few do hang
> Upon those boughs which shake against the cold—
> Bare ruined choirs, where late the sweet birds sang.
> > —WILLIAM SHAKESPEARE
>
> Silently one by one, in the infinite meadows of heaven
> Blossomed the lovely stars, the forget-me-nots of the angels.
> > —HENRY W. LONGFELLOW

The effect of simile and metaphor is the same. If we write "He acted like a cur" or "He was a cur," our readers will transfer the term *cur* to the term *he* (man). Or it may be said that the denotation of the first word, *he* (man) acquires the connotative meaning of the second, *cur*. In other words, simile and metaphor are connotative comparisons. As such, they may and should be used for their vividness and suggestiveness. A small child whose foot has gone to sleep tells us exactly and imaginatively, "My toes feel just like ginger ale." A little girl noticing the streaks and ribbons of color in a puddle of oil and grease said of them, "They look like a dead rainbow." Such figurative language is more than merely effective; it is well nigh perfect.

So, too, is this statement by a writer pinpointing the glitter and glamor of New York City's most resplendent street:

> This is the Park Avenue of poodles and polished brass; it is cab country, tip-town, glassville, and a window-washer's paradise.

Never underestimate the power of figurative language. You might say, for example, "I'm so restless I can't stand still" or "I'm so restless I feel I've got to scream or cry." You could say this. Or you might strive for an expression as effective as this figure of speech from the pen of Charles Dickens: "As restless as an evil conscience in a tumbled bed." Or for something like this from another writer: "As restless as willows in a windstorm." You will never know whether you can create this sort of language until you really try.

Personification is the giving of human attributes to inanimate objects or abstract ideas. In personification, we speak of the dead as though they were alive, of the inanimate as though it were animate, of animals as though they were human. Abstract ideas, such as Truth, Virtue, Death, and Love, are sometimes considered as persons, as, for example, "Truth fixed me with his naked eye."

Personification is more frequently used in poetry than in prose, although you may recall its frequent appearance in fairy stories as well as in Mother Goose rhymes. It is a stylistic device which will heighten reader interest only if employed fittingly and rarely. The following passage from Milton's "L'Allegro" provides several examples of personification:

> Sport that wrinkled Care derides,
> And Laughter holding both his sides.
> Come, and trip it as ye go,
> On the light fantastic toe;
> And in thy right hand lead with thee
> The mountain nymph, sweet Liberty.

Hyperbole is an extravagation, a deliberate overstatement designed to gain emphasis. "You look like a ghost" is an example of hyperbole (and simile, and triteness). "His voice thundered," "She was frightened to death," "I was insane from grief" are others. Hyperbole should be used sparingly and very cautiously. It can be effective but is frequently overdone.

The following examples of hyperbole will make clear why this stylistic device should be used rarely:

> Was this the face that launched a thousand ships,
> And burnt the topless towers of Ilium?
>
> —CHRISTOPHER MARLOWE

Take of London fog 30 parts; malaria 10 parts; gas leaks 20 parts; dewdrops gathered in a brick yard at sunrise, 25 parts; odor of honeysuckle 15 parts. Mix.

The mixture will give you an approximate conception of a Nashville drizzle. It is not so fragrant as a mothball nor as thick as pea-soup; but 'tis enough—'twill serve.

> —O. HENRY

Metonymy is the use of one word for another that it suggests. Sometimes metonymy consists of designating one thing by the name of another with which it is usually associated. Examples: "She sets a good table"; "addicted to the bottle"; "an old hand at the game"; "Have you read Kipling?"; "respect for gray hairs."

Metonymy is based on the principle of association of ideas. Frequently, it is effective in causing association of familiar ideas in the reader's mind, but you must be careful to use figures which are understandable and yet not hackneyed. It is difficult to steer between this Scylla and Charybdis (what figure of speech?); therefore, use metonymy sparingly. Its force is its pictorial appeal, its power to evoke images in your reader's minds. Used infrequently, it is an effective method of avoiding being abstract and general, of achieving concreteness. This result was obtained, for example, when in *Don Quixote*, Cervantes wrote "The pen is the tongue of the mind."

There are many other figures of speech: litotes, allegory, onomatopoeia, antithesis, and a dozen more. All these, as well as those which have been discussed, have their places in effective speaking and writing. But, once again, you are cautioned not to overuse figures of speech. They are a real part of the language but, like condiments, they must be used sparingly. Too much salt ruins the bread.

The following passages illustrate how effective the devices of simile and metaphor, personification, hyperbole, and metonymy may be. Identify the figure of speech which each passage employs; study the particular effectiveness of each figure of speech.

We have done a silly thing with our women. We have put modern high-powered engines into old antiquated vehicles.

—PEARL BUCK

In her housekeeping and domestic arrangements she seems to have been excellent. Her table is highly spoken of. . . .

The remote world in which he lived was but imperfectly accessible to the tinkle of the dinner bell. . . .

. . . he [Herndon] said that "melancholy dripped from him as he walked.". . .

While he was busy with such thought, the pistol of Wilkes Booth shattered the world of Mary Todd Lincoln into diminutive fragments, which no man ever again could piece together.

—GAMALIEL BRADFORD

Money is a lens in a camera.

—JAMES TRUSLOW ADAMS

But pleasures are like poppies spread,
You seize the flow'r, its bloom is shed;
Or like the snow falls in the river,
A moment white—then melts forever;
Or like the borealis race,
That flit ere you can point their place;
Or like the rainbow's lovely form
Evanishing amid the storm.

—ROBERT BURNS

Oblivion is not to be hired: the greater part must be content to be as though they had not been.

—SIR THOMAS BROWNE

Their starched blue blouses, shining as though varnished, ornamented at collar and cuffs with little patterns of white stitch-work, and blown up big around their bony bodies, seemed exactly like balloons about to soar, but putting forth a head, two arms, and two feet.

—GUY DE MAUPASSANT

The mobs of great cities add just so much to the support of pure government as sores do to the strength of the human body. It is the manners and spirit of a people which preserve a republic in vigour. A degeneracy in these is a canker which soon eats to the heart of its laws and constitution.

—THOMAS JEFFERSON

In the first place, gentlemen, you are to consider that a great empire, like a great cake, is most easily diminished at the edges. Turn your attention, therefore, first to your remotest provinces, that, as you get rid of them, the next may follow in order.

That the possibility of this separation may always exist, take special care the provinces are never incorporated with the mother country; that they do not enjoy the same common rights, the same privileges in commerce; and that they are governed by *severer* laws, all of your enacting, without allowing them any share in the choice of the legislators. By carefully making and preserving such distinctions, you will (to keep to my simile of the cake) act like a wise ginger-bread-baker, who, to facilitate a division, cut his dough half through in those places where, when baked, he would have it broken to pieces.

—BENJAMIN FRANKLIN

History is a stage where forces which are within human control contend and cooperate with forces which are not.

—R. H. TAWNEY

Mr. Webster, leaning back at his ease, telling stories, cracking jokes, shaking the sofa with burst after burst of laughter, or smoothly discoursing to the perfect felicity of the logical part of one's constitution, would illuminate an evening now and then. Mr. Calhoun, the cast-iron man, who looks as if he had never been born and never could be extinguished, would come in sometimes to keep our understandings upon a painful stretch for a short while, and leave us to take to pieces his close, rapid, theoretical, illustrated talk, and see what we could make out of it. . . . His speech abounds in figures, truly illustrative, if that which they illustrate were but true also.

—HARRIET MARTINEAU

Thus the spin is only the turn of the crank-handle which starts it: the hurricane itself is a vast motor, revolved by the energy generated by the condensation of water from the rising air.

—RICHARD HUGHES

Society is commonly too cheap. We meet at very short intervals, not having had time to acquire any new value for each other. We meet at meals three times a day, and give each other a new taste of that old musty cheese that we are.

—HENRY THOREAU

But I sprang upon them, like a black tempest, and fifty chariots I took, and beside each chariot two men bit the earth with their teeth, subdued beneath my spear.

—HOMER

The bow of God's wrath is bent, and the arrow made ready on the string, and justice bends the arrow at your heart, and strains the bow, and it is nothing but the mere pleasure of God, and that of an angry God, without any promise or obligation at all, that keeps the arrow one moment from being made drunk with your blood.

—JONATHAN EDWARDS

Society is a wave. The wave moves onward, but the water of which it is composed does not. The same particle does not rise from the valley to the ridge. Its unity is only phenomenal. The persons who make up a nation today, next year die, and their experiences die with them.

—RALPH WALDO EMERSON

SUMMARY

Adding to your stock of words is relatively easy; all that is required is that you be curious about those terms which you have not thoroughly mastered. If you become curious about words, you will then become a collector of words and have as much interest and fun as some people have in collecting stamps or autographs. Your curiosity will lead you to the dictionary for further information and, knowledge acquired, you will then be able correctly to use new words in your active vocabulary. It is not especially difficult to "lose" words, either. If you note carefully the errors which you make on your themes and which your instructor marks, you should make rapid progress in correct usage. The real difficulty lies in using words exactly and forcefully. Here you will need to exercise ingenuity, patience, effort. From the amazingly large resources of the dictionary you *can* choose the terms you wish, after careful thought and painstaking search. But the effort is worthwhile; once you have learned the pleasure that comes from "weaving thought to a gracious phrase," never again will you be content with the approximate word, the "just-as-good" term. Building and using a vocabulary is a life's work, but you are urged to take advantage of your unusual opportunities in college classes to make a real start on the difficult and fascinating study of words.

· EXERCISES ·

A. Define and use in sentences each of these words:

1. ominous	6. pervasive
2. trepidation	7. envisaged
3. idyllic	8. despotism
4. brainwashing	9. technological
5. plausible	10. nihilistic

B. Select in each series the word or word group which is closest in meaning to the word italicized in the phrase. Put your list on a separate sheet. Check it with your dictionary.

1. *lucidity* of explanation — vagueness/wordiness/fertility/brevity/clearness
2. an ugly *scowl* — boat/look/nose/statement/skull
3. an *irrelevant* remark — pertinent/cute/irreverent/unrelated/brilliant
4. never *procrastinate!* — forget/delay/hurry/prophesy/overeat
5. *exotic* perfumes — excellent/ordinary/sweet/expensive/foreign
6. an *orthodox* belief — ordinary/mistaken/religious/approved/pagan
7. to *obliterate* all traces — witness/destroy/investigate/emphasize/ignore
8. an *incredulous* person — insincere/kind/inefficient/unbelieving/skillful
9. to speak *monotonously* — tiresomely/alone/vigorously/effectively/clearly
10. financial *solvency* — saving/transaction/debt/soundness/contract
11. lost in a *maze* — amazement/marsh/confusion/mirth/surprise
12. *spontaneous* applause — unpremeditated/forced/insincere/loud/pleasing
13. a *synonymous* word — harsh/illiterate/difficult/easy/similar
14. to *tantalize* a child — tease/please/titillate/adopt/caress
15. to *assimilate* food — desire/need/buy/absorb/reject

16. a *somnolent* atmosphere   sleepy/clear/warm/cloudy/healthful
17. to *concoct* an alibi   destroy/prepare/ignore/insinuate/ concentrate on
18. a *potent* medicine   bitter/pleasant/patented/powerful/expensive
19. a *rendezvous* in New York   friend/appointment/apartment/show/ night club
20. reached the *zenith*   horizon/rim/top/zero point/goal
21. an unkind *allusion*   act/reference/insult/illusion/admission
22. the *limpid* water   cold/muddy/clear/obscure/purified
23. a *precarious* position   desirable/premeditated/perilous/elevated/ misunderstood
24. to be *arraigned* in court   invited/acquitted/accused/presented/ sentenced
25. all kinds of *vitality*   victuals/drink/people/necessities/vigor

C. The word *allow* has several synonyms, among them *let, permit, suffer,* and *tolerate.* Are there other synonyms for *let?*

D. The word *choice* has many synonyms. List at least five.

E. The following words have many meanings: *appeal, fix, point, keep, sweep.* Prepare for class an oral or written discussion of *one* of these words. Which meanings seem most common? Which seem most unusual? In what idiomatic phrases do these words appear?

F. Give one antonym for each of the following: *arrive, atrocious, arrogant, dark, latent, solitary, sophisticated, temporary, weak, wordy.*

G. Some words resemble others in sound and occasionally in spelling but differ in meaning. Use the following correctly in brief sentences:

accept, except	know, no
advice, advise	later, latter
affect, effect	lead, led
an, and	least, lest
angel, angle	lightening, lightning
are, our, or	loose, lose
biding, bidding	lose, loss
breath, breathe	medal, metal
capital, capitol	of, off
choose, chose, choice	on, one
cite, sight, site	passed, past
clothes, cloths	peace, piece
coarse, course	personal, personnel
conscience, conscious	precede, proceed
counsel, council, consul	principal, principle
dairy, diary	quiet, quite, quit
decent, descent	shone, shown
desert, dessert	shudder, shutter
dining, dinning	stationary, stationery
due, do	than, then
ever, every	their, there, they're
formally, formerly	therefor, therefore
forth, fourth	thorough, through
freshman, freshmen	though, thought, through
hear, here	to, too, two
hoping, hopping	want, wont, won't
human, humane	weak, week
its, it's (never *its'*)	weather, whether

were, where   woman, women
whose, who's   your, you're

H. Give the meaning of each of the following prefixes and list five common words containing each prefix: *bi-, cross-, non-, pre-, sub-*.

I. Give the meaning of each of the following suffixes and list five common words containing each suffix: *-al, -est, -less, -ist, -ment*.

J. From the final paragraph of Angle's "Gettysburg," p. 857, select those words which seem to you especially exact, concrete, and specific. Does the paragraph contain any diction which you consider ineffective?

K. For the first paragraph of "Lady Macbeth of Scarsdale," p. 777, follow the directions given for Exercise J.

L. The 10 words listed in Exercise A are from Lukacs' "It's Halfway to 1984," p. 761. Do you understand the meaning of each? Did you get this meaning from context? Know the words before reading the article? Did you look up any in a dictionary?

M. Locate at least five examples of figures of speech of different kinds in Eudora Welty's story, "A Worn Path," p. 962.

N. Follow directions given in Exercise M for Stevenson's "An Apology for Idlers," p. 739.

O. Follow directions given in Exercise M for Benét's "The Devil and Daniel Webster," p. 969.

CHAPTER 6

DEVELOPING A STYLE

If you were asked why you are taking freshman English, chances are good to excellent that you would give one of two answers: "Because it is required" or "To improve my writing style." Let the wisdom or stupidity of the requirement be debated elsewhere. Just what do we mean when we refer to "style in writing"? And indeed how *can* one improve the writing style he already has?

WHAT STYLE MEANS

The term *style* has been defined in many ways but never with universal satisfaction, since every speaker and writer has his own notion of its precise meaning. Do you agree with Lord Chesterfield that "Style is the dress of thought"? With Whitehead's comment that "Style is the ultimate morality of mind"? With Cardinal Newman's "Style is a thinking out into language"? With Jonathan Swift's suggestion that "Proper words in proper places make the true definition of a style"? Or with the most quoted definition of all, Buffon's "The style is the man himself" (*Le style est l'homme même*)? Do any of these definitions provide you with a useful, helpful concept?

Probably the word *style* means to you something more or less than any of these statements, or something entirely different. When you say, as frequently you may, that so-and-so has no style, or has poor style, rarely are you referring to his or her manner of writing and speaking. Probably you are commenting on a manner of acting or appearing or behaving (dressing, greeting someone, dancing), an individual's complex of attitudes and actions. If this is what is meant, then style for you refers to the *way* one does or expresses something. It singles out for notice or comment the particular and individual manner in which someone does or says something, whatever that something may be. Can we say that style consists, at least in part, of what a person adds to or subtracts from a particular activity: walking, eating, conversing, writing? Of the ways in which what one person does or says differ from the ways in which someone else does or says that same something? If style in general means "manner or mode," can we say that literary style is a way of putting thoughts into words, a characteristic manner of expression or construction in writing and speaking? A good many experts would agree that one can sensibly refer to style as the impress (influence) of personality upon subject matter. Your style is what you as an individual contribute to the expression of what you have in mind to say and write.

Perhaps even this passably clear and simple definition does not express what you mean by *style*. You may conceive of style as the removal from your work of so-called "errors" and infelicities rather than the addition of grace, strength, and other elements which you think should be reserved for professional writers. Style to you may mean correct spelling, suitable punctuation, the absence of errors in tense or agreement or the principal parts of verbs. That is, to some persons style implies writing which is relatively free of language impurity, which is aseptic, harmless because it is free of such "microorganisms" as comma faults and localisms. Many teachers and many more students would agree that attaining such a style—sterile, flat, and colorless though it usually is—is a laudable aim, one representing a distinct forward step, even though limited and largely negative.

To a college student, style should mean more than the negative aspects of writing and speaking—mere avoidance of mistakes in usage and mechanics. "Improving" one's style admittedly involves correctness and appropriateness, but it embraces far more than just this. To be truly effective, writing must be more than "adequate" in word choice and sentence structure. In addition to correctness, precisely what characteristics of style can a first-year college student reasonably hope to attain? And how can he go about acquiring these characteristics?

First, may we agree that the primary aim of writing, its only dominant purpose, is communicating ideas from the mind of the writer to that of the reader? If we agree, then it follows that anything and everything which blocks or slows down communication should be removed; anything and everything which facilitates or increases communication should be used. Therefore, we try to eliminate the errors—the faulty diction, illogical sentence structure, nonstandard usage—which distort or bury our meaning or which so attract our reader's attention that his mind is diverted from what we are trying to convey. In addition, we employ whatever devices of style we can in order to smooth and speed our message to our readers' minds.

Scores of devices have been used in the past and are currently being employed by competent writers for exactly this purpose. The overwhelming majority of the major attainable elements contributing to effective and pleasing style can somewhat loosely be classified under four headings:

Simplicity
Conversational quality
Individuality
Concreteness

Many other devices could be listed. But limited goals which have some prospect of attainment are more sensible than ambitious aims which might require a lifetime to achieve. Freshman English may seem interminable, but actually it lasts only one year.

SIMPLICITY

By *simplicity* is certainly not meant "writing down" to the reader, thus underestimating either his intelligence or his knowledge. Rather, the term involves expressing what one has in mind in terms that are clear, logical, and specifically geared to the level (age, education, etc.) of the persons for whom one is writing. If our subject is so technical that technical terms cannot be avoided, we use them—but define them without employing a tone or method insulting to the reader's intelligence. Furthermore, the level of the audience for whom we are writing would dictate how many such terms would be defined and in what detail. If we have a choice between a polysyllabic and a short word, we should use whichever is clearer and more exact—usually, but not always, the short word. More often than polysyllables, short words are clear and sharp, like signs chiseled from the face of a rock; in much writing, and especially in speaking, they are crisp and filled with zest, saying what they "mean" and leaving as little doubt as possible in the mind of reader or hearer. But whether we use long or short words, diction should be as simple and clear as we can make it so that our ideas will move smoothly "on stream."

In college, you hear and read many words previously unknown to you. Impressed, you may attempt what hundreds of thousands of your predecessors have done: to employ such expressions in speaking and writing not so much for their actual use value as to show others how smart you are, how "educated" you are becoming. Enlarging one's vocabulary and using new words purposefully are activities to be praised, but following either pursuit for reasons of vanity, self-esteem, or "culture climbing" is nonsensical. No truer statement about simplicity in style exists than this: "A book has one leg on immortality's trophy when the words are for children but the meanings are for men." Simplicity without substance is childish; but great thoughts, like great inventions of whatever kind, achieve much of their effectiveness and power through simplicity. Can you think of any great work of literature, of any great scientific discovery, which is deliberately and arbitrarily complex and involved? A good literary selection or an important scientific discovery may be beyond your understanding, but each is as simple as it can be and still be what it is.

Many other devices for achieving simplicity in style could be mentioned. In fact, a considerable number are discussed in Sections 17, 22, 23, 24, 25, 29, 30, 40, 41, 42, and 44 of the Handbook. Try to apply them in your own themes. In such selections as Thouless' "Emotional Meanings," p. 495, and "Why a Classic Is a Classic," p. 611, you can observe and analyze simplicity of diction, sentence structure, organization, and logic contributing powerfully to the process of communication.

CONVERSATIONAL QUALITY

Perhaps more than we sometimes realize, the *conversational* quality of what we read adds an appeal that helps us to grasp ideas being presented. Conversation is not necessarily informal and relaxed, but good conversation is never so elevated in tone, so "high and mighty," that one feels condescended to. Have you noticed that some essays, even ones considered great and timeless, by eighteenth- and nineteenth-century writers seem somewhat constrained, formal, and pontifical? That essays of more recent vintage are often more relaxed, less didactic and "preachy"? This difference in tone, in attitude, toward both subject and reader, is partly a matter of diction and sentence structure but perhaps even more a result of later authors' descending from their pedestals. Such a statement does not imply that only recent essays have a conversational quality and thus are enjoyable to read. Nor does it mean that a good writer, of whatever era, will figuratively remove his jacket and necktie and become "one of the boys in shirtsleeves." It does imply that most good writers of the past and present have tried not to sound stuffy and ponderous, that without losing their dignity they have labored to infuse a human, friendly, man-to-man quality into their writing. By conversational quality is meant ease of expression, not laxity of thought; consideration for the reader as one "thinking with" the author and not as a person both ignorant and stupid.

John R. Tunis, one of the more popular and esteemed professional writers of recent years, has said that he tries to write an essay or magazine article as though he were conversing with a dinner companion. By this, he explained, he meant that he attempted to use words and expressions that are not dull and stuffy, that he tried to anticipate and answer in his writing the questions his companion would actually raise in conversation, that he provided illustrations and examples designed to keep the attention of his listener and make him or her actually *see* what he was attempting to communicate. An even greater writer of an earlier time, Laurence Sterne, wrote in *Tristram Shandy:* "Writing, when properly managed"—and, being Sterne, he put in parentheses ("as you may be sure I think mine is")—"is but another name for conversation."

Huxley's "The Method of Scientific Investigation," p. 470, is notable for its conversational quality and so, obviously, is Bronowski's "The Creative Mind," p. 477. But conversational quality does not appear only in writing derived from lectures. These first two essays in Book Three are followed by scores of others with similar appeal. Notice the relaxed and even quietly intimate quality of Stevenson's "An Apology for Idlers," p. 739, and of Frost's "Mending Wall," p. 1163. Such selections most assuredly do not "descend to the level" of any reader whatever. Like many other selections in Book Three, they use the conversational device of "thinking with the reader" and thus achieve a degree of communication otherwise impossible.

INDIVIDUALITY

Closely related to the device of conversational tone is *individuality*, which is often a virtue and, occasionally, a vice in writing. Individuality implies "subjectivity"; when a writer is excessively subjective he is inward-centered and applies as far as possible only his own standards and judgments. A markedly subjective writer tends to ignore the needs and appeals of his readers and thinks exclusively of himself, his thoughts, his needs, his aspirations. Such a tendency—the direct opposite of the stylistic quality inherent in conversation—is a definite flaw. Arthur Schopenhauer has made this point clearly:

> A writer commits the error of subjectivity when he thinks it enough if he himself knows what he means and wants to say, and takes no thought of the reader, who is left to get at the bottom of it as best he may. This is as though the author were holding a monologue; whereas it ought to be a dialogue, too, in which he must express himself all the more clearly inasmuch as he cannot hear the questions of his interlocutor. The words should be so set down that they directly force the reader to think precisely the same thing as the author thought when he wrote them. Nor will this result be obtained unless the author has always been careful to remember that thought so far follows the law of gravity that it travels from head to paper much more readily than from paper to head; so that he must assist the latter passage by every means in his power.

Conversely, the individuality growing from subjectivity can be a genuine aid in developing a writing style which is effectively communicative. When we read nonfiction, such as essays and articles, we want and need to get the author's opinions, not merely a statement of facts, principles, and statistics. We may be dozing through a dull lecture, a flat recital of facts, but we tend to come awake when the lecturer begins to recount a personal experience, to give an eyewitness account, to express his opinions—in short, when he becomes a human being and stops being an automaton or robot.

No reader, and especially no instructor in freshman English, wishes to be confronted with lifeless, dry-as-dust material which possesses no spark of the writer's individuality, his personality, his subjective processes of thought and reasoning. (True, most encyclopedia articles and dictionary entries seem devoid of personality, but usually such selections are purposely cut-and-dried—and even here appear notable exceptions.) Nothing is more dull and hence less communicative than a theme which merely "goes through the motions" of setting down borrowed or plagiarized facts for the required number of words with no discernible stamp of the author's mind and personality. Even a research paper, one deliberately based on sources other than the writer's thought and experience, will communicate effectively only if and when it reveals to some degree the author's individual conclusions and judgments.

Prose can rarely be wholly objective (unless, of course, it is merely copied from reference sources). It will normally communicate to the reader only if it reveals at least something about its author. However, an excessively subjective composition can be as ineffective as a wholly objective one. If a writer parades his opinions to the exclusion of all other considerations, if his work is studded with "I," if he is self-centered and not in some respects reader-centered, he commits the error of subjectivity. At its height, subjectivity becomes *solipsism*, a firm belief that one's complete existence is within oneself. If one's writing is dull, lifeless, static, almost or totally devoid of emotion or personality, he commits the "error of objectivity." Both errors are serious, and striking a balance, a "golden mean," between them is not easy or simple.

But it can be done. Notice, for example, that "How Americans Choose Their Heroes," p. 548, is filled with the author's opinions, comments, and conclusions. Simultaneously, the article is loaded with facts, with concrete, verifiable statements which are woven into the fabric of the author's thesis. While reading this essay, we learn something about Davy Crockett, Daniel Webster, Abraham Lincoln, Andrew Jackson, other Americans of historical import—and Dixon Wecter. We may agree or disagree with the author's findings, but his opinions are stimulating without being "opinionated," and his subjective comments add movement, life, vigor, and even controversy to what in the hands of a less talented writer might have been dull history, a mere "think piece." Actually, none of the formal essays in Book Three lacks varying degrees of individuality. And, obviously, none of the informal essays, critical and biographical reports, short stories, plays, and poems would merit inclusion unless it possessed strong and identifiable elements of individuality.

Do such comments about individuality suggest that one must be *original* in his writing style? The answer, both "yes" and "no," depends upon what is meant by "originality." No one—teacher, student, college administrator, or even the coach of the football team—can reasonably be expected to come up with wholly new, entirely fresh ideas and with completely novel ways of conveying them. No one can do this often; perhaps no one now alive can do this *ever*. If he could, he would be as misunderstood as Galileo or Socrates and might lose his job or his life. But originality can and does also mean "independent thought," "individual insight," "constructive imagination." Each of these elements is attainable, at least on rare occasions, by nearly everyone. Goethe has wisely summed up this matter of individuality and originality:

> The most original authors of modern times are such not because they create anything new but only because they are able to say things in a manner as if they had never been said before.

You are yourself and no one but yourself, fortunately or unfortunately. If what you write, or say, bears at least to some slight degree the imprint of your own personality, your particular and inescapable individuality, then it will have "never been said before" in quite the same way. Bearing the marks of individuality, it will possess a genuinely important stylistic quality without which it would be dull and spiritless.

CONCRETENESS

Each of us has repeatedly read material which seemingly "made sense" but which left us with only a vague, fuzzy impression of what the author apparently intended us to absorb. Try as we might, we could not come to grips with the author's meaning and message. We felt that we were dealing with cotton wool or some other soft and flabby substance which we could not grasp, handle, and move about in our own thought processes. Discouraged or annoyed, we may have decided that the selection had no meaning and no message for us and thus gone on to something else, perhaps to a favorite television program.

One major cause of such a reaction is lack of *concreteness* in writing. The author we were trying unsuccessfully to read may have been using abstract words to express general ideas; he may have forgotten, if indeed he ever knew, that readers' minds respond most readily to the specific, the tangible, the concrete in writing just as entire personalities do in "real life." For example, when we are hungry we don't think of "nutrition" or "nourishment" or even of "food." We think of steak or baked potatoes or chocolate cake.

Actually, all that we know got into our heads as itemized bits of experience. When we were small, a parent or some other older person pointed out to us a dog, said "See the dog," and ever afterward, a d-o-g had some particular and special meaning for us. Your exact concept of a "dog" and that of anyone else will differ, but each item of experience in our private store of meanings has a definite, concrete application. For this reason, if no other, we respond most readily to concreteness in writing and feel baffled by abstract words and expressions which have no direct connection with our own backgrounds.

Abstract words are useful in discussing certain ideas and are especially common in such subjects as philosophy and the social sciences, but usually they are less exact, less meaningful, and consequently less effective than concrete words. Because they refer to specific and actual objects or concepts, concrete words have meanings more or less solidly established in the minds of both writer and reader. "Something worn on the human body between shoulders and chin" is rather vague but not entirely abstract. The concept can be made less vague by referring to a "collar" and more concrete by mention of a "ruff," "shawl collar," "wing collar," "tab collar," and "button-down." The word "neckwear" can refer to a "rather long narrow length of soft material such as silk or wool, worn about the neck and usually under a collar." If a speaker or writer uses "necktie," he is somewhat more specific; if he uses "four-in-hand," "bow-tie," "white tie," or "necktie party" he is being even more concrete.

Abstract words possess varying degrees of definiteness. Such words as *countryside*, *fear*, and *security* are not particularly specific, but they have more understandable connections with the experiences of most people than terms like *culture*, *duty*, *truth*, and *honor*. The word *carrier*, defined as a means of conveying and transporting, is somewhat abstract but can be made less so by using such terms as *motor vehicle*, *automobile*, *motorcycle*, and *handcar*, or by *mule*, *tank*, *bus*, *half-track*, and *kayak*.

Good writers sometimes use an abstract term because nothing else will fit and then immediately make it more communicative by providing a concrete example of what is meant or by translating its meaning into terms less abstract and vague. On p. 745, Robert Louis Stevenson uses several sentences to suggest that "the services of no single individual are indispensable." This idea is fairly clear despite the comparative abstractness of "services," "individual," and "indispensable." But Stevenson follows immediately with a figure of speech which masterfully enforces his idea: "Atlas was just a gentleman with a protracted nightmare." The concept—to anyone knowing the meaning of "protracted" and the identity of Atlas—is now unmistakable.

Or suppose you contend that government should intervene as little as possible in our economy and thus you employ the term "laissez-faire." Is this expression abstract or concrete? An effective writer, Stuart Chase, unwilling to take a chance on his readers' understanding of the term, used it but immediately equated it with a city which had "no traffic system," one where every driver was on his own. Chase then explained "enforced competition" as a system in which "traffic cops protect little cars"; "governmental regulation" as similar to "traffic cops advising drivers how to drive"; "government ownership" as a procedure in which "a traffic officer throws the driver out and gets behind the wheel himself." You may agree or disagree with the writer's definitions and analogies, but at least you know what he means and have been entertained while learning.

Much of what we remember from our reading of literature—especially of essays, articles, and biography—consists of incidents and anecdotes originally designed by the author to reinforce some possibly abstract concept. For example, once you have read it, you cannot forget "The Monster," p. 801, because the author uses one incident, anecdote, and illustration after another to drive home his concept of this particular "monster," Richard Wagner. Writing can rarely be more concrete than this—and hence more readable, understandable, and entertaining. Or examine Thoreau's essay beginning on p. 684. Ten years from now you may have forgotten much of what Thoreau here wrote, but you may think of the essay nearly every time you pick up a newspaper or hear a news report on television. And of course the appeal of short stories, plays, novels, and of much poetry lies in the fact that understandable, flesh-and-blood persons are involved in understandable problems and face understandable conflicts. What happens to people, why it happens, and what the results are seem real and exciting to us because happenings are narrated and described in concrete, specific terms which we can grasp as readily as we can observe or face problems in our own immediate lives.

Nine-tenths of all good writing consists of being concrete and specific. Perhaps the other tenth doesn't really matter.

ACHIEVING ONE'S OWN STYLE

Assuming that you now know something about style and a few of its desirable elements, what next? The only sensible answer is to ask: What is my style now and how do I go about improving it?

What your present style is is your concern and that of your instructor. The whole aim of freshman English is to make you aware of your stylistic assets and liabilities, to help you improve the former and decrease the latter. All the writing you and your classmates do, under the guidance of your teacher, is designed for the sole purpose of aiding you to remove flaws and increase clarity and effectiveness. The best method of improving your style —best because it is most direct, most specific, and most logical—is to write and keep writing under the practiced eye and hand of your instructor.

Two other methods of improving style require comment. Neither is as direct nor usually so effective as writing under supervision, but both none-theless are important. One method is *imitation;* the other is *analysis.*

IMITATION

Every writer must acquire his own style. Indeed, you have already achieved one, however much it may upset you and disturb your teacher. Your style, such as it is, already possesses qualities (good and bad) pecu-liarly your own. It has developed with you as you have grown and matured. Like it or not, your style reflects your personality, your character, your whole mode of thought. It may reflect these attributes improperly, unfairly, or obscurely, but reflect them it does. And yet your personality, character, and attitudes of thought have changed through the years and will continue to do so. Your style can be altered and improved to reflect these changes.

A mature style, such as you probably desire, is difficult to attain by conscious means. But one deliberate method of improving style is to select some writer, or writers, whose work you admire and attempt to model your own writing upon it. If you adopt the style of another slavishly, you become a mere imitator, an inevitable copycat and second-rater. But it may be possible through imitation to learn what characteristic qualities of style are most natural and effective for you and thus improve your own work. Some writer represented in Book Three may appeal strongly to you; if so, try to imitate his style, but not so closely that you become only a parodist. Your study should be interpretive rather than imitative; only thus can you be certain that your own approach is not obliterated by that of the writer being studied.

Many excellent writers claim to have become so by imitating the work of others. Robert Louis Stevenson, one of the all-time master stylists in English literature, once wrote:

> When I read a book or passage with some distinction, I must sit down at once and ape that quality. Thus I got practice in harmony, in rhythm, and in construction, playing the sedulous ape to Lamb, to Wordsworth, to Defoe, to Hawthorne, to Baudelaire.

Possibly, Stevenson would have become the great craftsman he was without imitating anyone, but obviously "playing the sedulous ape" did not impede his stylistic development.

In his *Autobiography,* Benjamin Franklin referred to his attempts to paraphrase some of the *Spectator* papers and then wrote:

But I found I wanted a stock of words, or a readiness in recollecting and using them, which I thought I should have acquired before that time if I had gone on making verses; since the continual occasion for words of the same import, but of different length, to suit the measure, or of different sound for the rhyme, would have laid me under a constant necessity of searching for variety; and also have tended to fix that variety in my mind, and make me master of it. Therefore I took some of the tales and turned them into verse; and, after a time, when I had pretty well forgotten the prose, turned them back again.

In a search for stylistic qualities apparent in the work of someone else, be careful to select only those qualities which seem natural and unforced for you. Avoid the tricks, artificial mannerisms, false or hearty breeziness, clipped dialogue, or witty understatement which enliven the work of an O. Henry, Hemingway, Oscar Wilde, or Thurber, but which seem contrived in your own work. Good style is natural; any out-and-out artifice is bad. Few writers can successfully imitate the flourishing sentences of an Addison or Pater, the tone and mood of an E. B. White, William Faulkner, or Thomas Wolfe.

ANALYSIS

Second only to actual writing as an effective method of improving one's style is careful analysis of good literary work. Such elements as figures of speech, transitional devices, length of sentences, polysyllabic words, and concrete or abstract nouns are easily discernible and even countable. Other qualities are more pervasive than these but can still be discovered and analyzed: humor, irony, slanginess, conciseness, rhythm, monotony, imagery, and quotable remarks such as epigrams and bons mots. Analyzing a competent writer's style for the occurrence or absence of such elements and qualities may help you to discover weaknesses and lacks in your own writing.

The analysis of a given selection should begin with careful, attentive reading. This should be followed by a second reading that is more analytical than the first. This time you should actually note, list, and count such matters as kinds of words and sentences, uses of figurative language, and the like. Hitherto unnoticed qualities of style will become apparent in such a reading. Finally, a third reading will enable you to see how the author achieves his effects because you now know the stylistic elements he employed. In this third reading you should be rewarded with specific ideas for improving your own style.

As a guide to your analysis of written work, keep in mind this list of six stylistic devices and elements. Not every one will appear in every selection, but many examples of each in Book Three await detection.

Sentence length. The shortest and longest sentences in a selection may range from one word to one hundred, or more. What is the average length? Are long and short sentences alternated? Does sentence length have a direct bearing on the rhythm or cadence of the selection?

Sentence type. Sentences may be simple, compound, complex, and compound-complex. They may be loose or periodic; declarative, interrogative, imperative, or exclamatory. What do sentence structure and type, both their variety and repetition, contribute to the style of the selection?

Figures of speech. How many figures of speech does the author employ? What kinds? What do they contribute to the connotation of words? to imagery? to the freshness (or staleness) of the selection? Are the figures of speech relatively simple? Elaborate? Forced and artificial? Fresh? Trite? What associations, connotations, attitudes, and emphases do they contribute to the tone of the selection and its central core of meaning?

Imagery. Some words have a "picture-forming" quality. Does the author use concrete words which call up sense impressions for you? Do verbal images employed represent appeals to the senses of sight, sound, taste, touch, and smell? Is the author prodigal or sparing in his use of imagery?

Conciseness. Is the style tightly knit, so taut that every word seems to count? Or is it leisurely, discursive, slow-moving, rambling? Do sentences seem to roll direct to the center pin as in a bowling strike or to pick off portions of ideas in more scattered fashion? Is the author sparing or lavish in his use of adjectives and adverbs? Is he more likely to write "a haze like the color of smoke" or "smoke-colored haze"? Does he use any disposable function words such as *the, a,* and *and*?

Sound. Part of the impression conveyed by a selection comes from its sound. Read aloud a part of any selection. Does the author use or overuse such stylistic elements as alliteration and assonance? Does the *rhythm* of a given selection derive from sentence length, the position of words requiring stress, the intonations and junctures necessarily involved in reading aloud? Does the selection exhibit euphony or any examples of cacophony?

Analysis of these six elements and of others possibly less obvious will enable you to "label" an author's style. With some reason, now that you have made a careful study, you can refer to a given author's style as breezy, labored, pompous, flowery, ironic, terse, and the like. All such terms are likely to have real meaning only for the user; it is common for students to disagree about the stylistic label or labels which should be attached to any particular selection. But any two persons who make a careful analysis of any selection are likely to agree, in general, that the style is (1) plain, or (2) elaborate, or (3) mixed. And most instructors, students, and contemporary professional writers will agree that a mixed style—now plain and unadorned, now elaborate and heightened, but always with a conversational base—is most suitable for most prose written today by most people.

Style and meaning are closely related. There are obvious relationships between the individuality of a writer and his style just as there are obvious traits of style characteristic of science fiction, advertising copy, and legal briefs. Qualities of language and elements of style directly affect the emphasis, tone, precision, suggestiveness, and intensity of the message being conveyed, the story being told, the idea being developed. Accurate understanding of a selection always depends to some degree upon an aware and sensitive response to the style in which it is presented. Analysis of effective style may not materially improve your writing but it will enormously improve your reading ability. This in itself is genuine progress.

CHAPTER 7

TRADITIONAL FORMS: EXPOSITION, ARGUMENT, DESCRIPTION, NARRATION

Let us assume that you are taking an automobile trip through a rural section of the United States. As you spin along the highway, you notice the farms, the growing crops, the farmhouses. When you stop at a filling station you converse briefly with the attendant; at lunch you talk with the waitress and comment on the varied foods served to you.

As you drive farther on that afternoon, you notice that trees and forests are becoming noticeably less plentiful, that broader and broader fields have been cleared for planting, and that the streams and rivers you cross are low. The sky does not appear so bright and clear as before; you seem to be moving through a thin, brown haze, and you have to hold a handkerchief over your nose or close all the windows of the car. You suddenly realize that you are in a dust storm and that the topsoil is being blown away. The grain no longer appears green, and the delicious smells floating up from the farm lands are shut out by the blanket of dust stretching all around you. At nightfall, you come to the outskirts of a city. The lights grow brighter as you approach the center of the town and finally you reach the hotel where you plan to spend the night. After registering and eating, you go up to your room. It is too late to go to a movie and thus, with nothing better to do, you decide to write a letter to a friend at home, telling him about your first day's travels.

What will you write? All day long you have been witnessing and hearing a moving, talking picture. Through all your five senses you have received myriad impressions. Suppose you write your friend a description of the countryside you have passed through, the people you have talked with, the food you have eaten, the dust storm, the hotel you are staying in—an account of the total effect which has been made on all your senses. If you write thus, selecting important details and playing upon the imaginative insight of your reader, you will succeed in composing what is technically called *description*.

Your friend does not care for details of this sort? Many people are bored, or say they are, by accounts of what others have seen, heard, smelled, tasted, and touched. Today when you were eating luncheon you started a conversation with the manager of the restaurant. He told you that he had been a farmer until recently but that he had had to leave his farm because of a series of "flash floods" which had endangered him and his wife and children. He recalled that heavily timbered areas surrounding his farm had been cleared and told how rains falling upon exposed lands rushed violently off to stream and river beds. For several hours one night he, his wife, and older children had feared that not only would their crops be ruined during a severe storm but that farm buildings and even their own home would be swept away. As he described the pouring rain and rushing torrents of water, his frightened children and terrified livestock, your attention and interest grew. Perhaps your friend would be interested, too? If you write him of that wild night the restaurant manager spoke of, the terror of the farm animals, the frenzied activity of mother, father, and children, you will write *narration*. It will have a descriptive background—nearly all narration has—but it will be what rhetoricians formally call narration. You and your reader will be concerned with an event, the happenings on a particular night and the characters involved.

The deep gullies you noticed beside the highway and the sudden dust storm of the afternoon start you thinking about the problem of erosion. Much of the richest soil in the United States, you recall, is being blown away or washed away by rivers and streams. You remember having read that in this country topsoil originally lay at an average depth of seven inches across the face of the land, but that it takes nature several hundred years to build a single inch of it. If your friend is a meditative person, you might write a letter which explains the process of erosion and tells what you know about the work of various agencies in dealing with reforestation, cover crops, soil conservation, flood control, etc. If you write this kind of letter you will be engaged in *exposition*.

Or you may decide that the problem of erosion is as important as the problem of international organization. You may argue that even after the questions of nations united or a world union or world peace with or without an international police force have been decided, the question of disappearing lands will remain to vex our descendants for generations to come. Land is important to all peoples, you observe, and erosion is prevalent in nearly all the countries of the world. If you marshal for your friend all the reasons for your belief in the great importance of erosion, you will be dealing with *argument*. You may describe and explain, but your primary purpose is to persuade your friend that the belief which you hold is logical.

If you are properly interested in communicating your thoughts and impressions, in writing a helpful, informative, interesting letter, you are not likely to be concerned with what name the rhetorician would give the material you are writing. These traditional forms of discourse—description, narration, exposition, and argument—are, indeed, little more than artificial divisions made for the purpose of analyzing composition. The good writer, whether amateur or professional, keeps his reader in mind, has a definite purpose and goal, and quite properly uses a bit of description here, of narration there, of exposition or argument in another place. He is content, and correctly so, if he succeeds in effectively conveying his thoughts and impressions. The labels his work bears are of little importance; if he stops to think at all, he will come to the realization that the four forms are nearly always used in combination.

In learning to write, however, it is necessary to learn to use all four forms, with special emphasis sometimes on one, sometimes on another. A brief review of the principles of expository, argumentative, descriptive, and narrative writing may be helpful; each of the forms has something to contribute to the effectiveness of writing. With this review out of the way, you can then be more intelligently concerned with the different forms in combination and have no further regard for rhetorical divisions.

EXPOSITION

Exposition is that type of writing which defines, explains, and interprets. Put another way, to distinguish it from the other traditional forms of discourse, exposition is all writing which does not primarily describe an object, tell a story, or maintain a position. It includes by far the greatest part of what we write and read: themes, textbooks, magazine articles, newspaper editorials, and all criticism of books, plays, motion pictures, radio and television programs, and musical compositions. Furthermore, it appears in most other forms of discourse and mediums of presentation; most novels, for example, explain and interpret; so do many motion pictures, radio speeches, picture magazines, and television programs.

Since the purpose of exposition is to make a subject comprehensible, expository writing must be well planned. The logical structure must be apparent at all times so that the reader will have a sense of progression, a knowledge that the writer is definitely taking him somewhere. Clarity and coherence are necessities, not merely virtues, of all good exposition. Chart your course in advance; making an outline (see Section 39) is the most practical way to secure proper organization. Be careful to define the terms you are using if they are capable of being misunderstood. Do everything possible to make your explanation clear. See Section 41.

Good expository writing is not only carefully planned and developed with a view to clarity; it is also *interesting*. Occasionally a reader will be interested in exposition because of its very clarity and logicalness. For example, a well-written encyclopedia article depends for its interest upon clearness as well as the reader's need for the information it contains. Similarly, exposition in technical and learned journals relies heavily upon clarity and the prior interest of the student in the subject matter. The general reader, however, ordinarily demands a greater aid to interest than mere clarity. The human mind, someone has remarked, has an extraordinary capacity for resisting information. Exposition, which has as its primary purpose the imparting of information, thus possesses limitations that other forms of discourse do not have. The storyteller has a chain of incidents and an emotional appeal to impart; the descriptive writer can appeal to the five senses; the debater has strong convictions to discuss and often can make a frank exploitation of his own personality. Since the expository writer has none of these aids to interest, he must be resourceful in achieving his ends. He must utilize narrative and descriptive material to make his information palatable; wherever possible, he must strive to get a new approach to the subject; he must make occasional use of humor and satire. Communication is the only proper test of exposition, as it is of the other forms of discourse. Expository material which is dull, dry, and commonplace is not really communicable to others.

Seldom do we remember a writer's or speaker's generalities or moralizings, but we recall vividly the stories he tells, the illustrative jokes, the revealing incidents, the re-creations of dialogue, the pertinent anecdotes he injects into his writing or speech. For more than 2,500 years, for example, we have enjoyed and remembered Aesop's fables. We may recall little of the Bible, but we are likely to keep forever in mind, once read, stories about Joseph, about David and Goliath, about Daniel in the den of lions, about the prodigal son, about the house built on sand and the parable of the lost sheep. Numerous specific methods of making exposition interesting and appealing are discussed in Chapter 6.

The two great problems in writing exposition are, therefore, to make it clear and to make it interesting.

One of the surest ways to obtain clarity and force in exposition is to arrange or order the materials in the form best suited to the substance of the essay and to the writer's purpose and the reader's needs. Several kinds of order may be used by the expository writer. He may proceed from something known to something unknown or from something simple to something complex. Again, he may employ *classification*, or a *time* or *space* order, *deduction* or *induction, analogy* or *contrast*. These are not the only possible orders in exposition, nor does the use of any one exclude the use of others in parts of the same essay or theme. A writer, for example, may arrange his illustrative materials in time or space at the same time that he develops his thesis (main idea) inductively. The first paragraph of Sir James Jeans' article on p. 121 provides an example of both *simple-to-complex* and *known-to-unknown* orders. Furthermore, analogy is apparent throughout this piece of exposition.

Three often used kinds of order are mentioned and briefly discussed in Section 33. A further comment on two of them and on other kinds of order mentioned in the preceding paragraph may be helpful to you in ordering expository paragraphs and themes.

Classification is simply division of a topic into various aspects. Such division may be arbitrary but usually is logical. For instance, the topic of *erosion* with which this chapter began can be classified or divided into its logical parts: erosion by water, erosion by wind, and erosion by glacier. A "research" theme on erosion might begin with a brief definition of the general process, proceed to a discussion (in separate paragraphs) of each of these three main kinds of erosion, and conclude with a statement about former and present methods for controlling erosion. Since this topic is too large for competent treatment in a single theme, one division of it might be classified for treatment: erosion by water may be ordered into discussion of running streams, rainwash, weathered rock, and rock waste. Or the subtopic of the removal of material by running water may be classified into hydraulic action, abrasion, and material in solution.

Almost any subject can be ordered by classification, as several of the articles in Book Three demonstrate. For example, the author of "Logic and Logical Fallacies," p. 486, classifies the kinds and forms of illogical thinking and discusses each.

A paper on the kinds of people in your home town may classify them on the basis of education, politics, religion, or background; the basis for the classification will depend upon the *theme* of your theme. Obviously, the main point of your theme should be determined before you decide upon classification or any other particular order.

Time or *space* organization is a special kind of order by classification. Chronological (time) order is the basis of almost all biographical and historical writing. In the explanation of a process, which will be discussed more thoroughly later in this chapter, the order is frequently chronological. Order in space may be geographical; the best-known example is the famous "All Gaul is divided into three parts," the opening of Caesar's *Gallic Wars*, which discusses in turn the parts of Gaul inhabited by the Belgae, the Aquitani, and the Gauls. An exposition of racial distinctions, of regional characteristics, of particular attitudes or habits in various countries might also most satisfactorily use order in space.

For an excellent example of both time and space order, study "Gettysburg," p. 849. Here *time* moves from "soon after the battle of Chancellorsville" to the battle of Gettysburg, to the making of plans for dedicating the battlefield, to the day of dedication itself, and on to an epilogue. In *space* this material moves from Virginia to Gettysburg, to Washington, back to Gettysburg, again to Washington, and finally to "many a country cottage over the land."

Deductive order moves from the general to the particular. The writer makes a general statement, or a series of general statements, about his topic and in the following paragraphs illustrates these general remarks with specific examples. He makes everything as clear as possible at the beginning by summarizing his position, supporting that summarization with the illustrations that follow. *Inductive* order, on the other hand, moves from the particular to the general. The writer may produce several examples which point toward the general idea of the theme and base his conclusions on the evidence which he has marshaled.

A good example of deductive order is the first part of McGuire's "The Human Community," p. 554. Notice carefully the first five paragraphs. Conversely, most of Thouless' "Emotional Meanings," p. 495, is developed in inductive order. Compare and contrast the order employed in the McGuire and Thouless essays.

Analogy and *contrast* are closely related. *Analogy* emphasizes similarities; an unfamiliar object or idea is explained by comparing it with another object or idea more familiar to the reader. *Contrast* emphasizes differences; both contrasted objects and ideas are made clearer than either would have been if described alone.

The writer's problem is always to choose the order most appropriate and effective for his particular purpose. For example, Sir James Jeans uses *analogy and contrast* in the selection just below. He also makes use of visual aids. Pictures, diagrams, and maps often increase your reader's understanding. Notice how clear the writer makes a phenomenon puzzling to most people:

> Imagine that we stand on any ordinary seaside pier, and watch the waves rolling in and striking against the iron columns of the pier. Large waves pay very little attention to the columns—they divide right and left and re-unite after passing each column, much as a regiment of soldiers would if a tree stood in their road; it is almost as though the columns had not been there. But the short waves and ripples find the columns of the pier a much more formidable obstacle. When the short waves impinge on the columns, they are reflected back and spread as new ripples in all directions.

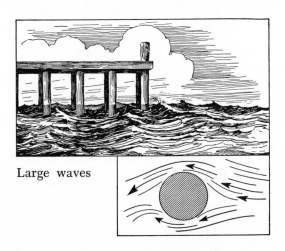

Large waves

To use the technical term, they are "scattered." The obstacle provided by the iron columns hardly affects the long waves at all, but scatters the short ripples.

We have been watching a sort of working model of the way in which sunlight struggles through the earth's atmosphere. Between us on earth and outer space the atmosphere interposes innumerable obstacles in the form of molecules of air, tiny droplets of water, and small particles of dust. These are represented by the columns of the pier.

The waves of the sea represent the sunlight. We know that sunlight is a blend of lights of many colours—as we can prove for ourselves by passing it through a prism, or even through a jug of water, or as Nature demonstrates to us when she passes it through the raindrops of a summer shower and produces a rainbow. We also know that light consists of waves, and that the different colours of light are produced by waves of different lengths, red light by long waves and blue light by short waves. The mixture of waves which constitute sunlight has to struggle through the obstacles it meets in the atmosphere, just as the mixture of waves at the seaside has to struggle past the columns of the pier. And these obstacles treat the light-waves much as the columns of the pier treat the sea-waves. The long waves which constitute red light are hardly affected, but the short waves which constitute blue light are scattered in all directions.

Thus, the different constituents of sunlight are treated in different ways as they struggle through the earth's atmosphere. A wave of blue light may be scattered by a dust particle, and turned out of its course. After a time a second dust particle again turns it out of its course, and so on, until finally it enters our eyes by a path as zigzag as that of a flash of lightning. Conse-

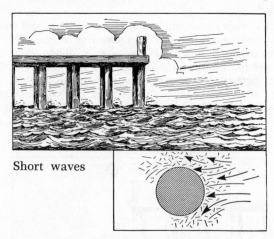

Short waves

quently the blue waves of the sunlight enter our eyes from all directions. And that is why the sky looks blue.[1]

Exposition usually does not stand alone, as has been pointed out, although most of our reading and much of our writing are of material which is expository in purpose. The précis and the paraphrase are forms

---

[1] From *The Stars in Their Courses* by Sir James Jeans. By permission of The Macmillan Company, publishers.

which, designed largely as exercises, are strictly expository. The investigative paper is also a form of explanation and interpretation which only too often consists of straight exposition with little or no narrative and descriptive material.

DEFINITION

An important type which is wholly expository in purpose and frequently so in form is the *definition*.

The typical dictionary definition has three parts: *term, genus, differentia*. From the standpoint of logic, a good definition is made only by placing the term to be defined in the class or kind to which it belongs (genus) and then giving a statement of the individual characteristics that distinguish the term from other members of the genus. Thus, "Braille [the term] is a system of printing or transcribing [the genus] in which the characters are represented by raised letters [the differentia]." Several logical cautions should be observed in making such definitions: (1) Use simple terms, (2) exclude all terms not in the genus, (3) include all terms that should be in the genus, (4) avoid using the term or any derivative of it.

In practice, most definitions are made less formally and exactly than this. Sometimes we use synonyms, explaining one term with the aid of other words which mean the same, or almost the same, thing. Thus we say that a *mendicant* is a *beggar,* or that *to pilfer* means *to steal.* Sometimes we wish to offer not a full, logical definition, but one which merely suggests genus or differentia. O. Henry in "A Municipal Report" "defined" Californians as "the Southerners of the West." Dr. Johnson "defined" a fishing pole as a rod with bait at one end and a fool at the other. The following definition, written by a student, is amusing rather than full and logical:

> To persons who have never taken freshman English, an English theme is "something" written for a course called "English Composition." To those who really know, this "something" often comes in weird sizes, colors, and shapes, but the editors of *Webster's New World Dictionary of the American Language* seem to agree with the outsiders: "a short essay, especially one written as an assignment in a school course."
>
> A student himself, when asked for a definition, usually quotes a handbook of English composition: he says that a theme is an exercise in the "principles of correct, clear, and effective communication of ideas from the writer to the reader." This is his definition when he's talking to his teacher. When he's not in the teacher's presence, his definitions vary.
>
> Alumni remember an English theme as a 10-minute-old composition, written in good English, which was handed in to the instructor two weeks late. There was always some bother about rewriting the theme, but if one bought the series of grade B themes for sale in the bookshop near the University, that slight inconvenience was done away with. (There were always a number of luckless students who were taught by an instructor young enough to remember the "tricks of the trade," but such instructors were few.)
>
> To me, a theme means working "on the hoof" for about three days; then I write the first draft with some enthusiasm and much speed. The draft "soaks" for about another three days and then the theme is trimmed and polished and given to the instructor on the date assigned.

Whether the assignment is for a profile, modeled after *The New Yorker,*
or a personal essay after E. B. White, I always accept the assignment silently.
The instructor is pleased to accept any fulfillment of any assignment to which
he can give a grade of C−!

On occasion, however, it is necessary to be more precise and full than
this. A definition does not have to be formal in order to define; a satisfactory
definition can overlook both genus and differentia. Such a definition can be
made by collecting examples or instances of the term. If asked to define a
laser, you could perhaps best define it for the lay reader by citing examples
of how it works. Or if asked to define *honesty,* you might well cite instances
of people who revealed honesty in their actions. You can also define satisfactorily by telling at some length what a thing is not, or by comparing and
contrasting the term with something known and familiar (extended simile
or metaphor). The following paragraphs from an article on the *whistle-punk*
show how instructive and yet entertaining this type of full, informal definition may be:

When I first went to work in a logging-camp in the Pacific Northwest
and heard mention of "whistle-punks," I thought the term had reference to
some mythical animal like the swamp-wogglers and side-hill badgers of the
East, or to some fabulous character of the Oregon timber. But I soon learned
that whistle-punks were very real, and very, very hard-boiled.

In the West any boy is known as a "punk," just why I haven't learned.
Whistle-punks are officially known on camp pay-rolls as signal boys. They
are the youthful loggers who, with jerk-wire or electric toots-ee, give the
signals for starting and stopping to engineers of donkey-engines that yard
the big Douglas fir timber, up and down the West Coast. They are automatons, standing throughout the day in one spot and yanking the whistle
wire once, twice, or in combinations, in answer to the hook-tender's orders.
The hook-tender has a log ready. He shouts, "Hi!" The punk jerks his
whistle-line and the whistle on the engine snorts. The engineer "opens her
up," and the log is brought in to the landing.

Despite his lowly job, which compares in dignity with that of the water-
boy of construction gangs, the punk is a well-known character in the Northwest. In Tacoma, Washington, the "Lumber Capital of America," a newspaper
has a daily column headed "The Whistle-Punk." I hold the punk to be well
worth a column.

When placed alongside the average whistle-punk, the so-called tough
kids of the Bowery and the gamins of Paris are like so many cherubim.
Punks are the "hardest" kids ever; or, at least, they *want* to be. They are so
tough they won't read even the *Police Gazette.* To hear one talk you would
suspect that he liked for breakfast nothing so much as a keg of iron bolts
soaked in gasoline, wood-alcohol, and snuff.

The vizor of the punk's cap is worn smooth where it has rested over an
ear. His best Sunday conversation sounds like extracts from Rabelais; and
when he is going *good* he can outcurse any cockney that ever mentioned the
King of England. When he spits, it is what learned men term a cosmic disturbance. . . . Yes, the punk is *hard.*

—STEWART H. HOLBROOK

You can find many excellent examples of definition in your collection
of readings. For one example, Cardinal Newman's entire brief essay, p. 701,

is an extended definition. As a matter of fact, every article in Book Three under the heading of "Thinking and Propaganda" consists in large part of definition: Huxley defines the method of scientific investigation; Bronowski explains what he means by "the creative mind"; Davis defines several kinds of illogical thinking processes; Thouless makes clear what the emotional meanings of certain words may be; Huff defines a statistic by revealing what one is and is not; Highet indicates what the thinking life of man is and clearly defines his idea of the free possession and use of knowledge. In a sense, each of these essays is one extended series of definitions.

EXPLANATION OF A PROCESS

Another kind of exposition consists of showing the steps or stages in the evolution of something which is being constructed. In a process exposition, you face the twin problems of substance and arrangement. The process itself helps to solve the first problem because it directs and limits the subject matter. If the process is complex, you must give full details; if it is simple, only a few details will be needed. Furthermore, if you are, for example, explaining the process of refining petroleum, you need not give a history of oil. Only the actual steps, the essential stages, of the process itself are necessary. You should plan the theme carefully so that each stage of the process will receive a proportionate amount of space.

The problem of order in writing expository processes is more difficult than that of substance. The reader must be able to understand each step of the process as it develops into the next. In general, the organization is chronological; the writer explains each step in the order in which it is performed in the whole process. As mentioned earlier, this order of occurrence can be used in the explanation of any process, although in any one stage it may be necessary to slow up the process exposition by defining the terms used. In explaining the production of cotton, for example, you might first tell how the soil is prepared, then how the seed is planted, then how the crop is fertilized and cultivated, how gathered, how ginned. In your explanation of any one of these five steps, it may be necessary to define the specific terms you use.

Clear and careful transition is of great importance in explaining a process. You must tell your reader when you start upon a new step and you must be careful not to allude to details not yet explained. Remember: *you* know all the stages, but you should assume that your reader knows only what you tell him in the order of your exposition.

In one sense, the explanation of a process involves the writing of a series of "paragraph themes." That is, each step in the process is explained and then linked to the next step. Your major problems are to make each paragraph as clear and readable as you can, arrange the paragraphs in a sequential order, and tie them into a coherent whole. Notice the organization and use of visual aids in this explanation of the function of the inner ear:

> In each of your inner ears is a part shaped like a snail shell and called the cochlea. That serves for hearing. Besides that there are two chambers and three horseshoe-shaped tubes, filled with a fluid and serving for balance or sense of movement.

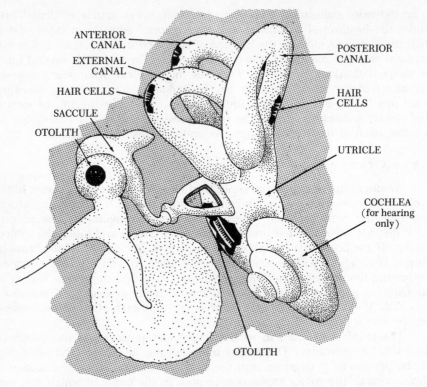

ANTERIOR CANAL
EXTERNAL CANAL
HAIR CELLS
SACCULE
OTOLITH
POSTERIOR CANAL
HAIR CELLS
UTRICLE
COCHLEA (for hearing only)
OTOLITH

Semicircular canals and otolith organs of the inner ear

The tubes, which are known as the semicircular canals, are in three different planes, one horizontal, and the other two upright but at right angles to each other, so that the three are in the same relative positions they would be if one were placed flat on the bottom of a box, a second stood up along the end and the third upright along the side.

Because of this arrangement, whichever way the head moves—forward or backward, to the right or left, or up or down—the fluid in at least one tube is disturbed.

Each semicircular canal has in it a set of hair cells with long hairs that project out into the fluid. The nerve-endings are in these cells.

When your head is spun around, the hair cells have to go along, but the fluid in the canal tends to lag behind. This pushes the hairs to one side, thus exciting the nerve-endings which in turn send their signals to your brain. This is how you know when you are spinning around, even with your eyes shut or in a fog. You know which way you are turning because the feeling is different when the fluid in different canals is disturbed, or when it is disturbed in different directions.

Horizontal rotation affects mostly the horizontal canal, but some canal in each ear would be affected by spinning in any direction. Many kinds of rotation affect all three canals. Of course, you also get clues from pressures on your body and from inside your body.

When you start spinning and then keep on going around at a constant speed, the fluid in the canals gets speeded up too. The hair cells then return to their normal position. This can fool you in a dangerous way. For the feeling that you are spinning stops completely, although actually you keep on going around.

A simple experiment will show you exactly how this works. Let a friend sit in a chair that you can spin around. Blindfold him and spin him. Keep him rotating, as nearly as you can, at a constant speed. After a while, he may be going around quite rapidly and yet feel sure that he is absolutely still—except for the vibration of the chair.

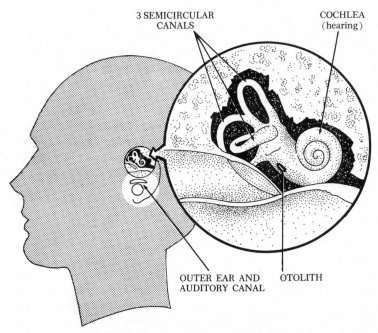

Position of the inner ear in the head

If you talk to him he will feel sure that *you* are sailing rapidly around his chair—very rapidly indeed if someone else spins the chair, and you are far away from him, for then you seem to be shooting around through a big circle at every rotation of his chair.

Now stop him. He will think he is going around in the opposite direction, although the chair is now still. That is because the fluid in the canals tends to coast on when the hair cells are stopped, thus pushing the hairs over in the opposite direction.

Now suppose he moves his head. The illusion he has of spinning will change. The direction in which he feels he is spinning changes. If you have been spinning him, actually, in a counter-clockwise direction, and he now puts his head over to the left until his ears are horizontal, he will have a startling experience.

He feels as if he were turning backwards, head under heels. It is an alarming experience. He thinks the chair is falling over backwards, and he will throw himself forward out of the chair in an effort to "right" himself—unless he is strapped in. His movement is just as quick as the cat's when she rights herself in falling.

This experiment gives you an idea of how an airplane pilot can sometimes make mistakes in flying his plane because of the tricks played upon
him by his inner ears.[2]

Do not feel disturbed or upset if you think that you cannot possibly
explain a process so involved as that dealing with the inner ear. You may
know little about the subject and care less. But, for example, you do have
habits, good and bad, and you give them some thought every day of your
life. You "could write a book" about some of them. What, then, is William
James' article, p. 595, but an explanation of habit in our lives, an exposition
of the process of making one's nervous system an ally instead of an enemy?

For another example of a process somewhat simpler than the functions
of the inner ear, consider once more the subject of *erosion*. Surely you have
witnessed the wind picking up and removing from an area fine particles
of soil and weathered rock. This process, known as *deflation*, is not difficult
to understand and explain. Erosion by wind (fine dust in suspension, particles as large as sand bounced along just above the ground, sand blast,
and wind abrasion, the forming of sand dunes and ventifacts) is a process
subject to study and then to clear and interesting explanation to others.

Scores of other and even more personal processes are observable in
everyone's daily life. Learning to write and talk about them is an important
segment of learning to communicate.

Narrative and Descriptive Exposition

The use of either narration or description, or both, is frequent in expository writing as a means of increasing clarity and holding reader interest.
Narrative exposition may tell how some process, operation, or experiment
is carried on; descriptive exposition may emphasize the appearance of an
object so that its purpose or principle or method of operation may be understood. In short, each method is exposition in combination with another form
of discourse. Some of the best exposition is both narrative and descriptive;
it explains how an object looks and how it works.

Examples of both narrative and descriptive exposition may be found
in popular science magazines, in photography manuals, and in accounts of
scientific research. The widely popular "how to" and personal experience
articles in general magazines contain much narrative exposition. Biographical sketches (profiles), social workers' case reports, and travel articles
usually contain a wealth of descriptive exposition.

An excellent example of the use of both narrative and descriptive elements in exposition is provided by Jeans' article beginning on p. 121. In
the first paragraph, for example, both action and physical details increase
reader interest and make the explanation clearer and more specific. Thoreau's celebrated account of the battle of the ants (p. 91) is an instance of
narrative and descriptive exposition with a couple of traces of argument.

For other examples of narrative and descriptive exposition in this
volume, see the first two paragraphs of this chapter. To the extent that the

---

[2] From "Psychology for the Fighting Man," *The Infantry Journal*, Washington, 1943.

writer was able, he attempted to combine descriptive details with a light admixture of narration (movement) in order to make the exposition as clear and as palatable as possible.

Better examples of this form may be noted in Van Wyck Brooks' "Helen Keller," p. 831; Clarke's "The Uses of the Moon," p. 564; Katz and Sanford's "Causes of the Student Revolution," p. 574; Feibleman's "What Happens in College," p. 658; Reston's "A Fable," p. 715; Ferril's "Freudian Football," p. 723; and McCarthy's "General Macbeth," p. 779. Each of these selections is fully expository in purpose, but each employs several narrative and descriptive aids to clearness, interest, and appeal.

SUMMARY

Defining terms and explaining processes or mechanisms are kinds of writing whose primary purpose is expository. They furnish excellent training in clear thinking and writing. So, also, do other forms of exposition treated elsewhere: the *informal essay*, p. 149; *criticism*, p. 154; the *profile*, p. 159, and the *formal essay*, p. 162.

Good exposition is difficult to write. Its essentials are clarity of plan and forcefulness of style. It requires definition of terms, especially of technical words and of common words used in a special sense. It demands an effective use of examples, comparisons, and contrasts. But, above all, its effectiveness depends upon the logic and the aids to interest which are employed. Exposition rarely stands alone as a pure form; but if the purpose is fundamentally expository, as it will be in most of your writing in freshman English, your work must be clear and interesting. Otherwise, your definition will not define, your explanation will not explain, your interpretation will not interpret.

Thumbnail explanations of some of the processes and terms discussed in preceding pages will be found under the heading *Exposition*, p. 377. Study of that entry may serve to help you focus upon a few of the important aspects of exposition as a form of writing.

ARGUMENT

There is no clear distinction between exposition and argument. The first explains, defines, and interprets; so does the second. What difference there is lies in the fact that exposition usually tries only to make something clear to the reader, whereas argument attempts not only to do that but also to convince, persuade, and even entice the reader or hearer. The end of argumentation is wholly practical; the reasoner wishes to persuade someone to act upon his suggestions or, at least, to accept his views. A salesman who explains the workings of a vacuum cleaner to a housewife is using exposition; but if he is a successful salesman, he is also trying to prevail upon her, to allure and entice her into buying a vacuum cleaner.

Like exposition, argument rarely appears in a pure form. Except when you debate in a literary society or intercollegiate contest, most of your arguing is highly informal. In the typical informal argument much use is made of the other three forms of discourse. If, for example, you are defending the position that college social fraternities are snobbish, you will define, explain, and interpret; you will probably cite instances of snobbishness; you will describe how fraternities are constituted and operated.

But whether formally or informally, you will argue much, both in college and later. Your mind is constantly being pulled about by propagandists; at home, at church, in the classroom, on the athletic field, over the radio, in newspapers and books and television programs, speakers and writers are and will be trying to get your attention so that they can convince you of the wisdom of their position. Every day you are called upon to accept, reject, or debate some point of view. All education, in fact, has been defined as learning what to believe and what to do. We shall never learn what is proper to believe and do unless we learn to think straight, to distinguish good argument from bad.

All arguments should be based on principles of logic. But much of the informal argument which we hear and use consists merely of name-calling. It deals with personalities rather than principles. It appeals to prejudice and passion, not to the intellect. Sarcasm and invective are, however, like fireworks—momentarily brilliant but without lasting effects.

It is true that we hear little good argument today from which we can learn, although the 1952 and 1956 presidential campaigns are considered by some experts to have produced much of the best political debating since the days of Lincoln and Douglas. Regardless of lack of opportunities for hearing good debating, we can at least try to be a little more precise and logical in the debates we engage in almost every day of our lives. We can learn to study and analyze evidence, to distinguish between that which bears on the subject and that which does not. We can strive to avoid thinking in a haphazard fashion and to keep prejudice and emotional bias from taking the place of sound reason. Acquiring honest habits of thought is the major problem of argument as well as a lifetime pursuit.

There are four major steps in formal argument: establishing the proposition to be debated; analyzing the proposition; formulating the argument; preparing the brief. Each deserves attention.

Establishing the Proposition

The proposition provides a point of contact; it should be a clear, definite, and exact statement of what is to be discussed.

Some propositions can be so established, but others cannot. Such an assertion as *Propaganda is prevalent today* is not arguable; no one can reasonably deny the truth of this statement. It would also be fruitless to argue the statement: *Man's normal span of life can be increased.* The truth of this assertion is readily apparent to any intelligent and informed person.

Propaganda is unfortunately prevalent today is not a well-stated proposition either. The word *unfortunately* does introduce difference of opinion so that the proposition is debatable: some may argue that propaganda is *fortunately* prevalent. But the proposition is not clear; precisely what is meant by *unfortunately*? Similarly, *Man's normal span of life can be tripled* is not well-stated. The findings of science are thus far inconclusive. Besides, the subject is so technical that it had best be left to scientists themselves.

A proposition should be stated in specific, affirmative terms and should be narrowed sufficiently to permit a definite point of contact. *Propaganda is undesirable because it deliberately influences opinions and actions with reference to predetermined ends* is a debatable proposition. It requires definition of terms (see below), but it is specific and affirmatively stated, and it suggests one major way in which, according to some, propaganda may be called undesirable. However, this statement is still not entirely suitable for debate; a proposition ideally contains no explicit argument such as the word *undesirable* suggests. Furthermore, it is still somewhat broad in its implications. *The type of propaganda employed in current newspaper advertisements for Sally's Soap should be prohibited* is a proposition which sets rather definite limits and is stated in unambiguous terms.

But even if we understand a proposition we are not necessarily ready to analyze and argue it. Some relatively simple or unimportant statements may not require background analysis, but many do. Some propositions may be fully understood only if we go into "the history of the question." That is, it may be necessary to know what brought the argument (proposition) into existence. In a debate on freight rates in this country, for example, it would be necessary to know something of their history, their application, and their present status. What has been the historic attitude of Eastern shippers? Of Southern shippers? Of those in the Far West? Without such knowledge it would be difficult or impossible to understand what is really at stake and what makes the argument significant at the present time.

ANALYZING THE PROPOSITION

Hardly less important than establishing a proposition is analyzing it. There is little point in arguing until you understand the precise meaning of what you are discussing. You must analyze the proposition for its intention and meaning. Who has not engaged in heated debate, only to discover at long last that he and his opponent were really in agreement all along, that they had misunderstood what they were arguing about? Careful definition of terms will bring out clearly the basis of disagreement and will remove the danger of not meeting on a common ground with your opponent. The term *propaganda,* for example, must be clearly defined. Once it was a reputable term; to what does it owe its sinister meaning today? Propaganda "deliberately influences opinions and actions with reference to predetermined ends." What of education? May it be called propaganda? What of advertising? Do not both education and advertising try to influence opinions and actions with reference to predetermined ends? Or would you not call education propagandic because it attempts to tell the whole truth and nothing but the truth for disinterested purposes? What of advertising —is it an attempt to tell the truth and nothing but the truth for interested purposes? If so, is it propagandic? Is propaganda in your debate to be restricted to conscious dishonesty and selfish aim?

In other words, you must indicate definitely the meanings and the limits of the proposition you intend to defend or attack. This analysis will combine definition of terms with a statement of the history of the question and the gathering of supporting material which will be logical evidence for your stating as you do the issues involved.

The Lincoln-Douglas debates have been mentioned. Note in this excerpt from Lincoln's Cooper Union speech how clearly he defines terms and states the issues involved:

> In his speech last autumn at Columbus, Ohio, as reported in *The New York Times*, Senator Douglas said:
>
> "Our fathers, when they framed the government under which we live, understood this question just as well as, and even better than, we do now."
>
> I fully endorse this, and I adopt it as a text for this discourse. I so adopt it because it furnishes a precise and an agreed starting-point for a discussion between Republicans and that wing of the Democracy headed by Senator Douglas. It simply leaves the inquiry: What was the understanding those fathers had of the question mentioned?
>
> What is the frame of government under which we live? The answer must be, "The Constitution of the United States." That Constitution consists of the original, framed in 1787, and under which the present government first went into operation, and twelve subsequently framed amendments, the first ten of which were framed in 1789.
>
> Who were our fathers that framed the Constitution? I suppose the "thirty-nine" who signed the original instrument may be fairly called our fathers who framed that part of the present government. It is almost exactly true to say they framed it, and it is altogether true to say they fairly represented the opinion and sentiment of the whole nation at that time. Their names, being familiar to nearly all, and accessible to quite all, need not now be repeated.
>
> I take these "thirty-nine," for the present, as being "our fathers who framed the government under which we live."
>
> What is the question which, according to the text, those fathers understood just as well as, and even better than, we do now?
>
> It is this: Does the proper division of local from Federal authority, or anything in the Constitution, forbid our Federal Government to control as to slavery in our Federal Territories?
>
> Upon this, Senator Douglas holds the affirmative, and Republicans the negative. This affirmation and denial form an issue; and this issue—this question—is precisely what the text declares our fathers understood "better than we." Let us now inquire whether the "thirty-nine," or any of them, ever acted upon this question; and if they did, how they acted upon it—how they expressed that better understanding.

Formulating the Argument

After you have analyzed the proposition to determine the points to be raised, you then need to arrange these points and their supporting proof to your own advantage. Fundamentally, this *formulation of proof* depends upon *reasoning*. Evidence alone will not convince; it must be arranged in a definite order so that it will make the greatest possible appeal to your hearers or readers. You will have to consider carefully the usual orders in exposition; which is best suited for the argument? Shall you make your point or points at the beginning and then elaborate upon them? Or shall you obtain suspense by withholding conclusions and by gradual disclosure convince the skeptical of the truth of your arguments? If you choose the former, you are proceeding deductively; if the latter, inductively. Or shall you use comparison and contrast, strengthening your argument and weakening your opponent's at the same time? Ultimately, of course, the choice of order will depend upon purpose, upon purpose which relates to your argument, which anticipates your opponent's position, and which takes your audience into account.

It is in formulating your argument that you will have greatest need to call on your knowledge of human nature. You will develop a certain point by reference to facts well known to your audience (readers), another by using proof appealing in itself but less familiar. You will remember the propensity of the mind to wander and will regain attention by the occasional use of an anecdote, incident, or report of dialogue. You will recall that the beginning and end of your argument are points of greatest emphasis and will not neglect to make telling assertions at these places.

It is also in formulating proof that you will have greatest need for clear reasoning. We think illogically much of the time, but a review of the fallacies discussed below should be of service.

P R E P A R I N G   T H E   B R I E F

Argument is almost wholly a matter of recognizing and revealing logical relationships between ideas. Any device which will clarify and emphasize these relationships is important because argument is prone to "jump the track" and take up unrelated issues. In argument, as in other forms of discourse, an outline is useful. The special form of outline used in argument is called a *brief*, but it has precisely the purpose and function that a topic or sentence or paragraph outline has in exposition (see p. 253). The brief differs from an ordinary outline only by using conjunctions (*for*, most notably) to reveal precise relationships between developing ideas. The brief is a complete statement of every phase of the argument, including definite indication of the proof that is to be supplied. Thus it may be called a "plan of attack."

In its simplest form, a brief consists of a stated conclusion followed by a statement of evidence, fact, or reason:

> A. John must have received his allowance this month, for
> 1. He has paid off his debt to me, and
> 2. He has bought a new pair of shoes.

A lengthy argument will require a lengthy series of interlocking statements, usually arranged under headings of *introduction, argument,* and *conclusion.* But the purpose of the brief is always the same: to present a close line of argument in a clearly revealed series of related ideas.

Thinking Logically

The four somewhat formal steps in argument which have been discussed are important. But each of them is dependent upon straight, logical thinking. In arguing especially, but also in explaining, describing, or narrating, we always find that we have to reason. Thinking clearly and honestly is one of man's most difficult and most important tasks. Some say it is his most important. This is the contention of the six articles headed "Thinking and Propaganda" in Book Three. It is also the thesis underlying many other selections in that collection of readings. Studying them, analyzing them, probing them will afford you an exciting opportunity to see good minds wrestling logically and entertainingly with important ideas.

For brief comment on thinking clearly and a summary of logical processes of thought and offenses against straight thinking, see Section 41d. Also, note the entry for *Logic* on p. 402. Of particular help should be the articles by Davis, "Logic and Logical Fallacies," and Sherwood, "Semantics: Denotation and Connotation."

SUMMARY

By now it is readily apparent that fallacies in logic are numerous, common, and overlapping. The specific names of these fallacies and of still others which could be mentioned are not really important. What is of utmost importance is that we try to find and analyze evidence; that we do not permit emotional bias and prejudice to take the place of sound reason or let unsound reason corroborate our prejudices. In short, we should attempt to acquire honest habits of thought. Colleges, which may fall far short of their goals in other respects, do provide unlimited opportunities and training in this significant endeavor. Our aim should be to arrive at beliefs which are solidly based on evidence of truth or some other form of assurance. As rational human beings we should, indeed *must*, hold some convictions. But those we attain and those we attempt to persuade others to hold should be based on straight, not crooked, thinking.

DESCRIPTION

Description is that kind of writing which tells how something looks, tastes, smells, sounds, feels, or acts. Every moment of every day we receive impressions through our five senses; whenever we try to tell someone how some thing or some person looks or sounds, for example, we are using description. It deals with things, people, places, scenes, animals, moods, and impressions. The primary purposes of description are to portray a sense impression and to indicate a mood. It tries to make the impression or mood as vivid, as real, as lifelike for the reader as it was for the writer when he received the impression or observed the mood.

Description is not often an independent form of writing. Except in travel "literature" and freshman themes, it never stands alone. Often, however, a paragraph of description appears in a longer work as does this one from O. Henry's "A Municipal Report":

Eight-sixty-one Jessamine Street was a decayed mansion. Thirty yards back from the street it stood, outmerged in a splendid grove of trees and untrimmed shrubbery. A row of box bushes overflowed and almost hid the paling fence from sight; the gate was kept closed by a rope noose that encircled the gate-post and the first paling of the gate. But when you got inside you saw that 861 was a shell, a shadow, a ghost of former grandeur and excellence.

Description is most effective when used in short passages as an aid in explaining or narrating something. But although its part is minor, its function is very important. The great value of description is that it brings something to life; it creates a vivid impression for the reader or hearer. All of us live in a world of images, not abstractions, and we respond to the graphic and the concrete. Good description is always both graphic and concrete. It is made so by the use of abundant details, as in this passage from O. E. Rölvaag's *Giants in the Earth*, previously quoted in part on pp. 93–94.

> Out on the sky line the huge plain now began to swell and rise, almost as if an abscess were forming under the skin of the earth. Although this elevation lay somewhat out of his course, Per Hansa swung over and held straight toward the highest part of it.
>
> The afternoon breeze lulled, and finally dropped off altogether. The sun, whose golden lustre had faded imperceptibly into a reddish hue, shone now with a dull light, yet strong and clear; in a short while, deeper tones of violet began to creep across the red. The great ball grew enormous; it retreated farther and farther into the empty reaches of the western sky; then it sank suddenly. . . . The spell of evening quickly crowded in and laid hold of them all; the oxen wagged their ears; Rosie lifted her voice in a long moo, which died out slowly in the great stillness. At the moment when the sun closed his eye, the vastness of the plain seemed to rise up on every hand— and suddenly the landscape had grown desolate; something bleak and cold had come into the silence, filling it with terror. . . . Behind them, along the way they had come, the plain lay dark green and lifeless, under the gathering shadow of the dim, purple sky.

The only person who should legitimately have difficulty in getting enough details into his description is one who is blind and deaf and without the ability to taste, touch, or smell. It is true that most of us go through life half-dead, not really seeing and hearing what is going on around us. A playwright once remarked that if the members of an audience were to pay on the basis of what each "got" from a play, some few should pay two or three times the regular admission price, some should pay nothing, and some should be paid for attending because they received less than nothing.

Few of us have trained ourselves to look carefully and accurately at objects and people around us and to see what we look at. Without this ability, we can never describe fully or effectively; with it, we have only the problem of selecting from a huge mass of details those which will most accurately indicate what we wish to convey. Guy de Maupassant, in telling of his apprenticeship as a writer and the assistance which Flaubert gave him, wrote:

> Talent is enduring patience. It is a matter of looking at that which one wishes to express long enough and with sufficient attention to discover in it an aspect no one has yet seen. Everything has its unexplored elements, because we are accustomed to see things with the eyes of others. The least

thing contains something of the unknown. Find it! To describe a blazing fire or a tree on the plain, let us live with that fire and that tree until they no longer resemble for us any other fire or tree. This is the way one becomes original.

Furthermore, having laid down the truth that in the entire world there are no two grains of sand, two flies, two hands, or two noses exactly alike, he [Flaubert] compelled me to describe an object so particularized as to distinguish it from all others of its species and class. He used to say, "When you pass a grocer seated on his doorstep, or a concierge smoking his pipe, or a cab stand, show me that grocer and that concierge in all their physical appearance and in all their moral nature so that I shall not mistake that grocer and that concierge for any other, and make me see by a single word wherein a cab horse differs from the fifty others that go before and come after him."

Depth and richness of description depend upon the ability of the writer to receive, select, and express details. Some details are based upon visual reproduction—color, movement, and form—and others convey impressions of tastes, touches, smells, and sounds. Without the use of all these, you can hardly expect to transmit the full imprint of what you yourself have, or should have, received. As a result, you may need to develop or to restore sharpness of sense impression and acuteness of observation. To become aware of the need, fully to understand the necessity, almost always suffices to increase sensitivity and keenness. Awareness followed by actual practice, by a real attempt to extract to the full the sense impressions and moods in experiences and occurrences, develops not only clear-cut perception and memory but also more lucid thinking.

Nevertheless, to catalogue all the pertinent details about an object is not to describe it. The result of this process is only a mass of raw material from which the reader must formulate his own impression. The writer of good description uses plentiful detail, but he tries to give a single effect, a dominant impression. His primary purpose is to convey the impressions he received when he saw or heard or felt or tasted or smelled whatever it is that he is describing. These impressions form a pattern, a dominant impression which must be supported by details but not obscured by them.

Notice the extraordinary amount of detail and the appeal to the senses used in this excellent piece of narrative, expository description:

A little after dawn, when the horizon looked like the pink stripe on a candy cane, the plant men, rubbing their eyes awake, entered the square, one-story brick structure on the outskirts of the city and threw some switches. A little before six, when the sky was the color of orange juice and the crisscross steel tower standing a couple of hundred yards away in the meadow had begun to cast a faint shadow, the three-foot radiotrons in the 5-kw. transmitter of station WWW were hot. A man sat down at a semicircular control board, slipped on a pair of earphones, and waited. Six miles away, in a small room on one of the upper floors of an office building another man also waited, his eyes watching the maddening progress of a long second hand around the face of a big clock. Once every revolution the shorter minute hand imperceptibly moved up a notch . . . five fifty-seven . . . five fifty-eight . . . five fifty-nine . . . five fifty-nine and one-half . . . A gesture passed between the man in the room and others, seen dimly behind a plate-glass panel in the wall. He moved closer to a diamond-shaped honeycomb of metal stand-ing the height of his nose on a thin steel stalk in the middle of the studio. The second hand swung from the vertical to the horizontal and then climbed to the vertical again, and for an instant all three hands were perpendicular across the clock. He took a breath and ran his tongue across his lips . . .

"Good morning, everybody! This is your announcer, Fred Spieler, wish-ing you all another day of health and happiness from the studios of WWW atop the Chamber of Commerce building in Smith City . . . I know that all you early birds are waiting to begin your setting-up exercises before break-fast, so I'll turn you over to your old friend Bill Bulgem. Are you ready, Bill?"

And as the milk-wagon horses plod quietly on rubber hoofs through the gray streets the city turns in its bed and gropes for the alarm. The feet of housewives patter across ten thousand floors, and, kitchen-bound, a thousand hands snap on the radio. The air, presently, is warm and sweet with bacon smells, and sweet, too, are the mingled sounds of cooking, the rhythmical scraping of razors against chins, and the energetic, yet mellifluous "All together now! One . . . two . . . three . . ." of Bill Bulgem.[3]

This piece of description is effective not alone because of its appeal to the senses. Like all good writing, it is *simple;* notice the extraordinary num-ber of one-syllable words. It is *clear;* as you read, you have the feeling that the writer has observed closely and knows thoroughly what he is writing about. There are no "purple passages" and elaborate subtleties to obscure the simple clarity of the description. Finally, the description is *narrative;* much more than a thread of action runs through it. Similarly, there is a thorough combination of narrative and descriptive elements in Stephen Crane's "The Snake":

Where the path wended across the ridge, the bushes of huckleberry and sweet fern swarmed at it in two curling waves until it was a mere winding line traced through a tangle. There was no interference by clouds, and as the rays of the sun fell full upon the ridge, they called into voice innumer-able insects which chanted the heat of the summer day in steady, throbbing, unending chorus.

A man and a dog came from the laurel thickets of the valley where the white brook brawled with the rocks. They followed the deep line of the path across the ridges. The dog—a large lemon and white setter—walked, tranquilly meditative, at his master's heels.

Suddenly from some unknown and yet near place in advance there came a dry, shrill whistling rattle that smote motion instantly from the limbs of the man and the dog. Like the fingers of a sudden death, this sound seemed to touch the man at the nape of the neck, at the top of the spine, and change him, as swift as thought, to a statue of listening horror, surprise, rage. The dog, too—the same icy hand was laid upon him, and he stood crouched and quivering, his jaw dropping, the froth of terror upon his lips, the light of hatred in his eyes.

Slowly the man moved his hands toward the bushes, but his glance did not turn from the place made sinister by the warning rattle. His fingers, unguided, sought for a stick of weight and strength. Presently they closed about one that seemed adequate, and holding this weapon poised before him,

---

[3] From "Radio: A $140,000,000 Art," *Fortune*. Reprinted by permission of the Editors of *Fortune*.

the man moved slowly forward, glaring. The dog with his nervous nostrils fairly fluttering moved warily, one foot at a time, after his master.

But when the man came upon the snake, his body underwent a shock as if from a revelation, as if after all he had been ambushed. With a blanched face, he sprang forward and his breath came in strained gasps, his chest heaving as if he were in the performance of an extraordinary muscular trial. His arm with the stick made a spasmodic, defensive gesture.

The snake had apparently been crossing the path in some mystic travel when to his sense there came the knowledge of the coming of his foes. The dull vibration perhaps informed him, and he flung his body to face the danger. He had no knowledge of paths; he had no wit to tell him to slink noiselessly into the bushes. He knew that his implacable enemies were approaching; no doubt they were seeking him, hunting him. And so he cried his cry, an incredibly swift jangle of tiny bells, as burdened with pathos as the hammering upon quaint cymbals by the Chinese at war—for, indeed, it was usually his death-music.

"Beware! Beware! Beware!"

The man and the snake confronted each other. In the man's eyes were hatred and fear. In the snake's eyes were hatred and fear. These enemies maneuvered, each preparing to kill. It was to be a battle without mercy. Neither knew of mercy for such a situation. In the man was all the wild strength of the terror of his ancestors, of his race, of his kind. A deadly repulsion had been handed from man to man through long dim centuries. This was another detail of a war that had begun evidently when first there were men and snakes. Individuals who do not participate in this strife incur the investigations of scientists. Once there was a man and a snake who were friends, and at the end, the man lay dead with the marks of the snake's caress just over his East Indian heart. In the formation of devices, hideous and horrible, Nature reached her supreme point in the making of the snake, so that priests who really paint hell will fill it with snakes instead of fire. These curving forms, these scintillant colorings create at once, upon sight, more relentless animosities than do shake barbaric tribes. To be born a snake is to be thrust into a place a-swarm with formidable foes. To gain an appreciation of it, view hell as pictured by priests who are really skilful.

As for this snake in the pathway, there was a double curve some inches back of its head, which, merely by the potency of its lines, made the man feel with tenfold eloquence the touch of the death-fingers at the nape of his neck. The reptile's head was waving slowly from side to side and its hot eyes flashed like little murder-lights. Always in the air was the dry, shrill whistling of the rattles.

"Beware! Beware! Beware!"

The man made a preliminary feint with his stick. Instantly the snake's heavy head and neck were bended back on the double curve and instantly the snake's body shot forward in a low, straight, hard spring. The man jumped with a convulsive chatter and swung his stick. The blind, sweeping blow fell upon the snake's head and hurled him so that steel-colored plates were for a moment uppermost. But he rallied swiftly, agilely, and again the head and neck bended back to the double curve, and the steaming, wide-open mouth made its desperate effort to reach its enemy. This attack, it could be seen, was despairing, but it was nevertheless impetuous, gallant, ferocious, of the same quality as the charge of the lone chief when the walls of white faces close upon him in the mountains. The stick swung unerringly again, and the snake, mutilated, torn, whirled himself into the last coil.

And now the man went sheer raving mad from the emotions of his forefathers and from his own. He came to close quarters. He gripped the stick with his two hands and made it speed like a flail. The snake, tumbling in the anguish of final despair, fought, bit, flung itself upon this stick which was taking his life.

At the end, the man clutched his stick and stood watching in silence. The dog came slowly and with infinite caution stretched his nose forward, sniffing. The hair upon his neck and back moved and ruffled as if a sharp wind was blowing; the last muscular quivers of the snake were causing the rattle to still sound their treble cry, the shrill, ringing war chant and hymn of the grave of the thing that faces foes at once countless, implacable, and superior.

"Well, Rover," said the man, turning to the dog with a grin of victory, "we'll carry Mr. Snake home to show the girls."

His hands still trembled from the strain of the encounter, but he pried with his stick under the body of the snake and hoisted the limp thing upon it. He resumed his march along the path, and the dog walked, tranquilly meditative, at his master's heels.[4]

Scientific description is given clarity and richness by expert selection of details. In the following paragraph George R. Stewart explains "Indian summer" by describing the movements of the air:

Indian summer is probably the best-loved part of fall. Along in October there is almost certain to come a short spell of sharply cooler weather, even with frost across the northern tier of States. But this influx of northern air drifts eastward over the Atlantic, and after a few days the high pressure may build up off Cape Hatteras. Then, as in summer, a great river of warm air flows up the Mississippi Valley and sweeps around to cover all the North Atlantic States. By this time even Louisiana and Arkansas have begun to cool off, so that the air which moves into New York and Pennsylvania is only warm enough to be pleasant. The same situation which in August would make a devastating heat wave, thus in October produces one of the finest times of the year—Indian summer. Just about then, also, the forces of the sun and air seem to come into a kind of balance, so that the idyllic interlude may linger for two weeks or more.[5]

The art of description not only can make you see what the writer has seen but can evoke reflection. George Moore, in *Avowals*, places in contrast pages from Rudyard Kipling and Pierre Loti. The Kipling passage, from *Kim*, reads:

By this time the sun was driving golden spokes through the lower branches of the mango trees; the parakeets and doves were coming home in their hundreds; the chattering grey-backed Seven Sisters, talking over the day's adventures, walked back and forth in twos and threes almost under the feet of the travelers; the shufflings and scufflings in the branches showed that the bats were ready to go out on the night picket. Swiftly the light gathered itself together, painted for an instant the faces and the cartwheels

---

[4] Reprinted from *Midnight Sketches* by Stephen Crane, by permission of and special arrangement with Alfred A. Knopf, Inc. Copyright 1898, 1902, 1926 by Alfred A. Knopf, Inc.

[5] From "The All-American Season," *The New York Times Magazine*. By permission of the author and the publisher.

and bullocks' horns as red as blood. Then the night fell, changing the touch of air, drawing a low, even haze like a gossamer veil of blue across the face of the country and bringing out, keen and distinct, the smell of wood smoke and cattle and the good scent of wheaten cakes cooked on ashes. The evening patrol hurried out of the police station with important coughings and reiterated orders, and a live charcoal ball in the cup of a wayside carter's hookah glowed red while Kim's eyes mechanically watched the last flicker of the sun on the brass tweezers.

This is a passage saturated with the recordings of the senses, yet we are left with the impression that Kipling has seen more than he felt. The passage from Loti, on the other hand, may not be the equal of Kipling's in sharpness of definition but, as Moore points out, it carries with it more of the essence of evening, more of the feeling produced by that hour:

> But evening comes, evening with its magic, and we relinquish ourselves to its charm once more.
> About our brave little encampment, about the rough horizon where all danger seems at present asleep, the twilight sky kindles an incomparable rose border, orange, then green; and then, rising by degrees to the zenith, it softens and quenches. It is the indecisive and lovely hour when, amid limpidities which are neither day nor night, our odorous fires begin to burn clearly, sending up their white smoke to the first stars; our camels, relieved of their burdens and their high saddles, sweep by the thin bushes, browsing on perfumed branches like great, fantastic sheep of slow, inoffensive demeanor. It is the hour when our Bedouins sit in a circle to tell stories and sing; the hour of rest and the hour of dream, the delicious hour of nomadic life.

Moore remarks that, factually, we learn more from the Kipling passage, but we are not moved as we are by Loti's.

One of the most famed of recent descriptive passages was written by the late Wilbur L. Cross. In 1938, when he was Governor of Connecticut, he began his annual Thanksgiving proclamation as follows:

> As the colors of Autumn stream down the wind, scarlet in sumach and maple, spun gold in the birches, a splendor of smoldering fire in the oaks along the hill, and the last leaves flutter away, and dusk falls briefly about the worker bringing in from the field a late load of its fruit, and Arcturus is lost to sight and Orion swings upward that great sun on his shoulder, we are stirred once more to ponder the Infinite Goodness that has set apart for us, in all this moving mystery of creation, a time of living and a home.

You should also note that this is an excellent example of a periodic sentence (see p. 62).

For an indication of just how important description can be in writing, turn to Eudora Welty's "A Worn Path," p. 962. Much of the beauty, pathos, and humor of this story derive from the author's exceptional handling of descriptive detail. Note, for instance, her commentary on the countryside, the central character, the small town. Here is local color made universal in its development. Or, for another example, consider Brodeur's "The Spoiler." Without clear, concise, vivid description of the countryside, the ski area, the focal character and his wife, the baby sitter, the group of "beatniks," this story would lose much of its effectiveness. For a third example, note that the appeal and effectiveness of Muir's selection (p. 696) come almost entirely from the author's superb handling of descriptive details.

S U M M A R Y

Description is that form of discourse by means of which we try to give vividness and reality to writing. It is effective only when it contains plentiful detail arranged so as to furnish a dominant impression presented from a logical and consistent point of view. Description is not the most important form of discourse—exposition is—but descriptive writing is the flesh and blood which cover the skeleton of prose; it is the form of writing that furnishes color, vividness, and reality to prose which, without it, would be pedestrian. Although it is only a tool of writing, description is of great importance.

N A R R A T I O N

Narration, like the other forms of discourse, rarely exists in a pure, or unmixed, state. News stories, history, biography, and autobiography always contain description and sometimes exposition and argument, as well as narration. Every account of an incident, every short story, play, or novel contains some description and exposition, and possibly some argument. But narration differs at least in purpose from exposition and argument; its primary and basic appeal is to the *emotions* of the reader or hearer rather than to the mind or the intellect. (It should be noted that history, biography, etc., are ordinarily more expository than narrative in purpose and hence do not always have a direct emotional appeal.) Narrative which does not move the reader, appeal to his emotions, make him eager to know "What happened next?" is poor narrative indeed. Because it does appeal primarily to the emotions, narrative is the easiest and most pleasant form of discourse to read and to listen to. It is an important medium of the prose artist for exactly this reason: It is more effective than either exposition or argument in that it appeals to the wellsprings of the reader's and hearer's emotions.

Both as a purveyor of pleasure and as a valuable aid in expository and descriptive writing, narration is worth studying. For purposes of analysis, in view of what you may be called upon to write or read in freshman composition, narrative writing can be divided arbitrarily into the following types: *anecdote, incident, sketch, short story, novel.*

A N E C D O T E

The *anecdote* is a narrative bit told or written to illustrate some specific point. Its chief characteristic is that it presents individuals in an action which illustrates some definite idea, illuminates some aspect of personality or character. Stuart Chase's "The Luxury of Integrity" illustrates its theme by the use of many anecdotes. Perhaps the most illuminating anecdote in the entire essay is of Jim and his mother, the housewife who could "afford the luxury of integrity":

> I recall the case of a brilliant young accountant who, shortly after winning his C.P.A., was given an opportunity to make a million dollars, more or less, in a few months' time. All he had to do was to approach certain corporations with an offer to split whatever rebates he might earn for them in their filed income tax returns. His share in turn was to be split with a government examiner who supplied the names of such corporations as had legitimate claims for rebates in past tax payments. He told his mother of the glittering opportunity. "Jim," she said, "you know when I come to wake you in the morning I shake you hard, and you don't stir?" "Yes," he said. "And then I shake you even harder, and you give a little moan?" "Yes." "And finally I shake as hard as I can, and you open one sleepy eye?" "Yes." "I'd hate to come in morning after morning and find you awake." He turned down the job and has been sleeping soundly ever since.

Every effective anecdote has a single point; in each, the dialogue, setting, and characters are subordinate to the main point. The anecdote rarely stands alone—except in poolrooms and smoking cars—but is a powerful method of making understandable a possibly difficult idea.

INCIDENT

An *incident* is a short narrative told for its own sake. Not concerned with making a point, it deals with a single, simple situation, an episode. Its primary emphasis is upon the character of the narrator or some person involved in the action, or upon the action itself. If you write of a simple event, such as buying a suit of clothes or having a haircut, you are creating an account of an incident. If you tell of a single occurrence at a summer camp or on a fishing trip—Heaven forbid!—you narrate an incident. The incident involves characters, setting, action, and dialogue, but it is simple in structure, brief, and without necessary emphasis upon dramatic conflict. Of these two incidents from the life of Samuel Johnson, the great eighteenth-century literary figure, the second is perhaps doubly interesting in that it is told by Gilbert Stuart himself, one of America's famous painters.

> Johnson spoke as he wrote. He would take up a topic, and utter upon it a number of the *Rambler*. On a question, one day, at Miss Porter's, concerning the authority of a newspaper for some fact, he related, that a lady of his acquaintance implicitly believed everything she read in the papers; and that, by way of curing her credulity, he fabricated a story of a battle between the Russians and Turks, then at war; and "that it might," he said, "bear internal evidence of its futility, I laid the scene in an island at the conflux of the Boristhenes and the Danube; rivers which run at the distance of a hundred leagues from each other. The lady, however, believed the story, and never forgave the deception; the consequence of which was, that I lost an agreeable companion, and she was deprived of an innocent amusement."
>
> Dr. Johnson called one morning on Mr. West to converse with him on American affairs. After some time Mr. West said that he had a young American living with him, from whom he might derive some information, and

introduced Stuart. The conversation continued (Stuart being thus invited to take a part in it), when the Doctor observed to Mr. West that the young man spoke very good English; and turning to Stuart rudely asked him where he had learned it. Stuart very promptly replied, "Sir, I can better tell you where I did not learn it—it was not from your dictionary." Johnson seemed aware of his own abruptness, and was not offended.

Numerous examples of incidents may be found in your collection of readings. What, for example, is "A Windstorm in the Forest," p. 696, but an enlarged incident? Both the McCarthy and Kennedy selections begin with incidents. Reston's "A Fable" is a form of incident in itself. Numerous other examples are easily uncovered. Why? Because skilled writers frequently use incidents to add life and vigor and memorability to what otherwise might be rather flat exposition or argument. Try to find other examples of this narrative device in expository material.

SKETCH

The *sketch* is usually a study of character, setting, or mood. It contains little action or plot and places emphasis on descriptive details. Unlike the anecdote, it is not concerned with making a point or illustrating a thesis; unlike the incident, it puts emphasis upon characterization to the virtual exclusion of action. The following, written by a college student, is a good illustration of a sketch of character analysis:

> She is thin and short and dark, of a peculiar kind of ugliness which comes and goes, suddenly terribly apparent as she laughs and talks vivaciously, oddly disappearing as she sits quietly, a queer lonely look on her face. What goes on inside a person such as she? Is she unhappy? *Can* she be happy? Does she ever pause to wonder whether she will be loved, whether someone will sit beside her and call her large beaked nose, her frizzed, lumpy hair, her black, un-pretty eyes beautiful?
>
> She is perhaps too obviously charming. Her face lights up as she talks; her conversation is pert and clever. Somehow one gets the feeling as one looks at her that from behind those darting black eyes a strange, lonely person is watching with deadly earnestness. If there is a person behind the lively, alert face it will be, or is already, warped and misshapen by the conditions of its existence. Sometimes she must think of theatres at night with their attractively dressed, perfumed women, men made mysterious by the dim lights and the silence. She must think of pale roads winding by dark country places. Of Fifth Avenue at night. Of dirty, poorly lit restaurants. Of walks along chilly, deserted streets. Perhaps she will feel some ache of longing in her small, immature body. And perhaps she will write a passionate love story of frustrated desire.
>
> It is easy to visualize her in later life. She will be thoroughly familiar with every new movement in art, literature, music. She will have seen the best shows when everyone else is still waiting for two tickets for that coming Saturday night. She will have read the best books before everyone else has had time to run into his bookstore to see if there is a copy in stock. At the parties to which her married friends will invite her, she will talk vivaciously to her friends' husbands, or to the young men who have been sent to sit with her. She will grow desperate with eagerness to keep this or that

man by her side, as she sees his eyes grow blank in uncomprehending politeness. And in her despair she will know that he is not worthy of her, that she is far finer, more intelligent, more interesting than 10 of such as he.

But when regard for appearances begins to disappear, she will embark on a long series of lunches with her girl friends, matinées with them, evening movies with her mother, or her sisters. She will perhaps continue writing. Her energies, directed solely at this one field, will fan her native talent into a certain blaze, and she will undoubtedly became a popular, if not an artistic success. Prosperity will agree with her. She will grow plump. Her angular face will lose its drawn, rouged hollows, and her figure will reveal some charm in its small, but pigeon-like contours. She will become more sure of herself—less anguished in her efforts to amuse. Perhaps when she is 35 or 40 she will marry, and continue to write, the habit having become ingrown. Her husband will sincerely admire her; her talent will be a constant source of pleasure to him. Such a little thing, and you should see how hard she works! She will be happy perhaps, but the feeling will come upon her again and again that she has missed something in her youth which she can never now replace. The bitterness which was hidden so well when she went to college will sink deeper and deeper behind the growing pudginess; gradually it may disappear. It was hard anyway to see any grand surge of emotion behind such spare angularity and tininess. But sometime she will write a nostalgic novel of young love and feel the better for it.

But all her bird-like motions, her bright little remarks, will be put to good use. All the things she dreamed of saying as a girl, all the little actions which she hoped men would see and admire, her smallness, now an asset, all these she will direct at her stout, slumberous husband, who will be pricked into laughter by the needle-like sharpness of her character.

For further illustration of the sketch, consider the third paragraph of "The Devil and Daniel Webster," p. 969. This is a well-nigh perfect example. Deems Taylor's "The Monster," p. 801, is actually an extended sketch. Van Wyck Brooks' "Helen Keller" is a series of sketches dealing with the mood and character of Miss Keller at varying times.

SHORT STORY, NOVEL

The *short story* is a type of narrative writing in which the simple elements of anecdote, incident, and sketch are expanded and shaped into a definite pattern of characterization and conflict. The fundamental principles of narration as they apply to the short story (and incidentally and superficially to the novel) are developed in Chapter 8.

SUMMARY

The traditional forms of discourse are arbitrary divisions of writing. They rarely exist alone, being nearly always found in combination. Making use of these divisions of composition is helpful only because each has certain principles exclusively its own. These forms have been isolated for analysis and discussion of principles; now it will be possible to consider more maturely (in Chapter 8) how the forms of discourse are welded into contemporary types of writing.

· EXERCISES ·

1. Examine several selections in your book of readings; determine how many of the four forms of discourse are contained in each selection.

2. From the vantage point of a window overlooking a busy street, indicate details which are primarily expository, descriptive, argumentative, and narrative.

3. Write a definition (logical or expanded) of one of the following:
Fascism; A Lowbrow; A Roommate; An English Composition Class; A College Library; Surrealism; A Country Fair; A Literary Tea; A Campus Widow; A Good Sport; The Ideal Wife (or Husband); Television; A Dirt Farmer; A Bore; Atheism; Religion; Football; Rewriting; A Campus Beatnik; Twist Dancing.

4. Write a theme explaining the processes or mechanisms involved in one of the following. If possible, illustrate with a sketch or diagram.
Ginning Cotton; Producing an Amateur Play; Making a Welsh Rabbit; Changing an Automobile Tire; Selling Clothing; Preparing for an Examination; Playing the Drums; Stealing Fruit; Making a Blueprint; Teaching Someone to Swim (or Dance or Kiss or Keep Quiet).

5. Write a theme for a named person on one of the following subjects. Begin each theme title with the words "So You Want To Learn To ———."
Tap Dance; Make a Strike (bowling); Play Offensive End; Do the Rumba; Row a Boat; Ride a Horse; Swim; Value Your Hand; Putt; Serve (tennis); Skin Dive.

6. Make a list of five debatable subjects. Try to establish (state) each proposition clearly enough to reveal the precise point of disagreement. One might deal with private or government ownership of utilities; another, freedom of the air waves; another, the influence of advertising. The important task is to make clear the *exact difference* of opinion or belief.

7. Analyze each of the following propositions, being careful to define the terms used. Make parallel lists of the points which can be used in support of each and the points which can be raised against each. Rephrase each proposition if necessary.

> All property should be taxed.
> Lobbying is a national menace.
> Women should never be allowed to hold public office.
> There is no such thing as a good war.
> The spoils system should be outlawed from politics.

8. Bring to class a selection from a newspaper or magazine which seems to mingle opinion and fact.

9. Point out fallacies in the following statements:

> Preachers' sons usually turn out badly.
> Red-haired people have quick tempers.
> Every man has his price.
> Too many cooks spoil the broth.
> Never believe a dishonest man.
> When in Rome you should do as the Romans do.
> Women always think intuitively.
> Falstaff, like all fat men, was humorous.
> A man is known by the company he keeps.
> A bad beginning makes a bad ending.

10. Copy from a guidebook a formal description of some place you have visited. Then write a brief description in which you try to convey to the reader some idea of the *impression* the place made on you. Use your five senses liberally.

11. Write a brief, literal description of one of the following:
A Hotel Room; A Soda Fountain; A Chemistry Laboratory; A Dentist's Office; A Bus Station; The College Cafeteria; A Professor's Office; An Incinerator; A Chain Grocery Store; A Skyscraper; An Old Well; A Filling Station; Backstage at a Theater; A Projection Booth; A Student's Notebook; A Dark Alley; A Block on a City Street; A Booth in a Beer Parlor.

12. Write a theme for a named person on one of the following subjects. Begin each theme title with the words "This Is a ———."
Town You Should Visit; Program You Should Hear; Meal You Would Enjoy; Girl (Boy) Whom You Should Know; Professor Whom You Should Have.

13. List five incidents which have recently occurred to you and which you think would be of general interest.

14. You believe that men are more honest (or dishonest) than women. Write an anecdote to "prove" your thesis.

15. Write an anecdote to "prove" or "disprove" any one of the following statements:

> Young people are no ruder than their elders.
> Relationships between the sexes are more honest today
>   than they were a century ago.
> Few people have the courage of their convictions.
> Informal education is more valuable than formal.
> Most important people have inferiority complexes.

16. Write a character sketch of one of the following:
A College Dean; A Typical Club Woman; A Member of Your Family; Your Best Friend; The Cashier at a Motion-Picture Theatre; A Camp Counselor; A Fraternity Brother; A Co-ed; A Typical "Lady-Killer"; An Actress as She Appears in the Part of a Specific Character; Your Family Physician.

17. Write a theme on one of the following subjects in which you use exposition, description, narration, and argument. (Some subjects should be limited.)
The United Nations; Democracy as a Way of Life; How We Celebrate Christmas; My Favorite Television Program; My Education Thus Far; How I Learned To Swim (Dance, Play Bridge); My Favorite Ancestor; How I Classify People; My Future as I See It; Opinions on Coeducation; The Most Important Thing in Life to Me Is ———.

18. From your book of readings select the three articles or essays which most appeal to you. Isolate their narrative, descriptive, argumentative, and expository elements. In each of the three, what form of discourse seems next important to exposition?

19. Select from your readings a short story which you think develops an argument as it unfolds a narrative.

20. Select from your readings a poem which you think is primarily expository; one which is primarily descriptive; one which is primarily argumentative. (The first 10 poems in the collection are primarily narrative.)

CHAPTER 8

MODERN METHODS AND TYPES

All writing, as Chapter 7 shows, may be classified according to purpose and form. Actually, however, writing tends to fall into types, each of which, properly executed, makes use of two or more of the traditional forms of discourse. Some of these types are clearly defined, others are vague in limitations and indefinite as to precise contents. For our purposes, the most important of these types are *autobiographical writing*, the *informal essay*, *criticism*, the *interview*, the *profile*, the *formal essay*, and the *short story*. The first three are well within any student's capacity to write, whereas the other four are somewhat more difficult. They are discussed so that you may be able to write more effectively at least the first three, possibly all of them. A careful study of these seven types will also enable you to deal more analytically and carefully with them when you read.

Modern methods and types are, fundamentally, adaptations of old ones. Autobiographical writing today leans heavily upon the work of Cellini, of St. Augustine, of Franklin and Rousseau. The modern-day informal essay is an outgrowth of the work of Montaigne, Lamb, Hazlitt, and Stevenson. Carlyle, Macaulay, Ruskin, Pater, Mill—all wrote formal essays which were the progenitors of the contemporary magazine article. So it is with the other types mentioned.

The discussion which follows is especially adapted to your needs, however, and indicates the changes in technique and emphasis which have come about fairly recently.

AUTOBIOGRAPHICAL WRITING

As was pointed out in Chapter 1, the first practical approach to the problem of learning to write is a consideration and evaluation of oneself. All writing, of whatever kind and type, is either composed of or influenced by the author's thoughts, feelings, and experiences. It is important, therefore, that we find out as much about ourselves as possible in order that we may form an accurate picture of the compound of mental, physical, and emotional elements and traits which each of us is. Because they recognize that students must learn something about themselves, English instructors frequently assign autobiographical themes in an attempt to encourage, and even to force, this process of evaluation.

Perhaps the most important thing to keep in mind when preparing autobiographical material is that you must distinguish between the trivial and the significant. An autobiography composed of *all* your memories of experiences, people, and places will be a hodgepodge. You must select those experiences which have really had some influence in shaping your life, write only of those places and people that have profoundly affected you. Remember, however, that some experience, seemingly slight, may have been quite important: a thwarted aim, a chance encounter, an overheard conversation.

Similarly, do not write an account of merely your physical existence. Relate not only *what* you have done and thought but also *why*. A completely bare "who's who" is not likely to disclose such interesting and significant details as an explanation of the forces behind your activities. You will reveal the character of your life more clearly by writing of mental and spiritual forces than by merely listing the facts of your ancestry, your schooling, the places you have lived in, the trips you have taken, etc. Somewhere in an autobiography such facts as these must be given. They should form a relatively minor part of the whole theme, however, and should serve merely as explanatory background material for more important details.

Good autobiographical writing is rare. Many autobiographical themes are unsucccessful because they are too largely concerned with such relatively unimportant items as are mentioned above. Another theme may fail because the writer feels too keenly the worthlessness of his life and makes only a half-hearted attempt to reveal its numerous and potentially interesting facets. Others are weak because their authors realize the impossibility of knowing, much less telling, the complete truth about themselves and thus relate half-truths or shun really important matters which could at best be only partly explained.

Unquestionably the most common cause of poor autobiographical writing is that the author fails to take enough time in "incubating" his thoughts. Some people would have you believe that it is a form of egotism to spend long hours in thinking of your experiences. But, actually, some of us are so accustomed to seeing everything through the eyes of others that it takes a long period of reflection for us to be able to distinguish any differences between our own attitudes and those of masses of people. If you think long enough about people, places, and events, however, you begin to understand that you are an individual and that your ideas do differ, no matter how slightly, from those of others. Without sufficient reflection you will never become aware of these differences. Individual characteristics, and explanations of them, are the prime requisites of all good autobiographical writing. Spend ample time in reflection and reverie and these differences will become apparent to you, apparent enough to put on paper. As Agnes M. MacKenzie has pointed out, "Your loving and my loving, your anger and my anger, are sufficiently alike for us to be able to call them by the same names; but in our experience and in that of any two people in the world, they will never be quite completely identical."

If you can discover how the world really looks to you, what you actually like, what you truly believe about some of the major matters of life, your autobiographical theme will be successful. Here are two suggestions for material to be included. You may combine or rearrange the items to suit your individual needs; in addition, consult the check list of questions given on pp. 5–6.

1. Give a brief account of your heredity and environment—ancestors, place of birth and place(s) of residence, early friends, school years, etc. This account does not necessarily come at the beginning of the theme; frequently it is more effective after a beginning in which the main idea and purpose of the composition have been stated.

2. Include a series of descriptions of people, places, and events which have genuinely influenced you. Do not hesitate to use anecdotes (see p. 141), incidents (see p. 142), and reports of conversation. Try to exclude relatively unimportant details.

Suggestions for methods of approach to autobiographical writing and ideas for elements to be included may be secured from several selections in your collection of readings. Also, be sure to read the section on "Self-Evaluation" in Chapter 1 and that part of Chapter 6 dealing with *individuality*.

THE INFORMAL ESSAY

More than any other expository or narrative type, the informal essay offers opportunity for self-expression. This kind of essay is closely allied to autobiographical writing, because most informal essays are either wholly or largely composed of personal observations and reflections, and autobiographical themes usually contain a series of embryonic informal essays.

It is difficult to define the informal essay, which also goes by the names of *personal, familiar,* and *light.* It has no set form, no obvious pattern; it may reflect any of a thousand moods and feelings; its subject matter is infinite. Rigid rules cannot be set down concerning either its structure or its style. Perhaps Montaigne, in the preface to his *Essais,* came as close as anyone ever has to defining the purpose and aim of this form of writing: "Reader, lo is here a well-meaning Book. . . . I have proposed unto myself no other than a familiar and private end. I have no respect or consideration at all, either to thy service, or to my glory. . . . I desire . . . to be delineated in mine own genuine, simple, and ordinary fashion, without contention, art, or study; for it is myself I portray. . . . Thus, gentle Reader, myself am the groundwork of my book; it is then no reason thou shouldest employ thy time about so frivolous and vain a subject." Thus Montaigne points out that the informal essay is interested in reflection for its own sake, is wholly personal (subjective), and has no pretensions toward learning and instruction.

Because the informal essay *is* informal, some writers get the idea that structure is wholly unimportant—that a series of random notes, strung together in any old fashion, constitutes an example of the type. It is true that the form of the essay may be varied, but every well-written essay does have a form, a definite plan and purpose of some sort. Many good familiar essays *seem* unorganized and disjointed, but there is no requirement that they be incoherent. Actually, disjointedness is no virtue unless it adds to the pleasure of reading the essay, as happens in some of the works of Charles Lamb, for example. Good personal essays written and published today have a definite plan and purpose, although their structure may differ from those of a hundred other essays. When you read informal essays, you will notice definite outlines. Actually, every one of the 14 informal essays reprinted in Book Three is so well and clearly structured that it can be put into a topic or sentence outline (see Section 39).

In writing the informal essay you will find that style is a far more important consideration than structure. In fact, style is everything in this type. Unfortunately, style, as such, cannot be taught; defined as the imprint of one's personality upon subject matter, it constitutes a well-nigh insuperable obstacle. No one can teach you to be humorous, or whimsical, or satirical. But it is true that if you possess some slight degree of humor, or whimsey, or satire, painstaking effort may bring it out vividly and effectively. The personal essay looks deceptively easy to write; actually it requires considerable effort by the writer to give the informal essay that high degree of polish which is its charm, its excuse for being.

Another popular misconception about the informal essay is that subject matter is unimportant—that the trivial, the insignificant, the unimportant may serve as "topic." Such a misconception is amusingly discussed—and corrected—in John P. Waters' "Little Old Lady Passes Away." Notice in the following excerpts that at the same time Waters condemns certain practices, he offers valuable suggestions either directly or by implication:

> The familiar essay, that lavender-scented little old lady of literature, has passed away. Search the magazines for her sparrowy whimseys, and in all but one or two of them you will find, in her stead, crisp articles, blatant exposés, or statistic-laden surveys. Even in the few that admit her pale ghost to their circle of economists, sociologists, and Washington correspondents, her position is decidedly subordinate: a scant column or two near the insurance advertisements at the back of the book. Her mourners—and there still are many—wonder why. There was a time . . .
>
> There was a time when the familiar essay was important; so important that The Atlantic Monthly Press issued four printings of a book explaining its characteristics and construction; so important that Christopher Morley, the little old lady's favorite American nephew, took time off to anthologize her for admiring high-school teachers and their victims in English I–II, who were often led to believe that all literature, like all Gaul, was divided into three parts: fiction, poetry (pronounced "poy'tree"), and the familiar essay, with the familiar essay far in the lead as a literary form.

At its best, the familiar essay was "a kind of improvisation on a delicate theme, a species of soliloquy; as if a man were to speak aloud the slender and whimsical thoughts that come to his mind when he is alone on a winter evening before a warm fire."

Intimacy, reverie, whimsey—these were the qualities that won it thousands of devoted readers, that made it kindly relief from frowning treatises, ramrod sermons, and all the high and mighty didacticism our fathers were flayed with before its advent. It was warm and human, unconcerned with life's granite problems but fascinated with the trifles, moods, and humors that colored the lives of its readers. It was comfortable literature, muddying no quiet pools with a stirred-up sense of sin, goading no laggard ambition to be something. Instead, it chatted easily and urbanely, graceful successor to the gradually dying art of conversation.

With so much in its favor, what caused its downfall? The answer is: the same qualities that made it popular—intimacy, reverie, whimsey. These qualities elicited so many gurgles of "How charming! What a delightfully helpless fellow the author must be!" from sisters, wives, and maiden aunts, that literarily inclined gentlemen who had not been gushed over for years immediately concluded that the way to become inundated in gush was to put themselves in print as quaint old fuss-budgets. As a consequence, starveling hacks raced bony clergymen to the mail-boxes with manuscripts that would make them "dears" and "darlings" to the petticoated portion of the populace.

They succeeded, of course, for the trick was easy. One had only to empty his mind of all knowledge, all common sense, all everything, except tender quotations from Horace and Tennyson, and start reacting. Anything was a fit subject, the simpler and more far-fetched the better. For example, Mr. Percival Biggs—a six-foot giant who had played tackle for Yale in the days when football was played with the feet—would suddenly develop all the cute physical attributes of a sissy when confronted by the relatively simple problem of stoking his hot-air furnace. Instead of being a harmless cylinder of sheet-metal, it became "an insatiable scarlet-mawed monster." His modest two tons of winter coal became "sable diamonds" to be "immolated thrice daily." He himself was transformed from a lazy suburbanite to a "quaking panderer to Zoroaster." He wallowed in self-pity.

There were other schools, too. The mellowists, for example, did not want to be darlings. They wanted to be ripe, winey. Young men of twenty, green as quinces, ripened overnight. No village attic lacked its fireside philosopher with his bowl of russet apples, his October cider, his Sherlock Holmes pipe, and his tin of Craven's Mixture—as unmellow a blend of grass and red-pepper, by the way, as Britain's abominable tobacconists ever foisted upon gullible Anglophiles. Reverie took the place of all other mental functions, and bookish archaisms from Evelyn and Pepys bade fair to drive out all other words from thesaurus and dictionary.

Worst of all, however, were the coy writers, the ones who defied death-by-strangulation with little tinklings called "An' Him Went Home to Him's Muvver." Others of these twitterers delighted in tickling the risqué with the feather end of their pens. Never boorishly, of course. A mild *damn*—in quotation marks—perhaps. Or the impish suggestion that they—pagans that they were—sometimes didn't quite close their shower-curtains all the way. This group was especially dear to schoolmarms from Brookline, Mass., who —during the months that Columbia Summer School was open—made life on the West Side subway utterly unbearable for native-born New Yorkers by staring them into nervous fits in an effort to gather first-hand material for hellish little papers on "The Typical New Yorker—Poor Thing."

At first, of course, these insect pests were few in number, and their buzzings were harmless enough. But when ever-increasing hordes discovered that writing the familiar essay was the ovaltine their egos needed, the end was near. No literature that is peopled exclusively with doddering loons afraid of sewing-machine flywheels, bewildered by the complex mechanics of hot-water faucets, and hero-stricken with such worthies as tympani thumpers, elevator starters, scissors grinders, and street cleaners can survive long.

The final ax fell when the high schools, with well-meaning but pitifully misdirected affection, took to teaching the fragile art to their fuzzy-lipped brats. Where there was one asinine but educated gush-hunter before, there were now whole herds of pubescent illiterates to annoy friends, relatives, and editors with misspelled masterpieces patterned after, or swiped from, the models their texts supplied.

What else, then, could the little old lady do but die as unobtrusively as possible? The children who had gathered around her hassock to hear her thin little musings had all grown up and gone away—or remained to mock her quaintness with their new-found wisdom. Radio, prohibition, and prosperity were stinging their senses with more peppery fare. A new and dizzyingly complex world had roared across the quiet hearth; and listeners once sure of their philosophies and content to roam in the pleasant meadows of reverie now groped bewildered for *facts*, explanations, anything to help them realign their lives before new discoveries, new techniques, drove out all meaning from life itself. Reverie, whimsey, and humor were out; they didn't get you anywhere.

Hence, gradually, the little old lady deserted her familiar haunts and faded away. Occasionally a sentimental editor, remembering her pleasant tea-table chatter, invites her fluttery ghost to visit his prim Caslon pages. There, politely baffled by the loud talk of collectivism and social trends and economic determinism all about her, she sits a while and muses with her old friends. Then she leaves and does not come back for months at a time. One day, perhaps, her pale ghost will not appear at all, and the hard young sociologists can have her pages all to themselves. But I hope not. For all their cocksure *-ologies*, they cannot comfort us the way she did—when she was at her best.[1]

The modern informal essay is often personal and often makes use of either humor or whimsy, but it is more likely to make use of irony. The ironic essay states one thing but makes it plain that something else is meant. Its purpose is not to deceive, but to make the real meaning more effective by having words convey the opposite meaning from that which they appear to have. The essayist is not contentious—on the contrary, his essay appears light, genial, breezy, witty. Underneath the surface, however, is criticism, frequently savage criticism. The ironic essay makes an attack, no matter how oblique, on some current stupidity, disagreeable trait, or generally believed fallacy. Irony has value because of its inherent humor and its obliqueness; a good-natured, indirect attack is often more effective than a straightforward, contentious approach. Not everyone can write humorously or whimsically, but all of us can be subtle, to varying degrees, in our attacks.

---

[1] From *Forum*, July, 1933.

It should be stressed that many good personal essays have an underlying significance which may be obscured by the brilliance of their style. *Personal* and *informal* are adjectives which may still be used in characterizing the modern essay, but rarely the adjective *light*. Stevenson, for example, has some very profound observations about life in "An Apology for Idlers," p. 739. Informal essays may be merely entertaining and amusing, but more often they deal with subject matter of intrinsic significance. Swift's "A Modest Proposal" and Defoe's "Shortest Way with the Dissenters" are diverting, but they are also thought-provoking. Just as there is no law that a personal essay must be disjointed, there is no requirement that its subject matter be trivial and insignificant.

There is little or nothing really trivial about Stinnett's attitude toward women in "On the Beach," p. 703. James Reston's "A Fable," p. 715, is amusing on the surface, but it contains some deadly shafts and barbs. Ferril's comments on "Freudian Football" are hilarious, but the essay is as pointed and meaningful in its way as is Stoke's "College Athletics: Education or Show Business?" There are both bite and irony in Bishop's "The Reading Machine," p. 720.

The following suggestions for writing informal essays may be helpful:

Keep a notebook. Ideas for essays come to us often but are quickly forgotten. If you will jot down ideas as they occur, you will be able to call upon them when needed. Also, if you are thinking about a certain essay you are planning to write, sentences and even paragraphs may come to you. Keep a notebook handy and write them down right away. After this process has gone on for some time, you will find that your essay is already "written" and all you have to do is to piece together and polish the fragments.

Keep your eyes and ears open. Excellent subjects for essays will come to you as you go about your daily tasks. That overheard conversation in the cafeteria; the sight of wads of chewing gum deposited in the drinking fountains; the girls who came to class dressed as though they were going to a barn dance or a formal party; the "Monday morning quarterbacks" whom you heard arguing in the corner drugstore—these are excellent subjects for discussion. Suggestions for the best personal essays are collected "on the hoof," while you are engaged in the routine of living. Ideas for informal essays will be scarce and dull if you sit down to "think them up." They will be plentiful and lively if you use your eyes and your ears every day and record your observations and findings in a notebook.

Always rewrite. After you have composed the first draft of your personal essay, lay it aside for a little while. Later, when reading it, you will note deficiencies and mistakes which you can remove. This phrase doesn't sound quite right—that word isn't the exact one. Revise. As has been pointed out, informal essays depend rather largely for their effectiveness on their degree of polish, their "high finish." Try out your essay on your friends, the members of your family, anyone who will listen. Their reactions may enable you to make improvements. At every rewriting you will find some way to increase its effectiveness. Informality and carelessness are not synonyms. Many of the most forceful phrases, the most entertaining sentences in your finished essay will come as the result of careful, time-consuming activity. The personal essay must be as stylistically perfect as you can make it.

A consideration of the following suggestions for informal essays may be fruitful. Notice that some of the topics may best be handled whimsically or humorously; others lend themselves to ironical development.

1. On Being the World's Amanuensis.
2. I Give a Red Apple to Teacher.
3. On Sophisticated Children.
4. The Smell of Old Clothes.
5. Our Educated Alumni.
6. The Disadvantages of Being a Woman.
7. "Visiting" by Telephone.
8. The Art of Rudeness.
9. "He-Men" on the Campus.
10. Why I Dislike Professors.
11. My Charming Roommate.
12. "Let's Talk About You," He Said.
13. On Living in a Fraternity House.
14. I'm Tired of Television.
15. Strong, Silent Men—They Bore Me.
16. What Every Professor Should Know.
17. On Entering Class Late.
18. Colleges Are Like Cafeterias.
19. I Give a Book-burning Party.
20. Hollywood and Hokum.
21. Music—Hot and Cold.
22. Dust on the Saddle—Atomic Dust, That Is.
23. Manners for Moderns.
24. Campus Styles in Dress.
25. Girls Who Are Cold (Cool, Warm, Hot).

CRITICISM

Criticism is a part of everyone's daily life. You exercise critical faculties every time you choose a meal in the cafeteria, decide how to spend the afternoon, or buy an article of clothing. You read one book in preference to another; you telephone Dorothy instead of Peggy; you choose the subway rather than the bus—all these are acts involving some sort of criticism.

In a broader and more exact sense, criticism is thoughtful, many-sided evaluation. The word *critic* comes from the Greek *kritikós*, meaning a *judge*. Thus, criticism is a process which weighs, evaluates, judges. Contrary to some opinion, it does not deal only with faults. Sound criticism mentions good qualities as well as bad, virtues as well as faults. It should not set out to praise or condemn; rather it weighs faults and excellencies and then passes a considered judgment.

In writing criticisms of books, plays, concerts and recitals, radio and television programs, and motion pictures, you should remember, therefore, that your comments must be based on knowledge. It is unfair to review a book or a motion picture, for example, without first having read (or listened and looked) with care and thoughtfulness. You must give whatever it is that you are reviewing a fair and thorough trial—as an impartial judge you can do no less. At some stage, the best criticism is thoughtful, detached, impersonal—not unreasoning and biased.

But critical writing is also emotional and highly personal. As individuals, we all have prejudices of some sort as a result of our heredity and environment—race, religion, occupation, politics, education, social position, etc. We must be on guard against our prejudices, but of course it is impossible for us not to react according to our individual traits. The best criticism is an amalgam of objectivity and subjectivity; it should be impersonal and yet it must be subjective. As Anatole France said:

> The good critic is he who recounts the adventures of his soul in the presence of masterpieces. Objective criticism no more exists than objective art, and those who suppose that they are putting anything but themselves into their work are the dupes of the most fallacious illusion. The fact is that one never escapes from himself. That indeed is one of our great misfortunes. What would we not give for the power to see, just for one moment, the heavens and earth as they appear to a fly, or to comprehend nature with the rude brain of an ape? But we are forever precluded from doing so. Unlike Tiresias, we are not able to be men and yet remember having been women. We are confined within our bodies as in a perpetual prison. The better part, it seems to me, is to admit unhesitatingly this deplorable condition and to avow that we speak of ourselves each time that we have not the resolution to remain silent.

Good criticism is subjective and is always biased to some degree, but the subjectivity and the bias should be predicated upon a sound knowledge of the material being criticized.

The foregoing remarks apply to criticism of all kinds, but it is likely that most of the reviewing you will do in college will be of books. Essentially, the principles of all criticism are the same, but these are the questions which a good book review should specifically answer:

1. What was the author trying to do?
2. How well did he succeed in his attempt?
3. What value has the attempt?

An answer to the first question should be a discussion of the scope and purpose of the book. What material is covered? What material is stressed? What was the author's apparent purpose in writing the book? These queries must be answered.

The second question requires comment not so much on material as on manner. What stylistic faults and excellencies does the book possess? Is it convincing, persuasive, dull? Would some readers find the book excellent, others think it inferior? What readers? Why?

The third question may be answered by a discussion of the theme and purpose of the book. Here you may legitimately criticize an author for having written a light romance instead of a novel of social significance, or vice versa. But remember: fairness demands that you first evaluate a book in terms of what it is designed to be. Later, if you wish, you may point out the worthiness or unworthiness of the attempt.

There are three different kinds, or methods, of book reviewing. The first is the method of the reporter; that is, the reviewer reports on the book as an item of news. He tells what the book contains, perhaps in the form of a précis or résumé; he tells something of the author and his method of handling material. Essentially, however, this type of review is not critical. It reports, in some detail, the observable facts about the author and contents of the book, and does little else. Book reviewers who conduct columns in daily newspapers are usually "book reporters" rather than critics.

Another method, the one most frequently expected by college instructors, is that of combining reportorial details with some critical comment. The writer of this kind of review not only reports but also explains, interprets, and evaluates the book in terms of its material, its style, its scope, and its purpose. Such a review is ordinarily composed of about 50 percent summary and 50 percent evaluation. This is the method often employed by professional reviewers in preparing copy for weekly magazines. The daily reviewer on a newspaper has time for little more than straight reporting, but the weekly reviewer has some opportunity for weighing and judging.

The third method has been called the "springboard review." This type of criticism deals only slightly with the actual book under consideration; the "reviewer" uses it merely as a convenient starting point from which he launches into a critical essay that ranges far afield. For example, a "springboard reviewer," in considering a book on war, may make a few comments about the book and then proceed to a discussion of other books on war, or the dominant psychology of war novels, or even to an analysis of the causes of international friction. Such critical essays may sometimes be found in monthly and quarterly magazines and in books of literary criticism.

The good review is usually a blend of these three methods. It contains some reportorial detail and some critical comment. It also compares and contrasts the book and its author with other similar or dissimilar books and authors, in an attempt to "place" the book and its special contribution.

The following suggestions for writing reviews may be helpful:

1. Always give some indication of the contents of the book. You do not wish to write your review wholly from a reportorial angle, but ordinarily you should assume that your review will be read by a person who has not read the book. Some indication of its contents is essential.

2. Select a controlling idea and mold your review around it. Obviously, it is impossible to comment on all the ideas contained in a book or to develop fully a large number of critical points. For purposes of unity and effectiveness, choose some major theme, or idea, or stylistic quality of the book and discuss it thoroughly; try also to relate other comments to your major point of attack by means of comparison and contrast.

3. Make some use of quotations from the book. Summarizing is helpful, indeed necessary, but it does not give any indication of the actual flavor of the book. A judicious and limited use of quotations will furnish the reader of your review with a good idea of the author's style and will also help to add compelling interest to your otherwise largely expository review. Neither the readers of your review who have read the book itself nor those who have not will be satisfied with a mere summary; well-chosen quotations appeal to everyone. Remember, however, to choose quotations carefully and use them sparingly.

4. Be specific. Do not use vague terms. If you say, for example, that

the style of an author is heavy, illustrate what you mean by quotation. If you say that the book is well-documented, give the names of some of the references the author has used. Your reader may be quite prepared to accept your general statements, but direct and specific illustration will more clearly convey your exact meaning.

5. Do not hesitate to inject yourself and your ideas into the review. Consciously or unconsciously, you will write subjectively, anyway. Relating the thoughts which occurred to you while you were reading the book, for example, possibly will serve to make the review more interesting, less wooden. After all, one function of a review is to describe a book in the light of the reviewer's own personality. Do not write only about your own opinions, but do not fail to give the reader an accurate and full account of your personal reactions.

6. Avoid contradictions and afterthoughts. If you have criticized a book severely, do not lamely end your review by writing, "But the book does have some good qualities" or "After all, the plot itself isn't bad." Fairness may demand the inclusion of such statements, but they should appear as thoughts, not afterthoughts. Above all, avoid ending your review with weak statements; end it instead on a positive reiteration of your dominant impression of the book, as, for example, Clifton Fadiman ended his review of *Moby Dick*, p. 747.

The examples of criticism in Book Three illustrate still other principles of good reviewing. Ciardi's analysis has become almost a classic in criticism of poetry because of its insight and informal, trenchant statement. Crowther's comment on *My Fair Lady* is a happy combination of motion-picture review and sage remarks on two actresses of importance on stage and screen. Atkinson largely restricts his statements to a consideration of music in this same motion picture. Both McCarten and McCarthy inject themselves into their reports with vigor and bite. None of the reviews in your collection exhibits every one of the principles mentioned in this section, but all are well above average and will repay careful study. Also, listen to television and radio comments about books, motion pictures, and plays whenever you can.

THE INTERVIEW

The formal interview has gradually gone out of fashion, even in the newspapers and magazines where it was once so prevalent. But a form of interview—a sort of clipped and truncated version—forms the basis of many current television and radio programs and in this way is known to many listeners and viewers. In this format and in its more formal one, the interview is a type of writing which has several advantages for the student writer. Interviewing a person and accurately recording his statement is difficult, but it is an efficient method of training the ear, the eye, and the memory. Truman Capote attributed much of the success of his *In Cold Blood* to the thoroughness and efficiency of the interviewing techniques which underlie most of this thriller.

Meeting and conversing with people is valuable, too, in developing a universally helpful knowledge of human nature. Also, the interview often serves as the base of the biographical sketch and the profile, other important types of modern writing.

You do not need to know and have access to important people in order to write interviews. A skillfully conducted conversation with a fellow student, or a college employee, or the proprietor of a nearby store, or a bus driver, or the cashier at a motion-picture theater may result in a genuinely interesting theme. Some of the reader's interest will center in the individual and some in what he has to say. If you describe the interviewee carefully and get him or her to talk about matters of general interest, you will engage the attention of your reader, never fear.

These suggestions may prove helpful:

1. Before interviewing someone, find out as much as you can about him. Thus you will know in advance something of his background and interests and will be able to ask pertinent questions. It is especially important to secure advance information if your interviewee is a prominent person; you should, for example, know a great deal about the career of a visiting lecturer before you talk to him.

2. Plan, in advance, the questions you are going to ask and the topics which you would like to have discussed. Nothing is so uncomfortable to a person being interviewed as to have to guess what his interviewer wants him to talk about. You should have at least enough questions and comments already planned to get the conversation started. The questions should deal with matters in which your readers are interested and which they will want discussed.

Sometimes, however, you must scrap your planned questions in order to fit in with the mood and temperament of your subject. You need to call upon all your ingenuity in dealing with an interviewee who talks rapidly, takes the conversation far afield from those matters in which your readers will be interested, and frequently "jumps the track" of the conversation.

Similarly exasperating is the noncommittal subject who answers in monosyllables such as "Yes" and "No," and who cannot or will not develop any ideas. Such people require great care in handling. A variety and abundance of planned topics and questions will be of real assistance to you.

3. Some people who are being interviewed become frightened when they see that you are actually recording in your notebook what they are saying. They tend to speak more guardedly or even refuse to make comments at all. In such instances, you should put away your notebook and rely on memory. As soon as you leave your subject, set down his comments as accurately as possible. Such a method will tax your memory, but it may, at times, be necessary. After a little experience, you will find that you can retain much of both the content and the spirit of the conversation; trained newspapermen are capable of obtaining and describing lengthy interviews without taking any but "mental" notes.

4. Avoid an exclusive use of a "question-and-answer" style in writing up the report of an interview. Often it is wise completely to avoid the idea of an interview, so far as the reader is concerned, because a monotonous series of questions and answers will prove wearisome. Combine several answers into a unified statement and omit mention of the specific questions themselves.

5. Give something of the background of the interviewee. Your reader will be interested in knowing a little of his biography, his appearance, his manner of speaking, and other similar human interest details. Possessing knowledge of these details, the reader will be more interested in what the interviewee says and more capable of understanding and evaluating it. At times, it is effective to "stage-manage" your subject: describe his movements as he talked, his reactions to interruptions of your conversation, etc. Such description serves to eliminate the possible monotony of straight dialogue and increases the interest of the reader in your interviewee.

6. Build your interview around some high point or central thesis of the conversation. Most conversations, no matter how well controlled, are rambling; not everything said is of equal importance. After an analysis of your notes, pick out the most striking statement or the topic of greatest interest and mold your report around it. Otherwise, your report may be a hodge-podge or merely a monotonous series of questions and answers.

7. Be careful to insure the mechanical accuracy of your interview. There are established rules for punctuating and paragraphing conversation. If you are in doubt, study Section 53.

THE PROFILE

The profile is a popular form of writing today; it combines strictly biographical material with character interpretation. That is, it is biographical writing done in the modern vein: superimposed upon an account of the subject's heredity, environment, and accomplishments is an attempted evaluation of his traits and characteristics. Such a definition is not completely satisfactory, but it indicates that the type requires "who's who" details plus anecdotal material plus character analysis. The modern profile differs from good biographical writing of the past only in the sense that it contains more anecdotes, human interest stories, and humorous or ironic comment. A profile, as its name indicates, is also not a full portrait; it merely seizes upon "highlights" and bears somewhat the relation to a full-length biography that a short story does to a novel.

You should, as a writer, be interested in all other people. The life of anyone is important to himself, and, indeed, certain phases of it will be interesting to others. We may sometimes tend to call someone a bore, thinking him completely dull and uninteresting, without trying to find out facts which would indicate that our judgments are hasty. The philosopher who said that "most men and women are merely one couple more" was expressing an opinion that many of us have about all people other than our friends and acquaintances. Robert Louis Stevenson, in trying to show that everyone's life was important, wrote: "The man who lost his life against a hen-roost is in the same pickle with the man who lost his life against a fortified place of the first order."

These statements indicate that we should be so interested in, and curious about, other people that we ought to take the trouble to find out the details of their life histories. They also indicate that we need not seek important men and women as subjects but that anyone, regardless of who he is,

is a potential subject for a profile. Robert Littell has admirably summed up
these ideas:

> Whether your success is destined to be in dollars or in praise only,
> other people will always be the thing most worth writing about. Keep your
> eye for them perpetually fresh. Nothing is more necessary than this almost
> moral attitude, and few things are more difficult. In effect, I am asking you
> never to allow yourself to be bored by other people. Boredom lumps them
> together, and classification is fatal in those who would write about them.
> They are all different; get that in your head and never let it get out. They
> are all worth writing about; get that into your head also. Learn to look at
> and listen to each one of them as if you were confronted by an entirely new
> specimen, unique in all the world, and learn to examine each one as if you
> had never seen him before.[2]

Like the interview, which is often used as a means of getting biographical material, the profile is a type of writing well worthy of our attention;
it forces us to meet, talk with, and try to understand other people; it requires
us to use our powers of observation and increases our knowledge of human
nature. The following suggestions for writing the profile may prove helpful:

1. A good profile contains much more than merely "who's who" detail.
It is important that the specific facts of heredity, training, etc., be given,
but ordinarily they should constitute a minor part of the whole. Dr. Johnson
once scornfully referred to purely factual biographical writing as "lives that
begin with a pedigree and end with a funeral." You will need to know many
"who's who" details about your subject, but in the actual writing of the
profile you should subordinate them to more important matters. A biographical sketch composed wholly of "mere facts" will not be nearly so
interesting and revealing as one which also deals with causes, reasons, and
motives.

2. Try to be thorough in getting information about your subject. You
can write best about a person when you know more details than you can
possibly use, because then you can select only the most interesting and
revelatory material which you have assembled. Talk not only to the subject
himself but also to his friends and acquaintances, the members of his
family, his roommate, his cook, his enemies, his teachers or students—in
short, to everyone who can furnish you with information. If possible, read
anything and everything he has written. In many instances, you will begin
to understand a person only after a thorough search for information. Take
time and pains in gathering material; to do so will pay you dividends later.
(If you are pressed for time, obviously you cannot follow all the suggestions
in this paragraph.)

3. Do not make your profile didactic. Intelligent readers can and will
form their own opinions; if you pass moral judgments on your subject, your
reader will lose interest. Naturally, what you write should influence your
reader's opinions, but that profile is effective which only *causes* judgments
and is somewhat subtle about actually stating them. Littell has even gone
so far as to say: "Approval or disapproval, like or dislike, must be rooted
out of your soul, where writing is concerned; entertain no moral or emo-

---

[2] From "Some Advice to Writers" by Robert Littell, *New Republic.*

tional judgments, but perceptions, facts, and understanding only." Such advice can never be completely followed, but at least you can influence opinion subtly and not make the profile a sermon, a moral lecture, or an unadulterated agency of propaganda.

You should try to be honest in writing the profile, of course. You can never learn and convey the whole truth about anyone, but you can make a sincere effort to get as much accurate information as you can and interpret it unbiasedly. Do not be worried about complete veracity, however. Gamaliel Bradford once said that there were only two classes of biographers—those who *thought* they were impartial and those who knew they were not. All that you can do is to make an honest effort to get the whole truth and interpret it fairly. No subject of a profile can ever be completely "whitewashed" or found wholly bad or unimportant.

4. Try to build the major portion of your profile around some dominant characteristic of the subject. It is obviously impossible to give all the details, all the personality traits which you have discovered. Furthermore, a sketch which is merely a random collection of factual details plus your own comments has no real unity and coherence. For example, in writing a profile of the Emperor of Japan, John Gunther wove most of the material about the concept of the emperor as a symbol of the Japanese state. Gamaliel Bradford's profile of Mary Lincoln develops only those characteristics which had some definite bearing upon her husband's life. Selective treatment enabled these writers to give a unity, coherence, and perspective to their articles which otherwise would have been missing.

Be on guard, however, against overemphasis. If you place too much stress on one characteristic, you may write a caricature rather than an honest profile. A caricature is effective for the cartoonist because it points up a dominant characteristic or feature, but, of course, it is not designed to give an accurate picture of the subject. The profile is.

5. Use many incidents (see p. 142) and anecdotes (see p. 141). Anecdotes, for example, make interesting reading and are a most excellent means of revealing character. Biographical articles are filled with anecdotal material; each narrative bit is included for the specific purpose of making the exposition of character both interesting and genuinely revelatory. Months after you have read biographical accounts you will remember some of their revealing and fascinating anecdotes, whereas much of the strictly expository material you will long since have forgotten—full proof of the effectiveness of narrative material.

6. No rule can be laid down concerning what details every profile should embrace. As a suggestion, however, a profile may contain, in addition to facts of heredity, environmental influences, and accomplishments, some or all of the following:

> Descriptions of the subject's personal appearance and characteristic actions—height, weight, clothing, manner of speaking and walking and sitting, gestures, etc.
>
> Direct quotations from the subject himself and from what others have said to you about him.
>
> Accounts of his philosophy—his opinions concerning important matters such as war, national and international politics, religion, contemporary

morals, and other also important questions such as college athletics, television, motion pictures, books and authors, or the cloak-and-suit business. Your whole aim is to reveal the subject as you think him to be and to tell how and why he "got that way."

7. You will notice that biographical articles may use different outlines (forms) of presentation. A good and typical profile, however, may be written as follows: First, give an account of your subject's physical appearance and follow with a few "flashes" of him or her in action—teaching a class, serving a customer, treating a patient, etc. After that, give a rapid story of the subject's life, stressing those details of heredity and environment which have had an important bearing upon him. Then come back to him as of the present, showing why he is important, interesting, amusing, or is bitter, frustrated, or happy, or whatnot. Here you will develop his guiding "philosophy of life," his primary motives, his aims and hopes, the worth of his actual achievements. Such an outline is merely a suggestion; rearrangement of the items is entirely permissible.

Several of the profiles and biographical sketches in Book Three will repay careful analysis. The article by Deems Taylor, p. 801, is somewhat more a character sketch than a profile; so, too, is the piece by Van Wyck Brooks on Helen Keller. Both are excellent examples of biography which put characterization and the subject's motives ahead of straight "who's who" details.

Brooks Atkinson's article on Thoreau, p. 805, is both more and less than a profile. In part it is a biographical sketch emphasizing influences upon the subject's life; also in part it is a critical evaluation of Thoreau's attitudes and work. In the book from which "Gettysburg," p. 849, is taken, the author has fashioned a narrative of Lincoln's life from birth to death by blending (synthesizing) various accounts written by various people. Paul Angle ties these separate accounts together with accurate and perceptive commentary.

THE FORMAL ESSAY, OR ARTICLE

The formal essay is a primarily expository type of writing which in recent years has been popularized by magazines and the Sunday supplements of newspapers. In fact, the essay as magazine article is the most widely published type of periodical literature in America today. For proof, note that every outstandingly successful American magazine started within the past five decades has been devoted wholly or mainly to publishing articles. The nonfiction of magazines includes, among other types, the profile and criticism, discussed previously in this chapter. But the article of fact and opinion is in itself a dominant type of contemporary writing.

The article, or formal essay (the terms are used interchangeably in this section), differs from the research paper in that it is usually written in a popular style and, although based on fact, is not accompanied by the paraphernalia of documentation (footnotes and bibliography; see pp. 379 and 358). The article of opinion, or of opinion based on fact, is likely to be more of a "think piece" than a research article and thus permits more individual interpretation and expression of personality. The formal essay is more clearly organized—and more directly concerned with significant material—than the informal essay. It may contain autobiographical elements, criticism, and even the results of interviews. Thus it possesses individual characteristics but bears some relationship to other expository forms.

The article, or essay, is to shorter forms of exposition what the short story is to incidents, anecdotes, and sketches. It represents a fusing of smaller expository types and, indeed, occasionally employs description, argument, and narration. Because it represents perhaps the highest form of art in relatively short expository composition, it is difficult to write. But you should understand something of the principles and techniques of article-writing. You will read many articles in college years and afterward; furthermore, you may have occasion to write a formal essay. For example, you may have read and thought much about some idea or problem which could be treated more communicatively in an article than in a formal research paper. The idea may not lend itself to such humorous or ironic treatment as the personal essay would demand. The idea cannot be developed in the form of criticism, or a profile, or an interview. The formal article should then be your medium.

Three basic problems are involved in the formal essay: (1) getting *ideas* for articles, (2) getting *material*, (3) *writing*.

GETTING IDEAS FOR FORMAL ESSAYS

There applies here all that is elsewhere said about choosing subjects from your own experience and observation, subjects about which you know something and in which you are genuinely interested. The only good idea for an article is the one which is significant for you, which means something to you, that you feel the need of expressing. You probably have within you ideas for numerous formal essays. You can write a full-length (2000–6000 words) account of the typical high-school education, its excellencies and faults. You may be able to write a description and criticism of the administration of your home town; of youth's hopes and fears for the future; of coeducation; the value of sports; woman's place in the professions; of reforestation or overpopulation or air pollution. You could conceivably write an article on armaments, methods of making money, the relations of the sexes, the contributions of television, radio, motion pictures, etc. *Any* idea is a good idea provided you are interested in it and will take the trouble to study and think about it thoroughly.

If you lack ideas, all you need do is study the titles of articles appearing in dozens of magazines each week and month. Here you may find a host of suggestions. A single copy of a magazine such as *The Reader's Digest* should give you several ideas for articles. Current motion pictures will do likewise. Television news programs are a particularly fertile source. Conversations and interviews ought to furnish you with still other suggestions. Your problem should be more to select one idea from a number than to find anything at all to write about. Choose the idea in which you are interested, which you think you can make interesting to others, and about which you can get sufficient developing information.

You probably will not be interested in all the formal essays reprinted in your book of readings, but it will be valuable for you to study the ideas with which they are concerned. Some of the subjects may be beyond your capacities, but each of the essays will give you suggestions for derivative articles which you could write.

GETTING MATERIAL FOR FORMAL ESSAYS

You will find that, in order to make an essay really sound and interesting, you must gather for it more material than you can use. Only from an overflowing stock of facts and ideas can you select those which will most effectively develop your thesis. The great fault with most student essays is that they are half-baked, not clearly thought through, not filled with supporting detail. Getting this detail requires time and effort.

First, you will probably need to discover and study whatever has been written before on your selected subject. In doing this you should consult the card catalog of your library and its periodical and newspaper indexes. You will need to talk to anyone and everyone who can give you ideas and materials. Perhaps your subject is one which has been treated in motion pictures. See them. Some radio or television program deals with the subject? Listen to it or watch it. Perhaps a questionnaire will give you needed information. Prepare and circulate one. Perhaps there are important people not living near you who could give you information. Write to them. Do everything you possibly can to get full developing detail for your essay. It may take days and weeks, but your article will be valueless unless it has plentiful detail and soundly factual information. Some of the best articles appearing today are in *Fortune*. A writer and at least one research person spend a *minimum* time of at least two months in getting material for every *Fortune* article. Your time will be limited, but you should make as thorough a search for material as you can.

After you have collected the material and before you begin to write, analyze it carefully. Single out the points of view which you wish to express; reject the material which is not sound or communicable; formulate a thesis for your article. In other words, do more than merely gather material: study it, evaluate it, assimilate it into your own thought processes.

WRITING THE FORMAL ESSAY

You have an idea and material for its development. Now you are faced with the problem of presenting your idea so that it will be most clearly and effectively communicated to your reader. As in all exposition, your first problem is to make the presentation *clear;* your second is to make it *interesting*.

As was pointed out in Chapter 1, you must keep your reader constantly in mind. It will not be sufficient if you yourself know what you have in mind; the reader must be shown also. Thoreau once said, "It takes two to speak truth, one to speak and another to hear."

Every *clear* essay has a definite pattern and purpose. The reader can tell just where the writer is going and can progress with him. Such a pattern is based on definite organization, usually in the form of an outline (see Section 39). It makes no difference what this pattern is, so long as it is both clear and logical. You may, for example, develop an idea *chronologically;* or you may use a *news story* pattern in which you begin with a graphic presentation (summary) of the entire article and then proceed to develop the idea chronologically. Or you may develop your essay *logically* on a basis of cause and effect. If the plan is *clear* to the reader, you will have taken a forward step in communicating your idea. See Section 33.

The diction of an essay should be as clear as its plan. If you use abstruse, or learned, or technical words, you must explain them to the general reader. If you make allusions to not generally known fields of knowledge, you must explain. If you refer to people not generally known, you must explain. Never forget that a word or a reference understood by you may be misunderstood by someone else. In both plan and diction, then, your essay must be completely clear.

Your article may be clear, however, and yet not be interesting. There are a few technical methods of gaining and holding the attention and interest of your reader.

1. One obvious method is to give your essay a good title, one which is both descriptive and arresting. As is mentioned in Chapter 2, a title should be more than a mere tag. It should have what is called "eye value"—that is, it should contain colorful words which have emotional connotations or which denote action; it should be fairly short. Who will deny that "The Gentle Art of Making Enemies" is more effective than the original title, "The Correspondence of James McNeill Whistler"? Or that "Vanity Fair" is a more interesting title than "Pencil Sketches of English Society"? The fact that the titles you use do not have to have "box-office value" is no excuse for their being dull and wordy. A study of the titles of essays in your anthology will prove enlightening.

2. The beginning and ending of the essay also offer opportunities for creating interest. A good beginning, or "lead" as it is sometimes called, should have "eye value," brevity, and action, too. You may begin your article with an incident of genuine interest, with an anecdote, or with dialogue. Each of these should be interesting in itself and should foreshadow the theme to follow.

The ending should be as effective as the beginning. Indeed, most well-written essays have beginnings and endings which are interchangeable. The ending may contain a restatement of the high point of the article; it may weave together the threads of the essay; or it may be a symbolizing incident, anecdote, or bit of dialogue which will reinforce and drive home the thesis of the article. Do not overlook the strategic value of the beginning and end positions of your paper. See p. 19.

3. Interest in your article will be enhanced by the use of both descriptive and narrative material. Exploitation of the writer's own personality, the use of humor, cynical subtlety, and satire, a fresh approach to an old subject—all these add to the forcefulness of your essay. But more effective than all other methods of achieving interest is *concreteness.* Someone has aptly said, "All that we know gets into our heads as itemized bits of experience."

From our own past lives we remember best specific conversations, definite places, actual situations. The readers of your essay will take the greatest interest in (and will remember longest) those parts of your writing where you give concrete, specific illustrations and relate definite anecdotes, incidents, and conversations. One well-told and apt story which illustrates a specific point is more effective than a dozen pages of straight exposition. You may, for instance, forget many of the ideas in formal essays which you read, but you will not soon forget extraordinarily effective anecdotes, incidents, and reports of conversation.

4. Be specific, be definite, be concrete in your writing—only thus can you effectively convey your ideas. Then, and only then, will the reader be able to see what is in the essay for him, what it means, and what significance it has.

In short, consider all the details which make effective and forceful the writing of the whole theme (see Chapter 2), all the traditional forms (see Chapter 7) which may contribute to successful expression of ideas, all the modern methods or types of writing which may be utilized in presentation of the topic. This, of course, is a counsel of perfection; yet the whole study of communication—of the word, the sentence, the paragraph, the theme, and the kinds of writing—is a cumulative process, a synthesis in which the writer brings to his idea all the devices, in their best forms, that he can command. See Chapter 6.

The writers of articles appearing in your collection of readings have employed many devices in their best forms. For example, what could possibly be clearer than the plan and purpose of Wecter's article on heroes, p. 548? Rarely has diction been more exact and effective than in Highet's "The Necessity for Reason," p. 510, or William James' article on habit, p. 595. All the titles of articles in the collection are exact and arresting. They vary in form and in length; study them carefully. None of the articles has a flat beginning or ending, and nearly all of them use some narrative and descriptive details as aids to clearness and concreteness. Each represents a synthesis of varied methods of communication. Each is probably beyond our abilities at the moment, but it is encouraging to realize that each was beyond the ability of the writer in his early stages of learning to communicate. We, too, can keep trying.

THE SHORT STORY

As was indicated in the discussion of narration on p. 141, the short story is a narrative type in which smaller elements such as the incident and sketch are expanded and molded into a definite pattern of artistic merit. Writing a good short story requires considerable skill, a thorough understanding of the principles of narration, and a great deal of time for planning, writing, and rewriting. Because the short story is an exacting form, you may never be able to write a fully satisfactory one in your freshman English course. Since, however, the short story does represent perhaps the greatest artistry to be achieved in any form of relatively short prose composition, try to understand something of the principles which apply to it in order to be able to write an acceptable story and read more understandingly and critically the great short stories of the past and present.

What Is a Short Story?

A short story may have any of a number of forms, and its subject matter may be concerned with any conceivable phase of human activity, mental or physical. A few principles applying to all narrative writing may, however, be mentioned.

First, all narration, whether in short-story or novel form, is designed to appeal primarily to the *emotions* of the reader. Its basic purpose is to make the reader feel rather than think, to reach him through his senses rather than through his intellect. Even this statement must be modified, for obviously the tools used in fiction must be those of the intellect; moreover, stories which appeal *only* to readers' emotions are always shallow and insignificant. But the *primary* aim of narration is to relate a story which will appeal to the feelings of the reader rather than try to convince him (argument), paint a picture (description), or impart knowledge (exposition). The good short story has a second (and always more important) purpose—to make the reader *think*. Guy de Maupassant once summed up the purposes of fiction clearly: "The public is composed of numerous groups who cry to us [writers]: '*Console* me, *amuse* me, make me *sad*, make me *sympathetic*, make me *dream*, make me *laugh*, make me *shudder*, make me *weep*, make me *think*.' " Your major problem, then, is to select material which will appeal to readers' emotions and to handle and manipulate this material so that it will most effectively stir their feelings. Your problem is one of *substance* and *form*, of material and technique.

What kinds of material will appeal to readers' emotions? The answer is simple and clear: any activity of any kind which reveals someone facing a problem. You may write narratively of ordinary people in ordinary, everyday situations, but your reader's interest will be quickened only when you place someone in a position where he has to face a problem. Life is, for all of us, a problem-solving business; our activities constantly involve *conflicts* of some kind. Problems, conflicts, struggles, dilemmas—call them what you will—these are the materials of fiction.

We may not always be interested in other people as such, but we become interested in them when we find that they are understandable characters who are in predicaments which we also have faced or could conceivably face. Each of us has a desire to live as fully as possible, either actually or in the experiences of others. In real life we act as we can or must; in fiction we can live vicariously in a sort of make-believe world. Characters in a short story must be understandable people with whom the reader can identify himself or his acquaintances.

As many writers have stated and as is acknowledged in the note in Book Three preceding the section devoted to short stories, no really adequate definition of a short story is possible. However, if you are going to try to write a story, or more than one, you need some kind of blueprint, some set of guidelines. Here, then, is an attempt at a "working" definition of the type—*a short story is a relatively short narrative which is designed to produce a single dominant effect and which contains the elements of drama.* That is, the short story is an account of recognizable, understandable people facing a recognizable, understandable problem, the solving or nonsolving of which produces an emotional effect upon the reader. The essentials of plot and purpose are to make the reader forget temporarily his own world and enter the world of the story. The writer creates or develops characters who will interest his reader—understandable people worthy of the reader's sympathy, admiration, hatred, etc. These characters must be placed in situations which cause the reader to become keenly eager to know "what happens next" or "how it turns out." Uncertainty, curiosity, and suspense are fed by obstacles, doubts, fears; finally, there is a solution of the problem, an ending of uncertainty and suspense.

Of course, it is difficult to carry out the steps in this recipe, so difficult that many who try never succeed. All failures in story-writing, however, are traceable to poor selection of story material or inadequate manipulation of that material.

THE SOURCES AND KINDS OF STORY MATERIAL

What is good story material? How can you be certain to get a good idea for a story? The first thing to remember is that story material must be *dramatic;* it must place people in understandable predicaments. You must set people whom you can convincingly portray and characterize in situations involving doubt and suspense. Successful short stories must be composed of material which gains the attention of the reader, arouses curiosity that grows naturally out of the characters or situations which have already gained attention, and sustains sympathy—causes the reader actually to become concerned about what is going to happen.

These functions of a short story are difficult to achieve because they require the use of material which the writer *knows thoroughly.* The first suggestion, then, for selecting a story idea is that you take something from your own experience or observation. If you do, you will presumably know enough about the characters involved, the conflict itself, the setting in which the action occurred, the meaning or thesis of the narrative to make them convincing to the reader. If you place people whose counterparts you have never known in situations which you have only imagined, your story will hardly be convincing. It will be merely fiction in the worst sense— imaginative material which has no reality, no significance.

Despite your possible disbelief, there have been numerous incidents and situations in your life or in the lives of people well known to you which will make good story material. Here, for example, are brief résumés of situations developed by college freshmen into short stories:

> A boy has made and saved some money. He wishes to go to college, but his father has recently died, his mother and his small sisters need financial help. What to do?
> A girl falls in love with another student, becomes engaged to him, and then finds out that his religion is so incompatible with her own that neither

her family nor his would ever sanction an engagement and marriage. What to do?

Mark and Henry are devoted friends of long years' standing. Then, one day, Henry finds out that Mark has been stealing money from him and engaging in several types of activity which Henry cannot condone. Henry is hurt and bewildered at his friend's actions. What to do?

Ruth and Margaret, two 15-year-old girls, are close friends. They share their secrets, confide in each other about everything. Ruth suddenly finds out that Margaret thinks her childish; that on the sly Margaret has been having surreptitious "dates" with older boys whose reputation is not good. What to do?

Two boys, swimming out beyond the breakers, begin to tire. One of them becomes utterly exhausted, calls to the other for help. The other realizes that he can barely make it to shore himself. Shall he try to hold up the other until help comes? Shall he swim in alone and seek help?

These five "ideas" are not the most effective which could be imagined, but each was taken from the writer's actual experience, each involved characters well known to the writer, and each possessed the necessary ingredient of conflict with its resultant suspense and doubt. Have you had no somewhat similar experiences? For illustration, when you were small did you ever feel neglected, cast off, alone? Match this feeling with the central statement of Chekhov's "Vanka," p. 909. Have you ever resented someone so much that you thought of hurting or even killing him? Read Poe's "The Cask of Amontillado," p. 860. Have you ever daydreamed, imagining all sorts of impossible things about yourself? Then read "The Secret Life of Walter Mitty," p. 916. Have you ever bought something made of such cheap materials and so poorly constructed that you felt cheated? Isn't this something of which Galsworthy wrote in "Quality"?

Surely you have experienced one or another of these situations. Select the one which had greatest significance for you, relate the action as it happened, people the story with characters well known to you, place the action in a setting which you can describe convincingly. Do this—and it is not impossible by any means—and you will have a satisfactory story idea. Execute it well and you will have created a satisfactory short story.

Of course the story should have some significance, some genuine meaning. We are so accustomed to reading slick little stories in popular magazines, stories which have no real theses or genuine meanings, that we may forget that a story should do more than convey merely an emotional appeal. Your stories, too, should give the reader something of significance as well as of entertainment. Write about a situation which not only was exciting but also had some genuine meaning for you, some real bearing upon your life.

Your greatest problem in selecting a story idea from your experience will be to choose one which has enough conflict in it to interest others. It is true that most of us live ordinary, run-of-the-mine lives, but it is also true that each of us faces problems of some kind at all times. These problems, or conflicts, are of three kinds; perhaps a brief discussion of them will reveal to you the drama inherent in certain experiences of your own.

The first type of conflict is *elemental*, or *physical:* a struggle between man and the physical world. It represents man versus the forces of nature: the difficulties and dangers faced by explorers, astronauts, aviators, auto-

mobile racers. Rain, cold, heat, wild beasts in the jungle, treacherous tides—
these are constant obstacles to mankind. Such elemental conflicts are frequently found in moving pictures, in melodramatic plays, in the pulp magazines. You may build a story around an account of yourself confronted by
cold, or sleet, or rain, or floods, or darkness, but it is not likely that you have
had many such conflicts. And, too, the story based wholly on a physical
conflict ordinarily appeals only to the emotions and not to the intellect and
is thus shallow and insignificant. Conrad's "Youth" is far more than merely
a story of physical conflict.

Another type of conflict is *social:* a struggle between man and man.
Much of popular fiction is based on social conflict: two men trying to win
the love of a girl; two classmates struggling for class honors; athletes trying
to outdo each other; the competition of businessmen; a girl having difficulties with her parents over her conduct, etc. It is likely that most of the conflicts about which you will care to write are social: your struggles with
conventions, other boys and girls, your parents, school regimen, etc.

The third kind of conflict is *internal,* or *psychological:* a struggle between two desires within the same person. For example, a man who does
not believe in war is called into the armed forces. He firmly believes in
pacifism and hates all war, but he is patriotic. What shall he do—go to jail
because of his convictions or go to war because of his love of country? A
woman is unhappily married and believes that both she and her husband
would be better off if they were separated. But she abhors the idea of separation or divorce and so do her friends and her church. She has an internal
struggle to decide what to do.

It should be obvious from each of these illustrations that conflicts are
rarely unmixed. Usually a social conflict involves an internal, and sometimes a physical, conflict. Psychological conflicts are nearly always influenced by social conflicts. As a matter of fact, there are traces of both social
and internal conflicts in nearly all short stories.

More important than being able to classify types of conflict is realizing
the need for making a conflict *intense.* Readers will not be interested in a
mild conflict. You must give maximum intensity to desires present in the
material and set against them maximum opposition. Sometimes you may
need to exaggerate the conflict involved in an actual experience; but always
try to make the conflict plausible; remember, too, that if it is overly intensified, your story will become melodramatic rather than dramatic. The moving-
picture serials in which the hero faces death several times in each "episode"
are frankly melodramatic. Get enough conflicts into your stories to make
them seem alive but not so much that they become ridiculous.

In considering material for a short story you need not only to single
out its type (or types) of conflict but also to determine what emphasis the
story will have. Since any phase of life may be used as material for a short
story, you may find that ideas come to you in chaotic form. Your problem is
to decide just where in a seemingly chaotic idea lies the most effective story.
You may place emphasis on the *characters* in a story, on the *action* of a
story, on the *setting* in which the action takes place, or on the *theme* of the
story. Every conceivable human activity is composed of people, events,
places, and thoughts about those people, events, and places. If you put

emphasis on character, you will write a story of characterization; if you place it on the action, you will write what is called a complication story; if on setting, a story of atmosphere; if on a general truth or theme, a thematic story.

A *character* story derives its major effect by centering attention on *who* is involved in the action rather than on *what* happens (action), or the place *where* the action occurred (setting), or the *theme* of the story. For example, Eudora Welty's "A Worn Path," p. 962, places emphasis on the character of Old Phoenix. There is description of setting, some action, and of course the story has genuine meaning and significance. Our interest in reading it, however, depends largely upon our reaction to Old Phoenix and our understanding of her patience, courage, and devotion.

The *method* of characterization is relatively unimportant. The thing to remember is that a story which relies upon treatment of character for its emotional effect simply must stress a personality trait or traits. It must "paint a portrait"; it must subordinate other considerations to that of making a character understandable to the reader.

A *complication* story is one which gains its emotional effect by emphasis upon *what happens*. Interest in Conrad's "Youth" is centered upon the action itself: the series of trials, mishaps, accidents, and misadventures of Marlow on his first trip to the East. This great story of the power of illusions to sustain man's steadfastness and courage in the face of physical and spiritual hardships is more than a moving romance of the sea, but it is undeniably built on complications. On a far lower level, motion pictures are frequently stories of straight action, the characters involved being merely types. Stories in adventure magazines are composed almost wholly of action; the same is true of many stories written for children, but it is not true of the best of these.

Probably the majority of the best modern short stories may be called *character-complication* stories. That is, they derive their emotional effects by some emphasis on character, some on action. Both the *what* and the *who* of the story are important. The stories you write will probably fall in this classification. Stories of complication only you are likely to find relatively insignificant, unless you have had some startlingly dramatic adventures. And it is very difficult for a beginner to write a straight story of character; his attempts are prone to develop into character sketches (see p. 143) rather than dramatic short stories.

The story of *atmosphere* derives its emotional effect from emphasis upon setting. Robert Louis Stevenson's "The Merry Men" is a good example. Purely atmospheric stories are scarce, for few of us have been so profoundly affected by some setting that we are capable of weaving it into a dramatic narrative. Considerable traces of atmospheric detail may be found in "A Rose for Emily," p. 901; "A Trip to Czardis," p. 926; "The Devil and Daniel Webster," p. 969, and "A Worn Path," p. 962. Every short story has some trace of atmospheric detail, but few depend upon setting for their primary effects.

The *thematic* story is one which gains its dominant emotional effect by emphasis upon a belief or a general truth. The author of a thematic story has an idea which he wishes to convey; he writes a story to prove or show his thesis, his point. You may, for example, believe that women are the intellectual superiors (or inferiors) of men. You may write a story, involving action and characters, to prove your thesis. In a sense, the thematic story is a "narrative article"; it puts exposition and argument into a narrative form. This is essentially what Galsworthy did in "Quality," p. 873. He felt strongly about a decline in workmanship and a lack of loyalty which he found rampant. He wrote a story to state his alarm and prove his point.

So much for the sources and kinds of story material and types of conflict. A few technical problems involved in writing the short story remain for discussion.

Short Story Writing Problems

1. *Beginning the story.* One of the most difficult problems in manipulating story material is to determine where and how to begin. Your story must immediately gain the attention of the reader and arouse his curiosity as to what happens next. It cannot begin slowly and dully; it must start off with an incident, or a bit of dialogue, or a piece of description which will seem *alive* to the reader. Because of this need for gaining interest at the beginning, some story-writers make use of what is known as the "flashback." This involves starting off with some dramatic incident or a bit of dialogue which chronologically belongs later in the story. After this beginning, the writer "flashes" or "loops" back to the logical beginning and proceeds with the narrative. This is, at best, an artificial method, and many good writers never use it. To be sure, they begin their stories interestingly, but they relate them in natural, logical, and usually chronological order. A good story containing sound elements of dramatic action does not need to depend upon artificial devices. Use a flashback if the logical and natural beginning of your story is dull and heavy. But do not use it thoughtlessly or unnecessarily. Good stories are "slices of life," and nothing can be more uncertain or more exciting than life itself. Most good stories can be told as they actually happened.

2. *Point of view.* Another technical problem is point of view. This means the position or slant from which the writer tells the story, the controlling vision which he has of his material. Selecting the best possible point of view is both troublesome and important. It will pay you to spend some time in deciding from just what focus the story can best be related. You must predetermine the answers to the questions "Whose story is it?" and "Who's going to tell the story?"

A preliminary consideration is grammatical form: should you use the first or third person? This consideration is relatively unimportant and is easily solved; use whichever seems more natural to you. If you yourself are a character in a story, use the first person unless you feel strained and cramped in doing so. If you feel more at home with the third person, give yourself a name and keep out the personal pronouns. There is no significant relationship between the point of view of a story and the use of "he," "she," or "I." It is wise not to use either the first or the third person in *all* your stories. Use each, on occasion, for variety.

A second consideration is more important. Should you tell the story from the position of a major character in the story, a minor character, or omnisciently? Each has its advantages and disadvantages; the use of each will be determined largely by what specific story material you have and what effect you wish to produce.

In using the major-character point of view, you identify yourself with a main character. What this main character thinks, says, hears, and feels will *be* your story. In this point of view, well adapted to stories based on internal conflict and to stories of characterization and complication generally, you can use either the first or the third person.

The minor-character point of view is more difficult to handle, and perhaps more artificial, than the other fictional points of view. As the author of a story, you assume that you do not know everything to be said; accordingly, you select some minor character whose knowledge is limited and tell the story from his slant. Thus, you might tell the love story of a boy and girl from the point of view of a restaurant proprietor in whose place of business they frequently meet. He will experience only part of the story and the reader's suspense will be heightened because the proprietor does not know all that is going on. The minor-character point of view is frequently employed in detective stories, for instance, just because of its suspense value.

The omniscient point of view places no restrictions on the author; he can assume that he knows all and can tell as much as he pleases. From this point of view, you can enter the mind of any character or relate what is happening simultaneously in Calcutta and Chicago. Obviously it requires you to use the third person.

The omniscient is perhaps the easiest of the three to use and is often employed in swiftly and chronologically developed action stories. It is, of course, weak in suspense. The major-character point of view is next easiest and is probably the one with which you should start, especially since you will be using material from your own experience or close observation. The minor-character point of view is the trickiest, most subtle, of the three and should, perhaps, be used only when you have a story whose suspense needs strengthening. Which of the three to use depends wholly upon your story material. It is always important, however, to have a focal character in answer to the question "Whose story is this?"

After you have decided on your point of view, stick to it. The reader will be confused, for example, if you start telling a story from one character's point of view and then suddenly interject some unuttered thought of another character. Your reader won't understand the shift.

3. *Dialogue.* Another difficult problem in short stories is the writing of dialogue. It is not true that every short story *must* contain dialogue, but most short-story writers do use it for specific reasons. What are the purposes of dialogue and the reasons for using it?

First, and perhaps most important, dialogue may aid in characterization. In actual life, you rarely know much about someone until you hear him talk. What he says and how he says it are a real indication of personality. Similarly, in a short story, the writer has his characters talk as a certain means of indicating their personalities to the reader. Dialogue furnishes an illusion of reality to imagined characters and makes them seem human and understandable, one of the prime essentials of narrative writing. An expert writer of dialogue can develop characterization adequately without the use of any other means; for example, Ernest Hemingway built up the central characters in several of his stories almost entirely by the use of dialogue.

It is not easy to write good dialogue. What you have characters say may seem wooden and stiff. Some writers have found that they must "talk" their dialogue, listen to it, before they can put it down on paper without artificiality. The heart of the matter is that you must know your characters thoroughly; only thus can you make talk come from them and not from yourself. It is not too much to say that if, after starting to write a story, you have to imagine what your characters will say, they are merely shadows, not real people. If through long observation or vivid imagination you have brought your characters alive, they will act and speak for themselves. Nearly all great writers have gone to great lengths to *learn* their story people; Conrad and Galsworthy, for example, have testified that they acted merely as amanuenses for their characters. Write about people whom you know well or have painstakingly evolved from your imagination and you should be able to set down their vivid, direct, character-revealing talk.

Try to make your characters sound natural. Naturalness is largely a matter of consistency. If you are describing a flighty co-ed who talks almost wholly in slang, do not suddenly make her speak sentences which sound oracular and philosophical. If you do so, you let her get "out of character." The reader will not object to the speech of any character so long as that speech is consistent within itself, keeps "in character," and is actually revelatory. Dialogue which is natural and comes from the character himself is a genuine aid in characterization.

A second reason for the use of dialogue is that, properly employed, it can swiftly advance the action of the story. Two of your characters, for example, may reveal in a brief conversation material which would otherwise require pages for development. Time and again an author can compress and speed up the action by revealing background detail in a few sentences of dialogue.

A third advantage in using dialogue is that it affords variety. Page after page of straight narration unbroken by the separate paragraphing required for individual speeches is likely to become monotonous. Not only that, but the speech of the various characters in a story may be quite dissimilar; the contrast itself affords variety and increases the reader's interest.

Write dialogue for any or all of these three reasons but never use it except to advance the action swiftly, to characterize, or to afford welcome variety If dialogue doesn't accomplish at least one of these purposes, it is useless.

Five problems, largely technical, are involved in the writing of dialogue. Brief mention of them may be helpful.

a. Don't write dialogue in a straight "question-and-answer" or "give-and-take" manner. Wherever possible, "stage-manage" your characters; that is, keep them as well as what they say in view. Throw in an occasional comment on the facial expression of a character as you have him speak; mention that so-and-so knocked out his pipe as he spoke; describe the gestures of someone as he talks, etc. Thus you will keep reminding your reader that not automatons but flesh-and-blood people are talking.

b. Eliminate as many "conversational tags" as you can—such dry and unemphatic phrases as "he said," "I replied," "she answered," etc. The only reason for using them at all is to make clear who is speaking. Since most of the conversation in your stories will probably involve only two people, use tags once or twice and then eliminate them until there is danger of the reader's forgetting who is talking. At best, such phrases are purely directive and, if used too much, merely clutter up the dialogue.

It is advisable, also, not to use tags which are too ornate. In a desire to get away from the dull "he said" or "she replied," you may be tempted to use other words. It is possible to *whisper* something, and perhaps even to *sigh* it, but many of the tags currently used are both flamboyant and illogical. Use sparingly such conversational tags as *ejaculated, hissed, breathed, gurgled, giggled, smiled, laughed, belched, grunted*, etc.

Furthermore, it is not necessary that every conversational tag contain one or more adverbs. In fact, adverbs should be used rarely because a series of expressions such as "he said *excitedly*," "he replied *quickly*," and "he grunted *loudly*" becomes boring and artificial. It is a good rule not to use an adverb with every tag and also never to use more than one adverb ending in *-ly* with any one directive expression.

c. Avoid long speeches in dialogue. "Talk as talk" *can* be made exciting, but ordinarily your reader will tire of a speech which runs for more than a page. It is different if you are having a character relate a story. He is carrying on a monologue; dialogue involves the speech of two people, who, if they are normal, make fairly brief statements. One of the major broadcasting stations has a standing rule that, in dialogue, no character shall speak more than 45 seconds at a time. In order to keep your story going and your readers interested, you should keep this rule in mind.

d. Do not use dialect in a story unless you are thoroughly familiar with it. Properly used, dialect is a powerful aid in characterization and also serves to interest the reader. But incorrectly or inconsistently used, it becomes annoying to the reader and defeats its purposes. Be very certain of your knowledge and your ear for language before you have your characters talk in broken English, or Scottish dialect, or with a New England accent. Ordinarily, you will be well advised to use only the dialect which you know intimately.

e. The content and quality of dialogue are far more important than its mechanics. There are, however, a few basic rules for paragraphing and punctuating dialogue. Unless you are thoroughly familiar with these rules, you should study Section 53.

There are 16 short stories in Book Three. By studying them carefully, you can and will learn much about different kinds of story materials and techniques. Some of them may provide ideas for your own attempts to write this highly developed form. And all of them should increase your awareness of the major differences between really good stories and cheap imitations which flood newsstands and television screens alike.

SUMMARY—MODERN METHODS AND TYPES

Each of the seven types of writing discussed in this chapter makes use of more than one of the four traditional forms of discourse. It is possible to write good examples of each type without conscious resort to these forms, but you must have noticed how much of this chapter is based on Chapter 7.

In freshman English you will probably have occasion to write autobiography, informal essays, and criticism—perhaps also the other four types which have been mentioned. All require careful planning and thought, painstaking writing and rewriting. The formal essay (article) and the short story are especially difficult and require your best efforts because they represent an artistic fusion of smaller types. Although these two types are on the professional level, you can learn much about their technique from attempting to write them. And, having made attempts, you may discover that your capacities for reading published articles and stories critically and understandingly will be increased. That in itself is no small gain.

BOOK TWO
REWRITING

A Handbook of Revision

TO THE STUDENT

When your themes are returned to you by your instructor with numbers in the margins, refer to the rules so numbered in this Handbook of Revision. Study the rules carefully in order to make the necessary revisions and also to avoid making the same errors in later themes.

Or your instructor may prefer to mark your themes using the symbols which appear in the end papers at the end of the book. He will explain which system or combination of systems will be followed.

Everyone makes mistakes of some sort in his writing. Only after a theme has been carefully planned, written, re-written, and proofread is it likely to be correct in all its details of grammar, punctuation, mechanics, spelling, diction (including idiom), and sentence and paragraph structure. You should keep a record of your most common errors in writing and thus make a sort of diagnosis of your major faults. After doing this, you should *systematically* and *conscientiously* study the Handbook sections dealing with your particular weaknesses so as to forestall making errors.

True ease in writing comes from art, not chance,
As those move easiest who have learned to dance.
—ALEXANDER POPE, *An Essay on Criticism*, Part II

PART I

THE SHORTER HANDBOOK

THE SENTENCE

All writing of whatever kind—paragraphs, themes, research papers, personal and business letters, reports, and answers to examination questions—is dependent upon that basic unit of expression, the sentence. Good sentences, in turn, depend upon (1) a knowledge of sentence structure, what might be called "sentence sense," and (2) experience and practice in reading effective sentences and in phrasing and developing your own.

Talking about the qualities of sentences is a necessary but somewhat artificial and involved activity. Actually, good sentences are fully as much a matter of personality and judgment as of rules and requirements. Good sentences will come easily when you know what you want to say, have some interest in what you know or think, and want to share that knowledge and understanding with your reader.

Naturalness and ease should be your goals in sentence writing, but it will help to recall, and to review, the three major characteristics of good sentences. A sentence should be *correct, clear,* and *effective.* These are somewhat vague and general qualities, but they can be pinpointed.

First, what in the structure, the form, of a sentence can prevent its being considered *correct* by customary standards? The three faults usually considered most glaring are *incompleteness* (Section 1), the *comma splice* (Section 2), the *fused sentence* (Section 3). Learning what these three offenses are and how to correct or avoid them will insure at least minimum correctness in, and acceptance for, your sentence structure.

Second, what in the form and phrasing of sentences can come between you and your reader, thwarting communication and leaving your reader baffled or annoyed, or both? *Clearness* in sentence structure is discussed under the following headings: *misplaced modifiers* (Section 4), *dangling modifiers* (Section 5), *split constructions* (Section 6), *faulty parallelism* (Section 7), *faulty coordination* (Section 8), *faulty subordination* (Section 9), *illogical constructions* (Section 10), *consistency* (Section 11), and *reference of pronouns* (Section 12).

If a sentence is *correct* in structure and *clear* in form and purpose, it is adequate, perhaps more than merely adequate. The first 12 sections of this book—which throughout is primarily concerned with correctness and clarity and with offenses against these qualities—contain somewhat overlapping discussions of these important topics.

And yet, correctness and clearness are but minimum characteristics of a good sentence. If you wish to achieve a varied, flexible, pleasing style that will always be appropriate to your purpose and your readers, you should consider other qualities which make writing more than just inoffensive and understandable. That is, you must learn also to write *effectively*. Three major violations of effectiveness are discussed in Section 13 (choppiness), Section 14 (lack of unity), Section 15 (wordiness). Avoiding these three kinds of sentence ineffectiveness is, again, a minimum achievement.

Other characteristics of genuinely effective sentences are adequate *transition* between sentences, *parallelism*, *variety* in length and form, and the *position* and *arrangement* of words in a sentence. Study each of these last-named topics in Part II of this book. Doing so will pay dividends as you acquire ease and naturalness in composing sentences that convey ideas and information with smoothness and grace. See Chapter 4 for additional comment.

For further discussion of the sentence as a basic unit of expression, see in Part II the following entries: *Sentence, arrangement of content; Sentence, grammatical structure of; Sentence, meaning and purpose of.*

1. INCOMPLETENESS (SENTENCE FRAGMENT)

The word *sentence* can mean "a stated opinion." By this definition, all words, or groups of words, which "make sense" to your reader or listener can be called sentences. But remember these two requirements for a *complete* sentence: (1) it must have both a subject and a predicate (verb) which actually appear or are clearly implied (understood); (2) it must not begin with a connecting word such as *although, as, because, before,* and *while* unless an independent clause follows immediately in the same construction.

This is a complete sentence: "Dick has bought a new jacket." Omit *Dick* (subject) or *has bought* (verb) and not enough remains to make a full sentence. Also, substituting for *has bought* a compound participle such as *having bought* produces an incomplete statement: "Dick having bought a new jacket." If a word such as *although* precedes *Dick*, the sentence is incomplete for another reason: the clause, "Although Dick has bought a new jacket," expresses an idea, but it depends on some other statement and is not capable of standing alone. If you don't like Dick, you might write: "Although Dick has bought a new jacket, he still looks like a hayseed."

1a. *Avoid setting off a phrase as a sentence.*

A phrase is only part of a full sentence. It should be attached to, or should be expressed within, the sentence of which it is a part. Or the phrase should be made complete in itself by adding what is needed, usually a subject, or verb, or both.

Incorrect	My last year in high school I studied for hours every night. *Getting ready for college entrance tests.*
Correct	My last year in high school I studied for hours every night, *getting ready for college entrance tests.*
	My last year in high school I studied for hours every night. *I was getting ready for college entrance tests.*
Incorrect	*Winter being mild last year.* I had to start mowing the lawn weeks earlier than usual.
Correct	*Winter being mild last year,* I had to start mowing the lawn weeks earlier than usual.
	Winter was mild last year, and I had to start mowing the lawn weeks earlier than usual.

1b. *Avoid setting off a dependent clause as a sentence.*

Adverbial and adjective clauses can never stand alone; they always *depend* upon something else for completeness. Correcting a dependent clause

Incorrect	I had no money for the trip. *When suddenly Jack paid me what he had borrowed.* [Adverbial]
	Because the course is difficult. We do not advise you to enroll in it. [Adverbial]
	Dick has talked with Coach Barnett. *Who thinks Dick's prospects for making the team are good.* [Adjective]
	Sue lived in Akron for five years. *From which her family moved to Atlanta.* [Adjective]
Correct	I had no money for the trip. Suddenly Jack paid me what he had borrowed.
	Because the course is difficult, we do not advise you to enroll in it.
	The course is difficult. We do not advise you to enroll in it.
	Dick has talked with Coach Barnett. He thinks Dick's prospects for making the team are good.
	Sue lived in Akron for five years, from which her family moved to Atlanta.

fragment often involves no change in wording; sometimes, changing a capital to a small letter and a period to a comma or to no mark at all will correct the error. Sometimes, you may prefer to make a dependent adverbial clause into an independent clause by omitting a subordinating conjunction and make an independent clause of an adjective clause by changing the relative pronoun to a personal one.

1c. *Avoid starting a statement with one construction and then stopping or shifting to another.*

You may begin a statement and then, forgetting where you and your thoughts are, change direction and construction, keep adding words, but stop before giving meaning to the words with which you started. In such an unfinished construction you must examine carefully what you have written to discover what is missing.

Incomplete	Some of the students from abroad, not being used to central heating, and also wearing heavy clothes.
Improved	Some of the students from abroad, not being used to central heating, and also wearing heavy clothes, were often uncomfortably warm.

1d. *Use only justifiable sentence fragments.*

Grammatically defined, a sentence consists of a subject and predicate (verb) and expresses a complete thought. However, many kinds of statements convey a full thought without an actual or implied subject or verb. Such expressions as *Ouch, Hello, Good-by, Never again, But to continue* can and do make clear, often effective, statements. Fragments often appear in short stories and novels because they are mirrors of normal conversation.

Context is frequently important in asking and answering questions and in providing details after a general statement. The following dialogue contains several fragments which are fully justifiable:

> "Where did you get those shoes?"
> "At Finchley's."
> "On sale?"
> "But of course."
> "How much?"
> "My secret, for now."
> "Be a clam, then."

You may complain that your instructor marks all fragments (also known as "period faults") as incorrect, even though you may claim to use them for some stylistic effect. Most teachers wish students to walk before they run; many will permit you to use fragments *after* you have clearly demonstrated your knowledge of sentence completeness.

2. COMMA SPLICE

Writing correctly is difficult now and always has been. You are required to write complete sentences with no fragments, not an easy task. But you are also expected to write full sentences *one at a time*. When your mind is racing or wandering, this is no simple chore.

Like the sentence fragment (period fault), the *comma splice* may be considered both an error in sentence construction and a flaw in punctuation. But the splice is no ordinary misuse of the comma; it consists of using a comma to join what really are two sentences. That is, a comma splices (joins) statements which should be separated by a period or joined by a semicolon, a colon, or a conjunction *and* a comma.

2a. *Avoid unjustifiable comma splices.*

The comma splice, or "comma fault," appears in several forms:

(1) Two statements which are related by content but which have little or no actual grammatical relationship.

(2) Two related statements, the second of which begins with a personal pronoun whose antecedent is in the first.

(3) Two related statements, the second of which begins with a demonstrative pronoun or adjective (*this, that, these*, etc.).

(4) Two statements, the second of which contains, or begins with, a conjunctive adverb (*however, then*, etc.).

In the order of faults given above, consider these comma splices:

> A meeting of the Sigma Society is scheduled for tonight, many important items are on the agenda.
> The physician examined the patient carefully, he did not say a word.
> Drive carefully when you near the bridge, this is very narrow.
> I was late for the lecture, however, Mr. James did not scold me.

The comma splice error can be corrected in several ways:

(1) Use a period after the first statement and a capital letter at the beginning of the second.

(2) Use a semicolon between the statements.

(3) Subordinate one of the statements and retain the comma.

(4) Insert a conjunction between statements, or as a substitute for the conjunctive adverb, and retain the comma.

Each of the four comma splices above can be corrected by more than one of these methods. However, you should avoid a series of short, jerky sentences; you should never attempt to show a cause-and-effect relationship where it does not exist and without proper subordination.

2b. *Use a justifiable comma splice only when it is effective and appropriate.*

An unjustifiable comma splice is a serious error, always confusing to your readers. An occasional comma splice, however, can be both suitable and stylistically valid. Many writers and professional editors carefully avoid all comma splices of whatever kind; your instructor may urge you to do likewise. Even so, a case can be made for using a comma in such constructions as these:

> I worked, I struggled, I failed.
> That is Alice, this is Betty.
> We are not going to the library, we are going to class.

3. FUSED SENTENCES

A sentence should express only one thought or a group of closely related thoughts. A violation of this principle is writing two complete sentences with no mark of punctuation whatever between them. This serious grammatical error confuses a reader because the writer of a fused sentence has not indicated in any way where one complete thought ends and another begins. Some instructors consider the fused sentence an even more serious flaw than the comma splice: the writer of a spliced sentence has at least realized the need for punctuation of some sort, even though what he uses is inadequate and incorrect.

3a. *Avoid writing two sentences with no punctuation between them.*

A sentence is, or should be, a complete and meaningful statement and must usually be followed by a terminal mark, a full stop: period, question mark, exclamation point.

Incorrect	Late that same month the dam broke thousands of people were left homeless in the resulting flood. After two days they left London for Copenhagen this city is the capital of Denmark.

It is possible to understand these two fused sentences, but lack of separation between their parts causes at least momentary confusion. Each may be written as two separate statements with a period between them. Or, if you wish to connect their ideas more closely, you may use punctuation which is not terminal.

Correct	Late that same month the dam broke. Thousands of people were left homeless in the resulting flood. After two days they left London for Copenhagen; this city is the capital of Denmark. After two days they left London for Copenhagen, the capital of Denmark.

3b. *Avoid correcting a fused sentence by placing a comma between its parts.*

Sentences should never be fused, run together. But to separate them with a comma is to make a "frying pan" error ("out of the frying pan into the fire"). A comma splice is almost as serious an offense as a fused sentence. A comma is insufficient in a sentence such as this: "He was in California last year he lived in San Diego." After the word *year* you may *not* use a comma. Your instructor may insist that you use a period or may permit a semicolon, colon, or dash. But do not use the "frying pan."

4. MISPLACED MODIFIERS

Words in an English sentence have meaning largely because of their position. That is, they have one meaning in one position, another meaning in another position, and little or no meaning in still another position. Some linguists maintain that the true basis of English grammar is word order. "My *first* roommate's name was Bill" has a meaning different from "My roommate's *first* name was Bill." Again, changing the position of only one word results in ideas quite unlike in these sentences: "I was invited to a dance *tonight.*" "I was *tonight* invited to a dance."

Try to keep related words together so that your readers may see the connection you have in mind; try to place every modifier so that logically and naturally it is associated with the word or phrase which it modifies.

4a. *Avoid a "squinting modifier."*

A modifier "squints" when it "looks both ways" and may refer to either of two parts of a sentence. Consider this sentence: "The person who can do this *well* deserves praise."

Well may modify either *can do* or *deserves*. You should revise. One way to clear up the confusion is to add *certainly* after *well*. Now the adverb *well* modifies *can do*, and the adverb *certainly* applies to *deserves*. Such a construction involves *juncture*, a term which you should consult in Part II.

Take another example: "The repairman who does his work quietly *from the point of view of the housewife* is worthy of praise." The "squinting" italicized phrases should appear at the beginning or end of the sentence, which will still be wordy and a little awkward but at least understandable.

4b. *Place clearly such words as* even, hardly, not, only, scarcely.

Words such as these are usually associated with the word or phrase immediately following or preceding. In this sentence, "He hardly has enough strength for the work," *hardly* may be thought to modify *has;* it should logically modify the adjective *enough*. To remove any possible doubt, write: "He has hardly enough strength for the work."

Here is a sentence containing eleven words: "Only the foreman told me to finish the job before noon." In it the word *only* can appear in every position from one through eleven: "The *only* foreman told me . . . ," "The foreman *only* told me . . . ," "The foreman told *only* me . . . ," "The foreman told me *only* . . . ," and so on. The position of *only* will provide eleven somewhat different meanings for the sentence. (Note that placing it in the sixth position causes a split infinitive, perhaps not a very sound idea. See Section 6a.)

4c. *Place clearly phrases and clauses.*

By failing to place phrases as near as they should have to words modified, writers of the following hardly expressed what presumably they intended to:

Last month the Capitol was closed for alterations to all visitors. [*To all visitors* should appear after *closed;* the resulting sentence will be no gem, but at least confusion will disappear.]

WANTED: A small apartment by two young businesswomen freshly painted and newly plastered. [True, the girls may have been both painted and plastered, but do you think that is what the writer meant to say?]

The President discussed everyday affairs and people whom you and I know *as simply as a little child.* [Place the italicized phrase after *discussed* or at the beginning of the sentence.]

5. DANGLING MODIFIERS

Any misplaced word, phrase, or clause dangles in the sense that it hangs loosely within a sentence. The word which another word or group of words is intended to modify should never be taken for granted; it should be expressed and it should be placed so that your readers can easily make the intended association.

The term *dangling* applies especially to verbal phrases and elliptical clauses, the correct position of which depends upon logical, careful thinking.

5a.   *Avoid dangling verbal phrases.*

Sentences containing dangling verbal phrases may be corrected in three ways: (1) by expanding the verbal phrase to a dependent clause; (2) by supplying the substantive (noun or pronoun) which the dangling phrase *should* modify; (3) by placing the construction so near the supplied substantive that no confusion is possible.

Incorrect	*Walking down the aisle,* the curtain rose. [Participial phrase]
	To play tennis well, a good racquet is needed. [Infinitive phrase]
	By exercising every day, your health will improve. [Gerund phrase]
Correct	While we were walking down the aisle, the curtain rose.
	Walking down the aisle, John saw the curtain rise.
	We, walking down the aisle, saw the curtain rise. [This revision is no great improvement because it widely separates subject and verb. See Section 6c.]

The two other incorrect sentences given may also be improved by one of the three methods suggested. Most of us don't too much mind making an error, but we do dislike being thought incoherent or ludicrous, both of which these sentences definitely are.

When a verbal phrase is used to denote a general action rather than a specific one, it is *not* considered a dangling modifier: "*Considering everything,* his suggestion was reasonable."

5b.   *Avoid dangling elliptical clauses.*

Ellipsis means "an omission." An elliptical clause is one without a subject, or verb, or both; it dangles unless the implied (understood) subject is the same as that of the main clause.

Incorrect	*When 19 years old,* my grandmother died . . .
	While working last night, the lights went out.
	Before thoroughly warmed up, you should not race a motor.

To correct such confused sentences, insert in the dangling clause the needed subject and verb, or change the subject (or subject and verb) in the main clause:

> When I was 19 years old, my grandmother died.
> When 19 years old, I grieved because my grandmother had died.

While I was working last night, the lights went out.
Before it is thoroughly warmed up, you should not race a motor.
You should thoroughly warm up a motor before you race it.

6. SPLIT CONSTRUCTIONS

Separating, or splitting, closely related parts in a sentence is not always incorrect. But splitting verbs in a verb phrase, the two parts of an infinitive, a preposition and its object, and other closely allied elements often results in awkwardness and lack of clarity. Whenever possible, you should keep logically related elements together.

6a. *Avoid splitting an infinitive.*

When a word, phrase, or clause comes between the sign of the infinitive, *to,* and a verb, the construction is called a *split infinitive.* Reputable speakers and writers occasionally split an infinitive; consequently, this error is no longer considered as grave as it once was. Also, on rare occasions, you must split an infinitive to make clear and exact what you have in mind. For example, in this sentence, "Martha wants *to really see* Tod in person," moving *really* to any other place in the sentence would change the meaning or weaken the effectiveness of the sentence.

Normally, however, no good reason exists for putting an adverb or phrase or other group of words between *to* and a verb. "He requested us to *as soon as possible* leave the building" would be clearer and more natural if the italicized words were moved to the end of the sentence.

6b. *Avoid separating the parts of a verb phrase.*

An auxiliary verb and main verb form a frequent pattern in English. Splitting such a verb phrase is rarely effective and usually results in an awkward construction. In sentences such as the following, the italicized words should be brought together:

There was the boy we *had* before we left *seen* in the park. (There was the boy we had seen in the park before we left.)
This building *has,* although it is hard to believe, *been* here for more than a century. (This building has been . . . *or* Although it is hard to believe, this building has been . . .)

6c. *Avoid the unnecessary separation of subject and verb, preposition and object, and other closely related sentence elements.*

Separation of such elements is occasionally justifiable. But in awkward and generally ineffective sentences like the following, the italicized elements should be brought together:

Jack, as soon as he heard the question, *raised his hand.*
Mabel crept *into,* although she was terrified, *the frail canoe.*
Mary *asked,* even before I could finish, *what I really meant.*

6d. *Place coordinate elements together.*

When two clauses or phrases of approximately equal strength and importance are used in a sentence, avoid putting one at the beginning of the sentence and the other at the end. The italicized phrases and clauses in these sentences should be brought together and be joined by *and:*

> *Although he was an ardent golfer,* he could never break 90, *although he practiced daily.*
> *With fair weather,* we should have a pleasant journey, *with good luck.*

7. FAULTY PARALLELISM

In writing, the word *parallelism* suggests "similarity," "close resemblance." When two or more ideas in a sentence are related in form and purpose, they can and should be phrased in the same grammatical form:

> Jill is *sweet* but *noisy.* [Words]
> Gray loves to read both *at home* and *at school.* [Phrases]
> Joy was shocked when she discovered *that one tire was flat* and *that the jack was missing.* [Clauses]

7a. *Sentence elements coordinate in rank should be parallel in structure.*

An infinitive phrase should be coordinate with an infinitive phrase, a dependent clause with a dependent clause, and so on:

> Harry liked *to swim* and *to fish.* [*Not* "Harry liked to swim and fishing." But the second *to* can be omitted, if desired.]
> Ned hoped *that he might earn a good reputation* and *that he might make a lot of money.* [*Not* "Ned hoped that he might earn a good reputation and to make a lot of money."]

7b. *Avoid partial parallelism.*

Make certain that *each* element in a series is similar in form and structure to *all* others in the same series:

> Steve has worked as a camp counselor, tennis coach, and has served as a bank teller. [Revise this sentence to read: "Steve has worked as a camp counselor, tennis coach, and bank teller."]
> That TV play was dramatic, exciting, and had an involved plot. [Revise this sentence to read: "That TV play was dramatic, exciting, and involved in plot."]

7c. *Avoid misleading parallelism.*

You should not use the same structural form for sentence elements of unequal value. If you do, you will mislead your readers. You should be especially careful in handling a series of elements which may appear to modify the same element when they are not actually parallel.

Ineffective	They left quickly, and they had a good automobile.
	For your sake, for $25 I will assist you.

	We bought that set from a local dealer and with a good walnut finish.
Improved	They left quickly in a good automobile.
	For your sake, I will assist you to the extent of $25.
	We bought that set from a local dealer; it has a good walnut finish.

7d. *Sentence elements following correlative conjunctions should be parallel in form.*

The four common pairs of correlatives are *both–and, either–or, neither–nor,* and *not only–but also.* Each member of each of these pairs should be followed immediately by the same grammatical form: two words, two similar phrases, two similar clauses.

Faulty	I *neither* have the time *nor* the money to make the trip.
	Either you can read the story at the library *or* in your own room.
	Not only when I am tired *but also* sick, I like to watch TV.
Improved	I have *neither* the time *nor* the money to make the trip.
	You can read the story *either* at the library *or* in your own room.
	Not only when I am tired *but also* when I am sick, I like to watch TV.

(See *Parallelism* in Part II.)

8. FAULTY COORDINATION

The adjective *coordinate* means "of equal importance or rank." If you think carefully, you can express your ideas in constructions which will show their varying importance; you should subordinate minor ideas so that important ones may be emphasized.

Avoid excessive coordination because it is monotonous, often childish, frequently ineffective. Avoid inaccurate and illogical coordination so as not to give your readers hazy and incorrect impressions of the relationship of your ideas and their relative degrees of significance.

8a. *Avoid stringy, "run-on" sentences.*

Do not overwork the compound sentence. An immature writer, such as a college student is striving not to be, might say "We bought a new TV set, and it was a beauty, and it had a 21-inch screen." Such a sentence is strung out, it runs on and on. As a mature writer, you should learn to reduce predication, that is, to convert an independent to a dependent clause, change a phrase to a word, etc.: "We bought a beautiful new TV set with a 21-inch screen." (See Section 15a.)

8b. *Avoid "seesaw" sentences.*

"Seesaw" sentences take their name from a familiar play device (a balanced plank or board) enjoyed by children and by some adults. Such sentences move alternately up and down and quickly become monotonous. A passage such as this cries out for reduced predication (see Section 8a):

> We thought of going to a dance, but we didn't have enough money. Next we decided to take a walk, but a heavy rain prevented that. We bought some soft drinks, and we went to John's house to watch TV. Soon John started snoring, and I became bored and restless.

8c. *Avoid inaccurate coordination.*

Use the *exact* coordinating conjunction required to relate two sentence elements. Do not use *and* if *but* is the exact connective, *but* for *or*, etc.:

> Joe wanted to go to the game, *but* [not *and*] he had to study.
> We had an interruption, *or* [not *but*] we would have finished sooner.

8d. *Avoid false coordination: do not join a relative clause to its principal clause by* and, but, *or* or.

And, but, or, and other coordinating conjunctions may properly connect only elements of equal rank. The most frequent and most distressing violation of this principle is the so-called "and which" construction. You should never use *and which, but which, and who, but who,* unless you have written a preceding "which clause" or "who clause."

> This is a beautiful tennis court, *and which* we enjoy using. [The simplest method of correcting this sentence is to omit *and* and also the comma, since the clause is restrictive. Or you can supply a preceding "which clause": "This is a beautiful tennis court which is open to all and which we enjoy using." Even better, cut out some of the deadwood: "We enjoy playing tennis on this beautiful court."]

8e. *Avoid overusing* so *as a conjunction.*

Even though *so* is a good and useful word, it comes to mind so easily and so often (have you noticed?) that it is often overused. You can avoid creating the juvenile effect caused by overuse of *so* if for it you occasionally substitute such a connective as *accordingly, so that, therefore, thus.* One or more of these connectives could substitute for *so* in such a series of monotonous statements as this:

> He didn't have a date, *so* he didn't plan to go to the dance.
> He began to feel lonely in his room, *so* he went to the library.
> He soon grew bored, fell asleep, and *so* got little work done.

9. FAULTY SUBORDINATION

The term *subordination* means "the act of placing in a lower class or rank." When a writer selects one idea for primary emphasis in a sentence, he automatically decides to subordinate others in the same sentence. If he doesn't, his sentences will appear in primer style like those of children just learning to talk. (See Section 8a and *Coordination* and *Subordination* in Part II.)

Being able to distinguish a main idea from a subordinate one is a genuine sign of maturity. Even though you can detect what is probably a main idea and what is subordinate, you will still have trouble unless you can distinguish between main and dependent clauses, between clauses and phrases, between phrases and single words. (See Section 15a.)

Careful, thoughtful, mature writing normally contains much subordination. But errors in the use of subordination are all too easy to make. The following are some major pitfalls to avoid.

9a. *Avoid putting a coordinate idea in a subordinate form.*

Undesirable	He was short and fat, *while* his sister was tall and slender.
	Born in Ohio in 1935, he became a resident of Utah in 1960.
Improved	He was short and fat, *but* his sister was tall and slender.
	He was short and fat; his sister was tall and slender.
	He was short and fat, *whereas* his sister was tall and slender.
	He was born in Ohio in 1935 *but* became a resident of Utah in 1960.
	He was born in Ohio in 1935 *and* became a resident of Utah in 1960.

9b. *Avoid putting the main idea of a sentence in a subordinate form; avoid putting a subordinate idea in a main clause.*

Upside-down subordination (an accurate, expressive term) exists when an idea of less importance is placed in a main clause and a more important idea in a subordinate clause. Sometimes it is difficult to determine which is which. Usually, the most dramatic incident and the effect, rather than the causes, are major ideas. Preliminaries, such as time and place, are usually minor (or at least less important) considerations.

Ineffective	We were getting tired of walking when suddenly we saw an oncoming car.
	I was halfway across the river when I saw a water moccasin.
Improved	When we were getting tired of walking, we saw an oncoming car.
	When (just as) I was halfway across the river, I saw a water moccasin.

9c. *Avoid excessive subordination.*

Sentence elements should be suitably linked but they should not be built like an accordion or, to vary the simile, like stairs—one step attached to the one just above.

Ineffective	These are orchids which were grown in Hawaii, where there is an excellent climate, and which were flown here today.
Improved	These orchids, grown in Hawaii where there is an excellent climate, were flown here today.
	These orchids, grown in Hawaii's excellent climate, were flown here today.

10. ILLOGICAL CONSTRUCTIONS

Construction in sentence writing means the grouping of words with other words or word formations. An *illogical construction* refers to a grouping of words which (1) is contrary to reason, (2) violates some principle of regularity, (3) fails to make good sense, (4) omits an important word or words, (5) adds an element which has no grammatical function, (6) substitutes a dependent clause functioning as one part of speech for another. No wonder there are so many types of illogical constructions: our minds are often inadequate, but they are all we have for thinking.

You can expect your readers to give careful attention, but you cannot expect them to untangle mixed and involved constructions or to correct your mistakes in logic. (Your instructor will do precisely this, but we are trying to avoid the penalty he will inflict for having to do so.)

The six kinds of illogical and mixed constructions just mentioned can be broken into 10 groups for careful examination.

10a. *Do not omit a necessary verb.*

In both speaking and writing, we often omit words without necessarily being illogical or unclear. "He always has worked hard and always will [work hard]" is understandable without the bracketed words. But it is doubtful that the following sentence could be considered complete: "The floor is swept and the dishes washed." In this sentence, *is* is understood to accompany *washed*. But "dishes is washed" is wrong. We should write: "The floor is swept and the dishes *are* washed."

> I never have and probably never will write good letters. [The word *written* should be added after *have*.]

10b. *Include all words essential for the clear expression of meaning.*

If a necessary article, pronoun, conjunction, or preposition is omitted, your meaning will not be clear or, worse, may be misinterpreted:

> The President and Chief Executive received us. [This sentence may mean that one person is both President and Chief Executive. If you mean to indicate two people, add *the* after *and*.]
> I have interest and regard for your work. [Add *in* after *interest*.]
> She asked that question be repeated. [Add another *that* before *question*.]

10c. *Do not omit words necessary in a comparison.*

Doubtful	He is so wealthy.
	Your theme was the greatest success.
	His feet are bigger than any boy in town.
Clearer	He is quite wealthy.
	He is so wealthy that he never needs to think about money.
	Your theme was a great success.
	Your theme was the greatest success of any received thus far.
	His feet are bigger than those of any other boy in town.

10d. *Avoid confusing "blends."*

Unless you are careful, certain blends may creep into your writing. *Regardless* and *irrespective* are good words but are often faultily blended into *irregardless. In spite of* and *despite* may be illogically blended into *despite of:* "Despite of what you say, I am not convinced." Blending *where* (meaning *at* or *in which*) with *at which* results in expressions such as "*Where* does she live *at?*" and "The town *where* I live *in.*"

10e. *Avoid a mixed or double comparison.*

A confused construction frequently occurs when a writer tries to include two comparisons in the same statement. Good usage permits a double comparison in the same sentence but only when the second appears after the first has been completed.

Illogical	The Battle of Stalingrad was *one of the greatest if not the greatest* single conflict of all time.
Preferable	The Battle of Stalingrad was *one of the greatest* single conflicts of all time, *if not the greatest.*

10f. *Make clear whether an object or term being compared is or is not part of a class or group.*

Avoid including within the class or group the object or term being compared, if it is part of the group. Use the word *other.*

Illogical	Helen is prettier than any girl in the school.
Clear	Helen is prettier than any other girl in the school.

When the superlative degree is involved, do not use *other;* this degree indicates that the object compared is included within the group.

Illogical	Helen is the prettiest of all the other girls in the school.
Clear	Helen is the prettiest of all the girls in the school.

10g. *Avoid confusing double negatives.*

Everyday speech is filled with such expressions as "haven't scarcely" and "can't help but." These are forms of what is called the *double negative,* two negative terms in the same statement. The double negative was used repeatedly by Chaucer, Shakespeare, and many other great writers of the past. It still appears regularly in correct French. Double negatives in English today, however, are considered out of style and unacceptable.

You are not likely to write, or often hear, such expressions as "I didn't see nobody" and "I didn't get none." You should avoid such commonly used and less obviously illiterate expressions as "I did *not* have *but* two," "one *can't* help *but*," "*not scarcely* enough," and "*not hardly* any."

10h. *Avoid using an adverbial clause as a noun clause.*

Dependent clauses function as parts of speech; to substitute an adverbial clause for a noun clause is as illogical as to use an adverb in place of a noun.

Dubious	*Because she had no new dress* was the reason Joy stayed at home.
	Eleanor noted *where the paper says* that it will snow tonight.
Correct	Joy stayed at home *because she had no new dress.*
	That she had no new dress was the reason Joy stayed at home.
	Eleanor noted *that the paper says* it will snow tonight.

10i. *Avoid using an adverbial clause in place of a noun or noun phrase.*

This suggestion is closely related to that given in Section 10h and is made for the same reason. *When, where,* and *because* clauses are chief offenders in this form of illogicality.

Dubious	Stealing is *when* (is *where*) one takes the property of another without permission and with stealth.
	My high fever was *because* I was in a weak condition.
Clear	Stealing is taking the property of another without permission and with stealth.
	Stealing is the act of taking the property . . .
	My weak condition caused my high fever.
	That I was in a weak condition was the cause . . .

10j. *Use a noun clause, not a sentence, as the subject or complement of* is *and* was.

A quotation may be the subject or complement of *is* and *was:*

"When I have fears that I may cease to be" is a line from Keats' famous poem.

Ordinarily, however, you should convert a sentence into a noun clause (or, rarely, a noun phrase) in this construction:

Illogical	I had lost my nerve was the reason I did not try.
	Fred's only hope is he will get his allowance today.
Improved	The reason that I did not try was that I had lost my nerve.
	Fred's only hope is that he will get his allowance today.
	Fred has only one hope: getting his allowance today.

11. CONSISTENCY

Consistency in a sentence means that its parts are in agreement, are similar, and that they must remain so unless there is good reason for shifting them. You should be consistent (avoid shifts) in tense, subject and voice, number, person or class of pronouns, and figures of speech.

11a. *Avoid unnecessary shifts in tense.*

Tense (see Section 67) indicates the time of a verb: past, present, future, present perfect, etc. Do not shift unnecessarily from past time to present or from present to past or back and forth between the two:

Jill was striding along when suddenly a motorcycle turned the corner. It *careens* wildly down the street, twisting as if its rider *is* unconscious. Jill leaped to the sidewalk. [Change *careens* to *careened, is* to *were.*]

11b. *Avoid aimlessly shifting the subject or voice in a sentence.*

Voice (see Section 68) is a term indicating whether the subject is acting (active) or is acted upon (passive). Consistency in voice within a sentence usually removes a major cause of shifts in subject. Ordinarily you should have one subject in a sentence and should use one voice (the active voice is usually more effective). After you select them, stay with them throughout the sentence.

| Faulty | The furnace burns little coal, and Joe says it is fully reliable. As you look across the street, lighted windows can be seen. |
| Improved | Joe says that the furnace burns little coal and is fully reliable. As you look across the street, you can see lighted windows. |

11c. *Avoid unnecessary shifts in number.*

A common error in the use of number is a thoughtless shift from plural to singular or from singular to plural, or failure to make pronouns and antecedents agree in number.

| Faulty | A small child can be a joy, but *they require* constant attention. [Change *they* to *it* or *he* or *she, require* to *requires*.] If men really try their best, *he is* bound to succeed. [Change *he* to *they* and *is* to *are*.] |

11d. *Avoid shifting the person or class of pronouns.*

A shift in pronoun reference violates the general rule that pronouns and antecedents must agree in person. The most common occurrence of this fault is shifting from the third person to the second.

| Faulty | If *one* tries hard enough, *you* will usually succeed. [*One* is an indefinite pronoun in the third person; *you* is a personal pronoun in the second person. The sentence should read: "If you try hard enough, you . . ." or "If one tries hard enough, he . . ."] |

11e. *Avoid shifts in figures of speech.*

You should not change suddenly from literal speech to figurative language, or vice versa (see Section 26). When you do use a figure of speech, you should not suddenly shift the figure. By not sustaining one figure of speech, we obtain such an inconsistent and confused statement as this:

She got into a rut and felt all at sea when she lost her job. [Whoever *she* is has trouble, but we can be of little help because we are laughing too hard at the weird description of her predicament. Perhaps this will be an improvement: "She felt depressed and uncertain when she lost her job."]

12. REFERENCE OF PRONOUNS

The word *reference* is used with pronouns and their antecedents to indicate the relationship between them. A pronoun *refers* to an antecedent; the latter is *referred* to by a pronoun. The relationship of a pronoun to its antecedent must be clear and unmistakable.

12a.   *Avoid double reference for a pronoun.*

Double reference occurs when there are two possible antecedents for a pronoun. Such ambiguous reference can be corrected by (1) repeating the antecedent, (2) using a synonym for the antecedent, (3) changing sentence construction.

Not clear	She took the eggs from the cartons and placed *them* on the counter.
Better	She took the eggs from the cartons and placed the cartons [or the *eggs*, if that is what you mean] on the counter.
	She took the eggs from the cartons and placed the latter on the counter.
	She removed the eggs and placed the cartons on the counter.

12b.   *Avoid implied reference for a pronoun.*

Implied reference occurs when an antecedent is not actually expressed and must be inferred from the context (what precedes or follows). The most common form of implied reference is using *this, that, what,* and *which* to refer to an entire preceding statement rather than to some specific word (usually a noun) in that statement. Such a fault may be corrected by (1) summing up the idea of a preceding statement in a noun which then becomes the antecedent, (2) making the statements coordinate, (3) rephrasing the sentence.

Not clear	Her sister is a nurse. *This* is the profession she intends to enter.
Better	Her sister is a nurse. *Nursing* is the profession she intends to enter.
	Her sister is a nurse; she intends to become one too.
	Because her sister is a nurse, she intends to study nursing also.

12c.   *Avoid vague reference for a pronoun.*

Every pronoun (especially *that, these, which, those, it*) should refer clearly to its antecedent or should be made clear by some other statement in the sentence.

Not clear	Janet's remark gave Joe *that* sinking feeling.
	In this editorial *it* states that taxes are increasing.
Better	Janet's remark gave Joe a sinking feeling.
	Janet's remark depressed Joe.
	Janet's remark gave Joe that sinking feeling which comes from despair.
	This editorial states that taxes are increasing.
	That taxes are increasing is the theme of this editorial.

12d.   *Avoid an indefinite use of* you, it, they.

In informal speech it is permissible to use such an expression as "*You* can always try harder," even though no particular person or group is addressed. Everyday speech is filled with statements such as "*It* says on the radio it will snow tonight" and "In this town *they* have plenty of fun."

In writing, however, it is preferable to use *one* or *person* rather than *you* if you wish to refer to no particular individual or group. Also, *it* should usually have an appropriate antecedent, unless you are using the impersonal *it* ("it is raining"). *They* should always have a definite antecedent.

Undesirable	When you become a Girl Scout, *you* learn many interesting facts. In this TV program *it* showed the horrors of drug addiction. *They* say that men prefer blondes.
Better	When one [or a *girl*] becomes a Girl Scout, *she* learns many interesting facts. This TV program showed the horrors of drug addiction. Some people say that men prefer blondes.

13. CHOPPINESS

An occasional short sentence is effective. A *series* of short sentences not only is monotonous but often gives unwanted emphasis to some comparatively unimportant ideas which should be subordinated. See *Variety in Sentence Structure*, p. 443.

13a. *Avoid writing a series of short, jerky sentences.*

The remedy: separate ideas should be properly coordinated and subordinated and placed together in a longer, unified sentence.

Faulty	It was dark. She was afraid to enter the room. She called her brother. He did not answer her. She was more terrified than ever.
Better	Because it was dark, she was afraid to enter the room. When she called her brother, he did not answer her, and consequently she was more terrified than ever.

13b. *Avoid writing a series of sentences containing short, jerky independent clauses.*

"Correcting" a series of short, jerky sentences by combining them into compound sentences is a "frying pan" error. Short, jerky clauses can be as ineffective as short, jerky sentences. (See Section 8b.)

Faulty	I work at a supermarket, and my job is stocking shelves. I have many friends there, but perhaps my best friend is Warren. He has a good disposition, which I don't.
Improved	I work at a supermarket where I stock shelves. Of all my friends there, Warren, who has the good disposition I lack, is perhaps the best.

14. UNITY

Unity means "oneness, singleness of purpose." A sentence should contain a single thought or a group of closely related thoughts. Unity has little to do with length; a long sentence may be unified and a short one ununified. This long sentence forms a unit of thought: "Although Lee liked her fellow employees, especially Mary Ellen and Harvey, she was tired of working and decided to resign and marry Henry." But this short sentence lacks unity: "Mary Ellen was a good worker, and she had a friend named Henry."

14a. *Avoid rambling sentences with too many details.*

Faulty	He was reared in Southport, a village in Connecticut, which has only about 1,000 inhabitants, but which has a famous yacht club, three churches, an excellent public library, several tree-lined residential streets, and a good motel, being located just off U. S. Highway 95.
Improved	He was reared in Southport, Connecticut, a village of about 1,000 inhabitants which is located just off U. S. Highway 95. Southport has several tree-lined residential streets, an excellent public library, a motel, three churches, and a famous yacht club.

14b. *Avoid placing unrelated ideas in the same sentence.*

You can sometimes achieve unity in a sentence containing unrelated ideas by showing some evidence of relationship or by subordinating one idea. If the ideas are not closely related and relationship cannot logically be indicated, place them in separate sentences. If no relationship whatever is evident, omit one of the ideas.

Faulty	His father was a jolly man, and he was a good doctor.
Improved	His father, a jolly man who cheered up his patients, was a good doctor.
	His father was a jolly man. He was also a good doctor.

15. CONCISENESS

Concise means "brief," "condensed." In sentence structure, *conciseness* implies that much is said in few words. Good writing results from a wealth of ideas and economy in words, not from scarcity of thought and a flood of words. Even fairly well-constructed sentences can be improved by removing nonessential words, by using direct word patterns, by economizing on modifiers. A sentence such as "My typing had the effect of making the boss regret the decision which had led him to hire me" can be shortened to "My typing made the boss regret hiring me"—a reduction from 19 words to eight.

Concise sentences are not necessarily effective, but a wordy sentence always loses some of its appeal and emphasis because of the extra load it carries. Particularly useless and ineffective is the thoughtless repetition of an idea already expressed: "audible to the ear," "complete monopoly," "four-cornered square," "fellow classmates," "endorse on the back," "six in number."

Our conversation is normally more wordy than formal writing should be because in speaking we do not have, or take, time to be economical and direct. Here are a few expressions which we probably use often in speaking but which should be made concise in writing:

Reduce these	*To these*
a certain length of time	a certain time
are of the opinion	believe
I would appreciate it if	please
in the event that	if
it is interesting to note that	[begin with the word after *that*]
on condition that	if
at the present time	now

Conciseness is such an important contribution to sentence effectiveness that it is also treated in several entries in Part II: *circumlocution, deadwood,* and *wordiness,* especially. But the single most helpful means of making sentences effectively concise is reducing predication. See *Conciseness,* Chapter 4, p. 58.

15a. *Learn to reduce predication.*

Reducing predication means decreasing the number of words used to make a statement. Consider these suggestions:

(1) Combine two short sentences into one.

From	He was a mechanic in a repair shop. He specialized in carburetor adjustment.
To	He was a garage mechanic, specializing in carburetor adjustment.

(2) Reduce a compound or complex sentence to a simple sentence.

From	Sarah Bernhardt was for many years an excellent actress, and everyone admired her talent.
	or
	Everyone admired the talent of Sarah Bernhardt, who was for many years an excellent actress.
To	Everyone admired the talent of Sarah Bernhardt, for years an excellent actress.

(3) Reduce a clause to a phrase.

From	. . . a haze which resembled the color of smoke.
To	. . . a haze the color of smoke.

(4) Reduce a phrase to a single word.

From	. . . a haze the color of smoke.
To	. . . a smoke-colored haze.

(5) Reduce two or more words to one.

From	. . . a foreman in the Department of Shipping.
To	. . . a shipping foreman.

15b. *Avoid adding unnecessary details.*

Using unnecessary details is known as *prolixity.* A prolix sentence obscures or weakens the main idea.

| Wordy | I decided to reward Phil at once with a mechanical toy which I had purchased at a low price only three weeks ago. [Omit mention of price entirely or place it in another sentence.] |

15c. *Avoid useless repetition of an idea.*

Useless repetition is called *tautology*.

| Faulty | Peggy was anxious for Jack to succeed and eager that he do so. In all necessary essentials the work is completed and finished. |
| Improved | Peggy was eager for Jack to succeed. In all essentials the work is completed. |

· EXERCISES ON THE SENTENCE ·

I

Sentence Recognition. In each of the numbered passages below, *printed here without internal punctuation,* you are to count the sentences. Some of the passages are incomplete (sentence fragments). In the space at the left of each item, put a capital letter indicating that the passage contains

> A   one sentence
> B   two sentences
> C   three sentences
> D   four or more sentences
> E   no sentence (a sentence fragment)

1. Ever since primitive man decided that it was easier to raise his own meat than to go out and hunt wild game there have been herdsmen and farmers who have had to build fences which moreover had to be maintained.

2. Fence building and fence repairing whether they concern stone walls living thorn hedges rail fences barbed wire or electric barriers to be installed and kept in good condition.

3. About the time young Abraham Lincoln was splitting oak and walnut logs into rails for "worm" fences middle western farmers began to hear of a small thorny tree native to the Arkansas River region which could be grown in dense hedges to enclose horses cattle sheep and hogs because the Osage (Wazhazhe or "war people") Indians inhabited that region it was called the Osage Orange.

4. The Osage orange is a medium-sized tree occasionally it reaches 50 feet in height and two feet in diameter it has glossy simple leaves they are about twice as long as broad.

5. The twigs armed with many straight stout sharp thorns about three-quarters of an inch long and orange-brown in color.

6. The large wrinkled orange-like green fruit four or five inches in diameter as well as the leaves and twigs contain a milky juice which is quite bitter commonly known as "hedge apples" these heavy and hard fruits are used by boys as missiles for mimic warfare and other purposes they are not edible.

7. The only tree of its kind in the world although it is distantly related to mulberries and figs and silkworms feed as readily on its leaves as on those of the mulberry.

8. Some of these trees have yellowish male flowers which bear pollen that is carried by bees to other trees with greenish female flower heads the ones which produce the "oranges."

9. Growing well on many kinds of soil throughout most of the United States sprouts from roots or shoots grown from seed or cuttings in nurseries are planted in one or two rows several inches apart where a hedge fence is wanted once or twice a year these are trimmed to form a dense hedge about four feet high and two feet wide the "whips" or sprouts being sometimes planted at an angle to create an interwoven lattice-like living fence.

10. If farmers neglect the trimming the hedges grow rapidly to become havens for birds and other wildlife the trees so produced however are valuable as posts for wire fences because Osage orange is more durable in the soil than any other wood many such fences having lasted more than 50 years without a single rotten post since they occupy and shade too much valuable cropland most such overgrown hedges have been removed in recent years.

II

Fragments, Comma Splices, Fused Sentences. In each pair of sentences, one is faulty. Faulty sentences are of three kinds: (1) sentence fragments; (2) comma splices; (3) fused sentences. Find the faulty sentences in the numbered items and on a separate sheet rewrite each in an acceptable form. Then indicate the nature of your revisions by inserting in the space on the left a capital letter showing that the item contains

A   a sentence fragment that could be best corrected by *changing the form of one word* (changing a participle to a finite verb, for example)

B   a sentence fragment that could be best corrected by *joining it* to the preceding or following sentence (with appropriate changes in punctuation and capitalization)

C   a sentence fragment that could be best corrected by *rewriting* (to make its structure complete)

D   a comma *splice* (to be corrected by changing the punctuation or by inserting a connective word)

E   a *fused* sentence (to be corrected by inserting appropriate punctuation or by inserting a connective word)

1. I was wrong in thinking the ice was thick enough to skate on, it was not. Fortunately the water was not very deep, and I scrambled ashore without much trouble.

2. Insurance statistics prove that women drive more safely than men. However, it will take more than statistics to convince me, in fact I just don't believe it.

3. It turns out you were right I forgot to return the book to the library. But I seldom make such mistakes, and I can't imagine how it happened.

4. The natives had a kind of lie-detector test, in which the suspected culprit was required to chew dry rice. The theory being that a bad conscience prevents or slows the flow of saliva.

5. An electric dryer is cheaper to buy than a gas dryer, however, it is more expensive to operate. So the salesman told me, at any rate.

6. Contrary to common belief, a bent stick always breaks first on the inside of the curve, not the outside. Because the tensile strength of wood is much greater than its compressive strength.

7. The use of silver rather than paper dollars was until recently common in the western states, especially for games of chance. "Iron dollars," as the old-timers called them.

8. People tend to hum or whistle tunes that were popular when they were about 20 years old. And are seldom conscious of doing so.

9. Ben and Sam often quarreled violently then they would make up and act as if nothing had happened. After I got to know them, I decided that they were just putting on a show, the customers having no suspicion of their intention.

10. A very interesting speech, whatever you may think of the opinions expressed. But most of the audience, I believe, came away unconvinced.

11. The bows of the plains Indians were designed for strength rather than marksmanship, they were accurate only at short range. In the hunting of buffalo, most arrows were shot from a distance of only a few feet, as near to actual contact as the horse could carry the rider.

12. The influence and prosperity of the family magazine devoted mainly to fiction crested in the first third of this century, before the competition of radio and television set in. Influence and prosperity which they are likely never to recover.

13. Many people think it is easy to tell the truth, actually it is one of the hardest things in the world. If you doubt it, read the reports turned in to the insurance company by people on opposite sides of a minor automobile accident.

14. We think of Canada as a very large country on the map it looks bigger than the United States. But in terms of settled population it is really a narrow transcontinental strip, easily driven across in one day.

15. Having seen only American-type windmills, pupils are puzzled by the story of Don Quixote. Wondering how he ever got his lance up high enough to attack the vanes.

III

Word Order and Dangling Elements. Each of the numbered sentences below is faulty, either in the order of words or in the way in which modifiers are attached to the remainder of the sentence. Find the faulty sentences and on a separate sheet rewrite each in acceptable form. Then, for each item, write in the space at the left a capital letter showing that the sentence contains

A   a word or phrase so placed as to give the sentence *two or more meanings*
B   separated *parallel* elements giving the sentence an *awkward* effect
C   a *split* construction: the separation of words which come together in normal speech patterns
D   a *dangling* modifier, although the thing modified is *named* in the sentence
E   an *elliptical dangling* modifier: the thing modified is *not named* in the sentence

1. I, after only a couple of days in Paris, was delighted to find my French coming back with a rush, although some of the slang baffled me, of course.

2. Fish are easy to catch in these waters when using the right bait.

3. After the first week, Professor White almost knows every student in his class.

4. Traveling by air all the way, the trip around the world was completed by Mallard in only eight days.

5. Although not trusting by nature, I gave Vic the loan because he seemed to be in dire want, although I didn't know him very well.

6. The woods were at last left behind, and, looking westward, an unbroken expanse of prairie sloped down to the river.

7. If I'm not imposing on your time, I'd like to take a look at the old Hackett house this afternoon, if you're willing to go with me.

8. I took hold of the sharp-finned fish that was struggling on the line with my bare hands.

9. We were stuck in the expressway jam for half an hour, and, while fuming helplessly in the line of cars, the airplane took off without us.

10. To play your best game, you have only to firmly keep in mind that your opponent is just as nervous as you are.

11. A man who has dates with girls wearing his heart on his sleeve is bound for trouble.

12. At that age I really meant, being simple enough to think it possible, to read all the books, see all the plays, hear all the music that existed, but there was never time.

13. To keep a car running reliably in those days a good deal of knowledge of machinery and mechanical aptitude was necessary.

14. When courses resumed in the fall, I found that I had nearly forgotten everything I knew about algebra.

15. Lying everywhere about the house I found an impressive collection of outgrown toys for the charity campaign.

IV

Parallelism and Word Order. Most of the numbered sentences below contain faults of parallelism. Some sentences are acceptably constructed. For each sentence, mark in the space at the left the capital letter indicating that in order to make the sentence acceptable you would have to

A   *insert* a necessary word or words
B   *take out* a superfluous word or words
C   change the form of one or more *verbs or verbals*
D   *change the order* of the words
E   *do nothing:* the sentence is acceptable as it stands

If so instructed, rewrite each faulty sentence on a separate sheet.

1. The problem these days is found not so much in choosing a college as gaining admittance to the college chosen.

2. Fired up by the hope that Father would be vastly impressed (and perhaps disposed to reward me accordingly), I swept the basement, cleaned out the garage, and then I carried all the trash to the alley.

3. In the debate on Latin American policy, he said that either we must gamble on supporting the noncommunist left or reconcile ourselves to alliances with military dictatorships.

4. Working on my stamp collection is in my opinion much more interesting than to watch television.

5. The most reliable sources of humor, as every jokesmith knows, are surprise at incongruity, the release of forbidden impulses (such as cruelty), and irreverence toward custom or authority.

6. Expressways not only cost far more than improved public transportation but often create more problems than they solve.

7. The referee tossed the coin, acted out the usual choices of the opposing field captains, and the all-important game was under way.

8. It is well to invest in a variety of enterprises rather than putting all your eggs in one basket.

9. Either one has to be 65 or blind in order to claim an extra personal exemption.

10. In navigation, finding your latitude is vastly easier than to determine your longitude, which depends on knowing exactly what time it is somewhere else.

11. In order to adjust the automatic choke, you wait until the motor is cold, remove the air filter, and loosen the set screws on the carburetor.

12. In the tradition of the cinema Western, a woman who has sinned is something like a horse with a broken leg—she either has to be shot or to meet some other violent end before the denouement.

13. I neither had the time nor the desire to cultivate his acquaintance.

14. The charm of a steam locomotive, both to adults and children, has never been fully explained.

15. Marcia dominates every committee she serves on, pointing out faults of logic and giving infallible advice; although you may dislike her now, when you get to know her better you will not so much dislike as loathe her.

V

Coordination and Subordination. Each numbered sentence below may present a problem in coordination or subordination of parts. Find the faults and on a separate sheet rewrite each item in an acceptable form. Then, for each sentence, insert in the space at the left the capital letter indicating that in order to make the sentence acceptable you would have to

A *subordinate* one or more of the parts, to correct an effect of monotony
B *change a conjunction,* to join the parts more logically or correctly
C put the main thought or idea in an *independent* instead of a dependent clause
D rearrange the dependent or subordinate elements, to correct an effect of *trailing off weakly*
E *do nothing:* the sentence is acceptable as it stands

1. The judge announced that my entry had won, after he had explained the points used in judging and had commended the runners-up in a manner satisfying to everybody.

2. I was a freshman, and I didn't know my way around, so my roommate drew a map of the campus for me, but I got lost on my way to my first class.

3. Quick reactions are important in driving, but actually the surest mark of a good driver is that he rarely has to do anything quickly.

4. They cause interference in television reception, which is the reason that high-speed motors in household appliances and tools were not employed after about 1950.

5. The idea of the Peace Corps at first met much criticism, but which virtually disappeared when the program was well under way.

6. The old-fashioned cooking stoves burned wood, so the temperature was difficult to control, but our grandmothers cooked wonderful meals on them, and they didn't complain.

7. We had been asked to bring the charcoal and lighting fluid, and in the hurry of packing the other picnic things I forgot them.

8. As much as I dislike his managerial tone of speaking, I have to admit that Harvey's ideas are usually sound and that we might have made a mess of the project without him.

9. People with an axe to grind often say that you can't legislate morality, though it must be obvious that a vast amount of traditionally accepted legislation has precisely that purpose.

10. The downed fliers were finally sighted and rescued, after they had spent 10 miserable days on the raft and had survived only through the ingenuity of Lieutenant Morrison, who devised a method of catching fish.

11. Vanilla flavoring is extracted from a tropical plant of great value, and which, surprisingly enough, is a member of the orchid family.

12. The kangaroo rat is ingeniously adapted to living in the desert, since it needs never to drink water, of which it produces all it needs internally by metabolizing carbohydrates that are found in the seeds it eats.

13. The ancient Greeks used a word meaning "of the smithy" as a term of contempt, because they regarded manual labor as degrading and fit only for slaves and thought that physical experiment was beneath the dignity of a scientist.

14. Nothing could be more frankly and personally revealing than Montaigne's essays, yet in which, surprisingly, we find virtually no genuine biographical information.

15. The deerfly is reported to be the fastest of living things, and some people claim it can fly at 300 miles per hour, but the evidence from films is contradictory, so the controversy will probably last a long time, and the whole idea may be a hoax.

VI

Illogical Constructions. Each numbered sentence below may contain one of the following faults: (1) an illogical construction (a faulty sentence plan or two sentence plans blended together); (2) an undesirable shift in person, number, tense, or voice; (3) a pronoun to which the reference is vague or missing. Some sentences are acceptable as they stand. For each sentence, write in the space at the left a capital letter indicating that in order to correct the sentence you would

A *insert* a necessary word or *take out* a superfluous word
B change the wording to effect consistency (correct an undesirable *shift* in point of view)
C rework the sentence to make the *reference* of a pronoun clear or correct
D change the *basic plan* of the sentence so that its parts are logically united
E *do nothing:* the sentence is acceptable as it stands

If so instructed, rewrite each faulty sentence on a separate sheet.

1. Just as Martin thought he had paid off his month's debts, they sent him another bill.

2. My chief criticisms of your story are that it has too little narrative interest and too many lush descriptions.

3. The subject which you are best in, you are likely to spend the most time on it.

4. When I serve my time in the Army, I hope they send me to Hawaii.

5. This is probably the only large city which you can pass between extremes of wealth and poverty by walking only a block or two.

6. We were much put out to discover that the boys had got into the refrigerator and drank almost all the cokes before the party started.

7. In this editorial it says that the first principle of foreign policy* is to refrain from doing what is clearly wrong.

8. One of the chief causes of rigidity in international relations is that every government becomes the prisoner of its own propaganda.

9. The tourist can now cross the Straits in a few minutes by bridge, whereas they often used to wait hours for a ferry.

10. The winter I won both the skating and skiing trophies was my greatest athletic achievement.

11. The reason why you are always slicing the ball is that you take too full of a backswing at the tee.

12. An intelligent Dalmatian is the kind of dog who can be trained easily.

13. It's true I don't care much for the food in the cafeteria, but at these prices I suppose you shouldn't complain.

14. I suppose I could select any of these magazines to read, but it must be illustrated.

15. My main objection to band practice was because we spent so much time walking around tracing out letters and diagrams on the field.

VII

Conciseness. Most of the sentences below contain deadwood of one kind or another that should be cut out or trimmed. Some sentences are already about as concise as they can be made. On a separate sheet, rewrite each wordy sentence in acceptable form. Then place in the space at the left a capital letter indicating that you have made the sentence more concise by

A   taking out something which *repeats* an idea already expressed
B   taking out a *qualifying tag* which adds no real information or interest
C   *reducing a predication* to a phrase or word
D   *doing nothing:* the sentence is already concise

1. The information which has been put together in this report should be immediately given to the sales department.

2. In the modern world of today, we are subject to many pressures unknown to our ancestors.

3. To me, this magazine contains an excess of advertising over other printed matter.

4. The most widespread and long-continuing use of competitive civil-service examinations occurred in the old Chinese Empire.

5. In the early sixties, intercollegiate athletics became not much more than an appendage, so to speak, of commercial television.

6. It was obvious to everyone that Violet resembled her maternal grandmother on her mother's side.

7. One of the reasons it took Odysseus many years to get home was that ships were then so rigged that they could sail only with a favoring wind.

8. Frankly, if I were in the situation that you are in, I would give the boss a piece of my mind and let him do whatever he liked about it.

9. Dixen turned out to be an abominable cook, and by the end of the week we had more or less decided to take turns at the job and give him something else to do.

10. The Schmidt camera, which combines the reflective and refractive principles and which was invented only a few years ago, is the first basic innovation in telescope design since the eighteenth century.

11. The courtship rituals and displays of many birds seem an exaggerated satire on human behavior and fashions.

12. The mental development of the mind is the subject of a course that I am now taking.

13. There are three sports that are played during the summer and that are popular.

14. In the summers we enjoy the rural life of the country, but in the fall we are glad to return to the urban life of the city.

15. The trouble with statistical reports, generally speaking, is that they often give an air of precision to conclusions which are in fact based on a long train of doubtful inferences.

THE WORD

The word is the smallest grammatical element which can stand alone as an utterance. Problems with words involve *spelling* and *diction;* of these, diction is considerably the more important and difficult.

Correct spelling is not yet old-fashioned, although comparatively little attention is currently paid to its teaching and its learning. But it is essential for intelligent communication. It is taken for granted and expected at all times. Yet many people realize their writing sometimes contains spelling errors, and they are embarrassed by doubts and fears about the correct spelling of difficult words. Distraction, confusion, and misunderstanding result from errors in spelling. Therefore, no one should be satisfied with anything less than perfection.

In Section 16 you will find treatment of seven specific attacks upon the problem of misspelling. In addition, Part II contains discussion of many groups of words (for example, those ending in *-able* and *-ible*) likely to cause spelling difficulties.

Although correct spelling is mandatory, it is less significant than diction. *Diction* is the choice of words (one word or a group of words) for the expression of ideas. The word comes from the Latin word *dictio* (meaning "saying," "a word") and its root, *dict*, adds meaning to familiar words such as *dictate, dictaphone, dictator,* and *dictionary.*

Because there are many words to choose from, because many ideas require expression in different shades of meaning and emphasis, and because errors must be avoided, diction is troublesome for most writers and speakers. And yet all good writing and speaking depend upon good diction.

Just as a sound builder carefully selects materials for the construction of a house, so must the writer make a real effort to choose carefully the words, the basic materials, which he uses. Effective communication, the primary aim of all writing and speaking, is impossible without effective choice and use of words. Chapter 5 is devoted to a study of the word.

Diction, like sentences, should be *correct, clear,* and *effective*. Sections 17–30 discuss these qualities as they apply to words, but no standards can be absolute. Our language is constantly changing. Also, diction, like fashions in dress, in food, in automobile design, in morals, is influenced by changes in taste. Again, what is acceptable in daily speech and conversation may be by no means suitable in written form. The use of this or that word cannot be justified by saying that it is often heard or seen in print. Advertisements, newspapers, magazines, and even well-considered books may exhibit poor diction.

In general, however, words should be in *present, national,* and *reputable* use. Section 17 considers words not in present use; Section 18 deals with words not in *national* use; Sections 19–28 treat "disreputable" words. Sections 29 and 30 provide suggestions for diction designed to be more than just correct and clear. As you study these sections, keep your dictionary constantly at your elbow. And, finally, be guided by the practices of standard authors and speakers of the past and present who command the respect of educated people. Such trust may seem blind and insubstantial, but is it any more so than our reliance upon arbiters of taste, of manners, of customs who regulate our daily lives?

16. SPELLING

Misspelling is not the most serious error a writer can commit, but many of your instructors, friends, acquaintances, or employers may consider it a major fault. Correct spelling is a significant phase of word study.

The first and most important step in correct spelling is to have the desire to learn, really to want to become a competent speller. The second is to devote the necessary time to learning. The third is to use all available means to learn. If you are, chronically and consistently, a poor speller, your instructor may recommend a special book which deals solely with spelling problems and provides spelling exercises.

In addition to *desire, time,* and *means,* it should be easy to improve if you habitually do these seven things:

1. Pronounce words correctly.
2. Mentally *see* words as well as hear them.
3. Use a dictionary to fix words in your memory.
4. Use memory devices (mnemonics) to help remember troublesome words.
5. Learn a few spelling rules.
6. Write words carefully in order to avoid errors caused not by ignorance but by carelessness.
7. *List* and *study* the words you most frequently misspell.

16a. *Pronounce words correctly.*

Actually, *mispronouncing* words causes more trouble than does a difference between the spelling and the sound of a correctly pronounced word. In other words, correct pronunciation is sometimes of little help in spelling, but mispronouncing often adds an additional hazard. It is probably improper pronunciation which would make you write "calvary" when you mean *cavalry*. *Affect* and *effect* look somewhat alike, but they do have different pronunciations as well as different meanings. A *dairy* is one thing; a *diary* is another and will be so indicated by correct pronunciation. There is some reason why, from the sound of the word, you might spell *crowd* as "croud" or *benign* as "benine." But there may be no reason except poor pronunciation for spelling *shudder* as "shutter," *propose* as "porpose," or *marrying* as "marring."

Spelling consciousness, an *awareness* of words, depends in part on correct pronunciation. Properly pronouncing the following words will help some persons to spell them correctly. Mispronouncing them will cause nearly everyone spelling trouble. Look at each word until you are fully aware of it. Pronounce each word correctly, consulting your dictionary often and carefully. This list is merely suggestive; many people mispronounce so many words in so many different ways that no list can be complete.

carton	concur	minister	sink
cartoon	conquer	minster	zinc
celery	elicit	pastor	specie
salary	illicit	pasture	species
color	finally	plaintiff	tenet
collar	finely	plaintive	tenant

Here are seven specific suggestions to keep in mind:

(1) Do not add vowels or consonants in pronouncing such words as *athletics, disastrous, height,* and *similar,* and you will not misspell them as "athaletics" or "atheletics," "disasterous," "heigth," and "similiar."

(2) Do not omit consonants in pronouncing such words as *environment, February, government,* and *library.*

(3) Do not omit syllables in pronouncing *accidentally, criticism, laboratory, miniature, sophomore,* and you will not misspell them as "accidently," "critcism," "labratory" or "labortory," "minature," and "sophmore."

(4) Carefully examine words which contain silent letters: *subtle, muscle, pneumonia, psychology, handsome, would, solemn, listen,* and many, many others.

(5) Watch the prefixes of words: *perform* and *perhaps* (not *preform* and *prehaps*), *prefix* (not *perfix*), *proposal* (not *porposal*).

(6) Beware of words containing lightly stressed syllables: *dollar, grammar, mathematics, professor.* Exaggerate the trouble spots: *dollAr, grammAr, mathEmatics, professOr.*

(7) Form the habit of pronouncing and spelling troublesome words syllable by syllable, writing them, and then pronouncing them aloud in order to relate the sound to the spelling.

16b. **Mentally see words as well as hear them.**

The ability to visualize words, to see them in the mind's eye, is the hall-mark of the good speller. When a word is mentioned, a proficient speller can "see" the word in full detail, every letter standing out, as though it were written on paper, or the floor, the wall, the sky—against whatever back-ground he calls to mind.

Here is a method of learning to see words mentally:

(1) With your eyes on the word being studied, pronounce it carefully. If you don't know the proper pronunciation, consult a dictionary.

(2) Study each individual letter in the word; if the word has more than one syllable, separate the syllables and focus on each one in turn.

(3) *Close your eyes* and pronounce and spell the word either letter by letter or syllable by syllable, depending upon its length.

(4) Look at the word again to make certain that you have recalled it correctly.

(5) Practice this alternate fixing of the image and its recall until you are certain that you can instantly "see" the word under any circumstances and at any time.

Such a procedure is especially valuable when dealing with tricky words which add or drop letters for no apparent reason, which contain silent letters, or which transpose or change letters without logical cause:

explain but *explanation*	*curious* but *curiosity*
proceed but *procedure*	*maintain* but *maintenance*
pronounce but *pronunciation*	*fire* but *fiery*

The most frequent error in visualizing words is mistaking one word for another which has some resemblance:

accept and *except; adapt* and *adopt; affect* and *effect; all together* and *alto-gether; beach* and *beech; breath* and *breathe; complement* and *compliment; council* and *counsel; envelop* and *envelope; formally* and *formerly; its* and *it's; loose* and *lose; pillar* and *pillow; stationary* and *stationery; statue, stature,* and *statute; want, wont,* and *won't*

Literally thousands of "look-alikes" and "sound-alikes" such as these demand that you become somewhat visual-minded if you wish to improve your spelling.

16c. **Use a dictionary to fix words in your memory.**

When you are doubtful about the spelling of any word, you should check it immediately in your dictionary. "Doubt + dictionary = good spell-ing" is a reliable formula. However, it is counsel that none of you is likely always to follow. On the other hand, your sense of doubt may be so great that you spend half your writing time flipping pages of the dictionary rather than communicating and thus grow bored and frustrated.

Nonetheless, the dictionary is a never-failing help in time of spelling trouble. Also, intelligent use of a dictionary can help to *prevent* trouble. That is, certain approaches to the vast amount of knowledge recorded in a dictionary can fix helpful principles and patterns in your mind so that you do not have to consult it for, at most, more than 5 percent of the words you use. Certain facts about word derivations, prefixes, suffixes, plurals, apostrophes, hyphens, and capitalization can be learned easily—facts which apply to large numbers and classes of words and help to improve your spelling in wholesale fashion. See *Dictionaries*, p. 371.

16d.   *Use memory devices to help remember troublesome words.*

One kind of memory device has the rather imposing name of *mnemonics*. The word is pronounced "ne-MON-iks" and comes from a Greek word meaning "to remember." A *mnemonic* is a special aid to memory, a memory "trick" based on what psychologists refer to as "association of ideas," remembering something by associating it with something else. You have been using mnemonics most of your life. The term applies to a basic characteristic of the human mind.

Any mnemonic is a sort of crutch, something you use until you can automatically spell a given word "without even thinking." But so is a rule a crutch, and, in a different sense, a dictionary is too. In time, you can throw away your spelling crutches except on rare occasions; until then you can use them to avoid staggering and falling.

A mnemonic will be most helpful when you base it upon some happening or some person meaningful in your life. That is, you must invent, or use, only mnemonics that have a *personal* association of ideas.

Here are a few examples of mnemonics. They may not help you because they have no personal association, but they will provide ideas for the manufacture of your own:

> *all right.*   Two words. Associate with *all correct* or *all wrong.*
> *compliment.*   A compliment is what *I* like to get.
> *piece.*   Have a *piece* of *pie.*
> *together.*   To + get + her.
> *vaccine.*   Vaccine is measured in *cubic centimeters* (*cc's*).

16e.   *Learn a few spelling rules.*

If you happen to study carefully a number of words which have similar characteristics, you can make some generalizations about their spelling. In fact, observers have been doing just this for more than a century, with the result that nearly 50 spelling rules have been formulated.

Generalizations about the groupings of letters which form classes of words definitely help some people to spell more correctly. Other writers apparently have a "psychological block" against spelling rules. But experience has shown that rules—or at least a few of the more basic ones—do help some people to spell correctly certain classes of words.

Given below are five rules of particular value.

WORDS CONTAINING *ei* OR *ie*

About 1,000 fairly common words contain *ei* or *ie*. It helps to know that *ie* occurs in about twice as many words as *ei*, but the problem is not thereby fully solved.

The basic rule may be stated in this well-known verse:

Write *i* before *e*
Except after *c*
Or when sounded like *a*,
As in *neighbor* and *weigh*.

This rule, or principle, applies only when the pronunciation of *ie* or *ei* is a long *e* (as in *he*) or the sound of the *a* in *pale*.

Here is another way to summarize the rule and its reverse: When the sound is long *e* (as in *piece*) put *i* before *e* except after *c*. When the sound is not long *e* (as it is not in *weigh*) put *e* before *i*.

Still another way to state the principle is this: When the *e* sound is long, *e* comes first after *c*, but *i* comes first after all other consonants:

ceiling	conceited	deceit	receipt
conceit	conceive	perceive	receive
achieve	cashier	handkerchief	reprieve
aggrieve	chandelier	hygiene	retrieve

This much of the rule is fairly simple: usually you write *ie* except after the letter *c* when you write *ei*—provided the sound is always long *e*. The last two lines of the doggerel verse refer to words in which *ei* sounds like *a*. Fortunately, only a few everyday words, such as the following, fall in this group:

chow mein	freight	reign	vein
eight	heinous	rein	weight
feint	neighbor	veil	weigh

A few words are exceptions to this basic *ei–ie* rule or are not fully covered by the four lines of doggerel. The best advice is to learn the following words by some method other than trying to apply the rule, which doesn't work:

either	financier	neither	sleight
Fahrenheit	height	protein	stein
fiery	leisure	seize	weird

In summary, then, keep the following in mind when you are faced with an *ei–ie* problem:

(1) Use *ie* generally when sounded as long *e* (*he*).
(2) Use *ei* after *c* when sounded as long *e* (*he*).
(3) Use *ei* when sounded as *a* (*eight*).
(4) Watch out for exceptions.

FINAL *e*

Hundreds of everyday words end in *e*, and thousands more consist of such words plus suffixes: *care, careful; hope, hopeful*, etc. In our pronunciation nearly all *e*'s at the ends of words are silent: *advice, give, live*, etc. Actually, the usual function of a final silent *e* is to make the syllable long: *rate* but *rat, mete* but *met, bite* but *bit, note* but *not*, etc. With these facts in mind, we can now proceed to a rule which covers more words than any other spelling rule, common words frequently misspelled.

Final silent *e* is usually dropped before a suffix beginning with a vowel but is usually retained before a suffix beginning with a consonant:

advise, advising	care, careful,	love, lovable
amuse, amusing,	careless	move, movable
amusement	come, coming	owe, owing
argue, arguing	desire, desirable	purchase, purchasing
arrive, arrival	dine, dining	safe, safety
bare, barely,	excite, exciting	sincere, sincerely
bareness	extreme, extremely	use, usable, useless
believe,	ice, icy	value, valuable
believable	like, likable	whole, wholesome

This basic rule is clear enough, but it does not cover all words ending in silent *e*. Here are additions and exceptions to the general principle.

1. Silent *e* is retained when *ing* is added to certain words, largely to prevent them from being confused with other words:

> *dye, dyeing,* to contrast with *die, dying*
> *singe, singeing,* to contrast with *sing, singing*
> *tinge, tingeing,* to contrast with *ting, tinging*

2. Silent *e* is retained in still other words before a suffix beginning with a vowel. Sometimes this is done for the sake of pronunciation, sometimes for no logical reason at all:

acre, acreage	line, lineage
cage, cagey	mile, mileage
courage, courageous	service, serviceable
here, herein	shoe, shoeing

FINAL *y*

The basic principle of spelling words ending in *y* is this:

1. Words ending in *y* preceded by a consonant usually change *y* to *i* before any suffix except one beginning with *i*:

angry, angrily	lovely, lovelier, loveliness
beauty, beautiful	lucky, luckier, luckily
carry, carries, carrying	marry, married, marriage
dignify, dignified,	pity, pitiful, pitying
dignifying	study, studied, studious
happy, happier, happiness	try, tried, trying

2. Words ending in *y* preceded by a vowel do not change *y* to *i* before suffixes or other endings:

annoy, annoyed, annoyance	employ, employer
betray, betrayal, betraying	pay, payable
buy, buyer, buying	stay, stayed, staying

Here are some everyday words which follow neither part of the "final *y*" principle:

baby, babyhood	pay, paid
busy, busyness (state of being busy)	say, said
day, daily	shy, shyly, shyness
lay, laid	wry, wryly, wryness

DOUBLING FINAL CONSONANT

Most words of one syllable and words of more than one which are accented on the last syllable, when ending in a single consonant (except *x*) preceded by a single vowel, double the consonant before adding an ending beginning with a vowel. This is a complicated rule but a helpful one, as may be seen: *run, running; plan, planning; forget, forgettable.* Several important exceptions, however, should be noted: *transfer, transferable; gas, gases, gaseous;* etc.

Note, also, that the rule applies only to words accented on the last syllable: *refer, referred,* but *reference; prefer, preferred,* but *preference.*

"ONE-PLUS-ONE" RULE

1. When a prefix ends in the same letter with which the main part of the word begins, be sure that both letters are included (see *Un-* in Part II).
2. When the main part of a word ends in the same consonant with which a suffix begins, be sure that both consonants are included.
3. When two words are combined, the first ending with the same letter with which the second begins, be sure that both letters are included.

accidentally	irresponsible	really
bathhouse	meanness	roommate
bookkeeping	misspelling	suddenness
cruelly	occasionally	unnecessary
dissatisfied	overrated	unnoticed
drunkenness	override	withholding

The only important exception to this rule is *eighteen,* which, of course, is not spelled "eightteen." Also, keep in mind that three of the same consonant are never written solidly together: *cross-stitch,* not "crossstitch"; *still life* or *still-life,* not "stilllife."

16f. *Do not carelessly misspell words.*

When writing, you concentrate on what you are trying to say and not on such matters as grammar, punctuation, and spelling. This concentration is both proper and understandable. But in your absorption you are quite likely to make errors of various sorts, including some in spelling, which result from haste or carelessness, not ignorance. When you discover a mistake of this kind, or when it is pointed out to you, you may reply: "Oh, I know better—I just wasn't watching" or "thinking" or "being careful" or whatever excuse you choose to make.

Isn't it fair to suggest that since many English words really are difficult to spell, we should be careful with those we actually know? And yet it is the simple, easy words nearly everyone *can* spell which cause over half the errors made. Listed below are 12 words or phrases repeatedly found misspelled. They are so easy that you are likely to look at them scornfully and say "I would never misspell any one of them." The fact is that you probably do misspell some of these words, on occasion, or other words just as simple.

a lot, *not* alot	research, *not* reaserch
all right, *not* alright	religion, *not* regilion
doesn't, *not* does'nt	surprise, *not* supprise
forty, *not* fourty	thoroughly, *not* throughly
high school, *not* highschool	whether, *not* wheather
ninety, *not* ninty	wouldn't, *not* would'nt

Errors of this sort are easy to make. Our pen or pencil slips; a finger hits the wrong typewriter key; our minds wander. Even excellent spellers often make silly mistakes. Be *careful.*

16g.   List and study the words you most frequently misspell.

Learning to spell is an individual, highly personal matter. One attack on correct spelling will work for one person but not for another. Also, the words whose spelling gives you trouble may not be the words which bother any of your friends and acquaintances. Perhaps it would be more precise to say that although certain words cause trouble for a majority of people, any list of commonly misspelled words will contain some that give you no difficulty and omit others that do. The best list of words for you to study is the one you prepare yourself to meet your own needs and shortcomings. Start making *your* list *now.*

17. OBSOLETE AND ARCHAIC WORDS

One of the many requirements of good usage is that words must be understandable to readers and listeners of the present time. Words do go out of style and out of use; you must have struggled with the meanings of words used by Shakespeare and other writers of earlier times. Except for doubtful purposes of humor, avoid using all antiquated expressions.

17a.   Avoid the use of obsolete words.

An *obsolete* word is one which has completely passed out of use; an *obsolescent* word is one in the process of becoming obsolete. One dictionary may label a word as "obsolete," another may call the same word "archaic." Whatever the label, avoid using such expressions as *gaol* for *jail, infortune* for *misfortune, garb* for *personal bearing, prevent* for *precede.*

17b.   Avoid the use of archaic words.

An *archaic* word is old-fashioned, one which has passed from ordinary language although it may still appear in legal and Biblical expressions. Certain archaic expressions may be labeled "poetic," but they, too, should be used sparingly, if at all. Good up-to-date writing will never contain expressions such as these: *enow* for *enough, gramercy* for *thank you, methinks* for *it seems to me, lief* for *willing, oft* or *ofttimes* for *often, wot* for *know.*

Unless you have some particular, and good, reason, avoid using *'tis* for *it is*, *'twas* for *it was*, and such archaic words as *dost, leadeth,* and *wouldst*.

18. LOCALISMS (PROVINCIALISMS) AND NATIONALISMS

A fundamental requirement of good usage is that words must be in national, not merely sectional, use. A *localism*, or provincialism, is a word or phrase used and generally understood in only a particular section or region of the country. See *National Use*, p. 86.

18a. *Avoid the use of localisms.*

Linguists differ among themselves on which expressions are localisms and which are merely colloquial (see Section 27). It may be difficult for you to detect certain localisms because you may have come to accept them and to assume they are nationally understood.

Avoid using such expressions as the following unless you have a specific stylistic intent:

> *chunk* and *chuck* for *throw, tote* for *carry, tote* [noun] for a *load, poke* for a *bag* or *sack, fatback* for *bacon, bunk into* for *bump into, reckon* for *think* or *suppose, choose* for *wish, heft* for *lift, trunk* for *tap, draw* for *gully, chuck* wagon for a *supply* wagon, *rustler* for a *cattle thief, selectman* for a *town official, to home* for *at home, loco* for *crazy*

18b. *Avoid the use of inappropriate nationalisms.*

A further extension of localism is *nationalism*, a term describing expressions common in or limited to English used by one of the English-speaking nations. *Americanism* and *Briticism* refer to words common in the United States and the British Isles. Ordinarily, it is an affectation for Americans to adopt such British vocabulary as the following: *tube* (for *subway*), *petrol* (for *gasoline*), *accumulator* (for *storage battery*), *stay-in strike* (for *sit-down strike*).

19. ILLITERACIES

19. *Avoid the use of illiterate words and phrases.*

Illiteracies are words and phrases not normally accepted in either colloquial or standard usage. Also called *barbarisms* and *vulgarisms, illiteracies* are characteristic of uneducated speech; they are to be avoided in writing unless put into the mouths of people being characterized. Illiteracies are not necessarily coarse and are frequently effective, but they should not be used without specific purpose.

Dictionary-makers apply different restrictive labels to "illiterate" or "vulgar" English. What may be marked *illiterate* in one dictionary may be termed *colloquial* in another. And because most dictionaries primarily record "standard" usage, many illiteracies are not listed at all.

The following words and phrases should be avoided:

acrossed, ain't, anywheres, being as, being as how, borned, boughten, brung, to burgle, concertize, couldn't of, dassent, disremember, drownded, drug [*past tense of* drag], fellers, hadn't ought, hisself, irregardless, kepted, losted, mistakened, nohow, nowheres, ourn, scairt, snuck [*past tense of* sneak], them's [*for* those are], them there, this here, vacationize

20. IMPROPRIETIES

Improprieties are recognized (standard) English words misused in function or meaning. The word constituting an impropriety is acceptable; its misuse causes the error.

20a. *Avoid improprieties in grammatical function.*

A word may be transferred from one part of speech to another, but it should not be employed in its new function until sanctioned by good use.

Verbs used as nouns: *eats, an invite, a fix, a think, a combine* (combination)
Nouns used as verbs: *to suspicion, to suicide, to author*
Adjectives used as adverbs: *real* pretty, *sure* big, *some* tall
Other examples: *seen* for *saw, done* for *did, except* for *unless, being how* for *because*

20b. *Avoid improprieties in meaning.*

A second class of improprieties includes words similar or somewhat similar to other words and used inexactly or wrongly for them. If you are in doubt about the meaning of a word or of two vaguely similar words, consult your dictionary (see also Section 16a.)

Pairs of words frequently confused in meaning may be illustrated:

aisle and *isle, allude* and *elude, altar* and *alter, climactic* and *climatic, complement* and *compliment, healthful* and *healthy, human* and *humane, imply* and *infer, later* and *latter, prophecy* and *prophesy*

21. SLANG

Slang is a particular kind of colloquialism or illiteracy; it consists of widely current terms having a forced, fantastic, or eccentric meaning. Slang is popular, but it has little place in standard English.

21. *Avoid slang in formal and in most informal writing.*

Slang does express feeling, although sometimes explosively and grotesquely. It also provides useful shortcuts and often prevents artificiality. But there are sound reasons for avoiding an excessive or thoughtless use of slang expressions.

First, many slang words and expressions last for a relatively brief time and then pass out of use, becoming unintelligible and violating the principle that words must be in current use. Who today uses such formerly popular expressions as "23 skiddoo" and "Ishkabibble"? How many people would understand them if they were used? Numerous currently popular slang expressions will be outmoded in a short time.

Second, the use of slang expressions prevents searching for exact words to express meaning. Many slang expressions are only rubber stamps; to refer to a person as a "jerk" hardly expresses exactly or fully any critical judgment or intelligent description. To argue that such a word conveys precisely the intended meaning is to reveal a poverty of vocabulary or careless thinking or laziness. The most serious charge against slang is that it becomes a substitute for thinking.

Finally, slang is not appropriate in most standard writing because it is not in keeping with the context. Words should be appropriate to the audience, the occasion, and the subject matter.

Note these typical slang expressions:

C-note, bang-up, beatnik, a bum hunch, to put it across, so what?, goof off, took the count, going some, put on the dog, have a heart, attaboy, mooch, cut no ice, fall for it, hard-boiled, get the goods on him, talk through your hat, cool, cool cat, goofy, wacky, to crab, let it ride, stow the gab, jitterbug, what's cooking?, you said it, in the groove, a smooth number, square, to get hep, to dig, swinging, to get with it, way out, man, sharp, a rat race, on the beam, sourpuss, cockeyed, egghead, mike, croak (*meaning* "die" *or* "kill"), slob, stuffed shirt, brass hat, brass (*high officials*), screwball, payola, psyched up, VIP *or* V.I.P., pad

22. TRITENESS

Triteness applies to words and expressions which are worn out from overuse. A trite expression is sometimes called *hackneyed language* or a *cliché*.

The origins of the words *triteness, hackneyed,* and *cliché* are illuminating: the first comes from the Latin word *tritus,* the past participle of *terere,* which means "to rub, to wear out"; *hackneyed* is derived from the idea of a horse, or carriage, let out for hire, devoted to common use, and thus worn out in service; *cliché* comes from the French word *clicher,* meaning "to stereotype."

Thus trite language resembles slang in that both are rubber stamps, "stereotyped plates" of thought and expression. Clichés may be tags from common speech, or overworked quotations, or outworn phrases from newspapers. They save the writer the task of stating exactly what he means, but their use results in writing which is both stale and ineffective. Such words and phrases may seem humorous; they are, indeed, often used for humor or irony. Used seriously, they suggest that the speaker or writer is naïve.

22. *Avoid trite language.*

Familiarity with trite words and expressions is likely to cause them to occur to us more readily than others which are more effective. Look suspiciously upon each word or phrase which leaps to mind until you can be certain that the expression is exact and unhackneyed. Words and phrases which do not seem trite to us may be clichés to any reader or listener more familiar than we with overworked expressions. Hundreds and hundreds of stale and jaded expressions could be cited, but here is a list of fifty to help alert you:

> aching void, acid test, all in all, along these lines, at a loss for words, believe me, blood is thicker than water, busy as a bee, by leaps and bounds, checkered career, conspicuous by its absence, depend upon it, depths of despair, each and every, equal to the occasion, few and far between, filthy lucre, first and foremost, fools rush in, goes without saying, green with envy, heartfelt thanks, he-man, in the last analysis, iron constitution, it stands to reason, last but not least, like an old shoe, method in his madness, Mother Nature, needs no introduction, no thinking man, paramount issue, powers that be, psychological moment, reigns supreme, sadder but wiser, sea of faces, sigh of relief, soul of honor, strong as an ox, sturdy as an oak, take my word for it, the time of my life, time marches on, too funny for words, wheel of fortune, where ignorance is bliss, words fail me, wry countenance

23. JARGON

Jargon is a somewhat general term. It is sometimes applied to mixed linguistic forms for communication between speakers who do not know each other's language, for example, *pidgin English* and *lingua franca*. It also refers to speaking and writing which contain a certain number of expressions unfamiliar to the general reader: the "jargon of sports," the "jargon of atomic physicists." The term *jargon* also applies to writing filled with long words (polysyllabication) and circumlocutions (indirect or roundabout expressions).

23a. *Avoid using indirect words and expressions.*

"Short words are words of might." This observation—wise but no truer than most generalizations—does not imply that long words should never be used; it does suggest that long words are more likely than short ones to be artificial, affected, pretentious, and high-flown. The user of jargon will write "The answer is in the negative" rather than "No." For him, "worked hard" is "pursued his tasks with great diligence"; "bad weather" is "unfavorable climatic conditions"; "food" becomes "comestibles"; "fire" becomes "devouring element"; "a meal" becomes "succulent viands" or "a savory repast." The jargoneer also employs what has been called "the trick of elegant variation": he may call a spade a spade the first time but will then refer to "an agricultural implement." In a paper on Lord Byron, he will use such variations as "that great but uneven poet," "the gloomy master of Newstead," and "the meteoric darling of society." Many of our most prominent sports figures today receive such jargonish names from sportswriters.

23b. *Avoid using vague, abstract words and expressions.*

It is impossible always to use concrete words (see Section 30), but be certain you mean precisely what you say in writing such usually vague words as *asset, case, character, condition, degree, factor, instance, nature, personality, persuasion, quality, state,* and *thing.* It is likely you will never really have to use these jargonistic expressions: *according as to whether, along the line of, in connection with,* and *in regard to.*

23c. *Use technical words appropriately.*

You should avoid introducing into ordinary, nontechnical writing words and expressions peculiar to, or understood only by, members of a particular profession, trade, science, or art. Legal jargon, medical jargon, and sports jargon, for example, have special meanings for people in those particular fields or occupations. So do more than 40 other classifications of words which have special subject labels: astronomy, entomology, marine, etc.

A specialist writing for specialists uses many technical words. If he is writing for others in the same general field, he will use fewer technical terms, or less difficult ones, and will define the more specialized terms. If he is writing for the nonspecialist and the general reader, he will use no technical terms at all or will at least define the ones he does use.

If you are a science major writing a class theme, do not introduce and leave unexplained such terms as *diastrophism* (geology), *stratus* (meteorology), *cuprous* (chemistry), *coniferous* (botany).

24. GOBBLEDYGOOK

Gobbledygook (or *gobbledegook*) is a special kind of jargon: generally unintelligible, wordy, inflated, and obscure verbiage. *Jargon* is always undesirable but is often understandable; *gobbledygook* is likely to be meaningless or quite difficult to decipher. The word was coined by a former United States congressman, grown weary of involved government reports, who apparently had in mind the throaty sound made by a male turkey. The term is increasingly applied to governmental and bureaucratic pronouncements which have been referred to as "masterpieces of complexity." For example, the phrase "the chance of war" in gobbledygook might be "in the regrettable eventuality of a failure of the deterrence policy." But gobbledygook is not confined to bureaucratic circles. Here is a direct quotation from a financial adviser concerning shares of stock: "Overall, the underlying pattern, notwithstanding periods of consolidation, remains suggestive of at least further selective improvement over the foreseeable future." What he meant: "Selected stocks will increase in price."

24. *Avoid the use of gobbledygook.*

A plumber, an often-told story goes, wrote to inform an agency of the United States government that he had found hydrochloric acid good for cleaning out pipes. Some bureaucrat responded with this gobbledygook: "The efficiency of hydrochloric acid is indisputable, but the corrosive residue is incompatible with metallic permanence." The plumber responded that he was glad the agency agreed. After several more gobbledygookish letters, an official finally wrote what he should have originally: "Don't use hydrochloric acid. It eats the inside out of pipes."

Here, in gobbledygook, are two well-known proverbs.

Feathered bipeds of similar plumage will live gregariously.
Too great a number of culinary assistants may impair the flavor of the consommé.

Can you translate this gobbledygook into the good, direct English of the originals?

25. EUPHEMISMS

Euphemisms, gobbledygook, and even to some extent certain forms of *jargon* are occasionally thought to be "fine" writing. They are anything but *fine,* and most pompous and insincere of them all are *euphemisms.* See *Reputable Use,* p. 87.

25. *Avoid using euphemisms in all your writing.*

Specifically, a *euphemism* is a softened, bland, totally inoffensive expression used in place of one which may suggest something unpleasant: *obsequies* for *funeral, expectorate* for *spit, mortician* for *undertaker, underprivileged* for *poor, prevaricate* for *lie.*

Good writers today condemn a roundabout way of expressing a supposedly uncouth idea. If an idea can be discussed at all—admittedly, some ideas and topics are in debatable taste—it should be treated directly, forthrightly.

26. MIXED FIGURES

A figure of speech is a method of expression in which words are used out of their literal sense, or out of ordinary ways of speaking, to suggest a picture or image. "She is an angel" and "eating like a pig" are illustrations of, respectively, the two most common figures of speech: *metaphor* and *simile.* Figurative language, often imaginative and picturesque, can add color and clarity to writing. But the images suggested by figures of speech can become mixed, with resulting confusion, distraction, or amusement.

26. *Avoid using mixed and inappropriate figures of speech.*

Do not perplex or attempt to amuse your reader by bringing in images which cannot possibly be related. Especially in the use of metaphor or simile, you should sustain one figure of speech and not shift to another (see Section 11e).

Here are examples of mixed and inappropriate figures:

At any party there is always a loud mouth who throws a monkey wrench in our dancing and food.

Although Judy can dance like a nymph, our ballet coach threw her out of the group like an old shoe.

By milking from Ned all the money we could, we killed the goose that lays the golden eggs.

Let us take the bull by the tail and look our future squarely in the face.

27. COLLOQUIALISMS

A *colloquialism* is a conversational word or phrase which is permissible in, and often indispensable to, an easy, informal style of speaking and writing. A colloquialism is *not* vulgar, not incorrect, not in bad taste, not substandard, not illiterate; it *is* an expression more often used in speech than in writing and more appropriate in informal than formal speech and writing.

27a. *Use colloquialisms appropriately.*

No objective rule or test will tell you when to use a colloquialism and when not to. In general, use a colloquialism when otherwise your writing would seem stiff and artificial.

Some words are colloquial in all their meanings; others are colloquial only in one or more of various meanings.

The following are examples of colloquialisms (as in dictionaries and linguistic studies, no attempt is made to indicate their comparative rank):

angel (*financial backer*), brass (*impudence*), freeze (*stand motionless*), don't, jinx, enthuse, phone, ad, gumption, cute, hasn't got any, brass tacks (*facts*), show up, try and, take a try at, alongside of, flabbergast

You might use any or all of these colloquialisms if you are reporting the conversation of a person who would characteristically speak them. You might use one or more of them in informal writing where the general tone is designed to be light or humorous or breezy. But degrees, or ranks, of colloquialisms range from "just below formal written English" to a low of "just above illiteracies." Suggestion: If you use any colloquialisms at all, use only a few and be certain that they are "in keeping" with the purpose and tone of your writing.

27b. *Avoid colloquialisms in formal writing.*

In formal, well-planned writing, avoid *all* colloquialisms unless you need them for some specific stylistic effect. In an analogy with clothing, formal writing without colloquialisms corresponds to the evening gown, white or black tie, dress suit or tuxedo. Informal writing with an occasional colloquialism corresponds to the business suit, the street dress. Writing filled with colloquialisms may be compared to slacks, sports shirts, and tennis shoes.

Contractions are a special kind of colloquialism, words from which an unstressed letter or syllable is dropped in speaking. Like other colloquialisms, contractions are appropriate in informal writing and even in formal and literary compositions where the writer wishes not to appear stilted and artificial in style. You probably will find no contractions in your textbooks on science or history, but you will find several in this book, which is written to appeal directly and simply to improving writers trying to use their language naturally and sincerely. In formal writing, prefer "have not" to "haven't" and "shall not" to "shan't"—but not if their use makes your writing seem affected and pompous. (See Section 58c and *Contraction* in Part II.)

28. IDIOM

English idiom means the usual way in which words of the English language are put together. *An idiom,* as distinct from *idiom,* is a structural form peculiar to a language. Frequently, idioms (idiomatic usage) are accepted words and phrases which violate logic, or "grammar," or both. Even so, to the native-born, an idiom is always familiar, deep-rooted, and immediately understood. "How do you do?" is, for example, an accepted idiom, although an exact answer would be absurd.

Idioms are necessary shortcuts in language and help to make writing vigorous and natural. Actually, idioms are the essential material of language: the widespread, everyday usage of people.

28. *Use acceptable idiomatic words and expressions.*

Your idiomatic usage should be confined to those word links generally acceptable. (A good desk dictionary contains statements of correct usage following most words which require comment.) The following idiomatic combinations are but a few of the thousands of similar expressions in our language:

> comply with, independent of, blame you for, adapted to, angry with, fond of, fondness for, as regards, entertain at dinner, plan to go, different from, differences between (two), differences among (three or more), take a dislike to, analogous to, listen to

Idiom, however, is more involved than this list indicates (at least for one not a native speaker). Certain words require different prepositions to express different meanings:

agree	{	to a proposal on a plan with a person
contend	{	for a principle with a person against an obstacle
differ	{	with a person from something else about or over a question
impatient	{	for something desired with someone else of restraint at someone's conduct

$$rewarded \begin{cases} \text{for something done} \\ \text{with a gift} \\ \text{by a person} \end{cases}$$

Also, the same word used with different prepositions and adverbs can form expressions with distinct meanings:

walk, walk about, walk around, walk away from, walk away with, walk back, walk down, walk into, walk off with, walk out on, walk over, walk past, walk through, walk within

Collecting idioms can be an enjoyable pastime. Analyzing their structure and meaning can be even more fun. What, for example, can you *make* of these idioms?

make a fool of, make a date, make a meal of, make as if, make heavy weather of, make it, make out, make off, make over, make up, make-up, make-ready

Or of these?

after one's own heart, change of heart, break one's heart, eat one's heart out, heart and soul, take to heart, wear one's heart on one's sleeve, have one's heart in the right place, set one's heart on

29. EXACT WORDS

Since the primary aim of writing is communication, you should try to use words which express exactly what you have in mind. For each idea there is a word, a phrase, or other group of words which will express your meaning more precisely than any other. Finding this exact expression takes time, causes trouble, and defeats many. But, as writers, we have an obligation to convey our thoughts clearly and specifically. See *Using Exact Words,* p. 92.

Sometimes the first word which comes to mind is the most nearly exact which can be used; more often it is not. Also, remember that a word means to the reader what the reader thinks it means, not necessarily what the writer thinks.

29a. *Do not misuse one word for another.*

Through carelessness or ignorance, it is easy to use a word which "looks like" the one which should be employed or which is somewhat related in meaning. Take your time, think, and use your dictionary (see Sections 16a, 20b). Doing so will prevent your using one word in the following pairs when you should use the other:

advise, inform	expect, suspect
amount, number	foreword, forward
beside, besides	genius, genus
capital, capitol	ingenious, ingenuous
convince, persuade	lightening, lightning
desert, dessert	loose, lose
disinterested, uninterested	marshal, martial

moral, morale	raise, rise
personal, personnel	respectfully, respectively
precede, proceed	stimulant, stimulus

29b. Use precise words.

Any of several words or phrases may convey a given idea in at least a general and understandable way. But if you will think, take your time, and perhaps consult a dictionary, you can come up with a word which more *precisely fits*. Is *happy* the most precise word you can use in "I was *happy* at the dance"? How about *rapturous, transported, ecstatic, blissful, entranced, jubilant, exultant*?

29c. Avoid excessive exaggeration.

To exaggerate is to misrepresent by overstatement: "I thought I'd die laughing"; "That professor is as old as Methuselah"; "She said she has a ghastly [or frightful or terrible] headache."

On occasion, exaggeration may be used effectively, but it is *never* exact and is not intended to be taken literally. It is more often misleading, inexact, and ludicrous than it is appropriate and picturesque. Be on guard when using such words as *amazing, awful, fantastic, gigantic, gorgeous, horrible, marvelous, overwhelming, phenomenal, staggering, terrible, thrilling, tremendous*, and *wonderful*. These words, and scores more like them, appear often in what is unkindly called "schoolgirl style"—a manner of writing characterized by gushiness, exaggeration, and overuse of intensifiers.

30. EMPHATIC DICTION

A word may be correct and clear but without much force and strength. Good writing is vigorous and positive and uses tame and colorless words only as necessary. Emphatic diction requires expressive nouns, verbs, adjectives, and adverbs; except for interjections, the other parts of speech are largely colorless anyway.

30a. Prefer specific to general words.

A specific word names a narrow concept; a general word names a broad concept. *House* is a general word, whereas *castle, chalet, lodge, mansion, shack*, and *villa* are specific. A "red" dress may be *carnelian, cerise, crimson, magenta, scarlet,* or *vermilion*. A conventional verb such as *walk* is general; more specific (and occasionally more effective) are such words as *flounce, mince, prance, saunter, shamble, stagger, stride, stroll, strut, totter,* and *traipse*.

One caution: do not strain for effects. You can overload your writing with such highly charged words that it becomes monotonously ineffective. But even this result is preferable to overusing such general, vague, and woolly words as *bad, fine, good, instrument, job, situation, thing, tired,* and *vital*.

30b. **Prefer concrete to abstract words.**

A concrete word expresses something tangible, usually perceivable by one or more of the senses: *encrusted, forsythia, gargle, guillotine, honeysuckle, lemony, waddle.* An abstract word suggests no really tangible image or impression: *duty, honor, leave, move, persuasion, slow, truth.*

Concrete words are specific, and specific words are frequently concrete; abstract words are general, and general words are often abstract. Ordinarily, and within reason, choose the specific, concrete word over the general, abstract one. See *Being Specific and Concrete*, p. 94.

30c. **Occasionally use words and phrases which paint a picture.**

A writer's obligation is to convey sensible comments clearly. But good writers, and even improving writers, search for words which suggest more than they say, which stimulate the reader's imagination. Such words have *connotative* values with suggestive associated meanings: *home*, not *house; baby sister*, not *girl; enigma*, not *problem; breechloader*, not *gun; mother*, not *woman.* By exact (*denotative*) definition, a *horse* is "a large, solid-hoofed, herbivorous mammal," but to anyone who has ever owned, loved, and cared for a horse, the word suggests many associated meanings. New Orleans is "an industrial and trade center," but its name suggests such images as "Crescent City," "Old French Quarter," "Mardi Gras," "Sugar Bowl," "Mid-Winter Sports Carnival," and "Dixieland Jazz." (See *Connotation* and *Denotation* in Part II.)

Use your imagination in writing, but try not to let it get out of hand. A profusion of specific, concrete, connotative words in one short theme will reduce its effectiveness.

Also, remember that many words have emotional values with overtones that convey attitudes from writer to reader. Nietzsche once wrote that "every word is a preconceived judgment." This is too strong a statement, because some words are colorless. But if you refer to someone as having a *positive* attitude or holding a *positive* opinion, your reader will be influenced by your choice of words from among the following: *opinionated, arbitrary, dogmatic, obstinate, stubborn, strong-willed, pigheaded, hardheaded, firm, unyielding, upright, incorruptible, hard-shelled.* Your reference to a *child* can convey quite a range of meanings, depending upon your choice from among these words: *brat, whelp, whippersnapper, urchin, tot, imp, toddler, lamb.* Words are indeed weapons and should be chosen and used with care.

· EXERCISES ON THE WORD ·

I

Spelling Rules. In each group of three words below, one is misspelled. Find the misspelled word; then decide which rule, if any, applies to it. In the space at the left, write the capital letter indicating that the correct spelling of the word falls under the rule treating

A *ei* or *ie*, according to preceding letter and pronunciation of the vowels

B final *e* or final *y* when a suffix is added

C   doubling the final consonant (or not) when a suffix is added
D   exceptional spelling required to preserve the pronunciation of the word
E   none of these: the correct spelling of the word is contrary to rule

1. conceive
   drooping
   changable

2. neighbor
   benefited
   sieze

3. briefing
   writing
   layed

4. beleiving
   looted
   lovable

5. annoyance
   alloted
   extremely

6. likelyhood
   weighing
   fighting

7. grievous
   forgetable
   happiness

8. kercheif
   reference
   meanness

9. canceled
   noticable
   luckily

10. leaving
    ladylike
    developed

II

Similar Words. Each sentence in the numbered pairs below may contain a word which does not mean what the writer intended it to mean because he has confused it with a similar word. In the space at the left, write the capital letter indicating that in this respect

A   the *first* sentence only is acceptable
B   the *second* sentence only is acceptable
C   *both* sentences are acceptable
D   *neither* sentence is acceptable

1. The prisoners effected an escape by digging a tunnel.
   The scolding had no apparent effect on Harry or Ned.

2. Both attorneys advised the principals in the lawsuit to compromise their differences.
   He is a man of very strict principals.

3. From his halting manner of speech I implied that he was keeping something back.
   His sly expression and covert gestures were obviously intended to infer that he would have more to tell us as soon as we got rid of the visitors.

4. For full understanding of an essay it is just as important to look up the literary illusions as to consult the dictionary about unfamiliar words.
   I distrust your explanation because I believe it is neither complete nor ingenuous.

5. His brilliant but unprincipled career came to an end when the Senate voted to censor his conduct.
   In this savage three-day action the infantry bore the blunt of the attack.

6. The recovery of Hicks and Bugasi from their injuries brought our squad back to its full complement.
   Science preens itself on being completely immoral.

7. Melville first gave full literary expression to the languorous enchantments of the South Sea aisles.
   Open housing is as much a social problem as an economical one.

8. I heartily thank you, ladies and gentlemen, for the fulsome reception that you have accorded me.

I felt sure that the game warden suspicioned the truth of our story.

9. His conduct was blameless in both his private and his officious life.

His administration was free of the venal practices which have brought many state governments into disrepute.

10. The healthful effects of citrus fruits were known for more than a century before they were understood.

All summer long the sheepherder tendered his flocks.

11. People who are cruel to animals are not human.

Telling young people that they are headed for trouble is one of those self-fulfilling prophesies which parents should avoid.

12. On the question of who leads whom to the altar, Butler said that in general women marry when they can, men when they can't help it.

After we had ridden out the storm, next afternoon's squall seemed anti-climactic.

13. The coroner is now examining the corps.

The fox cleverly eluded his pursuers.

14. My Irish setter ran off latter in the day.

The boat had founded on the rocks.

15. The overladen plane became air-born just a few feet before the end of the runway.

In a research paper it is better to site primary than secondary sources.

III

Levels or Areas of Usage. In this exercise, assume that the standard of word choice is that of careful but not overformal or affectedly "fine" American speech or writing. By this standard, each of the sentences below contains one or more questionable expressions. In the space at the left, write the capital letter indicating that in order to make the sentence acceptable, you would have to substitute (in one or more places)

A the correct *form* of a word or phrase (for an impropriety or illiteracy)
B a *current* American expression (for a regional, British, or old-fashioned one)
C a *more formal* expression (for slang, argot, or jocular usage)
D a *fresher or simpler* expression (for hackneyed language, journalese, or other professional or occupational jargon)
E a more *straightforward or frank* expression (for euphemism, would-be elegance, or affectedly fine writing)

(If the sentence fits more than one category, choose the first one it fits.)

1. In this crowning victory, the veteran left-hander gave everything he had.

2. I resent your calling me a dropout, being that actually I was thrown out.

3. In the little town where I grew up, a courthouse idler could achieve lasting distinction by unusual distance and accuracy of expectoration.

4. We made two stops to take on petrol during the race.

5. The gathering at Harold's was supposed to be a cram session, but I'm afraid we spent most of the time just goofing off.

6. Having finally reached the top of the divide, we all got out and left the car cool off.

7. All the girls wanted to ride with Claude to the game, because he really drives a boss car.

8. Mr. Powers is out of the office today, but I reckon you can see him tomorrow.

9. I have observed that fanatics or radicals in any political cause tend to prevaricate when it suits their purposes.

10. In response to your inquiry regarding our ability to supply earth-moving equipment immediately, I wish to state that the answer is in the affirmative.

11. The theme of your story is interesting, but your language is, methinks, too flippant and gossipy to fit it.

12. It was a terrific surprise to me to discover that the novel *Tom Jones* is far more interesting than the movie.

13. On returning to camp, we enjoyed an appetizing repast and, fatigued by the exertions of the trail, were glad to retire early.

14. At that period the college was forced by increased enrollments to expand its facilities greatly, irregardless of the expense.

15. At their return to the base, all the men were in the last stages of exhaustion, and even Morrison's iron constitution was a good deal the worse for wear.

16. I did not for a moment suspicion that John had it in for me, and was wholly surprised by his actions.

17. Miss Otis was extremely competent and industrious yet unusually pretty withal.

18. Mother said that we couldn't go to the game except we took little Herbie with us, and he was dead set against going.

19. Nobody admires originality and intellectual independence more than I do, but most of Bob's ideas are still too far out for me.

20. On this festive occasion the local gridiron hero was the center of attraction, and everybody else was green with envy.

IV

Figures of Speech. Each sentence below contains figurative language (metaphor or simile), which may and may not be effective. In the space at the left, write the capital letter indicating your judgment of the figurative language. (If the sentence fits more than one category, choose the first one it fits.)

A   bad because *mixed* (combines two or more incompatible images)
B   bad because *incongruous or absurd* (produces an effect not intended by the writer)
C   bad because *trite* (weakened by overuse)
D   reasonably *fresh and effective* (or at least not obviously faulty)

1. Collins took the pass over his shoulder and, running like a deer, covered the 50 yards to the goal line unmolested.

2. Many people are prevented by poverty from pursuing the higher fields of education.

3. While we talked, the kittens continued their intricate game, skittering back and forth over the floor like blown leaves.

4. Her smile disclosed a perfect row of teeth that shone like diamonds.

5. The social bridge between them was now so far apart that neither felt like keeping up the correspondence.

6. The poor schoolmaster was destined to be unlucky in love, and after a year his headlong pursuit of Miss Darby ended in flat disappointment.

7. Mrs. Peebles ruled her husband with an iron hand, and during her lectures the unfortunate man couldn't get a word in edgewise.

8. It was one of those stinging cold Arizona nights, with a sky full of the enormous desert stars shuddering and, I imagined, blowing on their hands.

9. From my experience as a player and coach, I would say that poor footwork is the greatest stumbling block in learning to play tennis.

10. The romantic intentions of the summer night were embarrassingly obvious—not a ripple on the dreaming lake, and a little mood music coming from the leaves overhead.

V

Improprieties and Mistaken Identities. Each sentence in the pairs below may contain careless or faulty diction. In the space at the left, write the capital letter indicating that of the two sentences

         A   the first only is acceptable
         B   the second only is acceptable
         C   both are acceptable
         D   neither is acceptable

1. I found the book rather *dissatisfying.*
I don't like the *hustling and bristling* to and from work in rush-hour crowds.

2. I have nothing to gain by the deal, and my curiosity is entirely *disinterested.*
There are usually many causes of an *economical* depression.

3. Football had a *derogative* influence on his study habits.
Whether you go or stay is *immaterial* to me.

4. Thanksgiving makes me conscious of *materialistic* things that I usually take for granted.
He easily passed the *entry* requirements of the college.

5. The movies supply *vicarious* pleasures.
I was interested in the close *contrast* exhibited by many details of their two lives.

6. I was embarrassed by that *phase* of the incident.
While in England he *frequented* the British Museum.

7. The two events are entirely *disassociated.*
Although you can't see it move, a glacier is in *continual* motion; it never stops.

8. A really accurate *translation* of a poem is impossible.
The conductor started the second movement with a *flourish* of his baton.

9. Information *achieved* from libraries is sooner forgotten than that from life.
It was truly a *pathetic* case.

10. He *obtained* his goal of getting a job in a circus.
He was too *reticent* to take part in sports.

11. The kind of reading he *indulged* in was mainly history and science.
The *commotion* of the waves had a bad effect on me.

12. Safety belts *avoid* many injuries in traffic accidents.
The desert Indians derived but a *meagre* existence from the soil.

13. Unfortunately the medicine only *added to* the complaint.
His only *repercussion* to this criticism was to call me names.

14. The only claim to interest in such art is its *novelty*.
Russian foreign policy *strove* in vain to gain access to the Straits.

15. The slum areas can be *remedied* only by complete removal.
New Orleans has many places of interest for excursions and *visitations*.

VI

Idiomatic Usage. Each sentence in the numbered pairs below may contain an example of nonstandard idiomatic usage. In the space at the left, write the capital letter indicating that

> A   the *first* sentence only is acceptable
> B   the *second* sentence only is acceptable
> C   *both* sentences are acceptable
> D   *neither* sentence is acceptable

1. I could not agree to his proposal that we nominate Sellers for vice-president.
He thought Sellers was the best candidate, but I could not agree with him.

2. I am often impatient with being delayed in expressway jams.
My father is often impatient with me.

3. Prior to the final test, we were given several review exercises to study.
Of approximately three subjects, he passed only English.

4. When John forgets a date with me, I get angry at him.
He is annoyed with me when I am late.

5. I prefer cooked breakfast food over the dry cereals.
I don't like this hat, and wish I hadn't bought it during a spur of the moment.

6. Obedience to the traffic laws saves a driver from tickets and fines.
Less and less original dramatic programs are broadcast on television.

7. Mother often tells me I am prone toward sloppiness in doing my chores.
She always adds that I seem oblivious to her criticism.

8. Statistics show that fewer licenses for horse-drawn vehicles are issued each year.
A well-trained horse is always obedient of commands given it.

9. Many people who are expert at swimming are not able to dive well.
He was angry that she was unmindful of his wishes.

10. Everybody was surprised to find him capable to play the piano so well.
She was astonished that he thought her careless about his feelings.

11. He was different than me in his study habits.
Most of his political views are different to mine.

12. As he held forth to the company on various topics, I couldn't help watching him.
He is very well-read, but as far as music, his taste is very limited.

13. I can't help but hope that he will accede to your request.
   You will save time by proceeding in conformity to the printed instructions.

14. After a brief hearing, he was acquitted from all blame in the accident.
   The evidence presented in court absolved her of any negligence.

15. That plant is peculiar to Central America and will not grow in this country.
   In accordance to the supervisor's instructions, the men left early.

16. Against my better judgment, he convinced me to look for another job.
   Experience has now convinced me that we were both wrong.

17. It doesn't matter if you like the course or not; you have to take it.
   The only subject at which I'm deficient is mathematics.

18. Several other products that cost less are equally as good.
   At last the work was completed to his entire satisfaction.

19. Contrasting my treatment of the subject with hers will show you how we differ.
   The assignment was to contrast Keats to Shelley.

20. No one is entirely independent of other people.
   Independence from Great Britain was the primary aim of the colonists.

VII

The Exact Word. In each of the following sentences you are to supply the missing word from the list given below it. In the space, write the capital letter indicating the word which most *exactly* fits the meaning and idiom of the context.

1. I have decided to ignore his criticism entirely, and nothing he can say will _____ me to make a reply.

   A   aggravate
   B   irritate
   C   provoke
   D   exasperate
   E   nettle

2. His failure to show up at the eight o'clock class was a rather frequent _____.

   A   event
   B   incident
   C   accident
   D   episode
   E   occurrence

3. Carrying the surveying equipment proved to be an awkward and exhausting task; before we had gone far I began to wish that I had chosen a less _____ load.

   A   heavy
   B   weighty
   C   ponderous
   D   massive
   E   cumbersome

4. It takes more courage to be patient and persevering under long-continuing _____ than to face a momentary danger boldly.

   A   calamity
   B   misfortune

C   disaster
D   mischance
E   catastrophe

5. Something was preventing the water from entering our part of the irriga-
tion system, and it took us several hours to locate and remove the _____.

A   obstacle
B   impediment
C   obstruction
D   hindrance
E   barrier

6. It was some comfort to him that nobody else would ever know, but for a
long time his conscience continued to _____ him with having betrayed his better
nature by a selfish act.

A   blame
B   censure
C   condemn
D   reprove
E   reproach

7. Having been left alone and with nothing in particular to do, he decided
to spend the afternoon in an aimless _____ through the surrounding fields and
woods.

A   excursion
B   ramble
C   tour
D   trip
E   jaunt

8. It is impossible to call a person or family _____ without implying that
there is something at least faintly absurd or pretentious about them.

A   polite
B   urbane
C   cosmopolitan
D   genteel
E   well-bred

9. These shameless elderly gossips were never known to spare an ounce of
charity for anybody outside their own circle, but they spent endless time on one
another's aches, pains, and operations in loud expressions of _____.

A   commiseration
B   sympathy
C   compassion
D   condolence
E   pity

10. This silly piece of criticism has neither seriousness of argument nor
decency of manner, and the writer's comments are to be dismissed as merely
_____.

A   trifling
B   playful
C   petty
D   frivolous
E   insignificant

THE PARAGRAPH

Writing is a process of building: letters form words; words are linked to form sentences; sentences are combined to make paragraphs. No theme can be better than its units of thought, *sentences*. No theme can be better than its groups of sentences, *paragraphs*.

A paragraph is a single sentence or a group, or bundle, of sentences developing either one single topic or idea or a specific and limited part of a larger topic. The purpose of a paragraph is to aid in communicating thought by *setting off* the single topic which it develops or by providing clear distinctions between the separate parts of a longer piece of writing.

Paragraphs have an effectiveness deriving from the fact that readers easily tire unless a page of writing is broken up into smaller units. The sign of the paragraph, *indention* (or *indentation*), is a helpful lure to the reader. He feels that he has finished a unit of writing and can go on to another. Many books, magazine articles, and even short stories are divided into chapters and sections quite as much to afford readers a "breathing space" as to keep closely related ideas or parts together. So it is with paragraphs, or should be.

If the paragraph develops only a single topic, as does a one-act play, it is, of course, independent; in a sense, it is a miniature theme. Some editorial writers, columnists, and advertising writers make frequent use of independent paragraphs. At the beginning of a term in freshman English, many instructors assign topics for development in single paragraphs. Later, they tend to assign larger topics which require development in a series of paragraphs.

Writing good paragraphs, whether independent or joined, is not easy. Several standards must be met, standards not attained without considerable mental effort. We are likely to seize upon an idea, attack it with a half-formed sentence or two and then, our minds "skittering around like water bugs," leap to another topic. Fragmentary and chaotic thought has never yet built a good paragraph.

A well-constructed paragraph should be correct, clear, and effective. For convenience, eight desirable characteristics of paragraphs may be indicated. The first three are mentioned below. A discussion of the remaining five makes up this entire division: substance, unity, order, proportion, and length.

1. A good paragraph contains a *topic sentence,* expressed or implied. (See pp. 36 and 440.)

2. A good paragraph contains *transitional aids* so that the thoughts within paragraphs make clear progress and so that there is clear passage from one paragraph to another. (See Section 44b and p. 46.)

3. A good paragraph is *mechanically correct:* it is properly indented; it contains the words which belong with it, not with a preceding or following paragraph; in dialogue it represents every change of speaker. (See Section 53b.)

31. SUBSTANCE

Themes frequently contain ineffective paragraphs not because the central ideas of paragraphs are weak but because their substance, their content, is thin, insipid, and meaningless. In other words, getting something to say about an idea, to flesh it out, requires genuine mental activity. "Betty is fun-loving and good-natured" is an adequate central thought, or topic sentence. Developing the idea in that sentence is something else again. Neither mere repetition of the central idea nor vague generalizations will build a good paragraph upon it and around it. What to do?

31a. *Gather material from your own thought and experience.*

Your own curiosity, observation, imagination, and reflection should provide useful developing details. You may think your experiences and thoughts are unimportant and worthless, but actually they are alive and significant precisely because they belong to you. They are not the second-hand comments and impressions of someone else but are really a part of the essential you. Only *you* know how, and in what ways, "Betty is fun-loving and good-natured." Your observations of Betty in action, your thoughts about her, can and will help you develop this concept by methods suggested in Section 31e. For example, you can *relate* how Betty "picked up" a dull party which seemed to be dying, how through sheer good spirits she got everyone into a receptive mood, ready and eager to enter into the spirit of a lively evening. Or you can *contrast* the good-natured reaction of Betty when made the butt of a practical joke with the angry or sour attitude of Lucile in a similar situation. Or you can *define* what you mean by "fun-loving" or "good-natured" or both, making specific references to Betty's mannerisms and personality as you do so.

31b. *Gather material from the thought and experience of others.*

Your own immediate resources will be insufficient for developing certain ideas with which you have had little or no experience and about which you may have thought not at all. But you can draw upon the experiences and observations of others as revealed in conversation, television and radio programs, books, motion pictures, newspapers, magazines, and lectures. You probably have had little direct contact with, say, the problems of emerging nations in Africa. But you can put others' ideas about these nations through the hopper of your own mind. Phrased in your own words, ideas picked up from outside sources will put flesh on the bare bones of a basic thought.

31c. *Avoid hazy generalizations.*

Adequate substance consists of specific, concrete ideas, impressions, and observations. Rambling generalizations are always trite, ineffective, and boring. Note how dull this paragraph is:

> Lying is bad policy. When you tell one lie, you usually have to tell a dozen more to cover up the first one. Even when you try your best to keep from getting caught, you usually wind up red-faced or red-handed. Sometimes the penalty for telling a lie can be severe. Telling the truth may hurt, but it's the only sure way to avoid trouble.

The student who wrote this paragraph improved it upon rewriting:

> Lying is bad policy. A friend of mine applied for a summer job last year and told a lie about his previous experience when he filed his application. A week after he had started work, his supervisor discovered my friend's claim was false and fired him instantly. My friend not only lost his job, but he couldn't bear to explain what had really happened. Furthermore, it was then too late to get another job and he was miserable all summer long. Now he knows, as I do, that lying is a bad and foolish policy.

31d. *Avoid ineffective repetition of the topic sentence.*

Repetition which adds nothing to the main idea is merely thought going around in circles, much like hazy generalizations. No matter how varied the words you use, meaningless repetition is flabby and monotonous. Notice how the topic sentence is echoed again and again in this ineffective paragraph:

> *Some people pay too much attention to material things.* They spend hours thinking about ways to make money and more hours about ways to spend it. Their greatest concern is clothes, meals, travel, and the money required to get these things. Giving so much attention to food, shelter, and clothing is plain silly. They should pay attention to more important matters.

That "some people pay too much attention to material things" is probably a fact, but it is also a generalization. Badly needed for the development of this general idea are specific *details* and definite *facts* (statements of occurrences that can be, and possibly have been, verified by others). For example:

1. A woman spends several days a week shopping for the latest styles and designs in imported clothes.
2. A man frankly says that he "lives to eat" and is more interested in a city's restaurants than in its libraries, museums, religious centers, sports spectacles, concerts, or anything else it has to offer.
3. A group of people, the so-called "jet set," wander from country to country in search of the latest and the smartest in clothes, food, and entertainment.

31e. *Follow a consistent method, or methods, in giving substance to a paragraph idea.*

Various methods of developing paragraph ideas (topic sentences) involve using different kinds of material. All methods of paragraph development have essentially the same purpose: making the reader see exactly and fully the thoughts contained in the implied or expressed topic sentence. The names which label different kinds of developing material are of little importance and less help to an experienced writer. He knows that a paragraph must communicate, and he usually lets the central idea determine the specific method best designed to "get across" to the reader his developing thoughts and impressions.

Often employed to develop a paragraph topic are (1) particulars and details, (2) illustration or example, (3) comparison or contrast, (4) division, (5) causes and effects, (6) reasons or inferences, and (7) definition.

(1) Development by *particulars and details* means expanding the idea contained in the topic sentence by a series of specific details or concrete particulars, arranged in some logical order. Since any topic is broader or more general than its supporting material, every paragraph in a sense is developed by particulars and details. Unlike other methods, however, this method uses ideas related to or suggested by preceding ideas.

(2) Development by *illustration or example* uses a series of sentences which furnish an instance representative of the more general statement in the topic sentence. The instance may be semi-specific, like "Consider a man who is jealous"; or, for greater effectiveness, it may be specific and concrete, like "Consider Shakespeare's Othello, who was overly jealous." An example familiar to the reader carries its own explanation and thus aids clearness.

(3) A topic may be made clear and effective by the use of *comparison or contrast*. Comparison shows the likeness between the topic and some idea or object familiar to the reader; contrast shows differences. Both comparison and contrast are often used within the same paragraph.

(4) Developing a topic by *division* means that the writer calls attention to two or more parts of the topic and discusses each one briefly within the same paragraph. Of course, if each part is expanded in some detail, separate paragraphs are preferable.

(5) Development by *cause (causes) or effect (effects)* is ordinarily used for topic statements regarded as facts and hence is common in much expository writing. The topic sentence gives the generalized statement or

conclusion drawn from the data; these data make up the supporting material of the paragraph, the causes or reasons. Or the supporting material tells what the various results or effects are of the general statement in the topic sentence.

(6) Development by *reasons or inferences* is a method usually used for topic statements regarded as opinions and hence is common in exposition of ideas and in argumentative writing. Supporting material gives the reasons used in establishing the opinion, or it gives the data from which the statement of the topic sentence was inferred.

(7) Development of a topic by *definition* involves the use of content which answers the implied question of the reader, "What do you mean by this?"

A good writer, or even a barely adequate one, is not likely to say to himself, "Now I shall give an illustration to develop the thought of this paragraph." Many writers would find it difficult to explain the kinds of substance they do use, the seven kinds listed. But a writer will *define* if he feels that the terms he is using are not clear. He will provide *particulars and details* if he judges the idea difficult for his readers to comprehend. He will give *illustrations and examples* that will clarify his idea and will relate to the reader's own experience. He will *compare or contrast* his topic idea with another which he is certain his readers already understand.

Above all, he is more likely to use several of these methods in combination than to rely upon any one alone. For example, Thomas Henry Huxley had the task of explaining "scientific investigation" to an audience of nonspecialists. In his opening paragraph he used as methods of development both *definition* and *comparison and contrast:*

> The method of scientific investigation is nothing but the expression of the necessary mode of working of the human mind. It is simply the mode at which all phenomena are reasoned about, rendered precise and exact. There is no more difference, but there is just the same kind of difference, between the mental operations of a man of science and those of an ordinary person as there is between the operations and methods of a baker or of a butcher weighing out his goods in common scales and the operations of a chemist in performing a difficult and complex analysis by means of his balance and finely graduated weights. It is not that the action of the scales in the one case and the balance in the other differ in the principles of their construction or manner of working; but the beam of one is set on an infinitely finer axis than the other and of course turns by the addition of a much smaller weight.

Analyze other paragraphs from your book of readings or from other sources. Careful study of their different kinds of substance will teach you more than further discussion here of this important problem. The discussion of paragraph substance beginning on p. 38 may also help you.

32. UNITY

If a paragraph contains one or more sentences, no matter how excellent in themselves, which do not bear upon the central idea, the paragraph is not unified. Lack of unity is ineffective because a reader, prepared for discussion of Topic A, is confused by detail concerning Topic B. Usually, he becomes confused in an attempt to see how the two topics are related. (Study carefully *Topic sentence* in Part II.)

32. *Omit material unrelated to the main thought of the paragraph.*

In planning and writing, our minds do not always work logically. Frequently, in composing a paragraph, you will think of an idea which may be important and necessary but which does not relate directly to the immediate topic. It should probably be used, but in another paragraph. Test each idea: does this material refer directly to the thought contained in the expressed or implied topic sentence of this paragraph? If the answer is "no," omit it entirely from your theme or place it elsewhere. Every paragraph should develop and communicate its own idea—and no other. See *Unity*, p. 42.

The italicized material in the following violates paragraph unity:

> Our government is primarily one of lawyers and bureaucrats who seem to feel that any attempt to root out gobbledygook is an attack upon their own livelihood. The present tax law, a creation of lawyers, is gleefully enforced by bureaucrats. *The Social Security Act was passed in 1935 and has had several major amendments since then.* Since nobody, including lawyers, knows exactly what our tax code means, lawyers can enjoy never-ending litigation.

33. ORDER

A paragraph containing detailed, interesting, unified material will lose much of its effectiveness if it is incorrectly or illogically arranged. A paragraph may contain five good sentences; a dinner may have five courses. Those five sentences should follow in logical, orderly sequence. The meal should do likewise: only an odd hostess indeed would serve dessert first or soup last.

Do not shuttle back and forth between sentences; keep related parts together; finish one phase of the central paragraph topic before you take up another. Because our minds are illogical, we tend to place ideas ahead of the spot where they belong or, temporarily forgetting, insert them later where they do not belong. Anyone telling a long story, or hearing one told, knows how difficult it is to present material in its proper order. See *Order*, p. 43.

33. *Arrange sentences in a paragraph in clear, orderly sequence.*

The arrangement of sentences within a paragraph depends upon the substance itself. But there is one requirement: order involves *progress*, a forward movement of some kind. Thought must go from some place to another.

Progress may be of several kinds: (1) *chronological* (time) order, with one sentence following another in the order that events discussed followed one another in time—as in narrative writing, expository processes, and some descriptive writing; (2) *point-of-view* (space) order, in which details are arranged from near to far, remote to near, outside to inside, inside to outside, top to bottom, etc.; (3) *logical* (mental) order, in which the writer makes a general statement and follows with details or states an effect and then cites causes.

Usually, sentences developing the most important phase of the paragraph idea should be placed at the beginning or end. Stylistic effectiveness can also be obtained by arranging the sentences (thoughts) in climactic order, keeping something in reserve. In most paragraphs, however, common sense—that rare commodity—will help you arrange your sentences properly. Anyone can detect the disorder in this jumbled paragraph:

> Viewed from the outside, the house seemed quite small. It was perched near a dam which backed up a large pond and therefore seemed dwarfed by its surroundings. But, inside, the rooms were larger than I had expected on all three floors. A converted mill, the house was painted a shade of brick red. The first floor consisted mainly of one huge room with two picture windows and an enormous fireplace; overhead was a gigantic beam from the original mill. Water pouring over the dam made a constantly refreshing sound. We were delighted with the house and its surroundings and immediately made the agent an offer to buy or rent it.

34. PROPORTION

The word *proportion* implies *symmetry*. A paragraph should be developed according to its relative idea value. Readers are likely to attribute importance to ideas on a basis of the length of paragraphs in which they are discussed. Often such emphasis is undue and causes out-of-proportion understanding. Ordinarily, length of paragraph and importance of idea should be related. But do not forget that a significant idea can *occasionally* be made doubly effective through brief, incisive handling. See *Proportion*, p. 45.

34. *Make sure that paragraphs are correctly proportioned.*

However much it appeals to you, dwelling at length upon some phase of the theme you are writing may distort its significance to the reader. Consider each paragraph in a composition both in its relationship to the whole and with anticipation of your reader's reaction. Here are some suggestions for proportioning paragraphs:

1. View the subject as a whole before writing.
2. Think of your reader: what central purpose will each paragraph have in communicating to him?
3. Assign a tentative number of words for the development of each paragraph. Alter this allotment as necessary.
4. Shorten a paragraph if it does not carry its weight, even though it appeals to you, even though revision will sacrifice valued wordage.
5. Lengthen a paragraph if its central idea seems to require amplification, definition, illustration, or any other kind of material needed to make fully clear to your reader what you have in mind.

35. LENGTH

Paragraph length, like proportion, is determined by the writer's purpose and by the significance of paragraph ideas. No specific rule for paragraph length can be stated except this: do not awkwardly and artificially avoid either long or short paragraphs. Some ideas demand lengthy treatment; short paragraphs are often effective in gaining emphasis. However, a *series* of paragraphs of approximately equal length is usually ineffective.

35a. *Avoid a series of short, choppy paragraphs.*

Paragraphs tend to be fairly short today, perhaps because of the influence of broadcasters and advertisers. In your own writing (presumably not intended to be broadcast or to advertise anything), avoid giving the impression that you have not fully and coherently developed the central ideas of a group of paragraphs. Note the choppy, unfinished effect of this series:

> When his alarm clock sounds, he sleepily turns it off and snuggles deeper under the covers.
> After a few minutes, he summons up his courage, erupts from the bed, and dashes to close the window.
> Then, sleepily rubbing his eyes, he slowly and dejectedly begins to think about the long day ahead.

A writer wished to develop the idea that although new knowledge is constantly being gained, old knowledge is being lost. The following short paragraphs represent concrete subdivisions of the topic idea, but the relationship among them is not made clear, and none is fully developed:

> North American Indians knew much about the curative value of herbs. But what they knew died with someone's grandmother a century ago, and present-day scientists must learn all over again for themselves.
> At one time, some lonely researcher must have discovered whether whiskers grow faster in hot weather or cold. But the knowledge gained has been lost, and the researcher may have died in despair.
> Time spent is time gone forever; knowledge once lost is rarely regained.

35b. *Avoid a series of long, heavy paragraphs.*

Lengthy paragraphs in succession may strain your reader's attention. He may finish one or two distended paragraphs, but he will lose interest, his attention will shift, unless he is furnished with a paragraph break which will afford an opportunity for him to "catch his breath," summarize the thought, and then proceed.

Still another objection to long paragraphs is that all too often they contain material which doesn't really belong, thus violating the important principle of paragraph unity. Usually, it is difficult to write an effective and unified paragraph of more than 200 words.

In today's popular magazines and some of the nation's better newspapers, average paragraph length is about 100 words. Remember, however, that paragraphs in such publications vary from 20 to 200 words and that, usually, several paragraphs of approximately the same length do not appear in sequence.

For further discussion of paragraph length, see the comment beginning on p. 45.

· EXERCISES ON THE PARAGRAPH ·

A wide variety of paragraph exercises will be found at the end of Chapter 3, beginning on p. 49. Tests involving all of the specific suggestions concerning paragraph substance, unity, order, proportion, and length given in that chapter and in Sections 31–35 are detailed and comprehensive. Your instructor will select exercises for you to do in accordance with your needs. Here are two supplementary exercises dealing with those important phases of paragraph study, paragraph analysis and paragraph development:

I. ANALYSIS

Circle the topic sentence (or write it on a separate sheet) in each of the following paragraphs. Indicate the order and kind of development in the spaces provided or on a separate sheet.

1. When you write a letter or a theme, or enter into a conversation, you *have* to have something to say and you *should* have some interest and purpose in expressing that something, whatever it is. Therefore, you "unlock your word-hoard," to use the picturesque phrase of the Anglo-Saxons, and select those words at your command which will most accurately convey your meaning to others. But nearly everyone feels the inadequacy of his vocabulary at times. All of us have had the experience of not being able to find the right words to express our thoughts, of being misunderstood, of not being able to make ourselves clear. Since there is an almost complete interdependence of thought and language— Oliver Wendell Holmes once said, "A word is the skin of a living thought"—it follows that by using the most effective words we possibly can we not only communicate our ideas more clearly to other people but also strengthen and clarify our own thinking.

.... *Order:* A, chronological; B, point of view; C, inductive; D, deductive

.... *Development:* A, definition; B, explanation; C, illustration; D, contrast

2. Like any other modern literary type, the novel evolved from various unsettled forms which preceded it. The professional teller of tales was an important figure for centuries before the invention of printing and still retains prominence in places where reading is not widespread. In ancient Egypt, in India and in Greece and in Rome, fables of beasts, fairy tales, and stories of adventure thrived. Italy and France produced many narrative writers, and for three centuries the medieval romance flourished in England. In Elizabethan England people began to turn to fiction as well as to drama for entertainment.

.... *Order:* A, chronological; B, point of view; C, inductive; D, deductive

.... *Development:* A, definition; B, explanation; C, illustration; D, contrast

3. This last method derived, of course, from improvements in scientific research: careful observation, minute and systematic analysis and synthesis. In a spirit of free inquiry, biographers and literary artists in other forms began late in the nineteenth century to uproot old moral conceptions and to view their fellow man with detachment, irony, and probing insistence. Among the first biographers to employ the Satanic approach was Strachey in *Eminent Victorians*

(1918), and some of his attitudes, at least, are evident also in the work of Gamaliel Bradford, Frank Harris, Thomas Beer, W. E. Woodward, William Bolitho, Harold Nicolson, and Philip Guedalla.

. . . .   *Order:* A, chronological; B, point of view; C, inductive; D, deductive
. . . .   *Development:* A, definition; B, explanation; C, illustration; D, contrast

4. Exposition is that type of writing which defines, explains, and interprets. Put another way, to distinguish it from the other traditional forms of discourse, exposition is all writing which does not primarily describe an object, tell a story, or maintain a position. It includes by far the greatest part of what we write and read: themes, textbooks, magazine articles, newspaper editorials, and all criticism of books, plays, motion pictures, television and radio programs, and musical compositions. Furthermore, it appears in most other forms of discourse and mediums of presentation: most novels, for example, explain and interpret; so do many motion pictures, radio speeches, and picture magazines.

. . . .   *Order:* A, chronological; B, point of view; C, inductive; D, deductive
. . . .   *Development:* A, definition; B, explanation; C, illustration; D, contrast

5. From a large picture window in the living room of our present home I can see a quiet, dreaming old millpond surrounded by weeping willows and waving marsh grass. As I turn to glance inside, I am again struck by the centuries-old beams and planking which were a part of this structure when it was a grist mill. As a reminder of bygone days, an ancient piece of mill gear, now a hatrack, hangs from steps leading up to the second floor. For more than a century the grinding of wheels and pouring of water have been stilled; the house is now as silent and calm as the old pond outside. I find it difficult either to understand or appreciate this quiet repose, because only two months ago we were living in a modern apartment on a traffic-laden street in a large city. There we looked out upon straining trucks, hooting taxis, and hurrying pedestrians. Our living room was as advanced as tomorrow with its mirrored walls, blue-and-gold color scheme, and wall-to-wall carpeting. Not even in the normally still watches of the night did street noises ever cease. Nothing about our former home suggested age or tranquillity; everything reminded of the bustling present.

. . . .   *Order:* A, chronological; B, point of view; C, inductive; D, deductive
. . . .   *Development:* A, definition; B, explanation; C, illustration; D, contrast

II. Development

Develop the following topic sentences through means suggested by your instructor. If you are left to your own devices, analyze the topic carefully before deciding upon a method of definition, contrast, etc.

1. One major difference between high school and college is _____.

2. Opportunities "equal to men's" sometimes work a hardship on women.

3. Students appreciate teachers who are "human" as well as capable.

4. Professional football is not a true sport.

5. Is one's conscience a really trustworthy guide to moral conduct?

6. It is clear that a monopoly may lead to a reduction in costs.

7. Her life was not dull; it was filled with joy and adventure.

8. The net worth of a corporation as shown by its records is referred to as "book value."

9. In Sophocles' *Antigone*, Creon is a highly controversial character.

10. Our first hero of the frontier was a superman, Davy Crockett.

11. Socrates was considered a heretic by many of his contemporaries.
12. Our country's natural resources correspond to money in the bank.
13. Urban life has its drawbacks.
14. Like everyone, I have some prejudices.
15. Scientists are not infallible.

THE THEME

No one can be said to write well until he can compose a completed whole, an entire theme. An automobile is considerably more than the sum of its parts: motor, electrical system, wheels, etc.; a theme is considerably more than the sum of its words, sentences, and paragraphs. Dependent though it is on its units of construction, a theme is dependent on more than these. This, fortunately or unfortunately for you, is a solid, hard fact.

Before writing a theme, while writing, and after you have written it, concentrate on the 12 questions which follow. Asking and answering these questions is taking a giant step on the way to becoming a soundly practical and effective handler of language.

1. Have I chosen a suitable subject and narrowed it so that in the number of words I have at my disposal I can provide a clear and reasonably complete account of what my reader expects or has a right to expect?

2. Have I followed an orderly plan in writing, working from either a mental or written outline? Have I divided the treatment into related parts and written at least one paragraph on each?

3. Is each of my paragraphs adequate in material, unified in substance, correctly proportioned?

4. Does my theme contain any unjustified sentence fragments?

5. Does my theme contain any fused sentences?

6. Have I avoided all comma splices?

7. Is all of the punctuation in my theme logical, necessary, and a clear aid to communication?

8. Have I checked to make sure that my theme contains no glaring

errors in grammar—agreement, reference of pronouns, correct verb forms, correct case of pronouns, etc.?

9. Is the sentence construction accurate and clear—no misplaced or dangling modifiers, split constructions, faulty parallelism, faulty coordination or subordination, illogical constructions, inconsistencies in tense, etc.? Have I avoided choppiness?

10. Is the diction as correct, clear, and effective as I can make it?

11. Have I checked the spelling of all words?

12. Have I proofread the theme carefully, checking painstakingly to eliminate all careless errors?

Is this too much to require? Take heart. Everyone can improve *from the very beginning* if he will really try. You and your teacher will soon find your standing on the chart on pp. 248–249. Try hard and you can raise your ranking a notch or two.

36. MANUSCRIPT FORM

What you have to say and the way you say that something, whatever it is, are the two really important elements in writing. But you should not overlook the importance of neatness, legibility, and orderly method in the papers you write. Teachers, being human, are often inclined to give a higher grade than it probably deserves to a theme which is neat, legible, and properly ordered. They are just as likely to assign a low grade to a theme which, despite its content, is slovenly and hard to decipher. Try to give to your ideas the outward form which will insure ready communication and a favorable response. At a party your body may be clean, your mind witty, your disposition genial; but what if your clothes need pressing, your fingernails and shoes need cleaning, your hair needs combing?

36a. *Conform to standards in preparing manuscript.*

If your instructor or department has given instructions for preparing manuscript, follow those directions carefully and exactly. Otherwise, use the following suggestions as a guide.

PAPER

Use prescribed paper or standard-sized stationery, 8½-by-11 inches, and no other. Use paper of good quality, preferably clean white bond which will take ink without blurring. Write on only one side of the sheet.

TITLE

Center the title on the first line or about two inches from the top of the page. Capitalize the first word and all other important words (see Section 55d). Do not use a period after the title but do use a question mark or exclamation point, if appropriate.

GRADING STANDARDS IN FRESHMAN COMPOSITION

	CONTENT	ORGANIZATION: RHETORICAL AND LOGICAL DEVELOPMENT
Superior (A–B)	A significant central idea clearly defined, and supported with concrete, substantial, and consistently relevant detail	Theme planned so that it progresses by clearly ordered and necessary stages, and developed with originality and consistent attention to proportion and emphasis; paragraphs coherent, unified, and effectively developed; transitions between paragraphs explicit and effective
Average (C)	Central idea apparent but trivial, or trite, or too general; supported with concrete detail, but detail that is occasionally repetitious, irrelevant, or sketchy	Plan and method of theme apparent but not consistently fulfilled; developed with only occasional disproportion or inappropriate emphasis; paragraphs unified, coherent, usually effective in their development; transitions between paragraphs clear but abrupt, mechanical, or monotonous
Unacceptable (D–F)	Central idea lacking, or confused, or unsupported with concrete and relevant detail	Plan and purpose of theme not apparent; undeveloped or developed with irrelevance, redundancy, or inconsistency; paragraphs incoherent, not unified, or undeveloped; transitions between paragraphs unclear or ineffective

From *Joint Statement on Freshman English in College, and High School Preparation,* by the Departments of English of Ball State Teachers College, Indiana

BEGINNING

Start the theme with an indented paragraph about one inch below the title on unruled paper. With ruled paper, skip one line. In the first sentence, avoid vague reference to the title.

MARGINS

Leave a frame of white space *all around each page.* On the left, the margin should be one inch or that shown by the printed vertical line on

	ORGANIZATION: SENTENCE STRUCTURE	DICTION	GRAMMAR, PUNCTUATION, SPELLING
Superior (A–B)	Sentences skillfully constructed (unified, coherent, forceful, effectively varied)	Distinctive: fresh, precise, economical, and idiomatic	Clarity and effectiveness of expression promoted by consistent use of standard grammar, punctuation, and spelling
Average (C)	Sentences correctly constructed but lacking distinction	Appropriate: clear and idiomatic	Clarity and effectiveness of expression weakened by occasional deviations from standard grammar, punctuation, and spelling
Unacceptable (D–F)	Sentences not unified, incoherent, fused, incomplete, monotonous, or childish	Inappropriate: vague, unidiomatic, or substandard	Communication obscured by frequent deviations from standard grammar, punctuation, and spelling

State Teachers College, Indiana University, and Purdue University. Used by permission.

standard theme paper. On the right and at the bottom of each page, the margins should be at least one-half inch. Keep the margins fairly uniform.

INDENTATION

Set in (indent) the first line of every paragraph a uniform distance; one inch is suggested. On the second and following pages, indent the first line only if it begins a paragraph.

Indicate a paragraph division not shown by placing the sign ¶ before the word beginning the paragraph. Cancel a paragraph division by placing "No ¶" in the left margin. Preferably, use neither mark; recopy the page, correcting the indentation.

INSERTIONS

Use a caret (∧) when inserting something omitted. Preferably, recopy the page. See Section 60c.

CANCELLATION

Draw a neat line through material you wish to omit. Do not use brackets or parentheses to cancel words. Preferably, recopy the page.

ORDER

Number pages with an Arabic numeral in the upper right-hand corner of each page. The first page is usually not numbered; if it is, place the number at the bottom center. Arrange the pages in correct sequence: 1, 2, 3, etc.

FOLDING AND ENDORSEMENT

Fold the pages lengthwise through the middle. On the right-hand side of the back of the last page, write (in the order desired by your instructor) your name, course, instructor's name, date, and number of the paper.

36b. *Make your handwriting legible.*

(1) Use a good pen with black or blue-black ink.

(2) Do not crowd your writing by running words together; do not write consecutive lines too closely together; leave ample margins.

(3) The consecutive letters in a word should be joined.

(4) Take your time. Most of us can form letters correctly and clearly if we take pains. Dot every lower-case *i* and *j* (with dots, not circles); cross every *t;* do not hurriedly write small letters for capitals, and vice versa.

36c. *Avoid numerous erasures and corrections.*

All of us are likely to make errors even in the final draft of a page. If the errors are numerous, correct them, of course. Preferably, recopy an entire page if it contains several erasures, blurs, and canceled or inserted words.

36d. *If possible, type your themes and other written work.*

Typescript is more legible than handwriting and, with rare exceptions, neater. In addition, you can detect mistakes in typescript more easily than in handwriting. If you do not know how to type, learning might be an excellent investment of time and money. If you do type, be certain to double-space all lines; quotations of more than four lines, however, should be single-spaced.

36e. *Proofread every theme before submitting it.*

Not even a professional writer can plan, compose, and correct in one operation. After you have completed a theme—and preferably some time after—reread it carefully, word by word. The changes you make as a result of doing so may raise your grade several points. See *Revision*, p. 26.

37. ANALYSIS OF SUBJECT

The logical first step in writing a theme should be to *examine* carefully the subject to be handled. You will need to know what the topic involves and what you intend to do with it. Since there is no such thing as good *purposeless* writing, you should set an objective for the theme; otherwise, you will merely be completing a routine assignment without much credit to yourself or any pleasure at all for your reader.

About any subject ask these four important questions:
1. What special characteristics distinguish my subject?
2. What am I trying to do with it?
3. For what specific reader(s) am I developing it?
4. How can I best convey my purpose and meaning to my reader(s)?

In addition, you must keep in mind the required length of the theme and the information needed to fulfill your purpose and meaning: How much do I know about the subject? Where can I get more information? In answering these two questions, remember that many subjects are too broad and too general for effective handling in a theme of normal length. After you have limited the subject to some phase which can be handled in manageable length, you can more easily state the central purpose you wish to achieve. See *What To Write About*, p. 13.

37a. *Determine the central purpose of your theme.*

In a single sentence (which may or may not be included in the actual theme), state your central purpose, your controlling idea. That is, what is the *theme* of the theme? A *thesis* sentence will enable you to grasp, identify, and state your central purpose.

On the general subject of "Part-Time Employment," you might try a plan like this:

Limited subject: "How I Got a Summer Job"
Possible title: "I Earn and Learn"
Reader: A next-door neighbor one year younger than you
Length: 500 words
Thesis sentence: Summer employment can be obtained by those who apply early and use a carefully planned approach.

This subject is still perhaps too broad for adequate treatment, but at least your tentative purpose is clearly stated: you can, largely through an account of your own experiences, show your neighbor how to get the summer job he or she wants.

37b. *List details that might be used.*

In determining your purpose, make an inventory of what you know and what you will need to find out. Your list might consist of ten or more items which could be used, arranged in no particular order:

1. Qualifications for getting a job
2. Timing the campaign
3. Discovering job opportunities (want ads, government bulletins)
4. People who can help
5. Making application
6. Preparation for interview
7. Carrying out the interview
8. Difficulties in being interviewed
9. Following up job prospects
10. Use of supporting letters

Such a listing provides an overview and suggests details to exclude. Your central purpose might be limited to a discussion of how to find out about jobs available (No. 3) or of being interviewed for a job (Nos. 6–8). If this is your decision, you would then revise both your title *and* thesis sentence. Limiting a subject to manageable proportions is one desired result of listing developing details.

37c. *Choose a consistent method of development.*

After limiting a subject and stating your central purpose, select a method of development which will most clearly and effectively accomplish the purpose of your thesis sentence for your chosen reader. Some subjects require definition of terms and a serious, critical approach. Some require argument: reasons for and against this or that cause or action. For the theme suggested in Section 37a, an informal, narrative approach is perhaps indicated.

Some subjects can be developed humorously; some require descriptive details; some require comparison and contrast. Whatever method you select —and remember that that is determined by subject *and* reader—be consistent in its use. Also, when you have finished writing, check to see that you have consistently maintained the method selected. A light, bantering tone in one paragraph should rarely be succeeded by a dignified, solemn approach in the next. (See Section 43b.)

38. CONTENT

"Sit down to write what you have thought; don't sit down to think what you will write."

A successful theme depends upon collecting material before you begin to write. You will need specific details to shore up the thesis you have chosen; you will need to avoid making general statements without having concrete material or evidence to support a central position or idea. See *Getting Material for Writing*, p. 16.

Since a theme is wholly composed of paragraphs, you should review what is said about substance in Section 31. If you can and will follow the suggestions given for developing paragraphs, the resultant theme will almost take care of itself. If you have trouble writing 500 words on any reasonably good topic, you probably have not taken enough time to gather material. In addition to the specific suggestions for gathering material given in Section 31, the following two recommendations may be made.

38a. *Select material with a specific reader, or readers, in mind.*

Always keep your prospective reader in mind. Usually, your readers will be your instructor and classmates, but on occasion you may be asked to write for someone else. Whoever your reader, how much does he already know about your topic? What can you write which will be freshly informative? Interesting? Appealing? If you are writing on a subject about which your reader likely knows little or nothing, what background information should you supply? What terms need defining? What technical material had best be omitted to avoid confusing your reader? What kinds of illustrations, examples, and descriptive details will help make the subject as clear to your reader as it is to you?

For further consideration of the interests and rights of readers, see p. 9.

38b. *Be honest about the material you gather.*

When you use an idea new to you, either in your own or in quoted words, state your indebtedness. Taking the ideas and words of another and passing them on as your own is *plagiarism*. In a short, ugly word, it is *thievery*. Sometimes, you can acknowledge a source with a mere phrase: "As Salinger suggests, ..." Sometimes you will need to make fuller acknowledgment in a footnote. But borrow, don't steal, and do indicate who the lender is.

It is equally important that in gathering content from others you think about it and try to state in your own words what you have learned. It is unnecessary to acknowledge every item of information you glean: you do not need to cite some authority if you write that water is wet or the earth is round. But you should always put information of whatever kind through your own thought processes and should express it in your own words. And again, if you quote directly or express an idea entirely new to you, state your source. Be honest. (See *Plagiarism* in Part II.)

39. OUTLINING

No one can write an orderly paper without having in mind or on paper some sort of outline, formal or informal. An outline may be thought of as a kind of blueprint for the builder of a theme, or as a recipe which specifies ingredients and the order in which they should be used.

Some students object to outlining; they insist that preparing a formal outline steals valuable time from actual writing and that an outline acts as a brake on the free flow of their ideas. Both objections make some sense. But time spent on an outline will be more than repaid when one begins to write. Also, nearly all of us think so illogically that we *need* some control over random ideas that pop into our heads.

An outline need not be detailed or elaborate. If you are writing a theme in class or an essay answer on an examination, only five minutes may be devoted to preparing a rough "sketch" outline which will certainly be informal and yet may pay big dividends. Nor need an outline be followed slavishly; it should be your servant, not your master. The outline you prepare may not be your completely final guide, because as you write you may see that certain changes in plan are necessary and effective. Work *from* an outline, not *for* it.

It is as illogical to say that you can't prepare an outline until after you read what you have written as it is to say you can't tell what you're going to say until after you have said it. Making a comment first and not thinking about it until later gets people into serious trouble every day. Trying to write a theme without some sort of advance plan will get you into a somewhat similar kind of difficulty every time you attempt it.

39a. *Use a thesis sentence in preparing an outline.*

As stated in Section 37a, a thesis sentence suggests the material to be developed. It need not be all-inclusive, but it should indicate something of the scope of what is to come and also your purpose. A thesis sentence carefully prepared in advance will make easier your task in preparing an outline. In addition, it will serve as a constant check against the unity and coherence of the outline and theme which follow. With thesis sentence written, start on your outline.

In addition to the quick "sketch" outline mentioned, three other kinds are often used: *topic, sentence,* and *paragraph* outlines.

39b. *Use a topic outline to make clear the arrangement of ideas.*

A topic outline, consisting of words and phrases, is perhaps more helpful to the writer than either of the other types of outlines discussed in Sections 39c and 39d. Such an outline may be quite simple:

MY FIRST DAY AT WORK

I. Sleeplessness the night before
II. Early morning preparation
III. The trip to work
IV. Getting started
V. How the day went

Such a scheme is really a "sketch" outline, but it may be made more elaborate. In fact, the expanded outline which follows could contain five or six main heads instead of the two shown.

MY FIRST DAY AT WORK

Thesis sentence: The first day at work is a nervous ordeal, but it can be endured because tension and worry pass away.

I. Prework jitters
  A. The night before
    1. Setting the alarm clock
    2. Sleeplessness
    3. Thoughts of failing
  B. The next morning at home
    1. Hurried dressing
    2. A bolted breakfast
II. The workday
  A. Getting to work
    1. A run for the bus
    2. My nervousness and other riders' composure
  B. The first hour
    1. Meeting the foreman
    2. Inability to understand
    3. Helpfulness of another worker
    4. Gradual easing of tension
  C. How the day went
    1. Slow passage of time
    2. Lunch hour
    3. Afternoon exhaustion
    4. Quitting time
    5. Satisfied feeling
    6. Readiness for tomorrow

39c. *Use a sentence outline to make clear to yourself and to your reader the arrangement of ideas.*

A sentence outline consists of complete sentences, not words and phrases. It is likely to be clearer to the writer than a topic outline and certainly is more helpful to a reader who wishes to make useful suggestions. For both of these reasons, many instructors insist upon sentence outlines.

For illustrative purposes, here is how Part I of the topic outline in Section 39b could appear in a sentence outline:

MY FIRST DAY AT WORK

I. I was nervous and jittery the night before I was to begin work.
  A. I set the alarm clock and turned in early.
  B. I could not get to sleep and tossed restlessly.
  C. My mind was tortured with fears of not being able to do the job.
II. The next morning I was tired and still nervous.
  A. I dressed hurriedly and clumsily.
  B. I did not feel like eating but bolted my breakfast.

39d. *Use a paragraph outline primarily for summarizing the work of others.*

A paragraph outline consists of groups of sentences (perhaps mainly topic sentences) indicating the contents of entire paragraphs. Such an outline may be used in planning your own theme. It is perhaps even more helpful in setting down summary sentences to indicate the thought of successive paragraphs in a selection being studied. Some students wisely make paragraph outlines in studying material difficult to grasp and master.

In the paragraph outline, material is not classified into major headings and subheadings; rather, the topic of each paragraph is simply listed in the order in which it is to appear. For illustration, here is a specimen paragraph outline of Part II of the topic outline in Section 39b:

1. Dashing from the breakfast table, I made a run for the bus.
2. My inner fears and worries had me in a turmoil, but other riders on the bus seemed calm and even casual.
3. The foreman was gruff, and my worries increased.
4. My hands were sweaty and my knees felt weak so that I couldn't catch on to what I was supposed to do.
5. A man nearby saw my confusion and kindly showed me, slowly and clearly, what my job was.
6. As I began to catch on, my hands stopped sweating and I began to feel easier in mind and body.
7. The morning passed slowly, and I thought lunchtime would never come.
8. During the afternoon, my muscles grew more and more tired, and I had to hang on until quitting time.
9. As I walked to catch the bus home, I felt satisfied that I had met the test of the first day and could meet the challenge of the next without fear.

39e. *An outline should be correct in form.*

Any outline which clearly reveals the structure of a theme is effective, so that "correctness" in form is more often a matter of convention and practice than of logic. Writers, however, have tended to follow certain conventions with which you should be familiar:

(1) Outlining is division; subdivision means division into at least two parts. If a single minor topic (subhead) must be mentioned, express it in its major heading or add another subhead.

(2) Use parallel phrasing. Do not use a word or phrase for one topic, a sentence for another. Topic, sentence, and paragraph outlines should be consistent in structure throughout.

(3) Avoid meaningless headings such as *Introduction, Conclusion, Reasons,* and *Effects.* If you feel they must appear, add specific explanatory subheads.

(4) The first main heading of the outline should not repeat the title of the theme. If the idea expressed in the title logically should appear in the outline, at least rephrase it.

(5) Avoid putting into a subhead any matter that should appear in a larger division; even more importantly, do not list in a main heading material belonging in a subdivision.

(6) Follow conventional uses of *indentation, symbols,* and *punctuation.*

Study the specimen outlines in this section. Note the use of Roman numerals beginning flush left in a topic outline. Observe that capital letters (A, B, C, etc.) indicate the first series of subdivisions and study their indentation. If needed, the next series of subdivisions is indicated by Arabic numerals (1, 2, 3, etc.). If still further subdivision is needed, use small letters (a, b, c, etc.). Observe that a period follows each numeral or letter and, in sentence and paragraph outlines, each sentence.

40. PROPORTION

Proportion requires that the development given each division of a theme be in accord with the relative importance of that paragraph or group of paragraphs. One major purpose of outlining (Section 39) is helping to achieve proportion in themes. Also, all of the discussion in Section 34 is pertinent to theme proportion.

Proportion in themes, like so many other problems in life, is *relative*. Importance is never *absolute*. In determining what parts of a theme should be expanded and which contracted, you must always keep in mind not only your subject but also your *purpose* and your *reader(s)*.

40. *Develop theme divisions in proportion to their importance.*

Do not overdevelop minor details of material already known to your reader. Similarly, give adequate attention (space) to the *thesis* (central idea) of your theme.

For example, if your purpose in writing a theme on "Football Scholarships at This College" is to prove to your classmates that such aid is a form of professionalism both costly and stupid, get quickly to the heart of your argument and develop it fully. You need no lengthy introduction, no discussion of the history of football or of professionalism in sports. Your readers have this background information; even if they do not, it is *relatively* unimportant.

For another example, if you wish to detail for your instructor the advances made recently in "Color Photography," you should assume that certain elementary details about cameras and picture-taking are either known to him or are relatively insignificant. Proceed to your point and stress it: advances in camera design, processes for developing, kinds of film, costs, and the like. Don't waste 400 words on the beginnings of photography and leave yourself only 100 for developing your thesis.

The basic principle of proportion in themes is simply this: "Render unto Caesar the things which are Caesar's."

41. CLEARNESS

Writing should be correct, clear, effective, and, if possible, appropriate. Most important of these desirable qualities is *clearness*. If you can adequately convey your thought to others, no matter how incorrectly or inappropriately, you will have achieved the major aim of writing—communication. Clarity is not all there is to good writing, but it is the *sine qua non* ("without which, nothing," "indispensable").

It is theoretically impossible for writing to be effective without being clear; but who has not read and reread material which was obviously "correct" and seemingly emphatic enough, without being able to understand its central meaning? Lack of understanding may be the reader's fault or the writer's, but regardless of whose it is, communication failure is present. Try to write correctly, appropriately, emphatically; above all, strive to be clear.

41a. *Define all terms which are not clear.*

You should never consider your reader entirely ignorant, but if you know enough to write about a subject—and you should—it is likely that you know some details which your reader does not. Certain terms familiar to you may be unknown to your reader. Even in context, he may be unable to guess the meaning of certain expressions. A reader should look up words he cannot define, but it is unwise to assume that he will always do so. Some slovenly readers never look up anything. Could this mean you, too?

As has been pointed out in Section 23c, you should define technical words for the general reader. If you use such terms as *bibb, idocrase, pegmatite,* and *tufa,* you should immediately define them; not one reader in a thousand will know what you are writing about, although each of those words is included in standard desk dictionaries. In fact, not all readers will understand even more commonly used words like *boldface, ecumenical, civil rights, exodontia,* and *logistics.* Always consider for whom you are writing: you need not explain *cosine* if you believe your readers have studied trigonometry.

Even more common words than these can cause confusion. What do you mean and what will your reader understand by *normal person, low income, freedom of speech, typical professor, un-American?* It is unwise to assume that the reader will have a conception like your own of the precise meaning of such terms.

41b. *Restate in simple language the meaning of any passage not fully clear.*

"The reader over your shoulder" may not understand a statement which seems clear to you. Put yourself in his place; at times he would like to ask, "Now just what do you mean by this?" A sentence can have a meaning playing over its surface and still be unclear. "After liquidating his financial obligations" means "after paying his debts." Why not say so in the first place?

41c. *Make every statement reasonable.*

"Since the beginning of time, no person has ever been reasonable at all times and in all circumstances." Most of us, perhaps all of us, would accept this as a true statement. But is it? Can we *prove* it?

It is all very well to recommend that every statement be reasonable, but this is a counsel of perfection. Reasoning is based upon facts or what are considered facts. But, for example, the *facts* of medicine or physics even ten years ago are hardly the *facts* today. Reasoning is also based upon conclusions drawn from facts. Yet the conclusions one reasonable man draws from a given set of facts may differ widely from those of another man.

Clearly, you cannot make your every statement reasonable. But at least you can avoid making statements which are obviously questionable; if you do make such a statement, you should be prepared to try to prove it. You should attempt to make your meaning clear by offering evidence which might be considered factual. You can usually avoid statements based on faulty premises, those based on false analogy, those involving mere generalizations. How logical are these statements?

> All automobiles should have governors limiting their speed to 50 miles an hour. [What about police cars? Ambulances? Traffic jams?]
>
> Since football is the most dangerous of all sports, my parents refused to allow me to play it. [Overlook the possible parental muddleheadedness: What about water polo? Bullfighting? Skin diving?]
>
> Ted knows all there is to know about stocks and bonds. [All? Absolutely nothing he doesn't know?]
>
> Gambling is a bad habit; everyone should avoid it because habits are bad. [Can you prove gambling is a bad habit? Are habits bad? All habits? What about the habit of paying your debts? Saying your prayers? Telling the truth?]

Errors in reasoning occur in fact-finding and process-describing papers and also in argumentative papers and speeches which try to establish a case, to prove a point. Our fallible minds are only too ready to ignore, twist, or exaggerate evidence. Some errors in reasoning involve logic; others violate that rare and valuable commodity, plain common sense.

41d. *Make every statement logical.*

Two common methods of thinking, used and abused every day, are *induction* and *deduction*. The former seeks to establish a general truth, an all embracing principle or conclusion. The inductive process begins by using observation of specific facts, which it classifies. From a sufficient number of these facts, or particulars, the inductive process leads into a general principle, a comprehensive conclusion. Movement of thought is from the *particular* to the *general*.

Deduction, conversely, seeks to show how a particular statement is true because it is part of, and leads down from, a general principle or truth. Movement of thought is from the *general* to the *particular*.

In *inductive reasoning* a set of individual particulars is studied experimentally and, from observations made, a general principle is drawn or formed. For example: "Every horse I have seen has four legs; therefore, I can expect all horses to have four legs."

In *deductive reasoning* an accepted general statement, which may be true or false, is applied to a particular situation or case. For example: "All horses are animals; this is a horse; therefore, this is an animal."

All of our thinking is basically inductive or deductive. But, as each of us knows only too well, we make mistakes in thinking and express many comments which are far from reasonable. Here is brief mention of 10 of the more common offenses against straight and clear thinking:

(1) *Hasty generalization:* observing only a few instances and then leaping to an unwarranted conclusion. You know a few athletes whom you consider stupid; does it follow that *all* athletes are mentally deficient?

(2) *Non sequitur:* the "it does not follow" error, an inference or con-

clusion which does not logically follow from the particulars upon which it is based. Some good professional writers admit to being poor spellers; are you justified in concluding that you, also a poor speller, are destined to be a good professional writer?

(3) *Biased* or *suppressed evidence:* selecting from questionable sources only what you need to prove a point, or omitting evidence that runs counter to your thesis. The testimony of dedicated sorority members is in itself not sufficient to prove that sorority membership promotes good scholarship. What do nonsorority members think; how does their scholarship rank?

(4) *Post hoc, ergo propter hoc:* a Latin phrase meaning "after this, therefore on account of this." This is a mistake in thinking that a happening which precedes another must necessarily be its cause, or that when one event follows another the latter event is the result of the first. The Roman Empire fell after the birth and spread of Christianity. Would anyone argue that Christianity *alone* directly *caused* the fall of Rome?

(5) *Distinguishing fact from opinion:* A *fact* is based on actuality of some sort, whereas *opinion* is a personal inference which may be mingled with a supposed fact. That Thomas Jefferson was President from 1801 until the inauguration of James Madison in 1809 is a fact. That Jefferson was the greatest of our presidents is an opinion.

(6) *Begging the question:* taking for granted a conclusion which has not yet been proved, or assuming in particulars what is to be proved in the conclusion. "Should a dangerous man like C. Lloyd Parker be allowed to run for office?" is a "loaded" question which assumes what needs to be proved.

(7) *Argumentum ad hominem:* a Latin phrase meaning "argument against the person." An attack upon the person who holds an opinion rather than upon the opinion itself. "Only a fool would believe that."

(8) *Evading the issue:* ignoring the point of discussion. If you tell a friend that he drives too fast and he responds that you are a poor driver, he has evaded the issue. He may be right, but he has neither met your objection nor won the argument.

(9) *Faulty analogy:* assuming that because two objects are similar in one respect they must be similar in another. The whipping post was a deterrent to crime in seventeenth-century New England; it is faulty analogy to hold that it would also be effective in the United States today.

(10) *Testimonials:* using the statement of a celebrity or historical figure to bolster one's argument. George Washington was a great president, the father of our country; but would his economic, social, and political views necessarily be valid for the twentieth century? Douglas MacArthur was a great military strategist, but something he said about gasoline motors may be less convincing than the words of a good mechanic.

As you consider and rewrite a theme, keep in mind these criticisms and suggestions which your instructor might make:

1. The statement needs qualification; it is too sweeping or dogmatic. (This comment refers to assertions which are *not* altogether false or irresponsible but simply cover too much ground too positively and need to be guarded with a limiting phrase or clause specifying the degree of certainty warranted, taking account of possible exceptions, or confining the generalization to what you are reasonably sure of.)

2. The facts cited are not such as are likely to be accepted on your bare assertion. You should supply informally in the current of your development some authority, occupational experience, or other reason why you should be believed.

3. Your argument is good so far as it goes, but it is unconvincing because you have failed to dispose of some obvious and overriding argument that can be made on the other side. Your case is strengthened when you evaluate your own argument and show that you have disposed of possible alternatives.

4. The evidence supplied is pertinent but falls far short of proof. One good reason does not build a case.

5. There is such a thing as being too specific, if you do not make clear what generalization is supported by the instances given. A well-developed train of thought works back and forth between the general and the specific, showing the connections and applications intended at each point.

6. Your treatment here is obviously marked by particular bias and prior emotional commitment. This does not necessarily make your conclusions false, but it does make them all suspect.

7. Your approach here is essentially moralistic and directive rather than analytical. No law exists against preaching, but distinguish preaching from investigation, analysis, and reasoning.

8. Here you are exploring religious or philosophical questions which have been canvassed for thousands of years by serious thinkers without being brought to an issue. You of course have a right to try your hand at them, but don't expect an easy success, and remember that no certain conclusions are possible when the assumptions with which you start out are untestable.[1]

Logic is an important study in itself, ranging all the way from a consideration of careless phrasing to detailed criteria of philosophical, literary, and scientific methods. A sampling such as is presented in this section should not lead you to think you are a master of logic. Study of a good book devoted to the subject will be rewarding. The following books, among several others, contain effective, extended treatments of methods for attaining clear thinking:

Altick, Richard D. "Patterns of Clear Thinking," chap. 3 in *Preface to Critical Reading*, 4th ed. New York: Holt, Rinehart and Winston, 1960.
Chase, Stuart. *Guides to Straight Thinking, with Thirteen Common Fallacies.* New York: Harper & Row, 1956.
Sherwood, John C. *Discourse of Reason: A Brief Handbook of Semantics and Logic*, 2nd ed. New York: Harper & Row, 1964.

Also, the articles by Sherwood, p. 618, and Davis, p. 486, should prove helpful to you.

---

[1] For these suggestions the individual largely responsible is Professor Macklin Thomas of the Department of Higher Education, Chicago.

42. CONSISTENCY

As applied to theme writing, *consistency* means "maintaining a uniform point of view, mood, and tone." The point of view of a writer is the physical and mental position that he takes relative to the object or subject under observation and consideration. Inconsistency in the physical point of view from which something is seen and the mental point of view from which specific details are considered can cause confusion for your reader. Of any theme you should ask: Have I shifted my point of view? If so, did I have a good reason for doing so? Are the shift and the reason for it made clear to my reader?

42a. *Be consistent in your physical point of view.*

Before beginning a theme, choose some point in *space* or *time* (hour, year, weather, season) from which you will consider your subject. For example, if you plan to describe a campus building, you can proceed from front to back, outside to inside, one floor to another. But do not shift your point of view without warning your reader; he will be confused if you are describing the outside of the building and suddenly begin to discuss heating facilities in the basement.

Shifts in time are equally bewildering. Do not thoughtlessly leap from one decade to another or give the impression it is night and suddenly mention noon sunlight the next day. If you are describing a New England snowstorm, do not abruptly add details about summer camps or trout fishing.

42b. *Be consistent in your mental point of view.*

You should assume a mental attitude toward your subject that will consistently reveal the mood, tone, and style of your treatment and also your personal attitude toward the topic. You can be subjective and let your feelings and emotions control your attitude, or you can try to be objective and impersonal. But you should not be both in the same theme. You can use a gay, breezy approach or a heavy, sad one, but do not shift suddenly from one mood and tone to the other. If you are explaining life insurance, you may present reasons for and against it, but you should make clear to your reader when you shift the argument. Also, if you are arguing against life insurance as a means of investment, present no arguments in favor of it unless you use them to further your thesis. In short, never confuse your reader about your mental point of view toward a topic.

42c. *Be consistent in your use of person.*

In treating a subject, you may use one of four personal points of view. The choice depends upon suitability to the subject and for your reader.

(1) The *first* person (*I, me, mine, we, ours*) is often used in telling about your own experiences and thoughts.

(2) The *second* person (*you, your, yours*) refers directly to your reader and is used in giving information or instructions, making requests, etc.

(3) The *third* person (*he, his, she, they, them*) is used when you are writing about some group or some person of either sex.

(4) The *impersonal* point of view (*one, everyone, a person*) is most often employed in expository, descriptive, and argumentative writing. In narrative writing, you should use the point of view of a major character, a minor character, or that of an all-knowing (omniscient) person or observer.

43. UNITY

Each paragraph in a theme may itself be unified (see Section 32), yet the theme as a whole may lack unity. The word *theme*, as applied to compositions (short papers), means a "single phase of one topic." A theme should clearly and fully develop this *one* phase and should not be "more than complete." A composition often lacks unity because one or more paragraphs within it, although unified, may not stick to the oneness of the central idea, the controlling purpose of the paper as a whole.

43a. *Discuss in a theme only one phase of a subject.*

The principle of unity in a theme is commonly violated in three ways:

(1) To meet a word quota, an irrelevant introduction or useless conclusion is tacked on.

(2) Material which has nothing to do with "the theme of the theme" pads out wordage. For example, a critical study of *Lord of the Flies* should contain no elaborate details about its author's background and experiences. A discussion of your favorite sport should not thoughtlessly slip into details about the high school you attended.

(3) Material is included which bears some relationship to your central idea and purpose but has little or no direct connection. If you are discussing your favorite academic subject in high school, include no paragraphs which describe school buildings—unless the latter are shown to have direct bearing upon your central purpose.

43b. *Give a theme unity of purpose and tone.*

Be consistent in your primary aim: to inform, or amuse, or satirize, or persuade, or ridicule, or whatever. Do not attempt to accomplish more than one purpose in one theme.

Decide on the basic form of writing you will use. If you wish to argue, omit narrative detail which adds nothing to your central purpose. If you wish to tell a story, use little argument and exposition—and none which has no direct relationship to your aim.

Try to make your theme unified in tone and mood. Tragedy and comedy, dignity and farce, pathos and ridicule are difficult to mingle in a short paper. A solemn page on President Kennedy's assassination probably should not contain any references at all to his lively undergraduate days. A farcical paper on night-club humor will lack unity if you add serious thoughts about the plights of minority groups. (See *Style* in Part II.)

44. COHERENCE AND TRANSITION

Coherence means "holding together." A theme is coherent when its parts have been so closely and clearly put together that a reader is never confused about the relationship of ideas. An outline (see Section 39) helps in achieving coherence but does not insure its presence. A careful writer *transfers* ideas from his own mind to that of a reader, trying at all times to show clear and orderly progress from beginning to end. In a really coherent paper, each paragraph grows out of the preceding one; each group of paragraphs dealing with one section of the theme is closely connected with other paragraph groups.

44a. *Leave no missing links in thought.*

The association of two ideas may seem clear and logical to you and quite illogical to your reader. He cannot see so readily as you can how ideas are related if you omit a necessary linking thought which was in your mind but not put on paper. For example, in a theme on "automation," one paragraph may deal with the effects of automation on jobs, and the next may discuss assembly line procedures. The relationship will not be clear to the reader unless you link the thoughts by commenting that, for example, innovations may seem to threaten work opportunities but eventually increase the number of jobs available. Your reader may disagree, but at least he will see the connection you have in mind.

44b. *Seek coherence by using transition.*

Transition means "passage or change from one position, place, or stage to another." In writing it involves *showing* evidence of the links, the bridges, between related units.

Shifts in thought will puzzle your reader unless he is prepared in advance for them. The most effective way to prepare your reader is to use transitional words, phrases, and sentences. Transitions resemble highway signs: "Slow Down: End of Pavement," "Detour: 100 Yards." Such signs prepare a motorist for changing conditions; transitional expressions have exactly the same design upon the reader. When you complete a group of paragraphs dealing with one phase of your topic, let the reader know what is to come next. Sometimes, you can sum up what has been written; more often you may point out the road ahead, a continuation in the same direction.

Transitions are important, but they should be brief and inconspicuous. You may, on rare occasions, need to use a complete sentence as a transitional aid. Frequently, a word or brief phrase will be sufficient. Among the most common transitional devices are these:

> *and, again, as an illustration, besides, but, by way of comparison* (or *contrast*), *for example, for instance, furthermore, however, in addition, in like manner, in the first place, nevertheless, otherwise, similarly, then, therefore, thus, while*

45. THE RESEARCH PAPER

The *research paper* (also called a *term paper* or *investigative theme*) is a report, usually from 1,500 to 6,000 words, assigned in nearly all college courses requiring outside reading. Its purpose is, or should be, to make a careful and reasonably thorough investigation of some subject and to present and interpret the source material unearthed. It is not, or should not be, a jumbled series of quotations from books and articles or paraphrases of them. It should be a carefully controlled study in as much depth as possible; it should set out with a definite purpose; it should state conclusions based upon your understanding and interpretation of the material read and studied.

The research paper, in short, is a time-consuming and mentally taxing exercise. You may complain about having to prepare one or more, but your protests are likely to be ignored: most instructors feel, with good reason, that preparing a research paper is excellent training which has value in the English classroom, in other college courses, and in still other outreachings of the mind. As you proceed, you may be astonished to find that seeking facts can be absorbing; you may discover that, once you really dig deep into a subject, you have talent for seeing the relationships of ideas and for interpreting them. The preparation of a research paper involves five major steps: (1) choosing and analyzing a subject, (2) investigating the subject carefully, (3) taking notes, (4) preparing an outline, (5) writing and revising.[2]

45a. *Choose and analyze your subject carefully.*

(1) Select a subject which is neither too large nor too small. Some subjects can be treated adequately in 1,000 words; trying to develop such subjects in 5,000 words results in padding and dull repetition. Even more importantly, select a subject which can be treated adequately in the assigned space. Subjects such as "Aviation," "The Social Security Act," and "Professional Basketball" are obviously too broad and inclusive. Trying to handle such a topic in 5,000 words is like using a teaspoon to catch rainwater.

(2) Select a subject in which you are already interested or in which you think you can become interested. Also, even though it interests you, do not select a subject so technical or abstruse that your readers cannot be interested in it.

(3) Select a subject about which sufficient material is available in your own college library. (See *Library, use of,* in Part II.)

(4) Select a subject from an investigation of which you can arrive at

---

[2] These steps constitute a complex operation. The pages which follow provide only a sketchy indication of the problems involved. Your instructor may supplement this section with classroom lectures and other specific teaching aids or may refer you to books dealing solely with research papers. If your instructor does assign one of a dozen such books, study it carefully, intensively. Preparing a research paper, and understanding fully what you are doing and the implications of your work, is one of the most valuable intellectual experiences college can offer.

a set of conclusions. A research paper, like an ordinary theme, should have a central thesis, a controlling idea. Any assembling of materials anticipates the support of some proposition, of some general idea or statement. The facts you gather should lead to conclusions, the most significant part of any research paper. (See Section 37.)

45b. *Make a thorough investigation of the subject.*

Pressed for time, or thinking that you are, you are not likely to collect more than a small part of the material available on any important subject. Amassing all that has been written on a fairly significant topic might require a year, a decade, a lifetime. But, within reason and time limitations, you should make a thorough search for information. A research paper is value-less if it merely dips into a subject. It is definitely an illusion that using an encyclopedia and investigating a topic are one and the same thing. Here are questions you should ask:

(1) *Where can I find a good résumé of this subject?*

It is sound practice to get an overall view of a subject, a general back-ground of information, in beginning an investigation. (Of course, if you start and stop here, you are shirking your task.) Most often you should start with an encyclopedia article. If your topic is not covered in a general or special subject encyclopedia, you may find the needed summary in a maga-zine article or chapter from a book.

But in starting with an encyclopedia article, do not assume that the *Britannica* is the final word, the source of all wisdom. It is a great and monumental general work, but the *Encyclopedia of the Social Sciences* or the *Dictionary of American History* might provide a better general view of your particular subject. No matter what the source, start with a nucleus of information to guide you in making the genuine investigation to follow.

(2) *What books are in the library on my topic?*

Begin your search in the card catalog for books mentioned in the bibli-ography following the résumé article just mentioned. If you will note the subject headings appearing at the bottoms of the cards you consult, you can choose those titles that seem useful. If a suitable *subject* heading eludes you, try looking in the catalog for a *title* card under the key word of your topic.

You have had some experience with card catalogs in libraries. Your college career will afford you many further opportunities to familiarize yourself with this extraordinary key for unlocking the fabulous resources of a library. It is probably true that some people attend school for a semester or a year without ever consulting the card catalog of their library. This could never be said of a real student. If you need help in familiarizing your-self with a card catalog, a librarian or your instructor will assist you and may even suggest one of a number of useful pamphlets or books dealing with this remarkable device. (See page 360.)

(3) *What reference materials will help?*

Try to prevent as much fumbling and waste of time as possible. Refer-ence materials, available in most libraries in large quantities, are excellent, time-saving aids. Spend some time in the reference room of your library, noting what is there. If you are genuinely confused, seek help from a librarian. A good reference librarian will suggest, for example, that if your topic has been discussed in Congress you should consult the *Congressional Quarterly;* that the *Harvard Guide to American History* is a timesaver in another area; that both *The Reference Shelf* and *Editorial Research Reports* treat topics of current public interest. *The Essay and General Literature Index* is a boon to harried researchers. Annual supplements to general encyclopedias such as the *Britannica* and the *Americana* provide invaluable reference materials. (See *Reference books* in Part II.)

(4) *How can I locate material recently written on my topic?*

You might begin this phase of your investigation by examining recent issues of the *Readers' Guide to Periodical Literature.* You can then compare what is listed there with entries in the *International Index to Periodicals* and *Bulletin of the Public Affairs Information Service* (P.A.I.S.). In addition, depending on your topic, you might consult entries in the *Art Index, Agricultural Index, Education Index, Applied Science and Technology Index,* and *Business Periodical Index.* (See page 415.)

Answering, and following up, the four questions just posed will provide a good start on your research. But the references listed above will not answer all your questions or provide all the guidelines needed; they represent only the beginning of your investigative processes. You have located some primary sources. Now you have to read and absorb what you have collected. As you read, you must take notes.

45c.   *Take careful notes from your reading.*

Note-taking should be a process of careful thinking, not a hasty scribbling of jumbled ideas or scratchy jottings here and there in a notebook. You should read carefully and thoughtfully when doing research; both the materials and methods of your notes should reflect equal care and thoughtfulness.

MATERIALS

Cards (3-by-5, preferably larger) can be easily shuffled into place according to subject outline; some students prefer to take notes on half-size or full-size sheets of paper. Whichever material you choose, place no more than one note on a card or sheet or half-sheet of paper. *Never* use both sides of the card or paper; if the quotation or the information needed requires more space than the card or sheet allows, continue on card or sheet 2, which should be clearly marked with the same heading.

METHODS

(1) Each book or other source used should be entered on a separate card or sheet, *in full bibliographical detail* giving full name of the author, title, place of publication, publisher, and date. Include the number of pages in the book or article on this master card. With this complete information about each source used, the reference on the individual notes can be somewhat shortened, and all of the information needed for your bibliography

Webster, Margaret
   Shakespeare Without Tears. New
York: McGraw-Hill Book Company,
Inc., 1942.   319 p.

Master card

The Elizabethan Stage
   "When Shakespeare came to London
around the year 1587... the Elizabethan
stage ... was in an extremely fluid
condition."
   Margaret Webster, Shakespeare
Without Tears, New York, McGraw-Hill,
1942, p. 19

The Elizabethan Stage
   James Burbage, about 1576, began
plans for a building to be used
primarily for plays.
   Marchette Chute, Shakespeare
of London, New York, E. P. Dutton,
1949, p. 29

will be assured. You will, then, have two files of cards: one, a master file which will include *all* bibliographical detail on each book or article used (this file can be arranged in order later for your bibliography); the other, a file containing notes taken for the body of your paper.

(2) *Before you begin to take notes on a book, study its Preface and Table of Contents.* Skim through each chapter or article first, then read carefully and take notes as needed. Often the index of a book saves time if you are careful not to overlook any possible entry for the subject being searched.

(3) *Record accurately and fully the details of the information you will need, and do it the first time.* Notes must be *legible*, so that they cannot be misinterpreted later, and *full*, so that repeated trips to the library to verify them will not be necessary. If you quote, *use quotation marks* to avoid wondering later whether your note represents your summary or whether it is in the author's words. Your notes should be *organized* under tentative headings; each should indicate its source by author, title, and page.

(4) *Condense your notes.* Make frequent use of topic sentences and summaries.

(5) *Rearrange and regroup your notes as work proceeds.* In effect, this regrouping and perhaps discarding (tentatively only, for it is a mistake to destroy what you may have second thoughts about later) amounts to making a preliminary outline.

(6) *Distinguish fact and opinion in your reading and in the notes made.* Consider the point of view of each author, judge whether he proves his points, note the date of publication. Not all cards will note material directly quoted; but all should be so worded that there will be no confusion in your mind later as to what *you* said or thought and what the *author* said or what his meaning was.

45d. *Prepare an adequate outline for your paper.*

You will probably make a number of tentative outlines as your work proceeds, but only after you have investigated thoroughly and taken notes carefully and fully can you make a final outline of your paper. When you are ready to state conclusions and have some idea of the framework of the entire structure, you can rearrange your notes (if carefully taken) under suitable headings. From these you can readily prepare a topic or sentence outline (see Section 39). Never, repeat *never*, attempt to write a research paper without some form of outline as a guide.

The following is a list of items which should appear in the majority of outlines for research papers. It is not an outline itself but merely an indication of contents a suitable outline will cover, a checklist of items to keep in mind.

(1) Purpose of investigation
(2) Importance (significance) of the subject
(3) Background (history) of the subject
(4) The investigation itself—chronological developments, description of apparatus, etc.
(5) Conclusions—generalized statements based on the findings of your study

Two conditions of special import help account for the violence of the attack upon witchcraft in colonial Massachusetts. One was the particular body of religious beliefs held by Puritans. The other traced from frontier conditions in early New England. I shall consider them in order.

First, it is noteworthy that intellectual leaders as well as the "common herd" among Puritans considered the Bible the infallible word of God.[1] They accepted without any question whatever such a Mosaic pronouncement as "Thou shalt not suffer a witch to live."[2] Few Puritans in New England, and hardly more in the mother country, even considered challenging current theology. Newton's law of gravitation was not used as an argument against the possibility of witches riding the sky on broomsticks. Many Puritans believed that individuals could, and did, enter into compacts with the Devil. They believed in a personal devil, as described by Phillips:

> A gentleman clothed in black with horns on his head,
> cloven hoofs, and a forked tail, whom you might meet by
> ill luck almost any dark night.[3]

Puritans listened and believed when Cotton Mather spoke these awesome words:

> We should every one of us be a dog and a witch, too,
> if God should leave us to ourselves. It is the
> mere grace of God, the chains of which refrain us
> from bringing the chains of darkness upon our souls.[4]

Such a pronouncement was similar to hundreds of others which filled the Puritan air and inclined hearers to hatred, fear, and persecution.

The other important condition intensifying the attack upon witches involves the hardships of frontier living in early New England...

---

[1] George Lyman Kittredge, Witchcraft in Old and New England (New York, 1929), pp. 329-330.

[2] Exodus, 22:18 (King James translation).

[3] James Duncan Phillips, Salem in the Seventeenth Century (Boston, 1933), p. 290.

[4] Cotton Mather, Memorable Providences, Relating to Witchcraft and Possessions (Boston, 1689). Quoted from David Levin, What Happened in Salem? (New York, 1960), pp. 96-97.

Specimen page

45e. ***Write and rewrite your paper correctly, clearly, interestingly.***

When you have read thoughtfully and taken adequate notes, your task is more than half-finished. Now you must write and revise until your paper "comes alive" in language that is your own. Most research papers are duller and more static than they need be. If you try hard enough, you can write both clearly and effectively. A good research paper is a living, tangible accomplishment; you may be pleasantly surprised at your delight in mastering one phase of a subject and communicating it with clarity, vigor, and appeal.

Nearly every section in this book is designed to help you write your paper. In addition, since your work must be documented, you should consult the entries for *Footnote* and *Bibliography* in Part II. Also, you should study in Part II the entries for *Card catalog; Library, use of; Periodical indexes;* and *Reference books.*

· EXERCISES ON THE THEME ·

A wide variety of exercises on the theme will be found beginning on p. 29; exercises there deal with major topics of theme writing discussed in Chapter 2. The exercises which follow here are concerned with other topics treated in the Handbook itself.

OUTLINES

A. Point out all the errors in the following outlines:

ARE COLLEGE BOYS STUDENTS?
I. Definition of word, *student.*
　a. Reference to several dictionaries.
II. Many boys come to college to engage in athletics.
　A. Some come to enjoy the social life.
　B. Others to keep from working.
III. A minority come to get a real education.
　1. Preparation for various professions.
　　a. Medicine, dentistry.
　　　1. Law, teaching.
IV. Summary and Conclusion.

THREE 4-H ACTIVITIES

I Junior leadership
　a) age
　b) experience
　C) girls' and boys' projects
II Clothing
　a) Age

B) experience
C) Time
D) Cost
III Freezing
　a) where purchased
　B) Cost

B. Make correct *topic* outlines of the material in Exercise A.

C. Make correct *sentence* outlines of material in Exercise A.

D. As your instructor directs, make a *sentence* or *topic* or *paragraph* outline of "How Americans Choose Their Heroes" by Dixon Wecter, p. 548.

PROPORTION

A. Study the amount of space given each division of one of your recent themes. Can you justify the proportion from the standpoint of both subject and reader?

B. Look up in a good dictionary these words: *perspective, distortion, proportion.* Illustrate them by reference to motion pictures, paintings, statuary, and architecture which you have seen.

CLEARNESS (LOGICAL THINKING)

How would you reply to the following questions or suppositions?

1. Suppose you hear a U. S. Government official quoted as saying, "The greatest enemy in America is the United States Government." What would you think?
2. What is your opinion when you learn that the official was speaking against Federal support of price controls for agricultural commodities, and his sentence, *in toto,* read: "The greatest enemy of free economic institutions in America is the United States Government"?
3. You receive through the mail material including a "Free Information Certificate" entitling you to receive free information on the White Cross Plan of hospitalization insurance. Give reasons why you think you would or would not receive this information if you wrote without referring to the "Free Information Certificate."
4. Mother once said to Father: "Honey, lend me 10 dollars. But just give me five now. Then you'll owe me five, and I'll owe you five, and we'll be even."
5. We students believe that we go to college to improve our faculties. Our faculties are our teachers. Therefore, we go to college to improve our teachers.
6. If you think I am dead, please awaken me thoroughly; I do not wish to be buried alive. (Note by the hotel bedside of an 80-year-old.)
7. If you do not receive this order, please write me and I shall send it to you again. (Letter to a mail-order house from a newly arrived immigrant.)
8. Three copies of this test are missing. Those who have them should make an A. Therefore, anyone who makes an A presumably is one of the three who has seen a copy of this test.
9. Mary loves Bill; Bill loves Sue; Sue loves Mike; Mike loves Sally; and Sally loves Henry. Therefore, Henry loves Mary.
10. Woman is an antonym for man, and man is an antonym for beast; therefore, woman is an antonym for beast.
11. When Professor Sheehan was asked how many students there were on our campus, he immediately replied, "About one out of 10."
12. Poison ivy won't hurt anybody. My brother and I have played in it often and never had any trouble.
13. Smoking isn't the least harmful; otherwise, there wouldn't be so many doctors that smoke.
14. I haven't acted like an old fool because an old fool must be at least 30, and I'm only 19.
15. It is either raining or not raining. It is *not* raining. Therefore, it must be raining.

POINT OF VIEW (CONSISTENCY)

A. Describe the *physical* point(s) of view of the author of "A Windstorm in the Forest," p. 696.

B. Describe the *mental* point of view of the author of "The Case for Greater Clarity in Writing," p. 654.

C. Comment on the *narrative* point of view revealed in "A Rose for Emily," p. 901.

Unity

A. Try to find places in a recent theme where you have dealt with more than one phase of a subject or where you have not confined yourself to one central purpose.

B. Show how a theme may lack unity even if all its component sentences and paragraphs are themselves unified.

C. Discuss violations of unity in the following plan for a theme:

MY ROOMMATE'S FATHER

I. My roommate's father is an excellent dentist.
II. He studied hard while he was in college and dental school and took many scholastic honors.
III. His mother died during his last year at dental school.
IV. My roommate is not a hard student; he is more interested in dancing and playing football.
V. After he was graduated, my roommate's father studied abroad for several years.
VI. He now has a large and lucrative practice in Houston.
VII. His health is poor, and he has engaged an assistant.
VIII. My roommate has many excellent characteristics.

Coherence and Transition

A. Comment on the paragraph order and transitional devices employed in "Definition of a Gentleman," p. 701.

B. Underscore the transitional words and phrases used in "Comfort," p. 707.

C. List all of the transitional devices you have used in one recent theme. Comment on their suitability, variety, and number.

The Research Paper

1. Using the Card Catalog (see card on p. 274)
    A. What is the call number of this book?
    B. What is the date of the author's birth?
    C. Where was this book published? By whom? In what year?
    D. How many pages does the book contain?
    E. The card contains two indications that this book would be very useful in a study of sociologists. What are they?
    F. Are there any portraits in this book?
    G. There are three other cards in the catalog for this book; what is the entry for each?
    H. In a card catalog following the word-by-word system of filing, what would be the proper entry for the following authors and titles? White, Alfred; *White April, and Other Poems;* White, Leonard B.; White Plains, New York; White House Conference; White-Williams foundation; Whitefield, George; Whitehall through the centuries; Whitehouse Collection.
    I. Arrange these subject headings in proper filing order: EDUCATION—

```
Soc.Sci.
HM19
 .E4    Ellwood, Charles Abram, 1873-
            The story of social philosophy, by Charles A. Ellwood ...
        New York, Prentice-Hall, inc., 1938.

            xiv p., 2 l., 3–581 p.   front., ports.,   21 cm.

            "We shall select outstanding individuals in the history of social
            thought, outline their doctrines, and briefly describe the conditions
            under which their thinking took place."—p. x.
            Published also in the Prentice-Hall sociology series under title:
            A history of social philosophy.


            1. Social sciences—Hist.  2. Sociologists.     I. Title.

            HM19.E4  1938                  309                         38—13162

            Library of Congress          [54t1]
```

ABSTRACTS; EDUCATION, AGRICULTURAL; EDUCATION—U. S.; EDUCA-
TION—QUOTATIONS; EDUCATIONAL PSYCHOLOGY; EDUCATION OF
ADULTS; EDUCATION—GREAT BRITAIN; EDUCATION, SECONDARY:
    (The rules to remember are that *place* follows other "dash" subdivisions;
all "dash" subdivisions precede the "comma" subdivisions, and phrase subject
headings follow both.)

2. *Periodical Indexes*

    Assuming that *Readers' Guide, Public Affairs Information Service* (P.A.I.S.),
*International Index, Art Index, Business Periodical Index, Engineering Index,
Applied Science and Technology Index* are all available in your library, which
would you choose to use in preference to others for each of these topics:
    A City Government
    B Automation (its technical aspects)
    C Automation (to locate again an article you remember having read in *Life*)
    D Automation (how it affects the grocer)
    E Landscape Architecture
    F Scholarly articles written about Edgar Allan Poe since 1950

3. *Choosing an Encyclopedia*

    Assuming that you have available the *Encyclopedia of the Social Sciences*
(E.S.S.), *Dictionary of American History, Literary History of the United States*
(L.H.U.S.), as well as a general encyclopedia (*Britannica, Americana,* or *Col-
lier's*), which would you prefer for each series below:

A The Purchase of Alaska   C Mushrooms
   Formation of the Republican Party   Olympic Games
   Building of the Erie Canal   Lumbering

B The Prophet Mohammed   D American Oratory
   Industrial Architecture   Brook Farm Experiment
   The Thrush (bird)   Transcendentalism

E	Probation and Parole	F	Drug Addiction
	Consumer's Coöperatives		Farm Tenancy
	City and Town Planning		Law Enforcement

4. *Footnotes*

Study the entry *Footnote* beginning on p. 379. Then arrange the following items in conventional footnote form and style:

A An article under the heading Jules Verne in the eleventh edition of the Encyclopaedia Britannica, volume 27, published in 1911. The article appears on page 1030.

B A reference to page 231 of a book entitled Magnificent Masquerade. The author is Charles Keats. Funk & Wagnalls Company, Inc., New York, published this 276-page book in 1964.

C A reference to page 100 of an article by Harold B. Meyers which appeared in Fortune in May, 1965. The title is Commuter Railroads Can Be Saved; the volume number of the magazine is 71.

D A reference which immediately follows on page 83 of the book mentioned in B (above).

E A reference to a chapter entitled The South Embraces Change which appears in a book entitled Seeds of Time. The author is Henry Savage, Jr. This 312-page book was published in 1959 by Henry Holt and Company, New York. The South Embraces Change appears on pages 242–274.

5. *Bibliographies*

Study the entry *Bibliography* beginning on p. 358. Then arrange the items given in Exercise 4 (above) in the form and order in which they should appear in a bibliography.

6. *Miscellaneous*

A. In *Bartlett* three or four quotations similar to this may be found: "A dwarf standing on the shoulders of a giant may see farther than the giant himself." Under what two key words would you be likely to find these quotations quickly?

B. Where would you look to find a brief biography of the governor of your state?

C. You neglected to make a note of who published the book when you used William F. Taylor, *The Story of American Letters.* How can you find the information in your library without using the book itself?

D. What would be a good source for a brief authoritative biography of John Jay, 1745–1829, first Chief Justice of the U. S. Supreme Court?

E. You believe Abraham Lincoln lived 1809–1865; what is the quickest way to verify the dates without using a book?

F. None of the sources available includes a biography of someone who began to figure prominently in the news about six months ago. Where would you look next?

G. An assignment requires you to read a biography of William Gladstone, 1809–1898, only a few pages long. But the article must be followed by a bibliography. Where would you find this?

PUNCTUATION AND
MECHANICS

Correct, clear, effective writing is impossible without proper punctuation. Our thoughts—and the relationships of our thoughts—are in considerable part dependent upon punctuation for their clear and orderly transmission to readers. Actually, punctuation originally developed because, without it, written language was unable to indicate or reproduce certain definite and clear qualities of speech. We can always tell, for example, from a person's voice whether he is making a statement or asking a question. But in writing we would not know which sentence made a statement and which asked a question unless we saw a period at the end of one and a question mark terminating the other. We also know that a pause, or a rising inflection, means something in speech.

These and other meanings and qualities in speech are reproduced in writing by certain marks of punctuation. In addition, since English is not a highly inflected language, the essential meaning of a sentence and the relationships of its parts are revealed primarily by word order (see *Inflection* and *Word order* in Part II). But word order is flexible, and punctuation is required to show or to suggest the grouping of words and phrases in a sentence which conveys meaning.

Punctuation is not entirely arbitrary and mechanical; it is truly an integral (or organic) part of writing. You cannot indiscriminately sprinkle your writing with punctuation marks and expect it to be fully understood. To be sure, punctuation usage varies with individual writers, but certain basic principles remain steadfast. These principles may be called "descriptive rules," since they have been formulated from hundreds and thousands of examples of punctuation as applied by reputable authors and, much more importantly, by professional editors and type compositors. When we have enough examples of one use of a certain mark of punctuation, we state this as a general principle or rule, beginning it thus: "Use the . . ." or "*Always* use the . . ." When most of our examples agree: "The mark is *usually* used . . ."; when examples are insufficient to make a generalization: "The mark is *occasionally* used . . ." Correct punctuation permits individuality only to the extent that communication of thought from writer to reader is aided, not impeded.

What is usually considered correct punctuation is about as fixed in usage as is correct spelling, and for a similar reason. Our punctuation usage is based upon the practice of editors and compositors who normally follow one or more of a group of standardized books of rules; spelling practices, too, are made rigid by the same professional groups relying upon standard guidebooks and dictionaries.

The most important marks of punctuation are

.	Period	,	Comma
?	Question mark	;	Semicolon
!	Exclamation point	:	Colon
—	Dash	" "	Double quotation marks
-	Hyphen	' '	Single quotation marks
'	Apostrophe	( )	Parentheses

The use, misuse, and overuse of each of these marks are discussed in the sections which follow. In addition, other items involving punctuation and the mechanics of writing are also discussed: *italics, capital letters, brackets, abbreviations, numbers,* and *miscellaneous marks.*

46. END STOPS

An *end stop* is a mark of punctuation used at the end of a sentence. Sometimes also referred to as *terminal marks,* end stops are usually a period, question mark, or exclamation point. More than 95 percent of all sentences end with a period, regardless of where they appear or who writes them. But the other two end stops have special, limited uses.

46a.　*Use a period at the end of a declarative sentence.*

His trip began with an inspection of the missile base.
Dick prefers winter to summer vacations.

46b.　*Use a period after most abbreviations.*

Mr. and Mrs. Richard Soule
Mary E. Bisacca, M.D. (b. 1905, d. 1960)
Oct. 15, Ariz., bbl., Ave., St., P.M.

46c. *Use periods properly in an outline.*

A period should appear after each number or letter symbol in an outline. Use no period at the end of a line in a topic outline, but do place one at the end of each sentence in a sentence or paragraph outline. (See Section 39.)

46d. *Use three spaced periods to indicate an intentional omission.*

Such periods, called *ellipses* or *ellipsis periods* or the *ellipsis mark*, indicate an omission of one or more words within a sentence or quotation. If the omission ends with a period, use four spaced periods.

> "Some books are to be tasted, others . . . swallowed, and some few . . . chewed and digested."
> The day wore on from sunrise to late afternoon. . . .

46e. *Use a period before a decimal, to separate dollars and cents, and to precede cents written alone.*

5.26 percent $4.38 $0.65

46f. *Use the exclamation point to end a forceful interjection or to indicate surprise or vigorous emotion.*

> So you have really decided to go!
> What an incredibly rude remark!
> May I ask you—please!—to help me now.

46g. *Use a question mark at the end of every direct question.*

> Does Ninki really love Henry?
> Pat asked, "May I go with you today?"
> You said—did I understand you?—that you were ill.

46h. *Use question marks to indicate a series of queries in the same sentence or passage.*

> Are you going? Is your sister? John? Mimi?
> Do you remember when car windshields opened to let in the breeze? When men wore garters? When grandmothers were elderly?

46i. *Distinguish carefully the purposes of end stops.*

(1) Use a period, not an exclamation point, after a mildly imperative sentence.

Take your time and work carefully.

(2) Use a period, not a question mark, after an indirect question.

Please tell me what he said and how he said it.

(3) Use a period, not a question mark, after a polite request or only superficially interrogative sentence.

"May I have your hat" is an expression more often prompted by courtesy than by curiosity.

46j. *Do not overuse end stops.*

(1) Do not use a period at the end of a theme title.

(2) Do not use end stops (especially the period) to punctuate sentence fragments (see Section 1).

(3) Avoid using a question mark enclosed in parentheses to indicate doubt, uncertainty, or a humorous meaning.

(4) Use the exclamation point sparingly. The emotion, surprise, or command expressed should be strong to warrant the exclamation point. Writing dotted with exclamation points is a form of "schoolgirl style." Also, an exclamation point after a long sentence looks silly; most of us don't have sufficient breath to exclaim more than a few words at a time.

47. THE COMMA

The comma serves many different purposes and is the most widely used of all punctuation marks. Because of its varied and distinct uses, it is also the most troublesome of the marks. And yet this mark of punctuation, more than any of the others, can and does help to make clear the meaning of writing. Its overuse and misuse also obscure meaning more than the mishandling of any other mark. If you can master even the basic uses of the comma—and you can—no other mark of punctuation can hold any terrors for you.

Always used within the sentence, the comma serves four purposes: to *introduce*, to *separate*, to *enclose*, to *show omission.*

Before undertaking study of these four purposes of the comma, it may help you to consider six basic, broad principles of comma use. Learning these six fundamental applications of the comma will not solve all your problems with this mark, but doing so will solve the majority of them.

1. Use a comma to separate long independent clauses in a compound sentence:

Jack has not replied to my letter, nor do I think that he ever will.
She tried to interest him in the stock, but he insisted that he would invest his money in real estate.

2. Use a comma to set off a long introductory phrase or clause from an independent clause which follows:

A retiring and unusually timid man, he refused even to consider the nomination.
When they had finished eating dinner and washing the dishes, they left for the theater.

3. Use a pair of commas to set off words and groups of words inserted within a sentence:

The manager did not say that, as you would know if you had listened carefully, nor did he even hint at it.
On that occasion, it seems, he was driving carelessly.

4. Use commas to divide elements in a series:

She blushed, stammered, and finally burst into tears.
Joe collected a change of clothing, shoes, and golf gear before he set off for
the day.

5. Use commas with transposed initials, with titles, in dates, etc.:

Both Smythe, H. M., and Smythe, J. W., were nominated for the position.
Dexter Lenci, M.D., and Francis Coffin, D.D., attended the services.
The boys sailed for Europe on June 22, 1962.

6. Use a comma, or commas, to prevent misreading:

The morning after a policeman came to the door.
In 1942 361 men from this town entered military service. [These two sentences *can* be unscrambled, but even momentary misreading will be prevented if commas follow *after* and *1942*.]

Learning these six principles of comma use will be an effective start;
each is more fully explained and illustrated in the sections which follow,
together with additional comment, exceptions, and still other examples of
comma usage.

Commas To Introduce

47a.   *Use a comma to introduce a word, phrase, or, on occasion, a clause.*

He needed only one thing, encouragement.
Only one course is left, to get a job.
She had an important decision to make, whether she should get married or
return to college.

47b.   *Use a comma to introduce a statement or question which is preceded
by a mental question or musing aloud.*

She thought to herself, I cannot afford to fail.
I wondered, should I tell the coach about my leg?

47c.   *Use a comma to introduce a short quotation.*

Sue replied, "I'll never speak to him again."

If the "Sue replied" or "she said" or an equivalent expression follows
the quotation, it is separated by a comma unless a question mark or exclamation point is needed:

"I'll never speak to him again," Sue replied.
"Do you think I'll ever speak to him again?" Sue replied.

If the "Sue replied" or its equivalent is inserted between two parts of a
quotation, it is enclosed by commas unless a stronger mark of punctuation is
called for:

"I'll never speak to him again," Sue replied, "unless he speaks to me first."
"I'll never speak to him again," Sue replied; "he insulted me."

When the quotation being introduced is either long or formal, use a colon rather than a comma (see Section 49b).

COMMAS TO SEPARATE

47d. *Use a comma to separate independent clauses joined by such conjunctions as* and, but, yet, neither, nor, or.

> She did not like her work, and her distaste for it was evident to everyone.
> It is one of the busiest streets in town, but motorists should avoid it because it is filled with potholes.
> The dancers wore few clothes, yet they were all wrapped up in themselves.

This use of the comma is one of the most frequently illustrated in all writing. However, its very frequency allows considerable flexibility in application. For example, if the clauses are short, the comma may be omitted before the conjunction. But "How short is short?" If each clause consists of only four or five words or less, obviously each is short. If the clauses consist of only subject and predicate, the comma is usually omitted:

> The grass grew and the flowers bloomed.
> Janet did not come nor did Harry.

Even long clauses connected by a conjunction are sometimes written without a comma if their thought relationship is close or if the subject of both clauses is the same:

> Stephen dressed as carefully as he could for he wished to make a good impression on the personnel manager.

47e. *Use a comma to separate an introductory modifying phrase or adverbial clause from the independent clause which follows.*

> By working hard and pleasing his employers, Steve got several promotions.
> When you have finished with this load, start on that one.

Note that the introductory phrase should be a modifying one *and* should contain a verb form in order to be followed by a comma. "Earning a big salary" contains a verb form, *earning*, but it does not modify in such a sentence as "Earning a big salary was his goal" and therefore does not require a following comma. Similarly, "Because of poor health" does not contain a verb form and, although it modifies in such a sentence as "Because of poor health the man could not work," it is not followed by a comma.

Also note that the comma follows only *introductory adverbial* clauses. Use no comma in a sentence such as "That you were late for work this morning is not my fault"; the noun clause, "that you were late for work this morning," is the subject of the verb *is*. As the subject of the verb it should not be separated from what follows. See Section 47t.

47f. *Use commas to separate words, phrases, and clauses in a series.*

> I chose a tray, selected my food, and paid the cashier.
> In the huge jail were what seemed miles of narrow, sunless, low-ceilinged corridors.

Because of his morbid curiosity he read all he could find about Jesse James, John Dillinger, Jumbo, two-headed calves, and the Cardiff Giant.

In this book Mark Twain revealed the gloom, pessimism, skepticism, and fury which darkened his last years.

Some writers omit the comma before the conjunction and punctuate such series as those illustrated as "A, B *and* C," "A, B *or* C." Greater clarity— the main purpose of punctuation—is usually achieved by the comma before the conjunction. For this reason its use is recommended, although it may be omitted.

A variation on this series is three or more items with the last two not joined by a conjunction. Commas are used after each member except the last:

This general store sells groceries, clothing, fishing supplies, camp equipment.

47g. *Use a comma to separate two or more adjectives when they equally modify the same noun.*

She wore an old, dirty dress and a new, pretty, expensive coat.

When the adjectives do not modify equally—that is, when they are not coordinate—use no commas:

A large green bug settled on the torn autumn leaf.

It is not always easy to determine whether modifying adjectives are really coordinate. One test is mentally to insert the coordinate conjunction *and* between adjectives; only if it naturally fits should you use a comma. In the illustrative sentence immediately above, you can fit *and* between *large* and *green* and between *torn* and *autumn,* but the fit does not seem natural. *Large,* for example, seems to modify *green bug.* Also, truly coordinate adjectives can be reversed: *torn autumn leaf* makes sense whereas *autumn torn leaf* does not.

47h. *Use commas to separate contrasted elements in a sentence.*

Such elements may be letters, numbers, words, phrases, or clauses:

The word begins with an *s,* not a *c.*
The answer should be 26, not 25.
Your error is due to carelessness, not ignorance.
Put your hat on the shelf, not on the floor.
The harder he tried, the less he succeeded.

47i. *Use a comma to separate words or other sentence elements that might be misread.*

Sentences in which commas are needed to prevent misreading are usually faulty in construction and should be rephrased. At times, however, a comma is essential to clarify meaning; without commas, the following sentences would be at least momentarily misunderstood:

The stock advanced five points, to 21. [The comma makes clear that the range of advance was 16 upward, not between five and 21.]

Instead of scores, hundreds telephoned the station.
He arrived on February 10, 1786.
The day after, the supervisor was absent himself.
In 1962, 331 people took this same test.
They prefer an education to drills and forced marches, and college dormitories to army barracks.
Soon after, she got up and left the house.

47j. *Use a comma, or commas, to separate thousands, millions, etc., in writing figures.*

In this contest 4,962 entries were received.
The deficit that year amounted to $8,786,983,000.

Commas are used with all numbers of four or more digits except telephone numbers, years, and house numbers:

Her number is 256-1847.
He was born in 1952.
She lives at 11002 Prospect Avenue.

The comma is also usually omitted from certain numbers in specialized use: motor number 136592; zip code number 10654; serial number 825364; 8.0946 inches; 8/1200 of an inch.

Commas To Enclose

47k. *Use commas to enclose parenthetical words, phrases, or clauses.*

A parenthetical expression (word, phrase, clause) may be omitted from a sentence without materially affecting meaning. Usually, but not always, a parenthetical expression may shift its position in a sentence without changing meaning:

However, the order was not filled that day.
The order, *however,* was not filled that day.
Oh, *yes,* I shall be glad to go.
You are, *on the other hand,* well suited for this work.
I believe, *whether or not you care for my opinion,*
    that our company was mistaken in its policy.

Parenthetical elements vary in intensity; you may indicate their relative strength by punctuation. Many expressions, for example, are so weak that they require no punctuation:

In fact I agree with you.
The foreman *also* believed that you tried.

47l. *Use commas to enclose inserted sentence elements.*

Inserted sentence elements are similar to parenthetical words, phrases, and clauses but normally are more essential to the meaning of the sentence than are the latter. They do not restrict the meaning of the sentence but they do add some degree of emphasis. Such emphatic expressions are set off by commas to indicate that they are to be considered forceful. Again, an inserted sentence element may interrupt or delay the meaning of a sentence, withholding (or suspending) important material until near the end of a sentence. Finally, an inserted sentence element may be transposed and thus require punctuation unnecessary in normal word order.

He is an honest man, a man of complete integrity, and has my full confidence. [Emphatic]
He is an honest man, not only because he keeps the letter of the law, but because he exceeds even the teachings of the Golden Rule. [Suspending]
A personable boy, tall and dark and handsome, was what she expected as an escort. [Transposed]

47m.   *Use commas to enclose nonrestrictive phrases and clauses.*

As a broad distinction, nonrestrictive phrases and clauses do not limit or actually restrict the word or words they modify, whereas restrictive phrases and clauses do. Observe what the identical clause does in each of these sentences:

Denver, *which is the capital of Colorado,* has an altitude of one mile.
The city *which is the capital of Colorado* has an altitude of one mile.

In the first of these sentences, the italicized clause may be omitted without materially affecting central meaning; the purpose of the clause is to supply additional information. The clear and controlling idea of the sentence is "Denver has an altitude of one mile." But the same clause in the second sentence is essential; it identifies, it tells *what* city "has an altitude of one mile." True, the italicized clause in the second sentence could be omitted and a grammatically complete sentence would remain, but it would lack full meaning.

Therefore we say that the clause in the first sentence is *nonrestrictive* and we enclose it in commas to set it off from the remainder of the sentence. The second is *restrictive* and should not be enclosed by commas or by any other mark of punctuation.

If you will carefully note comma usage in the following sentences, the principle of restrictive and nonrestrictive phrases and clauses should become clear:

Our son Stephen, *who was 17 last year,* hopes to become a physician.
Our son *who was 17 last year* hopes to become a physician.
The books *that I own* are all paperbacks.
The books, *those that I own,* are all paperbacks.
The suit *lying there on my bed* has had long wear.
The suit, *a blue one lying there on my bed,* has had long wear.
The girl *sitting in the front row* is a secretary.
The girl wearing a green dress and hat, *sitting in the front row,* is a secretary.

47n.   *Use commas to enclose absolute phrases.*

A phrase is called *absolute* when it stands apart and conveys only its own meaning. It *belongs* in a sentence but has no specific grammatical relationship to other words which it accompanies:

The performance over, we rose to leave.
He entered the office, *hat in hand,* to seek the job.
They were lonely that year, *their only son being away on military duty.*

470. Use commas to enclose words in apposition.

Words in apposition follow another word or group of words and serve to identify or explain them. A word in apposition, called an *appositive,* is a noun or pronoun, or a phrase acting as one of these two parts of speech, which provides explanation and is usually nonrestrictive in function. When the words in apposition actually limit or restrict meaning, then no enclosing commas are used:

> James Greene, *our foreman,* was a kindly man. [Nonrestrictive]
> Our foreman, *James Greene,* was a kindly man. [Nonrestrictive]
> *Foreman James Greene* was a kindly man. [Restrictive]
> Barry Smith, *Republican,* is a senator from Ohio.
> My assignment, *to wash all the dishes,* seemed endless.
> Here comes Mary Perry, *our gardening expert.*

47p. Use commas to enclose vocatives.

A vocative is a noun, pronoun, or noun phrase used in direct address. That is, a vocative indicates to whom something is said. A vocative may appear at various positions within a sentence:

> *Mr. Noble,* may I ask you a question?
> May I, *Mr. Noble,* ask you a question?
> May I ask you a question, *Mr. Noble?*
> Let me tell you, *all of you workers,*
>   that you have done a splendid job.

47q. Use commas to enclose initials or titles following a person's name.

> Joseph Clardy, Ph.D., and Robert Furth, D.D., are on the
>   school board.
> The letter was addressed to Marion High, Esq.
> Miriam Jones, chairman, was a handsome woman.
> Are you referring to Roosevelt, T., or Roosevelt, F. D.?
> James Exeter, Jr., was chosen as the first speaker.

47r. Use commas to enclose places and dates which explain preceding places and dates.

He left on July 20, 1964, for a trip around the world.
He lives in Columbia, Missouri, having been transferred there from Akron, Ohio.
Her new home is at 1607 Ravinia Road, Peru 29, Illinois.

(1) A comma is used *after* a postal zone number but never before it: "Sumter 5, Florida," *not* "Sumter, 5, Florida." No commas appear before or after zip code numbers.

(2) The second comma must be used when the state follows town or city and when the year follows both month and day. When only month and

year are used, employ either two commas or none at all: "In July, 1950, . . ." or "In July 1950 . . ."

(3) Punctuation in the date line of a letter is optional. Formerly it was common practice to write *June 6, 1966;* increasingly popular is the form *6 June 1966.* Both are acceptable. For the sake of clarity, always separate two numerals; where a word intervenes, the comma may be omitted, as shown, if you prefer.

COMMAS TO INDICATE OMISSION

47s. *Occasionally, use a comma to avoid wordiness or faulty repetition.*

Most sentences which require a comma to make clear that something has been left out are poorly constructed and should be rephrased. In rare instances, however, using a comma to show omission helps to avoid wordiness:

> In this office are 10 workers; in that one are 16.
> In this office are 10 workers; in that, 16. [The comma clearly and correctly replaces the words *one are.*]
> Smith is a collector of taxes; Jones, of stamps; Duane, of women.
> He takes his work seriously, himself lightly.
> A decade ago they were rich and powerful; only five years later, poor and weak.

UNNECESSARY COMMAS

47t. *Use no unnecessary commas.*

You should be able to justify the appearance of every comma you use. It is as great a sin against clarity to overuse or misuse commas as it is to omit them where they are needed as an organic part of writing. The most common misuses and overuses of the comma are discussed in the following "do not use" suggestions:

(1) Do not use a comma before the first or after the last member of a series.

> Chromatic colors include, red, green, purple, and brown.
> The tea was a cold, sweet, refreshing, drink.

Omit the first comma in the first sentence; the last in the second.

(2) Do not use a comma to separate a subject from its predicate. No comma is needed in any of these sentences:

> We requested that the road be paved.
> I quickly learned what sort of man he was.
> They soon found the weather to be too cold.

(3) Do not use a comma before the indirect part of a quotation. No comma is needed in a sentence such as this:

> The candidate stated that he was against higher taxes.

(4) Do not use a comma between two independent clauses where a stronger mark of punctuation (semicolon, period) is required (see Section 2).

This misuse, sometimes called the "comma fault" or "comma splice," always causes confusion. Use a semicolon or period for the misused comma in such a statement as this:

> The foreman told me to be there early, I told him I couldn't.

(5) Do not use a comma, or pair of commas, with words in apposition which are actually restrictive.

The italicized words which follow really limit, identify, or define; to enclose them with commas is a mistake:

> My sister *Margaret* is a lovely woman.
> Shakespeare's play *Macbeth* is one of his greatest.
> Eleanor *of Aquitaine* was the mother of Richard
>   *the Lion-Hearted.*

(6) Do not use a comma indiscriminately to replace a word omitted.

On occasion, a comma can correctly and clearly be substituted for a word or even a group of words, but rarely can it take the place of pronouns such as *that, who, whom, which.* In "Robin said, he would come to see me soon," the comma is incorrectly used for *that;* in "The person, I saw was a friend of mine," *whom* should replace the comma. "He thought, that child was sick" should be written "He thought that that child was sick." Actually, both comma and pronoun can be omitted in such constructions.

(7) Do not use a comma in any situation unless it adds to clarity and understanding.

This is a catchall suggestion. Admittedly vague, it should call attention to the fact that comma usage is slowly growing more and more "open" and less and less "closed." Every comma in the following sentences can be justified, but each could equally well be omitted since clarity is not affected in the slightest degree:

> Naturally, the first thing you should do, after reporting for work, is to see
>   the supervisor.
> After the play, Martha and I went home, by taxicab, because we wanted, at
>   all costs, to avoid subway crowds.

Commas are the most frequently used and most important-for-clarity of all marks of punctuation. Use them when necessary to make your meaning clear, but avoid using them when they interrupt or slow down thought or make a page of writing look as though someone had used a comma shaker.

48. THE SEMICOLON

The semicolon is a stronger mark of punctuation than the comma; it signifies a greater break or a longer pause between sentence elements. It is not, however, so forceful as terminal marks of punctuation. The semicolon has definitely established uses which are not difficult to master. Remember: the semicolon is used only between elements of equal rank; it is entirely a mark of *coordination.*

48a. *Use the semicolon to separate independent clauses not joined by a simple conjunction.*

In most contracts, the large print giveth; the small print taketh away.

"Children begin by loving their parents; as they grow older they judge them; sometimes they forgive them."

—WILDE

"If you make people think they're thinking, they'll love you; if you really make them think, they will hate you."

—MARQUIS

48b. *Use the semicolon to separate independent clauses joined by a conjunctive adverb.*

Conjunctive adverbs, special kinds of adverbs which can also be used as conjunctions, include *also, anyhow, as a result, besides, consequently, for example, furthermore, hence, however, in addition, indeed, in fact, instead, likewise, meanwhile, moreover, namely, nevertheless, otherwise, similarly, still, then, therefore, thus.*

He tried for two months to learn to use a comptometer; *then* he quit trying and admitted his failure.
This job is not simple; *however,* it is exciting and rewarding.
Jim's sister is a busy girl; *in fact,* she works harder than he does.

48c. *Use the semicolon between independent clauses which are lengthy or contain internal punctuation.*

"As long as war is regarded as wicked, it will have its fascination; when it is looked upon as vulgar, it will cease to be popular."

—WILDE

"Whatsoever thy hand findeth to do, do it with thy might; for there is no work, nor device, nor knowledge, nor wisdom, in the grave, whither thou goest."

—*Ecclesiastes*

"It is easy in the world to live after the world's opinion; it is easy in solitude to live after our own; but the great man is he, who, in the midst of the crowd, keeps with perfect sweetness the independence of solitude."

—EMERSON

48d. *Use the semicolon to separate phrases and clauses of considerable length and also series of words in which complete clearness is desired.*

Those chosen to receive awards were Shirley Blackman, who had not missed a day from work; Louise Wether, who had made the most suggestions for improving efficiency; Jack Smythe, who had the best record among all the salesmen.

48e. *Do not overuse the semicolon.*

The semicolon is a particular mark with quite definite uses which have been indicated in preceding sections. Like all other marks, it should be neither incorrectly used nor overused. Especially avoid using semicolons in the following ways:

(1) To set off phrases or dependent clauses unless for specific purposes indicated above.

Ordinarily, the semicolon has the same function as a period: it indicates a complete break, the end of one thought and the beginning of another. One fairly safe guide may be stated: *no period, no semicolon.* Setting off dependent clauses or phrases with semicolons will confuse your readers.

Wrong	Inasmuch as Joe has a fiery temper; we have to be careful what we say to him. [Dependent clause]
Wrong	Being careful to observe all traffic regulations; I am considered a good driver. [Participial phrase]
Wrong	The excitement of our mock political campaign having died down; we once again turned our attention to our jobs. [Absolute phrase]

To correct semicolon errors like these, use a comma or no punctuation; a comma is preferable.

(2) As a mark of introduction.

Wrong	My purpose is simple; to succeed in life.
Wrong	[In business letters] Dear Sir; Dear Mr. Woods; Gentlemen;

Substitute colons or commas for the semicolons.

(3) As a summarizing mark.

Wrong	Answering the phone, typing, filing; these were my duties that summer.

Use a dash or a colon, not a semicolon.

49. THE COLON

The colon is a mark of expectation or addition. Its primary function is to signal the reader to "watch for what's coming." That is, it signals to the reader that the next group of words will fulfill what the last group promised. What comes after the colon is usually explanatory or illustrative material which has been prepared for by a word, or words, preceding the colon.

Major uses of the colon are to introduce lists, tabulations, enumerations; to introduce a word, a phrase, or even a to-be-emphasized clause; to precede an example or clarification of an idea suggested before the colon; to introduce a restatement of a preceding phrase or clause; to spell out details of a generalization; to introduce a formal quotation.

49a. *Use the colon to introduce a word, phrase, or clause, or after an introductory statement which shows that something is to follow.*

My goal in this job is simple: success.
Only one course remains: to get out of here at once.
This is my problem: what do I do now?
Do this before you leave: check your passport, buy traveler's checks, have your smallpox vaccination.

49b. *Use the colon to separate introductory words from a long or formal quotation which follows.*

> Jefferson concluded his First Inaugural Address as follows: "And may that Infinite Power which rules the destinies of the universe lead our councils to what is best and give them a favorable issue for your peace and prosperity."

49c. *Use the colon as a separating mark in special situations.*

(1) *In business letters*, the salutation is separated from the body of the letter by a colon: *Dear Sir: Dear Mr. James: Gentlemen: My dear Mr. Burnside:*

It is customary to place a comma after the salutation of a friendly or personal letter (*Dear Jim,*), but the colon is not so formal a mark as to repulse friendship. Use either a colon or a comma after the salutation in such letters.

(2) *Titles and subtitles of books* may be separated by a colon: *The English Novel: A Panorama; Education for College: Improving the High School Curriculum.*

(3) *Hour and minute figures* in writing time may be separated by a colon: 10:15 A.M.; 4:46 P.M.

(4) *Acts and scenes of plays* may be separated by a colon: Shakespeare's *Twelfth Night*, II:v.

(5) *Chapters and verses of the Bible* may be separated by a colon: *Exodus*, 12:31.

(6) Volume and page references may be separated by a colon: *The History of the English Novel*, IV:77.

(7) *A publisher's location and name* may be separated by a colon: *New York: W. W. Norton & Company.*

(8) In stating proportions, both a single colon and double colon may be used: 2:4::4:8 (two is to four as four . . .).

49d. *Do not overuse the colon.*

The colon is a useful mark adding clarity to writing, but it should be employed to accomplish only the purposes suggested on p. 289. Used in other constructions, the colon becomes both obstructive and intrusive.

(1) Do not place a colon between a preposition and its object:

> I am fond *of: New Orleans, Seattle,* and *Denver*. [There is no need for the colon or any other mark of punctuation after *of*.]

(2) Do not place a colon between a verb and its object or object complement:

> He liked to *see: TV plays, movies,* and *football games*. [Use no mark of punctuation after *see*.]
> She likes a number of activities, *such as: swimming, dancing,* and *cooking*. [Use no mark of any kind after *such as*.]

50. THE DASH

The dash is a mark of punctuation most characteristically used to denote a sudden break or shift in thought. It has been described as "the interruption, the mark of abruptness, the sob, the stammer, and the mark of ignorance." The last epithet refers to the fact that although the dash is useful, its over-use reveals ignorance of other marks of punctuation and results in a choppy, incoherent style. Logically, some other mark can always be substituted for the dash, but its occasional use provides emphasis or surprise.

The dash is the only common mark of punctuation not on the standard typewriter keyboard. To type a dash, use two hyphens; no space precedes or follows the hyphens. Only in typing is the dash equal to two hyphens; the printed hyphen is smaller than half a dash.

50a. *Use a dash to indicate a break or shift in thought.*

> When I was in college—but I have already talked about that.
> Do we—can we—dare we ask for more money?
> I started to say, "But—" "But me no *but's!*" roared the supervisor.

50b. *Use a dash to introduce a word or group of words which you wish to emphasize.*

> What he needed most he never got—love.
> This is our most serious question—can we find
> a buyer for our product?

In such constructions as these, either a colon or comma could be used; the dash adds vigor, emphasis, and a tonal quality of emotion.

50c. *Use dashes to set off strongly distinguished parenthetical material.*

> I think—no, I am positive—that you should go.
> My mother can bandage that—she's a trained nurse, you know—so that it won't hurt at all.
> If you do succeed—and try hard!—telephone me promptly.
> Through clandestine channels—a small man wearing red suspenders—I discovered that the idea originated with one of the secretaries.

A pair of commas or two parentheses could replace the dashes in each of these sentences, but they would not so sharply set off and distinguish the parenthetical material.

50d. *Use a dash to indicate omission of letters and words and to connect combinations of letters and figures.*

> Senator S— was from my hometown.
> We were in one d— of a spot when that happened.
> June—October (June to or through October)
> She lived in that city 1960—1964.
> Ed used to fly a DC—8 on the New York—Dallas run.
> The speech was carried on a CBS—NBC—ABC hookup.

In typing or handwriting, a hyphen (-) might be substituted in each of the examples above except the first two, where a double dash could also be used.

Do not use a dash in such expressions as those above when the word *from* or *between* appears:

> From June to (or through) October [not *From June—October*]
> Between 1958 and 1962 [not *Between* 1958—1962]

A final word about the dash: use it sparingly. It is a strong and noticeable mark and should not be employed as a lazy substitute for more exact marks of punctuation or to indicate omitted ideas where you have nothing particular in mind.

51. THE HYPHEN

The hyphen is a mark of separation used between parts of a word. Although a separating mark, its most frequent use is to join two or more separate words to form a compound. As a largely mechanical device, serving as a mark of punctuation and as an aid in spelling, the hyphen is essential to correct, clear writing.

51a. *Use your dictionary to determine whether a word combination is written as a compound with a hyphen, as one word written solid, or as two separate words.*

The general principle of word-joining derives from actual usage. When two (or more) words first become associated with a single meaning, they are written separately. As they grow, through usage, to become more of a unit in thought and writing, they are usually hyphenated (spelled with a hyphen). Finally, they tend to be spelled as one word. This evolution may be seen in the following, the third word in each series now being the accepted form: *base ball, base-ball, baseball; rail road, rail-road, railroad.* This general principle, however, is not always in operation; many common expressions which one might think in the third stage are still in the first: *mother tongue, girl scout, in fact, high school.*

51b. *Use a hyphen to separate (actually, join) the parts of many compound words.*

There is neither a shortcut nor an all-inclusive rule for spelling compound words. It may help to know that the present-day tendency is to avoid using hyphens whenever possible. It may also help to know that seven groups, or classes, of words ordinarily require hyphens:

(1) Two or more words modifying a substantive (noun) and used as a single adjective: *fast-moving, bluish-gray, first-rate, un-American, wild-eyed.*

(2) Compound nouns: *by-product, sister-in-law, looker-on, ex-president.*

(3) Compound words with *half, quarter,* or *self* as the first element: *half-asleep, quarter-final, self-sacrifice.*

(4) Compound words made from a single capital letter and a noun or participle: *A-flat, F-sharp, T-shirt, X-ray.*

(5) Improvised compounds: *know-it-all, never-say-die, never-to-be-forgotten.*

(6) Compound numerals from *twenty-one* through *ninety-nine.*

(7) Compounds formed from the numerator and denominator of fractions: *three-fourths, two-thirds.*

51c. *Use a hyphen to indicate the division of a word broken at the end of a line.*

When using a division hyphen at the end of a line, keep the following rules in mind:

(1) Always divide according to pronunciation:

> knowl·edge, *not* know·ledge
> ste·nog·ra·pher, *not* sten·og·ra·pher
> sten·o·graph·ic, *not* ste·nog·ra·phic

(2) Place the hyphen at the end of the first line, never at the beginning of the second:

> The botanist deliberately used only two specimens in his demon-
> stration.

(3) Never divide a monosyllable. Write such words as *breath, ground, laughed, strength,* and *through* in their entirety on the first line; if this is not possible, carry the whole word over to the next line. Also, such parts of words as *-geous* (advantageous) and *-tious* (contentious) cannot be divided.

(4) Do not divide a one-letter syllable from the remainder of the word. A word such as *about* does have two syllables, a·bout, but it should not be broken up. Do not divide other two-syllable words such as *able, among, enough, item, many, unit, very.*

(5) Do not divide on a syllable with a silent vowel. The ending *-ed* is not fully pronounced in many words and should not be separated from the word of which it is a part. Avoid breaking up such words as *asked, attacked, climbed, massed, yelled.*

(6) Do not divide a word with only four letters. A word of only four letters can usually be crowded into the first line, if necessary. If space does not permit, carry over to the second line in their entirety such words as *also, into, only, open, real, veto.*

(7) Divide two consonants standing between vowels when pronunciation warrants. This principle is illustrated by words such as *alter·native, exis·ten·tialism, struc·ture, strin·gent.*

(8) Present participles may be divided before their *-ing* ending: *ask·ing, carry·ing, giv·ing, sing·ing, talk·ing, walk·ing.*

(9) Most prefixes and suffixes may be divided from main words.

(10) Do not divide sums of money.

(11) Do not divide initials in a name or in proper names.

(12) Do not divide units of time.

52. THE APOSTROPHE

The apostrophe, a mark of punctuation and a spelling symbol, has three uses: (1) to form the possessive (genitive) case of nouns and of certain pronouns; (2) to indicate omission of a letter or letters from words and of a figure or figures from numerals; (3) to indicate the plurals of letters, certain words, numerals, symbols, and some abbreviations.

52a. *Use an apostrophe and* s *to form the possessive case of a noun (singular or plural) not ending in* s:

> children, children's   horse, horse's
> doctor, doctor's   town, town's

> Children's shoes are often expensive.

52b. *Use only an apostrophe to form the possessive case of a plural noun ending in* s:

> boys, boys'   students, students'
> ladies, ladies'   weeks, weeks'

> The boys' coats are in the closet.

52c. *Use an apostrophe alone or an apostrophe and* s *to form the possessive of singular nouns ending in* s:

> Robert Burns, Robert Burns' (*or* Burns's)
> Charles, Charles' (*or* Charles's)
> She liked Francis' looks and Burns' (*or* Burns's) poems.

Usage varies, but the "standard rule" is that proper names of one syllable ending in an *s* sound add an apostrophe and *s*: "Marx's books," "Keats's poetry," "Robert Burns's songs." In words of more than one syllable ending in *s*, add the apostrophe only: "Demosthenes' orations," "Sophocles' plays."

52d. *In compound nouns add the apostrophe and* s *to the last element of the expression, the one nearest the object possessed:*

> my son-in-law's boat   King Henry IV's funeral
> somebody else's ticket   the city manager's duty

52e. *Use an apostrophe to show that letters or figures have been omitted:*

> aren't (are not)   they're (they are)
> don't (do not)   shouldn't (should not)

> The Civil War was fought 1861–'65 [1861 to 1865].

This use of the apostrophe is reflected in the most misspelled short and simple word in the English language. *It's* means "it is" and can never be correctly used for *its* in the possessive sense. "When a dog wags *its* tail, that is a sign *it's* happy." Never write the letters *i-t-s* without thinking whether or not you mean "it is."

52f. *Use an apostrophe and* s *to indicate the plurals of numerals, letters, and words considered as words.*

> Small children cannot always make legible 5's.
> Uncrossed *t*'s look like *1*'s.
> He uses too many *and*'s and *but*'s in speaking.

52g. *Never use an apostrophe in forming the plural of nouns and the possessive case of personal and relative pronouns.*

> The Browns [not *Brown's*] came to see us.

Correct	*ours, yours, his, hers, its, theirs, whose*
Incorrect	*our's, ours', your's, yours', his', her's, hers', it's, their's, theirs', who's* [unless you mean *who is*]

53. QUOTATION MARKS

Quotation marks, both double (". . .") and single ('. . .'), are marks of enclosure for words, phrases, clauses, sentences, and even paragraphs and groups of paragraphs. By definition, *quotation* means repeating (or copying) what someone else has said or written; *quotation marks* are a device used principally to indicate the beginning and end of material so repeated. These marks, often called *quotes*, consist of two (or one) inverted commas at the beginning (*open quote*) and two (or one) apostrophes at the closing of a quotation (*close quote*).

53a. *Use quotation marks to enclose every direct quotation and each part of an interrupted quotation.*

"What will my starting salary be?" I asked the manager.
"Well," he replied, "I'm not sure." Then, pausing, he inquired, "What do you think is fair?"

53b. *In dialogue use a separate paragraph for each change of speaker.*

> Mr. Gray was dressing for tennis when his young son, Ned, walked into the room.
> "Dad," announced Ned, "you have a very young figure."
> "Why, thank you, Ned," said Mr. Gray, feeling as though he wanted to embrace his son for the only really kind words he had heard in a week.
> Then Ned crushed him by adding, "But your face is *old*."

53c. *If a direct quotation extends for more than one paragraph, place quotation marks at the beginning of each paragraph but at the end of only the last.*

> "To measure and mark time has always been a concern of people. Early systems for noting the passage of time were based on the sun, stars, and moon.

"Egyptian priests established a year of 365 days as early as 4200 B.C. and based their calculations on the passage of the seasons, the sun's shadow, and the behavior of stars.

"Under Julius Caesar, astronomers prepared the Julian calendar in which 12 months were given arbitrary lengths and every fourth year was made a leap year."

53d. *Use quotation marks to enclose words with a widely different level of usage.*

No matter what its level of usage, if a word is appropriate use it with no quotation marks as a form of apology. In rare instances, however, you may wish to switch to an expression requiring enclosure:

If we judge that we "have it taped," we are not likely to be curious about the ways in which other races of man have answered questions that are also our questions.

The person who has "had it" so far as all religion is concerned looks with impatience on the role that religion has played in man's progress toward self-mastery.

53e. *Use quotation marks to enclose chapter headings and the titles of arti cles, short stories, and short poems.*

When both chapter heading and book are mentioned, or title of article (story, poem) and magazine, book and magazine names should be indicated by italics (underlining). (See Section **54.**)

He found the quotation from Longfellow's "The Children's Hour" in Bartlett's *Familiar Quotations.*

Grant Wood's famed painting, "American Gothic," was recently reproduced in *American Heritage.*

His most famous short story is called "The Devil and Daniel Webster." It first appeared in the *Saturday Evening Post* and was later published in a book entitled *Thirteen O'Clock.*

53f. *Use single quotation marks to enclose a quotation within a quotation.*

On rare occasions when you may have to punctuate a quotation within a quotation within a quotation, the correct order is double marks, single marks, double marks. If you need more sets than this, rephrase your sentence so as not to lose your reader entirely.

The coach said, "When you say, 'I'll be there on time,' I expect you to mean what you say."

The coach went on, "Then this player asked, 'What did the coach mean when he said, "Jim, be there on time"?' "

53g. *Place quotation marks correctly with reference to other marks.*

(1) The comma and the period *always* come *inside* quotation marks. This rule never varies and applies even when only the last word before the comma or period is enclosed (but not alphabetical letters or numerals).

(2) A question mark, exclamation point, or dash comes *outside* quotation marks unless it is part of the quotation. A single question mark comes

inside quotation marks when both the nonquoted and quoted elements are questions.

(3) The semicolon and colon come *outside* quotation marks.

Are you thoroughly confused by now? Perhaps these illustrations will help:

"Please lend me the money now," she said. "I won't need it tomorrow."
The pumpkin was rated "excellent," but I felt it was only "good."
She went to Gate "Y", but her proper entrance was "G".
Did Jim ask, "Have I enough money?"
What is meant by "an eye for an eye"?
The performance was an utter "flop"!
"My performance was a 'flop'!" she exclaimed.
"Well, I'll be—" she said and then blushed.
Study the following paragraphs in Stevenson's "Markheim": the first, third, and fifth.
Read Thoreau's "Brute Neighbors"; as a nature lover, you will appreciate it.

54. ITALICS

Words italicized in print (letters sloping to the right) should be underlined when you typewrite or write in longhand.

54a. *Underline once the following groups and classes of words.*

(1) Titles of books and magazines:

Foundations of Western Thought, All the King's Men, Saturday Review, The Atlantic Monthly

(2) Titles of plays, operas, long poems, and motion pictures:

Strange Interlude (play), *The Girl of the Golden West* (opera), *Paradise Lost* (long poem), *Duel in the Sun* (motion picture)

(3) Names of ships, trains, and aircraft:

the *Caronia* (steamship), the *City of Denver* (train), the *Bermuda Clipper* (aircraft)

(4) Names of newspapers:

The New York Times, The San Francisco Chronicle

Some style manuals, teachers, and other authorities recommend not italicizing the name of the city or the definite article in the titles of newspapers: the Denver *Post;* the New Orleans *Times-Picayune.* But the actual title itself is always italicized (underlined).

(5) Names of legal cases:

John Doe v. *Mary Doe* or John Doe *v.* Mary Doe

(6) Scientific names:

Ursus arctos (European brown bear), *Canis familiaris* (a plain *dog* to you and me)

54b. *Underline foreign words and phrases.*

Zeitgeist (German for "spirit of the time")
Honi soit qui mal y pense (French for "Shamed be he who thinks evil of it"
or "Evil to him who evil thinks")

Note that thousands of words and phrases have been so thoroughly absorbed into the English language that they need no longer be italicized. Such words as these can safely be written without italics (underlining):

alias	en route	matinee
billet doux	et cetera	mores
bona fide	ex officio	prima facie
carte blanche	gratis	sauerkraut
delicatessen	hors d'oeuvres	vice versa

54c. *Underline items for specific reference or emphasis.*

The word is spelled *dollar;* it should have been *collar.*
Your *l*'s look exactly like *t*'s. [Only the letter should be italicized, not the apostrophe or the *s*.]
Is this a *6* or a *9*?
The advertiser who wrote *Come Dye With Me* should have been a cleaner, not a funeral director.
Whatever you think, *whatever you even suspect,* keep to yourself for the present.
The late Will Rogers was genuinely humorous when he said: "Don't gamble. Take all your savings, buy some good stock, and hold it until it goes up. Then sell it. *If it doesn't go up, don't buy it.*"

55. CAPITALS

The use of capitals is so involved and debatable that universal rules and principles cannot be stated. The following suggestions, however, will serve as a guide.

55a. *Capitalize the first word of every sentence, including every quoted sentence.*

> The engine needs repair.
> He asked, "Does the engine need repair?"

When only a part of a direct quotation is included within a sentence, it is usually not begun with a capital letter:

The reporter told me that the official said he felt "fine" but thought that he should "take it easy" for a few weeks.

55b. *Capitalize proper nouns.*

(1) Names of people and titles used for specific persons:

George Washington, Theodore Roosevelt, the President, the Senator, the Treasurer, the General, Mr. Chairman, Father, Mother

(2) Names of countries, states, regions, localities, other geographic areas, and the like:

United States, England, Illinois, the Far East, the Dust Bowl, the Midwest, the Solid South, the Rocky Mountains, the Sahara Desert, the Connecticut River, Lake Michigan

(3) Names of streets:

Michigan Boulevard, Fifth Avenue, Old Mill Road

(4) Names of the Deity and personal pronouns referring to Him:

God, Heavenly Father, Son of God, Jesus Christ, Savior, His, Him, Thy, Thine

(5) Names for the Bible and other sacred writings:

Bible, the Scriptures, Book of Genesis, Revelations, Koran

(6) Names of religions and religious groups:

Protestantism, Roman Catholicism, Presbyterian, Jesuit, Unitarian

(7) Names of the days and the months (but *not* the seasons):

Monday, Tuesday, etc.; January, February, etc.; summer, winter, autumn, fall, spring

(8) Names of schools, universities, colleges:

Woodberry Forest School, California Institute of Technology, Davidson College, Boston University

(9) Names of historic events, eras, and holidays:

Revolutionary War, Christian Era, Middle Ages, Renaissance, Fourth of July, Labor Day

(10) Names of races, organizations, and members of each:

Indian, Negro, Malay, League of Women Voters, American Academy of Science, National League, San Francisco Giants, Big Ten Conference, an Elk, a Socialist

(11) Vivid personifications:

Fate, Star of Fortune, Destiny, the power of Nature, the paths of Glory, the chronicles of Time

(12) Trade names:

Ry-Krisp, Wheaties, Tide, Dreft, Sunkist

55c. *Capitalize the first word of every line of poetry.*

> How happy is he born and taught,
> That serveth not another's will;
> Whose armour is his honest thought,
> And simple truth his utmost skill!
> —WOTTON

55d. *Capitalize each important word in the title of a book, play, magazine, and musical composition:*

> *Romeo and Juliet, The Moonlight Sonata, Good Housekeeping, The Web of Earth, The Iceman Cometh*

Note: Do not capitalize prepositions, conjunctions, and articles except at the beginning or end of the title or unless they consist of five or more letters:

> *The Return of the Native, Caught Between Storms, Mr. Pim Passes By*

56. PARENTHESES

Parentheses are curved punctuation marks principally used to enclose explanatory matter in a sentence. They signal to a reader what a speaker means when he says "By the way" or "Incidentally."

56a. *Use parentheses to enclose material only remotely connected with its context.*

> This illustration (see p. 35) is quite clear.
> Your attitude (I am certain it is important) should be carefully explained.
> This issue of the magazine (September, 1964) is particularly interesting.
> This politician (about whom I shall have more to say later) is not worth your support.
> The general properties of sets of continuous real numbers (which exclude imaginary numbers such as those based on the square root of -1) are called mathematical analysis.

56b. *Use parentheses to enclose numerals or letters indicating divisions.*

Two parentheses are recommended, although some publications use only the second.

> The committee decided to (1) adopt the suggested budget, (2) set a date for the next meeting, (3) adjourn.

56c. *Use parentheses to enclose sums of money when accuracy is essential.*

> His total bill was four hundred dollars ($400.00).
> The wholesale price is eighty cents (80¢) per dozen.

Sums of money repeated for accuracy and enclosed in parentheses occur most often in business writing and in legal papers. Ordinarily, you need not resort to this device; either words or numerals will suffice.

57. BRACKETS

A bracket, [or], is one of two marks (brackets are always used in pairs) primarily for the purpose of enclosing the material which is not part of a quoted passage. That is, brackets are editorial marks used to enclose comments, corrections, or additions to *quoted* material.

57a. *Use brackets to enclose a comment inserted in a quoted passage.*

The speaker then said, "I am annoyed [obviously he was furious, not merely annoyed] by the neglect of our officials."
The foreman then remarked, "You may have the rest of the day off. [Cheers.] But you must report for work on time tomorrow."

57b. *Use brackets to enclose corrections in quoted matter.*

If the person whom you are quoting has made an error, or what you consider an error, you can add a correction and enclose it in brackets. If you wish not to make a correction but merely to call attention to the error, you may use the Latin word *sic,* which means "thus," and enclose it in brackets:

"In 1776 on the tenth [fourth] day of July, the Declaration of Independence was signed."
"I was born in 1938," the candidate wrote, "in Walthum [Waltham], Massachusatts [Massachusetts], and have lived there all my life."
"I am of English decent [*sic*] and am proud of my heritage."

57c. *Use brackets to add to a quoted passage.*

The advertisement read: "These shirts [oxford cloth, button-down collars] were designed by Oleg Rastrobi."
"The jury awarded £200 [$560] to the plaintiff."
"Later in the play," the lecturer continued, "he [Hotspur] is killed."
"They [the Germans] were not any more at fault than their collaborators [the Russians]," the speaker concluded.

58. ABBREVIATIONS

Abbreviations, shortened forms of words and phrases, help save time and space. Ordinarily, you will have more time and space than you know what to do with; in themes you should use abbreviations carefully and sparingly. Especially avoid using so many abbreviations that your writing appears telegraphic in style and offensive to your reader's eye: "N.Y.C. is a lg. place. Its central boro, Manhattan, lies E. of the Hudson R., W. of the E. Riv., and S. of the Bx."

Write out words in full, unless condensation seems necessary or the spelled-out words are unconventional, like *Mister* for *Mr.*

58a. *Use only acceptable abbreviations in formal writing.*

As a general rule, spell out all words and phrases which would be puzzling if abbreviated and abbreviate correctly all terms which are often encountered and readily understood in shortened form by everyone. In the following list are examples in various categories; avoid using most (not all) of them in formal themes:

> *Addresses:* Ave., Blvd., Rd., St.
> *Calendar divisions:* Mon., Mar., in the '90's
> *Geographic names:* U.S.A., Calif., St. Louis
> *Measurements:* mi., P.M., bbl., oz.
> *Money:* ¢, c., ct., $, dol.
> *Names and titles:* Mr., Mrs., Dr., Col., Litt.D.
> *School subjects:* chem., comp. lit., math

58b.   *Use a period after most abbreviations.*

Most standard abbreviations require a period, but note these exceptions:

> *Ordinal numbers:* 2nd, 4th, etc.
> *Shortened forms:* ad, phone, lab
> *Specialized forms:* TV, NBC, UNESCO, FBI
> *Contractions:* don't, haven't, isn't
> *Nicknames:* Joe, Al, Ned

58c.   *Avoid contractions in formal writing.*

Sometimes considered colloquial, contractions are questionable in unusually precise formal writing. Do not avoid such contractions as *won't*, *shouldn't*, and *can't* to the extent of making your writing seem artificial and pretentious; but seek to use them more often in reporting conversation than in your own formal writing. (See Section **27b** and *Contraction* in Part II.)

59. NUMBERS

The practice of writing words for numbers or of using figures is more a matter of convention and custom than of correctness. However, representing numbers *is* a matter of mechanics, and a troublesome one at that.

59a.   *Use words to represent numbers in special uses.*

(1) Isolated numbers less than 10:

> At least three men should be nominated for secretary.
> We can choose one of six magazines to read.

(2) Indefinite expressions or round numbers (figures are also acceptable, however):

> This theater will seat two thousand or three thousand persons.
> *or*
> This theater will seat 2,000 or 3,000 persons.

> The mid-fifties will probably be known as the atomic fifties.
> *or*
> The mid-50's will probably be known as the atomic 50's.

Right now I could use a hundred dollars.
or
Right now I could use $100.

(3) One number or related numbers at the beginning of a sentence:

Three of our officers are from Syracuse.
Twenty to thirty employees will be away on an inspection trip to Detroit.

(4) Numbers preceding a compound modifier containing a figure:

To line this wall, we need twelve ½-inch pieces of plywood.
Our tent is supported by two 8-foot poles.

(5) Fractions standing alone:

Be sure that the plywood is one-half inch thick.
I live about one-fourth of a mile from the highway.

59b. *Use figures to represent numbers in special uses.*

(1) Isolated numbers of 10 or more:

Only 35 parents attended the meeting at the school.
The amount is 12 times what it was in 1960.

(2) Dates, including the day or the day and the year:

Please report for duty by July 1.
I worked there from May 1 to October 15, 1964.

(3) House, room, telephone, and postal zone numbers:

She lives at 472 Old Mill Road; her telephone number is 534-6061.
She was in Room 2145 at the Ansonia Hotel, Columbia 6, North Dakota. (The appropriate zip code number would also appear in figures.)

(4) Highway and comparable numbers:

We were driving on Route 46.
The best programs will be found on Channel 20.

(5) Measurements:

Standard typewriter paper is 8½ by 11 inches in size.
The package weighed 6 pounds 4 ounces.
5-foot pole, ¼-inch wire, 2-inch margin

(6) Time:

9:00 P.M., 2:35 A.M., half past 5
11 o'clock [not *11 o'clock A.M.* or *11 A.M. in the morning*]
5 hours 8 minutes 12 seconds; 6 years 3 months 21 days

(7) Percentage:

8 percent, one-half of 1 percent, 5¼ percent return
You waste 5 to 10 percent of your lunch hour.

(8) Money:

$5.60, $0.60, 60 cents, $4 per dozen, 28¢ apiece

(9) Chapters and page numbers:

Chapter 7, p. 121, pp. 15–30, p. 1123

59c.   *Use figure-and-letter combinations appropriately.*

Occasionally, you will need to write figures and letters in combination, especially in expressing ordinal numbers (first, 1st; second, 2nd). Such combinations are correctly used in tables, sometimes in numbering items in a list, sometimes in dates (but not when the year immediately follows), and usually in expressing a numbered street from 10th on.

Your April 15th request (*or* your request of April 15) has been noted.
Your request of April 15, 1960, has been noted.
472 Old Mill Road; corner of 10th Street and Fifth Avenue; 105 Fifth Avenue; North 210th Street

60.   MISCELLANEOUS MARKS

Certain miscellaneous marks serve purposes in writing which are more concerned with spelling or pronunciation or mechanics than with punctuation as such.

60a.   *Use an accent mark where spelling requires it.*

In strictly formal and especially careful writing, each of these words and expressions would carry a special mark:

Acute accent (´): *blasé, début, éclair, fiancé, fiancée, passé*
Grave accent (`): *à la carte, frère, père, suède*
Circumflex (^): *bête noire, raison d'être, table d'hôte*
Cedilla (¸): *façade, Français, garçon, soupçon*
Dieresis (¨): *Chloë, naïve, preëxistent*
Tilde (˜): *cañon, mañana, señor*
Umlaut (¨): *Die Walküre, Tannhäuser*

60b.   *Use asterisks sparingly and never as substitutes for footnote numerals.*

A star-shaped figure, the asterisk is a conspicuous mark occasionally used to indicate omission or to call attention to something requiring comment in a footnote or elsewhere. Its purpose can usually be achieved more effectively by the ellipsis mark or by numerals.

60c.   *Use a caret to insert an omission.*

Place the caret below the line at the point of omission and write the inserted expression directly above or in the margin.

the spring of
The first building, now Old Main, was dedicated in ∧ 1865.

· EXERCISES ON PUNCTUATION ·

I

Periods and Related Marks. Each entry in the pairs below may contain a mistake in the use of periods, question marks, or exclamation points. In space at the left, write a capital letter indicating that of the two sentences

        A   the first only is acceptable
        B   the second only is acceptable
        C   both are acceptable
        D   neither is acceptable

1. Will you please refer to the Simmons file for the requested information.
    As I prepared to drive away, Father asked me if I hadn't forgotten something?

2. Mrs Ethel Richardson agreed to serve as secretary at the meeting.
    The skid marks measured 18 yd. 2 ft. 4 in.

3. The NASA announced a delay of the moon shot because of overcast skies.
    As soon as Porter arrived, he asked us if we had brought our diving equipment.

4. "Many provisions . . . for governmental intervention in the economy, once regarded as startling and dangerous, have now come to be commonplace and routine . . ."
    The FRB announced a rise in the bank discount rate to 5.5 percent.

5. The title of his theme, "The Can-Opener Culture.", seemed to me too comprehensive for a short essay.
    On your way out, would you please post this letter for me!

6. How many times have I asked you not to slam that door!
    Just as Bert had said, there was a good record player in the cabin, but his record collection contained nothing but—ugh!—country music.

7. Instead of addressing the letter to Mr. Henry Tripp, 1256 So. Euclid Ave., you would show your correspondent more respect by spelling out the address fully.
    A frequent and well-intended social query—haven't you lost some weight lately?—can never actually be pleasing, since it implies that the hearer was too fat before or is too thin now.

8. How can we make you comfortable? Something to eat? A magazine? Television? Or would you like just to be let alone?
    She was always asking her guests if they didn't believe in extrasensory perception?

9. Did the Weather Bureau say it will rain today?
    Isn't that a pity?

10. Will you kindly let me know as soon as Emerson returns to his office.
    You expect me to meet her plane at 2:30 AM? Impossible!

II

Commas To Introduce or To Separate. Each item below begins with a CORRECT sentence. You are to rewrite it as directed (in your head, on scratch paper, or in regular form for submission). Make only changes required by the directions. In space at the left, write a capital letter indicating that the rewritten sentence, compared with the original, has

> A   *lost* a mark of punctuation
> B   *gained* a mark of punctuation
> C   *changed* one mark of punctuation to another
>   (e.g., a comma to a semicolon)
> D   *more than one change in punctuation*
> E   the *same* amount and kind of punctuation as before

Example: As soon as I get home from work, I will wash the car.
                   (Start the rewritten sentence with the words /I will/.)

Explanation: The rewritten sentence reads: I will wash the car as soon as I get
                   home from work. (A comma has been *lost*, so the key answer
                   is *A*.)

1. I have arranged your interview with Adderley, and I will take you to see
him on Monday.
    (Take out the second /I/.)

2. I have arranged your interview with Adderley, and he will see you on
Monday.
    (Take out /and/.)

3. Adderley is the only man you have yet to interview.
    (Start the sentence: /There is only one man whom you/.)

4. Arrowheads were often made of obsidian (volcanic glass) in the absence
of metal.
    (Start the sentence: /In the absence/.)

5. Yesterday the Sioux City stockyards reported taking in 400 cattle and 300
sheep.
    (Multiply each figure by 10.)

6. He still owes more than $600.
    (Multiply the figure by 100.)

7. Willow bark contains various amounts of salicylic acid and was long used
as an analgesic before the discovery of aspirin.
    (Insert /it/ after /and/.)

8. "Should I really trust him with the secret?" I wondered aloud.
    (Start the sentence with /I wondered/ and take out /aloud/.)

9. Let me know as soon as the undercoat is dry, and I will finish painting the
car.
    (Start the sentence: /As soon as/.)

10. "For all I know," he said, "I may drive the old car for another year."
    (Change /For all I know/ to /I haven't decided yet/.)

11. The wind was driving ragged, swirling clouds across the sky.
    (Insert /massed/ after /driving/, and /storm/ after /swirling/.)

12. The apartment was furnished richly but not tastefully.
    (Take out /but/.)

13. As Harris read the letter, he looked around furtively; then he tore the
paper into small pieces and stuffed them in his pocket.
    (Take out /As/, the /he/ before /looked/, and /then he/.)

14. The ants have a perfect society—without nonconformists, radicals, or
criminals; it is surprising how many people would like us to take that system for
a model.
    (Insert /and/ after /criminals/.)

15. Psychologists have never been able to agree on what intelligence is, although they are continually engaged in measuring it.

(Start the sentence: /Although they/.)

III

Restriction and Nonrestriction. Each item below begins with a CORRECT sentence. You are to rewrite it as directed (in your head, on scratch paper, or in regular form for submission). Make no changes except those required by the directions. In space at the left, write a capital letter indicating that the rewritten sentence, compared with the original, has

    A   *lost* a comma
    B   lost *two* commas
    C   *gained* a comma
    D   gained *two* commas
    E   the *same* number of commas as before (possibly none)

1. A boat which leaks may be dangerous.

(Change /A/ to /John's/.)

2. The members of the senior class, who were wearing caps and gowns, were enjoying the mingled feelings of pride and absurdity usual on such occasions.

(By the management of punctuation alone, make it clear that some members of the senior class were *not* wearing caps and gowns.)

3. About a century ago, a lawless class of young bloods (called "scorchers") who burnt up the streets on high-wheeled bicycles were the subject of angry editorials.

(Insert /at speeds as high as 15 miles per hour/ after /bicycles/.)

4. I did not call on the Haskins just because Miriam was staying with them.

(Make it clear that the speaker did *not* call on the Haskins.)

5. The boys of Badger Patrol who had already crossed the creek signaled for the others to follow them.

(Make it clear that *all* the boys of Badger Patrol had crossed the creek.)

6. More than half the people who take up the doctor's time, it is said, have nothing specifically discoverable wrong with them.

(Change /people/ to /patients/.)

7. The protein-deficiency diseases which afflict the populations of many backward countries are often caused by lack of a single amino acid, lysine.

(Change /The protein-deficiency diseases/ to /Diseases associated with underconsumption of proteins/.)

8. Protein-deficiency diseases are often caused by lack of an amino acid, lysine, which is abundant in meat but scanty in some cereals.

(Put /lysine/ at the end of the sentence.)

9. Since Howard arrived, nobody at our summer hotel has lacked amusement, for he is infinitely diverting.

(Put /since Howard arrived/ after /amusement/.)

10. Since prices have increased along with them, recent increases in wages may not mean additional purchasing power.

(Shift the words preceding the comma to the end of the sentence.)

11. Some of the problems which initially motivated the slum-clearance movement have been shifted rather than remedied by high-rise building projects.

(Change /Some of the problems/ to /Problems of this first kind/.)

12. I hope you will let me use the car tonight as long as I need it.
(Change /I need it/ to /you're staying home anyway/.)

13. Incredible as it may seem, most college libraries suffer from the depreda-
tions of a small class of moral idiots who snip pages out of books and periodicals
in order to copy from them at leisure when writing term papers.
(Change /who/ to /some of whom/.)

14. Many a scientist has reported the odd experience of waking to find that
a problem that baffled him the day before had been solved during the night by
his subconscious mind.
(Change the second /that/ to /which/.)

15. The automated machine which takes the place of several employees may
create several new jobs—but probably not for the same people.
(Insert /here on the left/ after /machine/.)

IV

Commas To Enclose or Set Off. Each item below begins with a CORRECT sentence. You are to rewrite it as directed (in your head, on scratch paper, or in
regular form for submission). Make no changes except those required by the
directions. In space at the left, write a capital letter indicating that the rewritten
sentence, compared with the original, has

A   *lost* one comma
B   lost *two* commas
C   *gained* one comma
D   gained *two* commas
E   the *same* amount of punctuation as before

1. My uncle Harvey is a policeman.
(Insert /maternal/ after /My/.)

2.   Mr. Vertigo Spinn
                            Churn Agitators, Inc.
                            1313 Rolls Avenue
                            Centrifuge, Ohio
(To this address add the zip code number /43605/.)

3. The announced lineup for Tuesday's game had James Carter at second
base and Alvin Carter in left field.
(Insert the phrase /(no relation)/ after /Alvin Carter/.)

4. The new name in the lineup for Tuesday's game was J. Carter.
(Put Carter's initial *after* the surname.)

5. Mr. Larkin called while you were out, and in a very bad temper, too.
(Insert /you may as well know/ after /and/.)

6. The course in English composition is not addressed to a specific and generally agreed-on subject matter.
(Insert /like physics or chemistry/ after /not/.)

7. I had to stay home that afternoon and supervise the Two Demons, as we
call the twins, Mother having decided to get her hair done.
(Start the sentence: /Mother having decided/.)

8. The giant panda is not a bear or, for that matter, closely related to any
familiar animal.
(Insert /as many suppose/ after /not/.)

9. There is an association with members on both sides of the Atlantic whose sole purpose is to rescue the reputation of King Richard III from the calumnies of Tudor-minded historians.

(Insert /an earnest and active one/ after /association/.)

10. In this statement Mr. Tompkins has raised a question which deserves our earnest consideration.

(Change /has/ to /you have/.)

11. I bought a convertible because I already had a paisley scarf to go with it.

(Insert /not because I have a passion for fresh air but/ after /convertible/.)

12. The time of our first meeting was July 1964.

(Insert /16/ after /July/.)

13. Congressman Zebulon Tate of Iowa was named to fill the vacancy on the Rules Committee.

(Put /Congressman/ after /Tate/, and make any other necessary changes.)

14. The dominant philosophical modes of the West have been dialectical and rational; those of the East have been contemplative and mystical.

(Compress the clause following the semicolon to six words.)

15. The dreams that people can remember are usually those that occur just before waking.

(Change /usually/ to /in most instances/.)

V

Semicolon, Colon, Dash. Each item below begins with a CORRECT sentence. You are to rewrite it as directed (in your head, on scratch paper, or in regular form for submission). In space at the left, write a capital letter indicating that the shift from the original to the rewritten sentence requires you to

    A   insert, or change a mark to, a semicolon or semicolons
    B   insert, or change a mark to, a colon or colons
    C   insert, or change a mark to, a dash or dashes
    D   take out one of the marks above, or change it to a comma
    E   keep the same punctuation as in the original

1. The facts of her childhood were hardly ideal; she was born into poverty, abandoned at the age of six, and reared in an orphanage.

(Take out /she was/.)

2. At high school he starred in all the sports offered: football, basketball, and track.

(Take out /all the sports offered/.)

3. Now listen to this carefully: send word to me at once if the drill brings up any gravel or even coarse sand from the well.

(Put /now listen to this carefully/ after /me/.)

4. The wind had veered to the east and raised a scattering of whitecaps on the bay; a canoe crossing looked too dangerous to try.

(Change /had/ to /having/.)

5. Not all people, it has been found, can roll the tip of the tongue into the shape of a tube; this ability, being hereditary, cannot be acquired by practice— nor does it appear to be good for anything, for that matter.

(Insert /and/ after /tube/.)

6. A cat when lapping up milk cups its tongue backward, not, as many suppose, forward, in a rapid series of dipping and raking motions; this fact is one of the curious revelations of high-speed photography.

(Take out /this fact is/.)

7. You can hardly be a success in politics without being your own convinced disciple, but the reverse proposition is unfortunately not true.

(Change /but/ to /however/.)

8. The accident occurred at 12 minutes after three in the afternoon.

(Put the time in numerical and abbreviated form.)

9. The army expects of its rank and file one thing above all, and that is obedience.

(Take out /and that is/.)

10. Because of a rainy spell construction was halted for a week, so we were free from Monday through Friday.

(Change /so/ to /consequently/.)

11. One of the texts required in the course is *Western Art.*

(Lengthen the title by adding /*The Renaissance*/.)

12. The finalists in the competition for scholarships were Honor Blackmore, Bess Sanborn, and Stephen Dobbs.

(Reverse each name, putting the surname before the given name.)

13. Animals which prey on other animals move upwind when hunting, and for related reasons animals which are preyed on flee downwind when hunted.

(Take out /and/.)

14. The minister took his text from the third chapter, eleventh verse, of *Second Corinthians.*

(Put the citation in numerical notation.)

15. I can tell you in confidence that Mr. Snodgrass has been paying particular attention to me lately, and I really think the poor man is smitten.

(Give only the first letter of /Snodgrass/, the rest of the name being merely indicated.)

VI

Quotation Marks and Related Marks. Each sentence below may contain a mistake in the use of quotation marks, italics, or introducing marks. In space at the left, write a capital letter indicating that in the sentence

A　*quotation* marks are *missing, superfluous, or misplaced* with
　　respect to accompanying punctuation
B　*italics* indicators are missing or superfluous
C　*some other mark or letter* is missing or superfluous
D　a *wrong mark* is used (e.g., italics instead of quotation marks)
E　none of these: the sentence is *acceptable* as it stands

1. There is a favorable review of "The Nylon Jungle," an Italian movie now featured at the Araby Theatre, in today's Chicago *Spectator.*

2. "In those days," she said, "you had to send the children to school in Switzerland in order to qualify as a member of the *haute monde.*"

3. With an expression of intense hauteur, she said, "Do you really imagine that eating pie a la mode is the custom of all Americans"?

4. "Who was it," he asked, "that said, 'People will give up making war only when it comes to be regarded as vulgar.'?"

5. She replied, "I think it was Oscar Wilde;" then after a pause, "however, I'd better look it up to make sure."

6. Interviewed aboard the Queen Mary at his departure, the Prince said, "Americans are very clever people; they can understand my English but I can't understand theirs."

7. Paraphrasing William James, he said, "If you want to kick a bad habit, you should enlist pride in support of will power by announcing the decision publicly."

8. "Different as they look," said Professor Fitts, "the words sporran and purse are etymologically related."

9. The popular aphorism "nice guys finish last" is attributed to Leo Durocher.

10. "Are you absolutely sure," demanded the prosecutor, "that you heard the woman cry, 'It was Gerald—I *saw* him!'?"

11. As a bit of elephantine humor, the instructor in modern mathematics said, "You will find the old injunction to mind your p's and q's taking on new emphasis here."

12. Especially in "The New Republic," there was a tense controversy on the question whether Capote's factual novel, *In Cold Blood,* constituted a new form of narrative art.

13. When asked about the play, Don said that "he had never sat through such a boring performance."

14. A recently discovered poem, doubtfully ascribed to Wordsworth, is "The Barberry-Tree".

15. I liked his recent article, "The Uses of the Moon"; however, it was somewhat too speculative for many people.

VII

Marks of Enclosure. Each sentence below may contain a mistake in the use of parentheses, brackets, or punctuation associated with them (e.g., a comma used with a parenthesis). In space at the left, write a capital letter indicating that the sentence

A *lacks* a necessary mark or marks
B has a *superfluous* mark or marks
C uses a *wrong* mark or marks (some other mark[s] should have been used)
D *misplaces* a mark or marks with respect to accompanying punctuation or text
E is *acceptable* as it stands

1. It's an interesting coincidence that these same years of political jitteriness [the middle 50's] abounded also in sightings of saucers from outer space and other unidentified flying objects.

2. Professor White's exploits as a secret courier during World War II were recounted in an earlier issue of the same magazine [see January 26, 1958].

3. "It was with genuine regret," wrote the General, "that I then lay (*sic*) down the burdens of command."

4. Mrs. Hawkins is the recognized dictator of our little town's society (this is the same person, believe it or not, whom you knew in high school as Mary Trotter.)

5. Pentwater, Michigan, once a lumber shipping center and one of the busiest ports on the lake, is now a quiet resort community.

6. The short stories of Saki (Hector Hugh Munro), are among the wittiest ever written.

7. Writes Professor Bloch: "There can be little doubt that the Whig aristocracy of the eighteenth century led the best *all-around* [my emphasis] life ever enjoyed by any class anywhere."

8. "When Monroe uttered his famous Doctrine in 1822 (actually 1823), he can have had but little idea of the interpretations that subsequent administrations would put on it."

9. I know exactly where we left the car: it was just opposite a little shop with the sign, I'm not likely to forget it, "Antiques and Junque."

10. Although Timmy accepted my veto of his plan to trap old Mr. McDowell in an elephant pit, (I said it might break his neck), I could see that he privately regarded my objection as frivolous and cowardly.

VIII

Mechanics. Each sentence below may contain a mistake in the use of hyphens, apostrophes, capitals, abbreviations, numbers, or special marks such as the acute accent, circumflex, or cedilla. A "wrong mark" in the key list below includes also the wrong form, such as a capital instead of a small letter, written instead of Arabic numerals, etc. In space at the left, write a capital letter indicating that the sentence

A   *lacks* a necessary mark or marks
B   has a *superfluous* mark or marks
C   uses a *wrong* mark or form (some other should have been used)
D   *misplaces* a mark or marks
E   is *acceptable* as it stands

1. May'nt we come in now?

2. We visited the Trent's last night.

3. Among teen-agers, a passion for nonconformity can coexist very comfortably with passive submission to the mores of the clique or gang.

4. I told my Mother I would be home early.

5. There were 4 absentees on Monday.

6. The lowest temperature recorded for this day was on January 12th, 1940.

7. Professor Clark is preeminent in his field.

8. The President appoints the members of the cabinet.

9. It was an easily-forgotten novel.

10. Senora Madura was accompanied by her husband, the Ambassador.

11. He secured a loan at the rate of five and one-half percent.

12. Examples of highly visual writing are easily found in Keats's poetry.

13. You should be more self-reliant and not take second hand advice.

14. The store specializes in boys' and womens' wear.

15. Thucydides' history of the Peloponnesian war is fascinating reading.

16. The window measures 48 by 54 inches.

17. 51 members make up a quorum.

18. I was driving east on 113th Street at the time.

19. The Twins were wearing his-and-hers flannel jackets.

20. The Riviera is located in the South of France.

21. I finally figured out that he was my ex-brother-in-law's first cousin.

22. The Secretary stated in a hearing of the Senate Foreign Relations Committee that he had no ready-made solutions of our problems in the East.

23. According to Simmons' report, twenty-two cartons are missing.

24. Most under-developed countries lie south of the Tropic of Cancer.

25. Afterwards Father asked me where I had picked up such half-baked ideas.

GRAMMAR

Grammar is the science that deals with words and their relationships. It is a statement, or series of statements, of the way a language works; English grammar is "the English way of saying things." Defined another way, grammar includes discussion of the forms of words, their use in phrases, clauses, and sentences, their tenses, cases, and other changes in form. The word *grammar,* which derives from a Greek word *gramma* ("letter," "written symbol"), now refers to the basic structure of an entire given language.

The preceding paragraph defines grammar as the scientific, systematic *description* of a language. When grammar considers the evolution of words and compares present with former usage, it is called "historical." When the grammar of one language, say that of English, is compared with the grammar of another, say French, it is called "comparative."

Besides these types of scientific, analytical grammar—totally unconcerned with what is "right" or "wrong," "correct" or "incorrect"—we should consider *prescriptive* grammar. The latter is the application of so-called "rules" as guides to expression, as statements of how people *should* speak and write. Much prescriptive grammar is outmoded, illogical, and inconsistent. And yet a certain amount of prescription is needed if our speaking and writing are to conform to principles generalized from descriptive grammar. For example, description shows that the majority of speakers and writers naturally use the objective case after a preposition: *between him and me.* It is prescriptive grammar which suggests that *between he and I* is "incorrect" and that the use of such an expression may cost you embarrassment *or* money *or* a job. Prescriptive grammar which forbids ever ending a sentence with a preposition is absurd; prescriptive grammar which recommends that you use judgment and common sense in splitting infinitives is practical and sensible.

As a college student, you are expected to use language as do others with your educational and social advantages. Both in college and in later life, you should take pride in being able to use words and word combinations appropriate to your native language as it is spoken and written by educated people. As a native speaker of English, you know, and have known from an early age, much about the grammatical patterns of your language. Automatically you use certain structures without conscious thought or perhaps knowledge of what they involve. But in a college course in freshman English, you have an unrivaled opportunity to refresh your knowledge of grammar or to relearn what has slipped from your mind.

Sections 62–70 provide specific comments on major areas in which "violations" of generally accepted grammatical principles occur. Section 61 affords a summary of basic terms, the study of which should be supplemented by constant reference to definitions and explanations provided in Part II, pp. 345–447.

61. BASIC GRAMMATICAL TERMS

A knowledge of grammatical terms does not guarantee acceptable writing. In a truly formal sense, many gifted writers probably have forgotten "all the grammar" they ever knew. Ordinary mortals, striving to learn to write effectively, do need guidance. Perhaps "too much" guidance is as ineffective as "too little," but surely no one can improve his ease and surefootedness with language unless he knows at least what is meant by *parts of speech, verbals, phrases,* and *clauses.* Having an understanding of these terms, he can then proceed to an examination of that basic form in all writing, the sentence.

61a. **Learn to identify each word as a part of speech.**

A word is a letter or combination of letters, a sound or combination of sounds, forming a unit of thought capable of being used as an utterance.

Words are classified according to their use in larger units of thought— in phrases, clauses, and sentences. This functional (use) division results in eight so-called parts of speech. Every word in our language belongs to one or more parts of speech and is so labeled in every dictionary of decent quality and size. Words can also be grouped according to the purpose they serve:

Naming words	nouns and pronouns
Asserting words	verbs
Modifying words	adjectives and adverbs
Joining words	conjunctions and prepositions
Exclamatory words	interjections

Traditional and not entirely satisfactory definitions of the various parts of speech follow:

(1) A *noun* is the name of a person, place, thing, or idea:

girl　　country　　hat　　honor

(2) A *pronoun* is a substitute for a noun:

she　　it　　that　　somebody

(3) A *verb* expresses action, a state of being, or a condition; it says, or asserts, something:

come　　be　　run　　remain

(4) An *adjective* modifies (affects the meaning of) a noun or pronoun:

green　　some　　lively　　thirty

(5) An *adverb* modifies (affects the meaning of) a verb, adjective, or another adverb:

quickly　　strongly　　somewhat　　very

(6) A *conjunction* links (connects) words or groups of words:

and　　yet　　where　　while

(7) A *preposition* shows relationship between the noun or pronoun it precedes and some other word:

above　　between　　over　　within

(8) An *interjection* independently expresses feeling:

ah　　boo　　indeed　　ouch

61b. *Learn to distinguish between verbs and verbals.*

A verbal is a verb form incapable of acting as a predicate verb, whereas a predicate (or *finite*) verb can complete a statement about the subject of a sentence. Verbals consist of *participles, gerunds,* and *infinitives.*

(1) A *participle* is a verbal adjective, a word having the function of both verb and adjective. As a verb form, it can take an object and be affected in meaning by an adverb. As an adjective, it can modify a noun or pronoun and can itself be modified by an adverb.

Present participle: singing, speaking, asking
Past participle: sung, spoken, asked
Perfect participle: having sung, having been sung
The boy noisily *eating* popcorn is rude and thoughtless.
　[The participle *eating* modifies *boy* and has *popcorn* for an object; it is modified by the adverb *noisily.*]

(2) A *gerund* is a verbal noun, a word having the function of both verb and noun. As a verb form, it can take an object and be affected in meaning by an adverb. As a noun, it can be modified by an adjective and can be the subject of a verb and the object of a verb or preposition.

The present participle and the *-ing* gerund are spelled the same. Distinguish carefully between them:

> *Playing* golf vigorously can be good exercise. [*Playing*, a gerund, is the subject of the sentence in its capacity as a noun; as a verb form it takes an object, *golf*, and is modified by the adverb *vigorously*.]
> The boy *playing* golf is Warren Hibbard. [*Playing*, a participle, in its capacity as an adjective modifies *boy*; as a verb it takes an object, *golf*.]

(3) An *infinitive* has the function of both verb and noun, as does a gerund. But an infinitive may also be used as an adjective or adverb and is often introduced by *to*.

> *To drive* rapidly is a great thrill for her. [As a noun, the infinitive is the subject of the sentence; as a verb form, it is modified by *rapidly*.]
> The best time *to fish* is early in the evening. [The infinitive acts as an adjective modifying *time*.]
> The boys came *to swim*. [The infinitive is an adverbial modifier of *came*.]

61c. *Learn to identify phrases.*

A phrase, which usually serves as a part of speech, is a group of related words that does not contain a subject and predicate. Phrases may be classified as to use and form.

USE

(1) A *noun* phrase is used in a sentence as subject or object:

> *Making a lot of money* is his goal in life. [The italicized phrase is the subject of *is*.]
> He likes *making a lot of money*. [Here the phrase is the object of *likes*.]

(2) An *adjective* (*adjectival*) phrase is used in a sentence as a single adjective would be:

> The boys *in this dormitory* are noisy and thoughtless. [The italicized phrase modifies the noun *boys*.]

(3) An *adverb* (*adverbial*) phrase is used in a sentence to modify a verb, adjective, or adverb:

> We spent our vacation *on a farm*. [The italicized phrase modifies the verb *spent*; it answers the question "Where?"]

FORM

(1) A *prepositional* phrase is one beginning with a preposition; it may be used as adjective or adverb and, rarely, as a noun:

> The book *on the desk* is mine. [Adjective; what book?]
> He strode *into the room*. [Adverb; strode where?]
> *Without smiling* was his way of showing irritation. [Noun; subject of *was*.]

(2) A *participial* phrase takes its name from an initial or important word:

Racing like mad, we barely caught the bus.
Having run the last mile, we caught the bus.

(3) A *gerundial* phrase takes its name from the gerund it contains:

Playing at Forest Hills was his highest aim in sports.
The crowd enjoyed *her expert twirling of a baton.*

(4) An *infinitive* phrase takes its name from the infinitive it contains:

To make friends is a worthwhile endeavor.

(5) An *absolute* phrase is so-called because it is not directly attached to any other word in a sentence.

John left quickly, *his objection now being a matter of record.*

61d. *Learn to identify clauses.*

A clause is a group of words having a subject and predicate. Some clauses are *independent* (main, principal); others are *dependent* (subordinate).

(1) An *independent* clause is one that makes a complete grammatical statement and can stand alone. It may appear within a sentence or as a sentence itself:

A girl's greatest asset may be a boy's imagination.
Although only a cynic would say so, *a girl's greatest asset may be a boy's imagination.*

(2) A *dependent* clause is one that is incapable of standing alone and for its meaning depends upon the remainder of the sentence in which it appears. Dependent (subordinate) clauses function as nouns, adjectives, and adverbs.

Noun Clause

What you said is not true. [Subject of *is;* equivalent to "your remark"]
I do not believe *that you are my friend.* [Object of *believe*]
Your suggestion *that you are really lazy* surprises me. [In apposition with *suggestion;* see Section 470]

Adjective Clause

Girls *who have hair they consider their fortune* may have eyes which really draw interest. [The italicized clause modifies *girls.*]
The players think he is a coach *who should be taken with a grain of assault.* [Clause modifies *coach.*]

Adverbial Clause

How can I look up a word *when I don't know how to spell it?* [Clause modifies the verb *look up.*]
You can read more rapidly *than I can.* [Clause modifies the adverb *rapidly.*]
Steak is usually more expensive *than fish is.* [Clause modifies the adjective *expensive.*]

62. AGREEMENT OF SUBJECT AND PREDICATE

Agreement means "the state of being in accord," "conformity," "unison." As applied to grammar, the term means "correspondence in person, number, gender, or case." Thus when a subject "agrees" with its predicate, both subject and predicate verb have the same *person* (first, second, third) and *number* (singular or plural).

Few problems of agreement between subject and predicate arise, because English verbs (except *to be*) have only one form for singular and plural and for all persons except the third person singular present. But what few errors do occur are important. Usually, errors in agreement appear for two reasons: (1) the writer or speaker is confused about the *number* of the subject because of the presence of other words; (2) he uses a verb to agree not with the grammatical form of a subject but with its meaning. You need to know what the *true* subject is and whether it is singular or plural.

62a. *A predicate (verb) normally agrees with its subject in person and number.*

> The *owners* greedily *ask* too high a price. [*Owners* and *ask* are in the third person and are plural in number.]
> I *agree* to pay your asking price. [*I* and *agree* are in the first person and are singular in number.]
> He *agrees* to pay the asking price. [*He* and *agrees* are in the third person and are singular in number.]

Section 62a states the general rule. The following sections deal with variations and situations likely to cause trouble.

62b. *A verb should not agree with a noun which intervenes between it and the subject.*

Wrong	The *cause* for all the noise and confusion *were* not obvious. [Substitute *was* for *were*; *cause*, the subject, is singular.] I, together with *Eleanor* and *Sally*, *are* going. [Substitute *am* for *are*; *I* is the true subject.] The *child*, as well as the other members of the family, *were* frightened. [Substitute *was* for *were*; *child* is the true subject of the sentence.]

62c. *Singular pronouns require singular verbs.*

The following pronouns are singular: *another, anybody, anyone, anything, each, either, everybody, everyone, everything, neither, nobody, no one, one, somebody, someone.*

> Each *has* his duty to perform.
> No one *was* present at the time.
> One of you *is* mistaken.

None (literally *no one* and also meaning "not any") may be followed by either a singular or a plural verb. It is as frequently followed by a plural verb as by one in the singular, especially when the phrase which modifies *none* contains a plural noun (*none of the men*). The standard rule, however, is that *none* requires a singular verb.

Agreement based on meaning and agreement based on grammatical form sometimes conflict. In the sentence, "Each of the boys in this group *is* 16 years old," *each* and *is* are in grammatical agreement. But in "*Each* of the boys in this group *are* 16 years old," *are* is plural because the meaning of "each of the boys" is construed to be "all of the boys." A somewhat similar principle may be illustrated thus: "Everyone in the apartment house tuned *his* TV [or *their* TV's] to that channel." Careful speakers and writers follow grammatical agreement in such sentences; agreement based on meaning is widely employed but most appropriately in informal speech and writing.

62d. *For nouns plural in form but singular in meaning, use a singular verb.*

Authorities differ about the number of many such nouns. A good rule, according to usage, is "When in doubt, use a singular verb." The following are nearly always used with singular verbs: *physics, economics, mathematics, news, politics, whereabouts, mechanics, ethics, mumps, stamina, headquarters.*

> *Physics,* they were told, *is* the study of heat, light,
> sound, mechanics, and electricity.
> The sad *news was* broadcast at noon.

62e. *Subjects plural in form which indicate a quantity or number require a singular verb when the subject is regarded as a unit.*

> Four-fifths of the area *is* under water.
> Two from five *leaves* three.

62f. *Ordinarily use a plural verb with two or more subjects joined by* and.

> Both Ed and Bob *are* running for office.

When the two subjects form a single thought or have a very closely related meaning, a singular verb is frequently used:

> His kindness and generosity *is* well known.
> The sum and substance of his remarks *is* clear.

62g. *Singular subjects joined by* or *or* nor, either . . . or, *and* neither . . . nor *usually require a singular verb.*

> Either Mimi or Dick *is* at fault.
> Neither the boy nor his father *was* found guilty.

62h. *If the subjects differ in number or person, the verb agrees with the nearer subject.*

> Neither Phil nor the other boys *know.*
> Either they or I *am* liable for damages.

62i. *Relative pronouns referring to plural antecedents generally require plural verbs.*

> Each of *those* who *are* there should listen carefully.
> He is one of the most able *students* who *have* ever attended this school.

If *only* or some similar qualifying word precedes *one*, the verb in the subordinate clause is singular:

> He is the *only one* of those in this class who *listens* carefully.

62j. *A verb does not agree with a predicate noun.*

> The best part of a children's party *is* the ice cream and cake.
> Ice cream and cake *are* the best part of a children's party.

62k. *After the expletive* there, *the verb is singular or plural according to the number of the subject that follows. Always use a singular verb after the expletive* it.

> There *are* [not *is*] strong sentiments in his favor.
> There *were* [not *was*] baseball, tennis, and swimming.
> In the field there *stands* [not *stand*] a towering tree.
> It *is* [not *are*] the girls who must wash the dishes.

62l. *A collective noun takes a singular verb when the group is regarded as a unit, a plural verb when the individuals of the group are regarded separately.*

> The crew *has asked* him to help with coaching.
> The crew *are coming* on board in a few hours.
> The family *was named* Gregson.
> The family *were seated* at the dinner table.

63. AGREEMENT OF PRONOUN AND ANTECEDENT

A pronoun does not always agree with its antecedent in case, but it should agree in *gender, number,* and *person.*

> The *girl* picked up *her* books. [Feminine, singular, third]
> The *women* took off *their* coats. [Feminine, plural, third]
> The *man* removed *his* hat. [Masculine, singular, third]
> The *boys* raised *their* voices. [Masculine, plural, third]

63a. *Singular pronouns refer to singular antecedents.*

> Has anyone here forgotten *his* promise?
> Each passenger will have a berth to *himself*.
> Everybody is expected to do *his* share.

In the last sentence above, *everybody* may refer to men and women. Only in colloquial English could you say "Everybody is expected to contribute *their* share." You may write "Everybody is expected to contribute his or her share," although this construction sounds somewhat artificial. In grammar—and in few other situations and places—men are considered more important than women.

63b. *A pronoun agrees with the nearer of two antecedents.*

> He hated everything and everybody *who* caused his defeat.
> He hated everybody and everything *which* caused his defeat.
> Either Jack or his sisters will lose *their* chance to go.
> Either Jack's sisters or he will lose *his* chance to go.

63c. *A collective noun used as an antecedent takes either a singular or plural pronoun, depending upon the sense of the sentence.*

The group of girls was shouting *its* praises. [The group acted as a unit.]
The group of girls raised *their* umbrellas. [The group acted as individuals.]
The class *was* divided in *its* [not *their*] opinion of the speaker.
Members of the class *were* divided in *their* [not *its*] opinion of the speaker.

64. CASE

Case is one of the forms that a noun or pronoun takes to indicate its relationship to other words in the sentence. There are only three important cases in English: nominative (subjective); genitive (possessive); and objective (accusative).

A noun or pronoun is in the *nominative* case (subject of a sentence) when it indicates the person or thing acting; in the genitive (*possessive*) case when it denotes the person or thing owning or possessing; in the *objective* case when it indicates the person or thing acted upon.

There is no change in the *form* of a noun to denote the nominative and objective cases. Word order in the sentence provides the only clue:

The child rode his tricycle. [*Child* is in the nominative case, *tricycle* in the objective.]
The tricycle was ridden by the child. [*Tricycle* is in the nominative case, *child* in the objective.]

The possessive case does involve a change in the form of a noun. But the case of nouns usually causes little trouble.

Grammatical problems do often arise because many *pronouns*, unlike *nouns*, have distinct forms for the nominative and objective cases. Such problems appear most frequently with *personal* pronouns (*I, you, he, me, him*) and with *relative* and *interrogative* pronouns (*who, whom, whose*).

NOMINATIVE CASE

64a. *The subject of a sentence or a clause is in the nominative case.*

If the subject is a noun, rest easy; only an idiot could get its grammatical form wrong. If the subject is a pronoun, you still should have little trouble:

He and *I* [not *me*] volunteered to go.
Who [not *whom*] is speaking, please?

64b. *A predicate complement is in the nominative case.*

A *predicate complement* is a noun (no difficulty with case), a pronoun (nominative case, essentially), or a predicate adjective (no case involved) used after a linking verb (see Section **66**). After a linking (copulative, coupling) verb, use only the nominative case of a pronoun:

That was *she* [not *her*] calling on the telephone.
It was *they* [not *them*] who invited us to the dance.

In colloquial speech one often hears (and perhaps says) "It's me" or "This is me," or "That's him." Such expressions are growing more acceptable, but careful speakers and writers continue to use the nominative case in such constructions.

OBJECTIVE CASE

64c. *The object of a verb or preposition is in the objective case.*

All nouns and the pronouns *it* and *you* cause no difficulty in this construction. But carefully choose between *who* and *whom*, *I* and *me*, *she* and *her*, *he* and *him*, *they* and *them*, *we* and *us*:

Whom did the police blame for the accident?
The superintendent accused *me*.
That is a blow to *her*.
A group of *us* is going to the lecture.
Did you invite both *him* and *her* to our party?
To *whom* did you mention our party?

64d. *The indirect object of a verb is in the objective case.*

An *indirect object* is a noun or pronoun before which *to* or *for* is expressed or understood:

Give *me* a fuller explanation, please.
If you do *him* a favor, he will not be grateful.
Tell *whom* my bad luck? Didi? I certainly shall not.

64e. *The subject, object, or objective complement of an infinitive is in the objective case.*

Whom did you take him to be? [That is, you did take *him* to be *whom*?]
His father made *him* say that. [*Him* is the subject of *to say*.]
My eagerness to kiss *her* was great. [*Her* is the object of *to kiss*.]
Did Jack think him to be *me*? [*Me* is the objective complement of *to be*.]

NOMINATIVE OR OBJECTIVE CASE

So far, so good; now we come to the real trouble spots. If you do not fully understand the function of pronouns, particularly *who*, *whoever*, *whom*, and *whomever*, now is the time to learn them once and for all.

64f. Who and **whoever** *are used as subjects of verbs or as predicate pronouns.* **Whom** and **whomever** *are used as objects of verbs and of prepositions.*

(1) The following sentences illustrate correct use of *who* and *whoever:*

The question of *who* is eligible is unimportant. [*Who* is the subject of *is;* the entire clause *who is eligible* is the object of the preposition *of.*]

This article offers good advice to *whoever* will accept it. [*Whoever* is the subject of *will accept;* the clause *whoever will accept it* is the object of *to.*]

A stranger here, he does not know *who* is *who.* [The first *who* is the subject of *is;* the second *who* is a predicate pronoun.]

(2) These sentences illustrate proper use of *whom* and *whomever:*

That is the boy *whom* I saw at the beach last summer. [*Whom* is the direct object of *saw:* "I saw whom."]

Jack always tells his problems to *whomever* he meets. [*Whomever* is the direct object of *meets:* "He meets whomever."]

Give the present to *whomever* you wish. [*Whomever* is the object of the preposition *to.*]

(3) The case of a pronoun must not be affected by words which come between the pronoun and its antecedent. The case of a word always depends upon its *use* in a sentence:

Jill asked Gray *who* he thought would be elected. [Check by omitting *he thought.*]

Who do you think is responsible for that decision? [Check by omitting *do you think.*]

I winked at the girl *whom* no one thought we had invited. [Check by omitting *no one thought.*]

64g. *An appositive should be in the same case as the noun or pronoun it identifies or explains.*

> We, *you* and *I,* are silly to take this chance.
> The coach gave both of us, *Fred* and *me,* a stern lecture.
> A few of us, those *whom* you asked, are delighted to accept.

64h. *An elliptical clause of comparison, preceded by* **than** *or* **as,** *requires the case called for by the expanded construction.*

> You are as strong as *I* (am). [Nominative]
> This story interested you more than (it interested) *me.* [Objective]
> I do not love her as much as *he* (loves her). [Nominative]

Genitive (Possessive) Case

64i. *A noun or pronoun linked immediately with a gerund should preferably be in the possessive case.*

> She dislikes *your* being more attractive than she is.
> The coach praised John for *his* taking extra practice sessions.

When the use of a possessive with a gerund causes awkwardness, rephrase the sentence:

Awkward	No rules exist against *anyone's* in this class speaking his mind.
Improved	No rules exist against any class *member's* speaking his mind.

64j.   *Avoid using the possessive case of an inanimate object.*

Awkward	The *tree's* leaves were turning brown.
	This machine will quickly wax and polish the *dance hall's* floor.
Improved	The leaves *of the tree* were turning brown.
	This machine will quickly wax and polish the floor *of the dance hall* [or *the dance hall floor*].

64k.   *Use the possessive case in accordance with established idiom.*

Despite the suggestion given in Section **64j**, such expressions as the following are idiomatic and thus desirable:

a day's work, a moment's notice, a dime's worth, a stone's throw, a summer's work, at his wits' end, three years' experience, tomorrow's weather report, the law's delay, two semesters' study

65. PRINCIPAL PARTS OF VERBS

An English verb has three principal parts: *present tense* (present infinitive), *past tense, past participle* (go, went, gone). A good way to recall these parts is to substitute those of any verb for the following:

I play today.   I swim today.
I played yesterday.   I swam yesterday.
I have played every day this week.   I have swum every day this week.

65a.   *Do not misuse the past tense and past participle.*

The past tense and past participle of most English verbs are formed by adding -*d*, -*ed*, or -*t* to the present infinitive: *ask, asked, asked; deal, dealt, dealt.* Such verbs are called *regular*, or *weak*, verbs. Verbs which form the past tense and past participle by a vowel change as well as by the occasional addition of an ending are called *irregular*, or *strong*, verbs: *do, did, done; ride, rode, ridden.*

Wrong	The dog *has bit* the child seriously. [*has bitten*]
	Joe *drunk* a pint of cold milk. [*drank*]
	Snow *has fell* for 22 hours. [*has fallen*]

When in doubt about the correct forms of the past tense or past participle, consult your dictionary. If no additional forms follow the main entry, the verb is regular (formed with the endings -*d*, -*ed*, or -*t*).

65b.   *Do not carelessly omit the ending of a regular verb.*

We are *supposed* [not *suppose*] to arrive on time.
Yesterday I *asked* [not *ask*] for another examination.

65c. *Learn the principal parts of frequently used regular and irregular verbs.*

Following is a list of 50 troublesome verbs. Study them; put them into the three expressions suggested in the first paragraph of Section 65.

bear	bore	borne (born, *given birth to*)
begin	began	begun
bid	bid	bid (*as in an auction*)
bid	bade	bidden (*as in a command*)
bite	bit	bitten (bit)
blow	blew	blown
break	broke	broken
burst	burst	burst
catch	caught	caught
choose	chose	chosen
come	came	come
dig	dug	dug
dive	dived	dived
do	did	done
drag	dragged	dragged
draw	drew	drawn
drink	drank	drunk
drown	drowned	drowned
eat	ate	eaten
fall	fell	fallen
fly	flew	flown
forget	forgot	forgotten (forgot)
freeze	froze	frozen
get	got	got (gotten)
go	went	gone
hang	hung	hung (*object*)
hang	hanged	hanged (*person*)
know	knew	known
lay	laid	laid
lead	led	led
lend	lent	lent
lie	lay	lain (*recline*)
lie	lied	lied (*falsehood*)
lose	lost	lost
pay	paid	paid
raise	raised	raised
ride	rode	ridden
rise	rose	risen
run	ran	run
set	set	set
sing	sang	sung
sit	sat	sat
speak	spoke	spoken
swim	swam	swum
take	took	taken
tear	tore	torn
wake	waked (woke)	waked (woke)

wear	wore	worn
wring	wrung	wrung
write	wrote	written

66. LINKING AND AUXILIARY VERBS

Most verbs assert (indicate) action, but some few express a static condition or state of being, not of action. Nearly all such "inactive" verbs are *linking* verbs (also called *copulative* or *joining* verbs). A linking verb can "couple" two nouns or pronouns or a noun and an adjective: "This *is* my brother"; "The dog *looks* sick."

Another variety of verb which can cause trouble is the *auxiliary* verb: one which "helps out" another verb in forming tenses, voice, mood, and certain precise ideas. Usually an auxiliary verb has little meaning of its own, but it does change the meaning of the main verb which it accompanies:

> The man of the soil *has been* pushed more and more out of the American economy.
> A careful analysis of the oxygen content *should have been* made at the time.

The following are suggestions for handling linking and auxiliary verbs.

66a. *Distinguish between a linking verb and one that expresses action.*

The most common linking verb is *to be*. Other linking verbs are *appear, become, feel, grow, look, prove, remain, seem, smell, sound, stand, taste, turn*. Still other verbs occur in only a limited number of linking contexts: "*slam* shut," "*ring* true." Distinguish carefully between meanings of the same verb when it asserts action and when it does not:

> The sky *looks* overcast today. [Linking]
> Jane *looks* closely at every page she reads. [Action]
> We *felt* downcast over our defeat. [Linking]
> Marian *felt* her way through the dark room. [Action]

66b. *Use the correct auxiliary verb.*

The most common auxiliary verbs are *to be, to have,* and *to do*. Other auxiliaries are *can, could, dare, let, may, might, must, need, ought, shall, should, used, will, would*.

Meanings for these frequently used auxiliary verbs are given in your dictionary. Several of them are discussed in Part II, pp. 345–447. Be sure you know the right word. Do not, for example, use *should* if *would* is needed or *ought* if *must* is indicated. Also, do not confuse *of* with *have*.

Inaccurate	You *should of* told me about that.
	The child *might of* been seriously injured.
	Can I borrow your slide rule, please?
	I *had ought* to leave by now.
	Leave me think for a few minutes alone.

Accurate	You should *have* told me about that.
	The child might *have* been seriously injured.
	May I borrow your slide rule, please?
	I *ought to have* (should have) left by now.
	Let me think for a few minutes alone.

67. TENSE AND TONE

Tense indicates the time of the action or time of the static condition (state of being) expressed by a verb. The three divisions of time—past, present, future—are shown in English by six tenses. The three primary, or simple, tenses are the *present* tense, the *past* tense, the *future* tense. The three secondary, or compound, tenses are the *present perfect*, the *past perfect*, the *future perfect*.

Within some tenses, verbs also have certain *tones* which express precisely what the writer wishes to say: *simple* tone (I study); *progressive* tone (I am studying); and *emphatic* tone (I do study).

67a.   *Use the correct tense to express precise time.*

Unlike a highly inflected language, such as German, English has few tense forms; English verbs reveal change in tense only by inflection or by the use of auxiliary words (see Section 66). Difficulty with tense usage arises from not knowing the functions of the six tenses or from not thinking carefully about the exact time element involved. The following brief table and comments on each tense should help you to use the precise tenses needed to convey your ideas:

ACTIVE VOICE	
Present	I see (am seeing)
Past	I saw (was seeing)
Future	I shall see (shall be seeing)
Present perfect	I have seen (have been seeing)
Past perfect	I had seen (had been seeing)
Future perfect	I shall have seen (shall have been seeing)
PASSIVE VOICE	
Present	I am seen (am being seen)
Past	I was seen (was being seen)
Future	I shall be seen
Present perfect	I have been seen
Past perfect	I had been seen
Future perfect	I shall have been seen
VERBALS (NONFINITE VERB FORMS)	
Present infinitive	to see (to be seeing)
Perfect infinitive	to have seen (to have been seeing)
Present participle	seeing [none]
Past participle	seen [none]
Perfect participle	having seen (having been seeing)
Present gerund	seeing [none]
Perfect gerund	having seen (having been seeing)

(1) *Present tense* indicates that the action or condition is going on or exists now:

> He *walks* to his office every day.
> The truth *is* known.

(2) *Past tense* indicates that an action or condition took place or existed at some definite time in the past:

> She *mailed* the package yesterday.
> The summer of 1962 *was* hot.

(3) *Future tense* indicates that an action will take place, or that a certain condition will exist, in the future:

> We *shall leave* at noon tomorrow.
> Our glee club *will be singing* there next month.

The future may be stated by the present tense accompanied by an adverb (or adverbial phrase) of time. Such constructions as the following are common:

> I am going to San Diego soon.
> This Thursday the boat leaves for Honolulu.

(4) *Present perfect tense* indicates that an action or condition was begun in the past and has just been completed or is still going on. The time is past but it is connected with the present. The present perfect tense *presupposes* some relationship with the present:

> You *have been* a nuisance all of your life.
> The weather *has been* too cold for hiking in the woods.
> I *have* long *been* an Alfred Hitchcock addict.

(5) *Past perfect tense* indicates that an action or condition was completed at a time now past. It indicates action "two steps back." That is, the past perfect tense presupposes some relationship with an action or condition expressed in the past tense:

> The roads were impassable because ice sheets *had formed* during the night.
> He lived in Berkeley. He *had been* there for several months.

(6) *Future perfect tense* indicates that an action or condition will be completed at a future time:

> I *shall have died* by that time.
> The weather *will have moderated* before you leave.

The three secondary, or compound, tenses always indicate *completed* action, whether it be in the present (present perfect tense), in the past (past perfect tense), or in the future (future perfect tense).

67b. *Use the correct tone to express precise meaning.*

The *simple* tone is a concise statement of a "snapshot" or instantaneous action of a verb: I *talk* (present tense), I *talked* (past tense), I *shall talk* (future tense), I *have talked* (present perfect tense), I *had talked* (past perfect tense), I *shall have talked* (future perfect tense).

The *progressive* tone forms in each of the six tenses are built by using proper tense forms of the verb *to be* followed by the present participle of the main verb: I *am talking, was talking, shall be talking, have been talking, had been talking, shall have been talking.*

The *emphatic* tone forms are formed by the verb *to do* and the present infinitive of the main verb. The emphatic tone is used in only present and past tenses: I *do talk,* I *did talk.*

67c. *Watch carefully the sequence of tenses.*

When only one verb is used in a sentence, it should express the precise time involved. When two or more verbs appear in a sentence, they should be consistent in tense (see Section 11a). Most importantly, remember that the tense of a verb in a subordinate clause depends on the tense of the verb in the main clause.

(1) The present tense is used in a dependent clause to express a general truth:

> Some people did not believe that the earth *is* a planet.

The present tense is used alone to express a "timeless" truth.

> Thought *makes* the whole dignity of man.

Do not allow the tense of a verb to be attracted into the past when it should be present: "Last summer, I visited a small village in France; the houses *were* old and picturesque." (It is conceivable that the village has been destroyed, but is that what is meant?)

Passages in some short stories and novels are written in the present tense although the action occurred in time which is past. This use of what is called the *historical present* sometimes makes narrative more vivid, but it quickly becomes monotonous.

(2) Use a present infinitive except when the infinitive represents action completed before the time of the governing verb:

> I intended to *see* [not *to have seen*] you about it.
> Everyone is pleased to *have had* you as a visitor.

(3) A present participle indicates action at the time expressed by the verb; a past participle indicates action before that of the verb:

> *Traveling* all over the world, he *sees* many remarkable people.
> *Having been* a good student, he *was* able to get many letters of recommendation.

(4) When narration in the past tense is interrupted for reference to a preceding event, use the past perfect tense:

> In April they *pruned* the trees which *had been damaged* by sleet.
> He *told* me that he *had been* ill for a month.

As a summary, these two formulas for the sequence of tenses may be helpful to you:

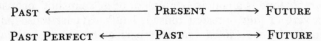

PAST ⟵——————— PRESENT ———————⟶ FUTURE

PAST PERFECT ⟵——— PAST ———————⟶ FUTURE

68. VOICE

Verbs are classified as to *voice*, active or passive.

A verb is in the *active* voice when the subject is the performer of the action or is in the condition or state named. In the *passive* voice, the subject does nothing, is inactive or passive, and has something done to it.

> The engineers *threw* a bridge across the river.
> A bridge *was thrown* across the river by the engineers.
>
> The lookout *sighted* the ship on the horizon.
> The ship on the horizon *was sighted* by the lookout.
>
> Tom *laid* the book on the table.
> The book *was laid* on the table by Tom.
>
> We *rested* on the beach.

In the first three examples above, the point of view and the emphasis are quite different. The verbs which are *active* stress the doers of the action —engineers, lookout, and Tom; the verbs which are *passive* stress the recipients of the action—bridge, ship, and book.

Choice of active or passive voice depends upon context, upon relative importance of the doer and the recipient of the action. Since intransitive verbs rarely fulfill the conditions which make verbs active or passive, only transitive verbs can have a passive voice (see *Transitive verb* in Part II).

In the last example above, *rested* is in the active voice because the subject, *we*, is in the state or condition named.

68a. *Never use an intransitive verb in a passive voice construction.*

Incorrect	Your books have been lain on the table.
	The puppy was sat on a chair.
Correct	Your books have been laid on the table.
	The puppy was made to sit on a chair.

68b. *Avoid frequent use of the passive voice.*

Doers and agents are usually more appealing than those who sit still and do nothing. Use of the active voice normally provides greater force, strength, and life than does the passive. Use the active voice whenever you wish to imply action, mental or physical; use the passive voice in impersonal writing ("These results *were noticed*") and as little elsewhere as possible. Your reader will prefer "Fred *kissed* Joy passionately" to "Joy *was kissed* passionately by Fred." Fred and Joy probably do not care what voice you use, and may be sorry you mentioned them, but it is likely that Joy was as "active" as Fred.

69. ADJECTIVES AND ADVERBS

Ordinarily, it is not difficult to determine when an adjective *or* adverb should be used. *Adjectives* "go with" nouns and pronouns; *adverbs* "go with" verbs, adjectives, and other adverbs. And yet misuse of adjectives and adverbs is common for three main reasons: (1) after linking verbs (see Section **66**), an adjective is used if reference is to the subject, an adverb if reference is to the verb itself; (2) idiomatic usage often violates the distinction between adjectives and adverbs; (3) some adjectives and adverbs have identical or similar forms. Keep in mind the following fundamental distinctions.

An *adjective* modifies a noun or pronoun by describing, limiting, or in some other closely related way making meaning more nearly exact. An adjective may indicate quality or quantity, may identify or set limits. Consequently, adjectives are of three general types: descriptive (a *red* hat, a *hard* lesson, a *damaged* thumb); limiting (the *fourth* period, her *former* home, *many* times); proper (an *American* play, a *Colorado* melon).

Some adjectives—indeed, most—have endings which mark them as adjectives. The more important of these include

-y: rocky, funny, dreamy, fussy, muddy
-ful: harmful, faithful, hurtful, sinful
-less: stainless, timeless, lawless, guiltless
-en: golden, wooden, given, hidden, rotten
-able (-ible): favorable, desirable, credible
-ive: obtrusive, submissive, impulsive
-ous: amorous, ridiculous, generous, marvelous
-ish: mannish, selfish, Danish, fortyish
-al: cordial, optional, experimental, judicial
-ic: metric, philosophic, authentic, artistic
-ary: primary, visionary, contrary, secondary
-some: meddlesome, tiresome, handsome, troublesome

An adjective may modify a noun directly ("this *yellow* light thrown upon the color of his ambitions") or indirectly ("the survivors, *weary* and *emaciated,* moved feebly toward the ship"). In sentences such as "The water felt *cold*" and "The corn is *ripe,*" each adjective is related to the subject, the word it modifies, by a linking verb. (A linking verb has little meaning of its own; it functions primarily as a connection between subject and predicate noun or predicate adjective.) In the sentences above, *cold* and *ripe* are called *predicate adjectives* or *complements.*

An *adverb* modifies a verb, adjective, or other adverb by describing or limiting to make meaning more exact. Adverbs usually tell *how, when, where, why, how often,* and *how much.* In "A low cry came *faintly* to our ears," the adverb modifies the verb *came* and tells *how.* In "We were *nearly* ready to leave," the adverb modifies the adjective *ready.* In "Close the door *very* softly," the adverb modifies the adverb *softly.*

Adverbs have the following characteristics:

1. Adverbs are commonly, but not always, distinguished from corresponding adjectives by the suffix *-ly: bad, badly; sure, surely; cold, coldly.*

2. Certain adverbs are distinguished from corresponding nouns by the suffixes *-wise* and *-ways: endways, sideways, lengthwise.*

3. Certain adverbs are distinguished from corresponding prepositions in not being connected to a following noun:

Adverb: He ran *up.*
Preposition: He ran *up* the street.

4. Like adjectives, but unlike nouns and verbs, adverbs may be preceded by words of the *very* group (intensifiers):

> The *most exotically* dressed girl . . .
> He went *right* by.

69a. *Do not use an adjective to modify a verb.*

The form of a word does not always reveal whether it is an adjective or adverb. Most words ending in *-ly* are adverbs, but *holy, sickly, fatherly,* and *manly* are adjectives. Also, some adjectives and adverbs have the same form: *quick, little, early, fast, kindly.* Finally, a few adverbs have two forms quite different in meaning: *late, lately; sharp, sharply.*

Wrong	He drives his car too *rapid.* [*Rapidly,* an adverb, should modify the verb *drives; rapid* is an adjective.] She dresses *neat* when she is going to a party. [Use *neatly.*] Shakespeare's Portia acted *womanly.* [Use *in a womanly way.*] The teacher spoke *abrupt* to me. [Use *abruptly.*]

69b. *Do not use an adjective to modify another adjective.*

Wrong	Judy is a *real* keen chess player. [Use *really,* an adverb.] That is a *sturdy* tailored overcoat. [Use *sturdily.*] Dick drove his convertible *plenty* fast. [Use *very,* or *quite,* or *exceedingly.*]

69c. *After such verbs as* appear, be, become, feel, look, seem, smell, taste, *the modifier should be an adjective if it refers to the subject, an adverb if it describes or defines the verb.*

Correct	This coffee tastes *good.* [Adjective] The dance hall looked *beautiful.* [Adjective] Jim appeared *sick* when he left the room. [Adjective] She looked at him *lovingly.* [Adverb] Karen feels *intensely* that she was slighted. [Adverb] Joe tasted *carefully* before he swallowed. [Adverb]

69d. *Be accurate in using words that may be either adjectives or adverbs.*

Correct	Sue was a *little* girl. [Adjective] Please come a *little* nearer. [Adverb] Bob was a *kindly* man. [Adjective] Bob spoke *kindly* to everyone. [Adverb] Get here quickly; be an *early* bird. [Adjective] I hope you will come *early.* [Adverb]

69e. *Be accurate in the use of comparatives and superlatives.*

Grammatically, *comparison* is the change in form of an adjective or adverb to indicate greater or smaller degrees of quantity, quality, or manner. The change is commonly indicated by the endings *-er* and *-est* or by the use of adverbial modifiers: *more, most, less, least*. The three degrees of comparison are *positive, comparative,* and *superlative*:

large	larger	largest
slow	slower	slowest
slowly	less slowly	least slowly
wise	wiser	wisest
wisely	more wisely	most wisely

Some comparisons are irregular: *good, better, best; little, less, least.*

Some adjectives are logically incapable of comparison because their meaning is absolute: *perpendicular, unique, round.* Only in informal speech and writing can something be *more impossible* or *more final* or *more fatal.* (See *Unique* in Part II.)

Comparative degree is used to show relationship between two persons, objects, or ideas:

> Fred is *taller* than I.
> This box contains *less* than the other one.

Superlative degree is used to show relationship among three or more:

> Alan is the *smartest* child in the class.
> This desk is the *most attractive* of the four on display.

70. CONJUNCTIONS

A *conjunction* is a linking word used to connect words or groups of words in a sentence. Conjunctions are of two main kinds: *coordinating,* which join words or groups of words of equal rank, such as *and, but, for, or nor, either, neither, yet;* and *subordinating,* which join dependent clauses to main clauses, such as *if, since, because, as, while, so that, although, unless.*

Certain coordinating conjunctions used in pairs are called *correlative* conjunctions. Most frequently used of these are *both . . . and, either . . . or, neither . . . nor, so . . . as, whether . . . or, not only . . . but also.*

Another kind of conjunction is the *conjunctive adverb,* a type of adverb that can also be used as a conjunction joining two independent clauses. Some examples are *accordingly, also, anyhow, besides, consequently, furthermore, hence, however, indeed, likewise, moreover, nevertheless, still, then, therefore, thus.*

70a. ***Distinguish among the meanings of conjunctions and conjunctive adverbs.***

Conjunctions, particularly those which are to join clauses, must be chosen with care, for they always show logical relationships of ideas. (See Sections 8, 9.) Often a careless writer will use *and* where the relationship of clauses needs to be more accurately expressed, probably by use of subordination. Compare emphasis and meaning in these sentences:

The search for the chemical formula has been rewarding *and* further investigation will make the rewards even greater.

Although the search for the chemical formula has been rewarding, further investigation will make the rewards even greater.

Depending upon your expressed purpose, you may coordinate or subordinate ideas in one of several ways. But unless you know the purpose (meaning) of conjunctions and conjunctive adverbs, you are likely to have trouble.

(1) Purpose: *along the same line or in the same direction of thought*

and, both . . . and, not only . . . but also, also, besides, furthermore, in addition, indeed, likewise, moreover, similarly, whereby, whereupon

(2) Purpose: *contrast*

although, but, however, instead, nevertheless, not only . . . but also, notwithstanding, still, whereas, yet

(3) Purpose: *affirmative alternation*

anyhow, either . . . or, else, moreover, or, still, whereas, whether

(4) Purpose: *negative alternation*

except that, however, instead, neither, neither . . . nor, nevertheless, nor, only, whereas

(5) Purpose: *reason, result, purpose, cause*

accordingly, as, as a result, because, consequently, for, hence, inasmuch as, in order that, since, so, so that, that, thereby, therefore, thus, whereas, why

(6) Purpose: *example*

for example, indeed, in fact, namely

(7) Purpose: *comparison*

indeed, in fact, moreover, so . . . as, than

(8) Purpose: *time*

after, as long as, as soon as, before, henceforth, meanwhile, once, since, then, till, until, when, whenever, while

(9) Purpose: *place*

whence, where, wherever, whither

(10) Purpose: *condition*

although, as if, as though, if, lest, once, provided, providing, though, unless

(11) Purpose: *concession*

although, insofar as, notwithstanding the fact that, though, unless, while

70b. *Use correlative conjunctions to correlate only two ideas.*

| Dubious | *Both* the wind, tides, heavy rain, *and* darkness conspired against us. [Delete *both* or two of the four subjects.] |

> *Neither* poverty, ill health, *nor* the indifference of others could keep John from entering college. [Delete one of the three subjects or otherwise rephrase the sentence.]

70c. *Avoid using a conjunctive adverb to join words or phrases or dependent clauses.*

Dubious	Ned's favorite foods are steak, broccoli, *also* ice cream. [. . . broccoli, *and* ice cream]
	At last report he was losing the decathlon; *still* was trying hard. [. . . *but* he was still trying hard]

70d. *Be careful in using* like *as a subordinating conjunction.*

In recent years the use of *like* in clauses of comparison has greatly increased ("It looks *like* he might succeed"). A popular cigarette tastes good "*like* a cigarette should"; we no longer avoid *like* "like we used to."

In standard English, however, *like* is used as a preposition with no verb following: "He looks like an athlete." For clauses of comparison, use *as* or *as if* in strictly formal English:

> My wet shoes felt *as if* [not *like*] they weighed a ton.
> I am named for my father *as* [not *like*] my father was named for his.
> You must do *as* [not *like*] I tell you.

· EXERCISES ON GRAMMAR ·

I

Parts of Speech, Grammatical Functions. In space at the left, write the capital letter indicating that the word, phrase, or clause italicized in each sentence below has the *grammatical function* of

    A   a noun (*naming* word)
    B   a finite verb (*asserting* word)
    C   an adjective (*modifying* word)
    D   an adverb (*modifying* word)
    E   a preposition or a conjunction

1. I mailed the letter *yesterday*.

2. Fish have a sixth *sense* which reports changes in water pressure.

3. Nothing of importance came up *during* the meeting.

4. I am ready for whatever changes in the situation *develop*.

5. I have told you but a *hundredth* part of the difficulties we faced.

6. I'*m* ready to help you at any time.

7. He was charged with driving too *fast* for road conditions.

8. I had *still* another reason for calling you.

9. It is of first importance in swimming *to learn* to take breath properly.

10. You read faster *than* I.

11. I don't want the people *sitting* over there to hear this.

12. You can *at least* try.

13. Who is *in charge* around here?

14. The best seats will go to *whoever comes first.*

15. *Insofar as* information is available, we will keep you posted.

16. Someone *has to have been monkeying* with this set, the way it works now.

17. *Doing* what other people expect you to do is his idea of morality.

18. *To whatever extent* I can help you, you can count on me.

19. The aphorism that truth lies *at the bottom of the cup* is often misleading.

20. *Whomever you want to invite* will be all right with me.

21. Courage *at two o'clock in the morning,* according to Napoleon, is the kind that counts.

22. To get up and *try* again, no matter how often you fail, is the mark of a hero.

23. I will repeat my last remark for the benefit of those *who came in late.*

24. These supplies, *however you came by them,* are going to prove useful.

25. We usually admire the people who like us; we do not always admire those *we like.*

II

Agreement and Case. In this exercise you are to apply the standards of edited English rather than those of informal speech. Word contractions are to be regarded as acceptable if they are in standard form. In space at the left, write a capital letter indicating that the sentence shows an error connected with

    A   agreement of the subject and predicate
    B   agreement of pronoun and antecedent
    C   case indicating subject or object
    D   case (genitive) indicating possession or attribution
    E   none of these: the sentence is acceptable as it stands

1. He is the only one of the people on this block who do not take the morning paper.

2. Aunt Tilda was really eloquent on the subject of Bert coming in late for dinner.

3. Either the operators or the foreman are to blame for the accident.

4. The spring series of lectures on Elizabethan dramatists was well attended.

5. We suspected the perpetrator of this joke to be either his sister or he.

6. You should keep the drainpipe's slant to about one-quarter inch to the foot.

7. Eight slices of pie divided by four make two apiece.

8. Everybody working on Sunday or a holiday will have their pay doubled.

9. I asked Sally if that was her brother or she who came in.

10. He said that whomever he stayed with would have to get used to him getting up early.

11. Father told Hy and me that we would be well rewarded for the weeks work.

12. The worst of my worries and difficulties was that nobody would believe me.

13. I finally collared the dog, after a week's watching, who had been digging up the garden.

14. It became clear to Mack and I that none of the fish in that pond was going to take a hook.

15. Either chemistry or physics is required in the third year.

16. Give these old skates to whomever you think can use them.

17. What I have written down here are the things you are to bring back from town.

18. Neither Parsons nor I am eligible for the scholarship.

19. Either you or Dolly swims better than her.

20. He is one of those people who have to be told everything twice.

21. I'm afraid this news has given you more dissatisfaction than me.

22. By this time more than half the crowd was standing and cheering.

23. The only furniture in the room are a single bed and a chest of drawers.

24. If you find that there isn't enough wieners to go around, fry some hamburgers.

25. He told those within hearing, John and I among others, that what we needed most were a couple of infielders and a catcher.

III

Verbs, Adjectives, Adverbs, Conjunctions. In this exercise, following current standard usage, *shall* and *will* or *should* and *would* are regarded as interchangeable forms in the 1st person; you will not be asked to distinguish them. In the 2nd and 3rd persons, *shall* still implies determination and *should,* obligation. In space at the left, write the capital letter indicating that the sentence contains an error involving

A   the *form* of a verb (confusion of principal parts, wrong mood, or use of a substandard form)
B   *tense or sequence* of tenses
C   use of *adjective for adverb* or vice versa, or the wrong form of either
D   misuse of *conjunctions* (preposition or coordinating conjunction used for subordination, etc.)
E   none of these: the sentence is *acceptable* as it stands

1. He looked as if he were about to explode, but with an apparent superhuman effort he controlled himself.

2. If I knew then what I know now, we would never have drifted apart.

3. I have never learned to play a piece of music, like you can, at first sight.

4. He has lived for several years in the Arctic before he settled down here, and has many fascinating stories to tell about his life there.

5. If I had had his experiences, I would write a book—maybe several books.

6. Before the party started, I made the irritating discovery that the boys had got into the refrigerator and drank most of the cokes.

7. He's a very retiring neighbor and never comes over without I ask him to call on us.

8. We would have liked to have Jed on our team, but he's too prejudice to join us.

9. If we keep very quiet and talk soft enough we may get close enough to take a picture.

10. Only in recent years was it discovered that the more distant galaxies seemed to be receding from us at enormous speeds.

11. If I would have known you were coming to town, I'd have got tickets for a play.

12. I had never swum in the ocean before, and I was surprised at how bitterly it tasted.

13. I can remember having the same experience; however, you'll get use to it.

14. I'm sorry the Petersons have already left; I should have liked to have seen them.

15. It's surprising how swiftly the time has passed, and I can hardly realize that at the end of the month I'll be here a whole year.

16. In the part of the country where I was born, every boy wanted to have a rifle, a pony, moreover a couple of good dogs.

17. If the fishing here turns out to be as good as I have heard of its being last year, I shall not have wasted my time in coming so far.

18. He was the wittiest and intelligentest speaker whom up to that time I had ever listened to.

19. After a long discussion that grew fairly warm at times, it was voted that the club president was directed to invite two speakers, on opposite sides of the question.

20. I wouldn't have tried to ride your bicycle, had I known the chain was broke.

IV

Exact Connectives. In each sentence below, a blank indicates the omission of a connective word or phrase. In space at the left, write a capital letter indicating the expression which fits the context and most precisely shows the relation between two parts of the sentence. Do not overlook correct punctuation.

1. Several teams on the Coast appear to be almost exactly balanced this year; _____ I wouldn't be surprised if the season ended in a three-way tie for the title.

    A   of course
    B   moreover,
    C   in fact,
    D   for example,
    E   anyway

2. A translation of a Latin passage into English is usually much longer than the original, _____ English uses separate words to express relations which in Latin are shown by inflections.

    A   primarily because
    B   chiefly for the reason that
    C   although
    D   consequently,
    E   in any case,

3. The difference is that the writer of ordinary fiction is permitted to introduce genuine surprises now and then, just as life does, _____ the writer of detec-

tive stories is required to play strictly fair with the reader and present only solutions which have been clued beforehand.

    A   but
    B   however,
    C   in contrast,
    D   whereas
    E   on the contrary,

4. It is a good rule of style to choose short, homely words instead of showy ones; _____ one should avoid an obviously affected, Hemingwayesque simplicity.

    A   in any case,
    B   at the same time,
    C   whenever possible,
    D   in contrast,
    E   notwithstanding,

5. Nobody knows how the public will react to the proposal of a guaranteed annual income; _____ I'm not sure how I feel about it myself.

    A   however that may be,
    B   in any event,
    C   consequently,
    D   for that matter,
    E   at the same time,

6. It is hard to say whether loneliness, hardship, or the awe of empty distances did most to form the quality of cowboy song and poetry; _____ what resulted was a compound of melancholy secular mysticism unique in literature.

    A   nevertheless,
    B   in any case,
    C   however,
    D   for all that,
    E   be that as it may,

7. The hardships of westward migration bore much more heavily on women than on men— _____ it was not uncommon for a pioneer husband to survive a series of wives.

    A   because
    B   consequently,
    C   so much so that
    D   therefore
    E   the proof being the fact that

8. It is not enough to say that the romantic village tradition ended when *Winesburg, Ohio*, exposed the pathology, and *Main Street* the boredom, of small-town life; _____ life in the Midwestern small town has always been marvelous for children and intolerable for adults.

    A   in either case,
    B   the reason is that
    C   however that may be,
    D   the fact is that
    E   in contrast,

9. Educators have traditionally assumed that whatever degree of ability the pupil brings to school will set upper limits to his education which even the most favorable environment cannot raise; _____ the advocates of programmed instruc-

tion maintain that with the right methods any healthy person can be taught literally anything.

A in comparison,
B however,
C in flat contradiction,
D nevertheless,
E at the same time,

10. Patriotism as a feeling of fondness and responsibility toward one's native terrain and its inhabitants may well be instinctive, and is generally wholesome; _____ patriotism as a belief that one's fellow nationals are superior to, and more valuable than, those of other nations has to be taught and is productive of endless misery.

A but
B in comparison,
C however,
D on the whole,
E on the other hand,

V

Review. Each item below consists of two sentences. You are to pick out the word (lettered) in the second sentence which has the same grammatical function as the italicized word in the first sentence. Use space at the left to insert the proper capital letter.

Example: I *am* tired of all this talking.
I think that he is willing to be on the team if we want him.
    A   B C   D   E

Explanation: The answer is B, because *am* is a finite linking verb and *is* is the only such verb in the second sentence. Answer A is wrong because "I am tired" is functionally quite different from "I think that . . ." Answer D is wrong because *be*, though a linking verb, is in infinitive form.

1. It *got* very cold last night.
If I don't get a job it will be pretty hard to keep up the payments on the
      A   B   C
car I bought before you came here.
    D   E

2. I do a lot of sailing *during* the summer.
We were loafing on the corner and talking of this and that while we waited
       A B   C
for Joe to show up.
D   E

3. She was combing her *tousled* red hair.
A little while later I saw an old man in a soiled, ragged jacket and wear-
    A   B   C
ing a hat with a green, sweaty band driving a wagon drawn by a sway-backed
            D   E
old horse.

4. I ran downstairs *when* I heard the telephone ringing.
Then he stopped paddling because he thought the canoe had struck a
    A   B

snag, and meanwhile the others, who had not noticed anything, drew some dis-
          C   D   E
tance ahead.

5. I sympathize with your motives; *all the same,* I think you are wrong.
    However early you start, it will be a long day's drive, yet it won't be too
          A   B   C
bad if you choose your route carefully and consequently don't waste time looking
  D   E
at the map.

6. I was *but* a child at the time.
    As I passed the window, I thought I saw somebody in the garden and
    A   B   C
turned to look again, but it was only a shadow.
           D   E

7. *It* is my turn to take the car.
    I looked for my scarf but could not find it because there were so many
    A   B   C   D
things on top of it in the drawer.
      E

8. It was I who gave *John* his first lessons in woodcraft.
    Nothing afforded me greater satisfaction in later life than the recollection
                  A   B   C
that I had paid my own way.
  D   E

9. Agricultural productivity has been greatly increased by corn *grown* from
hybrid seed.
    Ideas acquired in the course of reading are usually less well remembered
            A   B   C
than those which have been drawn from experience or picked up from observa-
                           D   E
tion.

10. I did not like to *do* the marketing unless Mother was with me.
    You want to keep an eye on Gardner during the game and watch every
           A   B
move he makes; you can learn a good deal if you do that.
    C   D   E

VI

Review. Each sentence below, continued through five lettered lines, contains an error in grammar. (You are to apply the standard of *edited* English rather than that of informal speech, but contractions are acceptable if they are in standard form.) In space at the left, write a capital letter indicating the line with the error.

1. A   Had I known that you were taking
      B   the same route to school as we,
      C   I'd have suggested you riding
      D   in the same car with
      E   John and me.

2. A   He lay looking like something
      B   the cat had dragged in,
      C   having swum too far and

    D   drank enough salt water
    E   to make anybody feel bad.

3. A   The latest of his exploits is
    B   to have caught four touchdown passes
    C   in one game, though he has been
    D   looking so good lately that I
    E   was not much surprise to hear of it.

4. A   He was an effective storyteller
    B   who we knew had traveled a great deal,
    C   and his account of adventures
    D   among savage tribesmen were
    E   thrilling to both Joey and me.

5. A   He failed in algebra because he is
    B   one of those people who begin to study
    C   too late, but if he had started earlier
    D   and worked harder,
    E   he may have passed the course with ease.

6. A   Once in possession of the house, I
    B   planned to make great changes, and
    C   would have completed them
    D   if I didn't run out of money
    E   before I had well begun.

7. A   We were held spellbound by the glass blower,
    B   marveling at how he could work so fast and careful
    C   in turning out little colored animals;
    D   there is not many an artist who combines
    E   so much speed and expertness.

8. A   They're now freshmen in college, and
    B   their chief worry is whether four years
    C   from now they're going to be as many jobs
    D   available to graduates as there are at present,
    E   but I think there're going to be plenty of jobs.

9. A   The intellectual level of foreign movies,
    B   according to many critics,
    C   are usually superior to
    D   that of those produced in America,
    E   especially in the category of satire.

10. A   The members of the early class
    B   and we in ours learned too late that
    C   if we had listened to the assignments
    D   and wrote up all the reports listed in them
    E   we might not have landed in the mess we're in now.

VII

Review. Each sentence below, continued through four lettered lines, may contain an error in grammar. (Apply the standard of *edited* English.) In the space at the left, write a capital letter indicating the line containing an error, if any. If there are no errors in the sentence, write key *E*.

1. A   The contract will be awarded to whoever
    B   submits the lowest estimate, and

      C   I hope it will effect a greater saving
      D   than last years economies.
      E   (No error)

2.   A   There is not many a girl
      B   who I have found believes
      C   that a simple yes or no
      D   are the best answers.
      E   (No error)

3.   A   It hardly seemed serious enough
      B   to Tom and me to justify
      C   us writing Dad to suggest that he
      D   attend the hearing.
      E   (No error)

4.   A   As soon as the lake appeared quiet
      B   enough, we swam out to the boat
      C   and began to dive for the motor,
      D   which had sunk in ten feet of water.
      E   (No error)

5.   A   The least of my fears was that
      B   I might lose my way, for although I
      C   had never taken this path in the dark before,
      D   I was use to every turn and dip in it.
      E   (No error)

6.   A   He has taught in this college
      B   for years before attracting
      C   national notice, but has since
      D   become our principal ornament.
      E   (No error)

7.   A   He is one of those people
      B   who find it easy to
      C   look wise and sound plausible
      D   on all sorts of topics.
      E   (No error)

8.   A   She told Ted and me that she would
      B   have had the apartment ready if we gave her a little
      C   earlier notice, since everybody knows that it
      D   takes time to get such a place looking neat.
      E   (No error)

9.   A   This short course of lectures
      B   on the new math have led us to conclude
      C   that such instruction proves ineffective unless
      D   the students' interest is enforced by regular tests.
      E   (No error)

10.   A   A state of ill-concealed hostility
      B   exist so far between these two new nations,
      C   and unless we can reconcile their demands,
      D   serious harm threatens both them and us.
      E   (No error)

PART II

GUIDE TO TERMS
AND USAGE

This Guide contains items in alphabetical order which fall into six sometimes overlapping groups:

1. Entries on particular words and expressions: *accept, except; quiet, quit, quite; to, too, two;* etc. These entries involve correct, effective, and appropriate diction.

2. Entries on grammatical constructions with recommendations for effective usage: *and which;* overuse of *so; should, would;* etc.

3. Entries for groups of words with similar spelling characteristics: *-able, -ible; -efy;* silent letters; etc.

4. Definitions and discussions of grammatical terms and expressions, treated at varying lengths. Where the term has been developed fully in Part I (adjective, adverb, etc.), there is no entry here and you should consult the index to Books One and Two, beginning on page 449. Certain items are here included which are not directly involved in the 70 sections of Part I. Occasionally, comment on a term or expression appearing in Part I is amplified in this Guide.

5. Brief articles, of somewhat general interest to the writer, bearing on problems of composition: conversation; dictionaries; history of English; lecture notes; listening; logic; use of the library; etc.

6. Brief comments on rhetorical matters: periodic sentence; schoolgirl style; variety in sentence structure; wordiness; etc.

A, an. The choice between *a* and *an* depends on the initial sound of the word which follows. *An* should be used before a vowel sound, *a* before a word beginning with a consonant sound: *an* adult, *a* picture; *an* honor, *a* hopeful suggestion.

Abbreviation. A shortened form of a word or phrase, such as *Mr.* for *Mister* and *S.C.* for *South Carolina.* Abbreviations, except such common ones as *Mr.* and *Dr.*, are normally unacceptable in standard writing and should never be overused. Also, periods are required with most of them. (See Section 58.)

Ability, capacity. *Ability* means the power to do something, physical or mental ("*ability* to speak in public"). *Capacity* is the ability to hold, contain, or absorb ("a room filled to *capacity*").

-able. 1. The ending should usually be *-able* if the base (root) is a complete word: *eat + able.*

acceptable	dependable	peaceable
available	detestable	predictable
breakable	drinkable	presentable
changeable	fashionable	profitable
comfortable	favorable	readable
commendable	laughable	seasonable
considerable	noticeable	taxable
creditable	passable	workable

2. The ending should usually be *-able* if the base (root) is a complete word lacking a final *e*: *desire + able = desirable.*

believable	excitable	sizable
deplorable	likable	usable
desirable	lovable	valuable

3. The ending should usually be *-able* if the base (root) ends in *i* (the original word may have ended in *y*): *enviable.* This principle of spelling makes more sense than most spelling "rules." If it were not followed, we would have a double *i* (*ii*), an unusual combination even in our weird spelling system.

appreciable	dutiable	reliable
classifiable	justifiable	sociable

4. The ending should usually be *-able* if the base (root) has other forms with the sound of long *a*: *demonstrate, demonstrable.* This principle will be helpful only if you actually sound out another form (or forms) of the root word to see whether it has (or they have) the long *a* sound: *abominate, abominable; estimate, estimable;* etc.

delectable	impregnable	inseparable
durable	inflammable	intolerable
flammable	innumerable	irritable

5. The end should usually be *-able* if the base (root) ends in hard *c* or hard *g*. Hard *c* is sounded like the *c* in *cat;* hard *g* has the sound of *g* in *get*. The following words illustrate this principle.

| amicable | implacable | irrevocable |
| applicable | indefatigable | practicable |

These five principles cover most of the fairly common words which have endings in *-able*. But if you wish to be able to spell all words ending with *-able*, study the following by some other method— rules won't help much:

affable	inevitable	palpable
equitable	inscrutable	portable
formidable	insuperable	probable
indomitable	memorable	vulnerable

(See *-ible*.)

Absolute expression.   An absolute expression (also called *nominative absolute*) is one which has a thought relationship, but no direct grammatical relationship, with the remainder of the sentence in which it occurs. (See Section 47n.) An absolute expression is usually composed of a noun or pronoun and a participle:

> *The game being lost,* we left the stadium.
> *The purpose of our field trip having been explained,* we set out resignedly.

Absolutely.   This word means "completely," "perfectly," "wholly." In addition to being greatly overused as an intensifier, it is both faulty and wordy in an expression such as "*absolutely* complete." Never use *absolutely* or any other such modifier with words like *complete, perfect, unique.* (See *Unique.*)

Abstract.   A word or phrase is *abstract* when it is not concrete (definite and specific) in meaning. It applies to a quality thought of as being apart from any material object: *honor, mercy, beauty.*

As a noun, *abstract* means a brief statement of the essential contents of an article, speech, book, etc. (See *Summary.*)

Abstract noun.   The name of a thing not evident to one of the senses, such as a quality or condition: *duty, happiness, glory, freedom.* (See *Concrete noun.*)

Accent.   This word has several meanings, two of which apply particularly to English speech or writing. We may say that someone has an *accent,* by which we mean his distinguishing regional or national manner of pronouncing or the tone of his voice ("a Southern *accent*"). Accent also means the emphasis (by pitch or stress or both) given to a particular syllable or word when speaking it. Thus we say "Please *accent* that word more clearly" or "The *accent* in the word *refer* is on the second syllable." As a noun, the first syllable of *accent* is stressed; as a verb, either syllable may be stressed, according to the use of the word.

Accent mark.   A mark used to distinguish between various sounds of the same letter. Thus we add a stroke above the letter *a* to show that it has a long sound as in the word *fāme.* Certain words in English require an acute accent, or grave accent, or circumflex accent, etc. An accent mark is related to *Diacritical mark,* which see. (See also Section 6oa.)

Accept, except.   *Accept* means "to receive" or "to agree with"; *except* means "to omit" or "to exempt." ("I will not *accept* your offer." "The men were punished but Ned was *excepted*.") As a preposition, *except* means "other than." ("Everyone *except* me was on time.")

Accidently. This "word" is an illiteracy. The word should be *accidentally*.

Accordion sentence. A sentence which, like an accordion, is alternately pulled out and pressed together. It is caused by faulty subordination. (See Section 9c.)

Accusative case. A term meaning the same as *objective case*. (See Section 64.)

Active voice. The form of an action-expressing verb which tells that the subject of the verb performs or does the action. (See Sections 11b and 68.)

Ad. A colloquial abbreviation, much used, for *advertisement*. In strictly formal writing, avoid such abbreviations as *ad*, *auto* for *automobile*, *phone* for *telephone*, *exam* for *examination*.

Ad-. This prefix, meaning "addition to," "motion toward," "nearness to," alters its form according to the root word to which it is attached. For example, before a root beginning with *sc* or *sp*, the *d* is dropped, as in *ascent* and *aspire*. Before *c*, *f*, *g*, *l*, *n*, *p*, and *t*, the *d* in *ad-* is assimilated (becomes the same as the following letter): *accommodate*, *affix*, *aggression*, *allegation*, *announce*, *appoint*, *attend*.

A.D., B.C. *Anno domini*, Latin for "in the year of the Lord," is represented by the letters *A.D.* "Before Christ" is abbreviated to *B.C.*

Added vowels. Some words are misspelled because in pronouncing them an extra vowel is added. Mispronouncing may cause you not only to misspell words but to be looked upon as careless in speech or uneducated or both. (See Section 16a.)

> *Athletic* (physically active and strong) should not be spelled "athaletic" or "atheletic."
> *Entrance* (act or point of coming in) should not be spelled "enterance."
> *Explanation* (interpretation) should not be spelled "explaination."
> *Grievous* (sad to hear, deplorable) should not be spelled "grievious."
> *Hindrance* (obstacle, impediment) should not be spelled "hinderance."
> *Hundred* (the number) should not be spelled "hundered."
> *Laundry* (washing of clothes) should not be spelled "laundery" or "laundary."
> *Mischievous* (prankish) should not be spelled "mischievious."
> *Monstrous* (huge, enormous) should not be spelled "monsterous."
> *Nervous* (emotionally tense) should not be spelled "nerveous."
> *Partner* (associate) should not be spelled "partener."
> *Remembrance* (souvenir, keepsake) should not be spelled "rememberance."
> *Spanish* (pertaining to Spain) should not be spelled "Spainish."
> *Umbrella* (a shade or screen) should not be spelled "umberella."

Ad lib. This verb, meaning "to improvise," "to extemporize," is both overused and colloquial. It is derived from the Latin phrase *ad libitum*, meaning "at pleasure," and is appropriately used in music to mean "freely." Avoid using *ad lib* to mean adding words and gestures not in the script or not intended to be said or otherwise expressed.

Advise. This word, meaning "to counsel," "to give advice to," is overused in business letters and other forms of communication for "tell," "inform." ("I am pleased to *inform* [not *advise*] you that the check has been received.")

Affect, effect.   As a verb, *affect* means "to influence," or "to assume." ("This book has *affected* my thinking.") *Effect* as a verb means "to cause" and as a noun means "result." ("Your good work will *effect* an improvement in your mark for the term." "This play will have a good *effect* on youth.")

Affectation.   Artificial behavior or manners intended to impress others. An *affectation* is a mannerism for effect which involves show or pretense. In language it is most evident in pronunciation and in the use of words or expressions not customary for the speaker or writer employing them. For most people "aren't I" is an affectation; so is the pronunciation of *been* as "bēn" (bean). Increasing the vigor and effectiveness of one's speech and writing is laudable, but deliberately trying to be different usually results in misinterpretation or confusion.

Affixes.   This is a term which embraces both *prefixes* and *suffixes*.

Prefixes are syllables added at the beginnings of words to alter or modify their meanings or, occasionally, to form entirely new words. For example, we add the prefix *de-* to the word *form* and make *deform*.

Suffixes are syllables added at the ends of words to alter their meanings, to form new words, or to show grammatical function (part of speech). Thus we add *-ly* to *like* and form *likely*.

The readiness with which prefixes and suffixes are tacked on to root words in the English language is an indication of the freedom in word formation which has characterized our language for many centuries. For example, consider the word *recession*. This is derived from a Latin word *cedere* (*cessus*), which has the general meaning of "go." To this base we add the prefix *re-*, which has a generalized meaning of "back" or "again," and the suffix *-ion*, an ending which shows that the word is a noun. Related to *recession* are many words with still other prefixes and suffixes but all with a similar root, or base: *recede, recess, recessive, concession, procession, secession,* etc. The prefix *re-* of *recession* occurs in such words as *reception* and *relation*.

A knowledge of the ways in which prefixes and suffixes are added to words will increase your vocabulary and improve your spelling. (See *Prefix* and *Suffix*.)

Agreement.   This word means "being in unison or concord." It involves correspondence, or sameness, in number, gender, and person. Thus, when a subject agrees with its verb, they are alike in having the same *person* (first, second, or third) and *number* (singular or plural). Pronouns agree not only in person and number but also in *gender* (masculine, etc.). (For more extended discussion, see Sections 11c, 62, 63.)

Ain't.   This contraction is considered illiterate, dialectal, or colloquial and is cautioned against in standard English, both written and spoken. The word, which stands for *am not*, is often informally used even by educated people, but it has not been accepted in the sense that *isn't* (for *is not*), *aren't* (for *are not*), and *weren't* (for *were not*) have been. (See *Contraction*.)

Alibi.   Used colloquially to mean "an excuse or any kind of defense," the word precisely and correctly should be used to mean "a plea or fact of having been elsewhere when an offense was committed." *Alibi* is often used in the loose sense mentioned above and is now a trite and jaded expression.

All right, alright.   The former expression is correct but has been overworked to mean "satisfactory" or "very well." *Alright* is analogous to *altogether* and *already* (both standard words) but is not yet an acceptable word in standard usage.

Alliteration.   Repetition of an initial sound in two or more words of a phrase, sentence, or line of poetry: "Ada ambled across the avenue." In poetry, alliteration is often effective; in prose, it is usually considered an *affectation*, which see.

-ally, -ly.   Because these endings appear so often in commonly used words, they account for a large number of misspellings.

1. The suffix *-ly* is used to form an adverb from an adjective: *poor + ly = poorly*. If the adjective ends in *l*, *-ly* is tacked on to the complete root, thus producing an *-lly* ending. Here is a list of frequently used, and occasionally misspelled, adverbs:

accidentally	fundamentally	personally
actually	generally	physically
annually	incidentally	practically
continually	individually	really
coolly	intentionally	skillfully
especially	logically	truthfully
exceptionally	morally	universally
finally	naturally	unusually
formally	occasionally	usually

2. The suffix *-ly* is added to basic words ending in silent *e*, the *e* being retained.

absolutely	entirely	scarcely
barely	immediately	severely
completely	infinitely	sincerely

3. If an adjective ends in *-ic*, its adverbial form ends in *-ally*. The only exception to this simple rule is *publicly;* you must fix this word in your visual memory. Here are examples of adverbs formed from adjectives with *-ic* endings:

academically	basically	grammatically
artistically	emphatically	lyrically
automatically	fantastically	systematically

The following adverbs do not completely follow the principles just enumerated. Fix them in your visual memory:

duly	possibly	truly
only	terribly	wholly

Almost.   See *Most, almost.*

Already, all ready.   The former means "earlier," "previously." ("When she arrived, her friend had *already* left.") *All ready* means "all are ready." ("They will leave when they are *all ready*.")

Altogether, all together.   Altogether means "wholly," "completely." ("He was not *altogether* pleased with his purchase.") *All together* means "all in company" or "everybody in one place." ("The family was *all together* for the holidays.")

Alumnus, alumna.   An *alumnus* is a male graduate; an *alumna* is a woman graduate. The respective plurals are *alumni* and *alumnae*. To refer to graduates of a school as *alum* or *alums* is colloquial or slangy.

A.M., a.m.; P.M., p.m.   The first expression, spelled with either capitals or lower-case letters, means "before noon" (from the Latin *ante meridiem*). P.M. or p.m. means "noon to midnight" (from the Latin *post meridiem*). Both are clear indicators of time. After them do not use such expressions as "in the morning," etc. Figures, not words, are conventionally used. ("We left at 7 A.M.") (See Section 59b.)

Ambiguity.   A word or other expression whose meaning is doubtful, uncertain, capable of being misunderstood or of being understood in more than one sense. Ambiguous expressions occur often in speech and writing: getting rid of them is one of the prime objects of all writers who wish to be effective. An antonym of ambiguity is *clearness* (clarity), which see. (See also Section 41.)

Americanism.   A word or phrase peculiar to the English language as developed in the United States. Americans use *er* in words such as *theater* and *center;* the English are much more likely to write *theatre* and *centre*. Americans double fewer consonants (*wagon, traveler*) than the English (*waggon, traveller*). We also write *favor* and *humor*, not *favour* and *humour*. In the United States we refer to an *elevator;* in England reference is to a *lift*.

Many minor differences exist between the language generally used in England and in the United States. For Americans to adopt British methods of pronunciation, British spelling, and British vocabulary is generally an *affectation*, which see.

Among, between.   The former shows the relationship of more than two objects; *between* refers to only two or to more than two when each object is considered in its relationship to others. ("We distributed the candy *among* the six children." "We divided the candy *between* Jill and Gray." "Understanding *between* nations is essential.")

Amount, number.   The former is used of things involving a unified mass —bulk, weight, or sums. ("What is the *amount* of the bill?") *Number* is used of things which can be counted in individual units. ("I have a *number* of hats and coats.")

Ampersand.   A mechanical mark (&) meaning *and*. It represents the letters of the Latin word for "and," *et*. Primarily designed and used to save space, it appears often in business writing, reference works, and company names. Except in these connections, its use is considered substandard in formal writing.

Analogy.   This word suggests "partial resemblance" and implies similarity in some respect between things otherwise unlike. In linguistics, *analogy* is the process by which new or less familiar words, constructions, or pronunciations conform with older ones. Thus we form *energize* from *energy* by analogy with *apologize* from *apology*.

Reasoning by analogy can cause serious blunders in logic (see Section 41c).

Analysis of a sentence.   Theoretically, you should be able to analyze a sentence both by words and by groups of words—*if you know grammar.*

Consider the following sentence:

> The little old lady across the street is carefully knitting a sweater for her grandson, who is a newsboy.

A grammatical analysis of this sentence is as follows:

The is a definite article modifying the noun *lady. Little* and *old* are adjectives modifying the noun *lady. Lady* is a noun used as *subject of the sentence. The little old lady* is the *complete subject* of *is knitting.*

Across is a preposition introducing the prepositional phrase; *the,* a definite article modifying the noun *street; street,* a noun used as object of the preposition *across.* The entire prepositional phrase, *across the street,* is used as an adjective modifying *lady.*

Is is an auxiliary verb which with the present participle *knitting* forms the present progressive tense, active voice, and is the *predicate of the sentence.*

Carefully is an adverb modifying the verb phrase *is knitting.*

A is an indefinite article modifying *sweater,* which is a noun used as direct object of the verb phrase *is knitting.*

For is a preposition; *her,* a possessive pronoun, third person singular feminine, refers to *lady* and modifies *grandson; grandson,* a noun, is the object of the preposition *for.* The entire prepositional phrase, *for her grandson,* is used as an adverb, modifying *is knitting,* if we think of the phrase as being closely associated with and tied to the verb phrase *is knitting;* if, however, we think of *for her grandson* as being closely associated with *sweater,* then both by logic and common sense we can call it a phrase used as an adjective modifying *sweater.*

Who is a relative pronoun, nominative case, referring to *grandson* and used as the subject of *is; is* is a linking verb; *a* is an indefinite article modifying *newsboy;* and *newsboy* is a predicate noun after a linking verb. The group of words, *who is a newsboy,* is an adjective clause modifying *grandson.*

The entire sentence is *complex* in its grammatical structure. (See *Diagraming.*)

-ance, -ence.   The suffixes *-ance* and *-ence* are added to root words (verbs) to form nouns: *attend, attendance; prefer, preference.* There is no single guiding principle in your choice of *-ance* or *-ence.* Correct pronunciation is of no help. Your only safe procedure is to consult your dictionary and try to form good visual images of *-ance* and *-ence* words.

One helpful principle, and one only, is this: if a verb ends in *r* preceded by a single vowel and is accented on the last syllable, it forms its noun with *-ence.*

abhorrence	concurrence	deference
coherence	conference	deterrence

| inference | preference | reference |
| occurrence | recurrence | transference |

The following are lists of frequently misspelled words ending in -*ance* and -*ence*. Study each until you have a total recall of its appearance.

FREQUENTLY MISSPELLED -*ANCE* WORDS

abundance	continuance	nuisance
acceptance	contrivance	observance
acquaintance	defiance	performance
admittance	deliverance	radiance
alliance	distance	relevance
allowance	endurance	reliance
ambulance	entrance	remembrance
annoyance	furtherance	remittance
appearance	grievance	resistance
arrogance	guidance	significance
assurance	instance	substance
attendance	insurance	temperance
balance	irrelevance	tolerance
brilliance	maintenance	vengeance

FREQUENTLY MISSPELLED -*ENCE* WORDS

absence	difference	obedience
audience	essence	patience
circumference	evidence	preference
coherence	excellence	presence
coincidence	existence	prominence
competence	experience	reference
conference	impudence	residence
confidence	inference	reverence
conscience	influence	sentence
convenience	innocence	silence
correspondence	insistence	subsistence
dependence	interference	violence

And etc.   A redundant expression. *Etc.* is an abbreviation for the Latin phrase *et cetera,* meaning "and so forth." Omit the *and* in "and etc."

And how!   A slang expression indicating strong feeling or approval. Avoid its use in standard English; it is both informal and trite.

And/or.   Primarily a business and legal expression, *and/or* is objected to by purists and other especially fastidious users of English. It is somewhat vague and also has business connotations objectionable to some people. Although it is a useful time-saver, in formal English you should avoid using it.

And which, and who, but which, but who.   Correct sentence structure provides that these phrases should appear in clauses only if preceded by clauses which also contain *which* or *who.* ("This is the first book *which* I bought *and which* I treasure," not "This is the first book I bought *and which* . . .") (See Section **8d.**)

Ante-, anti-.   The first of these prefixes is of Latin origin and means "before," "prior." *Anti-* is from the Greek and means "opposite," "against." Note these different spellings:

antebellum (*before the war*)	antiaircraft
antemeridian (*before noon, A.M.*)	antibiotic
antemortem (*before death*)	anticlimax
anteroom (*room before another room*)	antifreeze
antetype (*an earlier form*)	antisocial

Antecedent.   This word means literally "going before." The substantive (noun or pronoun) to which a pronoun refers is its antecedent (see Section 63).

> The *girl* has lost *her* gloves. [*Girl* is the antecedent of *her*.]
> *Men* were willing to stake *their* lives on the issue. [*Men* is the antecedent of *their*.]
> Remember that *pronouns* agree with *their* antecedents in gender, number, and person. [*Pronouns* is the antecedent of *their*.]

Antithesis.   This word means "opposition" or "contrast" of thoughts. "You are smart, but I am stupid" illustrates the meaning of the term. Shakespeare's "Fair is foul, and foul is fair" suggests what rhetorical power the device can have.

Antonym.   A word which is opposite in meaning to that of another word: *sad* is the antonym of *happy; small* and *little* are antonyms of *large*. (See *Synonym*.)

Anyway, anyways.   *Anyway* means "in any case," "anyhow." ("She was planning to go *anyway*.") *Anyways* has the same meaning as *anyway*, but it is considered either dialectal or colloquial when used to mean "in any case." ("*Anyway* [not *anyways*], I want to go too.")

Appositive.   A substantive added to another substantive to identify or explain it. The appositive signifies the same thing and is said to be "in apposition."

> One important product, *rubber,* this country has in short supply. [*Rubber* is in apposition with *product*.]
> More hardy than wheat are these grains—*rye, oats,* and *barley*. [*Rye, oats,* and *barley* are in apposition with *grains*.]

An appositive agrees with its substantive in number and case. It is set off by commas if its relationship is loose (nonrestrictive) and is used without punctuation if the relationship is close (restrictive). (See Section 470.)

Appropriateness.   In writing or speaking, this term means using words and constructions which are fit, suitable, proper. The appropriateness of language is determined by the subject being discussed, the situation or medium for discussion, the reader or listener, the writer or speaker. (For further discussion, see *Levels of usage, Standard English*.)

Apt, liable, likely.   *Apt* suggests fitness or tendency. ("She is *apt* in arithmetic.") *Liable* implies exposure to something burdensome or disadvantageous. ("You are *liable* for damages.") *Likely* means "expected," "probable." ("We are *likely* to have snow next month.") *Likely* is the most commonly used of the three terms. Distinction in meaning has broken down somewhat, but *apt* and *liable* used in the sense of "probable" are sometimes considered colloquial or dialectal.

-ar, -er, -or.   These suffixes have various origins, functions, and meanings. Their most common shared meaning denotes an actor, a doer, "one who." Following are lists of words ending in *-ar, -er,* and *-or* that are often misspelled.

FREQUENTLY MISSPELLED -AR WORDS

altar (*n.*)	grammar	popular
beggar	hangar	regular
calendar	liar	scholar
caterpillar	lunar	similar
cellar	molar	spectacular
circular	muscular	sugar
collar	particular	vinegar
dollar	peculiar	vulgar

FREQUENTLY MISSPELLED -ER WORDS

advertiser	consumer	messenger
affirmer	defender	minister
alter (*v.*)	diameter	murderer
announcer	disaster	observer
baker	employer	officer
beginner	examiner	partner
believer	foreigner	passenger
boarder	haberdasher	prisoner
border	jeweler	provider
boulder	lawyer	soldier
carrier	lecturer	teacher
commissioner	manager	traveler
condenser	manufacturer	writer

FREQUENTLY MISSPELLED -OR WORDS

accelerator	councillor	humor
actor	counselor	inferior
administrator	creditor	inventor
aggressor	debtor	investigator
anchor	dictator	janitor
auditor	director	legislator
author	distributor	manor
aviator	doctor	minor
bachelor	editor	monitor
behavior	educator	motor
benefactor	elevator	neighbor
cantor	emperor	odor
collector	escalator	pastor
commentator	executor	prior
competitor	factor	professor
conqueror	governor	protector
contributor	harbor	radiator

sailor	suitor	traitor
sculptor	supervisor	ventilator
senator	tenor	visitor

Arabic numerals.   See *Roman numerals.*

Argument.   A reason or reasons offered for or against something. Argument refers to a discussion in which there is disagreement and suggests the use of logic and a statement of facts to refute or support a position or point. *Argument* is one of the *forms of discourse,* the others being *narration, exposition,* and *description* (all of which see).

Articles.   The articles (*a, an, the*) may be classed as adjectives because they possess limiting or specifying functions. *A* and *an* are indefinite articles; *the* is the definite article: *a* phonograph, *an* error, *the* surgeon. (See *A, an.*)

-ary, -ery.   This suffix problem is simple. Many hundreds of English words end in *-ary.* Only eight fairly common words end in *-ery.* Learn these *-ery* words by whatever device works best for you; spell all others with *-ary.*

cemetery	every
confectionery	millinery
distillery	monastery
dysentery	stationery

Now, if you end all other words with *-ary,* you'll be right every time, unless you happen to use such a rare word as *philandery.* You will have no spelling problems with the endings of *auxiliary, boundary, dictionary, elementary, honorary, imaginary, library, secretary, voluntary,* and hundreds of other such everyday words.

As.   One of the most overworked words in the English language. It is a perfectly good word, but *since, because,* and *when* are more exact and effective conjunctions. ("*Since* [not *As*] it was snowing, we decided to stay indoors.") *As* is also often misused in place of *that* or *whether.* ("I doubt *that* [not *as*] I can go.") In negative comparisons some writers prefer *so . . . as* to *as . . . as.* ("He is not *so* heavy *as* his brother.") In general, use *as* sparingly; nearly always a more exact and effective word can be found. (See also Section 7od.)

As good as, if not better than.   A correctly phrased but awkward and mixed comparison. A statement will be more effective when "if not better" is put at the end. (*Awkward:* "My work is *as good as, if not better than,* your work." *Improved:* "My work is *as good as* yours, *if not better.*") (See Section 10e.)

Assonance.   A partial or approximate similarity of sound. *Assonance* occurs in words like *fate* and *make,* in which partial rhyme is achieved because the stressed vowel sounds are alike but the consonant sounds are different. (See *Rhyme.*)

Awful, awfully, abominably.   These and such other expressions as *terrible, ghastly,* and *horrible* are loose, overworked intensifiers. If you really need an intensifier, use *very* (which see).

Awkwardness.   A general term of disapproval which implies clumsiness, ungainliness, lack of grace and smoothness. Unfortunately, it applies to far too many phrases and sentences.

Bad, badly, ill.   *Bad* is an adjective meaning "not good," "not as it should be." *Badly* is an adverb meaning "harmfully," "wickedly," "unpleasantly," "inefficiently." *Ill* is both an adjective and an adverb and means "sick," "tending to cause harm or evil," or "in a malevolent manner," "wrongly." ("She was very *ill*.") *Bad* and *badly* are often incorrectly used with the verb *feel*. ("I feel bad today"—not *badly*, unless you mean that your sense of touch is impaired.)

Badly.   A colloquial expression for "very much." Avoid its use in this sense in formal writing and speaking.

Balance, remainder.   The latter term means "what is left over." *Balance* has many meanings, but its use as "remainder" is considered colloquial. ("He ate the *remainder* [not *balance*] of the meal.")

Balanced sentence.   A sentence so written that certain thoughts or ideas have similar phrasing for purposes of comparison, contrast, or emphasis. ("A wise man changes direction; a fool never does.") (See *Sentence, arrangement of content.*)

Bar.   In the meaning of "a short slanting stroke between two words," *bar* does not appear in most dictionaries. The preferred term is *virgule*, a pedantic word derived from the Latin *virgula,* "a rod." Whatever it is called—and typesetters call it a *bar*—it is a mark of punctuation showing that either of two words may be used in interpreting the sense of expressions such as *and/or*. It appears at the ends of lines of poetry when they are written solid rather than as separate verses (lines). It is also used in writing dates: 7/4/76 for July 4, 1776: 1/1/65 for January 1, 1965.

Barbarism.   A word or expression not standard in a language as, for example, "youse" for *you* (see Section 19).

B.C.   See *A.D.*

Beginning, ending sentence.   Do not begin or end a sentence with weak and relatively unimportant words or ideas. Sentences should usually be built with the most important idea at the beginning or end, the places of stress, places where the attention of the reader is most keen. You should remember, however, that transitional words and phrases, although seemingly colorless, are really significant and frequently deserve beginning positions.

Prepositions, parenthetical expressions, and most conjunctions are usually not "pivotal," or important, words. Thus you should place them within the sentence, although you should avoid artificiality and awkwardness in so doing. There is no rule against beginning a sentence with *and* or *but*. Normally, however, the beginning position should be given to a word more emphatic.

| Ineffective | He had no money to buy the meal *with*. (It is not incorrect to end a sentence with a preposition, but this sentence will be more effective if rearranged so that due emphasis is given the relatively important word *meal*: "He had no money with which to buy the meal.") |

Ineffective	*However,* he will pass, the professor says.
Better	The professor says, *however,* that he will pass.

Standard advice is never to begin a sentence with a numeral. This admonition seems largely a matter of typography or a printing convention. It is a good rule to follow, however, since beginning with a numeral sometimes causes momentary confusion.

To avoid monotony, do not begin a number of successive sentences with the same word or phrase. Avoid especially overuse of the outworn beginnings *there is, there are, it is, this, the, he,* and *we.*

Awkward	It is just the trip he had planned. It is just the day for the trip. It is the consummation of all his hopes.
Improved	It is just the trip he had planned and just the day for the trip, a consummation of all his hopes.

(See *Climactic order* and *Variety in sentence structure.*)

Being as.   A colloquial or illiterate substitute for *since, because, inasmuch as,* etc. ("*Since* [not *Being as*] I have some money, I'll lend you some.")

Beside, besides.   *Beside* is normally a preposition meaning "by the side of." *Besides* is an adverb meaning "moreover," and, infrequently, is a preposition meaning "except." ("The old man sat *beside* the stove." "I can't go because I have no money, and *besides* I don't feel well.")

Be sure and.   This expression is considered both colloquial and unidiomatic. ("When you get there, *be sure to* [not *sure and*] write to me.")

Between.   See *Among, between.*

Bibliography.   A list of books or articles, or both, relating to a particular subject. In a research paper, a bibliography is an alphabetical, sometimes classified, list containing the names of all works quoted from or generally used in preparation. Every formally prepared research paper should contain a bibliography placed at the end of the theme and begun on a separate page.

Bibliographical items should be arranged correctly and consistently. Usage varies, but unless your instructor rules otherwise, follow these suggestions:

1. Arrange items alphabetically by last names of the authors. Each surname is followed by a comma, then by the author's given name(s) or initials.
2. If the author's name is not given and not known, list the item by the first word (except *a, an, the*) in the title. List titles by the same author alphabetically, using a blank line about three-fourths of an inch long in place of the author's name after its first appearance.
3. A period follows the author's complete name.
4. The title of a book is followed by a period. (See also Section 54a.) Citing the publisher's name is optional.
5. Place and date of publication are separated by a comma and are not placed in parentheses.

The following are examples of citations of books and of articles from periodicals.

BIBLIOGRAPHY

BOOKS

> Chute, Marchette. *Shakespeare of London.* New York: E. P. Dutton & Co., 1949.
> Magill, Frank N., ed. *Masterpieces of World Literature in Digest Form.* First Series, 348–350. New York: Harper & Row, 1952.
> Partridge, Eric. *Shakespeare's Bawdy* (pp. 50–55). New York: E. P. Dutton & Co., 1948.

ARTICLES

> Hamblin, Dora Jane. "History's Biggest Literary Whodunit," *Life*, LVI (April 24, 1964), 69.
> Levy, Alan. "The Would-Be Writer Industry," *The Reporter*, XXIX (October 24, 1963), 48.
> Wilson, James Southall. "Devil Was in It," *American Mercury*, XXIV (October, 1931), 215–220.

Blame me for it, blame it on me. Both of these expressions are in everyday use, but only the former is considered idiomatically correct and proper. *Blame it on me* is either dialectal or colloquial.

Blend. This term refers to a mixing, fusing, or mingling of elements or varieties, as a *blend of tea.* In language, it means a word or construction formed by fusing two or more words: *motel* from *motor hotel*, *radioration* from *radio oration.* Some blends have been accepted in standard English; others have not. (See *Portmanteau word* and Section 10d.)

Boner. A slang term for "a stupid mistake," "a silly blunder." The person who referred to the "plastic" in his socks committed a blunder ("pulled a boner") by not writing "elastic." (See *Malapropism.*)

Brace. A mechanical device ({) used in printing and some writing to indicate that two or more words or lines are to be taken together.

Broke. This word has standard uses, but it is a colloquialism or slang when used to mean "out of money." To *go broke* (become penniless) and *go for broke* (dare or risk everything) are slangy expressions.

Bunch. A colloquialism for "a group of people," "crowd," or "set." ("Our set—or *group* or *crowd* or *gang*—was closely knit at that time.") A "bunch of grapes" is correct.

Business English. The forms, conventions, idioms, and customs peculiar to communication in trade and industry. Business English is, or should be, merely standard English applied to the specific needs of industry and trade. However, its mechanical forms are so fixed and standardized that reference to a book on the subject is required for thorough knowledge. (See *Letters.*)

But which, but who. See *And which*, etc.

Cacophony. A harsh, jarring sound. Generally considered discordant are words like *flak, clack, hiss, wrangle, gutter, gaseous, spinach,* and *squash.* The antonym of *cacophony* is *euphony* (which see).

Calculate, reckon, guess. These words are *localisms* for "think," "suppose," and "expect." Each of the words has standard and acceptable meanings, but in the senses indicated here they should always be avoided except in informal conversation.

Can, may, might. *Can* suggests "ability," physical and mental. ("He *can* make good progress if he tries hard enough.") *May* implies permission or sanction. ("The office manager says that you *may* leave.") The distinction between *can* and *may* (ability *v.* permission) is illustrated in this sentence: "Lee thinks that you *can,* and you *may* try if you wish." *May* also expresses possibility and wish (desire): "It *may* snow today" (possibility); "*may* you have a pleasant time" (wish, desire). *Might* is used after a governing verb in the past tense, *may* after a governing verb in the present tense: "He *says* that you *may* try"; "he *said* that you *might* try." (See Section 67c.)

Cancel out. Omit the *out.* This wordy expression is often used, perhaps by analogy with *cross out* or *strike out.*

Cannot help, cannot help but. The first of these expressions is preferable in such statements as "I *cannot help* talking about . . ." The *but* should be omitted since its addition results in a double negative: *cannot help* and *can but.* (See Section 10g.)

Can't hardly. Omit the *not* in the contraction. ("I *can* hardly hear you.") *Can't hardly* is a double negative. (See Section 10g.)

Capital, capitol. The first of these words may be employed in all meanings except that of "a building." A *capitol* is an edifice, a building. ("He raised new *capital* for the company." "The sight-seeing bus passed the state *capitol.*")

Card catalog. A library contains a vast amount of material of varied kinds. But the heart of any library is its collection of books and bound magazines. The key which will open this treasure to you is the *card catalog.* This index to a library consists of 3-by-5 cards filed alphabetically in long trays or drawers, in a series of filing cabinets. Book information may be found in a card catalog in three ways: (1) by author, (2) by title, (3) by subject. (A card is reproduced on p. 274.)

In all libraries, every nonfiction book is represented by at least three cards, usually identical except that certain lines giving subject headings and joint author may be typed across the top. If you know the author or the title of a book, you will most easily get the needed information from an author or title card. If you know the name of neither author nor title, you can consult the subject cards for books dealing with the subject upon which you are working.

In addition to revealing the resources of a library, the card catalog gives the call number by means of which each book is located on the shelves. Some libraries are so arranged that all or some of the books are placed on open shelves easily accessible to readers. In other libraries the main collection is shelved on closed stacks; to obtain a book, you must fill out a "call slip" furnished by the library and present it at the Circulation or Loan Desk.

The student who has access to the book collection will soon discover that books are arranged according to a definite system, the notational expression of which is the first part of the call number. The two classification systems commonly used in this country are the Dewey Decimal Classification and the Library of Congress Classification. Books classified by either system are arranged according to the subjects they treat.

In the Dewey Decimal Classification, fields of knowledge are arranged in 10 groups, including one group for reference or general books. Each major class and each subclass is represented by a three-digit number; further subdivisions are indicated by numbers following a decimal point. If you have access to the shelves in your library, you can quickly find your way around by noting that, in the Dewey system, books are classified and arranged as follows:

000	General works	500	Pure science
100	Philosophy	600	Applied science
200	Religion	700	Arts and recreation
300	Social sciences	800	Literature
400	Linguistics	900	History

An illustration: American literature has the subclassification 810–819; an edition of Longfellow's *Evangeline* has the call number 811.L86e. The *L* is the first letter of the author's name; the *e* is the first letter of the title.

The Library of Congress Classification uses letters of the alphabet followed by other letters or by Arabic numerals. Main classes are as follows:

A	General works	M	Music
B	Philosophy, religion	N	Fine arts
C	History, auxiliary sciences	P	Language and literature
D	History, topography (except American)	Q	Science
		R	Medicine
E, F	American history	S	Agriculture, husbandry
G	Geography, anthropology	T	Technology
H	Social sciences	U	Military science
J	Political science	V	Naval science
K	Law	Z	Bibliography, library science
L	Education		

In this system, PS 303–324 is devoted to American poetry; PS 700 on, to individual authors; PS 2250–2298, to Henry W. Longfellow. Longfellow's *Evangeline* has the call number PS 2263.

Those baffled and bewildered by myriad trays of cards filed in the card catalog see neither rhyme nor reason in the filing system. Some libraries follow a strictly alphabetical order, but the majority observe the rules outlined below.

All libraries file by entry, that is, according to what appears first on the card, whether author, subject, or title. Articles appearing as the first word of a title are ignored; most libraries file letter-by-letter to the end of the word. This means that the title card, *The American way*, would be filed in front of the subject card, AMERICANISMS, just as all cards beginning with "New York" would be filed in front of cards with "Newark" as the entry word. Libraries which file in strictly alphabetical order would, of course, place *-isms* before *way* and *-ark* before *York.* Incidentally, encyclopedias, as well as library catalogs, differ in this fundamental rule.

Books *about* an author (considered subject entries and typed in red or in black capitals) are filed before or after all books *by* that author.

Author cards having the same surname as the entry word are filed according to the given name; always make a note of the first name, or at least the initials, of an author and of the *exact* title of the book you wish.

Abbreviations and numerals are filed just as they would be if the words they represent were spelled out.

When the entry word is the same, all authors by that name precede all subjects, and all subjects precede all titles. For example, Washington, George (books by), WASHINGTON, GEORGE (books about), *Washington merry-go-round* (title) are entered in that order.

The regulations specific libraries establish for their users appear in various forms. Find out if your library has a guide or handbook which explains or interprets its organization.

Caret.   This is a mark ($\wedge$) used to show that something placed interlinearly or in a margin belongs in the space indicated. (See Section **6oc.**)

Case.   This word (other than indicating the forms of pronouns and nouns) has many vague meanings. *Case, phase, factor, instance, nature, thing* are prime examples of jargon (see Section **23b**). To *case,* in the sense of "examine carefully," is slang. Don't use "case the joint" in standard English.

-cede, -ceed, -sede.   These endings cause a large number of misspellings. But the problem they present is simple because so few words are involved. Only 12 words in the language end in the sound "seed," and not all of these are in common use.

First, only one word in English ends in *-sede: supersede.* It has this ending because of its origin; it comes from the Latin verb *sedere,* meaning "to sit." As with many other borrowed words in English, it maintains some connection with its source.

Second, only three of the 12 words ending with the "seed" pronunciation are spelled *-ceed: exceed, proceed,* and *succeed.*

Finally, the eight remaining words end in *cede,* and of these only half are in everyday use:

accede	cede	intercede	recede
antecede	concede	precede	secede

It won't help in spelling the *-ceed* and *-cede* words to know their origin, but it will help in avoiding a *-sede* ending: the 11 *-ceed* and *-cede* words derive not from *sedere* (as *supersede* does) but from the Latin *cedere,* meaning "to go." Thus *pre + cede* means "to go or come before," *inter + cede* means "to go or come between," and so on.

Circumlocution.   A lengthy, indirect, roundabout way of expressing something. An effective and clear synonym for this term is *deadwood;* a pedantic synonym is *periphrasis*. Vigorous and emphatic sentences are lean and direct; they contain no wordy expressions. "The sort of lightweight metal they employ in the making of kitchen utensils" can be more directly expressed by the single word *aluminum*. (See Section 15.)

Clearness.   One of the fundamental virtues of writing and speaking is *clearness*, but the term is not easy to discuss. Making your sentences clear involves such matters as *unity, completeness, coordination, word order, transition*, and the like. Each of these terms is discussed in its appropriate place in this Guide and should be consulted. And yet writing sentences which are free from muddiness, haziness, and cloudiness; which are easily and distinctly understood; which are entirely logical; which have no ambiguity or obscurity—such style results less from avoiding mistakes than from qualities of mind and heart which cannot readily be described or learned. This brief comment may not be helpful, or even *clear* to you. Now do you understand the problem of explaining *clearness*? (See Section 41.)

Climactic order.   Ideas arranged in the order of their importance so as to secure climax. Climax is attained when ideas in a sentence are so arranged that each succeeding idea has greater force than its predecessor. Avoid arranging the elements of a sentence so that it "sags," or loses force at the end.

Unemphatic	In this collision some died agonizing deaths; some received serious injuries; and a few were barely scratched.
Better	A few were barely scratched in this collision; but some received serious injuries; and some died agonizing deaths.
Unemphatic	We were frightened by the noises: the crashing of the thunder, the pouring of the rain, and the steady blowing of the wind.
Better	We were frightened by the noises: the steady blowing of the wind, the pouring of the rain, and the crashing of the thunder.

The effectiveness of a sentence depends not entirely on the *position* of any single word or idea but also on the arrangement of the whole sentence. The *sense* of the sentence must always be considered; the statement must be correct and clear. Effectiveness cannot be gained by a thoughtless or artificial attempt to employ the suggestion mentioned here; it will help to increase effectiveness only if its use does not destroy correctness, clearness, and naturalness. (See *Position and arrangement of words*.)

Close and open punctuation.   Writing in which as few marks of punctuation as possible are used is said to be punctuated in *open* style; writing which employs no incorrect marks but nevertheless omits none which could legitimately be used is called *close* in its punctuation. (See Section 47t, Part 7.)

The terms *open* and *close* have a somewhat specialized meaning when applied to business letters or, indeed, to correspondence of any kind. Punctuation of the heading and of both inside and outside addresses may follow the *open* or the *close* system. In the open system, no commas or final periods, except after abbreviations, are used after the separate lines, and some letter writers prefer also to omit the colon after the salutation and the comma after the complimentary close. In the closed system, commas are used after each line of the heading and inside address, except the last, at the end of which a period is used. Because of timesaving and convenience, most letter writers now use open punctuation. (See *Letters*.)

Commas. See *Close and open punctuation, Unnecessary commas*, and Section 47.

Common, mutual. The former means "belonging to many or to all." *Mutual* means "reciprocal." ("Airplanes are *common* carriers." "Our respect and love were *mutual*.") Avoid the redundancy of such a statement as "He and I entered into a mutual agreement."

Common noun. A noun referring to a member, or members, of a general group: *automobile, coat, hat, avenue*.

Compare, contrast. Compare is used to point out likenesses, similarities (used with the preposition *to*), and to examine two or more objects to find likenesses or differences (used with the preposition *with*). *Contrast* always points out differences. ("The poet *compared* his lady *to* a wood thrush." "The teacher *compared* my paper *with* Henry's and found no signs of copying." "In *contrast to* your work, mine is poor.")

Complected. This abomination may be considered an illiteracy or a dialectal expression. The standard word is "complexioned." ("Janet was dark-*complexioned*.")

Complement, compliment. *Complement* implies something which completes. ("This jewelry will *complement* your dress.") A *compliment* is flattery. ("Beulah enjoyed the *compliment* paid to her.")

Applied to grammar, *complement* has a quite specific meaning. It is a word or expression used to *complete* the idea indicated or implied by a verb. A *predicate complement* (sometimes called a *subjective complement*) may be a noun, a pronoun, or an adjective which follows a linking verb and describes or identifies the subject of the linking verb:

> This book is *a biography*.
> The leaves of this tree are *red*.

An *object complement* may be a noun or adjective which follows the direct object of a verb and completes the necessary meaning:

> We are painting our house *gray*.
> Our neighbors named their baby *Maryann*.
> The bowling team elected Schmidt *captain*.

Completeness. A sentence is *complete* when it lacks none of its parts; it is whole, entire, full. It contains a subject and predicate, both of them expressed or implied. It omits no words necessary to sense or structure. In short, it is perfect, rounded in its coverage. To achieve completeness in sentence structure without being wordy is far from simple. As a start toward achieving this goal, see Sections 1, 15.

Complex sentence. A sentence containing one independent clause and one or more dependent clauses (see *Sentence, grammatical structure of*).

Composition.   A *composition* is a literary, musical, or artistic product which usually reveals care in its formulation and plan. It may refer to any piece of writing with a definite *theme* (which see) and may be an *essay, short story, article,* or *book review.*

Compound-complex sentence.   A sentence containing two or more independent clauses and one or more dependent clauses (see *Sentence, grammatical structure of*).

Compound object.   See *Object.*

Compound predicate.   See *Predicate.*

Compound sentence.   A sentence containing two or more independent clauses (see *Sentence, grammatical structure of*).

Compound subject.   See *Subject.*

Conciseness.   This term refers to the quality of brevity, terseness. Writing is *concise* when it expresses much thought in few words. Succinct writing is both brief and comprehensive. The word *concise* comes from the Latin *concisus,* which means "cut off." Since all of us write somewhat wordily, we must edit (cut) our writing to make it concise. (See Section 15.)

Concrete noun.   A noun referring to an object evident to one of the senses of sight, hearing, taste, etc.: *trousers, hymn, tea.* This is contrasted with an *abstract noun* (which see).

Concreteness.   Concrete words, in contrast to abstract terms, are those that name objects or persons which can be seen, touched, etc.—*train, filing clerk, store, apple.* Each of these words has at least a slightly different meaning for each of us, but they have a "core" of reality which is readily understood. And yet your idea and mine of such abstract words as *goodness, duty,* and *sophistication* may differ widely. For this reason, concrete words are more exact than abstract ones, and concreteness is a highly valued quality in writing. (See Section 30b.)

Conjugation.   The changes in the form and uses of a verb to show *tense, mood, voice, number,* and *person.*

Connotation.   This word applies to the overtones of words—values and meanings which are suggested rather than specifically expressed in a dictionary definition. For example, San Francisco is "a seaport city in northern California," but the name itself has such connotations as "Golden Gate," "Chinatown," "Barbary Coast," "Gateway to the Orient," and "Earthquake of 1906." Connotative words have implied, suggestive, associated meanings, in contrast to *denotative* words. (See *Denotation* and Section 30c.)

Consonant.   In *phonetics* (which see) a *consonant* has a sound in which the breath is somewhat restricted or even stopped. Consonant sounds may be contrasted with *vowel* sounds, which are made with less friction and fuller resonance. The vowels in our alphabet are *a, e, i, o, u,* and sometimes *y.* All the other letters are consonants: *b, c, d, f,* etc. (See *Vowel.*)

Consonants dropped.   See *Dropped consonants.*

Contact, contacted.   Each of these words has perfectly proper uses, but as business terms they have been overworked. Possible substitutes are *communicate with, call, call upon, telephone.*

Context.   This word means the parts of a piece of writing or of speech which precede or follow a given word or passage with which they are directly connected. If we say that such and such a passage in a novel is obscene but that in its *context* it is essential and not shocking, we mean that what comes before or follows provides meaning that is important, even essential, to understanding and judgment.

Continual, continuous.   In some uses these words are interchangeable. A subtle distinction is that *continual* implies "a close recurrence in time," in "rapid succession," and that *continuous* implies "without interruption." ("The *continual* ringing of the doorbell bothers me." "The ticking of the watch was *continuous*.")

Continue on.   This is a wordy phrase. *Continue* means "to endure," "to last." Hence *on* is unnecessary to convey full meaning.

Contraction.   A shortened form of a word, such as *can't* for *cannot*, *I'll* for *I shall* or *I will*. Large numbers of contractions seem out of place in standard English except when used to convey the actual tone and flavor of dialogue. A few are used in this book to avoid stiffness and artificiality. (See Sections 27b, 58c.)

Contrast.   See *Compare, contrast.*

Conversation.   Undoubtedly the most universal form of social activity and our most important means of communicating with others is *conversation*. The good conversationalist—one who listens courteously and attentively and also has something interesting to say to his listeners—is welcomed everywhere. A lack of opportunities for such interchange can produce irritation, boredom, and even serious mental disorders; one of the most severe of all punishments is solitary confinement.

Conversation should be a genuine meeting of the minds. It has little in common with mere talkativeness, chattering about dates, clothes, or the weather. Good conversation is a stimulating pastime, especially when it concerns genuine ideas or problems and represents a frank interchange of information and opinion. Don't aim for mere glibness as a conversational goal; superficiality may enable you to "get by" in a group discussion, it may save you the trouble of defending your opinions, but it wastes your time and that of your companions.

How can you become a good conversationalist? First, be sincere and straightforward but also tactful and courteous. A group of people will seldom agree about anything of real consequence; and if they did, a conversation about it would probably be dull. A spirited discussion may be, and often is, argumentative. However, you can state your opinions and defend them firmly without hurting the feelings of those who differ with you. Frankness which verges on rudeness is never in good taste, nor is the brusque person welcome in a discussion. Flat contradiction is rude, but it is possible to differ with your neighbor and yet engage in a friendly discussion.

You will often engage in conversation with one person, even at a large party. You may be left with the guest of honor at a reception, a chaperon at a college dance, a professor at a college mixer, a stranger at a dinner party. If you are, don't try to interest him in yourself and your problems; instead, try to find out as much about him as you tactfully can. It is human to be flattered at another's interest in us, and few people fail to respond if that interest seems genuine.

Analyze every conversation you have an opportunity to hear or engage in. Notice that the best conversationalists are usually those who have the largest fund of interesting experiences or the greatest familiarity with the subjects of most interest to the people in your circle. Therefore, read, listen, and observe. Read as much as you can: a good daily paper, worthwhile magazines, books which are attracting attention. Keep informed about matters likely to be discussed among your acquaintances: current events, political affairs, personalities in the limelight, general economic and business conditions, important legislation recently enacted or pending, sporting events, current music, art, and literature. Try to remember good stories you hear or read, funny or interesting incidents which happen to you or your friends, amusing or significant happenings you see or read about. Above all, *practice* conversing; join in good conversation every chance you have. See *Oral communication, Group discussion.*

Convince, persuade. The former means "to overcome the doubts of." *Persuade* implies "influencing a person to an action or belief." ("I am *convinced* that you are right and you have *persuaded* me to help you.") *Convince to* is not idiomatic. (*Wrong:* "I *convinced* him *to* see the play." *Right:* "I *persuaded* him *to* see the play." "I *convinced* him *that* he should see the play.")

Cool. In the sense of "lacking warmth," "moderately cold," and several other meanings, *cool* is a useful and correct word. But it is informal or slangy when used to mean "actual" ("a *cool* million dollars"), "great," and "excellent." It is also highly informal in such debatable expressions as "cool jazz," "cool cat," and "cool customer."

Coordination. This word means "harmonious combination," "due ordering or proper relation." In grammar it involves the relationship between two or more elements of the same grammatical rank. (See Section **8.**)

Could of. An illiteracy. Probably because of its sound, it is sometimes written for *could have.* ("The rusty nail *could have* [not *could of*] hurt you.") (See *Would of, etc.*)

Council, counsel. *Council* means "an assembly," "a group." ("This is a *council* of citizens.") *Counsel* is both a noun and a verb and means "advice" or "to advise." ("The physician gave me expensive *counsel.*" "The manager will *counsel* fast action by the board of directors.")

Counter word. This expression means a term which is used in a vague sense of approval or disapproval but without any exact meaning. Many counter words are slang and all are trite: *swell, lousy, nice, terrible, ghastly, cool.* Counter words are prevalent in advertising and colloquial speech but are rarely suitable for standard writing. (See Section **29c.**)

Curve. A *curve* is a "continuously bending line without angles." The phrase, "throw someone a curve," meaning to confuse or upset someone, is informal and trite.

Cute. This is an overworked and somewhat vague word which generally expresses approval. Probably *charming, clever, attractive, winsome, piquant, pleasing, vivacious,* or one of a dozen other adjectives would come nearer the meaning you have in mind.

Data.   This word was originally the plural of the Latin *datum* and means "facts and figures from which conclusions may be drawn." Purists consider the word to be plural and use it with a plural verb, but its use with a singular verb is becoming more widespread. (*"These* data *are* not reliable." *"This* data *is* not reliable.")

De-, dis-, dys-.   These prefixes will cause spelling problems when you don't distinguish clearly between root words beginning with *s* and the prefixes themselves. Note these spellings:

> *describe* (write down), *de + scribe*
> *despoil* (strip, rob), *de + spoil*
> *dissemble* (disguise), *dis + semble*
> *dissimilar* (unlike), *dis + similar*

Only about 30 common words begin with *diss-*, but 10 times as many begin with *dis-*. Only three common words (and their derivatives) begin with *dys-*: *dysentery, dyspepsia, dystrophy* (as in "muscular dystrophy").

A simple rule: when the prefixes *dis-* and *mis-* are added to a root word beginning with *s*, neither *s* should be omitted: *dissatisfied, misstep.* When they are added to roots not beginning with an *s*, use only one *s: disappear, misfortune.*

Deadwood.   This word actually means, of course, dead wood on trees and, by extension, has come to mean anything which is useless or burdensome (see Section 15). In writing, it is a convenient label for wordiness and is applied to words and phrases which add little or nothing to the sentence in which they appear:

> *This is a topic that* may be written *This topic*
> *The fact that I came* may be written *My coming*
> *In the year of 1960* may be written *In 1960*

Declarative sentence.   A sentence which states a fact, a possibility, a condition (see *Sentence, meaning and purpose of*).

Declension.   The changes in the form or use of a noun or pronoun to indicate case, number, and person. *To decline* means to give these grammatical changes.

	SINGULAR			PLURAL		
Nominative	man	I	who	men	we	who
Possessive	man's	my, mine	whose	men's	our, ours	whose
Objective	man	me	whom	men	us	whom

Deductive reasoning.   This term comes from the word *deduction,* which means "the process of drawing a conclusion from something assumed or known." *Deductive reasoning* and *inductive reasoning* (which see) are alike in that they both refer to processes of reasoning, but they are quite different in meaning. (See *Logic* and Section 41c,d.)

Demonstrative pronoun.   A *demonstrative* pronoun points out and identifies.

It is declined (that is, inflected) for number but not for gender or case. The most important demonstrative pronouns are *this, that, these, those, such.*

> *This* is the way to clean a window.
> *That* is my new television set.
> *These* are your books; *those* on the table are mine.

Denotation. The exact, literal meaning of a word as contrasted with its *connotation,* or suggestive meaning. Thus, *home* has a denotative meaning of "house," "apartment," "fixed dwelling place." Its connotation might be "refuge," "place of peace," "retreat," "haven of rest." (See *Connotation.*)

Derivation. See *Origin of words.*

Description. To *describe* someone or something is to convey an impression or image which reveals the appearance, nature, and attributes of the person or thing under discussion. *Description* is one of the four *forms of discourse* (which see).

Des′ert, desert′, dessert′. These three words involve problems in spelling, pronunciation, and meaning. The first, with accent on the first syllable, means "barren ground." ("The *desert* is 100 miles wide.") *Desert* (with accent on the second syllable) means "to abandon." ("Don't ever *desert* your true friends.") *Dessert* (note the double *s*) is "the last course of a lunch or dinner." ("Apple pie is his favorite *dessert.*")

Diacritical mark. A diacritical mark, point, or sign is attached to a letter or character to distinguish it from another of the same form or to give it a particular phonetic value or indicate stress. For example, diacritical marks are used to show the sound of *a* as in *cär* and *a* as in *āble.* Every good dictionary employs diacritical marks; study those in your dictionary until you are thoroughly familiar with them.

Diagraming. A mechanical device to aid in identifying words as parts of speech, in identifying phrases and clauses, and in indicating in a sentence the uses or functions of these words, phrases, and clauses (see *Analysis of a sentence*). These purposes are accomplished through the use of lines: horizontal, perpendicular, slanting. See *The Grammar of Sentences,* p. 56.

The parts of a sentence are put on lines in the positions indicated in the following skeleton diagram. The three most important parts of the sentence (subject, predicate, object) are usually put on a horizontal line; any modifiers are appropriately placed on lines underneath.

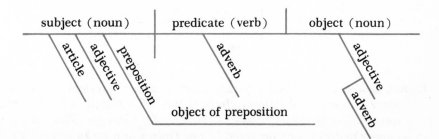

Filled in, such a diagramed sentence might read:

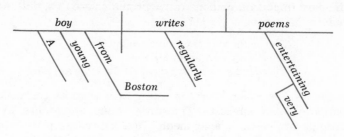

A young boy from Boston regularly writes very entertaining poems.

The simple subject, the simple predicate, the direct object, the object complement, the predicate noun or pronoun, and the predicate adjective are written on the main horizontal line. (If you have forgotten the meanings of these terms, look up each one at its appropriate place in this book.) Subject and predicate are separated by a perpendicular line intersecting the horizontal line. The direct object is separated from the verb by a short perpendicular line extending up from the horizontal line. The object complement, the predicate noun or pronoun, or the predicate adjective is set off by a short slanting line extending up to the left from the horizontal line. The following diagrams illustrate the principles just stated:

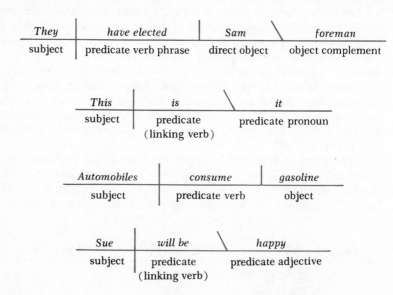

Dialect, dialectal. A *dialect* is the speech customs (pronunciation, vocabulary, grammatical habits) characteristic of a region. Thus we might refer to Scotch (Scots) dialect (*auld* for *old,* *bairn* for *child*) or mountaineer dialect (*poke* for *small bag* or *bonnet* or *a green vegetable*).

Dialectal is an adjective which applies to dialect words. An expression is dialectal when it attracts no notice in the region where it is used but seems out of place elsewhere. *Localisms* are dialectal words. (See Section 18.)

Dialogue. Conversation, talking together. *Dialogue* (also spelled *dialog*) refers to the passages of talk in a story, novel, or play. Fixed rules apply to the paragraphing and punctuation of dialogue. (See Sections 36 and 53a–c.)

Dictionaries. A *dictionary* is a book containing a selection of words, normally arranged alphabetically, concerning which information about meanings and a wealth of other material is given. In one sense, a reliable dictionary is a guide to standard English, "the practice of the socially accepted, those who carry on the important affairs of English-speaking people." But a dictionary is an authority largely in the sense that it *records* and *interprets* English words and phrases. Some carefully prepared dictionaries do not prescribe or dictate usage but rather indicate what is considered general language practice. As a record but not always as a final arbiter, a good dictionary is indispensable to *every* student. See *Building a Vocabulary*, p. 76.

Suitable dictionaries are what economists refer to as "durable goods." When you purchase a good dictionary, you should expect to keep and use it for many years. It is unwise to buy a "cheap" dictionary when an excellent one can be purchased for only a few dollars and its price can be amortized over a long period. A pocket dictionary is almost worthless, except as a flimsy guide to spelling and pronunciation. Equip yourself with a sufficiently large dictionary (approximately 100,000 entries), published by a reliable firm. Examples of such dictionaries are *The American College Dictionary, Webster's Seventh New Collegiate Dictionary, Webster's New World Dictionary, The Concise Oxford Dictionary, Funk & Wagnalls Standard College Dictionary.*

If you have never done so before, examine your dictionary carefully and critically. Read its table of contents; examine the information given on the inside of front and back covers; at least skim the prefatory pages as well as any supplementary materials at the back. Then read thoughtfully any editorial sections it contains: "general introduction," "guide to the use of this dictionary," "guide to pronunciation," or "explanatory notes." You may be astonished to discover resources of which you were previously unaware.

¹spell \'spel\ *n* [ME, talk, tale, fr. OE; akin to OHG *spel* talk, tale, Gk *apeilē* boast] **1 a :** a spoken word or form of words believed to have magic power **:** INCANTATION **b :** a state of enchantment **2 :** a strong compelling influence or attraction
²spell *vt* **:** to put under a spell **:** BEWITCH
³spell *vb* **spelled** \'speld, 'spelt\ **spell·ing** [ME *spellen*, fr. OF *espeller*, of Gmc origin; akin to OE *spell* talk] *vt* **1 :** to read slowly and with difficulty **2 a :** to find out by study **:** DISCOVER **b :** COMPREHEND, UNDERSTAND **3 a :** to name the letters of in order; *also* **:** to write or print the letters of in order **b :** to make up (a word) **:** FORM **4 :** MEAN, SIGNIFY ~ *vi* **:** to form words with letters
⁴spell *vb* **spelled** \'speld\ **spell·ing** [ME *spelen*, fr. OE *spelian*; akin to OE *spala* substitute] *vt* **1 :** to take the place of for a time **:** RELIEVE **2 :** to allow an interval of rest to **:** REST ~ *vi* **1 :** to work in turns **2 :** to rest from work or activity for a time
⁵spell *n* **1 a** *archaic* **:** a shift of workers **b :** one's turn at work **2 a :** a period spent in a job or occupation **b** *chiefly Austral* **:** a period of rest from work, activity, or use **3 a :** an indeterminate period of time **b :** a stretch of a specified type of weather **4 :** a time colored by some state of body or mind **:** FIT

Above all, learn to take your time when you look up a dictionary entry. It requires only a moment to learn the spelling, pronunciation, or one meaning of a word. But if you will *study* an entry carefully, you will derive much useful information about the word being considered and can make it a part of your active vocabulary. Time spent in studying words thoroughly will save time and errors later. For any word listed in a reliable dictionary, each of the first five of the following items is given; for many words, one or more of the next five kinds of information is also provided:

1. Spelling	6. Level(s) of meaning
2. Syllabication	7. Derivation
3. Pronunciation	8. Synonyms
4. Part(s) of speech	9. Antonyms
5. Meaning(s)	10. Other information

Most of these 10 items are discussed elsewhere in this book. Look them up so as to be better prepared to absorb some of the wonderful resources of your dictionary. Make it your business to make friends with a good dictionary. Few friendships you will ever form can be more rewarding.

Different from, than, to.   *Different than* and *different to* are considered colloquial by some authorities, improper and incorrect by others. Even so, these idioms have long literary usage to support them and certainly they are widely used. No one ever objects on any grounds to *different from*. Use *different from* and be safe, never sorry.

Direct address.   In this construction, also called the *vocative,* the noun or pronoun shows to whom speech is addressed. "*Jimmy,* where are you?" "What did you say, *Mother?*" (See Section 47p.)

Direct quotation.   A quotation which reproduces the exact words written or spoken by someone. (See Sections 47c, 53a.)

> "Please use your dictionary more often," the office manager said. "These letters will all need to be retyped."

Discourse, forms of.   See *Forms of discourse.*

Disinterested, uninterested.   The former means "unbiased," "not influenced by personal reasons." *Uninterested* means "having no interest in," "not paying attention." ("The minister's opinion was *disinterested.*" "I was completely *uninterested* in the play.") As a colloquialism, a somewhat inexact one, *disinterested* is often used in the sense of "uninterested," "indifferent."

Disregardless.   See *Irregardless, disregardless.*

Disremember.   An illiteracy. Never use this word in standard English.

Ditto marks.   The word *ditto* means "the same" or "a duplicate." Ditto marks (″) are used in itemized lists and tables to show that a word, figure, or passage above is to be repeated. (In typewritten manuscript use quotation marks to represent ditto marks.) Ditto marks are less used than formerly and are advised against in ordinary writing.

Done, don't.   The principal parts of this verb are *do, did, done. Done* is frequently used incorrectly as the past tense of *do.* ("We *did* [not *done*] our work early today.") *Don't* is often used incorrectly for *doesn't*. ("It *doesn't* [not *don't*] make much difference to me.")

Double negative.   This construction consists of the use of two negative words in the same statement: "He *couldn't* find his friend *nowhere*." Actually, a double negative can intensify and enforce a negative sense, but it is considered a colloquial or substandard form of expression in current English usage. (See Section 10g.)

Dropped consonants.   If our visual memory of words is stronger than our auditory image, well and good. But when a letter is incorrectly omitted in pronouncing a word, we have to be on guard. The following representative list of words should be studied carefully. In each word the "offending" consonant is set as a capital letter; try to pronounce it fully, sounding it out as an aid to your auditory memory. Admittedly, some of the consonants are really silent and are difficult to pronounce. Your pronunciation may offer a clue to the cause of some of your misspellings. (See Section 16a.)

accepT	emPty	kePt	slepT
aCquire	excepT	lanDlord	sofTen
anD	fasCinate	nesTle	swepT
authenTic	granDfather	ofTen	temPt
condemN	hanDful	promPt	tenTative
consumPtion	hanDle	pumPkin	tresTle
contemPt	idenTical	recoGnize	UseD to

Dropped vowels.   Educated speakers often drop vowels in pronouncing some words in the following list; even acceptable pronunciation is not always a sure guide. However, a few of these words could not be pronounced correctly from the faulty spellings shown—whole syllables would drop out. Only in uninformed or TV speech would *caramel*, for example, be pronounced "carmel." (See Section 16a.)

Check your pronunciation of the following words. Some people slur over the vowels shown in capital letters; some omit them entirely; some pronounce them with considerable stress. Pronounce each word as you normally do. If the letters in capitals are silent, or lightly stressed, in your speech, you are likely to omit them from your spelling.

accompanIment	defInite	liAble	opErate
accUracy	delivEry	luxUry	particUlar
aspIrin	diffErent	magAzine	privIlege
bachElor	famIly	mathEmatics	regUlar
boundAry	frivOlous	memOry	scenEry
casUalties	histOry	misEry	simIlar
considErable	ignOrant	mystEry	temperAture
crimInal	lengthEning	NiagAra	victOry

Due to.   Some authorities label this phrase "colloquial" when it is used to mean "because of." Nevertheless, it is widely used in this sense by capable speakers and writers. Purists prefer such expressions as *owing to, caused by, on account of,* and *because of*. If you wish your English to be above any possible criticism, avoid using *due to* as a preposition. ("Tension there was *caused by* [not *due to*] racial unrest which had been building for decades.") Most importantly, remember that *due to the fact that* is a wordy way of saying the short and simple word *since*. (See *Fact that*.)

Each . . . are.   *Each*, even if not followed by *one*, implies "one." Any plural words used in modifying phrases do not change the number. ("Each *is* [not *are*] expected to contribute *his* time." "*Each one* of you *is* a fraud.") (See Section **62c**.)

Effectiveness.   That quality in writing which enables a writer to produce results intended or expected. The primary aim of all writing is clear communication from writer to reader. Writing is most effective which most nearly meets this ideal.

It is possible to write sentences which are clear and correct and yet not effective. Effectiveness is a somewhat vague and elusive quality which is dependent upon many sentence characteristics. In general, effective sentences are those which produce desired results; they are efficient; they impress the reader with a sense of suitable form and adequate content. The qualities contributing most to effectiveness in sentences are *conciseness, parallelism, consistency, variety in structure,* and *position and arrangement of words.* (See each of these terms for specific discussion.)

-efy, -ify.   These two suffixes cause much spelling trouble, but the problem is simple when it is clearly looked at. Actually, only four words you are likely to use end in *-efy* (and you probably won't use them every day, either). All of the remainder, without exception, end in *-ify.*

Therefore, learn by whatever method seems best these four words and spell *all others* with *-ify:*

> *liquefy* (to make or become liquid)
> *putrefy* (to make or become rotten)
> *rarefy* (to make or become rare)
> *stupefy* (to make or become insensible)

Also, words built on these four tend to retain the *e* spelling: *liquefy, liquefies, liquefied, liquefying, liquefaction; putrefy, putrefies, putrefied, putrefying, putrefaction; rarefy, rarefies, rarefied, rarefying, rarefaction; stupefy, stupefies, stupefied, stupefying, stupefaction.*

E.g.   See *I.e.,* etc.

Either . . . or, neither . . . nor.   The former means "one of two." *Neither* means "not one of two." *Or* is used with *either, nor* with *neither.* The use of *either . . . or* and *neither . . . nor* in coordinating more than two words, phrases, or clauses is sanctioned by some dictionaries but not by others. ("*Either* of you *is* satisfactory for the role." "*Neither* the boys *nor* the girls wished to dance.") (See Sections **7d, 7ob**.)

Emigrate, immigrate.   The former means "to leave"; the latter means "to enter." ("Our janitor *emigrated* from Poland in 1938." "Many people have tried to *immigrate* to this country in the last decade.") The corresponding nouns, *emigration* and *immigration,* are similarly distinguished in meaning.

Emphasis.   Force of thought, feeling, action, or expression. In writing and speaking, emphasis depends less upon force than upon careful diction, position and arrangement of words, effective repetition, and the use of intensifiers. Emphasis is one of the most desired of all qualities in writing and speaking and one of the most difficult to define or attain.

The word *emphasis* suggests force or stress, but emphasis in sentence structure implies accurately conveying your ideas to your reader or listener. It involves leading your reader to see your thoughts in the same relative importance in which you see them.

Emphatic sentence structure may be attained in several ways. In sentence structure, *emphasis* and *effectiveness* mean much the same thing.

Enclosing punctuation.   See *Punctuation, purposes of.*

Ending sentence.   See *Beginning, ending sentence.*

English, history of.   The English we speak and write is descended from that spoken and written by immigrants from England, Scotland, and Ireland who founded the British colonies in this country in the seventeenth century. Their language, in turn, came from the dialects of ancient Germanic tribes.

For about 1,000 years before the Christian Era, our linguistic ancestors were semisavages wandering through northern Europe. These tribes, consisting of Angles, Saxons, and Jutes, spoke several dialects of what is known as Low German, or *Plattdeutsch.* They had some contact with the Roman Empire and promptly began a process which has continued unabated to the present day: they started borrowing words from Latin and placing them in their own vocabularies. We still use many everyday words borrowed by these tribes, such as *bishop, butter, cheese, plum, kettle, street, fork, cook.*

When the Roman Empire began to weaken, it had to give up its occupancy of what we now know as England, and the Germanic tribes, commonly called Anglo-Saxons, began to move in. We know little about the arrival of the Anglo-Saxons in England in the fifth century A.D., but we do know that after the year 600 they were partially converted to Christianity and that borrowing from Latin became even more pronounced. To what was then Anglo-Saxon, or Old English, were added many words which are in use today, such as *alms, anthem, martyr, palm, priest.*

England even then was considered an attractive and desirable place, and Norsemen from Denmark and the Scandinavian peninsula began a long series of hit-and-run raids. Forays of the Norsemen continued until the eleventh century, with the linguistic result that many Norse words were added to the language. Examples are *crawl, egg, law, race, scowl, tree.* Even our pronouns *they, them,* and *their* are of Norse origin. So is our suffix *-by,* the Danish word for "farm" or "town," which appears in names such as *Derby.*

Another event of great importance to our language was the Norman Conquest. The Normans, originally from Scandinavia, settled in northern France in the tenth century and adopted the French language. In 1066 they crossed the English Channel and became the masters of England. French became the language of the nobility, the court, and polite society, although the common people continued to use English. Our language was profoundly affected by the introduction of French; literally thousands of words were added to the English vocabulary between 1100 and 1500. A few examples will serve to show this borrowing: *bacon, baptism, biscuit, blanket, bucket, chess, curtain, fault, flower, government, grammar, incense, lamp, lemon, logic, parson, religion, scarlet, surprise, towel.*

Beginning about 1500, the discovery of new lands brought many thousands of other new words to the English language. Words from such remote regions as India, China, Africa, and North America enriched the language tremendously. Among familiar words borrowed, for example, from the North American Indians may be mentioned *Connecticut, Massachusetts, Monongahela, squaw, tomahawk, wampum.*

In short, during the past thousand years our language has far more than tripled its size. Words have come pouring into the language from French, Latin, Greek, Hebrew, Arabic, and a score of other tongues.

This brief comment on English is inadequate as linguistic history, but at least it may serve to make clear a dominant reason why spelling and pronunciation are so far apart. When these many thousands of words first arrived in English, they often appeared with the spellings, or phonetic (sound) approximations of the spellings, which they originally had and which did not always conform to the customs of English. Sometimes the spellings of words were modified to conform to the English tongue; many times they were not. The English language is a linguistic grab bag with tremendous range and flexibility.

English is truly a polyglot language. No such thing as "pure" English exists now or ever has. Edmund Spenser expressed a pious and patriotic thought when he referred to the purity of Chaucer's language as a "well of English undefyled," but for all practical purposes he was writing nonsense.

Enthuse. This word is a formation derived from "enthusiasm." Most dictionaries label *enthuse* as colloquial, although it is shorter and more direct than preferred locutions such as *be enthusiastic about* or *become enthusiastic over*. Even so, the word is greatly overused and somewhat "gushy"; do not use it in formal English.

Envelop, envelope. The verb *en-vel'op* (accent on second syllable) means "to cover," "to wrap." ("Fire will soon *envelop* the entire block.") *En'-vel-ope* (accent on first syllable) is a noun meaning "a covering." ("Put a stamp on this *envelope*.")

-er. See *-ar, -er, -or.*

-ery. See *-ary, -ery.*

Etc. *Etc.* is an abbreviation of the Latin *et cetera* and means "and so forth." It looks somewhat out of place in formal writing and tends to be overused. Furthermore, it cannot be pronounced in speech without sounding individual letters or giving the entire phrase. Sometimes we use *etc.* at the end of a list to suggest that much more could be added. But do we really have anything in mind? (See *And etc.*)

Etymology. The origin and development of a word; tracing a word back as far as possible by means of comparative *linguistics* (which see). (See also *Origin of words.*)

Euphemism. The substitution of a mild, bland, inoffensive expression for a blunt or harsh one. "To depart this life" is a *euphemism* for "to die." (See Section 25.)

Euphony. Agreeableness of sound; a speech sound pleasing to the ear. *Euphony* is largely a negative quality in English prose; it consists of avoiding unpleasant sounds such as sibilants, guttural expressions, and the like. Euphonious words selected by some writers: *vermilion, melody, nevermore, cuspidor, cellar door, moonlight.* The antonym of *euphony* is *cacophony* (which see).

Exaggeration. The act of unduly magnifying, overstating, going beyond the limits of truth. In writing, *exaggeration* is used not so much to deceive as to intensify or strengthen meaning: "starved" or "famished" for "hungry," "a million thanks," "abject adoration." (See *Hyperbole* and see Section 29c.)

Except. See *Accept, except.*

Exclamatory sentence. A sentence expressing strong feeling or surprise (see *Sentence, meaning and purpose of*).

Expletive. A word or phrase added either to fill out a sentence or to provide emphasis. The latter function is performed by expressions which are exclamatory or profane. The more frequently employed function of the expletive is complementary, however; in this sense, *surely, indeed, why,* and *yes* may be considered expletives. *It* and *there* are commonly used as expletives:

> *It* was Alice sitting there.
> *It* is a truism that men love freedom.
> *There* are 2400 people present.

Some grammarians further classify *it*. For example, Professor Paul Roberts[1] discusses "impersonal *it*," "situation *it*," and "expletive *it*," illustrating each as follows:

> *Impersonal:* It is raining.
> It is Wednesday.
> It snowed last night.
>
> *Situation:* It was Borg who started the trouble.
> It's Lois and the children.
> Was it the cat?
>
> *Expletive:* It is hard to believe that Clinton is 16.
> It is true that we were once great friends.

Exposition. A kind of writing that defines, explains, and interprets. As contrasted with other basic forms of discourse, *exposition* is all writing which does not primarily describe an object, tell a story, or maintain a position. It includes much of what we read: magazine articles, newspaper editorials, and textbooks. In addition, most of what we write consists of exposition.

---

[1] *Understanding Grammar* (New York, 1954).

Some of the more prominent kinds of exposition are these:

1. *Narrative exposition.* Explaining by telling a story and usually following a time order is commonly used in the explanation of a process. Subjects using the words *how, the method, the principle,* and the like, are developed by narrative exposition—for example, "How Petroleum Is Refined."

2. *Giving directions.* An important subdivision of narrative exposition is giving directions. Subjects may be impersonal, "How To Ride a Bicycle," or personal, "How I Learned To Ride a Bicycle." In either, directions should be so clear that your reader will have no trouble in following them.

3. *Descriptive exposition.* Explaining by describing, and ordinarily using space order, is commonly used to make clear the working of mechanical objects like a spark plug, the telephone receiver, a fishing reel. Frequently, descriptive exposition and narrative exposition are used together.

4. *Criticism.* Criticism is an estimation of worth or value, whether of a book, a magazine article, a movie, a radio or TV program, or a musical composition. Ordinarily, as critic, you answer four questions: What was the author's purpose? What methods did he use in accomplishing his purpose: scope, characters, setting, kind of plot, dialogue, point of view, style? Was the purpose successfully accomplished? Was it worth accomplishing?

5. *Informal and formal essays.* The informal or personal essay is usually a friendly and conversational explanation of the writer's attitudes, opinions, or moods toward a specific subject, using some dominant tone such as whimsy, satire, irony, humor.

The formal essay or article, commonly labeled "magazine article," is a dignified and usually impersonal treatment of a serious subject; it may be descriptive or argumentative, but it is mainly expository.

Fact that, the fact remains that.   Roundabout, wordy substitutes for *that* and *the fact is,* respectively (see *Due to*).

Farther, further.   These words are interchangeable in meaning, but unusually precise writers and speakers prefer *farther* to indicate space, a measurable distance. *Further* indicates "greater in degree, quantity, or time" and also means "moreover" and "in addition to." ("We walked two miles *farther.*" "Let's talk about this *further.*")

Faze.   This word, which means "to disturb" or "to agitate," is considered informal (colloquial) in this spelling by some authorities. Other spellings are *fease, feaze,* and *feeze.* The word *phase* has entirely different meanings.

Feature.   As both verb and noun, *feature* is an overworked colloquialism in the sense of "emphasize" or "emphasis." *Feature* is slang in the expression "Can you feature that?" meaning, presumably, "Can you imagine that?"

Fed up.   An expressive but slangy term meaning "to become disgusted, bored." Don't use it when you're trying to impress an intellectual.

Feel.   This useful word appears in several expressions which are colloquial or dialectal. In standard English avoid using *feel of* (for *feel*), *feel like* (for *wish to, desire*), *feel up to* (for *feel capable of*).

Female.   Fastidious usage restricts *female* to designations of sex in scientific contexts. If *female* is considered colloquial, and it is, then what word can we use to express "female human being of whatever age"? Correct usage can indeed be a nuisance at times.

Fewer, less.   Both of these words imply a comparison with something larger in number or amount. Although *less* is widely used in place of *fewer*, particularly in informal writing and in speech, the distinction between them seems useful. *Fewer* applies to number. ("*Fewer* horses are seen on the streets these days.") *Less* is used in several ways: *less* material in the dress, *less* coverage, *less* than a dollar. ("The *less* money we have the *fewer* purchases we can make.")

Figuratively.   This word means "metaphorically," "representing one thing in terms of another," "not literally." ("*Figuratively* speaking, you acted like a mouse.") (See *Literally.*)

Fine.   This word is much overused in the general sense of approval. It is colloquial when used as an adverb: "Mona sang *well* [not *fine* or *just fine*]." (See *Counter word.*)

Fine writing.   A term applied to writing which is incorrectly thought to be free of all impurities and blemishes because it has been made perfect. Actually, "fine" writing is artificial, affected, and overcareful. It results from the use of pompous and long words, from euphemism, from the use of too many modifiers, from the overuse of foreign words and Briticisms. (See Sections 18b, 23, 25.)

Firstly, secondly.   These words are acceptable, but most skilled users of the language prefer *first* and *second* because they are just as accurate and are shorter. *First of all* is a wordy expression.

First-rate, second-rate.   These words suggesting rank or degree of excellence are vastly overused. *First-rate* is colloquial in the sense of "very good" or "excellent" or "very well."

Fix.   This is a word of many meanings. In standard English it means "to make fast." As a verb, it is informal (colloquial) when used to mean "to arrange matters," "to get revenge on," "to repair." As a noun, it is used colloquially for "difficulty," "predicament."

Flunk.   A colloquialism for "to fail" and "failure," this word should not appear in standard English as either verb or noun.

Folks.   This word is colloquial when used to refer to "relatives" and "family." Both dialectal and colloquial is the expression *just folks*, meaning "simple and unassuming people." *Folksy* is a colloquial word for "sociable."

Footnote.   The purpose of a footnote is to mention the authority for some fact stated or to develop some point referred to in the body of a paper.

Generally known facts or quotations do not require footnotes, but you must avoid *plagiarism* (which see). Unless the idea and the phrasing are your own, refer the reader to some source for your statement. To be entirely honest, acknowledge every source of indebtedness even when no direct quotation is used.

On occasion, you may wish to develop, interpret, or refute some idea but not want an extended comment to clutter up the body of your paper. Use a footnote.

How many footnotes should appear in a research paper? One investigation may call for twice as many as another. Some pages of your paper may require a half-dozen or more footnotes; others may need none or only one or two. Acknowledge credit where it is due and supply discussion footnotes where they are needed for understanding.

Methods of footnoting are numerous, but whatever system you employ should be consistent throughout your paper and immediately clear to any intelligent reader.

For books, standard usage favors this form: (1) author's Christian name or initials followed by surname; (2) title of book (in italics) and number of edition; (3) place of publication; (4) name of publisher (optional); (5) date of publication; (6) volume and page reference.

In listing information about periodical material, place the title of the article or story after the author's name and before the name of the periodical. The title is put in quotation marks, the name of the magazine is italicized (underlined). The volume number, in Roman numerals, is placed immediately after the name of the periodical. By putting the volume number in Roman numerals and the page numbers in Arabic, you avoid the necessity for volume and page abbreviations. Study the correct forms for listing the following kinds of information:

BOOKS

[1] Henry Louis Mencken, *The American Language*, 4th ed. (New York, 1936), p. 168.

[1] John Tasker Howard and Arthur Mendel, *Our American Composers* (New York, 1941), p. 82.

[1] Douglas S. Freeman, *George Washington* (New York, 1948), II, 142.

[1] *Letters from W. H. Hudson*, ed. Edward Garnett (New York, 1923), p. 62.

[1] Homer, *The Odyssey*, trans. George Herbert Palmer (Boston, 1891), p. 46.

ARTICLES (ESSAYS, STORIES)

[1] Walter D. Edmonds, "Arrival of the Lily Dean," *The Saturday Evening Post*, CCX (May 7, 1938), 5.

[1] "Personality Tests," *Life*, XXI (October 7, 1946), 55.

[1] Katherine Mansfield, "Bliss," *A Study of the Short Story*, ed. Henry S. Canby and Alfred Dashiell (New York: Henry Holt and Company, Inc., 1935), p. 303.

Your instructor may prefer a shorter form or one in which the information is arranged differently. For example, he may require you to omit the author's first name, the place of publication, or the name of the publisher. After the form has been decided upon, be consistent in its use.

In documenting your research paper, you may be urged by your instructor to use abbreviations wherever possible for increased efficiency.

The main, or primary, forms shown above may well be used less often than short-cut versions. For example:

ibid.: The same. If a footnote refers to the same source as the one referred to in the footnote *immediately* preceding, the abbreviation *ibid.* (from the Latin *ibidem*, meaning "in the same place") may be used. If the volume, page, title, and author are the same, use *ibid.* alone. If the volume and page differ, use, for example, "*Ibid.*, III, 206." *Ibid.* usually comes at the beginning of a footnote and is capitalized for that reason only.

op. cit.: The work cited. After the first full reference to a given work, provided no other work by the same author is mentioned in the paper, succeeding references may be indicated by the author's surname followed by *op. cit.* (from the Latin *opere citato*, meaning "in the work cited") and the volume and page:

> Jones, *op. cit.*, IV, 19.
> Hasty, *op. cit.*, p. 94.

However, *op. cit.* does no real work and its use is being discarded in favor of a note containing only the author's last name and the page number involved: "Burke, p. 230."

passim: "Everywhere," "throughout." It is to be used when no specific page reference can be given.

loc. cit.: The place cited. If the reference is to the exact passage covered by an earlier reference not immediately preceding, use *loc. cit.* (from the Latin *loco citato*, meaning "in the place cited"). *Loc. cit.*, like *op. cit.*, seems wordy and is gradually being discarded in research writing. Actually, *ibid.* can do anything which *loc. cit.* can.

Some style manuals dealing with documentation recommend that *ibid.* and *passim* no longer be italicized (underlined). Two of the best and most influential manuals making this suggestion are *The MLA Style Sheet*, compiled by William R. Parker, formerly executive secretary of the Modern Language Association, first published in 1951 and revised in 1954; and *A Research Manual for College Studies and Papers*, by Cecil B. Williams, 3rd edition, 1963. You should follow the specific instructions given by your own instructor in this and other matters of documentation.

p. (*plural*, pp.): page (pages)
l. (*plural*, ll.): line (lines)
vol.: volume
ch. (*plural*, chs.): chapter (chapters)
ff.: following
v.: verse
ante: before
art.: article
sec. (*plural*, secs.): section (sections)
n. (*plural*, nn.): note (notes)

A footnote is indicated by an Arabic numeral placed above and to the right of the word to be commented upon. If the reference is to a quotation, place the numeral at the end of the passage. Before the actual footnote at the bottom of the page repeat the number used in the text. Do not use asterisks or other symbols in place of Arabic numerals.

Footnotes may be numbered consecutively throughout the manuscript or separately for each page. Follow the directions issued by your instructor.

Footnotes may be put at the bottoms of pages, between lines in the manuscript proper, or all together at the end of the paper. Most instructors prefer the first of these methods. If the footnotes are placed at the bottom of the page, they should not be crowded. Always leave a clearly defined space between the text and the footnotes. (See p. 270.)

Foreign plurals.   Certain nouns of foreign origin retain the plural of the language from which they were borrowed. Some borrowed words have gradually assumed plurals with the usual English -s or -es endings. Finally, some words have more than one plural form. Here is a brief list of fairly common nouns to fix in your mind:

agendum, agenda	focus, foci, focuses
alumna, alumnae	formula, formulas, formulae
alumnus, alumni	genus, genera, genuses
analysis, analyses	hypothesis, hypotheses
appendix, appendixes, appendices	index, indexes, indices
	larva, larvae
axis, axes	memorandum, memorandums, memoranda
bacterium, bacteria	
basis, bases	parenthesis, parentheses
cherub, cherubs, cherubim	phenomenon, phenomena
crisis, crises	radius, radii, radiuses
criterion, criteria, criterions	stimulus, stimuli
datum, data	thesis, theses
erratum, errata	vertebra, vertebrae, vertebras

Foreign words in English.   Our language has been borrowing words and expressions from other tongues for many centuries. Most borrowed words are now so much a part of our language that they can hardly be told from native expressions. Those not yet assimilated cause some trouble—in spelling, pronunciation, and forming of plurals. Words still considered to be foreign are so marked in dictionaries and should be underlined when you use them. Find out what system your dictionary employs for making this distinction. (See *English, history of.*)

Foreword, forward.   A *foreword* is a "preface" or "introduction." *Forward* suggests "movement onward." ("This book needs no *foreword.*" "The crowd surged *forward.*")

Formal English.   The language and speech of formal occasions. Its grammar and sentence structure are correct; diction and pronunciation are careful, precise, proper. (See *Levels of usage, Standard English.*)

Formally, formerly.   The first term means "in a formal manner," "precisely," "ceremonially." The latter means "in the past." ("The defendant bowed *formally* to the judge." "Betty was *formerly* an employee of that company.")

Former, latter.　　*Former* and *latter* refer to only two units. To refer to a group of more than two items, use *first* and *last* to indicate order.

Forms of discourse.　　It is conventional to divide writing into four forms of discourse (communication of thought by words). The forms—*description, exposition, narration, argument*—are rarely found in a pure or unmixed state; even a novel, which is basically narrative, usually contains much description and some exposition and argument. Each of the four forms is discussed at an appropriate place in this Guide.

Fort, forte.　　*Fort* means an "enclosed place," a "fortified building." *Forte* means "special accomplishment or ability." ("The Indians burned the settlers' *fort*." "His *forte* is playing the violin.")

Free from, free of.　　The former is idiomatically correct. *Free of* is considered either colloquial or dialectal.

Free gratis.　　*Gratis* means "without payment," "free." Use either *free* or *gratis*, not both.

"Frying pan error."　　A term used by some teachers to characterize an error resulting from an attempt to correct an original mistake. For example if you attempt to correct a fused sentence by inserting a comma, you have not improved matters much, if at all. The term is derived from an expression used by John Heywood and also in *Don Quixote*, "Lest we leap out of the frying pan into the fire," and generally implies "getting into even more serious trouble by trying to correct a mistake already made."

Funny.　　A common and useful word but one that is vastly overworked. Its use to mean "strange," "queer," "odd," "remarkable" is considered colloquial. Its primary meaning is "humorous" or "comical."

Further.　　See *Farther, further.*

Gender.　　The gender of nouns and pronouns is determined by sex. A noun or pronoun denoting the male sex is called *masculine: man, boy, lord, executor, he.* A noun or pronoun indicating the female sex is called *feminine: woman, girl, lady, executrix, she.* Nouns which denote no sex are referred to as *neuter: house, book, tree, desk, lamp, courage.* Some nouns and pronouns may be either masculine or feminine and are said to have *common* gender: *child, individual, friend, doctor, visitor, it, they.*

Genius, genus.　　The former refers to great ability. ("Bach was a man of *genius.*") *Genus* refers to class or kind. ("What is the *genus* of this plant?")

Gerund.　　A verbal noun ending in *-ing* (*speaking, singing*). Because the gerund has the same form as the present participle, note the difference in their functions: the participle is a *verbal adjective;* the gerund is a *verbal noun.* A gerund can take an object and be modified by an adverb, and, as a noun, it can be the subject or object of a verb or the object of a preposition. (See Section 61b.)

> *Playing* squash racquets is good exercise.
> All the campers enjoy *eating.*

Good, well.　　The former is an adjective with many meanings: a *good* time, *good* advice, *good* Republican, *good* humor. *Well* functions as both adjective and adverb. As an adjective it means "in good health," and as an adverb it means "ably" or "efficiently." ("I feel *well* once again." "The sales force worked *well* in this campaign.")

Got, gotten.   The principal parts of *get* are *get, got, got* (or *gotten*). Both *got* and *gotten* are acceptable words; your choice will depend upon your speech habits or on the rhythm of the sentence you are writing or speaking. *Got* is colloquial when used to mean "must," "ought," "own," "possess," and many other terms. ("I *ought* [not *got*] to go.") (See *Have got to.*)

Gourmand, gourmet.   These words have to do with eating, but they are different in meaning. A *gourmand* is a large eater. ("Diamond Jim Brady was a *gourmand,* often eating for three hours at a time.") A *gourmet* is a fastidious eater, an epicure. ("As a French chef, he considers himself a *gourmet.*")

Graduate.   This word has several meanings, all of which are in some way related to marking in steps, measuring. Idiom decrees that one *graduate from* (not *graduate*) a school.

Grand.   This word means "imposing," "magnificent," "noble." It is overused as a vague counter word meaning "delightful" or "admirable." *Grand* is colloquial in such expressions as *look grand, a grand time, feel grand.*

Gratis.   See *Free gratis.*

Group discussion.   Hundreds of thousands of Americans have received their first opportunity to speak in public through *group discussions*. The function of a group discussion, which may have varying degrees of formality and informality, is to pool the information of a group to find a satisfactory solution to the problem at hand.

Various types of public discussion are in general use today, but all call for the same type of preparation. A general topic is chosen and the specific problem for discussion is formulated. Possible solutions are usually presented by speakers assigned in advance. After more or less prolonged debate on these solutions, a plan of action or an agreement on policy is reached, if possible.

1. *The single-leader type.*

This kind of program often follows an important speech and always heightens interest in it. Here an open-forum period is allowed during which members of the audience may ask questions of the speaker or differ with him. The speaker himself may preside at the forum period, or the chairman may act as moderator and refer questions to the speaker. Or a meeting may be called to discuss a problem of local interest, such as a war memorial, and some elected or appointed member of the group may take charge of the meeting, acting as both chairman and discussion leader. His function is to state the problem or problems involved, to recognize speakers, to keep things going, to see that all important phases of the problem are considered, to insure that no one monopolizes the time, to prevent unpleasant conflicts, and to guide the discussion to some sort of conclusion. Most assemblies and parliamentary bodies follow a system of this type, usually governed by specific rules.

2. *The "town meeting" type.*

A group of experts—usually four—discusses opposing attitudes toward some important public question; each is given at least one opportunity to reply to the other's arguments, and the audience is then given an opportunity to enter the discussion and to question the speakers. A moderator presides over the meeting, introduces the speakers, and controls the audience discussion.

3. *The panel, or round-table, type.*

A group of experts, literally sitting around a table, discusses various aspects of the topic selected. The discussion is informal and resembles a spirited conversation. The speakers have no time limit when they speak, and they may speak as many times as they choose—unless they threaten to monopolize the discussion. The function of the chairman is to keep the discussion moving forward, to keep the various members of the panel participating, to sift out points of agreement if possible, and to summarize the argument for the audience at the end. Such panel discussions occur frequently on TV and radio programs.

4. *The debate.*

Formal debate has many characteristics in common with more informal panel discussions. But it is closely controlled by rules. The proposition for debate is carefully worded to provide a direct clash and to prevent ambiguity; opposing members are organized into teams, each with a captain; each speaker is allowed to speak twice in a prescribed order; a rigid time limit is imposed for each speech; and a judge, or board of judges, usually awards a decision to the team which has "played the game" more skillfully. Although this form of intellectual sport has unquestioned values for its participants, it is available only to relatively few students and has little direct application in everyday life. For further discussion of argument and debate, see pp. 129–134.

Guess. See *Calculate, reckon, guess.*

Guy. This word has several meanings but we most often use it colloquially to refer to a man, boy, or individual generally. Some experts regard this use of the word as slang; it should be avoided in standard English. To *guy* someone is a highly informal way to express the sense of teasing or joshing.

Gyp. This word, which probably derives from *gypsy*, is a slang term which refers to a swindler, a cheat, and to cheating or swindling. It is expressive enough but hardly dignified or tasteful; omit it from standard English.

Hang, hung. The principal parts of *hang* are *hang, hung, hung.* However, when the word refers to the death penalty, the parts are *hang, hanged, hanged.* ("The draperies are *hung.*" "The murderer was *hanged.*")

Have got to. A colloquial and redundant expression for "must," etc. ("I *must* [not *have got to*] do my laundry today.") (See *Got, gotten.*) *Have* is a useful verb and appears in many expressions we use constantly. In standard English we should avoid using such expressions as *have a check bounce, have cold feet, have a lot on the ball, have it in for* *someone.* In these expressions the *have* is only partly responsible for the colloquialism.

Head.　　This word of many meanings is colloquial in a variety of expressions. In formal speaking and writing you should avoid using such phrases as *to head for, heads up, out of one's head, to take a header, heady* (smart).

Healthful, healthy.　　These words are often used interchangeably, but *healthful* precisely means "conducive to health"; *healthy* means "possessing health." In other words, places and foods are *healthful,* people and animals are *healthy.* ("I wonder whether he is a *healthy* person because he lives in a *healthful* climate.")

Heap, heaps.　　*Heap* means a "mass," a "mound." Both *heap* and *heaps* are colloquial when used to mean "a great deal," "a large amount." ("He owns much [not *a heap of* or *heaps of*] real estate.")

Highbrow.　　See *Lowbrow, highbrow.*

Home, homey.　　Do not loosely use *home* for *house.* Do not omit the preposition in such an expression as *I am at home.* Most importantly, remember that *homey* is a colloquial word for *homelike.*

Homographs.　　Two words which have the same spelling but different meanings, origins, and perhaps pronunciations: *air* (atmosphere) and *air* (melody), *lead* (to conduct) and *lead* (metal).

Homonyms.　　Two words which have close or identical pronunciation but different meanings, origins, and frequently spellings: *pale* and *pail, sew* and *so, steal* and *steel.*

Human, humane.　　The word *human* refers to a person. Some especially careful or precise writers and speakers do not use the word alone to refer to man as man; they say or write "human being." However, the practice of using the word alone as a noun has a long and respectable background. *Humane* means "tender," "merciful," "considerate." (His treatment of the prisoners was *humane.*")

Hunch.　　This word has acceptable meanings as both verb and noun. In the sense of "a premonition or feeling that something is going to happen," it is informal and should be avoided in standard English.

Hyperbole.　　An extravagant expression not intended to be taken literally, an obvious and deliberate exaggeration: *as old as time.* (See *Exaggeration.*)

-ible.　　For comment on the problem of *-able* or *-ible,* see *-able.*

1. The ending should usually be *-ible* if the base (root) is not a complete word. Contrast this principle with Rule 1 under *-able:* if the base is a complete word, add *-able: mail* + *able* = *mailable.* If the base is not a complete word, we add *-ible: ris* + *ible* = *risible, poss* + *ible* = *possible.*

audible	feasible	negligible
combustible	horrible	plausible
compatible	indelible	tangible
credible	infallible	terrible
edible	intelligible	visible

2. The ending should usually be *-ible* if the base (root) ends in *ns: respons* + *ible* = *responsible.*

comprehensible	indefensible	ostensible
defensible	insensible	responsible
incomprehensible	irresponsible	sensible

3. The ending should usually be *-ible* if the base (root) ends in *-miss.* Comparatively few words belong in this category. Here are three examples:

| admissible | permissible | transmissible |

With roots not ending in *-miss,* but closely related, are such words with *-ible* endings as *accessible, compressible, irrepressible,* and *possible* (which also fits under Group 1, above).

4. The ending should usually be *-ible* if *-ion* can be added to the base (root) without intervening letters: *collect, collection, collectible.* A number of words (roots) form nouns by the immediate (nothing coming between) addition of *-ion.* All such words form adjectives ending in *-ible.*

accessible	convertible	inexhaustible
collectible	corruptible	reversible
connectible	digestible	suggestible

You should note that this principle is tricky: if *-ion* cannot be added to the root *immediately* (without intervening letters), the *-able* ending is more likely, as in *present, presentation, presentable.*

5. The ending should usually be *-ible* if the base (root) ends in soft *c* or soft *g.* This principle should be compared with Rule 5 under *-able.* A soft *c* sounds like an *s* (*force*); a soft *g* sounds like a *j* (*tangent*). The following words contain a soft *c* or a soft *g.* Also note that, with few exceptions, the roots are not complete words.

convincible	illegible	irascible
eligible	incorrigible	legible
forcible	invincible	negligible

Just as there are a few exceptions to the rules for *-able* endings, so are there for words ending in *-ible.* The commonly used words which are exceptions are not numerous. Among those words which, by rule, should end in *-able* but do not are the following:

| collapsible | discernible | inflexible |
| contemptible | gullible | irresistible |

Idiom. The forms or variety of expression of a language, the characteristic way in which it is put together. In speaking of French idiom, for example, we refer to such a distinct usage as putting the adjective after its noun or the fact that an adjective in French has forms for singular and plural and for masculine and feminine gender. (See Section 28.)

I.e., e.g., viz., N.B., P.S. These and many other abbreviations commonly appear in writing. Although abbreviations are not recommended for formal writing, many of them are useful shortcuts. For the Latin *id est,* meaning "that is," we use the abbreviation *i.e. E.g.* is an abbreviation for Latin *exempli gratia,* meaning "for example." *Viz.* is the abbreviation for the Latin *videlicet,* meaning "namely." *N.B.,* or *NB*, stands for Latin *nota bene,* meaning "note well." *P.S.,* or *p.s.,* is the abbreviation for "postscript"; *P.SS.,* or *p.ss.,* stands for "postscripts," from the Latin *postscripta.* (See also *Postscript.*)

If, whether.   In standard English, *if* is used to express conditions; *whether,* usually with *or,* is used in expressions of doubt and in indirect questions expressing conditions. ("*If* it doesn't snow, we shall go" [simple condition]. "We have been wondering *whether* we would reach our sales quota" [doubt]. "I asked *whether* the doctor had arrived" [indirect question].) In standard English *if* is not used with *or.* ("It does not matter *whether* [not *if*] you go or stay.")

-ify.   See *-efy, -ify.*

Immigrate.   See *Emigrate, immigrate.*

Imperative.   The mood (mode) of a verb expressing a command or a request. (See *Mood.*)

Imperative sentence.   A sentence expressing a command or a request (see *Sentence, meaning and purpose of*).

Impersonal construction.   A method of phrasing in which neither a personal pronoun nor a person as noun is stated as the actor. The passive voice is used, or words like *it* or *there.* (See *Expletive.*)

> I have four reasons for my decision. [Personal]
> There are four reasons for this decision. [Impersonal]
>
> We must consider two suggestions. [Personal]
> It is necessary to consider two suggestions. [Impersonal]
> There are two suggestions to be considered. [Impersonal]
> Two suggestions must be considered. [Impersonal]

Imply, infer.   To *imply* is to suggest a meaning hinted at but not explicitly stated. "Do you *imply* that I am not telling the truth?") To *infer* is to draw a conclusion from statements, circumstances, or evidence. ("After that remark, I *infer* that you no longer love me.") Do not confuse these two words in use.

Impractical, impracticable.   Distinctions in the meanings of these words have broken down somewhat, but the former means "theoretical" or "speculative." *Impracticable* means "not capable of being used," "unmanageable." ("His suggestions are *impractical* and his blueprints are *impracticable.*")

In, into.   The former is used to indicate motion within relatively narrow or well-defined limits. ("She walked up and down *in* her room for an hour.") *In* is also used when a place is not mentioned. ("The airplane came *in* for a landing.") *Into* usually follows a verb indicating motion to a place. ("When Marion strode *into* the room, everyone fell silent.")

In accordance to, with.   *In accordance with* is the preferred idiom. However, the phrase is wordy and trite.

In back ot.   This phrase is colloquial for "behind." However, *in the back of* and *in front of* are considered standard terms, although both are wordy. *Behind* and *before* are shorter and nearly always will suffice. ("*Behind* [not *in back of*] the office was the storeroom." "*Before* [or *in front of*] the house was a tree.")

Indefinite pronoun.   *Indefinite* pronouns are somewhat less exact in meaning than other pronouns. Among the more frequently used indefinite pronouns are *another, any, anyone, anything, everybody, everyone, everything, few, many, nobody, none, one, several, some, someone, something.* Compound forms built upon the pronoun *one* or the element *-body* take the possessive form (*anyone's, everybody's*). (See Section 52.)

Indicative.   The mood (or mode) of a verb expressing a fact or what seems to be a fact. (See *Mood.*)

Indirect object.   A noun or pronoun which precedes the direct object of a verb and before which the word *to* or *for* is understood. When an indirect object follows the direct object, a preposition (*to, for*) is actually used:

> Yesterday I bought *him* a coat.
> Yesterday I bought a coat for *him.*

Indirect question.   Restatement by one person of a direct question asked by another:

> When will you pay me? [Direct]
> Joe asked when I would pay him. [Indirect]

Individual.   See *Party, person, individual.*

Inductive reasoning.   Drawing a general conclusion or principle from a group of individual particulars or observations. (See *Deductive reasoning, Logic,* and Section 41c,d.)

Inferior than, to.   The former is not standard idiom; the latter is. ("This oil is *inferior to* [not *than*] that.")

Infinitive.   A word which has the function of both verb and noun and which also may be employed as an adjectival or adverbial modifier. The infinitive is usually introduced by the sign *to: to* speak, *to* sing.

Like a *gerund* (which see), an infinitive can take an object and be modified by an adverb. Also like a gerund, an infinitive, in its function as a noun, can be the subject or object of a verb and the object of a preposition. (See Section 61b.)

> I must *work* tonight. [Infinitive as part of predicate]
> *To succeed* in my job is my first aim. [Infinitive as adjective]
> The person *to see* is the manager. [Infinitive as adjective]
> She is going *to tell* us of her recent trip. [Infinitive as adverb]

Inflection.   A change in the form of a word to show a change in use or meaning. *Comparison* is the inflection of adjectives and adverbs. *Declension* (which see) is the inflection of nouns and pronouns. *Conjugation* (which see) is the inflection of verbs.

Ingenious, ingenuous.   *Ingenious* means "talented," "resourceful," or "tricky." ("This is an *ingenious* computation device.") *Ingenuous* means "innocent," "frank," or "naïve." ("Sally is an *ingenuous* little girl.")

In line, on line.   The first of these idiomatic terms is more widely used than the second throughout the United States. ("Jim stood *in line* with the other boys.") However, *on line* may be used if doing so causes no confusion to your reader or listener. The word *line* appears in several expressions which are considered colloquial or dialectal: *come into line* (meaning "to correspond" or "agree"), *get a line on* (meaning "to find out about").

In regards to.   Omit the *s* in *regards*. Better yet, substitute *concerning* or *about* for the entire phrase; one word is usually more effective than three. (See *Regard, regards.*)

In search for, in search of.   Both of these expressions are commonly used, but the latter is the preferred idiom.

Inserted k.   See *K inserted.*

Inside of, off of, outside of.   The *of* in each of these expressions is super-fluous. ("*Inside* [not *Inside of*] the barn the horses are eating hay." "The girl fell *off* [not *off of*] her tricycle." "Will you travel *outside* [not *outside of*] the state?") When these expressions are not prepositional, the *of* should be included: the *outside of* the house, the *inside of* the tent.

Intensifier.   A word or element used to strengthen, increase, or enforce meaning. For example, *certainly* and *tremendously* are adverbs used as intensifiers. (See *Awful, awfully, abominably.*)

Intensive pronoun.   A pronoun having the same form as the *reflexive pronoun* (which see).

Inter-.   This prefix, meaning "between," is frequently confused with *intra-*, which means "inside," "within."

intercollegiate (*between colleges*)	intramural (*within the walls*)
interfere (*come, carry between*)	intrastate (*within a state*)
interstate (*between, among states*)	intravenous (*within a vein or veins*)

Interjection.   The eighth part of speech, the *interjection*, has two distinguishing qualities: (1) it has no grammatical connection with the remainder of the sentence; (2) it expresses emotion—surprise, dismay, disapproval, anger, fear. Grammarians distinguish two kinds of interjections. First are those forms used only as interjections, never occurring otherwise in speech: *oh, ouch, tsk-tsk, psst, whew, alas.* Some of these contain sounds not used otherwise in English and consequently difficult to represent in writing: *tsk-tsk* is an inadequate representation of the clucking sound made to indicate disapproval. Second are the forms that occur sometimes as interjections and sometimes as other parts of speech: *goodness, well, my.* The two groups are hard to separate, since many words now used only as interjections originate from other parts of speech: *alas*, for example, has its root in a word meaning "wretched."

Interrogative pronoun.   An *interrogative* pronoun (*who, which, what,* occasionally *whoever, whichever, whatever*) introduces a question:

> *Who* shall demand that a pardon be granted?
> *Which* is the route we should take from Hammond?
> *What* do you have in mind?

Interrogative sentence. A sentence asking a question and followed by a question mark (see *Sentence, meaning and purpose of*).

Intonation. Rise and fall of the speaking voice. (See *Pitch.*)

Intransitive verb. See *Transitive verb.*

Introducing punctuation. See *Punctuation, purposes of.*

Inversion. Reversal of the usual or natural order of words. The most common inversion is placing the verb before the subject: "Came the depression and we . . ."

Irregardless, disregardless. Each of these words is an illiteracy. That is, neither is a standard word and neither should be used under any circumstances, formal or informal. The prefixes *ir-* and *dis-* are both incorrect and superfluous in these constructions. Use *regardless.* (See Section 10d.)

Irregular plurals. Given below is a representative list of words with irregular or nonsensical plurals which follow none of the principles stated under *Plurals* (which see):

alkali, alkalies, alkalis	goose, geese	scissors, scissors
bison, bison	grouse, grouse	series, series
brother, brothers, brethren	louse, lice	sheep, sheep
child, children	madame, mesdames	species, species
deer, deer	man, men	swine, swine
foot, feet	moose, moose	tooth, teeth
	mouse, mice	vortex, vortices, vortexes
	ox, oxen	

Is, was, were. Parts of the verb *to be.* It may help you to remember that *is* is singular in number, third person, present tense. ("*He* [or *She* or *It*] *is* in the room.") *Was* is singular, first or third person, past tense. ("*I* [or *He* or *She* or *It*] *was* in the room.") *Were* can be either singular or plural, second person in the singular and all three persons in the plural, and is in the past tense. ("*You* [both singular and plural] *were* in the room." "*We* [or *You* or *They*] *were* in the room.") The two most frequent errors in using *to be* are employing *was* for *were*, and vice versa, and using *is* in the first or second person instead of in the third, where it belongs.

Is when, is where. These terms are frequently misused, especially in giving definitions. Grammatically, the fault may be described as using an adverbial clause in place of the noun phrase or clause which is called for. "A subway *is where* you ride under the ground" can be improved to "A subway *is* [or *involves*] an electric railroad beneath the surface of the streets." "Walking *is when* you move about on foot" can be improved to "Walking *is the act of* [or *consists of*] *moving* about on foot." (See Section 10i.)

-ise, -ize, -yze. Some 500 fairly common words in our language end in *-ise*, *-ize*, or *-yze*. How can one master all these spellings, especially since correct pronunciation provides no help at all?

The best approach is to isolate the comparatively few words ending in *-yze* and *-ise* and to remember that *-ize* is by far the most common suffix and that the chances of its being correct are mathematically excellent.

These are the only four fairly common words in English ending in -*yze*, and of them you will normally use only two:

analyze, catalyze, electrolyze, paralyze

There are no clear "rules" for choosing between -*ise* and -*ize* endings. But although well over 400 words end in -*ize*, there are only one-tenth as many with an -*ise* suffix.

1. Combinations with -*cise*: *excise, exercise, exorcise, incise*. These -*cise* words are so spelled because they derive from Latin *incisus*, meaning "cut."

2. Combinations with *guise*: *disguise*.

3. Words ending in -*mise*: *compromise, demise, premise, surmise*.

4. Words ending in -*prise*: *apprise, comprise, emprise, enterprise, reprise, surprise*.

5. Combinations with -*rise*: *arise, moonrise, sunrise, uprise*.

6. Words ending in -*vise*: *advise, devise, improvise, revise, supervise*. These -*vise* words (except for *devise*) are derived from the Latin *visus*, "see," and hence retain a *v* and *s*.

7. Words ending in -*wise*: *contrariwise, lengthwise, likewise, otherwise, sidewise*.

8. Miscellaneous combinations with -*ise*: *advertise, chastise, despise, franchise, merchandise*.

This makes a total of less than 40 common words ending in -*yze* and -*ise*. All others with this suffix pronunciation end in -*ize*. Here are a few of the hundreds of words with this ending (in American spelling):

agonize	generalize	pasteurize
apologize	harmonize	patronize
authorize	humanize	plagiarize
baptize	legalize	realize
brutalize	liberalize	recognize
characterize	localize	reorganize
civilize	modernize	scandalize
colonize	monopolize	scrutinize
criticize	moralize	solemnize
demoralize	nationalize	specialize
economize	naturalize	subsidize
equalize	neutralize	symbolize
familiarize	organize	tantalize
fertilize	ostracize	utilize

It.   See *Expletive*.

It stands to reason.   A cliché.

Its, it's, its'.   This little three-letter combination causes more errors than any other grouping of letters in the English language. However, the distinctions among them are simple and easily learned. *Its* is the possessive form of *it*. ("The dress has lost *its* shape.") *It's* is a contraction of *it is* and should never be used unless it means precisely this. ("I think *it's* [*it is*] going to rain.") *Its'*? There is no such form or word in the language. (See Section **52e**.)

It's me.   Please turn immediately to Section **64b.**

Jealous, zealous.   The former means "resentful" or "envious"; idiom decrees that *jealous* should be followed by *of*, not *for*. ("Nancy is *jealous of* Anne's beauty.") *Zealous* means "diligent," "devoted." ("He was *zealous* in the duties of his office.")

Job.   This word is frequently and inexactly used in the sense of "achievement." The chief objection to it is its overuse to cover many general and vague meanings. Furthermore, *job* is colloquial when used to mean "affair" and slang when applied to a robbery. In short, *job* is a useful word, but it should be employed carefully and sparingly. Consult your dictionary.

Joining words.   The joining words among the parts of speech are *prepositions* and *conjunctions*.

Journalese.   A style of writing supposed to characterize newspaper usage. Good newspaper writing is terse, accurate, complete, and frequently employs relatively short sentences. Faults of some *journalese* are triteness, forced humor, neologisms (which see), and occasional resort to polysyllabication. Some newspaper writing is wordy and lazy, but much is vigorous and effective, remarkably so since it is prepared under pressure of time.

Juncture.   This word has several meanings, all of which involve the act or state of "joining" or "connecting." In linguistics, the term has a somewhat specialized meaning relating to the fact that words as we speak them are not usually separated to the extent that they are in writing. Our words tend to flow together without the pauses which, in writing, are shown by spaces. For example, consider the sentence quoted and discussed in Section 4a. If we speak the sentence, "The person who can do this well deserves praise," we would need briefly to interrupt our flow of sound after either *this* or *well* in order to be fully understood. Such interruptions vary in length and are frequently combined with variations in *pitch* (which see).

K inserted.   The letter *k* is usually added to words ending in *c* before a suffix beginning with *e, i,* or *y.* This is done in order to prevent mispronunciation; note the different pronunciations, for example, of *picnicking* and *icing.* Only a few common words are involved in this rule, but they are frequently misspelled:

colic, colicky	picnic, picnicked, picnicker
frolic, frolicked, frolicking	politic, politicking
mimic, mimicked, mimicking	shellac, shellacked, shellacking
panic, panicky	traffic, trafficked, trafficking

This rule must be applied carefully. Note, for example, the words *frolicsome* and *mimicry.* There is no reason to add *k,* since the *c* remains hard.

Kid.   This word means "a young goat," in which sense it is rarely used. But *kid* in two other senses is one of the most ubiquitous words in the language. We use it to refer to a "child or young person" and we use *to kid* when we mean "to tease, banter, jest with." In both uses the word is dubious in standard English.

Kind of a, sort of a.   In these phrases the *a* is superfluous. Logically, the main word (which can be *kind, sort,* or *type*) should indicate a class, not one thing. ("*What kind of* [not *what kind of a*] party is this?") Although *kind of* and *sort of* are preferred in this construction, these same phrases are often used colloquially to mean "almost," "rather," "somewhat." ("She was *rather* [not *kind of*] weary." "Martha was *almost* [not *sort of*] resigned to his leaving.")

Kinds of sentences.   Sentences may be classified and named in several ways: periodic, loose, and balanced; simple, compound, complex, and compound-complex; declarative, interrogative, imperative, and exclamatory (see *Sentence, arrangement of content; Sentence, grammatical structure of; Sentence, meaning and purpose of*).

Knock.   In the primary sense of "strike" and in several other meanings, *knock* is a legitimate word on any level of usage. We should avoid its use in such phrases and terms as *to knock* (colloquial for "to criticize"), *to knock about* (colloquial for "to wander"), and *to knock down* (colloquial in the sense of "to embezzle" or "to steal"). *Knock off*, meaning "to stop," as in "to knock off work," is ever more frequently heard, but it is still considered colloquial by most authorities.

Lab.   Colloquial for *laboratory* (see *Ad*).

Later, latter.   The spelling of these words is often confused. They also have different meanings. *Later* refers to time. ("He arrived at the office *later* than I did.") For *latter*, see *Former, latter*.

Lay.   See *Lie, lay, lye*.

Lead, led.   These words show the confusion that our language suffers because of using different symbols to represent one sound. *Lead* (pronounced *lēd*) is the present tense of the verb and causes little or no difficulty. *Led* (pronounced like the name of the metal) is the past tense and is often misspelled with *ea*. ("*Lead* the blind man across the street." "He *led* the blind man across the street yesterday.")

Learn, teach.   Standard English requires a distinction in meaning between these words. ("I'll *learn* the language if you will *teach* me.") *To learn* someone something is an illiteracy.

Least, lest.   The former means "smallest," "slightest." The latter means "for fear that." ("He did not give me the *least* argument." "Give me your picture *lest* I forget how you look.")

Leave, let.   Both words are common in several idiomatic expressions implying permission, but *let* is standard whereas *leave* is not. ("*Let* [not *leave*] me go with you.") (See Section **66b.**)

Lecture notes.   Naturally, you read extensively in college, but you listen even more often than you read. Perhaps it can be said that college primarily provides you with an *opportunity to listen*. Much of the listening you do will involve notetaking.

Many students fail at taking notes because they try to write down too much of what is being said. Some students feel that they should transcribe as many of the lecturer's words as possible in order to make a good set of notes. Or they feel that they should *outline* the lectures they hear. In either case, the notetaker cannot be effective. He concentrates too much on the mechanical process of writing when he should be listening and thinking about what he hears. As a result, the student receives some parts of a lecture, obtains garbled versions of other parts, and completely misses a large percentage of it.

The efficient notetaker spends most of his time listening and a minor amount in writing. A means of properly apportioning time between listening and writing during a lecture is found in the *précis* system of notetaking. To use it, you listen for the period of time it requires the speaker to make a point and then you write it down in a one-sentence summary. A lecture is usually organized so that the speaker makes a series of points (they might be compared with the topic sentences of written paragraphs) which support a main idea. If you catch these points and summarize them in a complete sentence, you will make efficient notes from the lectures you hear.

This kind of notetaking requires considerable practice. Actually, the time to listen and the time to write become more obvious as you learn to recognize how a lecture is organized. When you become adept at précis-writing, however, you will find your notes much more useful. Not only will they lead you to the central ideas contained in the lectures; they will also help you remember through mental association the facts and figures which should be in your mind simply because you were listening and not writing constantly during the lectures.

Here are a couple of worthwhile tips: Leave plenty of space around each sentence that you write in your notebook. As soon as possible after a lecture, review the précis notes and, if possible, expand them with whatever they bring to mind from the lecture. In this way you will produce a more complete set of notes depending less on memory, yet your notetaking will not have blocked your listening. (See also Section 45c and *Listening*.)

Led.   See *Lead, led*.

Legible, readable.   These terms are synonymous in the meaning of "capable of being deciphered or read with ease." *Readable* has the additional meaning of "interesting or easy to read." ("Your handwriting is *legible*." "This book is *readable*.")

Lend.   See *Loan, lend*.

Less.   See *Fewer, less*.

Lest.   See *Least, lest*.

Let.   This word, with a primary meaning of "allow," "permit," has many legitimate uses. Such phrases involving *let* as the following, however, are colloquial and should not be used in standard English: *let on* (in the sense of "pretend"), *let out* (as in "school let out"), *let up* (meaning "cease"). *To let one's hair down* is both colloquial and trite. (See also *Leave, let*.)

Letters.   During their college years, many students write more letters than all other forms of composition combined: examinations, themes, and reports. After leaving college, they are likely to write even more letters than they did in college—if they do any writing at all. So widely used a form of communication deserves careful attention: from the standpoint of utility only, training in no other kind of writing is more important.

As with all that you write, your letters unmistakably reflect and comment upon you. What you say and how you say that something, the paper you use, the appearance of your handwriting or typing, even the way you affix a postage stamp suggest your personality and your attitude, just as do your voice, diction, facial expression, and gestures.

Two comments may be helpful: (1) A good letter has the same characteristics as a good theme. In fact, a letter is, or should be, a theme governed by identical principles of correctness, clarity, and effectiveness. (2) Problems of form, presentation, and content in business letters are so detailed and involved that they can be handled adequately only in a course devoted to business correspondence or by close study of a book dealing only with this one subject.

Two main kinds of letters are *informal* (friendly) and *business* letters. Conventional patterns of *formal* correspondence (invitations to weddings and elaborate receptions and replies to such invitations, for example) might be considered a third form; however, such formal correspondence can usually be handled best through efficient stationers or engravers (who have standardized invitation forms) or through a counselor or standard reference work on etiquette.

Informal letters perhaps bulk larger in your correspondence than do business letters. Writing a friendly letter is, of course, a highly personal act. But since "the best way to have a friend is to be one," you should write letters which don't seem to say: "Here, take this. I owe you a letter, but what can I say in the limited time I have? It's messy and thin and almost incoherent—but I have a headache and also a test coming up. You should be glad to get anything." Suggestions:

1. *Take your time.* No one can write a careful, interesting letter in 10 minutes. Instead of writing *five* notes in 30 minutes, try writing only *one* letter-theme in the same length of time.

2. *Think about your reader, not only about yourself.* A personal letter has to use a number of *I*'s and *me*'s, but try also to express interest in what your reader is doing or seeing or thinking. Put a dot by the side of every *I, me, mine* in a letter you have written and then hold the page away from you for inspection. If you don't get the connection, your reader probably will.

3. *Give details.* Genuine information about one interesting conversation or one event might be more appealing to your reader than a series of hasty, unformed, kaleidoscopic, random comments about a dozen different matters. Even a personal letter should be a *theme*, not a group of disconnected and ununified sentences.

4. *Make your letters appropriate.* Do not thoughtlessly write the same thing to every correspondent. Ninki might be interested in one subject, Robin in another, Marion and Herbert in still a third. Keep in mind the tastes and interests of your reader.

5. *Write legibly.* No matter how close the friend to whom you are writing, he should not be told by the appearance of your letter: "Here, take it or leave it. If you can't read this, what do I care? I didn't want to take the trouble to write anything much, anyhow."

Business letters should (1) have a definite, specific purpose, (2)

Stenton College
Columbus, Illinois 10253
February 10, 19--

Mr. Joseph R. Stolpe, President
Stolpe Homes, Incorporated
180 Walnut Boulevard
Olympia, Illinois 10198

Dear Mr. Stolpe:

   Mr. Earl Winant, a member of the Olympia Realty Board, has
informed me that your firm plans this summer to build a number of
homes on the old Bloomfield estate, which you recently acquired,
and that you will need an additional builder's assistant.
I should like to apply for that position.

   A resident of Olympia, I am now at Stenton College, where I
plan to major in architecture. I am a graduate of the Hilltop School
in Cardiff, Pennsylvania, where as a student for three years I
completed one year of regular and two years of advanced mechanical
drawing. The small student body at Hilltop was responsible for
construction of the school itself, and so I participated in the
building, wiring, and plumbing of a 10-room dormitory, a science
building, and a farmhouse that was converted into classrooms.
I also was the designer and builder of the photography lab.

   During the past two summers, I have been employed by Hummel
Brothers, in nearby Darwin, as carpenter's helper. My duties with
the firm included roofing, insulating, digging foundations,
flooring, painting, and electrical work. I also drove their
2½-ton pick-up truck.

   My age is 19. I am in excellent health, am 5'10" tall, and
weigh 160 pounds. I own my own tools, and you can depend on my
working with them intelligently and skillfully.

   We shall have our mid-semester recess during the week beginning
March 15. I can come to your office then for an interview,
and shall do so at any time agreeable to you. When would be
most convenient?

                              Very truly yours,

                              Robert A. Dennison

                              Robert A. Dennison

References: Professor M. G. Farkes, Stenton College, Columbus,
                 Illinois 10253
            Mr. Rutherford Parsons, Hilltop School, Cardiff,
                 Pennsylvania (Director of Construction Activities)
            Mr. Conrad Hummel, Hummel Brothers, 120 Main Street,
                 Darwin, Illinois 10195
            Mr. Earl Winant, Olympia Realty Board, Olympia,
                 Illinois 10198

show consideration for the recipient, (3) be written in a natural, un-affected, clear style, (4) conform to the conventions of commercial correspondence, and (5) have an attractive appearance. Such require-ments involve the use of suitable stationery, careful typing or legible handwriting, adequate margins, and consistent and logical punctua-tion—as well as all other principles of clear and effective writing of whatever sort. More particularly, all good business letters are written in a form now standardized in six parts: the heading, the inside address, the salutation (greeting), the body of the letter, the complimentary close, and the signature. (See *Close and open punctuation.*) For com-ment on these elements of business correspondence and on varied kinds of letters (order letters, inquiries, adjustment letters, letters of applica-tion, and the like), see a good book dealing solely with business corre-spondence; a dozen or more will be available in your college library or bookstore.

Letters, silent.   See *Silent letters.*

Levels of usage.   Each of us employs a different level of usage depending upon whether we are speaking or writing, upon who are our audience and readers, and upon the kind of occasion. As Professor John S. Kenyon has pointed out, what are commonly grouped together in one class as different levels of language are false combinations of two cate-gories: cultural levels and functional varieties.

Among *cultural levels* may be included narrowly local dialect, un-grammatical speech, illiterate speech, slovenly vocabulary and con-struction, exceptional pronunciation, excessive and unskillful use of slang. On a higher level is the language used generally by cultured people over wide areas; it is both clear and grammatically correct. These two cultural levels are *substandard* and *standard*, respectively.

Among *functional varieties* not depending upon cultural levels, Professor Kenyon mentions colloquial language (itself existing in dif-fering degrees of formality or familiarity as in familiar conversation, private correspondence, formal conversation, familiar public address, formal platform or pulpit speech, public worship, legal writing, and so on). Functional varieties may be grouped in two classes: *familiar* and *formal* speaking or writing.

The term *level* does not properly apply to functional varieties: col-loquial, familiar, formal, legal, scientific. As Professor Kenyon suggests, these varieties are equally suitable for their respective functions and do not depend on the cultural status of the users. (See *Appropriateness* and *Standard English.*)

Liable.   See *Apt, liable, likely.*

Library, use of.   A library is a depository, a treasury of the written word and the graphic portrayal of thought preserved in manuscripts, pic-tures, and print. The heart of any library is its collection of books and bound magazines; in fact, the word *library* comes from the Latin word *liber,* meaning "book." But a library is much more than a static collec-tion of volumes. Finding out the resources of your college library and getting to know them is inseparable from the widening of intellectual horizons. Learning to use a library intelligently will lead to a more exciting, less monotonous, far richer life. Libraries are truly a symbol of civilization; thanks to them, we can stand on the shoulders of giant thinkers of the past and present.

Before losing time by a trial-and-error method of discovering the resources of your library, use a free hour for a tour of its physical arrangement. Examine the main reading room, reserved-book room, study alcoves, reference section, and periodical room. Your particular library may not be arranged to include such divisions, but it will have an equivalent organization. Learn what it is. Find out if your library or the Department of English has a pamphlet, handbook, or guide to the library explaining and interpreting its arrangement.

One primary reason for attending college, according to many students, is to make friends. If you will learn to use them intelligently, the best and longest-lasting friends you or anyone else is ever likely to make in college are the library and a good dictionary. (See Section 45 and the entries in this Guide for *Card catalog, Periodical indexes,* and *Reference books.*)

Lie, lay, lye.   The first of these words is the present tense (infinitive) of a verb meaning "to be in a recumbent or prostrate position." As a noun, it means a "falsehood." ("Please *lie* down." "Never tell a *lie*.") *Lay* has several meanings, but it is most often used as the past tense of *lie*. ("He *lay* down for a nap.") *Lye* is an alkaline substance. ("Some soaps contain *lye*.")

Lightening, lightning.   The former means "making less heavy." The latter means "discharge of electricity." ("Try *lightening* the load of wood on your wagon." "*Lightning* was flashing in the summer sky.")

Like.   See Section 70d.

Likely.   See *Apt, liable, likely.*

Line.   This standard word has several nonstandard uses. It is considered slang in such expressions as *come into line* (meaning both "agree" and "behave properly"); *get a line on; he gave* [or *fed*] *her a line.*

Linguistics.   The science of language. English linguistics is a study of the structure and development of the English language and its relationship to other languages. Involved in linguistics are *etymology, morphology, phonetics, semantics,* and *syntax* (all of which see). (See also *Juncture, Phoneme,* and *Pitch.*)

Linguistics is derived from the Latin word *lingua,* meaning "tongue," "language." The very origin of the word implies that linguistics and its practitioners, *linguists,* are more concerned with *speech* and its sounds than with language in written form; a tenet of linguistics is that language is primarily a matter of speech.

The word *structural* applied to linguistic study and analysis implies that a system, or series, of patterns in spoken language can be isolated and described. In structural grammar, emphasis is first placed on form (system) and secondarily on meaning. To a structuralist, words and their functions are classified by formal and structural means (changes in the form of a word, noting the ways it can be used in a sentence) with no particular regard for the meanings involved. That is, in structural grammar, "the cat's meow" and "the dat's meow" would receive similar attention because of the form and function of *cat* and *dat*, even though the latter is meaningless.

Structuralists recognize four *form classes* of words which correspond approximately to the parts of speech known as nouns, verbs, adjectives, and adverbs. All other words—mainly prepositions, pronouns, and interjections—are called *function* or *structure* words, since their purpose is to supply information about the relationships of parts of a sentence made up of the form classes of words. Function words, such as *a, the, enough,* and *after,* have little meaning by themselves but do provide clues to the structure of a sentence; they provide a framework into which "form class" words can be dropped. Such combinations of function words and form class words result in three kinds of structures: noun, verb, and modifier structures. All *substantives* are noun structures; verb structures consist of words of the verb form class together with such function words as linking verbs; modifier structures are words from adjective or adverb form classes.

Structural linguists classify sentences according to the structures they contain and the arrangement of these structures. Such classification results in several different kinds of *patterns* (subject–verb; subject–verb–predicate adjective, etc.).

Another kind of grammar, called *transformational,* attempts to outline the processes by which sentences are formed. Transformational grammar assumes that basic sentence patterns, called *kernel* sentences, can be transformed into more involved sentence patterns by combination or addition. This scientific approach to grammar provides rules for forming kernel sentences, for combining or otherwise altering kernel sentences into transformed sentences, and for making resultant transformations understandable and "pronounceable."

Regardless of its particular label or approach, each kind of "scientific," or "modern," linguistics emphasizes *word order* (which see) and the patterns of words and phrases. This emphasis on structure and pattern, on position and function, has resulted in terminology which is somewhat different from that of "traditional" grammar. For an example, study the entry for *Noun* on p. 407; the five characteristics given there of this part of speech constitute an approach to one form of modern linguistics, a form which may be called "scientific" since it is based on observation rather than upon formal Latin tradition.

At the present time, lack of agreement among linguists prevents any concrete, fully coherent description of modern linguistics—its undeniable achievements and its potential contribution to a study of language. But since description of our language should be as accurate as possible, hopefully some agreed-upon form of scientific linguistics will eventually improve, strengthen, or even replace our "traditional grammar" with its many inconsistencies, inaccuracies, and other shortcomings.

Freshman English seems a hardly suitable discipline for an introduction to linguistics and can ill afford time for more than a superficial grounding in a highly technical field. Perhaps some years from now, a course in college composition can be more securely based on modern linguistics than on the traditional approach with which we have been somewhat familiar almost from birth. Until then, we must "make do" with the inconsistencies and illogicalities of our present "grammar"—which, incidentally, has worked remarkably well for millions of people for several centuries.

Listening.   If you would like to improve your listening ability, you can make progress while listening to oral instruction in college. Unique advantages exist for a person who is willing to improve and apply his listening ability.

1. When you understand that listening is a learning tool, you find that almost everyone within hearing distance becomes a potential source of information. A friend in college may have a large store of knowledge to offer if you will only listen. The person who sits next to you on a bus or train or airplane may be an authority on a subject, and if you will give him your listening attention, he will often pass along a wealth of information. Your college staff has experts in many fields; most of them will take time outside of classes to pass on what they know to a good listener. This willingness of people to talk about what they know does not necessarily grow out of a generous nature; people usually are flattered and eager to share their knowledge.

2. Listening, as compared to reading, is sometimes a faster, more efficient means of gathering information. If you need to know something about a subject quickly you can often find an authority on it to ask. He is likely to speak in terms that you can understand. He may also select and consolidate information from his broad field of knowledge to give you an accurate, generalized view of the subject; for you to do the same through reading might take weeks or months of research. And, of course, if you don't understand his discourse, you can ask questions for immediate clarification; as a reader you cannot question the writer so easily. Also, many times a listener can obtain valuable information not easily found in written form.

3. Writing that may seem dull and difficult to understand as you read it can often be understood and appreciated if you listen to it. Shakespeare's plays are good examples. They were written to be heard and are at a disadvantage when presented simply as words on a page. However, if you can first hear one of the plays, and then read it, the visual experience is enhanced, and your chances of appreciating Shakespeare are much better. It's not difficult to find a friend who will join you in reading aloud. Also, if you have a record player, you might investigate the spoken-word records now produced in quantity. On these records famous authors read their own writings or accomplished actors read classical literature.

4. Good listening is one of the best-known ways for improving language facility. Perhaps this fact stems from early childhood when we learned to talk by listening to and imitating our elders. The principle remains at work for adults. You should listen to persons who are accomplished speakers, either in public-speaking situations or in conversation. At college you continually have such opportunities, and by doing a good job at listening, you will improve your oral language facility.

5. Your ability to listen is directly related to how much opportunity you have to learn by ear. When people talk to you, they are usually affected by how you listen. If you are attentive, you assist the speaker in saying exactly what he has on his mind. Inattentiveness acts as a damper on the person talking; he will sometimes stop, or at least he will find it more difficult to express his ideas. Try this simple experiment. In an empty room, try talking out loud to yourself about some simple fact. Your words may not flow smoothly, and you will undoubtedly become confused. Ask someone into the room and explain the same fact to him. You will find doing so far less difficult than before. We all need listeners; without them we are mentally lost as we talk. Therefore, when you are on the receiving end of oral information, you have a responsibility for producing effective communication. And, incidentally, the good listening called for here is not easily faked. Facial expressions, posture, eye movements, and gestures betray the poor listener or support the good one.

6. When you leave school, your ability to listen may become more important than ever. An adult spends nearly half his communication time in the act of listening. Throughout the business world it is being recognized that poor listeners are expensive employees. No matter who he is, the typical adult carries out much of his daily activity through spoken communication, the effectiveness of which is directly related to how people listen. Indeed, many of our most important affairs depend on listening. For example, the justice we deal by jury is related to people's listening abilities. What does a jury do? It listens, sometimes to millions of words of testimony, and then makes up its combined mind about the case on trial. Also, the way one votes in elections is affected by his ability to listen. This is to be expected in a nation that has many, many millions of television sets (with more to come) and more radios than bathtubs. (See *Lecture notes*.)

Literally.   This word not only is overused but also is confused with *figuratively*. It is an antonym of the latter and really means "not imaginatively," "actually." (See *Figuratively*.)

Loan, lend.   Many careful writers and speakers use *loan* only as a noun ("to make a *loan*") and *lend* as a verb ("to *lend* money"). Because of constant and widespread usage, *loan* is now considered a legitimate verb to be avoided only in strictly formal English.

Logic.   "The science of correct reasoning" is one definition of *logic* which may serve as well as any other. Specifically, logic is a science which deals with the requirements, the criteria, of valid (sound, true) thought. Perhaps, as some scholars say, logic is not really a science at all but a systematic study involving the principles of justified inferences (conclusions). Whether science or study or art, logic deals with the validity of thought.

If this all sounds too formidable, perhaps you would prefer the definition and illustration of logical reasoning given in *Alice's Adventures in Wonderland:*

"Contrariwise," continued Tweedledee, "if it was so, it might be; and if it were so, it would be; but as it isn't, it ain't. That's logic."

Section 41 contains comment on clear thinking, suggestions hopefully designed to enable you to be more nearly accurate, more *believable* in what you say and write. As a British author, Anthony Hope, once said, "Unless one is a genius, it is best to aim at being intelligible."

The origins and development of logic, from Aristotle on, are a fascinating subject but one obviously requiring a semester or a lifetime of hard study.

Loose, lose, loss. *Loose* means "not fastened tightly." ("This is a *loose* connection.") *Lose* means "to suffer the loss of." ("Don't *lose* your hard-earned money.") *Loss* means "a deprivation," "a defeat," "a reverse." ("The coach blamed me for the *loss* of the ball.")

Loose sentence. A sentence with its parts arranged so that its meaning is clear before the end of the sentence (see *Sentence, arrangement of content*).

Lots of, a lot of, a whole lot. These terms are colloquial for "many," "much," "a great deal." The chief objection to their use is that each is a vague, general expression.

Lousy. This word actually means "infested with lice." It is constantly used as a slang expression, however, to mean "dirty," "disgusting," "contemptible," "poor," "inferior," and "well supplied with" (as in "*lousy* with money"). Use it in only the most informal of informal conversations. You can startle or impress your friends by using *pediculous*.

Lowbrow, highbrow. These terms are being used so increasingly in both writing and speaking that presumably they will, in time, be accepted as standard usage. Their status now is that of either slang or colloquialisms, depending upon the authority consulted. For a while, at least, do not use them in formal writing and speaking. Need they be defined? For anyone who doesn't know, *lowbrow* refers to a person lacking, or considered to lack, cultivated and intellectual tastes. Naturally, *highbrow* is applied to those who do have such attainments. Both terms are frequently used in a derisive or derogatory manner.

Luxuriant, luxurious. The former term refers to abundant growth; *luxurious* pertains to luxury. ("The undergrowth was *luxuriant*." "The club's furnishings were *luxurious*.")

-ly. See *-ally, -ly*.

Macron. A short, straight, horizontal mark placed over vowels to denote their long quality: *ā* as in *dāme*, *ō* as in *ōld*, etc.

Mad. This short and useful word has many acceptable meanings such as "insane," "frantic," and "frenzied." Most authorities consider *mad* to be colloquial when it is used to mean "angry" or "furious." ("I was *angry with*—or *furious with*—[not *mad at*] him.")

Malapropism. Ridiculous misuse of words, usually resulting from confusion of words similar in sound but different in meaning: *progeny* for *prodigy*, *dual* for *duel*. The word comes from the name of a character in Sheridan's play, *The Rivals*—Mrs. Malaprop consistently misapplied words. (See *Boner*.)

Manuscript. Literally, a letter, report, document, or book written by hand (from Latin words for "hand" and "writing"). *Manuscript* is now used to mean composition prepared by hand or on the typewriter, as contrasted with type. The word may be abbreviated *MS.* (plural *MSS.*) or *ms.* (plural *mss.*).

May.　　See *Can, may, might.*

Maybe, may be.　　The former means "perhaps." ("*Maybe* you will finish your task early today.") *May be* (two words) is used to express possibility. ("It *may be* going to snow today.")

McCoy, the real.　　This term is supposedly derived from advertisements of prizefights stating that a celebrated boxer named McCoy would actually appear and not an inferior fighter with the same name. Whatever its origin, the phrase is both a cliché and slang.

Mechanics.　　The technical aspect of something as, in writing, the mechanical aspects of paragraphing, capitalization, use of italics, figures for numbers, and the like.

Memorandum.　　This word, which is of Latin origin and means "short note" or "record of events," has two plurals, both acceptable in standard English: *memoranda, memorandums.* Abbreviations are *memo* (singular) and *memos* (plural).

Metaphor.　　A figure of speech in which a term or phrase is applied to something to which it is not literally applicable. This is done in order to suggest a resemblance: "She is a perfect lamb." *Metaphor* and *simile* are allied in meaning; a *simile* expresses resemblance directly but does so by using *as, as if, like:* "She is like a delicate flower."

　　　　Unfortunately, most metaphors are either strained or trite. Many figures of speech are often "mixed"; standard advice is to sustain one figure and not suddenly shift to another: "We had the crankcase drained and thus nipped our trouble in the bud." (See *Simile* and Section 26.)

Metonymy.　　The use of the name of one thing for that of another to which it has some relationship: *The White House* for *office of the Presidency, bottle* for *milk* or *strong drink.*

Middle English.　　The English language spoken and written during the period from approximately A.D. 1100 to 1500. It differs markedly in pronunciation, spelling, and grammar from *Modern English* (our language since about 1500). (See *English, history of.*)

Might of.　　An illiteracy. ("If you had asked, I *might have* [not *might of*] accompanied you.") (See *Would of,* etc.)

Mighty.　　This word means "strong" or "powerful." When it is used to mean "very" or "extremely," it is considered a colloquialism. ("Tom was a *very* [not *mighty*] lucky boy.") (But see *Very.*)

Misspelling.　　See *Spelling* and Section 16.

Mixed metaphor.　　An incongruous assemblage of ideas, as "Pushing her along is the powerful magnet of advertising with its fangs of generalities." (See *Metaphor* and Section 26.)

Mode.　　A term meaning the same as *Mood* (which see).

Modify.　　To limit or describe or qualify a meaning in some other specific and closely related way, adjectives are used with nouns and pronouns and adverbs are used with verbs, adjectives, and other adverbs. Limiting: *five* acres, the *only* meal. Descriptive: *blue* skies, *large* houses, speak *rapidly*.

Monologue.   Talk or discourse by a single speaker is called a *monologue* (also spelled *monolog*). For example, an entire poem may consist of the thoughts (speech) of one person; in a play an actor may speak alone for a protracted period. (See *Dialogue*.)

Monosyllable.   A word of one syllable, such as *yes, no, through*. (See *Polysyllable*.)

Monotonous sentence structure.   Monotony in sentence structure means using groups of words which are so uniform and unvaried in style and structure as to become wearisome and dull. Monotony may be caused by using a series of short, simple sentences, by using a series of *seesaw sentences*, and in various other ways. (See *Variety in sentence structure*.)

Mood.   The mood (or mode) of a verb indicates the manner in which a statement is made. Thus, if we wish merely to express a fact or ask a question of fact, we use the *indicative* mood:

> The building *is* tall. [Statement]
> *Is* the building tall? [Question]

If we wish to express a desire or a condition contrary to fact, we use the *subjunctive* mood:

> Oh, how I wish I *were* in Austria! [Desire]
> If I *were* rich, I should give you your wish. [Contrary to fact]

If we wish to give a command, we use the *imperative* mood:

> *Shut* the gate, please.

The indicative and imperative moods are not troublesome, and the use of the subjunctive has largely disappeared. However, careful speakers and writers employ the subjunctive to express the precise manner in which they make their statements. *Were* and *be* are the only distinct subjunctive forms now in general use, although our speech still retains numerous subjunctive forms in sayings handed down from times when this mood was more widely used: Heaven *forbid*, if need *be*, *suffice* it to say, *come* what may.

1. As indicated above, use the subjunctive mood, not the indicative, to express a condition contrary to fact:

> If I *were* a senator, I would have you decorated.
> If you *were* I, would you try to go?

The subjunctive is used in expressions of *supposition* and to indicate that a condition is *highly improbable* even though not completely contrary to fact:

> He worked as if he *were* never going to have another opportunity.
> Suppose he *were* to ask you to go with him!
> If I *should* be too blunt, let me know.

2. Use the subjunctive in clauses introduced by *as though* or *as if* to express doubt or uncertainty:

> He talks as if he *were* the only clever person in the house.
> As though he *were* any wiser himself!

3. Use the subjunctive in *that* clauses expressing necessity or a parliamentary motion:

> It is essential that he *appear* at the meeting of the group.
> She insisted that I *come* to her house.
> I move that the contractors *be authorized* to proceed with the work.

4. As indicated above, use the subjunctive mood to express a desire (wish, volition):

> He wishes that he *were* a girl.
> I desire that you *be* given another chance.

5. In parallel constructions do not shift the mood of verbs:

> If I *were* in your position and *was* not prevented, I
>   should certainly speak up. [Change *was* to *were*.]

Differences between the indicative and subjunctive may be illustrated thus:

INDICATIVE	SUBJUNCTIVE
I take (am taken)	(if) I take (be taken)
you take (are taken)	(if) you take (be taken)
he, she, it takes (is taken)	(if) he, she, it take (be taken)
we take (are taken)	(if) we take (be taken)
I took (was taken)	(if) I took (were taken)
I am, we are	(if) I be, we be
you are, you are	(if) you be, you be
he is, they are	(if) he be, they be
I was, we were	(if) I were, we were

Moral, morale.   As an adjective, the former has a meaning of "good," "proper." ("Frances' *moral* code was high.") *Morale* refers to a condition, state of being, or attitude. ("The *morale* in this college is excellent.")

Morpheme.   Any word or part of a word not further divisible into smaller meaningful elements: *boy; -ish* in *boyish, ad-* in *advice.*

Morphology.   The patterns of word formation in a language, including derivation and inflection. *Morphology* and *syntax* (which see) together form a basic division of grammar.

Most, almost.   *Most* is the superlative of *many* and *much* and means "greatest in amount, quality, or degree." *Almost* means "very nearly," "all but." *Most* is colloquial when used for *almost.* ("He has *almost* [not *most*] finished his assignment.")

Muchly.   An illiteracy. Despite the fact that you may often hear the word, it really doesn't exist—at least not in standard English. Use *much* instead.

Must.   As a noun, this word is no longer considered slang by most authorities, but it is tiresomely overused to mean something essential or necessary, as in "This movie is a *must*."

Naming words. The parts of speech which are *naming words* are *nouns* and *pronouns*.

Narration. One of the *forms of discourse* (which see) that relates or recounts events: novels, short stories, plays.

N.B. See *I.e.*, etc.

Neither . . . nor. See *Either . . . or, neither . . . nor*.

Neologism. A new word or phrase or a known word or phrase employed in a new meaning. *Brunch* and *slanguage* are informal examples.

Newspaper English. Language thought to be characteristic of journalistic writing. (See *Journalese*.)

Nice. This is a word with many meanings, including "agreeable," "pleasant," "attractive," and "delightful." Its overuse indicates the need for more specific substitutes.

Nominative absolute. See *Absolute expression*.

No place, nowhere. The former is a perfectly sound phrase ("There's *no place* like home"), but in standard English it cannot be a synonym for *nowhere*. ("She could find her purse *nowhere* [not *no place*].") Be certain to spell *nowhere* correctly; *nowheres* is as dialectal as *no place*.

Noun. A *noun* names a person, place, or thing, a quality, idea, or action. Common nouns name all members of a common group: *woman, officer, city, building, state*. Proper nouns name particular members of a group: *Mr. Ward, Herbert Hoover, Dallas, Parthenon, California*. Some common nouns are concrete: *book, cake, hammer, sweater*—names of objects which can be perceived by the sense of touch, sight, taste, hearing, or smell. Some are abstract nouns: *sincerity, intelligence, grace, weakness*—names of things which cannot be perceived by the senses. Some are collective nouns: *team, family, squad, union*—names used for groups considered as units.

Nouns have the following characteristics:

1. Nouns can be, and usually are, preceded by such words as *the, a, my, his, this, some, each* (determiners).

2. Most nouns can express the meaning "more than one" by various formal devices, the regular one being the addition of *s* (in speech, *-s, -z*, or *-iz*): *caps, cabs, edges*. But note that in their uses *as proper*, proper nouns have no plurals; neither do such nouns as *fun, handwork*, and *furniture*.

3. Certain groups of nouns have typical endings—like *-tion, -ness, -ment, -ure*—which distinguish them from corresponding verbs (*determination, determine*) or from corresponding adjectives (*goodness, good*).

4. Many nouns are distinguished from corresponding verbs by stress: *ob'ject, object'*.

5. Nouns are also marked as such by their occurrence in a complicated but well-ordered set of positions: before the verb in statements, after prepositions, etc. Proper nouns are marked as nouns by position only. All other nouns are, or may be, marked by one of the other formal characteristics.

Nouns have *number,* singular or plural, *gender,* masculine, feminine, neuter, common; *person,* first, second, third; and *case,* a common form for both nominative and objective and a possessive form (genitive).

Noun clause.   In the sentence, *"What you paid* was too much," the dependent clause in italics is used as a noun, the subject of the verb *was.* The writer could have used a single noun instead of the clause to make the same statement: "The *price* was too much."

> He promised *that he would lend me his motorcycle.* [Noun clause used as the object of *promised*]
> I am fearful of *what he may do next.* [Noun clause used as the object of the preposition *of*]
> His remark *that he hated girls* surprised me. [Noun clause used as an appositive]
> His remarks usually were *whatever popped into his head.* [Noun clause used as a predicate complement]

Noun phrase.   A phrase can be used in a sentence as a noun is used—as subject, object, and so forth.

> *Playing on top of the shed* was his idea of fun.

Used as a noun, a phrase is called a noun phrase. It functions in a sentence exactly as a single noun functions. In the above example, the noun phrase "playing on top of the shed" serves as a name—a name for the particular activity which is an "idea of fun." It acts as the subject of *was.*

Number.   *Number* is slangy or colloquial in such expressions as *I get his number, a smart number, his number is up.*

Number also refers to the change in the form of a noun, pronoun, or verb to show whether one or more than one is indicated. (See *Amount, number* and Sections 11c, 62, 63.)

O, oh.   The former is usually part of a vocative (direct address), is normally capitalized, and is rarely followed by any mark of punctuation. *Oh* is an interjection, may be followed by a comma or exclamation point, and is capitalized according to the usual rules. ("O Mickey! You don't really mean that." "Yet, *oh,* what hatred we had for him!" "*Oh,* what a chance!")

Object.   The noun, pronoun, noun phrase, or noun clause following a transitive verb or a preposition.

> Your book is on the *floor.* [Object of preposition]
> She struck *him* with a newspaper. [Object of verb]
> I see *what you think.* [Object of verb]

A *simple object* is a *substantive* (which see) alone. A *complete object* is a simple object together with its modifiers. A *compound object* consists of two or more substantives.

> The Popes built the large yellow *house* on the slope. [Simple]
> The Popes built *the large yellow house on the slope.* [Complete]
> The Popes built *the house and the barn.* [Compound]

Object complement.   A word, usually a noun or adjective, used after the direct object of certain verbs and intended to complete the meaning of a sentence. ("We have chosen Margie *leader*." "Let me make this story *simple*.")

Of.   *Of* is an exceedingly common word with a variety of standard uses. However, it is not an allowable substitute for *have* after auxiliary verbs in such expressions as *could of, would of, might of, should of*. ("You *should have* [not *should of*] been here yesterday.") (See Section **66b.**)

Off of.   See *Inside of*, etc.

O.K.   This everyday term is colloquial or business English for "all right," "correct," "approved." It is occasionally spelled *OK, okay, okeh*. The terms *oke* and *okeydoke* are slang. For the debatable origin of *O.K.*, see any standard dictionary.

Old English.   The English language of the period before A.D. 1100. Often called *Anglo-Saxon*, it is as foreign to the native speaker and writer of Modern English as German or Latin. (See *English, history of*.)

Once-over.   A slang term meaning "a swiftly appraising glance," or what boys and girls, men and women, quite often give each other.

Onomatopoeia.   The formation of a word by imitating sound associated with the object or action named: *tinkle, buzz, whir, chickadee*.

Open punctuation.   See *Close and open punctuation*.

-or.   See *-ar, -er, -or*.

Oral, aural, verbal.   *Oral* means "spoken." ("The order was *oral*, not written.") *Aural* means "received through the ear," or "pertaining to the sense of hearing." ("After the concussion, Jane's *aural* sense was below normal.") *Verbal* means "of, in, or by means of words." In such a sentence as "Our contract was *verbal*," it means "unwritten." *Oral* and *verbal* are thus often confused in everyday use.

Oral communication.   Freshman English is concerned, and deeply concerned, with effective communication of ideas. The course properly emphasizes *written* work, but nearly everyone speaks far more than he writes. Though speaking and writing have many common characteristics, a brief consideration of how they differ may help us to improve both our written and oral communication. A speech is not merely "an essay walking on its hind legs." Here are some essential differences between oral and written composition:

1. The spoken message has only one hearing. The listener whose interest is not attracted immediately has lost it forever. The reader can always go back and reread.

2. The speaker is usually concerned with the attention of a group; the writer, of one individual at a time. A group is slower in getting meanings than the individual member, and the speaker must make allowances for this. Furthermore, each audience constitutes a special problem, and the speaker must take into account its size, average age, educational level, and special interests. Writing at its best is nearly universal in its appeal, but speaking is usually best when it is clearly adapted to immediate listeners.

3. Oral style differs from written style. The speaker must be instantly intelligible. His hearers cannot go back and meditate on a

sentence or try to figure out its meaning; if they do so, they are sure to lose what follows. The speaker's sentences, as a rule, are shorter and his language usually is simpler and more direct than the writer's. Reader and writer are separated, but speaker and listener are thrown into close association. The reader is usually alone, relatively comfortable, and free from distractions. The listener, on the other hand, is physically distracted by other members of the audience. Even when he is quietly at home listening to a speech over TV or the radio, it is more difficult for him to give close attention to it than to the printed page, which he can always reread if his attention wanders. Many more people are eye-minded than ear-minded.

4. The speaker's voice is an important consideration in oral communication, one which has no exact parallel in the written form.

5. The speaker's use of his body is important in establishing communication with his audience but has no bearing whatever upon writing. (See *Group discussion, Conversation.*)

Origin of words. An account of the history of a word, its origin and derivation, is known as its *etymology* (which see). Knowing what a word "comes from" is an aid in building vocabulary and in spelling. For example, the word *preparation* is derived from the Latin prefix *prae-* ("beforehand") plus *parare* ("to make ready"). Knowing this fact and accenting the first *a* in *parare* may help you to spell the word correctly: *preparation,* not "preperation."

Similarly, our word *dormitory* (a building containing sleeping rooms) is derived from the Latin word *dormitorium.* Noting the first *i* in this Latin word, and perhaps also knowing that the French word for sleep is *dormir,* may help you to spell *dormitory* with an *i* and not an *a.*

Here are simplified comments on the origins of five words to illustrate vocabulary building and spelling aids:

Calendar. This word is descended from the Latin word *calendarium,* meaning "account book." Note the *a;* we frequently misspell the word as *calender* (a perfectly good word with an entirely different meaning).

Consensus. This word comes from the same Latin root as *consent* (*con* + *sentire,* "to feel"). Note the *s* in *sentire* and you will not spell the word "concensus," as is frequently done. Omit "of opinion" in "consensus of opinion."

Equivalent. This word may be easier for you to spell if you remember that it means "equal in value" and is derived from the prefix *equi-* and the Latin verb *valere.* Accent the *val* sound in *valere* and connect it with *value.*

Extravagance. This word is composed of *extra-* ("beyond") and the Latin participle *vagans* (*vagari,* "to wander"). Extravagance means "wandering beyond limits." Accent the letters *v-a-g* in the root word to insure correct spelling.

Finis. This synonym for "end" has the same origin as the words *definite* and *finite.* Accent the *i* sound and remember the two *i*'s in this word.

Out loud.   *Aloud* is considered more nearly standard English. *Out loud* is colloquial and not entirely idiomatic.

Outside of.   See *Inside of*, etc.

Overuse of "so."   *So* is correctly used as a conjunctive adverb with a semicolon preceding, and it is frequently used between independent clauses with only a comma before it. The chief objection to *so* in such constructions is simply *overuse*. In constructions like those below, *so* can often be replaced by *therefore, thus, accordingly,* and the like, or predication may be reduced. (See Section 8e.)

Ineffective	The bridge was out on Route 8, *so* we had to make a long detour on Highway 20.
Improved	Since the bridge was out on Route 8, we had to make a long detour on Highway 20.

In correcting the overuse of *so*, guard against a worse error, that of using another conjunctive adverb with a comma before it and thus writing an unjustifiable comma splice (see Section 2):

Wrong	The bridge was out on Route 8, therefore we had to make a long detour on Highway 20. [Use a semicolon or a period.]

Sometimes *so* is misused when the writer means *so that* or *in order that*:

Ineffective	Do people want the legislators to spend more money *so* they themselves can pay higher taxes?
Improved	Do people want the legislators to spend more money *in order that* they themselves can pay higher taxes?

Paid, payed.   *Paid* is the past tense and past participle of the verb *pay*. ("He *paid* all his bills promptly.") *Payed* is used only in the sense of to *pay* out a cable or line. ("He *payed* out the anchor line slowly.")

Parallelism.   Parallelism means "like construction for like ideas." You will convey your precise meaning to your readers, surely and effectively, if you construct your sentences so that the reader can immediately see what ideas are of equal importance. Parallel construction for like ideas is indispensable to clear, grammatically correct, effective sentences. Parallel movement, correctly handled, is one means of attaining an emphatic, vigorous style. (See Section 7.)

The simplest form of parallelism involves two or more words in a series. Using more complex forms, the writer can make two or more phrases parallel, or two or more dependent clauses, or two or more independent clauses, or two or more sentences.

Words: Henry is *slow* but *thorough*. The American colors are *red, white,* and *blue*.

Phrases: Every afternoon my grandfather is at the barbershop *telling yarns about his youth* or *hearing the yarns that his cronies tell*.

Dependent clauses: I was desperate *when I arrived late in town* and *when I found there were no desirable rooms available*.

Independent clauses: Julius Caesar's most famous statement was this:
"*I came, I saw, I conquered.*"

Sentences: Alfred Lord Tennyson was the British poet who wrote lyrics
in his early life and dramas in his closing years. Robert Browning
was the British poet who wrote dramas in his early career and other
forms of poetry in his later life.

As an effective test for true parallelism, draw lines under parallel
elements. Then draw a corresponding number of lines in parallel form
and write the underlined words on these parallel lines. Examples from
the illustrations above:

Every afternoon my grandfather is at the barbershop
telling yarns about his youth

or

hearing the yarns that his cronies tell.

Julius Caesar's most famous statement was this:
I came,

I saw,

I conquered.

Paraphrase.   Not a form of *summary* (which see) but another type of
"report on reading" widely required in college work is the paraphrase.
A paraphrase is unlike a *précis* in that the latter is a digest of the
essential meaning of an original passage, whereas a paraphrase is a
full-length statement of that meaning. It is a free rendering of the sense
of a passage, fully and proportionately, but in different words.

The paraphrase is frequently used to make clear wording which
is vague and obscure, a process of simplification and modernization.
Each of you has read a particularly difficult poem or an especially
abstruse discussion in prose which you could not make sense of until
you put it into your own words. After you did so, its meaning was clear,
and you felt that you had actually translated the passage into your
own thought processes. Much of the discussion in English and social
science classrooms begins with a paraphrasing of the ideas expressed
in assignments from textbooks. In other words, every student has
almost daily need for reshaping source material to suit his purposes
and aims.

In making a paraphrase, follow these suggestions:

1. Read the original passage as often as necessary in order to
understand its full and exact meaning. It is impossible properly to
paraphrase a passage until you have mastered its essential content,
until you are familiar with its purposes, organization, and method of
getting at the central idea. Just as in making a précis, you must read
as well and think as consistently as you can. Some phrases and sentences you will probably have to reread several times, carefully and
reflectively, before their meaning will "come alive" for you. If the passage contains obscure words and allusions about which you are in
doubt, consult a dictionary or other reference book to determine their
meanings.

2. Use your own words. Try to find understandable equivalents for words and phrases which are obscure, but do not strain for synonyms. Repeat words whose meaning is unmistakably clear; restrict your changes to passages which actually require simplifying or modernizing. Do not fail to make necessary changes just because it is difficult to do so.

3. Leave out nothing of importance. A paraphrase is a restatement and, as such, should contain the essential thought of the original in its entirety. Omitting significant detail results in distortion.

4. Add nothing which is not in the original. Interpretation and explanation should be confined to making clear what the original author had in mind and should not convey the paraphraser's additional ideas. Whether you like or dislike what the writer has said, whether you agree or disagree with him, whether you think his logic is sound or faulty— these considerations do not enter into the making of the paraphrase. To make a paraphrase does not mean that you cease to think; it means that your thinking produces a full-length statement of another's meaning.

5. Keep as closely as clarity will permit to the form and tone of the original. If obscurity cannot otherwise be overcome, recast the passage, but be careful not to distort or to parody. Obviously, a paraphraser can hardly hope to achieve the same mood and tonal quality as the author of, say, a great poem, but he should try to preserve as much of these existing qualities as possible.

6. Use good English. Any paraphrase of a good poem or prose passage is worth far less than the original, but the better the paraphrase, the less the difference between it and the original. In addition to careful reading and constructive thinking, the making of a good paraphrase, just as of an effective précis, requires exact writing.

The following is a paraphrase made by a student. Criticize it in terms of the suggestions given above.

ON FIRST LOOKING INTO CHAPMAN'S HOMER

Much have I travell'd in the realms of gold,
And many goodly states and kingdoms seen;
Round many western islands have I been
Which bards in fealty to Apollo hold.
Oft of one wide expanse had I been told
That deep-brow'd Homer ruled as his demesne:
Yet did I never breathe its pure serene
Till I heard Chapman speak out loud and bold:
Then felt I like some watcher of the skies
When a new planet swims into his ken;
Or like stout Cortez, when with eagle eyes
He stared at the Pacific—and all his men
Look'd at each other with a wild surmise—
Silent, upon a peak in Darien.

—JOHN KEATS

PARAPHRASE

I have read widely in the great classics of literature and have noted many examples of great poetry. I had often been told of the work of Homer and the poetry which he had created, but I never really understood or appreciated its great beauty and power until I read Chapman's translation. Then I felt as awed as some astronomer who unexpectedly discovers a new planet, or as surprised and speechless as Cortez (Balboa) and his followers were when they saw the Pacific Ocean for the first time, from Panama.

Parenthetical statement. A word, phrase, clause, or sentence, by way of explanation, which is inserted in or added to a statement grammatically complete without it. Such a statement is usually enclosed by parentheses, commas, or dashes.

Participle. A *participle* is a word which has the function of both verb and adjective. The *present participle* always ends in -*ing* (*throwing, singing*). The *past participle* has various forms (*taken, sung, walked, set*). The *perfect participle* consists of *having* or *having been* plus the past participle (*having spoken, having been sung*); it is either active or passive in voice.

The participle, since it is a form of the verb as well as an adjective, can take an object and can be modified by an adverb. The participle resembles the adjective in that it can be modified by an adverb and can itself modify a noun or pronoun. (See Section 61b.)

> The ball *thrown* by the player went into the crowd.
> The boy expertly *taming* the horse is named Rudy.
> The tree *rustling* in the breeze is a willow.

Parts of speech. Words are classified according to their use in larger units of thought, that is, sentences. This functional division results in the so-called *parts of speech;* every word in the English language belongs to one or more of these parts of speech. There are eight such parts: *noun, pronoun, verb, adjective, adverb, conjunction, preposition, interjection.*

Many words are always used in a certain way, as a particular part of speech. But since our language is constantly changing, the functions of words reflect that change. *Chair,* for example, is almost always a noun, yet the poet A. E. Housman tells of carrying a victorious athlete "shoulder-high" in a parade through his hometown:

> The time you won your town the race
> We *chaired* you through the market-place.

Noun, verb, adjective, adverb name the four large form classes in English. They have the best title to the collective term "parts of speech."

1. The main parts of speech are large groups, each of them comprising thousands of words in the average vocabulary.
2. The membership of the main parts of speech is unstable and shifting. New nouns are constantly being formed, new prepositions seldom.
3. Words *name, assert, modify,* and *join.* To determine what part of

speech a given word is, observe how the word is used in a sentence of which it is a part. (See Section 61a.)

Party, person, individual.   Except in telephone and legal language, *party* implies a group and should not be used to refer to one person except in a colloquial sense. *Individual* refers to a single, particular person. As nouns, *individual* and *person* are synonymous. As an adjective, *individual* means "single," "separate," and is therefore unnecessary and repetitious when used to modify *person* or when "each" has been used. Both *individual person* and *each individual member* are wordy.

Passed, past.   The former is the past tense of the verb *to pass;* in its use as a verb, the latter is the past participle. ("The car *passed* us at 70 miles per hour." "Your troubles are now *past.*") *Pass* is not only a verb; it is also a noun. In one or the other of these two categories, it appears in many expressions which are either colloquial or slangy, among them *a pretty pass, make a pass at, pass out* (which see), *pass up, pass the buck.*

Pass out.   In the sense of "to faint" or "to become unconscious," *pass out* is a useful term but, as slang, should not appear in standard English.

Payed.   See *Paid, payed.*

Pep, peppy.   The former is an informal expression as both noun and verb. *Peppy,* an adjective, is fully as colloquial. Use some such standard word as *energy, briskness, spirit, vigor;* corresponding adjectives would be *energetic, brisk, spirited, vigorous.*

Percent, per cent.   This word (from Latin *per centum,* meaning "by the hundred") may be spelled as either one or two words. *Percent* is colloquial when used as a substitute for *percentage* (the noun). *Percentage* is colloquial when used in the meaning of "profit" or "advantage," as in "What's the percentage in hard work?"

Periodic sentence.   A sentence with its parts arranged so that its meaning is not clear or complete until the end is reached or nearly reached (see *Sentence, arrangement of content*).

Periodical indexes.   Current and recent issues of many magazines are often displayed in libraries, sometimes in a special periodical room. Older issues of magazines and of some newspapers are normally bound in book form; to find what you wish in them, you should consult *periodical indexes.* These are helpful guides to articles and other material which might lie buried except for the aid provided by indexes.

When you consult a periodical index, turn first to the front; here you will find lists of the periodicals indexed and helpful, full instructions for use of the volume.

Periodical indexes are of two kinds. *General* indexes list the contents of magazines and a few newspapers of widespread interest; *special* indexes, often more helpful than general ones, restrict themselves to coverage of one specific area: *Agricultural Index, Applied Science and Technology Index, Art Index, Chemical Abstracts, Education Index, Engineering Index, Psychological Abstracts,* etc. Among the more useful general indexes are these: *Readers' Guide to Periodical Literature, International Index to Periodicals, The New York Times Index, Facts on File.*

Most college libraries subscribe to many more periodical indexes than those mentioned here. Discover the resources of your library; speak to the reference librarian about your special needs and interests.

Person.   The change in the form of a pronoun or verb—sometimes merely a change in use, as with verbs—to indicate whether the "person" used is the person speaking (*first person*), the person spoken to (*second person*), or the person or thing spoken about (*third person*):

> *I*, Steve, testify that this is a true story. [First person]
> Please, *Steve,* try to tell the truth. [Second person]
> It is difficult for *him* [Steve] to tell the truth. [Third person]
> *I see, you see, he sees, she sees, it sees, we see, you see, they see*

Personal, personnel.   The former means "private," "individual." ("The employer granted me a *personal* interview.") *Personal* is a much overused word. Perhaps because we wish to belong, to show a close relationship with something, we say or write such sentences as "He is a *personal* friend of mine." Shouldn't the *personal* be omitted? How many friends does each of us have who are not personal? *Personnel* means "a body of persons," usually a group employed in any work, establishment, enterprise, or service. ("The *personnel* of this firm was [or possibly *were*] carefully chosen.")

Personal pronoun.   A direct substitute for a noun as subject or object: "Where did *you* buy it?" Like a noun, it has number, gender, person, and case, as is shown by the following table:

	SINGULAR		
	Nominative	*Possessive*	*Objective*
1st person	I	my, mine	me
2nd person	you	your, yours	you
3rd person			
masculine	he	his	him
feminine	she	her, hers	her
neuter	it	its	it
	PLURAL		
1st person	we	our, ours	us
2nd person	you	your, yours	you
3rd person	they	their, theirs	them

Grammatical problems frequently arise from the fact that, unlike nouns, both personal and relative pronouns have distinct forms for the nominative and objective cases.

Personal pronouns vary to show a change in person; other classes of pronouns do not. For example, *I* and *we*, representing a speaker, are in the first person. *You*, the person spoken to, is in the second person. Those spoken of (*she, he, it, they*) are in the third person.

Personal pronouns in the third person singular change to indicate gender. *He* is masculine, *she* is feminine, *it* is neuter. (See *Person.*)

Phoneme.   A class, or family, of closely related sounds regarded as a single sound. (These speech sounds are called *phones.*) For example, by contrast of the phoneme *p* with other phonemes, *pip* differs from *nip* and *tip*. Linguists differ in their analysis of the sounds of our language but are generally agreed that some 50 phonemes exist in the English language. No wonder many expressions are difficult to pronounce, since a phoneme is, by definition, the "simplest possible significant classification of sound."

Phonetics.   The science of speech sounds and their production.

Phony.   As both adjective and noun, this word is slang. As a quick and easy substitute for "not genuine," "fake," *phony* is so often used that, presumably, it will in time be acceptable in standard English. Until then, no.

Pitch.   The combination of *pitch, stress,* and *juncture* (which see) forms what is known as *intonation,* an important item in any analysis of the spoken language. In linguistic terms, intonation means "the significant speech pattern or patterns resulting from pitch sequences and pauses (juncture)." *Pitch* is closely connected with *stress;* the latter, which refers to loudness, may be primary, secondary, tertiary, or weak (neutral). One linguist (Paul Roberts) uses the sentence "The White House is a white house" to indicate the different emphases given *White House* and *white house.*

   Pitch is usually numbered from 1 to 4 (low to high or high to low, depending upon what linguist is speaking or writing). Pitch signals help in distinguishing spoken questions from statements just as question marks and periods do in writing.

Plagiarism.   The act of taking and passing off as one's own the thoughts and writings of someone else. It may be interesting to note that the word comes from a Latin term meaning "kidnaper." It might also be well to remember that "copying from one source is plagiarism; copying from two or more is research" is an inaccurate and dishonest observation. (See Section 38b.)

Plan on going, plan to go.   Both of these expressions are in everyday use, but the former is considered colloquial and idiomatically not so sound as *plan to go.*

Plenty.   This word is colloquial when used to mean "very," "fully." ("The water is *very* [not *plenty*] hot today.") But see *Very.*

Plurals.   You may find it fairly easy to spell the singular of a word (meaning "one") but have trouble forming and correctly spelling its plural (meaning "more than one"). This is quite understandable, since many English words form plurals in unusual ways. You can "look it up" in a dictionary when you are puzzled, but a few principles of plural-forming can easily be mastered. (See *Foreign plurals* and *Irregular plurals.*)

1. The plural of most nouns is formed by adding *s* to the singular:

bed, beds	cracker, crackers	hat, hats
book, books	dog, dogs	sheet, sheets

2. Nouns ending with a sibilant or *s* sound (*ch, sh, s, x, z*) form their plurals by adding *es:*

arch, arches	buzz, buzzes	mass, masses
box, boxes	church, churches	tax, taxes
bush, bushes	loss, losses	watch, watches

3. Nouns ending in *y* preceded by a consonant usually change *y* to *i* before adding *es:*

activity, activities	fly, flies	quantity, quantities
city, cities	library, libraries	sky, skies

4. Nouns ending in *y* preceded by a vowel usually add *s* without changing the final *y:*

alley, alleys	key, keys	toy, toys
chimney, chimneys	monkey, monkeys	turkey, turkeys

5. Nouns ending in *o* preceded by a vowel add *s* to form their plurals:

cameo, cameos	radio, radios
folio, folios	rodeo, rodeos

6. Nouns ending in *o* preceded by a consonant often add *es* to form their plurals:

cargo, cargoes	mosquito, mosquitoes
echo, echoes	Negro, Negroes
embargo, embargoes	potato, potatoes
fresco, frescoes	tomato, tomatoes
hero, heroes	tornado, tornadoes

7. Some nouns ending in *o* preceded by a consonant, including most musical terms, add *s* to form their plurals:

alto, altos	contralto, contraltos	silo, silos
banjo, banjos	dynamo, dynamos	solo, solos
canto, cantos	memento, mementos	soprano, sopranos
concerto, concertos	piano, pianos	zero, zeros

8. Nouns ending in *f* form their plurals in such variable ways that you should *always* consult your dictionary when in doubt. Nouns ending in *ff* usually add *s*. Most nouns ending in *fe* change *fe* to *ve* and add *s*. The following examples will be sufficient to make you remember the formula: *doubt + dictionary = correct spelling.*

belief, beliefs	life, lives	sheriff, sheriffs
chief, chiefs	loaf, loaves	staff, staves (or
grief, griefs	mischief, mischiefs	*staffs*)
half, halves (or *halfs*)	roof, roofs	tariff, tariffs
handkerchief, -chiefs	scarf, scarves	thief, thieves
leaf, leaves	self, selves	wife, wives

P.M.   See *A.M.*, etc.

Polysyllable.   A word having many, or more than three, *syllables* (which see). A *monosyllable* is a word of only one syllable. Good writing requires words of varying length, but "big words" should never be used merely to make an impression.

Portmanteau word.   A word made by telescoping or blending two or more words: *dandle* from *dance* and *handle, aquabelle* from *girl swimmer, aristobrat* from *aristocrat* and *brat*. (See *Blend.*)

Position and arrangement of words.   Effectiveness in sentence structure requires that words be so *chosen* and *arranged* that they have maximum impressiveness. Writers frequently attain correctness and clarity in their sentences, but only the more diligent or more gifted compose sentences which really "get across" decisively and emphatically.

Not all words or ideas in a sentence are of equal importance; consequently you must attempt to place elements of thought so that relatively unimportant items will remain in the background and important ones will achieve prominence. You can attain such effectiveness only by proper coordination and subordination. (See *Beginning, ending sentence; Climactic order; Periodic sentence; Variety in sentence structure;* and *Word order.*)

Postscript. A word meaning "a sentence or paragraph added to a letter after a writer's signature" or "any addition to a written or printed document." It comes from the Latin *post* ("after") and *scribere* ("to write"). The plural is *postscripts;* abbreviations are *P.S.* or *p.s.* (See *I.e.,* etc.)

Précis. A *précis* (the form is both singular and plural and is pronounced "pray-see") is a brief summary of the essential thought of a longer composition. It is a miniature of the original which reproduces in the same mood and tone the basic ideas of the original passage. The writer of a précis does not interpret or comment; his function is to provide a reduction of the author's exact meaning without omitting any important details.

In making a précis, follow these suggestions:

1. Select carefully the material to be condensed. Some selections can be reduced satisfactorily, but others are so tightly knit that condensation is virtually impossible. You can make précis of novels, short stories, speeches, or essays, but do not select material the style of which is especially compact and epigrammatic. Avoid material which has already been summarized, edited, or abridged; "continual distillation" cannot accurately indicate the essential thought of the original composition.

2. Read the selection carefully. The major purpose of a précis is to present faithfully, as briefly and clearly as possible, the important ideas of the selection being "cut down." In order to grasp the central ideas, you must read carefully, analytically, and reflectively. Look up the meanings of all words and phrases about which you are in doubt. Do not skim, but look for important or key expressions. Before starting to write, you must, to use Sir Francis Bacon's phrase, "chew and digest" the selection, not merely "taste" it or "swallow" it whole in a single gulp. You must see how the material has been organized, what devices the writer has used, what kinds of illustrations support the main thought. These suggestions are, of course, those which you would ordinarily follow every time that you attempt to read and to think as intelligently as you can.

3. Use your own words. Quoting sentences—perhaps topic sentences—from each paragraph results in a sentence outline, not a précis. You must use your own words for the most part, although a little quotation is permissible. Ordinarily, the phrasing of the original will not be suitable for your purposes. Once you have mastered the thought of

the selection, your problem is one of original composition. You are guided and aided by the order and wording of the material, but the précis itself represents your own analysis and statement of the main thought.

4. Do not use too many words. Nothing of real importance can be omitted, but you must remember that the central aim of a précis is condensation. The length of a condensation cannot arbitrarily be determined, but most prose can be reduced by two-thirds to three-fourths. Some verse is so compact that it can be condensed hardly at all; other verse can be shortened more than most good prose.

5. Do not alter the plan of the original. Thoughts and facts should not be rearranged; if they are, the essence of the original may be distorted. Give attention to proportion. Try to preserve as much as possible of the mood and tone of the original.

6. Write the précis in good English. The condensation should not be a jumble of disconnected words and faulty sentences. It should be a model of exact and emphatic diction and clear, effective sentence construction, because it must be intelligible to a reader who has not seen the original. The précis is not likely to be so well written as the original, but it should read smoothly and possess compositional merit of its own.

The following is a précis made by a student. Criticize it in terms of the suggestions given above.

ORIGINAL

But as for the bulk of mankind, they are clearly devoid of any degree of taste. It is a quality in which they advance very little beyond a state of infancy. The first thing a child is fond of in a book is a picture, the second is a story, and the third a jest. Here then is the true Pons Asinorum, which very few readers ever get over. (69 words)

—HENRY FIELDING

PRÉCIS

Most people lack taste; they remain childlike. Readers, like children, rarely ever get over the "bridge of asses" constituted by pictures, stories, and jokes. (24 words)

Predicate.   The verb or verb phrase in a sentence which makes a statement—an assertion, an action, a condition, a state of being—about the subject. A *simple predicate* is a verb or a verb phrase alone, without an object or modifiers; a *complete predicate* consists of a verb with its object and all its modifiers; a *compound predicate* consists of two or more verbs or verb phrases.

The next player drove the ball 200 yards down the fairway. [*Drove* is the simple predicate; *drove the ball 200 yards down the fairway* is the complete predicate.] I *wrote* the theme last night and *submitted* it this morning. [Compound predicate]

Predicate complement.   See *Complement.*

Prefix.   A *prefix* is an *affix* (which see) that is put before a word, stem, or word element to add to or qualify its meaning. Here is a brief list of prefixes which appear in a large number of words; approximate meanings are added as an aid to spelling and vocabulary improvement:

a-, ab- (from, away), as in *avert, absent*
ad- (toward, to), as in *adhere, adverb*
ante- (before), as in *antecedent, antedate*
anti- (against, opposite), as in *antidote, antitoxin*
com-, con- (with), as in *commit, confide*
de- (away, down), as in *decline, depressed*
di-, dis- (separation, reversal, apart), as in *divert, disappoint*
e-, ex- (out of, former), as in *elect, exclude, ex-president*
hyper- (over, above), as in *hyperacidity, hypercritical*
in- (not), as in *inexact, invalid*
inter- (between), as in *intercede, intervene*
mis- (wrong, bad), as in *misconduct, mistake*
non- (not, not one), as in *non-American, nonresident*
ob- (against), as in *object, obloquy*
poly- (many), as in *polygamy, polytechnic*
pre- (before), as in *predict, prenatal*
pro- (forward), as in *proceed, propel*
re- (again, back), as in *repay, restore*
sub- (under), as in *subscribe, submarine*
trans- (across), as in *transfer, transport*
ultra- (beyond), as in *ultramodern, ultraviolet*
un- (not), as in *unhappy, untruth*

Preposition. A linking word used to show the relationship of a noun or pronoun to some other word in the sentence. Prepositions show position or direction (*at, with, to, from*) or indicate cause or possession (*because of, of*).

The preposition is nearly always followed by a noun or pronoun (or the equivalent), with which it forms a unit. An exception is the use of prepositions in certain structures with *who* (*whom*), *which*, and *what: "Whom* are you going *with?" "What's* it made *of?"*

Prepositions in common use are *against, ahead of, along, alongside, amid, among, apart from, apropos, around, as far as, as to, at, back of, because of, before, behind, below, beneath, beside, besides, between, beyond, by, concerning, contrary to, despite, down, due to, during, for, from, in, in place of, inside, in spite of, into, in view of, like, near, of, off, on, on account of, onto, out of, over, owing to, past, per, round, since, through, throughout, till, to, toward, under, until, upon, up to, via, with, within.*

In common usage, certain prepositions are used with certain other parts of speech, forming idiomatic combinations (see Section 28).

Principal, principle. The former means "a sum of money" or "a chief person." As an adjective, *principal* means "main" or "chief." *Principle* is always a noun meaning "a governing rule or truth," "a doctrine." ("The *principal* of that school was a man of *principle*.")

Prior than, prior to. Both terms are in common use but only the latter has the sanction of accepted idiom.

Progressive verb form. A statement of continuing action or state of being within a tense, formed by the proper forms of the auxiliary *to be* followed by the present participle:

> We *are preparing* our reports today.
> Tommy *was playing* chess when I arrived.
> *Are* you *arriving* early? We *shall be leaving* before noon.

Prolixity.   The state or quality of being tedious, long, or wordy; speaking or writing at great length. (See *Circumlocution, Conciseness, Deadwood, Redundancy,* and *Tautology.*)

Pronoun.   A substitution for a noun or a noun-equivalent. Every pronoun refers directly or by clear implication to a noun or a noun-equivalent (called the *antecedent* of the pronoun) and agrees with that antecedent in person, number, and gender (but not necessarily in case): "Each boy present will please raise *his* hand."

Pronouns in common use are *I, me, mine, you, yours, he, him, his, she, her, hers, it, its, we, us, ours, they, them, theirs; myself, yourself, yourselves, himself, herself, ourselves, themselves; each other, one another; this, that, these, those, such; each, either, both, some, few, many, much, none, several, all, any, most, anybody, anyone, anything, everybody* (etc.), *nobody, nothing, one, two, three.*

Pronouns, which are used in all the grammatical functions of nouns (as object, subject, etc.), are of several kinds: *personal, relative, demonstrative, interrogative, reflexive (intensive), indefinite,* and *reciprocal* (all of which see). (See also Sections 11d, 12, 63.)

Pronunciation.   The act, or result, of producing the sounds of speech. *Pronunciation* is complex and many-faceted; it involves, among other things, levels of pronunciation, dialect, provincialisms, and spelling. Concerning pronunciation, the single best piece of advice is this: acquire a good dictionary and study its pronunciation key thoroughly.

Proofreading.   When we read, we usually see merely the outlines, or shells, of words. Only poor readers need to see individual letters as such; most of us comprehend words and even groups of words at a glance. As our eyes move along a line, we neither see nor recognize individual letters, and this, of course, is as it should be.

But have you ever noticed how much easier it is for you to detect errors in someone else's writing than in your own? This may be because in reading someone else's writing you are *looking* for mistakes. Or it may be that you look more carefully at the writing of someone else than at your own because you are unfamiliar with it and have to focus more sharply in order to comprehend.

Whatever the reason for closer scrutiny, in proofreading we narrow the range of our vision and thereby pick up mistakes hitherto unnoticed by the writer. In short, we detect careless errors not by reading but by *proofreading.* (See *Vision spread.*)

Proper name.   The name of a particular person, thing, or event: President Johnson, California, Christmas. Proper names and adjectives derived from them are always capitalized.

Proper noun.   A word which usually does not take a limiting modifier, is always capitalized, and is synonymous with *proper name.*

Proportion.   The comparative relationship between things or magnitudes as to size, quantity, number, emphasis, and the like. In writing, proportion usually refers to the relationship between length and emphasis of paragraphs or to the amounts of space given development of different ideas in a letter or report. (See Section 34.)

Proposition.   A mathematical term colloquially much overused for *affair, offer, project, undertaking, proposal,* and similar words.

P.S.   See *I.e.,* etc.

Punctuation.   See Sections 46–60 and *Close and open punctuation.*

Punctuation, purposes of.   Ordinarily you will apply a principle or specific rule of punctuation to a particular instance or sentence element. But it may be helpful in such application to remember that punctuation usually serves one of four purposes:

1. To *end* or *terminate* a statement (use a period, question mark, or exclamation point).

> The dance ended at midnight.
> Are you going home?
> What a play!

2. To *introduce* (use a comma, colon, or dash).

> This dish needs one thing, more salt.
> My purpose is simple: to pass this course.
> My goal in life is simple—success.

3. To *separate* parts of a sentence or word (use a comma, semicolon, dash, hyphen, or apostrophe).

> If you like me at all, try to come to the party.
> Some people prefer dinner at noon; others prefer it in the evening.
> Commas, periods, semicolons, and colons—these are common marks of punctuation.
> Mr. Proctor was elected secretary-treasurer.
> It isn't 9 o'clock yet.

4. To *enclose* parts of a sentence or a whole sentence (use commas, dashes, quotation marks, single quotation marks, parentheses, or brackets). Enclosure marks are used in pairs, except when the capital letter at the beginning of a sentence takes the place of the first or when a terminating mark at the end takes the place of the second.

> You are, my dear Jock, the first one I've asked.
> My dear Jock, you are the first one I've asked.
> You are not—and everyone knows this—a considerate person.
> You are not a considerate person—and everyone knows this.
> "The word 'lousy' is not in reputable use as a term in literary criticism," said the lecturer.
> You are referred to the United States Constitution (see especially Article VIII).
> "Later," the lecturer continued, "he [Hotspur] is killed."

Different marks to indicate these four principal purposes are, obviously, not necessarily interchangeable. The comma and the dash, for example, can serve three of the purposes. In applying to your writing general and specific principles of punctuation and mechanics, answer these questions when you have a problem:

1. What is it here which requires punctuation? That is, what kinds of sentences? What kinds of elements within sentences? What kinds of relationships between elements?

2. What purpose do I wish my punctuation to serve? Termination? Introduction? Separation? Enclosure? What kind of punctuation or mechanics will be correct? Will make for clearness? Add effectiveness?

3. What mark or marks of punctuation or mechanics will best accomplish that purpose?

Quiet, quit, quite.   *Quiet* means "still" or "calm." ("It was a *quiet* meeting.") *Quit* means "to stop," "to desist." ("Did you *quit* working?") *Quite* means "positively," "entirely." ("I am *quite* certain there is a burglar in the house.")

Quite a.   This phrase is colloquial when used to mean "more than." In standard English avoid using such phrases as *quite a few*, *quite a bit*, and *quite a party*.

Rabbit, rarebit.   A *rabbit* is a rodent of the hare family. In standard English there is no such word as *rarebit*. It frequently appears in the phrase *Welsh rarebit* (a dish of melted cheese on toast) but only because of faulty etymology; the correct phrase is *Welsh rabbit*. However, *rare* and *bit* can be correctly used as two words. ("That was a *rare bit* of comedy.")

Raise, raze, rise.   *Raise* means "to elevate," "to lift." ("Please *raise* your eyes and look at me.") *Raze* means "to tear down." ("The wreckers will *raze* this building.") *Rise* means "to get up." ("When the chairman enters, everyone should *rise*.") Strictly, the word *raise* is never a noun; therefore, a few purists consider it colloquial to refer to a *raise* in wages. The word, in standard English, should be *rise,* but *raise* is admittedly far more common. When referring to bringing up children, *rear, raise*, and *bring up* may all be used. *Rear* is preferred in this connection, although *bring up* is also standard; *raise* is colloquial. *To raise Cain, raise the roof, raise a rumpus*, and *raise the devil* are all slang. *To get a rise out of* someone or something is also slang.

Rang, wrung.   *Rang* is the past tense of the verb *ring*, meaning "to give forth a sound." ("He *rang* the bell for ten minutes.") *Wrung* is the past tense of the verb *wring*, "to press or squeeze." ("She *wrung* out the clothes before hanging them on the line.")

Real.   In the sense of "really" or "very," *real* is an impropriety. ("Are you *really*—or *very*—[not *real*] certain of your figures?") Adverbial use of *real* is increasing steadily. (See Section **69**.)

Rear.   See *Raise, raze, rise.*

Reason is because.   In standard English, the construction beginning "The reason is . . ." is followed by a noun or a noun clause usually introduced by *that.* Yet we often hear such a sentence as "I couldn't go; the *reason was because* I had to work." In spite of its form, the construction introduced by *reason was* is a noun clause rather than an adverbial one. But such a use should appear only in colloquial speech. Standard writing requires "I couldn't go; the *reason was that* I had to work." (See Section 10h.)

Reason why.   A redundant expression. Omit *why* and, in most constructions, also omit *reason*. "The *reason why* I like this job is the salary I get" can be improved by writing "I like this job because of the salary."

Receipt, recipe.   Both words mean "a formula" or "directions for making or preparing something." Fastidious users of the language prefer *recipe,* but in this meaning the terms are interchangeable. *Receipt* also means "a written acknowledgment of something received." It is considered badly overworked business jargon in such an expression as "We are in *receipt* of . . ."

Reciprocal pronoun.   A *reciprocal* pronoun indicates an interchange of actions suggested by the verb. This interchange may be seen in the following sentences involving the only two reciprocal pronouns in English:

> The blonde and the brunette complemented *each other.*
> The members of the group shouted at *one another.*

Reckon.   See *Calculate, reckon, guess.*

Redundancy.   An excess; too many words to express an idea; superabundance; superfluity. (See *Prolixity* and the entries there listed.)

Refer, refer back.   *Refer* means "to direct attention" or "to make reference"; therefore, *back* is superfluous. ("Please *refer* [not *refer back*] again to my statement.") The same kind of faulty diction is evident in *repeat again* and *return back.*

Reference books.   As is pointed out in Section 45, you might well begin your research on any subject by reading one or more articles in good reference books. Any book can be used for reference, but those which really merit the name are condensed, authoritative, conveniently arranged, and up to date. In most college libraries, reference books are available on open shelves or on tables in a special reference section or the main reading room.

Your instructor, or the reference librarian, can tell you which of the scores of reference books available to you are likely to be most helpful with a particular subject. In addition, you might examine the following titles for helpful comment on your reference problems:

American Library Association. *Ready Reference Collection.* Chicago: American Library Association, 1962.

Barton, Mary Neill. *Reference Books: A Brief Guide for Students and Other Users of the Library,* 5th ed. Baltimore: Enoch Pratt Free Library, 1962.

Hoffman, Hester R. *Reader's Adviser and Bookman's Manual,* 10th ed. New York: R. R. Bowker Co., 1964.

Murphey, Robert W. *How and Where To Look It Up.* New York: McGraw-Hill Book Co., 1958.

Winchell, Constance M. *Guide to Reference Books,* 7th ed. Chicago: American Library Association, 1951. Supplements.

Reference works are so numerous and so varied in content and quality that no adequate discussion can be provided here. But you should form at least a nodding acquaintance with such important works as these:

General encyclopedias: *Collier's Encyclopedia, Columbia Encyclopedia, Encyclopaedia Britannica, Encyclopedia Americana, Encyclopedia of the Social Sciences, New International Encyclopedia.*

Yearbooks: *Annual Register, Information Please Almanac, International Yearbook and Statesmen's Who's Who, Statistical Abstract of the United States, Who's Who in America, World Almanac and Book of Facts.*

In addition, your library probably has many other encyclopedias, handbooks, and dictionaries. Special reference works are available dealing with subjects such as biography, business and economics, education, drama and the theater, history, language, literature, music and the dance, painting and architecture, philosophy and psychology, religion, and science. Some of these special subject reference books will be useful and helpful. Ferret them out. Once again, a good reference book is the place where you should start—but only *start*—any research project you have.

Reflexive pronoun.　　A *reflexive (intensive)* pronoun is used for simple reference to the subject of a sentence. It is composed of one of the personal pronouns plus *-self* or *-selves.* Called *reflexive* because action of the verb is directed toward the subject, such a pronoun is construed as an adjective when it is used *intensively,* that is, when it emphasizes an antecedent. Most frequently employed reflexive (intensive) pronouns are *myself, yourself, himself, herself, itself, ourselves, yourselves, themselves.*

> His laboratory assistant burned *himself.* [Reflexive use]
> They appointed *themselves* as law enforcement officers. [Reflexive use]
> The nurse *herself* was at fault. [Intensive use]
> We employees *ourselves* are wholly responsible. [Intensive use]

Regard, regards.　　The former is used with *as* to mean "consider" or "think." ("I *regard* her *as* my best friend.") *In regard to* and *with regard to* are idiomatically sound, but both phrases are wordy and jargonistic. In these same phrases, *regards* is nonstandard. Restrict your use of *regards* to the plural form of the noun *regard* and the singular form of the verb.

Regular verb.　　Also called *weak verbs,* regular verbs usually form their past tense and past participle by adding *-d, -ed,* or *-t* to the present infinitive form: *move, moved, moved; help, helped, helped; mean, meant, meant.* (See *Strong verb* and Section **65**.)

Relative pronoun.　　A *relative* pronoun relates or connects a clause to its antecedent. It does have case but no forms distinctive of gender or number. However, the choice of a relative pronoun is determined in part by its antecedent: *who* (or *whom*) is used to refer only to persons; *which* is used in reference to things (inanimate objects, animals) and may be used for a group of persons considered as a group; *that* may refer to either things or persons.

The flyer *who* served in the Korean War is now an airline official.

Radar equipment *which* is to be used for ships must be installed carefully.

The group *which* collected the most old clothing was awarded a prize.

The dress *that* I bought last summer is now out of fashion.

The man *that* [or *whom*] I saw was named Ed Wolcott.

Who, which, and *that* are the most frequently used relative pronouns. *Whoever, whichever,* and *whatever* are less frequently employed compound forms; *whosoever, whichsoever,* and *whatsoever* have gone almost entirely out of current use.

Relative pronouns show the following changes:

Nominative case	who, that, which
Possessive case	whose
Objective case	whom, that, which

Remainder.   See *Balance, remainder.*

Repeat again.   See *Refer, refer back.*

Repetition.   Act of saying or writing again. In writing and speaking, some repetition is a genuine aid in achieving effectiveness; some is merely *deadwood* (which see). Discovering which is which is a large part of the process of learning to write.

Report.   An account presented or a statement made as the result of investigation or observation. A *report* may contain the results of research in office, field, or laboratory, or it may be a recommendation for action or decision. Basically it is an orderly presentation of data, carefully arranged for a specific purpose. Ease of reference and clearness should be its distinguishing characteristics.

Respectfully, respectively.   The former means "in a respectful manner." ("My detailed statement is *respectfully* submitted.") *Respectively* means "severally" or "in specified order." ("*Farewell, au revoir,* and *auf Wiedersehen* are ways of saying "good-bye" in, *respectively,* English, French, and German.")

Return back.   See *Refer, refer back.*

Rhetoric.   The art or science of literary uses of language, the body of principles and theory concerning the presentation of facts and ideas in clear, effective, and pleasing language. Rhetoric is only loosely connected with "grammar" and correctness and with specific details of the mechanics of writing. Substantial elements of rhetoric appear in Sections 13, 14, 15, 29, 30, 40 and in such entries in this Guide as *Beginning, ending sentence; Climactic order; Variety in sentence structure.*

Concern with the effectiveness and general appeal of oral and written communication and with methods of achieving literary quality and persuasive vigor has occupied mankind for many centuries. Along with logic and grammar, rhetoric made up the basic trivium of medieval study, but it had had a long and important career before this. The founder of rhetoric, Corax of Syracuse, laid down fundamental principles for public speech and debate in the fifth century B.C. Aristotle wrote a rhetoric more than 300 years before the Christian era in which he explained rhetoric as the art of giving effectiveness and persuasiveness to truth rather than to the speaker. (The word *rhetoric* comes from a Greek word, *rhetor*, meaning "orator.") Aristotle believed that rhetoric depended upon, and derived from, proof and logic and that its values could be taught as systematized principles. He distinguished between the appeal of rhetoric to man's intellect and the presentation of ideas emotionally and imaginatively which he discussed in his treatment of poetics.

However, many philosophers and orators through the centuries have tried to make rhetoric a mere tool of argumentation and persuasiveness without regard for truth or the validity of their points of view. Plato himself condemned rhetoric because he felt that many who practiced it used questionable techniques and had an unwholesome influence on public life; he also quoted Socrates as declaring rhetoric "superficial." One Greek philosopher referred to rhetoric as "the art of making great matters small and small things great." This tendency to downgrade rhetoric still persists as when we say that something is "mere rhetoric," meaning something empty, showy, without genuine substance.

It is undeniable that some modern politicians and writers use tricks of presentation to conceal bombast, paucity of thought, and outright dishonesty. But it is equally true that *how* we say or write something is important; that legitimate and time-tested rhetorical devices can increase the value and appeal of our writing and speaking; that although rhetoric without intellect is ineffective, so, too, are fact unadorned and opinion presented bare. (See, especially, Chapter 6.)

Rhetorical question.   A query designed to produce an effect and not to draw an answer. It is used to introduce a topic or emphasize a point; no answer is expected.

Rhyme.   Words or verses which agree in their terminal (end) sounds. Rhyme occurs when the accented vowels of two words and all succeeding sounds in the words are identical: *rain, stain*.

Rhythm.   Uniform recurrence of a beat or accent. In English prose, rhythm is marked by variety of movement. Reading aloud is the best method of detecting the rise and fall of prose and its repetition of stresses. Good prose writers achieve rhythmic patterns, but not, of course, in the metrical way which poets do. Among the many contributors to rhythm in prose are balanced sentences, variety in sentence length and structure, transitional devices, euphony, effective beginnings and endings of sentences.

Rise.   See *Raise, raze, rise*.

Roman numerals.   Our present numbers (1, 2, 3, 4, etc.) came to us from the Arabs and are called Arabic numerals. Although these are generally preferable, Roman numerals still find occasional use in current writing: numbering the preliminary pages of a book, marking year dates, and frequently indicating acts of plays, volume numbers of books and magazines, and chapter numbers of books.

George I, George II, and George III reigned in the eighteenth century, George V and George VI in the twentieth.

Prince Hal and Falstaff first appear in Act I, Scene 2, of Shakespeare's *Henry IV, Part I.*

This imposing building bears the date when it was constructed— MDCCCLXXIV.

Notice how Roman numerals are formed: a repeated letter repeats its value; a letter placed after one of greater value adds to it; a letter placed before one of greater value subtracts from it; a dashline over a letter denotes "multiplied by 1,000."

ROMAN NUMERALS

I	1	XXV	25	CD	400		
II	2	XXX	30	D	500		
III	3	XL	40	DC	600		
IV	4	L	50	DCC	700		
V	5	LXXXV	85	DCCC	800		
VI	6	LXXXIX	89	CM	900		
VII	7	XC	90	M	1,000		
VIII	8	XCV	95	MD	1,500		
IX	9	XCIX	99	MM	2,000		
X	10	C	100	MMM	3,000		
XV	15	CL	150	MMMM	4,000		
XIX	19	CC	200	$\overline{V}$	5,000		
XX	20	CCC	300	$\overline{M}$	1,000,000		

Root. In linguistics, the base of a word is a *root*, a morpheme to which may be added prefixes and suffixes. An approximate synonym for *base* and *root* in this sense is *stem;* all mean the part of a word to which suffixes and prefixes are added or in which phonetic changes are made. Thus we say that *love* is the root (stem or base) of the word *loveliness, form* of the word *reform,* and so on.

Sagging sentence. A sagging sentence loses force as it proceeds and tapers off at the end. This flaw results primarily from improper word order. (See *Climactic order.*)

Said, same, such. As an adjective, *said* is used in legal writing but is considered to be jargon in standard English. Unless you're a lawyer (or a lawyer's secretary), avoid such expressions as *said party, said person,* and *said proposal. Same* as a pronoun is also characteristic of legal and business use. Lawyers may insist upon its retention, but businessmen in general and you in particular should avoid such expressions as "check enclosed in payment for *same.*" *Such* may be an adjective, an adverb, and a pronoun—all with standard uses. It is considered colloquial, however, when used in place of a demonstrative. ("I could not tolerate *that* [not *such*].") *Such* is also colloquial when used as an intensifier. ("She is *a very* [not *such a*] charming person.")

Saw, seen. The principal parts of *to see* are *see, saw, seen. Seen* is improperly used as the past tense; *saw* is incorrect as the past participle. ("I *saw* [not *seen*] you yesterday." "I *have seen* [not *have saw*] you every day this week.")

Schoolgirl style.   A rather unchivalrous and unkind term for a manner of writing characterized by gushiness, exaggeration, and overuse of intensifiers. Counter words, triple underlinings, exclamation points, and dashes are used freely. As indicated, maturity and restraint are at a premium. Mechanical forms of emphasis are always self-defeating. (See Section 29c.)

Schwa.   See *Unstressed vowels*.

-sede.   See *-cede, -ceed, -sede*.

Semantics.   *Semantics* is the study of word meanings and changes of meaning. Specifically, semantics (1) refers to that branch of *linguistics* (which see) that deals with word meanings and historical changes in meaning and (2) involves a study of the relations among signs (words, symbols), their meanings, and the mental or physical actions called forth by them. As the science of meanings, semantics is contrasted with *phonetics*, the science of speech sounds and their production.

Man, so far as we now know, is the only creature capable of inventing symbol systems—such as mathematics and the English language—with which to record and evaluate his past and present and to plan his future. The conscious and systematic study of the role of human symbols in the lives of individuals and groups is known as "general semantics." The word "semantics" comes from the Greek *semainein*, "to mean," "to signify." But general semantics is concerned with meanings more than merely in their "dictionary sense." It involves several kinds of meaning, both verbal and nonverbal, and their importance in our private lives and our public affairs.

Like words, sentences, too, have meanings, and so do paragraphs, chapters, essays, songs, plays, poems, and books. But you cannot find the meaning of a paragraph or a poem by looking up in a dictionary the meaning of each of its words. Nor will you, as the late Wendell Johnson remarked, find the meaning of a particular sunset in the dictionary: you will find it only in yourself—in your own feelings and thoughts, in what you say and do. The meanings of words are no more in the words than is the meaning of a willow tree in a willow; the meanings of words are in the person who responds to them, or writes them, just as the meanings of "a green meadow are the children who chase butterflies across it, the artist who paints it, the cows who graze upon it, or the old soldier who remembers the battle that once was fought across its green slope" (Johnson).

To the general semanticist, the study of words is not simply the study of words, or paintings, or musical scores. Rather, the study of words includes a study of human beings and what words and paintings and musical scores mean to them. To discover what such things mean to people is to observe what people do to, with, and about them. Therefore, general semantics deals with *symbolic behavior*, its patterns, its principles, its effects on man and his world, and with the conditions of its changes from time to time in the lives of men and their societies.

In summary, general semantics is concerned not only with word meanings but also with a study of human beings and what words mean to them at different times and under different circumstances. (For further comment and clarification, see the Sherwood article beginning on p. 618.)

Sensual, sensuous. The former refers to gratification of the more gross bodily pleasures or appetites. *Sensuous* suggests the appeal of that which is pleasing to the senses. ("In his abandon he indulged in every *sensual* excess he could imagine." "He loved the *sensuous* music.")

Sentence, arrangement of content. Sentences may be classified according to the *arrangement* of their content.

A sentence in which the words are so set down that the meaning is not completed until the end or near the end is called *periodic*.

A sentence so constructed that the thought may be completed before the end is termed *loose*.

Our conversation and informal writing contain many more loose sentences than periodic. Yet a periodic sentence does provide suspense and variety; it holds the attention of reader or listener and contributes to stylistic effectiveness. Although a natural form of expression, the periodic sentence tends to become monotonous and forced and should not be overused.

Act quickly or you will be too late to buy the food you wish. [Loose]
He liked to play chess and bridge but more than either he enjoyed swimming and ice-skating. [Loose]
If you do not wish to pay this debt, please say so. [Periodic]
According to a former college president, to be at home in all lands and ages; to count Nature a familiar acquaintance and Art a familiar friend; to gain a standard for the appreciation of other men's work and the criticism of one's own; to make friends among men and women of one's own age who are to be the leaders in all walks of life; to lose one's self in generous enthusiasm and to cooperate with others for common ends; to learn manners from students who are gentlemen and gentlewomen; and to form character under professors who are dedicated—these are the returns of a college for the best four years of one's life. [Periodic]

A *balanced sentence* is so constructed that similar or opposing thoughts have similar structure. Such a sentence is sometimes used to make a statement especially emphatic and for comparisons and contrasts.

You can take a man out of the country; you can't take the "country" out of a man.
You may call him the man who invented evil, but I would say he is the man whom evil invented.

Sentence, grammatical structure of. Sentences may be classified according to grammatical structure as *simple, compound, complex,* or *compound-complex.*

A *simple sentence* contains only one subject (simple or compound) and one predicate (simple or compound) and expresses only one thought:

The road is dusty.
The boy and the girl ate and drank.

A *compound sentence* contains two or more independent clauses. The clauses of a compound sentence are grammatically capable of standing alone, but they are closely related parts of one main idea:

> She read and I listened to the radio.
> The nights are long but the days seem short.

A *complex sentence* contains one independent clause and one or more dependent (subordinate) clauses:

> Carol said that she had walked for several blocks.
> He is an athlete whose muscles are unusually pliant.

A *compound-complex sentence* contains two or more independent clauses and one or more dependent clauses:

> Since the day was unpleasant, we stayed indoors; Judy looked at TV and Ned wrote several letters.

Sentence, meaning and purpose of.   Sentences may be classified according to *meaning* and *purpose*.

A *declarative sentence* states a fact or makes an assertion:

> The car has eight cylinders.

An *interrogative sentence* asks a question:

> Does the car have eight cylinders?

An *imperative sentence* expresses an entreaty or command:

> Please lend me the money now.

An *exclamatory sentence* expresses strong feeling:

> Oh, if he were only my friend!
> Thank goodness, you are safe!

Sentence, sagging.   See *Sagging sentence* and also *Climactic order*.

Separating punctuation.   See *Punctuation, purposes of*.

Set.   See *Sit, set*.

Setup.   In the sense of "an easy victory," this term is slang. More importantly, *setup* is now being used widely to refer to anything related to organization, conditions, or circumstances. ("What's the new *setup*?") The term is vague, at best. Try to find something less used and more exact.

Shall, will.   Distinctions in the use of *shall* and *will* have largely broken down, but a few careful speakers and writers still observe them.

1. Use *shall* in the first person and *will* in the second and third persons to express *simple futurity*. ("I *shall* go." "You [or He] *will* go.")
2. For *emphasis*, to express *determination, command, intention,* or *promise,* use *will* in the first person and *shall* in the second and third persons. ("I *will* speak, no matter what the result may be." "You *shall* speak," meaning "You must speak.")

Shifts.   This is a term applied to *shifted constructions* and refers to elements which have the same relationship to the statement being made but not the same grammatical structure. Adjectives should be paralleled by adjectives, nouns by nouns, and so on; shifting from one form to another may confuse a reader. (See Section 11.)

Shoptalk. The specialized or technical vocabulary and idioms of those in the same work, the same way of life. That is, *shoptalk* is the colloquial language people use in discussing their particular line of work. To "talk shop" is the verb form of this expression. (See Section 23c.)

Should of. See *Of*.

Should, would. In general, use *should* and *would* according to the rules for *shall* and *will* (which see). The following may be helpful:

1. *Should*

Obligation—"I *should* read more than I do."

Expectation (a corollary of obligation)—"They *should* be here by this time."

Condition—"If he *should* speak, listen carefully."

Simple future (first person only)—"I *should* like to go."

2. *Would*

Habitual action—"He *would* walk in the woods every day."

Condition (*after* a conditional clause)—"If the weather were good, he *would* walk in the park."

Determination—"He *would* do it, no matter how much we protested."

Wish or desire—"*Would* I had gone with you!"

Simple future (second and third persons only)—"He said that he *would* go." (If the governing verb is in the past tense, use *would* to express futurity, as above. If the governing verb is in the present tense, use *will:* "He *indicates* that he *will* help us.") (See Section 67c.)

Silent letters. Some spelling authorities believe that the single greatest cause of misspelling connected with pronunciation is the silent letter. Sounds have been dropping out of our language for many centuries, but their disappearance has affected pronunciation much more than spelling. Actually, many letters no longer pronounced in certain words persist in our spelling "without rhyme or reason." For example, the *l* in such words as *could, would,* and *should* has been silent for hundreds of years.

The problem is compounded when we realize that the majority of the letters of our alphabet appear as silent letters in one word or another:

a is silent in *dead*	*l* is silent in *salmon*
b is silent in *doubt*	*m* is silent in *mnemonics*
c is silent in *scene*	*n* is silent in *column*
d is silent in *handsome*	*o* is silent in *too*
e is silent in *come*	*p* is silent in *raspberry*
f is silent in *off*	*t* is silent in *often*
g is silent in *sign*	*u* is silent in *guess*
h is silent in *honest*	*w* is silent in *answer*
i is silent in *weird*	*ch* is silent in *yacht*
k is silent in *knife*	*gh* is silent in *bough*

Most silent letters cause little difficulty in spelling. If you are visual-minded, you will automatically put a *k* in *knee* or a *g* in *gnat*. But some letters which are silent, or are so lightly sounded as to be almost unheard, do cause trouble. Here is a list of some common words which, in the pronunciation of most educated people, contain silent letters:

align	ghastly	knit	psychology
benign	ghost	knob	through
bomb	gnat	knock	thumb
comb	gnaw	knot	tomb
condemn	hymn	know	wrap
daughter	indebted	knuckle	wreck
dough	knack	plumber	wrench
dumb	knave	pneumonia	wretch
eight	knee	prompt	wring
fourth	kneel	psalm	write

Simile. A simile is a figure of speech by which are compared two things essentially different but thought to be alike in one or more respects. The point of resemblance is expressed by *like, as, as if:* "as sweet as candy." (See *Metaphor* and Section 26.)

Simple sentence. A sentence containing only one subject (simple or compound) and one predicate (simple or compound) and expressing only one thought (see *Sentence, grammatical structure of*).

Sit, set. *Sit,* predominantly an intransitive verb, not requiring an object, has the meaning of "to place oneself." *Set,* predominantly a transitive verb, requiring an object, means "to put" or "to place." ("*Set* the book on the table and come *sit* here.") *Set* used for *sit* in the meaning shown is dialectal or an impropriety. However, both words have several special meanings. For example, *set* has an intransitive use, as in "The sun *sets* early tonight."

Snafu. Military slang for "*s*ituation *n*ormal, *a*ll *f*ouled *u*p."

So. See *Overuse of "so."*

So as. See *As*.

Social correspondence. See *Letters*.

Sort of a. See *Kind of a, sort of a*.

Speech sounds. Scholars are agreed that the total number of speech sounds used by those who speak English is about 50. To express these sounds we have only 26 letters in our alphabet and they appear in about 250 spelling combinations. For example, there are 11 ways of spelling the sound of long *e*, the initial sound in *equal:*

1. eve	5. people	9. piece
2. seed	6. key	10. amoeba
3. read	7. quay	11. Caesar
4. receive	8. police	

This is entirely illogical, isn't it? Of course. But the situation is not hopeless.

Actually, some relationship often exists between sound and spelling; a large number of words are spelled exactly as they sound, and many others have sounds and spellings almost alike. The words *bat, red,* and *top* are spelled as they sound to most people. Many longer words are also spelled as they sound, especially if you break them into syllables: *lone-li-ness, mem-o-ry, part-ner.*

Moreover, many words which differ most in sound and spelling are those which you rarely use. Like almost everyone else, including good spellers, you look up such words in a dictionary before attempting to write them; they do not have to be learned. Few people can spell, on demand, such words as *flocculent* and *phthisic.* They consult a dictionary. So should you.

Spelling.   The one thing demanded of anyone who has had educational advantages is that he be able to spell. In your daily work or in social situations, you may not need to be able to add a column of figures. Few people will care. Not often will you be thought stupid if you don't know the dates of historical events—say, the Battle of Waterloo. Your knowledge of economics can be nil. You may not know the difference between an oboe and an ibis, an atom and a molecule. But if you can't spell, you're in trouble. Rightly or wrongly, fairly or unfairly, misspelling is the most frequently accepted sign of illiteracy.

Why is this? You can argue that the ability to think clearly is far more important than spelling. So are clear expression of thoughts, an attractive personality, and demonstrated ability in one's job. The fact remains that incorrect spelling is heavily penalized in our society—so heavily that it keeps people from getting jobs they want or prevents them from moving up to better positions. Inability to spell gives people complexes just as much as unsureness about grammar or proper methods of dress and social behavior.

The main reason for this somewhat illogical reliance on spelling as an index of intelligence and literacy is that correct spelling is the one fixed and certain thing about our language. The overwhelming majority of English words are spelled in only one way; all other ways are wrong. The accepted system *is* accepted. It is the system in which our business communications, our magazines, our newspapers, and our books have been written for generations. This uniformity applies to no other aspect of our language.

Study carefully all of Section **16.** Additional aids to spelling correctly will be found in the following entries in this Guide: *-able; Ad-; Added vowels; -ally; -ly; -ance, -ence; Ante-, anti-; -ar, -er, -or; -ary, -ery; De-, dis-, dys-; Dropped consonants; Dropped vowels; -efy, -ify; Foreign plurals; -ible; Inter-; Irregular plurals; -ise, -ize, -yze; K inserted; Plurals; Prefix; Silent letters; Speech sounds; Un-; Unstressed vowels; -wise.*

Standard English.   Language used in the conduct of public affairs, in various types of literature, in letters and documents carefully prepared, in magazines, speeches, and books. It is not necessarily overprecise and pedantic, nor does it rule out all colloquialisms and everyday expressions.

No standards of diction can be absolute, but it is safe to say that standard English is that which is used by reputable speakers and writers. Such usage is never fixed but changes constantly as the product of custom or of appropriateness of words to context. A writer's vocabulary is the *number* of words he can command; a writer's diction is the *kind* of words he uses. Words once considered not acceptable are now sanctioned, and vice versa. Diction ranges from philosophical abstractness to racy slang, from lofty utterances to the dialect of *Huckleberry Finn.* No single word is in itself standard, or substandard, for a word perfect in one context may be inappropriate in another. But general principles applying to standard usage have remained constant and may serve as guides: words should be in *present* use, in *national* use, and in *reputable* use. (See *Appropriateness, Levels of usage.*)

Stationary, stationery.   The former means "having a fixed or unmoving position." ("This rock is *stationary.*") *Stationery* means "paper for writing." ("This is new *stationery.*")

Statue, stature, statute.   A *statue* is a sculptured likeness. ("This is a *statue* of Robert E. Lee.") *Stature* is often used figuratively ("a man of moral *stature*"). A *statute* is a law. ("This *statute* forbids kissing in public.")

Stress.   See *Pitch.*

Strong verb.   Sometimes called *irregular,* strong verbs do not follow a regular pattern in forming their principal parts. Principal parts of irregular verbs are usually formed by vowel change: *see, saw, seen; drive, drove, driven; choose, chose, chosen.* Let the dictionary be your guide. (See *Regular verb* and Section **65.**)

Style.   This term has been defined in many ways but never satisfactorily, since every writer and speaker has his own notion of its meaning. In general, *style* is a "manner or mode of expression in language, a way of putting thoughts into words." It also refers to a specific or characteristic manner of expression or construction. An author's or speaker's style is the impress (influence) of his personality upon his subject matter.

Think of *mood* and *impression* as the mental or physical atmosphere that a writer creates to surround his reader and wants the reader to receive. Think of *style,* which occasionally may include mood and impression, as mainly the manner in which a writer expresses himself. In that expression, variety of phrase, clause, and sentence patterns is not only consistent but desirable. Consistency in style is also a matter of word choice. What kind of style are you aiming at? Formal? Dignified? Conversational? Simple? Archaic? Quaint? Whimsical? Flippant? Humorous? Breezy? Breathless? Concise? Whatever it is, be consistent in choosing and arranging words.

Subject.   The person or thing (noun, pronoun, noun phrase, noun clause) about which a statement or assertion is made in a sentence or clause. A *simple subject* is the noun or pronoun alone. A *complete subject* is a simple subject together with its modifiers. A *compound subject* consists of two or more nouns, pronouns, noun phrases, noun clauses.

The *bungalow* is for sale. [Simple subject]
The *yellow bungalow on the hill* is for sale. [Complete subject]

The *yellow bungalow and two acres of land* are for sale. [Compound subject]

What you think and what you want are no concern of mine. [Compound subject]

Subjunctive. The mood of a verb expressing desire, possibility, etc. (See *Mood.*)

Subordination. Like appropriate *coordination* (which see), appropriate subordination contributes to clear and effective writing by showing the relationship of less important to more important ideas.

Careful, thoughtful writing contains much subordination. Actually, the work of nearly all skilled writers abounds in subordination. Such work clearly communicates to readers because they can see what the relationships involved really are. Two important steps: (1) avoid faulty subordination (see Section 9); (2) reduce predication (see Section 15a).

Substantive. An inclusive term for noun, pronoun, verbal noun (gerund, infinitive), or a phrase or a clause used like a noun. The practical value of the word *substantive* is that it saves repeating all the words included in this definition. The following italicized words are examples of substantives:

My *hat* is three years old. [Noun]

They will leave tomorrow; in fact, *everyone* is leaving tomorrow. [Pronouns]

Your *leaving* is looked forward to. [Gerund]

To better myself is my *purpose*. [Infinitive, noun]

From Chicago to Los Angeles is a long distance. [Noun phrase]

What you think is *no problem of mine*. [Noun clause, noun phrase]

Do *you* know *that he is a thief*? [Pronoun, noun clause]

Suffix. A sound, syllable, or syllables added at the end of a word or word base to change its meaning, give it grammatical function, or form a new word: *-er* in *smaller*, *-ness* in *happiness*. (See *Affixes.*)

Summary. "You went to the movies last night, didn't you? What was the picture about?" "What did you do in the city this afternoon?" "Write a brief statement concerning the essential ideas in Thackeray's essay on Addison." All such questions, asked in conversation and on examinations, require summarizing answers—an indispensable form of communication in modern college life. Many times each day we are called upon to give, in written or oral form, condensed versions of events, ideas, or impressions.

In fact, the method of summary is generally prevalent. Such a popular magazine as *The Reader's Digest* is partly composed of summaries of more detailed articles in other magazines, and the editorial technique involved has been empolyed by dozens of imitative "digest" magazines. (Not all of these use straight condensation, not even *The Reader's Digest* itself: frequently the shortened article results from excerpting rather than from digesting.) Periodicals and clubs publish digests of entire books; TV and radio news commentators often furnish what are essentially summaries of the latest news developments. Magazines such as *Time* and *Newsweek* contain short articles which are, in one sense, condensations of events. Business executives frequently ask employees for brief reports concerning developments in departments or trends in business.

Such brief, comprehensive presentations of facts may be called summaries. A *summary* is a terse restatement of main points, as, for example, a summary of a chapter. It is related in meaning to *digest*, *résumé*, and *synopsis*, although the last-named is usually applied to a compressed statement of the plot of a play, story, or novel, rather than to expository prose.

Superlative degree.   The form of an adjective or adverb comparing three or more objects, persons, or ideas. (See Section 69e.)

> Of the three brothers, Albert is the *youngest*.
> In our family Mother is the one who drives *most recklessly*.

Sure.   This word is used as adjective or adverb, but it is colloquial in the sense of "surely," "certainly," "indeed." ("He was *certainly* [not *sure*] angry with the policeman.") *Sure* is also colloquial in such expressions as *sure enough* (meaning both "certainly" and "real") and *sure-fire* (meaning "certain to be successful"). (See *Be sure and*.)

Sure thing, a.   A slang expression.

Swell.   This word is not acceptable in standard English as a modifier. It is colloquial when used to mean "stylish," "fashionable," and it is slang when used as a general term of approval meaning "excellent." ("That was *an excellent* [not *a swell*] meal.") In the meaning of "conceited," *swelled head* is considered colloquial or slangy.

Syllable.   In phonetics, a *syllable* is a segment of speech uttered with one impulse of air pressure from the lungs. In writing, *syllable* refers to a character or set of characters (letters of the alphabet) representing one sound. In general, *syllable* refers to the smallest amount or unit of speech or writing.

Synonym.   A word having the same meaning, part of the same meaning, or nearly the same meaning as another: *cold, chill, chilling, chilly; hotel, inn, tavern; prevent, forestall, preclude, obviate, avert.* (See *Antonym*.)

Syntax.   The arrangement of words in a sentence to show their relationship. It is a rather vague and general term, but one for which our language has no adequate substitute. Although *syntax* is a branch of *grammar*, the latter term is more useful in referring to word order, parts of speech, and the like.

Take.   *Take* is a good, simple, useful word, but it appears in many expressions which are substandard. For example, *take and* is a colloquial and wordy expression. In the sentence, "He *took and* beat the horse unmercifully," *took and* should be omitted entirely. *Take* is colloquial or dialectal in *he took sick, she takes well* (she photographs well), *the day's take* (money or profit received), *take someone for* (cheat), *take it* (withstand difficulty, hardship), *take it lying down* (submit without protest), *take it on the chin* (undergo punishment or pain), *take it out of* (tire, exhaust), *take it out on* (make another suffer), *take on* (show emotion such as sorrow or anger), *take-in* (trickery), *take-off* (an amusing or mocking imitation), *taking* (contagious, said of a disease).

Take it easy. A trite expression which is used *ad nauseam*. So, also, is *take my word for it.*

Tasteful, tasty. The former means "having or showing good taste, sense, or judgment." *Tasty* means "flavorful," "savory," "having the quality of tasting good." ("The reception was a *tasteful* affair and the food served at it was *tasty*.") *Tasteful* for *tasty* is in rare or archaic use; *tasty* for *tasteful* is colloquial.

Tautology. Needless repetition of an idea in a different word, phrase, clause, or sentence. (See *Deadwood*.)

Technical terms. Terms which have special meanings for people in particular fields, occupations, or professions. Special subject labels are attached by dictionaries to such words in the fields of astronomy, engineering, psychology, and the like. Technical terms should be used sparingly in writing for the general public and, when so employed, may be enclosed in quotation marks—at least the first time they are used—and usually should be defined. (See Sections 23c, 41a.)

Telegraphic style. The clipped, abbreviated style employed in telegrams to save on words: "[Your] letter [has been] received. [I am] answering immediately. [Please accept my warm] regards."

Terminating punctuation. See *Punctuation, purposes of*.

Their, there, they're. These simple and common words cause much difficulty, but they are easy to keep straight. *Their* is a possessive pronoun. ("This is *their* house.") *There* means "in or at that place." ("Were you *there* when she arrived?") *They're* is a contraction of *they are*. ("We are disappointed because *they're* not coming.")

Theme. This word means "topic," "subject." When, for example, we speak of the *theme* of a play or a musical composition, we mean its controlling idea, its central subject matter and content. Also, a short, informal essay, such as a school composition, is known as a *theme*. (See Section 43.)

Then, than. These words are often confused in writing and sometimes in pronunciation. *Than* is a conjunction used in clauses of comparison. ("He worked better today *than* he did yesterday.") *Then* is an adverb of time. ("We *then* went to a restaurant.")

There. See *Expletive*.

These kind, those kind, these sort, those sort. *Kind* and *sort* are singular nouns; *these* and *those* are plural modifiers. Say and write *this kind, those kinds, this sort, those sorts*. (See *Kind of a, sort of a*.)

Thesis. A proposition stated or laid down and intended to be discussed, defended, and proved. *Thesis* is also a somewhat loose synonym for *theme* in the sense of "subject" or "content." (See Section 45a, Part 4.)

Throw a curve. See *Curve*.

Thusly. An illiteracy. Use *thus*.

Till, until, 'til. Each of these words means "up to the time of." *Till* and *'til* (a shortened form of *until*) have the same pronunciation and are more often used within a sentence than at the beginning. *Until* more often appears at the beginnings of sentences and is sometimes considered somewhat more formal than its two synonyms. All three terms are correct in standard English.

To, too, two.   Correct use of these words is largely a matter of careful spelling. *To* is a preposition (*"to* the store") and the sign of an infinitive (*"to* work"). *Too* is an adverb meaning "also" or "overabundance of." ("We *too* are working, but Jack is *too* lazy *to* get up.") *Two* is the number after one. ("The *two* secretaries were *too* tired *to* go.")

Tone.   The word *tone* has many different meanings, one of which refers to the general or prevailing character, trend, or quality of social or moral behavior: "this school's academic tone," "the moral tone of the city." In writing, *tone* is used to refer to the character or appeal or point of view of a given selection and of its author. Specifically, *tone* in this sense has approximately the meaning of *attitude* and refers to the approach of the writer to his material and to the effect he intends his work to have on his audience. When the tone of a piece of writing is serious or ironic, solemn, playful, formal, intimate, or informal, obviously the selection and its effect on readers are strongly influenced. The word is applied not only to an author but to the work itself and the various stylistic elements and devices (such as sentence structure, diction, imagery, and the like) which in combination contribute to character and appeal.

Two seventeenth-century poets, in dealing with the *carpe diem* theory (enjoy life today with no thought for tomorrow), exhibit markedly different *tones* in their point of view and in the stylistic devices they use. The former is gentle, relaxed, softly persuasive; even in such a poetic matter as assonance his appeal is happy and even gay:

> Gather ye rosebuds while ye may,
> Old time is still a-flying;
> And this same flower that smiles today
> Tomorrow will be dying.
> —ROBERT HERRICK

Notice the rough and strident sound, the passionate appeal, the urgent and even harsh call to action in these contrasting lines:

> Let us roll all our strength and all
> Our sweetness up into one ball,
> And tear our pleasures with rough strife
> Thorough the iron gates of life.
> —ANDREW MARVELL

In a quite different sense, the word *tone* distinguishes a characteristic of tenses of verbs, indicating within any one tense *emphasis* or *progress* or *simple* time: "I still *do* work." "I *was leaving* when you called." "I *mailed* the package." (See Section **67b.**)

Topic sentence.   A *topic sentence*, or statement, gives the subject of a paragraph. It states, suggests, or in some other way indicates the heart, the core, of the idea which is to be, is being, or has been developed. As the preceding sentence implies, a topic sentence may appear at various places within a paragraph.

Usually, the first sentence of a paragraph is the topic sentence. However, a topic sentence need not be a *sentence* at all: the subject of a paragraph may be suggested in a dependent clause, in a phrase, even in a single word. Also, a topic sentence need not be actually expressed; even so, every good, unified paragraph is so well knit that a reader, reflecting, can sum up the central thought of the paragraph in his own words.

As a check on the presence or absence of a paragraph topic, reread every paragraph you write. If you cannot locate or phrase a topic sentence to cover the contents of a paragraph, then rewriting is indicated. (See Section 32.)

Transition. Passage from one area, position, state, or stage to another. In writing and speaking, *transition* refers to methods by which writer and speaker bridge gaps between what has been covered and what is to come. (See Section 44b.)

Transitive verb. Verbs are classified as either transitive or intransitive. A *transitive* verb is regularly accompanied by a direct object; this direct object completes the meaning of the verb: "They *refused* his resignation." An *intransitive* verb requires no direct object: "He *will obey*." Whether a verb is transitive or intransitive depends upon meaning, upon the idea which the writer wishes to show: *will obey* in "He *will obey* our orders" is transitive.

Triteness. State of being worn out, overused, hackneyed by constant repetition (see Section 22).

Try and, try to. The correct idiom is *try to*. However, *try and* is in everyday use and has been for a century. Standard English would have you write "*Try to* [not *try and*] finish your work early."

Un-. When this prefix is added to a root word beginning with *n*, neither *n* is omitted (see Section 16e, *"One-plus-one" rule*).

unnamed	unneighborly	unnoticeable
unnatural	unnerved	unnoticed
unnecessary	unnoted	unnumbered

Uninterested. See *Disinterested, uninterested.*

Unique. This word means "having no like or equal" and expresses absoluteness as do words such as *round, square, perpendicular*. Logically, therefore, the word *unique* cannot be compared; something cannot be "more unique," "less unique," "more round," "less round." If a qualifying word such as *nearly* is used, the illogicality is removed. "This is the *most unique* painting in the museum" is not standard, but "This is the *most nearly unique* painting . . ." is. (See Section 69e.)

Unity. A term meaning "oneness." In writing and speaking, it refers to sentences, paragraphs, and themes which stick to their subjects and permit no extraneous material to filter in. *Unity* is a by-product of clear, careful thinking. (See Sections 14, 32, 43.)

Unmoral, amoral, immoral. *Unmoral* means "having no morality," "nonmoral," "unable to distinguish right from wrong." Thus we may say that an infant or a mentally disordered person is *unmoral*. *Amoral* means "not concerned with moral standards," "not to be judged by criteria or standards of morality." Morons and animals, for example, may be called *amoral. Immoral* means "wicked," "contrary to accepted principles of right and wrong." The acts of thieves, murderers, and embezzlers may be called *immoral*.

Unnecessary capitals.   Capitals are often overused or wrongly used. It is as great a mistake to use a capital letter when it is not called for as to fail to use one when it is needed. (See Section 55.)

1. If the reference is to *any one* of a class of persons or things rather than to a specific person or thing, do not capitalize the noun or the adjective:

> He is a general. He is General John Jones.
> I am going to a theater. I am going to the Bijou Theater.
> He is a vice-president of this company. This is Vice-president [*or* Vice-President] Samuel Jones.
> I attended high school. I attended Henry Hudson High School.

2. Do not carelessly make small (lower-case) letters so large that they resemble capitals (upper-case letters).

3. Do not capitalize names of points of the compass unless they refer to a specific geographical section:

Correct	He lives in the West.
	He walked south along the avenue.

4. Do not capitalize nouns such as *father* and *mother* if they are preceded by a possessive:

Correct	My father is a tall man.
	I love Mother very much.
	Your sister thinks I am quiet, but Grandma says I talk entirely too much.

Unnecessary commas.   Comma usage varies with different writers, but every comma used must be needed for sense construction. Modern punctuation usage omits more commas than formerly; therefore, be able to account for each comma you use. (See *Close and open punctuation* and Section 47t.)

Unpractical, impractical, impracticable.   The first two of these terms are interchangeable, although *impractical* is considered by some writers as being slightly more formal and refined. Each means "not practical," "lacking practical usefulness or wisdom." *Impracticable* means "not capable of being carried out, used, or managed." ("The piccolo player was a good man but thoroughly *impractical*." "The manager considered my plan *impracticable*.") (See *Impractical, impracticable*.)

Unstressed vowels.   No words in English are more often misspelled than those which contain unstressed (or lightly stressed) vowels. An unstressed vowel, like the *a* in *dollar*, is uttered with little force; its sound is faint, indistinct, blurred.

A technical name and symbol, *schwa* (ə), are used to indicate this sound of unstressed vowels. It resembles a kind of "uh," a quiet sound much less vigorous than the stronger "uh" sound found in such words as *flood* and *rush*.

This unstressed vowel sound may be represented in spelling by any one of the vowels: *a, e, i, o, u.*

> *a:* gramm*a*r, sof*a*, *a*bove, *a*go, *a*long
> *e:* corn*e*r, mod*e*l, *e*stablish, syst*e*m
> *i:* nad*i*r, per*i*l, or*i*gin, san*i*ty
> *o:* profess*o*r, spons*o*r, *o*ccur, gall*o*n
> *u:* murm*u*r, sulf*u*r, lux*u*ry, foc*u*s, circ*u*s

The letter *y* is sometimes a vowel also. Its unstressed sound is illustrated in the word *martyr.*

Although the schwa sound ("uh") is the most frequent unstressed vowel sound, it is not the only one. An unstressed *i* sound appears in such words as *solid* but is not always spelled as *i;* note, for example, such words as *private, women,* and *busy.* Still other unstressed vowel sounds occur in American speech, but isolating them is not helpful in learning to spell. Here is a representative list of everyday words often misspelled because of the unstressed vowels they contain:

academy	democracy	hangar	possible
accident	describe	humorous	private
actor	despair	hunger	privilege
applicant	develop	hypocrisy	propaganda
arithmetic	dilute	loafer	repetition
benefit	discipline	maintenance	respectable
busy	distress	martyr	ridiculous
calendar	dollar	mathematics	separate
category	ecstasy	medicine	solid
clamor	excellent	monastery	swindler
comparative	existence	optimism	terror
competitive	grammar	politics	vulgar

Until.   See *Till, until, 'til.*

Up.   This useful little word appears in many verb-adverb combinations (*grow up, give up, take up, use up*). In other phrases it adds nothing to the meaning of the verb; *up* is colloquial in such expressions as *choose up, divide up, finish up, increase up, wait up. On the up and up* is slang. *Up against* (meaning "face to face with") and *up against it* (meaning "in difficulty") are colloquial. *Up on* (meaning "informed about") and *up to* (meaning "scheming" or "plotting") are colloquial. *Up-and-coming* and *up one's alley* are other phrases to avoid in standard English. *Open up* is wordy in the sense of "give access to" and is colloquial when used to mean "speak freely."

Usage, levels of.   See *Levels of usage.*

Used to, used to could.   In the phrase *used to,* the *d* is often elided in speaking so that it sounds like *use to.* In writing, the *d* must be included. *Used to could* is an illiteracy; write *used to be able.*

Variety in sentence structure.   A series of sentences monotonous in structure is ineffective. We tire of reading a long succession of identical sentences, just as we tire of sameness in anything. Variety is much more than the spice of writing; it is a quality which reflects the mature processes of the writer's mind.

Revise sentences to make certain that they have *variety*. Vary their length and, occasionally, their normal word order. Vary the form of sentences (declarative, interrogative, etc.) and use periodic as well as loose sentences. Avoid a series of simple sentences and try to phrase more that are complex. Even simple sentences may be varied in structure.

The terms used in the preceding paragraph are discussed at appropriate places in this Guide; study them.

Verb.   See *Regular verb, Strong verb,* and Sections 65–68.

Verbal.   See *Oral, aural, verbal.*

Verbiage.   A somewhat learned word which means "wordiness," "an abundance of useless words." (See Sections 15, 24.)

Very.   *Very,* like *so, surely, too, extremely, indeed,* has been so overused that it has lost some of its value as an intensifier. Use these words sparingly and thoughtfully; consider whether your meaning isn't just as emphatic without them: "You are [very] positive about the matter." *Very* is used colloquially to qualify participles; formal use has adverbs like *much* or *greatly.*

Colloquial	I was *very annoyed* with myself.
Formal	I was *much annoyed* with myself.
Colloquial	I am *very torn* between the desire to speak my mind and the desire to keep out of trouble.
Formal	I am *greatly torn* between . . .

Video.   This word referring to the transmission of television images is rapidly growing in popularity. Purists insist that it is still colloquial, but general usage has decreed otherwise. Go ahead and use the word— even *look at video.* But read a good book now and then too.

Vision spread.   An important method of detecting errors in your writing is *proofreading* (which see). Much of the effectiveness of proofreading depends upon the spread of your vision.

The following triangle will show you how wide your vision (sight spread) is. Look at the top of the triangle and then down. How far down can you go and still identify each letter in each line at a *single* glance? Your central vision is as wide as the line above the one where you cannot identify each letter *without moving your eyes at all.*

a
a r
a r d
a r d c
a r d c f
a r d c f g
a r d c f g x
a r d c f g x y
a r d c f g x y z
a r d c f g x y z p
a r d c f g x y z p w

People differ in their range of vision as they do in nearly everything else. But many people have difficulty in identifying more than six letters at a single glance. Some have a span of vision embracing only three or four letters. Whatever your span, you should not try to exceed it when you are carefully checking for errors. If you do, you are reading—perhaps with excellent understanding—but you are not *proofreading*. And only proofreading will enable you to eliminate errors caused not by ignorance or stupidity but by carelessness.

Visual-mindedness. Each of us can form a *visual* image when a suggested idea calls to our minds a picture of some sort. When the word *tree* is mentioned to you, you can immediately "see in your mind" a vision, or representation, of some kind or shape of tree. The name of almost any object—*train, bus, church, child, cashier, rain*—will summon up a visual image. If you are visual-minded, you can readily call up such images. And if you are visual-minded, you are probably an above-average speller. When you need to spell any word, try to see it "in your mind's eye." (See Section 16b.)

Viz. See *I.e., etc.*

Vocative. See *Direct address.*

Vowel. In phonetics, a speech sound articulated so that there is a clear channel for the voice through the middle of the mouth. In spelling and grammar, a letter representing such a sound: *a, e, i, o, u,* and sometimes *y.* (See *Consonant.*)

Vowels added. See *Added vowels.*

Vowels dropped. See *Dropped vowels.*

Vowels unstressed. See *Unstressed vowels.*

Vulgarism. A term derived from the Latin *vulgus,* meaning "the common people." A *vulgarism* is a word or expression occurring only in common colloquial usage or in coarse speech. (See Section 19.)

Wait on. In the sense of "serve," this is an acceptable phrase. ("I have to *wait on* the customers now.") In the sense of "await" or "wait for," the phrase is dialectal or colloquial. ("Please hurry; I don't want to *wait for* [not *wait on*] you.")

Want for, want in, want out. The *for* in *want for* is dialectal. ("He *wants* [not *wants for*] to see the circus.") Neither *want in* nor *want out* is acceptable in formal English. ("The dog *wants to get out* [not *wants out*].")

Way, ways. The former is colloquial when used to mean "away." ("The mine is *away* [not *way*] across the state.") The following phrases involving *way* are also colloquial: *in a bad way, come my way* (achieve success), *act the way he does. Ways* is a dialectal substitute for *way* in such an expression as *a long ways to the river.*

Weak verb. See *Regular verb.*

Where. This is a useful word but it should not be substituted for *that* in standard English. ("We noted *that* [not *where*] the umpire made a mistake.")

Where at. As two words this phrase is redundant for *where.* In standard English avoid such a statement as "Janet did not know *where* she was *at.*"

Whether. See *If, whether.*

Who, whom. The former is the nominative case, the latter the objective.

When in doubt, try as a memory device the substitution of *he* for *who* and *him* for *whom,* since the proper use of *he* and *him* is more easily recognized: "I wonder *who* [or *whom?*] I should invite." I should invite *him.*" Therefore: "I wonder *whom* I should invite." (See Section **64f.**)

Who's, whose.   The former is a shortened form of *who is.* (*"Who's* ahead in the office pool?") *Whose* is the possessive case of *who.* (*"Whose* toes did I step on?")

Will, would.   See *Shall, will; Should, would.*

Wire.   This word (derived from *wireless*) is considered informal when used as a substitute for *telegram* or *telegraph.*

Wise.   This word is an acceptable adjective but is nonstandard in such expressions as a *wise guy, get wise to, get wise, put wise to, wise up, wisecrack.*

-wise.   This suffix has many standard uses and appears in such fully acceptable words as *clockwise* and *sidewise.* Unfortunately, it has been greatly overused in recent years and appears in scores of awkward and strained neologisms: *ideawise, travelwise, saleswise, laundrywise.*

Wordiness.   A sentence may be complete and unified and still be ineffective because it is wordy. Clear, effective sentences demand accuracy of thought and conciseness of expression. This does not mean that you should use a *telegraphic style* (which see). Nor does it mean that all sentences must be brief. A sentence of 100 words may be concise and one of 10 may be wordy. But sentences are rarely effective when they contain superfluous words or ideas.

In making sentences concise, you can eliminate unnecessary words, turn clauses into phrases, and use word-saving suffixes. For example, you would not refer to "a great, big, enormous man." Probably the last adjective alone would suffice. "Any typist who is qualified can become a member of the secretarial staff" may be shortened to "Any qualified typist can become a secretary." And a sentence such as "I was waiting for his telephone call until I became frantic" can be written "I was waiting frantically for his telephone call." If such condensation violates meaning, it should not be employed. But you hold readers only when your sentences are lean and vigorous. (See Sections 8a, 15.)

Word order.   An English sentence does not consist of a string of words in free relationship to each other but of groups of words arranged in patterns. Words in an English sentence have meaning because of their position. That is, they have one meaning in one position, another meaning in another position, and no meaning in still another position. Some linguists maintain that the basis of English grammar is word order. Certainly the order of words and of other locutions is a fundamental part of grammar and is basic in sentence construction. In addition, word order contributes to many effects of style, especially emphasis.

In highly inflected foreign languages, the relationships of words in a sentence are shown by their endings. English is not highly inflected, and confusion results when such functional words as prepositions and auxiliary verbs are not properly used. Even when they are, vagueness occurs in a sentence in which words are incorrectly placed. Try to keep related words together so that your reader may see their connection; try to place every modifier so that it is logically and naturally connected with the word or phrase it modifies. (See Sections **4, 5, 6.**)

Worst kind, worst sort, worst way. Slang terms for *very much, greatly, intensely,* and the like.

Would. See *Should, would.*

Would of, could of, might of, should of. These terms are all illiteracies probably resulting from attempts to represent what is pronounced. In rapid and informal speech, that is, *would have (would've)* has the sound of *would of.* In each phrase, *have* should replace *of.*

You all. In the sense of "all of you," this phrase has a recognized and standard plural meaning. When used to refer to one person, it may be considered either dialectal or an illiteracy.

-yze. See *-ise, -ize, -yze.*

Zeal. A word meaning "interest," "devotion," and "enthusiasm," *zeal* is what you need in learning to write correctly, clearly, effectively, and appropriately. You can learn if you will really try. Freshman English makes no demands beyond the ability of the average student. Hundreds of thousands of students before you have benefited from the course. With *zeal,* why not you?

INDEX

BOOK THREE

READING

A Collection of Readings for Writers

The world of books is the most remarkable creation of man. Nothing else that he builds ever lasts. Monuments fall; nations perish; civilizations grow old and die out; and, after an era of darkness, new races build others. But in the world of books are volumes that have seen this happen again and again, and yet live on, still young, still as fresh as the day they were written, still telling men's hearts of the hearts of men centuries dead.

—CLARENCE DAY, *The Story of the Yale University Press*

In anything fit to be called by the name of reading, the process itself should be absorbing and voluptuous; we should gloat over a book, be rapt clean out of ourselves, and rise from the perusal, our mind filled with the busiest kaleidoscopic dance of images, incapable of sleep or of continuous thought. The words, if the book be eloquent, should run thenceforward in our ears like the noise of breakers, and the story—if it be a story—repeat itself in a thousand colored pictures to the eye. It was for this last pleasure that we read so closely, and loved our books so dearly, in the bright, troubled period of boyhood. . . .

—ROBERT LOUIS STEVENSON, "A Gossip on Romance"

A NOTE
ON READING

Reading and writing are two aspects of the same process—the communication of thoughts, moods, and emotions. When you write effectively you convey your ideas and feelings to others; when you read well you receive from others their ideas and feelings. Since reading and writing are inseparably linked, it is important that in trying to learn to write well you learn to read well.

An American university president recently remarked that at one period in the history of this country our leaders "found time to read and demonstrated in their own lives and works the utility as well as the delight of reading. The four master-builders—Hamilton, John Adams, Jefferson, and Madison—were probably the four most widely read men of their age." Were they great because they were well-read, or well-read because they were great?

It has not been conclusively proved that all great writers have been efficient readers, but the experience of generations of college students has demonstrated a striking parallelism between efficient reading and effective writing. Furthermore, although the pervasive influence of motion pictures, radio, television, and varied audio-visual materials may eventually alter the situation, at least we know that a good general education cannot now be imparted to anyone unable to read both accurately and reflectively. In *Heroes and Hero-Worship*, Thomas Carlyle stated, "If we think of it, all that a university can do for us is still but what the first school began doing —teach us to *read*."

The process of learning to read efficiently is thus seen to be long and arduous. Perhaps it should be, for reading is almost miraculous when we consider that through it we have at our command and for our use much of the best that has been thought and written by the greatest minds of many centuries. Efficient reading demands the ability to concentrate, to use our intellectual curiosity, to visualize as we read so that images come to life and take on extra dimensions. Perhaps most importantly of all, efficient reading involves organizing and retaining ideas and impressions gained from the printed page.

Much of our reading is not accurate or reflective. When we read a light short story or novel, a mystery story or a comic book, we are usually seeking relaxation and quite naturally skip and skim. Ordinarily such reading fare neither deserves nor receives careful attention and subsequent reflection. But when we attempt similarly to read meaty fiction and drama, closely reasoned essays and biography, and carefully and concisely wrought poems, we become confused or receive all too little of the meaning intended. Desultory and inattentive reading is proper when applied to unimportant writing; the danger is that frequently we attempt to read anything and everything at the same speed and with the same degree of concentration.

The foregoing comment may stress the difficulty and burdensomeness of reading at the expense of the pleasure which it can and does afford many millions of readers. After all, reading is one of the few pure pleasures—some say the only one—known to mankind. Reading is a voluptuous delight for the initiated, a pastime which, in the words of Sir Philip Sidney, "holdeth children from play and old men from the chimney corner." Also, in fairness perhaps it should be said that some who feast on light fiction and comic books do not so much "skip and skim" as merely read without concentrated attention and following reflection. Finally, although you may not be among their number, many persons actually read for sheer pleasure works dealing with science, history, biography, philosophy, and the like. One's active sympathies and intellectual curiosity strongly affect *what* and *how* one reads.

Reading effectively is reading with both speed and comprehension. You will shortly discover, if you have not already done so, that one of the main differences between college and high-school work lies in the amount of reading required. It has been estimated that college students today have more than five times as much required reading as did those of 1900. You may feel that you are floundering in a sea of words: it has been estimated that as a college freshman you will be supposed to read some 4,000,000 words in textbooks, collateral volumes, and source books. Reading is required in all but about 10 percent of your college studies. Assignments of several thousand words each in such courses as history, economics, sociology, and political science will force you to increase your reading speed, even if you already are a rapid reader.

By a conspiracy of silence in high schools and colleges, until recently little attention was given to rapid reading. But the necessity for skipping and scanning at last has been recognized; one eminent educator recently remarked, "Success in college depends upon reading speed."

Our rate of reading is connected with the number of fixations that our eyes make as they move across a page. Our aim should be to reduce the number of fixations, to read not word-by-word but by thought phrases. As we lengthen the span of our eye movements, our reading rate will increase and so will our comprehension; then we will be reading not in isolated units but in context. A skillful reader infrequently has to refer to the beginning of a sentence he has finished; he will have carried the thought through in one rapid series of lengthened glances. The best advice, of course, is to "read with your head, not with your eyes"; so doing will increase comprehension by reducing fixations of the eyes and increasing concentration. Practice finding main ideas in a passage and separating them from subordinate thoughts; learn to find key words and key sentences and to distinguish them from merely illustrative material. Because of lengthy assignments in many of your courses you will have ample opportunity for such practice.

Certain hindrances to effective reading may exist for you. For example, if, after concentrated reading for a short time, your eyes feel tired or begin to smart, or your head begins to ache, you should consult an ophthalmologist or oculist. Again, good posture while reading will help to prevent muscular weariness and incorrect breathing. Also, you need a good light for reading, one that both illuminates the page without glare and does not shine directly into your eyes.

Speed in reading is important, but it is relatively easy to attain. Developing the power to deal thoroughly with a writer's ideas and to evaluate them is more difficult. Comprehension of reading is *thinking with the author*, absorbing his ideas. It involves re-creating the thought and experience of the author, forming images, and increasing vocabulary by constant use of a dictionary. Comprehension results from reading with concentration, slowly if necessary but always reflectively.

Remember that as an efficient reader you will read thought units, not word-by-word. You will read different types of material at different speeds and with varying degrees of concentration. You possess skill in getting the meanings of new words from context but will make frequent use of your dictionary. Above all, you will evaluate what you are reading, both during the process and later.

Considerable evidence indicates that the reading rate of the general literate population of this country over 16 years of age is about 250 words a minute, with approximately 70 percent comprehension. If this seems to be a rapid rate, remember that it is about the sixth-grade level for grammar school. As a college student you should be able to read much more rapidly, although, as is repeatedly stated in this book, different kinds of material require different speeds. Below is a sample of material of "average" difficulty. It is clear and well organized, but it does mention certain figures and it does make several key points. Therefore, it represents a difficulty and challenge typical of your college reading. It runs to slightly more than 400 words. Time yourself in reading it (number of seconds) and then immediately attempt to answer the 10 questions which follow. The results should indicate something of your rate of reading and of your comprehension.

Since the end of World War II, few communities have escaped the burden of building additional elementary schools and increasing their teaching staffs. Though this task is still far from completed, today the urgent need is for more high school classrooms and teachers. Within three more years the problem will have engulfed the colleges.

Merely to maintain the present quality of college education it will probably be necessary to double the number of college teachers within the 10 years from 1960 to 1970. We may have to duplicate the existing physical facilities that have been acquired slowly during 300 years. The cost of this will be many billions of dollars (one estimate: $15 billion). It is not surprising if leaders in education seem sometimes to stand disconcerted before this prospect, or to speak with confused voices, wondering where an answer is to be found.

The difficulties will not be over by 1980, for the road to which we are committed will still be broadening before us. Not then, any more than now, shall we be able to turn back from the vastly expanded educational operation to which we are being carried not only by the pressure of increasing population (76 million in 1900; by 1980 over 200 million), but also by technological advances. These advances continue to come at an accelerating pace. The process, based on the multiplication of scientific knowledge that is shaping our world, begins in education and, in turn, feeds on and demands more education. Thus there is a certain inevitability, a kind of compulsion, governing the development of education in America. As we look at the expanding technological future we should rejoice to be going ahead; but we may be excused, too, if at times we become quizzical about the end.

Whatever their professed aims in the past, colleges have usually been pathways to economic advance for those who attended them. It is statistically true today, for example, that the person who attends college may expect to earn upwards of $100,000 more during his lifetime than the one who does not. At present more than ever before our national life is motivated by economic calculations, and at the same time the expanding technology has contributed to making education almost unashamedly vocational. Applied science has created a technological society and, along with it, an almost insatiable demand for more and more recruits with more and more specialized, and technical, education. Industry tells us that 30,000 trained engineers are required each year to keep our machine society running. Obviously the vocational pressures on higher education, always formidable, will increase.

—NATHAN M. PUSEY, "The Exploding World of Education"

1. How greatly increased is the life income of one who attends college?

2. What increase in college teachers is predicted between 1960 and 1970?

3. What is the indicated population of the United States in 1980?

4. How many newly trained engineers are now required each year?

5. What burden have few communities escaped since World War II?

6. What increase is foreseen for existing educational facilities between 1960 and 1970?

7. What is one estimate of the cost of this increase (Question 6)?

8. What kind of compulsion is governing the development of American education?

9. What is suggested as the principal creation of applied science?

10. Why will vocational pressures on higher education increase?

Effective reading is an art, just as is good writing. Whether we read for relaxation or information, to escape or to learn, our aim should be to employ our time intelligently. More than three centuries ago, Francis Bacon commented as wisely as anyone ever has on the relationship of reading and writing:

> Read not to contradict and confute; nor to believe and take for granted; nor to find talk and discourse; but to weigh and consider. Some books are to be tasted, others to be swallowed, and some few to be chewed and digested; that is, some books are to be read only in parts; others to be read, but not curiously;[1] and some few to be read wholly, and with diligence and attention. Some books also may be read by deputy,[2] and extracts made of them by others; but that would be only in the less important arguments, and the meaner sort of books; else distilled books are like common distilled waters, flash[3] things. Reading maketh a full man; conference a ready man; and writing an exact man. And therefore, if a man write little, he had need have a great memory; if he confer little, he had need have a present wit; and if he read little, he had need have much cunning, to seem to know what he doth not.

Teachers and students themselves agree that a significantly large number of people are attempting college work with low-grade reading habits. Instructors have a right to expect that a freshman can read adult prose and poetry with reasonable speed sufficiently well to

1. gain and understand accurate information and ideas
2. recognize their organization and style of presentation
3. interpret them in terms of his own experience
4. analyze and evaluate them

If you cannot read sufficiently well to accomplish these aims, or if you read so painfully and slowly that reading is always a chore and never a pleasure, consider the following suggestions which summarize those already made and add a few new ones:

1. Inquire whether your college maintains special reading classes and consider the advisability of enrolling in one.
2. Practice reading "by phrases" rather than "by words."
3. Try to avoid pronouncing words as you read silently. (Few "lip movers" can read with adequate comprehension or speed.)
4. Think actively as you read. Daydreaming, napping, and just plain letting your mind "wander from the reservation" are enemies of efficient reading. Try to get the principal idea from each paragraph. Stop reading ever so often to consider what you have read; try to paraphrase it.
5. Do not ignore boldface paragraph, or section, topic headings; examine carefully all accompanying graphs, charts, tables, and photographs.
6. Practice reading against time. Borrow or buy a stop watch. Compare the speed with which you read and comprehend an assignment in biology or history with your reading speed of the college newspaper.

---

[1] carefully

[2] Modern-day "deputies" include many popular magazines which "digest" books and articles, as well as some publishing firms which issue abridged editions of longer works.

[3] insipid

READING AS A READER

When you read *as a reader* your purposes should be to acquire information, to form opinions, to draw conclusions. You endeavor to stock your mind with ideas for use in thinking, discussion, and writing. You look for new problems, answers to questions, visual details which widen your experience and understanding. Careful reading of any selection should help you to partial understanding of the author's life and background, to a statement of central theme and purpose, to a concept of the organization of main divisions and supporting material. This kind of reading must be painstakingly careful. In *Translating Literature into Life*, Arnold Bennett wrote:

> What is the matter with our reading is casualness, languor, preoccupation. We don't give the book a chance. We don't put ourselves at the disposal of the book. It is impossible to read properly without using all one's engine-power. If we are not tired after reading, common sense is not in us. How should one grapple with a superior and not be out of breath?
>
> But even if we read with the whole force of our brain, and do nothing else, common sense is still not in us, while sublime conceit is. For we are assuming that, without further trouble, we can possess, coordinate, and assimilate all the ideas and sensations rapidly offered to us by a mind greater than our own. The assumption has only to be stated in order to appear in its monstrous absurdity. Hence it follows that something remains to be done. This something is the act of reflection. Reading without subsequent reflection is ridiculous; it is equally a proof of folly and of vanity.

Bennett here used the word *reflection* to mean *evaluation*. Reading to absorb ideas is important in itself but it is not enough; we should also read to answer these questions: What is the author attempting to do? How well does he succeed in his attempt? What value has the attempt? In short, effective reading is critical reading, a many-sided evaluation of scope, material, and purpose.

READING AS A WRITER

When you read *as a writer* your attention should be focused not only upon the specific approaches already noted but also upon the author's technique, his methods of manipulating material. It should become habitual for you to study a writer's choice and use of words, his sentence and paragraph structure, even such relatively prosaic matters as punctuation and mechanics. Look consciously for the methods by which he secures his effects: aids to interest, such as humor, irony, anecdote; appeals to emotions; the logicalness of the presentation. Reading as a writer involves reading thoroughly, imaginatively, creatively. It implies a consideration of subject matter, style (the imprint of the author's personality on subject matter), and technique.

Thus far we have been considering general problems of reading which apply to all types of writing. Such problems apply with particular force and meaning to the formal and informal essays which you will examine. These are dominant types; much of your reading in college will be of materials which in substance and style resemble such essays, particularly the formal ones. Learning to read solid, meaty exposition should be one of the primary goals of every college student.

Reading biography, fiction, plays, and poems requires special attitudes and presents special opportunities in addition to those applying to reading in general. Consult the note on reading each of these separate types as it appears in the collection which follows.

THINKING

&

PROPAGANDA

THE METHOD OF
SCIENTIFIC INVESTIGATION

Thomas Henry Huxley

THOMAS HENRY HUXLEY (1825–1895) was born at Ealing, England. In 1846 after receiving his medical degree from the University of London, he made a four-year voyage on the British naval vessel *Rattlesnake*. During this voyage he began scientific studies which led him to accept, in later years, the conclusions which Darwin's *On the Origin of Species* (1859) established. An early believer in the theory of evolution, Huxley wrote and lectured to popularize Darwin's ideas and other scientific thought of his time.

1. The method of scientific investigation is nothing but the expression of the necessary mode of working of the human mind. It is simply the mode at which all phenomena are reasoned about, rendered precise and exact. There is no more difference, but there is just the same kind of difference, between the mental operations of a man of science and those of an ordinary person as there is between the operations and methods of a baker or of a butcher weighing out his goods

From *Man's Place in Nature and Other Essays*.

in common scales and the operations of a chemist in performing a difficult and complex analysis by means of his balance and finely graduated weights. It is not that the action of the scales in the one case and the balance in the other differ in the principles of their construction or manner of working; but the beam of one is set on an infinitely finer axis than the other and of course turns by the addition of a much smaller weight.

2. You will understand this better, perhaps, if I give you some familiar example. You have all heard it repeated, I dare say, that men of science work by means of induction and deduction, and that by the help of these operations they, in a sort of sense, wring from nature certain other things which are called natural laws and causes, and that out of these, by some cunning skill of their own, they build up hypotheses and theories. And it is imagined by many that the operations of the common mind can be by no means compared with these processes, and that they have to be acquired by a sort of special apprenticeship to the craft. To hear all these large words you would think that the mind of a man of science must be constituted differently from that of his fellow men; but if you will not be frightened by terms, you will discover that you are quite wrong and that all these terrible apparatus are being used by yourselves every day and every hour of your lives.

3. There is a well-known incident in one of Molière's plays where the author makes the hero express unbounded delight on being told that he had been talking prose during the whole of his life. In the same way I trust that you will take comfort and be delighted with yourselves on the discovery that you have been acting on the principles of inductive and deductive philosophy during the same period. Probably there is not one here who has not in the course of the day had occasion to set in motion a complex train of reasoning of the very same kind, though differing of course in degree, as that which a scientific man goes through in tracing the causes of natural phenomena.

4. A very trivial circumstance will serve to exemplify this. Suppose you go into a fruiterer's shop, wanting an apple. You take up one, and on biting it you find it is sour; you look at it and see that it is hard and green. You take up another one, and that too is hard, green, and sour. The shopman offers you a third; but before biting it you examine it and find that it is hard and green, and you immediately say that you will not have it, as it must be sour like those that you have already tried.

5. Nothing can be more simple than that, you think; but if you will take the trouble to analyze and trace out into its logical elements what has been done by the mind, you will be greatly surprised. In the first place you have performed the operation of induction. You found that in two experiences hardness and greenness in apples go together with sourness. It was so in the first case, and it was confirmed by the second. True, it is a very small basis, but still it is enough to make an induction from; you generalize the facts, and you expect to find sourness in apples where you get hardness and greenness. You found upon that a general law that all hard and green apples are sour; and that, so far as it goes, is a perfect induction. Well, having got your natural law in this

way, when you are offered another apple which you find is hard and green, you say, "All hard and green apples are sour; this apple is hard and green; therefore this apple is sour." That train of reasoning is what logicians call a syllogism and has all its various parts and terms— its major premise, its minor premise, and its conclusion. And by the help of further reasoning, which if drawn out would have to be exhibited in two or three other syllogisms, you arrive at your final determination, "I will not have that apple." So that, you see, you have, in the first place, established a law by induction, and upon that you have founded a deduction and reasoned out the special conclusion of the particular case. Well now, suppose, having got your law, that at some time afterwards you are discussing the qualities of apples with a friend. You will say to him, "It is a very curious thing, but I find that all hard and green apples are sour!" Your friend says to you, "But how do you know that?" You at once reply, "Oh, because I have tried them over and over again and have always found them to be so." Well, if we were talking science instead of common sense, we should call that an experimental verification. And if still opposed you go further and say, "I have heard from the people in Somersetshire and Devonshire, where a large number of apples are grown, that they have observed the same thing. It is also found to be the case in Normandy and in North America. In short, I find it to be the universal experience of mankind wherever attention has been directed to the subject." Whereupon, your friend, unless he is a very unreasonable man, agrees with you

and is convinced that you are quite right in the conclusion you have drawn. He believes, although perhaps he does not know he believes it, that the more extensive verifications are, that the more frequently experiments have been made and results of the same kind arrived at, that the more varied the conditions under which the same results have been attained the more certain is the ultimate conclusion, and he disputes the question no further. He sees that the experiment has been tried under all sorts of conditions as to time, place, and people with the same result; and he says with you, therefore, that the law you have laid down must be a good one and he must believe it.

6. In science we do the same thing; the philosopher exercises precisely the same faculties, though in a much more delicate manner. In scientific inquiry it becomes a matter of duty to expose a supposed law to every possible kind of verification, and to take care, moreover, that this is done intentionally and not left to mere accident as in the case of the apples. And in science, as in common life, our confidence in a law is in exact proportion to the absence of variation in the result of our experimental verifications. For instance, if you let go your grasp of an article you may have in your hand, it will immediately fall to the ground. That is a very common verification of one of the best established laws of nature, that of gravitation. The method by which men of science established the existence of that law is exactly the same as that by which we have established the trivial proposition about the sourness of hard and green apples. But we believe it in such an exten-

sive, thorough, and unhesitating manner because the universal experience of mankind verifies it, and we can verify it ourselves at any time; and that is the strongest possible foundation on which any natural law can rest.

7. So much by way of proof that the method of establishing laws in science is exactly the same as that pursued in common life. Let us now turn to another matter (though really it is but another phase of the same question), and that is the method by which from the relations of certain phenomena we prove that some stand in the position of causes towards the others.

8. I want to put the case clearly before you, and I will therefore show you what I mean by another familiar example. I will suppose that one of you, on coming down in the morning to the parlor of your house, finds that a teapot and some spoons which had been left in the room on the previous evening are gone; the window is open, and you observe the mark of a dirty hand on the window-frame; and perhaps, in addition to that, you notice the impress of a hobnailed shoe on the gravel outside. All these phenomena have struck your attention instantly, and before two seconds have passed you say, "Oh, somebody has broken open the window, entered the room, and run off with the spoons and the teapot!" That speech is out of your mouth in a moment. And you will probably add, "I know there has; I am quite sure of it." You mean to say exactly what you know; but in reality what you have said has been the expression of what is, in all essential particulars, an hypothesis. You do not *know* it at all; it is nothing but an hypothesis

rapidly framed in your own mind! And it is an hypothesis founded on a long train of inductions and deductions.

9. What are those inductions and deductions, and how have you got at this hypothesis? You have observed, in the first place, that the window is open; but by a train of reasoning involving many inductions and deductions, you have probably arrived long before at the general law—and a very good one it is—that windows do not open of themselves; and you therefore conclude that something has opened the window. A second general law that you have arrived at in the same way is that teapots and spoons do not go out of a window spontaneously, and you are satisfied that, as they are not now where you left them, they have been removed. In the third place, you look at the marks on the window and the shoe marks outside, and you say that in all previous experience the former kind of mark has never been produced by anything else but the hand of a human being; and the same experience shows that no other animal but man at present wears shoes with hobnails on them such as would produce the marks in the gravel. I do not know, even if we could discover any of those "missing links" that are talked about, that they would help us to any other conclusion! At any rate the law which states our present experience is strong enough for my present purpose. You next reach the conclusion that as these kinds of marks have not been left by any other animal than man, or are liable to be formed in any other way than by a man's hand and shoe, the marks in question have been formed by a man in

that way. You have, further, a general law founded on observation and experience, and that too is, I am sorry to say, a very universal and unimpeachable one—that some men are thieves; and you assume at once from all these premises—and that is what constitutes your hypothesis —that the man who made the marks outside and on the window sill opened the window, got into the room, and stole your teapot and spoons. You have now arrived at a *vera causa;* you have assumed a cause which it is plain is competent to produce all the phenomena you have observed. You can explain all these phenomena only by the hypothesis of a thief. But that is an hypothetical conclusion, of the justice of which you have no absolute proof at all; it is only rendered highly probable by a series of inductive and deductive reasonings.

10. I suppose your first action, assuming that you are a man of ordinary common sense and that you have established this hypothesis to your own satisfaction, will very likely be to go off for the police and set them on the track of the burglar with the view to the recovery of your property. But just as you are starting with this object, some person comes in and on learning what you are about says, "My good friend, you are going on a great deal too fast. How do you know that the man who really made the marks took the spoons? It might have been a monkey that took them, and the man may have merely looked in afterwards." You would probably reply, "Well, that is all very well, but you see it is contrary to all experience of the way teapots and spoons are abstracted; so that, at any rate, your hypothesis is less

probable than mine." While you are talking the thing over in this way, another friend arrives, one of that good kind of people that I was talking of a little while ago.

11. And he might say, "Oh, my dear sir, you are certainly going on a great deal too fast. You are most presumptuous. You admit that all these occurrences took place when you were fast asleep, at a time when you could not possibly have known anything about what was taking place. How do you know that the laws of nature are not suspended during the night? It may be that there has been some kind of supernatural interference in this case." In point of fact, he declares that your hypothesis is one of which you cannot at all demonstrate the truth and that you are by no means sure that the laws of nature are the same when you are asleep as when you are awake.

12. Well, now, you cannot at the moment answer that kind of reasoning. You feel that your worthy friend has you somewhat at a disadvantage. You will feel perfectly convinced in your own mind, however, that you are quite right, and you will say to him, "My good friend, I can only be guided by the natural probabilities of the case, and if you will be kind enough to stand aside and permit me to pass, I will go and fetch the police." Well, we will suppose that your journey is successful and that by good luck you meet with a policeman; that eventually the burglar is found with your property on his person and the marks correspond to his hand and to his boots. Probably any jury would consider those facts a very good experimental verification of your hypothesis touching the cause

of the abnormal phenomena observed in your parlor, and would act accordingly.

13. Now, in this supposititious case I have taken phenomena of a very common kind in order that you might see what are the different steps in an ordinary process of reasoning, if you will only take the trouble to analyze it carefully. All the operations I have described, you will see, are involved in the mind of any man of sense in leading him to a conclusion as to the course he should take in order to make good a robbery and punish the offender. I say that you are led, in that case, to your conclusion by exactly the same train of reasoning as that which a man of science pursues when he is endeavoring to discover the origin and laws of the most occult phenomena. The process is, and always must be, the same; and precisely the same mode of reasoning was employed by Newton and Laplace in their endeavors to discover and define the causes of the movements of the heavenly bodies as you, with your own common sense, would employ to detect a burglar. The only difference is that, the nature of the inquiry being more abstruse, every step has to be most carefully watched so that there may not be a single crack or flaw in your hypothesis. A flaw or crack in many of the hypotheses of daily life may be of little or no moment as affecting the general correctness of the conclusions at which we may arrive; but in a scientific inquiry a fallacy, great or small, is always of importance and is sure to be in the long run constantly productive of mischievous if not fatal results.

14. Do not allow yourselves to be misled by the common notion that an hypothesis is untrustworthy simply because it is an hypothesis. It is often urged in respect to some scientific conclusion that, after all, it is only an hypothesis. But what more have we to guide us in nine-tenths of the most important affairs of daily life than hypotheses, and often very ill-based ones? So that in science, where the evidence of an hypothesis is subjected to the most rigid examination, we may rightly pursue the same course. You may have hypotheses and hypotheses. A man may say, if he likes, that the moon is made of green cheese; that is an hypothesis. But another man, who has devoted a great deal of time and attention to the subject and availed himself of the most powerful telescopes and the results of the observations of others, declares that in his opinion it is probably composed of materials very similar to those of which our own earth is made up; and that is also only an hypothesis. But I need not tell you that there is an enormous difference in the value of the two hypotheses. That one which is based on sound scientific knowledge is sure to have a corresponding value; and that which is a mere hasty random guess is likely to have but little value. Every great step in our progress in discovering causes has been made in exactly the same way as that which I have detailed to you. A person observing the occurrence of certain facts and phenomena asks, naturally enough, what kind of operation known to occur in nature applied to the particular case, will unravel and explain the mystery. Hence you have the scientific hypothesis; and its value will be proportionate to the care and completeness with which its basis has

been tested and verified. It is in these matters as in the commonest affairs of practical life: the guess of the fool will be folly, while the guess of the wise man will contain wisdom. In all cases you see that the value of the result depends on the patience and faithfulness with which the investigator applies to his hypothesis every possible kind of verification.

· QUESTIONS ·

1. The lengths of the 14 paragraphs in this essay vary considerably. Does the length of each seem proportionate to the topic being treated? Is every paragraph fully unified?
2. Study carefully the seventh paragraph. What is the function of the first sentence? What clue does it offer to the organization of Huxley's essay? What is the function of the second sentence?
3. What is the difference between the mental operations "of a baker or of a butcher" and those of a scientist? By what specific device does Huxley make this clear?
4. Define inductive reasoning and deductive reasoning. Point out common examples of each.
5. Define and illustrate "syllogism."
6. Explain fully the meaning and importance of "experimental verification."
7. What are the implications of Huxley's statement that our confidence in a law "is in exact proportion to the absence of variation in the result of our experimental verifications"?
8. Analyze the inductions and deductions which lead to the hypothesis about the stolen spoons and teapot.
9. In "the case of the apples," why is the verification "mere accident"? How does scientific verification avoid being accident?
10. Show the importance of the two uses of the word "guess" in the next to last sentence of the essay.

Theme Subjects: (1) An Illustration of Deductive Reasoning; (2) Dangers in Syllogistic Reasoning; (3) Implications in the Study of a Science; (4) Reduction to Absurdity: Astounding Scientific Fiction; (5) A Limitation on the Scientific Method; (6) A Method of *Un*scientific Investigation! (7) James Bond (or Nero Wolfe or some favorite fictional character) and I Solve a Mystery; (8) Huxley's Simplistic View of Scientific Method.

THE CREATIVE MIND

J. Bronowski

JACOB BRONOWSKI (1908–   ) was born in Poland and came from Germany to England in 1920. He was graduated from Cambridge University in 1930 and continued his mathematical research there until 1933, when he became Senior Lecturer at the University of Hull. In 1942 he entered service with the British government, heading a unit to study the economic effects of bombing, and was scientific deputy to the British Chiefs of Staff Mission to Japan in 1945. Leaving the government in 1950, he joined the National Coal Board where he directed the eventual discovery of a process for making smokeless fuel and was Director-General of Process Development from 1959 to 1963. Visiting lecturer on science and human values at M.I.T. in 1953, he became in 1964 a Fellow of The Salk Institute for Biological Studies in San Diego, California, where he is currently Deputy Director. Among his books are *The Poet's Defense* (1939); *Insight* (1964); and *William Blake and England's Age of Revolution* (1965). He has also written numerous scientific articles.

There is a likeness between the creative acts of the mind in art and in science. Yet, when a man uses the word science in such a sentence, it may be suspected that he does not mean what the headlines mean by science. Am I about to sidle away to those riddles in the Theory of Numbers which Hardy[1] loved, or to the heady speculations of astrophysicists, in order to make claims for abstract science which have no bearing on its daily practice?

I have no such design. My purpose is to talk about science as it is, practical and theoretical. I define science as the organization of our knowledge in such a way that it commands more of the hidden potential in nature. What I have in

Reprinted by permission of Julian Messner, Division of Pocket Books, Inc., from *Science and Human Values* by J. Bronowski. Copyright © 1965 by J. Bronowski.
[1] G. H. Hardy, English mathematician, author of *A Mathematician's Apology*, Cambridge (England), 1940.

mind therefore is both deep and matter of fact; it reaches from the kinetic theory of gases to the telephone and the suspension bridge and medicated toothpaste. It admits no sharp boundary between knowledge and use. There are of course people who like to draw a line between pure and applied science; and oddly, they are often the same people who find art unreal. To them, the word *useful* is a final arbiter, either for or against a work; and they use this word as if it can mean only what makes a man feel heavier after meals.

There is no sanction for confining the practice of science in this or another way. True, science is full of useful inventions. And its theories have often been made by men whose imagination was directed by the uses to which their age looked. Newton turned naturally to astronomy because it was the subject of his day, and it was so because finding one's way at sea had long been a practical preoccupation of the society into which he was born. It should be added, mischievously, that astronomy also had some standing because it was used very practically to cast horoscopes. (Kepler used it for this purpose; in the Thirty Years' War he cast the horoscope of Wallenstein which wonderfully told his character, and he predicted a universal disaster for 1634 which proved to be the murder of Wallenstein.[2])

In a setting which is more familiar, Faraday worked all his life to link electricity with magnetism because this was the glittering problem of his day; and it was so because his society, like ours, was on the lookout for new sources of power. Consider a more modest example today: the new mathematical methods of automatic control, a subject sometimes called cybernetics, have been developed now because this is a time when communication and control have in effect become forms of power. These inventions have been directed by social needs, and they are useful inventions; yet it was not their usefulness which dominated and set light to the minds of those who made them. Neither Newton nor Faraday, nor yet Norbert Wiener, spent their time in a scramble for patents.

What a scientist does is compounded of two interests: the interest of his time and his own interest. In this his behavior is no different from any other man's. The need of the age gives its shape to scientific progress as a whole. But it is not the need of the age which gives the individual scientist his sense of pleasure and of adventure, and that excitement which keeps him working late into the night when all the useful typists have gone home at five o'clock. He is personally involved in his work, as the poet is in his, and as the artist is in the painting. Paints and painting too must have been made for useful ends; and language was developed, from whatever beginnings, for practical communication. Yet you cannot have a man handle paints or language or the symbolic concepts of physics, you cannot even have him stain a microscope slide, without instantly waking in him a pleasure in the very language, a sense of ex-

---

[2] Johann Kepler, German astronomer, 1571–1630; Albrecht Wallenstein, Duke of Friedland, general in the Thirty Years' War, lived 1583–1634.

ploring his own activity. This sense lies at the heart of creation.[3]

The sense of personal exploration is as urgent, and as delightful, to the practical scientist as to the theoretical. Those who think otherwise are confusing what is practical with what is humdrum. Good humdrum work without originality is done every day by everyone, theoretical scientists as well as practical, and writers and painters too, as well as truck drivers and bank clerks. Of course the unoriginal work keeps the world going; but it is not therefore the monopoly of practical men. And neither need the practical man be unoriginal. If he is to break out of what has been done before, he must bring to his own tools the same sense of pride and discovery which the poet brings to words. He cannot afford to be less radical in conceiving and less creative in designing a new turbine than a new world system.

And this is why in turn practical discoveries are not made only by practical men. As the world's interest has shifted, since the Industrial Revolution, to the tapping of new springs of power, the theoretical scientist has shifted his interests too. His speculations about energy have been as abstract as once they were about astronomy; and they have been profound now as they were then, because the man loved to think. The Carnot cycle and the dynamo grew equally from this love, and so did nuclear physics and the German V weapons and Kelvin's interest in low temperatures. Man does not invent by following either use or tradition; he does not invent even a new form of communication by calling a conference of communication engineers. Who invented the television set? In any deep sense, it was Clerk Maxwell who foresaw the existence of radio waves, and Heinrich Hertz who proved it, and J. J. Thomson who discovered the electron. This is not said in order to rob any practical man of the invention, but from a sad sense of justice; for neither Maxwell nor Hertz nor J. J. Thomson would take pride in television just now.

Man masters nature not by force but by understanding. This is why science has succeeded where magic failed: because it has looked for no spell to cast over nature. The alchemist and the magician in the Middle Ages thought, and the addict of comic strips is still encouraged to think, that nature must be mastered by a device which outrages her laws. But in four hundred years since the Scientific Revolution we have learned that we gain our ends

---

[3] As an example, consider the practice of mathematics. Mathematics is in the first place a language in which we discuss those parts of the real world which can be described by numbers or by similar relations of order. But with the workaday business of translating the facts into this language there naturally goes, in those who are good at it, a pleasure in the activity itself. They find the language richer than its bare content; what is translated comes to mean less to them than the logic and the style of saying it; and from these overtones grows mathematics as a literature in its own right. Mathematics in this sense, pure mathematics, is a form of poetry, which has the same relation to the prose of practical mathematics as poetry has to prose in any other language. This element of poetry, the delight in exploring the medium for its own sake, is an essential ingredient in the creative process. (Author's note.)

only *with* the laws of nature; we control her only by understanding her laws. We cannot even bully nature by any insistence that our work shall be designed to give power over her. We must be content that power is the byproduct of understanding. So the Greeks said that Orpheus played the lyre with such sympathy that wild beasts were tamed by the hand on the strings. They did not suggest that he got this gift by setting out to be a lion tamer.

What is the insight with which the scientist tries to see into nature? Can it indeed be called either imaginative or creative? To the literary man the question may seem merely silly. He has been taught that science is a large collection of facts; and if this is true, then the only seeing which scientists need do is, he supposes, seeing the facts. He pictures them, the colorless professionals of science, going off to work in the morning into the universe in a neutral, unexposed state. They then expose themselves like a photographic plate. And then in the darkroom or laboratory they develop the image, so that suddenly and startlingly it appears, printed in capital letters, as a new formula for atomic energy.

Men who have read Balzac and Zola are not deceived by the claims of these writers that they do no more than record the facts. The readers of Christopher Isherwood do not take him literally when he writes "I am a camera." Yet the same readers solemnly carry with them from their schooldays this foolish picture of the scientist fixing by some mechanical process the facts of nature. I have had of all people a historian tell me that science is a collection of facts, and his

voice had not even the ironic rasp of one filing cabinet reproving another.

It seems impossible that this historian had ever studied the beginnings of a scientific discovery. The Scientific Revolution can be held to begin in the year 1543 when there was brought to Copernicus, perhaps on his deathbed, the first printed copy of the book he had finished about a dozen years earlier. The thesis of this book is that the earth moves around the sun. When did Copernicus go out and record this fact with his camera? What appearance in nature prompted his outrageous guess? And in what odd sense is this guess to be called a neutral record of fact?

Less than a hundred years after Copernicus, Kepler published (between 1609 and 1619) the three laws which describe the paths of the planets. The work of Newton and with it most of our mechanics spring from these laws. They have a solid, matter of fact sound. For example, Kepler says that if one squares the year of a planet, one gets a number which is proportional to the cube of its average distance from the sun. Does anyone think that such a law is found by taking enough readings and then squaring and cubing everything in sight? If he does, then, as a scientist, he is doomed to a wasted life; he has as little prospect of making a scientific discovery as an electronic brain has.

It was not this way that Copernicus and Kepler thought, or that scientists think today. Copernicus found that the orbits of the planets would look simpler if they were looked at from the sun and not from the earth. But he did not in the first place find this by routine calculation. His first step was a leap of imagination—to lift himself from the earth, and put himself wildly, speculatively into the sun. "The earth conceives from the sun," he wrote; and "the sun rules the family of stars." We catch in his mind an image, the gesture of the virile man standing in the sun, with arms outstretched, overlooking the planets. Perhaps Copernicus took the picture from the drawings of the youth with outstretched arms which the Renaissance teachers put into their books on the proportions of the body. Perhaps he had seen Leonardo's drawings of his loved pupil Salai. I do not know. To me, the gesture of Copernicus, the shining youth looking outward from the sun, is still vivid in a drawing which William Blake in 1780 based on all these: the drawing which is usually called *Glad Day*.

Kepler's mind, we know, was filled with just such fanciful analogies; and we know what they were. Kepler wanted to relate the speeds of the planets to the musical intervals. He tried to fit the five regular solids into their orbits. None of these likenesses worked, and they have been forgotten; yet they have been and they remain the stepping stones of every creative mind. Kepler felt for his laws by way of metaphors, he searched mystically for likenesses with what he knew in every strange corner of nature. And when among these guesses he hit upon his laws, he did not think of their numbers as the balancing of a cosmic bank account, but as a revelation of the unity in all nature. To us, the analogies by which Kepler listened for the movement of the planets in the music of the spheres are farfetched.[4] Yet are they more so than the wild leap by which Rutherford and Bohr in our own century found a model for the atom in, of all places, the planetary system?

No scientific theory is a collection of facts. It will not even do to call a theory true or false in the simple sense in which every fact is either so or not so. Two thousand years ago the Epicureans held that matter is made of atoms, and we are now tempted to say that their theory was true. But if we do so we confuse their notion of matter with our own. John Dalton in 1808 first saw the structure of matter as we do today, and what he took from the ancients was not their theory but something richer, their image: the atom. Much of what was in Dalton's mind was as vague as the Greek notion, and quite as mistaken. But he suddenly gave life to the new facts of chemistry and the ancient theory together, by fusing them to give what neither had: a coherent picture of how matter is linked and built up from different kinds of atoms. The act of fusion is the creative act.

All science is the search for unity in hidden likenesses. The search may be on a grand scale, as in the modern theories which try to link the fields of gravitation and electromagnetism. But we do not need to be browbeaten by the scale of science. There are discoveries to be made by snatching a small like-

---

[4] The music of the spheres was itself a mathematical conception, which had been invented by Pythagoras in the sixth century B.C. Pythagoras taught that the distances between the heavenly bodies match the lengths of the strings that sound the different musical notes. It was deduced that the spheres that carry the heavenly bodies make music as they turn. (Author's note.)

ness from the air too, if it is bold enough. In 1935 the Japanese physicist Hideki Yukawa wrote a paper which can still give heart to a young scientist. He took as his starting point the known fact that waves of light can sometimes behave as if they were separate pellets. From this he reasoned that the forces which hold the nucleus of an atom together might sometimes also be observed as if they were solid pellets. A schoolboy can see how thin Yukawa's analogy is, and his teacher would be severe with it. Yet Yukawa without a blush calculated the mass of the pellet he expected to see, and waited. He was right; his meson was found, and a range of other mesons, neither the existence nor the nature of which had been suspected before. The likeness had borne fruit.

The scientist looks for order in the appearances of nature by exploring such likenesses. For order does not display itself of itself; if it can be said to be there at all, it is not there for the mere looking. There is no way of pointing a finger or a camera at it; order must be discovered and, in a deep sense, it must be created. What we see, as we see it, is mere disorder.

This point has been put trenchantly in a fable by Karl Popper. Suppose that someone wished to give his whole life to science. Suppose that he therefore sat down, pencil in hand, and for the next twenty, thirty, forty years recorded in notebook after notebook everything that he could observe. He may be supposed to leave out nothing: today's humidity, the racing results, the level of cosmic radiation and the stockmarket prices and the look of Mars, all would be there. He would have compiled the most careful rec-

ord of nature that has ever been made; and, dying in the calm certainty of a life well spent, he would of course leave his notebooks to the Royal Society. Would the Royal Society thank him for the treasure of a lifetime of observation? It would not. . . . It would refuse to open them at all, because it would know without looking that the notebooks contain only a jumble of disorderly and meaningless items.

Science finds order and meaning in our experience, and sets about this in quite a different way. It sets about it as Newton did in the story which he himself told in his old age, and of which the schoolbooks give only a caricature. In the year 1665, when Newton was twenty-two, the plague broke out in southern England, and the University of Cambridge was closed. Newton therefore spent the next eighteen months at home, removed from traditional learning, at a time when he was impatient for knowledge and, in his own phrase, "I was in the prime of my age for invention." In this eager, boyish mood, sitting one day in the garden of his widowed mother, he saw an apple fall. So far the books have the story right; we think we even know the kind of apple; tradition has it that it was a Flower of Kent. But now they miss the crux of the story. For what struck the young Newton at the sight was not the thought that the apple must be drawn to the earth by gravity; that conception was older than Newton. What struck him was the conjecture that the same force of gravity, which reaches to the top of the tree, might go on reaching out beyond the earth and its air, endlessly into space. Gravity might reach the moon: this was

Newton's new thought; and it might be gravity which holds the moon in her orbit. There and then he calculated what force from the earth (falling off as the square of the distance) would hold the moon, and compared it with the known force of gravity at tree height. The forces agreed; Newton says laconically, "I found them answer pretty nearly." Yet they agreed only nearly: the likeness and the approximation go together, for no likeness is exact. In Newton's sentence modern science is full grown.

It grows from a comparison. It has seized a likeness between two unlike appearances; for the apple in the summer garden and the grave moon overhead are surely as unlike in their movements as two things can be. Newton traced in them two expressions of a single concept, gravitation: and the concept (and the unity) are in that sense his free creation. The progress of science is the discovery at each step of a new order which gives unity to what had long seemed unlike. Faraday did this when he closed the link between electricity and magnetism. Clerk Maxwell did it when he linked both with light. Einstein linked time with space, mass with energy, and the path of light past the sun with the flight of a bullet; and spent his dying years in trying to add to these likenesses another, which would find a single imaginative order between the equations of Clerk Maxwell and his own geometry of gravitation.

When Coleridge tried to define beauty, he returned always to one deep thought: beauty, he said, is "unity in variety." Science is nothing else than the search to discover unity in the wild variety of nature —or more exactly, in the variety of our experience. Poetry, painting, the arts are the same search, in Coleridge's phrase, for unity in variety. Each in its own way looks for likenesses under the variety of human experience. What is a poetic image but the seizing and the exploration of a hidden likeness, in holding together two parts of a comparison which are to give depth each to the other? When Romeo finds Juliet in the tomb, and thinks her dead, he uses in his heartbreaking speech the words,

Death that hath suckt the honey of thy breath.

The critic can only haltingly take to pieces the single shock which this image carries. The young Shakespeare admired Marlowe, and Marlowe's Faustus had said of the ghostly kiss of Helen of Troy that it sucked forth his soul. But that is a pale image; what Shakespeare has done is to fire it with the single word honey. Death is a bee at the lips of Juliet, and the bee is an insect that stings; the sting of death was a commonplace phrase when Shakespeare wrote. The sting is there, under the image; Shakespeare has packed it into the word *honey;* but the very word rides powerfully over its own undertones. Death is a bee that stings other people, but it comes to Juliet as if she were a flower; this is the moving thought under the instant image. The creative mind speaks in such thoughts.

The poetic image here is also, and accidentally, heightened by the tenderness which town dwellers now feel for country ways. But it need not be; there are likenesses to conjure with, and images as powerful, within the man-made world. The poems of Alexander Pope belong to this world. They are not countrified, and therefore readers today find them unemotional and often artificial. Let me then quote Pope: here he is in a formal satire face to face, towards the end of his life, with his own gifts. In eight lines he looks poignantly forward towards death and back to the laborious years which made him famous.

Years foll'wing Years, steal something ev'ry day,
At last they steal us from our selves away;
In one our Frolicks, one Amusements end,
In one a Mistress drops, in one a Friend:
This subtle Thief of Life, this paltry Time,
What will it leave me, if it snatch my Rhime?
If ev'ry Wheel of that unweary'd Mill That turn'd ten thousand Verses, now stands still.

The human mind had been compared to what the eighteenth century called a mill, that is to a machine, before; Pope's own idol Bolingbroke had compared it to a clockwork. In these lines the likeness goes deeper, for Pope is thinking of the ten thousand Verses which he had translated from Homer: what he says is sad and just at the same time, because this really had been a mechanical and at times a grinding task. Yet the clockwork is present in the image too; when the wheels stand still, time for Pope will stand still for ever; we feel that we already hear, over the horizon, Faust's defiant re-

ply to Mephistopheles, which Goethe had not yet written—"let the clock strike and stop, let the hand fall, and time be at an end."

Werd ich zum Augenblicke sagen:
Verweile doch! du bist so schön!
Dann magst du mich in Fesseln schlagen,
Dann will ich gern zugrunde gehn!
Dann mag die Totenglocke schallen,
Dann bist du deines Dienstes frei,
Die Uhr mag stehn, der Zeiger fallen,
Es sei die Zeit für mich vorbei![5]

I have quoted Pope and Goethe because their metaphor here is not poetic; it is rather a hand reaching straight into experience and arranging it with new meaning. Metaphors of this kind need not always be written in words. The most powerful of them all is simply the presence of King Lear and his Fool in the hovel of a man who is shamming madness, while lightning rages outside. Or let me quote another clash of two conceptions of life, from a modern poet. In his later poems W. B. Yeats was troubled by the feeling that in shutting himself up to write, he was missing the active pleasures of life; and yet it seemed to him certain that the man who lives for these pleasures will leave no lasting work behind him. He said this at times very simply, too:

The intellect of man is forced to choose Perfection of the life, or of the work.

This problem, whether a man fulfills himself in work or in play, is of course more common than Yeats allowed; and it may be more com-

---

[5] Faust is addressing Mephistopheles in Part I of *Faust,* stating the terms of the contract and conditions on which his soul will become the devil's property: "If ever I say to the moment / 'Stay, you are so lovely!' / Then may you lock me in chains / Then will I gladly perish. / Then may the death knell ring / Then are you free from servitude / Let the clock strike and stop, let the hand fall / And time be at an end."

monplace. But it is given breadth and force by the images in which Yeats pondered it.

Get all the gold and silver that you
  can,
Satisfy ambition, or animate
The trivial days and ram them with
  the sun,
And yet upon these maxims meditate:
All women dote upon an idle man
Although their children need a rich
  estate;
No man has ever lived that had
  enough
Of children's gratitude or woman's
  love.

The love of women, the gratitude of children: the images fix two philosophies as nothing else can. They are tools of creative thought, as coherent and as exact as the conceptual images with which science works: as time and space, or as the proton and the neutron.

The discoveries of science, the works of art are explorations—more, are explosions, of a hidden likeness. The discoverer or the artist presents in them two aspects of nature and fuses them into one. This is the act of creation, in which an original thought is born, and it is the same act in original science and original art. But it is not therefore the monopoly of the man who wrote the poem or who made the discovery. On the contrary, I believe this view of the creative act to be right because it alone gives a meaning to the act of appreciation. The poem or the discovery exists in two moments of vision: the moment of appreciation as much as that of creation; for the appreciator must see the movement, wake to the echo which was started in the creation of the work. In the moment of appreciation we live again the mo-

ment when the creator saw and held the hidden likeness. When a simile takes us aback and persuades us together, when we find a juxtaposition in a picture both odd and intriguing, when a theory is at once fresh and convincing, we do not merely nod over someone else's work. We re-enact the creative act, and we ourselves make the discovery again. At bottom, there is no unifying likeness there until we too have seized it, we too have made it for ourselves.

How slipshod by comparison is the notion that either art or science sets out to copy nature. If the task of the painter were to copy for men what they see, the critic could make only a single judgment: either that the copy is right or that it is wrong. And if science were a copy of fact, then every theory would be either right or wrong, and would be so forever. There would be nothing left for us to say but this is so, or is not so. No one who has read a page by a good critic or a speculative scientist can ever again think that this barren choice of yes or no is all that the mind offers.

Reality is not an exhibit for man's inspection, labelled "Do not touch." There are no appearances to be photographed, no experiences to be copied, in which we do not take part. Science, like art, is not a copy of nature but a re-creation of her. We re-make nature by the act of discovery, in the poem or in the theorem. And the great poem and the deep theorem are new to every reader, and yet are his own experiences, because he himself re-creates them. They are the marks of unity in variety; and in the instant when the mind seizes this for itself, in art or in science, the heart misses a beat.

· QUESTIONS ·

1. What is Bronowski's principal thesis? Identify the steps through which he carries his development of this thesis.
2. How do you think Thoreau would have reacted to Bronowski's thesis?
3. Scientific activity is defined several times in this essay. Locate each instance of repetition. Does each seem faultily repetitious or does each clarify and extend meaning?
4. What is the tone of this essay? Be specific. For example, if you consider the tone "challenging" or "argumentative" or "controversial," cite instances of assumptions rebutted or popular attitudes denied.
5. Why is the story of Newton and the apple a "caricature"?
6. Define: abstract, kinetic, arbiter, horoscope, cybernetics, humdrum, alchemist, addict, analogies, meson, conceptual, juxtaposition, slipshod.
7. Explain the references to Faraday, Norbert Wiener, Industrial Revolution, Carnot cycle, Kelvin, Balzac, Zola, Christopher Isherwood, Leonardo, Rutherford, Bohr, Karl Popper.

Theme Subjects: (1) Once When My Heart Missed a Beat; (2) Fact and Theory (a concrete example from experience); (3) Creation and Appreciation: A Distinction; (4) The Theories of Huxley and Bronowski: A Comparison; (5) "The Love of Women, The Gratitude of Children."

LOGIC AND
LOGICAL FALLACIES

Robert Gorham Davis

ROBERT GORHAM DAVIS (1908–   ) was born in Northampton, Massachusetts. He received bachelor's and master's degrees from Harvard and has taught at his alma mater, at Rensselaer Polytechnic, and at Smith Col-

From *Handbook for English A*. Reprinted by permission of the author and the President and Fellows of Harvard College.

lege. He is now a professor of English at Columbia University. He is joint author of *Direct Communication: Written and Spoken* (1943) and editor of several other books, among them *Ten Modern Masters* (1953).

UNDEFINED TERMS

The first requirement for logical discourse is knowing what the words you use actually mean. Words are not like paper money or counters in a game. Except for technical terms in some of the sciences, they do not have a fixed face value. Their meanings are fluid and changing, influenced by many considerations of context and reference, circumstance and association. This is just as true of common words such as *fast* as it is of literary terms such as *romantic*. Moreover, if there is to be communication, words must have approximately the same meaning for the reader that they have for the writer. A speech in an unknown language means nothing to the hearer. When an adult speaks to a small child or an expert to a layman, communication may be seriously limited by lack of a mature vocabulary or ignorance of technical terms. Many arguments are meaningless because the speakers are using important words in quite different senses.

Because we learn most words—or guess at them—from the contexts in which we first encounter them, our sense of them is often incomplete or wrong. Readers sometimes visualize the Assyrian who comes down like the wolf on the fold as an enormous man dressed in cohorts (some kind of fancy armor, possibly) gleaming in purple and gold. "A rift in the lute" suggests vaguely a cracked mandolin. Failure to ascertain the literal meaning of figurative language is a frequent reason for mixed metaphors. We are surprised to find that the "devil" in "the devil to pay" and "the devil and the deep blue sea" is not Old Nick, but part of a ship. Unless terms mean the same thing to both writer and reader, proper understanding is impossible.

ABSTRACTIONS

The most serious logical difficulties occur with abstract terms. An abstraction is a word which stands for a quality found in a number of different objects or events from which it has been "abstracted" or taken away. We may, for instance, talk of the "whiteness" of paper or cotton or snow without considering qualities of cold or inflammability or usefulness which these materials happen also to possess. Usually, however, our minds carry over other qualities by association. See, for instance, the chapter called "The Whiteness of the Whale" in *Moby Dick*.

In much theoretic discussion the process of abstraction is carried so far that although vague associations and connotations persist, the original objects or events from which the qualities have been abstracted are lost sight of completely. Instead of thinking of words like *sincerity* and *Americanism* as symbols standing for qualities that have to be abstracted with great care from examples and test cases, we come to think of them as real things in themselves. We assume that Americanism is Americanism just as a bicycle is a bicycle, and that everyone knows what it means. We forget that before the question "Is

Arthur Godfrey sincere?" can mean anything, we have to agree on the criteria of sincerity.

When we try to define such words and find examples, we discover that almost no one agrees on their meaning. The word *church* may refer to anything from a building on the corner of Spring Street to the whole tradition of institutionalized Christianity. *Germany* may mean a geographical section of Europe, a people, a governing group, a cultural tradition, or a military power. Abstractions such as *freedom, courage, race, beauty, truth, justice, nature, honor, humanism, democracy* should never be used in a theme unless their meaning is defined or indicated clearly by the context. Freedom for whom? To do what? Under what circumstances? Abstract terms have merely emotional value unless they are strictly defined by asking questions of this kind. The study of a word such as *nature* in a good unabridged dictionary will show that even the dictionary, indispensable though it is, cannot determine for us the sense in which a word is being used in any given instance. Once the student understands the importance of definition, he will no longer be betrayed into fruitless arguments over such questions as whether free verse is "poetry" or whether you can change "human nature."

NAME-CALLING

It is a common unfairness in controversy to place what the writer dislikes or opposes in a generally odious category. The humanist dismisses what he dislikes by calling it *romantic;* the liberal, by calling it *fascist;* the conservative, by call-

ing it *communistic.* These terms tell the reader nothing. What is *piety* to some will be *bigotry* to others. *Non-Catholics* would rather be called *Protestants* than *heretics.* What is *right-thinking* except a designation for those who agree with the writer? Social security measures become *creeping socialism;* industrial organizations, *forces of reaction;* investigation into communism, *witch hunts;* prison reform, *coddling;* progressive education, *fads and frills.* Such terms are intended to block thought by an appeal to prejudice and associative habits. Three steps are necessary before such epithets have real meaning. First, they must be defined; second, it must be shown that the object to which they are applied actually possesses these qualities; third, it must be shown that the possession of such qualities in this particular situation is necessarily undesirable. Unless a person is alert and critical both in choosing and in interpreting words, he may be alienated from ideas with which he would be in sympathy if he had not been frightened by a mere name.

GENERALIZATION

Similar to the abuse of abstract terms and epithets is the habit of presenting personal opinions in the guise of universal laws. The student often seems to feel that the broader the terms in which he states an opinion, the more effective he will be. Ordinarily the reverse is true. An enthusiasm for Thomas Wolfe should lead to a specific critical analysis of Wolfe's novels that will enable the writer to explain his enthusiasm to others; it should not be turned into the argument that Wolfe is "the greatest American novelist," particularly if the writer's knowledge of American novelists is somewhat limited. The same questions of *who* and *when* and *why* and under what *circumstances* which are used to check abstract terms should be applied to generalizations. Consider how contradictory proverbial wisdom is when detached from particular circumstances. "Look before you leap," but "he who hesitates is lost."

Superlatives and the words *right* and *wrong, true* and *untrue, never* and *always* must be used with caution in matters of opinion. When a student says flatly that X is true, he often is really saying that he or his family or the author of a book he has just been reading, persons of certain tastes and background and experience, *think* that X is true. If his statement is based not on logic and examination of evidence, but merely reproduces other people's opinions, it can have little value or relevance unless these people are identified and their reasons for thinking so explained. Because many freshmen are taking survey courses in which they read a single work by an author or see an historical event through the eyes of a single historian whose bias they may not be able to measure, they must guard against this error.

SAMPLING

Assertions of a general nature are frequently open to question because they are based on insufficient evidence. Some persons are quite ready, after meeting one Armenian or reading one medieval romance, to generalize about Armenians and medieval romances. One ought, of course, to examine objectively as many examples as possible before making a generalization, but the number is far less important than the representativeness of the examples chosen. The *Literary Digest* Presidential Poll, sent to hundreds of thousands of people selected from telephone directories, was far less accurate than the Gallup Poll which questioned far fewer voters, but selected them carefully and proportionately from all different social groups. The "typical" college student, as portrayed by moving pictures and cartoons, is very different from the "average" college student as determined statistically. We cannot let uncontrolled experience do our sampling for us; instances and examples which impress themselves upon our minds do so usually because they are exceptional. In propaganda and arguments extreme cases are customarily treated as if they were characteristic.

If one is permitted arbitrarily to select some examples and ignore others, it is possible to find convincing evidence for almost any theory, no matter how fantastic. The fact that the mind tends naturally to remember those instances which confirm its opinions imposes a duty upon the writer, unless he wishes to encourage prejudice and superstition, to look carefully for exceptions to all generalizations which he is tempted to make. We forget the premonitions which are not followed by disaster and the times when our hunches failed to select the winner in a race. Patent medicine advertisements print the letters of those who survived their cure, and not of those who died during it. All Americans did not gamble on the stock exchange in the twenties, or become Marxists in the thirties, and all Vermonters are not thin-lipped and shrewd. Of course the search for negative examples can be carried too far. Outside of mathematics or the laboratory, few generalizations can be made airtight, and most are not intended to be. But quibbling is so easy that resort to it is very common, and the knowledge that people can and will quibble over generalizations is another reason for making assertions as limited and explicitly conditional as possible.

FALSE ANALOGY

Illustration, comparison, analogy are most valuable in making an essay clear and interesting. It must not be supposed, however, that they prove anything or have much argumentative weight. The rule that what is true of one thing in one set of circumstances is not necessarily true of another thing in another set of circumstances seems almost too obvious to need stating. Yet constantly nations and businesses are discussed as if they were human beings with human habits and feelings; human bodies are discussed as if they were machines; the universe, as if it were a clock. It is assumed that what held true for seventeenth century New England or the thirteen Atlantic colonies also holds true for an industrial nation of 160,000,000 people. Carlyle dismissed the arguments for representative democracy by saying that if a captain had to take a vote among his crew every time he wanted to do something, he would never get around Cape Horn. This analogy calmly ignores the distinction between the lawmaking and the executive branches of constitutional democracies. Moreover, voters

may be considered much more like the stockholders of a merchant line than its hired sailors. Such arguments introduce assumptions in a metaphorical guise in which they are not readily detected or easily criticized. In place of analysis they attempt to identify their position with some familiar symbol which will evoke a predictable, emotional response in the reader. The revival during the 1932 presidential campaign of Lincoln's remark, "Don't swap horses in the middle of the stream," was not merely a picturesque way of saying keep Hoover in the White House. It made a number of assumptions about the nature of depressions and the function of government. This propagandist technique can be seen most clearly in political cartoons.

DEGREE

Often differences in degree are more important than differences in kind. By legal and social standards there is more difference between an habitual drunkard and a man who drinks temperately, than between a temperate drinker and a total abstainer. In fact, differences of degree produce what are regarded as differences of kind. At known temperatures ice turns to water and water boils. At an indeterminate point affection becomes love and a man who needs a shave becomes a man with a beard. The fact that no men or systems are perfect makes rejoinders and counter-accusations very easy if differences in degree are ignored. Newspapers in totalitarian states, answering American accusations of brutality and suppression, refer to lynchings and gangsterism here. Before a disinterested judge could evaluate these mutual accusations, he would have to settle the question of the degree to which violent suppression and lynching are respectively prevalent in the countries under consideration. On the other hand, differences in degree may be merely apparent. Lincoln Steffens pointed out that newspapers can create a "crime wave" any time they wish, simply by emphasizing all the minor assaults and thefts commonly ignored or given an inch or two on a back page. The great reported increases in insanity may be due to the fact that in a more urban and institutionalized society cases of insanity more frequently come to the attention of authorities and hence are recorded in statistics.

CAUSATION

The most common way of deciding that one thing causes another thing is the simple principle: *post hoc, ergo propter hoc,* "After this, therefore because of this." Rome fell after the introduction of Christianity; therefore Christianity was responsible for the fall of Rome. Such reasoning illustrates another kind of faulty generalization. But even if one could find ten cases in which a nation "fell" after the introduction of Christianity, it still would not be at all certain that Christianity caused the fall. Day, it has frequently been pointed out, follows night in every observable instance, and yet night cannot be called the cause of day. Usually a combination of causes produces a result. Sitting in a draught may cause a cold, but only given a certain physical condition in the person sitting there. In such instances one may distinguish between necessary and

sufficient conditions. Air is a necessary condition for the maintenance of plant life, but air alone is not sufficient to produce plant life. And often different causes at different times may produce the same result. This relation is known as plurality of causes. If, after sitting in a stuffy theatre on Monday, and then again after eating in a stuffy restaurant on Thursday, a man suffered from headaches, he might say, generalizing, that bad air gave him headaches. But actually the headache on Monday may have been caused by eyestrain and on Thursday by indigestion. To isolate the causative factor it is necessary that all other conditions be precisely the same. Such isolation is possible, except in very simple instances, only in the laboratory or with scientific methods. If a picture falls from the wall every time a truck passes, we can quite certainly say that the truck's passing is the proximate or immediate cause. But with anything as complex and conditional as a nation's economy or human character, the determination of cause is not easy or certain. A psychiatrist often sees a patient for an hour daily for a year or more before he feels that he understands his neurosis.

Ordinarily when we speak of cause we mean the proximate or immediate cause. The plants were killed by frost; we had indigestion from eating lobster salad. But any single cause is one in an unbroken series. When a man is murdered, is his death caused by the loss of blood from the wound, or by the firing of the pistol, or by the malice aforethought of the murderer? Was the World War "caused" by the assassination at Sarajevo? Were the Navigation Acts or the ideas of John Locke more important in "causing" the American Revolution? A complete statement of cause would comprise the sum total of the conditions which preceded an event, conditions stretching back indefinitely into the past. Historical events are so interrelated that the isolation of a causative sequence is dependent chiefly on the particular preoccupations of the historian. An economic determinist can "explain" history entirely in terms of economic developments; an idealist, entirely in terms of the development of ideas.

SYLLOGISTIC REASONING

The formal syllogism of the type,

> All men are mortal
> John is a man
> Therefore John is mortal,

is not so highly regarded today as in some earlier periods. It merely fixes an individual as a member of a class, and then assumes that the individual has the given characteristics of the class. Once we have decided who John is, and what "man" and "mortal" mean, and have canvassed all men, including John, to make sure that they are mortal, the conclusion naturally follows. It can be seen that the chief difficulties arise in trying to establish acceptable premises. Faults in the premises are known as "material" fallacies, and are usually more serious than the "formal" fallacies, which are logical defects in drawing a conclusion from the premises. But although directly syllogistic reasoning is not much practiced, buried syllogism can be found in all argument, and it is often a useful clarification to outline your own or another writer's essay in syllogistic form. The two most frequent defects in the syllogism itself are the undistributed and the ambiguous middle. The middle term is the one that appears in each of the premises and not in the conclusion. In the syllogism,

> All good citizens vote
> John votes
> Therefore John is a good citizen,

the middle term is not "good citizens," but "votes." Even though it were true that all good citizens vote, nothing prevents bad citizens from voting also, and John may be one of the bad citizens. To distribute the middle term "votes" one might say (but only if that is what one meant),

> All voters are good citizens
> John is a voter
> Therefore John is a good citizen.

The ambiguous middle term is even more common. It represents a problem in definition, while the undistributed middle is a problem in generalization. All acts which benefit others are virtuous, losing money at poker benefits others, therefore losing at poker is a virtuous act. Here the middle term "act which benefits others" is obviously used very loosely and ambiguously.

NON-SEQUITUR

This phrase, meaning "it does not follow," is used to characterize the kind of humor found in pictures in which the Marx Brothers used to perform. It is an amusing illogicality because it usually expresses, beneath its apparent incongruity, an imaginative, associative, or personal truth. "My ancestors came over on the *Mayflower;* therefore I am naturally opposed to labor unions." It is not logically necessary that those whose ancestors came over on the *Mayflower* should be opposed to unions; but it may happen to be true as a personal fact in a given case. It is usually a strong personal conviction which keeps people from realizing that their arguments are non-sequiturs, that they do not follow the given premises with logical necessity. Contemporary psychologists have effectively shown us that there is often such a wide difference between the true and the purported reasons for an attitude that, in rationalizing our behavior, we are often quite unconscious of the motives that actually influence us. A fanatical antivivisectionist, for instance, may have temperamental impulses toward cruelty which he is suppressing and compensating for by a reasoned opposition to any kind of permitted suffering. We may expect, then, to come upon many conclusions which are psychologically interesting in themselves but have nothing to do with the given premises.

IGNORATIO ELENCHI

This means, in idiomatic English, "arguing off the point," or ignoring the question at issue. A man trying to show that monarchy is the best form of government for the British Empire may devote most of his attention to the charm of Elizabeth II and the affection her people feel for her. In ordinary conversational argument it is almost impossible for disputants to keep to the point. Constantly turning up are tempting side-issues through which one can discomfit an opponent or force him to irrelevant admissions that seem to weaken his case.

BEGGING THE QUESTION; ARGUING IN A CIRCLE

The first of these terms means to assume in the premises what you are pretending to prove in the course of your argument. The function of logic is to demonstrate that because one thing or group of things is true, another must be true as a consequence. But in begging the question you simply say in varying language that what is assumed to be true is assumed to be true. An argument which asserts that we shall enjoy immortality because we have souls which are immaterial and indestructible establishes nothing, because the idea of immortality is already contained in the assumption about the soul. It is the premise which needs to be demonstrated, not the conclusion. Arguing in a circle is another form of this fallacy. It proves the premise by the conclusion and the conclusion by the premise. The conscience forbids an act because it is wrong; the act is wrong because the conscience forbids it.

ARGUMENTS AD HOMINEM AND AD POPULUM

It is very difficult for men to be persuaded by reason when their interest or prestige is at stake. If one wishes to preach the significance of physiognomy, it is well to choose a hearer with a high forehead and a determined jaw. The arguments in favor of repealing the protective tariff on corn or wheat in England were more readily entertained by manufacturers than by landowners. The cotton manufacturers in New England who were doing a profitable trade with the South were the last to be moved by descriptions of the evils of slavery. Because interest and desire are so deeply seated in human nature, arguments are frequently mingled with attempts to appeal to emotion, arouse fear, play upon pride, attack the characters of proponents of an opposite view, show that their practice is inconsistent with their principles; all matters which have, strictly speaking, nothing to do with the truth or falsity, the general desirability or undesirability, of some particular measure. If men are desperate enough they will listen to arguments proper only to an insane asylum but which seem to promise them relief.

After reading these suggestions, which are largely negative, the student may feel that any original assertion he can make will probably contain one or several logical faults. This assumption is not true. Even if it were, we know from reading newspapers and magazines that worldly fame is not dimmed by the constant and, one suspects, conscious practice of illogicality. But generalizations are not made only by charlatans and sophists. Intelligent and scrupulous writers also have a great many fresh and provocative observations and conclusions to express and are expressing them influentially. What is intelligence but the ability to see the connection between things, to discern causes, to relate the particular to the general, to define and discriminate and compare? Any man who thinks and feels and observes closely will not want for something to express.

And in his expression a proponent will find that a due regard for logic does not limit but rather increases the force of his argument. When statements are not trite, they are usually controversial. Men arrive at truth dialectically; error is weeded out in the course of discussion, argument, attack, and counterattack. Not only can a writer who understands logic show the weaknesses of arguments he disagrees with, but also, by anticipating the kind of attack likely to be made on his own ideas, he can so arrange them, properly modified with qualifications and exceptions, that the anticipated attack is made much less effective. Thus, fortunately, we do not have to depend on the spirit of fairness and love of truth to lead men to logic; it has the strong support of argumentative necessity and of the universal desire to make ideas prevail.

· QUESTIONS ·

1. This article is closely reasoned and must be read and reread thoughtfully. Yet it is enlivened by humor, figures of speech, and allusions. Cite three examples of each of these stylistic devices.
2. This selection has 13 subheadings. List them and write a one-sentence definition of each. Use your own words.

3. Cite several examples of illogical thinking as heard by you in conversation. Give each a name according to the list supplied by Davis.
4. As suggested in Question 3, do the same with material heard on TV or radio.
5. As suggested in Question 3, do the same with material read in newspapers, magazines, or books.
6. Demonstrate your understanding of the word *context* by defining it in a paragraph comparable in length and method of treatment to any one you select from Davis' article.
7. Do you feel that some people go wrong in an argument more often because of a prior commitment or false information than because of formal fallacies?
8. Logic has been defined as "The mode of thinking followed by most people when the penalty for getting the wrong answer is immediate, obvious, and severe." Is this a fair definition? Do such conditions often obtain in bull sessions and student themes?

Theme Subjects: (1) My Love of Truth; (2) Thinking Straight Is Hard Work; (3) Illogicalities I've Been Guilty Of; (4) A Good Example of _____ (one of the fallacies cited; develop as an expository anecdote or as an incident); (5) Davis and Huxley (a comparison and contrast based on the articles in this section).

EMOTIONAL MEANINGS

Robert H. Thouless

ROBERT H. THOULESS (1894–   ) is a native of Norwich, England. He attended Cambridge University, took a degree in 1915, and soon afterward enlisted in the British Expeditionary Force. He later continued his studies in psychology at Cambridge. Thouless, formerly of the department of psychology at Glasgow University, is the author of several books on psychology. Among his related fields of interest are the psychology of religion and psychical research.

When we use a word in speech and writing, its most obvious purpose is to point to some thing or relation or property. This is the word's "mean-ing." We see a small four-footed animal on the road and call it a "dog," indicating that it is a member of the class of four-footed animals we call dogs. The word "dog" as we have used it there has a plain, straightforward, "objective" meaning. We have in no way gone beyond the requirements of exact scientific description.

Let us suppose also that one grandparent of the dog was a collie, another was an Irish terrier, another a fox terrier, and the fourth a bulldog. We can express these facts equally scientifically and objectively by saying that he is a dog of mixed breed. Still we have in no way gone beyond the requirements of exact scientific description.

Suppose, however, that we had called that same animal a "mongrel." The matter is more complicated. We have used a word which objectively means the same as "dog of mixed breed," but which also arouses in our hearers an emotional attitude of disapproval toward that particular dog. A word, therefore, can not only indicate an object, but can also suggest an emotional attitude toward it. Such suggestion of an emotional attitude does go beyond exact and scientific discussion because our approvals and disapprovals are individual—they belong to ourselves and not to the objects we approve or disapprove of. An animal which to the mind of its master is a faithful and noble dog of mixed ancestry may be a "mongrel" to his neighbor whose chickens are chased by it.

Similarly, a Negro may be indicated objectively as a "colored man" or he may be indicated with strong emotional disapproval and contempt as a "nigger." The use of the latter word debases any discussion in which it is used below the level of impartial and objective argument.

Once we are on the lookout for this difference between "objective" and "emotional" meanings, we shall notice that words which carry more or less strong suggestions of emotional attitudes are very common and are ordinarily used in the discussion of such controversial questions as those of politics, morals, and religion. This is one reason why such controversies cannot yet be settled.

There is a well-known saying that the word "firm" can be declined as follows: I am *firm,* thou art *obstinate,* he is *pigheaded.* That is a simple illustration of what is meant. "Firm," "obstinate," and "pigheaded" all have the same objective meaning—that is, following one's own course of action and refusing to be influenced by other people's opinions. They have, however, different emotional meanings: "firm" has an emotional meaning of strong approval, "obstinate" of mild disapproval, "pigheaded" of strong disapproval. . . .

Such thinking in wartime may do much harm by leading humane people to condone cruelty. When the ordinarily liberal-minded Swinburne wrote a poem during the Boer War on the death of a British officer who had been blamed for the bad condition of the camps in which the Boer women and children were interned, he said:

Nor heed we more than he what liars
    dare say
Of mercy's holiest duties left undone
Toward *whelps* and *dams* of *murderous* foes, whom none
Save we had spared or feared to starve
    and slay.

Whelps and *dams* clearly mean in objective fact *children* and *wives,* with the added meaning of the emotional attitude adopted toward the females and young of wild beasts, while *murderous* means no more in objective fact than that our foes killed us when they could (as we also killed them), with the added emotional meaning of an attitude toward them which is our attitude to those who are guilty of murder.

The use of emotionally toned words is not, of course, always to be condemned. They are always harmful when we are trying to think clearly on a disputable point of fact. In poetry, on the other hand, they have a perfectly proper place, because in poetry (as in some kinds of prose) the arousing of suitable emotions is an important part of the purpose for which the words are used.

In "The Eve of St. Agnes," Keats has written:

Full on this casement shone the wintry moon,
And threw warm gules on Madeline's fair breast.

These are beautiful lines. Let us notice how much of their beauty follows from the proper choice of emotionally colored words and how completely it is lost if these words are replaced by neutral ones. The words with strikingly emotional meanings are *casement*, *gules*, *Madeline*, *fair*, and *breast*. *Casement* means simply a kind of window with emotional and romantic associations. *Gules* is the heraldic name for red, with the suggestion of romance which accompanies all heraldry. *Madeline* is simply a girl's name, but one calling out favorable emotions absent from a relatively plain and straightforward name. *Fair* simply means, in objective fact, that her skin was white or uncolored—a necessary condition for the colors of the window to show—

but also *fair* implies warm emotional preference for an uncolored skin rather than one which is yellow, purple, black, or any of the other colors which skin might be. *Breast* has also similar emotional meanings, and the aim of scientific description might have been equally well attained if it had been replaced by such a neutral word as *chest*.

Let us now try the experiment of keeping these two lines in a metrical form, but replacing all the emotionally colored words by neutral ones, while making as few other changes as possible. We may write:

Full on this window shone the wintry moon,
Making red marks on Jane's uncolored chest.

No one will doubt that all of its poetic value has been knocked out of the passage by these changes. Yet the lines still mean the same in external fact; they still have the same objective meaning. It is only the emotional meaning which has been destroyed.

Now if Keats had been writing a scientific description for a textbook on physics instead of a poem, it would have been necessary for him to have used some such coldly objective terms as the ones into which we have just translated his lines. Such emotionally charged phrases as *warm gules* and *fair breast* would only have obscured the facts to which the scientist exactly but unbeautifully refers when he speaks of "the selective transmission of homogeneous light by pigmented glass."

The purpose of the present essay is to deal with the kind of problem in which cold and scientific thinking is required. Most of the practical problems of life are of this order. The fact that I shall abuse the use of emotional thinking in connection with such problems as tariffs, social ownership, revolution, and war does not mean that there is no place for emotional thinking. Poetry, romantic prose, and emotional oratory are all of inestimable value, but their place is not where responsible decisions must be made. The common (almost universal) use of emotional words in political thinking is as much out of place as would be a chemical or statistical formula in the middle of a poem. Real democracy will come only when the solution of national and international problems is carried out by scientific methods of thought, purged of all irrelevant emotion. Into the action which follows decision we can put all the emotion which we have refused to allow in our thinking. Let us think calmly and scientifically about war, and then actively oppose it with all the passion of which we are capable.

The growth of the exact thinking of modern science has been largely the result of its getting rid of all terms suggesting emotional attitudes and using only those which unemotionally indicate objective facts. It was not always so. The old alchemists called gold and silver "noble" metals, and thought that this emotionally colored word indicated something belonging to the metals themselves from which their properties could be deduced. Other metals were called "base." Although these terms have survived as convenient labels for the modern chemist, they carry none of their old emotional significance.

In popular biological discussions, on the other hand, such words are still used with their full emotional meaning, as when the "no-

bility" of man is contrasted with his alleged "base" origin. In this respect, popular biological discussion differs from that of the textbook and the laboratory, in which are used terms almost as devoid of emotional meaning as those of physics or chemistry.

Psychology is still younger in the ranks of the sciences, and the clearing away from it of emotional words has not gone very far. "Passion," "emotion," "sex" are all terms of our science which carry strong emotional meanings, so that it is difficult to discuss a controversial matter in psychology without using words which rouse strong emotions and confuse all issues. A beginning is being made. "Intelligence" was a subject on which it was difficult to think clearly because it carried so much emotional meaning. Now Professor Spearman has replaced it by what he calls "g" (or the "general factor"), which is a conception derived from the statistical analysis of a large collection of figures, and yet which is in its essence all that was really scientific in the old conception of intelligence. Some day a psychological genius will give us X or Z to replace the old emotional conception of sex, and we shall be able to discuss psychoanalysis as objectively as a mathematical physicist can discuss the quantum theory.

When we turn to politics and international questions, we are still further from straight scientific thinking. Such words as "Bolshevik," "Fascist," "reactionary," "revolutionary," "constitutional," "national honor," etc., are all words used in national and international political thinking which carry more of emotional than of any other meaning. So long as such words are the ordinary terms of rival politicians, how can we hope to think straight in national and international affairs? If a chemist doing an experiment depended on such thought processes as a nation uses in selecting its rulers or in deciding on peace or war with other nations, he would blow up his laboratory. This, however, would be a trivial disaster in comparison with what may result from emotional thinking in politics. Better have a hundred chemical laboratories blown up than the whole of civilization!

We must look forward to and try to help on the day when the thinking about political and international affairs will be as unemotional and as scientific as that about the properties of numbers or the atomic weights of elements. The spirit of impartial investigation of facts unswayed by irrelevant emotions has given us great advances in the sciences. Its triumphs will be even greater when it is applied to the most important affairs of life. We look forward to the day when we shall be able to discuss and settle such questions as Tariffs, Public *vs.* Private Ownership, and Disarmament Treaties as successfully as physicists have discussed and settled Einstein's theory of relativity.

Let us try to study a few more examples of the use of words with emotional meanings taken from various sources. Accounts of wars are rich sources of such material, so we are not surprised to find in a book on the French Commune the statement that large numbers of the regular troops were *assassinated* during the street fighting by the Communards, while a much larger number of the latter were *summarily executed* by the regulars. In order to reduce this to a statement of objective fact it is clear that the one word "killed" should be used in place both of *assassinated* and *summarily executed*. We have already noticed how such a choice of words with the same objective but opposite emotional meaning can be used to make us feel sympathetic to one and hostile to the other of two sides in warfare. During the Spanish Civil War, the supporters of the Government referred to themselves as the "Loyalists" and called Franco a "Rebel" or an "Insurgent." The supporters of Franco, on the other hand, called themselves "Nationalists" and referred to their opponents as "Reds." During the conflicts between Red and White forces in Russia and in China, our newspapers told us of the *atrocities* of the Bolsheviks and the *wise severity* of the White commanders. Examination of the details (often possible only long afterwards) shows that the objective facts of an *atrocity* and of *wise severity* are much the same, and that they are not the kind of objective facts which will call out an emotion of approval in a humane person.

A similar choice of words will be noticed in political discussion. A fluent and forcible speech delivered by one of our own party is *eloquent*, a similar speech by one of the opposite party is *fanatical;* again two words with the same objective meaning but with the opposite emotional meanings of approval and strong disapproval. The practical proposals of the opposition, moreover, are *panaceas*—a highly emotional word calling out the strongly disapproving emotions which we feel for those quack patent medicines which make extravagant claims. Those who show enthusiasm in support of proposals with which a speaker disagrees are *crackpots;*

while those showing similar enthusiasm on his own side are called *sound*. If a politician wishes to attack some new proposal he has a battery of these and other words with emotional meanings at his disposal. He speaks of "this suggested *panacea* supported only by *fanatical crackpots*"; and the proposal is at once discredited in the minds of the majority of people, who like to think of themselves as moderate, distrustful of panaceas, and uninfluenced by windy eloquence. Also, we may notice that it has been discredited without the expenditure of any real thought, for of real objective argument there is none—only the manipulation of words calling out emotion.

It is not, however, only in warfare and politics that such words are used in order to influence opinion more easily than can be done by words embodying real thought. Art criticism is also a good source for this kind of material. Ruskin said of Whistler's *Nocturnes:* "I have heard and seen much of *Cockney impudence* before now, but never expected to hear a *coxcomb* ask two hundred guineas for *flinging a pot of paint in the public's face.*" As in earlier passages, I have italicized the words or phrases with strongly emotional meanings. Stripped of these and reduced to a statement of objective fact, the passage would have to be paraphrased in some such way as follows: "I have heard and seen much of the behavior of Londoners before now, but never expected to hear a painter ask two hundred guineas for painting a picture which seemed to me to have no meaning." Plainly not much is left of Ruskin's criticism after this operation has been performed on it.

As a last example, we may take a part of an attack made by a newspaper on a novel. This runs: "Its *vicious* plea for the acknowledgment and *condonation* of *sexual perversity*, and the grounds on which it is based, loosen the very *sheet anchor of conduct.*" This passage calls out such strong emotions of abhorrence that most readers will be content to condemn the novel without further inquiry. Yet the effect is gained entirely by the choice of words with emotional meanings. It happens to deal with a subject on which emotions are strong, so a dispassionate examination is all the more necessary. We note that a *plea* is simply an argument, plus a suggestion of a repugnance for the kind of argument used; that *condonation* is tolerance plus an emotional suggestion that such toleration is indefensible; that *sexual* means something in the life of love of which we disapprove, and that a *perversity* is an unusualness plus an emotional suggestion of abhorrence. The loosening of a *sheet anchor* is a metaphor implying change and suggesting to a landsman the emotion of fear, while *conduct* is simply behavior of which we approve.

So reduced to its bare bones of statement of objective fact (ignoring for a moment the special difficulties raised by the word *vicious*), the passage becomes: "Its argument for the acknowledgment and tolerance of unusualness in the life of love, and the grounds on which it is based, change the principles of behavior." This clearly is an important statement if it is true, but is not enough in itself to condemn the book, because undoubtedly our principles of behavior do need changing from time to time. We can only decide intelligently whether or not they need changing in the particular case under discussion, when we have made a dispassionate statement of what the proposed changes are and why they are defended. As in all other cases, discussion of the question with emotionally charged words obscures the problem and makes a sensible decision difficult or impossible.

The word *vicious* has some special difficulties of its own. It arouses emotions of disapproval, but there is no word with the same objective meaning which would not. If we call the book bad, corrupt, or evil, the same emotions would be aroused. So we cannot perform the simple operation of replacing *vicious* by an emotionally neutral word with the same objective meaning. Can we then leave it out altogether, on the ground that it has no objective meaning, but that it is used merely to arouse emotion?

Here we are up against a problem about which there has been much dispute. Some people consider that all such words as "good," "bad," "beautiful," "ugly," only indicate one's own emotional reactions toward actions or things and in no sense properties of the actions or things themselves. But when we see a man steal a penny from a child and we call his action "bad," we are in fact saying something meaningful about the action itself and not merely about our own feelings. As to what that something is we may leave the philosophers to dispute; it may only be that the man's action has subtracted from the total amount of human happiness. So to say a book is *vicious* is not the same kind of thing as contrasting the *slaughter* of regular troops by Communards with the *execution* of the Communards by regular soldiers.

The statement that the book is *vicious* has a meaning which is not merely emotional, although, of course, the statement may not be true.

On the other hand, it is clearly not quite the same kind of meaning as a simple statement of outside fact such as "This is a book." Whether the book is good or bad is a real question, but it is a question peculiarly difficult to decide. Our own statement one way or the other is likely to be nothing but a reflection of our own personal prejudices and to have, therefore, no sort of scientific exactness. At the same time, such words certainly arouse strong emotions and should, therefore, be used sparingly in honest argument. The use of words implying moral judgments in the course of argument is very generally an attempt to distort the hearers' view of the truth by arousing emotions.

If we are trying to decide a simple question of fact, such words should be left out, because it is easier to settle one question at a time. If a man is accused of poisoning his wife, the prosecuting attorney should not say, "This *scoundrel* who hounded his wife to her grave." The question to be decided is whether the man did poison his wife. If he did, he is a "scoundrel" undoubtedly, but calling him a scoundrel does not help to decide the question of fact. On the contrary, it makes a correct decision more difficult by arousing emotions of hatred for the accused in the minds of the jury. Another obvious objection to the use of the word "scoundrel" before the man is convicted, which puts it in the ranks of "crooked thinking," is that it "begs the question" or assumes what is to be proved. The man is only a scoundrel if he is guilty, and yet the word has been used in the course of an argument to prove that he is guilty.

These two objections can be urged against the word "vicious" in the condemnation of a book quoted above. It calls up strong emotions making a just decision of the nature of the book difficult, and it assumes exactly what the article professes to prove—that the book is a bad one.

The aim of this essay has been to distinguish one kind of crooked thinking, in the hope that those who recognize how their opinions can be twisted away from the truth by the use of words with emotional meanings may be able to recognize this source of error and to guard themselves against it. Those of its readers who have found anything new to them in the ideas of this chapter should not, I suggest, be content simply to read the essay, but should try to do some practical work on its subject matter. If you were studying botany, you would not be content merely to read books on botany. If you were, that would not carry you far in botanical knowledge. Instead, you would gather plants from the hedges and weeds from your garden, dissecting them, examining them with a microscope or magnifying glass, and drawing them in your notebook. Psychology too should be studied by practical methods. Emotional thinking (like most of the other kinds of crooked thinking we shall be studying) is as common as a weed. It is to be found in the leading articles of newspapers, in the words of people carrying on discussions on political, religious, or moral

questions, and in the speeches made by public men when these deal with controversial matters. In order to understand it, we should collect specimens by putting them down on paper and then we should dissect them. Current political and social controversy in the United States abounds in such words and phrases as "crackpots," "economic royalists," "the abundant life," "bureaucracy" —or, on the street level—"scabs," "finks," "nigger-lovers." The New York *Herald Tribune* habitually referred to the child labor bill for New York State as the "youth control bill"; the Hearst press dubbed the New Deal the "Raw Deal"; Communists use the words "Trotskyite" and "Fascist" to cover a multitude of sinners; Secretary Ickes managed to get some powerful emotional undertones from Ferdinand Lundberg's phrase, "America's Sixty Families."

With these ideas and phrases in mind, it is not difficult to set forth on a practical search for truth. I suggest that readers should copy out controversial phrases from newspapers, books, or speeches which contain emotionally colored words. Then they should underline all the emotional words, afterwards rewriting the passages with the emotional words replaced by neutral ones. Examine the passage then in its new form in which it merely states objective facts without indicating the writer's emotional attitude toward them, and see whether it is still good evidence for the proposition it is trying to prove. If it is, the passage is a piece of straight thinking in which emotionally colored words have been introduced merely as an ornament. If not, it is crooked thinking, because the conclusion depends not on the objective meaning of the passage but on the emotions roused by the words.

When we condemn such a use of emotional words in writings and speeches, we must remember that this is a symptom of a more deep-seated evil—their prevalence in our own private, unexpressed thinking. Many of our highly colored political speakers whose speeches stir us as we are stirred by romantic poetry show themselves unable to think calmly and objectively on any subject. They have so accustomed themselves to think in emotionally toned words that they can no longer think in any other way. They should have been poets or professional orators, but certainly not statesmen.

It really does not matter much if we sometimes use emotional words. We all do when we are trying to produce conviction. What does matter is that we should not lose the power to think without them. So a more important exercise than any we can perform on written material is one we can perform on our own minds. When we catch ourselves thinking in emotional phraseology, let us form a habit of translating our thoughts into emotionally neutral words. So we can guard ourselves from ever being so enslaved by emotional words and phrases that they prevent us from thinking objectively when we need to do so—that is, whenever we have to come to a decision on any debatable matter.

· QUESTIONS ·

1. One paragraph begins "The purpose of the present essay is . . ." State the author's purpose in your own words.
2. In the fourth paragraph from the end of the essay, several allusions pertinent many years ago now seem dated. Supply current terms in lieu of "Trotskyite," etc.
3. What is the precise difference between emotional meaning and objective meaning? Is this difference clarified by the distinction between *denotation* and *connotation*? By Sherwood's article?
4. Why cannot controversies in politics, morals, and religion be settled when emotionally toned words are used? Is emotion irrelevant to discussion of national and international problems? Why?
5. Do you agree that if a word has no objective meaning, it should not be used in the "cold and scientific thinking" required for "the practical problems of life"? Why? Why not?
6. Do you believe that *good, bad, beautiful,* and *ugly* indicate only emotional reactions and never properties of actions or things?
7. Is there a distinction between *prejudice* and *opinion*? Between *knowledge* and *belief*?
8. What is the difference between a "moral judgment" and a "scientific judgment"?
9. From newspaper accounts of trials, select examples of the use of emotionally toned words.
10. Do either or both of the exercises which Thouless recommends in the last three paragraphs.
11. Does the author violate any of his own precepts?

12. Define: humane, devoid, quantum theory, trivial, manipulation, abhorrence, metaphor, moral judgments, prevalence, phraseology.

Theme Subjects: (1) Emotionally Toned Language in This Morning's Newspaper; (2) What the Term *Red* (Fascist, Beatnik, Great Society, Fink, Strikebreaker, Fundamentalist, Proletariat, Free Love, Conservative, Liberal) Means to Me; (3) My Reply to Thouless; (4) The Dominant Appeals of Advertising; (5) Emotionally Toned Language on TV; (6) My Own Emotional Phraseology.

HOW TO LOOK
AT A STATISTIC

Darrell Huff

DARRELL HUFF (1913–   ) was born in Gowrie, Iowa, and was graduated from the State University of Iowa with an M.A. degree in 1939. Starting as a reporter on *The Herald* (Clinton, Iowa) and *The Gazette* (Cedar Rapids), he has held editorial posts at *Look* (1939–1940), the D. C. Cook Publishing Company (1940–1941), as managing editor of *Better Homes and Gardens* (1942–1944), and executive editor of *Liberty* (1944–1945). His many books include *Pictures by Pete* (1944); *Twenty Careers of Tomorrow* (1945); *The Dog That Came True* (1944); *How To Lie with Statistics* (1954); *How To Take a Chance* (1959); and *Score: The Strategy of Taking Tests* (1961), as well as hundreds of articles in popular magazines.

Let's say you're in the business of making automobile tires. Tests on a type you've been making tell you it is good, on the average, for 20,000 miles. They tell you, further, that of every six tires you turn out, one will last less than 18,400 miles and one will run more than 21,600. The other two-thirds of your merchandise will fall somewhere between in durability.

You know this because you

have a quality-control department engaged in applying statistical method, which is in the main a use of probability theory.

Now comes your laboratory chief to tell you that a new rubber formula produces what seems to be a more durable tire. A sample of 64 has been run to destruction, showing a mean average life of 20,400 miles.

Is the new tire really better than the old? Or is the apparent improvement just a matter of chance, a lucky sample?

Your statistician will explain it all to you, probably in somewhat patronizing tones. What it will all come down to is that, by probability theory, there is 1 chance in 20 that a difference this size could be an accident. You can proceed with a changeover to the new rubber, having a reasonable certainty (19 to 1) that the new stuff actually is better than the old.

Sampling is one of our most useful techniques for studying a multitude of things. Polls sample public opinion because it would be hopelessly expensive to ask questions of the whole population. A manufacturer tests a sample of the light bulbs he makes to find out how long they will burn; if instead he tested them all, what would he have left to sell? An editor samples a manuscript because there are only so many hours in a day. And besides: "You don't have to eat all of an egg to know if it is bad."

In those words lies the basis of the theory of sampling. We can learn a little about the process by watching the editor at work. He reads a few lines here and a few there—large enough in number to get him an adequate sample, varied enough to protect him against a

writer whose skill improves after a bad opening scene. The less consistent the writer is and the more uneven his style, the more of the manuscript the editor will have to read to obtain a fair idea of its average quality.

So it is in scientific sampling. When you read of a conclusion that arises from sampling, as do a great many of the things you read or hear about these days, ask yourself two things. Is it a fair sample? Is it big enough?

This reminds us of a scene in a Chaplin movie: A customer offers his watch for a loan. Chaplin as pawnbroker examines the watch, knocks off the back, unscrews some innards, keeps on till the watch is completely dismembered. Then he hands the pieces back to the customer, shrugging his shoulders, refusing the loan.

Here, to sharpen your teeth on, are the first couple of paragraphs of a story carried in the *New York Times* under the head, "DOCTORS REPORTED FOR SECURITY PLAN."

"A recent poll in New Jersey indicates that most of the country's doctors would like to come under the Social Security old age and survivors insurance program, according to Representative Robert W. Kean, Republican of New Jersey.

"He announced today that the poll, conducted by the Essex County Medical Society, showed that New Jersey physicians favored inclusion by a 6-to-1 margin."

As you take a closer look at this poll and the facts behind the conclusion you will see how little it justifies any conclusion about "most of the country's doctors." Someone has assumed that Essex County accurately represents the nation as a whole. It may, but then again it may not. Essex County doctors may not even be typical of their New Jersey colleagues.

On top of that, as you would learn if you read the rest of the *Times* story, the 6-to-1 refers only to those doctors who returned a questionnaire postcard. Some 78% did not answer. Isn't there good reason to suspect that those in favor of the idea would be more inclined to mark a card and drop it into a mailbox than those who were opposed or indifferent?

For final consideration, here is a relevant fact that was omitted from the newspaper story. The questionnaire reached the physicians in an issue of the Bulletin of the Essex County Medical Society that contained, by no coincidence, an article by Congressman Kean arguing that Social Security should be extended to doctors.

We started with information from which it seemed we might reasonably draw this conclusion as to the probability: it is 6-to-1 that the next doctor you meet will favor extending Social Security to the medical profession. But in the end we find we can make this conclusion only about quite a special group. They can be realistically described not as U.S. doctors in general but merely as "the 22% of Essex County, N.J., doctors who replied to a questionnaire accompanying an article favoring one side of this controversial subject."

That's a sample of how far you can be misled by a sample cut on the bias.

But even knowing a sample is unbiased is not sufficient. You must also be sure it is big enough. The adequacy of the size of a sample can be measured only in terms of

chance, a word that comes into statistical discussions at all points.

The probability that a figure from a sampling study is true for the whole group from which the sample was selected is given as the degree of significance. This may refer to whether the figure is accurate within a given number of dollars or tons or hours or people. Or to whether what appears to be the greater of two quantities really is the greater.

When the Bureau of the Census tells you that its sampling reveals the average (median) income of American families to be $3,500, it will also tell you how far to trust this figure. To the report will be added some such information as that the chances are 19 out of 20 that the average is correct within a hundred-dollar range each way.

This 5% level of significance is good enough for some purposes. For much scientific work the required level is 1%, which means the odds are 99 to 1 that the apparent difference, or whatever, is a true one. Something as probable as this is often described as "practically certain."

You may also meet this important concept in the shape of what is called a probable error. Take an intelligence test and you may learn (if you can pry this secret data away from the psychometrician) that your I.Q. is 133. This means you're pretty bright, probably.

It also means your intelligence has been sampled rather than fully measured. Even a relatively good test like the Stanford-Binet requires only a few hours and obviously samples only a tiny part of the most limited intellect, even within the area of talent that it covers. Its makers have concluded that it has a probable error of about 3%. Since 3% of 133 is about 4, your level would be expressed as 133 ± 4.

This is an expression meaning that if you were to take a large number of tests exactly equal to this one, it's an even bet that your average score on them would come out within 4 points of 133, one way or the other. It means there is 1 chance in 4 that your I.Q. would turn out to be above 137. Dismally, it follows that the probability is also 1 in 4 that repeated testing would show your honest level to be below 129.

A probable-error table would enable you to figure out some more things. It would tell you that odds against a deviation of more than three probable errors either way are 21 to 1 against your really belonging to the below-113 intellectual set.

You can see why it is folly to regard such tests as precision instruments. Given two youngsters, a boy with an I.Q. rating of 125 and a girl with 133, what can you say about them? On the odds, there is 1 chance in 4 that the boy's true level is below 121. There is 1 chance in 4 that the girl's is above 137, as we have seen. So there is 1 chance in 16 that the girl stands at least 16 points higher than the boy. But the chance is equally good that he is just as clever as she is.

So it is with studies of magazine readership and advertising. If no figures estimating error or significance are to be found, better give the whole thing a big glassy stare. If they are there, take them to heart. You may avoid learning a remarkable lot that is not so.

Instead of the probable error you are likely to find something else, called the standard deviation or the standard error. It works much the same way but happens to be a good deal handier for mathematicians to work with. The difference is, one standard deviation each way will bracket almost exactly two-thirds of the cases instead of precisely one-half.

This part of statistics goes back, as a number of other useful ideas do, to Karl Gauss, the "prince of mathematicians," and his law of error. You won't be astounded to hear that it was derived from the theory of probability.

Suppose you clamp a rifle in a vise and fire thousands of rounds through it at a distant target that is just a big piece of cardboard. The bullets will not all go through the same hole, because arms and ammunition and air currents are not consistent. Instead they will form a pattern that seems at first to be highly irregular but which soon begins to take on form. There will be a heavy concentration of bullet holes, slowly fading off into a scattered few as the distance from its center increases.

The most remarkable thing about this pattern is how much you can predict about it without being anywhere in the vicinity or even knowing much of anything about firearms.

Fit a target-like series of concentric rings to the pattern. Make the center circle just big enough to take in one-half of the bullet holes. Draw the other circles so that each is the same distance from the next smaller one as the first is from the center point. Call the bullseye 10, the ring next to it 9, and so on.

Now here is what can be predicted through a knowledge of probabilities and nothing else: 7 out of each 22 bullet holes will be in the 9 ring, and 3 out of each 22 will be in the 8 ring. One in 26 will be in the next ring. The fraction will continue to shrink, reaching 2 in a million by the 4 ring.

Since these are probabilities, you can be practically certain that your predicted percentage will be very close to right for the rings that contain a large number of hits. Not so for the sparsely pinked outer rings; guessing them is like predicting the results of a mere handful of coin tosses.

Another thing you could do is chart the distribution of the bullet holes. First you'd draw a vertical bar of a height determined by the number of holes striking within one inch, let's say, of the center of the group. To the left, place another bar of a height proportional to the number of holes to be found between one and two inches away from the center in the left-hand half of the target. Continue this procedure to the left, and then do it to the right also. Connect the centers of the tops of the bars and you'll have a sweeping curve.

No matter what kind of rifle you've used or how far from the target it was, you'll get the same bell-shaped curve.

Graph the distribution of the heights of American men, and oddly enough you'll get just about exactly the same curve again. It will be high in the center, because there are more men of 5 feet 8 inches (or maybe the average is up an inch by now, but never mind) than any other height. The number who are 5'7" is slightly smaller, and so is the number who are 5'9". Shorter bars on either side of these three will represent the 5'6" group and

the 5'10". And so on. By the time you pass 5 feet in one direction and 6 feet 4 in the other, the bars will be pretty tiny.

If you were to ask quite a large number of people to heft a box and estimate its weight to the nearest ounce, their guesses would follow this same curve rather closely. If the greatest number should guess 22 ounces, there will probably be almost—but not quite—as many guesses of 21 and of 23 ounces, somewhat fewer of 20 and of 24, and so on.

Will the big bulge come at the right weight? Maybe, maybe not. The most popular guess will probably be close to right, but people can be wrong in the mass just as they can individually, and a box of one size or shape will be quite consistently guessed heavier than one of different appearance and same weight. An optimist named Condorcet discovered quite a time ago, to his final disillusionment, that individual errors do not always cancel each other out.

The chest measurements of Scottish soldiers have been shown to fit this same curve. So have the runs of a color or number on a roulette wheel, the velocities of molecules in a gas, and quite a lot of other things.

This fact so impressed many scientists and mathematicians in the days right after Gauss that they believed the normal curve to represent the nature of just about everything. They tried to force their data to fit it.

In fact, although it is remarkable how many and diverse things do fit this pattern, it is important to remember that there are many more distributions that do not. Human heights do, but human weights do not; nor do incomes. These two, by the way, form skew curves—the kind having one slope far steeper than the other. It's obvious that in a neighborhood where the mean (arithmetic average) income is $5,000 hardly any families will have incomes more than $3,000 under the average but a good many will receive in excess of $3,000 more than this average; and there will likely be a few with incomes many times the average.

This skewed or asymmetrical distribution produces a sad condi-tion: most of us have below-average incomes.

An average than which most of the constituent figures are less is likely to be rather misleading. That's precisely why the ordinary arithmetic average has been aban-doned for most statistical work with incomes. Used instead is the kind of average called a median, which is simply the figure that divides the whole distribution into two equal parts.

With a median, anyway, half of us can be above average.

· QUESTIONS ·

1. In a topic sentence, sum up the thesis of this article.
2. In what respects is this selection "dated"? Can you cite more recent events and names as substitutes for those used?
3. Comment on the diction of this article. Do you find it entertaining, breezy, chatty, offensive?
4. Explain what is meant by a "bell-shaped curve"; by the "degree of significance."
5. What bearing does the thesis of this selection have upon Maloney's "Inflexible Logic"?
6. Now is a suitable time to learn, once and forever, exact distinctions among *mean, median,* and *average.* Do you know them?
7. Define: durability, patronizing, coincidence, concentric, disillusionment, veloci-ties, asymmetrical.

Theme Subjects: (1) A Poll That Went Wrong; (2) I'm Above Average in _____; (3) I'm Below Average in _____; (4) My Opinion of Sampling Techniques; (5) TV Polls and Telephone Tests.

THE NECESSITY
FOR REASON

Gilbert Highet

GILBERT ARTHUR HIGHET (1906–   ) was born in Glasgow, Scotland, and was graduated from the University of Glasgow and from Oxford. He came to the United States in 1937. A naturalized citizen, he is Anthon Professor of the Latin Language at Columbia University and was chief book critic for *Harper's Magazine*, 1952–1954. Late in 1954 he became a member of the board of judges of the Book-of-the-Month Club, and, in 1958, chairman of the editorial advisory board of *Horizon*. Among his many books are *The Classical Tradition* (1940); *The Art of Teaching* (1950); *People, Places, and Books* (1953); *Man's Unconquerable Mind* (1954); *Talents and Geniuses* (1957); *The Powers of Poetry* (1960); and *The Anatomy of Satire* (1962).

With all its limitations, with all its dangers, reason is still one of the essential powers of man. It is not his sole essence. He is not a thinking machine, nor should he try to become one. He is not a thinking animal. He is something much more, something greater and more complex. "How noble in reason!" says the greatest of poets, and goes on "how infinite in faculty!" before adding one more of his inimitable, unforgettable phrases, "this quintessence of dust." But thinking is one of the necessary activities that make him human. He must think.

Day and night, from childhood to old age, sick or well, asleep or awake, men and women think. The brain works like the heart, ceaselessly pulsing. In its three pounds' weight of tissue are recorded and stored billions upon billions of memories, habits, instincts, abilities, desires and hopes and fears, patterns and tinctures and sounds and inconceivably delicate calculations and brutishly crude urgencies, the sound of a whisper heard thirty years ago, the resolution impressed by daily practice for fifteen thousand days, the hatred cherished since childhood, the delight never experienced but incessantly imagined, the complex structure of stresses in a bridge, the exact pressure of a single finger on a single string, the development of ten thousand different games of chess, the precise curve of a lip, a hill, an equation, or a flying ball, tones and shades and glooms and raptures, the faces of countless strangers, the scent of one garden, prayers, inventions, crimes, poems, jokes, tunes, sums, problems unsolved, victories long past, the fear of Hell and the love of God, the vision of a blade of grass and the vision of the sky filled with stars.

It is curious to be awake and watch a sleeper. Seldom, when he awakes, can he remember anything of his sleep. It is a dead part of his life. But watching him, we know he was alive, and part of his life was thought. His body moved. His eyelids fluttered, as his eyes saw moving visions in the darkness. His limbs sketched tiny motions, because his sleeping fancy was guiding him through a crowd, or making him imagine a race, a fight, a hunt, a dance. He smiled a little, or looked anxious, or turned angrily from one side to the other. Sometimes (like Lord Byron) he ground his teeth in rage, and still slept. Sometimes he spoke, in a scarcely articulate shout or a gentle murmur sounding strong in his mind. His heart beat fast with excitement, or slow with despair. He sweated. He felt the passage of time and was making himself ready for the morning with its light and noise. And all that time he was thinking—vaguely and emotionally if he was intellectually untrained, in symbols, animals, and divinities if he was a primitive man, often in memories, sometimes in anticipations of the future, and, far oftener than he himself would believe, forming intricate and firm decisions on difficult problems carried over from his waking life. He will say "I never dream, I only sleep"; but he arises with eight hours of thought written on the records of his brain as surely as another strain of grey has grown on his hair or a new firmness in the muscles of his shoulder. He may call the result a vision or a determination, a revelation or a whim, but it is a thought, worked out by his brain while he slept as surely as his heart was beating and his pancreas secreting digestive juices. Awake or asleep, man thinks. Sometimes it seems as though the chief distinction between powerful and ineffective men lay in the control and direction of their thoughts: the wise and energetic man contrives to use his mind even while his body sleeps; the stupid and helpless man dreams half his life away, even when his eyes are open. Almost every man of affairs acknowledges this when he says "That is a difficult decision: I'll sleep on it." Poincaré the mathematician knew it well. Just before going to sleep, he wrote down his hardest problems, and often woke with them solved, clarified during the night hours by his unsleeping brain.

Day and night, throughout their entire lives, men think. They think as naturally and inevitably as they breathe. It is a crime to deny them the best material for thought, as it is a crime to deprive them without just cause of health, liberty, and life. And it is one of their duties to themselves to think as copiously and richly as they can, to exercise and enjoy their minds as they exercise and enjoy their bodies, making them part of the total harmony which is their life.

Anthropologists sometimes seem to talk as though they believed it impossible to compare one society with another, calling one "superior" and another "inferior." Yet they would agree, like the rest of us, that a nation whose children died in infancy or grew up weak and sickly was inferior physically to a nation which kept its children alive and contrived for them a long and healthy life. In the same way, there can be no doubt that a superior nation is one which uses the minds of its people, giving them a constant flow of interesting ideas to think about, ensuring that no class or group is kept from acquiring knowledge because of sex, color, caste, religion, or poverty, stimulating the free, fresh production of ideas, respecting those who record and transmit knowledge, keeping open many channels of communication within the frontiers of the country, and beyond them throughout the world, and not only across geographical distances but through the long ranges of historical time. There have been too few nations such as that. It is for the encouragement of knowledge, that fertility and interchange of ideas, that we admire republican Athens, Augustan Rome, Renaissance Italy, and the France, England, and Germany of the nineteenth century. It is sad, nevertheless, to think through history, and to see how many millions of men and women, in so many hundreds of societies, have lived and died ignorant and thought-benumbed, as though born deaf and blind.

Knowledge to their eyes her ample page
　Rich with the spoils of time did ne'er unroll;
Chill penury repressed their noble rage
　And froze the genial current of the soul.

It is sobering to think that we ourselves, our children or their children, might be thrust into the same numbness, imprisoned in the narrow limits of daily routine, or suffering, or (even worse) pleasure. Against such dangers we must constantly assert the right to knowledge, its free possession and use.

· QUESTIONS ·

1. The phrase, "this quintessence of dust," is from Shakespeare's *Hamlet*, II:2. Locate the quotations which precede this phrase.
2. The stanza above is from Gray's "Elegy Written in a Country Churchyard." Does "noble rage" mean *anger* or an *excited sense of inspiration*?
3. What are the dates usually given for republican Athens; Augustan Rome; Renaissance Italy?
4. In what respects do you consider man more than a thinking animal?
5. Give an example from your own experience of "sleeping on" a problem.
6. Has recent scientific research invalidated any of the author's comments on sleep?

7. The second paragraph is notable for its sentence structure and sustained rhythm. Analyze these qualities. Is the third sentence of this paragraph unified, clear?

Theme Subjects: (1) "I Never Dream, I Only Sleep"; (2) Why I Am Not a Thinking Machine; (3) The Best-Remembered Incident of My Childhood; (4) I Watch My Sleeping Roommate; (5) Reason Is Not So Important As _____.

PROBLEMS

&

POINTS OF VIEW

FAITH IN SCIENCE

I. I. Rabi

IsIDOR ISAAC RABI (1898–   ) was born in Austria and was brought to the United States in infancy. A graduate of both Cornell and Columbia universities, Dr. Rabi has studied extensively in Europe and holds several honorary degrees. He has taught at many universities and served on several scientific and cultural commissions of the United States government and the United Nations. He received the Nobel Prize in physics in 1944. He is the author of *My Life and Times as a Physicist* (1960).

1. Mankind is puny and feeble under the heavens as long as it is ignorant. It is ignorant in so far as it is self-limited by dogma, custom, and most of all by fear—fear of the unknown. To science the unknown is a problem full of interest and promise; in fact science derives its sustenance from the unknown; all the good things have come from that inexhaustible realm. But without the light of science the unknown is a menace to be avoided by taboo or propitiated by incantation and sacrifice. The scientific tradition rests first of all on a faith in mankind, in the ability of humans to understand, and ultimately, within

From *The Atlantic Monthly*, January, 1951. Reprinted by permission of the author.

certain limits, which are in the nature of things, to control, the environment in which we live in all its aspects: physical, biological, and social.

2. This optimistic faith has always permeated and energized the American way of life. The scientific tradition should help us to renew and reaffirm our faith. In recent years, however, ominous symptoms of moral hypochondria have disturbed the development of our institutions. Under the threat of impending conflict with the Russian empire some sections of the public have reacted with blind, irrational fear. The action of Congress in overriding the presidential veto of the anti-Communist bill and the arrogant dismissal of a large number of professors by the regents of the University of California are the newest examples of what I would call moral hypochondria. A healthy awareness of grave danger should lead to clear, considered, decisive action. Hysterical fear results in the setting up of taboos around emotionally charged words and symbols. The real objective, security for the free development of our institutions, becomes hazy and possibly perverted when panic takes over.

3. The greatest enemy of the scientific tradition is superstition. By superstition I do not mean merely a belief in goblins, gremlins, and the malevolent power of Friday the 13th. The superstition which is completely incompatible with the scientific tradition usually comes as a plausible system of ideas founded on premises which defy exact formulation. They may be words without a definite meaning or inferences from events inexactly described or unique and nonrepetitive.

4. An attempt to study a superstition in an external, objective fashion usually encounters emotional and often physical opposition from its proponents. Mankind seems to have a genius for the invention of superstition. As science advances, superstition makes more and more use of the terminology of science; it becomes in fact a parody of the scientific method, a deft mixture of the true and the false, which often has a fatal fascination.

5. The best examples of this sort of thing can probably be found within the realm of the Soviets. The whole Nazi movement in Germany was founded on this kind of superstition. Superstitions arise everywhere and there is no force which can hope to combat them successfully except science.

6. Even science itself has not been wholly free from superstition. Science strives for understanding, but how can one distinguish understanding from mere plausibility? The scientific tradition, although affirmative in spirit, polices itself by a profound skepticism. There are many examples where scientists have made mistakes, where they have been fooled or have fooled themselves. However, all their work passes under the scrutiny of friendly but skeptical minds.

7. Individual authority no longer possesses any force in the scientific tradition. No scientist, however great his renown, can mislead his fellow scientists for longer than it takes to check his observations or verify his conclusions and their consequences. Whether the individual scientist acknowledges his error or not is of little consequence as long as the tradition is kept pure. Controversy and polemic are now outmoded forms of scientific publication except possibly within the

Soviet Union. Even there the appeal is hardly meant for fellow scientists.

8. I dwell on this point not only to show something of the reason for the great authority of established scientific doctrine, but also to indicate the way of life of science when it is free. If some of the customs and tradition of science could be transferred to the halls of our Congress or the United Nations, how beautiful life could become.

9. It is a truism to say that the application of science to technology is the basis of modern life in the United States. I refer not only to the products in everyday use, from the automobile parked in the street to the detergent in the kitchen, but more to the living social integration of our economy. Cut a relatively few electric power lines and the larger gasoline pipes which cross the country from west to east and south to north and keep them cut for a while. The effect on the life of the country would be like a thumb on the windpipe of a baby. Even the proud independent farmer would be unable to cultivate his acres without gasoline. His horses are gone and his wife is not inured to pulling the plow.

10. The development of new means of communication, production, transportation, and control have not merely added new possibilities to an existing way of living: they have so altered our basic patterns of organization that national life as of today would be impossible without them. We consider ourselves exponents of individualism and free enterprise, and national planning is on the whole unpopular. Yet we live under a degree of integration of social effort comparable to that of the cells in our bodies. I doubt very much whether we would have dared to build a social structure which is so vulnerable to attack from without, and to social disorganization from within, if it were actually planned from the very beginning.

11. On the other hand, if we consider the assimilation of science into our way of thought we find that our general public—and even our educated public—is as ignorant of science as a healthy Hottentot is of physiology. We are like the city boy who likes milk but is afraid of cows.

12. It is one of the paradoxes of our age that our general public, our lawmakers, our molders of public opinion, novelists, columnists, labor leaders, and administrators, have not devoted themselves more to understanding this force which is shaping our present and our future. Wise decisions in which science is involved cannot be reached merely by consulting experts. The very aims and ideals which condition these decisions come from the intellectual and spiritual background of the people who are in positions of responsibility. These ideals come from within and are a part of the culture of the nation. We do not ask an expert to tell us what should be our heart's desire. We only ask him how it is to be attained.

13. Barring war or other catastrophe, our standard of living, and therefore our dependence on science, will increase rather than decrease. Even if our population were decentralized, our dependence on science would not be lessened, but rather increased, if we wish to maintain and better our standards of health and comfort. Is it not folly to believe that a complex organism like our society, dependent as it is on science for its life-blood and development, can continue to be man-

aged properly by people whose education is not imbued with the living tradition of science, who have never experienced the influence of a scientific discipline?

14. For what science has to offer, and for what the country needs, a mere interest in the so-called scientific method, without specific knowledge of some part of some science, is as devoid of content as moral principle without moral action.

15. Over and above our lives as citizens, we also live our lives as individuals. What has science to offer as a guide to conduct and to the enrichment of one's inner life?

16. Fundamental to the existence of science is a body of established facts which come either from observation of nature in the raw, so to speak, or from experiment. Without facts we have no science. Facts are to the scientist what words are to the poet. The scientist has a love of facts, even isolated facts, similar to the poet's love of words. But a collection of facts is not science any more than a dictionary is poetry. Around his facts the scientist weaves a logical pattern or theory which gives the facts meaning, order, and significance. For example, no one can look at a brilliant night sky without emotion, but the realization that the earth and planets move in great orbits according to simple laws gives proportion and significance to this experience.

17. Theory may be qualitative and descriptive like Darwin's theory of the origin of species, or quantitative, exact, and mathematical in form like Newton's theory of the motions of planets. In both cases the theory goes far beyond the facts because it has unforeseen consequences which can be applied to new facts or be tested by experiment.

18. A scientific theory is not a discovery of a law of nature in the sense of a discovery of a mine or the end result of a treasure hunt or a statute that has been hidden in an obscure volume. It is a free creation of the human mind. It becomes a guide to new discovery and a way of looking at the world—which gives it meaning.

19. A successful theory goes far beyond the facts which it was made to fit. Newton in his laws of motion and theory of universal gravitation essentially created a universe which seemed to have the same properties as the existing universe. But it is hardly to be expected that the creation of a finite human mind would duplicate existing nature in every respect. The history of science indicates that it can't be done. Newton's theory has given place to Einstein's theory of relativity and gravitation. The Darwinian theory has been greatly modified by the geneticists.

20. The great scientific theories enable us to project our knowledge to enormous distances in time and space. They enable us to penetrate below the surface to the interior of the atom, or to the operation of our bodies and our minds. They are tremendously strong and beautiful structures, the fruit of the labors of many generations. Yet they are man-made and contingent. New discoveries and insights may modify them or even overthrow them entirely. However, what was good in them is never lost, but is taken over in the new theory in a different context. In this respect the scientist is the most conservative of men.

21. More than anything else, science requires for its progress opportunity for free, untrammeled, creative activity. The scientist must

follow his thought and his data wherever they may lead. A new and fundamental scientific idea is always strange and uncomfortable to established doctrine and must have complete freedom in its development; otherwise it may be strangled at birth. Ever since the time of Galileo the progress of science has continued without a break and at an accelerated rate in spite of war, revolution, and persecution. However, this progress has not always been in the same country. When science faltered in Italy, it began to bloom in England and Holland, then in France and Germany. Now that scientific progress is unfortunately slowing down in Europe, science in the United States after an incredibly long period of quiescence has burst out with tremendous vigor.

22. The great contributions to science in any country have usually come during or close to a period of great vigor in other fields, in periods of optimism, expansion, and revolutionary creative activity. In England it was right after the Elizabethan period. Newton's great contributions came within fifty years after the death of Shakespeare. The other great period in British science was between the Napoleonic Wars and the First World War. It was also a period of great poetry. In the United States the giant figure of Benjamin Franklin had no equal down to the most recent times; his period also produced the greatest statesmen in our history.

23. I do not wish to imply any necessary causal connection between important achievements in different fields of activity, but no one will deny that certain intellectual, moral, and spiritual climates are more conducive to creative activity than others. No one can deny that the continuity of a living tradition can be broken by the murder, exile, or ostracism of its chief exponents, or that a culture which is sterile can be kept so indefinitely by rigorous police action which prevents the intrusion of alien ideas. We have seen all too many examples of the self-preservation of sterility in recent years.

24. Fortunately for the scientific tradition it carries with it many gifts, some of which are more practical than spiritual, and therefore it has never lacked a new home when the time came to move. Science has never become localized in any place or in any culture. It is merely human and universal. French science and German science, Russian, English, Japanese, and American, do not exist separately as does poetry or some other arts such as law and government. They all speak the same universal language of science and say the same things when they have something to say. When another mode is imposed from without, science either quietly dies or goes away, leaving the field to the charlatan and pseudo-scientist.

25. What then are our conclusions? What does the tradition of science teach us?

26. It teaches us moderation and tolerance of ideas, not because of lack of faith in one's own belief, but because every view is subject to change and every truth we know is only partial. The strange thought or custom may still be valid.

27. It teaches cooperation not only among people of the same kind, but also of the most diverse origins and cultures. Science is the most successful cooperative effort in the history of mankind.

28. Science inspires us with a feel-

ing of hopefulness and of infinite possibility. The road ahead may be invisible, but the tradition of science has shown that the human spirit applied in the tradition of science will find a way toward the objective. Science shows that it is possible to foresee and to plan and that we can take the future into our own hands if we rid ourselves of prejudice and superstition.

29. The tradition of science teaches us that no vested interests in institutions or systems of thought should escape continual re-examination merely because they have existed and have been successful. On the other hand it also teaches us to conserve what is operative and useful.

30. Science teaches us self-discipline. One must continually look for the mote in one's own eye. The his-tory of science shows that it is always there.

31. These lessons can be multiplied to cover almost the entire range of human activity, because science is itself a contemporaneous living thing made by men for man's edification and entertainment.

32. I will close with one last point. Science is fun even for the amateur. Every scientist is himself an amateur in another field of science which is not his specialty, but the spirit is the same. Science is a game that is inspiring and refreshing. The playing field is the universe itself. The stakes are high, because you must put down all your preconceived ideas and habits of thought. The rewards are great because you find a home in the world, a home you have made for yourself.

· QUESTIONS ·

1. Make a sentence outline of the 32 paragraphs in this article.
2. Is the effect of superstition always negative? Answer carefully.
3. How can ignorance act as a stimulus to mankind?
4. Has the advent of the sputniks and the "space age" caused this article to become "dated"? Be specific.
5. "We are like the city boy who likes milk but is afraid of cows." What other figures of speech in this article can you list?
6. Dr. Rabi lists five major lessons which the tradition of science can teach us. Name and explain them. Do you accept these statements about the lessons of science?
7. In the second paragraph, the author cites two examples of "moral hypochondria." What does this term mean? Can you give several other more up-to-date examples?
8. Compare and contrast this essay with those by Huxley and Bronowski.

Theme Subjects: (1) A Lesson in Self-Discipline; (2) Rabi Versus Krutch (a debate); (3) Science Is (Is Not) Fun for Me; (4) My Own Faith (Lack of Faith) in Science; (5) An investigative paper on the career of I. I. Rabi; (6) I Am a "Healthy Hottentot."

THE NATURE
OF SCIENCE

Ralph Ross and Ernest van den Haag

RALPH ROSS (1911–   ) was born in New York City. He received his
bachelor's degree from the University of Arizona and his doctorate from
Columbia University. He is a professor at the University of Minnesota and
chairman of the Humanities Program. In addition to *The Fabric of Society*
he has written *Skepticism and Dogma* (1950) and *Society and Politics*
(1964).

ERNEST VAN DEN HAAG (1914–   ) was born in The Hague and educated
in France, Germany, and Italy. He has a master's degree from the University
of Iowa and a Ph.D. degree from New York University. Since 1946 he has
taught at N.Y.U. Dr. van den Haag is the author of many articles and of
Education as an Industry (1956) and *Passion and Social Constraint* (1963).

Science is often defined inade-
quately as "an organized body of
knowledge." This would make cook-
books, Sears, Roebuck catalogues,
and telephone books science, which
they are not. Sometimes science is
defined simply as rationality, but
that would make much of theology
and metaphysics science, which
they are not. *Rationality* is logical
consistency, lack of contradiction.
It is to be distinguished from *reasonableness*, the quality of a mind
open to arguments and evidence
opposed to its beliefs: a willingness
to reconsider. Rationalists can be
quite unreasonable or dogmatic. Ra-
tionalist metaphysicians and theolo-
gians are often certain about premises which come from intuition or
revelation. Even paranoiacs may be
thought of as rationalists, for they
are commonly most rigorous in reasoning. But their premises, which
they cling to in spite of all evidence,
are absurd.

WHAT SCIENCE IS

Science is empirical, rational, general, and cumulative; and it is all

four at once. Science is *empirical* in that all its conclusions are subject to test by sense experience. Observation is the base on which science rests, but scientific observation is more than keeping one's eyes open. It is observation made by qualified observers under controlled conditions of those things which confirm or disconfirm, verify or refute a theory. Sherlock Holmes could tell by the stains on a vest what a man had eaten for breakfast. From a number of such observations he arrived at a theory about why and how a particular crime was committed. This procedure is excellent for detection but insufficient for science, because it yields only knowledge of particular events. Science would go on to ask why and how crime, not a particular crime, is committed. Science uses facts to test general theories and general theories to make predictions about particular facts.

Scientific observation may be made of things as they exist, like the color of an apple or the temperature of the air, or it may be made of what results from an experiment. An experiment is the deliberate manipulation of conditions in order to bring about what we want to observe. If we want to test the hypothesis that a new plastic can withstand two hundred pounds of pressure without crumbling, we may have to create a situation in which such pressure is applied to a piece of the plastic, because it is unlikely that the situation already exists anywhere in the world, or if it does, that all other factors are kept constant. In some sciences, like astronomy, we do not sufficiently control the subject matter to experiment on it—although we do control the conditions of observation—and we dis-

tinguish those sciences from others, like chemistry, in which experiment is possible, by calling the latter "experimental sciences."

Although all scientific thought *ultimately* rests on observation, there are vast portions of it which are entirely *rational:* analysis of the meanings of terms, deductions from existent theories, explorations of the logical relations among concepts and among theories. Logic is applied to science constantly because logic contains the rules of valid thinking. The application of mathematics is often thought, erroneously, to be an index of the status of any science. Of course, the more it can be applied usefully within a science, the more advanced the science. For mathematics functions both as a language in which scientific laws are stated, giving them the utmost precision, elegance, and economy, and as the basis of measurement. Many of the most significant advances in physics, astronomy, and chemistry have depended on advances in and application of mathematics. Without calculus the work of Isaac Newton would have been impossible. Yet great scientific work in other fields, performed by men like Pasteur, Darwin, and Pavlov (with whose names pasteurization, evolution, and conditioned response in psychology are associated), has used little or no mathematics. This is true also of important contributions to social science, like those of Weber, Veblen, and Mosca. Nothing is gained by the use of mathematics when a subject is not measurable or sufficiently precise.

If observation is the base of science, *general laws* are its crown. The body of any science is a set of general laws, logically connected, from which the occurrence of particular events is predictable. Young sciences, like nineteenth-century biology, are chiefly taxonomic; that is, they organize and classify a subject matter so that there will be enough order in it for laws to be sought. Even less-advanced sciences, like contemporary anthropology and sociology, still record a host of particular and often isolated observations so that there will be material from which to generalize. One goal of science is the creation of a unified body of knowledge which will relate all the sciences to one another; thus from laws of physics and chemistry—which deal with matters that are basic to all things, organic and inorganic—one could move logically to laws of biology, psychology, and society. Ideally, all science would be logically deducible from a single law general enough to apply to everything.

Of course, we are so far from a single set of laws for all the sciences that we can scarcely go logically from physics to chemistry. We are closer to—though still far enough from—more limited ideals of the unity of science: unity on the basis of terms or of methods. There have been relatively successful attempts to create a common body of terms for the sciences, so that propositions of one science can be meaningful in others. And, despite great differences in the procedures and apparatus of the particular sciences, it is possible to approximate a statement of the most general methods of science so that they are applicable to all science.

Science is *cumulative* in that present knowledge is based on past knowledge, even when the new supersedes the old. The dullest freshman in an introductory physics course knows more about physics than Aristotle did, not because he is brighter than Aristotle but, among other things, because of the work of Aristotle. Scientific conclusions are held tentatively; if they were regarded as certainly true, inquiry would be terminated and mistakes would be enshrined as dogma. But science is self-corrective; its mistakes are eliminated by more science. This is perhaps the basic criterion that distinguishes science from all other ways proposed for attaining truth: intuition, authority, tradition, for example. Different intuitions, authorities, and traditions may contradict each other, but each will remain firmly convinced of its own truth. These methods can be corrected only from outside themselves, especially by logical criticism and new evidence. But science is corrigible by its own practice, through continued application of its method. And the recurrent criticism that science is unreliable because it is always changing misses the point. Science is reliable *because* its conclusions change in a successive approximation of truth. It does not claim absolute truth for any of its conclusions, but only probability. And at any time we can expect the probability of a scientific law to be greater than knowledge about the same subject from any other source. Further, science does not correct itself only by recognition of mistakes. Solving one problem opens a path to others, and they in turn may lead back to a reconsideration of the earlier problem. When we learn that something previously called an instinct, for example, is actually the result of cultural conditioning, we promptly ask whether the same is true of other "instincts." And what we discover about conditioning as a result of this new inquiry may lead to greater understanding of the first "instinct."

Of course, scientific growth is not always direct; there are many blind alleys, and errors may last for years. But many errors have worked out well in the end because they led to the study of related problems or accidental discovery of some truth. Examples include the political doctrine of a state of nature,[1] which led to the isolation of specifically social and political characteristics of human behavior; the theory of humors, which pointed the way to discovery of a relationship between glandular secretions and temperament; and alchemy, which in the search for ways of transmuting other substances into gold helped found the science of chemistry. As Augustus De Morgan, a nineteenth-century English mathematician, said, "Wrong hypotheses, rightly worked, have produced more useful results than unguided observation."

Many scientists rule out of court all vague and fuzzy notions. Yet science has often advanced because of, not despite, just such notions when they were bold and imaginative or were metaphors which called attention to a previously neglected relationship. Max Planck wrote:[2]

. . . If a new idea were to be admitted only when it had definitely proved its justification, or even if we merely demanded that it must have a clear and definite meaning at the outset, then such a demand might gravely hamper the progress of science. We must never forget that ideas devoid of a clear meaning frequently gave the strongest impulse to the further development of science. The idea . . . of perpetual motion gave rise to an intelligent comprehension of energy; the idea of the absolute velocity of the earth gave rise to the theory of relativity, and the idea that the electronic movement resembled that of the planets was the origin of atomic physics. These are indisputable facts, and they give rise to thought, for they show clearly that in science as elsewhere fortune favors the brave. In order to meet with success it is well to aim beyond the goal which will eventually be reached.

Looked at in this light the ideas of science wear a new aspect. We find that the importance of a scientific idea depends, frequently enough, upon its value rather than on its truth. This applies, e.g., to the concept of the reality of an external world or to the idea of causality. With both the question is not whether they are true or false, but whether they are valuable or valueless.

Planck's distinction between the value and the truth of scientific ideas is not absolutely exclusive; truth, too, is a value, and in science it is the ultimate value. But there

[1] This is the belief that men were at first nonsocial creatures who behaved on instinct and impulse. Living together in society was thought to be the result of a rational decision which was embodied in a "social contract," stating that men would give up certain of their "natural rights" or powers to each other or to a sovereign. Some political writers knew that there probably never was a state of nature, but they continued to talk about it because it provided a useful contrast to the way men live in society, and it allowed them to distinguish the specifically social elements in human behavior from those they regarded as natural, or biological.

[2] From *Philosophy of Physics* by Max Planck. Reprinted by permission of George Allen & Unwin, Ltd., London, 1936, pp. 111 ff.

are other scientific values and they are not inconsistent with truth. If we distinguish between science as a product and science as a process, we can see that as a product—as a body of propositions about the world—what we value are answers, and we want them to be true. But as a process, what we value are questions and methods, with their attendant insights and new concepts. And the truth of the presuppositions on which questions are based may be irrelevant to the value of the questions themselves, or of the concepts that go with them. Here the chief values are those of stimulating and guiding further inquiry.

The cumulative character of science becomes clearer in contrast with art, which does not necessarily improve. We know more about art and artistic technique than artists of the past did, but our poets, playwrights, sculptors, and musicians are not superior to Dante, Shakespeare, Michelangelo, and Bach. The reasons are simple. Every artist, no matter what he has learned from his masters, really starts from scratch. He may not only refuse to build on past artistic achievements—which make up no single body of work, anyway—but he may have to reject much of the past for the sake of his own vision. The scientific novice, however, starts his thinking with the conclusions of past science. Although he may correct some of it, he accepts most of it and goes further. And he enters a laboratory complete with instruments which his predecessors did not have, instruments making new and more exact observation and measurement possible. The artist has no such aid from instruments, for a typewriter will write no better sonnets than a quill.

· QUESTIONS ·

1. Make an outline (topic or sentence, as directed) of this selection.
2. What technical device (stylistic method) contributes to the effectiveness of the opening paragraph? The closing paragraph?
3. Show that you understand science is empirical; rational; general; cumulative.
4. Compare and contrast "The Nature of Science" with those articles in this volume by T. H. Huxley, Rabi, and Bronowski.
5. Define: paranoiacs, manipulation, hypothesis, taxonomic, transmuting, causality, irrelevant, quill.
6. Explain the references to Pasteur, Darwin, Pavlov, Veblen, Dante, Michelangelo, Bach, Planck, Weber, Mosca, Sherlock Holmes, Aristotle.
7. In the first paragraph, *rationality* and *reasonableness* are distinguished. Write an anecdote or incident making clear this distinction.
8. What kind of person do you prefer: one who is rational or one who is reasonable?
9. The final paragraph is developed largely by *contrast* and *comparison*. Write a paragraph using the same method but dealing with a *baseball player* and a *biologist* (or two other types of your selection).

Theme Subjects: (1) My Own Disorganized Body of Knowledge; (2) My Love of (Aversion to) Mathematics; (3) My Decision To Become a Scientist; (4) Science Is My *Bête Noire;* (5) One of My Own Blind Alleys.

THE IDEA OF PROGRESS

Charles A. Beard

CHARLES A. BEARD (1874–1948), historian and political scientist, was educated at DePauw University and at Oxford, Cornell, and Columbia; at the last-named institution he became a professor of politics in 1915. In addition to active participation in political and economic affairs of his own country, he was an adviser in Japan and in Belgrade. A prolific writer, Beard first attracted the attention of historians and political scientists with *An Economic Interpretation of the Constitution* (1913), and then remained a controversial figure among his contemporaries. Among his most popular and influential books are *The Rise of American Civilization* (1933, with his wife, Mary R. Beard); *The Republic* (1943); and *Basic History of the United States* (1944, also with Mrs. Beard).

Although hailed in some circles of conceit as a glorious symbol of more speed and bigger machines, and in others as a covering for cruel materialism, the concept of progress is one of the most profound and germinal ideas at work in the modern age. It is at the same time an interpretation of the long history of mankind and a philosophy of action in this world of bewildering choices. It gives a clue of meaning to the rise of civilization out of the crudities of primitive barbarism and offers a guide to the immense impending future. Briefly defined, it implies that mankind, by making use of science and invention, can progressively emancipate itself from plagues, famines, and social disasters, and subjugate the materials and forces of the earth to the purposes of the good life—here and now. In essence the idea of progress belongs to our own times, for it was unknown to the ancients and to the thinkers of the Middle Ages. It is associated, therefore, with every phase of the vast intellectual, economic, and rational movement which has transformed the classical and medieval heritage into what is called, for the sake of convenience, Western civilization.

Hence it is closely affiliated with democracy, natural science, technology, and social amelioration, and shares with them the strength of universality. It is more than a theory. It has achievements to its credit on every hand—diseases stamped out, pain silenced or assuaged, the span of life lengthened, famine made obsolete, comforts and conveniences established, sanitation supplied to multitudes, knowledge made popular through amazing instrumentalities of transmission and reproduction. And it suggests a faith of power, faith that the world, as Emerson said, "is all gates, all opportunities, strings of tension to be struck." Rejecting resignation as a philosophy of life, it confronts obstacles with assurance. Where the pessimist sees the worst, it proposes a search for the best and advances toward perfection by increments. The suffering, ignorance, and folly which drive the timid to the Nirvana of doubt and oblivion are, under the light of progress, calls to action, to research, to planning, and to conquest. Touched by the genius of universal emancipation, the idea cuts across the barriers of caste, class, race, and nationality, breaks through rigid boundaries, and regards the substances and forces of nature as potential instruments of humane purposes. Everywhere it makes its way, dissolving the feudal institutions of Europe, disturbing the slumbers of the Orient, arousing lethargic Russia, and finding a naked avowal in the United States of America: the earth may be subdued to the security, welfare, and delight of them that dwell therein. . . .

All through the nineteenth century the idea of progress continued to work as a powerful ferment in the opinions of the world. In America, the extension of the suffrage beyond the boundaries of the propertied classes, the adoption of universal education, and the growth of a leveling freedom in the agrarian West helped to widen its scope to include the whole population, to democratize it, in a word, and make it a guiding principle for a civilization. In previous times and in other circumstances, privileged classes and individuals could lift themselves to a position of comfort, security, and prosperity by law and economic advantage and thus enjoy the benefits and delights of culture; now at last in a vast natural theater, it was thought, a whole people could, through progressive development, enjoy the blessings of science, industry, and art, and become civilized. The hewers of wood and drawers of water were to rise above the level of serfdom and sit at the banquet prepared by applied science. Here civilization was conceived not as a beautiful fairyland of delight surrounded by brutalizing labor, illiteracy, and margin-of-subsistence living for the masses. The actualities of American life, it was easy to show, were far from the ideal held up to the faithful, but the concept of progress, once let loose in our democracy, continued to act as a dynamic force, transforming every aspect of American civilization.

With inescapable fatality the mass production made possible by machinery and nourished by our unparalleled natural resources accelerated the leveling democracy implied in the idea of progress. Gigantic industries could not flourish without an immense market. And where was that market to be found? In a small privileged class enriched by the profits of capitalism? Only one answer was possible.

The few craftsmen of the Middle Ages might sell the choice products of loom, forge, kiln, and chisel to lords, ladies, bishops, princes, and kings, but masters of huge industries turning out commodities by the ton and the million could thrive in no such limited area of demand. Markets for mass production simply could not be found unless the masses themselves rose above the historic margin of subsistence and were able to buy by the ton and the million. Only when the standard of life for the multitude is constantly rising and buying capacity is expanding can widening outlets be found for the goods which pour in swelling streams from the vast industries made possible by science and machinery. If the American bourgeois were as indifferent, on moral grounds, to the lot of the masses as the French nobility of the eighteenth century to the plight of their laborious peasants, still their enterprises could not develop without a continuous enlargement of the popular market—without a steady growth in the capacity of the masses to buy and enjoy goods once confined to the classes.

Herein, no doubt, lies one of the main sources of the European criticism which is directed against the idea of progress as powerfully expressed in American civilization. Every quest for the inner nature of that criticism and for the roots of its inspiration leads immediately to an opposition of class ideals. True culture, we are told, is inevitably confined to "the superior minority" and cannot exist when boundaries are widened to include millions of nameless and unknown. This is the theme of one school of writers which had its origins in ancient Greece and survives in the latest hour, finding new spokesmen as the old are forgotten. Consciously or unconsciously, it is dominated by one secret wish or conviction: Democracy operating under the idea of progress is incompatible with "culture."

This concept and the antithesis were clearly and eloquently set forth long ago in the writings of Amiel.[1] "In society," he remarks, "people are expected to behave as if they lived on ambrosia and concerned themselves with no interests except such as are noble. Care, need, passion do not exist. All realism is suppressed as brutal. In a word, what is called *le grand monde* [the world at large] gives itself for the moment the flattering illusion that it is moving in an ethereal atmosphere and breathing the air of the gods. For this reason all vehemence, any cry of nature, all real suffering, all heedless familiarity, any genuine sign of passion, are startling and distasteful in this delicate *milieu* and at once destroy the collective work, the cloud-palace, the imposing architectural creation raised by common consent. It is like the shrill cockcrow which breaks the spell of all enchantments and puts the fairies to flight. These select gatherings produce without intending it a sort of concert for the eye and ear, an improvised work of art. By the instinctive collaboration of everybody concerned, wit and taste hold festival, and the associations of reality are exchanged for the associations of imagination. So understood, society is a form of poetry; the cultivated classes deliberately recompose the idyll of the past, and the buried

---

[1] Henri Frédéric Amiel, 1821–1881, Swiss philosopher and poet.

world of Astraea.[2] Paradox or not, I believe that these fugitive attempts to reconstruct a dream, whose only end is beauty, represent confused reminiscences of an age of gold haunting the human heart; or rather, aspirations toward a harmony of things which everyday reality denies to us, and of which art alone gives us a glimpse." Undoubtedly this is a fair statement of the idealized case; although a student of the world's social memoirs may be inclined to believe that such a *grand monde* never existed, save perhaps in the Tokugawa era of Japan at the height of its glory.

Having drawn his perfect picture of *le grand monde* supplied by Europe, Amiel presents the contrast afforded by the United States: "For the Americans, life means devouring, incessant activity. They must win gold, predominance, power; they must crush rivals, subdue nature. They have their hearts set on the means and never for an instant think of the end. They confound being with individual being, and the expansion of self with happiness. This means that they do not live by the soul, that they ignore the immutable and eternal, bustle at the circumference of their existence, because they cannot penetrate to its center. They are restless, eager, positive, because they are superficial. To what end all this stir, noise, greed, struggle? It is all a mere being, stunned and deafened." In short, without stopping now to dispute the correctness of Amiel's contentions, Americans do not live on ambrosia, dispense with care, move in an ethereal atmosphere, breathe the air of the gods, escape from the world, and reconstruct a dream whose only end is beauty; they are incessantly engaged in subduing nature and in seeking to develop an ordered economy which will establish security, continuity in high productive output, and the widest possible distribution of the benefits flowing from efficient industry.

When once the antithesis presented by Amiel is clearly recognized and its implications understood, the issue of civilization before us becomes perfectly evident. Whether and how long European countries will continue to maintain superior minorities concerned only with "noble" interests, with cloud palaces and associations of the imagination, is an appropriate matter for speculation. Assuming their virtues to be all that their advocates claim, it may be appropriately asked, "At what price glory?" Bent backs, knotted hands, and numbed minds must pay for parties at which such wit and taste hold festival and the idyll of the past is recovered for the delight of the participants. If, when the balance sheet is struck, the credits outweigh the debits, still it may be surmised that the knowledge released by science, the demands of industry for markets, the awakening insistence of the multitude on sharing the fruits of the earth, have made forever obsolete *le grand monde* of the lotos-eaters. Esthetes may regret it, but there is something Promethean in the vast upward thrust of the masses under the banner of progress, and those who have occasion to think, teach, or direct in the coming years will have to reckon with that invincible fact. Iron gates are closing on the

---

[2] During the Golden Age (antiquity), Astraea lived on earth, was later metamorphosed into the constellation Virgo. The name represents "innocence."

dreams of privilege, and those who cherish the ideals of that order will have to look beyond this world for their lost Atlantis.[3] This seems to inhere in the nature of things, even though poignant Americans will long continue to pay large honoraria to Europeans for the privilege of listening to deprecatory estimates respecting the very heart and dynamic of civilization in the United States.

If critics of progress fail to grasp its cosmic nature, friends of the idea often make it appear petty and ridiculous by the undiscriminating zeal with which they espouse it. As in the case of every other fruitful concept, a lunatic fringe is associated with the idea. To these shortsighted spectators at the great show, all movement is progress, means are ends, and the worth of a personality is to be measured by the number of motor-cars, telephones, radios, and bathtubs he possesses. The idea of progress thus becomes purely numerical. J. P. Morgan had more things than Dante; therefore he was superior. Jim Fiske had more diamond rings than Francis of Assisi; accordingly, his rating in civilization must be higher. Zenith has more miles of paved streets than Athens, a single apartment house in New York will hold the entire population of that ancient city; evidently America transcends in achievement the best of the Greeks. Thus a noble concept of humanity is made both absurd and contemptible, obnoxious in the house of its friends, and a shining target for abuse at the hands of its opponents.

Yet when the critics and scof-fers, writing under soft lamps or lecturing for fees to well-fed audiences, in comfortable rooms electrically lighted, venture to speak of an alternative, they can offer only a return to agriculture and handicrafts. Overlooking the fact that they can themselves go at any time to any one of a thousand waste places awaiting the plow or the hoe, they prefer to advise others to incur the risk. When asked for a bill of particulars, they become hazy and vague. Are we merely to surrender the tractor and return to the steel plow? Why not to the wooden plow? Or better still, to the forked stick hardened by fire? Each advance on the most primitive instrument is a gain in efficiency, a transfer of labor from man to a tool. In the process of retreat are surgery and dentistry to go into the discard? Sanitation, antiseptics, and anesthetics? Each of these gains has marked a step in progress, or rather a long series of steps, and each art steadily advances in our own time as masters of the test tube and microscope penetrate deeper and deeper into the mysteries of nature. Fundamentally the machine differs from the tool in degree, not in kind, and the chemist works in materials no less than did the most primitive woman herbalist. His knowledge is wider, his skill is greater, but his ends may well be fundamentally the same—the relief of human suffering. Where then is the line to be drawn? To what point in the long upward progress of mankind is the return to be made? To ask these questions is to answer them. The severest critic of progress is forced to admit, when cornered, that the

---

[3] Atlantis, a large mythical island supposed to have existed somewhere in the Atlantic Ocean, first mentioned by Plato.

problem is not one of retreat, but of ends and methods, of choices and uses.

If in the hands of its superficial champions the idea of progress seems to emphasize means rather than ends, an examination into the history and nature of the concept shows that this notion is without basis. Although selfish men have seized upon the instrumentalities of progress and have left in the train of their exploits hideous industrial cities, slums, poverty, and misery, that upshot is no more to be attributed to the idea itself than the cruelties of the Inquisition to the teachings of Jesus. An inquiry into the writings of those who originated and developed the theory of progress shows at the center of their thought the concept of the good life as the end of progressive endeavor, the genius which is to preside over the searches and labors of explorers and experimenters. The good life for the multitude, not for a superior minority living in a land of illusion on the sweat of the "ignoble"—this is the kernel germinating in the heart of the concept of progress. To see life whole and to see it steadily, to sound its deeps, to illuminate its possibilities, and to make the noblest and wisest use of material resources in realizing its purposes, this is the sum total of the idea of progress— a grand end, conceived in the light of universality, appealing to a mankind seeking high destiny and striving for mastery over the instrumentalities to be employed by the way. Anything less than this is a caricature of the idea.

Wrongly identified with capitalism, communism, or particular systems of economy, though standing at the very threshold of the great analysis and inquest, the idea of progress nevertheless clearly reveals the method by which ends are to be attained. Its method is that of science and technology—rationality, in short. And that method implies many things. It implies an open-eyed and open-minded attitude toward tasks in hand and problems to be solved. Working with concrete materials under positive law, technology is as indifferent to the emotional idiosyncrasies of individuals and classes as the elements themselves. Universal in its reach, as transcendent as the gods, it cannot be monopolized by any nation, period, class, government, or race. Its catholicity surpasses that of all religions. Essentially objective in its manipulations, dealing with materials, quantities, and known laws, technology is leveling and democratic in its effects; it is not a closed cult handed down by a few masters to a few students in cloistered universities. Rational in nature, corresponding to the mathematics of physical things and forces, this method is necessarily planful. It cannot begin anything without a goal, project, or purpose. To proceed at all it must stake out a field of work, a problem to be solved, and then it must proceed according to plan, on the assumption of predictable results, to predetermined ends. Inexorably, therefore, it cuts across the wild welter of unreasoned actions, irrelevant sentiments, and emotional starts and fits which have so long characterized human life in historic politics, industry, agriculture, and esthetics. Rational and planful, working in the unity of all things, this method is centripetal, drawing all arts, economies, and sciences inward toward the unity of the world—with implications so vast, so in harmony with mankind's noblest dreams, that the imagination is staggered by them.

Since the rationality of progress imposes limitations on inner impulses and cuts across external arrangements, it inevitably involves all departments of human activity —pure science, invention, industry, transportation, agriculture, government, finance, medicine, social adjustments, the work of women, education, arts, and letters. As the first carved gates of ancient Egypt celebrated the purpose of the ruling monarch, so the latest skyscraper in New York reflects the functions of its inhabitants. All branches of civilization mirror the dominant idea. If the escape of negation be sought, it will be found blocked at the exit. All arts, sciences, and crafts are drawn into the movement of regnant thought and practice. And when the thought of the thinker, the dream of the artist, and the aspiration of the practitioner draw together under a common principle of unification, the light and heat required for heroic endeavor are generated, giving to each the power of the whole, suffusing all with a sense of elevation and movement, supplying energy to the weak, and providing for the strong and willful who make history that social dynamic without which even Napoleon himself might have been a Corsican lawyer or Genoese scrivener.

· QUESTIONS ·

1. State succinctly what Beard means by "the idea of progress." Does he over-extend the literal meaning of *progress*?
2. In what respects has the United States outstripped the remainder of the world? In what has it lagged or been over-zealous?
3. Define: Nirvana, technology, bourgeois, agrarian, Promethean, poignant, cosmic, lotos-eaters, herbalist, milieu, idiosyncrasies, honoraria, cloistered, regnant, scrivener.
4. Compare and contrast this essay with those in this volume by Ross and van den Haag and Bishop.
5. Name some other "germinal ideas" of Western civilization in addition to that of *progress*.
6. What spiritual and moral counterarguments to Beard's thesis can you advance? What political rebuttals? What of existentialism?
7. How skilled a debater do you consider the author of this selection? Is he logical? Fair? Forceful?

Theme Subjects: (1) Progress Is (Is Not) Illogical; (2) Beard and Krutch (or Bishop) Debate Progress; (3) Progress and Atomic Fission; (4) I Am (Am Not) a Lotos-Eater; (5) "To See Life Whole and To See It Steadily . . ."; (6) My Idea of Progress.

SNAPSHOT OF AMERICA

AN ANTHROPOLOGIST LOOKS
AT THE UNITED STATES

Clyde Kluckhohn

CLYDE KLUCKHOHN (1905–   ) was born in Iowa and graduated from the University of Wisconsin in 1928. He has also studied at the University of Vienna, at Oxford as a Rhodes Scholar, and at Harvard (Ph.D., 1936). His distinguished teaching career in anthropology and archeology includes duty at the University of New Mexico and at Harvard. As director of the Russian Research Center, 1947–1954, at the latter institution, as consultant to the United States Indian Service, and as director of the Institute of Ethnic Affairs, Mr. Kluckhohn is admirably equipped to provide a "snapshot" of American life. His published works include *Beyond the Rainbow* (1933); *The Navaho* (1946); *Personality in Nature, Society, and Culture* (1948); *Mirror for Man* (1949); and *Culture and Behavior* (1962).

American culture has been called a culture of paradoxes. Nevertheless, national advertising and a national moving-picture industry would be impossible were there not certain terms in which one can appeal to the vast majority of this capturable people. Though sectional, economic, and religious differences are highly significant in some respects, there are certain themes that transcend these variations. Some life goals, some basic attitudes tend to be shared by Americans of every region and of all social classes.

To start with the commonplace: even the most bitter critics of the United States have conceded us material generosity. In spite of the romanticism of "public-spirited disinterestedness" most Americans are outgoing and genuinely benevolent. Sometimes, to be sure, American humanitarianism is linked with the missionary spirit—the determination to help others by making the world over on the American model.

Perhaps no huge society has ever had such generalized patterns for laughter. In older civilizations it is commonly the case that jokes are fully understood and appreciated only by class or regional groups. It is true that it is some distance from the sophisticated humor of *The New Yorker* to the slapstick of popular radio programs. But the most widespread formulas reach all Americans. Some of the most characteristic of these are related to the cult of the average man. No one becomes so great that we cannot make fun of him. Humor is an important sanction in American culture. Probably the ridicule of Hitler did more than all the rational critiques of Nazi ideology to make the man in the street contemptuous of Nazism.

All European travelers are struck by American attitudes toward women. They often note that "Americans spoil their women," or that "America is dominated by petticoats." The truth is more complicated. On the one hand, it is clear that a very large number of American women of privileged economic position are freed by labor-saving devices from much household drudgery—particularly after their few children have entered school. Their abundant leisure goes into women's clubs, community activities, "cultural" organizations, unhealthy devotion to their children, other mildly or seriously neurotic activities. It is also true that many American men are so wrapped up in pursuit of the success goal that they largely abdicate control over their children's upbringing to their wives. The responsibility of American women for moral and cultural questions is tremendous. On the other hand, it is too often forgotten that almost every girl who graduates from high school or college has had some job training. We interest

women in careers but make it difficult for them to attain a full life in one. In a culture where "prestige" is everything we have felt it necessary to set aside Mother's Day as a symbolic atonement for the lack of recognition ordinarily given to domestic duties.

In Japan a year ago Japanese of many classes complained to me that it was difficult to understand American democracy because Americans seemed to lack an explicit ideology that they could communicate. The Japanese contrasted the Russians who could immediately give a coherent account of their system of beliefs. Various Americans have remarked that what the United States needed more than a good five-cent cigar was a good five-cent ideology. Such explicit ideology as we have derives largely from the political radicalism of the late eighteenth century. We repeat the old words, and some of the ideas are as alive now as then. But much of this doctrine is dated, and a new latent ideology inherent in our actual sentiments and habits is waiting for popular expression.

Particularly since the drastic disillusionment that followed the fine Wilsonian phrases of World War I, Americans have been shy at expressing their deepest convictions and have been verbally cynical about Fourth of July oratory. Yet devotion to the American Way has been none the less passionate. It is significant that aviators in this past war who were under narcotics in the course of psychotherapy would not only talk freely about personal emotional problems but were equally articulate on the ideological reasons for American participation in the war.

The pattern of the implicit

American creed seems to embrace the following recurrent elements: faith in the rational, a need for moralistic rationalization, an optimistic conviction that rational effort counts, romantic individualism and the cult of the common man, high valuation of change—which is ordinarily taken to mean "progress," the conscious quest for pleasure.

Mysticism and supernaturalism have been very minor themes in American life. Our glorification of science and our faith in what can be accomplished through education are two striking aspects of our generalized conviction that secular, humanistic effort will improve the world in a series of changes, all or mainly for the better. We further tend to believe that morality and reason must coincide. Fatalism is generally repudiated, and even acceptance seems to be uncongenial—though given lip service in accord with Christian doctrine.

The dominant American political philosophy has been that the common man would think and act rationally. The same premises are apparent in typical attitudes toward parental responsibility. The individual, if "let alone" and not "corrupted by bad company," will be reasonable. If a child does not turn out well, the mother or both parents tend to blame themselves or to explain the failure by "bad blood"—as if action-guided-by-reason could of itself always produce well-adjusted children when the biological inheritance was adequate.

While many Americans are in some senses profoundly irreligious, they still typically find it necessary to provide moral justifications for their personal and national acts. No people moralizes as much as we do. The actual pursuit of power, pres-

tige, and pleasure for their own sakes must be disguised (if public approval is to be obtained) as action for a moral purpose or as later justified by "good works." Conversely, a contemplative life tends to be considered "idleness."

The American mother offers her love to her child on the condition of his fulfilling certain performance standards. No conversational bromides are more characteristically American than "Let's get going"; "Do something"; "Something can be done about it." Although during the thirties there was widespread devaluation of present and future and though pessimism and apathy about the atomic bomb and other international problems are certainly strong currents in contemporary national thinking, the dominant American reaction is still—against the perspective of other cultures—that this is a world in which effort triumphs. A recent public opinion study showed that only 32 percent of Americans were concerned about social security—for themselves.

Countless European observers have been impressed by "enthusiasm" as a typically American quality. During the war military analysts noted repeatedly that the British were better at holding a position but the Americans at taking one. As Margaret Mead has observed, the British cope with a problem; Americans start from scratch and build completely anew.

Americans are not merely optimistic believers that "work counts." Their creed insists that anyone, anywhere in the social structure, can and should "make the effort." Moreover, they like to think of the world as man-controlled. This view about the nature of life is thus intimately linked with that conception of the individual's place in society which may be called "romantic individualism."

In the English-speaking world there are two principal ideologies of individualism. The English variety (which may be tagged with the name of Cobden) is capitalistic in its basic outlook. American individualism has agrarian roots and may be associated with Jefferson. To this day Americans hate "being told what to do." They have always distrusted strong government. The social roles most frequently jibed at in comic strips are those that interfere with the freedom of others: the dog-catcher, the truant officer, the female social climber (Mrs. Jiggs) who forces her husband and family to give up their habitual satisfactions. "My rights" is one of the commonest phrases in the American language. This historically conditioned attitude toward authority is constantly reinforced by child-training patterns. The son must "go farther" than his father, and revolt against the father in adolescence is expected.

However, as de Tocqueville pointed out, Americans are characteristically more interested in equality than in liberty. "I'm as good as the next man" seems at first a contradiction of the American emphasis upon success and individual achievement within a competitive system. It is true that there are relatively few places at the top in a social pyramid—*at any one time*. But the American faith that "there is always another chance" has its basis in the historical facts of social mobility and the fluidity (at least in the past) of our economic structure. "If at first you don't succeed, try, try again." The American also feels that if he himself does not "get a break," he has a prospect for vicarious achievement through his children.

American individualism centers upon the dramatization of the individual. This is reflected in the tendency to personalize achievement, good or bad. Americans prefer to attack men rather than issues. Corporations are personified. Public power projects were advertised as much as a means of beating the Utility Devil as a way of getting better and cheaper service.

The less opportunity the greater the merit of success. "You can't keep a good man down." Conversely, failure is a confession of weakness, and status distinctions and even class lines are rationalized on such grounds as "he got there by hard work," "it's his own fault that he didn't get on." Such attitudes— and the idealization of the "tough guy" and the "red-blooded American" and the fear of "being a sucker"—derive both from the Puritan ethic and from the American pioneer era. Aggressive activity and rapid mobility were effectual in the rapid development of a new country, and it made sense then that the rewards in money and status should be high.

The worship of success has gone farther than in any known culture, save possibly prewar Japan. This is reflected in countless staple phrases such as "bettering yourself," "getting ahead," and "how are you getting on?" The opposition to Roosevelt's proposal for a taxation program that would limit net income to $25,000 attests to the depth of feeling for slogans like "the sky's the limit." But the striving for money is not simply the pursuit of purposeless materialism. Money is primarily a symbol. The deeper competition is for power and prestige. "Aggressive" is, in American culture, a descriptive adjective of high praise when applied to an individual's personality or character. "You have to be aggressive to be a success." The obvious crudities of aggression are, as Lynd says, explained away by identifying them .with the common good.

But there is a defensive note in this aggressiveness which is also symptomatic. Competitive aggressiveness against one's fellows is not just playing a part in a drama. The only way to be safe in American life is to be a success. Failure to "measure up" is felt as deep personal inadequacy. In a phrase, the American creed is equality of opportunity, not equality of man.

The cult of the average man might seem to imply disapproval of outstanding individuals of every sort. Certainly it is true that a great deal of hostility is directed upward. However, under the influence of the dramatic and success aspects of the "romantic individualism" orientation, the typical attitude toward leaders may best be described as one of mixed feelings. On the one hand, there is a tendency to snipe at superior individuals with a view to reducing them to the level of their fellows. On the other hand, their very success is a dramatic vindication of the American way of life and an invitation to identification and emulation.

The cult of the average man means conformity to the standards of the current majority. To de Tocqueville this was "enfeeblement of the individual." A more recent observer, Fromm, who also looked at the American scene from a European viewpoint, likewise finds this conformity repressive to self-expression. But he fails to see that the American is not a passive automaton submitting to cultural compulsives like European provincials. The American voluntarily and consciously seeks to be like others of his age and sex—without in any way becoming an anonymous atom in the social molecule. On the contrary, all the devices of the society are mobilized to glamorize the individual woman and to dramatize every achievement of men and women that is unusual—but still within the range of approved aspirations of the conforming majority. "Miss America" and "the typical American mother" are widely publicized each year, but an announced atheist (no matter of what brilliance and accomplishment) cannot be elected President.

American devotion to the underdog must be linked to this attitude. As Lynd points out, we worship bigness yet we idealize "the little man." "Griping" is a characteristic American trait, but the griping of American soldiers against the officer caste system is to be understood in terms of American egalitarian notions and especially of the cult of the average man. The fact that officers and enlisted men do not have equal access to various facilities for recreation and transportation enraged what were felt to be the most basic sentiments in the American code. To some extent this aspect of the cult of the average man doubtless represents a refuge for those who fail "to rise," a justification for envy of those who do.

Because of the cult of the average man, superficial intimacy is easy in America. People of every social class can talk on common topics in a way that is not so easy in Europe where life is based more on repetition of patterns of early family routines that are differentiated by class. However, American friendships tend to be casual and transitory.

Thanks to our expanding economy and to national folklore created by various historical accidents, the nineteenth-century faith in "progress" became intrenched in the United States as nowhere else. As Lovejoy and Boas have pointed out, America's golden age has been located mainly in the future rather than in the past. To some extent, to be sure, the future has been brought into the present by installment plan buying, the philosophy of "spend, don't save," etc. But the basic underlying notions have been well made explicit by Carl Becker.

By locating perfection in the future and identifying it with the successive achievements of mankind, the doctrine of progress makes a virtue of novelty and disposes men to welcome change as in itself a sufficient validation of their activities.

Western Europeans and Americans tend to be fundamentally different in their attitudes toward conforming. Americans believe in conforming only to the standards of one's own age group, and change-in-time is a strong value; Europeans believed—or have believed—in conforming to a past society and have found security in traditional behavior; yet conformity to a contemporary society is only incidental and not a value. There are, to be sure, wide disparities in American hospitality to change. We take pride in material change but are, on the whole, more hostile than contemporary Europeans to changes in our institutions (say the Constitution or the free enterprise system). In some

ways the conformity of middle-class Englishmen, for instance, is more rigid than that of Americans—but in other ways it is less so. American attitudes toward change make generational conflicts more serious. These very generational conflicts, however, make certain types of social change possible. As Mead points out, children can be more "successful" than their parents, hence "better."

Americans publicly state that having a good time is an important part of life and admit to craving "something new and exciting." In terms of this ideology we have created Hollywood, our Forest of Arden type of college life, our National Parks, Monuments, and Forests. Leaders of our entertainment industry are the best paid men and women in the United States. We spend as much for moving pictures as for churches, more for beauty shops than for social service. However, because of the Puritan tradition of "work for work's sake," this devotion to recreation and material pleasure is often accompanied by a sense of guilt—another instance of the bipolarity of many features of American culture. The pleasure principle attains its fullest development in American youth culture. Youth is the hero of the American Dream. Most especially, the young girl ready for marriage is the cynosure of American society.

We have borrowed ideas and values from countless sources. If one takes single features, one can match almost every instance in a dozen or more cultures, including the primitive. For example, during the last war many of our soldiers carried magic amulets, such as a miniature wooden pig which was said to have raised fogs, smoothed

out a high sea, commuted an execution, or cured assorted cases of illness. But if one looks at the total
combination of premises and attitudes one sees a pattern that has its
own special flavor, even though this
description is too brief to take account of regional, class, ethnic
group, and generational variations.

An anthropological snapshot
of the American way of life cannot catch all the details, but, with
other cultures in the background,
it should highlight some meaningful interplay of light and shadow.
And the attempt is needed. No

amount of knowledge of Russian or
Chinese culture will avail in the
solution of our international problems unless we know ourselves also.
If we can predict our own reactions
to a probable next move in the Russian gambit and have some clues
as to why we shall react in that
manner, the gain to self-control and
toward more rational action will be
tremendous. Because of our tradition of assimilating immigrants and
because of our overweening pride
in our own culture, it is particularly
difficult to get Americans to understand other cultures.

· QUESTIONS ·

1. In a paragraph or more for each, the author comments on American generosity, humor, attitude toward women, etc. Make a topical outline of the essay,
   using such listings.
2. Indicate your agreement or disagreement with the comments Kluckhohn makes
   on each of the topics listed (Question 1, above). Are your attitudes based on
   sound knowledge, observation?
3. Summarize the "pattern of the implicit American creed" as the author develops it.
4. Explain the references to Wilsonian phrases, Mrs. Jiggs, de Tocqueville, Lynd,
   Fromm, Boas, Mead, Forest of Arden, the American Dream.
5. Define: paradoxes, capturable, sophisticated, ideology, latent, rational, moralistic, secular, humanistic, apathy, status, symptomatic, generational, cynosure, gambit, culture, neurotic, abdicate, atonement, egalitarian, bipolarity.
6. Why does the author believe it essential for Americans to know themselves and
   be able to predict their reactions? To what extent are these aims possible?
7. What contradictory elements do you discern in this essay? Among various
   groups and kinds of Americans?
8. Compare and contrast Kluckhohn's comments on progress with Beard's "The
   Idea of Progress."
9. In what specific areas are the author's references and allusions now somewhat
   "dated"? Are his central theses thus invalidated?

Theme Subjects: (1) Standards of the Current Majority in My Home Town; (2)
My Attitude Toward Women (Men); (3) My Favorite Brand of Humor; (4) "Let's
Get Going"; (5) "You Can't (Can) Keep a Good Man Down"; (6) Griping in My
Dormitory (House, etc.); (7) "Don't Tell Me What To Do"; (8) Forest of Arden
Colleges; (9) The Magic Amulets in My Life; (10) Kluckhohn Is Wrong About

A VISION OF THE YEAR 2000

Clare Boothe Luce

CLARE BOOTHE LUCE (1903–   ) was born in New York City and was edu-
cated at St. Mary's, in Garden City, L.I., and at The Castle, Tarrytown, New
York. She holds degrees from Colby College and from Fordham, Temple,
Creighton, and Georgetown universities. An associate editor of *Vogue* maga-
zine in 1930, she became associate and then managing editor of *Vanity
Fair* (1931–1934), was a newspaper columnist in 1934, and since 1935 has
been a playwright whose works include *The Women* (1937); *Kiss the Boys
Goodbye* (1938); *Margin for Error* (1939); and *Child of the Morning*
(1951). Mrs. Luce was a Connecticut representative to the 78th and 79th
Congresses and U. S. Ambassador to Italy, 1953–1957. She is a trustee of the
Carnegie Endowment for International Peace and a director of the Museum
of Modern Art. Her other writings include *Stuffed Shirts* (1933) and *Europe
in the Spring* (1940).

As we enter the new year 1966, it
is time to take stock of the fact that
we are living through the greatest
revolution in the history of mankind. It is not ideological in character, though modern ideologies—
capitalism, Communism, fascism,
and socialism—have all played their
parts in advancing or delaying it.
Its origins are rooted in the ancient
past—and in man's ancient yet ever
modern thirst for knowledge and
for power over his environment.

This world-shaking revolution is the
scientific and technological revolution of the twentieth century.

The pace of science and of
technology in the West had begun
to quicken well before World War
II. But it is their explosive rate of
progress since then, especially in
America, that now gives them their
revolutionary character.

For example, the New York
World's Fair of 1939 chose as its
theme "The World of Tomorrow."

From *McCall's Magazine*, January, 1966. Reprinted by permission of the
author and the publisher.

Its most spectacular exhibit was a scale model of a futuristic civilization in which mankind had intercontinental rocketry and atomic power. Guides who conducted open-mouthed visitors through the exhibit informed them that the scientists and technologists who had designed it were confident rockets would come in one or two generations, though atomic power probably would be a matter of several centuries. Five years later, America had both.

During my first term in Congress (1942–44), if any Congressman had predicted that the United States would be spending billions within fewer than twenty years to land on the moon, the moonstruck solon might have landed back in private life after the next election. Unmanned spacecraft orbiting Mars; men walking in space, digging through the earth's crust on the ocean floor, perfecting "death rays" (lasers); submarines capable of firing intercontinental missiles from under water and cruising below polar floes; robot machines that not only could calculate production needs and consumer demands, but program their own work, make decisions, correct their own errors, digest and memorize millions of facts and figures and produce them in the twinkling of an eye—all such things, as we reached the midcentury mark, were still to be found only in science fiction and in Buck Rogers and Superman comic strips. Today they, and much else that was incredible a few years ago, are realities.

In the past quarter of a century, the scientific and technological revolution has radically changed our life. It has changed our landscape and architecture, our domestic politics, foreign policies, economics, sociology, manners, morals, ethics—the entire character and quality of our culture.

And yet scientists (and their computers) are telling us that the revolution has scarcely begun and that its rate of progress will be sixteen times greater each year than the year before.

Our wildest speculations, as 1966 is ushered in, may seem merely timid predictions as we near the end of this century. Submarines that can fly? Vertical passenger-plane takeoffs? Planes carrying a thousand people? These are already on the drawing boards. A device to supply man with "gills," so he can breathe as easily in the ocean as he does on land? Sport submarines that can cruise for a week-end on the ocean's bottom? Engineering methods that will permit us to erect houses and hotels on the bosom of the sea? Accurate medical checkups and diagnoses made by computers? New eyes for old? New ears, hearts, kidneys, livers, bones for outworn or diseased ones? A life expectancy of a hundred years? All quite possible in the lifetime of millions of Americans. The great breakthrough —the discovery of how to dissolve the field of gravity, so man can hover above the earth in giant aircraft or sky houses and observatories? A way to control volcanoes, so they will create new islands for our constantly expanding population to inhabit? Maybe not for centuries—but maybe before our children become grandparents.

Only one thing can we predict with any certainty: If the revolution is *not* stopped, life in America in the year 2000 will be as different from life here today as life today differs from life in 1800. And over fifty percent of our population will be living in the super-revolutionary year 2000!

We know, as free men who are (or ought to be) the masters of our machines, that the revolution *can* be stopped dead in its tracks—any time we deliberately choose to stop it. We could today launch a nuclear holocaust that would end the revolution with a billion-trillion-horse-power bang.

There is another way we can turn the revolution into a nightmare for America, if not for the rest of the world. That is to continue to fail (as we are presently failing) to take charge of it firmly, at the political, sociological, and physical levels where it is affecting our lives adversely.

How should a free and democratic people set about controlling this prodigious revolution? That is a subject too vast for a columnist's limited pen. But already many American leaders are arguing the urgent need for control. The problem—and paradox—of crushing poverty in an age of potentially limitless plenty challenges even the dullest political minds.

We are beginning to realize that unemployment among unskilled and semiskilled workers must steadily increase as automation and cybernation phase out their jobs. We know it is daily more necessary to plan jobs now for millions of idle hands who will otherwise be employed by the Devil. We suspect that if we are to keep consumer dollars flowing into industry, we may have to guarantee an annual income for all our adults and may even have to pay our young people to go to college, so they won't turn to crime, for want of job opportunities. We are beginning to realize that we will have to shorten the workweek by days, not hours, if we are to maintain even nominal full employment.

But as a nation we are still far from aware of how tragically we have failed to control some of the pernicious physical side effects of the revolution.

We have let our superb industrial plants dump their refuse into all our river systems and inland-ocean lakes, turning even the mighty Hudson and Mississippi into poisonous sewers and our Great Lakes into cesspools. We have let our industrial machines and proliferating automobiles fill the skies over our cities with noxious gases and industrial dirt of every kind. In a technological age that could easily provide disposal plants and filter systems for air and water pollutants, we have supinely permitted the revolution to filter its noisome wastes through our stomachs and lungs.

We have refused to make government, industry, or ourselves responsible for disposing decently of the corpses of our worn-out mechanical household slaves—refrigerators, television sets, and other equipment destined for the junkyard. The ugly, rusty, twisted bodies of our most idolized machine, the automobile, have piled up along our highways. We have increased the scandal of the automobile graveyard with the scandal of roadside litter. Every day, tons of bottles, cans, boxes, papers, food remnants, cigarette butts, and other rubbish are thrown out of car windows onto the roadside. (And to all this we annually contribute to our highways the bloody litter of more than 50,000 smashed bodies.)

It is as though, having a genie under our national roof, a prodigious Santa Claus who showers us with luxuries and comforts and toys, we allow him to poison us with his breath and bury us in his filth, while we enjoy his gifts.

It has been estimated (by those miraculous computers) that an adequate program to provide clean air, clean water, and clean highways for citizens of the future will cost 50 billion dollars. But if we do not very soon undertake this program, by the year 2000, Americans will be living in an Augean stable. At this point, the country is likely to become a nation of emigrants. The tremendous population shift to the West in the past ten years is partially due to the desire of millions to escape the disgusting side effects of the revolution. But when, even in the West, people no longer can see the stars at night for the smog, they will begin to leave America itself—

Looking in the New Year's crystal ball, I see two pictures forming for the year 2000. In one, thousands of Americans are leaving in thousand-passenger planes (and hover ships) for lands—any lands, however "backward"—where there are green hills and blue skies and sweet waters. Australia, New Zealand, Africa, Latin America, islands where the winds broom white clouds and where birds sing in occasional parks and forests—such lands are beckoning Americans, in full flight from the vast slum made of their own country by their parents' indifference to the side effects of history's greatest revolution.

In the second picture, I see a fair land, full of shining buildings and extraordinary new machines and artifacts, whose uses I am unable to imagine—any more than I could have imagined what a radio or television set was for, had I seen their forms in a crystal ball in my youth. In this picture, I also see sights I once was familiar with: old men fishing and young people swimming in the wide, clean rivers that flow through cities—small children playing in the shade of great trees along flower-bordered highways—lovers walking through green city parks under a clear midnight moon, unafraid of muggers.

But I also see a new sight: magnificent universities with garden campuses, where the youth of our land is being trained to direct the revolution for the betterment of mankind. And I seem to hear a professor explaining that, along about 1966, the American people began energetically to fight the war against poverty. Not against material poverty only, but against poverty of spirit. "America," this professor is saying, "awoke somewhat late to the fact that it is not enough for a great nation of free men to be strong and rich in material things. It must be rich in spirit, rich in imagination, rich in courage— and it must desire to create a beautiful as well as a prosperous country. So, about 1966, the American people began to control the scientific and technological revolution. This revolution is still presenting us with many problems; but thanks to the actions begun thirty years ago, we of the twenty-first century know we can solve them."

· QUESTIONS ·

1. This is a clearly ordered essay. As your instructor directs, make a sentence or paragraph outline of it.
2. Give the gist of the fifth paragraph in your own words and then amplify your summary. Do the same for the seventh paragraph.
3. What are your comments on Mrs. Luce's remarks about the side effects of the revolution as they are apparent today?
4. Is the author's vision for the future too hopeful, too idealistic? What steps do you know of that have been taken to correct some existing eyesores and headaches?
5. This essay was written in 1965 for appearance early in 1966. Is it in any sense "dated" today or is it an evergreen article? If it is "evergreen," is the country doomed along the lines the author suggests?
6. Define: solon, laser, cybernation, phase out, pernicious, proliferating, noxious, supinely, noisome, genie, Augean stable, mugger.

Theme Subjects: Select any one problem or condition which the author mentions and develop it in terms of your own experience, observation, and reading. This essay is a gold mine of ideas for theme writing and bull sessions.

LOYALTY

AND FREEDOM

Archibald MacLeish

ARCHIBALD MACLEISH (1892–   ) was born in Glencoe, Illinois, and was graduated from Yale in 1915. He also holds a law degree from Harvard and honorary doctorates from many colleges and universities. He was Librarian of Congress, 1939–1944, and was Boylston Professor of Rhetoric at Harvard from 1949 until 1962. Best known as a poet, Mr. MacLeish received the National Book Award for his *Collected Poems, 1917–'52*, in 1953, the

From *The American Scholar*, Autumn, 1953. Reprinted by permission.

same year in which he was awarded the Pulitzer Prize for poetry. Six years later, in 1959, his book *J.B.: A Play in Verse* (1957) won both the Antoinette Perry award and the Pulitzer Prize for drama. *Poetry and Experience* was published in 1961.

Two things become increasingly evident as the sickness of our American democracy approaches its inevitable crisis: one is the surpassing genius of the founders of this Republic; the other is the transience of even the greatest of political resolutions. It was the supreme achievement of the generation of the American Revolution that it solved the most difficult of all constitutional problems, the problem of the reconciliation within one society of the conflicting human desires for freedom and for community. It may well be the ultimate shame of our generation that with us that resolution fails.

A free society is, of course, a contradiction in terms. Freedom means individual freedom: above all, freedom of conscience and freedom of mind. Society means community of some sort: not only membership in the community, but loyalty to the community. Only where all men think and believe alike does the contradiction disappear; and such societies, as history has demonstrated over and over again, are not alive but dead. Elsewhere, a resolution must be found not in conformity, but in the very nature of human difference. It was there that the authors of the American Constitution found it. They rejected as unworkable and offensive the notion of an established creed or an official doctrine or a national belief to be held in common by all Americans. Conformity of belief has, from time to time in the history of the world, overrun whole populations like a plague, flinging them into fanatical religious wars upon unbelievers everywhere; but it is not by chills and fevers such as these that nations are established or that nations endure. Nations are created, nations endure, by the men who compose them—the actual men, the individual men. And it was in the individuality of the individual men, in their differences from each other, that the founders of this Republic put their trust.

Men were to create a community in America not because they were to belong to the same race, not because they were to subscribe to the same political doctrines, not because they were to worship in the same church, but because they were to share a common experience, the experience of being free together. They were to be free to be men and so to share freedom and so to become a community and a nation. Their loyalty was to be a loyalty to the right of each one of them, and so of all of them, to be free. It was the conviction of our ancestors—a conviction which they wrote into their Constitution in the form of an explicit limitation on the law-making power of the central government—that loyalty to the liberty of every man to believe what he chooses would outlast loyalty to any formulation of belief whatever. That that conviction was well grounded, the history of the American people down to our own time has conclusively demonstrated.

But though the American resolution has proved itself under varying conditions over a considerable period of time, it was never more than a balancing of conflicting human needs. A shift in either direction—toward a more passionate assertion of the demands of individual freedom, or a more jealous insistence upon the precedence of the community—was always possible and did, of course, from time to time occur. There was always, in consequence, the danger that one emotional need might so overbalance the other that the underlying structure would collapse. What has been happening in the United States over the period of the past five years or more makes it tragically evident that that danger is now both real and present. There has been a massive, almost glacial, shift away from the passion for individual freedom and toward a desire for security of association, of belonging, of conformity.

The change is not a purely American phenomenon. It has been observed elsewhere during recent years and, in some parts of the world, in the most extreme forms. In eastern Europe and in Asia, a cancerous aggravation of the natural human desire for community and association has sent millions of human beings to march in Red Flag parades and Brown Shirt parades and Fascist triumphs—millions of human beings who have found in the community of shouting voices, the community of hatred for the outsiders, the community of persecution and murder, something their sick hearts required. We have not come to that in this Republic, but it is only too clear that the emotions which move us are emotions capable, if similarly perverted, of similar consequences. The same perplexity and hatred and fear which have formed the Communist herds and the Fascist gangs in other countries have already produced their herds and gangs in the United States; and conformity of opinion and belief, the first demands of the mob everywhere, has been secured by methods which differ only in degree from the methods of the Moscow and Berlin streets. When loyalty is put before freedom, and when loyalty is made to mean loyalty not to the right to be free, but to the demands of the majority, with economic and social destruction as the penalty for dissent, the drums of Moscow and Berlin are near enough to hear.

What has been happening in American schools and universities in the past few months is plain enough for any eye to read. The explanation of the successful intrusion of government—or of a group of politicians acting in the name of government—into an area from which the American tradition, if not the American Constitution, excludes it, is to be found in the changed attitude of the American people. We Americans have become increasingly convinced that unless we can believe in something in common, the Communists will take us over. To the Russians, we tell ourselves, communism is a faith. How, then, can we hope to confront it with nothing but the freedom of each one of us to believe what he pleases? And how, unless our educational institutions produce likeminded men and women, can we hope to become a like-minded people? And unless we become a like-minded people, how, in this iceberg age of gigantic floating lumps of national mentality, can our nation survive? We can think of no answer either in our own history or elsewhere; and the longing for conformity so overwhelms us that we look on in silence, if not in active approval, while the one freedom which underlies all others—the freedom of the mind—is attacked at the point where its protection is most essential to the Republic, and by methods of hypocrisy and intimidation which shame us all.

It is our silence as a people, far more than the mischievousness of the politicians engaged in this foray, which should give concern to those who truly love the country. There have always been cynical and ambitious politicians, ignorant of the American tradition or contemptuous of its meaning, who would gladly lead the mob against the individual for political advantage. What is new is the encouragement given men of this character by the indifference of the citizens. The eight or ten great newspapers which still maintain their integrity have protested. The leaders of the learned professions and of the American churches and of liberal and labor organizations have condemned the whole campaign of censorship and suppression. But the country is silent when it does not openly applaud. If attacks on individual liberty are conducted in the name of "loyalty," they are justified without more argument. It makes no difference that the "loyalty" asserted is not the loyalty Americans have understood in the past—loyalty to the right of each individual to think and speak as he chooses, loyalty to the ideal of freedom. It makes no difference that the "loyalty" is loyalty to the economic and social and political and military and diplomatic views of the inquisitors. "Loyalty" is in question, and "loyalty" comes before freedom in a time like this.

If "loyalty" continues to come before freedom in the American scale of values, there can be little doubt as to the ultimate outcome. The delicate balance upon which the Republic has maintained itself for almost two hundred years will be destroyed, and the United States will follow Nazi Germany and Communist Russia into that frozen world in which everything coheres and conforms, and the life of the individual mind and soul is of no more significance than the life of a single drop of frozen water in an ice floe. No one who believes in the vitality of the American people— no one who recalls the passionate indignation with which they have defended their personal liberties in the past—can suppose that this will happen. But as time goes by and the expected revulsion of opinion against the censors and inquisitors fails to materialize, there is an anxious questioning in many hearts. What has befallen us as a people? Have we truly changed, or have we only forgotten for a time the history out of which we come? Is it our fear of communism, sedulously played upon by the perpetrators of these evils, which destroys our faith in freedom, or has our faith in freedom itself decayed?

History, if honest history is written in the world ahead, perhaps will find an answer. We ourselves can only guess at one. We would guess, I think, that fear of communism is not the entire explanation. There is a limit to the extent to which a virile and sanguine people, united in a contempt for Communist theory and Communist practice, can be terrified by cries that they are about to be converted to communism by secret operatives and darkling conspiracies. We would guess also, I suppose, that the explanation is not to be found in any conscious decline in our devotion to the ideas of freedom. Those who now attack personal freedom at its roots in the universities, and who threaten to attack it in the churches and the press, are themselves obliged to use the vocabulary of freedom to justify their activities. What would seem to us to have changed, I think, is not our belief in freedom but our *faith* in freedom—our faith that freedom will really work—that it can, itself, and by its own means, survive the attacks of enemies as gigantic, as closely integrated, as disciplined, as controlled as the enemy it faces now.

But to say this is to say, at the same time, something more. Faith in freedom rests necessarily upon faith in man. The American belief in man was the condition precedent to the existence of the American Republic. It was because men like John Adams and Franklin and Jefferson believed in man that they believed in the possibility that men might govern themselves: the possibility, that is to say, of freedom. A *loss* of faith in freedom results, by the same logic, from a *loss* of faith in man. And it is that, almost certainly, which has occurred in the United States. We no longer wholly trust the power of the institutions of freedom to defend themselves by the methods of freedom because we no longer wholly believe in the capacity of men to live as men in a world such as our technicians and scientists have revealed to us. Our symbol—the symbol which made us

the nation we were—has shriveled.

If this, or something like it, is the explanation of our tragic loss of heart, then at least part of the responsibility can be allocated readily enough. The underlying failure is a failure of education. We have increasingly ignored the human things, the things of the mind and spirit, the proofs of man's dignity and worth, in the teaching of our schools and even in our universities; and we are paying the inevitable price. Generations of schoolboys taught only techniques and tools produce generations of men to whom only techniques and tools are important, men who have no comprehension of their own resources or those of their neighbors, men who know nothing of those great conceptions of human destiny, those patterns of life and death, which our kind has produced over countless generations.

In the struggle for the defense of human freedom, everything depends on the vitality of the belief in man, on the health and vigor of the human things; and there is no way to maintain the human things but to know them. A man of morality in Rome was a man who knew and respected the mores, the acknowledged human ways, the forms and orders; and it is not otherwise with us. A free man is a man who knows and loves the things of which a man in freedom is capable. Only those who know what a man can be at his best, in his arts, in his conceptions, in his imagination and his realization, are capable of valuing freedom, and only those who are capable of valuing freedom are likely to defend it.

· QUESTIONS ·

1. What are the two things which MacLeish says are now becoming increasingly evident?
2. Why is "a free society" a contradiction in terms?
3. What is your understanding of "the experience of being free together"?
4. Have events since MacLeish wrote this article (1953) accelerated the "loss of faith in man" which is discussed? Do you think that a more powerful central government in Washington increases or decreases man's individual freedom?
5. To what extent do you feel that *loyalty* and *freedom* are incompatible?
6. What opposing groups and movements might be mentioned now in addition to those cited in this article?
7. Define: transience, fanatical, explicit, sanguine.
8. Can you give any examples of the intrusion of government into college life?
9. Does MacLeish confuse the American and French revolutions?
10. State the thesis of this essay in a paragraph.

Theme Subjects: (1) The Best Way To Fight Communism; (2) Democracy Is a _____ Faith; (3) My Definition of Loyalty; (4) What MacLeish Overlooks; (5) Modern Witch-Hunters; (6) Man at His Best.

HOW AMERICANS CHOOSE
THEIR HEROES

Dixon Wecter

DIXON WECTER (1906–1950) was born in Houston, Texas, and held A.B. and Litt.D. degrees from Baylor University and M.A. and Ph.D. degrees from Yale. As a Rhodes Scholar he earned the degree of B.Litt. from Oxford. A teacher of both history and English, he was Margaret Byrne Professor of History at the University of California, 1949–1950, and literary editor of

From Dixon Wecter, *The Hero in America*, Charles Scribner's Sons, 1941. Reprinted by permission.

the Mark Twain estate from 1946 to his death. Among his numerous books are *The Saga of American Society* (1937); *The Hero in America* (1941); *When Johnny Comes Marching Home* (1944); *Report from Paradise* (1949); *The Love Letters of Mark Twain* (1950); and *Sam Clemens of Hannibal* (1952).

The sort of man whom Americans admire, trust, and are willing to follow can be sketched with a few lines. East and west, north and south, his portrait is familiar. At the basic level he must be self-respecting, decent, honorable, with a sense of fair play; no Machiavelli nor Mussolini need apply. He must be firm and self-confident in leadership: Davy Crockett's "Be always sure you're right, then go ahead!" is approved American doctrine, whether in the headstrong and cocksure types we sometimes follow, like Old Hickory and Theodore Roosevelt, or in the great characters of our imagination like Paul Bunyan and Huckleberry Finn. Mother wit and resourcefulness we love. But a reputation for "genius" is unnecessary and may do the hero harm. Brilliantly clever men like Alexander Hamilton and John Randolph of Roanoke, and pure intellectuals like John Quincy Adams (by the guess of educators given the highest I.Q., 165, of all Americans in the Hall of Fame), are not major idols. An able man must not glory in his cleverness. By our standards one is sometimes allowed to "put over a fast one"—Benjamin Franklin and Abraham Lincoln did, repeatedly—but he must not appear to relish the coup for its own sake. Art must conceal art. A clodhopper politician like Huey Long, boasting "There are not many people in the United States who are smarter than I am, and none in Louisiana," did not understand this restraint. Long's scornful assertion that he could buy votes in his Legislature "like sacks of potatoes" to the country at large was equally bad politics. Uncle Sam allows his favorites to be shrewd in a good cause, but there must be no avowal of cynicism in principle. (In modern movies, the hero may pull a fast one for the sake of his mother, or his girl friend, or some worthy ideal, but not for himself.) The backwoods always has a certain admiration for rustic rascality, and the metropolis loves a flippant wise-crack—but in America at large there is a pretty strong prejudice against the wise guy.

Vanity or personal arrogance in any form is taboo. The dandy in public life—accepted more tolerantly in the England of Disraeli and Lord Curzon—is disliked by Americans. Meriwether Lewis, a great explorer of the West, was handicapped by the nickname of "The Sublime Dandy" and his manners of a Beau Nash. William Pinkney, one of the most brilliant lawyers of a century ago, was ridiculed because of his fawn-colored gloves and corsets and the vanity that led him to begin a speech all over again when he saw ladies enter the visitors' gallery of the Supreme Court.

Effeminacy is fatal. Martin Van Buren failed of re-election in 1840 after the public had grown tired of his lace-tipped cravats and morocco shoes and a ribald Whig politician had exposed his use of a lotion called "Essence of Victoria." In the West, the dude was a traditional villain. (Ironically, in 1860 Lincoln's campaign manager worked hard to get him photographed in a boiled shirt with pearl studs, to make a better impression in the East.)

The arrogance of caste is equally deadly in American hero-worship. Hancock, Jay, Gouverneur Morris were snobs who never won the sway, with even a seasoning of popular admiration, that some Tory statesmen have enjoyed in England. The public can never forget that Hamilton once exclaimed, "Your people, sir, is a great beast!" (These words, quoted in the second decade of this century in school texts on American history by William B. Guitteau, McLaughlin and Van Tyne, and Albert Bushnell Hart, were omitted, after protests from school boards and patrons, from subsequent editions in the 1920's, when the Hamiltonian philosophy was in favor during the era of Republican prosperity.) Harding paid Hamilton the dubious compliment of saying, in 1921, "No man's life ever gave me greater inspiration than Hamilton's"; and bankers have often praised the first Secretary of the Treasury. But the people at large have repaid his scorn with neglect.

Even Daniel Webster—for all his adoration in New England and among the propertied classes—has failed, for like reasons, to make the upper rungs of hero-worship. All else favored him: a head so noble that it was often said "no man could be as great as Webster looked," a record of success from barefoot boy on a New Hampshire farm to the United States Senate and Cabinet, a superb voice that made the blood pound in men's temples. But he was known as "the pensioner of Wall Street," who spent his days so ex-clusively around mahogany tables in clubs and directors' rooms—where the smoke of Havana cigars hung blue, and "mountain dew" Scotch regaled his fine palate—that in the end he became not the idol of the People but of the Best People. There are apparent exceptions. The rich man's friend is sometimes elected President—as in the days of McKinley, Harding, and Coolidge —when the voters look upon themselves as potential rich men, but his popularity strikes no roots in the substratum of affection and legend.

Within limits, the mores of the hero may vary with his times. Emerson, living in the day of Old Hickory, Clay, and Webster, remarked that to the great man, "doing for the people what they wish done and cannot do, of course, everything will be permitted and pardoned—gaming, drinking, fighting, luxury . . . everything short of infamous crime will pass." Hadn't Jackson run off with another man's wife? Didn't he and Clay fight duels and bet on racehorses? Weren't Clay and Webster notoriously heavy drinkers—even though Webster was said to concede enough to appearances on the platform to refresh himself with white brandy out of a water-glass? Emerson's conclusion was probably too sweeping: in the first place he forgot that the capital of Puritanism had already moved from New England into insular America, and secondly he failed to reckon with the merely regional popularity of Clay and Webster which even then was fading. Only Jackson endured, a greater democrat as well as a man of higher personal integrity. The hero of a democracy—unlike the Stuarts, Bourbons, and Napoleons of the

Old World—cannot invite public opinion to go to hell. He must pay tribute to conformity.

Through most of our cultural history, for the average man sex and religion have been life's two most serious subjects, and irregularity even in the mighty leader must not go too far. Aaron Burr's "one hundred bastards" belong to the legend of villainy, along with Thaddeus Stevens' alleged mistresses, white and black; while Tom Paine's agnostic mockery made him in spite of his great patriotic services an object of folk hate. As for the hero, debunkery by sensational writers has usually addressed itself to secret nips at the bottle, failure to attend church, or flirtation with a neighbor's wife—rather than to matters of rightful public concern, like soundness of military strategy, foresight, or statesmanly wisdom.

The great man who wins acceptance as a hero will find his vagaries and skepticisms trimmed down by convention. Nevertheless, it is surprising how few of the American great, in comparison with those of the Old World, have cultivated lush private lives, though their individual views on religion have often shown more independence than orthodoxy. To a man's man, the sturdy profanity of Washington and Old Hickory, like the earthy jokes of Franklin and Lincoln, will be forgiven and, in the main, forgotten. Fundamentally the hero is required to be chaste, loyal, honest, humble before duty and before God. He is apt to have a dash of Puritan conscience, but the beauty of holiness is no more expected than is a sense of poetry.

The people's choice of heroes for America has been prevailingly sound; our major favorites are those any nation might be proud of. They go far toward vindicating the whole democratic theory of careers open to talents. We believe that character is more important than brains. Hard work, tenacity, enterprise, and firmness in the face of odds are the qualities that Americans most admire, rather than originality or eloquence of tongue and pen.

The hero must be a man of good will and also a good neighbor, preferably something of a joiner. Of the solitudes and lonely isolations of a great man like Lincoln the public has little conception. It likes to think of its idol as simple in greatness. Manliness, forthright manners, and salty speech are approved. Love of the soil, of dogs and horses and manual hobbies and fishing is better understood than absorption in art, literature, and music. (The public distrusts Presidents who are photographed fishing in their store clothes.) The hero must not lose touch with his birthplace and origins, however humble; the atmosphere of small towns and front-porch campaigns, cultivated by so many candidates for President, pays tribute to this demand. "I really believe there are more attempts at flattering the farmers than any other class," Lincoln as candidate for President remarked at the Wisconsin State Fair, "the reason for which I cannot perceive, unless it be that they cast more votes than any other."

Also, the touch of versatility and homely skill is applauded in a hero. Thomas Jefferson is remembered less as the eighteenth-century virtuoso than as an inventor of gadgets from which he plainly got a great deal of fun. "Tinkering" is American. European lads—like Henrich Steffens growing up in Denmark, and Michael Pupin in a Serbian village—have testified to the fascination that Franklin, "wiser than all the wise men of Idvor," held for them. The hero must do things better than the common folk, but his achievements (unlike those of the artist, philosopher, and pure scientist) must lie open to every-man's comprehension. It is well, too, that the labels of the hero conform to those of the group, so that iden-tification between him and the ma-jority can more easily be made: for example, all of our major idols have been both Anglo-Saxon and Prot-estant.

Bravery, honesty, strength of character are the stuff for hero-worship. At the boy's level, this worship gravitates toward the doer of spectacular deeds; on the average adult level, toward the wielder of power; and in the eyes of a more critical judgment, toward idealism and moral qualities. The most uni-versal hero is he who can fill all these specifications. This, by the many shapes of their courage, in-tegrity, and strength, Washington and Lincoln and Lee are able to do. When the dust of partisanship has settled, another leader in two great crises, economic and military— Franklin D. Roosevelt—will prob-ably join their august company. But Jefferson the sedentary man, Ben Franklin the opportunist, and Andrew Jackson the rough-hewn soldier fail to satisfy everybody. Upon a still lower rank, men like Daniel Boone and Crockett and Buffalo Bill and Edison remain al-most juvenile heroes. They do not have all the dimensions of our few supreme symbols. Was it not Emer-son who suggested that we Ameri-cans were the shattered pieces of a great mould?

Our most powerful hero epics center about our leaders. What, then, in the final analysis do Wash-ington, Franklin, Jefferson, Jackson, Lincoln, and in the provisional ver-dict Wilson and the Roosevelts have in common? Among them lie many differences. In heredity, economic origins, training, skill, tempera-ment, party affiliations, and attach-ment to specific policies they may seem as diverse as we could find by sifting the nation from Atlantic to Pacific. All save perhaps Wash-ington were "liberals" by the gauge of their times—and Washington, one must not forget, was an arch political rebel, who even in old age sought to balance his conservatism by an honest effort to be nonpar-tisan. (And even Washington has slowly waned before the warmer humanity of Lincoln.) What is their common denominator?

All of them, the people believe, loved America more deeply than any selfish consideration. The hero as made in America is a man who has the power and yet does not abuse it. He is the practical demon-stration of romantic democracy. Washington is most sublime be-cause, after winning our freedom, he refused a crown, military dic-tatorship, and every personal re-ward. Lee is grandest because he did what he thought was his duty, failed under heartbreaking odds, and then with gentleness did his best to repair all hate and malice. Lincoln is most appealing because, in the conduct of that same desper-ate war which gave him the power of a czar, he never forgot his love for the common people of North and South.

More clearly than the great

heroes of Europe, military and political, ours stand for a progress concept. They spring from stock that has bred schemes both wise and foolish—with its talk about the pursuit of happiness, the more abundant life, and the American Dream. None of these epic leaders left the Republic as he found it—although to avoid disturbing a single stick or stone seems to have been the policy of men like James Buchanan, Chester A. Arthur, William McKinley, and Calvin Coolidge. At times, to be sure, the people themselves have wanted no change, felt no urge to take on fresh responsibility in the national sphere. In eras like theirs, nothing is added to the stature of American ideals—such as civil liberty, equality of opportunity, faith in the average man, social justice, respect for the rights of weaker nations and for the good estate of democracy throughout the earth. A Chief Executive may then be called to office who rules as a minor Augustus over a gilded age or serves as the genial host at a great barbecue. But ten years hence he is not likely to be remembered as a great man or even as a symbol worth keeping.

Our heroes, we believe, are cast in a different mould. Their ruling passion, as we see it, is a sense of duty, alert to the best among the stirring impulses of their time and able to make that impulse effective. They translate the dream into act. The supreme leader is he who can hitch the great bandwagon to the star of American idealism.

· QUESTIONS ·

1. List the adjectives (paragraph 1) which, according to the author, best describe the American hero. Do you disagree with any of these findings?
2. What are the qualities which are taboo (paragraphs 2 ff.)? Do you disagree with any of the author's comments?
3. Cite illustrations, other than those given by Wecter, of how "the mores of the hero may vary with his times."
4. Do the selections in this volume by Benét and Kennedy offer additional explanations of Webster's failure to become a national hero?
5. For what reasons, as listed by Wecter, do you feel that the following are, or are not, national heroes: Herbert Hoover, Truman, Adlai Stevenson, Eisenhower, J. F. Kennedy, Nixon, Helen Keller, Jane Addams?
6. Define: ribald, substratum, mores, conformity, vagaries.
7. Wecter states "All of our major idols have been both Anglo-Saxon and Protestant." He might have added "white." Are all our heroes of today and of the past really WASPs (White, Anglo-Saxon, Protestant)?
8. What is meant by "a progress concept"? Does the idea this phrase represents find an echo in Kluckhohn's "Snapshot of America"?
9. Write a one-paragraph summary of the positive and negative attributes of the typical American hero as described by Wecter.

Theme Subjects: (1) My Idea of America's Greatest Hero (past or present); (2) The Greatest Man (Woman) Who Ever Lived Was (Is) _____; (3) A Comparison of the Ideas of Wecter and Kluckhohn; (4) America's Greatest Villain (see Benét's short story, "The Devil and Daniel Webster"); (5) America's Favorite Heroes of Sport (Theater, Screen, etc.).

THE HUMAN COMMUNITY

Paul McGuire

PAUL McGUIRE (1903–   ) was born in Peterborough, South Australia, and educated at the Christian Brothers College (Adelaide) and at the University of Adelaide. After serving as an extension lecturer for his university, he became a newspaper correspondent. Mr. McGuire lectured extensively in the United States just before and immediately after World War II. During the war he served in the Royal Australian Navy. In 1954 he became Australia's Minister to Italy; he served his country as Ambassador to Italy in 1958–1959. Among his numerous books are *The Two Men and Other Poems* (1933); *The Poetry of Gerard Manley Hopkins* (1934); *Funeral in Eden* (1938); *Australia: Her Heritage, Her Future* (1939); *Westward the Course!* (1942); *Experiment in World Order* (1948); and *There's Freedom for the Brave* (1949).

1.   Every man belongs to many communities. As Presbyterian, storekeeper, Republican, golfer, husband, Rotarian, stockholder, in his desire for a good 25-cent cigar, as a regular patron of the Interborough Subway, a man belongs to different communities of interest and purpose.

2.   We live within a marvelous complexity of communities and interests. Of most, we take little thought; many we take entirely for granted until they fail us, as we take the operations of our skin and viscera for granted until something goes wrong. We mark the ills and conflicts of the social body much more than its normal and healthy operation; but the harmony of nature which organizes cells for the miracles of life and strangely feeds and sustains them by the incorporation of elements of air, earth, and water is a more fundamental phenomenon. Marx insists on the class conflict; but though a man breed and nurse every conceivable grievance, he is still constantly sustained through life by his community, his countless cords to his fellows.

3.   We are most conscious of the communities which touch our emotions and responsibilities, and to which we actively contribute: our

family and the immediate groups in which we work or take our pleasure; the near, dear, and local. We are more alive to our office on Main Street and our home on Elm Avenue and our local associations than to our membership in the Commonwealth of Massachusetts or the Federal Union or the world communities. But these bear on us increasingly as the world grows smaller and the flights of bombers longer, and as our daily livelihood is influenced by the movements of world trade.

4. A human being rising at morning in Bayswater or the Bronx is an expression of a vast economy which reaches to the ends of the earth and back to the remotest depths of time. The fruit, cereal, bread, butter, milk, and eggs which have grown into him are come from acres he may never see and by processes of production, distribution, and exchange to which he seldom need attend. His bones, flesh, and blood are transmutations perhaps of the grass, soil, and airs of Texas, Argentina, Australasia, Iowa, and Manitoba. His shoes once walked the range in Montana or the plains of Western Queensland. The modern man of the cities is a testimony in flesh to the nature and necessity of a world economy. But he seldom applies to his political opinions the evident and intimate facts declared by his stomach, unless his stomach is pinched.

5. A girl in Omaha belongs to countless associations, local and universal. As she puts on her lipstick she enters an economic pattern which embraces the Solomon Islander knocking coconuts for copra from his palm trees. The New Yorker, as the saying runs, is fifteen hundred miles from his breakfast. The Englishman may reach fifteen thousand miles to bring in his joint of mutton. The American who at last sensibly wears wool in his winter socks may have it from the Woomera or the Transvaal. The British loaf is compounded from Australia and Canada. There is all Africa, as Sir Thomas Browne remarked, and a great deal else within us.

6. Our tools and instruments are derived from associations and communities reaching far into space and time. The breakfast in the Bronx is eaten with an instrument that once caught Tom Coryate's eye in Italy and earned him the splendid cognomen, Furcifer. Our ideas and values are drawn from the whole range of mankind. Breakfast in the Bronx or Bayswater is accompanied by news from all the world, screened by countless habitual attitudes and responses and traditions and prejudices. It is organized into the corpus of knowledge and experience which each of us has developed from our cultural inheritance. The breakfaster may eat to a rhythm derived from the Hottentot. He may even have earlier said a prayer learned from a prophet of Israel or the Angel of the Annunciation. Across the table, Junior may be spoiling his digestion trying to recall demonstrations first developed by a Greek of Alexandria, dust these twenty-two hundred years; and certainly the design of the breakfast room owes something to Euclid.

7. The morning journey from the Bronx or Bayswater moves on the works of countless men: on the application of scientific knowledge grown from the first dawn of wonder at the world; on a synthesis of human contributions which in-

cludes the work of Volta, Stephenson, miners, seamen, ticket-punchers, and the millions more.

8.   We all, in brief, live in and by miracles of community and collaboration. We belong to communities and societies whose threads are woven into the whole pattern of the world since its beginnings. This complex of common interests and purposes and acts and ideas is the most massive fact of man's existence as a social being. Yet it is one of the most neglected in our daily concern with the world. The most formidable political and economic theories of our times take the fact of conflict as the prime mover of history. Our politics are now dominated by the accidents of conflict rather than by our substantial community. We have organized accidents, local in time and place, to declare principles which we now treat as universals. We shall not make sense of our world while we thus misread its evidence.

· QUESTIONS ·

1. State the thesis of this essay. Do you accept it? How does it differ from the central thought of "Loyalty and Freedom"?
2. Is conflict the "prime mover" in our national life? What of political campaigns, campus rivalries, love affairs, business competition, sports?
3. Define: class conflict, world economy, corpus of knowledge, viscera.
4. Analyze the structure of paragraph 8. Then show that it is a summary of the entire essay. Do you agree that we "misread" the evidence all about us?
5. Explain the structural methods and kinds of substance used in developing paragraphs 4–6, inclusive.
6. Using paragraph 1 as a guide, write a paragraph beginning "I belong to many communities. . . ."

Theme Subjects: (1) The Communities I Belong To; (2) "No Man Is an Iland" (Donne); (3) Where My Breakfast (Clothing, News) Came From; (4) McGuire Is Right, But _____; (5) My Countless Cords to _____.

WHY I AM NOT GOING
TO THE MOON

Joseph Wood Krutch

JOSEPH WOOD KRUTCH (1893–   ) was born in Knoxville, Tennessee, and was graduated from the University of Tennessee, later taking his master's and doctorate at Columbia University. He has had a distinguished career as professor and lecturer in English and journalism at Columbia University, Polytechnic Institute of Brooklyn, Vassar, and the New School for Social Research. From 1943 to 1952 he served as Brander Matthews Professor of Dramatic Literature at Columbia. Dramatic critic and associate editor of *The Nation*, 1924–1932, he was on the board of editors, 1932–1937, and drama critic until 1952. A member of many literary and philosophical societies, he is on the board of editors for the American Men of Letters Series. Among his many books are *Comedy and Conscience After the Restoration* (1924); *Edgar Allan Poe—A Study in Genius* (1926); *Experience and Art* (1932); *Henry David Thoreau* (1948); *The Measure of Man* (recipient of National Book Award) (1954); *Human Nature and the Human Condition* (1959); *The World of Animals* (1961); and *Herbel* (1965).

It was, I believe, a mountain climber who invented the phrase "because it is there" to explain why he wanted to climb a particular peak. Because ours is an age devoted to all sorts of unexamined enterprises, his phrase has passed into popular speech and the very frequency with which it is invoked is a striking indication of the fact that many of the things we do, many of the ends we pursue, cannot be justified except by saying that, after all, these things can be done and these ends can be pursued.

Yet we cannot, after all, study everything that could be studied or do everything that could be done. Wisdom would seem to suggest that we ask, not only what can be done, but what is most worth doing

From *The Saturday Review*, November 20, 1965. Reprinted by permission of the author and the publisher.

—but that is exactly what the "because it is there" philosophy refuses to recognize. As Thoreau said, it is not worthwhile to go half way round the world to count the cats in Zanzibar. But there are, I presume, cats in Zanzibar and they could be counted. Better yet, the number could be pretty accurately estimated by a scientifically planned sampling. But before approving such an enterprise as one we ought to undertake, I would want some sounder reason than simply the fact that the cats are, presumably, there.

When President Kennedy was asked why our government was so eager to get someone to the moon, even he could think of no better answer than the catch-phrase "because it is there." Now, I am willing to believe that there may be better reasons. They may be military, and if there are sound military reasons I somewhat reluctantly yield to them. But I dismiss as mere foolish excuses most of the others I have heard—such as the prestige value of beating the Russians or, most farfetched of all, von Braun's suggestion that colonization of the bodies in outer space is the best solution to the population problem.

At the risk of provoking the scorn of all the proponents of pure science, fundamental research, and so forth (as well as of all the "because it is there" boys), I would like to say that I have not yet heard any argument that seemed to me to justify the enormous expenditure of time, money, and brains upon this particular enterprise. Henry Adams said that the Middle Ages believed building cathedrals the thing most worth doing, just as the mid-nineteenth century in the United States gave the same sort of priority to railroad building. In our own time, exploration of space seems to have won a similar priority. We seem to regard it as not only worth doing but even more worth doing than anything else and, therefore, worth anything it may cost. But there is, it seems to me, no doubt that this inevitably means less time, less money, and less available brainpower to be spent on other things that, in addition to being there, seem to have stronger claims upon our attention.

That we should be dazzled by the sheer wonder of what man has been able to do is not surprising. The technical problems solved are surely the most difficult ever attacked by science. Out of nowhere has suddenly appeared a whole new race of experts who seem to move easily in a realm of thought and of practice that most of us cannot even enter. Within a few years they have accomplished what the most extravagant follower of Jules Verne would not have dared imagine except for some distant future. Yet the very wonder of it makes it difficult for us to maintain any sense of proportion. To question its value is likely to seem mere impudence. Yet it ought to be, at least, questioned.

I am not thinking exclusively in terms of the argument that the money spent might be better used to relieve the sufferings of the poor, although that is itself an argument not quite so easily disposed of as Philip Morrison, professor of physics at Cornell and formerly a group leader at Los Alamos, assumed when he wrote recently in *The New Leader*: "The claim of each act we carry out in common must rest on its merit and not on the general thesis that no rich, strange, useless thing can justly be bought while some men lack necessities. . . . Those who built the Acropolis forgot the Helots; those who sailed the Indies thought nothing of the landless peasants."

The poor we have always with us and those who cite that text do not always seem to remember the context—which might seem to make it support Professor Morrison's thesis. The comment was made as a reply to those of the disciples who had rebuked a stranger woman for pouring upon the head of Jesus a rich ointment which, they pointed out, might have been sold and the proceeds given to the poor. "The poor ye have always with you but me you have not always with you." But the question is not merely whether *any* rich, interesting, or beautiful thing can justifiably be bought while some men lack necessities. It is whether, in this particular case, the enormous expenditure is justified when it means neglecting, not only many men, but many other things with at least as much claim to being "rich, strange and (possibly) useful" as well.

Like the poor, this problem has always been with us and in one form or another probably always will be. But in times past men did have one guide in deciding *which* rich and strange thing was worth spending time and brains and money to create or do: They believed (as we do not) that one thing was intrinsically and absolutely better, wiser, or more to be admired than something else. They did not have to fall back on any "because it is there" argument because they had not, like us, been reduced by moral and cultural relativism to a sort of impotence that leaves us powerless to defend one

choice as opposed to another and that therefore encourages us to do whatever can be done and to offer no reason more persuasive than the simple "because it is there to be done."

If we do indeed do some things that should have been left undone and do others less worth doing than those we neglect, none of that can be blamed on science itself. The great but limited field of its competence is knowing (pure science) and doing (technology). It cannot —as the wiser of its practitioners admit—evaluate. Though it can teach us how to get to the moon, we need something else to tell us whether or not we ought to go there.

Hence it is that if science is not to blame, some scientists are— just insofar as they encourage the now almost universal belief that science is omnicompetent and that any problems that cannot be solved by the scientific method (and that means all questions involving evaluation) are simply unsolvable or, essentially, meaningless. The tendency to fall back upon "because it is there" as the only answer to the question why a certain thing should be done is simply a demonstration of the inadequacy of science alone as a guide for either society or for the life of an individual.

Three centuries and a half ago Francis Bacon wrote in *The Advancement of Learning:* "We are much beholden to Machiavelli and others, that write what men do, and not what they ought to do." This was perhaps a useful observation at the time; but the situation in the intellectual world is now by no means what it was in Bacon's day. And of all the threats to civilization perhaps none is greater than that which leads sociology to ask only what men do do and technology only what can be done, or, to use again the popular phrase, "what is there." By banishing "ought" from the vocabulary of our sociology, and by asking of our technologists only what they can do rather than what is worth doing, we are making ourselves passengers in a vehicle over which no critical intelligence pretends to exercise any control and which may, indeed, take us not only to the moon but to destinations even less desirable.

Some will no doubt answer that many of the advances of science are due to boundless curiosity concerning things that seem to have no possible application. But such curiosity is much safer when it leads us to know whatever we can know rather than to do whatever we can do. We have a tendency to rush from knowing to doing without pausing for reflection. Technology, if not science, has sometimes entailed penalties when it has taught us how to do things better left undone. This fact was seldom noted even by a few until quite recently when even a minority began to wonder whether or not it would have been better for everybody if the secret of the atom had never been penetrated. Curiosity, even scientific curiosity, can open a Pandora's box as well as a treasure chest.[1] And one should use a certain amount of caution in lifting the lid of any box whose contents are unknown.

Primitive man suffered from both a lack of knowledge and a lack of know-how. He believed a great many absurd and often troublesome things that were not true. He had a very limited knowledge of how to do what he wanted to do. But this last limitation was also something of a safeguard, even if a rather unsatisfactory one. He could not destroy his environment as disastrously as we can destroy ours, and he could not kill as many of his neighbors as he would have been glad to kill if he had known how. Perhaps his intentions and desires were even worse than ours, but he didn't know as well as we how to implement them. We know only too well. Know-how continues to leave know-what and know-whether further and further behind.

I do not know just how military expenditures compare with those incurred in connection with the exploration of space. But except for defense, no other single enterprise of the government is financed on so lavish a scale. This surely suggests that those responsible for giving it this unquestioned priority assume that of all the achievements possible in our generation this is the one most important. But does anyone seriously believe that this is true? That if a good fairy should grant us one wish we should say, "Let me get to the moon, and beyond"?

Consider, for example, the population explosion and not only what it has already done to make life difficult and ugly but also what it threatens to do in the future. In the minds of many thoughtful people it is a danger to mankind that may be as great as that of atomic warfare—the one threatening us

---

[1] In classical mythology, the gift of a box or jar by Zeus to Pandora, the first mortal woman, containing all human ills, resulted in her opening it with dire results. In another version, the box contained all blessings, every one of which escaped upon Pandora's act except *hope*.

with too many people, the other with a world in which there will be none at all. One could easily fill a book full of statements by responsible persons that say just this in one way or another. One moderate comment from Dr. Walter Hoagland, president of the American Academy of Arts and Sciences, will suffice. In a recent *Bulletin of the Atomic Scientists* he described experiments that demonstrate to his satisfaction that in animal populations overcrowding produces various pathological conditions including a fatal adrenal malfunction called the "Stress Syndrome." He believes that the same thing will happen to human beings under similar circumstances, and this seems to dispose of the assurance that the feeding of a monstrously overgrown population will present no serious problems to an ever-advancing technology.

Dr. Hoagland went on to suggest that we can "do nothing and just wait for the Stress Syndrome or a new virus to do its work," or we can "leave the solution to some trigger-happy dictator with a suitable stockpile of atomic weapons." On the other hand, so he suggests, we might just possibly "decide on an optimum population for the world and by education and social pressure try to see that it is not exceeded."

Admittedly, that last suggestion, though the only sensible one, involves problems to which the solutions are not at the moment by any means obvious. But it is to President Johnson's credit that he has given, more clearly than any other high government official ever has, recognition to the fact that the population explosion should be reckoned with somehow, sometime.

Not long after his inauguration the foreign aid bill contained this sentence: "Funds available to carry out this provision may be used to conduct research into the problems of population growth." True, the implication seems to be that no such problems exist in our own country. And the very fact that so timid a statement should mark an epoch is itself enough to demonstrate how casually, almost as a parenthetical afterthought, we approach what is, in actual fact, the second if not the first greatest threat to the future of mankind. Suppose that we had got no further in our plans to explore space than the provision in an omnibus bill for funds "to conduct research into the problem of space travel." Would that not suggest that we didn't think it very important— just something that might be looked into some day and at leisure?

Historians of ancient Egypt say that what we would call its "national income" was, during its days of greatness, very high. But the standard of living endured by the majority of its population was very low indeed because all of the income above what was essential to the barest existence went into the pyramids and other extravagances.

Now, no one could say that such a situation exists today in the United States. A good deal of our national income goes, not only into welfare, but into the pockets of citizens who buy with it what they like—whether that be education for their children, books and pictures and music for themselves, or (in somewhat more numerous instances) the most expensive automobiles their income (plus available credit) will get them. But future historians (if there are any) may wonder that we put into our rocket motors and all that goes into the making of them so large a slice of the national income.

Once, for several centuries, the Western world was united in the belief that the most important task it could possibly accomplish would be the recovery of the Holy Sepulcher.[2] It sacrificed thousands of lives, to say nothing of vast wealth and a large part of its manpower, in the attempt to achieve something that few of us today can regard as having been more than an irrational obsession. Yet to a large section of the intelligent men of that time the enterprise must have seemed as obviously important as landing on the moon seems to us. But is not the moon, like the Holy Sepulcher, a mere symbol? It is not even in the hands of the infidel—though I suppose that if the Russians get there first it will be considered to be. And I wonder if, at some not too distant date, our crusade will not have come to seem no less incomprehensible than that of our forefathers.

Why don't we devote to the problem of overpopulation an effort as determined as that we are making to get to the moon before the Russians? Why, even at long last, do we do no more than to say that a small part of a large fund may be used to "conduct research into the problem" but not even to take any action?

The most important of the answers to this question is not the opposition of moralists or the indifference of those who see in what they call a "bumper crop of babies" an ever-increasing market for the baby foods it will eat and, a little later, for the cigarettes it will smoke. The most important reasons are, first, the fact that this problem is far more difficult than the problem (stupendous though it is) of how to get to the moon; and, second, that the solution, if there is one, cannot be reached by the methods that have yielded such astonishingly successful results when applied to all the problems that do not involve human nature and that therefore yield to mechanical solutions. That the technological problem of birth control has been solved, that our so triumphant know-how includes the know-how of contraception, is quite typical of our age's greatest strength. That we do not know how our know-how can be applied to promote a good life is equally so. If a Cousteau suggests that we build undersea cities and a von Braun gives the even more preposterous suggestion that we colonize the planets; if, moreover, these are taken seriously by some, it can only be because these are purely technological solutions and it is upon technology that most of us rest whatever hopes we may have for a decent future.

I remember having read, some fifteen or more years ago, a book by Willy Ley in which was discussed the conditions that would have to be created before a rocket could break away from the earth's gravity and proceed indefinitely toward whatever object in space it had been pointed at. To do that, if I remember correctly, the rocket would have to be capable of a speed twice what it had been possible to achieve up to that time. This critical speed was named "the escape velocity."

---

[2] The sepulcher (tomb, burial place) in which the body of Jesus lay between His burial and His resurrection.

And though the ironic implications of the term did not strike me then, they do strike me now. Perhaps one of the reasons we are so attracted by the problems of space exploration is that absorption in them helps us forget the more difficult problems lying right at our feet and that an "escape velocity" is precisely what we have achieved.

A good many science fiction stories have been written about the survivors, sometimes the last surviving couple, on a depopulated earth. If I were to try my hand at that kind of fiction I should imagine a pair of astronauts who had escaped to the moon and who looked back at an earth where the Stress Syndrome produced by overcrowding had at last involved, not only the exchange of the Russian and American overkill stockpile, but also the smaller but effective contributions from what are now called —but by then wouldn't be—the undeveloped countries. Our astronauts had brought along the equipment necessary for the return journey. But it did not take them long to decide not to use it.

· QUESTIONS ·

1. Point out the specific ways in which this essay and that by Clarke contradict each other. Which essayist do you feel has the stronger argument? Whom do you believe? Whom would you rather believe?
2. Krutch considers the problem of overpopulation greater than that of reaching and colonizing the moon; Clarke refers to dominating the earth as a *triviality*. Do you agree with the implied importance of overpopulation? Would Lilienthal agree?
3. "If the secret of the atom had never been penetrated"—discuss some probable effects of this unreality.
4. Explain the references to von Braun, Cousteau, Willy Ley.
5. Define: relativism, impotence, omnicompetent, adrenal, implications, epoch, stupendous.

Theme Subjects: (1) My Vote Goes to _____ (Krutch or Clarke); (2) Another Pandora's Box That I Know; (3) Krutch Is (Is Not) a Mossback; (4) Clarke Is (Is Not) a Wild Visionary; (5) My Own Space Calendar.

THE USES OF THE MOON

Arthur C. Clarke

ARTHUR CHARLES CLARKE (1917–   ) was born in Somerset, England, and served as an auditor in the British Civil Service from 1936 until World War II, when he joined the Royal Air Force and became a radar instructor and technical officer in charge of the first Ground-Controlled Approach System. Fascinated by matters relating to space flight, he proposed the use of satellites for communications as early as 1945, in an article in *Wireless World,* and in 1951 became a full-time scientific and science fiction writer. Lecturer, undersea explorer, and photographer, he is a member of, among others, the British Interplanetary Society, International Academy of Astronautics, the American Rocket Society, and the British Sub-Aqua Club, and was the winner of the 1952 International Fantasy Award, the 1961 Kalinga Prize for the popularization of science, and the Stuart Ballantine Medal of the Franklin Institute in 1963. He is author of many books, including *Interplanetary Flight* (1950, 1951, 1960); *The Exploration of Space* (1951), which became a Book-of-the-Month in this country; *The Coast of Coral* (1956); *The Challenge of the Spaceship* (1959); and *Profiles of the Future* (1962), and has written more than 300 articles and short stories for popular magazines.

The two greatest nations in the world are now preparing to land men on the Moon within the next decade. This will be one of the central facts of political life in the years to come; indeed, it may soon dominate human affairs. It is essential, therefore, that we understand the importance of the Moon in our future; if we do not, we will be going there for the wrong reasons and will not know what to do when we arrive.

Many people imagine that the whole project of lunar exploration is merely a race with the Russians —a contest in conspicuous consumption of brains and material, designed to impress the remainder of mankind. No one can deny the strong element of competition and national prestige involved, but in the long run, this will be the least important aspect of the matter. If the race to the Moon were nothing more than a race, it would make good sense to let the Russians bankrupt themselves in the strain of winning it, in the calm confidence that their efforts would collapse in recriminations and purges some time during the 1970's.

There are some shortsighted people (including a few elderly, but unfortunately still influential, scientists) who would adopt just such a policy. Why spend tens of billions of dollars, they ask, to land a few men on a barren, airless lump of rock, nothing more than a cosmic slagheap, baked by the Sun during the daytime and frozen to subarctic temperatures in the long night? The polar regions of this Earth are far more hospitable; indeed, the deep oceans could probably be exploited and even colonized for a fraction of the sum needed to conquer the Moon.

All this is true; it is also totally irrelevant. The Moon *is* a barren, airless wasteland, blasted by intolerable radiations. Yet a century from now it may be an asset more valuable than the wheatfields of Kansas or the oil wells of Oklahoma. And an asset in terms of actual hard cash—not the vast imponderables of adventure, romance, artistic inspiration, and scientific knowledge. Though, ultimately, these are the only things of real value, they can never be measured. The conquest of the Moon, however, can be justified to the cost accountants, not only to the scientists and the poets.

Let me first demolish, with

considerable pleasure, one common argument for going to the Moon— the military one. Some ballistic generals have maintained that the Moon is "high ground" that could be used for reconnaissance and bombardment of the Earth. Though I hesitate to say that this is complete nonsense, it is as near to it as makes very little practical difference.

You cannot hope to see as much from 250,000 miles away as from a TV satellite just above the atmosphere, and the use of the Moon as a launching site makes even less sense. For the effort required to set up one lunar military base with all its supporting facilities, at least a hundred times as many bases could be established on Earth. Also it would be far easier to intercept a missile coming from the Moon, and taking many hours for the trip in full view of telescopes and radar, than one sneaking round the curve of the Earth in twenty minutes. Only if, which heaven forbid, we extend our present tribal conflicts to the other planets will the Moon become of military importance.

Before we discuss the civilized uses of our one natural satellite, let us summarize the main facts about it. They may be set down quite briefly:

The Moon is a world a quarter the diameter of Earth, its radius being just over a thousand miles. Thus its area is one-sixteenth of our planet's—more than that of Africa, and almost as much as that of both the Americas combined. Such an amount of territory is not to be despised: it will take many years (and many lives) to explore it in detail.

The amount of material in the Moon is also impressive; if you would like it in tons, the figure comes to 750,000,000,000,000,000,-000,000, which is millions of millions of times more than all the coal, iron, minerals and ores that man has shifted in the whole of history. It is not enough mass, however, to give the Moon much of a gravitational pull; as everyone now knows, a visitor to the Moon has only a fraction (actually one-sixth) of his terrestrial weight.

This low gravity has several consequences, almost all of them good. The most important is that the Moon has been unable to retain an atmosphere; if it ever had one, it long ago escaped from the Moon's feeble clutch and leaked off into space. For all practical purposes, therefore, the lunar surface is in a perfect vacuum. (*This* is an advantage? Yes: we'll see why in a moment.)

Because there is no atmosphere to weaken the Sun's rays, or to act as a reservoir of heat during the nighttime, the Moon is a world of very great temperature extremes. On our Earth, in any one spot, the thermometer seldom ranges over as much as a hundred degrees even during the course of a year. Though the temperature can exceed 100°F in the tropics, and drop to 125° *below* zero in the Antarctic, these figures are quite exceptional. But every point on the Moon undergoes twice this range during the lunar day; indeed, an explorer could encounter such changes within seconds, merely by stepping from sunlight into shadow or vice versa.

This obviously presents problems, but the very absence of atmosphere which causes such extremes also makes it easy to deal with them —for a vacuum is one of the best possible heat insulators, a fact familiar to anyone who has ever taken along hot drinks on a picnic.

No air means no weather. It is hard for us, accustomed to wind and rain, cloud and fog, hail and snow to imagine the complete absence of all these things. None of the meteorological variations which make life interesting, unpredictable, and occasionally impossible on the surface of this planet take place on the Moon: the only change which ever occurs is the regular, utterly unvarying cycle of day and night. Such a situation may be monotonous but it simplifies, to an unbelievable extent, the problems facing architects, engineers, explorers, and indeed everyone who will ever conduct operations of any kind on the surface of the Moon.

The Moon turns rather slowly on its axis, so that its day (and its night) are almost thirty times longer than ours. As a result, the sharp-edged frontier between night and day, which moves at a thousand miles an hour on the Earth's equator, has a maximum speed of less than ten miles an hour on the Moon. In high lunar latitudes, a walking man could keep in perpetual daylight with little exertion. And because the Moon turns on its axis in the same time as it revolves around the Earth, it always keeps the same hemisphere turned toward us. Until the advent of Lunik III, this was extremely frustrating to astronomers; in another generation, as we shall see, they will be very thankful for it.

So much for the main facts; now for a few assumptions which most people would accept as reasonable now, though they would have laughed at them before 1957.

The first is that suitably protected men can work and carry out engineering operations on the face of the Moon, either directly or by remote control through robots.

The second is that the Moon consists of the same elements as the Earth, though doubtless in different proportions and combinations. Most of our familiar minerals will be missing: there will be no coal or limestone, since these are the products of life. But there will be carbon, hydrogen, oxygen, and calcium in other forms, and we can evolve a technology to extract them from whatever sources are available. It is even possible that there may be large quantities of free (though frozen) water not too far below the Moon's surface; if this is the case, one of the chief problems of the lunar colonists will be solved.

In any event, without going into details of mining, ore processing, and chemical engineering, it will be possible to obtain all the materials needed for maintaining life. The first pioneers will be content with mere survival, but at a later stage they will build up a self-supporting industry based almost entirely on lunar resources. Only instruments, specialized equipment, and men will come from Earth; the Moon will supply all the rest—ultimately, of course, even the men.

There have been many studies and books on the subject of lunar colonization (I have written one myself) and all those who have gone into the subject are agreed on the general picture. The details vary, as they must until we have much more exact knowledge of conditions on the Moon, but that is of no importance. It may take as little as fifty years (the interval between the Wright biplane and the B-52!)

to establish a viable lunar colony; it may take a hundred. But if we wish, it can be done; on the Moon, to borrow the words of William Faulkner's Nobel Prize speech, "Man will not merely endure—he will prevail."

Now for the reasons why it is worth the expense, risk, and difficulty of prevailing on the inhospitable Moon. They are implicit in the question: what can the Moon offer that we cannot find on Earth?

One immediate but paradoxical answer is Nothing—millions of cubic miles of it. Many of the key industries in the modern world are based on vacuum techniques; electric lighting and its offspring radio and electronics could never have begun without the vacuum tube, and the invention of the transistor has done little to diminish its importance. (The initial steps of transistor manufacture have themselves to be carried out in vacuum.) A great many metallurgical and chemical processes, and key stages in the production of such drugs as penicillin, are possible only in a partial or virtually complete vacuum; but it is expensive to make a very good vacuum and impossible to make a very large one.

On the Moon, there will be a "hard" vacuum of unlimited extent outside the door of every airlock. I do not suggest that it will be worthwhile switching much terrestrial industry to the Moon, even if the freight charges allowed it. But the whole history of science makes it certain that new processes and discoveries of fundamental importance will evolve as soon as men start to carry out operations in the lunar vacuum. Low-pressure physics and technology will proceed from rags to riches overnight; industries which today are unimagined will spring up on the Moon and ship their products back to Earth. For in that direction, the freight charges will be relatively low.

And this leads us to a major role that the Moon will play in the development of the solar system: it is no exaggeration to say that this little world, so small and close at hand (the very first rocket to reach it took only thirty-five hours on the journey) will be the stepping stone to all the planets. The reason for this is its low gravity; it requires twenty times as much energy to escape from the Earth as from the Moon. As a supply base for all interplanetary operations, therefore, the Moon has an enormous advantage over the Earth—assuming, of course, that we can find the materials we need there. This is one of the reasons why the development of lunar technology and industry is so important.

From the gravitational point of view, the Moon is indeed high ground, while we on Earth are like dwellers at the bottom of an immensely deep pit out of which we have to climb every time we wish to conduct any cosmic explorations. No wonder that we must burn a hundred tons of rocket fuel for every ton of payload we launch into space—and on a one-way trip at that. For return journeys, thousands of tons would be needed.

This is why all Earth-based plans for space travel are so hopelessly uneconomic, involving gigantic boosters with tiny payloads. It is as if, in order to carry a dozen passengers across the Atlantic, we had to construct a ship weighing as much as the *Queen Elizabeth* but costing very much more. (The development costs for a large space vehicle are several billion dollars.) And, to make the whole thing completely fantastic, the vehicle can be used only once, *for it will be destroyed in flight*. Of the tens of thousands of tons that leave the Earth, only a small capsule will return. The rest will consist of boosters dropped in the ocean or discarded in space.

When nuclear power is harnessed for rocket propulsion, the position will be improved from the preposterous to the merely absurd. For even nuclear rockets must carry hundreds or thousands of tons of reaction mass, to provide a thrust when it is ejected. Every rocket, nuclear or chemical, has to have something to push against; that something is not the surrounding air, as many people once believed, but the rocket's own fuel.

However, the nuclear rocket will use the very simplest of fuels —plain hydrogen. There must be plenty of this on the Moon, combined in water (which is 11 percent hydrogen) or in some other form. The first order of business in lunar exploration will be to locate sources from which hydrogen may be obtained; when this has been done, and it is possible for ships to refuel on the Moon, the cost, difficulty, and complexity of all space operations will be reduced at least tenfold.

Since spacecraft need not carry fuel for the return trip (imagine where transatlantic flying would be today, if it operated on this basis!) it will no longer be necessary to build and jettison ten-thousand-ton vehicles to deliver ten-ton payloads. Instead of monstrous, multistaged boosters, we can use relatively small rockets that can be refueled and flown over and over again. Space flight would emerge from its present status as a fantastically expensive stunt and would start to make economic—perhaps even commercial—sense.

This, however, would be only a beginning. The big breakthrough toward really efficient space operations may depend upon the fortunate fact that the Moon has no atmosphere. The peculiar (by our standards—they are normal by those of the universe) conditions prevailing there permit a launching technique much more economical than rocket propulsion. This is the old idea of the "space gun," made famous by Jules Verne almost a hundred years ago.

It would probably not be a gun in the literal sense, powered by chemical explosives, but a horizontal launching track like those used on aircraft carriers, along which space vehicles could be accelerated electrically until they reached sufficient speed to escape from the Moon. It is easy to see why such a device is completely impractical on Earth but might be of enormous value on the Moon.

To escape from the Earth, a body must reach the now familiar speed of 25,000 miles an hour. At the fierce acceleration of ten gravities, which astronauts have already withstood for very short periods of time, it would take two minutes to attain this speed—and the launching track would have to be *four hundred miles* long. If the acceleration were halved to make it more endurable, the length of the track would have to be doubled. And, of course, any object traveling at such a speed in the lower atmosphere would be instantly burned up by friction. We can forget all about space guns on Earth.

The situation is completely different on the Moon. Because of the almost perfect vacuum, the lunar escape speed of a mere 5,200 m.p.h. can be achieved at ground level without any danger from air resistance. And at an acceleration of ten gravities, the launching track need be only 19 miles long—not 400, as on Earth. It would be a massive piece of engineering, but a perfectly practical one, and it would wholly transform the economics of space flight.

Vehicles could leave the Moon *without burning any fuel at all;* all the work of take-off would be done by fixed power plants on the ground, which could be as large and massive as required. The only fuel that a space vehicle returning to Earth need carry would be a very small amount for maneuvering and navigating. As a result, the size of vehicle needed for a mission from Moon to Earth would be reduced tenfold; a hundred-ton spaceship could do what had previously required a thousand-tonner.

This would be a spectacular enough improvement; the next stage, however, would be the really decisive one. This is the use of a Moon-based launcher or catapult to place supplies of fuel where they are needed, in orbit round the Earth or indeed any other planet in the solar system.

It is generally agreed that long-range space flight—particularly voyages beyond the Moon—will become possible only when we can refuel our vehicles in orbit. Plans have been drawn up in great detail for operations involving fleets of tanker rockets which, perhaps over a period of years, could establish what are virtually filling stations in space. Such schemes will, of course, be fantastically expensive, for it requires about fifty tons of rocket fuel to put a single ton of payload into orbit round the Earth, only a couple of hundred miles up.

Yet a Moon-based launcher could do the same job—from a distance of 250,000 miles!—for a twentieth of the energy and without consuming any rocket fuel whatsoever. It would launch tanks of propellants "down" toward Earth, and suitable guidance systems would steer them into stable orbits where they would swing around endlessly until required. This would have as great an effect on the logistics of space flight as the dropping of supplies by air has already had upon polar exploration; indeed, the parallel is a very close one.

Though enormous amounts of power would be required to operate such lunar catapults, this will be no problem in the twenty-first century. A single hydrogen bomb, weighing only a few tons, liberates enough energy to lift a hundred million tons completely away from the Moon. That energy will be available for useful purposes when our grandchildren need it; if it is not, we will have no grandchildren.

There is one other application of the lunar catapult that may be very important, though it may seem even more far-fetched at the present time. It could launch the products of the Moon's technology all the way down to the surface of the Earth. A rugged, freight-carrying capsule, like a more refined version of today's nose cones and re-entry vehicles, could be projected from the Moon to make an automatic landing on the Earth at any assigned spot. Once again, no rocket fuel would be needed for the trip, except a few pounds for maneuvering. All the energy of launching would be provided by the fixed power plant on the Moon; all the slowing down would be done by the Earth's atmosphere. When such a system is perfected, it may be no more expensive to ship freight from Moon to Earth than it is now to fly it from one continent to another by jet. Moreover, the launching catapult could be quite short, since it would not have to deal with fragile human passengers. If it operated at fifty gravities acceleration, a four-mile-long track would be sufficient.

I have discussed this idea at some length for two reasons. The first is that it demonstrates how, by taking advantage of the Moon's low gravity, its airlessness, and the raw materials that must certainly be there, we can conduct space exploration far more economically than by basing our operations on Earth. In fact, until some revolutionary new method of propulsion is invented, it is hard to see any other way in which space travel will be practical on the large scale.

The second reason is the slightly more personal one that, to the best of my knowledge, I was the first to develop this idea in a 1950 issue of the *Journal* of the British Interplanetary Society. Five years earlier I had proposed the use of satellites for radio and TV communications; I did not expect to see either scheme materialize in my lifetime, but one has already happened and now I wonder if I may see both.

The subject of communications leads us to another extremely important use of the Moon. As civilization spreads throughout the solar system, the Moon will provide the main link between Earth and her scattered children. For though it is just as far to the other planets from the Moon as from the Earth, sheer distance is not the only factor involved. The Moon's surface is already in space, while the surface of the Earth—luckily for us—is shielded from space by a whole series of barriers through which we have to drive our signals.

The best known of these barriers is, of course, the ionosphere, which reflects all but the shorter radio waves back to Earth. The shortest waves of all, however, go through it with little difficulty, so the ionosphere is no hindrance to space communications.

What *is* a serious barrier—and this has been realized only during the past year—is the atmosphere itself. Thanks to the development of an extraordinary optical device called the laser, which produces an intense beam of almost perfectly parallel light, it now appears that the best agent for long-distance communications is not radio, but *light*. A light beam can carry millions of times as many messages as a radio wave and can be focused with infinitely greater accuracy. Indeed, a laser-produced light beam could produce a spot on the Moon only a few hundred feet across, where the beam from a searchlight would be thousands of miles in diameter. Thus colossal ranges could be obtained with very little power; calculations show that with lasers we can think of signaling to the stars, not merely to the planets.

But we cannot use light beams to send messages through the Earth's erratic atmosphere; a passing cloud could block a signal that had traveled across a billion miles of space. On the airless Moon, however, this would be no problem, for the sky is perpetually clear to waves of all frequencies, from the longest radio waves, through visible light, past the ultraviolet and even down to the short X-rays which are blocked by a few inches of air. This whole immense range of electromagnetic waves will be available for communications or any other use— perhaps such applications as the broadcasting of power, which has never been practical on Earth. There will be enough "band width" or ether space for all the radio and TV services we can ever imagine, no matter how densely populated the planets become and however many messages the men of the future wish to flash back and forth across the solar system.

We can thus imagine the Moon as a sort of central clearing house for interplanetary communications, aiming its tightly focused light beams to the other planets and to ships in space. Any messages that concerned Earth would be radioed across the trivial 250,000-mile gulf on those wavelengths that penetrate our atmosphere.

There are several other reasons why the Moon might almost have been designed as a base for interplanetary communications. Everyone is now familiar with the enormous radio telescopes which have been built to reach out into space and to maintain contact with such distant probes as our Pioneers and Explorers (and the Rangers, Mariners, and Prospectors that will follow them). The most ambitious of these was the ill-fated 600-foot giant at Sugar Grove, West Virginia —abandoned when partly built, after some scores of millions of dollars had been spent on it.

The 600-foot telescope was an expensive failure because it was too heavy; the planned weight was about 20,000 tons, but design changes later brought it up to 36,000 tons. But on the Moon, both the cost and weight of such a structure would be enormously reduced —perhaps by more than 90 percent. For thanks to the low gravity, a very much lighter construction could be used than is necessary on Earth. And the Moon's airlessness pays another dividend, for a terrestrial telescope has to be designed with a substantial safety factor so that it can withstand the worst that the weather can do. There is no need to worry about gales on the Moon, where there is not the slightest breeze to disturb the most delicate structures.

Nor have we yet finished with the Moon's advantages from the view of those who want to send (and receive) signals across space. It turns so slowly on its axis that the problem of tracking is much simplified; *and it is a quiet place.*

Or, to be more accurate, the far side of the Moon is a quiet place —probably the quietest that now exists within millions of miles of the Earth. I am speaking, of course, in the radio sense; for the last sixty years, our planet has been pouring an ever increasing racket into space. This has already seriously inconvenienced the radio astronomers, whose observations can be ruined by an electric shaver a hundred miles away.

But the land first glimpsed by Lunik III is beyond the reach of this electronic tumult; it is shielded from the din of Earth by two thousand miles of solid rock—a far better protection than a million miles of empty space. Here, where the earthlight never shines, will be the communications centers of the future, linking together with radio and light beams all the inhabited planets. And one day, perhaps, reaching out beyond the solar system to make contact with those other intelligences for whom the first search has already begun. That search can hardly hope for success until we have escaped from the braying of all the radio and TV stations of our own planet.

What has already been said should be enough to convince any imaginative person—anyone who does not believe that the future will be a carbon copy of the past—that the Moon will be a priceless possession and its exploration far more than the expensive scientific stunt that some foolish people have called it. At the same time it should be emphasized that the most important and valuable uses of the Moon will be ones that nobody has thought of today. This has always been true in the past of exploration and scientific discovery, and it will be equally true in the future. I will merely hint at a few possibilities here.

In a recent discussion of space exploration plans, Professor Harold Urey made the point that the Moon is one of the most interesting places in the solar system—perhaps more so than Mars or Venus, even though there may be life on these planets. For the face of the Moon may have carried down through the ages, virtually untouched by time, a record of the conditions that existed billions of years ago, when the universe itself was young. On Earth, all such records have long been erased by the winds and the rains and other geological forces. When we reach the Moon, it will be as if an entire library of lost volumes, a million times older than that destroyed at Alexandria, was suddenly thrown open to us.

Quite beyond price will be the skills we will acquire during the exploration—and ultimately, colonization—of this new land in the sky. I suspect, though only time will tell whether this is true, that we will learn more about unorthodox methods of food production on the Moon within a few years than we could in decades on the Earth. Can we, in an almost literal sense of the phrase, turn rocks into food? We must master this art (as the plants did, aeons ago) if we hope to conquer space. Perhaps most exciting of all are the possibilities opened up by low-gravity medicine and the enormous question: "Will men live longer on a world where they do not wear out their hearts fighting against gravity?" Upon the answer to this will depend the future of many worlds and of nations yet unnamed.

Much of politics, as of life, consists of the administration of the unforeseen. We can foresee only a minute fraction of the Moon's potentialities, and the Moon itself is only a tiny part of the universe. The fact that the Soviet Union is making an all-out effort to get there has far deeper implications than have been generally faced.

The Russians, whatever else they may be, are realists. And as Sir Charles Snow has pointed out in his highly influential book, *Science and Government,* between 35 and 45 percent of their top men have some technical and scientific training. (It is doubtful if the proportion is a quarter of this in the West.) As a result, they have often made correct choices—for example, the decision to develop the lithium bomb and giant rocket boosters—when the United States wasted its energies in such technological dead ends as tritium bombs and air-breathing missiles.

They may have done so again in the most important field of all. I wonder if any of the "Leave it to the Russians" school of anti-space flight critics seriously imagines that Soviet science is outward bound merely to impress the uncommitted nations. That could be achieved in a dozen less expensive ways.

No, the Russians know exactly what they are doing. Perhaps they are already laughing at the shortsighted prophets who have said: "Anyone who owns the Moon can dominate the Earth."

They may no longer be concerned with such trivialities. They realize that if any nation has mastery of the Moon, it will dominate not merely the Earth, but the whole accessible universe.

· QUESTIONS ·

1. In what respects is this article, written in 1961, already "dated"? As a prophet and seer, can you predict other ways in which it will become still more "dated" as time passes?
2. Does this article stretch your imagination and your concept of life more than you are willing to accept? Are you excited about the prospects held forth by Clarke? Do you long for "the good old days"?
3. Make a list of the main arguments *for* conquest of the moon which the author rebuts.
4. Summarize the arguments *against* conquest of the moon which Clarke attempts to puncture.

5. Make a précis of the principal arguments for conquest of the moon which the author develops and defends.
6. Summarize the principal known facts about the moon as they are set forth in this article.
7. What is the tone of this article? What examples of irony or humor can you cite? What of the diction? Debating style?
8. Do you tend to side with Clarke or with Krutch in their "argument" about the moon? Are they discussing the same issues? Be specific.

Theme Subjects: (1) Reston's "A Fable" and the Russian Space Program; (2) Going Somewhere for the Wrong Reasons; (3) Clarke and Krutch: A Debate; (4) My Life in an "Immensely Deep Pit"; (5) Dominating the Earth Is a Triviality?

CAUSES OF THE
STUDENT REVOLUTION

Joseph Katz
and
Nevitt Sanford

JOSEPH KATZ (1920–   ) was born in Swikau, Germany, and was graduated from the University of Pennsylvania (1942). Becoming a fellow at Columbia University (1943–1944), he was awarded his doctorate in 1948. He has been lecturer and professor at Cornell University and at Amherst and Vassar colleges. In 1961 he assumed his present posts as resident director of Student Development Study and visiting professor of philosophy at Stanford University. Winner of Columbia's Woodbridge Prize in 1949, he is author of, among others, *Plotinus' Search for the Good* (1950); *The American College* (1962); and coauthor of *Writers on Ethics* (1962).

From *The Saturday Review*, December 18, 1965. Reprinted by permission of the authors and the publisher.

NEVITT SANFORD (1909–   ) was born in Chatham, Virginia, and was graduated from the University of Richmond and Columbia. Taking his Ph.D. in psychology at Harvard in 1934, he stayed on until 1940 to do research. Following World War II, during which he served in the O.S.S., he became professor of psychology at the University of California (Berkeley) until 1961. He is now professor of psychology and education and director of the Institute for the Study of Human Problems at Stanford. He is a coauthor of *Physique, Personality and Scholarship* (1943) and *The Authoritarian Personality* (1950) and has contributed numerous articles to professional journals.

To those of us who have worked with college students, revolution has come as no surprise. We are aware how far from the truth is the stereotype of the happy-go-lucky, golden college years. The time between seventeen and twenty-one is often one of nagging self-doubt, of intense conflict in relations with other people, of painful and sometimes rebellious struggles for independence from one's parents, of an uneasy search for one's eventual occupational and sexual roles. Such emotional struggles and discomforts upset the individual's equilibrium and thus free considerable energy for either creative or destructive acts. As a social institution, the American college has traditionally been quite successful in channeling such wild energy. By providing the avenue for entrance into the adult occupational and social world, and by requiring a reasonable output of hard work, it has been able to bind energies through having students sit down and study. For those students, and there always have been many, who found that the curriculum provided insufficient outlet for creative energy, extracurricular activities of all sorts were available. Moreover, there has always been a ready tolerance for more blind or destructive outlets for student energies. Although disciplinary measures have sometimes been used for student pranks, no university has been thrown into crisis, no public outcries have been heard, even in connection with the more violent student panty-raids or the annual spring festival at Fort Lauderdale, Florida.

Adolescence is the time of life when a new generation defines itself. Not only does it have to find its own values and come naturally into some conflict with the older generation, but there are implicit expectations on the part of the older that the one coming along will do something different—and, we hope, better. Adults are ambivalent about youth: we hold them down and at the same time we urge them on. Thus adolescence is a time when we may expect major attacks upon the established order. For the individual, adolescence offers perhaps the best chance that he will ever have to define himself in new ways, different from those with which he has been brought up.

In spite of all these internal forces pressing for change, adolescents in college have until recently been able to maintain an external appearance of apathy. Hence some further explanations must be given for the occurrence of the student revolution.

As is well known, the conditions of the post-Sputnik era have led to a tightening of standards of academic performance and an increased demand upon quantity of work by students. The resulting pressure is felt by good students as well as poor ones. In the more selective schools, all the students are able and well prepared, yet they still feel an enormous amount of pressure, because of the grading curve and the inclination of the faculty to assign more reading than anyone can do. People usually ascribe these pressures to the intellectual competition of the Cold War, but another factor is the higher birth rate, which has considerably increased the number of students applying to colleges and has thus provided both an economic and a moral base for increased selectivity.

These increased demands are not limited to the college years but extend far back into the years before college. It is no longer uncommon for even nine-year-olds to have some anxious concern about getting into a college of their choice. Certainly during the high school years the anxieties of teachers, parents, and students conspire to create a sense of pressure about whether one is going to measure up.

When students are finally admitted to college, they feel they "have it made," they now expect to enter a freer community devoted to the pursuit of knowledge and other objectives, no longer so hampered by the need to be tested and graded. They soon find, of course, that the grading system is lying in wait for them, more demanding than ever. Performance that in high school was graded top level now gets only a passing grade—and sometimes not even that. Yet as larger and larger numbers are preparing to go on to either graduate or professional schools, the need for

good examination performance is as crucial as ever. Moreover, it becomes clear that being tested and measured is going to continue for years, even into the life beyond college.

Those of us who have studied college students know that the work demanded of them cannot be fulfilled in a usual forty-hour week. Most students do not mind hard work, however; work is good for them, and they know it. The problem is that too often they cannot feel that the work is leading to any worthy purpose. Owing to the increasing accent on specialization in higher education and the tendency for undergraduate courses to be increasingly pre-professional, students at the beginning of their college careers must do a great deal of work that is essentially meaningless to them. They start out on the lowest rungs of four or five professional ladders with the expectation that, after they have learned the basic concepts and methods, they will eventually reach a place where the work will become interesting and they will be able to use their minds actively. But so elaborate and specialized have the disciplines become that the time when a student can participate in his profession's concerns has to be postponed to later and later years. Undergraduate studies consist more and more of memorizing by hard work a mass of abstract material mostly untied to anything in the student's experience.

This burden of meaningless labor creates not so much work pressures as psychological pressures, weariness, and resentment. The undergraduate is somewhat like a child who can discharge an enormous amount of physical energy but feels suddenly tired when someone suggests that he mow the lawn. Compounding the pressure is the sense of forever being tested and evaluated, a source of special anxiety during the college years when the question of how one is going to measure up as a man or woman is always hauntingly present.

The effects of the testing and grading system have not been limited to the individual student; the pressures that it engenders have altered the social and psychological ecology of the college world. Several recent studies, covering many different types of colleges, seem to agree that only about 20 percent of all students can be classified as academicians. What, then, becomes of the 80 percent whose primary orientation is not toward the academic aspect of the college? In the past those students have had ample opportunity to express their skills and inclinations in many other activities: student government, fraternities, drama groups, athletics, literary and religious and political clubs, and so forth. Even though what was learned in these activities was not officially classified as education, many students received valuable training for their future occupations. Regardless of future utility, extracurricular pursuits helped to make one's passage through the college personally meaningful. With the growing dominance of the academic sector, with its demands for a speeded-up work output and tougher grading requirements, this natural ecology has been profoundly disturbed.

The indications are that increased work demands, competitiveness, and a resultant pervasive guilt when one is not occupied with studying have also considerably diminished the opportunities for forming friendships with other students, at least the kind of deep and meaningful friendships that require time and freedom from psychological encumbrance in order to grow. It is no accident that the revolutionary student puts great emphasis on community—what he calls "communitarianism." It springs from his wish to declare that development of warm, intimate relationships is not easy in college today.

The lack of community seems more acute because the faculty and administration rarely relate to the student as an individual. He is conceived rather as an aggregate of different functions, categorically separable from each other, for the management of which different sets of machinery have been set up. Registering, advising, counseling, disciplining, lecturing, grading papers—all are handled by different people who attend strictly to the function rather than to the student.

Interestingly enough, the student soon lends himself to this way of doing things. In the advisory situation, for example, a professor might on some occasion decide that he had five minutes to spare and ask the student a question about himself that would invite the beginning of a personal relationship. But the chances are that the student has other functions to be performed that day and is eager to be on his way, with the result that the two people do not relate. This lost opportunity, multiplied many times, adds up to the dehumanization of the campus.

Just as they rarely perceive students as individuals, professors or administrators do not themselves often act as individuals in relations with students. They are occupants of social roles or performers of functions. The same professor might within the space of a few days speak as a classroom teacher, as a member of a faculty committee, and as a spokesman for his department. Through the inconsistency of these several comments he might give students the impression that he has no integrity, lending support to their saying, "You can't trust anyone over thirty." But, in actuality, the professor's individual integrity was never involved because he was not required or expected to act as an individual. Rather, he was expected to say and to do what was required by his role. His words and deeds were probably very similar to those of any other person who might have acquired that role.

This depersonalization is an expression of the involvement of the university in our technology. Many people comment on it at the intellectual level, but students are its real victims.

Another factor in student unrest is the decline of the college function *in loco parentis*. Traditionally, *in loco parentis* has meant that the college was more or less a complete substitute for parents; it would offer positive attention to the student's development and active care for his needs, as well as necessary restraints and punishments. In recent years all the nurturing functions of the college have been eroded or neglected while the control and punishment functions have been maintained. This in itself creates a revolutionary climate. In family life, the child who is ignored except when it is necessary to punish him is soon on the road to becoming a rebel or delinquent. Students for many years surrendered their rights as citizens in exchange for the special care and developmental attention that parents or college were expected to offer. Now, with the care and nurturance gone, students not inappropriately demand their rights. This is not because students are more mature than they used to be or because they are any less in need of what colleges might do to develop them. It is because they find themselves in a situation that is essentially unfair and would induce rebellious feelings in people of any age.

The conditions thus far mentioned constitute negative reasons for the student revolution. They describe the discontent and the frustration that have provided some of the fuel. To them one could add other factors, such as the increasing distance of the teacher from his student, particularly because of a reward system that makes research rather than teaching a primary incentive for the college professor. But negative factors alone would not have taught the student revolution. On the contrary, they would have resulted only in apathy and depression. Let us look, then, for the positive factors that have touched off the current uprisings.

While the colleges in recent years have unwittingly, and quite against their better intentions, been encouraging a passive conformity and acrobatic work-mindedness in students, other social institutions and events have gone in the opposite direction by encouraging a more active role for people of undergraduate age. The most dramatic of these has been the civil rights movement, which has made it possible for students to give much more than a verbal commitment to a socially relevant course. It has opened to them a realm of social action which often requires a high degree of courage and purposeful activity. On a less dramatic level there have been various tutorial programs springing up on college campuses all over the nation. Through these, students teach children of the underprivileged or work in families of the psychotic or the jailed. There they soon discover that the kind of teaching which they have received is utterly inadequate to reach the children and families under their responsibility. They have to devise new approaches—and are often rewarded with a considerable expansion of their own personalities.

Such activities do more than appeal to students' idealism. They provide a natural escape valve. Students who have tasted the satisfaction of doing socially relevant and often useful work have developed a sense of their own usefulness. What they have been denied because of a specialized curriculum they have been finding for themselves in involvement on the social front.

As a result of our national affluence, more students are traveling, too, either as individuals or as part of the overseas programs of their colleges. With travel have come contacts with cultures different from their own and the opportunity to develop new resources within themselves for dealing with these differences.

All these non-college activities have unwittingly raised a corps of student activists. Not only have the participants already experienced roles in which they counted for something, but some have received extensive training in the arts of civil conflict, civil disobedience, even active revolutionism. (The Peace Corps, too, is training some-

what older people for a more reformist conception of their social roles.) When these students return to their campuses and survey the conditions under which they are being educated, many find it increasingly unbearable to be treated like passive containers into which information is to be poured.

In his discontent, the undergraduate has received support from a hitherto most unpredictable source: the graduate student.

Until recently, the time sense of the undergraduate has been short. During his first year, he was usually preoccupied with sizing up the situation and learning the ropes of being a student. During his last year, he was involved with the problems of life after graduation and no longer much interested in affairs at the college. This left only two years in the middle when the student could be actively concerned, and he was easily convinced that this acquaintance was too transitory for him to have much to say about how the school should be run. Neither administration nor faculty were particularly inclined to disagree with that impression.

All this has been changed now by the intense involvement of the graduate student in the cause of undergraduate education. The graduate student brings to the undergraduate's cause the authority that "older" people carry, plus the prestige of having mounted another selection hurdle and the benefit of a wider temporal view of the educational establishment.

This interest of graduate students in education, and the interest of some of them in becoming good college teachers, is one of the most striking features of the contemporary educational scene. Not so long ago it would have been impossible to budge graduate students from the library or the lab where they were pursuing a life dedicated to their specialty and the challenge of carving out a secure academic career in it.

Today, however, graduate students in many departments of our universities suffer from the same kinds of pressures and constraints, the same burden of meaningless work, as do undergraduates or even high school students. As departments have grown larger and more professionalized, traditional communities of scholars, embodying graduate students and professors with whom they worked closely, have been disappearing. The graduate student is being put through a series of tests that involve even more serious consequences than do undergraduate tests and is required every minute of his day to think and act within the confines of his profession's requirements. He must, in effect, surrender himself to his profession. He cannot investigate what he is curious about but only what can be investigated by approved methods. He has little time to explore other fields, or even to get beyond a specialized area of his own field, because whoever is in charge of his work often demands more than can reasonably be done. He cannot ask questions of a sort that might broaden his mind because he cannot afford to display any ignorance. He cannot converse in the language of educated men because this might be interpreted as professional impurity.

Graduate students are pretty cynical about this system. They say that they will stay with it only until they get their "union card"; then they will be free to inquire as they please. But even before they receive their degrees, they begin to be aware that the constraints will be nearly as great after they have actually entered the profession. Acceptance of graduate school requirements brings about an identification with the system that is very difficult to shake off later.

Graduate students also have many occasions to lament their wasted years as undergraduates. They specialized in those years, thinking that in graduate school they would find freedom. Now, when they look back from their new vantage point, they see that they lost the best opportunity to pursue their genuine interests and explore new ones when they were undergraduates. Hence they have a natural inclination to relive their own undergraduate years vicariously through the students who are now entering college. Or if they had a good undergraduate experience they feel sympathy for their younger brothers in the large universities.

In sum, graduate students have been changing sides. Finding the channels into "management" too narrow, the effort to negotiate them too costly in other values, the rewards of belonging to the governing body too remote or otherwise dubious, they have been casting their lot with the "workers." The new alliance of graduate with undergraduate has given the student movement unprecedented security and vigor.

No revolution is made by the totally deprived. A certain measure of well-being is necessary for people to have the energy and vision to seek an improvement of their lot. In some sense the current student revolution thus credits the educational system that already exists.

For years, American parents and schools have been striving to develop people who are capable of emotional and intellectual independence. Had there not been a good basis for self-direction and management of their own affairs, this generation would not have been capable of taking affairs so much into their own hands and creating discomfort among the very elders who equipped them with this capacity.

Where is the student movement heading? Clearly students are asking for the right to have a share in their own education. This is an event unique in the history of American education, and perhaps all education. There have been student movements at other times such as the liberal and leftist movements during the Thirties, but the object of these was social change; they came into conflict with the university only incidentally when students felt that their freedom of expression was inhibited. Today's revolution is on a different level. Now students want to have a voice in the fundamental organization of instruction and extracurricular affairs. (One is reminded of the University of Bologna in the late Middle Ages when such an arrangement existed only to be superseded by the control of the faculty.) This demand for participation does not stem from any desire to make college life easier. Rather it springs from a profound attempt to seek answers as to how one might achieve such ends as a reliable personal identity, community with other people, and social objectives that will bring comfort and justice to those largely bereft of them in our society. There is, moreover, a desire among many students for a level of intellectual investigation and discussion that will bring professors and students into the same intellectual community.

The student movement does not yet have a detailed program for educational reform. (Neither of course have their elders.) But some of the elements of a program are already at hand, such as creating smaller units of instruction, establishment of more meaningful student communities, the relation of theory to social practice and experience, teaching of students by older students, experimentation with different curricular arrangements. No doubt their ideas, as well as those of faculty members who take a critical stand, are going to become firmer and more detailed in the days ahead. In any event, the signs seem to be clear that we are not dealing with an isolated or transitory movement. One might make an analogy to the growth of the labor movement, in which another segment of society awoke to a consciousness of its own power and worth. From the time of that awakening, the eventual participation of labor in running the overall commercial enterprise was almost inevitable. The student movement has, as a matter of fact, resorted to means quite like those used by the labor movement. Students feel, as workers did, that their power and the legitimacy of their demands are not confined to any one campus but are universal. Quite naturally students from one campus are carrying their ideas to other campuses, where a fertile soil is ready for them.

The student movement appears to be carried forward by the élan of a small minority. Our research indicates that the socially involved students total not more than 15 percent. But the movement can no longer be controlled by dealing with the minority alone, because it is expressing the frustrations and aspirations now shared by the majority of students.

The next question, of course, is how trustees, administration, and faculty are going to handle the student revolution. All three segments generally are unprepared for the task. First of all, none of the three is very familiar with students' attitudes and aspirations. Second, many administrators and professors lack the psychological skills, and sometimes the tough-mindedness, that are required for dealing with the idealism, ambivalences, and conflicting emotions of youth in the late adolescent or early adult years. Third, faculty do not readily give up their own orientation toward research and academic careerism, in the light of which students' demands seem like an unwelcome intrusion.

College authorities, for their part, feel threatened when the bases of their power are attacked. Those of us who have worked or talked with students in the movement, find, however, that for all their apparent ferociousness and rebelliousness—and even the more extreme anarchism of some of them—underneath they are still reasonably pliable. Their search is for identity, meaning, community, and, by no means least, a response from the adult world. When this response is forthcoming, most of the rebelliousness vanishes, and in its place there is often an almost touching desire for adult leadership. This is not to say, of course, that the students can be handled with any kind of psychological manipulations. They are aware and tough enough to resent and fight off attempts to compromise their integrity.

Far from presenting a threat, these students actually represent to college authorities a unique opportunity. At one time it looked like a hard fight to get either graduate or undergraduate students interested in the process of education. Now they have both become involved on their own, even at the expense of personal sacrifice. These students are *asking* to be educated and to be one with the intellectual community if only we show them the way. Administrators therefore who can find some way to respond to what is human, though sometimes chaotically expressed, in these undergraduate students, will find that they are going to be part of a truly revolutionary phase in the history of education. While the eighteenth century discovered that good government depends upon the consent of the governed, our generation has the opportunity of discovering and bringing to fruition a system of education that is based upon the consent of the educated.

· QUESTIONS ·

1. List and discuss the negative and positive causes of the student revolution as the authors present them.
2. Are these causes fairly and objectively stated? Do you disagree with any of them? Have you encountered some or all of them in your own experience? Are they restricted to large university campuses?
3. Can you list causes for revolution other than those presented here?

4. On your campus is less or more than 15 percent of the student body "socially involved"?
5. What is the tone of this article? Do you feel that you would like to have the authors as advisers in college?

Theme Subjects: (1) Gaddis Smith and Katz-Sanford: A Comparative View; (2) My Education Has (Does Not Have) My Consent; (3) Colleges Are for Study, Not Revolution; (4) "I never dared to be radical when young for fear it would make me conservative when old."—Robert Frost; (5) My Opinion of "Activists" on This Campus; (6) What's a Teacher Really For, Anyway? (7) One Thing That Should Be Changed on This Campus; (8) My Role in the Student Protest Movement.

RADIO, TV,
AND THE COMMON MAN

Gilbert Seldes

GILBERT (VIVIAN) SELDES (1893–   ) was born in Alliance, New Jersey, and was graduated from Harvard in 1914. After graduation he became music critic for the Philadelphia *Evening Ledger* and was a newspaper correspondent during World War I. After years of work as an editor, critic, and columnist for several magazines and newspapers, he served as director of experimental television programs for the Columbia Broadcasting System, 1937–1945. Among his books are *The Seven Lively Arts* (1924, and later reissued); *The Great Audience* (1950); *The Public Arts* (1956). Mr. Seldes, an acknowledged authority on television, radio, and motion pictures, has an uncanny ability to project ideas and tendencies of the future. This article was written in 1954, but it raises searching questions about radio and television which are fully as much with us now as they were then. His

Reprinted from *Is the Common Man Too Common? An Informal Survey of Our Cultural Resources and What We Are Doing About Them* by Joseph Wood Krutch and others. Copyright 1954 by the University of Oklahoma Press. Used by permission.

primary concern is not with radio and television fads of the moment but with standards of public taste—a topic which changes from time to time but never disappears.

In the Thirty Years' War between the broadcasters and their critics the heavy battalions and God—as represented by the public—have been on the broadcasters' side. If television hadn't revived some ancient misgivings and made some early blunders, serious criticism of the broadcasting industry might have disappeared entirely; the critics had become fretful and ineffective, and the broadcasters—who had been occasionally apologetic—were so secure in public favor that they showed few symptoms of the guilt complex that had haunted them in their earlier phases. As far as the public was concerned the critics were asking irrelevant questions, withholding praise where it was clearly due, and setting themselves up as the enemy of whatever was popular. The coming of television gave the critics a second chance to ask the right questions and thereby arrive at a useful relation to the industry.

The question being asked by *The Saturday Review* is one of the right ones. It is part of a general inquiry into the relation between the communicative arts and the public, and as it applies to broadcasting it can be put in simple terms: Is it true, as has often been said, that the broadcasters underestimate the taste, intelligence, and maturity of the public? Are the masses ahead of the media?

Oversimplified like this, the question is also overloaded. The critics are asking the broadcasters, "How much longer do you intend to go on beating your wives?" and the broadcasters' answer is usually a combination of "We aren't legally married" and "They love it."

Obviously you can't discuss the relationship between broadcasters and audience until you know what an audience is. If you dig down to the bedrock on which the industry is founded, these solid facts become apparent: (1) an audience is what the sponsor buys; (2) an audience is what the broadcasters deliver; (3) an audience is a measurable fraction of *the* audience; (4) all the fractional audiences put together fall short of being "the public." Not at all apparent, but confirmed by experience, is the hypothesis that audiences are created by broadcasting.

The fundamental attitudes toward audiences are all simple. Broadcasters (including sponsors) attempt to satisfy the current wants of large sections of the total audience; critics assert that the people making up these audiences have other interests and curiosities, perhaps not intense enough to be called wants, but legitimate; they also assert that the definite wants of smaller, but sizable, audiences should also be satisfied. And the Government, representing us as the third party in the discussion, licenses broadcasters to operate "in the public interest," which transcends all partial interests and is greater than their sum. It is, for instance, in the public interest that a vast number of citizens should be alert and intelligent enough to meet the successive crises of the world today, and it is therefore against the public interest if broadcasting fails to contribute to our awareness of problems and our capacity to solve them. But the individual broadcaster can be and usually is absolved of this responsibility.

The fact that an audience is a commodity to be bought and sold is usually concealed, because technically sponsors buy "time on the air." But both the jargon of the trade and some recent rulings of the FCC indicate that what is actually bought is the time and attention given by the audience. To attract sponsors, broadcasters often promise to *build* an audience for the time-period chosen, and there is ample evidence that audiences have been prevented from coming into existence. The hypothesis stated above can be expanded: audiences are created by broadcasts and exist only at those times and in those places that the broadcasters want them to exist. . . .

Several years ago CBS issued an effective promotion piece called "Our Sixty-ninth-Most-Popular-Program"; it pointed out that, although 68 other programs on the network had higher ratings, "Invitation to Learning" still had an impressive audience of over a million listeners. At about the same time (according to FCC records) "Invitation to Learning" was being heard on only 39 CBS stations; 97 other affiliates of the network did *not* carry the program. No proof exists that any significant number of people in these 97 other cities demanded to hear "Invitation to Learning," but common sense rejects the idea that *nobody* in 97 average cities would be glad to hear a program that a million people in 39 other cities listened to with pleasure. That an audience in the 97 cities did not come into being was simply because the creative act, making the program available, was not performed. . . .

Parallel and opposite is the case of symphonic music. The precarious lives of great orchestras in pre-radio days, their constant "drives" for endowment funds, indicate that at most a few hundred thousand musical individuals actively wanted to hear the classics. This hardly constituted a demand by broadcasting standards. It is a matter of record that when William S. Paley proposed to broadcast the concerts of the New York Philharmonic Symphony he knew that an audience for them did not exist and declared his intention of creating one. He was successful; eventually the Philharmonic even acquired a sponsor, and its audience was at one time estimated at about ten million. The demand is so intense that an attempt to broadcast the concerts by transcription, at various hours, brought violent objections and was abandoned after a single season.

The effect of symphonic broadcasts and other musical programs on concert-going and the sale of classical records—some $50,000,000 a year spent on the first and 40 percent of all record sales for the latter—are in a sense secondary proofs of the creative power of broadcasting. The primary effect is radio's own audience. In creating this audience sponsors were unable to afford the long pull; they paid for orchestral music but withdrew support after a short time, so that it required a network with all its resources (and the happy coincidence of unsold time on the air) to sustain the programs long enough to let the audience form, to let enough people know that they didn't dislike "longhair" music as much as they thought they did. Again, considering broadcasting only, and not cultural effects, it should be noted that the significance of this entire episode lies not in the fact that the music was good and serious, but that the broadcasters offered all kinds of music, widening the area of choice; if the prevalent mode had been classical and the broadcasters had created an audience for hot music, the moral would still be the same: audiences are created by programs.

There is a more significant but less spectacular case in which the broadcasters acted in the public interest far ahead of public demand. They began to supply international news and commentary of a high order in the 1930's, at a time when the people at large preferred not to be troubled by such matters, a period of marked self-absorption in domestic affairs and strong isolationism. These programs were unsponsored for many years, and almost without exception they demanded real mental activity on the part of the listener to match the alert intelligence of the correspondents abroad. These broadcasts were a specific case of giving the public what the public ought to have—and no damned nonsense about what the public wants; and I believe that the high level of emotional stability of the American people after Pearl Harbor is largely due to the creation of an audience, of substantial size, aware of the international situation. This is one of the most honorable services radio has rendered to our country, and I think the industry ought to be proud of it, without reservation.

But the industry does make a reservation, in principle. It cannot accept the Paley principle of creative broadcasting because of the responsibility that principle implies. For you cannot logically say, "We created the audience for great music and for the discussion of public affairs, but in the case of neurotic daytime serials and sadistic murder playlets we weren't creative at all, we were merely satisfying a demand that already existed." Demand is generalized and diffuse—for entertainment, for thrills, for vicarious sadness, for laughs; it can be satisfied by programs of different types and different qualities; and only after these programs have been offered is there any demand for them. Supply comes first in this business and creates its own demand. . . .

Our mass media, the movies as well as radio and television, offer a variety of entertainments, but they are for the most part aimed at the same intellectual level and call for the same emotional responses, the level and the responses being relatively low. The challenge to the mind comes infrequently, and we are being conditioned to make frequent emotional responses of low intensity—the quick nervous reaction to melodrama and the quick laugh at everything else. . . .

Statistical evidence exists that actually the audience—the public, to be more accurate—wants more. I place few bets on the automatic answer given to researchers, "Yes, we would like more serious programs on the air," because, for one thing, some of the respondents call quiz shows educational and because this "want" is a pious aspiration as diffused and uncertain as what the broadcasters say they get from the public. Yet it is noteworthy that *all* the researches point in the same direction: people at every level of education, in significant numbers, do imply some dissatisfaction with the programs they are getting, and among these there are ten million people, not habitual book readers, not college graduates, who consistently ask for programs of a higher intellectual content. (Book readers and college graduates make the same request twice as often, but they are numerically less important. All these figures come from studies made for the industry.)

The evidence favorable to the broadcasters (in music, for instance) and the unfavorable evidence (the prevalence of third-rate crime programs, let us say) come together at this point. If the broadcasters accept their social responsibility, they can continue to pile up huge profits without corrupting the taste and undermining the mental activity of the audience. Sponsors, agencies, packagers, stations, and networks taken together have created the kinds of wants they could satisfy, and while broadcasting has not lost audiences—as the movies have—by repeating the sure thing over and over again, there have always been vast untouched segments of the public. . . .

It is at this point that the broadcasters share responsibility with other manipulators of the public. They dodge it by the ancient excuse of giving the public what it wants, conceiving the public as a mass with tastes already formed. Once they admit that the media can raise or lower the public taste, in the very act of satisfying the public demand, they will come closer to their function, which is defined legally as operating in the public interest, and which, morally, does not insist on raising the public taste but demands, as a minimum, that the public be given every opportunity to find its own level of taste by having access to the best as well as to the mean—which, in this case, is far from golden.

· QUESTIONS ·

1. In what respects have events in television and radio broadcasting during recent years accentuated the problems raised by Seldes? Cite specific examples to prove your points.
2. Phrase the central thesis of this selection in not more than two unified sentences.
3. Are you generally satisfied or generally dissatisfied with the TV and radio fare available to you?
4. Is Seldes fair and impartial in his comments? Biased and shortsighted? Is he an astute and objective observer of the TV and radio scene or an intellectual snob? Be specific in your answers.

Theme Subject: (1) What Broadcasting (TV or Radio) Means to Me; (2) My Favorite TV (or Radio) Program; (3) An Educational Program (TV or Radio) Now on the Air; (4) What Mr. Seldes Overlooks; (5) I Like (Dislike) Soap Operas; (6) Mass Media and the Taste of the Majority (limit to some specific phase and develop as an investigative theme); (7) Needs I Have That Mass Media Ignore; (8) My Opinion of _____ (some specific radio or TV program).

300,000,000 AMERICANS WOULD BE WRONG

David E. Lilienthal

DAVID ELI LILIENTHAL (1899–   ) was born in Morton, Illinois, and won his A.B. at DePauw University in 1920 and his LL.B. at Harvard in 1923. He was founding director of the Tennessee Valley Authority and served as its chairman, 1941–1946. From 1946 until 1950 he was chairman of the board of the U. S. Atomic Energy Commission. He is cofounder and chairman of the board of the Development and Resources Corporation, holds many honorary degrees, and was the recipient of the Freedom Award (1949) and the Public Welfare Medal, National Academy of Sciences (1951). He is the author of *TVA: Democracy on the March* (rev. 1953); *This I Do Believe* (1949); *Big Business: A New Era* (1953); and *Change, Hope and the Bomb* (1963), as well as *The Journals of David E. Lilienthal* (3 vols., 1964, 1966).

1. By the year 2000, just one generation away, the population of the United States will probably be about 300 million—100 million higher than it is now and 200 million higher than it was in 1920. Yet, in comparison with many underdeveloped nations, population growth would not seem to be a serious problem in America.

2. Certainly this vastly increased population will not lack for food. While population growth in Latin America, for example, has brought per capita food production below pre-World War II levels, we in the U.S. worry about overweight, spend huge sums to restrict farm production, and give away enough food to prevent famine in poor nations throughout the world. In contrast to less developed nations, we have enough space, too. Just fly over this country and see the huge, sparsely populated areas that could easily accommodate additional tens of millions.

3. Great differences in resources,

technology, and education help explain why Americans regard overpopulation as a menace only to other peoples. It can't happen here, they think. I used to think so, too; I don't any more.

4. During the past 10 years, much of it spent overseas, I came to the easy conclusion that if we succeeded in tripling or quadrupling food production in hungry nations—and in some areas in which I worked we did just that—the problem of overpopulation could be solved. But gradually I learned I was mistaken to believe that increased food production was the complete answer to the crisis of population abroad. Gradually, I also learned that America's overflowing cornucopia has obscured a deeper crisis developing here: a population of at least 300 million by 2000 will, I now believe, threaten the very quality of life of individual Americans.

5. An additional 100 million people will undermine our most cherished traditions, erode our public services, and impose a rate of taxation that will make current taxes seem tame. The new masses, concentrated (as they will be) in the already strangling urban centers, cannot avoid creating conditions that will make city life almost unbearable. San Francisco, to take a still tolerable example, once was one of my favorite cities—cosmopolitan, comfortable, lovely. Now the highrise buildings have sprouted like weeds and suburban blight is advancing on the Golden Gate. The value of real estate has increased while people's enjoyment of life declines.

6. Historically, the United States owes much of its vigor and power to population growth. (Only 50 million people rattled around in Amer-

ica in 1880.) Large markets, skilled manpower, huge factories, a country able to spend billions on war, space, and social welfare—all this, plus 75 million passenger cars—is surely a consequence of rising population. But no economy and no physical environment can sustain infinite population growth. There comes a point at which a change in quantity becomes a change in quality—when we can no longer speak of "more of the same." And another 100 million people will, I fear, make just that change in the joy of life in America.

7. It is probably true that as the population will grow, so will the dollar value of our output. U.S. wealth, measured by Gross National Product, is now $670 billion; barring a major economic setback, total output will be doubled in about two decades. With G.N.P. climbing at the rate of $40 billion a year, the U.S. probably can afford to build the schools, housing projects, roads, and other necessities of life for 300 million Americans.

8. But if our resources are mainly spent merely to survive, to cope with life in a congested America, then where is the enjoyment of living? Our teeming cities are not pleasant places today; imagine them by the middle of the next century when the areas of some might be 100 times larger than they are now. This is the real possibility envisioned by Roger Revelle, director of the newly established Center for Population Studies at the Harvard School of Public Health. And it will be to the cities that tomorrow's millions will flock. Or consider the picture, drawn with characteristic wit, by economist John Kenneth Galbraith: "It is hard to suppose that penultimate Western man, stalled in the ultimate traffic jam

and slowly succumbing to carbon monoxide, will be especially enchanted to hear from the last survivor that in the preceding year Gross National Product went up by a record amount."

9. Nor does the nightmare consist only of traffic jams and a bumper-to-bumper way of life. As we have seen in the history of the last 25 years, public services only the Federal Government can provide will continue to expand. Moreover, state governments, until now unable (or unwilling) to pay their share of the bills, show signs of awakening to their responsibilities. But bigger government efforts do not produce better results for human beings; they are simply a way of getting a job done when no more feasible methods exist.

10. Even today, most of the nation's most serious problems are caused largely by the pressures of a too rapidly rising population. In the next generation, the problems may become unmanageable. Take four basic needs: education, water, air, and power.

11. The quality of education is closely related to the problem of numbers. Within the next five years, we are told, the number of high school students will rise to 15 million (a 50 percent increase over 1960), forcing hundreds of communities to consider imposing stiff new taxes. Many taxpayers will refuse to accept the added burden and their children will attend even more crowded classes. Far-sighted citizens will approve new school bond issues, but the increased financial drain probably will not result in an improved education.

12. Our standard of democracy entitles everyone to free schooling through high school. But our educational standards are rising. Two-year junior colleges, many of them supported by cities and states, loom as the next step in our system of free, universal education. Along with the surge in enrollment at traditional four-year colleges and universities, higher education is expected to attract about 12 million students in 1980 (triple the 1960 figure).

13. Merely building the physical facilities for such huge increases is a formidable prospect. Creating a sympathetic atmosphere for education, and filling the need for qualified teachers is a much more staggering problem. Of course, we may argue for the radical reform of U.S. education. We may plead for overhauling the existing system of teacher training, as James B. Conant has eloquently done. But I see few signs we are about to undertake such vast changes in the machinery of U.S. education; nor does it seem possible, even if the mood for drastic reform was overwhelming, simply to order new procedures, new goals, and new solutions and then put them into practice. Good teachers cannot be turned out by fiat. We do not live in a planner's paradise.

14. With increased urbanization and industrialization, demands on the water supply will be much greater than most Americans have remotely imagined. The drought in the northeast United States was an indication of shortages even greater to come. And though engineers and scientists can, and will, tap new sources of water and devise ways to purify polluted rivers like the Hudson, the cost will be fantastic— hundreds of billions of dollars. Add to the current strain the pressure of a 50 percent increase in population

and the result may well be a chronic water shortage that can hardly be solved at any tolerable price.

15. Imaginative but impractical water schemes have been proposed, such as one to bring to the United States the almost limitless supply of far northern water, carrying it a thousand miles and more to our own boundaries. Assuming that Canada would agree to the politically prickly diversion of her waters, the cost is estimated in the neighborhood of $100 billion. But it has taken more than a generation of hot dispute and interminable litigation to decide priorities of water among our own sister states of the West. How much greater the difficulties of diverting Canada's water to care for U.S. needs?

16. As for nuclear-powered desalination plants, quite apart from the cost of constructing the huge installations we would need and the pipelines to carry the water inland, there is the additional problem of safety in disposing of radioactive waste. Technicians may solve the problem, but at what social cost? The conversion of precious open spaces into atomic garbage dumps?

17. Just as easily accessible water supplies dwindle, air pollution will increase. Air pollution is the result of congestion, industrialization, and the multiplication of automobiles—factors in direct relation to population density in urban areas. Los Angeles is not an industrial city, yet at times its air is hardly fit to breathe. And with the spread of industry in the sprawling cities of the nation, more and more places will be Los Angelized.

18. We have long assumed that at least the air we breathe is free. It won't be for much longer as we expand our efforts to purify the atmosphere. In California, for example, an aroused public finally insisted that automobile manufacturers install exhaust filters to trap toxic chemicals. Keeping automobile fumes and industrial poisons out of the air we breathe is going to be an increasingly costly business. By the year 2000 the high cost of breathing will be a real issue, not just a phrase.

19. Packing too many people into an urban area increases the cost of providing still another essential of everyday living: electric power. Even more serious, such concentrations of people may make absolutely reliable electric service more and more difficult to maintain. I doubt if it was a mere coincidence, for example, that New York City needed 10 hours to restore electricity after the Northeast power failure in 1965, while smaller communities were able to turn on their lights in a much shorter time. Growth is desirable up to a point; then the advantage of size diminishes and the multiplication of complexity multiplies the headaches. And by 1980 we can expect at least a 300 percent increase in the nation's electrical energy needs. Most of this will flow into urban areas. The present difficulties of maintaining absolutely reliable service to such concentrations of people and industry, and holding down costs, will thus be magnified.

20. As chairman of TVA and the Atomic Energy Commission, and in my present work in Asia and Latin America, I have become familiar with the problems of producing and distributing electricity on a large scale. Indeed, it was TVA a generation ago that pioneered the concept that the greater the use of electricity the lower the cost per

kilowatt hour. This is still generally true. But for great cities the exact contrary is coming to pass. To *distribute* electricity in a large, densely populated area such as New York is more costly than in smaller urban markets. Huge generating power plants produce ever lower generating costs; but to bring this power to the consumer in massive concentrations of population grows more and more expensive. Consequently, the price of this essential of modern life probably will go up in the great cities as population growth continues.

21. Without realizing it, we are fast approaching what may be called the population barrier beyond which lie unpredictability and, I fear, problems of unmanageable size. Consider, for example, the relationship between population growth and the poor.

22. The Federal Aid to Dependent Children program has doubled to more than four million cases during the last decade, while the costs have soared from about $600 million to more than $1.8 billion. Even more depressing than the numbers of families who cannot survive without welfare assistance is the phenomenon known as the "cycle of dependency."

23. More than 40 percent of parents whose children receive A.D.C. funds themselves had parents who received relief checks. This cycle is sad but not surprising. Poor people tend to have more children than they want or can afford, and the children have less chance to receive the education and training they need to break the pattern. Thus, even the third generation appears on relief rolls in the United States, the most socially mobile nation in the world. In America, reports the

National Academy of Sciences in a recent study, "The Growth of U. S. Population," "the burden of unwanted children among impoverished and uneducated mothers . . . is much like that experienced by mothers in underdeveloped countries."

24. Since the poor cannot contribute their share of the mounting costs of education, medical care, public housing, and similar necessary government enterprises, the money must be supplied by the rest of the population through taxation. But the most painful loss is not measured in dollars but in human resources. And one measure of the potential loss is the fact that one-fourth of America's children are the offspring of poor parents.

25. Belatedly, we are helping poor couples who need and want financial and medical help in family planning. The White House Conference on Health in November, 1965, gave high priority to birth control as part of Federal efforts to halt the cycle of dependency and poverty. Tax-supported activities in 40 states, combined with such large-scale private efforts as Harvard's Center for Population Studies and the $14.5 million grant by the Ford Foundation for basic research by the Columbia-Presbyterian Medical Center and the Population Council, herald new progress in a long-neglected field.

26. We tend to patronize the poor by preaching to them about birth control; though poverty-stricken parents with four, five, or six children are the most publicized aspect of population growth, they are by no means the most important numerical aspect of the problem. As a matter of simple arithmetic, the four-fifths of the nation's families

who earn more than the poverty-line income of $3,000 a year—and who can afford two, three, or four children—produce a greater total of children than the one poor couple out of five which may have six youngsters.

27. In fact, the latest census information reveals that though poor families may have more children than do better-off families, the difference is much smaller than many people believe. According to the National Academy of Sciences analysis, in 1960 married women 40 to 44 years old in families with incomes below $4,000 and above $4,000 differed in the average number of children by less than one. The postwar baby boom, for example, was more pronounced among middle- and upper-income families than among the poor.

28. Thus, these relatively well-off families are the ones mainly responsible for our rapidly rising population curve. They and their children are the ones who will account for most of the 100 million additional Americans by the end of the century.

29. How many children a couple should have is a decision only they should make; a government inducement or deterrent—a tax, for example—is morally repugnant and politically impossible. We cannot penalize the poor in order to limit the size of their families while we allow more prosperous parents to have as many children as they want. The large majority of middle- and upper-class parents need no birth-control help from government, nor will they welcome outside advice on so personal a matter. Yet it is this group of families who will want to have three, four, or more children for the very natural reason that they

like children and can afford to support them. The question is, can the *country* support them?

30. Any notion that The Pill or some other scientific device is the sole and complete answer is very dubious. At a symposium on birth control not long ago, Dr. Stephen J. Plank, a professor in the Harvard School of Public Health, cautioned against "the facile assumption . . . that we may be able to contracept our way to the Great Society." Birth control, he said, is a question of motivation rather than technology alone.

31. The neglected arithmetic of the population problem facing us is depressing. Look at these tables showing the birth and death rates over the past quarter-century in the United States:

	BIRTHS	RATE (PER 1,000 POP.)
1940	2,360,399	17.9
1945	2,735,456	19.5
1950	3,554,149	23.6
1955	4,047,295	24.6
1960	4,257,850	23.7
1964	4,027,490	21.0

	DEATHS	RATE (PER 1,000 POP.)
1940	1,417,269	10.8
1945	1,401,719	10.6
1950	1,452,454	9.6
1955	1,528,717	9.3
1960	1,711,982	9.5
1964	1,798,051	9.4

32. Although the birth rate has been declining since the mid-50's, while the death rate has remained relatively stable, the drop in the birth rate is too little and too late to prevent an oversized population. The surge in the number of births

over deaths continues (2.3 million were added to the population in 1964).

33. Or examine these low and high population projections prepared by the Census Bureau:

	LOW	HIGH
1970	206,000,000	211,000,000
1985	248,000,000	276,000,000
2010	322,000,000	438,000,000

34. The high figure would be reached if birth rates returned to the levels of the early 1950's. The low estimate—enormous as it is—is based on the possibility that the rates may decline by 1985 to the comparatively low levels of the early World War II years.

35. One theoretical way out of the dilemma would be to say that since America can no longer sustain complete "family freedom," some form of compulsory birth control is, regrettably, necessary. It would not be the first time in our history that government intervened to restrain individual impulse in the name of collective welfare. Yet, where children and parents are concerned, I do not believe we can yet advocate the sacrifice of one freedom for the sake of preserving another. Such a "solution" would make no sense at all, theoretically, practically, or ethically.

36. Government policies and private programs must make plain the kind of life we all face if economically comfortable families reproduce at rates they personally can afford. With equal urgency we must make plain the dangers if poor families have children in numbers they cannot afford.

37. Obviously, a stationary population—one in which the birth rate matches the death rate—is out of the question for many years to come. It is probably not feasible, nor even desirable. All we can hope to achieve is a slower rise in the size of our population rather than the present steep increase. What is needed is a far more drastic cut in the birth rate—a voluntary curtailment of the right to breed. It is needed, but I have no great conviction that it will happen.

38. For though scientific ingenuity may be able to solve many of the technological problems, we are only beginning to understand people always change more slowly than technology. It is easier, after all, to design a new industrial process than redesign a cultural tradition. Yet that is the order of change we face if we are to preserve life's dignity and quality. Confronted by the crisis of population growth, we must, at present, appeal to private conscience for the sake of the general good.

· QUESTIONS ·

1. As your instructor suggests, prepare a paragraph or sentence outline of the 38 paragraphs in this essay.
2. Name the four basic needs cited by the author, a discussion of which occupies paragraphs 11 through 20.
3. In what way is paragraph 5 a *thesis paragraph* for the entire essay?
4. Name any specific ways in which your "enjoyment of living" has been hampered by population growth.

5. Is Lilienthal an alarmist? For example, is continuous physical growth of any kind at a constant rate actually possible? (See the Letters column of the *New York Times Magazine*, February 6, 1966, p. 6.)
6. Define: cornucopia, penultimate, feasible, fiat, mobile, inducement, deterrent, motivation, voluntary.
7. Can you cite examples in American life where "individual impulse in the name of collective welfare" has been restrained?
8. How effective do you feel would be the appeal to "private conscience" for which the author calls?

Theme Subjects: (1) My Answer to Lilienthal; (2) My Solution to the Problem of Overpopulation; (3) Overpopulation Is Really No Problem; (4) The Greatest Problem in American Life Today Is _____; (5) Science Will (Will Never) Find a Solution to Overpopulation.

HABIT

William James

WILLIAM JAMES (1842–1910) was born in New York City and spent much of his boyhood with his brother Henry (the novelist) in travel and private study in Europe. After work at Harvard (he received his M.D. degree in 1869) he began his long teaching career in 1872. Among his most widely read books are *The Will To Believe and Other Essays* (1897); *The Varieties of Religious Experience* (1902); and *Pragmatism* (1907).

"Habit a second nature! Habit is ten times nature," the Duke of Wellington is said to have exclaimed; and the degree to which this is true no one can probably appreciate as well as one who is a veteran soldier himself. The daily drill and the years of discipline end by fashioning a man completely over again, as to most of the possibilities of his conduct.

There is a story, which is credible enough, though it may not be true, of a practical joker, who, seeing a discharged veteran carrying home his dinner, suddenly called out, "Attention!" whereupon the man instantly brought his hands down, and lost his mutton and potatoes in the gutter. The drill had been thorough, and its effects had become embodied in the man's nervous structure.[1]

Riderless cavalry-horses, at many a battle, have been seen to come together and go through their customary evolutions at the sound of the bugle-call. Most trained domestic animals, dogs and oxen, and omnibus- and car-horses, seem to be machines almost pure and simple, undoubtingly, unhesitatingly doing from minute to minute the duties they have been taught and giving no sign that the possibility of an alternative ever suggests itself to their mind. Men grown old in prison have asked to be readmitted after being once set free. In a railroad accident to a traveling menagerie in the United States sometime in 1884, a tiger, whose cage had broken open, is said to have emerged but presently crept back again, as if too much bewildered by his new responsibilities, so that he was without difficulty secured.

Habit is thus the enormous flywheel of society, its most precious conservative agent. It alone is what keeps us all within the bounds of ordinance and saves the children of fortune from the envious uprisings of the poor. It alone prevents the hardest and most repulsive walks of life from being deserted by those brought up to tread therein. It keeps the fisherman and the deck-hand at sea through the winter; it holds the miner in his darkness and nails the countryman to his log-cabin and his lonely farm through all the months of snow; it protects us from invasion by the natives of the desert and the frozen zone. It dooms us all to fight out the battle of life upon the lines of our nurture or our early choices and to make the best of a pursuit that disagrees, because there is no other for which we are fitted and it is too late to begin again. It keeps different social strata from mixing. Already at the age of twenty-five you see the professional mannerism settling down on the young commercial traveler, on the young doctor, on the young minister, on the young counsellor-at-law. You see the little lines of cleavage running through the character, the tricks of thought, the prejudices, the ways of the "shop," in a word, from which the man can by-and-by no more escape than his coat-sleeve can suddenly fall into a new set of folds. On the whole, it is best he should not escape. It is well for the world that in most of us, by the age of thirty, the character has set like plaster and will never soften again.

If the period between twenty and thirty is the critical one in the formation of intellectual and professional habits, the period below twenty is more important still for the fixing of *personal* habits, properly so called, such as vocalization and pronunciation, gesture, motion, and address. Hardly ever is a language learned after twenty spoken without a foreign accent; hardly ever can a youth transferred to the society of his betters unlearn the nasality and other vices of speech bred in him by the associations of his growing years. Hardly ever, indeed, no matter how much money there be in his pocket, can he even learn to *dress* like a gentleman-born. The merchants offer their wares as

---

[1] "Huxley's *Elementary Lessons in Physiology, Lesson XII.*" (James's note.)

eagerly to him as to the veriest "swell," but he simply *cannot* buy the right things. An invisible law, as strong as gravitation, keeps him within his orbit, arrayed this year as he was the last; and how his better-bred acquaintances contrive to get the things they wear will be for him a mystery till his dying day.

The great thing, in all education, is to *make our nervous system our ally instead of our enemy*. It is to fund and capitalize our acquisitions and live at ease upon the interest of the fund. *For this we must make automatic and habitual, as early as possible, as many useful actions as we can* and guard against the growing into ways that are likely to be disadvantageous to us, as we should guard against the plague. The more of the details of our daily life we can hand over to the effortless custody of automatism, the more our higher powers of mind will be set free for their own proper work. There is no more miserable human being than one in whom nothing is habitual but indecision, and for whom the lighting of every cigar, the drinking of every cup, the time of rising and going to bed every day, and the beginning of every bit of work are subjects of express volitional deliberation. Full half the time of such a man goes to the deciding, or regretting, of matters which ought to be so ingrained in him as practically not to exist for his consciousness at all. If there be such daily duties not yet ingrained in any one of my readers, let him begin this very hour to set the matter right.

In Professor Bain's chapter on "The Moral Habits" there are some admirable practical remarks laid down. Two great maxims emerge from his treatment. The first is that in the acquisition of a new habit, or the leaving off of an old one, we must take care to *launch ourselves with as strong and decided an initiative as possible*. Accumulate all the possible circumstances which shall re-enforce the right motives; put yourself assiduously in conditions that encourage the new way; make engagements incompatible with the old; take a public pledge, if the case allows; in short, develop your resolution with every aid you know. This will give your new beginning such a momentum that the temptation to break down will not occur as soon as it otherwise might; and every day during which a breakdown is postponed adds to the chances of its not occurring at all.

The second maxim is: *Never suffer an exception to occur till the new habit is securely rooted in your life.* Each lapse is like the letting fall of a ball of string which one is carefully winding up; a single slip undoes more than a great many turns will wind again. *Continuity* of training is the great means of making the nervous system act infallibly right. As Professor Bain says:

The peculiarity of the moral habits, contradistinguishing them from the intellectual acquisitions, is the presence of two hostile powers, one to be gradually raised into the ascendant over the other. It is necessary, above all things, in such a situation, never to lose a battle. Every gain on the wrong side undoes the effect of many conquests on the right. The essential precaution, therefore, is so to regulate the two opposing powers that the one may have a series of uninterrupted successes, until repetition has fortified it to such a degree as to enable it to cope with the opposition, under any circumstances. This is the theoretically best career of mental progress.

The need of securing success at the *outset* is imperative. Failure at first is apt to dampen the energy of all future attempts, whereas past experience of success nerves one to future vigor. Goethe says to a man who consulted him about an enterprise but mistrusted his own powers: "Ach, you need only blow on your hands!" And the remark illustrates the effect on Goethe's spirits of his own habitually successful career. Professor Baumann, from whom I borrow the anecdote, says that the collapse of barbarian nations when Europeans come among them is due to their despair of ever succeeding as the newcomers do in the larger tasks of life. Old ways are broken and new ones not formed.

The question of "tapering-off," in abandoning such habits as drink and opium-indulgence, comes in here, and is a question about which experts differ within certain limits, and in regard to what may be best for an individual case. In the main, however, all expert opinion would agree that abrupt acquisition of the new habit is the best way, *if there be a real possibility of carrying it out.* We must be careful not to give the will so stiff a task as to insure its defeat at the very outset; but, *provided one can stand it,* a sharp period of suffering, and then a free time, is the best thing to aim at, whether in giving up a habit like that of opium, or in simply changing one's hours of rising or of work. It is surprising how soon a desire will die of inanition if it be *never* fed.

One must first learn, unmoved, looking neither to the right nor left, to walk firmly on the straight and narrow path, before one can begin "to make one's self over again." He who every day makes a fresh resolve is like one who, arriving at the edge of the ditch he is to leap, forever stops and returns for a fresh run. Without *unbroken* advance there is no such thing as *accumulation* of the ethical forces possible, and to make this possible, and to exercise us and habituate us in it, is the sovereign blessing of regular *work*.[2]

A third maxim may be added to the preceding pair: *Seize the very first possible opportunity to act on every resolution you make and on every emotional prompting you may experience in the direction of the habits you aspire to gain.* It is not in the moment of their forming, but in the moment of their producing *motor effects,* that resolves and aspirations communicate the new "set" to the brain. As the author last quoted remarks:

The actual presence of the practical opportunity alone furnishes the fulcrum upon which the lever can rest, by means of which the moral will may multiply its strength and raise itself aloft. He who has no solid ground to press against will never get beyond the stage of empty gesture-making.

No matter how full a reservoir of *maxims* one may possess, and no matter how good one's *sentiments* may be, if one have not taken advantage of every concrete opportunity to *act,* one's character may remain entirely unaffected for the better. With mere good intentions hell is proverbially paved. And this is an obvious consequence of the

---

[2] "J. Bahnsen, *Beiträge zu Charakterologie* (1867), Vol. I, p. 209." (James's note.)

principles we have laid down. A "character," as J. S. Mill[3] says, "is a completely fashioned will"; and a will, in the sense in which he means it, is an aggregate of tendencies to act in a firm and prompt and definite way upon all the principal emergencies of life. A tendency to act only becomes effectively ingrained in us in proportion to the uninterrupted frequency with which the actions actually occur and the brain "grows" to their use. Every time a resolve or a fine glow of feeling evaporates without bearing practical fruit is worse than a chance lost; it works so as positively to hinder future resolutions and emotions from taking the normal path of discharge. There is no more contemptible type of human character than that of the nerveless sentimentalist and dreamer, who spends his life in a weltering sea of sensibility and emotion but who never does a manly concrete deed. Rousseau, inflaming all the mothers of France by his eloquence to follow Nature and nurse their babies themselves, while he sends his own children to the foundling hospital, is the classical example of what I mean. But every one of us in his measure, whenever, after glowing for an abstractly formulated Good, he practically ignores some actual case, among the squalid "other particulars" of which that same Good lurks disguised, treads straight on Rousseau's path. All Goods are disguised by the vulgarity of their concomitants in this work-a-day world; but woe to him who can only recognize them when he thinks them in their pure and abstract form! The habit of excessive novel-reading and theatre-going will produce true mon-

sters in this line. The weeping of a Russian lady over the fictitious personages in the play, while her coachman is freezing to death on his seat outside, is the sort of thing that everywhere happens on a less glaring scale. Even the habit of excessive indulgence in music, for those who are neither performers themselves nor musically gifted enough to take it in a purely intellectual way, has probably a relaxing effect upon the character. One becomes filled with emotions which habitually pass without prompting to any deed, and so the inertly sentimental condition is kept up. The remedy would be never to suffer one's self to have an emotion at a concert without expressing it afterward in *some* active way. Let the expression be the least thing in the world—speaking genially to one's aunt or giving up one's seat in a horse-car, if nothing more heroic offers—but let it not fail to take place.

These latter cases make us aware that it is not simply *particular lines* of discharge, but also *general forms* of discharge, that seem to be grooved out by habit in the brain. Just as, if we let our emotions evaporate, they get into a way of evaporating, so there is reason to suppose that if we often flinch from making an effort, before we know it the effort-making capacity will be gone; and that, if we suffer the wandering of our attention, presently it will wander all the time. Attention and effort are, as we shall see later, but two names for the same psychic fact. To what brain-processes they correspond we do not know. The strongest reason for believing that they do depend on

---

[3] John Stuart Mill (1806–1873), English philosopher and economist.

brain-processes at all, and are not pure acts of the spirit, is just this fact, that they seem in some degree subject to the law of habit, which is a material law. As a final practical maxim, relative to these habits of the will, we may, then, offer something like this: *Keep the faculty of effort alive in you by a little gratuitous exercise every day.* That is, be systematically ascetic or heroic in little unnecessary points, do every day or two something for no other reason than that you would rather not do it, so that when the hour of dire need draws nigh, it may find you not unnerved and untrained to stand the test. Asceticism of this sort is like the insurance which a man pays on his house and goods. The tax does him no good at the time and possibly may never bring him a return. But if the fire *does* come, his having paid it will be his salvation from ruin. So with the man who has daily inured himself to habits of concentrated attention, energetic volition, and self-denial in unnecessary things. He will stand like a tower when everything rocks around him and when his softer fellow-mortals are winnowed like chaff in the blast.

The physiological study of mental conditions is thus the most powerful ally of hortatory ethics. The hell to be endured hereafter, of which theology tells, is no worse than the hell we make for ourselves in this world by habitually fashioning our characters in the wrong way. Could the young but realize how soon they will become mere walking bundles of habits, they would give more heed to their conduct while in the plastic state. We are spinning our own fates, good or evil, and never to be undone. Every smallest stroke of virtue or of vice leaves its never so little scar. The drunken Rip Van Winkle, in Jefferson's play,[4] excuses himself for every fresh dereliction by saying, "I won't count this time!" Well! he may not count it, and a kind Heaven may not count it; but it is being counted none the less. Down among his nerve-cells and fibres the molecules are counting it, registering and storing it up to be used against him when the next temptation comes. Nothing we ever do is, in strict scientific literalness, wiped out. Of course, this has its good side as well as its bad one. As we become permanent drunkards by so many separate drinks, so we become saints in the moral, and authorities and experts in the practical and scientific spheres by so many separate acts and hours of work. Let no youth have any anxiety about the upshot of his education, whatever the line of it may be. If he keep faithfully busy each hour of the working-day, he may safely leave the final result to itself. He can with perfect certainty count on waking up some fine morning to find himself one of the competent ones of his generation, in whatever pursuit he may have singled out. Silently, between all the details of his business, the *power of judging* in all that class of matter will have built itself up within him as a possession that will never pass away. Young people should know this truth in advance. The ignorance of it has probably engendered more discouragement and faint-heartedness in youths embarking on arduous careers than all other causes put together.

---

[4] Joseph Jefferson (1829–1905), American actor.

· QUESTIONS ·

1. Compare and contrast this essay with Osler's "A Way of Life."
2. What does James mean when he calls habit "the enormous fly-wheel of society"?
3. What, according to the author, is the "great thing" in all education?
4. List five of your "most useful" habits.
5. List five of your "most useless" habits.
6. Name the three maxims for forming new habits.
7. How can a "character" be "a completely fashioned will"?
8. What does the author mean by the "power of judging"?
9. Define: ordinance, cleavage, automatism, volitional, momentum, concomitants, gratuitous, hortatory, dereliction.
10. This essay is "dated" in its allusions. Is it also "old-fashioned" in its advice, its "value judgments"? If you think it old-fashioned, do you feel that it is valueless today or, conversely, invaluable as a guide to conduct?

Theme Subjects: (1) My Worst Habit; (2) How To Stop _____; (3) How To Live in Moderation; (4) My Hell Is Paved with _____; (5) "Habit Is Ten Times Nature."

A WAY OF LIFE

William Osler

SIR WILLIAM OSLER (1849–1919), a Canadian physician, was graduated from McGill University in 1872, later to become one of the greatest medical figures of his time. He taught at his alma mater and at Pennsylvania, Johns Hopkins, and Oxford. Among his better-known works are *The Principles and Practice of Medicine* (1893) and *A Concise History of Medicine* (1919).

What each day needs that shalt thou
  ask,
Each day will set its proper task.
        —GOETHE

Fellow students:
    Every man has a philosophy of life in thought, in word, or in deed, worked out in himself uncon-

From *A Way of Life,* published 1937 by Paul B. Hoeber, Inc., a division of Harper & Brothers. Reprinted by permission.

sciously. In possession of the very best, he may not know of its existence; with the very worst he may pride himself as a paragon. As it grows with the growth it cannot be taught to the young in formal lectures. What have bright eyes, red blood, quick breath and taut muscles to do with philosophy? Did not the great Stagirite[1] say that young men were unfit students of it?— they will hear as though they heard not, and to no profit. Why then should I trouble you? Because I have a message that may be helpful. It is not philosophical, nor is it strictly moral or religious, one or other of which I was told my address should be, and yet in a way it is all three. It is the oldest and the freshest, the simplest and the most useful, so simple indeed is it that some of you may turn away disappointed as was Naaman the Syrian when told to go wash in Jordan and be clean. You know those composite tools to be bought for 50 cents, with one handle to fit a score or more of instruments. The workmanship is usually bad, so bad, as a rule, that you will not find an example in any good carpenter's shop; but the boy has one, the chauffeur slips one into his box, and the sailor into his kit, and there is one in the odds-and-ends drawer of the pantry of every well-regulated family. It is simply a handy thing about the house, to help over the many little difficulties of the day. Of this sort of philosophy I wish to make you a present—a handle to fit your life tools. Whether the workmanship is Sheffield[2] or shoddy, this helve will fit anything from a hatchet to a corkscrew.

My message is but a word, *a Way,* an easy expression of the experience of a plain man whose life has never been worried by any philosophy higher than that of the shepherd in *As You Like It.* I wish to point out a path in which the wayfaring man, though a fool, cannot err; not a system to be worked out painfully only to be discarded, not a formal scheme, simply a habit as easy—or as hard!—to adopt as any other habit, good or bad.

I

A few years ago a Christmas card went the rounds, with the legend, "Life is just one 'derned' thing after another," which, in more refined language, is the same as saying, "Life is a habit," a succession of actions that become more or less automatic. This great truth, which lies at the basis of all actions, muscular or psychic, is the keystone to the teaching of Aristotle, to whom the formation of habits was the basis of moral excellence. "In a word, habits of any kind are the result of actions of the same kind; and so what we have to do is to give a certain character to these particular actions" (*Ethics*). Lift a seven months' old baby to his feet— see him tumble on his nose. Do the same at twelve months—he walks. At two years he runs. The muscles and the nervous system have acquired the habit. One trial after another, one failure after another, has given him power. Put your finger in a baby's mouth and he sucks

---

[1] Aristotle was born at Stagira in the fourth century B.C.

[2] Sheffield is a manufacturing town in England famous for its steel and cutlery.

away in blissful anticipation of a response to a mammalian habit millions of years old. And we can deliberately train parts of our body to perform complicated actions with unerring accuracy. Watch that musician playing a difficult piece. Batteries, commutators, multipliers, switches, wires innumerable control those nimble fingers, the machinery of which may be set in motion as automatically as in a pianola, the player all the time chatting as if he had nothing to do in controlling the apparatus—habit again, the gradual acquisition of power by long practice and at the expense of many mistakes. The same great law reaches through mental and moral states. "Character," which partakes of both, in Plutarch's words, is "long-standing habit."

Now the way of life that I preach is a habit to be acquired gradually by long and steady repetition. It is the practice of living for the day only, and for the day's work, *life in day-tight compartments.* "Ah," I hear you say, "that is an easy matter, simple as Elisha's advice!" Not as I shall urge it, in words which fail to express the depth of my feelings as to its value. I started life in the best of all environments—in a parsonage, one of nine children. A man who has filled Chairs in four universities, has written a successful book, and has been asked to lecture at Yale, is supposed popularly to have brains of special quality. A few of my intimate friends really know the truth about me, as I know it! Mine, in good faith I say it, are of the most mediocre character. But what about those professorships, etc.? Just habit, a way of life, an outcome of the day's work, the vital importance

of which I wish to impress upon you with all the force at my command.

Dr. Johnson remarked upon the trifling circumstances by which men's lives are influenced, "not by an ascendant planet, a predominating humour, but by the first book which they read, some early conversation which they have heard, or some accident which excited ardour and enthusiasm." This was my case in two particulars. I was diverted to the Trinity College School, then at Weston, Ontario, by a paragraph in the circular stating that the senior boys would go into the drawing-room in the evenings and learn to sing and dance—vocal and pedal accomplishments for which I was never designed; but like Saul seeking his asses, I found something more valuable, a man of the White of Selborne type, who knew nature, and who knew how to get boys interested in it. The other happened in the summer of 1871, when I was attending the Montreal General Hospital. Much worried as to the future, partly about the final examination, partly as to what I should do afterwards, I picked up a volume of Carlyle, and on the page I opened there was the familiar sentence— *"Our main business is not to see what lies dimly at a distance, but to do what lies clearly at hand."* A commonplace sentiment enough, but it hit and stuck and helped and was the starting point of a habit that has enabled me to utilize to the full the single talent entrusted to me.

II

The workers in Christ's vineyard were hired by the day; only for this day are we to ask for our daily bread, and we are expressly bidden to take no thought for the morrow. To the modern world these commands have an Oriental savour, counsels of perfection akin to certain of the Beatitudes, stimuli to aspiration, not to action. I am prepared on the contrary to urge the literal acceptance of the advice, not in the mood of St. James—"Go to now, ye that say, to-day or to-morrow we will go into such a city, and continue there a year, and buy and sell and get grain; whereas ye know not what shall be on the morrow"; not in the Epicurean spirit of Omar with his "jug of wine and thou," but in the modernist spirit, as a way of life, a habit, a strong enchantment at once against the mysticism of the East and the pessimism that too easily besets us. Change that hard saying "sufficient unto the day is the evil thereof," into "the goodness thereof," since the chief worries of life arise from the foolish habit of looking before and after. As a patient with double vision from some transient unequal action of the muscles of the eye finds magical relief from well-adjusted glasses, so, returning to the clear binocular vision of to-day, the over-anxious student finds peace when he looks neither backward to the past nor forward to the future.

I stood on the bridge of one of the great liners, ploughing the ocean at 25 knots. "She is alive," said my companion, "in every plate; a huge monster with brain and nerves, an immense stomach, a wonderful heart and lungs, and a splendid system of locomotion." Just at that moment a signal sounded and all over the ship the water-tight compartments were closed. "Our chief factor of safety," said the captain. "In spite of the *Titanic*," I said. "Yes," he replied, "in spite of the *Titanic*." Now each one of you is a much more marvellous organization than the great liner, and bound on a longer voyage. What I urge is that you so learn to control the machinery as to live with "day-tight compartments" as the most certain way to ensure safety on the voyage. Get on the bridge and see that at least the great bulkheads are in working order. Touch a button and hear, at every level of your life, the iron doors shutting out the Past—the dead yesterdays. Touch another and shut off, with a metal curtain, the Future—the unborn tomorrows. Then you are safe—safe for today! Read the old story in the *Chambered Nautilus*, so beautifully sung by Oliver Wendell Holmes, only change one line to "Day after day behold the silent toil." Shut off the past. "Let the dead past bury its dead." So easy to say, so hard to realize! The truth is, the past haunts us like a shadow. To disregard it is not easy. Those blue eyes of your grandmother, that weak chin of your grandfather have mental and moral counterparts in your make-up. Generations of ancestors, brooding over "Providence, foreknowledge, will and fate, fixed fate, free will, foreknowledge absolute," may have bred a New England conscience, morbidly sensitive, to heal which some of you had rather sing the 51st Psalm than follow Christ into the slums. Shut out the yesterdays, which have lighted fools the way to dusty death, and have no concern for you personally, that is, consciously. They are there all right, working daily in us, but so are our livers and our stomachs. And the past, in its unconscious action on our lives, should bother us as little as they do. The petty annoyances, the real and fancied slights, the trivial mistakes, the disappointments, the sins, the sorrows, even the joys—bury them deep in the oblivion of each night. Ah! but it is just then that to so many of us the ghosts of the past,

> Night-riding Incubi[3]
> Troubling the fantasy,

come in troops, and pry open the eyelids, each presenting a sin, a sorrow, a regret. Bad enough in the old and seasoned, in the young these demons of past sins may be a terrible affliction, and in bitterness of heart many a one cries with Eugene Aram, "Oh God! Could I so close my mind, and clasp it with a clasp." As a vaccine against all morbid poisons left in the system by the infections of yesterday, I offer "a way of life." "Undress," as George Herbert says, "your soul at night," not by self-examination, but by shedding, as you do your garments, the daily sins whether of omission or of commission, and you will wake a free man, with a new life. To look back, except on rare occasions for stock-taking, is to risk the fate of Lot's wife.[4] Many a man is handicapped in his course by a cursed combination of retro- and intro-spection, the mistakes of yesterday paralysing the efforts of to-day, the worries of the past hugged to his destruction, and the worm Regret allowed to canker the very heart of his life. To die daily, after the manner of St. Paul, ensures the resurrection of a new man, who makes each day the epitome of life.

III

The load of to-morrow added to that of yesterday, carried to-day, makes the strongest falter. Shut off the future as tightly as the past. No dreams, no visions, no delicious fantasies, no castles in the air, with which, as the old song so truly says, "hearts are broken, heads are turned." To youth, we are told, belongs the future, but the wretched tomorrow that so plagues some of us has no certainty, except through to-day. Who can tell what a day may bring forth? Though its uncertainty is a proverb, a man may carry its secret in the hollow of his hand. Make a pilgrimage to Hades with Ulysses, draw the magic circle, perform the rites, and then ask Tiresias[5] the question. I have had the answer from his own lips. The future is to-day—there is no to-morrow! The day of a man's salvation is *now*—the life of the present, of to-day, lived earnestly, intently, without a forward-looking thought, is the only insurance for the future. Let the limit of your horizon be a twenty-four hour circle. On the title page of one of the great books of science, the *Discours de la Methode* of Descartes (1637), is a vignette showing a man digging in a garden with his face toward the earth, on which rays of light are streaming from the heavens; above him is the legend "*Fac et Spera.*" 'Tis a good attitude and a good motto. Look heavenward, if you wish, but never to the horizon—that way danger lies. Truth is not there, happiness is not there, certainty is not there, but the falsehoods, the frauds, the

---

[3] Incubi are imaginary demons, evil spirits.

[4] Lot's wife, niece of Abraham by marriage, was changed into a pillar of salt for looking back during the flight from Sodom. See *Genesis*, 13:1–12, 19.

[5] Tiresias was a blinded seer who had prophetic vision. See Sophocles' *Antigone*.

quackeries, the *ignes fatui*[6] which have deceived each generation—all beckon from the horizon and lure the men not content to look for the truth and happiness that tumble out at their feet. Once while at College climb a mountain top and get a general outlook of the land and make it the occasion perhaps of that careful examination of yourself, that inquisition which Descartes urges every man to hold once in a lifetime—not oftener.

Waste of energy, mental distress, nervous worries dog the steps of a man who is anxious about the future. Shut close, then, the great fore and aft bulkheads and prepare to cultivate the habit of a life of Day-Tight Compartments. Do not be discouraged—like every other habit, the acquisition takes time, and the way is one you must find for yourselves. I can only give general directions and encouragement, in the hope that while the green years are on your heads, you may have the courage to persist.

IV

Now, for the day itself! What first? Be your own daysman! and sigh not with Job for any mysterious intermediary, but prepare to lay your own firm hand upon the helm. Get into touch with the finite and grasp in full enjoyment that sense of capacity in a machine working smoothly. Join the whole creation of animate things in a deep heartfelt joy that you are alive, that you see the sun, that you are in this glorious earth which nature has made so beautiful and which is yours to conquer and to enjoy. Realize, in the words of Browning, that "There's a world of capability for joy spread round about us, meant for us, inviting us." What are the morning sensations?—for they control the day. Some of us are congenitally unhappy during the early hours; but the young man who feels on awakening that life is a burden or a bore has been neglecting his machine, driving it too hard, stoking the engines too much, or not cleaning out the ashes and clinkers. Or he has been too much with the Lady Nicotine, or fooling with Bacchus, or, worst of all, with the younger Aphrodite—all "messengers of strong prevailment in unhardened youth." To have a sweet outlook on life you must have a clean body. As I look on the clear-cut, alert, earnest features, and the lithe, active forms of our college men, I sometimes wonder whether or not Socrates and Plato would find the race improved. I am sure they would love to look on such a gathering as this. Make their ideal yours—the fair mind in the fair body. The one cannot be sweet and clean without the other, and you must realize, with Rabbi Ben Ezra, the great truth that flesh and soul are mutually helpful! This morning outlook—which really makes the day—is largely a question of a clean machine—of physical morality in the wide sense of the term. *"C'est l'estomac qui fait les heureux,"* as Voltaire says; no dyspeptic can have a sane outlook on life; and a man whose bodily functions are impaired has a lowered moral resistance. To keep the body fit is a help in keeping the mind pure, and the sensations of the first few hours of the day are the best test of its normal state. The clean

---

[6] *Ignes fatui* are flitting phosphorescent lights seen at night, commonly considered misleading or deluding.

tongue, the clear head, and the bright eye are birthrights of each day. Just as the late Professor Marsh would diagnose an unknown animal from a single bone, so can the day be predicted from the first waking hour. The start is everything, as you well know, and to make a good start you must feel fit. In the young, sensations of morning slackness come most often from lack of control of the two primal instincts—biologic habits—the one concerned with the preservation of the individual, the other with the continuance of the species. Yale students should by this time be models of dietetic propriety, but youth does not always reck the rede[7] of the teacher; and I dare say that here, as elsewhere, careless habits of eating are responsible for much mental disability. My own rule of life has been to cut out unsparingly any article of diet that had the bad taste to disagree with me or to indicate in any way that it had abused the temporary hospitality of the lodging which I had provided. To drink, nowadays, but few students become addicted, but in every large body of men a few are to be found whose incapacity for the day results from the morning clogging of nocturnally-flushed tissues. As moderation is very hard to reach, and as it has been abundantly shown that the best of mental and physical work may be done without alcohol in any form, the safest rule for the young man is that which I am sure most of you follow—abstinence. A bitter enemy to the bright eye and the clear brain of the early morning is tobacco when smoked to excess, as it is now by a large majority of students. Watch it, test it, and if need be, control it. That befogged, woolly sensation reaching from the forehead to the occiput, that haziness of memory, that cold fish-like eye, that furred tongue and last week's taste in the mouth—too many of you know them—I know them—they often come from too much tobacco. The other primal instinct is the heavy burden of the flesh which Nature puts on all of us to ensure a continuation of the species. To drive Plato's team taxes the energies of the best of us. One of the horses is a raging, untamed devil, who can only be brought into subjection by hard fighting and severe training. This much you all know as men; once the bit is between his teeth the black steed Passion will take the white horse Reason with you and the chariot rattling over the rocks to perdition.

With a fresh, sweet body you can start aright without those feelings of inertia that so often, as Goethe says, make the morning's lazy leisure usher in a useless day. Control of the mind as a working machine, the adaptation in it of habit, so that its action becomes almost as automatic as walking, is the end of education—and yet how rarely reached! It can be accomplished with deliberation and repose, never with hurry and worry. Realize how much time there is, how long the day is. Realize that you have sixteen waking hours, three or four of which at least should be devoted to making a silent conquest of your mental machinery. Concentration, by which is grown gradually the power to wrestle successfully with any subject, is the secret of successful study. No mind however dull can escape the bright-

---

[7] Reck the rede: heed the advice.

ness that comes from steady application. There is an old saying,
"Youth enjoyeth not, for haste"; but
worse than this, the failure to cultivate the power of peaceful concentration is the greatest single cause
of mental breakdown. Plato pities
the young man who started at such
a pace that he never reached the
goal. One of the saddest of life's
tragedies is the wreckage of the
career of the young collegian by
hurry, hustle, bustle and tension—
the human machine driven day and
night, as no sensible fellow would
use his motor. Listen to the words
of a master in Israel, William
James: "Neither the nature nor the
amount of our work is accountable
for the frequency and severity of
our breakdowns, but their cause
lies rather in those absurd feelings
of hurry and having no time, in
that breathlessness and tension;
that anxiety of feature and that
solicitude of results, that lack of
inner harmony and ease, in short,
by which the work with us is apt
to be accompanied, and from which
a European who would do the same
work would, nine out of ten times,
be free." *Es bildet ein Talent sich
in der Stille,* but it need not be for
all day. A few hours out of the sixteen will suffice, only let them be
hours of daily dedication—in routine, in order and in system, and
day by day you will gain in power
over the mental mechanism, just as
the child does over the spinal marrow in walking, or the musician
over the nerve centres. Aristotle
somewhere says that the student
who wins out in the fight must be
slow in his movements, with voice
deep, and slow speech, and he will
not be worried over trifles which
make people speak in shrill tones
and use rapid movements. Shut

close in hour-tight compartments,
with the mind directed intensely
upon the subject in hand, you will
acquire the capacity to do more and
more, you will get into training;
and once the mental habit is established you are safe for life.

Concentration is an art of slow
acquisition, but little by little the
mind is accustomed to habits of
slow eating and careful digestion,
by which alone you escape the
"mental dyspepsy" so graphically
described by Lowell in the *Fable
for Critics.* Do not worry your
brains about that bugbear Efficiency, which, sought consciously
and with effort, is just one of those
elusive qualities very apt to be
missed. The man's college output
is never to be gauged at sight; all
the world's coarse thumb and finger
may fail to plumb his most effective work, the casting of the mental
machinery of self-education, the
true preparation for a field larger
than the college campus. Four or
five hours daily—it is not much to
ask; but one day must tell another,
one week certify another, one month
bear witness to another of the same
story, and you will acquire a habit
by which the one-talent man will
earn a high interest, and by which
the ten-talent man may at least save
his capital.

Steady work of this sort gives
a man a sane outlook on the world.
No corrective is so valuable to the
weariness, the fever and the fret
that are so apt to wring the heart
of the young. This is the talisman,
as George Herbert says,

> The famous stone
> That turneth all to gold,

and with which, to the eternally
recurring question, What is Life?
you answer, I do not think—I act

it; the only philosophy that brings you in contact with its real values and enables you to grasp its hidden meaning. Over the Slough of Despond, past Doubting Castle and Giant Despair, with this talisman you may reach the Delectable Mountains and those Shepherds of the Mind—Knowledge, Experience, Watchful and Sincere. Some of you may think this to be a miserable Epicurean doctrine—no better than that so sweetly sung by Horace:—

Happy the man—and Happy he alone,
He who can call to-day his own,
He who secure within can say,
To-morrow, do thy worst—for I have lived to-day.

I do not care what you think, I am simply giving you a philosophy of life that I have found helpful in my work, useful in my play. Walt Whitman, whose physician I was for some years, never spoke to me much of his poems, though occasionally he would make a quotation; but I remember late one summer afternoon as we sat in the window of his little house in Camden there passed a group of workmen whom he greeted in his usual friendly way. And then he said: "Ah, the glory of the day's work, whether with hand or brain! I have tried

To exalt the present and the real,
To teach the average man the glory of his daily work or trade."

In this way of life each one of you may learn to drive the straight furrow and so come to the true measure of a man.

v

With body and mind in training, what remains?

Do you remember that most touching of all incidents in Christ's ministry, when the anxious ruler Nicodemus came by night, worried lest the things that pertained to his everlasting peace were not a part of his busy and successful life? Christ's message to him is His message to the world—never more needed than at present: "Ye must be born of the spirit." You wish to be with the leaders—as Yale men it is your birthright—know the great souls that make up the moral radium of the world. You must be born of their spirit, initiated into their fraternity, whether of the spiritually-minded followers of the Nazarene or of that larger company, elect from every nation, seen by St. John.

Begin the day with Christ and His prayer—you need no other. Creedless, with it you have religion; creed-stuffed, it will leaven any theological dough in which you stick. As the soul is dyed by the thoughts, let no day pass without contact with the best literature of the world. Learn to know your Bible, though not perhaps as your fathers did. In forming character and in shaping conduct, its touch has still its ancient power. Of the kindred of Ram and sons of Elihu, you should know its beauties and its strength. Fifteen or twenty minutes day by day will give you fellowship with the great minds of the race, and little by little as the years pass you extend your friendship with the immortal dead. They will give you faith in your own day. Listen while they speak to you of the fathers. But each age has its own spirit and ideas, just as it has its own manners and pleasures. You are right to believe that yours is the best University at its best period. Why should you look back to be shocked at the frowsiness and dullness of the students of the seventies or even of the nineties? And cast no thought forward, lest you reach a period where you and yours will present to your successors the same dowdiness of clothes and times. But while change is the law, certain great ideas flow fresh through the ages and control us effectually as in the days of Pericles. Mankind, it has been said, is always advancing, man is always the same. The love, hope, fear and faith that make humanity and the elemental passions of the human heart remain unchanged, and the secret of inspiration in any literature is the capacity to touch the chord that vibrates in a sympathy that knows nor time nor place.

The quiet life in day-tight compartments will help you to bear your own and others' burdens with a light heart. Pay no heed to the Batrachians[8] who sit croaking idly by the stream. Life is a straight, plain business, and the way is clear, blazed for you by generations of strong men into whose labours you enter and whose ideals must be your inspiration. In my mind's eye I can see you twenty years hence— resolute-eyed, broad-headed, smooth-faced men who are in the world to make a success of life; but to whichever of the two great types you belong, whether controlled by emotion or by reason, you will need the leaven of their spirit, the only leaven potent enough to avert that only too common Nemesis to which the Psalmist refers: "He gave them their heart's desire, but sent leanness withal into their souls."

I quoted Dr. Johnson's remark about the trivial things that influence. Perhaps this slight word of mine may help some of you so to number your days that you may apply your hearts unto wisdom.

· QUESTIONS ·

1. What is the thesis of this essay?
2. Do you subscribe to this thesis? Why? Why not?
3. This essay is more than half a century old. In what respects is it "dated"?
4. Do you believe that "every to-day well lived makes every yesterday a dream of happiness"?
5. This essay is filled with allusions and references. Can you identify at least the following: Naaman the Syrian, the River Jordan, Plutarch, Elisha, the Beatitudes, Omar, George Herbert, Descartes, Rabbi Ben Ezra, Goethe, John Bunyan, Pericles? (A good Bible dictionary and a short history of English literature will provide information in most instances.)
6. Compare and contrast the style and substance of this essay-lecture with the selection from William James.
7. The "one day at a time" or "24-hour" method is often successfully used in helping alcoholics and narcotics addicts. Does Osler's comment explain why?

Theme Subjects: (1) My Way of Life; (2) Concentration: Key to Success; (3) "Tomorrow Is Only a Vision"; (4) "Look to This Day!"; (5) My Worst Habit; (6) The Glory (?) of My Daily Work; (7) What I Live For; (8) What Dr. Osler Overlooks; (9) Nicotine and Bacchus Are My _____; (10) My Night-Riding Incubi.

---

[8] Batrachians: a term applying to the Amphibia, a class of vertebrates that comprises frogs and salamanders.

READING, WRITING

&

EDUCATION

❧

WHY A CLASSIC
IS A CLASSIC

Arnold Bennett

(ENOCH) ARNOLD BENNETT (1867–1931) was born near Hanley, England, identified as "Hanbridge" of the Five Towns, the setting of many of his best novels. The son of a solicitor, he was educated at the "Middle School" of Newcastle, and as a solicitor's clerk he went to London at the age of 22. Bennett soon entered journalism, lived in France from 1900 to 1908, and returned to England to become one of the most important and prolific writers of his time. He was recognized as an "editor, novelist, dramatist, and connoisseur of all the arts." According to Bennett, he "was able to buy a new hat" with the profits from his first novel, *A Man from the North*, published when he was 31. Generally considered his greatest works, however, are *The Old Wives' Tale* (1908); *Clayhanger* (1910); *Hilda Lessways* (1911); and *Riceyman Steps* (1923).

From *Literary Taste: How To Form It* by Arnold Bennett. Reprinted by permission of Doubleday & Company, Inc.

The large majority of our fellow citizens care as much about literature as they care about aëroplanes or the program of the Legislature. They do not ignore it; they are not quite indifferent to it. But their interest in it is faint and perfunctory; or, if their interest happens to be violent, it is spasmodic. Ask the two hundred thousand persons whose enthusiasm made the vogue of a popular novel ten years ago what they think of that novel now, and you will gather that they have utterly forgotten it, and that they would no more dream of reading it again than of reading Bishop Stubbs's *Select Charters*. Probably if they did read it again they would not enjoy it—not because the said novel is a whit worse now than it was ten years ago; not because their taste has improved—but because they have not had sufficient practice to be able to rely on their taste as a means of permanent pleasure. They simply don't know from one day to the next what will please them.

In the face of this one may ask: Why does the great and universal fame of classical authors continue? The answer is that the fame of classical authors is entirely independent of the majority. Do you suppose that if the fame of Shakespeare depended on the man in the street it would survive a fortnight? The fame of classical authors is originally made, and it is maintained, by a passionate few. Even when a first-class author has enjoyed immense success during his lifetime, the majority have never appreciated him so sincerely as they have appreciated second-rate men. He has always been reënforced by the ardor of the passionate few. And in the case of an author who has emerged into glory after his death, the happy sequel has been due solely to the obstinate perseverance of the few. They could not leave him alone; they would not. They kept on savoring him, and talking about him, and buying him, and they generally behaved with such eager zeal, and they were so authoritative and sure of themselves, that at last the majority grew accustomed to the sound of his name and placidly agreed to the proposition that he was a genius; the majority really did not care very much either way.

And it is by the passionate few that the renown of genius is kept alive from one generation to another. These few are always at work. They are always rediscovering genius. Their curiosity and enthusiasm are exhaustless, so that there is little chance of genius being ignored. And, moreover, they are always working either for or against the verdicts of the majority. The majority can make a reputation, but it is too careless to maintain it. If, by accident, the passionate few agree with the majority in a particular instance, they will frequently remind the majority that such and such a reputation has been made, and the majority will idly concur: "Ah, yes. By the way, we must not forget that such and such a reputation exists." Without that persistent memory-jogging the reputation would quickly fall into the oblivion which is death. The passionate few have their way only by reason of the fact that they are genuinely interested in literature, that literature matters to them. They conquer by their obstinacy alone, by their eternal repetition of the same statements. Do you suppose they could prove to the man in the street that Shakespeare was a great artist? The said man would not even understand the terms they employed. But when he is told ten thousand times, and generation after generation, that Shakespeare was a great artist, the said man believes—not by reason, but by faith. And he, too, repeats that Shakespeare was a great artist, and he buys the complete works of Shakespeare and puts them on his shelves, and he goes to see the marvelous stage-effects which accompany *King Lear* or *Hamlet*, and comes back religiously convinced that Shakespeare was a great artist. All because the passionate few could not keep their admiration of Shakespeare to themselves. This is not cynicism, but truth. And it is important that those who wish to form their literary taste should grasp it.

What causes the passionate few to make such a fuss about literature? There can be only one reply. They find a keen and lasting pleasure in literature. They enjoy literature as some men enjoy beer. The recurrence of this pleasure naturally keeps their interest in literature very much alive. They are forever making new researches, forever practicing on themselves. They learn to understand themselves. They learn to know what they want. Their taste becomes surer and surer as their experience lengthens. They do not enjoy today what will seem tedious to them tomorrow. When they find a book tedious, no amount of popular clatter will persuade them that it is pleasurable; and when they find it pleasurable no chill silence of the street-crowds will affect their conviction that the book is good and permanent. They have faith in themselves. What are the qualities in a book which give keen and lasting pleasure to the passion-

ate few? This is a question so difficult that it has never yet been completely answered. You may talk lightly about truth, insight, knowledge, wisdom, humor, and beauty. But these comfortable words do not really carry you very far, for each of them has to be defined, especially the first and last. It is all very well for Keats in his airy manner to assert that beauty is truth, truth beauty, and that that is all he knows or needs to know. I, for one, need to know a lot more. And I never shall know. Nobody, not even Hazlitt or Sainte-Beuve, has ever finally explained why he thought a book beautiful. I take the first fine lines that come to hand—

> The woods of Arcady are dead,
> And over is their antique joy—

and I say that those lines are beautiful because they give me pleasure. But why? No answer! I only know that the passionate few will broadly agree with me in deriving this mysterious pleasure from these lines. I am only convinced that the liveliness of our pleasure in those and many other lines by the same author will ultimately cause the majority to believe, by faith, that W. B. Yeats is a genius. The one reassuring aspect of the literary affair is that the passionate few are passionate about the same things. A continuance of interest does, in actual practice, lead ultimately to the same judgments. There is only the difference in width of interest. Some of the passionate few lack catholicity, or, rather, the whole of their interest is confined to one narrow channel; they have none left over. These men help specially to vitalize the reputations of the narrower geniuses, such as Crashaw. But their active predilections never contradict the general verdict of the passionate few; rather they reenforce it.

A classic is a work which gives pleasure to the minority which is intensely and permanently interested in literature. It lives on because the minority, eager to renew the sensation of pleasure, is eternally curious and is therefore engaged in an eternal process of rediscovery. A classic does not survive for any ethical reason. It does not survive because it conforms to certain canons, or because neglect would kill it. It survives because it is a source of pleasure and because the passionate few can no more neglect it than a bee can neglect a flower. The passionate few do not read "the right things" because they are right. That is to put the cart before the horse. "The right things" are the right things solely because the passionate few *like* reading them. Hence—and I now arrive at my point—the one primary essential to literary taste is a hot interest in literature. If you have that, all the rest will come. It matters nothing that at present you fail to find pleasure in certain classics. The driving impulse of your interest will force you to acquire experience, and experience will teach you the use of the means of pleasure. You do not know the secret ways of yourself; that is all. A continuance of interest must inevitably bring you to the keenest joys. But, of course, experience may be acquired judiciously or injudiciously, just as Putney may be reached via Waltham Green or via St. Petersburg.

· QUESTIONS ·

1. In the light of today, how would you rewrite Bennett's first sentence?
2. Who in your acquaintance are members of the "passionate few"?
3. Who, says Bennett, make and keep alive the fame of a classical author?
4. Do you approve of the simile in "They enjoy literature as some men enjoy beer"?
5. David Riesman, a noted teacher and author, has referred to books as "gunpowder of the mind." Do you agree with this figure of speech? Would Arnold Bennett have agreed?
6. What is Bennett's definition of a classic? Are "intensely" and "permanently" relative or absolute terms? Do you agree or disagree with the definition?
7. Who was Bishop Stubbs? Crashaw? Hazlitt? Sainte-Beuve? W. B. Yeats?
8. Substitute place names of your own choosing for those in the last sentence.

Theme Subjects: (1) The Best-sellers of Yesteryear; (2) When Doctors Disagree; (3) Everyone to His Own Taste; (4) A Reply to Bennett; (5) My Definition of a Classic; (6) The Lost Art of Reading; (7) The Verdict of the Crowd; (8) Literary Taste: How Not To Form It; (9) A Classic Which Bores Me; (10) A TV Treatment of _____ (a classic).

HOW TO FIND
TIME TO READ

Louis Shores

LOUIS SHORES (1904–   ) was born in Buffalo and received his A.B. degree from the University of Toledo in 1926. He also holds degrees from Columbia (in library science) and George Peabody College. He has been dean of the Library School at Florida State University since 1946. He was made editor-in-chief of *Collier's Encyclopedia* in 1960.

If you are an average reader you can read an average book at the rate of 300 words a minute. You cannot maintain that average, however, unless you read regularly every day. Nor can you attain that speed with hard books in science, mathematics, agriculture, business, or any subject that is new or unfamiliar to you. The chances are you will never attempt that speed with poetry or want to race through some passages in fiction over which you wish to linger. But for most novels, biographies, and books about travel, hobbies or personal interests, if you are an average reader you should have no trouble at all absorbing meaning and pleasure out of 300 printed words every 60 seconds.

Statistics are not always practicable, but consider these: If the average reader can read 300 words a minute of average reading, then in 15 minutes he can read 4,500 words. Multiplied by 7, the days of the week, the product is 31,500. Another multiplication by 4, the weeks of the month, makes 126,000. And final multiplication by 12, the months of the year, result in a grand total of 1,512,000 words. That is the total number of words of average reading an average reader can do in just 15 minutes a day for one year.

Books vary in length from 60,000 to 100,000 words. The average is about 75,000 words. In one year of average reading by an average reader for 15 minutes a day, 20 books will be read. That's a lot of books. It is 4 times the number of books read by public-library borrowers in America. And yet it is easily possible.

One of the greatest of all modern physicians was Sir William Osler. He taught at The Johns Hopkins Medical School. He finished his teaching days at Oxford University. Many of the outstanding physicians today were his students. Nearly all of the practicing doctors of today were brought up on his medical textbooks. Among his many remarkable contributions to medicine are his unpublished notes on how people die.

His greatness is attributed by his biographers and critics not alone to his profound medical knowledge and insight but to his broad general education, for he was a very cultured man. He was interested in what men have done and thought throughout the ages. And he knew that the only way to find out what the best experiences of the race had been was to read what people had written. But Osler's problem was the same as everyone else's, only more so. He was a busy physician, a teacher of physicians, and a medical-research specialist. There was no time in a 24-hour day that did not rightly belong to one of these three occupations, except the few hours for sleep, meals, and bodily functions.

Osler arrived at his solution early. He would read the last 15 minutes before he went to sleep. If bedtime was set for 11:00 P.M., he read from 11:00 to 11:15. If research kept him up to 2:00 A.M., he read from 2:00 to 2:15. Over a very long lifetime, Osler never broke the rule once he had established it.

We have evidence that after a while he simply could not fall asleep until he had done his 15 minutes of reading.

In his lifetime, Osler read a significant library of books. Just do a mental calculation for half a century of 15-minute reading periods daily and see how many books you get. Consider what a range of interests and variety of subjects are possible in one lifetime. Osler read widely outside of his medical specialty. Indeed, he developed from this 15-minute reading habit an avocational specialty to balance his vocational specialization. Among scholars in English literature, Osler is known as an authority on Sir Thomas Browne, seventeenth-century English prose master, and Osler's library on Sir Thomas is considered one of the best anywhere. A great many more things could be said about Osler's contribution to medical research, to the reform of medical teaching, to the introduction of modern clinical methods. But the important point for us here is that he answered supremely well for himself the question all of us who live a busy life must answer: How can I find time to read?

The answer may not be the last 15 minutes before we go to sleep. It may be 15 minutes a day at some other time. In the busiest of calendars there is probably more than one 15-minute period tucked away somewhere still unassigned. I've seen some curious solutions to the problem of finding time for reading.

During army days in the last year of the war I discovered a Pfc. in my squadron who seemed unusually well-read. I found in his 201 file a remarkable civilian and military biography. His four years of service included two overseas, all meritorious but without heroics. Had all of his recommendations for promotion gone through he would have had not only his commission, but probably the rank of captain. But here he was, still a private first-class—because, despite the military emphasis on education, efficiency, loyalty, and all other criteria for determining promotion, accident plays a most important part. Every time this Pfc. had been recommended for promotion, except once, he had been transferred, or come up against a table of organization limitations, or a new change in regulations, or a superior officer who had filled out the forms incorrectly or forgotten them in his third right-hand drawer. And so he had remained a Pfc., and had taken his reward in reading. The amount he did in the army was prodigious.

I was curious about his method. And one day, before I asked him, I found a partial answer. Every day the enlisted men put in an hour of drill and formations. During that time at least one fairly long period of rest was called. Imagine my surprise on my first visit to the drill field when, at the command "rest!" I saw one man in the whole long line pull out a paper pocket book and begin to read, standing up.

When I talked with him, I found that from boyhood he had developed the habit of carrying a little book in his pocket from which he read every minute he was not doing something else. He found a book especially useful and relaxing during the periods of waiting which all of us experience daily—waiting for meals, buses, doctors, hair cuts, telephone calls, dates, performances to begin, or something to happen. There were his 15 minutes a day, or more. There were his 20 books a year—1,000 in a lifetime.

No universal formula can be prescribed. Each of us must find our own 15-minute period each day. It is better if it is regular. Then all additional spare minutes are so many bonuses. And, believe me, the opportunity for reading-bonuses are many and unexpected. Last night an uninvited guest turned up to make five for bridge. I had the kind of paper book at hand to make being the fifth at bridge a joy.

The only requirement is the will to read. With it you can find the 15 minutes no matter how busy the day. And you must have the book at hand. Not even seconds of your 15 minutes must be wasted starting to read. Set that book out in advance. Put it into your pocket when you dress. Put another book beside your bed. Place one in your bathroom. Keep one near your dining table.

You can't escape reading 15 minutes a day, and that means you will read half a book a week, 2 books a month, 20 a year, and 1,000 or more in a reading lifetime. It's an easy way to become well read.

· QUESTIONS ·

1. Compare and contrast this article with "Habit" by William James.
2. What advice given in Osler's "A Way of Life" is reflected in Shores' comment on the famous physician?
3. Make an analysis of your reading habits. How much time each day do you

spend on magazines? Newspapers? Books other than those assigned? Radio? Television?

4. Aside from textbooks, are your life and attitudes toward life being influenced by books?

5. Name five books you would most like to read "if you had time."

6. By Shores' calculation, how long would it take you to read these five books?

Theme Subjects: (1) Books Are (Are Not) Stupid Stuff; (2) TV Is (Is Not) More Educational Than Books; (3) I Don't Like Treadmill Reading; (4) My Reading Program and How I Propose To Fulfill It; (5) Life Is Too Short for Reading.

SEMANTICS:

DENOTATION AND

CONNOTATION

John C. Sherwood

JOHN COLLINGSWOOD SHERWOOD (1918–   ) was born in Hempstead, New York, and was graduated from Lafayette College (1941) and Yale University, taking his Ph.D. in 1945. Instructor in English at Cornell University from 1944 to 1946, he joined the faculty of the University of Oregon, where he is professor of English. He is author of *Discourse of Reason* (1964); coauthor of *Reading and Rhetoric from Harper's* (1963); and *A Writer's Reader* (1950).

A convenient scheme for classifying the problems of language is one which distinguishes in terms of the relationships which words by their nature possess. A given word may be regarded as having three rela-

Adapted from *Discourse of Reason: A Brief Handbook of Semantics and Logic,* second edition, by John C. Sherwood. Copyright © 1960, 1964 by John C. Sherwood. Reprinted by permission of Harper & Row, Publishers.

tionships: (1) a relationship with the other words with which it is used, (2) a relationship with the persons who utter and hear it, and (3) a relationship with the thing it represents (the *referent*). The relationships of words with each other are a matter of grammar, for grammar is not primarily a set of prohibitions (though it may be so taught) but a set of rules for combining the different classes of words into intelligible sequences. The relationship of a word to the thing or things it represents is the primary and proper area of concern for academic semantics, but some semanticists have also concerned themselves very usefully with the relationships between words and people. Here semantics tends to overlap rhetoric, but with this significant difference: rhetoric is traditionally an art of persuasion, a set of devices to enable us to move the emotions of others with words, whereas this type of semantics has been concerned partly with studying the emotional effects of language theoretically, and partly with helping us to understand the emotional effects of words in order to resist those effects when others attempt to employ them on us—a purpose almost opposite to the aims of rhetoric. Understandably, the more philosophical semanticists have tended to be concerned with the first aspect, and the more popular writers with the second.

For our present purposes it is enough to notice that the meaning of most words has two overlapping yet distinguishable aspects. A word has its *denotation*, a certain set of things in the world which it stands for and points to; but it also has its *connotation*, a set of feelings and associations which it arouses in the people who use it. The word "traitor" denotes the kind of person who has "given aid and comfort to the enemy in time of war," but it has in addition all sorts of unpleasant associations based on our natural attitudes toward traitors. The discussion of semantics included here is built around these two aspects. . . .

DENOTATION

Words as Symbols

At first glance it might seem that a study of denotation would be superfluous and that no educated user of language could ever forget that words stand for things: how otherwise could they be of use to us? Still it is well to remind ourselves, first, that words are signs, objects whose real value lies in the fact that they *point* to something else; and, second, that they are the particular kind of sign called a *symbol.* Symbols differ from certain other types of signs in that the connection between the sign and the thing it points to is entirely a matter of human convention. A cloud is a sign of rain because it brings the rain, and a weathervane is a sign of the wind because the wind controls it, but there is no special reason why a tool used for digging should have the sign "spade," except that speakers of English, through long usage and custom, have chosen to make it so. Verbal symbolism is even more arbitrary than some other kinds of symbolism. A cross naturally suggests Christianity, just as a sword suggests war, or a skull death, but there is no natural reason why we should say "dog" when the Frenchman says "chien." Words, then, are symbols of things—but two qualifications are in order. Certain types of words are perhaps not strictly symbolic or are symbolic only in a very special way; such are prepositions and conjunctions, whose real function is syntactical, the function of joining other words together. Furthermore, the things symbolized—the referents—are of the most various kinds.

Words may stand for existing objects such as bathing suits and unabridged dictionaries; for possible or imagined objects, such as Martians and unicorns; for qualities, both physical and moral, such as hardness and goodness; for thoughts and feelings, states, actions, and events, classes and groups, abstractions, concepts, and relations. Often the thing represented is quite complex, or may have existence only in our own minds. What is the "thing" to which the name "England" corresponds—a plot of ground, a people, a government, a culture, or the sum of all? And if we feel that we can easily define England in terms of measured boundaries, what about such a term as "Western Civilization," whose chronological and geographical limits we could never define with any exactitude? What, too, are the things to which the poet's "imagination" and the psychoanalyst's "id" correspond? Can we point to the section of the brain that contains them? Now all these terms are useful and even necessary, and we should not hold them suspect because we cannot feel or handle their referents. We must keep in mind, however, that behind words lie not merely tangible objects, but a miscellaneous collection of physical and mental phenomena of differing degrees and kinds of material reality, and that the existence of a word is no assurance of the exist-

ence of a corresponding object outside the mind.

It is equally important to remember that no mystic bond connects the word to its referent. A few words only seem to have a natural appropriateness, chiefly onomatopoeic words like "hiss" and "murmur." Yet not only the ordinary people who shout at foreigners to make them understand but great thinkers often speak as if each thing had one word which belonged to it by right and to no other. Plato argues that the letters composing a word are (or ought to be) an indication of the thing represented; while Bacon, in order to arrive at the nature of heat, analyzes all the objects to which men have applied the term "hot," from fire to pepper, and Aristotle believes that, even when a word has several senses, there is something common to them all. Actually the relationship is rather shifty and unstable business. One word may serve to designate a series of quite unrelated objects; a railroad train is something very different from the train of a wedding gown, though the idea of towing or pulling is present in both. Words also shift their meanings in the process of time. "Marshal" once meant a farrier, but now designates the highest kind of military officer; "prove" once meant "test" and now usually means "establish." A "knight" is a nobleman, but the German cognate "Knecht" now means a servant. A guinea pig is not a pig and does not come from Guinea. Any lingering illusion about a natural correspondence between words and things should disappear if we have occasion to translate from one language to another. Sometimes there are words in one language for which the other has no equivalent; we cannot express our idea of "home" with any single French word, while for the expressive French "patrie" we can only offer the clumsy German-sounding "fatherland." Foreign words for colors may not even correspond to ours; Whatmough reports that Welsh, Navaho, and Latin do not distinguish green from blue, and to Homer the sea is the color of wine. Mark Twain laments comically that the German "Zug" and "Schlag" can mean anything, but what would a German say of our "get" and "case"? Beginning students may attempt word-for-word translations, but scholars know better.

In the seventeenth century certain thinkers dreamed of a language in which the correspondence of words and things would be stable and reliable; Swift makes fun of them in his picture of a group of scientists who have lost all faith in words and communicate by pointing at objects. The dream, we know now, is futile. The world around us does not consist of a definite number of easily distinguishable objects to be named as Adam named the animals. It is, as William James called it, a "booming, buzzing confusion" out of which we select a certain number of phenomena considered worthy enough for the assignment of words. Whether a thing will have a name or not depends on our feelings and interests and the framework of our thinking. A vocabulary that covered the whole of existence would be infinitely large or at least beyond the capacity of human memory; it would be as useless as a map made to the same scale as the area it represented. *Punch* imagines a Greek word meaning "chalk under the fingernails of

sixth form masters," but this seems a trivial object to have a word to itself, and most of the time we are more selective. Because domestic animals have been so important to human economy, we frequently devise, for a given animal, not merely a name for the species, but names for different sexes, ages, and types—horse, stallion, mare, gelding, colt, Percheron. In naming dinosaurs we are content with a name for the species; it seems unnecessary to have a special term for a baby female *tricerotops*. The existence of a word is usually attributable to our need for it.

Largely by necessity, then, words (other than proper nouns) stand not for individual objects but for classes of objects; hence to use a certain word is to indicate that the object which it denotes belongs to the same class as certain other objects, which by accepted usage are called by the same name. To speak of a "bat" is to say that the object of discussion is a mammal that can fly and has certain other known characteristics; if we are careful, that is all we understand it to mean. Some words classify in terms of more characteristics than others. To call a creature a "dog" is to say more about it than to call it a "mammal"; the latter word designates a very large class of beings with relatively few qualities in common.

By the nature of things words classify, and by the nature of things they also abstract. When we call an animal a "dog" we do so because it has certain biological characteristics —four legs, warm blood, certain kinds of teeth, and so on; when we call it a "domestic animal" we mean that it is kept for use by human beings; when we call it "man's best friend" we are talking about its loyalty. In each case we abstract, that is, we isolate certain aspects of the denoted object, leaving others out of account. To call a man a "criminal" is to consider him solely with reference to his conduct on certain occasions, without reference to anything else in his character or situation.

The classifications which common words make, unlike the classes marked out by scientific terminology, are often very unsystematic and illogical. The words we use to designate ethnic groups other than our own show this lack of system: sometimes they classify in terms of geography or nationality (Swiss), sometimes by language (Bantu), sometimes by real or supposed physical characteristics (Indian). Classification varies in extent and in kind from language to language as well. In the language of the Cuna, a Central American Indian group, animals have different names by day and by night; in English we do not make such distinctions. Sometimes we decide to alter our classifications, and a whale ceases to be a fish, though if we classified solely on the basis of shape and habitat it would remain a fish. Sometimes we have difficulty deciding whether the word applies or not: is a Neanderthal man or an unborn child a human being? No one disputes the salient characteristics of a cave man or an embryo, but we may not all agree that they are properly denoted by the term "human being."

General, Vague, and Ambiguous Terms

Normally we answer the questions of *word choice* by advising a careful use of the dictionary, a respect for correct usage, and the use of concrete terms. (A semanticist would add: Keep your eye on the referent!) Teachers tend to emphasize these points and with good reason, since the beginning writer often tends to be careless and vague; but emphasizing these points alone oversimplifies the matter. Words may be general, they may be vague, or they may be ambiguous. A word is general if it designates a very large number of objects with little in common: words like "animal," "vehicle," or "tool." A word is vague if the boundaries of its denotation are indistinct: we could hardly hope to frame an ironclad distinction between "hill" and "mountain," or between "large" and "small." A small elephant is larger than a large ant, and our idea of a small car has changed a good deal in the last few years. A word is ambiguous if it has several accepted meanings: we must decide from the context whether "table" means a piece of furniture or a column of figures. The word "plant" is general because it refers to half the living creation, the word "similar" is vague because we are not sure of the degree and kind of resemblance intended between compared things, and the word "ash" is ambiguous because it might refer to a tree or the residue of a fire. It would be easy to suggest that we avoid such words but hard to do so in practice. We would hardly wish to avoid general terms anyway; they are the means by which we indicate broad relations and large classes. We need the general term "institution" to cover in a broad way the social units which we describe more specifically as colleges, prisons, asylums, and so on;

they have something in common which the name serves to suggest. Vague words too have their uses; we can never define absolutely the words "some" or "several," but we need such words all the same. In general, we say, we should be as definite and concrete as is possible and appropriate. Merely as a matter of vividness we may prefer the particular to the general, but the specific term is not necessarily more exact and may even be less clear than the inclusive general term. We can sometimes escape from vagueness by statistics and speak of a six-footer instead of a tall man, but too much precision would be pedantic. Often a vague word becomes specific in context; we could not say how tall "tall" is, but we could say within a few inches how tall a tall man is. Context tends to take care of ambiguous words also. The term "buffalo" is somewhat ambiguous, since our early settlers applied the term (which in the old world designates what we call a "water buffalo") to an animal equivalent to the European bison, and in a scientific or legal context we should have to be pedantic and call it a "bison"; but in such specific sentences as "The Sioux hunted the buffalo" there is no ambiguity. Moderate care and exactness, varying with the occasion, is what is needed, not a deep suspiciousness of all but the most concrete terms.

Words as Labels

The failure to understand the symbolic nature of language and to distinguish clearly between words and the things they stand for can have serious practical consequences. To be able to call something by its right name is satisfying, for it makes us feel that we understand the situation. The feeling of satisfaction may not always be justified. We are ill and experience a series of well-defined symptoms; the doctor comes and gives a name to them: pneumonia, endocarditis, neurasthenia, and we feel comforted by knowing the name of what is annoying us. Perhaps the comfort is justified, because the doctor's use of the term means that he understands the nature of the disorder and the proper method of treatment; but perhaps the name is a mere *label* for the symptoms, and we know no more than we did before. (Sometimes too a term that is meaningful to the doctor is a mere label to the patient.) Early chemistry had a term "phlogiston," designating a substance supposed to be weightless, odorless, and intangible; it was thought to be the cause of fire. We know today, of course, that phlogiston has no existence at all; but the early chemist, equipped with his label, thought he had understood the cause of fire. In literary criticism and the social sciences we are in special danger of confusing labeling with analysis or investigation, and to throw about terms such as "urban," "unconscious," "irony," and "empathy," instead of looking at the thing itself. Such labeling is not entirely futile; it communicates something of the speaker's opinion but not always much information.

Even when labeling is moderately informative, it may do us a disservice by stopping thought; having applied the label, we do not feel obliged to go further. The driver is a "woman," hence erratic; the professor is a "Red," hence dangerous; the girl is "Irish," hence black-haired, blue-eyed, charming, warm-hearted, and impulsive. There is a special danger when we use racial designations in that way. Terms like "wog" are hardly a *cause* of prejudice. Rather they serve to express the prejudices we already feel on the basis of economic or political rivalry or our primitive fears of the strange and unknown; yet even so they can do a great deal of damage by helping to confirm or continue prejudices we might otherwise outgrow and by infecting others with the same feelings. Even the ordinary, neutral names for races have to be used with care. A term such as "German" is, to begin with, ambiguous; it may refer to present or former citizenship, to language, to place of residence, or possibly to race, assuming that it is possible to identify a German race as distinct from inhabitants of Germany or people who speak German. To call a person "German" is to say one of these things and (if we are careful) to do no more. There is a German culture differing somewhat from ours, and we could probably make a fairly plausible list of ways in which the average German differs from the average American, but the differences among individuals are so great that we could never assume that the person we have labeled will have all the average characteristics of his class. *Life* magazine reports the case of a man who, once classified as "feeble-minded," remained imprisoned in an institution for fifty-nine years, though he could play eight musical instruments, was a skilled printer, and was gentle and amiable. If we can keep in mind that words classify and abstract, we may come closer to avoiding such errors. . . .

ARGUING ABOUT WORDS

Another pitfall in the use of words is the tendency to argue about terms when there is no real dispute about the facts of the case. William James illustrates the point with the following puzzle: A man is pursuing a squirrel around a tree. The squirrel circles, clinging to the bark, so that the trunk always conceals him from the man. Both man and squirrel are going around the tree; is the man going around the squirrel? Here there is no dispute about the movements of man or squirrel, but only about the relevance of the term "around": the argument is, in a practical sense at least, quite trivial. Such quibbling is common in literary criticism. John Dryden wonders whether *The Faerie Queene* is a genuine epic, Samuel Johnson doubts whether Shakespeare's plays are true tragedies, and some modern editors try to call the Book of Job a drama; in none of these cases is there a question of what the work is really like or even of its literary merit but only of the definition of a term. Necessarily verbal disputes sometimes acquire practical consequences, especially when the disputed words occur in a law or regulation. In Ellis Parker Butler's "Pigs Is Pigs," the express agent and his customer argue as to whether a shipment of guinea pigs should pay the rate for *pets* or the higher rate for *pigs*. The dispute can hardly be called pointless, since money is involved, though the agent is obviously more concerned with words than facts, or he would see that for all practical purposes the animals are pets. Disputes about important questions of fact or value may take the *form* of disputes about words; it is only the dispute in which nothing is at stake but the term which is idle and foolish.

A final error is the failure, accidental or deliberate, to keep to the same meaning of a term throughout a discussion. The hedonist argues that pleasure is the only motive for human action and that the philanthropist and the martyr give up their possessions and lives because sacrifice is what gives them pleasure. Before we give ourselves up to cynicism, however, let us notice that, although in the beginning of the argument "pleasure" seems to have its normal meaning of pleasant satisfactions, by the end of the argument it seems to mean simply whatever line of conduct we voluntarily choose. The argument is not only cynical but nearly meaningless or at best tautological, saying that we do what we wish to do because we wish to do it. A television program celebrated what passes in mass-communication circles for "faith." The theme was illustrated by three examples: a minister's faith that his bankrupt church would be able to stay open (an eccentric millionaire subsequently sent him a million dollars), his faith that a little boy run over by a truck had achieved immortality, and his faith that an untested pneumonia vaccine just invented by his prospective son-in-law would cure, not kill, his ailing daughter (needless to say, it cured her). The second variety of faith we recognize as normal Christian faith, but the "faith" in the vaccine is either a calculated risk based on a rational appraisal of the doctor's character and scientific stature, or it is no better than the faith that keeps cancer quacks in business. As for a faith that depends for its fulfillment on the generosity of eccentric millionaires, it has neither a rational nor a theological basis and is bound to be frequently disappointed.

DEFINITION

One obvious escape from verbal disputes is the careful definition of terms. Definition often consists merely in offering a synonym, but since there are few exact synonyms in English, careful definition requires something more. A convenient formula, though open to certain logical objections (it really defines the thing rather than the word), is Aristotle's *genus* and *differentia*. We tell to what general class (*genus*) the referent of the word belongs and then enumerate the characteristics (*differentia*) which distinguish it from other members of the class. Consider, for instance, the following definitions from the *New English Dictionary;* the genus is in italics, the remainder of the definition constituting the differentia:

VESSEL: Any *structure* designed to float upon and traverse the water for the carriage of persons or goods.
SHIP: A large sea-going *vessel.*
WARSHIP: A *ship* armed and manned for war.
BATTLESHIP: A *warship* of the largest and most heavily armored class.

The "extended definition," in which a term is defined at length in a short essay, though a useful exercise, is rather a description than a definition, since it goes far beyond what is necessary to show the correct use of the word or to identify the referent.

The necessity for defining terms in controversy arises from

the fact that so many words in English have more than one accepted meaning; the definition serves to inform the reader as to which of the possible meanings the writer intends to use. A discussion of the "teaching of English" can only lead to futility if the writer means by "English" the teaching of composition and the reader assumes that he is referring to the whole field of "English," including literature.

Not infrequently in controversy we encounter definitions which cannot honestly be regarded as corresponding to ordinary usage, but which are obviously manufactured especially to support the argument, as in the following instance:

Vivisection is experimenting with living beings, and that's just what "liberals" are doing today—carrying out experiments on living people to see if they can stand them. Progressive education, socialized medicine, stealing money from the taxpayer to support bureaucracy—it's all vivisection.

If "vivisection" were used in the ordinary sense, it would obviously not be applicable to progressive education or socialized medicine; the definition has been distorted in order to get a certain effect. . . .

Conclusions

Words, then, are symbols whose arbitrary relationships to the things they represent must always be kept in mind if we are to avoid the pitfalls that interfere with rational discourse. Not only must we be very careful in using vague and general terms; we must scrupulously refrain from substituting labeling for learning, from quarreling about terms, and from allowing shifts of meaning to unsettle our arguments.

CONNOTATION

In discussing denotation we covered what we normally think of as the *meaning* of a word; but denotation is seldom the whole story. "Lot" and "homesite" might refer to the same patch of ground, and yet a realtor might regard the latter word as more enticing and thus better suited to his purposes. The words "booze" and "liquor" designate the same fluid, but they do not at all have the same impact on the hearer or reader. What makes the difference in each case is that area of meaning called *connotation,* by which we mean the feelings and associations that cluster around all but a very few neutral, sterile words. Connotation cannot always be adequately covered by dictionaries, for it is a shifting, vague area of meaning which does not lend itself to sharp definition. Sometimes, for example, connotations are personal or local (the word "Yankee" would have very different connotations in New England and in the South). But most connotations are commonly associated with their words by enough people so that communication of feeling can take place. For, consciously or unconsciously, we express our feelings about the world through connotations; to use a word with a certain connotation is to pass judgment on the thing designated. If we are sensitive to connotations we can better express our own feelings, we can better appreciate the skillful handling of connotation in literature, and we can be on our guard against allowing our opinions to be molded against our better judgment by the impact of emotional language. "Speech in its essence is not neutral," says Kenneth Burke; "it is intensely moral—its names for objects contain the emotional overtones which give us the cues as to how we should act toward those objects."

To be sure, a word often evokes certain feelings only because of our attitudes toward the *object* being designated. It is natural that the terms "brainwash" and "concentration camp" should have unpleasant overtones, since the things themselves are thoroughly unpleasant. The words "Quaker" (meaning literally one who quakes) and "Methodist" (meaning a person of methodical habits) were originally mocking nicknames bestowed on those religious groups by their critics and carried derogatory associations; but once the organizations themselves had gained respectability, the terms became simply the names of the organizations and lost their original derisive meanings: at each stage, the feelings evoked by the words were conditioned by prevailing attitudes toward the *thing* being designated.

But in much connotation, feelings are suggested more by *words* than things. As we have already noted, we frequently find more than one word for the same object, each one suggesting a different range of feelings, so that the feelings seem to belong to the word rather than to the object itself. "Foam suggests the sea, froth suggests beer," says Fowler; it would be hard to describe objectively how foam differs from froth. A young girl would rather be called "slim" (or better "svelte") than "skinny." In dealing with the unpleasant facts of life, we are fond of manufacturing *euphemisms*— neutral or pleasant-sounding terms that somehow do not arouse the feelings that naturally go with the object. So to die becomes to "pass away," a prison becomes a "reformatory" or even a "home," old people become "senior citizens," inferior students become "exceptional learners," and the school principal in the *New Yorker* cartoon reassuringly tells the anxious parent, "There's no such thing as a bad boy. Hostile, perhaps. Aggressive, recalcitrant, destructive, even sadistic. But not *bad*." It is as if we thought we could magically change the nature of the object by changing the name it bears.

CONNOTATION AND SPECIAL VOCABULARIES

Some words take all or part of their connotation from the circumstances of use; slang terms, illiterate or dialect forms may have somewhat disagreeable or comic connotations because they are associated with the lower levels of society. Many slang terms seem to exist to express irreverent or unorthodox feelings and are perhaps called slang because they are felt as subversive not only of good English but of standard moral values as well. If someone calls the church a "gospel factory," the minister a "hallelujah peddler," and the members "amen-snorters," he is probably not very pious; if he calls his wife a "ball-and-chain," a "help-spend," or a "loud speaker," he has probably a rather cynical view of marriage. Such terms as "eye burner," "grade grabber," and "greasy grind" do not sound as if they had been invented by the members of Phi Beta Kappa. If such a slang term undergoes promotion and becomes part of the standard vocabulary, it is likely to shed its picturesque connotations in the process.

At the opposite extreme from

slang, we have formal vocabularies whose use is reserved for special topics and occasions. It is natural for an English-speaking Protestant to resort, in religious services, to the vocabulary and rhythms of the King James Bible and the Book of Common Prayer.

Man that is born of a woman, hath but a short time to live and is full of misery. He cometh up, and is cut down like a flower; he fleeth as it were a shadow, and never continueth in one stay.

In the midst of life we are in death: of whom may we seek for succour but of thee, O Lord, who for our sins art justly displeased? (The Burial of the Dead)

Generations of use have given this basically fine language an additional magic, and more modern translations of scripture are likely to seem somewhat flat by comparison, however valuable they may be in communicating to the reader untrained in Elizabethan English the plain sense of the text.

METAPHOR

Slang is likely to be metaphorical; and in general metaphor is one of the most effective devices for extending connotation when, in poetry or some other context which demands concentration and the precise expression of emotion, we wish to express a feeling that has not become attached to any of the words normally used to describe the object we are discussing. The metaphor, we remember, is a condensed simile; we call one object by the name of another, meaning not that they are identical but that there is some significant point of comparison. "House of God" not only names a church but suggests the divine presence the worshiper feels there; "family tree" suggests not only the branching form which the genealogy takes on paper but also the ideas of growth and strength; "ship of state" (for government) suggests the ideas of order and subordination, of striving toward a goal, of courage in the face of danger. Metaphor is, in fact, one of the chief means by which language grows.

CONTROL OF CONNOTATION

The control of connotation is particularly important in artistic works, but the problem has likewise its grossly practical side. All too many writers and speakers tend to confuse the communication of information with the expression of feeling. Writers of advertising are notoriously skillful at this sort of thing. The slogan "pure as the tear that falls upon a sister's grave" pretended to describe the quality of a brand of port wine, but if interpreted literally is not very complimentary; what the advertiser hoped to accomplish was to get an uncritical, sentimental response to emotionally charged words like "pure" and "sister" and somehow attach these emotional responses to his product, however remote the actual connection between wine and a deceased sister. It is possible to talk at considerable length without doing much more than play with emotions. . . .

The problem is especially complex when we deal with *value words* —words like "good," "evil," "lovely," "pretty," "useful," "elegant," and the like, whose principal function is to indicate the approval or disapproval of the speaker. By some writers such words are regarded as purely emotive—as "snarl" and "purr" words which do nothing but indicate an attitude. Generally, however, such words can be regarded as at least vaguely descriptive; they say or imply that a thing has certain characteristics and that as a consequence it merits our approval or disapproval. Even "good," one of the most general of our value words, can be concrete in context: we have a fair idea of what is meant by a good used car, or the long-dreamed-of good five-cent cigar, or even Perelman's good five-cent psychiatrist. A good doctor cures the sick and a good lawyer wins cases—the context makes the specific meaning clear. Many value words, such as "chaste," "blasphemous," "neat," "helpful," are quite descriptive. If value words were not descriptive, we should not need so many of them; a small set, expressing various grades of approval or disapproval, would be enough. (Some people of limited imagination do manage to get along with a few words like "nice," "lousy," or "cool.") In using such words we want to select the term which most exactly describes both the object and our feeling.

Unhappily, value words are not always used either carefully or without design, the misuse being especially common in politics and advertising. Certain words often used in controversy become after a while so charged with emotion that they are, in Hayakawa's phrase, "loaded," and hence dangerous to use, even when in origin fairly descriptive; at least one should be on one's guard when one hears them in controversy. Political terms such as "social-ist," "Communist," "fascist," or even "totalitarian" are capable of moderately exact definition in terms of party membership or acceptance of a particular belief: neither the socialist nor his enemy doubts that he believes in "public ownership of the means of production." Terms like "liberal" and "conservative" are harder to define because they are essentially relative, like "large" and "small," and change with the times, so that today's "conservative" is a conservative because he holds to the beliefs of the nineteenth-century liberal; and yet among careful users in proper context the terms are informative. But all these terms are used more often than not as mere terms of praise or abuse, so that a man may qualify as a socialist for wanting cheap electrical power and as a fascist for opposing racketeering in labor. Fluoridation, health insurance, desegregation—all pass for "Communist plots" in the language of modern political oratory. Even words fairly neutral and innocent in themselves may become loaded in certain contexts; modern worship of science makes the term attractive, and hence we get such phrases as "scientific grammar" and "scientific criticism" to designate studies that could not possibly apply the true scientific method to their purposes nor attain the mathematical exactitude of the physical sciences. A "people's democracy" is likely to be a dictatorship. The cheapest and hence most standardized model of one contemporary automobile used to be called "Custom," though "custom" ought to refer to something made to order; the corresponding model of another make was called "Plaza," suggestive of fine hotels and limousines. All this is innocent enough, since no one buys a car sight unseen, but the orator who calls his mildly conservative opponent a "fascist" is far from innocent.

SLANTING

So far we have been considering connotation with reference to single words and phrases, but there is also what we might call the *connotation of the whole*, the emotional import of the whole passage, which is not merely the sum total of the connotations, but the result of the complex interaction of the material presented, the vocabulary, and even such subtle qualities as sentence rhythm. Here as always we, as writers, must be careful to give exactly the feeling we wish to convey, and as readers we must avoid being improperly influenced by the artful manipulation of language. Let us take the following passage from Thorstein Veblen:

As it finds expression in the life of the barbarian, prowess manifests itself in two main directions—force and fraud. In varying degrees these two forms of expression are similarly present in modern warfare, in the pecuniary occupations, and in sports and games. Both lines of aptitudes are cultivated and strengthened by the life of sport as well as by the more serious forms of emulative life. Strategy or cunning is an element invariably present in games, as also in warlike pursuits and in the chase. In all of these employments strategy tends to develop into finesse and chicane. Chicane, falsehood, browbeating, hold a well-secured place in the method of procedure of any athletic contest and in games generally. The habitual employment of an umpire, and the minute technical regulations governing the limits and details of permissible fraud and strategic advantage, sufficiently attest the fact that fraudulent practices and attempts to overreach one's opponents are not adventitious features of the game. In the nature of the case habituation to sports should conduce to a fuller development of the aptitude for fraud; and the prevalence in the community of the predatory temperament which inclines men to sports connotes a prevalence of sharp practice and callous disregard of the interests of others, individually and collectively. Resort to fraud, in any guise and under any legitimation of law or custom, is an expression of a narrowly self-regarding habit of mind. It is needless to dwell at any length on the economic value of this feature of the sporting character.[1]

What this passage says in effect is that since both force and strategy are necessary for success in war, business, and sport, sport is a good preparation for business. This proposition (except for the implication that force is commonly used in business) is one that many businessmen and most coaches would applaud, yet it is expressed in such a way as to make both business and sport seem not only evil but a little ridiculous. For the strategy which is a perfectly legitimate part of most competitive games, Veblen uses extremely derogatory terms—"fraud," "chicane," "falsehood," "sharp practice." Skill in play becomes "aptitude for fraud"; the umpire instead of enforcing fair play settles "the limits and details of permissible fraud"; and an interest in sports shows a "predatory temperament." If we can analyze such passages and

---

[1] Thorstein Veblen, *The Theory of the Leisure Class*, New York, 1931, pp. 273–274.

can distinguish clearly between the information conveyed and the tone which has been given to the facts by the use of words having certain connotations, we shall be better able to protect ourselves from improper verbal influences.

This process by which an emotional tone is given to facts in order to influence the reader's attitude is aptly called *slanting*. With sufficient ingenuity, one can do remarkable tricks with facts and give a completely false impression without stating any outright falsehood. Here is a British description of the battles of Lexington and Concord:

. . . The Troops now combated with fresh Ardour, & marched in their return with undaunted countenances, receiving Sheets of fire all the way for many Miles, yet having no visible Enemy to combat with, for they never would face 'em in an open field, but always skulked & fired from behind Walls, & trees, & out of Windows of Houses, but this cost them dear for the Soldiers entered those dwellings, & put all the Men to death. Lord Percy has gained great honor by the conduct thro' this day of severe Service he was exposed to the hottest of the fire & animated the Troops with great coolness & spirit. Several officers are wounded & about 100 soldiers. The killed amount to near 50, as to the Enemy we can have no exact acct. but it is said there was about ten times the Number of them engaged, & that near 1000 of 'em have fallen.

Except for the exaggeration of the Colonial casualties, the details here are accurate enough, but one gets the impression that the "return" of the troops to their refuge in Boston was a victory of some kind. Notice, for instance, how much more of the passage is concerned with the courage of the troops than is concerned with the outcome of the action,

and how the Colonists' prudence in fighting from shelter becomes "skulking."

Conclusions

One should avoid the easy position that the use of language to arouse or control emotion is dangerous and that as far as possible we ought to limit ourselves and others to the neutral expression of verifiable facts. Modern logicians have in fact managed to escape from emotional language through the use of symbolic logic, a kind of algebra of propositions. But we can hardly hope to escape from emotion in our everyday use of words, no matter how much we sharpen our perception of connotations. Nor would we wish to escape; having feelings, we wish to express them, get others to share them, even at times to impose them on others. We should not wish to violate reason or morality in our use of words. We shall always reject this sort of thing:

Can we endure four more years of political cannibalism at the hands of a predatory, power-hungry conglomeration of third-rate bosses and bureaucrats who can only stay in power by buying the votes of the nonproductive elements in society? Can we put up with a moron government whose stupidity, rigidity, and cupidity are leading us to the abyss of totalitarian tyranny?

But what about this?

With malice toward none; with charity for all; with firmness in the right as God gives us to see the right, let us strive on to finish the work we are in; to bind up the nation's wounds; to care for him who shall have borne the battle, and for his widow, and his orphan—to do all which may achieve and cherish a just and lasting peace among ourselves, and with all nations.

Surely we regard the sentiments from Lincoln's Second Inaugural Address as worthy ones; surely we would wish that more people in Reconstruction days had been moved by his rhetoric. Insofar as feeling is a legitimate part of human life, it is necessarily a part of language.

And just so far as we strive in other areas to make feeling subservient to reason and law, just so far do we strive to control emotional language. A knowledge of semantics and of the kindred discipline of rhetoric can help us to exercise this control; and it is no flaw in the disciplines themselves if they can be utilized by a Hitler as well as a Lincoln.

· QUESTIONS ·

1. Explain clearly what the author means (in this essay) by *denotation, connotation, referent, abstract* (v.), *slang, euphemism, metaphor,* and *slanting.* (If you can't do this, you had better read again this idea-packed, closely reasoned essay.)
2. Two important sections of this essay are labeled "Conclusions." Summarize the ideas presented in each.
3. Does this selection suggest why "the pen is mightier than the sword"? Or do you think it is not?
4. Discuss (or write a theme about) the verbal technique of some essay, speech, or newspaper article which reveals an obvious use (or misuse) of emotional language.
5. Compare and contrast this essay with that by Robert H. Thouless.
6. Your understanding of this article will be enriched if you can identify some or all of the following: Bacon, Aristotle, Whatmough, Swift, William James, *Punch,* John Dryden, Fowler, Perelman, Hayakawa.
7. Your understanding of this essay will be similarly enriched if you can define the following: id, onomatopoeic, farrier, ethnic, ambiguous, relevance, tautological, impact, derogatory, subversive, emotive, chicane, adventitious, predatory, pecuniary. (Some, perhaps not all, of these words you may wish to add to your active vocabulary.)

Theme Subjects: (1) Like Fire, Language Should Not Be Played With; (2) Why Bull Sessions Are (Are Not) a Waste of Time; (3) What I Feel About Slang; (4) A Language Pitfall I Now Try To Avoid; (5) My Report on a Slanted Argument.

LANGUAGE INFLATION

Robert Cluett

ROBERT CLUETT (1932–   ) was born in New York and received his secondary school education at Lawrenceville. He holds B.S. and M.A. degrees from Columbia University. After service in the U. S. Coast Guard, he began teaching at the Kent School, Kent, Connecticut, where he is now an English master. He has published a number of articles and is coauthor of *Effective English Prose* (1965).

Some years ago, in one of his wittier columns, James Reston pointed out that the American language is suffering from inflation. He deplored our tendency to elevate the janitor to the post of Custodial Engineer and the file clerk to the position of Records Supervisor.

He neglected to indicate that all he had touched on was inflation of nomenclature. The analogy is apt but misleading, for the inflation in mere nomenclature is like the rise in the consumer price index: It is only a symptom, and it should not be mistaken for the substantive facts that it represents. Just as the rise of that index is but one symptom of altered values, of a changed relationship between the government and our economy, and of a radically transformed credit structure, so is the inflation of our no-menclature but one symptom of what we are doing to ourselves and to our values in the cause of progress. Our real linguistic inflation lies in an almost entirely new use of language that is the fruit of the social sciences, of new social forms, and of modern technology.

The inflation of nomenclature could be grouped with other inflationary phenomena under a heading called *the failure of language to correspond to the truth as we have known it.* Quite obviously we know that the janitor is no engineer and that the file clerk supervises very little indeed, and we recognize that the inflationary euphemisms by which we now name them are but a kind of balm to their vanity; technology having eliminated much of our menial work, we give to the remaining menial jobs names that

From *Teachers College Record*, March, 1965. This article is reprinted with the author's permission and has been adapted by him for this edition of this book.

make them sound like something they are not. Surely it is no sin, we say, to spend more verbal coin on these jobs than they are worth; surely in the interests of better labor relations, we say, such small lies are perfectly innocuous.

There are, however, other forms of overexpenditure that are less easily recognized and are far less innocuous. I herewith offer one man's view of what our real linguistic inflation is and of what it means to us.

THE MODERN STYLE

The two principal forms of the new linguistic inflation, denial of personhood and the annihilation of fact, both work to produce the modern style—sometimes jointly, sometimes singly. By comparing it with the style of Thomas Macaulay, we can see what the qualities of the modern style are.

Consider Macaulay:

Those members—a numerous body—who envied and dreaded Montague readily became the unconscious tools of the cunning malice of Sunderland, whom Montague had refused to defend in Parliament, and who, though detested by the opposition, contrived to exercise some influence over that party through the instrumentality of Charles Duncombe. Duncombe, indeed, had his own reasons for hating Montague, who had turned him out of the place of Cashier of the Excise. A serious charge was brought against the Board of the Treasury, and especially against its chief. He was the inventor of Exchequer Bills, and they were popularly called Montague's notes. He had induced the Parliament to enact that those bills, even when at a discount in the market, should be

received at par by the collectors of Revenue. . . .

Notice that with three exceptions, the grammatical subject of each of the verbs above is a *person;* those men that are acted upon are acted upon by other men. In each of his sentences, Macaulay implies that men are acting through a conscious choice between clear alternatives—and this in a discussion of an economic phenomenon, the monetary and credit crisis of 1698.

Consider another economist, writing recently about our monetary troubles:

Due to pressure of savings available for real estate investment, there is little doubt that over a period of the last few years there have been considerable excesses in certain types of construction and in specific areas. This overbuilding is perhaps most apparent in motels, hotels, and high-rise, high-price apartment houses. Evidence at the present time is to the effect that construction will remain at a high level in 1964, but a serious slow-up in business brought about by the type of boom conditions mentioned above could create serious problems in the real estate field by some time in 1965.

Each of these men is trying to describe an economic phenomenon as he sees it; there are significant differences. Notice that between 1861 and now, the view of cause-and-effect has completely changed. In Macaulay's passage, men are hating, refusing, using each other as tools, and turning one another out. Because these men, who should know better, are behaving badly, *they* are creating an economic crisis. In his bumptious nineteenth-century liberalism, Macaulay refuses to assign any part of the crisis to the law of supply and demand or to any other abstract force. In the second passage, by marked contrast, there is not a single discernible human being acting by conscious choice: It is not that *speculators have stupidly erected too many buildings;* it is rather that "there have been considerable excesses." Moreover, the problem is not that *men will continue to act stupidly*, but that "construction will remain at a high level." Doubtless in economics and sociology Macaulay was naive and made an egregious overestimate of the importance of man in relation to his circumstances. In his account, *men* did things; events and trends followed.

The second account, equally honest and probably much more in keeping with the facts, gives us men and their individual decisions functioning as bits of froth on a tidal wave of savings, investment, overbuilding, and boom conditions. Dealing with abstract forces, our modern economist takes abstractions as the subjects of his sentences. The qualities of his style are thoroughly modern: The sentences are anti-rhythmical; the diction, unlike Macaulay's, strives to be entirely flat and denotative; words or short phrases, such as "recently" or "since 1959," are inflated into "over a period of the last few years"; in the modification of nouns, other words customarily used as nouns displace both the adjective ("boom conditions" for "inflationary conditions") and the prepositional phrase ("real estate field" for "field of real estate"); above all, the subjects of the sentences are all abstractions,

and the verbs, unlike Macaulay's *envy, dread, contrive,* and *hate,* are neutral.

When a man is telling the truth as he sees it, the only objection to this style is an aesthetic one. But what of the man who says, "Outside the peer-group, manifestations of hostility occur," instead of, "People tend to dislike those who are unlike themselves"? Here we have not an abstract occurrence being described in abstract terms, but a matter of relatively free choice being described as though it were something as irresistible as the laws of physics. In shifting the main actor of the sentence from "people" to "manifestations," we have not only expressed our idea in inflated verbal coin but have nearly obliterated the notion that individual people have any free will in the matter. And herein lies a major objection to the inflated style: It does not tell the truth, for it ascribes to abstract forces the responsible acts of individual men. In the inflated style, the idea that *we need honest and intelligent men if we are to build a good society* becomes, "The validity and proper use of concepts might play a basic part in the safety of our country and society." Similarly, in dealing with a person learning something, the inflated style gives us, "Patterns and skills in thinking thus become outcomes of instruction along with substantive outcomes derived from subject matter, and also with personal-social-moral developments from experience."[1]

In each of these examples, the writer has attributed an act of human choice to an abstract force.

---

[1] W. H. Burton, R. B. Kimball, and R. L. Wing, *Education for Effective Thinking,* New York, Appleton-Century-Crofts, 1960.

What are the implications of this kind of style? What do we do when we speak of the bombing of a church as "a manifestation of inter-racial tension," when we speak of the gunning down of Hungarian students as "expansionist tendencies within the Soviet bloc," or when on hearing a man call the President of the United States a communist we respond in our most enlightened and unbiased way, "Diction with high emotive content is character-istic of dogmatic political group-ings"? By divesting the acts we perceive of any human origin, we suggest that nowhere along the line did anyone make a choice, and a wicked choice at that. And having denied the human origin of the act, having attributed the act to an ab-stract force, we find it easy not to react to it morally at all.

INFLATIONARY FORCES

Doubtless much of the abstraction in our discourse comes from the findings of the social sciences over the last 100 years. Unlike Macaulay, modern man is acutely aware of abstract forces—both inside and outside himself—that are beyond his control, and doubtless we owe much to the social sciences for putting man in his place. In the modern style, however, abstraction becomes not one of several forces interacting with man, but the mainspring and sole source of reality; we see in modern American prose a world peopled not by men but a species of

neo-Calvinist deities, whose visita-tions and elections are made mani-fest in our language with terms like "hostility," "aggression," "adjust-ment." In so annihilating person-hood, we divest man not only of his free will, but of all the possibilities of good and evil that we know him to possess. In short, we corrupt and debase our own relationship with the world as we perceive it.[2]

Besides the misuse of the so-cial sciences, there are other perva-sive inflationary forces at work, chiefly modern technology and the effects and causes that attach to it. The fruits of technology certainly include both television and the computer. With the former, we con-front ourselves daily with an unend-ing stream of infelicitous linguistic models. With the latter, we have managed to devise means of com-munication that annihilate tradition entirely. Also with the latter and its possibilities in automation, we have managed to remove people farther and farther from the actual produc-tive business of day-to-day life, and it is only by substantial aid from modern machinery that we have managed to inflict upon ourselves the large modern corporation.

Impelled by our tax laws and by our technology, men have cre-ated in the large modern corporation something that is much newer than most of us suspect and far more important. The large corporation is the major area outside elective poli-tics where a man can acquire a considerable amount of personal power; and if the power he acquires is largely illusory, he can still within

---

[2] Doubtless an agile and widely-read scholar, with world enough and time, could trace the beginning of man's elimination from the real world back to Gali-leo's discrimination between primary and secondary qualities, perhaps back well before him. As a major and comprehensive trend in *style*, however, it is mainly a contemporary phenomenon.

the "corporate context" rise very high on a very large and very elaborate command chart. To the ambitious and materialistic young man, the large corporation is as natural an avenue to success today as the founding of one's own business was two generations ago. But it is more than this. It is the model for most of our government agencies; it is the source of most of our governmental talent; it is the generator of most of our wealth. In 1961, the nation's 500 largest corporations accounted, directly and indirectly, for $260 billion worth of economic activity, some 52 percent of our gross national product; various levels of government, most of them modeled on the large corporation, accounted for $130 billion, or 26 percent. Thus, 78 percent of our economic activity was the outgrowth of large, corporate-style organizations of one kind or another. Because it feeds us, because it clothes us, because through trusteeships and foundations it guides much of our education, it is, whether we like it or not, the key feature of our lives. As the key feature, it may well have the most profound and far-reaching influence on our mode of expression.

The principal—the antihero, if you will, or the unprotagonist—of the modern corporation is a man that we shall call the career manipulator, of whom much has already been said by William H. Whyte in *The Organization Man*. The gifts of the manipulator have little or nothing to do with the article or service that his company produces. They lie in other areas. This man can juggle books, convene committees, listen to subordinates. Outside the company compound, he can give you sunburn by the way he radiates the corporate image. Tempted by "the skills of human relations," he finds himself both the master and slave of "a tyranny more subtle and more pervasive"[3] than that which he has come to supplant.

On September 15, 1963, the American Management Association took, as an advertisement for itself, a whole extra section of the Sunday *New York Times* in order to survey the accomplishments of management in the last forty years. Of the arts of the manipulator, the AMA says, "Management is the responsibility for accomplishing results through the efforts of other people." Note the emphatic position of the term, "other people." It goes on to say that among the functions of management are "Integrating the viewpoints of people with functions," "Instilling the service motive," "Making the organization dynamic and adaptable," "Relating the organization's affairs to the community," and "Providing human satisfactions in work output." The interesting feature of management's *own* description of its functions is that not once in the 28-page *Times* supplement is there any mention of the thing produced. Nor is there any mention of the manipulator's need to be acquainted with either the product or the productive process. There is, moreover, an almost total neglect of those who do the actual work. The picture of management here is of a process wherein one manipulator, armed with a battery of psychological tests in one hand and a womb-to-tomb welfare plan in the other, manipulates other

---

[3] W. H. Whyte, *The Organization Man*, Garden City, N.Y., Doubleday Anchor, 1957.

manipulators in such a way that at the end of the fiscal year, the books will show a large paper profit and the command chart will show a fearful symmetry.

But sarcasm, alas, can dismiss neither the importance of the manipulator nor his effects on style. He lives in a world far removed from the traditional reality of people and actions, as far removed indeed as the world of the automated production worker is from that of the alleged artisan of sixty years ago. He no longer lives in a world of real people, real things, or real actions; instead he lives in a world the major realities of which are "functions and echelons," "products" (what they are matters not to him), and "norms." Quite naturally, his style is a reflection of the abstract non-realities of his world; if people ever appear in his sentences, they have usually been admitted by virtue of their membership on some committee or other. Similarly, this is not a style in which men make decisions; it is one in which "propositions are held" (by whom, it is rarely said) or one in which—in the case of the daring—"it is the feeling of the committee that . . ." It is a depopulated style dominated by euphemism and by what James Koerner calls "the forward passive."[4]

These men are not part of a consciously organized movement to undermine the culture; nor do I feel that more than a very few of them have a sense of even mild wrongdoing. Far from being an organized conspiracy, they are merely a group of men with an ingrained penchant for responding with alacrity to trends and norms and to the opinions of others. The trend that they are riding in our own time, one set in motion by taxes and technology, is a trend toward fewer and larger and more amorphous corporate groupings: "Diversify and consolidate; consolidate and diversify"— this is the operating principle of any successful modern corporation. It is the principle which drives tobacco firms to buy out razor manufacturers and drives chemical companies to buy up textile mills. It is also the principle which has reduced the number of American auto manufacturers from ten to four in little over a decade and the number of firms producing 90 percent of America's blankets from nine to four in the same amount of time. In an age where technology can make one product obsolete overnight, diversification is only a matter of common sense.

Consolidation is similar, but more complex. Because the tax laws make individual accretions of capital nearly impossible; and because they have driven the existing concretions of capital into trusts, foundations, and other committee-managed institutions, there is much less "free" capital than there used to be for new ventures. Furthermore, technology has developed productive machinery to the point where any new plant facility demands two and a half times the capital per production worker needed in 1947. Because of technology's insatiable appetite for capital, and because committee capital (or 90 percent of that available) goes only to the outfit with proven success, new ventures are seldom born, and old ones combine in order to have

---

[4] James D. Koerner, Executive Secretary, Council for Basic Education, and editor of *The Case for Basic Education*, 1959. (Editor's note.)

the resources to stay alive. And when they do combine, they form groupings so diverse and far-flung that their management must be an end in itself. Thus the manipulator is not a conspirator at all, but a mere respondent, a man who has entered a door opened by certain features of the times.

As much as they have decreed his entry, taxes and technology have decreed the how and the why of his remaining and flourishing. With such massive sums of money at stake, with individual decision annihilated, and displaced by the voice of the committee, safety and security—made respectable by our welfare credo—become the dominant values not only in the management of any company, but in its relationships with its employees, relationships that end as a species of lock-in. Our income tax laws have made it cheaper, both for the company and for the individual, to work out a concealed—and deferred—income plan than to have the company pay the employee enough for him to work out his own savings, his own pension, his own insurance. Thus, a man who wants to leave a big company nowadays must often give up a huge deferred vested interest in a pension; he may also be in for a whopping increase in his health and life insurance premiums.[5] In addition to this deterrent to individualism, there are a number of others.

THE LUXURY OF INDIVIDUALISM

First of these deterrents is that the odds against a man who strikes out on his own are colossal: The greater need for capital and the sources of new capital have served to increase those odds perhaps tenfold in the last fifteen years. A second deterrent is that there are fewer "other firms" to flee to, and even these are much more likely than they would have been forty years ago to be exactly like the firm a man flees from. In these circumstances, the employee is more inclined to hold his tongue than he ever has been before. If he should say something that commits him strongly to a given policy or idea, especially if his is a minority view, he will not be popular with his colleagues and superiors, who are consensus-directed and do not deviate much from committee views. Given this unpopularity, he will pay heavily for any false steps. To be sure, he won't be fired; such a turn would be contrary to the policy that seeks, as one company put it, to "establish maximum security in all personnel" (the metaphor is extremely apt). No, instead he will be frozen in grade and given the most isolated, non-essential job possible.

A man with vigorous ideas that threaten his colleagues had better change either his ideas or his style of expression. If he is to keep his

---

[5] In chapter 13 of *The Organization Man*, Whyte cites a recent survey indicating that there are increasing numbers of job transfers because differing organizations are coming to have increasingly interchangeable parts. As Whyte himself points out, however, the chief reason for such transfers is an increase in responsibility, and the "lost" pension benefits are made up by the new company. This kind of transfer comes to a man as a kind of reward for his having conformed better than his peers; as such, it has the same stultifying effect on people's ability and will to express themselves frankly and vigorously as the other features of organization life do.

place on the monkey mountain of corporate committees, if he is looking to some degree of "responsibility" in the future, and if he doesn't want to give up thousands of dollars in deferred compensation, either he will keep those dirty little deviationist thoughts inside his head or he will learn to swap "we are wrong . . ." for "in the present circumstances, market forces suggest that further earnings might be realized from some reorientation of product suitability. . . ." Notice how neatly the original idea is caught up and annihilated in a great vat of linguistic mush. Notice also how the inflated style has managed to sterilize the original thought: Human agents, with the attendant suggestions of human error and human responsibility, have been completely removed from the sentence. The inflated style has now given us a safe, secure thought for which nobody will be held responsible.

In short, the imperatives of organization life establish a kind of thought control through control of expression. And the control applies to matters that should legitimately be quite outside the purview of the company's authority. Forty years ago, an honest crank who could do a good job would not be a bad employee in many companies. In the '20s and '30s, a man who off the job was a Bull Mooser, a temperance fanatic, or a part-time taxidermist, could find employment so long as he was a competent man in his job. Nowadays, however, with technology diminishing the number of working hours and with modern management theory expanding the number of hours of enforced recreation within the corporate family, well . . . temperance and taxidermy

keep a fellow out of things. Likewise *any* pronounced political ideas: A man who subscribes to *Human Events, The Nation, The National Review,* or *The New Republic* is going to ruffle the other fellows on the committee. Perhaps I should say, "Disruption of the consensus will take place." For middle-management job openings, people who express pronounced ideas of any kind need not apply.

Let me be clear that my view of this transformation is no romantic "golden-age-to-age-of-iron" formula. The old-style boss was no doubt amply unpleasant—indeed, a good deal more so than his successor, the manipulator—but his criteria were spelled out with abundant clarity. Furthermore, he was only one of many, and the many came in all shapes, sizes, and political hues. Pleasing him was a matter of not violating standards announced in advance, usually at the time of one's employment; vigorous expression that did not violate those standards was perfectly acceptable. The manipulator, by contrast, cannot spell out standards or criteria; all he can do is put forth a series of shadowy "norms" in which *any* pronounced opinion or unusual activity is frowned on. And things are constricted further by virtue of the diminishing number of companies in any given field and of the increasing similarity of one personnel manager to another.

Thus vigorous utterance within the company compound is annihilated by a combination of "enlightened pre-selection," example, and shadowy fear. Outside the compound, it is treated with considerable severity. In this regard, three recent cases of "resignation" are instructive.[6] A vice-president of Petrofina "resigned" because of an article he wrote for *Look* about the political climate of Dallas. A supervisor of municipal services for Bethlehem Steel likewise "resigned" because "it was felt" (by whom?) that his membership in the Bethlehem (Pennsylvania) Civic League might imply that the town's largest employer was less than celestially fair in its hiring practices. An advertising executive in the midwest met a similar fate because some lectures he had given on Communist propaganda techniques might sound "sort of right-wing." Naturally, there are many other such cases, but this is a sufficient sampling to make the lesson clear: Don't let any dissenting or even concrete thoughts into your discourse, or you will be on the receiving end of the next forward passive.

While the career manipulator, with his abundant and amorphous committees, has been filing the high and low spots off our thoughts, while he has been abstractionizing our nouns and verbs, he has also been emerging as the senior corporate officer, both in business and in government. For a look at what his emergence at this level means, let us consider, as the ad boys have instructed us, the before and after pictures. Many of us can remember the television image of an enraged Charles Wilson, pointing at some Senator and saying, "What's good for the country is good for GM and vice versa." We can also remember Mr. Wilson, at a hearing on unemployment two years later, saying

that he had always liked hunting dogs better than house dogs and that a man who won't go out and seek work doesn't deserve our help. Even those who smile at the nineteenth-century quaintness of Mr. Wilson's idea of personal responsibility must admire his directness and candor; after all, this is a man trying in honest and forceful language to express reality as he perceives it. Not so with his Defense Department successors. Consider our recent use of B-26s in Vietnam.

The B-26 was a flying coffin even in its palmiest days years ago, but Mr. Zuckert informs us that it had been "selected with precise mission suitability in view." Notice the vigorous use of the forward passive: In Mr. Zuckert's sentence, it is not an instance of responsible men making a responsible decision; it is rather a case of some airplanes having "been selected," presumably by an unperson or by a group of unpeople. Notice also the hurdle provided by the terminal noun pile: Is it that the mission was suitable for the war or that the planes were suitable for the mission? Evidently Mr. Zuckert would prefer us not to know: he assures us that the B-26s "have been withdrawn."

The apotheosis of the modern, inflated style occurs when it passes from being a mode of expression to being a mode of looking at the world. In this stage, the inflated style, like Newspeak,[7] is a means not only of expressing bureaucratic orthodoxy but of making all other modes of thought impossible. For example, consider the recent testi-

---

[6] See the *Wall Street Journal,* "Jobs and Controversy," May 5, 1964.

[7] A term coined by George Orwell to refer to a form of communication. See "It's Halfway to 1984" by John Lukacs. (Editor's note.)

mony of a prominent industrial executive appearing before a Senate committee. This man testified that the truest competition exists when differing companies put identical price tags on similar products. In other words, this man *said* that true competition will exist in, say, the toothpaste business when all the manufacturers charge 59 cents for a seven-ounce tube, 89 cents for a ten-ounce tube, and so forth. And this was an impeccably honest man who believed what he said. The significance of his testimony is that it could be given only by a man who lives in a culture the linguistic habits of which have been designed to conceal or distort reality rather than to express it. In a complex world, truth is hard enough to apprehend. But if we deny ourselves the means of giving it voice, if with our language we teach ourselves to disbelieve all the evidence of sense, the senses, and the intuition, then how much longer will we be able to apprehend the truth at all?

Progress, in its effect on language, has given us a new style wherein man is meaningless and wherein traditional, tangible reality is all but unrecognizable. The principal actors in our cosmic drama of technology and bureaucracy are trends, factors, machines. For the time being, the inflated style is but a mode of expression, a kind of convention for looking in a distorted way at ourselves and the things around us. But the style is habit forming, and after a while it could come to dominate our thoughts, with the consequence that we end like that biographer of Sam Johnson who so fervently believed himself the reincarnation of his subject that he contracted scrofula. After speaking too long of a reality in which man does not count, we might find ourselves in thirty years ready to yield up our world to the machines and abstract forces that we have heretofore been able, in our clumsy way, to resist and sometimes to control.

· QUESTIONS ·

1. What are the two forms of linguistic inflation discussed by Cluett? Show that you understand what is meant by each.
2. Is the final paragraph a fair summary of the thesis of this article?
3. How would you characterize the tone of this selection? Is the style reasoned? Angry? Overly argumentative? Vigorous but fair?
4. What does Cluett write about the effects of television, computers, and modern corporations on linguistic inflation? Can you name other influences?
5. Are you now more interested, or feel that you may become more interested, in "safety and security" than in "being yourself"?
6. In your own noninflated language, summarize the thesis of this essay in approximately 100 words.
7. Compare and contrast the discussion of "progress" in this essay with the views of Charles A. Beard's "The Idea of Progress."
8. Define: nomenclature, substantive, innocuous, egregious, illusory, penchant, amorphous, accretion, respondent, deterrent, deviationist, constricted, apotheosis, scrofula.

Theme Subjects: (1) My Own Inflated Verbal Coin; (2) Annihilation of Fact in _____ (an essay, editorial, news story, etc.); (3) The Luxury of Trying To Be an Individual; (4) I'm a Company Man Myself; (5) An Answer to Cluett.

THE EDUCATED IMAGINATION

Northrop Frye

NORTHROP FRYE (1912–   ) was born in Sherbrooke, Quebec, was graduated from the University of Toronto (1933) and Oxford University (1940), and holds honorary degrees from several Canadian and American universities. Professor of English and Principal of Victoria College at the University of Toronto, he has visited and taught at many American universities, including Harvard, Columbia, Princeton, Indiana, and Washington. Dr. Frye is author of *The Well-Tempered Critic* (1963); *Anatomy of Criticism* (1957); *Fearful Symmetry: A Study of William Blake* (1947); *T. S. Eliot* (1963); and *Fables of Identity* (1963), as well as articles, critical reviews, and contributions to some 30 other books.

When you stop to think about it, you soon realize that our imagination is what our whole social life is really based on. We have feelings, but they affect only us and those immediately around us; and feelings can't be directly conveyed by words at all. We have intelligence and a capacity for reasoning, but in ordinary life we almost never get a chance to use the intellect by itself. In practically everything we do it's the combination of emotion and intellect we call imagination that goes to work. Take, for example, the subject that in literary criticism is called *rhetoric*, the social or public use of words. In ordinary life, as in literature, the way you say things can be just as important as what's said. The words you use are like the clothes you wear. Situations, like bodies, are supposed to be decently covered. You may have some social job to do that involves words, such as making a speech or preaching a sermon or teaching a lesson or presenting a case to a judge or writing an obituary on a dead skinflint or reporting a murder trial or greeting visitors in a public building or writing copy for an ad.

In none of these cases is it your job to tell the naked truth: we realize that even in the truth there are certain things we can say and certain things we can't say.

Society attaches an immense importance to saying the right thing at the right time. In this conception of the "right thing," there are two factors involved, one moral and one aesthetic. They are inseparable, and equally important. Some of the right things said may be only partly true, or they may be so little of the truth as to be actually hypocritical or false, at least in the eyes of the Recording Angel.[1] It doesn't matter: in society's eyes the virtue of saying the right thing at the right time is more important than the virtue of telling the whole truth, or sometimes even of telling the truth at all. We even have a law of libel to prevent us from telling some truths about some people unless it's in the public interest. So when Bernard Shaw remarks that a temptation to tell the truth should be just as carefully considered as a temptation to tell a lie, he's pointing to a social standard beyond the merely intellectual standards of truth and falsehood, which has the power of final veto, and which only the imagination can grasp. We find rhetorical situations everywhere in life, and only our imaginations can get us out of them. Suppose we're talking to somebody, let's say a woman, who's in a difficult mood. We're faced at once with the problem: does what she is saying represent her actual meaning, or is it just a disguised way of representing her emotional state of mind? Usually we assume the latter but pretend to

be assuming the former. This is a problem in rhetoric, and our decision is an act of literary criticism. The importance of rhetoric proves, once again, that the imagination uses words to express a certain kind of social vision. The social vision of rhetoric is that of society dressed up in its Sunday clothes, people parading in front of each other, and keeping up the polite, necessary and not always true assumption that they are what they appear to be.

In our use of words in ordinary life we are all bad poets. We read stories in our newspapers about Britain and Russia and France and India, all doing that and thinking that, as though each of these nations was an individual person. We know, of course, that such a use of language is a figure of speech, and probably a necessary figure, but sometimes we get misled by such figures. Or we get into the opposite habit of referring to the government as "they," forgetting that they're our own employees and assuming that "they" are carrying out plans and pursuing interests of their own. Both of these habits are forms of misapplied mythology or personification.

The central place of the imagination in social life is something that the advertisers suddenly woke up to a few years ago. Ever since, they've been doing what they call projecting the image and hiring psychologists to tell them what makes the most direct appeal to the imagination. I spoke of the element of illusion in the imagination, and advertising is one example, though a very obvious one, of the deliberate creation of an illusion in the middle

---

[1] An angel in Heaven who, in the view of some, writes down in a large book all of man's deeds and misdeeds while he is on earth.

of real life. Our reaction to advertising is really a form of literary criticism. We don't take it literally, and we aren't supposed to: anyone who believed literally what every advertiser said would hardly be capable of managing his own affairs. I recently went past two teen-age girls looking at the display in front of a movie which told them that inside was the thrill of a lifetime, on no account to be missed, and I heard one of them say: "Do you suppose it's any good?" That was the voice of sanity trying to get its bearings in a world of illusion. We may think of it as the voice of reason, but it's really the voice of the imagination doing its proper job. You remember that I spoke of irony, which means saying one thing and meaning another, as a device which a writer uses to detach our imaginations from a world of absurdity or frustration by letting us see around it. To protect ourselves in a society like ours, we have to look at such advertising as that movie display ironically: it means something to us which is different from what it says. The end of the process is not to reject all advertising but to develop our own vision of society to the point at which we can choose what we want out of what's offered to us and let the rest go. What we choose is what fits that vision of society.

This principle holds not only for advertising but for most aspects of social life. During an election campaign, politicians project various images on us and make speeches which we know to be at best a carefully selected part of the truth. We tend to look down on the person who responds to such appeals emotionally: we feel he's behaving childishly and like an irresponsible

citizen if he allows himself to be stampeded. Of course there's often a great sense of release in a purely emotional response. Hitler represented to Germany a tremendous release from its frustrations and grievances by simply acting like a three-year-old child: when he wanted something he went into a tantrum and screamed and chewed the scenery until he got it. But that example shows how dangerous the emotional response is and how right we are to distrust it. So we say we ought to use our reason instead. But all the appeals to us are carefully rationalized, except the obviously crackpot ones, and we still have to make a choice. What the responsible citizen really uses is his imagination, not believing anybody literally, but voting for the man or party that corresponds most closely, or least remotely, to his vision of the society he wants to live in. The fundamental job of the imagination in ordinary life, then, is to produce, out of the society we have to live in, a vision of the society we want to live in. Obviously that can't be a separated society, so we have to understand how to relate the two.

The society we have to live in, which for us happens to be a twentieth-century middle-class society, presents our imagination with its own substitute for literature. This is a social mythology, with its own folklore and its own literary conventions, or what corresponds to them. The purpose of this mythology is to persuade us to accept our society's standards and values, to "adjust" to them, as we say. Every society produces such a mythology: it's a necessary part of its coherence, and we have to accept some of it if we're to live in it, even things that we don't believe. The more slowly a society changes, the more solidly based its mythology seems to be. In the Middle Ages the mythology of protection and obedience seemed one of the eternal verities, something that could never change. But change it did, at least all of it that depended on a certain kind of social structure. A hundred years ago a mythology of independence, hard work, thrift, and saving for a rainy day looked equally immortal, but, again, everything that was based on weak social services and stable values of money had to go. If a society changes very rapidly, and our society certainly does, we have to recognize the large element of illusion in all social mythology as a simple matter of self-protection. The first thing our imaginations have to do for us, as soon as we can handle words well enough to read and write and talk, is to fight to protect us from falling into the illusions that society threatens us with. The illusion is itself produced by the social imagination, of course, but it's an inverted form of imagination. What it creates is the imaginary, which is different from the imaginative.

The main elements of this social mythology will be familiar to you as soon as I mention them. I spoke of advertising, and what's illusory about that is the perverted appeal it so often makes to the imagination: the appeals to snobbery and to what are called "status symbols," the exploiting of the fear of being ridiculed or isolated from society, the suggestion of an easy way of getting on the inside track of what's going on, and so on. Then there's the use of cliché, that is, the use of ready-made, prefabricated formulas designed to give those who are too lazy to think the illusion of

thinking. The Communists of course have made a heavy industry of clichés, but we have our own too. Hard-headed business man; ivory tower; longhair; regimentation; togetherness; airy-fairy. Anybody who believes literally what these clichés express, as far as any thinking for himself is concerned, might just as well be in Moscow reading about fascist hyenas and the minions of imperialist aggression.

Then there's the use of what we call jargon or gobbledygook, or what people who live in Washington or Ottawa call federal prose, the gabble of abstractions and vague words which avoids any simple or direct statement. There's a particular reason for using gobbledygook which makes it a part of social mythology. People write this way when they want to sound as impersonal as possible, and the reason why they want to sound impersonal is that they want to suggest that the social machine they're operating, usually a government agency, is running smoothly, and that no human factors are going to disturb it. Direct and simple language always has some force behind it, and the writers of gobbledygook don't want to be forceful; they want to be soothing and reassuring.

I remember a report on the classification of government documents which informed me that some documents were eventually classified for permanent deposition. The writer meant that he threw them away. But he didn't want to say so, and suggest that somebody was actually tearing up paper and aiming it at a wastebasket; he wanted to suggest some kind of invisible perfect processing. We get similar euphemisms in military writing, where we read about "antipersonnel bombs," meaning bombs that kill men, designed not to give us any uncomfortable images of legs torn off and skulls blown open. We can see here how the ordinary use of rhetoric, which attempts to make society presentable, is becoming hypocritical and disguising the reality it presents beyond the level of social safety.

Then there's all the mythology about the "good old days," when everything was simpler and more leisurely and everybody was much closer to nature and got their milk out of cows instead of out of bottles. Literary critics call these reveries pastoral myths, because they correspond to the same kind of convention in literature that produces stories about happy shepherds and milkmaids. Many people like to assume that the society of their childhood was a solid and coherent structure which is now falling apart, as morals have become looser and social conditions more chaotic and the arts more unintelligible to ordinary people, and so forth. Some time ago an archaeologist in the Near East dug up an inscription five thousand years old which told him that "children no longer obey their parents, and the end of the world is rapidly approaching." It's characteristic of such social myth-making that it can swing from one extreme to the other without any sense of inconsistency, and so we also have progress myths, of the kind that rationalize the spreading of filling stations and suburban bungalows and four-lane highways over the landscape. Progress myths come into all the phony history that people use when they say that someone is a "Puritan," meaning that he's a prude, or that someone else is "medieval" or "mid-Victorian," meaning

that he's old-fashioned. The effect of such words is to give the impression that all past history was a kind of bad dream, which in these enlightened days we've shaken off.

I mentioned the various diagrams and doodles that people carry around in their minds to help them sort things out. Sometimes they sort things the wrong way. For instance, there's the diagram of left-wing and right-wing in politics, where you start with Communism at the extreme left and go around to Fascism at the extreme right. We use this diagram all the time, but suppose I were to say: "the Conservatives are nearer to being Fascists than the Liberals, and the Liberals are nearer to being Communists than the Conservatives." You recognize that statement to be nonsense; but if it's nonsense, the diagram it's founded on is more misleading than it is useful. The person it's useful to is the person who wants to turn abusive, which is my next point.

Ordinary speech is largely concerned with registering our reactions to what goes on outside us. In all such reactions there's a large automatic or mechanical element. And if our only aim is to say what gets by in society, our reactions will become almost completely mechanical. That's the direction in which the use of clichés takes us. In a society which changes rapidly, many things happen that frighten us or make us feel threatened. People who can do nothing but accept their social mythology can only try to huddle more closely together when they feel frightened or threatened, and in that situation their clichés turn hysterical. Naturally that doesn't make them any less mechanical. Some years ago, in a town in the United States, I heard somebody say "those yellow bastards," meaning the Japanese. More recently, in another town, I heard somebody else use the same phrase, but meaning the Chinese. There are many reasons, not connected with literary criticism, why nobody should use a phrase like that about anybody. But the literary reason is that the phrase is pure reflex: it's no more a product of a conscious mind than the bark of a dog is.

We said that the person who is surrounded with advertisers, or with politicians at election time, neither believes everything literally nor rejects everything, but chooses in accordance with his own vision of society. The essential thing is the power of choice. In wartime this power of choice is greatly curtailed, and we resign ourselves to living by half-truths for the duration. In a totalitarian state the competition in propaganda largely disappears, and consequently the power of imaginative choice is sealed off. In our hatred and fear of war and of totalitarian government, one central element is a sense of claustrophobia[2] that the imagination develops when it isn't allowed to function properly. This is the aspect of tyranny that's so prominently displayed in George Orwell's *1984*. Orwell even goes so far as to suggest that the only way to make tyranny permanent and unshakable, the only way in other words to create a literal hell on earth, is deliberately to debase our language by turning our speech into an automatic gabble. The fear of being reduced to such a life is a genuine fear, but of course as soon as we express it in hysterical clichés we are in the same state ourselves. As the poet William Blake says in

describing something very similar, we become what we behold.

Too often the study of literature, or even the study of language, is thought of as a kind of elegant accomplishment, a matter of talking good grammar or keeping up with one's reading. I'm trying to show that the subject is a little more serious than that. I don't see how the study of language and literature can be separated from the question of free speech, which we all know is fundamental to our society. The area of ordinary speech, as I see it, is a battleground between two forms of social speech, the speech of a mob and the speech of a free society. One stands for cliché, ready-made idea, and automatic babble, and it leads us inevitably from illusion into hysteria. There can be no free speech in a mob: free speech is one thing a mob can't stand. You notice that the people who allow their fear of Communism to become hysterical eventually get to screaming that every sane man they see is a Communist. Free speech, again, has nothing to do with grousing or saying that the country's in a mess and that all politicians are liars and cheats, and so on and so on. Grousing never gets any further than clichés of this kind, and the sort of vague cynicism they express is the attitude of somebody who's looking for a mob to join.

You see, freedom has nothing to do with lack of training; it can only be the product of training. You're not free to move unless you've learned to walk, and not free to play the piano unless you practice. Nobody is capable of free speech unless he knows how to use language, and such knowledge is

---

[2] A morbid dread of closed or narrow places.

not a gift: it has to be learned and worked at. The only exceptions, and they are exceptions that prove the rule, are people who, in some crisis, show that they have a social imagination strong and mature enough to stand out against a mob. In the row over desegregation in New Orleans, there was one mother who gave her reasons for sending her children to an integrated school with such dignity and precision that the reporters couldn't understand how a woman who never got past grade six learned to talk like the Declaration of Independence. Such people already have what literature tries to give. For most of us, free speech is cultivated speech, but cultivating speech is not just a skill, like playing chess. You can't cultivate speech, beyond a certain point, unless you have something to say, and the basis of what you have to say is your vision of society. So while free speech may be, at least at present, important only to a very small minority, that very small minority is what makes the difference between living here and living in East Berlin or South Africa. The next question is: where do the standards of a free society come from? They don't come from that society itself, as we've just seen.

Let us suppose that some intelligent man has been chasing status symbols all his life, until suddenly the bottom falls out of his world and he sees no reason for going on. He can't make his solid gold cadillac represent his success or his reputation or his sexual potency any more: now it seems to him only absurd and a little pathetic. No psychiatrist or clergyman can do him any good, because his state of mind is neither sick nor sinful: he's wrestling with his angel. He discovers immediately

that he wants more education, and he wants it in the same way that a starving man wants food. But he wants education of a particular kind. His intelligence and emotions may quite well be in fine shape. It's his imagination that's been starved and fed on shadows, and it's education in that that he specifically wants and needs.

What has happened is that he's so far recognized only one society, the society he has to live in, the middle-class twentieth-century society that he sees around him. That is, the society he does live in is identical with the one he wants to live in. So all he has to do is to adjust to that society, to see how it works and find opportunities for getting ahead in it. Nothing wrong with that: it's what we all do. But it's not all of what we all do. He's beginning to realize that if he recognizes no other society except the one around him, he can never be anything more than a parasite on that society. And no mentally healthy man wants to be a parasite: he wants to feel he has some function, something to contribute to the world, something that would make the world poorer if he weren't in it. But as soon as that notion dawns in the mind, the world we live in and the world we want to live in become different worlds. One is around us, the other is a vision inside our minds, born and fostered by the imagination, yet real enough for us to try to make the world we see conform to its shape. This second world is the world we want to live in, but the word "want" is now appealing to something impersonal and unselfish in us. Nobody can enter a profession unless he makes at least a gesture recognizing the ideal existence of a world beyond his own interests: a world of health for the doctor, of justice for the lawyer, of peace for the social worker, a redeemed world for the clergyman, and so on.

I'm not wandering away from my subject, or at least I'm trying not to. My subject is the educated imagination, and education is something that affects the whole person, not bits and pieces of him. It doesn't just train the mind: it's a social and moral development too. But now that we've discovered that the imaginative world and the world around us are different worlds, and that the imaginative world is more important, we have to take one more step. The society around us looks like the real world, but we've just seen that there's a great deal of illusion in it, the kind of illusion that propaganda and slanted news and prejudice and a great deal of advertising appeal to. For one thing, as we've been saying, it changes very rapidly, and people who don't know of any other world can never understand what makes it change. If our society today is different from what it was in 1942, it can't be real society, but only a temporary appearance of real society. And just as it looks real, so this ideal world that our imaginations develop inside us looks like a dream that came out of nowhere and has no reality except what we put into it. But it isn't. It's the real world, the real form of human society hidden behind the one we see. It's the world of what humanity has done, and therefore can do, the world revealed to us in the arts and sciences.

A hundred years ago the Victorian poet and critic Matthew Arnold pointed out that we live in two environments, an actual social one and an ideal one, and that the ideal one can only come from something

suggested in our education. Arnold called this ideal environment *culture*, and defined culture as the best that has been thought and said. The word culture has different overtones to most of us, but Arnold's conception is a very important one, and I need it at this point. We live, then, in both a social and a cultural environment, and only the cultural environment, the world we study in the arts and sciences, can provide the kind of standards and values we need if we're to do anything better than adjust.

I spoke of three levels of the mind, which we have now seen to be also three forms of society and three ways of using words. The first is the level of ordinary experience and of self-expression. On this level we use words to say the right thing at the right time, to keep the social machinery running, faces saved, self-respect preserved, and social situations intact. It's not the noblest thing that words can do, but it's essential, and it creates and diffuses a social mythology, which is a structure of words developed by the imagination. For we find that to use words properly even in this way we have to use our imaginations, otherwise they become mechanical clichés, and get further and further removed from any kind of reality. There's something in all of us that wants to drift toward a mob, where we can all say the same thing without having to think about it, because everybody is all alike except people that we can hate or persecute. Every time we use words, we're either fighting against this tendency or giving in to it. When we fight against it, we're taking the side of genuine and permanent human civilization.

This is the world revealed by

philosophy and history and science and religion and law, all of which represent a more highly organized way of using words. We find knowledge and information in these studies, but they're also structures, things made out of words by a power in the human mind that constructs and builds. This power is the imagination, and these studies are its products. When we think of their content, they're bodies of knowledge; when we think of their form, they're myths, that is, imaginative verbal structures. So the whole subject of the use of words revolves around this constructive power itself, as it operates in the art of words, which is literature, the laboratory where myths themselves are studied and experimented with.

The particular myth that's been organizing this talk, and in a way the whole series, is the story of the Tower of Babel in the Bible.[3] The civilization we live in at present is a gigantic technological structure, a skyscraper almost high enough to reach the moon. It looks like a single worldwide effort, but it's really a deadlock of rivalries; it looks very impressive, except that it has no genuine human dignity. For all its wonderful machinery, we know it's really a crazy ramshackle building, and at any time may crash around our ears. What the myth tells us is that the Tower of Babel is a work of human imagination, that its main elements are words, and that what will make it collapse is a confusion of tongues. All had originally one language, the myth says. That language is not English or Russian or Chinese or any common ancestor, if there was one. It is the language of human nature, the language that makes both Shakespeare and Pushkin authentic poets, that gives a social vision to both Lincoln and Gandhi. It never speaks unless we take the time to listen in leisure, and it speaks only in a voice too quiet for panic to hear. And then all it has to tell us, when we look over the edge of our leaning tower, is that we are not getting any nearer heaven, and that it is time to return to the earth.

· QUESTIONS ·

1. The author's own imagination is fertile and far-ranging. Can you make a topic or paragraph outline of his argument?
2. Do you agree that imagination is a combination of emotion and intellect? If not, why not?
3. Had you ever connected a knowledge and understanding of English with the principles of free speech? Do you do so now after reading this essay?
4. Aside from Frye's own references, what other internal indications are there that this essay was originally prepared as a talk?
5. Comment on the tone of this essay-speech. Is the diction too racy and colloquial for such a serious subject? Does the varied diction increase interest and readability?
6. "The fundamental job of the imagination in ordinary life, then, is to produce, out of the society we have to live in, a vision of the society we want to live in."

---

[3] In *Genesis* (11:4–9) is an account of an ancient city (Babylon) where the building of a tower designed to reach heaven was begun. A confounding of the language of the people occurred.

Relate this profound statement to your feelings about your home, your parents, your college life, a boy or girl whom you love, your plans for a career. Where does reality (intellect) stop and where do your feelings (emotion) take over?

Theme Subjects: (1) Only a Fool Tells (Doesn't Tell) the Truth; (2) The Current Advertisement I Most Dislike (Like); (3) My Educated (Uneducated) Imagination; (4) The Rhetoric of Telephoning for a Date; (5) Imagination Is Only Lies; (6) "Do You Suppose It's Any Good?"

MAN WILL PREVAIL

William Faulkner

For brief comment on the life and writing career of William Faulkner, see "A Rose for Emily."

I feel that this award was not made to me as a man, but to my work—a life's work in the agony and sweat of the human spirit, not for glory and least of all for profit, but to create out of the materials of the human spirit something which did not exist before. So this award is only mine in trust. It will not be difficult to find a dedication for the money part of it commensurate with the purpose and significance of its origin. But I would like to do the same with the acclaim too, by using this moment as a pinnacle from which I might be listened to by the young men and women already dedicated to the same anguish and travail, among whom is already that one who will some day stand here where I am standing.

Our tragedy today is a general and universal physical fear so long sustained by now that we can even bear it. There are no longer problems of the spirit. There is only the question: When will I be blown up? Because of this, the young man or woman writing today has forgotten the problems of the human heart in conflict with itself which alone can make good writing because only that is worth writing about, worth the agony and the sweat.

He must learn them again. He must teach himself that the basest of all things is to be afraid; and, teaching himself that, forget it forever, leaving no room in his workshop for anything but the old verities and truths of the heart, the old universal truths lacking which any story is ephemeral and doomed— love and honor and pity and pride and compassion and sacrifice. Until he does so, he labors under a curse. He writes not of love but of lust, of defeats in which nobody loses anything of value, of victories without hope and, worst of all, without pity or compassion. His griefs grieve on no universal bones, leaving no scars. He writes not of the heart but of the glands.

Until he relearns these things, he will write as though he stood among and watched the end of man. I decline to accept the end of man. It is easy enough to say that man is immortal simply because he will endure: that when the last ding- dong of doom has clanged and faded from the last worthless rock hanging tideless in the last red and dying evening, that even then there will still be one more sound: that of his puny inexhaustible voice, still talking. I refuse to accept this. I believe that man will not merely endure: he will prevail. He is immortal, not because he alone among creatures has an inexhaustible voice, but because he has a soul, a spirit capable of compassion and sacrifice and endurance. The poet's, the writer's, duty is to write about these things. It is his privilege to help man endure by lifting his heart, by reminding him of the courage and honor and hope and pride and compassion and pity and sacrifice which have been the glory of his past. The poet's voice need not merely be the record of man, it can be one of the props, the pillars to help him endure and prevail.

· QUESTIONS ·

1. This, of course, is the now famed speech which the late author gave when he was awarded the Nobel Prize for literature in Stockholm on December 10, 1950. What do you think of its tone? How do you characterize its style?
2. The author has often been criticized for his involved, intricate style, for the unclear structure of his sentences. Do you find this speech easy or difficult to follow?
3. Analyze the length, type, and structure of the sentences in the first paragraph. How does their pattern vary in the next three paragraphs?
4. Do you call this statement an "affirmation of faith," a "cry of doom," or a "denial of inevitable defeat"? (It has been called all of these. It has also been termed a "majestic, noble, and impassioned utterance transcending time and place.")

Theme Subjects: (1) When I Expect To Be Blown Up; (2) _____ (a novelist) "Writes Not of the Heart but of the Glands"; (3) "The Basest of All Things Is To Be Afraid"; (4) What Might Help Me To Endure and Prevail.

THE CASE FOR
GREATER CLARITY
IN WRITING

Ivor Brown

Ivor John Carnegie Brown (1891–   ) is one of London's most accomplished men of letters. His first novel was published when he was only 24; since then he has composed many books on politics, drama, and the art of writing. Among his better-known titles are *A Word in Your Ear* (1942); *No Idle Words* (1948); *Chosen Words* (1955); *London* (1960); *How Shakespeare Spent the Day* (1963); *What Is a Play?* (1964).

The literary fashion of these days is not to know what you mean and, if challenged, to shrug a careless shoulder and say that you write what you write and the reader must make his own interpretation. The author's observations are presumed to be pregnant; the reader is to be midwife and bring the child to birth. It is no business of genius to make itself plain.

    This was the line taken up by T. S. Eliot in an interview given after the first production of *The Cocktail Party* at the Edinburgh Festival of Arts in 1949. The play later acted with immense success in London and New York was, I think, a simplified and improved version of the original. But that does not affect Eliot's reply to the charge of being obscure and his tenet that the artist is under no obligation to be explicit. He projects his thoughts, feelings, and fancies: on the task of interpretation the public must bring its own wits to bear.

    I suggest in return that this attitude betrays either laziness or affectation. It is the abdication of authorship. It is the business of the literary artist to know his mind and

From the *New York Times Book Review*, July 30, 1950. Reprinted by permission.

to speak it. Mr. Eliot, after all, was dramatizing certain problems of conduct and of human relations and he presented a Psychotherapeutic Sage as moral preceptor. He was not just fetching up thoughts that lie too deep for tears; he was informing us about destiny and salvation, important matters on which we have a right to clear instruction. In that case we surely are entitled to know what his opinions on these great matters are. The fact that the play was written in what might be called conversational verse does not affect the proposition that an author is evading his responsibilities if he is not intelligible.

Swift shrewdly said that the true definition of style is "proper words in proper places." To this I would add "proper thoughts in proper order." There is nothing impossible about that. The greatest prose writers of our time are in my estimation Bernard Shaw and Somerset Maugham. Did either of them ever write a sentence that was vague?

If you are anti-Shavian you can accuse Shaw of writing every sort of nonsense, but you need never pause for a moment to wonder what sort of nonsense he intends. And as a model of lucid scrutiny of a life's experience and a life's conclusions Maugham's *The Summing-Up* is unsurpassed. Again, you need not agree with his judgments and valuations, but you know precisely what those judgments are.

Now let us have some examples of the muddled writing for which in my opinion there is no excuse. Mr. Henry Green's novels are now very much in the intellectual fashion, presumably because he so loftily disdains syntax, grammar, and punctuation. Here is a typical sentence from page 1 of his much-praised story, modestly called "Nothing":

It was wet then, did she remember he was saying, so unlike this he said, and turned his face to its dazzle of window, it had been dark with sad tears on the panes and streets of canals as he sat by her fire for Jane liked dusk, would not turn on the lights until she couldn't see to move, while outside a single street lamp was yellow, reflected over a thousand raindrops on the glass, the fire was rose, and Penelope came in.

Could anything be untidier? A schoolboy would be in trouble for such infantile, turbid, ill-punctuated stuff, with its flood of commas and contempt of all the rules of composition; those rules were not made to be a nuisance to writers but for the advantage of readers. As a reader I object to having this mess thrown at my head.

Then we have Mr. T. S. Eliot writing "Notes Towards a Definition of Culture." Note the timidity of the title. He is not offering to define culture; he is going to devote 124 pages to fidgeting round the edges of a definition. He includes sentences like this:

The way of looking at culture and religion which I have been trying to adumbrate is so difficult that I am not sure I grasp it myself except in flashes or that I comprehend all its implications.

Now if an author can only "try to adumbrate" an opinion and then admits his own inability to understand his own point of view, I suggest that he should keep quiet until he has cleared up his own confusion. Can one imagine a master of thought and English faltering and fumbling in this way! But to cut one's way through mental fog is now to be called obvious, or trivial; to founder in it, confessing one's impotence, is taken to be profound.

Nobody can pretend that much of the poetry written in the last quarter of a century has not been obscure. That is one reason why in Great Britain the bulk of it has become unsalable. London publishers protest that, with the exception of Eliot and one or two others, it is ruin to print poetry, and the Arts Council, appealed to for help by the distraught bards, is busily considering what to do about the wilting Muse. Shall it endow with public funds publication of the poetry which the public is now so unwilling to read?

The defense of the Obscure poets who defy grammar, syntax, and meaning as they eject their strained imagery is a mixed one. Some pleaders merely deny the charge; those who do not understand the tangled products of the Spasmodist Singers are accused of being lazy or stupid or both. The blame is laid on the boneheaded reader who will not puzzle the stuff out and work away at the verbal jigsaw provided. Another plea is that the contemporary world is so confused in its complex of economic, political, ethical, and psychological problems that nobody who is true to his time can be expected to be lucid in the exposition of the age and its dilemmas.

The first excuse is a mere denial of guilt, which gets nowhere in a court of law. The second is an affirmation and defense of artistic impotence. Once more it is the abdication of the author. The more intricate the mass of our difficulties

the greater is the need of minds able to cut into them like knives, get rid of jargon and give us meaning.

One habit of those unable to express themselves is to take cover under a long word which happens to be in vogue. Existentialism is an obvious case in point. Whenever somebody tells me that So-and-So is an Existentialist, with the implication that I am therefore to bow my head in awe and admiration, I immediately challenge him for a definition of Existentialism. I have never had the beginnings of a satisfactory reply.

Producers and actors of Existentialist plays are completely flummoxed if asked to cut the cackle and say exactly what they mean. So, in my experience, are literary critics. They wander off into some vague profundities about Essence and when asked to say exactly what that means they do not know.

To be vague may often be a short cut to a certain kind of popularity. It provides a debating point, and man is an argumentative animal. To write a poem, a play, or a book which will become a dinner-table topic may be a profitable occupation. It is jam for the intellectual snobs who relish telling you what the author was really getting at. Because you do not know, and do not pretend to know, you are supposed to be a crude simpleton. The history of the Snob-Value of the Obscure deserves a book in itself. When Browning remarked that only the author knew the meaning of his "Sordello" and that he had forgotten it, he gave enormous joy to the Browning Societies of his day, who then got to work on unravelment and so displayed their own surpassing acumen and ingenuity.

Admittedly the poet is not quite in the same position as the writer of prose. He is working more on percept than on concept, more on feeling than on dialectic. But there is no reason why he should not be able to give an exact image in words of his perceptions and his emotions. The best poets have managed to do so. Do we know just what Keats felt about the nightingale or the Grecian urn? We do. He did not have to make war on syntax or turn his odes into a grammarian's funeral.

I have never had to scratch my head over the sweet melancholy of A. E. Housman or put wet towels round an aching brain in order to excavate the meanings from a poem of Tennyson. Sometimes a creative mind works so rapidly that his thought outruns his hand and the images become telescoped like the railway carriages in an accident: Shakespeare's immense fecundity sometimes led to this. But no great poet, at his best, is obscure.

The public as a whole—that is, the public barring the Intellectual Snobs—shows its sensible preference for having its artists in sufficient possession of their faculties to put us all, and immediately, in possession of their meaning. The artist who does not know his own intentions is a pretender. If he does know them and cannot express them he is merely incompetent.

I hope I have made myself plain.

· QUESTIONS ·

1. Do you believe that the primary purpose of writing is communication? If not, what is?
2. A popular satirist has said: "If you can't communicate, the least you can do is shut up." What do you think of his advice?
3. What obligations does the reader have to an author?
4. What twentieth-century poems have you read, understood, and enjoyed? What modern poems (or poets) seem confusing to you?
5. Compare and contrast this essay with those in this volume by Robert Cluett and George Orwell.

Theme Subjects: (1) A Review of *The Cocktail Party* (or Eliot's *The Confidential Clerk*); (2) What the Word "Style" Means to Me; (3) It's Not Easy To Be Clear; (4) I Write as I Please; (5) "The Snob-Value of the Obscure"; (6) Most Writers Are Pretenders; (7) A Work of Art Should Be, Not Mean.

WHAT HAPPENS
IN COLLEGE

James Feibleman

JAMES KERN FEIBLEMAN (1904–   ) was born in New Orleans and has combined careers in business and teaching. A partner in the Leopold Investment Company since 1954, he has also been acting assistant professor of English at the College of Arts and Sciences, Tulane University (1943–1944), acting assistant professor of philosophy (1944–1946) and, since 1946, graduate professor and (1956) chairman of the university's department of philosophy. A radio broadcaster and lecturer at many universities and foundations, he is author of, among others, *Death of the God in Mexico* (1931); *Christianity, Communism and the Ideal Society* (1937); *In Praise of Comedy* (1939); *The Theory of Human Culture* (1946); *Aesthetics* (1949); *Inside the Great Mirror* (1958); *The Foundations of Empiricism* (1962); and *Mankind Behaving: Human Needs and Material Culture* (1963).

Every fall on every college campus you can see them—the hordes of incoming freshmen. In the excitement, the welter of new experiences and sensations, they are not aware that they are beginning the four most traumatic years of their lives.

College life is a series of shocks, some pleasant, some not, some clearly defined, some vaguely sensed. But they are shocks none the less; nothing in the experience of a high school student has prepared him for life at college.

What are the students like? They come from all sorts of backgrounds: the very wealthy, who sport Cadillacs (if cars are allowed on the campus), fur coats, impressive allowances; the poor, with the tired determined look of odd-hour jobs and too little sleep. They are tall and short, handsome and ugly, bright and dull. They come (at any

From *The Saturday Review*, October 20, 1962. Reprinted by permission of the author and the publisher.

fair-sized university) from all parts of the country and even from all parts of the world. Some come from fine secondary schools, some from woefully inadequate ones.

Only one thing they are certain to have in common: they are roughly in the same age group. (The older freshmen, so common under the G. I. Bill, have virtually disappeared.) Thus a similar set of biological maturations is occurring in them. They are at once callous and sensitive, baffled and intuitive, mystified and understanding, bored and interested. They are full of conflicts, fresh awakenings, contradictions and oppositions. They are basically terribly confused, because they are encountering powerful influences for the first time and are preparing to meet them first and interpret them later.

Why do they come to college? I am well acquainted with the usual reasons advanced by young people to account for their presence in college. Occasionally what they say is true, if sententious. Mostly it is not —perhaps because they themselves do not know what impels them. (To see the swarm of freshmen descend on campuses in the fall is an impressive experience; a bit, I imagine, like watching the migration of the salmon.) During years of teaching I think I have seen a well-defined set of motives reappear with each class. And these (one or a combination of them) are why young people come to college.

(1) They come because it is assumed that they will come, because almost everyone they know does. After all, there are 4.5 million people in college right now and there are supposed to be another 3 million more by 1970. The herd instinct is strong in young peo-

ple, and the desire to be considered a regular fellow means that if the gang goes, so do you. I've known young men to turn down a really fine school for a fourth- or fifth-rate one—to be with their friends.

Very little depends on the situation of their parents. In many less privileged groups, having a child in college is a mark of success, a public sign that the children are having a better chance than their parents ever did. The current word for this, I believe, is "status symbol."

Among other people, people of wealth, sending children to college is a foregone conclusion: educational advantages are also cultural advantages, and people of wealth, it is thought, should look and sound like people of wealth. Many young men give no thought to the selection of a college. They have been taught to assume that they will go to the college their father, their grandfather, and, in many cases, their great-grandfather attended. The reasons are usually more familial and dynastical than practical.

(2) A second and related reason why students come is to make good contacts. (There is no one more cynical than a freshman.) After all, if your roommate happens to be a boy whose father is president of a shoe manufacturing company, you may have a good opening in business when you graduate.

Such attitudes are not confined to the poor but ambitious youth. The American hierarchy is largely (even though not exclusively) a matter of money. Immediately after the question of whether or not there is money comes the question of how long it has been in the family. The older fortunes look down on the *nouveau riche,* but nobody ever asks how the older fortunes were first acquired and whether the circumstances surrounding such acquisition were moral. The passage of a few generations removes a great many stains.

Thus everybody has some reason for wanting to ascend the social scale: the poor wish to associate with the rich, the rich with the still richer, and the new rich with the old rich. The older rich send their children to acquire polish and to learn how to retain the fortunes they will inherit. Good contacts mean contacts with those higher in the social scale.

(3) Then there is sheer laziness. So very often a parent says to a child: "I will support you until you have finished college. After that you will have to support yourself." For the indolent this leaves little choice; who, under these circumstances, would refuse? They come to college with the very simple intent of avoiding work just a little longer, and they behave accordingly when there. I once had a roommate whose interests were confined to athletics. He spent the entire morning playing the tenor saxophone in bed. He arose only for lunch and the afternoon at the gym.

(4) There is another group of students who have come to college to bide their time, but not out of laziness. They are waiting until they can make a decision about the choice of a profession. To many high-schoolers there is nothing more frightening than the well-meant question: "What are you going to become?" They don't know. They have little idea of the requirements of the different careers open to them. They have even less understanding of themselves. They simply have not found out what they want to do, how they would enjoy making a living, and how they could make the best living. They do not know what their equipment is, what they are best suited for, or what sort of work will be the most congenial.

The university is a good place to come in that frame of mind. There are so many types of activities going on simultaneously, so many professions laid out side by side, so many branches of knowledge readily available. The decision concerning a career can often best be hastened by easy and quick familiarity with a few aspects of several.

(5) To escape or at least postpone military service is another reason. Under the present draft law, students may be deferred as long as they do well in college. Thus they have a very practical motive: they prefer an education to drills and forced marches, and college dormitories to army barracks. The more honest of the group will admit this fact quite readily.

(6) Many come simply to learn to make a living. The idea is about that most of the good positions in the business world are awarded to college graduates. A Bachelor of Arts or a Bachelor of Science degree is today the equivalent of a high school diploma fifty years ago; in our technological civilization there is not much that can be done without training. Young people realize that the chance of making money, or of making more money, lies through a formal education, including often the earning of a graduate degree in medicine, law, engineering, or architecture.

(7) To have fun is still another motive. Quite a few undergraduate colleges and some univer-

sities do not require more than lip service to the curriculum, and resemble country clubs a great deal more than they do centers of higher learning. (Some of the illustrated brochures they send out seem to indicate, in fact, that they are quite proud of the similarity.) Even in the best of schools there are programs which are not demanding, and one of the courtesies extended by the older students to the new is the precise listing of every easy course in the curriculum.

Here is an opportunity to extend the protected world of childhood a bit longer. Many students seem to attend college only for the extracurricular activities, including those which are approved officially, such as athletics and the supervised social diversions of the fraternities and sororities, as well as those which are not approved: drinking, gambling, and a general sowing of wild oats at the risk of life and limb.

(8) To obtain an education. There are students who actually come because they want to learn, because they are curious about many things. These are the students who will tell you: "There are thousands of books I want to read." They are aware of their own lack of information and they want to do something about it. Often these are the brighter students—but this is not necessarily so. Some are the unfortunate drones, men and women who possess the best of motives and an instinctive, strong drive in the direction of learning, but who unfortunately lack the requisite imagination and intelligence to go with it.

What happens to students in college? The teaching institution is faced with an onslaught of fresh-

men who are impelled toward the campus for a great variety and complexity of reasons. What happens to them there is something not even they can predict or expect. They enter college as adolescents; when they leave some four years later, with or without a degree, they are young adults. Some of this is simple maturation, of course, but some is also the direct result of their college experience. College experience itself is partly the experience of learning, the acquisition of a certain amount of ordered knowledge. It is also a combination of other forces not directly related to the classroom and the library, forces whose impact is more diffused but no less important. They are essentially part of the hurly-burly of campus life.

It is the students' first meeting, most likely, with a national and perhaps international group of men and women of their own age. Excepting those fortunate enough to have attended a very superior and international prep school (and only a tiny minority have), a high-schooler's contacts are likely to have been restricted to other inhabitants of the same town, even of the same neighborhood in a larger town. It is small wonder, then, that living in a dormitory with and attending class with, say, a Pakistani, an Italian, or a Norwegian, makes students overwhelmingly aware of a difference of lives, opinions, values.

Even the shift in the kind of curriculum is upsetting. The students are used to having the day arranged for them from, say, nine to three, high school fashion. They now find themselves attending classes for only fifteen hours or so a week. The concentration in depth on a few subjects is a new idea to them. The requisite self-discipline is often something they learn only after painful experience.

Furthermore, college is the students' first encounter with live intellectuals. They meet individual members of the faculty who have written important books or completed important pieces of research. The various intellectual fields become matters of personal experience. The students learn that work does not just happen to get done. They find that the productive intellectual is not a superman but an everyday figure. They will also make the discovery that there are those who consider intellectual pursuits reason enough for an entire life. Students are nearly always surprised to find such pursuits valued so highly.

Students are surprised, too, at their first meeting with really violent political opinion of all possible varieties. Their parents and/or their friends may have held violent political preferences, but it isn't until college that they see the full range of political possibility. Through student organizations and student publications, they meet for the first time with Democrats *and* Republicans, with conservatives *and* radicals. They are urged to take sides, if not as voters, then at least as partisans.

It is in college, too, that the sharp, bitter sting of failure is first experienced to any appreciable extent. A good high school student may find himself only a passing college scholar. Inequalities become painfully obvious. It is perhaps a matter of capacities. Those who develop long legs could become runners; those with short legs could not. Some are born with excellent intellectual capacities; some are not.

One student will make good grades without any effort; another will fail even though he sits up most of the night with his books. The recognition of native inequalities is often hard for students to accept.

What does the student learn? At the end of his four years, what can be fairly listed as the acquisition of the average student?

On the simplest level he has acquired a considerable amount of information and has learned something of the vast range of knowledge. He has become a bit intellectualized—generically, an intellectual is simply one who is at home among the classic abstractions. If he is astute he can acquire not only a familiarity with them, but also a considerable degree of manipulative skill. Further, he will have found the way he wants to go —whether it is out into the world of business or on into the world of graduate education.

He will also have learned to question. He was born into and grew up within one state, one set of institutions, one moral code, one church, one set of fixed views held by his parents, one determinate set of preferences of his group of friends. He learns in college that, for every one of these influences, there is a multiple set of possible alternatives. There are other cultures, other customs; the way things are done is not necessarily the way they have always been done or the way they have to be done. Some alternatives seem better, some much worse; but all are worthy of consideration. And, indeed, the abstract consideration of possible alternatives in every field is precisely what the universities provide. The net effect on the student is to challenge the authorities on whom he has always relied for support. Henceforth he must rely upon his own abilities to ascertain the facts and upon his own reason as the safest guide.

This is what the educational system has given him. It is also worth seeing what the system has *not* given him. If a student has taken seriously the things he hears in college, there is one great gap in his preparation. The world of abstractions is orderly, neat, and perfectly formed. Its rules are those of necessity and determinism. The world of practical affairs, into which the student emerges after four or more years of college, is governed to some extent by laws, but it is also a jungle, full of accident, chance, and opportunism, a brutal struggle for survival where the competition is so fierce that not much stands in the way of the ruthless and the ambitious. Fail, and you starve alone; succeed, and you dine with many friends.

There is no course in college designed to prepare the student for what he will encounter in the way of brute facts, and to this extent all college training is inadequate and even misleading. It is cruel to send students out to meet the world so well equipped in some ways and so ill prepared in others. We teach the ideal conditions of possible worlds passingly fair, but we do not teach the crude conditions of the actual world at all. Thus when we look at what a student learns in the university, we find that it is chiefly confined to what ought to be and is not extended to what actually is. What the student does not learn is appalling and raises the question of how well selected is the information concerning what ought to be, when the selection of what ought to be rests on a knowledge of the limitations of what is. The *theory* of practice is a theory as well as a practice, and so it can justify itself in the academic curriculum, but it is at the same time a theory of *practice,* and so is capable of arming the innocent for what he will encounter outside the academic curriculum.

· QUESTIONS ·

1. This essay may be divided into four sections: reasons for entering college, what happens in college, what one learns there, what one doesn't learn. Show that you understand the author's comments on each of these divisions in this clearly ordered article.
2. Which of the four sections of this essay most appeals to you? Why?
3. Do you disagree with any of the author's comments? Which ones? Why?
4. Can you think of any reasons for coming to college not mentioned by the author?
5. Can you expand the author's comments in the final two sections of the article (what one learns and what one doesn't learn in college)?
6. Define: welter, traumatic, maturation, callous, sententious, familial, dynastical, hierarchy, *nouveau riche*, indolent, drone, diffused, generically, manipulative, determinism.

Theme Subjects: (1) Why I Think I Came to College; (2) College Is (Is Not) Just a Nursery; (3) Why This College Seems Right (Wrong) for Me; (4) One Thing College Cannot Prepare Me For; (5) What's Happened to Me in College So Far; (6) College Is a Poor (Excellent) Place in Which To Get an Education.

MONEY IS NOT ENOUGH

Claude M. Fuess

CLAUDE MOORE FUESS (1885–1963) was born in Waterville, New York. He took his bachelor's degree at Amherst College and held many honorary degrees from his alma mater and other colleges and universities. He became an English instructor at Phillips Academy, Andover, Massachusetts, in 1908; he later served as headmaster there for 15 years. He was the author of numerous books and edited several collections of poetry and prose.

Erect more school buildings, hire more teachers, endow more scientists, let Congress appropriate a few more billions and—rich as America is—we can't help winning the Cold War in general and the crisis in education in particular. That seems to be the cry today.

This is indeed a superficial view of the current emergency. We shall soon discover, what some have learned already, that anger is not enough. Political fulmination is not enough. And money is not enough. The issue goes deep into the very heart of our civilization, of our philosophy as a people, of our motivations and desires. I am a schoolmaster, and I prefer to stick here to the educational side of this problem, but much of what I have to say equally relates to the other aspects of our national community life.

Until our national attitude has changed, no expenditure of mere money will enable us to hold our own with the Russians. They have realized for some years the necessity of guiding every child as far along the educational path as he is qualified to go, of identifying talent early and cultivating it to the utmost, of rewarding scholarship and research, and making teaching a reputable, dignified profession. Meanwhile, American men and women who might have been contributing to the Space Age have been designing new and better television sets, automobiles, and the countless gadgets which are part of the daily life of every American. We have been voting ourselves and our children longer and longer holidays at precisely the moment when we need to utilize more profitably all the

From *The Saturday Review*, February 1, 1958. Reprinted by permission of the publisher.

time available. We have become so enervated by prosperity that, according to accurate testimony from sportswriters, more and more spectators are watching fewer and fewer athletes. According to Harold Kaese, athletic clubs are vanishing because the average boy "won't stick to anything tough." Child for child and man for man we read fewer books proportionately than almost any so-called cultured country in the world. Sweden, with a population of 7 million, has nearly as many public libraries as the United States. And now we delude ourselves into believing that, by increasing the budget, we can quickly redeem ourselves and demonstrate our superiority!

All over the country modern public schools are being dedicated, many of them impressively beautiful, well-lighted, with gymnasiums and swimming pools and auditoriums, located where passing motorists can look and admire. Buildings are desirable, of course. But teachers are much more important. A school may be great without perfect equipment. It cannot be great without inspiring instructors. Our emphasis has been, and still is, on show rather than on substance. In his provocative book, *This Is Goggle, or The Education of a Father*, Bentz Plagemann describes his experiences with his recalcitrant son, who was a hellion until he came under the influence of an understanding teacher. Said the father, "It was then that we learned, once and for all, what it takes to make a man out of a boy. It's very simple. It takes a man." We must cease thinking of our schools as primarily bricks and granite and glass and regard them as hives of human personality. Money does help to secure

dynamic instructors, but it still is not enough. We shall have to give them also respect, encouragement, and some deserved applause.

Another inescapable fact is that these Russian "barbarians," in education as in other areas, work longer and harder than we do. No economy-minded American can look at these magnificent regional schools, empty during the summer months, without being conscious of the waste involved. For long periods their superb facilities are being put to no effective use. The number of holidays has been so increased by legislation that many boys and girls, like their parents, are at a loss how to spend their spare time. Let us face the truth. Most schoolteachers no more need thirteen weeks of summer vacation than doctors or bankers or librarians. If any boys and girls are sincerely eager to learn and move along faster, why not let them receive the instruction for which they hunger? If vacations were shorter and teachers were paid more accordingly, the profession would be for many of them more attractive, and thousands of ambitious adolescents would welcome the opportunity for acceleration. This is not just an "egghead pipedream." Some independent schools which have undertaken such an experiment have been well satisfied with the results. A summer session of this type at Phillips Academy, Andover, has been in operation for more than twenty years, enabling pupils to cover an entire year's work in a subject like French or to make up a previous failure in chemistry or English. I have talked with many of the summer students. They are glad to be doing something directly profitable instead of loafing on beaches or street-corners.

Still another hampering factor is the soft attitude of parents towards their offspring, their unwillingness to subject them, or to have them subjected, to severe discipline in behavior or study. Philip Wylie touched a sensitive spot in our social organism when he framed his comprehensive indictment of "Mom." But "Pop" is often just as culpable as "Mom." Many a father who has achieved success through strenuous labor and grim self-sacrifice says quite openly, "My son must never work as hard as I did," forgetting that it was this very struggle which made him what he is. When the Progressives evolved the fascinating idea that no marks should be given to students, they rejoiced the hearts of millions of "Moms" and did a disservice to America. "Competition gives the losers a sense of inferiority; therefore let's abolish it," they said. No expenditure of money can revive the competitive spirit which was once such an incentive to so many healthy-minded children.

In some ways our current problem is one of sentimentality versus discipline. I suspect that parents will have to make their children lead more exacting lives, to make more demands upon them, to teach them in the home the elementary principles of law, order, and occasional renunciation. This requires no money—only a change of heart.

Corollary to all this is the fact that we have been spending millions on retarded children just to keep them contented, or at least alive. This is, of course, a moral obligation of the state, and no one would wish to change the policy. Meanwhile, however, we have been doing very little to enable the bright children to realize their potentials. In most of our public schools the standards have been adjusted to the average pupils, with the inevitable consequence that the more brilliant who find the assignments easy lose their drive. Byron S. Holinshead pointed out at least six years ago that thousands of exceptionally gifted young Americans never reached college, at the same time that our college campuses were teeming with wealthy "wasters" out for nothing but a good time. Here money can help, but it must be backed by sympathetic community interest. The Russians, latecomers in many cultural areas, have discovered that progress is dependent on a very small number of research scholars who, under proper encouragement, may be of service to a national program. Mass education should not mean mass mediocrity, but it needs to be supplemented by special attention to the talented.

That such a system of advanced education for exceptionally able children is not undemocratic is proved by the advocacy of Thomas Jefferson, that practical visionary who left so few areas of knowledge unexplored. He early recognized that any society advances chiefly through the utilization of the capabilities of its best-endowed citizens. His proposals for Virginia called for education of the young on three levels—elementary, grammar, and collegiate. On his theory, the most promising boys in each grammar school were to be sent to the university by the state. Jefferson saw nothing undemocratic in this recognition of the fact that some children are mentally superior to their mates and therefore, if rightly trained, are likely to become leaders. In a letter to John Adams in 1813 he mentioned particularly those who early excel in what he called "virtue and talents," who would "thus have been sought out from every condition of life, and completely prepared by education for defeating the competition of wealth and birth for public trust."

For measuring aptitudes we have had for some time machinery more accurate than the subjective judgments used in Jefferson's day. Our mechanism is not infallible, but aptitude and achievement tests do exist through which we can identify talent at an early age and thus select from among the candidates those who seem likely to profit by further and more intensive instruction. Already this is being done in some degree through the generosity of private industry. It might well become a function of government, with necessary precautions against the possible intrusion of Washington bureaucracy.

For such a program we need money, but we also require popular approval of the principle involved. If what we believe to be our American culture is to be preserved, it will be through the research, the resourcefulness, and the influence of a comparatively small group of talented persons. Subjecting a larger and larger proportion of our youth to elementary mathematical and scientific instruction will not accomplish what we are after. It is essential that every American child should learn to read and write and cipher. But it is even more desirable at the moment that the best should get the best. For the moment we should be more concerned with the uncommon than with the average. Selecting the best-qualified, educating them to the highest level of which they are capable, and then using them as their genius directs—

this is the policy which might conceivably save us from destruction. Someone said recently, "A keen mind has become a resource more valuable than uranium . . . The crying need of our country today is the trained mind, the skilled worker, the creative thinker." We shall have to support such a far-reaching plan not only with taxation but with unceasing cooperation.

Indeed, our present problem can be solved only in part by the expenditure of vast sums of money. Deep in the consciousness of a large percentage of Americans is an anti-intellectualism almost sinister in its manifestations, an emotional distrust of the human mind whenever it functions above the twelfth-grade level. Our only half-concealed contempt for or indifference to the operations of scholars and teachers has brought them into disrepute. How can we help being dismayed when we learn from a recent survey that six out of every ten Americans hadn't read a book—not a single book—in the preceding year?

The national habit of measuring success by cash income has inevitably affected the popular judgment on educators. Higher salaries, such as those just announced at Harvard, will naturally improve a professor's status in the community. But it will certainly take some time for public-school teachers, who in the long run must guide every step towards improvement, to attain the living standards of most members of school committees and Parent-Teacher Associations. Here again money cannot do everything. The values of the American people will have to become more spiritual and intellectual and less material.

All this has to some people always seemed important, but it is now important for everybody. We are in direct rivalry with nations which may not possess our money but which have an amazing constructive vitality. Every American should be familiar with Voltaire's oft-quoted aphorism, "History is only the pattern of silken slippers descending the stairs to the thunder of hobnailed boots climbing upward from below"—which is just as appropriate for nations as it is for classes of society. It is nothing new for a vigorous race, adventurous and imaginative, industrious and stoical, to win a place in the sun and have visions of world domination. The pattern from then on is familiar. With prosperity, play and pleasure seem more attractive than hard work, and a drop in morale is inevitable. Then is precisely the moment when a fresh people, barbarian perhaps but willing to endure hardships and make sacrifices, has so often risen and overthrown the enervated and demoralized older society.

The symptoms of deterioration are all around us in our apprehensions, our frequent hysteria, our willingness to think that all our sins can be redeemed by an increased budget. In education we have been repeatedly warned by specialists who know their stuff. We need new school buildings and better salaries for teachers, but we need even more some comprehension of the way in which education on the highest levels may be utilized to make us safe and strong. Let us spend money where it is needed, but let us go further. Let us through every possible agency determine just where we stand and just what is required to restore the pioneer spirit. Only by drastic measures can we reverse a trend so reminiscent of what has happened to earlier empires.

· QUESTIONS ·

1. Paragraph one states a suggested course of action. How much of the article is devoted to refuting this course?
2. Phrase Fuess' thesis. Do you agree with it?
3. Just how effective do you consider your precollege education?
4. Are school and college vacations too long?
5. In school was your progress impeded by "retarded" classmates?
6. Do you believe in grouping students in sections according to their abilities? Is this an undemocratic step?
7. Precisely what does Fuess mean by "the pioneer spirit"?
8. Define: enervated, egghead, culpable, corollary, infallible, anti-intellectualism, stoical.
9. Compare the thesis of this essay with that of James Reston's "A Fable."
10. In what respects is this essay "dated"? For example, is research today so lavishly endowed that the teaching Fuess requests has become "a lost art"?

Theme Subjects: (1) The Best Teacher I Ever Had; (2) My School Was a Hive of Human Personality; (3) My Plan for Bright Children; (4) College Work Is (Is Not) Hard Enough; (5) The Status of School Teachers in My Community; (6) What the PTA Meant to My School; (7) An Example of Wastefulness in My High School.

COLLEGE ATHLETICS:
EDUCATION OR
SHOW BUSINESS?

Harold W. Stoke

HAROLD WALTER STOKE (1903–   ) was born in Bosworth, Missouri, and holds earned degrees from Marion (Indiana) College, the University of Southern California, and Johns Hopkins. After a distinguished teaching career he became president of the University of New Hampshire in 1944. Dr. Stoke was president of Louisiana State University, 1947–1951, and dean of the Graduate School at the University of Washington, 1951–1955. From 1955 to 1958 he was dean of the Graduate School of Arts and Science, New York University, and he was president of Queens College, New York City, 1958–1964. He has contributed widely to journals of political science and education and is author of *The American College President* (1959).

I

On the morning of December 7, 1951, in the General Sessions Court in New York City, fourteen tall young men stood before Judge Saul S. Streit. The scene was the climax of the notorious basketball scandals in which players had been convicted of receiving bribes from professional gamblers for throwing basketball games in Madison Square Garden. The judge was stern, but for the culprits he tempered justice. Jail sentences and fines were few and light. Judge Streit then looked over the heads of the defendants and hurled angry words at the colleges and universities they represented. He charged that these institutions had so far forgotten their educational mission and had so over-emphasized athletics that they themselves had made this scene in his courtroom all but inevitable.

Addressing himself to the colleges, Judge Streit demanded imme-

From *The Atlantic Monthly*, March, 1954. Reprinted by permission of the author.

diate and drastic reforms. Among these were the restoration of athletic responsibilities to faculties and to the academic administrative authorities; the revitalization of the National Collegiate Athletic Association; the establishment of an amateur code and of a capable, well-financed policing authority.

While there was some dismay (if little surprise) in university circles at the basketball scandals, there was genuine puzzlement about the judge's suggestions for reform. The point that had escaped him was that all his proposals had been tried for years—uniformly without success. If Judge Streit and the countless educators who have tackled this problem had asked themselves why Bradley University, Kentucky, New York University, North Carolina State, or any other university should ever play basketball in Madison Square Garden, they would have started on a line of inquiry which would have brought about a better understanding. Obviously it was no educational interest that brought the teams there, no huge concentration of alumni, no essential training program. It wasn't wholly a matter of money. They were there in response to a far more complex and subtle compulsion: to assist their schools as a part of the system of American higher education to carry out that system's latest and growing responsibility—namely, to provide public entertainment.

In our American society the need for entertainment is an inevitable consequence of the changing conditions of our lives—the lengthening life span, the shorter work week, speed and mobility, industrialization and prosperity. These changes create social vacuums, and for filling social vacuums the American system of education—and particularly higher education—is one of the most efficient devices ever invented. It is flexible, highly varied, and in touch with virtually the entire population; furthermore, it is characterized by a genuine spirit of service. It is manned by aggressive and accommodating people; it is suffused with a thoroughly practical philosophy. Hence, to its already great and growing array of services —its teaching, research, adult education, military training, and general public service—it has added another, public entertainment. This responsibility has been accepted in some instances eagerly, in some instances reluctantly, but nonetheless accepted. Drama, music, radio, and television widen the educational as well as the entertainment services of the universities; wherever these touch the public they possess more of the characteristics of entertainment than of education. Yet of all the instrumentalities which universities have for entertaining the public, the most effective is athletics.

What educational institutions thus far have not seen is that the responsibility for supplying public entertainment is a responsibility different in kind from those they have previously performed. The failure to understand this fact has led to endless strain in the management of athletics, to bewilderment among educators and the public, and even to outright scandal. Conceived as education, athletics is inexplicable, corrupting, and uncontrollable; as public entertainment, and even as public entertainment to be provided by educational institutions, athletics becomes comprehensible and manageable.

The most essential distinction between athletics and education lies in the institution's own interest in the athlete as distinguished from its interest in its other students. Universities attract students in order to teach them what they do not already know; they recruit athletes only when they are already proficient. Students are educated for something which will be useful to them and to society after graduation; athletes are required to spend their time on activities the usefulness of which disappears upon graduation or soon thereafter. Universities exist to do what they can for students; athletes are recruited for what they can do for the universities. This makes the operation of the athletic program in which recruited players are used basically different from any educational interest of colleges and universities.

The fundamental distinctions between athletics and education are somewhat obscured by several arguments frequently heard. The first is that athletics has "educational values." This is the familiar "character building," "team spirit," "sportsmanship" argument. Anyone who knows the actual operations of athletics will admit that such values could be realized far better if athletics were handled as recreation and physical education. The second argument is that many fine athletes make fine scholastic records—implying that there must not, after all, be any conflict between athletics and education. Again the answer can be short. Big-time athletics requires 20 to 28 hours per week of its devotees, aside from the time spent away from the campus; hence it is bound to detract from an athlete's education. But how can an impoverished athlete get a chance at a college education? I'll answer that question with another: Is he

any more entitled to it than anyone else?

II

College athletics *is* public entertainment. Last year football audiences numbered 40 million, and now basketball is outstripping football in attendance. It is estimated that the public pays $100 million a year to the colleges for admission tickets, and television has added enormously to the number of spectators and to the revenue. Public interest as measured in publicity, newspaper coverage, and attention is far beyond that given to any educational activity. In no major school does the attention given to the appointment of a president compare with that given to the appointment of a coach, and the general public can name many more coaches than presidents.

The organization of this public entertainment is intricate. Most of the larger colleges and universities, private and public, are organized into athletic conferences managed by highly paid commissioners. Through them, complicated athletic schedules are worked out with all the finesse of the international bargaining table, and considerations of finance, publicity, the prospective careers of coaches and even of presidents are balanced in equations which would baffle electronic computers. Stadiums, field houses, and playing fields are constructed with the entertainment-seeking public primarily in mind. At the time the Yale Bowl was built it would have seated the entire adult population of New Haven, while Michigan could have put twice the population of Ann Arbor into its stadium. The University of Southern California and the University of California at

Los Angeles are big schools, but even they would scarcely need the Memorial Stadium for their students and faculty. Obviously the real underwriters of bonds which build athletic plants are not students, but the public. Many an athletic director caught in a squeeze of high costs and inadequate gate receipts wishes to heaven he had all of the student tickets to sell to the people willing to pay more for them.

The same force lies back of the other features of athletics—the numerous and high-priced coaching specialists, the elaborate half-time shows, the colorful bands (supported almost as completely by scholarships as are the athletes and for the same purpose), the frolicsome majorettes, the carefully planned and executed spontaneous student rallies and demonstrations, the food, drink, and program concessions. None of these could possibly serve any educational purpose for which a college or university exists, but they are wonderful aids to public entertainment.

Perhaps most significant of all is the fact that the rules of the games themselves are now constructed and reconstructed with their entertainment value uppermost. Like dramatic coaches and directors bringing into being a Broadway production, the coaches and athletic directors gather each year to adjust the rules of football and basketball for the purpose of heightening the dramatic and entertainment value. The substitution rule, who may run with the ball, what may be allowed to happen within the ten-yard line or within the last four minutes, the nature of the penalties, and, currently, the one- or two-platoon system in football are matters which are governed by their effect upon the entertainment and upon the welfare of the enterprise. In basketball the rules have been changed to encourage high scoring, constant running and action, alternate chances at scoring in order to provide the murderously exciting finishes which now characterize the game. Revisions are made each year only after the most elaborate study and consideration and with a wariness which would do credit to the fuse workers in a munitions factory.

Consider the Bowl games. They are important influences on athletic policies and at the same time irrefutable evidence that athletics, so far as the Bowls are concerned, have no educational significance whatsoever. So far as I know, no one seriously claims that they do.

All of the Bowls for obvious reasons are located in the South or in winter vacation areas. They are immensely successful business promotions; there is nothing about them remotely related to education. As one man put it: "Rose Bowl, Sugar Bowl, Orange Bowl—all are gravy bowls!" A half-million people saw the games in the eight major bowls last January 1, and it is estimated 70 million more heard them on radio or saw them on television. Receipts were almost $2.5 million. The distribution of the money follows a kind of formula in each conference—a large percentage to each school participating in the Bowl, a smaller percentage to each school in the conference and to the conference treasury itself. A more subtle formula to ensure support for Bowl games could hardly be devised. Participation in one of the Big Four Bowls—Rose, Sugar, Cotton, and Orange—may bring each participating school as much as $125,000. Everyone profits—except the players, whose amateur status has thus far confined them to such grubby rewards as gifts of gold watches, blankets, free tickets which can be scalped, sometimes a little cash—the last usually secretly. Under pressure from the players and perhaps from a sense of institutional guilt at the indefensible exploitation, the rewards to players are improving but they still are far below the A.S.C.A.P. and Equity pay scales for big-time entertainers.

III

How is all this to be made compatible with the nation's educational system? Most troubles arise from the failure of colleges to see that in supplying public entertainment they have embarked upon an operation which is different from their educational functions—and one that requires different management. Colleges have acted as if athletics were merely an extension of student recreation. Since athletes come from the same high schools as other students, are about the same age, and do get a kind of education, it has been assumed that the academic regulations applicable to the general run of students should also apply to athletes. We overlook completely the different reasons for which each is there. Hence schools have prescribed the same formal academic requirements for both the athlete and the nonathlete—a minimum number of hours must be taken, a certain number of courses must be passed, systematic progress, however slow, must be made toward a degree, and a host of other regulations must be followed.

Yet athletics, like a corrosive acid, has eaten through every academic regulation—to the great frustration, bewilderment, and cynicism of the educational community. It has defeated faculties, forced the resignations of presidents, wrecked coaches, and undercut the support of institutions where the efforts to apply academic regulations have been insistent. Where such regulations have been successfully applied they have all but killed the athletic programs, or put them in abeyance, as at New York University, Fordham, or Pittsburgh, until a more "understanding" attitude permits revival. There are, of course, many schools—Oberlin, Swarthmore, Haverford, Bowdoin, to name a few—that attract little attention from the entertainment-seeking public because they make little attempt to supply public entertainment.

The truth is that the appetite of the public cannot be satisfied by the quality of entertainment which can be provided by athletics governed by academic regulations. Consequently, at institutions which are meeting the public's demands, academic regulations must be ignored, compromised, or eliminated. Admission requirements for athletes have become less formidable than they used to be, and usually an arrangement can be made for the boys to make up high school deficiencies. The requirements as to courses, progress toward degrees, and even grades can generally be met by either a flexible elective system or the "tailored curriculum" leading to a highly specialized "degree" in which many hours of handball, swimming, and coaching can be included. Where this does not suffice, every athletic department of any size provides at its own expense counseling and tutoring service for any of its men likely to get into trouble. Not all athletes need these negations of educational regulations, but the point is that when required the negations must be available. How compelling the necessity is can be estimated by the situations which come to light when these compromises are not sufficient —the wholesale cheating at West Point, the alteration of records at William and Mary, special examinations, and countless other devices involving various degrees of accommodation or even fraud and misdemeanor. No matter what the regulation, if it prevents athletics from supplying the public entertainment for which it exists, a way around must be found. This has been the fate which has uniformly attended the regulative efforts of faculties, administrators, code committees, accrediting associations, and even the N.C.A.A. itself.

Why should this conflict be so irreconcilable? There are many reasons, but perhaps the most compelling is that adequate entertainment can be provided only by winning teams. No amount of gushy sentiment about "playing the game" will conceal the fact that the public wants its teams to win. Victory is a part of the total titillation. If the public can't have it from one source it will transfer its loyalties and money to some other. Chick Meehan filled Yankee Stadium with football fans roaring for N.Y.U., but when de-emphasis came, N.Y.U. found that 6000 was a good crowd to watch it play Fordham, the archrival. "When Michigan loses, someone has to pay" may be a slogan at Ann Arbor, but it sums up the attitude of all schools with athletic entertainment: the schools must get the entertainers.

The recruitment of players is the key to most of the athletic anxi-

eties of college presidents, the desperation of coaches, the pressure of alumni, and the activities of outside influences, business and otherwise. A chain reaction of undesirable consequences follows. The school must get the player, and the best one; the player knows this, and the bidding starts. Sometimes negotiations are carried on by a parent or other relative in order that the player may be technically free of all nonamateur bargains; otherwise he becomes a part of a corrupt bargain about which, if questions arise, he must lie or forever keep silent. Gradually the "board, room, and tuition" formula—plus a little extra, if necessary—has won acceptance. Sometimes the myth of employment persists as the justification for such payments, but it is now generally acknowledged to be a myth. The effort to limit the number of such scholarships is actually an effort to equalize competition between schools. The conferences often set a limit—but there are ways around it, the junior college "farm system" for one.

The bidding, of course, is highest for the best. In this field rumor is rife. There is the cartoon of the coach who angrily turns to one of his players and says: "Jones, you're through! Turn in your suit and your convertible." The deal may have a hundred variations, from a pledge to help the ambitious athlete on through medical school to assistance to various relatives. My own experience leads me to believe that the bizarre bargain is less frequent than educators and the public think, but is crucial nonetheless. One or two stars can transform a team into a winner and are worth what they cost. Schools bargain with all kinds of appeals—the prestige of the Ivy

League may appeal to the boy from the Middle West; religious affiliation may take a boy to Notre Dame; the lavish dormitory facilities for athletes may tip the scales for Louisiana State or Texas. Most conferences have rules which prevent an athlete who has signed with one school from leaving it to join another, even though he later discovers the immense advantages of the second school. Conferences resent scouts from outside their territory, yet raiding is universal. By a dozen devices high school coaches are encouraged to become feeders for particular colleges and universities, sometimes by the flattering appointment to a coaching school staff, support for a bigger job, or even cash. Thus the web is widespread, subtle, and effective.

The services of the American educational system in the field of public entertainment cannot be taken lightly—least of all by the educational institutions themselves. It may not be an ideal use of an educational institution to supply public entertainment, but the public interest exists; and for the institutions, either the necessity or the willingness to supply it also exists. The schools which would like to refuse will be compelled to supply it to keep up with their willing rivals. Their only choice is whether they will manage the entertainment in such a way as to prevent damage to themselves as educational institutions—damage which the present methods certainly entail. These methods frequently create financial obligations which imperil educational development because they have contractual priority over educational budgets. Those who recruit players and the players who are recruited are too often corrupted not because of the bargains they strike, but because the bargains are in violation of pledges all have agreed to uphold. Influences outside universities are encouraged to seek control of educational operations—influences which are seldom willing to confine their interests to athletics. Athletics requires an atmosphere of academic accommodation to its necessities, to the great cynicism of faculties and students. It has bred a kind of humiliating schizophrenia in educational administrators who are compelled to defend with platitudes what they do not believe or to keep an uneasy silence. It has created a kind of amused tolerance toward institutions on the part of the very public which buys the entertainment—a tolerance which says that whatever the virtues and respectability of higher education on all other scores, it must be given the privilege of this secret sin.

IV

At the risk of scornful disagreement let me outline how, it seems to me, the great strain in our educational institutions can be reduced. The first and most crucial step is purely intellectual: to make the admission, both inside and outside the universities, that our programs of intercollegiate athletics are operated primarily as public entertainment and not as educational responsibilities. This will lay a foundation for entirely new solutions to the problem.

With the acceptance of this concept most of the undesirable stresses and strains will begin to disappear. Athletics—that is, *winning* athletics—now becomes a legitimate university operation. Recruiting becomes not only legal but justifiable. To get the best athletes becomes not only understandable but commendable in exactly the same way that one seeks for excellence in any department of the university. One gives the athlete what the resources will allow—just as Illinois offers the graduate assistant in history or chemistry what it can to attract the best. No one thinks the less of Illinois because it can outbid Montana for graduate students. In short, athletic practices which are not at all appropriate to "educational" activities become acceptable and legitimate as parts of a program of public entertainment.

The same principle clarifies the position and character of the coaching staff. Let it be the best that can be obtained, as large and specialized as the situation requires. Let it be freed to meet its obligations without the moral strain imposed by the necessity to circumvent impossible requirements. The financial situation likewise becomes manageable. Since athletics is to be managed as entertainment, it need not in logic or in fact be a charge on the educational budget; and just as no educational institution expects to support itself from athletics, so athletics should not expect to be a charge on education. Self-support for athletics as public entertainment is at once a financial liberation and a restraint.

And why should there be concern about the academic record of a young man who comes to a university primarily to play on a team and whom the university has brought for exactly that purpose? I submit that nothing is lost by relieving all athletes of the obligation to meet academic requirements, if they cannot or do not wish to do so. Let us be courageous enough to admit that the university's interest in them is that they be good athletes, not that

they be good students. It is the insistence that they be students which creates the problem both for the faculty and for the athletic managers, and to the detriment of both. Of course, if a boy wishes to be a student as well as an athlete, by all means encourage him, but in that case the fact that he is an athlete need not enter into his status as a student any more than his grades as a student should be made to affect his effectiveness as an athlete. The athlete will then for the first time be on a par with every other student who works his way through school. His academic progress will be exactly proportional to the time and interest he has beyond the demands of his employment.

What if the athlete has no interest whatsoever in his further education? A team entirely made up of professionals is not the solution for the colleges. The best solution is a prescription of academic work suited to the tastes and talents of the athlete but with the clear understanding by professors and athletes alike that the record as a student will be neither a hindrance nor a help to athletic success.

What! someone says. Have unbridled bidding for athletes? No eligibility rules? No discipline? By no means—but let these things arise, as they will, from athletic and not from academic sources and necessities. Let eligibility rules be drawn and enforced by those who are most concerned about them—the athletic managements—not by faculties. Who can be counted on to expose infractions of eligibility rules? Opponents! Every roster of players is exchanged between coaches—why should a faculty committee bother? Who is hurt if the ineligible player plays? The opposition! Who is the best insurance that he won't? The opposition! No, faculties and administrators have gratuitously assumed a lot of unnecessary burdens —and to what purpose or to what effect it is hard to see.

The relinquishment of formal academic—not institutional—control over athletics will have very substantial advantages both for athletics and for education. The first is the restoration of institutional and personal integrity. Gone will be the necessity to keep up the pretense that at the present time suffuses the discussion of athletics as a part of an educational program. The establishment of single-mindedness will be the greatest advantage, for educational institutions are basically devoted to intellectual honesty. Such honesty will free athletics as well as education from the schizophrenia from which they both now suffer.

A very valuable outcome will also be the dissipation of the sentimentality which currently surrounds college athletics in the mind of the public. This myth is carefully preserved not for its truth but for its utility. Listen to any major coach talk about his team and you will see how little such sentimentality is justified. He refers to his "material," not to boys; he discusses weakness at end and tackle and backfield, completely oblivious of the feelings of his men. There is not a player whom he will not instantly displace if he can get a better one. One of the most unhappy tasks that athletic managements must perform is to get rid of players to whom scholarships have been given—commitments made—but who can't quite make the grade on the field. Perhaps the public which sees the universities as operating departments of public entertainment and sees athletes as assistants in the department will come to think of the whole matter a little differently—to the great relief of everyone concerned.

When doctors find that a given treatment results in no improvement, they re-examine their diagnosis; when scientists find that experiments produce no anticipated results, they revise their basic hypothesis. Educators now find that what was once the recreation of students in school has been transformed into a responsibility of the educational system to supply the public with entertainment. It is essential that educators carry through a fundamental revision of concepts of athletic management appropriate to this transformation.

· QUESTIONS ·

1. State in one or two sentences the essential argument of this essay.
2. Can you cite any statements which are not supported? For example, does *no* school actually give to the appointment of a president attention comparable to that given the appointment of a coach?
3. What do you think should be the bases of scholarship grants?
4. Is your school more interested in athletes than students? Substantiate your answer.
5. What new football rules promote or lessen the entertainment value of the game?
6. In section IV, the author outlines a series of steps. What are they?

7. Define: tempered, intricate, spontaneous, irreconcilable, myth, crucial, entail, dissipation, schizophrenia, transformation.

8. Since this article was published in 1954, much has occurred to support the author's recommendations. What, for example? Even more has occurred to increase the "public entertainment" features of college athletics. What, for example?

Theme Subjects: (1) Why I Received My Scholarship; (2) This College Is (Is Not) a True Educational Institution; (3) The Great Sports Myth; (4) My Opinion of Intramural Sports; (5) Dr. Stoke Is Wrong (Right); (6) How To Recruit Athletes; (7) A Valid Athletic Policy for This College; (8) A Curriculum for Football Players.

LO, THE OLD
COLLEGE SPIRIT

G. Gaddis Smith

G. GADDIS SMITH (1932–   ) received his bachelor's degree from Yale in 1954. He was chairman (editor-in-chief) of the *Yale Daily News* when he originally wrote "Lo, the Old College Spirit." He is now a professor of history at Yale University and has published *Britain's Clandestine Submarines* (1964) and *American Diplomacy During the Second World War* (1965).

The scene: a college football stadium anywhere in the United States. *The time:* a Saturday afternoon in the fall. From his seat on the 50-yard line, portly Joe Alumnus, class of 1928, pouts as his team gives up another touchdown and sinks deeper into infamy. Along the sidelines cheerleaders strain their hoarse voices: "Come on, gang, let's have a little noise!" But from the undergraduates comes only silence.

This article originally appeared in *The New York Times Magazine*, January 17, 1954, and is reprinted here by permission of author and publisher. Mr. Smith has revised the article expressly for this book.

To Joe Alumnus, class of 1928, it is clear that the Old College Spirit is gone. Here are the results: the players are soft, the students don't care, and the college itself probably hasn't educated a *real* man in thirty years.

Elsewhere that afternoon Joe Alumnus could have found more evidence to support his conclusion. Half the students were not even at the football game. A few were studying, some were enjoying an autumn game of tennis or golf, others had gone home or were at work on a part-time job. What horror, what heresy! When Joe Alumnus was an undergraduate, four freshmen were once caught playing cards in a dormitory during a football game. That night they were driven ten miles out into the country and left to walk back in their underwear.

Joe Alumnus is right. The Old College Spirit is dead, just as dead as near beer, the Stutz Bearcat, and the goldfish-swallowing tournament. But that doesn't mean today's student is a dull, lifeless cog in a spiritless community. It means he has become a quiet, more mature individual seldom given to flamboyance and exhibitionism of the do-or-die-for-dear-old-Rutgers variety.

The old grad who remembers his hip flask and raccoon coat and likes to call the undergraduates of today a bunch of humorless jellyfish should join the superficial critic who denounces this generation as "silent." At least the two can agree with each other. Today's college student has more genuine spirit and a better sense of humor than his father or his grandfather. He doesn't make as much noise and he doesn't lavish as much foolish attention on athletic spectacles and boyish

pranks because his spirit goes deeper and means more to the school he loves and to higher education itself.

Humor is one of the best indicators of how a generation thinks. Let's see what sort of thing is considered humorous in college today:

At one college, a junior recently succeeded in planting a story in a local newspaper to the effect that two campus buildings were moving toward each other because of a geologic fault and would collide in 500 years.

A few years ago, Yale's 130-pound football manager, no football player, was sent in to catch a pass for the final extra point against Harvard. "It stinks," said the Harvard captain, but he was in the minority; even Harvard men admitted the incident was pretty funny.

At a big university the august former state governor was "kidnapped" by a bogus student political group. He spoke for two hours before an attentive but fake audience while the real audience waited impatiently in a near-by hall.

Compare these stunts with those of the past when the Old College Spirit reigned: fraternity letters painted in indelible red on the white marble of the courthouse, chapel bell stolen from a rival college, cows in the girls' dormitory, head-shaving raids on unsuspecting freshmen, train tracks greased along the grade outside of town. Compare the two and you will see a pattern. The college sense of humor today is more subtle and restrained. It makes fun of the times and of human nature. It does not depend on the grotesque or on what might be called over-stimulated "alma matriotism."

In the football stadium, where some old grads seem to think the only worthwhile part of education is found, the undergraduate of today may appear overly dignified, but he enjoys his football just the same. Unlike some alumni he knows that only a game and not the honor and reputation of the school is being fought for on the field. He probably doesn't know all the cheers or the college song (last fall a small band of Boy Scouts out-yelled an entire student cheering section), but he says he is there to watch and not join in mob hysteria.

The place of the football player has also changed with the passing of the Old College Spirit. No longer is he worshipped as the hero of college, America, all manhood. Today he is either a true amateur mildly admired for his skill or a virtual professional taken for granted as just another chap earning an honorable living.

Traditional college bravado has been replaced by an unobtrusive sense of pride in what is best in American education coupled with a determination in a perilous time to make the good better, something which can't be done by waving pennants. The football team may be headed for a bowl bid or have lost every game in the Conference. So what? How can that mean anything at all to the quality of education? Since World War II and increasingly in very recent years, the college student has placed the emphasis of his spirit increasingly on first things, on education for a free society and not on meaningless prestige in sports or anything else.

This attitude was put another way by one old grad, class of 1904, who remarked that "effusive demon-stration has been replaced by a deeper pride in one's college and a personal interest in her permanent welfare." The old grad could well have gone further and said that the focus of pride is less on the single college or university as the *only* good school in the country and more on the idea of college education and on its strivings for improvement.

The changes are obvious in every section of the land, in big university and small college, state school and private. The customs of the past are gone or going fast: the absurdly intricate and often unpleasant fraternity and sorority initiation escapades, the week-long victory celebrations, freshman beanies, hazing, town-gown riots, and so on. Behind the changes are many causes.

Foremost is the fact that today's undergraduate has almost no leisure time; his existence has been accurately described as "lurching from crisis to crisis." On top of a more demanding academic schedule than his father ever knew he has piled an amazing proliferation of extracurricular activities. Instead of spending half the day in unhurried conversation, smoking a pipe and sipping beer, the average college student of the mid-twentieth century wants to do things: compete strenuously in intramural athletics instead of watching the varsity, edit a newspaper or magazine, engage in dramatics or sing with the glee club, perhaps run a little money-making business on the side. Every day he is launching new enterprises, inventing new schemes. There is no time to think about college-spirit traditions—much less learn and practice them. Unfortunately—and here's the rub—all too many undergraduates find too little time to think deeply and study at leisure either.

Second, America's colleges have undergone a revolution in the relations of the sexes. When the legendary Dink Stover came to Yale in 1911, a wise upper classman advised: "And another thing: no fooling around women; that isn't done here—that'll queer you absolutely." And Stover echoed his generation by replying, "Of course." Twenty years later the shrill cry of "Fire" still resounded through the dormitories of Yale whenever a female appeared in view. As one alumnus says, "gals were as scarce as Indians" except at one or two big football games.

What a change has taken place! Today, American college education is overwhelmingly co-educational, and rightly so. Even the schools of the Ivy League, once stodgy bastions of the isolated male animal, have begun to open their gates. Thanks to the automobile, half the undergraduates in the Ivy League have at least one date a week, a performance undreamed of a generation ago. Harvard and Radcliffe are virtually one co-educational institution. Yale, under a special program, admitted a few girls to undergraduate classes for the first time in 1958. The natural result of the coming of women has been the abandonment of the stag folderol that once was such an integral part of the Old College Spirit. No one wants to stay in Princeton or New Haven on a weekend when he can be in Northampton or Poughkeepsie.

Another aspect of the new age is the great increase in the number of married students. Before World War II most colleges had standing rules against marriage: get hitched and get fired. But since 1945 the rules have bowed before the reality, first, of the influx of veterans, and now of the lower marriage age and better economic resources of the average American. Married students have in turn contributed their bit to the demise of the Old College Spirit. Who feels like screaming oneself silly over a football game when back in the apartment is a baby who will soon be screaming for his bottle?

Other reasons are more serious. Leading the list is general apprehension about the state of the world. One senior recently put it this way: "Education is supposed to make one inquire into the nature of things and form value judgments. Let's assume that it is successful. For a student who has benefited by that education, it is difficult to get overly worked up about any football team, defeated or undefeated. As such a student, I am just too conscious of the real problems of the world. Things are a little too gray; in some ways they seem to be about as messed up as they can be. And most guys know that problems can't be solved on a grassy field 100 yards long."

This increased awareness of the world is evident everywhere you look in college. One of the first things which most alumni notice when they return to visit college is the great number of students who daily read a metropolitan newspaper. "When I was in college," one alumnus said, "I didn't read a newspaper from September to June. We just didn't care what was happening in the world." But, for that matter, neither did most Americans in the Twenties.

The terrific competition for places in each freshman class at almost every college and university (the more popular schools can accept only about one fourth of all those who apply for admission) has had a direct effect on college spirit in the old style. The energetic alumnus who now enrolls his new-born son for the class of 1980 has little assurance that the boy will be accepted when the time comes. As for the boy, he will doubtless be glad of acceptance at any one of many colleges—not just Dad's alma mater. Furthermore, whatever college the boy attends there is an increasing chance that it will be only a way station on his educational road. In many colleges today more than half the students go on to do some advanced graduate or professional studying, almost always at another school. Such conditions make it impossible for the fanatical one-college loyalty of the past to survive.

The Old College Spirit at its worst had strong overtones of social snobbery and thus is now out of place in a more balanced social system. With the opportunity of a college education now readily open to almost all social and economic groups, the wealthy Eastern prep school aristocracy of old has dwindled to relative unimportance in the college population. One result is a diluting of old family college ties— another of the great defenders of outmoded tradition.

Finally, there is the great educational awakening going on throughout the country—a movement which began at the end of World War II, long before the nation's startled surprise over the Russian sputniks. You can see the ferment at work in scores of ambitious new experiments, and you can sense it even more in the bull sessions where today's undergraduates are constantly questioning the purpose and content of what they study. Someone will say: "I don't want to be like my father. He went through college and was graduated as an uneducated man. All he did learn was useless facts which he forgot overnight." And others will agree. No longer is the "gentleman's 70" a fashionable mark, or a safe one as the colleges face the oft-described approaching tidal wave of students, and graduate schools and employers demand far more than mediocrity. The myth that the well-rounded good fellow with low grades is a better man than the scholar has gone the way of the Old College Spirit to which it was related. In its place is the knowledge that the well-rounded scholar is best of all.

The Old College Spirit is no more—no one will deny that. But gone, too, are some things of value: the spontaneous lack of reserve, the boundless enthusiasm, and, often, the fun. The new spirit is a bit pretentious, it is condescending, and it is too often stone-faced. The reaction against the excesses of the Twenties is occasionally so extreme that some undergraduates will have no part of it. They, like their fathers, still long for the glory of Dink Stover or the champagne springtime of Scott Fitzgerald. They wish that Frank Merriwell were more than a ghost that flitted quietly along the sidelines once or twice during the football season. These people are uneasy; they are suffering the pains of transition.

But if the new spirit is not entirely accepted and if it is impossible to define with precision, its broad outlines are emerging as it spreads beyond the colleges and through much of the present generation. The new spirit has deep implications and three chief qualities (and here perhaps an apology is due for ending on a too-serious note):

1. The new spirit is composed of faith mingled with criticism. A previous generation moved wildly from the exaltation of 1917–18 to the disillusionment of 1919, from the boundless optimism of the late Twenties to the black despair of the Thirties. In each moment, according to the present generation's interpretation of recent history, there was foolish faith untempered by criticism, or total criticism of life and society without faith. Today's generation hopes to acquire and preserve both.

2. The new spirit is soundly conservative in the best meaning of the word. Mere change will not be confused with progress and reform; but tradition will not be embellished with false sanctity.

3. Finally, it is a spirit of leadership seeking both courage and tolerance: the courage to search for truth and speak it even when, especially when, it pains; and the tolerance to understand that good and evil in human relationships, from the personal to the international, are not absolutes.

· QUESTIONS ·

1. Comment on the stylistic effect of the first three paragraphs.
2. Demonstrate that the fourth paragraph states the entire thesis of the article.
3. What specific incidents and anecdotes are used to develop the thoughts of the first four paragraphs?
4. This article is developed largely by contrast. Make parallel columns of contrasted topics and ideas. (Short phrases will suffice.)
5. Do you agree or disagree with the ideas set forth in the final three paragraphs?
6. Does your campus reflect the statements made by Smith?
7. What is the *tone* of this essay? Compare it with the tone of "College Athletics: Education or Show Business?"
8. Does this essay foreshadow some of the results indicated in an article published a dozen years later, "Causes of the Student Revolution"?

Theme Subjects: (1) What College Means to Me; (2) I'm Proud (Not Proud) of My College; (3) My Post-College Plans; (4) What Mr. Smith Overlooks; (5) College Is for Fun; (6) My Awareness of the World (not less than 1000 words); (7) A Recent College Prank on This Campus; (8) I'm a Married Student; (9) Women on This Campus; (10) Stoke and Smith (a comparison of ideas expressed by these two writers in articles in this volume); (11) My Faith in Education.

INFORMAL ESSAYS

WHERE I LIVED

AND

WHAT I LIVED FOR

Henry David Thoreau

HENRY DAVID THOREAU (1817–1862) was born in Concord, Massachusetts, and was educated in the woods of that town and at Harvard. After his graduation in 1837, he taught school in Concord for some time. Thoreau built himself a hut at nearby Walden Pond and lived there from July 4, 1845, to September 6, 1847, the period of which he wrote in his famous book, *Walden,* from which this selection is made.

I went to the woods because I wished to live deliberately, to front only the essential facts of life, and see if I could not learn what it had to teach, and not, when I came to die, discover that I had not lived. I did not wish to live what was not life, living is so dear; nor did I wish to practice resignation, unless it was quite necessary. I wanted to live deep and suck out all the marrow of life, to live so sturdily and Spartan-like as to put to rout all that was not life, to cut a broad swath and shave close, to drive life into a corner, and reduce it to its lowest terms, and, if it proved to be mean, why then to get the whole and genuine meanness of it, and publish its meanness to the world; or if it were sublime, to know it by experience, and be able to give a true account of it in my next excursion. For most men, it appears to me, are in a strange uncertainty about it, whether it is of the devil or of God, and have *somewhat hastily* concluded that it is the chief end of man here to "glorify God and enjoy him forever."

Still we live meanly, like ants; though the fable tells us that we were long ago changed into men; like pygmies we fight with cranes; it is error upon error, and clout upon clout, and our best virtue has for its occasion a superfluous and evitable wretchedness. Our life is frittered away by detail. An honest man has hardly need to count more than his ten fingers, or in extreme cases he may add his ten toes, and lump the rest. Simplicity, simplicity, simplicity! I say, let your affairs be as two or three, and not a hundred or a thousand; instead of a million count half a dozen, and keep your accounts on your thumb-nail. In the midst of this chopping sea of civilized life, such are the clouds and storms and quicksands and thousand-and-one items to be allowed for, that a man has to live, if he would not founder and go to the bottom and not make his port at all, by dead reckoning, and he must be a great calculator indeed who succeeds. Simplify, simplify. Instead of three meals a day, if it be necessary eat but one; instead of a hundred dishes, five; and reduce other things in proportion. Our life is like a German Confederacy, made up of petty states, with its boundary forever fluctuating, so that even a German cannot tell you how it is bounded at any moment. The nation itself, with all its so-called internal improvements, which, by the way, are all external and superficial, is just such an unwieldy and overgrown

establishment, cluttered with furniture and tripped up by its own traps, ruined by luxury and heedless expense, by want of calculation and a worthy aim, as the million households in the land; and the only cure for it, as for them, is in a rigid economy, a stern and more than Spartan simplicity of life and elevation of purpose. It lives too fast. Men think that it is essential that the Nation have commerce, and export ice, and talk through a telegraph, and ride thirty miles an hour, without a doubt, whether *they* do or not; but whether we should live like baboons or like men, is a little uncertain. If we do not get out sleepers[1] and forge rails, and devote days and nights to the work, but go to tinkering upon our *lives* to improve *them*, who will build railroads? And if railroads are not built, how shall we get to heaven in season? But if we stay at home and mind our business, who will want railroads? We do not ride on the railroad; it rides upon us. Did you ever think what those sleepers are that underlie the railroad? Each one is a man, an Irishman, or a Yankee man. The rails are laid on them, and they are covered with sand, and the cars run smoothly over them. They are sound sleepers, I assure you. And every few years a new lot is laid down and run over; so that, if some have the pleasure of riding on a rail, others have the misfortune to be ridden upon. And when they run over a man that is walking in his sleep, a supernumerary sleeper in the wrong position, and wake him up, they suddenly stop the cars, and make a hue and cry about it, as if this were an exception. I am glad to know that it takes a gang of

---

[1] railway ties

men for every five miles to keep the sleepers down and level in their beds as it is, for this is a sign that they may sometime get up again.

Why should we live with such hurry and waste of life? We are determined to be starved before we are hungry. Men say that a stitch in time saves nine, and so they take a thousand stitches today to save nine tomorrow. As for *work*, we haven't any of any consequence. We have the Saint Vitus's dance, and cannot possibly keep our heads still. If I should only give a few pulls at the parish bell-rope, as for a fire, that is, without setting the bell, there is hardly a man on his farm in the outskirts of Concord, notwithstanding that press of engagements which was his excuse so many times this morning, nor a boy, nor a woman, I might almost say, but would forsake all and follow that sound, not mainly to save property from the flames, but, if we will confess the truth, much more to see it burn, since burn it must, and we, be it known, did not set it on fire,— or to see it put out, and have a hand in it, if that is done as handsomely; yes, even if it were the parish church itself. Hardly a man takes a half-hour's nap after dinner, but when he wakes he holds up his head and asks, "What's the news?" as if the rest of mankind had stood his sentinels. Some give directions to be waked every half-hour, doubtless for no other purpose; and then, to pay for it, they tell what they have dreamed. After a night's sleep the news is as indispensable as the breakfast. "Pray tell me anything new that has happened to a man anywhere on this globe,"—and he reads it over his coffee and rolls, that a man has had his eyes gouged out this morning on the Wachito

River; never dreaming the while that he lives in the dark unfathomed mammoth cave of this world, and has but the rudiment of an eye himself.

For my part, I could easily do without the post-office. I think that there are very few important communications made through it. To speak critically, I never received more than one or two letters in my life—I wrote this some years ago— that were worth the postage. The penny-post is, commonly, an institution through which you seriously offer a man that penny for his thoughts which is so often safely offered in jest. And I am sure that I never read any memorable news in a newspaper. If we read of one man robbed, or murdered, or killed by accident, or one house burned, or one vessel wrecked, or one steamboat blown up, or one cow run over on the Western Railroad, or one mad dog killed, or one lot of grasshoppers in the winter,—we never need read of another. One is enough. If you are acquainted with the principle, what do you care for a myriad instances and applications? To a philosopher all *news*, as it is called, is gossip, and they who edit and read it are old women over their tea. Yet not a few are greedy after this gossip. There was such a rush, as I hear, the other day at one of the offices to learn the foreign news by the last arrival, that several large squares of plate glass belonging to the establishment were broken by the pressure,—news which I seriously think a ready wit might write a twelvemonth, or twelve years, beforehand with sufficient accuracy. As for Spain, for instance, if you know how to throw in Don Carlos and the Infanta, and Don Pedro and Seville and Granada, from time to time in the right proportions,—they may have changed the names a little since I saw the papers,—and serve up a bullfight when other entertainments fail, it will be true to the letter, and give us as good an idea of the exact state or ruin of things in Spain as the most succinct and lucid reports under this head in the newspapers: and as for England, almost the last significant scrap of news from that quarter was the revolution of 1649; and if you have learned the history of her crops for an average year, you never need attend to that thing again, unless your speculations are of a merely pecuniary character. If one may judge who rarely looks into the newspapers, nothing new does ever happen in foreign parts, a French revolution not excepted.

What news! how much more important to know what that is which was never old! "Kieou-he-yu (great dignitary of the state of Wei) sent a man to Khoung-tseu to know his news. Khoung-tseu caused the messenger to be seated near him, and questioned him in these terms: What is your master doing? The messenger answered with respect: My master desires to diminish the number of his faults, but he cannot come to the end of them. The messenger being gone, the philosopher remarked: What a worthy messenger! What a worthy messenger!" The preacher, instead of vexing the ears of drowsy farmers on their day of rest at the end of the week,—for Sunday is the fit conclusion of an ill-spent week, and not the fresh and brave beginning of a new one,—with this one other draggle-tail of a sermon, should shout with thundering voice, "Pause! Avast! Why so seeming fast, but deadly slow?"

Shams and delusions are es-teemed for soundest truths, while reality is fabulous. If men would steadily observe realities only, and not allow themselves to be deluded, life, to compare it with such things as we know, would be like a fairy tale and the Arabian Nights' Entertainments. If we respected only what is inevitable and has a right to be, music and poetry would resound along the streets. When we are unhurried and wise, we perceive that only great and worthy things have any permanent and absolute existence, that petty fears and petty pleasures are but the shadow of the reality. This is always exhilarating and sublime. By closing the eyes and slumbering, and consenting to be deceived by shows, men establish and confirm their daily life of routine and habit everywhere, which still is built on purely illusory foundations. Children, who play life, discern its true law and relations more clearly than men, who fail to live it worthily, but who think that they are wiser by experience, that is, by failure. I have read in a Hindoo book, that "there was a king's son, who, being expelled in infancy from his native city, was brought up by a forester, and, growing up to maturity in that state, imagined himself to belong to the barbarous race with which he lived. One of his father's ministers having discovered him, revealed to him what he was, and the misconception of his character was removed, and he knew himself to be a prince. So soul," continues the Hindoo philosopher, "from the circumstances in which it is placed, mistakes its own character, until the truth is revealed to it by some holy teacher, and then it knows itself to be *Brahme*." I perceive that we inhabitants of New England live this mean life that we do because our vision does not penetrate the surface of things. We think that that *is* which *appears* to be. If a man should walk through this town and see only the reality, where, think you, would the "Milldam" go to? If he should give us an account of the realities he beheld there, we should not recognize the place in his description. Look at a meeting-house, or a courthouse, or a jail, or a shop, or a dwelling-house, and say what that thing really is before a true gaze, and they would all go to pieces in your account of them. Men esteem truth remote, in the outskirts of the system, behind the farthest star, before Adam and after the last man. In eternity there is indeed something true and sublime. But all these times and places and occasions are now and here. God himself culminates in the present moment, and will never be more divine in the lapse of all the ages. And we are enabled to apprehend at all what is sublime and noble only by the perpetual instilling and drenching of the reality that surrounds us. The universe constantly and obediently answers to our conceptions; whether we travel fast or slow, the track is laid for us. Let us spend our lives in conceiving then. The poet or the artist never yet had so fair and noble a design but some of his posterity at least could accomplish it.

Let us spend one day as deliberately as Nature, and not be thrown off the track by every nutshell and mosquito's wing that falls on the rails. Let us rise early and fast, or break fast, gently and without perturbation; let company come and let company go, let the bells ring and the children cry,—determined to make a day of it. Why should we knock under and go with the stream? Let us not be upset and overwhelmed in that terrible rapid and whirlpool called a dinner, situated in the meridian shallows. Weather this danger and you are safe, for the rest of the way is down hill. With unrelaxed nerves, with morning vigor, sail by it, looking another way, tied to the mast like Ulysses. If the engine whistles, let it whistle till it is hoarse for its pains. If the bell rings, why should we run? We will consider what kind of music they are like. Let us settle ourselves, and work and wedge our feet downward through the mud and slush of opinion, and prejudice, and tradition, and delusion, and appearance, that alluvion which covers the globe, through Paris and London, through New York and Boston and Concord, through Church and State, through poetry and philosophy and religion, till we come to a hard bottom and rocks in place, which we can call *reality*, and say, This is, and no mistake; and then begin, having a *point d'appui*,[2] below freshet and frost and fire, a place where you might found a wall or a state, or set a lamppost safely, or perhaps a gauge, not a Nilometer, but a Realometer, that future ages might know how deep a freshet of shams and appearances had gathered from time to time. If you stand right fronting and face to face to a fact, you will see the sun glimmer on both its surfaces, as if it were a cimeter,[3] and feel its sweet edge dividing you through the heart and marrow, and so you will happily conclude your mortal career. Be it

---

[2] point of support, resting point
[3] properly, "scimitar" or "scimeter"

life or death, we crave only reality. If we are really dying, let us hear the rattle in our throats and feel cold in the extremities; if we are alive, let us go about our business.

Time is but the stream I go a-fishing in. I drink at it; but while I drink I see the sandy bottom and detect how shallow it is. Its thin current slides away, but eternity remains. I would drink deeper; fish in the sky, whose bottom is pebbly with stars. I cannot count one. I know not the first letter of the alphabet. I have always been regretting that I was not as wise as the day I was born. The intellect is a cleaver; it discerns and rifts its way into the secret of things. I do not wish to be any more busy with my hands than is necessary. My head is hands and feet. I feel all my best faculties concentrated in it. My instinct tells me that my head is an organ for burrowing, as some creatures use their snout and fore paws, and with it I would mine and burrow my way through these hills. I think that the richest vein is somewhere hereabouts; so by the divining-rod and thin rising vapors I judge; and here I will begin to mine.

· QUESTIONS ·

1. This is a truly rebellious essay. Do you agree or disagree with its central thesis?
2. How do you interpret Thoreau's comment that we should "spend one day as deliberately as Nature"?
3. Is it as easy, and as fashionable, to be a rebel as a conformist?
4. What is a poseur? Was Thoreau one? Why? Why not?
5. How much time do you daily devote to the news—in newspapers and through radio and television? Is your time well spent?
6. Do you live "with . . . hurry and waste of life"? How? Why?
7. Thoreau's advice was considered "impossible" and "impractical" even in his own day. What do you think of it today?
8. What would be the economic and physical effects on American life if the suggestions in this essay were literally followed out? See "The Idea of Progress."

Theme Subjects: (1) I Do (Do Not) Wish To Live Deeply; (2) What I Really Want from Life; (3) Life That Is Merely Existence; (4) The Marrow of Life; (5) What Dr. William Osler Would Say About Thoreau; (6) My Idea of an Honest Man; (7) Read the News and Get Ulcers; (8) The Stream I Go A-Fishing In.

WALDEN

E. B. White

ELWYN BROOKS WHITE (1899–   ) was born in Mount Vernon, New York. After his graduation from Cornell in 1921, Mr. White traveled about and held several positions, including a reporter's job on the Seattle *Times* and work as a production assistant in an advertising agency. He is well known for his contributions to *The New Yorker* and for such books as *The Lady Is Cold* (1929); *Is Sex Necessary?* (1929 and 1950, with James Thurber); *Every Day Is Saturday* (1934); *The Fox of Peapack* (1938); *One Man's Meat* (1942 and 1944); *Charlotte's Web* (1952); *The Second Tree from the Corner* (1953); *The Points of My Compass* (1962). Mr. White now spends part of his time in New York, part in Maine.

Miss Nims, take a letter to Henry David Thoreau. Dear Henry: I thought of you the other afternoon as I was approaching Concord doing fifty on Route 62. That is a high speed at which to hold a philosopher in one's mind, but in this century we are a nimble bunch.

On one of the lawns in the outskirts of the village a woman was cutting the grass with a motorized lawn mower. What made me think of you was that the machine had rather got away from her, although she was game enough, and in the brief glimpse I had of the scene it appeared to me that the lawn was mowing the lady. She kept a tight grip on the handles, which throbbed violently with every explosion of the one-cylinder motor, and as she sheered around bushes and lurched along at a reluctant trot behind her impetuous servant, she looked like a puppy who had grabbed something that was too much for him. Concord hasn't changed much, Henry; the farm implements and the animals still have the upper hand.

I may as well admit that I was journeying to Concord with the deliberate intention of visiting your woods; for although I have never knelt at the grave of a philosopher nor placed wreaths on moldy poets, and have often gone a mile out of my way to avoid some place of historical interest, I have always wanted to see Walden Pond. The account which you left of your sojourn there is, you will be amused to learn, a document of increasing pertinence; each year it seems to gain a little headway, as the world loses ground. We may all be transcendental yet, whether we like it or not. As our common complexities increase, any tale of individual simplicity (and yours is the best written and the cockiest) acquires a new fascination; as our goods accumulate, but not our well-being, your report of an existence without material adornment takes on a certain awkward credibility.

My purpose in going to Walden Pond, like yours, was not to live cheaply or to live dearly there, but to transact some private business with the fewest obstacles. Approaching Concord, doing forty, doing forty-five, doing fifty, the steering wheel held snug in my palms, the highway held grimly in my vision, the crown of the road now serving me (on the righthand curves), now defeating me (on the lefthand curves), I began to rouse myself from the stupefaction which a day's motor journey induces. It was a delicious evening, Henry, when the whole body is one sense, and imbibes delight through every pore, if I may coin a phrase. Fields were richly brown where the harrow, drawn by the stripped Ford, had lately sunk its teeth; pastures were green; and overhead the sky had that same everlasting great look which you will find on page 144 of the Oxford Pocket Edition. I could feel the road entering me, through tire, wheel, spring, and cushion; shall I have intelligence with earth too? Am I not partly leaves and vegetable mold myself?—a man of infinite horsepower, yet partly leaves.

Stay with me on 62 and it will take you into Concord. As I say, it was a delicious evening. The snake had come forth to die in a bloody S on the highway, the wheel upon its head, its bowels flat now and exposed. The turtle had come up too to cross the road and die in the attempt, its hard shell smashed under the rubber blow, its intestinal yearning (for the other side of the road) forever squashed. There was a sign by the wayside which announced that the road had a "cotton surface." You wouldn't know what that is, but neither, for that matter, did I. There is a cryptic ingredient in many of our modern improvements—we are awed and pleased without knowing quite what we are enjoying. It is something to be traveling on a road with a cotton surface.

The civilization round Concord today is an odd distillation of city, village, farm, and manor. The houses, yards, fields look not quite suburban, not quite rural. Under the bronze beech and the blue spruce of the departed baron grazes the milch goat of the heirs. Under the porte-cochère stands the reconditioned station wagon; under the grape arbor sit the puppies for sale. (But why do men degenerate ever? What makes families run out?)

It was June and everywhere June was publishing her immemorial stanza: in the lilacs, in the syringa, in the freshly edged paths and the sweetness of moist beloved gardens, and the little wire wickets that preserve the tulips' front. Farmers were already moving the fruits of their toil into their yards, arranging the rhubarb, the asparagus, the strictly fresh eggs on the painted stands under the little shed roofs with the patent shingles. And though it was almost a hundred years since you had taken your ax and started cutting out your home on Walden Pond, I was interested to observe that the philosophical spirit was still alive in Massachusetts: in the center of a vacant lot some boys were assembling the framework of a rude shelter, their whole mind and skill concentrated in the rather inauspicious helterskelter of studs and rafters. They too were escaping from town, to live naturally, in a rich blend of savagery and philosophy.

That evening, after supper at the inn, I strolled out into the twilight to dream my shapeless transcendental dreams and see that the car was locked up for the night (first open the right front door, then reach over, straining, and pull up the handles of the left rear and the left front till you hear the click, then the handle of the right rear, then shut the right front but open it again, remembering that the key is still in the ignition switch, remove the key, shut the right front again with a bang, push the tiny keyhole cover to one side, insert key, turn, and withdraw). It is what we all do, Henry. It is called locking the car. It is said to confuse thieves and keep them from making off with the laprobe. Four doors to lock behind one robe. The driver himself never uses a laprobe, the free movement of his legs being vital to the operation of the vehicle; so that when he locks the car it is a pure and unselfish act. I have in my life gained very little essential heat from laprobes, yet I have ever been at pains to lock them up.

The evening was full of sounds, some of which would have stirred your memory. The robins still love the elms of New England villages at sundown. There is enough of the thrush in them to make song inevitable at the end of the day, and enough of the tramp to make them hang round the dwellings of men. A robin, like many another American, dearly loves a white house with green blinds. Concord is still full of them.

Your fellow-townsmen were stirring abroad—not many afoot, most of them in their cars; and the sound which they made in Concord at evening was a rustling and a whispering. The sound lacks steadfastness and is wholly unlike that of a train. A train, as you know who lived so near the Fitchburg line, whistles once or twice sadly and is gone, trailing a memory in smoke, soothing to ear and mind. Automobiles, skirting a village green, are like flies that have gained the inner ear—they buzz, cease, pause, start, shift, stop, halt, brake, and the whole effect is a nervous polytone curiously disturbing.

As I wandered along, the *toc toc* of ping-pong balls drifted from an attic window. In front of the Reuben Brown house a Buick was drawn up. At the wheel, motionless, his hat upon his head, a man sat, listening to Amos and Andy on the radio (it is a drama of many scenes and without an end). The deep voice of Andrew Brown, emerging from the car, although it originated more than two hundred miles away, was unstrained by distance. When you used to sit on the shore of your pond on Sunday morning, listening to the church bells of Acton and Concord, you were aware of the excellent filter of the intervening atmosphere. Science has attended to that, and sound now maintains its intensity without regard for distance. Properly sponsored, it goes on forever.

A fire engine, out for a trial spin, roared past Emerson's house, hot with readiness for public duty. Over the barn roofs the martins dipped and chittered. A swarthy daughter of an asparagus grower, in culottes, shirt, and bandanna, pedalled past on her bicycle. It was indeed a delicious evening, and I returned to the inn (I believe it was your house once) to rock with the old ladies on the concrete veranda.

Next morning early I started afoot for Walden, out Main Street and down Thoreau, past the depot and the Minuteman Chevrolet Company. The morning was fresh, and in a bean field along the way I flushed an agriculturalist, quietly studying his beans. Thoreau Street soon joined Number 126, an artery of the State. We number our highways nowadays, our speed being so great we can remember little of their quality or character and are lucky to remember their number. (Men have an indistinct notion that if they keep up this activity long enough all will at length ride somewhere, in next to no time.) Your pond is on 126.

I knew I must be nearing your woodland retreat when the Golden Pheasant lunchroom came into view—Sealtest ice cream, toasted sandwiches, hot frankfurters, waffles, tonics, and lunches. Were I the proprietor, I should add rice, Indian meal, and molasses—just for old time's sake. The Pheasant, incidentally, is for sale: a chance for some nature lover who wishes to set himself up beside a pond in the Concord atmosphere and live deliberately, fronting only the essential facts of life on Number 126.

Beyond the Pheasant was a place called Walden Breezes, an oasis whose porch pillars were made of old green shutters sawed into lengths. On the porch was a distorting mirror, to give the traveler a comical image of himself, who had miraculously learned to gaze in an ordinary glass without smiling. Behind the Breezes, in a sun-parched clearing, dwelt your philosophical descendants in their trailers, each trailer the size of your hut, but all grouped together for the sake of congeniality. Trailer people leave the city, as you did, to discover solitude and in any weather, at any hour of the day or night, to improve the nick of time; but they soon collect in villages and get bogged deeper in the mud than ever. The camp behind Walden Breezes was just rousing itself to the morning. The ground was packed hard under the heel, and the sun came through the clearing to bake the soil and enlarge the wry smell of cramped housekeeping. Cushman's bakery truck had stopped to deliver an early basket of rolls. A camp dog, seeing me in the road, barked petulantly. A man emerged from one of the trailers and set forth with a bucket to draw water from some forest tap.

Leaving the highway I turned off into the woods toward the pond, which was apparent through the foliage. The floor of the forest was strewn with dried old oak leaves and *Transcripts*. From beneath the flattened popcorn wrapper (*granum explosum*) peeped the frail violet. I followed a footpath and descended to the water's edge. The pond lay clear and blue in the morning light, as you have seen it so many times. In the shallows a man's waterlogged shirt undulated gently. A few flies came out to greet me and convoy me to your cove, past the No Bathing signs on which the fellows and the girls had scrawled their names. I felt strangely excited suddenly to be snooping around your premises, tiptoeing along watchfully, as though not to tread by mistake upon the intervening century. Before I got to the cove I heard something which seemed to me quite wonderful: I heard your frog, a full, clear *troonk*, guiding me, still hoarse and solemn, bridging the years as the robins had bridged them in the sweetness of the village evening. But he soon quit, and I came on a couple of young boys throwing stones at him.

Your front yard is marked by a bronze tablet set in a stone. Four small granite posts, a few feet away, show where the house was. On top of the tablet was a pair of faded blue bathing trunks with a white stripe. Back of it is a pile of stones, a sort of cairn, left by your visitors as a tribute, I suppose. It is a rather ugly little heap of stones, Henry. In fact the hillside itself seems faded, browbeaten; a few tall skinny pines, bare of lower limbs, a smattering of young maples in suitable green, some birches and oaks, and a number of trees felled by the last big wind. It was from the bole of one of these fallen pines, torn up by the roots, that I extracted the stone which I added to the cairn—a sentimental act in which I was interrupted by a small terrier from a nearby picnic group, who confronted me and wanted to know about the stone.

I sat down for a while on one of the posts of your house to listen to the bluebottles and the dragonflies. The invaded glade sprawled shabby and mean at my feet, but the flies were tuned to the old vibration. There were the remains of a fire in your ruins, but I doubt that it was yours; also two beer bottles trodden into the soil and become part of earth. A young oak had taken root in your house, and two or three ferns, unrolling like the ticklers at a banquet. The only other furnishings were a DuBarry pattern sheet, a page torn from a picture magazine, and some crusts in wax paper.

Before I quit I walked clear round the pond and found the place where you used to sit on the northeast side to get the sun in the fall, and the beach where you got sand for scrubbing your floor. On the eastern side of the pond, where the highway borders it, the State has built dressing rooms for swimmers, a float with diving towers, drinking fountains of porcelain, and rowboats for hire. The pond is in fact a State Preserve, and carries a twenty-dollar fine for picking wild flowers, a decree signed in all solemnity by your fellow-citizens Walter C. Wardell, Erson B. Barlow, and Nathaniel I. Bowditch. There was a smell of creosote where they had been building a wide wooden stairway to the road and the parking area. Swimmers and boaters were arriving; bodies splashed vigorously into the water and emerged wet and beautiful in the bright air. As I left, a boatload of town boys were splashing about in mid-pond, kidding and fooling, the young fellows singing at the tops of their lungs in a wild chorus:

Amer-i-ca, Amer-i-ca, God shed his
   grace on thee,
And crown thy good with brotherhood
From sea to shi-ning sea!

I walked back to town along the railroad, following your custom.

The rails were expanding noisily in the hot sun, and on the slope of the roadbed the wild grape and the blackberry sent up their creepers to the track.

The expense of my brief sojourn in Concord was

Canvas shoes ...	$1.95	
Baseball bat	.25	gifts to take
Left-handed fielder's glove	1.25	back to a boy
Hotel and meals	4.25	
In all	$7.70	

As you see, this amount was almost what you spent for food for eight months. I cannot defend the shoes or the expenditure for shelter and food: they reveal a meanness and grossness in my nature which you would find contemptible. The baseball equipment, however, is the sort of impediment with which you were never on even terms. You must remember that the house where you practiced the sort of economy which I respect was haunted only by mice and squirrels. You never had to cope with a shortstop.

· QUESTIONS ·

1. Comment on the diction of the essay. For example, how many examples of *onomatopoeia* can you find?
2. What are the implications of the sixth paragraph? (The sentences in parentheses are from Thoreau.)
3. What specific parts of this essay are direct or implied criticism of people today?
4. Is there any direct or implied criticism of Thoreau?
5. What is the tone of this essay? How do you account for it?
6. Define: transcendental, polytone, contemptible, impediment, cope.
7. What additional light does Atkinson's "Thoreau" shed upon this essay? The selection from Thoreau's *Walden*?

Theme Subjects: (1) Write a theme describing changes you observe on a second visit to a place; show clearly which changes are physical or material, which are changes in the writer; (2) A Letter to _____; (3) Mechanical Gadgets and the Man; (4) A Nimble Bunch; (5) The Cryptic Ingredient.

A WINDSTORM
IN THE FOREST

John Muir

JOHN MUIR (1838–1914) was born in Scotland and came to the United States in 1849. He was educated at the University of Wisconsin, where he majored in science. Interested in botany and geology especially, he made lengthy trips through the United States, many of them on foot. His expedition from Indiana to the coast is fully detailed in *A Thousand-Mile Walk to the Gulf* (1916). For years he lived in California, studying the forests and glacial formations of the West and actively assisting in the movement to conserve our forest preserves. Among his best-known books are *My First Summer in the Sierra* (1911) and *The Story of My Boyhood and Youth* (1913).

One of the most beautiful and exhilarating storms I have ever enjoyed in the Sierra occurred in December, 1874, when I happened to be exploring one of the tributary valleys of the Yuba River. The sky and the ground and the trees had been thoroughly rain-washed and were dry again. The day was intensely pure, one of those incomparable bits of California winter, warm and balmy and full of white sparkling sunshine, redolent of all the purest influences of the spring, and at the same time enlivened with one of the most bracing windstorms conceivable. Instead of camping out, as I usually do, I then chanced to be stopping at the house of a friend. But when the storm began to sound, I lost no time in pushing out into the woods to enjoy it. For on such occasions Nature has always something rare to show us, and the danger to life and limb is hardly greater than one would experience crouching deprecatingly beneath a roof.

It was still early morning when I found myself fairly adrift. Delicious sunshine came pouring over the hills, lighting the tops of the pines and setting free a stream of summery fragrance that contrasted strangely with the wild tones of the storm. The air was mottled with pine-tassels and bright green plumes, that went flashing past in the sunlight like birds pursued. But there was not the slightest dustiness, nothing less pure than leaves, and ripe pollen, and flecks of withered bracken and moss. I heard trees falling for hours at the rate of one every two or three minutes; some uprooted, partly on account of the loose, water-soaked condition of the ground; others broken straight across, where some weakness caused by fire had determined the spot. The gestures of the various trees made a delightful study. Young Sugar Pines, light and feathery as squirrel-tails, were bowing almost to the ground; while the grand old patriarchs, whose massive boles had been tried in a hundred storms, waved solemnly above them, their long, arching branches streaming fluently on the gale, and every needle thrilling and ringing and shedding off keen lances of light like a diamond. The Douglas Spruces, with long sprays drawn out in level tresses, and needles massed in a gray, shimmering glow, presented a most striking appearance as they stood in bold relief along the hilltops. The madroños in the dells, with their red bark and large glossy leaves tilted every way, reflected the sunshine in throbbing spangles like those one so often sees on the rippled surface of a glacier lake. But the Silver Pines were now the most impressively beautiful of all. Colossal spires 200 feet in height waved like supple goldenrods chanting and bowing low as if in worship, while the whole mass of their long, tremulous foliage was kindled into one continuous blaze of white sun-fire. The force of the gale was such that the most steadfast monarch of them all rocked down to its roots with a motion plainly perceptible when one leaned against it. Nature was holding high festival, and every fiber of the most rigid giants thrilled with glad excitement.

I drifted on through the midst of this passionate music and motion, across many a glen, from ridge to ridge; often halting in the lee of a rock for shelter, or to gaze and listen. Even when the grand anthem had swelled to its highest pitch, I could distinctly hear the varying tones of individual trees— Spruce, and Fir, and Pine, and leafless Oak—and even the infinitely gentle rustle of the withered grasses at my feet. Each was expressing itself in its own way—singing its own song, and making its own peculiar gestures—manifesting a richness of variety to be found in no other forest I have yet seen. The coniferous woods of Canada, and the Carolinas, and Florida, are made up of trees that resemble one another about as nearly as blades of grass, and grow close together in much the same way. Coniferous trees, in general, seldom possess individual character, such as is manifest among Oaks and Elms. But the California forests are made up of a greater number of distinct species than any other in the world. And in them we find, not only a marked differentiation into special groups, but also a marked individuality in almost every tree, giving rise to storm effects indescribably glorious.

Toward midday, after a long, tingling scramble through copses of hazel and ceanothus, I gained the summit of the highest ridge in the neighborhood; and then it occurred to me that it would be a fine thing to climb one of the trees to obtain a wider outlook and get my ear close to the Æolian music of its topmost needles. But under the circumstances the choice of a tree was a serious matter. One whose instep was not very strong seemed in danger of being blown down, or of being struck by others in case they should fall; another was branchless to a considerable height above the ground, and at the same time too large to be grasped with arms and legs in climbing; while others were not favorably situated for clear views. After cautiously casting about, I made choice of the tallest of a group of Douglas Spruces that were growing close together like a tuft of grass, no one of which seemed likely to fall unless all the rest fell with it. Though comparatively young, they were about 100 feet high, and their lithe, brushy tops were rocking and swirling in wild ecstasy. Being accustomed to climb trees in making botanical studies, I experienced no difficulty in reaching the top of this one, and never before did I enjoy so noble an exhilaration of motion. The slender tops fairly flapped and swished in the passionate torrent, bending and swirling backward and forward, round and round, tracing indescribable combinations of vertical and horizontal curves, while I clung with muscles firm braced, like a bobolink on a reed.

In its wildest sweeps my treetop described an arc of from twenty to thirty degrees, but I felt sure of its elastic temper, having seen others of the same species still more severely tried—bent almost to the ground indeed, in heavy snows—without breaking a fiber. I was therefore safe, and free to take the wind into my pulses and enjoy the excited forest from my superb outlook. The view from here must be extremely beautiful in any weather. Now my eye roved over the piny hills and dales as over fields of waving grain, and felt the light running in ripples and broad swelling undulations across the valleys from ridge to ridge, as the shining foliage was stirred by corresponding waves of air. Oftentimes these waves of reflected light would break up suddenly into a kind of beaten foam, and again, after chasing one another in regular order, they would seem to bend forward in concentric curves, and disappear on some hillside, like sea-waves on a shelving shore. The quantity of light reflected from the bent needles was so great as to make whole groves appear as if covered with snow, while the black shadows beneath the trees greatly enhanced the effect of the silvery splendor.

Excepting only the shadows there was nothing somber in all this wild sea of pines. On the contrary, notwithstanding this was the winter season, the colors were remarkably beautiful. The shafts of the pine and libocedrus were brown and purple, and most of the foliage was well tinged with yellow; the laurel groves, with the pale undersides of their leaves turned upward, made masses of gray; and then there was many a dash of chocolate color from clumps of manzanita, and jets of vivid crimson from the bark of the madroños, while the ground on the hillsides, appearing here and there through openings between the groves, displayed masses of pale purple and brown.

The sounds of the storm corresponded gloriously with this wild exuberance of light and motion. The profound bass of the naked branches and boles booming like waterfalls; the quick, tense vibrations of the pine needles, now rising to a shrill, whistling hiss, now falling to a silky murmur; the rustling of laurel groves in the dells, and the keen metallic click of leaf on leaf—all this was heard in easy analysis when the attention was calmly bent.

The varied gestures of the multitude were seen to fine advantage, so that one could recognize the different species at a distance of several miles by this means alone, as well as by their forms and colors, and the way they reflected the light. All seemed strong and comfortable, as if really enjoying the storm, while responding to its most enthusiastic greetings. We hear much nowadays concerning the universal struggle for existence, but no struggle in the common meaning of the word was manifest here; no recognition of danger by any tree; no deprecation; but rather an invincible gladness as remote from exultation as from fear.

I kept my lofty perch for hours, frequently closing my eyes to enjoy the music by itself, or to feast quietly on the delicious fragrance that was streaming past. The fragrance of the woods was less marked than that produced during warm rain, when so many balsamic buds and leaves are steeped like tea; but, from the chafing of resiny branches against each other, and the incessant attrition of myriads of needles, the gale was spiced to a very tonic degree. And besides the fragrance from these local sources there were traces of scents brought from afar. For this wind came first from the sea, rubbing against its fresh, briny waves, then distilled through the redwoods, threading rich ferny gulches, and spreading itself in broad undulating currents over many a flower-enameled ridge of the coast mountains, then across the golden plains, up the purple foothills, and into these piny woods with the varied incense gathered by the way.

Winds are advertisements of all they touch, however much or little we may be able to read them; telling their wanderings even by their scents alone. Mariners detect the flowery perfume of land-winds far at sea, and sea-winds carry the fragrance of dulse and tangle far inland, where it is quickly recognized, though mingled with the scents of a thousand land-flowers. As an illustration of this, I may tell here that I breathed sea-air on the Firth of Forth, in Scotland, while a boy; then was taken to Wisconsin, where I remained nineteen years; then, without in all this time having breathed one breath of the sea, I walked quietly, alone, from the middle of the Mississippi Valley to the Gulf of Mexico, on a botanical excursion, and while in Florida, far from the coast, my attention wholly bent on the splendid tropical vegetation about me, I suddenly recognized a sea-breeze, as it came sifting through the palmettos and blooming vine-tangles, which at once awakened and set free a thousand dormant associations, and made me a boy again in Scotland, as if all the intervening years had been annihilated.

Most people like to look at mountain rivers, and bear them in mind; but few care to look at the winds, though far more beautiful and sublime, and though they become at times about as visible as flowing water. When the north winds in winter are making upward sweeps over the curving summits of the High Sierra, the fact is sometimes published with flying snow-banners a mile long. Those portions of the winds thus embodied can scarce be wholly invisible, even to the darkest imagination. And when we look around over an agitated forest, we may see something of the wind that stirs it, by its effect upon the trees. Yonder it descends in a rush of water-like ripples, and sweeps over the bending pines from hill to hill. Nearer, we see detached plumes and leaves, now speeding by on level currents, now whirling in eddies, or, escaping over the edges of the whirls, soaring aloft on grand, upswelling domes of air, or tossing on flamelike crests. Smooth, deep currents, cascades, falls, and swirling eddies, sing around every tree and leaf, and over all the varied topography of the region with telling changes of form, like mountain rivers conforming to the features of their channels.

After tracing the Sierra streams from their fountains to the plains, marking where they bloom white in falls, glide in crystal plumes, surge gray and foam-filled in boulder-choked gorges, and slip through the woods in long, tranquil reaches—after thus learning their language and forms in detail, we may at length hear them chanting all together in one grand anthem, and comprehend them all in clear inner vision, covering the range like lace. But even this spectacle is far less sublime and not a whit more substantial than what we may behold of these storm-streams of air in the mountain woods.

We all travel the milky way together, trees and men; but it never occurred to me until this storm-day, while swinging in the wind, that trees are travelers, in the ordinary sense. They make many journeys, not extensive ones, it is true; but our own little journeys, away and back again, are only little more than treewavings— many of them not so much.

When the storm began to abate, I dismounted and sauntered down through the calming woods. The storm-tones died away, and, turning toward the east, I beheld the countless hosts of the forests hushed and tranquil, towering above one another on the slopes of the hills like a devout audience. The setting sun filled them with amber light, and seemed to say, while they listened, "My peace I give unto you."

As I gazed on the impressive scene, all the so-called ruin of the storm was forgotten, and never before did these noble woods appear so fresh, so joyous, so immortal.

· QUESTIONS ·

1. To what senses does the author appeal? Explain your answer with quotations.
2. Show how the author mingles elements of narration and description. Does this mingling add to the dramatic effect of the essay?
3. In what ways does Muir draw parallels between people and natural objects?
4. One student after reading this essay remarked that he felt as if he had had a refreshing bath. Does it similarly affect you?

5. How do you think Thoreau and Muir would have liked each other's attitude toward nature?

Theme Subjects: (1) The Most Beautiful (Thrilling, Terrible) Storm I've Experienced; (2) "The World Is Too Much with Us"; (3) Smells I Like; (4) I'm a City Boy (Girl) Myself; (5) When Nature Held High Festival; (6) Nature Is for the Birds.

DEFINITION OF A GENTLEMAN

John Henry Newman

JOHN HENRY NEWMAN (1801–1890) was one of the truly notable literary and religious figures of the nineteenth century. Originally an Anglican vicar, he was received into the Roman Catholic Church in 1845 and in 1879 was created a Cardinal by Pope Leo XIII. His *Apologia Pro Vita Sua* (1864, 1865) is a well-wrought autobiography; many volumes of his sermons have continued to wield influence; his *The Idea of a University* (1852) is the rich outcome of his work as Rector of Catholic University, Dublin.

Hence it is that it is almost a definition of a gentleman to say he is one who never inflicts pain. This description is both refined and, as far as it goes, accurate. He is mainly occupied in merely removing the obstacles which hinder the free and unembarrassed action of those about him; and he concurs with their movements rather than takes the initiative himself. His benefits may be considered as parallel to what are called comforts or conveniences in arrangements of a personal nature: like an easy chair or a good fire, which do their part in dispelling cold and fatigue, though nature provides both means of rest and animal heat without them. The true gentleman in like manner carefully avoids whatever may cause a jar or a jolt in the minds of those with whom he is cast—all clashing of opinion, or collision of feeling, all restraint, or suspicion, or gloom, or resentment, his great concern being to make every one at their ease and at home. He has his eyes on all his company; he is tender towards the bashful, gentle towards the distant, and merciful towards the absurd; he can recollect to whom he is speaking; he guards against unseasonable allusions, or topics which may irritate; he is seldom prominent in conversation, and never wearisome. He makes light of favors while he does them, and seems to be receiving when he is conferring. He never speaks of himself except when compelled, never defends himself by a mere retort; he has no ears for slander or gossip, is scrupulous in imputing motives to those who interfere with him, and interprets everything for the best. He is never mean or little in his disputes, never takes unfair advantage, never mistakes personalities or sharp sayings for arguments, or insinuates evil which he dare not say out. From a long-sighted prudence he observes the maxim of the ancient sage, that we should ever conduct ourselves towards our enemy as if he were one day to be our friend. He has too much good sense to be affronted at insults; he is too well employed to remember injuries, and too indolent to bear malice. He is patient, forbearing, and resigned, on philosophical principles; he submits to pain because it is inevitable, to bereavement because it is irreparable, and to death because it is his destiny. If he engages in controversy of any kind, his disciplined intellect preserves him from the blundering discourtesy of better, perhaps, but less educated minds, who, like blunt weapons, tear and hack instead of cutting clean, who mistake the point in argument, waste their strength on trifles, misconceive their adver-

sary, and leave the question more involved than they find it. He may be right or wrong in his opinion, but he is too clear-headed to be unjust; he is as simple as he is forcible, and as brief as he is decisive. Nowhere shall we find greater candor, consideration, indulgence; he throws himself into the minds of his opponents, he accounts for their mistakes. He knows the weakness of human reason as well as its strength, its province, and its limits. If he be an unbeliever, he will be too profound and large-minded to ridicule religion or to act against it; he is too wise to be a dogmatist or fanatic in his infidelity. He respects piety and devotion; he even supports institutions as venerable, beautiful, or useful, to which he does not assent; he honors the ministers of religion, and it contents him to decline its mysteries without assailing or denouncing them. He is a friend of religious toleration, and that, not only because his philosophy has taught him to look on all forms of faith with an impartial eye, but also from the gentleness and effeminacy of feeling, which is the attendant on civilization.

Not that he may not hold a religion too, in his own way, even when he is not a Christian. In that case his religion is one of imagination and sentiment; it is the embodiment of those ideas of the sublime, majestic, and beautiful, without which there can be no large philosophy. Sometimes he acknowledges the being of God, sometimes he invests an unknown principle or quality with the attributes of perfection. And this deduction of his reason, or creation of his fancy, he makes the occasion of such excellent thoughts, and the starting-point of so varied and systematic a teach-

ing, that he even seems like a dis- | all, and he appears to others to feel
ciple of Christianity itself. From the very accuracy and steadiness of his logical powers he is able to see what sentiments are consistent in those who hold any religious doctrine at and to hold a whole circle of theological truths which exist in his mind no otherwise than as a number of deductions.

· QUESTIONS ·

1. Explain the structure of this essay.
2. The selection consists of only two paragraphs. Are both unified?
3. List a half-dozen adjectives best describing Cardinal Newman's definition of a gentleman.
4. Is this definition of a gentleman timeless or more than a century out of date? Is the word *gentleman* itself dated?
5. Is Cardinal Newman's gentleman "too good to be true"? Why? Why not?
6. Define: concur, allusions, scrupulous, irreparable, candor, embodiment.

Theme Subjects: (1) My Definition of a Gentleman (Lady); (2) When It's Hard To Be Gentlemanly; (3) Tolerance Is a "Weasel" Word; (4) The Finest Gentleman I Know.

ON THE BEACH

Caskie Stinnett

CASKIE STINNETT (1911–   ) was born in Remington, Virginia, and was graduated from the College of William and Mary in 1932. He began his career as a reporter for the Staunton, Virginia, *News-Leader* and in 1936 served with the U.S. government in Washington as an information specialist. In 1945 he entered magazine work and is presently on the staff of *The Saturday Evening Post*. He is author of *Will Not Run Feb. 22nd* (1956); *Out of the Red* (1960); and *Back to Abnormal* (1963). He contributes articles to many popular magazines and is a lecturer on humor.

For a long time (too long, it now appears) we watched with strained tolerance the struggle between men and women which, in retrospect, seems to have left the cold-war stage right after World War II. For a while it was fun to watch, the women being absurdly arrogant as they got a better grip on their authority and the men being petulant as they discovered no one was impressed any longer with their Clarence Day attitudes, when suddenly the laughter left and the whole thing took on a life-and-death character. We used to think one of our finest moments was to lean an arm on a mantelpiece, swirl the olive in our glass, and tell our fellow dinner guests—in a first-rate Peter DeVries manner—how we felt about the thing: "In the war between the sexes," we would say owlishly, "we are a conscientious objector." It was a good line, all right, but we don't say it any more, for the same reason, perhaps, that Chamberlain suddenly stopped saying that all Hitler wanted to do was to take back the Fatherland. One day Man was the stronger sex, the next day he was just bewildered, groping through the reference books to see where nature, God, and his own philosophers had let him down.

In the first flush of their victory, the Women were generous. All they wanted was Equality, they said, nothing more. When they reached that point, though, they didn't pause long enough to touch up their lipstick. Oh, some things that were well established could go on, the victors said. Men could continue to die younger than women, the incidence of widowhood could continue its ascent, construction work and stoop-labor could remain the right of man, and, if they wanted to, they could continue to paint the greatest pictures, write the greatest books, compose the greatest symphonies, and think the loftiest thoughts. None of that would be disturbed, they promised, if man recognized his place and kept in it. Any student of history knew this couldn't work; the victor can't grant the vanquished equality. It didn't work, and Women soon dropped the pretense.

Well, we've brooded about this a good bit, along with some other poor losers, and we're willing to concede the battle lost but hope something can be salvaged from the reconstruction period that lies ahead. To that end, we've been reading the works of our leading traitors—D. H. Lawrence, Ashley Montagu, and others who have supported Woman in her belief that she must control the world. From our reading has come a sort of pleasant confusion—exactly the kind of confusion which makes men so lovable and so frightening (wanting to believe what they read, but at the same time fighting every idea). More than anything else, the thing that really halts our progress is the image which emerges from these writings of Woman as a special creature, a creature of uncommon prescience, of understanding of such depth that man can only estimate it, of such vision that, by comparison, Man is little more than a Cub Scout, of masterful intrigue and diplomacy, and, above all, a creature who is a victim of almost total misunderstanding.

It's that last we balk at. Women are understood much better than they think. It's an old stunt, when you're trying to get away with something, to take on an aura of mystery. Kids do it all the time, but with only moderate success, because other kids see through the trick instantly. We know what women want: they want tenderness, warmth, kindness, and compassion. But they shouldn't take it by force.

· QUESTIONS ·

1. Some readers think this is a charming, lighthearted, and amusing informal essay; others consider it ironic, biting, and even vicious. Is it either or both?
2. Which would be the better alternative title for this selection: "Why I Hate Women" or "Men Are Such Fools"? Why the present title?
3. List the charges cited for and against women and for and against men in this essay. Do you think the author really meant any or all of them?
4. Even in so light and seemingly frivolous a topic as this, you miss much unless you understand the allusions which an author makes. For example, Clarence Day was a noted wit, the genial but sardonic author of *Life with Father;* DeVries is a somewhat satirical contemporary novelist. Can you identify D. H. Lawrence and Ashley Montagu? And do you associate Chamberlain with an umbrella?

Theme Subjects: (1) Select one of the two topics mentioned in Question 2, above; (2) I Am a Conscientious Objector in the War Between _____; (3) I Am a Traitor to My Sex; (4) One Thing Women (or Men) Have Taken by Force; (5) A review of *Back to Abnormal.*

THE

COSMONAUTS' WHISKERS

Russell Baker

RUSSELL BAKER (1925–   ) was born in Loudon County, Virginia, and grew up in New Jersey and Maryland. He served with the Naval Air Force during World War II and was graduated from Johns Hopkins University in 1947. He began his career with the *Baltimore Sun* and later joined the Washington Bureau of the *New York Times*. Since 1962 he has been writing "Observer," a column of criticism and wit for the *Times* which also appears in newspapers throughout the country. Mr. Baker is author of *An American in Washington* (1961); *No Cause for Panic* (1964); and *All Things Considered* (1965).

When the Russian cosmonauts Nikolayev and Popovich made the first overnight orbit around the earth and returned from space, they needed a shave. It was too bad. These 5 o'clock shadows from the Buck Rogers future proved conclusively, for those who still had hopes, that something cosmic out there is grinning at us.

When two men strike out for that wonderful universe next door, it is depressing to know that they are going to arrive with the same old burdens of trouble and sorrow they carried back here. And that is clearly the message of the cosmonauts' beards.

After all, if a man can't even expect to leave the shaving miseries back on earth, what likelihood is there that anything else is going to be better once he gets to the other worlds?

All the evidence of both Soviet and American space travel to date indicates that instead of solving anything, travel around the cosmos is only going to make the routine problems of coping with life harder than ever. John Glenn's experiment with eating in space showed that cookies out there crumble just as cookies crumble down here. Down here they at least settle into sofa chinks and bedclothes. Out there, without gravity, they float suspended in space, where they can drift under eyelids and into delicate machinery. Add to the paraphernalia required for future space ships: a cookie-crumb net.

Schoolboys everywhere will think twice about space careers since the Russians have shown that space travel is no excuse for ignoring their homework. Colonel Popovich reported that he was studying his English after his 500,000th mile and planned to get on with his physics after dinner.

Again these are difficult earth burdens made harder. Physics and English are hard enough to master under the most comfortable campus conditions. Imagine trying to come to grips with the dangling participle and adiabatic expansion while encumbered with a pressurized suit, gloves, and glass helmet. And while watching a telephone that might ring any minute with a personal call from Leonid Brezhnev or Lyndon B. Johnson.

A Congressional committee has recently held hearings on the feasibility of giving the ladies a role in the American astronaut program. It takes little imagination to guess the problems this will raise when the day comes, as it surely will. Powder blending with the cookie crumbs suspended in mid-capsule, bobby pins floating into the yaw stabilizer, gloves lost on remote planets.

Add to the paraphernalia required for future space ships: an interplanetary ladies' glove-finder.

The technologists can probably supply the gadgets needed to whip these problems. If they can shave sandpaper on television, they can shave an astronaut in weightless space without scattering whiskers all through the cookie crumbs.

They can probably devise ways to clear the cabin air of crumbs, bobby pins, face powder, and even man-woman tensions. On the grander level they can probably think up ways to transport all the commonplaces of earth life, from politics to war to traffic congestion, all over the solar system.

What they cannot do, however, is build man an escape hatch to that wonderful universe next door.

As the cosmonauts' beards have shown, they can only help man lug his troubles along on the search.

No one can disparage the instinct behind the search. It would be too bad, however, if it ended by blotting out the Milky Way with a curtain of celestial debris composed of old whiskers, bobby pins, and face powder dumped from spaceship garbage ejectors.

· QUESTIONS ·

1. What is the stylistic effect gained by the last four words of the first sentence?
2. The thesis sentence of this essay is stated several times in the first three paragraphs and beginning of the fourth. Which statement do you prefer in style and content? Phrase your own thesis sentence for this selection.
3. What two items does the author say must be added to requirements for future space ships?
4. What is the tone of this essay? The purpose? How serious is this purpose?

Theme Subjects: (1) Something Cosmic Out There Is Grinning; (2) My Opinion of Buck Rogers; (3) Eating Crackers in Bed—or in Space; (4) How To Ignore Your Homework; (5) My Favorite Escape Hatch.

COMFORT

Aldous Huxley

Aldous (Leonard) Huxley (1894–1963), English novelist, essayist, and poet, was a grandson of Thomas Henry Huxley and a grandnephew of Matthew Arnold. Undaunted by his imposing heritage, Aldous Huxley wrote

From *Proper Studies* by Aldous Huxley, Harper & Row. Copyright 1927, 1955 by Aldous Huxley. Reprinted by permission of Harper & Row and Chatto & Windus.

a series of brilliantly satiric novels, including *Crome Yellow* (1921); *Mortal Coils* (1922); *Antic Hay* (1923); *Point Counter Point* (1928); *Brave New World* (1932); and *Ape and Essence* (1948). He also published a large number of trenchant essays and several distinguished volumes of poetry. The best single-volume collection of his writings is *The World of Aldous Huxley* (1947). Among more recent books are *The Devils of Loudun* (1952); *The Doors of Perception* (1954); *Tomorrow and Tomorrow and Tomorrow* (1956); *Collected Essays* (1960); and *Island* (1962).

French hotel-keepers call it *Le confort moderne,* and they are right. For comfort is a thing of recent growth, younger than steam, a child when telegraphy was born, only a generation older than radio. The invention of the means of being comfortable and the pursuit of comfort as a desirable end—one of the most desirable that human beings can propose to themselves—are modern phenomena, unparalleled in history since the time of the Romans. Like all phenomena with which we are extremely familiar, we take them for granted, as a fish takes the water in which it lives, not realizing the oddity and novelty of them, not bothering to consider their significance. The padded chair, the well-sprung bed, the sofa, central heating, and the regular hot bath—these and a host of other comforts enter into the daily lives of even the most moderately prosperous of the Anglo-Saxon bourgeoisie. Three hundred years ago they were unknown to the greatest kings. This is a curious fact which deserves to be examined and analysed.

The first thing that strikes one about the discomfort in which our ancestors lived is that it was mainly voluntary. Some of the apparatus of modern comfort is of purely modern invention; people could not put rubber tyres on their carriages before the discovery of South America and the rubber plant. But for the most part there is nothing new about the material basis of our comfort. Men could have made sofas and smoking-room chairs, could have installed bathrooms and central heating and sanitary plumbing any time during the last three or four thousand years. And as a matter of fact, at certain periods they did indulge themselves in these comforts. Two thousand years before Christ, the inhabitants of Knossos were familiar with sanitary plumbing. The Romans had invented an elaborate system of hot-air heating, and the bathing facilities in a smart Roman villa were luxurious and complete beyond the dreams of modern man. There were sweating-rooms, massage-rooms, cold plunges, tepid drying-rooms with (if we may believe Sidonius Apollinaris) improper frescoes on the walls and comfortable couches where you could lie and get dry and talk to your friends. As for the public baths, they were almost inconceivably luxurious. "To such a height of luxury have we reached," said Seneca, "that we are dissatisfied if, in our baths, we do not tread on gems." The size and completeness of the thermae was proportionable to their splendour. A single room of the baths of Diocletian has been transformed into a large church.

It would be possible to adduce many other examples showing what could be done with the limited means at our ancestors' disposal in the way of making life comfortable. They show sufficiently clearly that if the men of the Middle Ages and early modern epoch lived in filth and discomfort, it was not for any lack of ability to change their mode of life; it was because they chose to live in this way, because filth and discomfort fitted in with their principles and prejudices, political, moral, and religious.

COMFORT AND THE SPIRITUAL LIFE

What have comfort and cleanliness to do with politics, morals, and religion? At a first glance one would say that there was and could be no causal connection between armchairs and democracies, sofas and the relaxation of the family system, hot baths and the decay of Christian orthodoxy. But look more closely and you will discover that there exists the closest connection between the recent growth of comfort and the recent history of ideas. I hope in this essay to make that connection manifest, to show why it was not possible (not materially, but psychologically impossible) for the Italian princes of the quattrocento, for the Elizabethan, even for Louis XIV to live in what the Romans would have called common cleanliness and decency, or enjoy what would be to us indispensable comforts.

Let us begin with the consideration of armchairs and central heating. These, I propose to show, became possible only with the breakdown of monarchical and feudal power and the decay of the old family and social hierarchies. Smoking-room chairs and sofas

exist to be lolled in. In a well-made modern armchair you cannot do anything but loll. Now, lolling is neither dignified nor respectful. When we wish to appear impressive, when we have to administer a rebuke to an inferior, we do not lie in a deep chair with our feet on the mantelpiece; we sit up and try to look majestical. Similarly, when we wish to be polite to a lady or show respect to the old or eminent, we cease to loll; we stand, or at least we straighten ourselves up. Now, in the past, human society was a hierarchy in which every man was always engaged in being impressive towards his inferiors or respectful to those above him. Lolling in such societies was utterly impossible. It was as much out of the question for Louis XIV to loll in the presence of his courtiers as it was for them to loll in the presence of their king. It was only when he attended a session of the Parlement that the King of France ever lolled in public. On these occasions he reclined in the Bed of Justice, while princes sat, the great officers of the crown stood, and the smaller fry knelt. Comfort was proclaimed as the appanage of royalty. Only the king might stretch his legs. We may feel sure, however, that he stretched them in a very majestic manner. The lolling was purely ceremonial and accompanied by no loss of dignity. At ordinary times the king was seated, it is true, but seated in a dignified and upright position; the appearance of majesty had to be kept up. (For, after all, majesty is mainly a question of majestical appearance.) The courtiers, meanwhile, kept up the appearances of deference, either standing, or else, if their rank was very high and their blood peculiarly blue, sitting, even in the royal presence, on stools. What was true of the king's court was true of the nobleman's household; and the squire was to his dependents, the merchant was to his apprentices and servants, what the monarch was to his courtiers. In all cases the superior had to express his superiority by being dignified, the inferior his inferiority by being deferential; there could be no lolling. Even in the intimacies of family life it was the same: the parents ruled like popes and princes, by divine right; the children were their subjects. Our fathers took the fifth commandment very seriously—how seriously may be judged from the fact that during the great Calvin's theocratic rule of Geneva a child was publicly decapitated for having ventured to strike its parents. Lolling on the part of children, though not perhaps a capital offence, would have been regarded as an act of the grossest disrespect, punishable by much flagellation, starving, and confinement. For a slighter insult—neglect to touch his cap— Vespasiano Gonzaga kicked his only son to death; one shudders to think what he might have been provoked to do if the boy had lolled. If the children might not loll in the presence of their parents, neither might the parents loll in the presence of their children, for fear of demeaning themselves in the eyes of those whose duty it was to honour them. Thus we see that in the European society of two or three hundred years ago it was impossible for any one—from the Holy Roman Emperor and the King of France down to the poorest beggar, from the bearded patriarch to the baby—to loll in the presence of any one else. Old furniture reflects the physical habits of the hierarchical society

for which it was made. It was in the power of mediaeval and Renaissance craftsmen to create armchairs and sofas that might have rivalled in comfort those of to-day. But society being what, in fact, it was, they did nothing of the kind. It was not, indeed, until the sixteenth century that chairs became at all common. Before that time a chair was a symbol of authority. Committee-men now loll, Members of Parliament are comfortably seated, but authority still belongs to a Chairman, still issues from a symbolical Chair. In the Middle Ages only the great had chairs. When a great man travelled, he took his chair with him, so that he might never be seen detached from the outward and visible sign of his authority. To this day the Throne no less than the Crown is the symbol of royalty. In mediaeval times the vulgar sat, whenever it was permissible for them to sit, on benches, stools, and settles. With the rise, during the Renaissance period, of a rich and independent bourgeoisie, chairs began to be more freely used. Those who could afford chairs sat in them, but sat with dignity and discomfort; for the chairs of the sixteenth century were still very throne-like and imposed upon those who sat in them a painfully majestic attitude. It was only in the eighteenth century, when the old hierarchies were seriously breaking up, that furniture began to be comfortable. And even then there was no real lolling. Armchairs and sofas on which men (and, later, women) might indecorously sprawl, were not made until democracy was firmly established, the middle classes enlarged to gigantic proportions, good manners lost from out of the world, women emancipated, and family restraints dissolved.

CENTRAL HEATING AND THE FEUDAL SYSTEM

Another essential component of modern comfort—the adequate heating of houses—was made impossible, at least for the great ones of the earth, by the political structure of ancient societies. Plebeians were more fortunate in this respect than nobles. Living in small houses, they were able to keep warm. But the nobleman, the prince, the king, and the cardinal inhabited palaces of a grandeur corresponding with their social position. In order to prove that they were greater than other men, they had to live in surroundings considerably more than life-size. They received their guests in vast halls like roller-skating rinks; they marched in solemn processions along galleries as long and as draughty as Alpine tunnels, up and down triumphal staircases that looked like the cataracts of the Nile frozen into marble. Being what he was, a great man in those days had to spend a great deal of his time in performing solemn symbolical charades and pompous ballets—performances which required a lot of room to accommodate the numerous actors and spectators. This explains the enormous dimensions of royal and princely palaces, even of the houses of ordinary landed gentlemen. They owed it to their position to live, as though they were giants, in rooms a hundred feet long and thirty high. How splendid, how magnificent! But oh, how bleak! In our days the self-made great are not expected to keep up their position in the splendid style of those who were great by divine right. Sacrificing grandiosity to comfort, they live in rooms small enough to be heated. (And so, when they were off duty, did the great in the past; most old palaces contain a series of tiny apartments to which their owners retired when the charades of state were over. But the charades were long-drawn affairs, and the unhappy princes of old days had to spend a great deal of time being magnificent in icy audience-chambers and among the whistling draughts of interminable galleries.)

Driving in the environs of Chicago, I was shown the house of a man who was reputed to be one of the richest and most influential of the city. It was a medium-sized house of perhaps fifteen or twenty smallish rooms. I looked at it in astonishment, thinking of the vast palaces in which I myself have lived in Italy (for considerably less rent than one would have to pay for garaging a Ford in Chicago). I remembered the rows of bedrooms as big as ordinary ballrooms, the drawing-rooms like railway stations, the staircase on which you could drive a couple of limousines abreast. Noble *palazzi*, where one has room to feel oneself a superman! But remembering also those terrible winds that blow in February from the Apennines, I was inclined to think that the rich man of Chicago had done well in sacrificing the magnificences on which his counterpart in another age and country would have spent his riches.

BATHS AND MORALS

It is to the decay of monarchy, aristocracy, and ancient social hier-

archy that we owe the two components of modern comfort hitherto
discussed; the third great component—the bath—must, I think, be
attributed, at any rate in part, to
the decay of Christian morals.
There are still on the continent of
Europe, and, for all I know, elsewhere, convent schools in which
young ladies are brought up to believe that human bodies are objects
of so impure and obscene a character that it is sinful for them to
see, not merely other people's nakedness, but even their own. Baths,
when they are permitted to take
them (every alternate Saturday)
must be taken in a chemise descending well below the knees. And they
are even taught a special technique
of dressing which guarantees them
from catching so much as a
glimpse of their own skin. These
schools are now, happily, exceptional, but there was a time, not so
long ago, when they were the rule.
Theirs is the great Christian ascetic
tradition which has flowed on in
majestic continuity from the time
of St. Anthony and the unwashed,
underfed, sex-starved monks of the
Thebaid, through the centuries, almost to the present day. It is to the
weakening of that tradition that
women at any rate owe the luxury
of frequent bathing.

The early Christians were by
no means enthusiastic bathers; but
it is fair to point out that Christian
ascetic tradition has not at all times
been hostile to baths as such. That
the Early Fathers should have found
the promiscuity of Roman bathing
shocking is only natural. But the
more moderate of them were prepared to allow a limited amount of
washing, provided that the business
was done with decency. The final
decay of the great Roman baths was
as much due to the destructiveness
of the Barbarians as to Christian
ascetic objections. During the Ages
of Faith there was actually a revival
of bathing. The Crusaders came
back from the East, bringing with
them the oriental vapour bath,
which seems to have had a considerable popularity all over Europe.
For reasons which it is difficult to
understand, its popularity gradually
waned, and the men and women of
the late sixteenth and early seventeenth centuries seem to have been
almost as dirty as their barbarous
ancestors. Medical theory and court
fashions may have had something
to do with these fluctuations.

The ascetic tradition was always strongest where women were
concerned. The Goncourts record in
their diary the opinion, which seems
to have been current in respectable
circles during the Second Empire,
that female immodesty and immorality had increased with the
growth of the bath habit. "Girls
should wash less" was the obvious
corollary. Young ladies who enjoy
their bath owe a debt of gratitude
to Voltaire for his mockeries, to the
nineteenth-century scientists for
their materialism. If these men had
never lived to undermine the convent school tradition, our girls
might still be as modest and as
dirty as their ancestresses.

COMFORT AND MEDICINE

It is, however, to the doctors that
bath-lovers owe their greatest debt.
The discovery of microbic infection
has put a premium on cleanliness.
We wash now with religious fer-
vour, like the Hindus. Our baths
have become something like magic

rites to protect us from the powers of evil, embodied in the dirt-loving germ. We may venture to prophesy that this medical religion will go still further in undermining the Christian ascetic tradition. Since the discovery of the beneficial effects of sunlight, too much clothing has become, medically speaking, a sin. Immodesty is now a virtue. It is quite likely that the doctors, whose prestige among us is almost equal to that of the medicine men among the savages, will have us stark naked before very long. That will be the last stage in the process of making clothes more comfortable. It is a process which has been going on for some time—first among men, later among women—and among its determining causes are the decay of hierarchic formalism and of Christian morality. In his lively little pamphlet describing Gladstone's visit to Oxford shortly before his death, Mr. Fletcher has recorded the Grand Old Man's comments on the dress of the undergraduates. Mr. Gladstone, it appears, was distressed by the informality and the cheapness of the students' clothes. In his day, he said, young men went about with a hundred pounds' worth of clothes and jewellery on their persons, and every self-respecting youth had at least one pair of trousers in which he never sat down for fear of spoiling its shape. Mr. Gladstone visited Oxford at a time when undergraduates still wore very high starched collars and bowler hats. One wonders what he would have said of the open shirts, the gaudily coloured sweaters, the loose flannel trousers of the present generation. Dignified appearances have never been less assiduously kept up than they are at present; informality has reached an unprecedented pitch. On all but the most solemn occasions a man, whatever his rank or position, may wear what he finds comfortable.

The obstacles in the way of women's comforts were moral as well as political. Women were compelled not merely to keep up social appearances, but also to conform to a tradition of Christian ascetic morality. Long after men had abandoned their uncomfortable formal clothes, women were still submitting to extraordinary inconveniences in the name of modesty. It was the war which liberated them from their bondage. When women began to do war work, they found that the traditional modesty in dress was not compatible with efficiency. They preferred to be efficient. Having discovered the advantages of immodesty, they have remained immodest ever since, to the great improvement of their health and increase of their personal comfort. Modern fashions are the most comfortable that women have ever worn. Even the ancient Greeks were probably less comfortable. Their under-tunic, it is true, was as rational a garment as you could wish for; but their outer robe was simply a piece of stuff wound round the body like an Indian *sari*, and fastened with safety-pins. No woman whose appearance depended on safety-pins can ever have felt really comfortable.

COMFORT AS AN END IN ITSELF

Made possible by changes in the traditional philosophy of life, comfort is now one of the causes of its own further spread. For comfort has now become a physical habit, a fashion, an ideal to be pursued for its own sake. The more comfort is brought into the world, the more it is likely to be valued. To those who have known comfort, discomfort is a real torture. And the fashion which now decrees the worship of comfort is quite as imperious as any other fashion. Moreover, enormous material interests are bound up with the supply of the means of comfort. The manufacturers of furniture, of heating apparatus, of plumbing fixtures, cannot afford to let the love of comfort die. In modern advertisement they have means for compelling it to live and grow.

Having now briefly traced the spiritual origins of modern comfort, I must say a few words about its effects. One can never have something for nothing, and the achievement of comfort has been accompanied by a compensating loss of other equally, or perhaps more, valuable things. A man of means who builds a house to-day is in general concerned primarily with the comfort of his future residence. He will spend a great deal of money (for comfort is very expensive: in America they talk of giving away the house with the plumbing) on bathrooms, heating apparatus, padded furnishings, and the like; and having spent it, he will regard his house as perfect. His counterpart in an earlier age would have been primarily concerned with the impressiveness and magnificence of his dwelling—with beauty, in a word, rather than comfort. The money our contemporary would spend on baths and central heating would have been spent in the past on marble staircases, a grand façade, frescoes, huge suites of gilded rooms, pictures, statues. Sixteenth-century popes lived in a discomfort that a modern bank manager would consider unbearable; but they had Raphael's frescoes, they had the Sistine chapel, they had their galleries of ancient sculpture. Must we pity them for the absence from the Vatican of bathrooms, central heating, and smoking-room chairs?

I am inclined to think that our present passion for comfort is a little exaggerated. Though I personally enjoy comfort, I have lived very happily in houses devoid of almost everything that Anglo-Saxons deem indispensable. Orientals and even South Europeans, who know not comfort and live very much as our ancestors lived centuries ago, seem to get on very well without our elaborate and costly apparatus of padded luxury. I am old-fashioned enough to believe in higher and lower things, and can see no point in material progress except in so far as it subserves thought. I like labour-saving devices, because they economize time and energy which may be devoted to mental labour. (But then I enjoy mental labour; there are plenty of people who detest it, and who feel as much enthusiasm for thought-saving devices as for automatic dishwashers and sewing-machines.) I like rapid and easy transport, because by enlarging the world in which men can live it enlarges their minds. Comfort for me has a similar justification: it facilitates mental life. Discomfort handicaps thought; it is difficult when the body is cold and aching to use the mind. Comfort is a means to an end. The modern world seems to regard it as an end in itself, an absolute good. One day, perhaps, the earth will have been turned into one vast feather-bed, with man's body dozing on top of it and his mind underneath, like Desdemona, smothered.

· QUESTIONS ·

1. Show how the fourth sentence of the first paragraph is virtually a one-sentence outline of the entire essay.
2. Do you fully agree with all of Huxley's argument? If not, where do you differ?
3. Can you name items of comfort other than those cited by the author?
4. Are Huxley's comments on modern dress for men and women less pertinent today than when they were written? Think carefully before answering.
5. Explain the references to Knossos, Sidonius Apollinaris, Seneca, Diocletian, Louis XIV, Calvin, the Apennines, St. Anthony, the Goncourts, Voltaire, Desdemona.
6. Define: quattrocento, hierarchies, appanage, theocratic, flagellation, indecorously, ascetic, assiduously.
7. What is the tone of this essay? How would you characterize Huxley's style?

Theme Subjects: (1) My Idea of Solid Comfort; (2) The High Cost of Modern Comfort; (3) What Huxley Overlooks; (4) Garaging a Ford in _____; (5) The Best Way To Take a Bath; (6) The Lures of Modern Advertising.

A FABLE

James Reston

JAMES BARRETT RESTON (1909–   ) was born in Scotland, was brought to the United States in 1910, and then returned to Scotland from 1914 to 1920 to attend school. A graduate of the University of Illinois (1932), he holds degrees from Colgate, Oberlin, Rutgers, Dartmouth, and New York University. Beginning his career on the Springfield, Ohio, *Daily News* in 1932, he did publicity work for Ohio State University and the Cincinnati Baseball Club, and in 1934 became a reporter for the Associated Press, based first in New York City and then in London. In 1939 he joined the London bureau of *The New York Times*, was transferred to its Washington bureau in 1941, and has served as its chief since 1953. Mr. Reston won the 1945 Pulitzer

Prize for news reporting; his other awards include la Légion d'Honneur, Order of St. Olav (Norway), and Order of Merit (Chile).

Once upon a time, all the creatures in the animal kingdom got to lying around drinking Olde Mead (120 proof) and making goo-goo eyes at every cute chick in the forest. All, that is, except the Bears.

The Beavers wouldn't cut down trees unless they had power saws, and the Rabbits wouldn't eat anything except icebox lettuce with thousand island dressing, and pretty soon the Bears started going around gobbling up all the other animals.

After a while, a horse named Gallup took a poll which showed that 97.3 percent of the animals left were against being gobbled up, so the King Lion called them all together and made them a big speech about the need for sacrifices.

"Ask not what the forest can do for you," he said, "but what you can do for the forest." Everybody from the Elephant to the Jackass was deeply impressed and began asking exactly that.

"What can we do to help?" asked the Chief Worker among the Ants.

INCENTIVES, ANYBODY?

"The trouble with you," replied the Lion, "is that you need more incentives. You are not getting paid enough for your labor. I'm going to see to it that your minimum wage is raised from a dollar an hour to a dollar and a quarter an hour right away."

"But it is jobs we need more than anything else," said the Chief Ant.

"I know," replied the Lion. "It is a terrible thing to be an unemployed Ant, so I'm going to increase your unemployment compensation and stretch it out over a longer period."

"What about us?" asked the Fat Cat. "What can we do to help?"

"Produce," replied the Lion. "Production is what we need, and I promise that your depletion allowances will be maintained at a high level so that you continue to have more cream than anybody else."

"And what about us?" asked the farmer Jackass. "What shall we do?"

"Don't produce," said the Lion. "Farm production is what we don't need. Please don't produce any more and we'll pay you well. We'll do anything, but please take it easy."

Up then strode the Tiger, who had been watching the Bears from a missile gap on the fringe of the forest. "Give us our orders," said the Tiger. "We have seen the enemy and we want to help."

"I want you to be happy," said the Lion. "I know how it is out there without your women folk and your cubs. Go back to your post in peace and I'll send them all out to you at Government expense."

THE BEARS ARE HEARD FROM

At this point, there was a ghastly roar from the Bears in the forest. "Hearken to that," said the Lion. "We have never been in greater danger. The outcome of this struggle is very much in doubt. Where are the volunteers?"

First to step up was a very old British Lion. "We must be sensible about this," he said. "We must talk things over with the Bears. It is all very tiresome, but we must not be rash or beastly in our attitude."

Next came the French Giraffe who said he hated Bears but pointed out that the Giraffes were all fighting among themselves and did not really have time to watch the Bears.

Finally, a German Police Dog offered to watch the Bears but complained that he could not afford to do very much and besides did not trust himself to get too close to the Bears. Whereupon the Lion called once more for volunteers.

"Let us help," said all the female animals. "You treat us like a bunch of useless ninnies while all the female Bears are working over there like mad."

"This is a male's world," said the Lion. "You are consumers, not fighters. You must consume more useless things, so that the workers can produce more useless things."

"What about us?" said all the young Oxen. "We are strong and willing."

"But you are dumb," roared the Lion. "You must educate yourselves. Everybody who is not dumber than an Ox must have a college education."

"But I am poor," said the Church Mouse.

"Don't give it a thought," said the Lion. "I'll get you a scholarship at Oberlin, or a Government job in Washington under the Harvard faculty."

So saying, the Lion lay down with the Lamb, and the Bears laughed and laughed, and the wise old Owl flew off in search of a safer perch.

MORAL: ASK AND YE SHALL RECEIVE; ASK NOT, AND YE SHALL RECEIVE ANYWAY.

· QUESTIONS ·

1. Explain fully the meaning of the word *fable.*
2. Explain fully the meaning of "A Fable." Is this essay entirely fictitious? Does it enforce a useful truth? Can you suggest names of persons and countries for those of animals mentioned?
3. State the central thesis of this essay in about 50 words.
4. Is the point of view of this essay progressive and enlightened? Conservative, reactionary? (Before answering, you might investigate the author's reputed political leanings and his general reputation and then follow this "research" with a careful rereading of the selection.)
5. What is the tone of this selection? Comment on its diction, allusions, and clipped sentence structure.

Theme Subjects: (1) Reston Is Unfair in "A Fable"; (2) Straight Talk (use real names and your own sentences in a rewriting of this essay); (3) Americans Are (Are Not) Growing Ever More Socialistic; (4) What I Expect from My Government (narrow to one phase only); (5) A Fable (using Reston's essay as a model, write on some other problem of American life).

GAMESMANSHIP

Stephen Potter

STEPHEN (MEREDITH) POTTER (1900–   ) was born in London. He attended Westminster School and Merton College, Oxford University. For several years he was a part-time lecturer in literature at various English universities; in 1935 he began a ten-year stint as a writer and producer for the British Broadcasting Company (BBC). Among his books are *The Muse in Chains* (1936); *Gamesmanship* (1948); *Lifemanship* (1951); *One-Upmanship* (1952); *Sense of Humor* (1955); and *Steps to Immaturity* (1959).

ORIGINS

What is gamesmanship? Most difficult of questions to answer briefly. "The Art of Winning Games Without Actually Cheating"—that is my personal "working definition." What is its object? There have been five hundred books written on the subject of games. Five hundred books on play and the tactics of play. Not one on the art of winning.

I well remember the gritty floor and the damp roller-towels of the changing-room where the idea of writing this book came to me. Yet my approach to the thing had been gradual.

There had been much that had puzzled me—I am speaking now of 1928—in the tension of our games of ping-pong at the Meynells'. Before that there had been the ardours and endurances of friendly lawn tennis at the Farjeons' house near Forest Hills, where Farjeon had wrought such havoc among so many visitors, by his careful construction of a "home court," by the use he made of the net with the unilateral sag, or with a back line at the hawthorn end so nearly, yet not exactly, six inches wider than the back line at the sticky end. There had been a great deal of hard thinking on both sides during the wavering tide of battle, ending slightly in my favour, of the prolonged series of golf games between E. Lansbury and myself.

8TH JUNE 1931

But it was in that changing-room after a certain game of lawn tennis in 1931 that the curtain was

---

From *Gamesmanship, or The Art of Winning Games Without Actually Cheating* by Stephen Potter. Reprinted by permission of Henry Holt and Company, Inc.

lifted, and I began to see. In those days I used to play lawn tennis for a small but progressive London College—Birkbeck, where I lectured. It happened that my partner at that time was C. Joad, the celebrated gamesman, who in his own sphere is known as metaphysician and educationist. Our opponents were usually young men from the larger colleges, competing against us not only with the advantage of age but also with a decisive advantage in style. They would throw the service ball very high in the modern manner: the back-hands, instead of being played from the navel, were played, in fact, on the backhand, weight on right foot, in the exaggerated copy-book style of the time—a method of play which tends to reduce all games, as I believe, to a barrack-square drill by numbers; but, nevertheless, of acknowledged effectiveness.

In one match we found ourselves opposite a couple of particularly tall and athletic young men of this type from University College. We will call them Smith and Brown. The knock-up showed that, so far as play was concerned, Joad and I, playing for Birkbeck, had no chance. U.C. won the toss. It was Smith's service, and he cracked down a cannon-ball to Joad which moved so fast that Joad, while making some effort to suggest by his attitude that he had thought the ball was going to be a fault, nevertheless was unable to get near with his racket, which he did not even attempt to move. Score: fifteen-love. Service to me. I had had time to gauge the speed of this service, and the next one did, in fact, graze the edge of my racket-frame. Thirty-love. Now Smith was serving again to Joad—who this time, as the ball

came straight towards him, was able, by grasping the racket firmly with both hands, to receive the ball on the strings, whereupon the ball shot back to the other side and volleyed into the stop-netting near the ground behind Brown's feet.

Now here comes the moment on which not only this match, but so much of the future of British sport was to turn. Score: forty-love. Smith is about to cross over to serve to me. When Smith gets to a point *not less than one foot and not more than two feet* beyond the centre of the court (I know now what I only felt then—that timing is everything in this gambit), Joad called across the net, in an even tone:

"Kindly say clearly, please, whether the ball was in or out."

Crude to our ears, perhaps. A Stone-Age implement. But beautifully accurate gamesmanship for 1931. For the student must realise that these two young men were both in the highest degree charming, well-mannered young men, perfect in their sportsmanship and behaviour. Smith stopped dead.

SMITH: I'm so sorry—I *thought* it was out. (*The ball had hit the back netting twelve feet behind him before touching the ground.*) But what did you think, Brown?

BROWN: I *thought* it was out—but do let's have it again.

JOAD: No, I don't want to have it again. I only want you to say clearly, if you will, whether the ball is in or out.

There is nothing more putting off to young university players than a slight suggestion that their etiquette or sportsmanship is in question. How well we know this fact, yet how often we forget to make use of it. Smith sent a double fault to me, and another double fault to

Joad. He did not get in another ace service till halfway through the third set of a match which incidentally we won.

That night I thought hard and long. Could not this simple gambit of Joad's be extended to include other aspects of the game—to include all games? For me, it was the birth of gamesmanship.

· QUESTIONS ·

1. Is the prevailing tone of this selection one of mock seriousness? Dry humor? Understatement? Select and defend your answer or supply a more accurate term.
2. This essay contains several sentence fragments (period faults). Are they stylistically effective or do they lessen effectiveness?
3. It is abundantly clear that the time in this selection is 1931. Has the passage of time altered the "lesson" of this essay?
4. From internal evidence in this essay, demonstrate that Potter is English.
5. How effective do you consider the dialogue in this selection?

Theme Subjects: (1) **My Idea of Gamesmanship**; (2) **It's Dirty Pool, Just the Same**; (3) **The Worst Loser(s) I Ever Faced**; (4) **The American Credo of Fair Play**; (5) **". . . But How You Played the Game"**; (6) *Gamesmanship* (a review of the entire book).

THE

READING MACHINE

Morris Bishop

Morris (Gilbert) Bishop (1893–   ) was born in Willard, New York, and educated at Cornell University, where he taught romance languages until 1960 and now is university historian. He has written several books, among them *A Gallery of Eccentrics* (1928); *Pascal, the Life of Genius*

(1936); *Spilt Milk* (1942); and *A Bowl of Bishop* (1954). Mr. Bishop is also editor of *A Treasury of British Humor* (1942) and author of *A History of Cornell* (1962).

"I have invented a reading machine," said Professor Entwhistle, a strident energumen whose violent enthusiasms are apt to infect his colleagues with nausea or hot flashes before the eyes.

Every head in the smoking room of the Faculty Club bowed over a magazine, in an attitude of prayer. The prayer was unanswered, as usual.

"It is obvious," said Professor Entwhistle, "that the greatest waste of our civilization is the time spent in reading. We have been able to speed up practically everything to fit the modern tempo—communication, transportation, calculation. But today a man takes just as long to read a book as Dante did, or—"

"Great Caesar!" said the Professor of Amphibology, shutting his magazine with a spank.

"Or great Caesar," continued Professor Entwhistle. "So I have invented a machine. It operates by a simple arrangement of photoelectric cells, which scan a line of type at lightning speed. The operation of the photoelectric cells is synchronized with a mechanical device for turning the pages—rather ingenious. I figure that my machine can read a book of three hundred pages in ten minutes."

"Can it read French?" said the Professor of Bio-Economics, without looking up.

"It can read any language that is printed in Roman type. And by an alteration of the master pattern on which the photoelectric cells operate, it can be fitted to read Russian, or Bulgarian, or any language printed in the Cyrillic alphabet. In fact, it will do more. By simply throwing a switch, you can adapt it to read Hebrew, or Arabic, or any language that is written from right to left instead of from left to right."

"Chinese?" said the Professor of Amphibology, throwing himself into the arena. The others still studied their magazines.

"Not Chinese, as yet," said Professor Entwhistle. "Though by inserting the pages sidewise . . . Yes, I think it could be done."

"Yes, but when you say this contrivance reads, exactly what do you mean? It seems to me—"

"The light waves registered by the photoelectric cells are first converted into sound waves."

"So you can listen in to the reading of the text?"

"Not at all. The sound waves alter so fast that you hear nothing but a continuous hum. If you hear them at all. You can't, in fact, because they are on a wave length inaudible to the human ear."

"Well, it seems to me—"

"Think of the efficiency of the thing!" Professor Entwhistle was really warming up. "Think of the time saved! You assign a student a bibliography of fifty books. He runs them through the machine comfortably in a weekend. And on Monday morning he turns in a certificate from the machine. Everything has been conscientiously read!"

"Yes, but the student won't remember what he has read!"

"He doesn't remember what he reads now."

"Well, you have me there," said the Professor of Amphibology. "I confess you have me there. But it seems to me we would have to pass the machine and fail the student."

"Not at all," said Professor Entwhistle. "An accountant today does not think of doing his work by multiplication and division. Often he is unable to multiply and divide. He confides his problem to a business machine and the machine does his work for him. All the accountant has to know is how to run the machine. That is efficiency."

"Still, it seems to me that what we want to do is to transfer the contents of the book to the student's mind."

"In this mechanized age? My dear fellow! What we want is to train the student to run machines. An airplane pilot doesn't need to know the history of aerodynamics. He needs to know how to run his machine. A lawyer doesn't want to know the development of theories of Roman law. He wants to win cases, if possible by getting the right answers to logical problems. That is largely a mechanical process. It might well be possible to construct a machine. It could begin by solving simple syllogisms, you know— drawing a conclusion from a major premise and a minor premise—"

"Here, let's not get distracted. This reading machine of yours, it must *do* something, it must make some kind of record. What happens after you get the sound waves?"

"That's the beauty of it," said Professor Entwhistle. "The sound waves are converted into light waves, of a different character from the original light waves, and these are communicated to an automatic typewriter, working at inconceivable speed. This transforms the light impulses into legible typescript, in folders of a hundred pages each. It tosses them out the way a combine tosses out sacked wheat. Thus, everything the machine reads is preserved entire, in durable form. The only thing that remains is to file it somewhere, and for this you would need only the services of a capable filing clerk."

"Or you could read it?" persisted the Professor of Amphibology.

"Why, yes, if you wanted to, you could read it," said Professor Entwhistle.

An indigestible silence hung over the Faculty Club.

"I see where the Athletic Association has bought a pitching machine," said the Assistant Professor of Business Psychology (Retail). "Damn thing throws any curve desired, with a maximum margin of error of three centimeters over the plate. What'll they be thinking of next?"

"A batting machine, obviously," said Professor Entwhistle.

· QUESTIONS ·

1. Apply Beard's comments concerning the "lunatic fringe" to Entwhistle's proposal. What remarks does Aldous Huxley make which are applicable to this essay?
2. What proposals can you make comparable to that for a reading machine?
3. Do automation and teaching machines, so-called, have any bearing on the thesis of this little essay?
4. Which predominates in Bishop's essay: wit, whimsy, or satire?
5. Define: energumen, photoelectric, synchronized, contrivance, premise.

Theme Subjects: (1) Entwhistles I Have Known; (2) This Mechanized Age; (3) Science and My Comfort; (4) Lunatic Innovations; (5) Professor Entwhistle: Mankind's Greatest Benefactor; (6) I Am an Obstructionist.

FREUDIAN FOOTBALL

Thomas Hornsby Ferril

THOMAS HORNSBY FERRIL (1896–   ) was born in Denver and received an A.B. degree from Colorado College. Except for service during World War I he has spent his entire life in Denver, but his fame as poet and editor is national and even international. Copublisher (with his wife, Helen R. Ferril) of the famed *Rocky Mountain Herald*, he contributes an urbane and thoughtful weekly column to it. The paragraphs which follow illustrate the quality of his fertile, roving mind. His best-known volume of prose is *I Hate Thursday* (1946); his best collection of poetry is *New and Selected Poems* (1952). He was one of 31 poets commissioned by the Steuben Glass Company to participate in its "Poetry in Crystal" exhibition in New York City in 1963.

As I look back over the intellectual caprices of the past quarter century, I am amazed that neither the Marxists nor the Freudians ever took out after football. There's not a single book on the subject. It is now too late. In olympian cerebration, Marx and Freud are obsolete; the atom has taken over, and football, for the moment, seems reasonably safe from encroachment, although we may still see a few flurries; cobalt tracers, perhaps, for the study of the parabolas of flat passes, but it won't amount to much because the atom is cut out for graver duties.

If the Marxists had been more alert, they could have made something out of football as brutal capitalistic exploitation of the working class. They might have noted a few strikes for higher pay and a court decision entitling a college football player to workman's compensation benefits following injury.

But it was the Freudians who

From *The Rocky Mountain Herald*, Denver, Colorado. Reprinted by permission of the author.

made the colossal blunder. You could argue that they overlooked football on the grounds that it was just too big to be noticed on those Saturday afternoons when the college library was free for their invasion of fiction, drama, poetry, painting, sculpture, music, and economics.

Yet why, when the whole town was roaring over their heads, did they pay no attention to the emotional frenzy? Frankly, I think they must have, but the Freudians were notoriously selfish fellows; they wanted everything whole-hog; they were always extremely jealous of anthropologists, and, as you look back on their dilemma as far as football was concerned, their dog-in-the-manger attitude was perhaps justified, for no self-respecting Freudian could ever have done a full-dress job on football without cutting some detested anthropologist in on the gravy.

But had the Freudians been less self-centered and had they welcomed a bit of anthropological assistance, just think of the monumental treatises by which the scientific literature of the period might have been enriched, great books wedding the wisdom of "Gesammelte Schriften" with the profundity of "The Golden Bough."

Let me set down, in nostalgic summary, some of the findings that might have been made, had the Freudians not been sulking in their tents.

Obviously, football is a syndrome of religious rites symbolizing the struggle to preserve the egg of life through the rigors of impending winter. The rites begin at the autumn equinox and culminate on the first day of the New Year with great festivals identified with bowls of plenty; the festivals are associated with flowers such as roses, fruits such as oranges, farm crops such as cotton, and even sun-worship and appeasement of great reptiles such as alligators.

In these rites the egg of life is symbolized by what is called "the oval," an inflated bladder covered with hog skin. The convention of "the oval" is repeated in the architectural oval-shaped design of the vast outdoor churches in which the services are held every Sabbath in every town and city, also every Sunday in the greater centers of population where an advanced priesthood performs. These enormous roofless churches dominate every college campus; no other edifice compares in size with them, and they bear witness to the high spiritual development of the culture that produced them.

Literally millions of worshipers attend the Sabbath services in these enormous open-air churches. Subconsciously, these hordes of worshipers are seeking an outlet from sex-frustration in anticipation of violent masochism and sadism about to be enacted by a highly trained priesthood of young men. Football obviously arises out of the Oedipus complex. Love of mother dominates the entire ritual. The churches, without exception, are dedicated to Alma Mater, Dear Mother. (Notre Dame and football are synonymous.)

The rites are performed on a rectangular area of green grass orientated to the four directions. The grass, symbolizing summer, is striped with ominous white lines representing the knifing snows of winter. The white stripes are repeated in the ceremonial costumes of the four whistling monitors who control the services through a time period divided into four quarters, symbolizing the four seasons.

The ceremony begins with colorful processions of musicians and semi-nude virgins who move in and out of ritualized patterns. This excites the thousands of worshipers to rise from their seats, shout frenzied poetry in unison, and chant ecstatic anthems through which runs the Oedipus theme of willingness to die for love of Mother.

The actual rites, performed by 22 young priests of perfect physique, might appear to the uninitiated as a chaotic conflict concerned only with hurting the oval by kicking it, then endeavoring to rescue and protect the egg.

However, the procedure is highly stylized. On each side there are eleven young men wearing colorful and protective costumes. The group in so-called "possession" of the oval first arrange themselves in an egg-shaped "huddle," as it is called, for a moment of prayerful meditation and whispering of secret numbers to each other.

Then they rearrange themselves with relation to the position of the egg. In a typical "formation" there are seven priests "on the line," seven being a mystical number associated not, as Jung purists might contend, with the "seven last words" but, actually, with sublimation of the "seven deadly sins" into "the seven cardinal principles of education."

The central priest crouches over the egg, protecting it with his hands while over his back quarters hovers the "quarter-back." The transposition of "back quarters" to "quarter-back" is easily explained by the Adler school. To the layman the curious posture assumed by the "quarter-back," as he hovers over the central priest, immediately suggests the Cretan origins of Mycenaean animal art, but this popular view is untenable. Actually, of course, the "quarter-back" symbolizes the libido, combining two instincts, namely (a) Eros, which strives for even closer union and (b) the instinct for destruction of anything which lies in the path of Eros. Moreover, the "pleasure-pain" excitement of the hysterical worshipers focuses entirely on the actions of the libido-quarter-back. Behind him are three priests representing the male triad.

At a given signal, the egg is passed by sleight-of-hand to one of the members of the triad who endeavors to move it by bodily force across the white lines of winter. This procedure, up and down the enclosure, continues through the four quarters of the ritual.

At the end of the second quarter, implying the summer solstice, the processions of musicians and semi-nude virgins are resumed. After forming themselves into pictograms, representing alphabetical and animal fetishes, the virgins perform a most curious rite requiring far more dexterity than the earlier phallic Maypole rituals from which it seems to be derived. Each of the virgins carries a wand of shining metal which she spins on her fingertips, tosses playfully into the air, and with which she interweaves her body in most intricate gyrations.

The virgins perform another important function throughout the entire service. This concerns the mystical rite of "conversion" following success of one of the young priests in carrying the oval across the last white line of winter. As the moment of "conversion" approaches, the virgins kneel at the edge of the grass, bury their faces in the earth, then raise their arms to heaven in supplication, praying that "the uprights will be split." "Conversion" is indeed a dedicated ceremony.

Freud and Breuer in 1895 ("Studien über Hysteria") described "conversion" as hysterical symptoms originating through the energy of a mental process being withheld from conscious influence, and this precisely accounts for the behavior of the virgins in the football services.

The foregoing, I confess, scarcely scratches the surface. Space does not permit interpretation of football as related to dreams, or discussion of the great subconscious reservoirs of thwarted American energy that weekly seek expression through vicarious enjoyment of ritualized violence and infliction of pain. To relate football to the Oedipus complex alone would require, as it well deserves, years of patient research by scholarly men such as we find in the Ford Foundation.

I only regret that these studies were not undertaken a quarter century ago, when the Freudians were in full flower. It's just another instance, so characteristic of our culture, of too little and too late.

· QUESTIONS ·

1. Is the tone of this article humorous, sardonic, satirical, or all three?
2. Comment on the diction of this essay. If you think some of it slangy and trite, does it seem in keeping with the tone, purpose, and substance of the essay?
3. This now-famous article has been reprinted many times. As an investigative study, compare the original version reprinted here with treatments as they have appeared in *Harper's Magazine* (December, 1957), *Reader's Digest,* and numerous anthologies. Which version do you prefer?
4. This may be a "fun" article, but your understanding and appreciation of it will be enhanced (as will your general knowledge) by an awareness of some of the contributions of Freud, Jung, and Adler. What do you know of their work?
5. Define: caprices, olympian cerebration, parabola, exploitation, treatise, Sabbath (careful, now), Cretan, Mycenaean, libido, Eros, triad, fetish, Maypole, gyrations, Oedipus.

Theme Subjects: (1) What Ferril Overlooks; (2) Freudian Dancing (or Basketball, or Baseball, or Dating, or some other popular activity); (3) One of the topics suggested in the penultimate paragraph of the essay; (4) The Freudian Behavior of Returning Alumni.

ON GOING TO BED

Christopher Morley

CHRISTOPHER MORLEY (1890–1957) was born in Haverford, Pennsylvania, and attended Haverford College. From 1910 to 1913 he was a Rhodes Scholar at Oxford and in 1933 received an honorary Litt.D. from Haverford. Morley was a popular and versatile writer of novels, essays, plays, and poems, and also did editorial work for New York and Philadelphia newspapers. His informal, frequently whimsical essays have appeared in many volumes, among them *Pipefuls* (1920); *Plum Pudding* (1921); and *The Old Mandarin* (1947). Among his better-known novels are *Parnassus on Wheels* (1917); *The Haunted Book Shop* (1919); *Where the Blue Begins* (1922); *Thunder on the Left* (1925); and *Kitty Foyle* (1939). Mr. Morley was editor-in-chief of the revised edition of *Bartlett's Familiar Quotations* (1948) and published *The Ballad of New York* (1950).

One of the characters in *The Moon and Sixpence*[1] remarked that he had faithfully lived up to the old precept about doing every day two things you heartily dislike; for, said he, every day he had got up and he had gone to bed.

It is a sad thing that as soon as the hands of the clock have turned ten the shadow of going to bed begins to creep over the evening. We have never heard bedtime spoken of with any enthusiasm. One after another we have seen a gathering disperse, each person saying (with an air of solemn resignation): "Well, I guess I'll go to bed." But there was no hilarity about it. It is really rather touching how they cling to the departing skirts of the day that is vanishing under the spinning shadow of night.

This is odd, we repeat, for sleep is highly popular among human beings. The reluctance to go to one's couch is not at all a reluctance to slumber, for almost all of us will doze happily in an armchair or on a sofa, or even festooned on the floor with a couple of cushions. But the actual and formal yielding to sheets and blankets is to be postponed to the last possible moment.

The devil of drowsiness is at his

From *Forty-four Essays*, 1925. Reprinted by permission.
[1] By Somerset Maugham.

most potent, we find, about 10:30 P.M. At this period the human carcass seems to consider that it has finished its cycle, which began with so much courage nearly sixteen hours before. It begins to slack and the mind halts on a dead centre every now and then, refusing to complete the revolution. Now there are those who hold that this is certainly the seemly and appointed time to go to bed and they do so as a matter of routine. These are, commonly, the happier creatures, for they take the tide of sleep at the flood and are borne calmly and with gracious gentleness out to great waters of nothingness. They push off from the wharf on a tranquil current and nothing more is to be seen or heard of these voyagers until they reappear at the breakfast table digging lustily into their grapefruit.

These people are happy, aye, in a brutish and sedentary fashion, but they miss the admirable adventures of those more embittered wrestlers who will not give in without a struggle. These latter suffer severe pangs between 10:30 and about 11:15 while they grapple with their fading faculties and seek to reëstablish the will on its tottering throne. This requires courage stout, valour unbending. Once you yield, be it ever so little, to the tempter, you are lost. And here our poor barren clay plays us false, undermining the intellect with many a trick and wile. "I will sit down for a season in that comfortable chair," the creature says to himself, "and read this sprightly novel. That will ease my mind and put me in humour for a continuance of lively thinking." And the end of that man is a steady nasal buzz from the bottom of the chair where he has collapsed, an unsightly object and a disgrace to humanity. This also means a big bill from the electric light company at the end of the month. In many such ways will his corpus betray him, leading him by plausible self-deceptions into a pitfall of sleep, whence he is aroused about 3 A.M. when the planet turns over on the other side. Only by stiff perseverance and rigid avoidance of easy chairs may the critical hour between 10:30 and 11:30 be safely passed. Tobacco, a self-brewed pot of tea, and a browsing along bookshelves (remain standing and do not sit down with your book) are helps in this time of struggle. Even so, there are some happily drowsy souls who can never cross these shadows alone without grounding on the Lotus Reefs. Our friend J— D— K—, magnificent creature, was (when we lived with him) so potently hypnophil that, even erect and determined at his bookcase and urgently bent upon Brann's *Iconoclast* or some other literary irritant, sleep would seep through his pores and he would fall with a crash, lying there in unconscious bliss until someone came in and prodded him up, reeling and ashamed.

But, as we started to say, those who survive this drastic weeding out which Night imposes upon her wooers—so as to cull and choose only the truly meritorious lovers—experience supreme delights which are unknown to their snoring fellows. When the struggle with somnolence has been fought out and won, when the world is all-covering darkness and close-pressing silence, when the tobacco suddenly takes on fresh vigour and fragrance and the books lie strewn about the table, then it seems as though all the rubbish and floating matter of the day's thoughts have poured away and only the bright, clear, and swift current of the mind itself remains, flowing happily and without impediment. This perfection of existence is not to be reached very often; but when properly approached it may be won. It is a different mind that one uncovers then, a spirit which is lucid and hopeful, to which (for a few serene hours) time exists not. The friable resolutions of the day are brought out again and recemented and chiselled anew. Surprising schemes are started and carried through to happy conclusion, lifetimes of amazement are lived in a few passing ticks. There is one who at such moments resolves, with complete sincerity, to start at one end of the top shelf and read again all the books in his library, intending this time really to extract their true marrow. He takes a clean sheet of paper and sets down memoranda of all the people he intends to write to, and all the plumbers and what not that he will call up the next day. And the next time this happy seizure attacks him he will go through the same gestures again without surprise and without the slightest mortification. And then, having lived a generation of good works since midnight struck, he summons all his resolution and goes to bed.

· QUESTIONS ·

1. In what specific ways does the author personalize his material? Does he overuse this stylistic device?
2. Explain the references to Lotus Reefs and Brann's *Iconoclast*. Why are both references particularly apt in this essay?
3. Analyze the sentence structure of the first four paragraphs. Does the variety you find partially explain the charm of the essay?
4. Define: sedentary, hypnophil, friable, mortification.

Theme Subjects: (1) The Two Things I Most Dislike; (2) Sleep, Blessed Sleep; (3) After Midnight Strikes; (4) Evening Resolution, Morning Forgetfulness; (5) My Brutish and Sedentary Roommate; (6) Recipes for Getting to Sleep.

TWISTED TALES: "MACBETH"

Richard Armour

RICHARD WILLARD ARMOUR (1906–   ) was born in San Pedro, California. He received his bachelor's degree at Pomona College and his master's and doctorate at Harvard. He has taught English at the University of Texas, Northwestern, College of the Ozarks, Wells College, and at Scripps College and Claremont Graduate School, where he is now Balch Lecturer in English literature. He is best known as a contributor of light verse to magazines in the United States and England. Among his more popular books are *It All Started with Columbus* (1953); *It All Started with Eve* (1956); *Golf Is a Four-Letter Word* (1962); *The Medical Muse, or What To Do Until the Patient Comes* (1963); *Through Darkest Adolescence* (1963); and *American Lit Relit* (1964).

INTRODUCTION

As is frequently pointed out by the critics, *Macbeth* was probably written in haste. No one knows why Shakespeare was in a hurry, unless he was nauseated by all the bloodshed. At any rate this explains the unusually large number of tragic flaws in the play.

It is the shortest of Shakespeare's major tragedies.* According to one theory, it was long in its original version and subsequently cut. Most of the cutting was doubtless left in the capable hands of Macbeth and the hired murderers, with Lady Macbeth cheering them on.

Shakespeare, who never could think up a plot all by himself, found this one in Holinshed's *Chronicles*, changing it just enough so that no one would recognize the source.**

* Some don't consider this a flaw.

** He didn't count on the resourcefulness of modern scholars, who have to discover things like this to become associate professors.

If, as researchers say, Shakespeare took liberties with Scottish history, most of us who love liberty applaud him for it.

As Kittredge observes, Shakespeare at the beginning of the play "plunges, as usual, *in medias res.*" Whatever this is, he doesn't come up for air until the play is over. Few Elizabethan dramatists had such powers of endurance as Shakespeare, and few modern theatergoers have such powers of endurance as the Elizabethans.

The play is full of atmosphere, which helps the characters breathe. Of the characters, the most interesting are Macbeth and Lady Macbeth. The latter is not only her husband's wife but his evil genius.* According to G. B. Harrison, "Lady Macbeth is at the same time greater and less than her husband," which is about as neat a trick as you will find in all Shakespeare. Cruel and heartless as they appear, both Macbeth and Lady Macbeth are said to have a gentle, loving side. It must be the side away from the audience.

There are some beautiful passages. One of them is the hallway in Macbeth's castle, where Lady Macbeth loved to finger-paint on the wall with other people's blood.

MACBETH AND THE WITCHES

Three witches, extremely weird sisters, are having a picnic amidst thunder and lightning somewhere in Scotland. Judging from their appearance, they placed one-two-three in the Edinburgh Ugly Contest.

"When shall we three meet again in thunder, lightning, or in rain?" asks one of them. They hate nice weather and are happiest when they are soaking wet and their hair is all stringy.

"When the hurly-burly's** done, when the battle's lost and won," another replies. A battle is going on between the forces of Duncan, the King of Scotland, and some Norwegians, assisted by the rebel Thane of Cawdor. At the moment it's looking good for Duncan, because two of his generals, Macbeth and Banquo, have cunningly put bagpipes into the hands of the enemy, who are blowing their brains out.

The witches hear some dear friends† calling, and depart. "Fair is foul, and foul is fair," they comment philosophically as they leave. This must have been pretty upsetting to any moralists, semanticists, or baseball umpires who chanced to overhear them.

Shortly afterward, the battle having been won by Macbeth, and the weather having turned bad enough to be pleasant, the witches meet again.

"Where hast thou been, Sister?" asks one.

"Killing swine," the second replies. All three of them have been busy doing similarly diverting things, and one of them happily shows the others the thumb of a drowned sailor which she is adding to her thumb collection.††

Macbeth and Banquo come by

---

* All in all, quite a helpmate.
** See also hurdy-gurdy, hunky-dory, and okey-dokey.
† A cat and a toad. Witches have to make friendships where they can.
†† In a comedy, this would be considered tragic relief.

at this point, on their way to inform the King that they have defeated the rebels. They would rather tell him in person than render a report in triplicate.

"Speak, if you can," says Macbeth boldly to the hags. "What are you?" He rather thinks they are witches, but would like to hear it from their own skinny lips.

The witches start hailing.* They hail Macbeth as Thane of Glamis and Thane of Cawdor and say he will be King Hereafter. Not to leave Banquo out, they hail him as "lesser than Macbeth, and greater." (The witches are masters of gobbledyspook.) He won't be a king, they say, but he'll beget kings, and now they have to begetting along.

Macbeth knows he is Thane of Glamis, but has no idea (or didn't have until now) of becoming Thane of Cawdor or King Hereafter. "Stay, you imperfect speakers, tell me more," he commands. But the witches, perhaps not liking the way he refers to their elocution, vanish into thin air, making it slightly thicker.

While Macbeth is meditating about what the witches have forecast for him, a couple of the King's henchmen, straight from a busy day of henching, ride up. They bring word that Duncan is liquidating the Thane of Cawdor and giving his title to Macbeth, it being an inexpensive gift. (Duncan, as King of Scotland, was Scotcher than anybody.)

"Look how our partner's rapt," remarks Banquo, noticing that Macbeth, stunned with all the good news, acts as if he has been struck on the noggin. But Macbeth is only lost in thought, and will find his way out presently. Thus far the witches have been batting 1.000, and Macbeth is beginning to take more than a casual interest in Duncan's health.**

DUNCAN IS DONE IN

Back at Macbeth's castle, Lady Macbeth receives a letter in which her husband tells about the witches and how prophetic their prophecies are proving. However, Lady Macbeth knows that her husband is a Weak Character. He would like to be king, but is embarrassed by any social unpleasantness, such as murdering a friend. Sometimes Lady Macbeth thinks there's something wrong with his circulatory system.

"It is too full o' the milk of human kindness," she mutters, remembering how easily his blood curdles. As for herself, she would ask nothing better than to be filled "from the crown to the toe, top-full of direst cruelty." She already has a good deal of the stuff in her, but thinks there is room for more.

Word comes that Duncan, on his way home from the battle and wanting to save the price of a hotel room, plans to spend the night with the Macbeths. Lady Macbeth rubs her hands with Glee, a Scottish detergent of those days, and prepares to entertain the royal guest. She seems to hear a raven croaking, and that's a sure sign of death.†

---

* Until now it has been raining.
** Henceforth when he says "How are you?" to the King it will be a bona fide question.
† At least of the raven.

"Come, you spirits that tend on mortal thoughts," she cries out to whatever unseen spirits may be lurking in the murk, "unsex me here. Come to my woman's breasts and take my milk for gall." It is to the credit of the spirits that they do not accept her invitation.

By the time Macbeth arrives, Lady Macbeth has it all figured out. She tells her husband that they will wait until Duncan has gone to bed, ply his guards with drink, and then stab Duncan to death with the guards' daggers, thus not bloodying any of their own utensils.

Knowing that he shows everything on his face, including what he has eaten for breakfast, Lady Macbeth instructs her husband how to act. "Look like th' innocent flower," she says craftily, "but be the serpent under 't." Her last words are spoken with a menacing hiss.

Macbeth at first has misgivings, wondering whether this is quite the sort of thing for him to do as Duncan's host. Also he is scared, but not as scared as he is of Lady Macbeth.

"If it were done when 'tis done, then 'twere well it were done quickly," Macbeth rattles off to his wife, hoping to confuse her.

"Screw your courage to the sticking-place," Lady Macbeth tells him, handing him his tool box. Macbeth finally agrees to go along, but he doesn't sound any too enthusiastic.

That night Macbeth finds himself on his way to the guest room, about to dispatch Duncan. Lady Macbeth has given the guards a Mickey MacFinn and taken their weapons, which she thoughtfully lays out for her partner in crime.*

"Is this a dagger which I see before me, the handle toward my hand?" Macbeth asks himself. (It is.) He hears a wolf howl, starts, and keeps going.

In a few moments an owl begins hooting, crickets cry,** and bells ring. Duncan, whom Macbeth has stabbed, is the only one who keeps still. Then Macbeth imagines he hears someone cry out, "Macbeth does murder sleep—the innocent sleep, sleep that knits up the raveled sleave† of care." This has become an FSQ†† although carpers contend that it is nothing but a Mixed Metaphor.

Anyhow, he is too upset to put the bloody daggers by the guards, and Lady Macbeth takes over from her lily-livered husband.

"Infirm of purpose!" she addresses him tenderly, using a nickname she employs only when the two are alone together. "Give me the daggers." She carries them off, plants them by the guards, and is back in an instant, bloody but unbowed.

"I dare do all that may become a man," Macbeth says to her plaintively; "who dares do more is none." What he means is that it takes a woman to tackle the really dirty jobs.

Just then a knocking is heard. At first Lady Macbeth thinks it's

---

* She thought at first of murdering Duncan herself. But as he lay sleeping, his mouth wide open and his teeth in the glass on the chair, he looked too much like her dear old father.

** Usually they chirp, but not in a situation like this.

† "Sleave," the scholars insist, is not the same as "sleeve," but no one is convinced.

†† Famous Shakespearean Quotation.

her husband's knees, but then she realizes the doorbell isn't working and somebody wants in.

"Retire we to our chamber," she whispers to Macbeth, who is staring at his hands as if he has never seen them before.* Her idea is not to come out of retirement until they have removed all the tell-tale blood and climbed into their nighties. They exeunt.

The knocking continues, and a porter goes to the gate. He takes his time,** being busy speculating about Hell. (Shakespeare's porters are invariably Philosophers.) "Anon, anon," he calls to the persons outside, not knowing their names.

The knockers, who are really boosters, are two of Duncan's henchmen—Macduff (in some texts Macduffel) and Lennox. They ask for Macbeth, and when he comes in, pretending to have been awakened by the uproar, they inquire about Duncan.

"Is he stirring?" asks Macduff.

"Not yet," Macbeth replies, having a hard time keeping a straight face. "'Twas a rough night," he adds, trying to explain his rather rumpled appearance.

Macduff goes into Duncan's room, and shortly thereafter dashes out looking as if he has seen a corpse.

"O horror, horror, horror!" he screams. As soon as he can think of another word, he cries, "Awake, awake!" Quickly he turns the place into bedlam. "Ring the bell! Come, look on death itself!" People begin to queue up. When Lady Macbeth enters and is told that Duncan is murdered, her reaction is studied.† "What, in our house?" she says, simulating horror at the choice of locale. "Help me hence, ho," she cries, confident that some courteous courtier will offer his arm. But too much else of interest is going on. Not until she swoons and lies stretched out on the floor does anyone pay her heed†† and carry her out.

Naturally enough, the finger of suspicion points at the two guards, and Macbeth promptly kills them both before it swings around his way. Malcolm and Donalbain, Duncan's sons, don't like the look of things and light out for England and Ireland, respectively, before somebody puts the finger on *them*.

So Macbeth ascends the throne, and Lady Macbeth is terribly proud of her husband and the way he is going up in the world.

THE GHOSTLY GUEST

Macbeth should be happy as a king, but Banquo and his son Fleance disturb him. He remembers the witches' prophecy that Banquo is going to beget kings, and doesn't like the idea of having gone to all this trouble just to set up the throne for someone else's brats. Macbeth himself is the end of his line, and, although he doesn't know it yet, near the end of his rope. Besides, he suspects Banquo of suspecting him of foul play.‡

So he invites Banquo to dine

---

* "What hands are here?" he asks.
** He is a porter, isn't he?
† Especially by young tragic actresses.
†† A small sum, or carrying charge.
‡ By coincidence, "Foul play" is precisely what a contemporary reviewer, writing in the London *Tymes*, said of *Macbeth*.

one evening at the castle. While Banquo and Fleance are out on a horseback ride, getting up an appetite,* Macbeth calls in a couple of professional and fully licensed murderers.** Any more murders on his own, he fears, will lose him his amateur standing. The murderers, who are described as "without," though we never know what it is they lack, are quickly employed to practice their trade on Banquo and Fleance. They are despicable, heartless characters, and Macbeth is delighted to have made their acquaintance. "Your spirits shine through you," he says to them, trying to be complimentary but not knowing quite how to put it. Then he waves them on their way and bids them Godspeed, although it seems a little inappropriate.

Banquo and Fleance are riding around and around in the park, still feeling none too hungry. The murderers wait until their victims have dismounted,† and then set upon Banquo and stab him fatally. Before he dies, however, he warns Fleance.

"Fly, good Fleance, fly, fly, fly!"

Obediently, Fleance takes off. Although he gains elevation only by leaps and bounds, he is soon out of sight. The murderers have accomplished only half the job, but for once it was the little one that got away.

That night, at the banquet, Macbeth is just sitting down†† when one of the murderers sticks his bloodstained face in, explaining that he cut himself while shaving. He reports to Macbeth that Banquo is done for, with twenty gashes in his head. But while they were counting the gashes, Fleance escaped, and they'll settle for fifty cents on the dollar.

Macbeth goes back to the table, intending to enjoy his mead and potatoes, but when he gets to his chair he sees the ghost of Banquo sitting in it. He is disconcerted, to say the least.

"See! Behold! Look! Lo!" he cries,‡ but no one knows what's troubling him. They think he must be seeing things, which he is. Finally the ghost leaves, and Macbeth sits down, mopping his brow with a slab of roast beef. Lady Macbeth tries to calm everyone.

"My lord is often thus," she says soothingly, but creating an unfortunate picture of their home life. "The fit is momentary." Then she whispers into his ear, "Take care, my lord, thou 'rt about to spill the beans."

Macbeth is just beginning to relax and regain his color, when Banquo's ghost reenters.

"Avaunt, and quit my sight!" Macbeth screams. The ghost avaunts, but not before some of the guests.‡‡ Lady Macbeth suddenly yearns to be alone with her husband.

---

* Banquo has eaten at the castle before, and sitting at the same table with Lady Macbeth dries up his gastric juices.

** Later joined by a third, thought by some scholars to be Macbeth in disguise, but more likely an apprentice murderer, getting experience.

† Shakespeare was part owner of the theater, and well aware that the cleanup crew charged extra if a horse was brought onstage.

†† "You know your own degrees," he says to his guests, all of them college men.

‡ A speech rich in ideas for the publishers of American picture magazines.

‡‡ Macbeth is acting so insanely that he resembles Hamlet, and they fear they have stumbled into the wrong play.

"Stand not upon the order of your going," she hints to those who are still gossiping in the doorway, giving them a slight push and turning off the porch light.

Alone, Macbeth and Lady Macbeth look at each other disconsolately. It will be hard to win back their reputation for gay dinner parties. The evening is ruined, and there is nothing left to do but go to bed and have a few nightmares.

THE WITCHES AGAIN

Macbeth is in deep now, and knows it. It was all caused by the rosy picture, now turned blood-red, painted by the witches. Maybe, thinks Macbeth, he can ask the weird sisters a few more questions and find out what's going to happen in the fifth act.

Alone he strides the heath and, sure enough, comes upon the witches. These beauties are standing around a boiling caldron, fixing supper.

"Double, double toil and trouble," they moan as they stir the bubbling brew. Apparently they dislike cooking. As they stir, they toss in such ingredients as newts' eyes, goats' gall, poisoned entrails, bats' wool, lizards' legs, dragons' scales, and now and then the finger of a birth-strangled babe or a dash of baboon's blood for seasoning. They take care to follow the recipe* exactly, and, not surprisingly, seem in no rush to eat.

As Macbeth walks up, he hails them cheerily. "How now, you secret, black, and midnight hags!"

He wants to ingratiate himself so they will answer his questions.

He seems to have said just the right thing, for they give him all sorts of interesting information. They advise him to look out for Macduff but otherwise not to worry, since (1) nobody born of woman shall harm him and (2) he won't be defeated until Birnam Wood comes to Dunsinane Hill. From this he gathers that he is an excellent insurance risk.

The only thing that disturbs Macbeth is a little pantomime staged by the witches shortly before they vanish. In it, Banquo's ghost points to a long row of kings, and grins sickeningly. Since the ghost may have been sampling the witches' bat and lizard stew, this is understandable. Macbeth correctly interprets the show to mean that Banquo has outfoxed and outbegot him. However, he still doesn't see how he can be defeated by the present generation. Though no student of obstetrics, he is afraid of no man not born of woman, and it is his considered opinion that Birnam Wood will stay put.

"Who can bid the tree unfix his earth-bound root?" he asks of no one in particular, and receives no answer.

MACBETH GETS HIS

Although unable to get at Macduff, who is vacationing in England, Macbeth hires some murderers to slay Macduff's wife and son.** Fortunately most of this domestic slaughter takes place offstage.

---

* You can find this dish in Greta Ghoul's "Recipes for Retching" or in almost any diet cookbook.
** The ready availability of murderers is a boon to Macbeth and to the plot.

When Macduff learns that his family has been wiped out, he is sore annoyed, which is an ugly combination. Teaming up with Duncan's son, Malcolm, he raises an army. This takes time—you know how long it takes to raise a family.

"Front to front bring thou this fiend of Scotland and myself," he implores MacJove and the other Scottish gods, shuddering to think of Macbeth creeping up on him from behind.

Meanwhile Lady Macbeth, who has been trying to remove Duncan's blood from her hands for weeks, keeps washing them without any luck.* When she isn't washing them, she is wringing them.**

"Out, damned spot!" she shrieks, losing her temper and foolishly thinking an imprecation will succeed where cleaning fluid has failed. Self-possessed as she was in the first act, she is now a bundle of nerves, and none too securely tied together.

Night after night she walks in her sleep, muttering about blood and Banquo's ghost. Unfortunately the Court Doctor hasn't even a love seat, much less a couch, in his office. He is therefore "unable to minister to a mind diseased," and stands helplessly by.

"What's done cannot be undone," Lady Macbeth mutters, struggling with a knot in her stomach. As she sleepwalks, she carries a candle in her hand, leaving a trail of tallow drippings.† Finally she dies, this being the only way she can give up the ghost.

Macduff, Malcolm, and their army are now at Birnam Wood, while Macbeth remains at his castle at Dunsinane. "Tomorrow, and tomorrow, and tomorrow," he says over and over and over to himself, rather liking the sound.

Alarum clocks commence to go off, signaling the beginning of the battle. Macbeth rushes to the field, still thinking he leads a charmed life. Only when the enemy soldiers camouflage themselves with trees from Birnam Wood and start branching out toward Dunsinane does Macbeth realize that the witches have played False with him. Then, when he gets into hand-to-hand, toe-to-toe conflict with Macduff, and Macduff casually mentions that he wasn't born of woman, or at least not in the usual way—he was "from his mother's womb untimely ripp'd" by some impatient obstetrician—Macbeth is ready to quit.

"Lay off, Macduff, I've had enuff"†† is his unforgettable cry. But Macduff, warming to his task and sensing the final curtain, taunts his opponent.

"Yield thee, coward," he suggests, forgetting that Shakespearean heroes go down swinging.

Indeed, Macbeth has taken about all the guff from Macduff he can stand. "Lay *on*," he snarls, in a memorable change of prepositions.

The fighting is terrible, and it

---

* See Glee, above.

** Sometimes she sniffs them. "All the perfumes of Arabia will not sweeten this little hand," she says sourly.

† "Out, brief candle!" commands Macbeth, addressing an inanimate object (as do so many of Shakespeare's characters) in the full knowledge that it can't talk back.

†† Another version, no less authentic, is: "Lay ough, Macdough, I've had enough."

is fortunate for the audience that, like the slaughter of Lady Macduff and her son, it is offstage. They thrust, parry, and lunge as if their lives depend on it. At last Macbeth begins to tire. He is bored* by Macduff, who also cuts off his head. This he gives to Malcolm, who is now King of Scotland and likely to get all sorts of unusual presents.

As the curtain is rung down, Malcolm invites everyone to come and see him crowned at Scone. The invitation does not apply to members of the audience, who at this point are too exhausted, anyhow, for further festivities.

QUESTIONS ON MACBETH

1. Have you a weird sister? An odd brother?
2. Comment on the following quotation: "'Aroint thee, witch!' the rump-fed ronyon cries." Discuss the advantages of rump-fed over spoon-fed and intravenous.
3. Was Macbeth thane? How does he compare in this respect with Hamlet?
4. Would you trust Lady Macbeth as a wet nurse? Keep in mind her expression of solicitude for her own infant: "I would, while it was smiling in my face, have pluck'd my nipple from his boneless gums and dash'd the brains out."
5. Which would you prefer in your stew:
   a. Newts' eyes?
   b. Dragons' scales?
   c. A dash of baboon blood?
6. Continue and bring to an interesting conclusion Lady Macbeth's unfinished poem:

   > "The thane of Fife
   > Had a wife. . . ."

7. If you have trouble remembering lines, take the part of one of the witches in the following scene:

   > 1ST WITCH. Hail!
   > 2ND WITCH. Hail!
   > 3RD WITCH. Hail!

8. "Upon my head," said Macbeth, "they placed a fruitless crown." What did he expect, a bowl of grapes and bananas?
9. Did you realize that a hautboy is not a male child but a musical instrument?
10. Try to piece together the history of Scotland. Use Scotch Tape if necessary.

· QUESTIONS ·

Professor Armour has supplied his own questions for this selection. They seem eminently well suited to this delightfully absurd paraphrase; others might be superfluous.

Theme Subjects: If you like paraphrases and parodies, tackle one of Shakespeare's other plays or some selection in this volume. The editor does not feel that he should encourage you strongly; you and your instructor may do your own conniving.

---

* Through the heart.

AN APOLOGY
FOR IDLERS

Robert Louis Stevenson

ROBERT LOUIS STEVENSON (1850–1894) was born in Edinburgh, Scotland, and studied engineering and law at Edinburgh University. He had no real liking for either profession, however, and against his father's wishes he began writing. Of himself he has said: "I imagine nobody had ever such pains to learn a trade as I had; but I slogged at it day in and day out; and I frankly believe (thanks to my dire industry) I have done more with smaller gifts than any man in the world." Stevenson's romantic stories and gallantry in the face of ill health (he was an almost continuous invalid from weak lungs) have served to make him one of the most beloved of modern authors. His constant travels in search of health resulted in such books as *An Inland Voyage* and *Travels with a Donkey in the Cevennes*. He is well known as a novelist (*Kidnapped, Treasure Island*), short story writer ("Markheim," "Dr. Jekyll and Mr. Hyde"), poet (*A Child's Garden of Verses*), and essayist (*Familiar Studies of Men and Books, Virginibus Puerisque*). He lived for a time in the United States, married an American, and spent the last years of his life in the South Sea Islands (Samoa).

BOSWELL: We grow weary when idle. JOHNSON: That is, sir, because others being busy, we want company; but if we were idle, there would be no growing weary; we should all entertain one another.

Just now, when every one is bound, under pain of a decree in absence convicting him of *lèse*-respectability, to enter on some lucrative profession, and labor therein with something not far short of enthusiasm, a cry from the opposite party who are content when they have enough, and like to look on and enjoy in the meanwhile, savors a little of bravado and gasconade. And yet this should not be. Idleness so-called, which does not consist of doing nothing, but in doing a great deal not recognized in the dogmatic formularies of the ruling class, has as good a right to state its position as industry itself. It is admitted that the presence of people who refuse to enter in the great handicap race for sixpenny pieces is at once an insult and a disenchantment for those who do. A fine fellow (as we see so many) takes his determination, votes for the sixpences, and, in the emphatic Americanism, "goes for" them. And while such an one is plowing distressfully up the road, it is not hard to understand his resentment when he perceives cool persons in the meadows by the wayside, lying with a handkerchief over their ears and a glass at their elbow. Alexander is touched in a very delicate place by the disregard of Diogenes. Where was the glory of having taken Rome for these tumultuous barbarians who poured into the Senate house and found the Fathers sitting silent and unmoved by their success? It is a sore thing to have labored along and scaled the arduous hilltops, and, when all is done, find humanity indifferent to your achievement. Hence physicists condemn the unphysical; financiers have only a superficial toleration for those who know little of stock; literary persons despise the unlettered; and people of all pursuits combine to disparage those who have none.

But, though this is one difficulty of the subject, it is not the greatest. You could not be put in prison for speaking against industry, but you can be sent to Coventry for speaking like a fool. The greatest difficulty with most subjects is to do them well; therefore, please to remember this is an apology. It is certain that much may be judiciously argued in favor of diligence; only there is something to be said against it, and that is what, on the present occasion, I have to say. To state one argument is not necessarily to be deaf to all others, and

that a man has written a book of travels in Montenegro is no reason why he should never have been to Richmond.

It is surely beyond a doubt that people should be a good deal idle in youth. For though here and there a Lord Macaulay may escape from school honors with all his wits about him, most boys pay so dear for their medals that they never afterward have a shot in their locker, and begin the world bankrupt. And the same holds true during all the time a lad is educating himself, or suffering others to educate him. It must have been a very foolish old gentleman who addressed Johnson at Oxford in these words: "Young man, ply your book diligently now, and acquire a stock of knowledge; for when years come upon you, you will find that poring upon books will be but an irksome task." The old gentleman seems to have been unaware that many other things besides reading grow irksome, and not a few become impossible by the time a man has to use spectacles and cannot walk without a stick. Books are good enough in their own way, but they are a mighty bloodless substitute for life. It seems a pity to sit, like the Lady of Shalott, peering into a mirror, with your back turned on all the bustle and glamour of reality. And if a man reads very hard, as the old anecdote reminds us, he will have little time for thoughts.

If you look back on your own education, I am sure it will not be the full, vivid, instructive hours of truantry that you regret; you would rather cancel some lackluster periods between sleep and waking in the class. For my own part, I have attended a good many lectures in my time. I still remember that the spinning of a top is a case of kinetic stability. I still remember that emphyteusis is not a disease, nor stillicide a crime. But, though I would not willingly part with such scraps of science, I do not set the same store by them as by certain other odds and ends that I came by in the open street while I was playing truant. This is not the moment to dilate on that mighty place of education, which was the favorite school of Dickens and of Balzac and turns out yearly many inglorious masters in the Science of the Aspects of Life. Suffice it to say this: if a lad does not learn in the streets, it is because he has no faculty of learning. Nor is the truant always in the streets, for, if he prefers, he may go out by the gardened suburbs into the country. He may pitch on some tufts of lilacs over a burn and smoke innumerable pipes to the tune of the water on the stones. A bird will sing in the thicket. And there he may fall into a vein of kindly thought and see things in a new perspective. Why, if this be not education, what is? We may conceive Mr. Wordly Wiseman accosting such an one and the conversation that should thereupon ensue:

"How now, young fellow, what dost thou here?"

"Truly, sir, I take mine ease."

"Is not this the hour of the class? and shouldst thou not be plying thy Book with diligence, to the end thou mayest obtain knowledge?"

"Nay, but thus also I follow after Learning, by your leave."

"Learning, quotha! After what fashion, I pray thee? Is it mathematics?"

"No, to be sure."

"Is it metaphysics?"

"Nor that."

"Is it some language?"

"Nay, it is no language."

"Is it a trade?"

"Nor a trade neither."

"Why, then, what is't?"

"Indeed, sir, as a time may soon come for me to go upon Pilgrimage, I am desirous to note what is commonly done by persons in my case, and where are the ugliest Sloughs and Thickets on the Road; as also, what manner of Staff is of the best service. Moreover, I lie here, by this water, to learn by root-of-heart a lesson which my master teaches me to call Peace, or Contentment."

Hereupon Mr. Wordly Wiseman was much commoved with passion; and, shaking his cane with a very threatful countenance, broke forth upon this wise: "Learning, quotha!" said he; "I would have all such rogues scourged by the Hangman!"

And so he would go his way, ruffling out his cravat with a crackle of starch, like a turkey when it spreads its feathers.

Now this, of Mr. Wiseman's, is the common opinion. A fact is not called a fact, but a piece of gossip, if it does not fall into one of your scholastic categories. And inquiry must be in some acknowledged direction, with a name to go by, or else you are not inquiring at all, only lounging; and the workhouse is too good for you. It is supposed that all knowledge is at the bottom of a well or the far end of a telescope. Sainte-Beuve, as he grew older, came to regard all experience as a single great book in which to study for a few years ere we go hence; and it seemed all one to him whether you should read in chapter xx, which is the differential calculus, or in chapter xxxix, which is hearing the band play in the gardens. As a matter of fact, an intelligent person, looking out of his eyes and harkening in his ears, with a smile on his face all the time, will get more true education than many another in a life of heroic vigils. There is certainly some chill and arid knowledge to be found upon the summits of formal and laborious science; but it is all round about you, and for the trouble of looking, you will acquire the warm and palpitating facts of life. While others are filling their memory with a lumber of words, one-half of which they will forget before the week be out, your truant may learn some really useful art: to play the fiddle, to know a good cigar, or to speak with ease and opportunity to all varieties of men. Many who have "plied their book diligently" and know all about some one branch or another of accepted lore come out of the study with an ancient and owl-like demeanor and prove dry, stockish, and dyspeptic in all the better and brighter parts of life. Many make a large fortune, who remain underbred and pathetically stupid to the last. And meantime there goes the idler, who began life along with them—by your leave— a different picture. He has had time to take care of his health and his spirits; he has been a great deal in the open air, which is the most salutary of all things for both body and mind; and, if he has never read the great Book in very recondite places, he has dipped into it and skimmed it over to excellent purpose. Might not the student afford some Hebrew roots, and the business man some of his half-crowns, for a share of the idler's knowledge of life at large and Art of Living? Nay, and the idler has another and

more important quality than these. I mean his wisdom. He who has much looked on at the childish satisfaction of other people in their hobbies will regard his own with only a very ironical indulgence. He will not be heard among the dogmatists. He will have a great and cool allowance for all sorts of people and opinions. If he finds no out-of-the-way truths, he will identify himself with no very burning falsehood. His way takes him along a by-road, not much frequented, but very even and pleasant, which is called Commonplace Lane and leads to the Belvedere of Common Sense. Thence he shall command an agreeable if not very noble prospect; and while others behold the East and West, the Devil and the Sunrise, he will be contentedly aware of a sort of morning hour upon all sublunary things, with an army of shadows running speedily and in many different directions into the great daylight of Eternity. The shadows and the generations, the shrill doctors and the plangent wars, go by into ultimate silence and emptiness; but, underneath all this, a man may see out of the Belvedere windows much green and peaceful landscape; many firelit parlors; good people laughing, drinking, and making love as they did before the Flood or the French Revolution; and the old shepherd telling his tale under the hawthorn.

Extreme *busyness,* whether at school or college, kirk or market, is a symptom of deficient vitality; and a faculty for idleness implies a catholic appetite and a strong sense of personal identity. There is a sort of dead-alive, hackneyed people about, who are scarcely conscious of living except in the exercise of some conventional occupation. Bring these fellows into the country, or set them aboard ship, and you will see how they pine for their desk or their study. They have no curiosity; they cannot give themselves over to random provocations; they do not take pleasure in the exercise of their faculties for its own sake; and, unless Necessity lays about them with a stick, they will even stand still. It is no good speaking to such folk; they cannot be idle, their nature is not generous enough, and they pass those hours in a sort of coma which are not dedicated to furious moiling in the gold-mill. When they do not require to go to the office, when they are not hungry and have no mind to drink, the whole breathing world is a blank to them. If they have to wait an hour or so for a train, they fall into a stupid trance with their eyes open. To see them, you would suppose there was nothing to look at and no one to speak with; you would imagine they were paralyzed or alienated; and yet very possibly they are hard workers in their own way, and have good eyesight for a flaw in a deed or a turn of the market. They have been to school and college, but all the time they had their eye on the medal; they have gone about in the world and mixed with clever people, but all the time they were thinking of their own affairs. As if a man's soul were not small to begin with, they have dwarfed and narrowed theirs by a life of all work and no play until here they are at forty, with a listless attention, a mind vacant of all material of amusement, and not one thought to rub against another, while they wait for the train. Before he was breeched he might have clambered on the boxes; when he was twenty he would have stared at the girls; but now the pipe is smoked out, the snuff-box empty, and my gentleman sits bolt upright upon a bench, with lamentable eyes. This does not appeal to me as being Success in Life.

But it is not only the person himself who suffers from his busy habits, but his wife and children, his friends and relations, and down to the very people he sits with in a railway carriage or an omnibus. Perpetual devotion to what a man calls his business is only to be sustained by perpetual neglect of many other things. And it is not by any means certain that a man's business is the most important thing he has to do. To an impartial estimate it will seem clear that many of the wisest, most virtuous, and most beneficent parts that are to be played upon the Theater of Life are filled by gratuitous performers, and pass, among the world at large, as phases of idleness. For in that Theater not only the walking gentlemen, singing chambermaids, and diligent fiddlers in the orchestra, but those who look on and clap their hands from the benches do really play a part and fulfil important offices toward the general result. You are no doubt very dependent on the care of your lawyer and stockbroker, of the guards and signalmen who convey you rapidly from place to place, and the policemen who walk the streets for your protection; but is there not a thought of gratitude in your heart for certain other benefactors who set you smiling when they fall in your way, or season your dinner with good company? Colonel Newcome helped to lose his friend's money; Fred Bayham had an ugly trick of borrowing shirts; and yet they were better people to fall among than Mr. Barnes. And, though Falstaff was neither sober nor very honest, I think I could name one or two long-faced Barabbases whom the world could better have done without. Hazlitt mentions that he was more sensible of obligation to Northcote, who had never done him anything he could call a service, than to his whole circle of ostentatious friends; for he thought a good companion emphatically the greatest benefactor. I know there are people in the world who cannot feel grateful unless the favor has been done them at the cost of pain and difficulty. But this is a churlish disposition. A man may send you six sheets of letter-paper covered with the most entertaining gossip, or you may pass half an hour pleasantly, perhaps profitably, over an article of his; do you think the service would be greater if he had made the manuscript in his heart's blood, like a compact with the devil? Do you really fancy you should be more beholden to your correspondent if he had been damning you all the while for your importunity? Pleasures are more beneficial than duties because, like the quality of mercy, they are not strained, and they are twice blest. There must always be two to a kiss, and there may be a score in a jest; but wherever there is an element of sacrifice, the favor is conferred with pain, and, among generous people, received with confusion.

There is no duty we so much underrate as the duty of being happy. By being happy, we sow anonymous benefits upon the world, which remain unknown even to ourselves, or, when they are disclosed, surprise nobody so much as the benefactor.

The other day a ragged, bare-foot boy ran down the street after a marble with so jolly an air that he set every one he passed into a good humor; one of these persons, who had been delivered from more than usually black thoughts, stopped the little fellow and gave him some money with this remark: "You see what sometimes comes of looking pleased." If he had looked pleased before, he had now to look both pleased and mystified. For my part, I justify this encouragement of smiling rather than tearful children; I do not wish to pay for tears anywhere but upon the stage; but I am prepared to deal largely in the opposite commodity. A happy man or woman is a better thing to find than a five-pound note. He or she is a radiating focus of goodwill; and their entrance into a room is as though another candle had been lighted. We need not care whether they could prove the forty-seventh proposition; they do a better thing than that—they practically demonstrate the great Theorem of the Livableness of Life. Consequently, if a person cannot be happy without remaining idle, idle he should remain. It is a revolutionary precept; but, thanks to hunger and the workhouse, one not easily to be abused; and, within practical limits, it is one of the most incontestable truths in the whole Body of Morality. Look at one of your industrious fellows for a moment, I beseech you. He sows hurry and reaps indigestion; he puts a vast deal of activity out to interest and receives a large measure of nervous derangement in return. Either he absents himself entirely from all fellowship, and lives a recluse in a garret, with carpet slippers and a leaden inkpot; or he comes among people swiftly and bitterly, in a contraction of his whole nervous system, to discharge some temper before he returns to work. I do not care how much or how well he works, this fellow is an evil creature in other people's lives. They would be happier if he were dead. They could easier do without his services in the Circumlocution Office than they can tolerate his fractious spirits. He poisons life at the wellhead. It is better to be beggared out of hand by a scapegrace nephew than daily hag-ridden by a peevish uncle.

And what, in God's name, is all this pother about? For what cause do they embitter their own and other people's lives? That a man should publish three or thirty articles a year, that he should finish or not finish his great allegorical picture, are questions of little interest to the world. The ranks of life are full; and, although a thousand fall, there are always some to go into the breach. When they told Joan of Arc she should be at home minding women's work, she answered there were plenty to spin and wash. And so even with your own rare gifts! When nature is "so careless of the single life," why should we coddle ourselves into the fancy that our own is of exceptional importance? Suppose Shakespeare had been knocked on the head some dark night in Sir Thomas Lucy's preserves, the world would have wagged on better or worse, the pitcher gone to the well, the scythe to the corn, and the student to his book, and no one been any the wiser of the loss. There are not many works extant, if you look the

alternative all over, which are worth the price of a pound of tobacco to a man of limited means. This is a sobering reflection for the proudest of our earthly vanities. Even a tobacconist may, upon consideration, find no great cause for personal vainglory in the phrase; for, although tobacco is an admirable sedative, the qualities necessary for retailing it are neither rare nor precious in themselves. Alas and alas! you may take it how you will, but the services of no single individual are indispensable. Atlas was just a gentleman with a protracted nightmare! And yet you see merchants who go and labor themselves into a great fortune and thence into the bankruptcy court; scribblers who keep scribbling at little articles until their temper is cross to all who come about them, as though Pharaoh should set the Israelites to make a pin instead of a pyramid; and fine young men who work themselves into a decline, and are driven off in a hearse with white plumes upon it. Would you not suppose these persons have been whispered, by the Master of the Ceremonies, the promise of some momentous destiny; and that this lukewarm bullet on which they play their farces was the bull's-eye and center point of all the universe? And yet it is not so. The ends for which they give away their priceless youth, for all they know, may be chimerical or hurtful; the glory and riches they expect may never come, or may find them indifferent; and they and the world they inhabit are so inconsiderable that the mind freezes at the thought.

· QUESTIONS ·

1. In what sense does Stevenson use "apology"? What is his central thesis?
2. How does this statement summarize the essay: "There is no duty we so much underrate as the duty of being happy"?
3. Explain the references to Boswell, Johnson, Alexander, Diogenes, Coventry, Lord Macaulay, Lady of Shalott, Dickens, Balzac, Sainte-Beuve, Colonel New-come, Falstaff, Barabbas(es), Hazlitt, Joan of Arc, Atlas, Pharaoh.
4. Summarize the thought of the final paragraph. Is this paragraph different in tone from the remainder of the essay? If so, why?
5. How does the style of this essay differ from that of other personal essays in this volume? Be specific in your answer.
6. Define: lucrative, disparage, kinetic stability, stillicide, arid, recondite, sublunary, gratuitous, ostentatious, allegorical, chimerical.

Theme Subjects: (1) A Reply to Stevenson; (2) Modern Atlases; (3) Experience Is a Great Teacher; (4) On Playing Hooky; (5) Productive Idleness; (6) An Apology for "Busyness."

CRITICISM

HERMAN MELVILLE

Clifton Fadiman

CLIFTON FADIMAN (1904–   ) was born in New York City and received an A.B. from Columbia in 1925. After graduation he taught English in a New York City high school for two years. During undergraduate days he began contributing articles to newspapers and periodicals. Since 1925 he has been a lecturer, at various times, at the People's Institute, at Columbia and at New York University, and in many cities throughout the United States. At present he is a member of the editorial boards of the Book-of-the-Month Club and *Encyclopaedia Britannica* as well as essayist for *Holiday* Magazine. Among his books are *Party of One* (1955); *Fantasia Mathematica* (1958); *The Lifetime Reading Plan* (1959); and *Enter Conversing* (1962).

I

1. Some twenty-odd years ago, on May 18, 1921, Justice Oliver Wendell Holmes, then eighty, in a letter to his lifelong friend, Sir Frederick Pollock, wrote: "Did I mention *Moby Dick*, by Herman Melville? I remember him in my youth. It seemed to me a great book—as ten years later may some of George Borrow's things, possibly influenced by him—but I should think a much greater man. It shook me up a good deal. It is wonderful already that a book published in 1851 doesn't seem thin, now. Hawthorne did when last I read *The Scarlet Letter*. Not so *Moby Dick*."

2. Holmes, a man given to wide and impartial decisions, made no judicial error here. By common consent—but, interestingly enough, a consent given only during the last

Reprinted by permission of The Limited Editions Club, for whose edition of *Moby Dick* this article was written as an introduction.

two decades—*Moby Dick* is one of
the great books of the world. It does
not "seem thin, now" any more than
in 1921 it seemed thin to the lucky
Balboas and Columbuses who then
rediscovered its Pacific rhythms and
Atlantic rages.

3. A minor proof of its greatness
lies in the circumstance (always
true of masterpieces) that, while
there seems nothing new to say
about it, we are forever trying our
hands at further commentary. In
the case of a minor work, no matter
how interesting, critics sooner or
later, happily, have their say, the
river of annotation dribbles off, and
the position of the work is more or
less firmly established. But men and
women will always attempt the
seemingly impossible task of writing
something new about Shakespeare
and Dante—and Melville. That is,
of course, because the meaning of a
good minor work is clear and single
while the meaning of a great major
work is multiplex.

4. The greatest books rise from a
profound level of wonder and terror, a level common to all humanity
in all times and climes, but a level
so deep that we are only at times
aware of it. From time to time a
man—Cervantes or Dostoevski or
Melville—lets down into this deep
well the glorious, pitiful bucket of
his genius, and he brings up a
book, and then we read it, and dimly
we perceive its source, and know
that source to be something profound and permanent in the human
imagination.

5. The mysterious liquid drawn
from this well is never crystalline.
Rather does each man, looking into
it, see mirrored a different set of
images, reflections, points of light,
and layers of shadow. All great

books are symbolical myths, over-
laid like palimpsests with the meanings that men at various times assign to them.

6. *Moby Dick* is a book about Evil.
Melville, with his characteristic
irony, said of it, "I have written a
wicked book and feel as spotless as
the lamb." At no time in his life
was Melville ever notably happy,
but at thirty-two, when he sat down
to the composition of his masterpiece, he was notably miserable, a
sick, worried, and unhappily married man. Some of the poison of his
personal life was undoubtedly discharged, veiled in symbols, into the
book. But if this were the only impulse behind *Moby Dick,* it would
be but a subjective work of the second order, like *Childe Harold.* Melville's despair was metaphysical as
well as personal; his awareness of
evil goes beyond his own constricted
circumstances. His book is not a
lament but a vision.

7. Yet we must not lose ourselves
in generalities, but remember always the kind of man Melville was
—a magnificent Gloomy Gus, unquestionably ill at ease in his time
and place, a romantic metaphysician whose affinities were with the
Elizabethans rather than with his
perky nineteenth-century contemporaries. He was by nature a solitary
—not a half-and-half solitary like
Thoreau, but a simon-pure one, akin
to a Thebaid ascetic. It must have
been hard to live with Melville. Perhaps such men as he should be excused from the amenities of ordinary intercourse.

8. He was not a "literary man" in
the sleek professional sense. His
work was forced out of him; it is a
kind of overflow of his vast interior
silence. "Seldom have I known any

profound being that had anything to say to this world, unless forced to stammer out something by way of getting a living." Again he says, "This whole book is but a draught—nay, but the draught of a draught."

9. A pessimism as profound as Melville's, if it is not pathological, —and his is not,—can exist only in a man who, whatever his gifts, does not possess that of humor. There is much pessimism in Shakespeare but with it goes a certain sweetness, a kind of radiance. His bad men—Macbeth, Iago—may be irretrievable, but the world itself is not irretrievable. This sense of balance comes from the fact that Shakespeare has humor, even in the plays of his later period. Melville had none. For proof, reread Chapter 100, a labored, shrill, and inept attempt at laughter. Perhaps I should qualify these strictures, for there is a kind of vast, grinning, unjolly, sardonic humor in him at times—Ishmael's first encounter with Queequeg is an example. But this humor is bilious, not sanguine, and has no power to uplift the heart.

10. I said that *Moby Dick* was a book about Evil; and so it is. It is the nearest thing we have to an un-Christian (though not an anti-Christian) epic. It is the other face of the Divine Comedy—the product of unfaith, as Dante's epic was the product of faith. But to believe in Evil's reality is not to espouse it. Melville is as far removed from a pure champion of evil, like Hitler, as he is from a pure champion of good, like St. Francis. Ahab knows that Good exists in the world, he even has his own moments of softening of the heart, but basically he is mesmerized by what is negative and disas-

trous. He cannot turn his mind away from Moby Dick.

II

11. The relationship between Ahab and the White Whale forms the central line of the story. Superficially this relationship is the same as that which animates any number of bloody Elizabethan tragedies of revenge. Ahab's leg has been torn off by Moby Dick; therefore he hates the whale; he pursues it to the death and is dragged down, in the very middle of his vengeance, to his own destruction: a sufficiently familiar pattern. But any grown-up reader of *Moby Dick* understands at once that this pattern is a mere blind, a concession to the brute fact that at bottom we still have no better way of portraying the storms of the soul than by means of physical action.

12. The subsurface meaning of the Ahab-Moby Dick relationship is that the two are one. Moby Dick is a monster thrashing about in the Pacific of Ahab's brain. It is as much a part of him as is his leg of ivory. The struggle that takes place on the vast marine or at the ends of a hundred harpoons is but Melville's method of exteriorizing the combat in the arena of Ahab's own chiaroscuro spirit.

13. The White Whale swam before him as the monomaniac incarnation of all those malicious agencies which some deep men feel eating in them till they are left living on with half a heart and half a lung. That intangible malignity which has been from the beginning; to whose dominion even the modern Christians ascribe one-half of the worlds; which the ancient Ophites of the east reverenced in

their statue devil;—Ahab did not fall down and worship it like them; but deliriously transferring its idea to the abhorred white whale, he pitted himself, all mutilated, against it. All that most maddens and torments; all that stirs up the lees of things; all truth with malice in it; all that cracks the sinews and cakes the brain; all the subtle demonisms of life and thought; all evil, to crazy Ahab, was visibly personified, and made practically assailable in Moby Dick. He piled upon the whale's white hump the sum of all the general rage and hate felt by his whole race from Adam down; and then, as if his chest had been a mortar, he burst his hot heart's shell upon it.

14. Like his cousins, Faust and Hamlet, Ahab is a divided man, at odds with his own mortality, at odds with all the grief in the world, at odds with his own incapacity to enjoy the world's fair show, and therewith be content. The whole complex narrative of *Moby Dick*, with all its cetology and its digressions, is but the cunningly disguised soliloquy of a man in direst pain— pain which can cease only with suicide. And suicide is the true end of *Moby Dick*, the whale and the man, being one, turning upon each other simultaneously. There are certain men who are artists in suicide, who carve out for themselves, over many years, careers which have as their goal self-destruction. Ahab is such a man, and all his adventures, rages, conversations, soliloquies are but the joists and floorings of an immense structure of self-ruin.

15. If there is one grand type of character Melville knows to the last fiber and droplet of blood, it is the type self-dedicated to disaster. This self-dedication is a convoluted thing, never direct, never simple.

Hamlet needs five acts and hundreds of lines of anguished poetry to achieve it. Ahab, in whom masochism is a complex art, cannot kill himself save in a roundabout manner, through the instrumentality of the White Whale. If there were no Moby Dick, it would be necessary for Ahab to invent one. In a sense, he is an invention, a white floating cancer in Ahab's own mind.

16. In the same way, to make sure that he will never deviate from this road, however curving, to disaster, Ahab strips himself of all associations that might waylay him into joy. He throws away his pipe in fury because it might bring him pleasure. Gifted, as he bitterly reflects, "with the high perception," he lacks "the low, enjoying power; damned, most subtly and most malignantly! damned in the midst of Paradise."

17. Just why he lacks "the low, enjoying power" Melville never tells us. He presents us with a fixed type; the causes of its fixity do not concern him. To give a certain surface rondure of motivation to Ahab's pessimism, he offers us the amputated leg, but we are not taken in by it; we know that this lightning-seared soul was deep in hell even in the days when he stood upon two feet of living bone. Moby Dick is a pretext, or, as Melville would say, a symbol.

18. Why do his men fear Ahab? Compare their emotion with that felt by the sailors toward Wolf Larsen in *The Sea-Wolf*. In Jack London's novel the men are afraid of Larsen, another man, another creature; and therefore their fear is overcomable. But no one on the *Pequod*, however brave he be, can overcome his fear of Ahab, because the fear is seated in himself. His Ahab-fear

is a fear of *himself*, or rather of the pit of blackness, the central dark motherlode of despair which every man at times knows to be within him. But we are afraid to confess this primordial horror. When we come upon one who, like Ahab, *does* confess it, exulting in his confession, we shrink back, as if we had looked in the mirror and seen there the horrid head of the Gorgon. It is this self-fear that explains Ahab's unholy domination of his crew. It explains too the desperate joy with which the men pursue Moby Dick, as if they felt that, by killing the monster, they could exorcise the fear and dispel with their puny harpoons the gathered and oppressive malice of the world.

III

19. It is generally recognized that the canons of the ordinary novel do not apply to *Moby Dick*. If we applied them we should be forced to put it down as an inept, occasionally powerful, but on the whole puzzling affair. This was the conventional opinion up to two decades ago. During those decades we have discovered *Moby Dick* to be a masterpiece. What caused this shift in perspective? To put it simply, we discovered how *Moby Dick* should be read. We must read it not as if it were a novel but as if it were a myth. A novel is a tale. A myth is a disguised method of expressing mankind's deepest terrors and longings. The myth uses the narrative form and is often mistaken for true narrative. Once we feel the truth of this distinction, the greatness of *Moby Dick* becomes manifest: we have learned how to read it.

20. *Moby Dick* is a myth of Evil and Tragedy, as the Christian epic is a myth of Good and Salvation.

"Both the ancestry and posterity of Grief go further than the ancestry and posterity of Joy," thinks Ahab; and this central brooding conviction threads every page of the story, even when it seems most concerned with trypots, harpoons, and sperm oil.

21. The note is struck in the very opening sentence—surely the most magical first sentence in literature: "Call me Ishmael." Who is Ishmael? He is the narrator but he is also Ahab (as all the characters of the book are partially Ahab) and he is also you and I, considered as eternal outcasts, which we are, the experience of birth being in a sense the casting-off of the moorings that attach us quite literally to mankind.

22. The *Pequod* seems a crowded world. Indeed it is a microcosm, with its philosophers, its men of action, its lunatics, its African savages and Polynesian cannibals. Yet, for all the shapes that man its boats or raise its sails, the *Pequod* is a heaving hell of lonely and grief-touched souls, whose solitudes are gathered up and made manifest in the figure of Ahab. Melville underlines this perception in the very abode of community itself, in the Whaleman's Chapel, where "each silent worshipper seemed purposely sitting apart from the other, as if each silent grief were insular and incommunicable."

23. The symbolic values of the book are not allegorically plain, as in *The Pilgrim's Progress*, for Melville does not have Bunyan's Protestant certitude. They waver, shadowlike, at times emerging into the world of reality, at times descending into the subterranea of myth. For instance, Fedallah and his Malays do not merely "represent" the evil spirits conjured up by Ahab's nec-

romantic power. They are in truth these very spirits. Yet at the same time they fulfill a solid and specific function aboard the *Pequod*. They are at one and the same time part of a whaling cruise and of Hell. It is this extraordinary ambiguity that gives *Moby Dick* its special murky atmosphere and which may have been responsible for the lack of understanding that was its portion for so many years.

24. Yet there should have been no misunderstanding, for Melville in a dozen passages reiterates that his story is not to be taken literally. The symbolism is not simple, no mere system of correspondences. It is rather the subtle atmosphere the whole story breathes. It is not imposed (except occasionally, and then the effect is creaky). "All visible objects," says Ahab, "are but as pasteboard masks. But in each event—in the living act, the undoubted deed—there, some unknown but still reasoning thing puts forth the moulding of its features from behind the unreasoning mask."

25. The poet is one, it has been said, who sees resemblances. Then Melville is all poet, for he sees little else, the world being for him a shadow-show, a whale-line but the halter round all men's necks, the very earth itself but the "insular Tahiti," in the soul of man, encompassed by the "appalling ocean" of "the horrors of the half-known life."

26. This vivid sense of an extra, invisible dimension in all things makes it possible for Melville's alembicating mind to mix such incongruities as angels and spermaceti, and distill an essence of beauty.

27. Finally, *Moby Dick* is America's most unparochial great book, less delivered over to a time and place than the work of even our freest minds, Emerson and Whitman. It is conceived on a vast scale, it shakes hands with prairie seas and great distances, it invades with its conquistador prose "the remotest secret drawers and lockers of the world." It has towering faults of taste, it is often willful and obscure, but it will remain America's unarguable contribution to world literature, so many-leveled is it, so wide-ranging in that nether world which is the defiant but secretly terror-stricken soul of man, alone and appalled by his aloneness.

· QUESTIONS ·

1. By use of a specific example, show that you agree or disagree with Fadiman's main point in paragraph 3.
2. Explain thoroughly the meaning of the last two sentences in paragraph 6.
3. What does Fadiman mean by "the kind of man Melville was—a magnificent Gloomy Gus"? Do you think that the comparison is well chosen?
4. Do you agree with Fadiman's statement on pessimism and humor (paragraph 9)? Be specific in showing why you do or do not.
5. Expand as fully as you can the distinction that Fadiman draws between novel and myth.
6. Explain why "Call me Ishmael" is, for Fadiman, "the most magical first sentence in literature" (paragraph 21). Do you agree that the sentence is "magical"? Can you recall any other "magical" first sentences in books or stories you have enjoyed?
7. Vocabulary study: metaphysical, affinities, ascetic, amenities, inept, mes-

merized, rondure, exorcise, canons, microcosm, allegorically, ambiguity, alembicating, symbolism, necromantic.

8. Show that paragraph 27 is both a masterful summary of the entire review and an excellent example of appealing, rhythmic, balanced structure.

Theme Subjects: (1) A Review of Another of Melville's Novels; (2) Magical First Sentences; (3) One Chapter in Melville's Biography; (4) Pessimism and Humor; (5) Write a review of Bunyan's *The Pilgrim's Progress*, emphasizing the distinction between novel and myth which Fadiman makes in this essay.

ROBERT FROST:

THE WAY TO THE POEM

John Ciardi

JOHN CIARDI (1916–   ) was born in Boston and studied at Bates College and Tufts University. He received his master's degree from the University of Michigan in 1939. He has taught at the University of Kansas City, Harvard, and Rutgers. He has published several volumes of poetry and has been poetry editor of *The Saturday Review* since 1956. Among several recent books he has published is *Person to Person* (1964).

STOPPING BY WOODS ON A SNOWY EVENING[1]

Whose woods these are I think I know.
His house is in the village though;
He will not see me stopping here
To watch his woods fill up with snow.

My little horse must think it queer
To stop without a farmhouse near
Between the wood and frozen lake
The darkest evening of the year.

He gives his harness bells a shake
To ask if there is some mistake.
The only other sound's the sweep
Of easy wind and downy flake.

The woods are lovely, dark and deep.
But I have promises to keep,
And miles to go before I sleep,
And miles to go before I sleep.

The School System has much to say these days of the virtue of reading widely, and not enough about the virtues of reading less but in depth. There are any number of reading lists for poetry, but there is not enough talk about individual poems. Poetry, finally, is one poem at a time. To read any one poem carefully is the ideal preparation for reading another. Only a poem can illustrate how poetry works.

Above, therefore, is a poem—one of the master lyrics of the English language, and almost certainly the best-known poem by an American poet. What happens in it?—which is to say, not *what* does it mean, but *how* does it mean? How does it go about being a human re-enactment of a human experience? The author—perhaps the thousandth reader would need to be told—is Robert Frost.

Even the TV audience can see that this poem begins as a seemingly-simple narration of a seemingly-simple incident but ends by suggesting meanings far beyond anything specifically referred to in the narrative. And even readers with only the most casual interest in poetry might be made to note the additional fact that, though the poem suggests those larger meanings, it is very careful never to abandon its pretense to being simple narration. There is duplicity at work. The poet pretends to be talking about one thing, and all the while he is talking about many others.

Many readers are forever unable to accept the poet's essential duplicity. It is almost safe to say

that a poem is never about what it seems to be about. As much could be said of the proverb. The bird in the hand, the rolling stone, the stitch in time never (except by an artful double-deception) intend any sort of statement about birds, stones, or sewing. The incident of this poem, one must conclude, is at root a metaphor.

Duplicity aside, this poem's movement from the specific to the general illustrates one of the basic formulas of all poetry. Such a grand poem as Arnold's "Dover Beach" and such lesser, though unfortunately better known, poems as Longfellow's "The Village Blacksmith" and Holmes's "The Chambered Nautilus" are built on the same progression. In these three poems, however, the generalization is markedly set apart from the specific narration, and even seems additional to the telling rather than intrinsic to it. It is this sense of division one has in mind in speaking of "a tacked-on moral."

There is nothing wrong-in-itself with a tacked-on moral. Frost, in fact, makes excellent use of the device at times. In this poem, however, Frost is careful to let the whatever-the-moral-is grow out of the poem itself. When the action ends the poem ends. There is no epilogue and no explanation. Everything pretends to be about the narrated incident. And that pretense sets the basic tone of the poem's performance of itself.

The dramatic force of that performance is best observable, I believe, as a progression in three scenes.

In scene one, which coincides with stanza one, a man—a New England man—is driving his sleigh somewhere at night. It is snowing, and as the man passes a dark patch of woods he stops to watch the snow descend into the darkness. We know, moreover, that the man is familiar with these parts (he knows who owns the woods and where the owner lives), and we know that no one has seen him stop. As scene one forms itself in the theatre of the mind's-eye, therefore, it serves to establish some as yet unspecified relation between the man and the woods.

It is necessary, however, to stop here for a long parenthesis: Even so simple an opening statement raises any number of questions. It is impossible to address all the questions that rise from the poem stanza by stanza, but two that arise from stanza one illustrate the sort of thing one might well ask of the poem detail by detail.

Why, for example, does the man not say what errand he is on? What is the force of leaving the errand generalized? He might just as well have told us that he was going to the general store, or returning from it with a jug of molasses he had promised to bring Aunt Harriet and two suits of long underwear he had promised to bring the hired man. Frost, moreover, can handle homely detail to great effect. He preferred to leave his motive generalized. Why?

And why, on the other hand, does he say so much about knowing the absent owner of the woods and where he lives? Is it simply that one set of details happened-in whereas another did not? To speak of things "happening-in" is to assault the integrity of a poem. Poetry cannot be discussed meaningfully unless one can assume that everything in the poem—every last comma and variant spelling—is in

it by the poet's specific act of choice. Only bad poets allow into their poems what is haphazard or cheaply chosen.

The errand, I will venture a bit brashly for lack of space, is left generalized in order the more aptly to suggest *any* errand in life and, therefore, life itself. The owner is there because he is one of the forces of the poem. Let it do to say that the force he represents is the village of mankind (that village at the edge of winter) from which the poet finds himself separated (has separated himself?) in his moment by the woods (and to which, he recalls finally, he has promises to keep). The owner is he-who-lives-in-his-village-house, thereby locked away from the poet's awareness of the-time-the-snow-tells as it engulfs and obliterates the world the village man allows himself to believe he "owns." Thus, the owner is a representative of an order of reality from which the poet has divided himself for the moment, though to a certain extent he ends by reuniting with it. Scene one, therefore, establishes not only a relation between the man and the woods, but the fact that the man's relation begins with his separation (though momentarily) from mankind.

End parenthesis one, begin parenthesis two.

Still considering the first scene as a kind of dramatic performance of forces, one must note that the poet has meticulously matched the simplicity of his language to the pretended simplicity of the narrative. Clearly, the man stopped because the beauty of the scene moved him, but he neither tells us that the scene is beautiful nor that he is moved. A bad writer, always ready to overdo, might have written: "The vastness gripped me, filling my spirit with the slow steady sinking of the snow's crystalline perfection into the glimmerless profundities of the hushed primeval wood." Frost's avoidance of such a spate illustrates two principles of good writing. The first, he has stated himself in "The Mowing": "Anything *more* than the truth would have seemed too weak" (italics mine). Understatement is one of the basic sources of power in English poetry. The second principle is to let the action speak for itself. A good novelist does not tell us that a given character is good or bad (at least not since the passing of the Dickens tradition): he shows us the character in action and then, watching him, we know. Poetry, too, has fictional obligations: even when the characters are ideas and metaphors rather than people, they must be *characterized in action*. A poem does not *talk about* ideas; it *enacts* them. The force of the poem's performance, in fact, is precisely to act out (and thereby to make us act out empathically, that is, to *feel out,* that is, to *identify with*) the speaker and why he stopped. The man is the principal actor in this little "drama of why" and in scene one he is the only character, though as noted, he is somehow related to the absent owner.

End second parenthesis.

In scene two (stanzas two and three) a *foil* is introduced. In fiction and drama, a foil is a character who "plays against" a more important character. By presenting a different point of view or an opposed set of motives, the foil moves the more important character to react in ways that might not have found expression without such opposition.

The more important character is thus more fully revealed—to the reader and to himself. The foil here is the horse.

The horse forces the question. Why did the man stop? Until it occurs to him that his "little horse must think it queer" he had not asked himself for reasons. He had simply stopped. But the man finds himself faced with the question he imagines the horse to be asking: what *is* there to stop for out there in the cold, away from bin and stall (house and village and mankind?) and all that any self-respecting beast could value on such a night? In sensing that other view, the man is forced to examine his own more deeply.

In stanza two the question arises only as a feeling within the man. In stanza three, however (still scene two), the horse acts. He gives his harness bells a shake. "What's wrong?" he seems to say. "What are we waiting for?"

By now, obviously, the horse —without losing its identity as horse—has also become a symbol. A symbol is something that stands for something else. Whatever that something else may be, it certainly begins as that order of life that does not understand why a man stops in the wintry middle of nowhere to watch the snow come down. (Can one fail to sense by now that the dark and the snowfall symbolize a death-wish, however momentary, i.e., that hunger for final rest and surrender that a man may feel, but not a beast?)

So by the end of scene two the performance has given dramatic force to three elements that work upon the man. There is his relation to the world of the owner. There is his relation to the brute world of the

horse. And there is that third presence of the unownable world, the
movement of the all-engulfing snow
across all the orders of life, the
man's, the owner's, and the horse's
—with the difference that the man
knows of that second dark-within-
the-dark of which the horse cannot,
and the owner will not, know.

The man ends scene two with
all these forces working upon him
simultaneously. He feels himself
moved to a decision. And he feels a
last call from the darkness: "the
sweep / Of easy wind and downy
flake." It would be so easy and so
downy to go into the woods and let
himself be covered over.

But scene three (stanza four)
produces a fourth force. This fourth
force can be given many names. It is
certainly better, in fact, to give it
many names than to attempt to limit
it to one. It is social obligation, or
personal commitment, or duty, or
just the realization that a man cannot indulge a mood forever. All of
these and more. But, finally, he has
a simple decision to make. He may
go into the woods and let the darkness and the snow swallow him
from the world of beast and man.
Or he must move on. And unless he
is going to stop here forever, it is
time to remember that he has a
long way to go and that he had best
be getting there. (So there is something to be said for the horse, too.)

Then and only then, his question driven more and more deeply
into himself by these cross-forces,
does the man venture a comment
on what attracted him: "The woods
are lovely, dark and deep." His
mood lingers over the thought of
that lovely dark-and-deep (as do
the very syllables in which he
phrases the thought), but the final
decision is to put off the mood and

move on. He has his man's way to
go and his man's obligations to tend
to before he can yield. He has miles
to go before his sleep. He repeats
that thought and the performance
ends.

But why the repetition? The
first time Frost says "And miles to
go before I sleep," there can be little
doubt that the primary meaning
is "I have a long way to go before
I get to bed tonight." The second
time he says it, however, "miles to
go" and "sleep" are suddenly transformed into symbols. What are
those "something-elses" the symbols
stand for? Hundreds of people have
tried to ask Mr. Frost that question
and he has always turned it away.
He has turned it away *because he
cannot answer it.* He could answer
some part of it. But some part is
not enough.

For a symbol is like a rock
dropped into a pool: it sends out
ripples in all directions, and the
ripples are in motion. Who can say
where the last ripple disappears?
One may have a sense that he
knows the approximate center point
of the ripples, the point at which
the stone struck the water. Yet even
then he has trouble marking it
surely. How does one make a mark
on water? Oh, very well—the center
point of that second "miles to go" is
probably approximately in the
neighborhood of being close to
meaning, perhaps, "the road of life";
and the second "before I sleep" is
maybe that close to meaning "before
I take my final rest," the rest in darkness that seemed so temptingly
dark-and-deep for the moment of
the mood. But the ripples continue
to move and the light to change on
the water, and the longer one
watches the more changes he sees.
Such shifting-and-being-at-the-same-

instant is of the very sparkle and life of poetry. One experiences it as one experiences life, for every time he looks at an experience he sees something new, and he sees it change as he watches it. And that sense of continuity in fluidity is one of the primary kinds of knowledge, one of man's basic ways of knowing, and one that only the arts can teach, poetry foremost among them.

Frost himself certainly did not ask what that repeated last line meant. It came to him and he received it. He "felt right" about it. And what he "felt right" about was in no sense a "meaning" that, say, an essay could apprehend, but an act of experience that could be fully presented only by the dramatic enactment of forces which is the performance of the poem.

Now look at the poem in another way. Did Frost know what he was going to do when he began? Considering the poem simply as an act of skill, as a piece of juggling, one cannot fail to respond to the magnificent turn at the end where, with one flip, seven of the simplest words in the language suddenly dazzle full of never-ending waves of thought and feeling. Or, more precisely, of felt-thought. Certainly an equivalent stunt by a juggler— could there be an equivalent— would bring the house down. Was it to cap his performance with that grand stunt that Frost wrote the poem?

Far from it. The obvious fact is that *Frost could not have known he was going to write those lines until he wrote them.* Then a second fact must be registered: *he wrote them because, for the fun of it, he had got himself into trouble.*

Frost, like every good poet, be-gan by playing a game with himself. The most usual way of writing a four-line stanza with four feet to the line is to rhyme the third line with the first, and the fourth line with the second. Even that much rhyme is so difficult in English that many poets and almost all of the anonymous ballad makers do not bother to rhyme the first and third lines at all, settling for two rhymes in four lines as good enough. For English is a rhyme-poor language. In Italian and in French, for example, so many words end with the same sounds that rhyming is relatively easy—so easy that many modern French and Italian poets do not bother to rhyme at all. English, being a more agglomerate language, has far more final sounds, hence fewer of them rhyme. When an Italian poet writes a line ending with "vita" (life) he has literally hundreds of rhyme choices available. When an English poet writes "life" at the end of a line he can summon "strife, wife, knife, fife, rife," and then he is in trouble. Now "life-strife" and "life-rife" and "life-wife" seem to offer a combination of possible ideas that can be related by more than just the rhyme. Inevitably, therefore, the poets have had to work and rework these combinations until the sparkle has gone out of them. The reader is normally tired of such rhyme-led associations. When he encounters "life-strife" he is certainly entitled to suspect that the poet did not really want to say "strife"—that had there been in English such a word as, say, "hife," meaning "infinite peace and harmony," the poet would as gladly have used that word instead of "strife." Thus, the reader feels that the writing is haphazard, that the rhyme is making the poet say things he does not really feel, and which, therefore, the reader does not feel except as boredom. One likes to see the rhymes fall into place, but he must end with the belief that it is the poet who is deciding what is said and not the rhyme scheme that is forcing the saying.

So rhyme is a kind of game, and an especially difficult one in English. As in every game, the fun of the rhyme is to set one's difficulties high and then to meet them skillfully. As Frost himself once defined freedom, it consists of "moving easy in harness."

In "Stopping by Woods on a Snowy Evening" Frost took a long chance. He decided to rhyme not two lines in each stanza, but three. Not even Frost could have sustained that much rhyme in a long poem (as Dante, for example, with the advantage of writing in Italian, sustained triple rhyme for thousands of lines in "The Divine Comedy"). Frost would have known instantly, therefore, when he took the original chance, that he was going to write a short poem. He would have had that much foretaste of it.

So the first stanza emerged rhymed a-a-b-a. And with the sure sense that this was to be a short poem, Frost decided to take an additional chance and to redouble: in English three rhymes in four lines is more than enough; there is no need to rhyme the fourth line. For the fun of it, however, Frost set himself to pick up that loose rhyme and to weave it into the pattern, thereby accepting the all but impossible burden of quadruple rhyme.

The miracle is that it worked. Despite the enormous freight of rhyme, the poem not only came out as a neat pattern, but managed to do so with no sense of strain. Every word and every rhyme falls into place as naturally and as inevitably as if there were no rhyme restricting the poet's choices.

That ease-in-difficulty is certainly inseparable from the success of the poem's performance. One watches the skill-man juggle three balls, then four, then five, and every addition makes the trick more wonderful. But unless he makes the hard trick seem as easy as an easy trick, then all is lost.

The real point, however, is not only that Frost took on a hard rhyme-trick and made it seem easy. It is rather as if the juggler, carried away, had tossed up one more ball than he could really handle, and then amazed himself by actually handling it. So with the real triumph of this poem. Frost could not have known what a stunning effect his repetition of the last line was going to produce. He could not even know he was going to repeat the line. He simply found himself up against a difficulty he almost certainly had not foreseen and he had to improvise to meet it. For in picking up the rhyme from the third line of stanza one and carrying it over into stanza two, he had created an endless chain-link form within which each stanza left a hook sticking out for the next stanza to hang on. So by stanza four, feeling the poem rounding to its end, Frost had to do something about that extra rhyme.

He might have tucked it back into a third line rhyming with the *know-though-snow* of stanza one. He could thus have rounded the poem out to the mathematical symmetry of using each rhyme four times. But though such a device might be defensible in theory, a rhyme repeated after eleven lines is so far from its original rhyme sound that its feeling as rhyme must certainly be lost. And what good is theory if the reader is not moved by the writing?

It must have been in some such quandary that the final repetition suggested itself—a suggestion born of the very difficulties the poet had let himself in for. So there is that point beyond mere ease in handling a hard thing, the point at which the very difficulty offers the poet the opportunity to do better than he knew he could. What, aside from having that happen to oneself, could be more self-delighting than to participate in its happening by one's reader-identification with the poem?

And by now a further point will have suggested itself: that the human-insight of the poem and the technicalities of its poetic artifice are inseparable. Each feeds the other. That interplay is the poem's meaning, a matter not of *what does it mean,* for no one can ever say entirely what a good poem means, but of *how does it mean,* a process one can come much closer to discussing.

There is a necessary epilogue. Mr. Frost has often discussed this poem on the platform, or more usually in the course of a long-evening-after a talk. Time and again I have heard him say that he just wrote it off, that it just came to him, and that he set it down as it came.

Once at Bread Loaf, however, I heard him add one very essential piece to the discussion of how it "just came." One night, he said, he had sat down after supper to work at a long piece of blank verse.

The piece never worked out, but Mr. Frost found himself so absorbed in it that, when next he looked up, dawn was at his window. He rose, crossed to the window, stood looking out for a few minutes, and *then* it was that "Stopping by Woods" suddenly "just came," so that all he had to do was cross the room and write it down.

Robert Frost is the sort of artist who hides his traces. I know of no Frost worksheets anywhere. If someone has raided his wastebasket in secret, it is possible that such worksheets exist somewhere, but Frost would not willingly allow anything but the finished product to leave him. Almost certainly, therefore, no one will ever know what was in that piece of unsuccessful blank verse he had been working at with such concentration, but I for one would stake my life that could that worksheet be uncovered, it would be found to contain the germinal stuff of "Stopping by Woods"; that what was a-simmer in him all night without finding its proper form, suddenly, when he let his still-occupied mind look away, came at him from a different direction, offered itself in a different form, and that finding that form exactly right the impulse proceeded to marry itself to the new shape in one of the most miraculous performances of English lyricism.

And that, too—whether or not one can accept so hypothetical a discussion—is part of *how* the poem means. It means that marriage to the perfect form, the poem's shapen declaration of itself, its moment's monument fixed beyond all possibility of change. And thus, finally, in every truly good poem, "How does it mean?" must always be answered "Triumphantly." Whatever the poem "is about," *how* it means is always how Genesis means: the word become a form, and the form become a thing, and—when the becoming is true—the thing become a part of the knowledge and experience of the race forever.

· QUESTIONS ·

1. This article is "analysis in depth." Does it contribute to, or detract from, your appreciation of Frost's poem?
2. Ciardi states that Frost's poem is best described as "a progression in three scenes." Explain these scenes.
3. What is the effect upon you of the narrative epilogue?
4. With what conclusions of Ciardi do you agree? Disagree?

Theme Subjects: (1) Mr. Ciardi Has Ruined My Supper (Appreciation, Delight in Frost, etc.); (2) My Analysis of _____ (a short poem from this volume); (3) "Letter to Letter-Writers" (a report on the Ciardi sequel, *The Saturday Review,* May 17, 1958); (4) What "Stopping by Woods . . ." Means to Me; (5) Detailed Analysis Is the Bunk; (6) My Favorite Poem, and Why; (7) The Duplicity of _____.

IT'S HALFWAY TO

1984

John Lukacs

JOHN LUKACS (1924–   ) was born in Hungary, received his education there and in England, and came to the United States in 1946. He has been professor of history at Chestnut Hill College in Philadelphia since 1947 and visiting professor at La Salle College (Philadelphia) since 1949. He has taught at Columbia University (1954–1955), the University of Pennsylvania (1964), and the University of Toulouse, France (1964–1965). In 1963,

1964, and 1966 he was honors examiner at Swarthmore College. He has written four books, *The Great Powers and Eastern Europe* (1953); *The Tocqueville-Gobineau Correspondence* (1959); *A History of the Cold War* (3 vols., 1961, 1962, 1966); and *Decline and Rise of Europe* (1965), as well as many historical articles, reviews, essays, and poems. An American citizen, he now lives in Chester County, Pennsylvania.

We are now halfway to 1984. George Orwell, the author of *1984*, finished his book in 1948. That was 18 years ago, and it is not more than another 18 years before that ominous date rolls around.

It is *ominous*, in every sense of that antique adjective. There is reason to believe that 18 years from now thousands of people will experience a feeling of uneasiness, perhaps a light little shudder of trepidation, as they first encounter that new year's numerals in print. In the English-speaking world, at least, "1984" has become a household term, suggesting some kind of inhuman totalitarian nightmare. And since millions who have not read the book now recognize the term, it is reasonable to assume that both the theme and the title of the book have corresponded to an emerging consciousness among many people in the otherwise progressive-minded, English-speaking democracies, to the effect that things are *not* getting better all the time—no, not at all.

The plot of *1984* is well-known but it may be useful to sum it up briefly. By 1984 most of the world has been divided by three super-states—Oceania, Eurasia, and Eastasia. They are perpetually at war with one another, but no one of them is completely able to subdue the others. This state of war enables the rulers of these states (the ruler of Oceania being Big Brother) to keep their peoples both ignorant and submissive. This is achieved by totalitarian and technical methods, by the absoluteness of one-party rule, and by a kind of censorship that controls not only the behavior but even the thinking process of individuals. The hero of *1984*, Winston Smith, born in 1945 (both the date and the first name are significant), is a simple party member and a functionary of the Ministry of Truth in London, which is the chief city of Airstrip One, for that is what Britain became after she had been absorbed by the United States to form Oceania. (Continental Europe, having been absorbed by the Soviet Union, had become Eurasia.)

Winston is a weak and forlorn intellectual who, however, is sickened not only by the dreary living conditions in 1984 but by the prevalence of official lying and the almost complete absence of personal privacy. One day he stumbles into a love affair, which in itself is a dangerous thing since the party punishes illicit relationships severely. Winston experiences happiness and a sense of personal fulfillment, especially as Julia shares his hatred of the existing system.

There is a high official in the Ministry of Truth, O'Brien, whom Winston instinctively trusts. He and Julia confide in O'Brien. They are deceived. All along, O'Brien has set a trap for them: they are arrested in their secret little room. They are tortured. Winston, despite his strong residue of convictions, not only confesses to everything imaginable, but in the end, faced by an especially horrible torture, he even betrays Julia. He is finally released; he is a completely broken man; he has even come to believe in the almightiness and goodness of Big Brother.

But it is not this plot, it is rather Orwell's description of everyday life in 1984 that is the principal matter of the novel and, one may suppose, the principal matter of interest to its readers. Life in 1984 is a mixture of horror and dreariness. What is horrible is not so much war as the shriveling of personal freedoms and privacy with the planners of the superstate controlling vast portions of once-independent lives. What is dreary is that within these totalitarian conditions the living standards of masses of people in what were once civilized and prosperous countries are reduced: Food and drink are little better than standardized slop; mass entertainments are primitive and vulgar; personal property has virtually disappeared.

One of the profound differences between *1984* and Aldous Huxley's *Brave New World* (published in 1932, the latter still had many of the marks of the light-headed twenties; its philosophy compared with that of *1984* is a rather irresponsible *jeu d'esprit*) lies in Orwell's view of the past rather than of the future. Looking back from 1984, conditions in the early, capitalistic portion of the twentieth century seem romantic and almost idyllic to Winston Smith, so much so that on a solemn occasion he offers a toast "to the past." Unemployment, revolutions, Fascism and, to some extent, even Nazism and Communism are lesser evils than what is going on in Oceania in 1984, since by that time the rulers of the state have perfected brainwashing and thought-control to the point that the memories of entire generations, and hence their opinions about the past, have been eliminated.

This, of course, does not happen overnight: It is a brutal but gradual development. In *1984,* Orwell set the decisive turning point in the middle sixties, "the period of the great purges in which the original leaders of the Revolution were wiped out once and for all. By 1970 none of them was left, except Big Brother himself."

Let us keep in mind that *1984* is the work of a novelist and not of a prophet; Orwell ought not be criticized simply because some of his visions have not been borne out. On the other hand, Orwell was concerned in the late forties with certain tendencies of evil portent; and *1984* was a publishing success because around 1950, for great numbers of people, the picture of a society such as he described was not merely fantastic but to some extent plausible.

It is still plausible today, but not quite in the way in which Orwell envisaged the future 18 years ago. Halfway to 1984 we can say, fortunately, that most of Orwell's visions have proved wrong. It is true that the United States, the Soviet Union, and China correspond to some extent to the superpowers Oceania, Eurasia, and Eastasia. But the United States has not annexed Britain, the Soviet Union has fallen far short of conquering all of Europe, and even China does not extend much beyond her traditional boundaries.

What is more important, the superpowers are not at war with one another. It is true that during the so-called cold war between the United States and the Soviet Union many of the practices of traditional and civilized diplomacy were abandoned; but the cold war has given place to something like a cold peace between these two superpowers. Even the dreadful and ominous war in Asia is marked by the reluctance of the United States and China directly to attack each other.

Orwell proved correct in saying that "war . . . is no longer the desperate, annihilating struggle that it was in the early decades of the twentieth century. It is a warfare of limited aims between combatants who are unable to destroy one another. . . ." Yet Orwell was interested principally not in international but in internal developments. For example, in *1984* the peoples of Oceania are isolated; travel is forbidden except for a small minority of the élite; and the press is controlled to the extent that no meaningful information from the outside world is available to the public.

But now, halfway to 1984, the opposite has been happening. It is not warfare but torrents of automobiles and mass tourism that threaten to destroy entire landscapes and cityscapes; great amounts of information are available to us about an undigestible variety of matters; and at times it seems that the cultural traditions of great Western nations are endangered less by the persistence of isolationism than by a phony internationalism drummed up by a kind of pervasive publicity that drowns out the once truer music of the arts.

Also, in the world of *1984* most people are ill-fed, badly clothed, run-down. But this, too, has not happened. Now, halfway to 1984, almost everywhere in the world, living standards have risen, and the danger is not, as Orwell envisaged it, that entire generations of once-prosperous countries will no longer know such things as wine, oranges, lemons, and chocolate; it is, rather, that our traditional tastes and table habits may be washed away by a flood of frozen and synthetic foods of every possible kind, available to us every hour of the day.

The reasons why Orwell's visions of 1984 have been wrong seem to be bound up with the time and the circumstances of the book's conception. About the circumstances Orwell himself was supposed to have said that *1984* "wouldn't have been so gloomy if I had not been so ill." He wrote most of the book in self-imposed isolation on a rain-shrouded Scottish island, finishing it in an English country hospital in late 1948. Shortly thereafter, he was moved to a hospital in London, where in January, 1950, he died. As for the time of writing, in the late nineteen-forties Orwell's imagination succumbed, at least in part, to the temptation of conceiving the future as an increasingly acute continuation of what seems to be going on at the present. (In one of his earlier essays, Orwell had criticized the American writer James Burnham for this very fault.) Around 1949, when most intellectuals had come around to recognizing that Stalin's tyranny was hardly better than Hitler's, many of them concluded that it is in the nature of totalitarianism to become more and more tyrannical as time goes on. Indeed, some of them established their reputations by the ponderous books they produced on this theme. (Hannah Arendt's *The Origins of Totalitarianism* is an example.) Yet only a few years later, events in Eastern Europe and in Russia showed that history is unpredictable and that the projections of intellectuals are often oversimplified. But this Orwell did not live to see.

He foresaw the horrible features of 1984 as the consequences of totalitarianism, of political tyranny, of the despotism of a dictator. But halfway to 1984 we can see, for example, that the era of totalitarian dictatorship is sliding away, into the past. Even the Soviet Union seems to be moving in the direction of what one may call "post-totalitarian"; all over Eastern Europe (though not yet in Asia) we can perceive regimes that, though dictatorial, are no longer totalitarian. The danger for us is, rather, the obverse: the possibility of totalitarian democracy.

Totalitarian democracy? The words seem paradoxical; our eyes and ears are unaccustomed to the sight and the sound of them in combination. Yet I believe that we ought to accustom our imaginations to the possibility of a democratic society in which universal popular suffrage exists while freedom of speech, press, and assembly are hardly more than theoretical possibilities for the individual, whose life and ideas, whose rights to privacy, to family autonomy and to durable possessions are regimented by government and rigidly molded by mass production and by mass communications.

Let me, at this point, fall back on a personal illustration. For a long time the term "1984" evoked, to me, the image of a police state of the Eastern European type. But when I think of 1984 now, the image that swims into my mind is that of a gigantic shopping center

and industrial complex—something like the one which has been erected a few miles from where I live in eastern Pennsylvania.

The undulating rural landscape around Valley Forge, with its bright dots of houses and its crossroads, has been transformed. There is now the eerie vastness of the General Electric Space Center whose square edifices spread across hundreds of acres. Beyond it stand other flat windowless blocks of buildings— the King of Prussia shopping center, around the trembling edges of which bulldozers roar from morning to night, boring their brutal tracks into the clayey soil which they must churn to mud before it can be covered by concrete. The predominant material is concrete, horizontal and vertical concrete. Twice a day, thousands of people pour into and out of this compound, in a tremendous metallic flow. But no one lives there. At night and on Sundays, these hundreds of acres resemble a deserted airport, with a few automobiles clustering here and there, or slowly cruising on one of the airstrips, occasionally peered at by uniformed guards. Why fly to the moon? Stand on a cold January night in the middle of a parking lot in a large shopping center in the American North. It is a man-made moonscape. This is how the moon will look after our Herculean efforts, after we reach it, colonize it, pour concrete over it.

This is how 1984 looks to me, in the middle sixties, but I know and feel that this view is neither solitary nor unusual. There are millions of Americans who, passing a similar space-age complex of buildings, will say "1984," covering up their resignation with a thin coat of defensive humor. What strikes us is not just the ugliness of the buildings but something else, something that is not so much the reaction of middle-aged earthmen against brave new worlds as it is the expression of a feeling which is, alas, close to the Orwellian nightmare vision: a sense of impersonality together with a sense of powerlessness.

The impersonality is there, in the hugeness of the organization and in the anonymous myriads of the interchangeable human beings who make up most of their personnel. The powerlessness is the feeling which I share with so many of my neighbors—that we cannot stop what in America is called the March of Progress, the cement trucks coming toward us any day from across the hill; the knowledge that our voices, our votes, our appeals, our petitions amount to near-nothing at a time when people have become accustomed to accepting the decisions of planners, experts, and faraway powerful agencies. It is a sickening inward feeling that the essence of self-government is becoming more and more meaningless at the very time when the outward and legal forms of democracy are still kept up.

Let us not fool ourselves: Now, halfway to 1984, with all of the recent advances of civil rights, with all of the recent juridical extensions of constitutional freedoms, we *are* facing the erosion of privacy, of property and—yes—even of liberty. This has nothing to do with the Communist Conspiracy or with Ambitious Government Bureaucrats— that is where our New Conservatives go wrong. It has nothing to do with Creeping Socialism. It has very much to do with Booming Technology. The dangers which our modern societies in the West, and particularly the United States, face now, halfway to 1984, are often new kinds of dangers, growing out of newly developing conditions. What ought to concern us is the rootlessness of a modern, technological, impersonal society, with interchangeable jobs and interchangeable people, on all levels of education.

We ought to dwell less on the possibility of unemployment arising out of automation, in a society which, after all, feels obligated to produce full employment; rather, we ought to consider the growing purposelessness of occupations in a society where by now more people are employed in administration than in production. And in such a society we ought to prattle less about the need for more "creative leisure" when the problem is that work becomes less and less creative. We ought to worry not about the insufficient availability of products but about the increasing impermanence of possessions. We ought to think deeply not so much about the growth of the public sectors of the public economy at the expense of private enterprise (which, at any rate, is no longer very "private"), but rather, about the cancerous growth of the public sectors of our existence at the expense of the private autonomy of our personal lives.

We ought to concern ourselves less with the depreciation of money and more with the depreciation of language; with the breakdown of interior, even more than with the state of exterior, communications— or, in other words, with the increasing practices of Orwell's Doubletalk and Doublethink, and with their growing promotion not so much by political tyrannies as by all kinds of techniques, in the name of Progress.

I cannot—and, perhaps, I need not—explain or illustrate these concerns in greater detail. They are, in any event, 1966 concerns about the future, not 1948 ones. Still, while many of the phantoms that haunted Orwell's readers 18 years ago have not materialized, the public currency of the term "1984" has lost none of its poignancy. The tone of our literature, indeed of our entire cultural atmosphere, is far more pessimistic than it was 18 years ago. "Alienation" and "hopelessness" are no longer Central European words; they are very American. This broad, and often near-nihilistic, cultural apathy and despair is relatively new on the American (and also on the British) scene. Its existence suggests that, despite the errors of Orwell's visions, the nightmare quality of *1984* continues to obsess our imagination, and not merely as the sickly titillation of a horror story. It haunts millions who fear that life may become an Orwellian nightmare even without the political tyranny that Orwell had predicted.

"It is by his political writings," Bertrand Russell once wrote, "that Orwell will be remembered." If this is so—and at this moment, halfway to 1984, it still seems so—he will be remembered for the wrong reasons, and one can only hope that the slow corrective tides of public opinion in the long run will redress the balance.

Orwell was not so much concerned with the degeneration of justice as with the degeneration of truth. For Orwell, both in the beginning and in the end was The Word. This is true of *1984*, too, which had three levels. On the top level there is the "plot," the love affair of Winston and Julia, which is really flat and inconsequential. On the second level there is the political vision which, as we have seen, sometimes holds up, sometimes not. It is the third level, of what is happening to words and to print, to speech and to truth in 1984, which agitated Orwell the most. Indeed, this spare and economical writer chose to end the novel *1984* by adding an appendix on "The Principles of Newspeak." Orwell was frightened less by the prospects of censorship than by the potential falsification of history and by the mechanization of speech.

The first of these protracted practices would mean that the only possible basis for a comparison with conditions other than the present would disappear; the second, that the degeneration of traditional language would lead to a new kind of mechanical talk and print which would destroy the meaning of private communications between persons. This prospect haunted Orwell throughout the last 12 years of his life. Some of his best essays dealt with this theme of falsifications of truth—even more than totalitarianism, this was his main concern. As long as people can talk to one another meaningfully, as long as they have private beliefs, as long as people retain some of the qualities of Winston Smith's mother (she had not been an "unusual woman, still less an intelligent one; and yet she had possessed a kind of nobility, a kind of purity, simply because the standards she obeyed were private ones. Her feelings were her own, and could not be altered from the outside . . ."), tyranny was vulnerable; it could not become total.

Orwell was wrong in believing

that the development of science was incompatible with totalitarianism (by 1984, "science, in the old sense, has almost ceased to exist. In Newspeak there is no word for science"). As we have seen, he foresaw a decay of technology ("the fields are cultivated by horse-ploughs while books are written by machinery"). This is not what has happened; now, halfway to 1984, the fields are cultivated by bulldozers while books are written by machine-men. But Orwell was right in drawing attention to Doublethink, "the power of holding two contradictory beliefs in one's mind simultaneously, and accepting both of them," and to the desperate prospects of Doubletalk, of the degeneration of standards of language through varieties of super-modern jargon, practiced by political pitchmen as well as by professional intellectuals. There is reason to believe that, were he alive today, Orwell would have modified his views on the nature of the totalitarian menace; and that, at the same time, he would be appalled by many of the present standards and practices in mass communications, literature, and publishing, even in the West, and perhaps especially in the United States.

In short, the 1984 that we ought to fear is now, in 1966, different from the 1948 version. Politically speaking, Tocqueville saw further in the eighteen-thirties than Orwell in the nineteen-forties. The despotism which democratic nations had to fear, Tocqueville wrote, would be different from tyranny: "It would be more extensive and more mild; it would degrade men without tormenting them. . . . The same principle of equality which facilitates despotism tempers its rigor." In an eloquent passage Tocqueville described some of the features of such a society: Above the milling crowds "stands an immense and tutelary power, which takes upon itself alone to secure their gratifications and to watch over their fate. That power is absolute, minute, regular, provident, and mild. . . ." But when such a government, no matter how provident and mild, becomes omnipotent, "what remains but to spare [people] all the care of thinking and all the trouble of living?"

Orwell's writing is as timely as Tocqueville's not when he is concerned with forms of polity but when he is concerned with evil communication. In this regard the motives of this English Socialist were not at all different from the noble exhortation with which Tocqueville closed one of his chapters in *Democracy in America:* "Let us, then, look forward to the future with that salutary fear which makes men keep watch and ward for freedom, not with that faint and idle terror which depresses and enervates the heart." Present and future readers of *1984* may well keep this distinction in mind.

· QUESTIONS ·

1. In what sense is this a "springboard review"? In what sense is it an article about major American problems today?
2. State Lukacs' thesis in about 100 words. Do you generally agree with him? Disagree? Why?
3. The paragraph beginning "We ought to dwell less . . ." is a cogent summary

of much of this article-review. Analyze it for content and balanced sentence structure.

4. What is your concept of "totalitarian democracy"? Do you agree or disagree that this country is nearing it?
5. Can you cite examples in which internationalism is proving itself "phony"?
6. From your own experience and observation, cite a dozen examples of "Booming Technology."
7. Are you as pessimistic as Lukacs? Less so? More so? Why?
8. Define: ominous, trepidation, illicit, *jeu d'esprit*, élite, pervasive, edifice, juridical, poignancy, nihilistic, apathy, titillation, tutelary, salutary.

Theme Subjects: (1) A Review of "It's Halfway to 1984"; (2) A Review of *1984;* (3) My Concept of Personal Privacy; (4) My Concept of Personal Freedom; (5) A Shopping Center (Industrial Complex) Near My Home.

"MY FAIR LADY"

Henry Hewes

HENRY HEWES (1917–   ) was born in Boston and educated at Columbia University. He was a staff writer on *The New York Times*, 1949–1952, and, since 1953, has done drama criticism for *The Saturday Review*. He has lectured on drama at Sarah Lawrence College and, since 1956, at Columbia University. He was editor of *The Best Plays of 1961–62* and continues to adapt and direct plays here and abroad.

My Fair Lady is a delightful, lean musical frolic. This happy state of affairs is in good part attributable to the tough-minded dialogue of George Bernard Shaw's *Pygmalion*. The only significant changes from the movie (and the movie itself differs slightly from the play) are the addition of scenes that give Alfred Doolittle a chance to carouse with the proletariat, thus slightly blurring the individualistic qualities which led Shaw to label him the most original moralist in England; a shifting of Eliza Doolittle's first conversational test from Mrs. Higgins's salon to a club tent at Ascot (her *faux pas* has been appropriately revised from "Not bloody likely!" to "C'mon, Dover, move your bloomin'

From *The Saturday Review,* March 31, 1956. Reprinted by permission of the publisher.

arse!"); and the inclusion of a comic scene in which Colonel Pickering telephones Scotland Yard to report Eliza's flight from Higgins's Wimpole Street flat.

While Shaw's relatively unmangled text is the important factor in the success of *My Fair Lady*, Alan Jay Lerner's lyrics and Frederick Loewe's music do their share of the work, too. Following the example set by Brecht and Weill in *The Threepenny Opera* and Marc Blitzstein in *Regina,* they have written this score with the notion that each song should be for the purposes of the dramatic situation rather than to be a "number."

From this kind of show they have borrowed the device of a violently contrasting verse and chorus. For example, in *My Fair Lady* the song "I'm an Ordinary Man" is sung calmly and relaxedly by Higgins until he comes to the refrain beginning "But let a woman in your life. . . ." At this point the music becomes as stormy and frenetic as life with a woman can be. As Mr. Lerner points out:

You want to talk of Keats or Milton;
She only wants to talk of love.
You go to see a play or ballet
And spend the evening searching for
      her glove.

Another dramatic use of song comes in "You Did It." This number, celebrating Higgins's winning of his bet that he could pass a flower-girl off as a duchess, presents Higgins's smugly modest protestations in antiphony with Pickering's overinsistent praise, while the real heroine stands in the corner overlooked.

Many of the songs are loosely based on specific lines from *Pyg-*

malion. "With a Little Bit of Luck" is a bouncy refrain describing Alfred Doolittle's freedom from middle-class morality. Sings the Falstaffian Doolittle:

The gentle sex was made for man to
      marry;
To tend his needs and see his food is
      cooked.
But with a little bit of luck
You can have it all and not get hooked.

Then there is Eliza's "Just You Wait," in which she anticipates the moment when the King of England offers her anything she wishes and she replies " 'enry 'iggins's 'ead." The latter recalls "The Black Freighter" song from *The Threepenny Opera,* in which a prostitute sings about the revenge she will take on her oppressors when she comes into power.

The familiar "Rain in Spain" speech-exercise has been set to a tango in which Higgins, Pickering, and Eliza burst into joyous back-and-forth response at Eliza's victory over phonetics. This leads to a mock bullfight in a spirit of childish hysteria which is the quintessence of musical comedy. "Without You" becomes a sarcastic song of defiance to Higgins. And "I've Grown Accustomed to Her Face" is an alternately romantic, alternately vitriolic song in which Higgins's ego argues with his id.

Since a complete evening of functional music is perhaps a bit too austere for a Broadway audience, Lerner and Loewe have sagely included in their score at least one conventional show tune. Their intoxicating "On the Street Where You Live" may well become a musical-comedy standard, and only purists will complain that the number as sung by Freddy makes him a rather more poetic figure than Shaw intended him. The song for Freddy should have implied the famous sequel where Shaw has Eliza—preferring a lifetime of having her slippers fetched rather than a lifetime of fetching slippers for someone else—go on to marry Freddy rather than Higgins.

Under Moss Hart's sharp comic direction the performances are delicious. Rex Harrison, playing what Shaw described as a man whose affections and sense of beauty are disengaged from his specifically sexual impulses, manages to be an unsexy Rexy a good part of the way. Much of the time he is capricious and cocky, performing such antics as balancing a cup and saucer on top of his hat. Much of the time he is contemptuously rude to Eliza. And the first time he does release his extraordinarily magnetic passion it is for the English language rather than for a woman. But near the end when he finally does express his feelings for Eliza (the motion-picture ending in which she returns to his flat is used) the voltage between them is so overpowering that Shaw's unromantic sequel becomes preposterous. The audience *has* its happy ending to "misfit" Shaw's deliberately didactic drama.

Maybe this is best for the spirit of musical comedy, although one of the greatest of all, *Pal Joey*, did manage to get away with a more hard-boiled denouement. The audience wants Higgins to be Prince Charming and Eliza to be Cinderella. And Julie Andrews, whose first successful role was Cinderella in a London pantomime, is ideal as a self-made rather than a lucky rags-to-riches heroine. Though she sells violets she is not one herself, as she makes a sweeping snubbing turn and anticipates her father's appeal for funds with "Not a brass farthing." Her beauty, like her speech and manners, improves in gradual stages and, although the twenty-year-old star's external fire is still in the process of developing, she achieves magnificent inner intensity in the quiet scenes. Robert Coote plays Pickering a bit more like Dr. Watson than as Shaw's scholar, but his performance is solid. Holloway provides a swaggering music-hall version of Alfred Doolittle, and Cathleen Nesbitt with her own innate graciousness saves the part of Mrs. Higgins from the snobbish caricature the authors have tended to make her.

Oliver Smith's settings are appropriately light, and he has sketched particularly bright backgrounds of Covent Garden, Ascot, the London flower-market, and Mrs. Higgins's conservatory. Cecil Beaton's costumes are at their glorious best when he is dealing with the *haut-monde*. He makes the crowd at Ascot a glittering étude in black and gray. Hanya Holm's dances are pleasant and brief.

In short, *My Fair Lady*, while lacking the absolute faithfulness to purpose that one finds in a masterpiece like *The Threepenny Opera* or *The Boy Friend* or even the show-stopping high-spots one finds in *Pal Joey, South Pacific,* and *Guys and Dolls,* is nevertheless an intelligent wedding of musical-comedy and musical-play techniques enchantingly performed. It is not only the best new musical production of the season. It is—and this is more pertinent than superlatives—an enormously eupeptic treat.

· QUESTIONS ·

1. Make a paragraph outline of this review. Do some of the paragraph topics overlap?
2. What phases of a musical drama does the reviewer not discuss?
3. Comment on the diction in Hewes's statement, ". . . the performances are delicious."
4. Define: carouse, proletariat, moralist, unmangled, frenetic, antiphony, Falstaffian, vitriolic, id, denouement, eupeptic.
5. Compare and contrast this review with those by Crowther and Atkinson. (The
   movie referred to in the first paragraph of Hewes's review is an earlier version,
   one which preceded the "musical frolic" under discussion here.)

Theme Subjects: (1) The Music in *My Fair Lady;* (2) The Best Musical Play I
Ever Saw (stage, motion picture, television); (3) A Review of *Pygmalion;* (4)
_____ Is an Enormously Eupeptic Treat.

WELCOMING TWO

FAIR LADIES

Bosley Crowther

BOSLEY CROWTHER (1905–   ) was born in Lutherville, Maryland, and
was graduated from Princeton in 1928. He has been with *The New York
Times* his entire professional life, beginning as a general reporter. Screen
critic and editor for the *Times* since 1940, Mr. Crowther is widely regarded
as one of America's most trenchant and intelligent commentators on motion
pictures. He is the author of *The Lion's Share* (1957), a well-received and
authoritative study of Metro-Goldwyn-Mayer and the rest of the motion-
picture industry; of *Hollywood Rajah* (1960); and *Great Films* (1965).

Thank goodness, Julie Andrews had scored a magnificent hit as the nursemaid in *Mary Poppins* before the film of *My Fair Lady* had its triumphant opening. For now no one can feel too angry that Miss Andrews didn't get to do the role of the girl in *My Fair Lady* that she so winningly brought forth on the stage, and all can join in clearest conscience in hailing Audrey Hepburn for the crisp, the wondrous, and enchanting Eliza Doolittle that she gives us in the film.

Somehow the bare-faced enrollment of Miss Hepburn to play the role, when the two other top stars of the stage show, Rex Harrison and Stanley Holloway, were brought over for the film, became the most talked-about aspect in the public's consideration of the rendering into motion picture of the most successful musical comedy ever done. The payment by Jack L. Warner of $5.5 million for the rights was a detail beside the substitution of Miss Hepburn for the popular English star.

So was the natural employment of Alan Jay Lerner to do the script. He had adapted the show from Shaw's *Pygmalion* and had done the lyrics for the music of Frederick Loewe. Likewise, the use of Cecil Beaton to do the costumes and settings for the film: he had brilliantly performed that function for *My Fair Lady* on the stage. A $17 million budget? That was inconsequential. What was impressive and disturbing was that the darling Miss Andrews had been scratched.

Well, now everyone can breathe easily and join in a jolly hands-around in honor of Mr. Warner and Walt Disney, who happily took him off the hook. For Mr. Disney's grabbing of Miss Andrews to play the title role in the film he intended producing from the popular "Mary Poppins" children's books has resulted in a livelier introduction for the youthful and bell-voiced star than if she had simply come forth and repeated her "Fair Lady" role from the stage. And Mr. Warner's calculation that Miss Hepburn could wonderfully expand the dramatic and emotional possibilities of that complex and difficult role, under George Cukor's seasoned direction, has proved remarkably sound.

So now we have two fair ladies where we might have had only one, and the screen has suddenly burgeoned with music, romance, and charm.

This, indeed, is the cheeriest significance of the coincidence of these two films: qualities which had seemed to be dissolving have been abundantly returned. In a medium which has lately been conspicuous for vulgarity, "sickness," and bad taste, two beautifully wholesome and refreshing entertainments have emerged and two delightfully fetching female characters have encouragingly come into their own.

By now, everyone who is remotely a "Mary Poppins" fan—that is, an addicted reader of P. L. Travers' books—should have raced to see her as Miss Andrews brings her forth in this richly endowed production from the Disney studio. And everyone who loves a genuine charmer should see her before she goes.

For here is Miss Travers' stalwart nanny working her off-hand miracles with a beguilingly dry, decisive deftness and in a newly acquired delightful voice. No one dares defy her when she flies out of the sky into the home of the Bankses in Edwardian London and takes their two enraptured children under her wing—no one, that is, until the master (David Tomlinson) tries to intrude. Then a brisk confrontation of practicality with the magic of fantasy occurs—and anyone who knows Mary Poppins and her wizardry can guess which wins.

And anyone who knows Mr. Disney can guess what lively and free felicities of staging and animation have been added to make the whole thing spin. There are wonderfully casual feats of magic worked with trick photography, some fine musical numbers and dances, especially a ballet of chimney sweeps on a London roof. And there is one prolonged animated sequence in which Miss Andrews and Dick Van Dyke as a Cockney sidewalk artist lead the children through a world of caricatures of Edwardian English fascinations that is simply out of this world.

Yes, in *Mary Poppins*, Miss Andrews is provided a spinning vehicle, and already she is projected into a surely successful screen career.

On the other hand, Miss Hepburn, who is fully familiar and admired, adds further cubits to her stature with her acting of the *My Fair Lady* role. For even with Marni Nixon ghosting her singing voice, which delivers some well-nigh perfect renderings of the lovely Lerner-Loewe songs, she applies her dramatic talents and her extraordinarily sensitive face and eyes to making much more than a vocal heroine of the transplanted waif of Mr. Shaw.

Amidst all the splendor of scenery and staging that is got upon the screen in this faultlessly tasteful production, Miss Hepburn evolves the bright Eliza from a shabby and

squalling guttersnipe into a trim, finely modulated woman with profound human feeling and a soul.

Obviously, Mr. Cukor has sensed that the secret of this show is in the subtle and complex relations of two contrasting social beings. On the one hand, there is the unfeeling and mechanical-minded master of perfect speech whose habitual concept of people is that of well-mannered talking machines. And, on the other hand, there is the vulgar and untutored girl of the streets who aspires to the artificial graces but is intuitively benevolent and warm.

Thus Mr. Cukor has directed his most sensitive attention in this film to the intimate verbal confrontations and emotional abrasions of these two. And he has got the most true and touching values out of the simple dialogic scenes between Rex Harrison as the hard Professor Higgins and Miss Hepburn as the basically soft girl.

To be sure, the musical phrases are important and contribute much to the excitement of humor and sentiment in the audience. Peaks of eloquence are accomplished when Eliza melodically proclaims her capacity for nocturnal dancing or when Higgins chants his fondness for her face. And many of the supplemental song scenes, such as the dustman's wild surrender to marriage ("Get Me to the Church"), add comment and sensuous excitement to the film.

Likewise there are many other factors that make this a stimulating show: Mr. Holloway's playing of the dustman, Mr. Beaton's exquisite décor, the prescient and finished performing of all the members of the cast. But it is in the collisions of the characters that Miss Hepburn and Mr. Harrison so well define that the sparks of *My Fair Lady* are so brilliantly and burningly struck.

The arrival of this delightful picture—and of *Mary Poppins,* too —in these grave times is an incalculable manifestation of the irrepressible optimism of films.

· QUESTIONS ·

1. This article is a tribute to "two fair ladies," two motion pictures, a play, and a series of books. Does Crowther weave his material smoothly while presenting a consistent thesis, or does the review attempt too much?
2. The final paragraph provides a clue to the logical method of this article. Is the plan deductive or inductive?
3. Does this commentary make you wish to see (see again) either of the pictures discussed? If so, can you tell why?
4. What examples can you give of "vulgarity, sickness, and bad taste" in recent motion pictures which you have seen?
5. Do you think that American films are generally on a par with or superior or inferior to Italian films? French? English? Does this essay-report-review by Crowther refute or buttress your belief?

Theme Subjects: (1) The Best Film I Have Ever Seen; (2) I Don't (Do) Like Wholesome Films; (3) Some Thoughts on Current Motion Pictures; (4) The Irrepressible Optimism (Stupidity, Gullibility, Poignancy, Power) of Moving Pictures.

"MY FAIR LADY'S"

MUSIC

Brooks Atkinson

For brief comment on the life and writing career of Brooks Atkinson, see "Thoreau."

Asked for his opinion of the film version of *My Fair Lady*, one of the licensed critics in this emporium replied: "Too great."

It was a perceptive remark. Too many grandly dressed British swells pour out of the opera house in the opening scene. There are too many too ponderous dray horses in the Covent Garden sequences and too many local characters in a jolly mood. There is too much realistic detail, including a street excavation with real dirt tossed up on real shovels. The voice-recording machines in Professor Higgins's laboratory are too spectacularly efficient and the charts are too omniscient and grim.

Even the $5.5 million that Jack Warner paid for *My Fair Lady* was apparently too reckless, for the program ($1 a copy) says that the price paid "rocked an industry unprepared for such a courageous gesture of economic confidence." In other words, Mr. Warner regarded it as a good gamble. Ultimately, the box office will decide whether he has been too munificent with cash.

But Mr. Warner and a stable of geniuses, like George Cukor and Cecil Beaton, have not been able to overwhelm this musical masterpiece. Hollywood's childish need to top everything else in the world has not subdued the glow of the story or the rapture of the music, which is literally haunting. To see *My Fair Lady* in another form is to find one's self silently humming the melodies for several cheerful days afterward, for the music that Frederick Loewe wrote eight years ago with a Viennese flavor comes as close to immortality as any theater score of the century.

Which is the finest melody: "Wouldn't It Be Loverly?" "Why Can't the English?" "With a Little Bit of Luck," "I Could Have Danced All Night," "Ascot Gavotte," "Without You," "Get Me to the Church on Time," "I've Grown Accustomed to Her Face"? It is impossible to choose among them, or among the others not itemized here, because each song expresses eloquently a particular mood. The only banal song is "On the Street Where You Live." All the others have the style and freshness, the cadence and melody of enchanting theater music.

If Bernard Shaw were still around, peering at the world from under those ferocious eyebrows, he would complain that Alan Jay Lerner, author of *My Fair Lady*, has taken the word "romance" too literally from the title page of the original *Pygmalion—A Romance in Five Acts*. After *Pygmalion* became a success, Shaw insisted that Eliza does not marry Professor Higgins; she marries Freddy. Although Mr. Lerner does not specifically plight the troth of Eliza and the professor in the last act, he leaves no doubt that they are going to live together one way or the other—preferably the first.

Mr. Lerner is right. In view of the sentimental last act of *Pygmalion*, it was sheer perversity on the part of Old Beelzebub to turn Eliza out of the professor's house. Having foregone romance by making a celibate marriage himself, Shaw forbade romance in *Pygmalion*.

Casting Audrey Hepburn in the part that Julie Andrews originated makes Mr. Lerner's romantic conclusion obligatory because Miss Hepburn is one of the movie's superlatives. In the last act she is too exquisitely beautiful—slender, dainty, reserved, fastidious. Even the impeccably insufferable Higgins by Rex Harrison could not resist her. Today's comments come from one theatergoer who thinks that Miss Andrews was the better Eliza, especially in the first act, because she was simpler. Her speech and manners were less obviously contrived, and her last-act Eliza was a genuine transfiguration. It is an effort for Miss Hepburn to act down to the bedraggled guttersnipe of the first act. The last act is her moment of personal truth—Ondine in a London setting.[1]

But her beauty in those ravishing costumes from Mr. Beaton's sewing machine is so dazzling that comments on the craft of acting are probably irrelevant. Miss Hepburn may be too great for *My Fair Lady*. But who's complaining?

---

[1] *Ondine* is a play in which Audrey Hepburn once played the leading role.

· QUESTIONS ·

Topics for discussion and for writing given after the reviews by Henry Hewes and Bosley Crowther will also serve here. Actually, a comparison and contrast of these three reviews—their substance, purpose, and tone—would make an interesting topic for debate and for writing. In addition, a careful reading (or rereading) of *Pygmalion* will provide you with further ideas and with something concrete to say about each of these reviews of material based upon the original play.

LADY MACBETH
OF SCARSDALE

John McCarten

JOHN McCARTEN (1916–   ) was born in Philadelphia and attended the Shippen School there. He has been an editor and writer for *Fortune, Time, American Mercury,* and other publications and is currently on the staff of *The New Yorker.*

England's Old Vic Company, which has afforded us so much pleasure, entertainment, excitement, and enlightenment in the past, is with us once again, at the New York City Center, and it has begun its visit with a presentation of *Macbeth*. It is my hope that our guests, who in this instance have reduced a great tragedy to the proportions of a high-school elocution exercise, will get a grip on themselves, forget all about fancy enunciation, and, during the rest of their stay, give us some genuinely visceral drama. Lord knows, the introductory offering afforded them every chance to do this, since the principal characters in *Macbeth* are never sure at the end of day whether the night will bring sleep or slaughter.

What the company has done here is to tone down the raging emotional content of the play and reduce the frightening gore to Hollywood ketchup. It was probably an unfortunate accident of makeup that made me think of John Clements, who portrays Macbeth, as a sort of well-barbered Schweppesman, more or less slumming around primitive Scotland, and reading immortal lines with a kind of pedagogical weariness. He has as his consort Barbara Jefford, who is gentle, beautiful, and obviously too kind to encourage her husband to set a trap for a mouse, let alone goad him into annihilating all possible successors to the throne of Scotland. But no matter how softly we approach *Macbeth* we must have a good deal of bloodletting; unhappily, in the present production this is done by murderers got up in clerical black who go for their victims as if they were about to administer the last rites rather than speed the poor souls to their doom.

None of the performers on view, with the exception of William Sylvester and Irene Sutcliffe, who depict the Macduffs, seem to be aware that they are supposed to convey to the audience that "their pangs must be extreme who spill life's sacred stream." As for the three witches, they look much too substantial to vanish into the air, and one has a face as round and harmless as an autumn moon.

I guess the main difficulty with this *Macbeth* is the direction, by Michael Benthall. What the play demands is alarums and excursions, but Mr. Benthall seems to think that if everybody will just lower his voice and stop getting all worked up, Shakespeare's poetry will have a chance to come through. The only trouble with this notion is that Shakespeare was writing dramatic poetry.

· QUESTIONS ·

1. What is the tone of this review? Would you say that the reviewer is "letting off spleen" or that, if the performance was as he reports, it deserved what it here gets?
2. The diction in this brief report-review is nimble and incisive. Cite three or four examples of word choice which seem worth comment.
3. What does McCarten imply when he refers to *Macbeth* as being not so much poetry as *dramatic* poetry?

Theme Subjects: (1) The Frightening Gore of Hollywood Ketchup; (2) "A Well-Barbered Schweppesman" Whom I Know; (3) A High-School Elocution Exercise

That I Remember; (4) I Like (Dislike) Bloodletting Drama; (5) McCarten's Implied Opinion of *Macbeth;* (6) Shakespeare in the Suburbs. (Scarsdale is a "typical commuting town" near New York City.)

GENERAL MACBETH

Mary McCarthy

MARY THERESE MCCARTHY (1912–   ) was born in Seattle, Washington, and was graduated from Vassar College in 1933. Editor of *Partisan Review* from 1937 to 1948, she has taught literature at Bard College and was instructor in English at Sarah Lawrence in 1948. She was 1949 winner of the *Horizon* prize, and in 1964 was nominated for the National Book Award for her novel, *The Group* (1963). Among other books are *The Company She Keeps* (1942); *The Oasis* (1949); *Cast a Cold Eye* (1950); *The Groves of Academe* (1952); *A Charmed Life* (1955); *Venice Observed* (1956); *The Stones of Florence* (1959); *On the Contrary* (1961); and *Theatre Chronicles, 1937–1962* (1963).

He is a general and has just won a battle; he enters the scene making a remark about the weather. "So fair and foul a day I have not seen." On this flat note Macbeth's character tone is set. "Terrible weather we're having." "The sun can't seem to make up its mind." "Is it hot/cold/wet enough for you?" A commonplace man who talks in commonplaces, a golfer, one might guess, on the Scottish fairways, Macbeth is the only Shakespeare hero who corresponds to a bourgeois type: a murderous Babbitt, let us say.

You might argue just the opposite, that Macbeth is over-imaginative, the prey of visions. It is true that he is impressionable. Banquo, when they come upon the witches, amuses himself at their expense, like a man of parts idly chaffing a fortune-teller. Macbeth, though, is deeply impressed. "Thane of Cawdor and King." He thinks this over aloud. "How can I be Thane of Cawdor when the Thane of Cawdor is alive?" When this mental stumbling block has been cleared away for him (the Thane of Cawdor has received a death sentence), he turns his thoughts *sotto voce* to the next question. "How can I be king when Duncan is alive?" The answer comes back, "Kill him." It does fleetingly occur to Macbeth, as it would to most people, to leave matters alone and let destiny work it out. "If chance will have me king, why, chance may crown me, without my stir." But this goes against his grain. A reflective man might wonder how fate would spin her plot, as the Virgin Mary wondered after the Angel Gabriel's visit. But Macbeth does not trust to fate, that is, to the unknown, the mystery of things; he trusts only to a known quantity—himself—to put the prophecy into action. In short, he has no faith, which requires imagination. He is literal-minded; that, in a word, is his "tragedy" and his tragedy.

It was not *his* idea, he could plead in self-defense, but the witches', that he should have the throne. *They* said it first. But the witches only voiced a thought that was already in his mind; after all, he was Duncan's cousin and close to the crown. And once the thought has been put into *words*, he is in a scrambling hurry. He cannot wait to get home to tell his wife about the promise; in his excitement, he puts it in a letter, which he sends on ahead, like a business-man briefing an associate on a piece of good news for the firm.

Lady Macbeth—has this been noted?—takes very little stock in the witches. She never pesters her husband, as most wives would, with questions about the Weird Sisters: "What did they say, exactly?" "How did they look?" "Are you sure?" She is less interested in "fate and meta-physical aid" than in the business at hand—how to nerve her husband to do what he wants to do. And later, when Macbeth announces that he is going out to consult the Weird Sisters again, she refrains from comment. As though she were keeping her opinion—"O proper stuff!" —to herself. Lady Macbeth is not superstitious. Macbeth is. This makes her repeatedly impatient with him, for Macbeth, like many men of his sort, is an old story to his wife. A tale full of sound and fury signifying nothing. Her contempt for him perhaps extends even to his ambition. "Wouldst not play false, And yet wouldst wrongly win." As though to say, "All right, if that's what you want, have the courage to get it." Lady Macbeth does not so much give the impression of coveting the crown herself as of being weary of watching Macbeth covet it. Macbeth, by the way, is surely her second husband (she has "given suck" and Macbeth "has no children"), and either her first husband was a better man than he, which galls her, or he was just another general, another superstitious golfer, which would gall her too.

Superstition here is the opposite of reason on the one hand and of imagination on the other. Macbeth is credulous, in contrast to Lady Macbeth, to Banquo, and, later, to Malcolm, who sets the audience an example of the right way by mistrusting Macduff until he has submitted him to an empirical test. Believing and knowing are paired in Malcolm's mind; what he *knows* he believes. Macbeth's eagerness to believe is the companion of his lack of faith. If all works out right for him in this world, Macbeth says, he can skip the next ("We'd jump the life to come"). Superstition whispers when true religion has been silenced, and Macbeth becomes the butt of his own know-nothing materialism incarnate in the jeering witches on the heath.

As in his first interview with them he is too quick to act literally on a dark saying, in the second he is too easily reassured. He will not be conquered till "Great Birnam Wood to High Dunsinane shall come against him." "Why, that can never happen!" he cries out in immediate relief, his brow clearing.

It never enters his mind to examine the saying more closely, test it, so to speak, for a double bottom, as was common in those days (Banquo even points this out to him) with prophetic utterances, which were known to be ambiguous and tricky. Any child knew that a prophecy often meant the reverse of what it seemed to say, and any man of imagination would ask himself how Birnam Wood *might* come to Dunsinane and take measures to prevent it, as King Laius took measures to prevent his own death by arranging to have the baby Oedipus killed. If Macbeth had thought it out, he could have had Birnam Wood chopped down and burned on the spot and the ashes dumped into the sea. True, the prophecy might still have turned against him (since destiny cannot be avoided and the appointment will be kept at Samarra), but that would have been another story, another tragedy, the tragedy of a clever man not clever enough to circumvent fate. Macbeth is not clever; he is taken in by surfaces, by appearance. He cannot think beyond the usual course of things. As with "No man of woman born." All men, he says to himself, sagely, are born of women; Malcolm and Macduff are men; therefore I am safe. This logic leaves out of account the extraordinary: the man

brought into the world by Caesarean section. In the same way, it leaves out of account the supernatural— the very forces he is trafficking with. He might be overcome by an angel or a demon, as well as by Macduff.

WHO KNOWS REMORSE?

Yet this pedestrian general sees ghosts and imaginary daggers in the air. Lady Macbeth does not, and this tendency in her husband grates on her nerves; she is sick of his terrors and fancies. A practical woman, Lady Macbeth, more a partner than a wife, though Macbeth treats her with a trite domestic fondness—"Love," "Dearest love," "Dearest chuck," "Sweet remembrancer." These endearments, this middle-aged, middle-class cuddliness, as though he called her "Honeybunch" or "Sweetheart," as well as the obligatory "Dear," are a master stroke of Shakespeare's and perfectly in keeping with the prosing about the weather, the heavy credulousness.

Naturally, Macbeth is dominated by his wife. He is old Iron Pants in the field (as she bitterly reminds him), but at home she has to wear the pants; she has to unsex herself. No "chucks" or "dearests" escape her tightened lips, and yet she is more feeling, more human at bottom than Macbeth. She thinks of her father when she sees the old King asleep, and this natural thought will not let her kill him. Macbeth has to do it, just as the quailing husband of any modern virago is sent down to the basement to kill a rat or drown a set of kittens. An image of her father, irrelevant to her purpose, softens this monster woman; sleepwalking, she thinks of Lady Macduff. "The Thane of Fife had a wife. Where is she now?" Stronger than Macbeth, less suggestible, she is nevertheless imaginative, where he is not. She does not see ghosts and daggers; when she sleepwalks, it is simple reality that haunts her—the crime relived. "Who would have thought the old man to have had so much blood in him?" Over and over, the details of the crime repeat themselves on the screen of her consciousness. This nightly reliving is not penitence but more terrible—remorse, the agenbite of the restless deed. Lady Macbeth's uncontrollable imagination drives her to put herself in the place of others—the wife of the Thane of Fife—and to recognize a kinship between all human kind: the pathos of old age in Duncan makes her think, "Why, he might be my father!" This sense of a natural bond among men opens her to contrition—sorrowing with. To ask whether, waking, she is "sorry" for what she has done is impertinent. She lives with it and it kills her.

Macbeth has absolutely no feeling for others, except envy, a common middle-class trait. He *envies* the murdered Duncan his rest, which is a strange way of looking at your victim. What he suffers on his own account after the crimes is simple panic. He is never contrite or remorseful; it is not the deed but a shadow of it, Banquo's spook, that appears to him. The "scruples" that agitate him before Duncan's murder are mere echoes of conventional opinion, of what might be *said* about his deed: that Duncan was his king, his cousin, and a guest under his roof. "I have bought golden opinions," he says to himself (note the verb), "from all sorts of people";

now these people may ask for their opinions back if they suspect him of the murder. It is like a business firm's being reluctant to part with its "good will"—an asset. The fact that Duncan was such a good king bothers him, and why? Because there will be universal grief at his death. But his chief "scruple" is even simpler. "If we should fail?" he says timidly to Lady Macbeth. Sweet chuck tells him that they will not. Yet once she has ceased to be effectual as a partner, Dearest love is an embarrassment. He has no time for her; she should have died hereafter. That is, when he was not so busy. Again the general is speaking.

The idea of Macbeth as a conscience-tormented man is a platitude as false as Macbeth himself. Macbeth has no conscience. His main concern throughout the play is that most selfish of all concerns: to get a good night's sleep. His invocation to sleep, while heartfelt, is perfectly conventional; sleep builds you up, enables you to start the day fresh. Thus the virtue of having a good conscience is seen by him in terms of bodily hygiene, as if it were a Simmons mattress or an electric blanket. Lady Macbeth shares these preoccupations. When he tells her he is going to see the witches, she remarks that he needs sleep.

A WOMAN UNSEXED

Her wifely concern is mechanical and far from real solicitude. She is aware of Macbeth; she *knows* him (he does not know her at all, apparently), but she regards him coldly as a thing, a tool that must be oiled and polished. His soul-states do not interest her; her attention is narrowed on his morale, his public conduct, the shifting expressions of his face. But in a sense she is right, for there is nothing to Macbeth but fear and ambition, both of which he tries to hide, except from her. This naturally gives her a poor opinion of the inner man.

Why is it, though, that Lady Macbeth seems to us a monster while Macbeth does not? Partly because she is a woman and has "unsexed" herself, which makes her a monster by definition. Also because the very prospect of murder quickens an hysterical excitement in her, like the discovery of some object in a shop—a set of emeralds or a sable stole—which Macbeth can give her and which will be an "outlet" for all the repressed desires he cannot satisfy. She behaves as though Macbeth, through his weakness, will deprive her of self-realization; the unimpeded exercise of her will is the voluptuous end she seeks. That is why she makes naught of scruples, as inner brakes on her throbbing engines. Unlike Macbeth, she does not pretend to harbor a conscience, though this, on her part, by a curious turn, *is* a pretense, as the sleepwalking scene reveals. After the first crime, her will subsides, spent; the devil has brought her to climax and left her.

Macbeth is not a monster, like Richard III or Iago or Iachimo, though in the catalogue he might go for one because of the blackness of his deeds. But his deeds are only the wishes and fears of the average, undistinguished man translated halfheartedly into action. Pure evil is a kind of transcendence that he does not aspire to. He only wants to be king and sleep the sleep of the just, undisturbed. He could never have been a good man, even if he had not met the witches; hence we cannot see him as a devil incarnate, for the devil is a fallen angel. Macbeth does not fall; if anything, he somewhat improves as the result of his career of crime. He throws off his dependency and thus achieves the "greatness" he mistakenly sought in worldly symbols.

The isolation of Macbeth, which is at once a punishment and a tragic dignity or honor, takes place by stages and by deliberate choice; it begins when he does not tell Lady Macbeth that he has decided to kill Banquo and reaches its height in the final action. Up to this time, though he has cut himself off from all human contacts, he is relying on the witches as a substitute. When he first hears the news that Macduff is not "of woman born," he is unmanned; everything he trusted (the literal word) has betrayed him, and he screams in terror, "I'll not fight with thee!" But Macduff's taunts make a man of him; he cannot die like this, shamed. His death is his first act of courage, though even here he has had to be pricked to it by mockery, Lady Macbeth's old spur. Nevertheless, weaned by his very crimes from dependency, nursed in a tyrant's solitude, he meets death on his own, without metaphysical aid. "Lay on, Macduff."

THE TREPIDANT EXECUTIVE

What is modern and bourgeois in Macbeth's character is his wholly *social* outlook. He has no feeling for others, and yet until the end he is a vicarious creature, existing in his own eyes through others, through what they may say of him, through what they tell him or promise him.

This paradox is typical of the social being—at once a wolf out for himself and a sheep. Macbeth, moreover, is an expert buck-passer; he sees how others can be used. It is he, not Lady Macbeth, who thinks of smearing the drunken chamberlains with blood, so that they shall be caught "red-handed" the next morning when Duncan's murder is discovered. At this idea he brightens; suddenly, he sees his way clear. It is the moment when at last he decides. The eternal executive, ready to fix responsibility on a subordinate, has seen the deed finally take a *recognizable* form. Now he can do it. And the crackerjack thought of killing the grooms afterwards (dead men tell no tales—old adage) is again purely his own on-the-spot inspiration; no credit to Lady Macbeth.

It is the sort of thought that would have come to Claudius in *Hamlet,* another trepidant executive. Indeed, Macbeth is more like Claudius than like any other character in Shakespeare. Both are doting husbands; both rose to power by betraying their superior's trust; both are easily frightened and have difficulty saying their prayers. Macbeth's "Amen" sticks in his throat, he complains, and Claudius, on his knees, sighs that he cannot make what priests call a "good act of contrition." The desire to say his prayers like any pew-holder, quite regardless of his horrible crime, is merely a longing for respectability. Macbeth "repents" killing the grooms, but this is strictly for public consumption. "O, yet I do repent me of my fury, That I did kill them." In fact, it is the one deed he does *not* repent (i.e., doubt the wisdom of) either before or after. This hypo-

critical self-accusation, which is his sidelong way of announcing the embarrassing fact that he has just done away with the grooms, and his simulated grief at Duncan's murder ("All is but toys; renown and grace is dead; The wine of life is drawn," etc.) are his basest moments in the play, as well as his boldest; here is nearly a magnificent monster.

The dramatic effect, too, is one of great boldness on Shakespeare's part. Macbeth is speaking pure Shakespearean poetry, but in his mouth, since we know he is lying, it turns into facile verse, Shakespearean poetry parodied. The same with "Here lay Duncan, his silver skin lac'd with his golden blood. . . ." If the image were given to Macduff, it would be uncontaminated poetry; from Macbeth it is "proper stuff"— fustian. This opens the perilous question of sincerity in the arts: is a line of verse altered for us by the sincerity of the poet (or speaker)? In short, is poetry relative to the circumstances or absolute? Or, more particularly, are Macbeth's soliloquies poetry, which they sound like, or something else? Did Shakespeare intend to make Macbeth a poet, like Hamlet, Lear, and Othello? In that case, how can Macbeth be an unimaginative mediocrity? My opinion is that Macbeth's soliloquies are not poetry but rhetoric. They are tirades. That is, they do not trace any pensive motion of the soul or heart but are a volley of words discharged. Macbeth is neither thinking nor feeling aloud; he is declaiming. Like so many unfeeling men, he has a facile emotionalism, which he turns on and off. Not that his fear is insincere, but his loss of control provides him with an excuse for histrionics.

These gibberings exasperate Lady Macbeth. "What do you mean?" she says coldly after she has listened to a short harangue on "Methought I heard a voice cry 'Sleep no more.'" It is an allowable question—what *does* he mean? And his funeral oration on *her,* if she could have heard it, would have brought her back to life to protest. "She should have died hereafter"— fine, that was the real Macbeth. But then, as if conscious of the proprieties, he at once begins on a series of bromides ("Tomorrow and tomorrow . . .") that he seems to have had ready to hand for the occasion like a black mourning suit. All Macbeth's soliloquies have that ready-to-hand, if not hand-me-down, air, which is perhaps why they are given to schoolchildren to memorize, often with the result of making them hate Shakespeare. What children resent in these soliloquies is precisely their sententiousness—the sound they have of being already memorized from a copybook.

Macbeth's speeches often recall the Player's speech in *Hamlet*— Shakespeare's example of how-not-to-do-it. He tears a passion to tatters. He has a rather Senecan rhetoric, the fustian of the time; in the dagger speech, for example, he works in Hecate, Tarquin, and the wolf— recherché embellishment for a man who is about to commit a real murder. His taste for hyperbole goes with a habit of euphuism, as when he calls the sea "the green one." And what of the remarkable line just preceding, "the multitudinous seas incarnadine," with its onomatopoeia of the crested waves rising in the *t*'s and *d*'s of "multitudinous" and subsiding in the long swell of the verb? This is sometimes cited as an example of pure poetry, which it would be in an anthology of isolated lines, but in the context, dramatically, it is bombast, a kind of stuffing or padding.

The play between poetry and rhetoric, the *conversion* of poetry to rhetoric, is subtle and horrible in *Macbeth,* being itself a subversive process or treasonous manipulation. The suggestion seems to be that poetry used for an ulterior purpose (as Macbeth uses it) turns into rhetoric. Macbeth is the perfect utilitarian. If an explanation is needed, you might say he learned to *use* words through long practice in haranguing his troops, whipping them and himself into battle frenzy. Up to recent times a fighting general, like a football coach, was an orator.

But it must be noted that it is not only Macbeth who rants. Nor is it only Macbeth who talks about the weather. The play is stormy with atmosphere—the screaming and shrieking of owls, the howling of winds. Nature herself is ranting, like the witches, and Night, black Hecate, is queen of the scene. Bats are flitting about; ravens and crows are hoarse; the house-martins' nests on the battlements of Macbeth's castle give a misleading promise of peace and gentle domesticity. "It will be rain tonight," says Banquo simply, looking at the sky (note the difference between this and Macbeth's pompous generality), and the First Murderer growls at him, striking, "Let it come down." The disorder of Nature, as so often in Shakespeare, presages and reflects the disorder of the body politic. Guilty Macbeth cannot sleep, but the night of Duncan's murder, the whole house, as if guilty too, is restless; Malcolm and Donalbain talk and laugh in their sleep; the drunken porter, roused, plays that he is gatekeeper of hell.

NATURE TWO-SIDED

Indeed, the whole action takes place in a kind of hell and is pitched to the demons' shriek of hyperbole. This would appear to be a peculiar setting for a study of the commonplace. But only at first sight. The fact that an ordinary philistine like Macbeth goes on the rampage and commits a series of murders is a sign that human nature, like Nature, is capable of any mischief if left to its "natural" self. The witches, unnatural beings, are Nature spirits, stirring their snake-filet and owl's wing, newt's eye and frog toe in a camp stew: earthly ingredients boil down to an unearthly broth. It is the same with the man Macbeth. Ordinary ambition, fear, and a kind of stupidity make a deadly combination. Macbeth, a self-made king, is not kingly, but simply the original Adam, the social animal, and Lady Macbeth is Mother Eve.

There is no play of Shakespeare's (I think) that contains the words *Nature* and *natural* so many times, and the word *Nature* within the same speech can mean first something good and then something evil, as though it were a pun. Nature is two-sided, double-talking, like the witches. "Fair is foul and foul is fair," they cry, and Macbeth enters the play unconsciously echoing them, for he is never original but chock-full of the "milk of human kindness," which does not mean kindness in the modern sense but simply human "nature," human

kind. The play is about Nature, and its blind echo, human nature.

Macbeth, in short, shows life in the cave. Without religion, animism rules the outer world, and without faith, the human soul is beset by hobgoblins. This at any rate was Shakespeare's opinion, to which modern history, with the return of the irrational in the Fascist nightmare and its new specters of Communism, Socialism, etc., lends support. It is a troubling thought that Macbeth, of all Shakespeare's characters, should seem the most "modern," the only one you could transpose into contemporary battle dress or a sport shirt and slacks.

The contemporary Macbeth, a churchgoer, is indifferent to religion, to the categorical imperative or any group of principles that may be held to stand above and govern human behavior. Like the old Macbeth, he'd gladly skip the future life, not only for himself but for the rest of humanity. He listens to soothsayers and prophets and has been out on the heath and in the desert, interfering with Nature on a grand scale, lest his rivals for power get ahead of him and Banquo's stock, instead of his, inherit the earth— why this should have seemed such a catastrophe to the real Macbeth, who had no children, is a mystery the scholars never mention. Unloosing the potential destructiveness that was always there in Nature, as Shakespeare understood, the contemporary Macbeth, like the old one, is not even a monster, though he may breed monsters, thanks to his activities on the heath; he is timorous, unimaginative, and the prayer he would like to say most fervently is simply "Amen."

· QUESTIONS ·

1. This essay is *iconoclastic*. Define this term and prove (or disprove) the entire statement by *specific* references to the selection.
2. What is the *tone* of this essay? What do you infer is the author's real opinion of Macbeth, of Lady Macbeth, of Shakespeare as a dramatist?
3. Define: fairways, Babbitt, impressionable, reflective, metaphysical, credulous, pedestrian, agenbite, transcendence, bourgeois, trepidant, gibberings, hyperbole, philistine, timorous.
4. Do you feel that in paragraph 1 a veiled allusion is made to a highly placed American? That in several other passages this same individual is somewhat ridiculed?
5. What adjectives would you apply to the style of this selection?

Theme Subjects: (1) Generals Do (Do Not) Make Good Political Leaders; (2) Macbeth Was (Was Not) a Walter Mitty; (3) A Dominating Woman I Know; (4) My Most Ambitious Moment; (5) Macbeth: A Toothless Monster; (6) Miss McCarthy Is (Is Not) Fair.

ON THE KNOCKING

AT THE GATE IN

"MACBETH"

Thomas De Quincey

THOMAS DE QUINCEY (1785–1859) was an essayist who, in flowing prose, revealed his profound scholarship and critical insight. Like Samuel Taylor Coleridge, his contemporary, De Quincey was addicted to the use of opium, that "dread agent of unimaginable pleasure and pain." But De Quincey turned to excellent account his experiences with the "eloquent" drug, drawing upon them, as he did, for the substance of his masterpiece, *The Confessions of an English Opium Eater.*

From my boyish days I had always felt a great perplexity on one point in *Macbeth*. It was this:—The knocking at the gate which succeeds to the murder of Duncan produced to my feelings an effect for which I never could account. The effect was that it reflected back upon the murderer a peculiar awfulness and a depth of solemnity; yet, however obstinately I endeavoured with my understanding to comprehend this, for many years I never could see *why* it should produce such an effect.

Here I pause for one moment, to exhort the reader never to pay any attention to his understanding when it stands in opposition to any other faculty of his mind. The mere understanding, however useful and indispensable, is the meanest faculty in the human mind, and the most to be distrusted; and yet the great majority of people trust to nothing else,—which may do for ordinary life, but not for philosophical purposes. Of this out of ten thousand instances that I might produce I will cite one. Ask of any person whatsoever who is not previously prepared for the demand by a knowledge of the perspective to draw in the rudest way the commonest appearance which depends upon the laws of that science,—as, for instance, to represent the effect of two walls standing at right angles to each other, or the appearance of the houses on each side of a street as seen by a person looking down the street from one extremity. Now, in all cases, unless the person has happened to observe in pictures how it is that artists produce these effects, he will be utterly unable to make the smallest approximation to it. Yet why? For he has actually seen the effect every day of his life. The reason is that he allows his understanding to overrule his eyes. His understanding, which includes no intuitive knowledge of the laws of vision, can furnish him with no reason why a line which is known and can be proved to be a horizontal line should not *appear* a horizontal line: a line that made any angle with the perpendicular less than a right angle would seem to him to indicate that his houses were all tumbling down together. Accordingly, he makes the line of his houses a horizontal line, and fails, of course, to produce the effect demanded. Here, then, is one instance out of many in which not only the understanding is allowed to overrule the eyes, but where the understanding is positively allowed to obliterate the eyes, as it were; for not only does the man believe the evidence of his understanding in opposition to that of his eyes, but (what is monstrous) the idiot is not aware that his eyes ever gave such evidence. He does not know that he has seen (and therefore *quoad*[1] his consciousness has *not* seen) that which he *has* seen every day of his life.

But to return from this digression. My understanding could furnish no reason why the knocking at the gate in *Macbeth* should produce any effect, direct or reflected. In fact, my understanding said positively that it could *not* produce any effect. But I knew better; I felt that it did; and I waited and clung to the problem until further knowledge should enable me to solve it. At

[1] As regards

length, in 1812, Mr. Williams[2] made his *début* on the stage of Ratcliffe Highway, and executed those unparalleled murders which have procured for him such a brilliant and undying reputation. On which murders, by the way, I must observe that in one respect they have had an ill effect, by making the connoisseur in murder[3] very fastidious in his taste, and dissatisfied by anything that has been since done in that line. All other murders look pale by the deep crimson of his; and, as an amateur once said to me in a querulous tone, "There has been absolutely nothing *doing* since his time, or nothing that's worth speaking of." But this is wrong; for it is unreasonable to expect all men to be great artists, and born with the genius of Mr. Williams. Now, it will be remembered that in the first of these murders (that of the Marrs) the same incident (of a knocking at the door soon after the work of extermination was complete) did actually occur which the genius of Shakspere has invented; and all good judges, and the most eminent dilettanti, acknowledged the felicity of Shakspere's suggestion as soon as it was actually realized. Here, then, was a fresh proof that I was right in relying on my own feeling, in opposition to my understanding; and I again set myself to study the problem. At length I solved it to my own satisfaction; and my solution is this:—Murder, in ordinary cases, where the sympathy is wholly directed to the case of the murdered

person, is an incident of coarse and vulgar horror; and for this reason,—that it flings the interest exclusively upon the natural but ignoble instinct by which we cleave to life: an instinct which, as being indispensable to the primal law of self-preservation, is the same in kind (though different in degree) amongst all living creatures. This instinct, therefore, because it annihilates all distinctions, and degrades the greatest of men to the level of "the poor beetle that we tread on,"[4] exhibits human nature in its most abject and humiliating attitude. Such an attitude would little suit the purpose of the poet. What then must he do? He must throw the interest on the murderer. Our sympathy must be with *him* (of course I mean a sympathy of comprehension, a sympathy by which we enter into his feelings, and are made to understand them,—not a sympathy of pity or approbation). In the murdered person, all strife of thought, all flux and reflux of passion and of purpose, are crushed by one overwhelming panic; the fear of instant death smites him "with its petrific mace."[5] But in the murderer, such a murderer as a poet will condescend to, there must be raging some great storm of passion,—jealousy, ambition, vengeance, hatred, —which will create a hell within him; and into this hell we are to look.

In *Macbeth,* for the sake of gratifying his own enormous and teeming faculty of creation, Shak-

---

[2] In 1812 Williams murdered two families, the Marrs and the Williamsons, in London.

[3] See De Quincey's essay, "Murder Considered as One of the Fine Arts," in which De Quincey gives an account of Williams's crimes.

[4] From *Measure for Measure,* III, i, 79.

[5] From *Paradise Lost,* X, 294.

spere has introduced two murderers: and, as usual in his hands, they are remarkably discriminated: but,— though in Macbeth the strife of mind is greater than in his wife, the tiger spirit not so awake, and his feelings caught chiefly by contagion from her,—yet, as both were finally involved in the guilt of murder, the murderous mind of necessity is finally to be presumed in both. This was to be expressed; and, on its own account, as well as to make it a more proportionable antagonist to the unoffending nature of their victim, "the gracious Duncan," and adequately to expound "the deep damnation of his taking off,"[6] this was to be expressed with peculiar energy. We were to be made to feel that the human nature, —i.e., the divine nature of love and mercy, spread through the hearts of all creatures, and seldom utterly withdrawn from man,—was gone, vanished, extinct, and that the fiendish nature had taken its place. And, as this effect is marvellously accomplished in the *dialogues* and *soliloquies* themselves, so it is finally consummated by the expedient under consideration; and it is to this that I now solicit the reader's attention. If the reader has ever witnessed a wife, daughter, or sister in a fainting fit, he may chance to have observed that the most affecting moment in such a spectacle is *that* in which a sigh and a stirring announce the recommencement of suspended life. Or, if the reader has ever been present in a vast metropolis on the day when some great national idol was carried in funeral pomp to his grave, and, chancing to walk near the course through which it passed, has felt powerfully, in the silence and desertion of the streets, and in the stagnation of ordinary business, the deep interest which at that moment was possessing the heart of man,—if all at once he should hear the death-like stillness broken up by the sound of wheels rattling away from the scene, and making known that the transitory vision was dissolved, he will be aware that at no moment was his sense of the complete suspension and pause in ordinary human concerns so full and affecting as at that moment when the suspension ceases, and the goings-on of human life are suddenly resumed. All action in any direction is best expounded, measured, and made apprehensible, by reaction. Now, apply this to the case in *Macbeth*. Here, as I have said, the retiring of the human heart and the entrance of the fiendish heart was to be expressed and made sensible. Another world has stept in; and the murderers are taken out of the region of human things, human purposes, human desires. They are transfigured: Lady Macbeth is "unsexed"; Macbeth has forgot that he was born of woman; both are conformed to the image of devils; and the world of devils is suddenly revealed. But how shall this be conveyed and made palpable? In order that a new world may step in, this world must for a time disappear. The murderers and the murder must be insulated—cut off by an immeasurable gulf from the ordinary tide and succession of human affairs—locked up and sequestered in some deep recess; we must be made sensible that the world of ordinary life is suddenly arrested, laid asleep, tranced, racked into a dread armistice; time must be annihilated, rela-

---

[6] From *Macbeth*, I, vii, 20.

tion to things without abolished; and all must pass self-withdrawn into a deep syncope and suspension of earthly passion. Hence it is that, when the deed is done, when the work of darkness is perfect, then the world of darkness passes away like a pageantry in the clouds: the knocking at the gate is heard, and it makes known audibly that the re-action has commenced; the human has made its reflux upon the fiendish; the pulses of life are beginning to beat again; and the re-establishment of the goings-on of the world in which we live first makes us profoundly sensible of the awful parenthesis that had suspended them.

O mighty poet! Thy works are not as those of other men, simply and merely great works of art, but are also like the phenomena of nature, like the sun and the sea, the stars and the flowers, like frost and snow, rain and dew, hailstorm and thunder, which are to be studied with entire submission of our own faculties, and in the perfect faith that in them there can be no too much or too little, nothing useless or inert, but that, the farther we press in our discoveries, the more we shall see proofs of design and self-supporting arrangement where the careless eye had seen nothing but accident!

· QUESTIONS ·

1. What is the central argument of this critical essay?
2. Do you agree that "understanding . . . is the meanest faculty of the human mind"?
3. Have you tried the experiment mentioned in paragraph 2? With what results?
4. How would you characterize the style of the final paragraph?
5. In this essay, what is the author trying to do? How well does he succeed? Of what value is his attempt?
6. Compare and contrast this essay with "General Macbeth."

Theme Subjects: (1) "My Careless Eye"; (2) A Review of *Macbeth;* (3) "The Primal Law of Self-Preservation"; (4) Feeling Versus Understanding—An Incident; (5) My Short-lived Career as an Artist.

AUTOBIOGRAPHY PROFILE & PORTRAIT

A NOTE ON READING

Biography has been a popular form of reading from its beginnings. Sketches of kings and members of the ruling class thrilled readers some 2000 years ago with their emphasis on martial and other adventurous deeds. Readers vicariously experienced activity, securing release and a form of escape apparently no less popular then than they are today. Curiosity about others is as old as the human race, and its potency and prevalence have increased rather than decreased through the centuries. Within the past century our curiosity about others, great and small, has resulted in both a major industry and a major literary type. Biography and autobiography in books, magazines, motion pictures, television, and radio are a twentieth-century flood which shows no signs of receding.

To be sure, modern readers are not always so absorbed with literal accounts of striking deeds as readers and listeners were 20 centuries ago. But eagerness to know the intimate details of others' lives, curiosity about people's attainments, about their strengths and weaknesses, their ways of speaking and thinking and acting, their human and their inhuman qualities are as dominant now as man's urge to escape or live vicariously through fiction. This fascination with the lives of others has been cultivated as biography has become a more settled type, as it has come to be more appealingly written, as it has dealt more and more with "ordinary" people and less and less with contemporary kings and princes.

The present-day popularity of biographical writing also traces to the fact that readers have come to realize that truth is actually "stranger than fiction." Perhaps it would be more correct to say that "truth is stranger than fiction *dares* to be," for some of the complications, ironies, and coincidences in almost anyone's life would have to be discarded by a competent narrative writer. Put into fiction they would seem either impossible or improbable. The biographer is restrained by no such consideration. His whole work, if properly handled, seems authentic and credible, and its reader will willingly accept more hair-raising and heart-stopping episodes than any novelist or story writer could hope to employ. Good biographical and auto-biographical writing is narrative and has not only appropriated the appealing techniques of narration but added to them.

It should be noted, however, that biography and autobiography have a distinct limitation. Philip Guedalla was unduly cynical when he remarked that biography is "a region bounded on the north by history, on the south by fiction, on the east by obituary, and on the west by tedium." But it is true that every age writes its own biography and emphasizes its own villains and heroes. Thus it is necessary to remember that a biography may not deal with timeless truth, that it often merely reflects an attitude or point of view of an earlier day. Other types—essays, stories, poems, novels, plays—can and often do state essential and ever-green truths. Biography may reveal such truths, but there are few undisputed and documented facts in anyone's life, and probably no biography or autobiography has ever been complete, unprejudiced, or impartial. "The proper study of mankind is man," but study unadorned and unaided by artistic creativeness may be faulty and fragmentary. And a long list of autobiographies, St. Augustine's, Cellini's, Casanova's, Rousseau's, and Franklin's among them, attest that it is even more difficult to know—and to tell—the truth, the whole truth, about oneself. Novelist, short story writer, poet, and dramatist—under no such compulsion—create characters or narrate events which are a synthesis and which, at their best, seem "truer than truth." Thackeray once wrote that "fiction carries a greater amount of truth in solution than the volume which purports to be all true."

An attempt to view man's mind from the inside may be considered as appealing more to morbid inquisitiveness than to healthy curiosity. Guedalla has likened the new biography to a sport such as big-game hunting and suggests that it is as unfair as only such a sport can be. In an attempt not to become mythmakers, some biographers tend to become exhibitionists. Spice, not truth; abuse, not use; realism, not a single reticence—these are the credo of those whose aim is sensationalism and resulting sales. However this may be, the penetrating discernment and urbane detachment of the new school of biographers have made the type a serious rival of fiction. Actually, modern biography at its best is as dramatic as a play, as absorbing as a short story, as reflective as an essay, and, in the hands of a master like Sandburg, as beautiful as a poem.

A PAINTER
AND A PAGE

Lincoln Steffens

(JOSEPH) LINCOLN STEFFENS (1866–1936) was born in San Francisco, was graduated from the University of California in 1889, and then studied in Berlin, Heidelberg, Leipzig, Paris, and London. Returning to America in 1892, he became a successful reporter on *The New York Evening Post*. His intelligent curiosity gained the confidence of important men in New York civic and financial circles and started him on his career as a journalist. As managing editor of *McClure's Magazine,* Steffens began his famous muckraking investigation of unsavory facts in politics and business. A series of articles interpreting his extensive study of boss rule and reform movements in midwestern cities during the Theodore Roosevelt period was collected in *The Shame of the Cities* (1904). Other volumes dealing with social and political practices are *The Struggle for Self-Government* (1908); *Upbuilders* (1909); *The Least of These* (1910).

My father brought home to dinner one Sunday a painter, W. M. Marple, an artist from "the City," as we called San Francisco. I was excited. I had read about the famous painters; art was one way of being great; and I had been taken to the Crocker Art Gallery in Sacramento. All very interesting, but there was some mystery about pictures. Those that I liked best were scenes in mining-camps or on ranches and, generally, from the life about me.

I could not discover anything very great in them. It seemed to me that they weren't even true; they didn't see things as I saw them. It was evident that in art, as in everything else, there was something to learn. And this visiting artist was my chance to learn it.

"I can't tell you anything about art," he said when I put to him at table my eager questions. "Nobody can. But I can show you."

He proposed after dinner to go

out and make some sketches. He meant that he was going to paint a picture! And I could watch him at it! Where? What was there to paint in Sacramento? I guessed that he would paint the Capitol; that was the greatest thing in town. But no, I had a triumph, but it was not on my guess of the Capitol.

My father, mother, and others always wondered why I spent so much time over on the American River bottom: a washed-out place, where no one else ever went. Why not ride in the streets or the good country roads? I could not explain very well. The river bottom was all gravel and sand, cut up by the seasonal floods and left raw and bare of all but dead, muddied brush and trees. I remembered how it disappointed me the first time I saw it, the day I rode over there on my new pony. Since then I had filled it up with Indians, Turks, beavers, and wild beasts and made it a beautiful scene of romance and adventure. But I could not tell everybody that! I was ashamed of my taste in natural scenery.

And yet that was Mr. Marple's choice. He asked my father to take him there. He said he had passed by it on a train one afternoon and had seen something he wanted to paint. To my father's astonishment and mine, we had to lead the great painter to my playground. I was the guide, of course, a troubled but a very proud leader; I could not think myself what Mr. Marple would like to see and paint there. A hole, where I swam because the water was warm, did not suit him. He pushed on deeper into the brush and, forgetting us in a most fascinating way, he moved about, here, there, till, satisfied at last, he unpacked his stuff, set up his easel, put a

small square of boarded canvas on it, and went to work without a word.

How I watched! His first movements I could imitate, and I did, to the bridge-tender the next day. That painter looked at the scene in which I could see nothing to paint; nothing; just brush, miles and miles of mud-stained brush and leafless, drowned scrub willows. He studied this with one eye, held up the handle of his brush, and measured something which he dabbed off on his canvas. Then he looked some more, long, hard, while he pinched paints in little piles on his already mixed-up board of many colors. What was he doing? I asked. "Getting the colors right," he said, and with that, he began suddenly to paint. Fast. I lost track of what he was doing, though I did not take my eyes off that easel and the scene. I could not make out what was going on. Whatever it was, he was quick about it, so quick that in a very few minutes he had the whole canvas covered, and then, as he stepped back and I looked, suddenly it became a picture, a picture of the scene; only—

"What is it?" I asked him.

"Oh, the name of it when the sketch is painted," he said, "will be, say, 'A Sunset.' "

Yes, that was right. The sun was burning a golden hole in the top line of the brush and the brush under and around the hole was gold, too, old gold; the whole was a golden picture. But—he was looking at it himself, squinting, with his head on one side, then on the other; he touched it here, there, and finally, backing far away, he said, "Not so bad, eh? Not bad."

It was beautiful, I thought, but it wasn't good; it wasn't true. It was bad of the brush; it wasn't brush at all. And I said as much. He laughed, and he answered me with a saying I never forgot.

"You see the brush and the baked mud. All right. They are there. Many things are there, and everybody sees what he likes in this and in every other scene. I see the colors and the light, the beautiful chord of the colors and the light."

Now I did not see the brush either; it was not the baked mud that made me come and play over there; and I told him so. I admitted that I had seen that the first time I rode out there, but after that—after that—

"Well," he encouraged me, "what did you see after that?"

I was caught. I owned up to the Indians, Saracens, elephants, and—he did not laugh. My father did; not the painter. Mr. Marple said that if I were an artist, I should paint Indians or wild animals—"You should paint a princess in the brush if you see her there." I could understand that.

"But your golden light is really there," I said, "and my Indians aren't."

"Your Indians are where my gold is," he answered, "where all beauty is, in our heads. We all paint what we see, as we should. The artist's gift is to see the beauty in everything, and his job is to make others see it. I show you the gold, you show me the romance in the brush. We are both artists, each in his line."

My father bought that picture, and my mother arranged to have me take drawing lessons. I was going to be a great painter for a while and fill the American River bottom with—what I saw there. But my drawing teacher did not teach

me the way Mr. Marple did; I could not learn to copy other drawings; all I ever did that was called good was a group of horses' heads. My mother held me to it; she made me take drawing lessons as she made me take music lessons long after I had lost all desire and interest in them. That was her guiding principle of education: that her children were to have a chance at everything; no talent was to be overlooked in us. None.

The proper fruit of Mr. Marple's visit was of another, a similar sort. I was to have a lesson, not in drawing, but in seeing. Mr. Marple's son, Charlie, came to live with us. Maybe that was the purpose of the painter's visit. Anyway, after him came Mrs. Marple, and from her I learned that her son, a boy a little older than I was, had a promise of an appointment to be a page at the next session of the Legislature. She was looking for a place for him to live, a house where he would be cared for. "Would I like a playmate?"

Would I? I was delighted. I could show him all the places I knew, and he could show me the Legislature. But what was a page? There were pages in my books; they were little boys at court or in the service of knights and ladies. But a page in a Legislature, what was that? A messenger, they said, a boy that carried bills and letters and notes from one member to another on the floor of the House or Senate. I became interested in the Capitol, the Legislature, the government. I read up on, I asked everybody questions about these things, I visited the Capitol, and as always with me, I formed some sort of picture of the machinery of government. Yes, and I had made in my mind also a portrait of Charlie Marple, made it up out of what I had read of stories and pictures of pages at court.

When Charlie came he was no more like my picture than his father's sketch was like my river bottom, and as for the Legislature . . . Charlie was a homely fellow—and weak, physically—not graceful and pretty, and he wasn't so eager for politics as he was to use my pony. He had been told about that; he had been looking forward to riding it; and when we went together out to the stable, his expectations were satisfied. He put his hand cautiously on the pony's rump, and the face he turned to me was alight with pleasure.

"But," he said, "I can't ride; never was on a horse in my life."

"It's easy," I reassured him, and I boosted him up on the pony's back there in the stall. When he found that easy, I untied the horse and led him out around the yard until Charlie learned to sit him without hanging on too hard to his mane. A happy boy he was at the end of his first lesson, and I was proud. I got on and showed how I could ride, up and down, around the block, at any gait. "Easy, see?"

We had to go to the Capitol and to the hotel lobbies to inquire about his appointment, which was only promised; and I worried: I knew what promises were. I went with him and it was his turn to show me things. He seemed to know as much about politics as I did about my riding, but he was more interested in riding than he was in that Legislature. He made me tell him over and over where he would ride: down the river, up the river, out in the country, to the trestle bridge, to the beaver traps. There was a long

delay of his appointment, and I wondered why. The legislators were in town; Sacramento was filled with them; and the Legislature did not meet. Why?

Charlie explained indifferently that they were "organizing." There were committees to "fix up" and a lot of fat jobs to be distributed; not only pages to appoint, but clerks, sergeants-at-arms—everything; hundreds of them, and yet not enough to go around. There were, for instance, three times as many boys promised pageships as there were pages; and a pageship was a petty job. The page got only $10 a day. Some places paid much more than this in salaries, besides what you could make out of them.

"It all depends on who gets the speakership," said Charlie. "Let's go riding."

"But aren't you afraid you'll get left?" I asked anxiously.

He wasn't. His "member" was the San Francisco leader of the Republican railroad crowd which was sure to capture the speakership and thus the whole organization of the House. They could fill any job, but of course they had to give something good to the Democratic railroad gang and "chicken-feed" to the opposition Republicans. That was "good politics."

So we went riding, both of us on the one horse. I rode in front, Charlie holding on to my waist behind. He was glad of the delay. Until the sessions began, we could play all day every day together, and his salary was cumulative—$10 a day! The amount of it impressed me. A boy getting $10 a day was a wonder to a boy like me, who never had more than a dime at a time. Charlie hardly thought of it. His thoughts were on the pony, on learning to ride, seeing the rivers and the country, or playing Indians and crusaders, and trapping beavers.

I wish I could recall all that I went through that winter. It was a revelation: it was a revolution to me. Charlie was appointed a page; we all went to the opening session, where, with a formal front, the Speaker was elected (just as if it had not been "fixed"), speeches made (just as if spontaneously), and the committees and the whole organization read off (just as if it had not been "settled" days and nights before). Then I saw why Charlie wasn't interested in his salary: he got none of it; it all went home; and he had no more money in his pocket than I had in mine. But also I saw that the Legislature wasn't what my father, my teachers, and the grown-ups thought; it wasn't even what my histories and the other books said. There was some mystery about it as there was about art, as there was about everything. Nothing was what it was supposed to be. And Charlie took it as it was; my father took it as it seemed to be; I couldn't take it at all. What troubled me most, however, was that none of them had any strong feeling about the conflict of the two pictures. I had. I remember how I suffered; I wanted, I needed, to adjust the difference between what was and what seemed to be. There was something wrong somewhere, and I could not get it right. And nobody would help me.

Charlie was forever for getting away from the Capitol. So were the legislators. They kept adjourning, over every holiday, over Sundays, over Saturdays and Sundays, over Saturdays, Sundays, and Mondays.

We could ride, therefore, and we did. We made long trips out to the ranches, up and down and across the rivers. Charlie never wearied; he never got enough of our exploration and of our romance. He entered into the spirit of my games of "playing" knight or cowboy. He learned to ride; he could go off alone, but I liked riding, too, and he preferred that we stay together. It was more fun to talk and think together about dangers ahead; it was safer to meet them shoulder to shoulder. I enjoyed our many, many days of free play.

But I enjoyed also the sessions of the House when Charlie had to be on the floor. He found me a seat just back of the rail where I could sit and watch him and the other pages running about among the legislators in their seats. Charlie used to stand beside me, he and the other small pages, between calls, and we learned the procedure. We became expert on the rules. The practices of debate, quite aside from the legislation under consideration, fascinated me. I wished it were real. It was beautiful enough to be true. But no, speeches were made on important subjects with hardly anyone present but the Speaker, the clerks, and us boys. Where were the absent members? I did not ask that question often; not out loud. The pages laughed; everybody laughed. Charlie explained.

"The members are out where the fate of the measure debated here is being settled," and he took me to committee rooms and hotel apartments where, with the drinks and cigars, members were playing poker with the lobbyists and leaders. "The members against the bill are allowed to win the price agreed on to buy their vote."

Bribery! I might as well have been shot. Somewhere in my head or my heart I was wounded deeply.

Once, when the Speaker was not in the chair and many members were in their seats, when there was a dead debate in an atmosphere of great tension, I was taken down a corridor to the closed door of a committee room. There stood reporters and a small crowd of others watching outside. We waited awhile till, at last, the Speaker came out, said something, and hurried with the crowd back to the Assembly. Charlie held me back to point out to me "the big bosses" who had come "up the river" to "force that bill through"; they had "put on the screws." I was struck by the observation that one of the bosses was blind. We went back to the House, and quickly, after a very ordinary debate of hours, the bill was passed on the third reading and sent to the Senate, where, in due course, it was approved. It was a "rotten deal," the boys said, and I remember my father shook his head over it. "The rascals!" he muttered.

And that, so far as I could make out from him and from all witnesses—that was the explanation. The Legislature, government— everything was "all right," only there were some "bad men" who spoiled things—now and then. "Politicians" they were called, those bad men. How I hated them, in the abstract. In the concrete—I saw Charlie Prodger often in the lobby of the Legislature, and I remember that some one said he was "one of them," a "politician." But I knew Charlie Prodger, and I knew he was not a "bad man."

And the sergeant-at-arms, who was called "bad"—one of the San Francisco gang—he was one of the kindest, easiest-going men I ever met. He looked out for me; he took care of all the boys. Many a time he let Charlie Marple off to have a free day with me. And there were others: every "crook" I met seemed to me to belong in a class with the bridge-tender, Mr. and Mrs. Stortz, and all the other grown men and women who "understood a fellow"— did not stick at rules; did not laugh at everything a boy said and frown at every little thing he did.

When the Legislature closed and Charlie Marple went home, I was left to ride around the country alone, thinking, thinking. I asked questions, of course; I could not think out alone all that I had been learning that winter; I could not easily drop the problem of government and the goodness and badness of men. But I did not draw from my friends any answers that cleared my darkness. The bridge-tender said that all Legislatures were like that. And Jim Neely said so too; Ah Hook[1] was not interested.

"What for you askem me fool question," he said. "Chinaman he findee out long time allee government allee samee—big clook."

But there was an answer of a sort about that time, an answer to one of my questions: Why didn't somebody challenge the rascals— if they were so bad? The boss of Sacramento, Frank Rhodes, the gambler, was having one of his conventions of the local ringleaders in a room under his gambling-house. It was at night. There were no outsiders present, none wanted, and the insiders were fighting, shooting

---

[1] A farmhand and a Chinese farmer, friends of young Steffens.

men. During the meeting Grove L. Johnson, a well-known attorney in the town, walked in with his two sons, Albert and Hiram, both little more than boys, and both carrying revolvers. They went up to the front, and with one of his boys on one side of him, the other on the other, Mr. Johnson told those crooks all about themselves and what they were doing. He was bitter, fearless, free-spoken; he insulted, he defied those politicians; he called upon the town to clean them out and predicted that their power would be broken some day. There was no answer. When he had finished, he and his sons walked out.

Something in me responded to that proceeding. It was one way to solve my problem. There was no other response, so far as I could see or hear. People said unpleasant things about Grove L. Johnson, and the Rhodes ring went right on governing the town. Later, much later,

the boss disappeared, and still later Grove L. Johnson himself was one of the bosses of the Legislature. Albert Johnson died. But Hiram Johnson became a reform Governor of California and a United States Senator.

What struck and stunned me at the time was that this courageous attack by the Johnsons—especially by the boys—had no effect upon the people I knew. I was trying to see the Legislature and government as Mr. Marple saw the sunset through the brush in the river bottom; not the mud but—the gold, the Indians —some beauty in them. The painter said there always was something beautiful to see. Well, Mr. Johnson and his two boys—their defiance was beautiful; wasn't it? I thought so, and yet nobody else did. Why? I gave it up, or, better, I laid the question aside. I had other things to think of, wonderful things, things more in my line.

· QUESTIONS ·

1. From what you know of Steffens' character, explain the final paragraph of this selection.
2. Is your own state legislature comparable to the one described by Steffens? How? How not?
3. Was Steffens an idealist or a realist? Consider your answer carefully.
4. How do you account for many people's lack of interest in government? What would serve to increase your own interest?
5. How many politicians do you know? What sort of people are they?
6. Would Mr. Johnson qualify for a "profile in courage," as developed by the late President Kennedy?

Theme Subjects: (1) My Taste in Natural Scenery; (2) "Organizing" the Campus; (3) The Hard Facts of Politics; (4) Why People Don't Vote; (5) Defiance Is Beautiful; (6) The Courage of Hiram Johnson; (7) A Review of Steffens' *Autobiography;* (8) What a Muckraker Would Find in My Town.

THE MONSTER

Deems Taylor

(JOSEPH) DEEMS TAYLOR (1885–1966) was a composer and critic who, after graduation from New York University, became a journalist. His love for music prevailed, and he became a music critic and editor of *Musical America*. As a composer he first won serious attention with cantatas based on the well-known poems, "The Highwayman" (Noyes) and "The Chambered Nautilus" (Holmes). Other compositions include "Through the Looking-Glass," an impressionistic suite based on Carroll's fantasy; *The King's Henchman*, a romantic opera of medieval England with libretto by Edna St. Vincent Millay; and *Peter Ibbetson*, an operatic work based on Du Maurier's novel. He also wrote music for plays by George S. Kaufman, Marc Connelly, and Elmer Rice. Books of criticism largely collected from Mr. Taylor's radio talks include *Of Men and Music* (1937), *The Well-Tempered Listener* (1940), and *Music to My Ears* (1949). Two later books are *Some Enchanted Evenings* (1953) and *The One-Track Mind* (1953).

He was an undersized little man, with a head too big for his body—a sickly little man. His nerves were bad. He had skin trouble. It was agony for him to wear anything next to his skin coarser than silk. And he had delusions of grandeur.

He was a monster of conceit. Never for one minute did he look at the world or at people, except in relation to himself. He was not only the most important person in the world, to himself; in his own eyes he was the only person who existed. He believed himself to be one of the greatest dramatists in the world, one of the greatest thinkers, and one of the greatest composers. To hear him talk, he was Shakespeare, and Beethoven, and Plato, rolled into one. And you would have had no difficulty in hearing him talk. He was one of the most exhaustive conversationalists that ever lived. An evening with him was an evening spent in listening to a monologue. Sometimes he was brilliant; sometimes he was maddeningly tiresome. But whether he was being brilliant or dull, he had one sole topic of conversation: himself. What *he* thought and what *he* did.

He had a mania for being in the right. The slightest hint of disagreement, from anyone, on the most trivial point, was enough to set him off on a harangue that might last for hours, in which he proved himself right in so many ways, and with such exhausting volubility, that in the end his hearer, stunned and deafened, would agree with him, for the sake of peace.

It never occurred to him that he and his doings were not of the most intense and fascinating interest to anyone with whom he came in contact. He had theories about almost any subject under the sun, including vegetarianism, the drama, politics, and music; and in support of these theories he wrote pamphlets, letters, books . . . thousands upon thousands of words, hundreds and hundreds of pages. He not only wrote these things, and published them—usually at somebody else's expense—but he would sit and read them aloud, for hours, to his friends and his family.

He wrote operas; and no sooner did he have the synopsis of a story, but he would invite—or rather summon—a crowd of his friends to his house and read it aloud to them. Not for criticism. For applause. When the complete poem was written, the friends had to come again, and hear *that* read aloud. Then he would publish the poem, sometimes years before the music that went with it was written. He played the piano like a composer, in the worst sense of what that implies, and he would sit down at the piano before parties that included some of the finest pianists of his time, and play for them, by the hour—his own music, needless to say. He had a

composer's voice. And he would invite eminent vocalists to his house, and sing them his operas, taking all the parts.

He had the emotional stability of a six-year-old child. When he felt out of sorts, he would rave and stamp, or sink into suicidal gloom and talk darkly of going to the East to end his days as a Buddhist monk. Ten minutes later, when something pleased him, he would rush out of doors and run around the garden, or jump up and down on the sofa, or stand on his head. He could be grief-stricken over the death of a pet dog, and he could be callous and heartless to a degree that would have made a Roman emperor shudder.

He was almost innocent of any sense of responsibility. Not only did he seem incapable of supporting himself, but it never occurred to him that he was under any obligation to do so. He was convinced that the world owed him a living. In support of this belief, he borrowed money from everybody who was good for a loan—men, women, friends, or strangers. He wrote begging letters by the score, sometimes groveling without shame, at others loftily offering his intended benefactor the privilege of contributing to his support, and being mortally offended if the recipient declined the honor. I have found no record of his ever paying or repaying money to anyone who did not have a legal claim upon it.

What money he could lay his hands on he spent like an Indian rajah. The mere prospect of a performance of one of his operas was enough to set him to running up bills amounting to ten times the amount of his prospective royalties. On an income that would reduce a more scrupulous man to doing his own laundry, he would keep two servants. Without enough money in his pocket to pay his rent, he would have the walls and ceiling of his study lined with pink silk. No one will ever know—certainly he never knew—how much money he owed. We do know that his greatest benefactor gave him $6,000 to pay the most pressing of his debts in one city, and a year later had to give him $16,000 to enable him to live in another city without being thrown into jail for debt.

He was equally unscrupulous in other ways. An endless procession of women marches through his life. His first wife spent twenty years enduring and forgiving his infidelities. His second wife had been the wife of his most devoted friend and admirer, from whom he stole her. And even while he was trying to persuade her to leave her first husband he was writing to a friend to inquire whether he could suggest some wealthy woman—*any* wealthy woman—whom he could marry for her money.

He was completely selfish in his other personal relationships. His liking for his friends was measured solely by the completeness of their devotion to him, or by their usefulness to him, whether financial or artistic. The minute they failed him —even by so much as refusing a dinner invitation—or began to lessen in usefulness, he cast them off without a second thought. At the end of his life he had exactly one friend left whom he had known even in middle age.

He had a genius for making enemies. He would insult a man who disagreed with him about the weather. He would pull endless wires in order to meet some man who admired his work and was able and anxious to be of use to him— and would proceed to make a mortal enemy of him with some idiotic and wholly uncalled-for exhibition of arrogance and bad manners. A character in one of his operas was a caricature of one of the most powerful music critics of his day. Not content with burlesquing him, he invited the critic to his house and read him the libretto aloud in front of his friends.

The name of this monster was Richard Wagner. Everything that I have said about him you can find on record—in newspapers, in police reports, in the testimony of people who knew him, in his own letters, between the lines of his autobiography. And the curious thing about this record is that it doesn't matter in the least.

Because this undersized, sickly, disagreeable, fascinating little man was right all the time. The joke was on us. He *was* one of the world's great dramatists; he *was* a great thinker; he *was* one of the most stupendous musical geniuses that, up to now, the world has ever seen. The world did owe him a living. People couldn't know those things at the time, I suppose; and yet to us, who know his music, it does seem as though they should have known. What if he did talk about himself all the time? If he talked about himself for twenty-four hours every day for the span of his life, he would not have uttered half the number of words that other men have spoken and written about him since his death.

When you consider what he wrote—thirteen operas and music dramas, eleven of them still holding the stage, eight of them unquestionably worth ranking among the world's great musico-dramatic masterpieces—when you listen to what he wrote, the debts and heartaches that people had to endure from him don't seem much of a price. Eduard Hanslick, the critic whom he caricatured in *Die Meistersinger* and who hated him ever after, now lives only because he was caricatured in *Die Meistersinger*. The women whose hearts he broke are long since dead; and the man who could never love anyone but himself has made them deathless atonement, I think, with *Tristan und Isolde*. Think of the luxury with which for a time, at least, fate rewarded Napoleon, the man who ruined France and looted Europe; and then perhaps you will agree that a few thousand dollars' worth of debts were not too heavy a price to pay for the *Ring* trilogy.

What if he was faithless to his friends and to his wives? He had one mistress to whom he was faithful to the day of his death: Music.

Not for a single moment did he ever compromise with what he believed, with what he dreamed. There is not a line of his music that could have been conceived by a little mind. Even when he is dull, or downright bad, he is dull in the grand manner. There is greatness about his worst mistakes. Listening to his music, one does not forgive him for what he may or may not have been. It is not a matter of forgiveness. It is a matter of being dumb with wonder that his poor brain and body didn't burst under the torment of the demon of creative energy that lived inside him, struggling, clawing, scratching to be released; tearing, shrieking at him to write the music that was in him. The miracle is that what he did in the little space of seventy years could have been done at all, even by a great genius. Is it any wonder that he had no time to be a man?

· QUESTIONS ·

1. Describe the structure of this biographical sketch. Were you prepared for the sharp contrast provided in the last four paragraphs?
2. Which of Wagner's shortcomings seems to you most heinous? Most "forgivable"?
3. "Is it any wonder that he had no time to be a man?" Can you accept the implied forgiveness of this question? Why? Why not?
4. In what sense does the author mean that Wagner was "right all the time"? Do you know or have you read of anyone else so infallible? Can you name any persons the record of whose lives "doesn't matter in the least"?
5. What is your understanding of the true meaning of *tolerance*? (Perhaps the derivation of the word will help to clarify your definition.)
6. Define: delusions, exhaustive, monologue, harangue, vegetarianism, synopsis, groveling, rajah, scrupulous, arrogance, libretto, trilogy, compromise.

Theme Subjects: (1) No Time To Be a Man; (2) Wagner Was a Great Composer, But _____; (3) The Most Conceited (Tiresome, Dull) Person I Know; (4) An Evening with a Monologist; (5) My Own Emotional Stability; (6) One Good Way To Make Enemies; (7) Nothing Succeeds Like Success; (8) The Beam in My Own Eye.

THOREAU

Brooks Atkinson

(JUSTIN) BROOKS ATKINSON (1894–   ) was born in Melrose, Massachusetts. After his graduation from Harvard in 1917, Atkinson became a reporter and reviewer for the *Boston Transcript*, at the same time editing the *Harvard Alumni Bulletin*. In 1922 he began reviewing books for the *New York Times* and from 1925 to 1960 was drama critic for that paper, except while serving as a foreign correspondent during World War II. He is presently the *Times* critic at large. A sensitive and scholarly writer, Atkinson published in 1927 *Henry Thoreau: The Cosmic Yankee*. Two years earlier he had published *Skyline Promenade*, reflections on mountain climbing and kindred interests. In 1940 he published in *The Atlantic Monthly* a moving tribute to his much-loved police dog, "Cleo for Short." Later books are entitled *Tuesdays and Fridays* (1963) and *Brief Chronicles* (1966).

I

Thoreau was the genius of Concord, where he was born on July 12, 1817. Although that venerable and tranquil town was sheltering two other eminent men of letters—Emerson and Hawthorne—and at least two minor literary notables—Alcott and Channing—Thoreau was bone of Concord's bone and flesh of Concord's flesh, and he could never be torn away from the town where he was born. Several other New England towns might have nourished him well; he was a man of infinite resource and could find all truth within himself. There are towns in the White Mountains or on Cape Cod that would have provided a career for him; if he had lived in them his healthy prose would have caught their rhythm and his character would have taken shape in their image, for he was the poet of New England locality. But if Concord was fortunate in numbering him amongst her subjects, he was fortunate in Concord where the meadows were fertile, the hills gentle, the woods hospitable, and where the natural resources were rich without being wild. For there was a pond in Concord—Walden

Pond—which all the world recognizes now as a masterpiece, and two pleasant rivers flowed through the bosom of the town, filled with fluvial treasures and offering passage to other parts of the universe.

Nor was that all Concord had to offer a man of original mind and great personal character. Lying close to Boston, where the intellectual life of America was most resolute, Concord was simmering with ideas. When Thoreau was a young man, Emerson was already the fountainhead of Concord's intellectual and spiritual life. Transcendentalism, which believed in the infinity of man, flowed out of Emerson's books, lectures, neighborhood relationships, and walks in the fields. Everything Emerson said and did was part and parcel of his faith. But he was no solitary in Concord. Concordians in general were alert. People discussed religion, philosophy, and politics in the parlors, church vestries, at the stores and even along the streets. Already famous in national history, Concord was making spiritual history by the interest it cultivated in the vague, aspiring ideas of the time. It was a fine place for a man whose curiosity about life was unlimited.

Having chosen a good town for his nativity, Thoreau also chose good parents and relatives. His father was descended from sea captains and merchants from the Channel island of Jersey; his grandfather had accumulated moderate wealth from privateering and storekeeping in Boston. His mother had descended from a wealthy and notable Tory family whose estates had been confiscated during the Revolution. By the time of Thoreau's generation the wealth on both sides had dwindled to almost nothing; his

immediate family was always hard-pressed. But his parents were people of independent mind, probity, and vigor of spirit, and they were capable of hard work. Although their means were limited, they sent Henry to Harvard College, class of 1837, for they believed in cultivating the mind. Being practical people, they may have hoped to have him succeed in one of the established professions, as other good students generally did. But the profession he practiced was a strange one that he evoked from his private character, and it paid him nothing but his self-respect. If his parents, his brother and sisters were disappointed, there is no record of regret or rebuke. They were people of intelligence and principle; probably they always understood his potentialities and admired his vital integrity, and it is certain that they loved him with the warm affection of a family that lived on intimate terms.

To some of his neighbors Thoreau seemed austere. But his family had all the best of him, which was affectionate, kind, and loyal; and whenever Thoreau wrote to his mother from Staten Island or to his sisters in Roxbury or Bangor, the thoughts were homely, the style was glowing, and the concern with family affairs was anxious. When his father died he dropped in large part the career he had carved out of himself and Concord and took over the responsibilities of the head of the family. Although that burden must have involved a considerable sacrifice, he accepted it calmly and discharged his duty, for the Thoreaus were in the habit of regarding personal honor as a natural part of their lives.

He was a writer. He was the

author of thirty-nine manuscript volumes, only two of which were published during his lifetime; and it is doubtful if he ever earned much more from his writings than they cost him. For the volumes of which he was author were almost entirely the journals where he industriously assembled his thoughts and observations and tried to extract the basic truth of the cosmos. In fact, his journals were the core of his life; he confessed to them and then drew sustenance from them, "as a bear sucks his claws in winter"; and all his published works were made out of them. "Henry Thoreau—Writer of Journals" might well be the description of his profession. *Walden* and *A Week on the Concord and Merrimack Rivers* are only parts of the treasures buried in his copybooks.

When he was graduated from college he might have had hopes of a less private career. He was a serious young man. He had already made up his mind that most of the ways by which men earn a living are degrading and that men sell themselves into perpetual bondage by conforming to the traditional ways of the world. Most of his principles that developed into passionate accusations in his mature philosophy are to be found in his college essays, for the life of Thoreau was a straight, firm line of moral development from youthful introspection into the militant wisdom of his last years. At first he tried to teach school, which was the ordinary profession of college graduates. In association with his brother, who was an attractive, high-spirited young man with considerable ability, Thoreau did teach school in Concord for a year or two, much to the delight of the students and their parents. Like everything with which he was connected, it was no routine scheme for earning a living, but a forward-looking school that gave full value in book education and that tried to enrich the lives of the students by personal association with the teachers during walks in the fields and picnics on the river where some of the more luxuriant facts about life could be learned. All his life Thoreau had a winning way with children; more than some of their elders they could appreciate the kindliness and frankness of a naturally upright man. But his brother died, a particularly agonizing death that left its mark on everyone who loved him, and Thoreau gave up the school.

For a few years he had no settled employment. He lived in Emerson's home, taking charge of all those practical things to which the grand old man of Concord was so conspicuously unsuited; he toiled over his thoughts, which was his lifetime occupation, and wrote for *The Dial,* which was the Pierian Spring of Transcendentalism. For a few months he lived with William Emerson's family on Staten Island, New York, as a tutor, meanwhile apparently looking around in New York for a literary association where he could find a market for his wares. But the magazines and newspapers in New York in 1843 were not ready to pay cash for the kind of fiercely independent thoughts Thoreau struggled with in his journals. Presently he was back in Concord, which he regretted having left, and settled down with his family in their pencil business. Probably he knew, what he had long suspected, that the world was not ready to receive him on his own exacting terms.

If Thoreau had never gone to live alone in a hut at Walden Pond it is possible that he would never have been celebrated. That was the most dramatic thing he ever did; the chronicle of his adventure is a classic. In 1845, the time was ripe for a bold move. He was at loose ends; his brother's death was still a source of misery. Furthermore, he was a romantic youth, under the mask of truculent sobriety; he was only 28 years of age, a lover of nature and an honest and capable workman with his hands. As it happened, a friend of his had lived one winter in a hut on the shore of a pond in the next township and Thoreau very likely helped him build the camp. As Thoreau's bosom companion, Ellery Channing, wrote in the spring of 1845: "It seems to me you are the same old sixpence you used to be, rather rusty, but a genuine piece. I see nothing for you in this earth but that field which I once christened 'Briars'; go out upon that, build yourself a hut and there begin the process of devouring yourself alive."

By the end of March he borrowed an axe from Alcott, cut down some white pine timber beside Walden Pond to frame a hut, and on Independence Day, which was highly propitious, he moved in and lived there alone for two years. Watching and listening, studying, thinking, dreaming, attending to the varying moods of the pond, writing in his journals, trying the virtue of the great world outside by the simple truths of his secluded existence— all that brought his career to fruition. Although he left the hut in 1847 and supported himself by surveying, pencil-making, and other homely crafts, he had found the path to a wise approach to life at

Walden Pond, and from that time on he was a man whose destiny was in full view. Sometimes Thoreau seemed needlessly morose in his responses to human society; it was late in life before he threw down his guards and took men as good companions with human gusto. But the opening up of his career began at Walden; after that camping experience with its philosophical, economic, and romantic aspects he wrote with confidence, force, and clarity; he understood and rejoiced in his place in the world.

The rest of his career is quickly stated. In 1849 he published at his own expense *A Week on the Concord and Merrimack Rivers,* which was the record, with glorious discursions, of a boat voyage he had made with his brother into New Hampshire ten years earlier. In 1854 he published *Walden,* which slowly brought his original rebellion to the notice of the world. Meanwhile, in various contemporary periodicals he published "On the Duty of Civil Disobedience," which is an insurgent essay that has helped to reshape the world; also his savory records of journeys to Canada, the Maine woods and Cape Cod, and many other minor essays. All his life he and the other members of his family had been ardent abolitionists, and at times took part in helping Negro slaves to escape. In 1845 he had personally seceded from the Union as the most earnest protest he could make against a government that tolerated slavery, and he spent a night in jail to make his point public. When John Brown defied the government at Harper's Ferry, Thoreau, who was eminently a practical man, found a concrete cause that illuminated all he had ever thought and written about freedom; suddenly he was transfigured into a man of action. His several speeches on John Brown are grand summonses to battle—angry, rebuking, and founded on principle.

Soon after this inspiring episode in his career, his health began to fail rapidly. Although he made one desperate attempt to recover it by a futile journey to Minnesota, he soon realized that he was doomed, and he patiently spent the last two frail years of his life getting his myriad papers in order, compiling articles from his journals for *The Atlantic Monthly*—sometimes riding out with his sister to look on the beauties of Concord which he had devoted his life to discovering and describing. His submissive death was the surest proof that he wholly believed the faith he had lived. He had no regrets or misgivings. "One world at a time," he said to Channing, who was speculating on the hereafter. When someone else inquired whether he had made his peace with God, he answered, "We have never quarreled." On May 6, 1862, when he was almost 45 years of age and when the fruit blossoms were out and the fragrance was coming in at the window, he died, as he had lived, with complete faith in the wisdom of nature. His sister remarked that he was the most upright man she had ever known.

II

As a writer, Thoreau embraced so many subjects that it is still difficult to catalogue him. He was "poet-naturalist," as Channing described him; but he was also philosopher, historian, economist, rebel, revolutionary, reporter. Apart from its poetic record of an idyllic adventure, *Walden* is the practical philosophy of rebellion against the world's cowardly habits of living. Most formless of his books and yet most winning and light-hearted, the *Week* is a compound of thought, scholarship, speculation, and narrative. *The Maine Woods* is the most pungent and profound study of woods and camping that has ever been written. "On the Duty of Civil Disobedience" is an eloquent declaration of the principles that make revolution inevitable in times of political dishonor. The John Brown papers are political pamphleteering. Large portions of the journals are character studies of the people in Concord whom Thoreau most admired. Although he rarely left Concord and seldom read the newspapers, he was well informed about the life of his times and had fiery opinions about slavery and justice. His achievements in those fields have somewhat overshadowed the range of his scholarship and the brilliance of his detached portraits of people. Almost nothing escaped the keen eyes and mind of this tireless writer; there is a bewildering variety in his work.

Although it is impossible to catalogue him neatly, there is in everything he did a concrete point of view that gives a clear-cut unity to the abundance and disarray of his writing. Primarily he was a moral philosopher. From those first tentative college essays, which are touching in their youthful fortitude, to the fulminating John Brown polemics there was a grave, responsible, pure-minded attitude toward life in all his work. He had a passion for wise and honorable living. As a whole, the Transcendentalists were not systematic philosophers, bent on arranging the pattern of life into a logical sequence. Quite the contrary: they believed in living by inspiration. Believing that man and the universe were God, they worshipped Him by trying to live in spiritual harmony with the great laws of nature—trying humbly to be good men. Their philosophy was little more than a collection of "thoughts," of individual aspirations and manifestations distilled from the sunshine and the mist over the river. They believed that they were living the good life, not by accumulating knowledge or acquiring possessions, but by quickening their awareness of the beauties of nature and human nature. Thoreau yearned to be as pure and innocent as the flowers in the field. Although the Transcendentalists were not as a whole consistent churchgoers in a period when churchgoing was an integral part of community life, they were nevertheless deeply religious people. In a humble way, they represented God on earth; they were His agents because they were trying to live in His image and they believed that men might yet found Heaven on earth by looking into their own hearts for the rules of life and by following the direction of their finest instincts.

Thoreau was the most enduring of the lot because he had the most intimate knowledge and understanding of nature and was, accordingly, practical and concrete. That was the source of what Emerson admired as "the oaken strength" in his writing. For Thoreau did not merely write verses to the evanescent beauties of the out-of-doors and stroll placidly through the fields after a stuffy day in the study; he made it his business to know everything that he could about nature from personal observation. He wanted to know the cold by the

tingle in his finger-tips and the darkness by stumbling through the woods at night, and he felt most elated when his senses were as alert as those of the woodchuck and the loon. He felt that his whole life was on the most solid footing when his boots were deep in the river-bank muck in the springtime. Although he acquired an enormous fund of knowledge by the persistence of his goings forth in all kinds of weather and by the extraordinary capacity he had for observation, he was not a modern scientist. On the contrary, he suspected science because he believed that it dealt in specimens rather than in life. No one has ever given himself to nature so passionately, so confidently, so privately. It was a rich, turbulent, exhausting life he led. Although the world was at loose ends and his neighbors lived lives of "quiet desperation," he believed that he was on the right track and had nothing but immortality to fear when he was present to greet the first bluebird in late February or early March and to find the first hepatica blooming among the late snowdrifts. Spring always convinced him that he could live forever on the lavish bounty of God. God was good: he knew because he listened to the song of God in the woods.

Everything remarkable about Thoreau sprang directly from his devotion to nature. It was nature more than man, it was the out-of-doors more than books or political discussions that taught him the necessity for independence. A free man himself—free by his own principle and vigilance—he despised the cowards who conformed. He had a poor opinion of his townsmen who mortgaged their lives for a farm and pushed a house, barn, and sixty-acre woodlot down through the long years before them. He disliked the gentlemen who had isolated themselves from life by civil employment or social artifice. He was contemptuous of the million compromises men make with their governments to acquire wealth or to preserve the peace on a false basis. As for himself, he knew the fundamentals of life so thoroughly from personal association with the flowers he ministered unto and the woodlots he surveyed for his neighbors, that he had no intention of making any compromises with his genius whatsoever, and he swore that he at least should be a free man though everyone else sold his soul to comfort and convenience.

That is why he refused to pay a poll tax to a government that tolerated slavery, and that is why John Brown was his man. All his life he had been conducting an individual rebellion against the slavery of thought, commerce, and manners. When John Brown rebelled against Negro slavery at Harper's Ferry on principle alone at the certain risk of his life, Thoreau completely understood him. It was his sort of thing on a greater scale. It was what he had been waiting for. Although some of his neighbors counselled caution, Thoreau took the initiative into his own hands, summoned a village meeting, and pled with his townsmen for justice and action with more cogency and eloquence than he had ever imparted to a speech before. He carried the John Brown defense to Boston at considerable personal risk. Although the militant John Brown episode may seem alien to the life of a solitary philosopher, it was really the logical and brilliant climax to his philosophy. To love nature was to

worship freedom. To believe in nature was to rebel.

Certainly it was no passport into good society. Especially in his early years before his philosophy was fully formed and when perhaps he felt a little wounded by the world's indifference to his talents, he had a truculent way with people and it annoyed or grieved them according to their natures. There was in those days a taciturn or forbidding streak in his deportment. One of his neighbors said she could love him but that she could not like him. Emerson said: "Henry is— with difficulty—sweet." For the brazenly independent life he had set his mind on living put him on the defensive in a town accustomed to the amenities. Being shy and abnormally sensitive, Thoreau protected himself by erecting around him a high wall of reserve, skepticism, and external misanthropy. To those who had never glanced down into the ringing depths of his character he was an odd stick, and many people resented him.

That rasp in his social relations was a defect in personality rather than the truth of his character. Fundamentally, he was a man of abiding affections. Although he distrusted gentlemen and hated impostors, he had such exalted standards of friendship that his friends sometimes had difficulty in meeting his requirements. For the simple, honest folks of the town he had great relish, and he liked to talk to them and keep well posted on their affairs. He admired an honest farmer more than a clever publican and made no secret of his preference. When he believed that he was among friends he could be an exuberant comrade on occasions. With Channing, his familiar companion out-of-doors, he was on terms of long-suffering and humorous affection; there was "an inexhaustible fund of good fellowship" in Channing, to use Thoreau's own words of appreciation. Although his moral philosophy had given him an austere appearance, he had a Yankee sense of humor; he liked puns and ludicrous incongruities and comic turns of phrase.

When the secret of his life was fairly published in *Walden* and people began to seek him out as a leader of thought, his defenses began to drop one by one. He had made many friends and did them the honor of taking them seriously. The last eight years of his life were conspicuously social. He visited and was visited. He enjoyed the companionship of congenial people at home, in the woods, and on journeys to the White Mountains and the Maine woods. When his health began to fail, there was a need for companionship greater than he had experienced before; and when he planned to go to Minnesota in search of his health he was reluctant to go alone. For Thoreau was no misanthrope. He required, as he said, "broad margins to his leisure," so that his thoughts might grow freely. His perceptions were so acute, his understanding of men was so penetrating that he was unhappy in company that misjudged him. A person who was spiritually coarse wounded him grievously. But he was always civil, courteous, and kind in his ordinary relationships around town; he had abundant affection for his family and his friends; he was generous with his talents; and in those last ten years of his life, when his private battle with life was won, he overflowed with good will toward good

men. It may have surprised him a little to discover how glorious life can be in the company of good people. Certainly it expanded his horizons enormously.

Since he was all of one piece—man, matter, and spirit—it is impossible to discuss his style of writing apart from himself. At his best he wrote the most vigorous and pithy prose in American literature; and no wonder, for his training was extraordinarily complete. On the one hand, he was a remarkable classical scholar; all his life he read Greek and Latin poetry and translated into English poetry the classic verses he admired most. On the other hand, he had learned out-of-doors the great truth of fresh simplicity. There are no literary flourishes in his style; everything grows out of nature. "Simplicity, simplicity, simplicity," were the three great maxims of his life; and they stood guard over the notes he scribbled in the field and the sentences he developed out of them when he expanded them in his journal, rewriting more than once until they carried his thought with the greatest strength and directness of statement he could master. "The one great rule of composition—and if I were a professor of rhetoric I should insist on this—is to speak the truth," he said. He approached his subject as though he were the first man to write about this world which has been so long inhabited and so carelessly spattered with ink. Since his mind was clear, the facts are accurately stated, and the thoughts and impressions endure in words that feel concrete—a part of old Mother Earth.

It is noticeable that his writing improved according to his familiarity with a subject. When he first went into the Maine woods he was in new territory, which put him on his guard, and his Ktaadn essay shows the reserve of a stranger who had not shed his Concord experience. After his third journey, described in the Allegash essay, he wrote with the assurance and enthusiasm of a man who had conquered his subject and enjoyed the labor of recording it. When he first went to Cape Cod he felt uneasy and a little hostile to such meagre land; after his third visit he was writing with the humorous, genial relish of an old inhabitant. There is no better prose in American literature than the clear, sinewy, fragrant writing in *Walden* which discusses the homely details of house-building and kitchen economy and rejoices in the romantic loveliness of sounds at night and bird notes by day and speculates on the beauties of good living—all in plain images and simple phrases that do not change pace with the change of subject. Although his writing looks easy, only a man of keen mind and remarkable skill could have made a sentence carry so much baggage and have given living form to impulses of the imagination.

But that was Thoreau—a man with the skill of an artisan and the aspiration of a poet. He had disciplined himself so that the two were perfectly mated. What he was as a man looks sternly out of every page he wrote; it represents his deliberate conviction. When Thoreau was dying, Bronson Alcott described him in a familiar letter as "the most sagacious and wonderful Worthy of his time, and a marvel to coming ones." That was the generous thought of a neighbor who was moved by the prospect of losing a noble friend. But perhaps it was not unreasonably excessive. For by faith and works Thoreau learned how to live a life, which is a thing rarely heard of; and his writings have helped thousands of his kinsmen to make their lives more rich and honest and able.

· QUESTIONS ·

1. Why are Atkinson's opening sentence and first paragraph particularly effective?
2. What is the purpose of the first sentence of the third paragraph?
3. Why was it "highly propitious" that Thoreau went to live in his hut at Walden Pond on Independence Day?
4. In what ways does E. B. White's "Walden" substantiate Atkinson's commentaries on Thoreau?
5. Explain why Atkinson says that Thoreau "was not a modern scientist."
6. Identify: Emerson, Hawthorne, Alcott, Channing, Transcendentalism, John Brown.
7. Explain why Thoreau refused to pay his poll tax.
8. Write a paragraph developing and explaining Thoreau's "one great rule of composition."
9. Does Thoreau's own life make more significant the meaning of the following sentence from *Walden:* "It is not worth the while to go round the world to count the cats in Zanzibar"?
10. Define: integrity, cosmos, degrading, fruition, morose, gusto, transfigured, myriad, submissive, idyllic, fulminating, evanescent, "quiet desperation," lavish.

Theme Subjects: (1) Two Views of Thoreau (see E. B. White's "Walden"); (2) Walden Pond and the World Today; (3) Thoreau's Poll Tax; (4) An Answer to Thoreau; (5) The Necessities of Life; (6) What Thoreau Forgot (Ignored, Overlooked).

DANIEL WEBSTER, AMERICAN

John F. Kennedy

JOHN FITZGERALD KENNEDY (1917–1963) was born in Brookline, Massachusetts, attended Princeton University, and was graduated *cum laude* from Harvard University in 1940. Before and directly after World War II he was a correspondent for *The Chicago Herald-American* and for the International News Service, covering the San Francisco United Nations Conference, the Potsdam Conference, and the British elections of 1945. Entering politics, he was a member of the 80th–82nd Congresses, and from 1953–1961 was U. S. Senator from Massachusetts. In 1961 he took office as the thirty-fifth President of the United States, and on November 22, 1963, was assassinated. Among his many writings are *While England Slept* (1940); *Profiles in Courage* (1956), which won the Pulitzer Prize for biography in 1957; *Strategy of Peace* (1960); and *To Turn the Tide* (1962), a selection of his public statements as President.

The blizzardy night of January 21, 1850, was no night in Washington for an ailing old man to be out. But wheezing and coughing fitfully, Henry Clay made his way through the snowdrifts to the home of Daniel Webster. He had a plan—a plan to save the Union—and he knew he must have the support of the North's most renowned orator and statesman. He knew that he had no time to lose, for that very afternoon President Taylor, in a message to Congress asking California's admission as a free state, had only thrown fuel on the raging fire that threatened to consume the Union. Why had the President failed to mention New Mexico, asked the North? What about the Fugitive Slave Law being enforced, said the South? What about the District of Columbia slave trade, Utah, Texas boundaries? Tempers mounted, plots unfolded, disunity was abroad in the land.

But Henry Clay had a plan—a plan for another Great Compromise to preserve the nation. For an hour he outlined its contents to Daniel Webster in the warmth of the latter's comfortable home, and together they talked of saving the Union. Few meetings in American history have ever been so productive or so ironic in their consequences. For the Compromise of 1850 added to Henry Clay's garlands as the great Pacificator; but Daniel Webster's support which insured its success resulted in his political crucifixion, and, for half a century or more, his historical condemnation.

The man upon whom Henry Clay called that wintry night was one of the most extraordinary figures in American political history. Daniel Webster is familiar to many of us today as the battler for Jabez Stone's soul against the devil in Stephen Vincent Benét's story. But in his own lifetime, he had many battles against the devil for his own soul—and some he lost. Webster, wrote one of his intimate friends, was "a compound of strength and weakness, dust and divinity," or in Emerson's words "a great man with a small ambition."

There could be no mistaking he was a great man—he looked like one, talked like one, was treated like one, and insisted he was one.

With all his faults and failings, Daniel Webster was undoubtedly the most talented figure in our Congressional history: not in his ability to win men to a cause—he was no match in that with Henry Clay; not in his ability to hammer out a philosophy of government—Calhoun outshone him there; but in his ability to make alive and supreme the latent sense of oneness, of Union, that all Americans felt but which few could express.

But how Daniel Webster could express it! How he could express almost any sentiments! Ever since his first speech in Congress—attacking the War of 1812—had riveted the attention of the House of Representatives as no freshman had ever held it before, he was the outstanding orator of his day—indeed, of all time—in Congress, before hushed throngs in Massachusetts, and as an advocate before the Supreme Court. Stern Chief Justice Marshall was said to have been visibly moved by Webster's famous defense in the Dartmouth College case—"It is, sir, as I have said, a small college—and yet there are those who love it." After his oration on the two hundredth founding of Plymouth Colony, a young Harvard scholar wrote:

I was never so excited by public speaking before in my life. Three or four times I thought my temple would burst with the rush of blood. . . . I was beside myself and I am still so.

And the peroration of his reply to Senator Hayne of South Carolina, when secession had threatened twenty years earlier, was a national rallying cry memorized by every schoolboy—"Liberty and Union, now and forever, one and inseparable!"

A very slow speaker, averaging hardly a hundred words a minute, Webster combined the musical charm of his deep organ-like voice, a vivid imagination, an ability to crush his opponents with a barrage of facts, a confident and deliberate manner of speaking, and a striking appearance to make his orations a magnet that drew crowds hurrying to the Senate chamber. He prepared his speeches with the utmost care, but seldom wrote them out in a prepared text. It has been said that he could think out a speech sentence by sentence, correct the sentences in his mind without the use of a pencil, and then deliver it exactly as he thought it out.

Certainly that striking appearance was half the secret of his power and convinced all who looked upon his face that he was one born to rule men. Although less than six feet tall, Webster's slender frame when contrasted with the magnificent sweep of his shoulders gave him a theatrical but formidable presence. But it was his extraordinary head that contemporaries found so memorable, with the features Carlyle described for all to remember: "The tanned complexion, the amorphous crag-like face; the dull black eyes under the precipice of brows, like dull anthracite furnaces needing only to be blown; the mastiff mouth accurately closed." One contemporary called Webster "a living lie, because no man on earth could be so great as he looked."

And Daniel Webster was not as great as he looked. The flaw in the granite was the failure of his moral senses to develop as acutely as his other faculties. He could see nothing improper in writing to the President of the Bank of the United States—at the very time when the Senate was engaged in debate over a renewal of the Bank's charter—noting that "my retainer has not been received or refreshed as usual." But Webster accepted favors not as gifts but as services which he believed were rightly due him. When he tried to resign from the Senate in 1836 to recoup speculative losses through his law practice, his Massachusetts businessmen friends joined to pay his debts to retain him in office. Even at his deathbed, legend tells us, there was a knock at his door, and a large roll of bills was thrust in by an old gentleman, who said that "At such a time as this, there should be no shortage of money in the house."

Webster took it all and more. What is difficult to comprehend is that he saw no wrong in it—morally or otherwise. He probably believed that he was greatly underpaid, and it never occurred to him that by his own free choice he had sold his services and his talents, however extraordinary they might have been, to the people of the United States, and no one else, when he drew his salary as United States Senator. But Webster's support of the business interests of New England was not the result of the money he obtained, but of his personal convictions. Money meant little to him except as a means to gratify his peculiar tastes. He never accumulated a fortune. He never was out of debt. And he never was troubled by his debtor status. Sometimes he paid, and he always did so when it was convenient, but as Gerald W. Johnson says, "Unfortunately he sometimes paid in the wrong coin —not in legal tender—but in the confidence that the people reposed in him."

But whatever his faults, Daniel Webster remained the greatest orator of his day, the leading member of the American Bar, one of the most renowned leaders of the Whig party, and the only Senator capable of checking Calhoun. And thus Henry Clay knew he must enlist these extraordinary talents on behalf of his Great Compromise. Time and events proved he was right.

As the God-like Daniel listened in thoughtful silence, the sickly Clay unfolded his last great effort to hold the Union together. Its key features were five in number: (1) California was to be admitted as a free (nonslaveholding) state; (2) New Mexico and Utah were to be organized as territories without legislation either for or against slavery, thus running directly contrary to the hotly debated Wilmot Proviso which was intended to prohibit slavery in the new territories; (3) Texas was to be compensated for some territory to be ceded to New Mexico; (4) the slave trade would be abolished in the District of Columbia; and (5) a more stringent and enforceable Fugitive Slave Law was to be enacted to guarantee return to their masters of runaway slaves captured in Northern states. The Compromise would be condemned by the Southern extremists as appeasement, chiefly on its first and fourth provisions; and by the Northern abolitionists as 90 per cent concessions to the South with a meaningless 10 per cent sop thrown to the North, particularly because of the second and fifth provisions. Few Northerners could stomach any strengthening of the Fugitive Slave Act, the most bitterly hated measure—and until prohibition, the most flagrantly disobeyed —ever passed by Congress. Massa-chusetts had even enacted a law making it a crime for anyone to enforce the provisions of the Act in that state!

How could Henry Clay, then hope to win to such a plan Daniel Webster of Massachusetts? Was he not specifically on record as a consistent foe of slavery and a supporter of the Wilmot Proviso? Had he not told the Senate in the Oregon Debate:

I shall oppose all slavery extension and all increase of slave representation in all places, at all times, under all circumstances, even against all inducements, against all supposed limitation of great interests, against all combinations, against all compromises.

That very week he had written a friend: "From my earliest youth, I have regarded slavery as a great moral and political evil. . . . You need not fear that I shall vote for any compromise or do anything inconsistent with the past."

But Daniel Webster feared that civil violence "would only rivet the chains of slavery the more strongly." And the preservation of the Union was far dearer to his heart than his opposition to slavery.

And thus on that fateful January night, Daniel Webster promised Henry Clay his conditional support, and took inventory of the crisis about him. At first he shared the views of those critics and historians who scoffed at the possibility of secession in 1850. But as he talked with Southern leaders and observed "the condition of the country, I thought the inevitable consequences of leaving the existing controversies unadjusted would be Civil War." "I am nearly broken down with labor and anxiety," he wrote his son, "I know not how to meet the present emergency, or with what weapons to beat down the Northern and Southern follies now raging in equal extremes. . . . I have poor spirits and little courage."

Two groups were threatening in 1850 to break away from the United States of America. In New England, Garrison was publicly proclaiming, "I am an Abolitionist and, therefore, for the dissolution of the Union." And a mass meeting of Northern Abolitionists declared that "the Constitution is a covenant with death and an agreement with hell." In the South, Calhoun was writing a friend in February of 1850, "Disunion is the only alternative that is left for us." And in his last great address to the Senate, read for him on March 4, only a few short weeks before his death, while he sat by too feeble to speak, he declared, "The South will be forced to choose between abolition and secession."

A preliminary convention of Southerners, also instigated by Calhoun, urged a full-scale convention of the South at Nashville for June of that fateful year to popularize the idea of dissolution.

The time was ripe for secession, and few were prepared to speak for Union. Even Alexander Stephens of Georgia, anxious to preserve the Union, wrote friends in the South who were sympathetic with his views that "the feeling among the Southern members for a dissolution of the Union . . . is becoming much more general. Men are now beginning to talk of it seriously who twelve months ago hardly permitted themselves to think of it . . . the crisis is not far ahead. . . . A dismemberment of this Republic I now consider inevitable." During the critical month preceding

Webster's speech, six Southern states, each to secede ten years later, approved the aims of the Nashville Convention and appointed delegates. Horace Greeley wrote on February 23:

There are sixty members of Congress who this day desire and are plotting to effect the idea of a dissolution of the Union. We have no doubt the Nashville Convention will be held and that the leading purpose of its authors is the separation of the slave states . . . with the formation of an independent confederacy.

Such was the perilous state of the nation in the early months of 1850.

By the end of February, the Senator from Massachusetts had determined upon his course. Only the Clay Compromise, Daniel Webster decided, could avert secession and civil war; and he wrote a friend that he planned "to make an honest truth-telling speech and a Union speech, and discharge a clear conscience." As he set to work preparing his notes, he received abundant warning of the attacks his message would provoke. His constituents and Massachusetts newspapers admonished him strongly not to waver in his consistent antislavery stand, and many urged him to employ still tougher tones against the South. But the Senator from Massachusetts had made up his mind, as he told his friends on March 6, "to push my skiff from the shore alone." He would act according to the creed with which he had challenged the Senate several years earlier:

Inconsistencies of opinion arising from changes of circumstances are often justifiable. But there is one sort of inconsistency that is culpable: it is the inconsistency between a man's conviction and his vote, between his conscience and his conduct. No man shall ever charge me with an inconsistency of that kind.

And so came the 7th of March, 1850, the only day in history which would become the title of a speech delivered on the Senate floor. No one recalls today—no one even recalled in 1851—the formal title Webster gave his address, for it had become the "Seventh of March" speech as much as Independence Day is known as the Fourth of July.

Realizing after months of insomnia that this might be the last great effort his health would permit, Webster stimulated his strength for the speech by oxide of arsenic and other drugs and devoted the morning to polishing up his notes. He was excitedly interrupted by the Sergeant at Arms, who told him that even then—two hours before the Senate was to meet—the chamber, the galleries, the anterooms and even the corridors of the Capitol were filled with those who had been traveling for days from all parts of the nation to hear Daniel Webster. Many foreign diplomats and most of the House of Representatives were among those vying for standing room. As the Senate met, members could scarcely walk to their seats through the crowd of spectators and temporary seats made of public documents stacked on top of each other. Most Senators gave up their seats to ladies and stood in the aisles awaiting Webster's opening blast.

As the Vice President's gavel commenced the session, Senator Walker of Wisconsin, who held the floor to finish a speech begun the day before, told the Chair that "this vast audience has not come to hear me, and there is but one man who can assemble such an audience. They expect to hear him, and I feel it is my duty, as it is my pleasure, to give the floor to the Senator from Massachusetts."

The crowd fell silent as Daniel Webster rose slowly to his feet, all the impressive powers of his extraordinary physical appearance— the great, dark, brooding eyes, the wonderfully bronzed complexion, the majestic domed forehead—commanding the same awe they had commanded for more than thirty years. Garbed in his familiar blue tailed coat with brass buttons, and a buff waistcoat and breeches, he deliberately paused a moment as he gazed about at the greatest assemblage of Senators ever to gather in that chamber—Clay, Benton, Houston, Jefferson Davis, Hale, Bell, Cass, Seward, Chase, Stephen A. Douglas and others. But one face was missing—that of the ailing John C. Calhoun.

All eyes were fixed on the speaker; no spectator save his own son knew what he would say. "I have never before," wrote a newspaper correspondent, "witnessed an occasion on which there was deeper feeling enlisted or more universal anxiety to catch the most distinct echo of the speaker's voice."

In his moments of magnificent inspiration, as Emerson once described him, Webster was truly "the great cannon loaded to the lips." Summoning for the last time that spellbinding oratorical ability, he abandoned his previous opposition to slavery in the territories, abandoned his constituents' abhorrence of the Fugitive Slave Law, abandoned his own place in the history and hearts of his countrymen, and abandoned his last chance for the goal that had eluded him for over twenty years—the Presidency. Daniel Webster preferred to risk his career and his reputation rather than risk the Union.

"Mr. President," he began, "I wish to speak today, not as a Massachusetts man, nor as a Northern man, but as an American and a Member of the Senate of the United States. . . . I speak today for the preservation of the Union. Hear me for my cause."

He had spoken for but a short time when the gaunt, bent form of Calhoun, wrapped in a black cloak, was dramatically assisted into his seat, where he sat trembling, scarcely able to move, and unnoticed by the speaker. After several expressions of regret by Webster that illness prevented the distinguished Senator from South Carolina from being present, Calhoun struggled up, grasping the arms of his chair, and in a clear and ghostly voice proudly announced, "The Senator from South Carolina *is* in his seat." Webster was touched, and with tears in his eyes he extended a bow toward Calhoun, who sank back exhausted and feeble, eyeing the Massachusetts orator with a sphinx-like expression which disclosed no hint of either approval or disapproval.

For three hours and eleven minutes, with only a few references to his extensive notes, Daniel Webster pleaded the Union's cause. Relating the grievances of each side, he asked for conciliation and understanding in the name of patriotism. The Senate's main concern, he insisted, was neither to promote slavery nor to abolish it, but to preserve the United States of America. And with telling logic and remarkable foresight he bitterly attacked the idea of "peaceable secession":

Sir, your eyes and mine are never destined to see that miracle. The dismemberment of this vast country without convulsion! Who is so foolish . . . as to expect to see any such thing? . . . Instead of speaking of the possibility or utility of secession, instead of dwelling in those caverns of darkness, . . . let us enjoy the fresh air of liberty and union. . . . Let us make our generation one of the strongest and brightest links in that golden chain which is destined, I fondly believe, to grapple the people of all the states to this Constitution for ages to come.

There was no applause. Buzzing and astonished whispering, yes, but no applause. Perhaps his hearers were too intent—or too astonished. A reporter rushed to the telegraph office. "Mr. Webster has assumed a great responsibility," he wired his paper, "and whether he succeeds or fails, the courage with which he has come forth at least entitles him to the respect of the country."

Daniel Webster did succeed. Even though his speech was repudiated by many in the North, the very fact that one who represented such a belligerent constituency would appeal for understanding in the name of unity and patriotism was recognized in Washington and throughout the South as a *bona fide* assurance of Southern rights. Despite Calhoun's own intransigence, his Charleston *Mercury* praised Webster's address as "noble in language, generous and conciliatory in tone. Mr. Calhoun's clear and powerful exposition would have had something of a decisive effect if it had not been so soon followed by Mr. Webster's masterly playing." And the New Orleans *Picayune* hailed Webster for "the moral courage to do what he believes to be just in itself and necessary for the peace and safety of the country."

And so the danger of immediate secession and bloodshed passed. As Senator Winthrop remarked, Webster's speech had "disarmed and quieted the South [and] knocked the Nashville Convention into a cocked hat." The *Journal of Commerce* was to remark in later months that "Webster did more than any other man in the whole country, and at a greater hazard of personal popularity, to stem and roll back the torrent of sectionalism which in 1850 threatened to overthrow the pillars of the Constitution and the Union."

Some historians—particularly those who wrote in the latter half of the nineteenth century under the influence of the moral earnestness of Webster's articulate Abolitionist foes—do not agree with Allan Nevins, Henry Steele Commager, Gerald Johnson, and others who have praised the Seventh of March speech as "the highest statesmanship . . . Webster's last great service to the nation." Many deny that secession would have occurred in 1850 without such compromises; and others maintain that subsequent events proved eventual secession was inevitable regardless of what compromises were made. But still others insist that delaying war for ten years narrowed the issues between North and South and in the long run helped preserve the Union. The spirit of conciliation in Webster's speech gave the North the righteous feeling that it had made every attempt to treat the South with fairness, and the defenders of the Union were thus united more strongly against what they felt to be Southern violations of those compromises ten years later. Even from

the military point of view of the North, postponement of the battle for ten years enabled the Northern states to increase tremendously their lead in popularity, voting power, production, and railroads.

Undoubtedly this was understood by many of Webster's supporters, including the business and professional men of Massachusetts who helped distribute hundreds of thousands of copies of the Seventh of March speech throughout the country. It was understood by Daniel Webster, who dedicated the printed copies to the people of Massachusetts with these words: "Necessity compels me to speak true rather than pleasing things. . . . I should indeed like to please you; but I prefer to save you, whatever be your attitude toward me."

But it was not understood by the Abolitionists and Free Soilers of 1850. Few politicians have had the distinction of being scourged by such talented constituents. The Rev. Theodore Parker, heedless of the dangers of secession, who had boasted of harboring a fugitive slave in his cellar and writing his sermons with a sword over his ink stand and a pistol in his desk "loaded and ready for defense," denounced Webster in merciless fashion from his pulpit, an attack he would continue even after Webster's death: "No living man has done so much," he cried, "to debauch the conscience of the nation. . . . I know of no deed in American history done by a son of New England to which I can compare this, but the act of Benedict Arnold." "Webster," said Horace Mann, "is a fallen star! Lucifer descending from Heaven!" Longfellow asked the world: "Is it possible? Is this the Titan who hurled mountains at Hayne years ago?" And Emerson proclaimed that "Every drop of blood in that man's veins has eyes that look downward. . . . Webster's absence of moral faculty is degrading to the country." To William Cullen Bryant, Webster was "a man who has deserted the cause which he lately defended, and deserted it under circumstances which force upon him the imputation of a sordid motive." And to James Russell Lowell he was "the most meanly and foolishly treacherous man I ever heard of."

Charles Sumner, who would be elevated to the Senate upon his departure, enrolled the name of Webster on "the dark list of apostates. Mr. Webster's elaborate treason has done more than anything else to break down the North." Senator William H. Seward, the brilliant "Conscience" Whig, called Webster a "traitor to the cause of freedom." A mass meeting in Faneuil Hall condemned the speech as "unworthy of a wise statesman and a good man," and resolved that "Constitution or no Constitution, law or no law, we will not allow a fugitive slave to be taken from the state of Massachusetts." As the Massachusetts Legislature enacted further resolutions wholly contrary to the spirit of the Seventh of March speech, one member called Webster "a recreant son of Massachusetts who misrepresents her in the Senate"; and another stated that "Daniel Webster will be a fortunate man if God, in his sparing mercy, shall preserve his life long enough for him to repent of this act and efface this stain on his name."

The Boston *Courier* pronounced that it was "unable to find that any Northern Whig member of Congress concurs with Mr. Webster"; and his old defender, the Boston *Atlas*, stated, "His sentiments are not our sentiments nor we venture to say of the Whigs of New England." The New York *Tribune* considered it "unequal to the occasion and unworthy of its author"; the New York *Evening Post* spoke in terms of a "traitorous retreat . . . a man who deserted the cause which he lately defended"; and the Abolitionist press called it "the scarlet infamy of Daniel Webster. . . . An indescribably base and wicked speech."

Edmund Quincy spoke bitterly of the "ineffable meanness of the lion turned spaniel in his fawnings on the masters whose hands he was licking for the sake of the dirty puddings they might have to toss to him." And finally, the name of Daniel Webster was humiliated for all time in the literature of our land by the cutting words of the usually gentle John Greenleaf Whittier in his immortal poem "Ichabod":

So fallen! so lost! the light withdrawn
   Which once he wore!
The glory from his gray hairs gone
   Forevermore! . . .

Of all we loved and honored, naught
   Save power remains;
A fallen angel's pride of thought,
   Still strong in chains. . . .

Then pay the reverence of old days
   To his dead fame;
Walk backward, with averted gaze,
   And hide the shame!

Years afterward, Whittier was to recall that he penned this acid verse "in one of the saddest moments of my life." And for Daniel Webster, the arrogant, scornful giant of the ages who believed himself above political rancor, Whittier's attack was especially bitter. To some extent he had attempted to shrug off his attackers, stating that he had expected to be libeled and abused, particularly by the Abolitionists and intellectuals who had previously scorned him, much as George Washington and others before him had been abused. To those who urged a prompt reply, he merely related the story of the old deacon in a similar predicament who told his friends, "I always make it a rule never to clean up the path until the snow is done falling."

But he was saddened by the failure of a single other New England Whig to rise to his defense, and he remarked that he was

engaged in a controversy in which I have neither a leader nor a follower from among my own immediate friends. . . . I am tired of standing up here, almost alone from Massachusetts, contending for practical measures absolutely essential to the good of the country. . . . For five months . . . no one of my colleagues manifested the slightest concurrence in my sentiments. . . . Since the 7th of March there has not been an hour in which I have not felt a crushing weight of anxiety. I have sat down to no breakfast or dinner to which I have brought an unconcerned and easy mind.

But, although he sought to explain his objectives and reassure his friends of his continued opposition to slavery, he nevertheless insisted he would

stand on the principle of my speech to the end. . . . If necessary I will take the stump in every village in New England. . . . What is to come of the present commotion in men's minds I cannot foresee; but my own convictions of duty are fixed and strong, and I shall continue to follow those convictions without faltering. . . . In highly excited times it is far easier to fan and feed the flames of discord, than to subdue them; and he who

counsels moderation is in danger of being regarded as failing in his duty to his party.

And the following year, despite his seventy years, Webster went on extended speaking tours defending his position: "If the chances had been one in a thousand that Civil War would be the result, I should still have felt that thousandth chance should be guarded against by any reasonable sacrifice." When his efforts—and those of Clay, Douglas, and others—on behalf of compromise were ultimately successful, he noted sarcastically that many of his colleagues were now saying "They always meant to stand by the Union to the last."

But Daniel Webster was doomed to disappointment in his hopes that this latent support might again enable him to seek the Presidency. For his speech had so thoroughly destroyed those prospects that the recurring popularity of his position could not possibly satisfy the great masses of voters in New England and the North. He could not receive the Presidential nomination he had so long desired; but neither could he ever put to rest the assertion, which was not only expressed by his contemporary critics but subsequently by several nineteenth-century historians, that his real objective in the Seventh of March speech was a bid for Southern support for the Presidency.

But this "profound selfishness," which Emerson was so certain the speech represented, could not have entered into Daniel Webster's motivations. "Had he been bidding for the Presidency," as Professor Nevins points out, "he would have trimmed his phrases and inserted weasel-words upon New Mexico and the fugitive slaves. The first precaution of any aspirant for the Presidency is to make sure of his own state and section; and Webster knew that his speech would send echoes of denunciation leaping from Mount Mansfield to Monamoy Light." Moreover, Webster was sufficiently acute politically to know that a divided party such as his would turn away from politically controversial figures and move to an uncommitted neutral individual, a principle consistently applied to this day. And the 1852 Whig Convention followed exactly this course. After the pro-compromise vote had been divided for fifty-two ballots between Webster and President Fillmore, the convention turned to the popular General Winfield Scott. Not a single Southern Whig supported Webster. And when the Boston Whigs urged that the party platform take credit for the Clay Compromise, of which, they said, "Daniel Webster, with the concurrence of Henry Clay and other profound statesmen, was the author," Senator Corwin of Ohio was reported to have commented sarcastically, "And I, with the concurrence of Moses and some extra help, wrote the Ten Commandments."

So Daniel Webster, who neither could have intended his speech as an improvement of his political popularity nor permitted his ambitions to weaken his plea for the Union, died a disappointed and discouraged death in 1852, his eyes fixed on the flag flying from the mast of the sailboat he had anchored in view of his bedroom window. But to the very end he was true to character, asking on his deathbed, "Wife, children, doctor, I trust on this occasion I have said nothing unworthy of Daniel Webster." And to the end he had been true to the Union, and to his greatest act of courageous principle; for in his last words to the Senate, Webster had written his own epitaph:

I shall stand by the Union . . . with absolute disregard of personal consequences. What are personal consequences . . . in comparison with the good or evil which may befall a great country in a crisis like this? . . . Let the consequences be what they will, I am careless. No man can suffer too much, and no man can fall too soon, if he suffer or if he fall in defense of the liberties and Constitution of his country.

· QUESTIONS ·

1. State in one sentence your understanding of Webster's "act of courage."
2. What is the stylistic effect gained by the narrative opening of this profile?
3. What parallels and contrasts do you find in this biographical sketch and "The Devil and Daniel Webster"?
4. Comment on the author's technique in playing up the drama of Webster's actual delivery of the famed speech.
5. Have you ever heard a speaker who moved, excited, and aroused you? Who? Why? How?
6. What can you find out about Webster's "peculiar tastes"?
7. "Few meetings in American history have ever been so productive or so ironic in their consequences." Can you comment on meetings other than the Clay-Webster one which were probably highly dramatic, whether or not productive and ironic?

8. What do *you* think of Webster, his oratory, his character, his place in American history?

Theme Subjects: (1) Webster Was (Was Not) Really a Courageous Man; (2) Here's Someone More Courageous Than Daniel Webster; (3) A Review of *Profiles in Courage;* (4) The Seventh of March Speech (an investigative paper); (5) What I Consider the Most Courageous Act in American History; (6) The Most Courageous Act I Ever Witnessed.

THE STORY OF MY LIFE

Helen Keller

HELEN (ADAMS) KELLER (1880–   ) was born in Tuscumbia, Alabama. As a consequence of illness she has been blind and deaf since the age of 19 months, but as the result of long training (the beginning of which is recounted in the selection which follows) she has become a lecturer on behalf of the blind and deaf throughout the world. One of the great women of the twentieth (or any other) century, Miss Keller holds numerous honorary degrees and has received the acclaim of millions of people, high and low, during her long and useful lifetime.

The most important day I remember in all my life is the one on which my teacher, Anne Mansfield Sullivan, came to me. I am filled with wonder when I consider the immeasurable contrasts between the two lives which it connects. It was the third of March, 1887, three months before I was seven years old.

On the afternoon of that eventful day, I stood on the porch, dumb, expectant. I guessed vaguely from my mother's signs and from the hurrying to and fro in the house that something unusual was about to happen, so I went to the door and waited on the steps. The afternoon sun penetrated the mass of honeysuckle that covered the porch, and fell on my upturned face. My fingers lingered almost unconsciously on the familiar leaves and blossoms which had just come forth to greet the sweet southern spring. I did not know what the future held of marvel or surprise for me. Anger and bitterness had preyed upon me continually for weeks, and a deep languor had succeeded this passionate struggle.

Have you ever been at sea in a dense fog, when it seemed as if a tangible white darkness shut you in, and the great ship, tense and anxious, groped her way toward the shore with plummet and sounding-line, and you waited with beating heart for something to happen? I was like that ship before my education began, only I was without compass or sounding-line and had no way of knowing how near the harbour was. "Light! give me light!" was the wordless cry of my soul, and the light of love shone on me in that very hour.

I felt approaching footsteps. I stretched out my hand as I supposed to my mother. Some one took it, and I was caught up and held close in the arms of her who had come to reveal all things to me, and, more than all things else, to love me.

The morning after my teacher came she led me into her room and gave me a doll. The little blind children at the Perkins Institution had sent it and Laura Bridgman had dressed it; but I did not know this until afterward. When I had played with it a little while, Miss Sullivan slowly spelled into my hand the word "d-o-l-l." I was at once interested in this finger play and tried to imitate it. When I finally succeeded in making the letters correctly I was flushed with childish pleasure and pride. Running downstairs to my mother I held up my hand and made the letters for doll. I did not know that I was spelling a word or even

that words existed; I was simply making my fingers go in monkey-like imitation. In the days that followed I learned to spell in this uncomprehending way a great many words, among them *pin, hat, cup* and a few verbs like *sit, stand,* and *walk.* But my teacher had been with me several weeks before I understood that everything has a name.

One day, while I was playing with my new doll, Miss Sullivan put my big rag doll into my lap also, spelled "d-o-l-l" and tried to make me understand that "d-o-l-l" applied to both. Earlier in the day we had had a tussle over the words "m-u-g" and "w-a-t-e-r." Miss Sullivan had tried to impress it upon me that "m-u-g" is *mug* and that "w-a-t-e-r" is *water,* but I persisted in confounding the two. In despair she had dropped the subject for the time, only to renew it at the first opportunity. I became impatient at her repeated attempts and, seizing the new doll, I dashed it upon the floor. I was keenly delighted when I felt the fragments of the broken doll at my feet. Neither sorrow nor regret followed my passionate outburst. I had not loved the doll. In the still, dark world in which I lived there was no strong sentiment or tenderness. I felt my teacher sweep the fragments to one side of the hearth, and I had a sense of satisfaction that the cause of my discomfort was removed. She brought me my hat, and I knew I was going out into the warm sunshine. This thought, if a wordless sensation may be called a thought, made me hop and skip with pleasure.

We walked down the path to the well-house, attracted by the fragrance of the honeysuckle with which it was covered. Someone was drawing water, and my teacher placed my hand under the spout. As the cool stream gushed over one hand she spelled into the other the word *water,* first slowly, then rapidly. I stood still, my whole attention fixed upon the motions of her fingers. Suddenly I felt a misty consciousness as of something forgotten —a thrill of returning thought; and somehow the mystery of language was revealed to me. I knew then that "w-a-t-e-r" meant the wonderful cool something that was flowing over my hand. That living word awakened my soul, gave it light, hope, joy, set it free! There were barriers still, it is true, but barriers that could in time be swept away.

I left the well-house eager to learn. Everything had a name, and each name gave birth to a new thought. As we returned to the house, every object which I touched seemed to quiver with life. That was because I saw everything with the strange, new sight that had come to me. On entering the door I remembered the doll I had broken. I felt my way to the hearth and picked up the pieces. I tried vainly to put them together. Then my eyes filled with tears; for I realized what I had done, and for the first time I felt repentance and sorrow.

I learned a great many new words that day. I do not remember what they all were; but I do know that *mother, father, sister, teacher* were among them—words that were to make the world blossom for me, "like Aaron's rod, with flowers." It would have been difficult to find a happier child than I was as I lay in my crib at the close of that eventful day and lived over the joys it had brought me, and for the first time longed for a new day to come.

I recall many incidents of the summer of 1887 that followed my soul's sudden awakening. I did nothing but explore with my hands and learn the name of every object that I touched; and the more I handled things and learned their names and uses, the more joyous and confident grew my sense of kinship with the rest of the world.

When the time of daisies and buttercups came, Miss Sullivan took me by the hand across the fields, where men were preparing the earth for the seed, to the banks of the Tennessee River, and there, sitting on the warm grass, I had my first lessons in the beneficence of nature. I learned how the sun and the rain make to grow out of the ground every tree that is pleasant to the sight and good for food, how birds build their nests and live and thrive from land to land, how the squirrel, the deer, the lion, and every other creature finds food and shelter. As my knowledge of things grew, I felt more and more the delight of the world I was in. Long before I learned to do a sum in arithmetic or describe the shape of the earth, Miss Sullivan had taught me to find beauty in the fragrant woods, in every blade of grass, and in the curves and dimples of my baby sister's hand. She linked my earliest thoughts with nature and made me feel that "birds and flowers and I were happy peers."

But about this time I had an experience which taught me that nature is not always kind. One day my teacher and I were returning from a long ramble. The morning had been fine, but it was growing warm and sultry when at last we turned our faces homeward. Two or three times we stopped to rest under a tree by the wayside. Our last halt was under a wild cherry tree a short distance from the house. The shade was grateful, and the tree was so easy to climb that with my teacher's assistance I was able to scramble to a seat in the branches. It was so cool up in the tree that Miss Sullivan proposed that we have our luncheon there. I promised to keep still while she went to the house to fetch it.

Suddenly a change passed over the tree. All the sun's warmth left the air. I knew the sky was black, because all the heat, which meant light to me, had died out of the atmosphere. A strange odour came up from the earth. I knew it, it was the odour that always precedes a thunderstorm, and a nameless fear clutched at my heart. I felt absolutely alone, cut off from my friends and the firm earth. The immense, the unknown, enfolded me. I remained still and expectant; a chilling terror crept over me. I longed for my teacher's return; but above all things I wanted to get down from that tree.

There was a moment of sinister silence, then a multitudinous stirring of the leaves. A shiver ran through the tree, and the wind sent forth a blast that would have knocked me off had I not clung to the branch with might and main. The tree swayed and strained. The small twigs snapped and fell about me in showers. A wild impulse to jump seized me, but terror held me fast. I crouched down in the fork of the tree. The branches lashed about me. I felt the intermittent jarring that came now and then, as if something heavy had fallen and the shock had traveled up till it reached the limb I sat on. It worked my suspense up to the highest point, and just as I was thinking the tree and I should fall together, my teacher seized my hand and helped me down. I clung to her, trembling with joy to feel the earth under my feet once more. I had learned a new lesson—that nature "wages open war against her children, and under softest touch hides treacherous claws."

After this experience it was a long time before I climbed another tree. The mere thought filled me with terror. It was the sweet allurement of the mimosa tree in full bloom that finally overcame my fears. One beautiful spring morning when I was alone in the summerhouse, reading, I became aware of a wonderful subtle fragrance in the air. I started up and instinctively stretched out my hands. It seemed as if the spirit of spring had passed through the summer-house. "What is it?" I asked, and the next minute I recognized the odour of the mimosa blossoms. I felt my way to the end of the garden, knowing that the mimosa tree was near the fence, at the turn of the path. Yes, there it was, all quivering in the warm sunshine, its blossom-laden branches almost touching the long grass. Was there ever anything so exquisitely beautiful in the world before! Its delicate blossoms shrank from the slightest earthly touch; it seemed as if a tree of paradise had been transplanted to earth. I made my way through a shower of petals to the great trunk and for one minute stood irresolute; then, putting my foot in the broad space between the forked branches, I pulled myself up into the tree. I had some difficulty in holding on, for the branches were very large and the bark hurt my hands. But I had a delicious sense that I was doing something unusual and wonderful, so I kept on climbing higher and higher, until I reached a little seat which somebody had built there so long ago that it had grown part of the tree itself. I sat there for a long, long time, feeling like a fairy on a rosy cloud. After that I spent many happy hours in my tree of paradise, thinking fair thoughts and dreaming bright dreams.

I had now the key to all language, and I was eager to learn to use it. Children who hear acquire language without any particular effort; the words that fall from others' lips they catch on the wing, as it were, delightedly, while the little deaf child must trap them by a slow and often painful process. But whatever the process, the result is wonderful. Gradually from naming an object we advance step by step until we have traversed the vast distance between our first stammered syllable and the sweep of thought in a line of Shakespeare.

At first, when my teacher told me about a new thing I asked very few questions. My ideas were vague, and my vocabulary was inadequate; but as my knowledge of things grew, and I learned more and more words, my field of inquiry broadened, and I would return again and again to the same subject, eager for further information. Sometimes a new word revived an image that some earlier experience had engraved on my brain.

I remember the morning that I first asked the meaning of the word *love*. This was before I knew many words. I had found a few early violets in the garden and brought them to my teacher. She tried to kiss me: but at that time I did not like to have any one kiss me except my mother. Miss Sullivan put her arm gently round me and spelled into my hand, "I love Helen."

"What is love?" I asked.

She drew me closer to her and said, "It is here," pointing to my heart, whose beats I was conscious of for the first time. Her words puzzled me very much because I did not then understand anything unless I touched it.

I smelt the violets in her hand and asked, half in words, half in signs, a question which meant, "Is love the sweetness of flowers?"

"No," said my teacher.

Again I thought. The warm sun was shining on us.

"Is this not love?" I asked, pointing in the direction from which the heat came. "Is this not love?"

It seemed to me that there could be nothing more beautiful than the sun, whose warmth makes all things grow. But Miss Sullivan shook her head, and I was greatly puzzled and disappointed. I thought it strange that my teacher could not show me love.

A day or two afterward I was stringing beads of different sizes in symmetrical groups—two large beads, three small ones, and so on. I had made many mistakes, and Miss Sullivan had pointed them out again and again with gentle patience. Finally I noticed a very obvious error in the sequence and for an instant I concentrated my attention on the lesson and tried to think how I should have arranged the beads. Miss Sullivan touched my forehead and spelled with decided emphasis, "Think."

In a flash I knew that the word was the name of the process that was going on in my head. This was my first conscious perception of an abstract idea.

For a long time I was still—I was not thinking of the beads in my lap, but trying to find a meaning for "love" in the light of this new idea. The sun had been under a cloud all day, and there had been brief showers; but suddenly the sun broke forth in all its southern splendour.

Again I asked my teacher, "Is this not love?"

"Love is something like the clouds that were in the sky before the sun came out," she replied. Then in simpler words than these, which at that time I could not have understood, she explained: "You cannot touch the clouds, you know; but you feel the rain and know how glad the flowers and the thirsty earth are to have it after a hot day. You cannot touch love either; but you feel the sweetness that it pours into everything. Without love you would not be happy or want to play."

The beautiful truth burst upon my mind—I felt that there were invisible lines stretched between my spirit and the spirits of others.

From the beginning of my education Miss Sullivan made it a practice to speak to me as she would speak to any hearing child; the only difference was that she spelled the sentences into my hand instead of speaking them. If I did not know the words and idioms necessary to express my thoughts, she supplied them, even suggesting conversation when I was unable to keep up my end of the dialogue.

This process was continued for several years; for the deaf child does not learn in a month, or even in two or three years, the numberless idioms and expressions used in the simplest daily intercourse. The little hearing child learns these from constant repetition and imitation. The conversation he hears in his home stimulates his mind and suggests topics and calls forth the spontaneous expression of his own thoughts. This natural exchange of ideas is denied to the deaf child. My teacher, realizing this, determined to supply the kinds of stimulus I lacked. This she did by repeating to me as far as possible, verbatim, what she heard, and by showing me how I could take part in the conversation. But it was a long time before I ventured to take the initiative and still longer before I could find something appropriate to say at the right time.

The deaf and the blind find it very difficult to acquire the amenities of conversation. How much more this difficulty must be augmented in the case of those who are both deaf and blind! They cannot distinguish the tone of the voice or, without assistance, go up and down the gamut of tones that give significance to words; nor can they watch the expression of the speaker's face, and a look is often the very soul of what one says.

· QUESTIONS ·

1. It is difficult to keep remembering that the author of this selection is blind. What internal evidence is there that, although she is blind, she actually "sees"?
2. This autobiography is largely narrative and descriptive. Point out specifically expository elements.
3. Comment on the stylistic effectiveness of the incident of the storm.
4. What, if anything, do you find remarkable in the incident concerning the mimosa?
5. Make an outline (topic or sentence, as directed) of this selection.

6. What kind of order does Miss Keller use in this portion of her autobiography?
7. What is your reaction to Miss Sullivan?
8. Does Miss Keller qualify for a "profile in courage," as developed by John F. Kennedy?

Theme Subjects: (1) "A Look Is Often the Very Soul of What One Says"; (2) A Blind Person Whom I Know; (3) Blindness Is Not the Worst Handicap, _____ Is; (4) Van Wyck Brooks' Opinion of Miss Keller; (5) The Results of Miss Keller's Work for the Blind (an investigative theme); (6) A School for the Blind-Deaf; (7) Helen Keller and Albert Schweitzer (parallel character sketches); (8) My Definition of Love.

HELEN KELLER

Van Wyck Brooks

VAN WYCK BROOKS (1886–1963) was born in Plainfield, New Jersey, and educated at Harvard. The holder of honorary doctorates from several colleges and universities, he was a distinguished literary and social historian and critic. The author of many important books, he is perhaps best known for his five-volume history of literary life in America: *The Flowering of New England* (1936); *New England: Indian Summer* (1940); *The World of Washington Irving* (1944); *The Times of Melville and Whitman* (1947); and *The Confident Years* (1951). Later works are *Scenes and Portraits* (1953); *Days of the Phoenix* (1957); *From the Shadow of the Mountain* (1961); and *Fenollosa and His Circle* (1962).

I

When I was in St. Augustine, Florida, in the winter of 1932, Helen Keller appeared at the Cathedral Lyceum, and I went to see and hear her there, drawn by curiosity, such as one feels for any world-famous person. For Helen Keller was not only famous but she had been so from the age of ten, when she had sat on Edward Everett Hale's knee and Queen Victoria asked Phillips Brooks about her. A ship was named after her in 1890, and, while Oliver Wendell Holmes had published a letter of hers in one of his books,

From *Harper's Magazine*, May, 1954. Reprinted by permission of the author.

she had visited Whittier in his house on the Merrimac River. President Grover Cleveland had received her in the White House, as other presidents were to do in after years, and Mark Twain had said that the two most interesting characters of the nineteenth century were, quite simply, Napoleon and Helen Keller. Yet there she was in St. Augustine, still young, in 1932, and here she continues to be twenty-two years later.

I remember one phrase she uttered then, interpreted by her companion (for, never having heard her own voice, her speech was turbid): a phrase referring to the subway in New York that "opened its jaws like a great beast," which struck me at the moment as reminiscent of the prophets in the Bible. I was not aware then how steeped she was in the language of the Bible, which I later heard her expound with Biblical scholars; nor did I know how familiar she was, literally, with the jaws of beasts, for she had once stroked a lion's mouth. The lion, it is true, was young and well fed in advance, but nevertheless she entered its cage boldly; for her "teacher," as she always called Anne Sullivan, the extraordinary woman who developed her mind, wished her to meet experiences of every sort.

The daughter of a Confederate officer, Miss Keller was born on an Alabama farm and knew cows, mules, and horses from her earliest childhood; they had eaten apples from her hand and never harmed her; and her teacher, feeling that she should know wild animals as well, introduced her early to the zoo of a circus. She shook hands with a bear, she patted a leopard, she was lifted up to feel the ears of a giraffe. She encouraged elephants to wind their trunks about her neck, and big

snakes wrapped their coils about her, so that Helen Keller, for this reason partly, grew up without fear, and she has remained both physically and morally fearless. The only animals she has not touched are the panther and the tiger, for the tiger is "wanton," as I once heard her say, an appropriate word but characteristic of a mind that has been fed from books instead of the give-and-take of everyday talk.

At that time I knew little of Helen Keller's life and mind, and I could not have guessed that a few years later I was to be her neighbor, seeing her often. My old friend the sculptor Jo Davidson brought us together, just as her own feeling for sculpture had drawn her to Jo Davidson, because Helen Keller "saw" with her hands. She has "ten eyes for sculpture," as Professor Gaetano Salvemini said when, in 1950, she visited Florence, and he arranged for her to see Michelangelo's Medici tombs and the sculpture of Donatello in the Bargello. Salvemini had movable scaffolds set up so that she could pass her hands over the Medici heads and St. John the Baptist, the figures of Night and Day and the Madonna and Child; and our friend Jo, who was present, said he had never seen these sculptures before as when he watched her hands wandering over the forms. She peered as it were into every crevice and the subtlest modulations; exclaiming with pleasure as she divined the open mouth of the singing youth and murmuring over the suckling infant, "Innocent greed!" She had quoted in *The World I Live In* a saying of Ghiberti about some sculptured figure he had seen in Rome, that "its most exquisite beauties could not be discovered by the sight but only by the touch of the hand passed over it." To how much else and to how many others her "seeing hand" has led her first or last! It has been her passport to the world outside her.

For the world in which she lives herself is built of touch-sensations, devoid of physical color and devoid of sound, and she has written much about the hand by which she lives and which takes the place of the hearing and sight of others. Exploring the faces of her friends and people whom she has just met, she reads them as if she were clairvoyant, and she can distinguish the Yankee twang and the Southern drawl she has never heard by touching two or three spots on the throats of the speakers.

She says that hands are quite as easy to recognize as faces and reveal the secrets of the character more openly, in fact, and she can tell from hands at once whether people have large natures or whether they have only "dormouse valor." In the soft smooth roundness of certain hands, especially of the rich who have never known toil, she feels a certain chaos of the undeveloped; and, in her land of darkness and silence, she can feel with her own hands the beautiful, the strong, the weak, the comic.

She had early learned geography from maps that her teacher made out of clay or sand on the banks of the Tennessee River, feeling mountains and valleys and following the course of other rivers, and she relates in *The Story of My Life* how, in 1893, she virtually saw with her fingers the World's Fair in Chicago. It is true that the inventor of the telephone, Alexander Graham Bell, one of her early admirers, was there with her and described to her some of the sights in the deaf-and-dumb "system," but he had arranged for her to touch all the objects in the bazaars, the relics of ancient Mexico, the Viking ship. She had taken in with her finger tips the Arabian Nights of the fair as she had learned to read from the raised letters of Braille.

It is natural that Helen Keller has dwelt at length in her books on the hand by which alone the blind are able to see. She very early dedicated her own life to the cause of the education of the blind—doubly handicapped as she was and the only one so handicapped who has ever become a thoroughly well-educated person. (The only possible exception is Robert Smithdas, who graduated from St. John's University in 1952.) Because she was handicapped, because two of her senses were cut off, nature augmented her three remaining senses, not the sense of touch alone but the sense of taste and the sense of smell, which others regard, she says, as a "fallen angel."

In her these are all exceptionally acute and alert. She tells in her *Journal* how in London, passing through a gate, she knew at once by the smell of burning leaves, with the smell of the grass, that she was in Green Park, and she says she can always distinguish Fifth Avenue from humbler New York streets by the odors issuing from the doors as she walks past. She knows the cosmetics that women are using and the kind of coffee they are roasting within and whether they use candles and burn soft coal or wood, just as she recognized St. Louis from the smell of the breweries miles away and Peoria from the smell of the whisky stills. "Listening" with her feet, she says, in a hotel dining-room, she knows the moods and characters of people who walk past her, whether they are firm or indecisive, active or lazy, careless, timid, weary, angry, or sad; and she will exclaim, "What lovely white lilacs!", knowing they are white by touch or smell, for in texture and perfume white lilacs differ from purple. Sometimes, hearing her say these things, I have thought of Edward Sheldon, my blind friend who remarked to Cornelia Otis Skinner, "Your hair is dark, isn't it? I can tell from your voice." Helen Keller, who cannot hear voices, feels vibrations. When an orchestra plays, she follows the music waves along the floor; and, detecting on her desk upstairs the vibration of the bell from the pantry below, she answers with a shuffle of the feet, "Coming down!"

All this gave rise in early years to legends of a "wonder girl" that always annoyed Helen Keller—for she is the embodiment of humor and simple good sense—as well as to rumors in Europe that she was the last word in "American bluff," which led to various efforts to discredit and expose her. The girl who had "found the Blue Bird," as Maeterlinck put it, was said never to be tired or discouraged or sad, and all sorts of supernatural faculties were attributed to her, especially the gift of making uncanny predictions.

But, while Anne Sullivan took pains to keep her from being a prodigy, and no one found anything to expose, it was impossible to conceal the fact that she had a remarkable mind and even perhaps a still more remarkable will. Speaking of this, Emma Goldman said she proved that the human will had "an almost illimitable power"; and what could one say of an intellect as handicapped as hers that, at eighteen, carried her so far in so many directions? If she did not master, she learned much of geometry, algebra, physics, with botany, zoology, and the philosophy that she knew well, while she wrote good letters in French, as later she spoke German, reading Latin too when she went to college. Unable to hear lectures or take notes, she graduated with honors at Radcliffe, where she wrote her autobiography in the class of Mr. Copeland, the famous "Copey" who said she showed that she could write better, in some of her work, than any other man or woman he had had as a pupil.

It was Anne Sullivan who had invented the methods of connecting mind with mind that made all this possible, of course—and that seemed to be "superhuman," as Einstein remarked; although Helen all but outstripped her perceptive teacher and retained all that she took in. Few of the required books were printed for the blind, and she had to have whole books spelled into her hand, while, always examining, observing, reflecting, surrounded by darkness and silence, she wrote that she found music and brightness within. Through all her thoughts flashed what she supposed was color. With her native traits of pluck and courage, energy, tenacity, she was tough-minded and independent also, and her only fear was of writing something that she had been told or that she had read, something that was not out of her own life and mind.

II

This was the girl who had evolved from the headstrong child whom Anne Sullivan had found in Alabama and whom she had taken at the age of eight to the Perkins Institution in Boston where Helen afterward visited off and on. There she encountered Laura Bridgman, the first deaf-and-dumb person who had ever been taught to communicate with her fellow-creatures, Dr. Howe's celebrated pupil whom Dickens had written about and who was a contrast indeed to the "young colt" Helen. Laura Bridgman was shocked, in fact, by her impulsive movements and rebuked her for being too forward, robust as she was, while the statue-like motionless Laura, with her cool hands, struck Helen as like a flower that has grown in the shade.

A much more interesting personality, and ruddily healthy from the start, Helen herself was to grow up fond of sports, riding a horse and a bicycle tandem, playing cards and chess and all but completely self-reliant. Moreover, she was never guarded from the knowledge of evil, and, fully informed as she always was about the seamy sides of life, the mind that she developed was realistic. Nothing could have been more tonic than Helen Keller's bringing up, under the guidance of Anne Sullivan, on the farm in Alabama. They read and studied out of doors on the river bank, in the woods, in the fields, in the shade, as Helen remembered, of a wild tulip tree, and the fragrance of the mimosa blossoms, the pine needles, and the grapes were blended with all her early lessons. She learned about the sun and rain, and how birds build their nests, about squirrels, frogs, wild flowers, rabbits, and insects; and, as it came back to her, everything that sang or bloomed, buzzed or hummed as part of her education.

It might have been supposed, meanwhile, that the Perkins Institution also influenced Helen in various ways, for she carried through life what seemed to be the stamp of the reformist mind that the great Dr. Howe represented. An old Yankee abolitionist, Samuel Gridley Howe was concerned for all the desolate and all the oppressed, and Helen has written with the same indignation and grief about lynching and anti-Semitism and the case of Sacco and Vanzetti. Usually on the unpopular side, and for years a follower of Debs, she was almost a social outcast in certain circles when Mark Twain, who hated injustice— and was a special friend of hers —said there were worse things than being blind. It was worse to have eyes and not to see. Helen liked Mark Twain all the better because, as she wrote in *Midstream,* he did not temper his words to suit feminine ears, because "his talk was fragrant with tobacco and flamboyant with profanity," while, with his tender heart, he matched her tough mind. It pleased her when, bidding her good night, he said she would find in the bathroom not only bourbon and Scotch but plenty of cigars.

Helen's realism, along with her social imagination, developed in her the planetary mind, so that on her tours to help the blind in all the six continents she has read in every country the signs of the times. With an outlook that was molded more or less by Emerson and Whitman, along with the New Church doctrines that are her religion—for she was early convinced by Swedenborg's writings—she has become a world citizen who stands for the real America that public men so often misrepresent. She has understood Japan and Greece and especially perhaps the Bible lands, Egypt,

Lebanon, Syria, Israel, where she has lectured at universities from Cairo to Jerusalem and where new schools for the blind have risen as she passed. Reaching out to meet the minds of all sorts and conditions of men, she comprehends their needs and aspirations, so that she is a true spokesman of our multiracial country that is already a vestibule of the coming "one world."

III

Now it happens that, living myself in Connecticut, not far from Helen Keller, I have taken a few notes about her in recent years, jotting down chance remarks of hers and other memoranda, comments that from time to time she has suggested. I offer some of these, unconnected as they are, as follows:

July 1945

Helen has been out picking blueberries today. She has only to touch them to know when they are ripe.

The paths and garden at her house are all so perfectly kept that I exclaimed over them. Helen does it. In summer she is up at five every morning, edging the driveway and the paths. She asks Herbert [Herbert Haas, who drives the car and runs the house] what she should do next. Then she weeds the flower beds. She distinguishes by touch between the flowers and the weeds.

Helen comes to dinner, bringing her checkerboard for a little game.

I had happened on a poem, "To Helen Keller" by Edmund Clarence Stedman, published in 1888, fifty-seven years ago. Richard Watson Gilder also addressed a poem to her, and both these poets had written sonnets and odes to Lincoln at the time of his death. Now, halfway through another century, Helen looks at

times, and even very often, like a young girl. How many poems were written to her by Robert Frost and others in the good old days when poetry was still "public."

Dinner with Helen and Salvemini at Professor Robert Pfeiffer's. Our Florentine hostess Mrs. Pfeiffer played an Italian song. Helen stood by with her left hand on the piano top, waving her right hand, keeping time. In this way she knows by heart Beethoven's "Ninth Symphony" and recognizes many other compositions.

Someone asked her how she tells the difference between day and night. "Oh," she said, "in the day the air is lighter, odors are lighter, and there is more motion and more vibration in the atmosphere. At night there is less vibration; the air is dense and one feels less motion in things."

With Helen and Polly Thomson [Anne Sullivan's successor] in New York, at a small political meeting in the Hotel Astor. Maury Maverick was with us, just back from England, marveling over the work of the English surgeons in the war. Vice-President Truman had come up from Washington to make a short speech, and we were all introduced to him.[1] Later Helen said, "He has an open hand. There are no crooks in his fingers." She grasps character instantly. Truman was deeply touched by Helen. He was in tears when she spoke to him.

September 1945

Today, more than usually, an air of Scotland pervades Helen's house. In the first place, it is called Arcan Ridge after an old farmhouse in the Scottish Highlands, and Polly Thomson, who has been with Helen since 1914, speaks with a livelier than ever Scottish accent. But this evening William Allan Neilson comes to dinner, the president of Smith College who was one of Helen's professors at Rad-

---

[1] Actually, Truman had become President on April 12, 1945. (Editor's note.)

cliffe and learned the manual alphabet to talk with her there. (He was one of my old professors at Harvard too, and now he is the only person living who, meeting me, aged sixty, invariably addresses me as "Boy.") Neilson still speaks broad Scots, almost every word with "hair on it," as Rudolph Ruzicka said of another Scotsman.

After dinner the talk fell on Scottish songs. Helen went upstairs to her study—for she knows her way perfectly about the house—and brought down a two-volume collection of Scottish songs in Braille which the publishers in Edinburgh had sent her. She read the table of contents with her fingers rapidly, found a song she wanted, turned the pages and read it out to us—a Highland "wail from Skye," as Polly put it.

With Helen and Polly to the harvest festival at the Jewish Theological Seminary far uptown in New York. Midday meal in the Sukkah, the festival tent set up in the quadrangle. The walls were hung with all the fruits of the season, or all the fruits of the Holy Land that are mentioned in the Bible. We sat with the president of the Seminary, Dr. Louis Finkelstein, and the famous Hebrew scholar, Dr. Saul Lieberman. For a moment I thought of the New Testament scene in the Temple at Jerusalem, for Helen surprised these great Jewish doctors with her knowledge of the Bible. I remembered what she wrote in *Midstream:* she had read her Braille Bible so often that in many places the dots had been rubbed off.

Listening to the Hebrew grace with her fingers on Dr. Finkelstein's lips, she said, "It is like the voice of the Lord upon many waters, the Lord of Glory, thundering."

Then she said, "The Bible is the only book that reaches up to the times in which we live. It speaks knowingly of the sun, the skies, the sea, and the beauty of distant stars. . . . There are no differences in men.

Differences are only as the variation in shadows cast by the sun."

After lunch we rode downtown in a Broadway bus to the Grand Central Station. Helen likes to feel the crowd around her. Suddenly she said, "There is a painter in the bus." I looked around and, sure enough, there was a house painter sitting in a corner at the other end of the bus, twenty feet away.

July 1946

Dinner at Helen's. She is ready for any adventure. We talked about the gypsies and Conrad Bercovici, and I told her how Bercovici had taken me through the East Side one night where the gypsies were camping out in the cellars of old warehouses. Obliged to come into the city so that their children could go to school, they lived in these abandoned cellars just as they lived on the road in summer. They even set up tents and built campfires on the concrete floors, while their young women told fortunes on the streets.

In Polly's hand Helen's fingers rippled with excitement. She asked me to remind Bercovici of his promise to take her through the East Side and show her the gypsies.

October 1949

Helen comes to dinner. . . . One of our friends asked Helen how she had come to understand abstractions. She said she had found that good apples were sweet and that there were also bad apples that were bitter. Then she learned to think of the sweetness and bitterness apart from the apples. She grasped the idea of sweetness and bitterness in themselves. Sir Alfred Zimmern, at dinner with us, my friend since the days when he wrote *The Greek Commonwealth* forty years ago, listening to Helen, exclaimed, "She is exactly following the method of Plato's dialogues." And indeed her words and their rhythm were Platonic.

The fact is that Helen has a philosophic mind. She relates in her little book, *My Religion*, how, when she was twelve or so, she suddenly said to her teacher, "I have been in Athens." She meant, of course, in imagination, for she had been reading about Greece, but observe what followed in her thinking. She instantly perceived that the "realness" of her mind was independent of conditions of place and body, that she had vividly seen and felt a place thousands of miles away precisely because she had a mind. How else could one explain this being "in Athens"? From that moment, she continued, "Deafness and blindness were of no real account. They were to be relegated to the outer circle of my life."

Is not that real philosophy, the life of reason?

Christmas 1951

Helen has a way of bursting out with the most surprising remarks at table. Today she was full of Thucydides and the Peloponnesian war, about which she had been reading this Christmas morning. "What a stupid war!—the stupidest war in history," she said, shaking her head in mournful disapproval. She had been brooding and grieving over this war, which destroyed the democracy of Athens. For the rest, she was sure there was nothing about war that Thucydides did not know.

The other day she burst out about a certain Evelyn Cheesman, an English entomologist who had written wonderful things, she said, about insects. Helen had read her in one of the Braille magazines, no doubt— whether English, American, French, or German, for Helen reads them all.

Polly took her up. "What's this, Helen? Who is this Evelyn Cheesman?" Polly likes to tease her, and she is sometimes severe with her. For instance, if Helen makes a mistake in typewriting one of her letters, Polly makes her copy the page again. (Usually Helen's typing is like an expert stenographer's, but the other day

there were a few dim lines in one of her letters and she added this postscript: "Polly says the writing of this machine doesn't please her critical eye. My apologies. H.K.")

To return to the lady entomologist, Helen is charmingly eager about these shining new bits of knowledge. She has the earnest innocence of a ten-year-old child. Often, on the other hand, she speaks like an oracle, or, as one might say, an Asiatic sage. In spite of her incessant work, much of her life is still spent in solitary meditation, alone in the dark with her own thoughts, or with the Bible or the classics; and, as she lives in her way as the old prophets lived in the desert, many of her words inspire a kind of reverential wonder. She naturally uses archaic and poetic expressions of the sort that children pick up in their reading, words that are seldom heard in the ordinary talk that she hears only when the ever-alert Polly passes it on to her.

(I must add, what all their friends know, that Polly is in her way as extraordinary a person as Helen. Without her vitality and her diplomatic sense, what could Helen do in her journeys about the world? And what inexhaustible buoyancy both of them have! I have seen them together on a midnight train, when everyone else was asleep, smiling and chatting like birds on a branch in the morning.)

June 1953

Helen is seventy-three years old today. She lives much in eternity and much in history, but she only lives in time when she is able to keep up with the news. This week she returned from a two-months' absence in South America, and she has not had a moment yet to catch up with the newspapers and magazines. Unable to talk politics, she talks at table about Pepys's Diary, which our host Stuart Grummon is reading. She fishes up two or three facts about Pepys that I had forgotten or never knew, remembered from her own reading twenty years ago.

What variety there is in her mind! She is interested in everything. One day she recalled to me the dancing of La Argentina, though how she conceived of this so well I cannot imagine. Another day she quoted at length from a poem by Robinson Jeffers, who once told me he had seen Helen's name in the register of a hotel in the Orkney Islands. And what happy phrases come to her mind. Some children spelled words into her hand and she said their small fingers were like "the wild flowers of conversation."

About Helen Keller, it seems to me, William James uttered the last word when he wrote, "The sum of it is that you are a *blessing*"; a verdict that has been ratified in hundreds of hospitals throughout the world where she has all but raised the dead. Some day the story will be told of the miracles she has performed, or what would have passed for miracles in less case-hardened ages, when the blind have opened inward eyes and really seen life for the first time after Helen Keller has walked and talked with them.

How many, meanwhile, may have thought of her while reading the colonel's soliloquy at the end of Arthur Koestler's *The Age of Longing,* observing that American women are all too busy "playing bridge" to be "cut out for the part of martyrs and saints. . . . American womanhood," the colonel went on, "has produced no Maid of Orleans, no Rosa Luxembourgs or Madame Curies, no Brontës or Florence Nightingales or Krupskayas," and one might add that it seldom produces anyone as rash as various people who generalize about it. For how many types there are in our teeming population! One might easily suggest a list to set beside the list this fictional colonel has drawn from three or four countries. The names of Jane Addams and Emily Dickinson would appear somewhere on such a list, and I dare say that for not a few the name of Helen Keller would figure as leading all the rest.

· QUESTIONS ·

1. Does this selection make you wish to know more about Helen Keller? About Van Wyck Brooks and his work?
2. Explain how incidents and anecdotes enhance the appeal of nearly all writing. Cite examples from this selection to make your points.
3. The final paragraph is a remarkable tribute. Compare its quiet appeal with that of the final paragraph from De Quincey's essay.
4. Compare this sketch with the autobiographical material by Miss Keller in this volume.

Theme Subjects: (1) The Greatest "Blessing" Whom I Know; (2) The Most Handicapped Person Whom I Know; (3) The "Polly Thomson" in My Life; (4) My Too, Too Dull Senses; (5) What Is a Life of Reason?; (6) Jane Addams: An Appreciation.

"SUCH, SUCH WERE THE JOYS . . ."

George Orwell

"GEORGE ORWELL" was the pseudonym of ERIC BLAIR (1903–1950), who was born at Motihari, Bengal, and was educated at Eton. In 1922 he entered service with the British government in Burma, but left in 1927 to pursue a writing career. He lived in Paris for about two years, supporting himself meagerly with such jobs as dishwasher and private tutor, and then moved to London. Later, he contributed a London letter to *Partisan Review* and wrote for the *London Observer*. In 1949 he was winner of the first Annual Award by *Partisan Review*. Among his many books are *Down and Out in Paris and London* (1933); *Burmese Days* (1934); *Keep the Aspidistra Flying* (1936); *Homage to Catalonia* (1938); *Animal Farm: A Fairy Story* (1945); *Nineteen Eighty-four* (novel) (1949); *Shooting an Elephant* (essays) (1950); and *Such, Such Were the Joys* (essays) (1953). After his death, *Animal Farm* was made into a cartoon motion picture (1954), and *Nineteen Eighty-four* was produced on television.

The various codes which were presented to you at Crossgates—religious, moral, social, and intellectual—contradicted one another if you worked out their implications. The essential conflict was between the tradition of nineteenth-century asceticism and the actually existing luxury and snobbery of the pre-1914 age. On the one side were low-church Bible Christianity, sex puritanism, insistence on hard work, respect for academic distinction, disapproval of self-indulgence: on the other, contempt for "braininess" and worship of games, contempt for foreigners and the working class, an almost neurotic dread of poverty, and, above all, the assumption not only that money and privilege are the things that matter, but that it is better to inherit them than to have to work for them. Broadly, you were bidden to be at once a Christian and a social success, which is impossible. At the time I did not perceive that the various ideals which were set before us cancelled out. I merely saw that they were all, or nearly all, unattainable, so far as I was concerned, since they all depended not only on what you did but on what you *were*.[1]

Very early, at the age of only ten or eleven, I reached the conclusion—no one told me this, but on the other hand I did not simply make it up out of my own head: somehow it was in the air I breathed—that you were no good unless you had £100,000. I had perhaps fixed on this particular sum as a result of reading Thackeray. The interest on £100,000 a year (I was in favour of a safe 4 percent), would be £4,000, and this seemed to me the minimum income that you must possess if you were to belong to the real top crust, the people in the country houses. But it was clear that I could never find my way into that paradise, to which you did not really belong unless you were born into it. You could only *make* money, if at all, by a mysterious operation called "going into the City," and when you came out of the City, having won your £100,000, you were fat and old. But the truly enviable thing about the top-notchers was that they were rich while young. For people like me, the ambitious middle class, the examination passers, only a bleak, laborious kind of success was possible. You clambered upwards on a ladder of scholarships into the Home Civil Service or the Indian Civil Service, or possibly you became a barrister. And if at any point you "slacked" or "went off" and missed one of the rungs in the ladder, you became "a little office boy at forty pounds a year." But even if you climbed to the highest niche that was open to you, you could still only be an underling, a hanger-on of the people who really counted.

Even if I had not learned this from Sim and Bingo,[2] I would have learned it from the other boys. Looking back, it is astonishing how intimately, intelligently snobbish we all were, how knowledgeable about names and addresses, how swift to detect small differences in accents and manners and the cut of clothes. There were some boys who seemed to drop money from their pores even in the bleak misery of the middle of a winter term. At the beginning and end of the term, especially, there was naively snobbish chatter about Switzerland, and Scotland with its ghillies and grouse moors,[3] and "my uncle's yacht," and "our place in the country," and "my

---

[1] Eric Blair (George Orwell) was the son of a Customs and Excise official who retired early on a small pension. When young Eric was sent to "Crossgates" at the age of eight, family financial resources were extremely modest. As the author points out in this selection, he was accepted at this pseudofashionable school at a reduced rate in hopes that he would win a scholarship at Eton and thus be a credit to "Crossgates." This young Blair (Orwell) finally accomplished when he was 14. Eton is a famed public school, so-called to distinguish this type of collective education from training by a "private" tutor.

[2] Sim was the students' nickname for the headmaster of "Crossgates." Bingo was Sim's wife.

[3] Ghillie (or gillie) is a Scottish and Irish term for a fishing and hunting guide. Grouse are game birds somewhat resembling pheasants.

pony" and "my pater's touring car." There never was, I suppose, in the history of the world a time when the sheer vulgar fatness of wealth, without any kind of aristocratic elegance to redeem it, was so obtrusive as in those years before 1914. It was the age when crazy millionaires in curly top hats and lavender waistcoats gave champagne parties in rococo houseboats on the Thames, the age of diabolo and hobble skirts, the age of the "knut" in his grey bowler and cutaway coat, the age of *The Merry Widow*, Saki's novels, *Peter Pan*, and *Where the Rainbow Ends*, the age when people talked about chocs and cigs and ripping and topping and heavenly, when they went for divvy weekends at Brighton and had scrumptious teas at the Troc. From the whole decade before 1914, there seems to breathe forth a smell of the more vulgar, un-grown-up kinds of luxury, a smell of brilliantine and crème de menthe and soft-centred chocolates—an atmosphere, as it were, of eating everlasting strawberry ices on green lawns to the tune of the Eton Boating Song. The extraordinary thing was the way in which everyone took it for granted that this oozing, bulging wealth of the English upper and upper-middle classes would last forever and was part of the order of things. After 1918 it was never quite the same again. Snobbishness and expensive habits came back, certainly, but they were self-conscious and on the defensive. Before the war the worship of money was entirely unreflecting and untroubled by any pang of conscience. The goodness of money was as unmistakable as the goodness of health or beauty, and a glittering car, a title or a horde of servants was mixed up in people's minds with the idea of actual moral virtue.

At Crossgates, in term time,[4] the general bareness of life enforced a certain democracy, but any mention of the holidays, and the consequent competitive swanking about cars and butlers and country houses, promptly called class distinctions into being. The school was pervaded by a curious cult of Scotland, which brought out the fundamental contradiction in our standard of values. Bingo claimed Scottish ancestry, and she favoured the Scottish boys, encouraging them to wear kilts in their ancestral tartan instead of the school uniform, and even christened her youngest child by a Gaelic name. Ostensibly we were supposed to admire the Scots because they were "grim" and "dour" ("stern" was perhaps the key word), and irresistible on the field of battle. In the big schoolroom there was a steel engraving of the charge of the Scots Greys at Waterloo, all looking as though they enjoyed every moment of it. Our picture of Scotland was made up of burns, braes, kilts, sporrans, claymores, bagpipes, and the like, all somehow mixed up with the invigorating effects of porridge, Protestantism, and a cold climate. But underlying this was something quite different. The real reason for the cult of Scotland was that only very rich people could spend their summers there. And the pretended belief in Scottish superiority was a cover for the bad conscience of the occupying English, who had pushed the Highland peasantry off their farms to make way for the deer

---

[4] The time during an academic year; that is, while school is in session.

forests, and then compensated them by turning them into servants. Bingo's face always beamed with innocent snobbishness when she spoke of Scotland. Occasionally she even attempted a trace of Scottish accent. Scotland was a private paradise which a few initiates could talk about and make outsiders feel small.

"You going to Scotland this hols?"[5]

"Rather! We go every year."

"My pater's giving me a new gun for the twelfth. There's jolly good black game where we go. Get out, Smith! What are you listening for? You've never been in Scotland. I bet you don't know what a black-cock looks like."

Following on this, imitations of the cry of a black-cock, of the roaring of a stag, of the accent of "our ghillies," etc., etc.

And the questionings that new boys of doubtful social origin were sometimes put through—questionings quite surprising in their mean-minded particularity, when one reflects that the inquisitors were only twelve or thirteen!

"How much a year has your pater got? What part of London do you live in? Is that Knightsbridge or Kensington? How many bathrooms has your house got? How many servants do your people keep? Have you got a butler? Well, then, have you got a cook? Where do you get your clothes made? How many shows did you go to in the hols? How much money did you bring back with'you?" etc., etc.

I have seen a little new boy, hardly older than eight, desperately

lying his way through such a catechism.[6]

"Have your people got a car?"

"Yes."

"What sort of car?"

"Daimler."

"How many horse-power?"

(Pause, and leap in the dark.) "Fifteen."

"What kind of lights?"

The little boy is bewildered.

"What kind of lights? Electric or acetylene?"

(A longer pause, and another leap in the dark.) "Acetylene."

"Coo! He says his pater's car's got acetylene lamps. They went out years ago. It must be as old as the hills."

"Rot! He's making it up. He hasn't got a car. He's just a navvy.[7] Your pater's a navvy."

And so on.

By the social standards that prevailed about me, I was no good, and could not be any good. But all the different kinds of virtue seemed to be mysteriously interconnected and to belong to much the same people. It was not only money that mattered: there were also strength, beauty, charm, athleticism and something called "guts" or "character," which in reality meant the power to impose your will on others. I did not possess any of these qualities. At games, for instance, I was hopeless. I was a fairly good swimmer and not altogether contemptible at cricket, but these had no prestige value, because boys only attach importance to a game if it requires strength and courage. What counted was football, at which I was

---

[5] holidays

[6] a set of formal questions put as a test

[7] unskilled laborer; a shortened form of "navigator," which sometimes means, in England, a laborer

a funk.[8] I loathed the game, and since I could see no pleasure or usefulness in it, it was very difficult for me to show courage at it. Football, it seemed to me, is not really played for the pleasure of kicking a ball about, but is a species of fighting. The lovers of football are large, boisterous, nobbly boys who are good at knocking down and trampling on slightly smaller boys. That was the pattern of school life—a continuous triumph of the strong over the weak. Virtue consisted in winning: it consisted in being bigger, stronger, handsomer, richer, more popular, more elegant, more unscrupulous than other people— in dominating them, bullying them, making them suffer pain, making them look foolish, getting the better of them in every way. Life was hierarchical[9] and whatever happened was right. There were the strong, who deserved to win and always did win, and there were the weak, who deserved to lose and always did lose, everlastingly.

I did not question the prevailing standards, because so far as I could see there were no others. How could the rich, the strong, the elegant, the fashionable, the powerful, be in the wrong? It was their world, and the rules they made for it must be the right ones. And yet from a very early age I was aware of the impossibility of any *subjective* conformity. Always at the centre of my heart the inner self seemed to be awake, pointing out the difference between the moral obligation and the psychological *fact*. It was the same in all matters, worldly or other-worldly. Take religion, for instance. You were supposed to love

God, and I did not question this. Till the age of about fourteen I believed in God and believed that the accounts given of him were true. But I was well aware that I did not love him. On the contrary, I hated him, just as I hated Jesus and the Hebrew patriarchs. If I had sympathetic feelings towards any character in the Old Testament, it was towards such people as Cain, Jezebel, Haman, Agag, Sisera: in the New Testament my friends, if any, were Ananias, Caiaphas, Judas, and Pontius Pilate. But the whole business of religion seemed to be strewn with psychological impossibilities. The Prayer Book told you, for example, to love God and fear him: but how could you love someone whom you feared? With your private affections it was the same. What you *ought* to feel was usually clear enough, but the appropriate emotion could not be commanded. Obviously it was my duty to feel grateful towards Bingo and Sim; but I was not grateful. It was equally clear that one ought to love one's father, but I knew very well that I merely disliked my own father, whom I had barely seen before I was eight and who appeared to me simply as a gruff-voiced elderly man forever saying "Don't." It was not that one did not want to possess the right qualities or feel the correct emotions, but that one could not. The good and the possible never seemed to coincide.

There was a line of verse that I came across, not actually while I was at Crossgates, but a year or two later, and which seemed to strike a sort of leaden echo in my heart. It was: "The armies of unalterable

---

[8] coward
[9] by order or rank

law." I understood to perfection what it meant to be Lucifer,[10] defeated and justly defeated, with no possibility of revenge. The schoolmasters with their canes, the millionaires with their Scottish castles, the athletes with their curly hair—these were the armies of the unalterable law. It was not easy, at that date, to realise that in fact it *was* alterable. And according to that law I was damned. I had no money, I was weak, I was ugly, I was unpopular, I had a chronic cough, I was cowardly, I smelt. This picture, I should add, was not altogether fanciful. I was an unattractive boy. Crossgates soon made me so, even if I had not been so before. But a child's belief of its own shortcomings is not much influenced by facts. I believed, for example, that I "smelt," but this was based simply on general probability. It was notorious that disagreeable people smelt, and therefore presumably I did so too. Again, until after I had left school for good I continued to believe that I was preternaturally ugly. It was what my schoolfellows had told me, and I had no other authority to refer to. The conviction that it was *not possible* for me to be a success went deep enough to influence my actions till far into adult life. Until I was about thirty I always planned my life on the assumption not only that any major undertaking was bound to fail, but that I could only expect to live a few years longer.

But this sense of guilt and inevitable failure was balanced by something else: that is, the instinct to survive. Even a creature that is weak, ugly, cowardly, smelly, and in no way justifiable still wants to stay alive and be happy after its own fashion. I could not invert the existing scale of values, or turn myself into a success, but I could accept my failure and make the best of it. I could resign myself to being what I was and then endeavour to survive on those terms.

To survive, or at least to preserve any kind of independence, was essentially criminal, since it meant breaking rules which you yourself recognized. There was a boy named Johnny Hall who for some months oppressed me horribly. He was a big, powerful, coarsely handsome boy with a very red face and curly black hair, who was forever twisting somebody's arm, wringing somebody's ear, flogging somebody with a riding crop (he was a member of the Sixth Form), or performing prodigies of activity on the football field. Bingo loved him (hence the fact that he was habitually called by his Christian name), and Sim commended him as a boy who "had character" and could "keep order." He was followed about by a group of toadies who nicknamed him Strong Man.

One day, when we were taking off our overcoats in the changing-room, Hall picked on me for some reason. I "answered him back," whereupon he gripped my wrist, twisted it round, and bent my forearm back upon itself in a hideously painful way. I remember his handsome, jeering red face bearing down upon mine. He was, I think, older than I, besides being enormously stronger. As he let go of me a terrible, wicked resolve formed itself in my heart. I would get back on him by hitting him when he did not expect it. It was a strategic mo-

---

[10] a fallen angel, or archangel; sometimes referred to as the Devil

ment, for the master who had been "taking"[11] the walk would be coming back almost immediately, and then there could be no fight. I let perhaps a minute go by, walked up to Hall with the most harmless air I could assume, and then, getting the weight of my body behind it, smashed my fist into his face. He was flung backwards by the blow and some blood ran out of his mouth. His always sanguine[12] face turned almost black with rage. Then he turned away to rinse his mouth at the washing-basins.

"All right!" he said to me between his teeth as the master led us away.

For days after this he followed me about, challenging me to fight. Although terrified out of my wits, I steadily refused to fight. I said that the blow in the face had served him right, and there was an end of it. Curiously enough he did not simply fall upon me then and there, which public opinion would probably have supported him in doing. So gradually the matter tailed off, and there was no fight.

Now, I had behaved wrongly, by my own code no less than his. To hit him unawares was wrong. But to refuse to fight afterwards, knowing that if we fought he would beat me—that was far worse: it was cowardly. If I had refused because I disapproved of fighting, or because I genuinely felt the matter to be closed, it would have been all right; but I had refused merely because I was afraid. Even my revenge was made empty by that fact. I had struck the blow in a moment of mindless violence, deliberately not looking far ahead and merely deter-

mined to get my own back for once and damn the consequences. I had had time to realise that what I did was wrong, but it was the kind of crime from which you could get some satisfaction. Now all was nullified. There had been a sort of courage in the first act, but my subsequent cowardice had wiped it out.

The fact I hardly noticed was that although Hall formally challenged me to fight, he did not actually attack me. Indeed, after receiving that one blow he never oppressed me again. It was perhaps twenty years before I saw the significance of this. At the time I could not see beyond the moral dilemma that is presented to the weak in a world governed by the strong: Break the rules, or perish. I did not see that in that case the weak have the right to make a different set of rules for themselves; because, even if such an idea had occurred to me, there was no one in my environment who could have confirmed me in it. I lived in a world of boys, gregarious animals, questioning nothing, accepting the law of the stronger and avenging their own humiliations by passing them down to someone smaller. My situation was that of countless other boys, and if potentially I was more of a rebel than most, it was only because, by boyish standards, I was a poorer specimen. But I never did rebel intellectually, only emotionally. I had nothing to help me except my dumb selfishness, my inability—not, indeed, to despise myself, but to *dislike* myself —my instinct to survive.

It was about a year after I hit Johnny Hall in the face that I left

---

[11] supervising, taking charge of
[12] highly colored, ruddy

Crossgates for ever. It was the end of a winter term. With a sense of coming out from darkness into sunlight I put on my Old Boy's tie as we dressed for the journey. I well remember the feeling of that brandnew silk tie round my neck, a feeling of emancipation, as though the tie had been at once a badge of manhood and an amulet[13] against Bingo's voice and Sim's cane. I was escaping from bondage. It was not that I expected, or even intended, to be any more successful at a public school than I had been at Crossgates. But still, I was escaping. I knew that at a public school there would be more privacy, more neglect, more chance to be idle and selfindulgent and degenerate. For years past I had been resolved—unconsciously at first, but consciously later on—that when once my scholarship was won I would "slack off" and cram no longer. This resolve, by the way, was so fully carried out that between the ages of thirteen and twenty-two or -three I hardly ever did a stroke of avoidable work.

Bingo shook hands to say goodbye. She even gave me my Christian name for the occasion. But there was a sort of patronage, almost a sneer, in her face and in her voice. The tone in which she said good-bye was nearly the tone in which she had been used to say *little butterflies*. I had won two scholarships, but I was a failure, because success was measured not by what you did but by what you *were*. I was "not a good type of boy and could bring no credit on the school. I did not possess character or courage or health or strength or money, or even good manners, the power to look like a gentleman."

"Good-bye," Bingo's parting smile seemed to say; "it's not worth quarrelling now. You haven't made much of a success of your time at Crossgates, have you? And I don't suppose you'll get on awfully well at a public school either. We made a mistake, really, in wasting our time and money on you. This kind of education hasn't much to offer to a boy with your background and outlook. Oh, don't think we don't understand you! We know all about those ideas you have at the back of your head, we know you disbelieve in everything we've taught you, and we know you aren't in the least grateful for all we've done for you. But there's no use in bringing it all up now. We aren't responsible for you any longer, and we shan't be seeing you again. Let's just admit that you're one of our failures and part without ill-feeling. And so, goodbye."

That at least was what I read into her face. And yet how happy I was, that winter morning, as the train bore me away with the gleaming new silk tie round my neck! The world was opening before me, just a little, like a grey sky which exhibits a narrow crack of blue. A public school would be better fun than Crossgates but at bottom equally alien. In a world where the prime necessities were money, titled relatives, athleticism, tailor-made clothes, neatly brushed hair, a charming smile, I was no good. All I had gained was a breathing-space. A little quietude, a little self-indulgence, a little respite from cramming—and then, ruin. What kind of ruin I did not know: perhaps the colonies or an office stool, perhaps prison or an early death. But

---

[13] protective charm

first a year or two in which one could "slack off" and get the benefit of one's sins, like Doctor Faustus.[14] It is the advantage of being thirteen that you cannot only live in the moment, but do so with full consciousness, foreseeing the future and yet not caring about it. Next term I was going to Wellington. I had also won a scholarship at Eton, but was uncertain whether there would be a vacancy, and I was going to Wellington first. At Eton you had a room to yourself—a room which might even have a fire in it. At Wellington you had your own cubicle, and could make cocoa in the evenings. The privacy of it, the grown-upness! And there would be libraries to hang about in, and summer afternoons when you could shirk games and mooch about the countryside alone, with no master driving you along. Meanwhile there were the holidays. There was the .22 rifle that I had bought the previous holidays (the Crackshot, it was called, costing twenty-two and sixpence), and Christmas was coming next week. There were also the pleasures of overeating. I thought of some particularly voluptuous cream buns which could be bought for twopence each at a shop in our town. (This was 1916, and food-rationing had not yet started.) Even the detail that my journey-money had been slightly miscalculated, leaving about a shilling over—enough for an unforeseen cup of coffee and a cake or two somewhere on the way—was enough to fill me with bliss. There was time for a bit of happiness before the future closed in upon me. But I did know that the future was dark. Failure, failure, failure—failure behind me, failure ahead of me—that was by far the deepest conviction that I carried away.

· QUESTIONS ·

1. This portion of Orwell's autobiography is considered remarkably frank and revealing. Do you think he could have been so forthright had he not allowed many years to elapse between experience and writing?

2. The title of this selection comes from a poem by William Blake, "The Echoing Green," one of a group published in *Songs of Innocence*. Find the volume and see whether these poems dealing with the wonder and joy of early childhood have any relationship to Orwell's days at "Crossgates."

3. The first paragraph is a masterful statement of the thesis of this entire section of autobiography. Analyze it. Are the mood and tone of this paragraph echoed in the final two sentences of the selection?

4. What experiences have you had which match those of Orwell? Are all children snobbish? Sadistic? Herd-minded?

5. In "It's Halfway to 1984" and in any of Orwell's own work which you have read do you find lingering traces of the author's bitter experiences at "Crossgates"?

6. Did the unfairness and downright meanness he found at school tend to make him a lifelong rebel? What do you think such experiences would have done to you?

---

[14] Faust, a German astrologer and magician, was said to have sold his soul in exchange for youth, worldly experiences, wealth, and power.

Theme Subjects: (1) I Am (Am Not) Capable of Subjective Conformity; (2) I Am (Am Not) a Rebel and Proud of It; (3) The Meanest Teacher (Principal, Headmaster) I Ever Knew; (4) An Example of Snobbery on This Campus; (5) It's Embarrassing To Tell the Truth About Myself; (6) This Is My Life (a small segment of your autobiography).

GETTYSBURG

Paul McClelland Angle

PAUL McCLELLAND ANGLE (1900–   ) is a noted Lincoln scholar and director of the Chicago Historical Society. Among his books are *Mary Lincoln, Wife and Widow* (with Carl Sandburg, 1932); *Here I Have Lived—A History of Lincoln's Springfield* (1935); *A Handbook of Illinois Society* (1943); *A Shelf of Lincoln Books* (1946); *The Living Lincoln* (with Earl S. Miers, 1955); *Tragic Years, 1860–1865* (1960); and *Crossroads, 1913* (1963).

Soon after the Battle of Chancellorsville, Lee took the exultant Army of Northern Virginia across the Potomac and started north. Perhaps his ultimate objective was Washington, perhaps it was the rich cities of Pennsylvania, where dwindling supplies might be replenished. No one knew. Hooker, whose army had not been demoralized by defeat, started north at the same time, skillfully disposing his troops so that they would stand as a shield between the Confederates and the national Capital.

Early in the morning of June 28, 1863, George Gordon Meade, commanding Hooker's Fifth Corps, was awakened by a messenger from the President placing him in command of the Army of the Potomac. Four days later his forward ele-

ments stumbled into Lee's advance guard, and the Battle of Gettysburg began. For three days Lee sent troops hitherto invincible against blue lines that at first yielded and then stood firm. When it was over, his army, bled by 20,000 casualties, had lost one of the decisive battles of history.

I

Carl Sandburg recounts the first great victory of the Army of the Potomac:

From day to day neither Meade nor Lee had been certain where the other was. Lee would rather have taken Harrisburg, its stores and supplies, and then battled Meade on the way to Philadelphia. In that case Lee would have had ammunition enough to keep his artillery firing with no letup, no orders during an infantry charge that ammunition was running low and must be saved.

Lee rode his horse along roads winding through bright summer landscapes to find himself suddenly looking at the smoke of a battle he had not ordered nor planned. Some of his own marching divisions had become entangled with enemy columns, traded shots, and a battle had begun that Lee could draw away from or carry on. He decided to carry on. He said Yes. His troops in their last two battles and on general form looked unbeatable. Against him was an untried commander with a jealous staff that had never worked as smoothly as his own. If he could repeat his performances with his men at Fredericksburg and Chancellorsville, he could then march to Harrisburg, use the State Capitol for barracks, replenish his needs, march on to Philadelphia,

Baltimore, and Washington, lay hold of money, supplies, munitions, win European recognition and end of the war.

The stakes were immense, the chances fair. The new enemy commander had never planned a battle nor handled a big army in the wild upsets of frontal combat on a wide line. Also, fifty-eight regiments of Northern veterans who had fought at Antietam, Fredericksburg, Chancellorsville, had gone home, their time up, their places filled by militia and raw recruits.

One factor was against Lee: he would have to tell his cannoneers to go slow and count their shells, while Meade's artillery could fire on and on from an endless supply. Another factor, too, was against Lee: he was away from his Virginia, where he knew the ground and the people, while Meade's men were fighting for their homes, women, barns, cattle, and fields against invaders and strangers, as Meade saw and felt it.

To Lee's words, "If the enemy is there, we must attack him," Longstreet, who now replaced Stonewall Jackson, spoke sharply, "If he is there, it will be because he is anxious that we should attack him —a good reason, in my judgment, for not doing so." This vague and involved feeling Longstreet nursed in his breast; attack was unwise, and his advice rejected. It resulted in hours of delay and wasted time that might have counted.

Lee hammered at the Union left wing the first day, the right wing the second day, Meade on that day sending word to Lincoln that the enemy was "repulsed at all points." On the third day, July 3, 1863, Lee smashed at Meade's center. Under Longstreet's command,

General George Edward Pickett, a tall arrow of a man, with mustache and goatee, with long ringlets of auburn hair flying as he galloped his horse, headed 15,000 men, who had nearly a mile to go up a slow slope of land to reach the Union center. Pickett might have had thoughts in his blanket under the stars some night that week of how long ago it was, twenty-one years, since he, a Virginia boy schooled in Richmond, had been studying law in his uncle's office in Quincy, Illinois, seeing men daily who tried cases with the young attorney Abraham Lincoln. And the Pickett boy had gone on to West Point, graduated at the bottom of his class, the last of all, though later he had been first to go over the parapets at Chapultepec in 1847, and still later, in 1859, had taken possession of San Juan Island at Puget Sound on the delicate mission of accommodating officials of the Buchanan administration in bringing on a war with Great Britain, with the hope of saving his country from a threatened civil war by welding its divided sections. British diplomacy achieved joint occupation of the island by troops of two nations and thus averted war. On the Peninsula, Pickett's men had earned the nickname of "The Game Cock Brigade," and he considered love of woman second only to the passion for war.

Before starting his men on their charge to the Union center, Pickett handed Longstreet a letter to a girl in Richmond he was to marry if he lived. Longstreet had ordered Pickett to go forward and Pickett had penciled on the back of the envelope, "If Old Peter's (Longstreet's) nod means death, good-by, and God bless you, little one!" An officer held out a flask of whiskey to Pickett: "Take a drink with me; in an hour you'll be in hell or glory." And Pickett said No; he had promised "the little girl" he wouldn't.

Across the long rise of open ground, with the blue flag of Virginia floating ahead, over field and meadow Pickett's 15,000 marched steadily and smoothly, almost as if on a drill ground. Solid shot, grape and canister, from the Union artillery plowed through them, and later a wild rain of rifle bullets. Seven-eighths of a mile they marched in the open sunlight, every man a target for the Union marksmen behind stone fences and breastworks. They obeyed orders; Uncle Robert had said they would go anywhere and do anything.

As men fell, their places were filled, the ranks closed up. As officers tumbled off horses it was taken as expected in battle.

Perhaps half who started reached the Union lines surmounting Cemetery Ridge.

Then came cold steel, the bayonet, the clubbed musket. The strongest and last line of the enemy was reached. "The Confederate battle flag waved over his defenses," said a Confederate major, "and the fighting over the wall became hand to hand, but more than half having already fallen, our line was too weak to rout the enemy."

Meade rode up white-faced to hear it was a repulse and cried, "Thank God!" Lee commented: "They deserved success as far as it can be deserved by human valor and fortitude. More may have been required of them than they were able to perform." To one of his colonels, Lee said, "This has been a sad day for us, a sad day, but we cannot expect always to gain victories."

As a heavy rainfall came on

the night of July 4, Lee ordered a retreat toward the Potomac.[1]

II

Cemeteries mark battlefields. How that at Gettysburg came to be created, and how Lincoln was invited to dedicate it, are related by Clark E. Carr, the Illinois member of the cemetery commission.

Scarcely had the reverberations of the guns of the battle died away when the Honorable David Wills, a citizen of Gettysburg, wrote to the Honorable Andrew G. Curtin, the great war Governor of Pennsylvania, suggesting that a plot of ground in the midst of the battlefield be at once purchased and set apart as a soldiers' national cemetery, and that the remains of the dead be exhumed and placed in this cemetery. He suggested that the ground to be selected should be on what was known as Cemetery Hill, so called because adjoining it is the local cemetery of Gettysburg. . . .

Governor Curtin at once approved of the recommendation of Mr. Wills, and correspondence was opened with the governors of the loyal States whose troops had engaged in the battle, asking them to co-operate in the movement. The grounds proposed by Mr. Wills . . . were at once purchased. . . .

It was proposed, as the work proceeded, that memorial dedicatory exercises be held to consecrate this sacred ground, which was finally determined upon. The day first fixed upon for these exercises was the twenty-third of October, 1863.

The Honorable Edward Everett, of Massachusetts, was then regarded as the greatest living American orator, and it was decided to invite him to deliver the oration; and this was done. But he replied that it was wholly out of his power to make the necessary preparation by the twenty-third of October. So desirous were we all to have Mr. Everett that the dedication was postponed to Thursday, the nineteenth of November, 1863—nearly a month—to suit Mr. Everett's convenience. The dedication took place on that day.

A formal invitation to be present was sent to the President of the United States and his Cabinet, to Major General George G. Meade . . . and to the officers and soldiers who had participated in, and gained, the memorable victory. Invitations were also sent to the venerable Lieutenant General Winfield Scott and to Admiral Charles Stewart, the distinguished and time-honored representatives of the army and navy, to the diplomatic corps, representing foreign governments, to the members of both Houses of Congress, and to other distinguished personages.

All these invitations and all arrangements for the dedicatory exercises—as was the case with everything relating to the cemetery—were considered and decided upon by our Board of Commissioners, and were, insofar as he was able, under the direction of the Board, carried into effect by Mr. Wills, our president. As we were all representing and speaking for the governors of our respective States, by whom we were appointed, we made all the invitations in their names.

The proposition to ask Mr. Lin-

---

[1] From *Abraham Lincoln: The War Years* by Carl Sandburg, copyright 1939 by Harcourt, Brace and Company, Inc.

coln to speak at the Gettysburg ceremonies was an afterthought. The President of the United States had, like the other distinguished personages, been invited to be present, but Mr. Lincoln was not, at that time, invited to speak. In fact, it did not seem to occur to anyone that he could speak upon such an occasion.

Scarcely any member of the Board, excepting the member representing Illinois, had ever heard him speak at all, and no other member had ever heard, or read from him, anything except political discussions. When the suggestion was made that he be invited to speak, while all expressed high appreciation of his great abilities as a political speaker, as shown in his debates with Senator Douglas, and in his Cooper Institute address, the question was raised as to his ability to speak upon such a grave and solemn occasion as that of the memorial services. Besides, it was said that, with his important duties and responsibilities, he could not possibly have the leisure to prepare an address for such an occasion. In answer to this it was urged that he himself, better than anyone else, could determine as to these questions, and that, if he were invited to speak, he was sure to do what, under the circumstances, would be right and proper. . . .

It was finally decided to ask President Lincoln "after the oration" (that is to say, after Mr. Everett's oration), as Chief Executive of the nation, "to set apart formally these grounds to their sacred use by a few appropriate remarks." This was done in the name of the governors of the States, as was the case with

others, by Mr. Wills; but the invitation was not settled upon and sent to Mr. Lincoln until the second of November, more than six weeks after Mr. Everett had been invited to speak, and but a little more than two weeks before the exercises were held.[2]

III

Tardy as it was, the invitation to speak was promptly accepted by the President. On November 18, 1863, he and his party proceeded from Washington to Gettysburg by special train. Of that trip and the preliminaries of the dedicatory exercises, John Hay preserved much in his diary, at the same time demonstrating that a man with a finely developed literary instinct does not always recognize a masterpiece when he hears it.

On our train were the President, Seward, Usher and Blair; Nicolay and myself; Mercier and Admiral Reynaud; Bertinatti and Capt. Isola and Lt. Martinez and Cora; Mrs. Wise; Wayne MacVeagh; McDougal of Canada, and one or two others. We had a pleasant sort of trip. . . .

At Gettysburg the President went to Mr. Wills, who expected him, and our party broke like a drop of quicksilver spilled. MacVeagh, young Stanton, and I foraged around for a while—walked out to the college, got a chafing dish of oysters, then some supper, and finally, loafing around to the Court House where Lamon was holding a meeting of marshals, we found Forney and went around to his place, Mr. Fahnestock's, and drank a little whisky with him. He had

---

[2] Carr, *Lincoln at Gettysburg*, 8–10, 18–25.

been drinking a good deal during
the day and was getting to feel a
little ugly and dangerous. He was
particularly bitter on Montgomery
Blair. MacVeagh was telling him
that he pitched into the Tycoon
coming up, and told him some
truths. He said the President got a
good deal of that from time to time
and needed it. . . .

We went out after a while following the music to hear the sere-
nades. The President appeared at
the door and said half a dozen
words meaning nothing and went
in. Seward, who was staying around
the corner at Harper's, was called
out, and spoke so indistinctly that
I did not hear a word of what he
was saying. Forney and MacVeagh
were still growling about Blair.

We went back to Forney's
room, having picked up Nicolay,
and drank more whisky. Nicolay
sang his little song of the "Three
Thieves," and we then sang "John
Brown." At last we proposed that
Forney should make a speech and
two or three started out, Shannon
and Behan and Nicolay, to get a
band to serenade him. I stayed with
him. So did Stanton and MacVeagh.
He still growled quietly and I
thought he was going to do something imprudent. He said, "If I
speak, I will speak my mind." The
music sounded in the street, and
the fuglers came rushing up im-
ploring him to come down. He
smiled quietly, told them to keep
cool, and asked, "Are the recorders
there?" "I suppose so of course,"
shouted the fugler. "Ascertain," said
the imperturbable Forney. "Hay,
we'll take a drink." They shouted
and begged him to come down. The
thing would be a failure—it would
be his fault, etc. "Are the recorders

congenial?" he calmly insisted on
knowing. Somebody commended
prudence. He said sternly, "I am always prudent." I walked downstairs
with him.

The crowd was large and clamorous. The fuglers stood by the door
in an agony. The reporters squatted
at a little stand in the entry. Forney
stood on the threshold, John Young
and I by him. The crowd shouted as
the door opened. Forney said, "My
friends, these are the first hearty
cheers I have heard tonight. You
gave no such cheers to your President down the street. Do you know
what you owe to that great man?
You owe your country—you owe
your name as American citizens."

He went on blackguarding the
crowd for their apathy and then
diverged to his own record, saying
he had been for Lincoln in his heart
in 1860—that open advocacy was
not as effectual as the course he
took—dividing the most corrupt organization that ever existed—the
proslavery Democratic party. He
dwelled at length on this question
and then went back to the eulogy
of the President, that great, wonderful, mysterious, inexplicable man
who holds in his single hands the
reins of the Republic; who keeps his
own counsels; who does his own
purpose in his own way, no matter
what temporizing minister in his
cabinet sets himself up in opposition to the progress of the age.

And very much of this.

After him Wayne MacVeagh
made a most touching and beautiful
speech of five minutes and Judge
Shannon of Pittsburgh spoke effectively and acceptably to the people.

"That speech must not be
written out yet," says Young. "He
will see further about it when he

gets sober," as we went upstairs. We sang more of "John Brown" and went home.

In the morning I got a beast and rode out with the President's suite to the Cemetery in the procession. The procession formed itself in an orphanly sort of way and moved out with very little help from anybody, and after a little delay, Mr. Everett took his place on the stand—and Mr. Stockton made a prayer which thought it was an oration; and Mr. Everett spoke as he always does, perfectly—and the President, in a fine, free way, with more grace than is his wont, said his half dozen words of consecration, and the music wailed and we went home through crowded and cheering streets. And all the particulars are in the daily papers.[3]

IV

Here are the "half dozen words of consecration."

Fourscore and seven years ago our fathers brought forth on this continent a new nation, conceived in liberty, and dedicated to the proposition that all men are created equal.

Now we are engaged in a great civil war, testing whether that nation, or any nation so conceived and so dedicated, can long endure. We are met on a great battlefield of that war. We have come to dedicate a portion of that field as a final resting-place for those who here gave their lives that that nation might live. It is altogether fitting and proper that we should do this.

But in a larger sense, we can-not dedicate—we cannot consecrate—we cannot hallow—this ground. The brave men, living and dead, who struggled here, have consecrated it far above our poor power to add or detract. The world will little note nor long remember what we say here, but it can never forget what they did here. It is for us, the living, rather, to be dedicated here to the unfinished work which they who fought here have thus far so nobly advanced. It is rather for us to be here dedicated to the great task remaining before us—that from these honored dead we take increased devotion to that cause for which they gave the last full measure of devotion; that we here highly resolve that these dead shall not have died in vain; that this nation, under God, shall have a new birth of freedom; and that government of the people, by the people, for the people, shall not perish from the earth.

V

In prose only less memorable than Lincoln's own, Carl Sandburg has written the epilogue to Gettysburg:

After the ceremonies at Gettysburg, Lincoln lunched with Governor Curtin, Mr. Everett, and others at the Wills home, held a reception that had not been planned, handshaking nearly an hour, looking gloomy and listless but brightening sometimes as a small boy or girl came in line, and stopping one tall man for remarks as to just how high up he reached. At five o'clock he attended a patriotic meeting in

---

[3] Reprinted by permission of Dodd, Mead & Company from *Lincoln and the Civil War* by Tyler Dennett. Copyright 1939 by Dodd, Mead & Company, Inc.

the Presbyterian church, walking arm-in-arm with old John Burns, and listening to an address by Lieutenant Governor-elect Anderson of Ohio. At six-thirty he was on the departing Washington train. In the dining car his secretary, John Hay, ate with Simon Cameron and Wayne MacVeagh. Hay had thought Cameron and MacVeagh hated each other, but he noted: "I was more than usually struck by the intimate jovial relations that existed between men that hate and detest each other as cordially as do the Pennsylvania politicians."

The ride to Washington took until midnight. Lincoln was weary, talked little, stretched out on one of the side seats in the drawing room and had a wet towel laid across his eyes and forehead.

He had stood that day, the world's foremost spokesman of popular government, saying that democracy was yet worth fighting for. He had spoken as one in mist who might head on deeper yet into mist. He incarnated the assurances and pretenses of popular government, implied that it could and might perish from the earth. What he meant by "a new birth of freedom" for the nation could have a thousand interpretations. The taller riddles of democracy stood up out of the address. It had the dream touch of vast and furious events epitomized for any foreteller to read what was to come. He did not assume that the drafted soldiers, substitutes, and bounty-paid privates had died willingly under Lee's shot and shell, in deliberate consecration of themselves to the Union cause. His cadences sang the ancient song that where there is freedom men have fought and sacrificed for it, and that freedom is worth men's dying

for. For the first time since he became President he had on a dramatic occasion declaimed, howsoever it might be read, Jefferson's proposition which had been a slogan of the Revolutionary War—"All men are created equal"—leaving no other inference than that he regarded the Negro slave as a man. His outwardly smooth sentences were inside of them gnarled and tough with the enigmas of the American experiment.

Back at Gettysburg the blue haze of the Cumberland Mountains had dimmed till it was a blur in a nocturne. The moon was up and fell with a bland golden benevolence on the new-made graves of soldiers, on the sepulchers of old settlers, on the horse carcasses of which the onrush of war had not yet permitted removal. The New York *Herald* man walked amid them and ended the story he sent his paper: "The air, the trees, the graves are silent. Even the relic hunters are gone now. And the soldiers here never wake to the sound of reveille."

In many a country cottage over the land, a tall old clock in a quiet corner told time in a tick-tock deliberation. Whether the orchard branches hung with pink-spray blossoms or icicles of sleet, whether the outside news was seedtime or harvest, rain or drouth, births or deaths, the swing of the pendulum was right and left and right and left in a tick-tock deliberation.

The face and dial of the clock had known the eyes of a boy who listened to its tick-tock and learned to read its minute and hour hands. And the boy had seen years measured off by the swinging pendulum, and grown to man size, had gone away. And the people in the cottage knew that the clock would stand there and the boy never again come into the room and look at the clock with the query, "What is the time?"

In a row of graves of the Unidentified the boy would sleep long in the dedicated final resting place at Gettysburg. Why he had gone away and why he would never come back had roots in some mystery of flags and drums, of national fate in which individuals sink as in a deep sea, of men swallowed and vanished in a man-made storm of smoke and steel.

The mystery deepened and moved with ancient music and inviolable consolation because a solemn Man of Authority had stood at the graves of the Unidentified and spoken the words "We cannot consecrate—we cannot hallow—this ground. The brave men, living and dead, who struggled here, have consecrated it far above our poor power to add or detract. . . . From these honored dead we take increased devotion to that cause for which they gave the last full measure of devotion."

To the backward and forward pendulum swing of a tall old clock in a quiet corner they might read those cadenced words while outside the windows the first flurry of snow blew across the orchard and down over the meadow, the beginnings of winter in a gun-metal gloaming to be later arched with a star-flung sky.[4]

· QUESTIONS ·

1. This selection employs a unique biographical method. Do you agree that "scholarliness, intimacy, and vigorous movement" result from its use?
2. What significant characteristics of Lincoln are revealed in this selection? Be specific in your answer.
3. Which of the five sections of "Gettysburg" most appeals to you? Why?
4. The sentence structure of Lincoln's address is notable. Analyze it.
5. Give a brief description of the address delivered by Edward Everett. Contrast it with Part IV of this selection.
6. Why was Lincoln called "the world's foremost spokesman of popular government"? Who were other similar spokesmen in 1863?

Theme Subjects: (1) Greatness and Simplicity; (2) A Review of *The Lincoln Reader;* (3) The Captains and the Kings Depart; (4) Lincoln and Lee: A Comparison.

---

[4] From *Abraham Lincoln: The War Years* by Carl Sandburg, copyright 1939 by Harcourt, Brace and Company, Inc.

SHORT STORIES

A NOTE ON READING

Although little more than a century old, the short story traces its ancestry to earlier forms of prose fiction. The type as we know it has evolved not only from the novel but, like the novel itself, from brief tales told by cavemen in the long ago, from the fables of Aesop, and from ancient Oriental episodes and stories. Quite probably the oldest of all literary forms in origin, the short story certainly owes something to that famous medieval potpourri, the *Gesta Romanorum*, to Chaucer and *The Canterbury Tales*, to Boccaccio's *Decameron* and Cervantes' *Don Quixote*, to "novels" and "histories" of the Elizabethan age, and to many other influences.

From these precursors of the short story has evolved a definite type of literature, a type really founded by Edgar Allan Poe (1809–1849). When Poe discarded the leisurely narrative methods of earlier writers, Washington Irving among them, and began to construct narratives notable for unity and compression, the modern short story was born. It should be remembered, however, that Poe did not "invent" the short story. His contribution was the shaping and arranging of materials and elements known and used for centuries. When Nathaniel Hawthorne (1804–1864) shortly followed Poe's stories with his somber, reflective, slowly paced fiction, the type may be said to have been both born and weaned. It rapidly grew to adulthood, first in America and somewhat later in England.

It is impossible to give a satisfactory definition of the short story. Although many attempts have been made, all have failed, some less conspicuously than others. The definitions have been too narrow or too broad. One that is too restricting puts the short story form into a strait jacket that inevitably hampers its freedom of movement so that it does not include, as it must, certain types of successful experimental stories which do not conform to a rigid pattern. And a definition that is too broad is likely to mean little or nothing.

Instead of trying to define a short story in precise terms, it is more helpful to study its possibilities and its limitations—what it can do and what it cannot do. The following suggestions introduce some of the possibilities and limitations of the type.

The limitation of the short story is the limitation of space: it must be short. The average story, because generally it must not exceed 5000–6000 words, has not the range of the novel. The short-story writer paints miniatures; the novelist paints murals. Because he must confine himself to a small canvas, the writer of the short story ordinarily observes certain principles. He knows, because his story must be short, that he must limit the number of characters in it and that usually its focus must fall on one character, or at most on a limited group of characters. He must similarly restrict the number of settings he uses; within a short space of time he cannot with impunity move his characters from place to place. Also he must not allow his story to consume any more time than is necessary. And, finally, he knows that he must focus the reader's attention on a single situation, the climax of his story. Whereas a novel can build up an infinite number of scenes before the climax is reached, the short story is proportionately restricted; its climax must be reached quickly.

The possibilities of the short story are the outgrowth of its limitations. Its assets capitalize on its liabilities. Although a story cannot deal with subjects suitable for a novel, conversely it can deal with certain situations that a novel could not handle effectively. Just because a story *is* short, the writer can concentrate his material most effectively, whereas the novelist may be more diffuse. A short story is like a newspaper editorial on a local tax problem; a novel resembles a treatise on economics. Each serves a need, but in a different way.

The great advantage of the short story is that it can focus sharply on a single character (or a very limited group of characters) in a single situation. Even a casual reading of the stories in this volume will reveal the fact that each builds to a single climactic situation. All the incidents in the forepart of each story are calculated nicely to focus the reader's attention on the ending. The novel, too, adopts this method of construction; but its subject is likely to be wider, its scope broader, its characters more numerous, its situations, comparatively speaking, more varied and unrelated.

We may well conclude that the guiding principle of the short story is *unity*. The stories concentrate on a single unified situation; the characters are reduced to a minimum number, and the author usually focuses on only one. Even when the spotlight of our attention is almost equally divided between two or more, the focus is shared, not divided.

Unity, then, is the basic principle of the short story: a story concentrates whenever possible on a single character in a single situation at a single moment.

Here are some hints on what to look for in short stories. All these questions will not apply to every narrative; furthermore, they are designedly general. Intelligent and continued reading will suggest further and more specific questions. But these basic questions will serve as a starting point for analysis.

1. Who is the central character of the story? (Or is there more than one central character? If so, how does the author preserve the unified focus?)

2. What are the dominant traits of the central character?

3. What forces make up the main conflict of the story?

4. How is this conflict resolved? If it is not resolved, what prevents a resolution?

5. What part does setting play in the story?

6. What is the theme, or idea, that underlies the story?

7. From what point of view is the story told? How does the author economize by shortening the actual elapsed time of the story?

8. Which of the four basic elements of fiction dominates the story—character, action (plot), setting, and theme?

THE CASK OF
AMONTILLADO

Edgar Allan Poe

EDGAR ALLAN POE (1809–1849), whose sinister tales are reflective of his tragic life, was born in Boston and orphaned less than three years later. His unhappiness in the foster home of the Allans of Richmond, his brief attendance at the University of Virginia and West Point, his poverty-stricken and unstable later life are familiar legends. Poe's reputation as the founder of the modern short story stems from the meticulously fashioned, unified "single effect" which he devised. His stories and many of his poems are sustained studies in mystery and horror. Among his most famous short stories are "Ligeia," 1838; "The Fall of the House of Usher," 1839; "The Murders in the Rue Morgue," 1841; "The Masque of the Red Death," 1842; "The Black Cat," 1843; "The Gold-Bug," 1843; "The Tell-Tale Heart," 1843; and "The Purloined Letter," 1845.

The thousand injuries of Fortunato I had borne as I best could; but when he ventured upon insult, I vowed revenge. You, who so well know the nature of my soul, will not suppose, however, that I gave utterance to a threat. *At length* I would be avenged; this was a point definitively settled—but the very definitiveness with which it was resolved precluded the idea of risk. I must not only punish, but punish with impunity. A wrong is unredressed when retribution overtakes its redresser. It is equally unredressed when the avenger fails to make himself felt as such to him who has done the wrong.

It must be understood that neither by word nor deed had I given Fortunato cause to doubt my good will. I continued, as was my wont, to smile in his face, and he did not perceive that my smile *now* was at the thought of his immolation.

He had a weak point—this Fortunato—although in other regards he was a man to be respected and even feared. He prided himself on his connoisseurship in wine. Few Italians have the true virtuoso spirit. For the most part their enthusiasm is adopted to suit the time and opportunity, to practice imposture upon the British and Austrian millionaires. In painting and gemmary,[1] Fortunato, like his countrymen, was a quack, but in the matter of old wines he was sincere. In this respect I did not differ from him materially;—I was skillful in the Italian vintages myself, and bought largely whenever I could.

It was about dusk, one evening during the supreme madness of the carnival season, that I encountered my friend. He accosted me with excessive warmth, for he had been drinking much. The man wore motley. He had on a tight-fitting parti-striped dress, and his head was surmounted by the conical cap and bells. I was so pleased to see him that I thought I should never have done wringing his hand.

I said to him—"My dear Fortunato, you are luckily met. How remarkably well you are looking today. But I have received a pipe[2] of what passes for Amontillado,[3] and I have my doubts."

"How?" said he. "Amontillado? A pipe? Impossible! And in the middle of the carnival!"

"I have my doubts," I replied; "and I was silly enough to pay the full Amontillado price without consulting you in the matter. You were not to be found, and I was fearful of losing a bargain."

"Amontillado!"

"I have my doubts."

"Amontillado!"

"And I must satisfy them."

"Amontillado!"

"As you are engaged, I am on my way to Luchresi. If anyone has a critical turn, it is he. He will tell me—"

"Luchresi cannot tell Amontillado from Sherry."

"And yet some fools will have it that his taste is a match for your own."

"Come, let us go."

"Whither?"

"To your vaults."

"My friend, no; I will not impose upon your good nature. I perceive you have an engagement. Luchresi—"

"I have no engagement; come."

"My friend, no. It is not the

---

[1] knowledge of precious gems
[2] a large cask
[3] a pale-colored Spanish sherry

engagement, but the severe cold with which I perceive you are afflicted. The vaults are insufferably damp. They are encrusted with nitre."

"Let us go, nevertheless. The cold is merely nothing. Amontillado! You have been imposed upon. And as for Luchresi, he cannot distinguish Sherry from Amontillado."

Thus speaking, Fortunato possessed himself of my arm; and putting on a mask of black silk and drawing a *roquelaure*[4] closely about my person, I suffered him to hurry me to my palazzo.

There were no attendants at home; they had absconded to make merry in honor of the time. I had told them that I should not return until the morning, and had given them explicit orders not to stir from the house. These orders were sufficient, I well knew, to insure their immediate disappearance, one and all, as soon as my back was turned.

I took from their sconces two flambeaux, and giving one to Fortunato, bowed him through several suites of rooms to the archway that led into the vaults. I passed down a long and winding staircase, requesting him to be cautious as he followed. We came at length to the foot of the descent and stood together upon the damp ground of the catacombs of the Montresors.

The gait of my friend was unsteady, and the bells upon his cap jingled as he strode.

"The pipe," he said.

"It is farther on," said I; "but observe the white web-work which gleams from these cavern walls."

He turned towards me and looked into my eyes with two filmy orbs that distilled the rheum of intoxication.

"Nitre?" he asked, at length.

"Nitre," I replied. "How long have you had that cough?"

"Ugh! ugh! ugh!—ugh! ugh! ugh!—ugh! ugh! ugh!—ugh! ugh! ugh!—ugh! ugh! ugh!"

My poor friend found it impossible to reply for many minutes.

"It is nothing," he said, at last.

"Come," I said, with decision, "we will go back; your health is precious. You are rich, respected, admired, beloved; you are happy, as once I was. You are a man to be missed. For me it is no matter. We will go back; you will be ill, and I cannot be responsible. Besides, there is Luchresi—"

"Enough," he said; "the cough is a mere nothing; it will not kill me. I shall not die of a cough."

"True—true," I replied; "and, indeed, I had no intention of alarming you unnecessarily—but you should use all proper caution. A draught of this Médoc[5] will defend us from the damps."

Here I knocked off the neck of a bottle which I drew from a long row of its fellows that lay upon the mold.

"Drink," I said, presenting him the wine.

He raised it to his lips with a leer. He paused and nodded to me familiarly, while his bells jingled.

"I drink," he said, "to the buried that repose around us."

"And I to your long life."

He again took my arm, and we proceeded.

"These vaults," he said, "are extensive."

"The Montresors," I replied,

---

[4] a cloak reaching to the knees
[5] a claret wine produced in southwestern France

"were a great and numerous family."

"I forget your arms."

"A huge human foot d'or, in a field azure; the foot crushes a serpent rampant whose fangs are embedded in the heel."

"And the motto?"

"Nemo me impune lacessit."[6]

"Good!" he said.

The wine sparkled in his eyes and the bells jingled. My own fancy grew warm with the Médoc. We had passed through long walls of piled skeletons, with casks and puncheons intermingling, into the inmost recesses of the catacombs. I paused again, and this time I made bold to seize Fortunato by an arm above the elbow.

"The nitre!" I said; "see, it increases. It hangs like moss upon the vaults. We are below the river's bed. The drops of moisture trickle among the bones. Come, we will go back ere it is too late. Your cough—"

"It is nothing," he said; "let us go on. But first, another draught of the Médoc."

I broke and reached him a flagon of De Graves.[7] He emptied it at a breath. His eyes flashed with a fierce light. He laughed and threw the bottle upwards with a gesticulation I did not understand.

I looked at him in surprise. He repeated the movement—a grotesque one.

"You do not comprehend?" he said.

"Not I," I replied.

"Then you are not of the brotherhood."

"How?"

"You are not of the masons."

"Yes, yes," I said, "yes, yes."

"You? Impossible! A mason?"

"A mason," I replied.

"A sign," he said, "a sign."

"It is this," I answered, producing from beneath the folds of my *roquelaure*, a trowel.

"You jest," he exclaimed, recoiling a few paces. "But let us proceed to the Amontillado."

"Be it so," I said, replacing the tool beneath the cloak, and again offering him my arm. He leaned upon it heavily. We continued our route in search of the Amontillado. We passed through a range of low arches, descended, passed on, and, descending again, arrived at a deep crypt, in which the foulness of the air caused our flambeaux rather to glow than flame.

At the most remote end of the crypt there appeared another less spacious. Its walls had been lined with human remains, piled to the vault overhead, in the fashion of the great catacombs of Paris. Three sides of this interior crypt were still ornamented in this manner. From the fourth the bones had been thrown down, and lay promiscuously upon the earth, forming at one point a mound of some size. Within the wall thus exposed by the displacing of the bones, we perceived a still interior recess, in depth about four feet, in width three, in height six or seven. It seemed to have been constructed for no especial use within itself, but formed merely the interval between two of the colossal supports of the roof of the catacombs, and was backed by one of their circumscribing walls of solid granite.

It was in vain that Fortunato,

---

[6] No one attacks me with impunity.

[7] a French wine

uplifting his dull torch, endeavored to pry into the depth of the recess. Its termination the feeble light did not enable us to see.

"Proceed," I said; "herein is the Amontillado. As for Luchresi—"

"He is an ignoramus," interrupted my friend, as he stepped unsteadily forward, while I followed immediately at his heels. In an instant he had reached the extremity of the niche, and finding his progress arrested by the rock, stood stupidly bewildered. A moment more and I had fettered him to the granite. In its surface were two iron staples, distant from each other about two feet, horizontally. From one of these depended a short chain, from the other a padlock. Throwing the links about his waist, it was but the work of a few seconds to secure it. He was too much astounded to resist. Withdrawing the key I stepped back from the recess.

"Pass your hand," I said, "over the wall; you cannot help feeling the nitre. Indeed, it is *very* damp. Once more let me *implore* you to return. No? Then I must positively leave you. But I must first render you all the little attentions in my power."

"The Amontillado!" ejaculated my friend, not yet recovered from his astonishment.

"True," I replied; "the Amontillado."

As I said these words I busied myself among the pile of bones of which I have before spoken. Throwing them aside, I soon uncovered a quantity of building stone and mortar. With these materials and with the aid of my trowel, I began vigorously to wall up the entrance of the niche.

I had scarcely laid the first tier of the masonry when I discovered that the intoxication of Fortunato had in a great measure worn off. The earliest indication I had of this was a low moaning cry from the depth of the recess. It was *not* the cry of a drunken man. There was then a long and obstinate silence. I laid the second tier, and the third, and the fourth; and then I heard the furious vibrations of the chain. The noise lasted for several minutes, during which, that I might hearken to it with the more satisfaction, I ceased my labors and sat down upon the bones. When at last the clanking subsided, I resumed the trowel, and finished without interruption the fifth, the sixth, and the seventh tier. The wall was now nearly upon a level with my breast. I again paused, and holding the flambeaux over the mason-work, threw a few feeble rays upon the figure within.

A succession of loud and shrill screams, bursting suddenly from the throat of the chained form, seemed to thrust me violently back. For a brief moment I hesitated, I trembled. Unsheathing my rapier, I began to grope with it about the recess; but the thought of an instant reassured me. I placed my hand upon the solid fabric of the catacombs, and felt satisfied. I reapproached the wall; I replied to the yells of him who clamored. I re-echoed, I aided, I surpassed them in volume and in strength. I did this, and the clamorer grew still.

It was now midnight, and my task was drawing to a close. I had completed the eighth, the ninth and the tenth tier. I had finished a portion of the last and the eleventh; there remained but a single stone to be fitted and plastered in. I struggled with its weight; I placed it partially in its destined position. But now there came from out the niche a low laugh that erected the hairs upon my head. It was succeeded by a sad voice, which I had difficulty in recognizing as that of the noble Fortunato. The voice said—

"Ha! ha! ha!—he! he! he!—a very good joke, indeed—an excellent jest. We will have many a rich laugh about it at the palazzo—he! he! he!—over our wine—he! he! he!"

"The Amontillado!" I said.

"He! he! he!—he! he! he!—yes, the Amontillado. But is it not getting late? Will not they be awaiting us at the palazzo, the Lady Fortunato and the rest? Let us be gone."

"Yes," I said, "let us be gone."

"*For the love of God, Montresor!*"

"Yes," I said, "for the love of God!"

But to these words I hearkened in vain for a reply. I grew impatient. I called aloud—

"Fortunato!"

No answer. I called again—

"Fortunato!"

No answer still. I thrust a torch through the remaining aperture and let it fall within. There came forth in return only a jingling of the bells. My heart grew sick—on account of the dampness of the catacombs. I hastened to make an end of my labor. I forced the last stone into its position; I plastered it up. Against the new masonry I re-erected the old rampart of bones. For the half of a century no mortal has disturbed them. *In pace requiescat.*[8]

· QUESTIONS ·

1. This story is so compressed that much is left out. For example, we do not know what were "the thousand injuries." What else is omitted in the interests of economy?
2. How effective would this story be if narrated in the third person? What would be gained or lost?
3. Poe wrote concisely but used effective repetition of word and phrase. The sardonic echoing of what one word especially contributes to this story?
4. Define: definitiveness, impunity, unredressed, wont, immolation, connoisseurship, virtuoso, motley, explicit, gesticulation, aperture.

Theme Subjects: (1) The Arrogance of Pride; (2) I Am a Connoisseur of _____; (3) The Most Cruel Deed I Ever Witnessed; (4) Poe's Review of Hawthorne's *Twice-Told Tales* (a review); (5) Poe's "The Philosophy of Composition" (a review).

---

[8] May he rest in peace.

THE AMBITIOUS GUEST

Nathaniel Hawthorne

The Puritan heritage of his Salem, Massachusetts, family was a dominant influence on the work of NATHANIEL HAWTHORNE (1804–1864), but his concern is with moral conflicts rather than formal theological and ethical systems. His novel and short-story writing, begun in 1825, denies the optimism of other writers of his generation and reflects a thoughtful interest in moral and psychological problems. *The Scarlet Letter*, 1850, for example, is a tragic study of the effect of sin on the lives of four people; in *The House of the Seven Gables*, 1851, he traces the decline of a Puritan family; *The Blithedale Romance*, 1852, contains a satire on the Brook Farm experiment in community living.

One September night a family had gathered round their hearth and piled it high with the driftwood of mountain streams, the dry cones of the pine, and the splintered ruins of great trees that had come crashing down the precipice. Up the chimney roared the fire and brightened the room with its broad blaze. The faces of the father and mother had a sober gladness; the children laughed; the eldest daughter was the image of Happiness at seventeen; and the aged grandmother, who sat knitting in the warmest place, was the image of Happiness grown old. They had found the "herb, heart's-ease," in the bleakest spot of all New England. This family were situated in the Notch of the White Hills, where the wind was sharp throughout the year and pitilessly cold in the winter,—giving their cottage all its fresh inclemency before it descended on the valley of the Saco. They dwelt in a cold spot and a dangerous one; for a mountain towered above their heads, so steep that the stones would often rumble down its sides and startle them at midnight.

The daughter had just uttered some simple jest that filled them all with mirth, when the wind came through the Notch and seemed to pause before their cottage—rattling the door, with a sound of wailing and lamentation, before it passed into the valley. For a moment it saddened them, though there was nothing unusual in the tones. But the family were glad again when they perceived that the latch was lifted by some traveler, whose footsteps had been unheard amid the dreary blast which heralded his approach, and wailed as he was entering, and went moaning away from the door.

Though they dwelt in such a solitude, these people held daily converse with the world. The romantic pass of the Notch is a great artery, through which the lifeblood of internal commerce is continually throbbing between Maine, on one side, and the Green Mountains and the shores of the St. Lawrence, on the other. The stagecoach always drew up before the door of the cottage. The wayfarer, with no companion but his staff, paused here to exchange a word, that the sense of loneliness might not utterly overcome him ere he could pass through the cleft of the mountain or reach the first house in the valley. And here the teamster, on his way to Portland market, would put up for the night; and, if a bachelor, might sit an hour beyond the usual bedtime and steal a kiss from the mountain maid at parting. It was one of those primitive taverns where the traveler pays only for food and lodging but meets with a homely kindness beyond all price. When the footsteps were heard, therefore, between the outer door and the inner one, the whole family rose up, grandmother, children, and all, as if about to welcome someone who belonged to them and whose fate was linked with theirs.

The door was opened by a young man. His face at first wore the melancholy expression, almost despondency, of one who travels a wild and bleak road, at nightfall and alone, but soon brightened up when he saw the kindly warmth of his reception. He felt his heart spring forward to meet them all, from the old woman, who wiped a chair with her apron, to the little child that held out its arms to him. One glance and smile placed the stranger on a footing of innocent familiarity with the eldest daughter.

"Ah, this fire is the right thing!" cried he; "especially when there is such a pleasant circle round it. I am quite benumbed; for the Notch is just like the pipe of a great pair of bellows; it has blown a terrible blast in my face all the way from Bartlett."

"Then you are going toward Vermont?" said the master of the house, as he helped to take a light knapsack off the young man's shoulders.

"Yes; to Burlington, and far enough beyond," replied he. "I meant to have been at Ethan Crawford's to-night; but a pedestrian lingers along such a road as this. It is no matter; for, when I saw this good fire and all your cheerful faces, I felt as if you had kindled it on purpose for me and were waiting my arrival. So I shall sit down among you, and make myself at home."

The frank-hearted stranger had just drawn his chair to the fire when something like a heavy footstep was heard without, rushing down the steep side of the mountain, as with long and rapid strides, and taking such a leap in passing the cottage as to strike the opposite precipice. The family held their breath, because they knew the sound, and their guest held his by instinct.

"The old mountain has thrown a stone at us, for fear we should forget him," said the landlord, recovering himself. "He sometimes nods his head and threatens to come down; but we are old neighbors and agree together pretty well upon the whole. Besides, we have a sure place of refuge hard by if he should be coming in good earnest."

Let us now suppose the stranger to have finished his supper of bear's meat; and, by his natural felicity of manner, to have placed himself on a footing of kindness with the whole family, so that they talked as freely together as if he belonged to their mountain brood. He was of a proud, yet gentle spirit —haughty and reserved among the rich and great; but ever ready to stoop his head to the lowly cottage door, and be like a brother or a son at the poor man's fireside. In the household of the Notch he found warmth and simplicity of feeling, the pervading intelligence of New England, and a poetry, of native growth, which they had gathered when they little thought of it from the mountain peaks and chasms, and at the very threshold of their romantic and dangerous abode. He had traveled far and alone; his whole life, indeed, had been a solitary path; for, with the lofty caution of his nature, he had kept himself apart from those who might otherwise have been his companions. The family, too, though so kind and hospitable, had that consciousness of unity among themselves, and separation from the world at large, which, in every domestic circle, should still keep a holy place where no stranger may intrude. But this evening a prophetic sympathy impelled the refined and educated youth to pour out his heart before the simple mountaineers and constrained them to answer him with the same free confidence. And thus it should have

been. Is not the kindred of a common fate a closer tie than that of birth?

The secret of the young man's character was a high and abstracted ambition. He could have borne to live an undistinguished life, but not to be forgotten in the grave. Yearning desire had been transformed to hope; and hope, long cherished, had become like certainty that, obscurely as he journeyed now, a glory was to beam on all his pathway,— though not, perhaps, while he was treading it. But when posterity should gaze back into the gloom of what was now the present, they would trace the brightness of his footsteps, brightening as meaner glories faded, and confess that a gifted one had passed from his cradle to his tomb with none to recognize him.

"As yet," cried the stranger,— his cheek glowing and his eye flashing with enthusiasm,—"as yet, I have done nothing. Were I to vanish from the earth to-morrow, none would know so much of me as you: that a nameless youth came up at nightfall from the valley of the Saco and opened his heart to you in the evening and passed through the Notch by sunrise and was seen no more. Not a soul would ask, 'Who was he? Whither did the wanderer go?' But I cannot die till I have achieved my destiny. Then, let Death come! I shall have built my monument!"

There was a continual flow of natural emotion, gushing forth amid abstracted revery, which enabled the family to understand this young man's sentiments, though so foreign from their own. With quick sensibility of the ludicrous, he blushed at the ardor into which he had been betrayed.

"You laugh at me," said he, taking the eldest daughter's hand, and laughing himself. "You think my ambition as nonsensical as if I were to freeze myself to death on the top of Mount Washington, only that people might spy at me from the country round about. And, truly, that would be a noble pedestal for a man's statue!"

"It is better to sit here by this fire," answered the girl, blushing, "and be comfortable and contented, though nobody thinks about us."

"I suppose," said her father, after a fit of musing, "there is something natural in what the young man says; and if my mind had been turned that way I might have felt just the same. It is strange, wife, how his talk has set my head running on things that are pretty certain never to come to pass."

"Perhaps they may," observed the wife. "Is the man thinking what he will do when he is a widower?"

"No, no!" cried he, repelling the idea with reproachful kindness. "When I think of your death, Esther, I think of mine, too. But I was wishing we had a good farm in Bartlett, or Bethlehem, or Littleton, or some other township round the White Mountains; but not where they could tumble on our heads. I should want to stand well with my neighbors and be called Squire and sent to General Court for a term or two; for a plain, honest man may do as much good there as a lawyer. And when I should be grown quite an old man and you an old woman, so as not to be long apart, I might die happy enough in my bed and leave you all crying around me. A slate gravestone would suit me as well as a marble one—with just my name and age, and a verse of a hymn, and something to let people know that I lived an honest man and died a Christian."

"There now!" exclaimed the stranger; "it is our nature to desire a monument, be it slate or marble, or a pillar of granite, or a glorious memory in the universal heart of man."

"We're in a strange way to-night," said the wife, with tears in her eyes. "They say it's a sign of something, when folks' minds go a-wandering so. Hark to the children!"

They listened accordingly. The younger children had been put to bed in another room, but with an open door between them, so that they could be heard talking busily among themselves. One and all seemed to have caught the infection from the fireside circle and were outvying each other in wild wishes and childish projects of what they would do when they came to be men and women. At length a little boy, instead of addressing his brothers and sisters, called out to his mother.

"I'll tell you what I wish, Mother," cried he. "I want you and Father and Grandma'm, and all of us, and the stranger, too, to start right away and go and take a drink out of the basin of the Flume!"

Nobody could help laughing at the child's notion of leaving a warm bed and dragging them from a cheerful fire, to visit the basin of the Flume,—a brook which tumbles over the precipice, deep within the Notch. The boy had hardly spoken when a wagon rattled along the road and stopped a moment before the door. It appeared to contain two or three men, who were cheering their hearts with the rough chorus of a song, which resounded, in broken notes, between the cliffs, while the singers hesitated whether to continue their journey or put up here for the night.

"Father," said the girl, "they are calling you by name."

But the good man doubted whether they had really called him and was unwilling to show himself too solicitous of gain by inviting people to patronize his house. He therefore did not hurry to the door; and the lash being soon applied, the travelers plunged into the Notch, still singing and laughing, though their music and mirth came back drearily from the heart of the mountain.

"There, Mother!" cried the boy again. "They'd have given us a ride to the Flume."

Again they laughed at the child's pertinacious fancy for a night ramble. But it happened that a light cloud passed over the daughter's spirit; she looked gravely into the fire and drew a breath that was almost a sigh. It forced its way in spite of the struggle to repress it. Then, starting and blushing, she looked quickly round the circle, as if they had caught a glimpse into her bosom. The stranger asked what she had been thinking of.

"Nothing," answered she, with a downcast smile. "Only I felt lonesome just then."

"Oh, I have always had a gift of feeling what is in other people's hearts," said he, half seriously. "Shall I tell the secrets of yours? For I know what to think when a young girl shivers by a warm hearth and complains of lonesomeness at her mother's side. Shall I put these feelings into words?"

"They would not be a girl's feelings any longer if they could be put into words," replied the mountain nymph, laughing, but avoiding his eye.

All this was said apart. Perhaps a germ of love was springing in their hearts, so pure that it might blossom in Paradise, since it could not be matured on earth; for women worship such gentle dignity as his; and the proud, contemplative, yet kindly soul is oftenest captivated by simplicity like hers. But while they spoke softly, and he was watching the happy sadness, the lightsome shadows, the shy yearnings of a maiden's nature, the wind through the Notch took a deeper and drearier sound. It seemed, as the fanciful stranger said, like the choral strain of the spirits of the past, who in old Indian times had their dwelling among these mountains and made their heights and recesses a sacred region. There was a wail along the road, as if a funeral were passing. To chase away the gloom, the family threw pine branches on their fire, till the dry leaves crackled and the flame arose, discovering once again a scene of peace and humble happiness. The light hovered about them fondly and caressed them all. There were the little faces of the children, peeping from their bed apart, and here the father's frame of strength, the mother's subdued and careful mien, the high-browed youth, the budding girl, and the good old grandma, still knitting in the warmest place. The aged woman looked up from her task, and, with fingers ever busy, was the next to speak.

"Old folks have their notions," said she, "as well as young ones. You've been wishing and planning and letting your heads run on one thing and another, till you've set my mind a-wandering too. Now what should an old woman wish for, when she can go but a step or two before she comes to her grave?

Children, it will haunt me night and day till I tell you."

"What is it, Mother?" cried the husband and wife at once.

Then the old woman, with an air of mystery which drew the circle closer round the fire, informed them that she had provided her graveclothes some years before,— a nice linen shroud, a cap with a muslin ruff, and everything of a finer sort than she had worn since her wedding day. But this evening an old superstition had strangely recurred to her. It used to be said, in her younger days, that if anything were amiss with a corpse, if only the ruff were not smooth, or the cap did not set right, the corpse in the coffin and beneath the clods would strive to put up its cold hands and arrange it. The bare thought made her nervous.

"Don't talk so, Grandmother!" said the girl, shuddering.

"Now,"—continued the old woman, with singular earnestness, yet smiling strangely at her own folly,—"I want one of you, my children,—when your mother is dressed in the coffin—I want one of you to hold a looking-glass over my face. Who knows but I may take a glimpse at myself and see whether all's right."

"Old and young, we dream of graves and monuments," murmured the stranger youth. "I wonder how mariners feel when the ship is sinking, and they, unknown and undistinguished, are to be buried together in the ocean—that wide and nameless sepulcher?"

For a moment, the old woman's ghastly conception so engrossed the minds of her hearers that a sound abroad in the night, rising like the roar of a blast, had grown broad, deep, and terrible, before the fated group were conscious of it. The house and all within it trembled; the foundations of the earth seemed to be shaken, as if this awful sound were the peal of the last trump. Young and old exchanged one wild glance and remained an instant, pale, affrighted, without utterance or power to move. Then the same shriek burst simultaneously from all their lips. "The Slide! The Slide!"

The simplest words must intimate, but not portray, the unutterable horror of the catastrophe. The victims rushed from their cottage and sought refuge in what they deemed a safer spot—where, in contemplation of such an emergency, a sort of barrier had been reared. Alas! they had quitted their security and fled right into the pathway of destruction. Down came the whole side of the mountain, in a cataract of ruin. Just before it reached the house, the stream broke into two branches—shivered not a window there, but overwhelmed the whole vicinity, blocked up the road, and annihilated everything in its dreadful course. Long ere the thunder of the great Slide had ceased to roar among the mountains, the mortal agony had been endured, and the victims were at peace. Their bodies were never found.

The next morning, the light smoke was seen stealing from the cottage chimney up the mountain side. Within, the fire was yet smoldering on the hearth, and the chairs in a circle around it, as if the inhabitants had but gone forth to view the devastation of the Slide and would shortly return, to thank Heaven for their miraculous escape. All had left separate tokens, by which those who had known the family were made to shed a tear for each. Who has not heard their name? The story has been told far and wide, and will forever be a legend of these mountains. Poets have sung their fate.

There were circumstances which led some to suppose that a stranger had been received into the cottage on this awful night and had shared the catastrophe of all its inmates. Others denied that there were sufficient grounds for such a conjecture. Woe for the high-souled youth, with his dream of Earthly Immortality! His name and person utterly unknown; his history, his way of life, his plans, a mystery never to be solved, his death and his existence equally a doubt! Whose was the agony of that death moment?

· QUESTIONS ·

1. What use does Hawthorne here make of dramatic suspense? Did you anticipate the ending?
2. Does the beginning of a love interest add to the pathos of the story? If so, how?
3. Would a modern short-story writer employ the last three sentences? Might he omit the entire final paragraph? The last two paragraphs? Account for your answers.
4. State the central meaning of this story. What does the grandmother add to this meaning?
5. This story, which deals with the futility of human effort in a world where the lot of man is considered foreordained and where death is inexorably final, has been compared to the book of *Ecclesiastes* in the Old Testament. Read *Ecclesiastes* and point out parallels between its reflections on life and the thematic development of "An Ambitious Guest."

Theme Subjects: (1) Man Proposes, God Disposes; (2) My Greatest Disappointment in Life; (3) The Monument I Should Like To Build; (4) The Pride of Youth; (5) The Preface to Hawthorne's *Twice-Told Tales* (a review); (6) A Premonition I Once Had.

QUALITY

John Galsworthy

JOHN GALSWORTHY (1867–1933) was born in Surrey, England, and edu-cated at Harrow and New College, Oxford. The son of a prominent London attorney, he himself studied law but never cared for practice. Wide reading, extensive traveling, and his own instincts led him to writing. His fame rests upon his work as a dramatist and novelist, but his fecundity and versatility resulted in many short stories, essays, and poems as well. His plays, usually marked by social criticism, are numerous—among the more powerful are *The Silver Box* (1906); *Strife* (1909); *Justice* (1910); *Loyalties* (1922); *Old English* (1924). The great series of novels known as *The Forsyte Saga* (1906–1928) is probably his major contribution to literature. Always a meticulous craftsman, Galsworthy was awarded the Nobel Prize for liter-ature in 1932.

I knew him from the days of my extreme youth, because he made my father's boots; inhabiting with his elder brother two little shops let into one, in a small by-street—now no more, but then most fashionably placed in the West End.

That tenement had a certain quiet distinction; there was no sign upon its face that he made for any of the Royal Family—merely his own German name of Gessler Broth-ers; and in the window a few pairs of boots. I remember that it always troubled me to account for those unvarying boots in the window, for he made only what was ordered, reaching nothing down, and it seemed so inconceivable that what he made could ever have failed to fit. Had he bought them to put there? That, too, seemed inconceiv-able. He would never have tolerated in his house leather on which he had not worked himself. Besides, they were too beautiful—the pairs of pumps, so inexpressibly slim, the patent leathers with cloth tops, making water come into one's mouth, the tall brown riding-boots

From *The Inn of Tranquillity* by John Galsworthy. Reprinted by permission of Charles Scribner's Sons.

with marvelous sooty glow, as if, though new, they had been worn a hundred years. Those pairs could only have been made by one who saw before him the Soul of Boot—so truly were they prototypes, incarnating the very spirit of all footwear. These thoughts, of course, came to me later, though even when I was promoted to him, at the age of perhaps fourteen, some inkling haunted me of the dignity of himself and brother. For to make boots—such boots as he made—seemed to me then, and still seems to me, mysterious and wonderful.

I remember well my shy remark, one day, while stretching out to him my youthful foot:

"Isn't it awfully hard to do, Mr. Gessler?"

And his answer, given with a sudden smile from out of the sardonic redness of his beard: "Id is an Ardt!"

Himself, he was a little as if made of leather, with his yellow crinkly face, and crinkly reddish hair and beard, and neat folds slanting down his cheeks to the corners of his mouth, and his guttural and one-toned voice; for leather is a sardonic substance, and stiff and slow of purpose. And that was the character of his face, save that his eyes, which were gray-blue, had in them the simple gravity of one secretly possessed by the Ideal. His elder brother was so very like him—though watery, paler in every way, with a great industry—that sometimes in early days I was not quite sure of him until the interview was over. Then I knew that it was he, if the words, "I will ask my brudder," had not been spoken, and that, if they had, it was the elder brother.

When one grew old and wild and ran up bills, one somehow never ran them up with Gessler Brothers. It would not have seemed becoming to go in there and stretch out one's foot to that blue iron-spectacled face, owing him for more than—say —two pairs, just the comfortable reassurance that one was still his client.

For it was not possible to go to him very often—his boots lasted terribly, having something beyond the temporary—some, as it were, essence of boot stitched into them.

One went in, not as into most shops, in the mood of: "Please serve me, and let me go!" but restfully, as one enters a church; and, sitting on the single wooden chair, waited —for there was never anybody there. Soon—over the top edge of that sort of well—rather dark, and smelling soothingly of leather— which formed the shop, there would be seen his face, or that of his elder brother, peering down. A guttural sound, and the tip-tap of bast slippers beating the narrow wooden stairs, and he would stand before one without coat, a little bent, in leather apron, with sleeves turned back, blinking—as if awakened from some dream of boots, or like an owl surprised in daylight and annoyed at this interruption.

And I would say: "How do you do, Mr. Gessler? Could you make me a pair of Russia leather boots?"

Without a word he would leave me, retiring whence he came, or into the other portion of the shop, and I would continue to rest in the wooden chair, inhaling the incense of his trade. Soon he would come back, holding in his thin, veined hand a piece of gold-brown leather. With eyes fixed on it, he would remark: "What a beaudiful biece!" When I, too, had admired it, he would speak again: "When do you wand dem?" And I would answer: "Oh! As soon as you conveniently can." And he would say: "Tomorrow fordnighd?" Or if he were his elder brother: "I will ask my brudder!"

Then I would murmur: "Thank you! Good-morning, Mr. Gessler." "Goot-morning!" he would reply, still looking at the leather in his hand. And as I moved to the door, I would hear the tip-tap of his bast slippers restoring him, up the stairs, to his dream of boots. But if it were some new kind of footgear that he had not yet made me, then indeed he would observe ceremony—divesting me of my boot and holding it long in his hand, looking at it with eyes at once critical and loving, as if recalling the glow with which he had created it, and rebuking the way in which one had disorganized this masterpiece. Then, placing my foot on a piece of paper, he would two or three times tickle the outer edges with a pencil and pass his nervous fingers over my toes, feeling himself into the heart of my requirements.

I cannot forget that day on which I had occasion to say to him: "Mr. Gessler, that last pair of town walking-boots creaked, you know."

He looked at me for a time without replying, as if expecting me to withdraw or qualify the statement, then said:

"Id shouldn'd 'ave greaked."

"It did, I'm afraid."

"You goddem wed before dey found demselves?"

"I don't think so."

At that he lowered his eyes, as if hunting for memory of those boots, and I felt sorry I had mentioned this grave thing.

"Zend dem back!" he said; "I will look at dem."

A feeling of compassion for my creaking boots surged up in me, so well could I imagine the sorrowful long curiosity of regard which he would bend on them.

"Zome boods," he said slowly, "are bad from birdt. If I can do noding wid dem, I dake dem off your bill."

Once (once only) I went absent-mindedly into his shop in a pair of boots bought in an emergency at some large firm's. He took my order without showing me any leather, and I could feel his eyes penetrating the interior integument of my foot. At last he said:

"Dose are nod my boods."

The tone was not one of anger, nor of sorrow, not even of contempt, but there was in it something quiet that froze the blood. He put his hand down and pressed a finger on the place where the left boot, endeavoring to be fashionable, was not quite comfortable.

"Id 'urds you dere," he said. "Dose big virms 'ave no self-respect. Drash!" And then, as if something had given way within him, he spoke long and bitterly. It was the only time I ever heard him discuss the conditions and hardships of his trade.

"Dey get id all," he said, "dey get id by adverdisement, nod by work. Dey dake id away from us, who lofe our boods. Id gomes to this—bresently I haf no work. Every year id gets less—you will see." And looking at his lined face I saw things I had never noticed before, bitter things and bitter struggle—and what a lot of gray hairs there seemed suddenly in his red beard!

As best I could, I explained the circumstances of the purchase of those ill-omened boots. But his face and voice made a so deep impression that during the next few minutes I ordered many pairs! Nemesis fell! They lasted more terribly than ever. And I was not able conscientiously to go to him for nearly two years.

When at last I went I was surprised that outside one of the two little windows of his shop another name was painted, also that of a bootmaker—making, of course, for the Royal Family. The old familiar boots, no longer in dignified isolation, were huddled in the single window. Inside, the now contracted well of the one little shop was more scented and darker than ever. And it was longer than usual, too, before a face peered down, and the tip-tap of the bast slippers began. At last he stood before me, and, gazing through those rusty iron spectacles, said:

"Mr. ____, isn'd id?"

"Ah! Mr. Gessler," I stammered, "but your boots are really *too* good, you know! See, these are quite decent still!" And I stretched out to him my foot. He looked at it.

"Yes," he said, "beople do nod wand good boods, id seems."

To get away from his reproachful eyes and voice I hastily remarked: "What have you done to your shop?"

He answered quietly: "Id was too exbensif. Do you wand some boods?"

I ordered three pairs, though I had wanted only two, and quickly left. I had, I know not quite what feeling of being part, in his mind, of a conspiracy against him; or not perhaps so much against him as against his idea of boot. One does not, I suppose, care to feel like that; for it was again many months before my next visit to his shop, paid, I remember, with the feeling: "Oh!

well, I can't leave the old boy—so here goes! Perhaps it'll be his elder brother!"

For his elder brother, I knew, had not character enough to reproach me, even dumbly.

And, to my relief, in the shop there did appear to be his elder brother, handling a piece of leather.

"Well, Mr. Gessler," I said, "how are you?"

He came close, and peered at me.

"I am breddy well," he said slowly; "but my elder brudder is dead."

And I saw that it was indeed himself—but how aged and wan! And never before had I heard him mention his brother. Much shocked, I murmured: "Oh! I am sorry!"

"Yes," he answered, "he was a good man, he made a good bood; but he is dead." And he touched the top of his head, where the hair had suddenly gone as thin as it had been on that of his poor brother, to indicate, I suppose, the cause of death. "He could nod ged over losing de oder shop. Do you wand any boods?" And he held up the leather in his hand: "Id's a beaudiful biece."

I ordered several pairs. It was very long before they came—but they were better than ever. One simply could not wear them out. And soon after that I went abroad.

It was over a year before I was again in London. And the first shop I went to was my old friend's. I had left a man of sixty, I came back to find one of seventy-five, pinched and worn and tremulous, who genuinely, this time, did not at first know me.

"Oh! Mr. Gessler," I said, sick at heart; "how splendid your boots are! See, I've been wearing this pair nearly all the time I've been abroad; and they're not half worn out, are they?"

He looked long at my boots— a pair of Russia leather, and his face seemed to regain its steadiness. Putting his hand on my instep, he said:

"Do dey vid you here? I 'ad drouble wid dat bair, I remember."

I assured him that they had fitted beautifully.

"Do you wand any boods?" he said. "I can make dem quickly; id is a slack dime."

I answered: "Please, please! I want boots all round—every kind!"

"I vill make a vresh model. Your food must be bigger." And with utter slowness, he traced round my foot, and felt my toes, only once looking up to say:

"Did I dell you my brudder was dead?"

To watch him was quite painful, so feeble had he grown; I was glad to get away.

I had given those boots up, when one evening they came. Opening the parcel, I set the four pairs out in a row. Then one by one I tried them on. There was no doubt about it. In shape and fit, in finish and quality of leather, they were the best he had ever made me. And in the mouth of one of the town walking-boots I found his bill. The amount was the same as usual, but it gave me quite a shock. He had never before sent it in until quarter day. I flew downstairs and wrote a check, and posted it at once with my own hand.

A week later, passing the little street, I thought I would go in and tell him how splendidly the new boots fitted. But when I came to where his shop had been, his name was gone. Still there, in the window, were the slim pumps, the patent leathers with cloth tops, the sooty riding-boots.

I went in, very much disturbed. In the two little shops—again made into one—was a young man with an English face.

"Mr. Gessler in?" I said.

He gave me a strange, ingratiating look.

"No, sir," he said, "no. But we can attend to anything with pleasure. We've taken the shop over. You've seen our name, no doubt, next door. We make for some very good people."

"Yes, yes," I said, "but Mr. Gessler?"

"Oh!" he answered; "dead."

"Dead! But I received these boots from him only last Wednesday week."

"Ah!" he said; "a shockin' go. Poor old man starved 'imself."

"Good God!"

"Slow starvation, the doctor called it! You see he went to work in such a way! Would keep the shop on; wouldn't have a soul touch his boots except himself. When he got an order, it took him such a time. People won't wait. He lost everybody. And there he'd sit, goin' on and on—I will say that for him—not a man in London made a better boot! But look at the competition! He never advertised! Would 'ave the best leather, too, and do it all 'imself. Well, there it is. What could you expect with his ideas?"

"But starvation—!"

"That may be a bit flowery, as the sayin' is—but I know myself he was sittin' over his boots day and night, to the very last. You see, I used to watch him. Never gave 'imself time to eat; never had a penny in the house. All went in rent and leather. How he lived so long

I don't know. He regular let his fire
go out. He was a character. But he
made good boots."

"Yes," I said, "he made good
boots."

· QUESTIONS ·

1. This selection has been called an essay, a short story, and "a brief for the defense." Explain.
2. The younger brother is characterized largely in dialogue. Are the subject matter and diction of this dialogue appropriate and effective? Comment on the dialect.
3. What is the author's attitude to each of the brothers? To the young clerk? What is your attitude?
4. Is the tone of the story sentimental or critical or both? Explain your answer.
5. State the conflict of the story. Is it fully understandable?

Theme Subjects: (1) Mass Production and Standards of Workmanship; (2) An Honest Workman Whom I Know; (3) People Don't Appreciate Quality; (4) Handicraft Versus Factory Methods; (5) It Pays To Advertise; (6) Pride in Craftsmanship; (7) Outmoded Methods Should Be Discarded!

YOUTH

Joseph Conrad

One of the most remarkable achievements in literature is that of JOSEPH
CONRAD (1857–1924), whose writing, begun at the age of 38, was done
entirely in a language learned comparatively late in life. Born of Polish
parents in the Ukraine, Conrad (Teodor Józef Konrad Korzeniowski) left
Poland at 17 and voyaged for 20 years before settling permanently in England. His intimate knowledge of the sea is evident in all of his stories and
novels, in which the ocean is often used metaphorically to symbolize life
itself. His philosophical view embodies the individual's need for positive
virtues—duty, loyalty, courage, honor—in a chaotic and unstable world.
Among Conrad's outstanding fictional works are *Almayer's Folly* (1895);

The Nigger of the Narcissus (1897); *Lord Jim* (1900); *Heart of Darkness* (1902); *Nostromo* (1904); *Under Western Eyes* (1911); *Chance* (1914); *Victory* (1915); and *The Arrow of Gold* (1919).

This could have occurred nowhere but in England, where men and sea interpenetrate, so to speak—the sea entering into the life of most men, and the men knowing something or everything about the sea, in the way of amusement, of travel, or of bread-winning.

We were sitting round a mahogany table that reflected the bottle, the claret glasses, and our faces as we leaned on our elbows. There was a director of companies, an accountant, a lawyer, Marlow, and myself. The director had been a *Conway* boy, the accountant had served four years at sea, the lawyer —a fine crusted Tory, High Churchman, the best of old fellows, the soul of honor—had been chief officer in the P. & O. service in the good old days when mailboats were square-rigged at least on two masts, and used to come down the China Sea before a fair monsoon with stun'sails set alow and aloft. We all began life in the merchant service. Between the five of us there was the strong bond of the sea, and also the fellowship of the craft, which no amount of enthusiasm for yachting, cruising, and so on can give, since one is only the amusement of life and the other is life itself.

Marlow (at least I think that is how he spelt his name) told the story, or rather the chronicle, of a voyage:

"Yes, I have seen a little of the Eastern seas; but what I remember best is my first voyage there. You fellows know there are those voyages that seem ordered for the illustration of life, that might stand for a symbol of existence. You fight,

work, sweat, nearly kill yourself, sometimes do kill yourself, trying to accomplish something—and you can't. Not from any fault of yours. You simply can do nothing, neither great nor little—not a thing in the world—not even marry an old maid, or get a wretched 600-ton cargo of coal to its port of destination.

"It was altogether a memorable affair. It was my first voyage to the East, and my first voyage as second mate; it was also my skipper's first command. You'll admit it was time. He was sixty if a day; a little man, with a broad, not very straight back, with bowed shoulders and one leg more bandy than the other, he had that queer, twisted-about appearance you see so often in men who work in the fields. He had a nutcracker face—chin and nose trying to come together over a sunken mouth—and it was framed in iron-gray fluffy hair, that looked like a chinstrap of cotton-wool sprinkled with coal-dust. And he had blue eyes in that old face of his which were amazingly like a boy's, with that candid expression some quite common men preserve to the end of their days by a rare internal gift of simplicity of heart and rectitude of soul. What induced him to accept me was a wonder. I had come out of a crack Australian clipper, where I had been third officer, and he seemed to have a prejudice against crack clippers as aristocratic and high-toned. He said to me, 'You know, in this ship you will have to work.' I said I had to work in every ship I had ever been in. 'Ah, but this is different, and you gentlemen out of them big ships; . . . but there!

I dare say you will do. Join to-morrow.'

"I joined tomorrow. It was twenty-two years ago; and I was just twenty. How time passes! It was one of the happiest days of my life. Fancy! Second mate for the first time—a really responsible officer! I wouldn't have thrown up my new billet for a fortune. The mate looked me over carefully. He was also an old chap, but of another stamp. He had a Roman nose, a snow-white, long beard, and his name was Mahon, but he insisted that it should be pronounced Mann. He was well connected; yet there was something wrong with his luck, and he had never got on.

"As to the captain, he had been for years in coasters, then in the Mediterranean, and last in the West Indian trade. He had never been round the Capes. He could just write a kind of sketchy hand, and didn't care for writing at all. Both were thorough good seamen, of course, and between those two old chaps I felt like a small boy between two grandfathers.

"The ship also was old. Her name was the *Judea*. Queer name, isn't it? She belonged to a man Wilmer, Wilcox—some name like that; but he has been bankrupt and dead these twenty years or more, and his name don't matter. She had been laid up in Shadwell basin for ever so long. You may imagine her state. She was all rust, dust, grime —soot aloft, dirt on deck. To me it was like coming out of a palace into a ruined cottage. She was about 400 tons, had a primitive windlass, wooden latches to the doors, not a bit of brass about her, and a big square stern. There was on it, be-low her name in big letters, a lot of scrollwork, with the gilt off, and

some sort of a coat of arms, with the motto 'Do or Die' underneath. I remember it took my fancy im-mensely. There was a touch of ro-mance in it, something that made me love the old thing—something that appealed to my youth!

"We left London in ballast— sand ballast—to load a cargo of coal in a northern port for Bangkok. Bangkok! I thrilled. I had been six years at sea, but had only seen Melbourne and Sydney, very good places, charming places in their way—but Bangkok!

"We worked out of the Thames under canvas, with a North Sea pilot on board. His name was Jermyn, and he dodged all day long about the galley drying his handkerchief before the stove. Apparently he never slept. He was a dismal man, with a perpetual tear sparkling at the end of his nose, who either had been in trouble, or was in trouble, or expected to be in trouble— couldn't be happy unless something went wrong. He mistrusted my youth, my common sense, and my seamanship, and made a point of showing it in a hundred little ways. I dare say he was right. It seems to me I knew very little then, and I know not much more now; but I cherish a hate for that Jermyn to this day.

"We were a week working up as far as Yarmouth Roads, and then we got into a gale—the famous October gale of twenty-two years ago. It was wind, lightning, sleet, snow, and a terrific sea. We were flying light, and you may imagine how bad it was when I tell you we had smashed bulwarks and a flooded deck. On the second night she shifted her ballast into the lee bow, and by that time we had been blown off somewhere on the Dogger Bank.

There was nothing for it but go below with shovels and try to right her, and there we were in that vast hold, gloomy like a cavern, the tallow dips stuck and flickering on the beams, the gale howling above, the ship tossing about like mad on her side; there we all were, Jermyn, the captain, everyone, hardly able to keep our feet, engaged on that gravedigger's work, and trying to toss shovelfuls of wet sand up to windward. At every tumble of the ship you could see vaguely in the dim light men falling down with a great flourish of shovels. One of the ship's boys (we had two), impressed by the weirdness of the scene, wept as if his heart would break. We could hear him blubbering somewhere in the shadows.

"On the third day the gale died out, and by and by a north-country tug picked us up. We took sixteen days in all to get from London to the Tyne! When we got into dock we had lost our turn for loading, and they hauled us off to a pier where we remained for a month. Mrs. Beard (the captain's name was Beard) came from Colchester to see the old man. She lived on board. The crew of runners had left, and there remained only the officers, one boy and the steward, a mulatto who answered to the name of Abraham. Mrs. Beard was an old woman, with a face all wrinkled and ruddy like a winter apple, and the figure of a young girl. She caught sight of me once, sewing on a button, and insisted on having my shirts to repair. This was something different from the captains' wives I had known on board crack clippers. When I brought her the shirts, she said: 'And the socks? They want mending, I am sure, and John's—Captain Beard's—things are all in order

now. I would be glad of something to do.' Bless the old woman. She overhauled my outfit for me, and meantime I read for the first time *Sartor Resartus* and Burnaby's *Ride to Khiva*. I didn't understand much of the first then; but I remember I preferred the soldier to the philosopher at the time; a preference which life has only confirmed. One was a man, and the other was either more —or less. However, they are both dead and Mrs. Beard is dead, and youth, strength, genius, thoughts, achievements, simple hearts—all dies. . . . No matter.

"They loaded us at last. We shipped a crew. Eight able seamen and two boys. We hauled off one evening to the buoys at the dock gates, ready to go out, and with a fair prospect of beginning the voyage next day. Mrs. Beard was to start for home by a late train. When the ship was fast we went to tea. We sat rather silent through the meal—Mahon, the old couple, and I. I finished first, and slipped away for a smoke, my cabin being in a deckhouse just against the poop. It was high water, blowing fresh with a drizzle; the double dock gates were opened, and the steam colliers were going in and out in the darkness with their lights burning bright, a great splashing of propellers, rattling of winches, and a lot of hailing on the pierheads. I watched the procession of headlights gliding high and of green lights gliding low in the night, when suddenly a red gleam flashed at me, vanished, came into view again, and remained. The fore end of a steamer loomed up close. I shouted down the cabin, 'Come up, quick!' and then heard a startled voice saying afar in the dark, 'Stop her, sir.' A bell jingled. Another voice cried warningly, 'We are going right into that bark, sir.' The answer to this was a gruff 'All right,' and the next thing was a heavy crash as the steamer struck a glancing blow with the bluff of her bow about our fore-rigging. There was a moment of confusion, yelling, and running about. Steam roared. Then somebody was heard saying, 'All clear, sir.' . . . 'Are you all right?' asked the gruff voice. I had jumped forward to see the damage, and hailed back, 'I think so.' 'Easy astern,' said the gruff voice. A bell jingled. 'What steamer is that?' screamed Mahon. By that time she was no more to us than a bulky shadow maneuvering a little way off. They shouted at us some name—a woman's name, Miranda or Melissa—or some such thing. 'This means another month in this beastly hole,' said Mahon to me, as we peered with lamps about the splintered bulwarks and broken braces. 'But where's the captain?'

"We had not heard or seen anything of him all that time. We went aft to look. A doleful voice arose hailing somewhere in the middle of the dock, '*Judea* ahoy!' . . . How the devil did he get there? . . . 'Hallo!' we shouted. 'I am adrift in our boat without oars,' he cried. A belated water-man offered his services, and Mahon struck a bargain with him for a half crown to tow our skipper alongside; but it was Mrs. Beard that came up the ladder first. They had been floating about the dock in the mizzly cold rain for nearly an hour. I was never so surprised in my life.

"It appears that when he heard my shout 'Come up' he understood at once what was the matter, caught up his wife, ran on deck, and across, and down into our boat, which was fast to the ladder. Not bad for a sixty-year-old. Just imagine that old fellow saving heroically in his arms that old woman—the woman of his life. He set her down on a thwart, and was ready to climb back on board when the painter came adrift somehow, and away they went together. Of course in the confusion we did not hear him shouting. He looked abashed. She said cheerfully, 'I suppose it does not matter my losing the train now?' 'No, Jenny—you go below and get warm,' he growled. Then to us: 'A sailor has no business with a wife—I say. There I was, out of the ship. Well, no harm done this time. Let's go and look at what that fool of a steamer smashed.'

"It wasn't much, but it delayed us three weeks. At the end of that time, the captain being engaged with his agents, I carried Mrs. Beard's bag to the railway station and put her all comfy into a third-class carriage. She lowered the window to say, 'You are a good young man. If you see John—Captain Beard—without his muffler at night, just remind him from me to keep his throat well wrapped up.' 'Certainly, Mrs. Beard,' I said. 'You are a good young man; I noticed how attentive you are to John—to Captain—' The train pulled out suddenly; I took my cap off to the old woman: I never saw her again. . . . Pass the bottle.

"We went to sea next day. When we made that start for Bangkok we had been already three months out of London. We had expected to be a fortnight or so—at the outside.

"It was January, and the weather was beautiful—the beautiful sunny winter weather that has more charm than in the summertime, because it is unexpected, and crisp, and you know it won't, it can't, last long. It's like a windfall, like a godsend, like an unexpected piece of luck.

"It lasted all down the North Sea, all down Channel; and it lasted till we were three hundred miles or so to the westward of the Lizards; then the wind went round to the sou'west and began to pipe up. In two days it blew a gale. The *Judea*, hove to, wallowed on the Atlantic like an old candle-box. It blew day after day: it blew with spite, without interval, without mercy, without rest. The world was nothing but an immensity of great foaming waves rushing at us, under a sky low enough to touch with the hand and dirty like a smoked ceiling. In the stormy space surrounding us there was as much flying spray as air. Day after day and night after night there was nothing round the ship but the howl of the wind, the tumult of the sea, the noise of water pouring over her deck. There was no rest for her and no rest for us. She tossed, she pitched, she stood on her head, she sat on her tail, she rolled, she groaned, and we had to hold on while on deck and cling to our bunks when below, in a constant effort of body and worry of mind.

"One night Mahon spoke through the small window of my berth. It opened right into my very bed, and I was lying there sleepless, in my boots, feeling as though I had not slept for years, and could not if I tried. He said excitedly:

" 'You got the sounding rod in here, Marlow? I can't get the pumps to suck. By God! It's no child's play.'

"I gave him the sounding rod and lay down again, trying to think of various things—but I thought only of the pumps. When I came on deck they were still at it, and my watch relieved at the pumps. By the light of the lantern brought on deck to examine the sounding rod I caught a glimpse of their weary, serious faces. We pumped all the four hours. We pumped all night, all day, all the week—watch and watch. She was working herself loose, and leaked badly—not enough to drown us at once, but enough to kill us with the work at the pumps. And while we pumped the ship was going from us piecemeal: the bulwarks went, the stanchions were torn out, the ventilators smashed, the cabin door burst in. There was not a dry spot in the ship. She was being gutted bit by bit. The longboat changed, as if by magic, into matchwood where she stood in her gripes. I had lashed her myself, and was rather proud of my handiwork, which had withstood so long the malice of the sea. And we pumped. And there was no break in the weather. The sea was white like a sheet of foam, like a caldron of boiling milk; there was not a break in the clouds, no—not the size of a man's hand—no, not for so much as ten seconds. There was for us no sky, there were for us no stars, no sun, no universe—nothing but angry clouds and an infuriated sea. We pumped watch and watch, for dead life; and it seemed to last for months, for years, for all eternity, as though we had been dead and gone to a hell for sailors. We forgot the day of the week, the name of the month, what year it was, and whether we had ever been ashore. The sails blew away, she lay broadside on under a weather cloth, the ocean poured over her, and we did not care. We turned those handles, and had the eyes of idiots. As soon as we had crawled on deck I used to take a round turn with a rope about the men, the pumps, and the mainmast, and we turned, we turned incessantly, with the water to our waists, to our necks, over our heads. It was all one. We had forgotten how it felt to be dry.

"And there was somewhere in me the thought: By Jove! This is the deuce of an adventure—something you read about; and it is my first voyage as second mate—and I am only twenty—and here I am lasting it out as well as any of these men, and keeping my chaps up to the mark. I was pleased. I would not have given up the experience for worlds. I had moments of exultation. Whenever the old dismantled craft pitched heavily with her counter high in the air, she seemed to me to throw up, like an appeal, like a defiance, like a cry to the clouds without mercy, the words written on her stern: '*Judea*, London. Do or Die.'

"O youth! The strength of it, the faith of it, the imagination of it! To me she was not an old rattle-trap carting about the world a lot of coal for a freight—to me she was the endeavor, the test, the trial of life. I think of her with pleasure, with affection, with regret—as you would think of someone dead you have loved. I shall never forget her. . . . Pass the bottle.

"One night when tied to the mast, as I explained, we were pumping on, deafened with the wind, and without spirit enough in us to wish ourselves dead, a heavy sea crashed aboard and swept clean over us. As soon as I got my breath I shouted, as in duty bound, 'Keep on, boys!' when suddenly I felt something hard floating on deck strike the calf of my leg. I made a grab at it and missed. It was so dark we could not see each other's

faces within a foot—you understand.

"After that thump the ship kept quiet for a while, and the thing, whatever it was, struck my leg again. This time I caught it—and it was a saucepan. At first, being stupid with fatigue and thinking of nothing but the pumps, I did not understand what I had in my hand. Suddenly it dawned upon me, and I shouted, 'Boys, the house on deck is gone. Leave this, and let's look for the cook.'

"There was a deckhouse forward, which contained the galley, the cook's berth, and the quarters of the crew. As we had expected for days to see it swept away, the hands had been ordered to sleep in the cabin—the only safe place in the ship. The steward, Abraham, however, persisted in clinging to his berth, stupidly, like a mule—from sheer fright, I believe, like an animal that won't leave a stable falling in an earthquake. So we went to look for him. It was chancing death, since once out of our lashings we were as exposed as if on a raft. But we went. The house was shattered as if a shell had exploded inside. Most of it had gone overboard—stove, men's quarters, and their property, all was gone; but two posts, holding a portion of the bulkhead to which Abraham's bunk was attached, remained as if by a miracle. We groped in the ruins and came upon this, and there he was, sitting in his bunk, surrounded by foam and wreckage, jabbering cheerfully to himself. He was out of his mind; completely and forever mad, with this sudden shock coming upon the fag-end of his endurance. We snatched him up, lugged him aft, and pitched him headfirst down the cabin companion. You understand there was no time to carry him down with infinite precautions and wait to see how he got on. Those below would pick him up at the bottom of the stairs all right. We were in a hurry to go back to the pumps. That business could not wait. A bad leak is an inhuman thing.

"One would think that the sole purpose of that fiendish gale had been to make a lunatic of that poor devil of a mulatto. It eased before morning, and next day the sky cleared, and as the sea went down the leak took up. When it came to bending a fresh set of sails the crew demanded to put back—and really there was nothing else to do. Boats gone, decks swept clean, cabin gutted, men without a stitch but what they stood in, stores spoiled, ship strained. We put her head for home, and—would you believe it? The wind came east right in our teeth. It blew fresh, it blew continuously. We had to beat up every inch of the way, but she did not leak so badly, the water keeping comparatively smooth. Two hours' pumping in every four is no joke— but it kept her afloat as far as Falmouth.

"The good people there live on casualties of the sea, and no doubt were glad to see us. A hungry crowd of shipwrights sharpened their chisels at the sight of that carcass of a ship. And, by Jove! they had pretty pickings off us before they were done. I fancy the owner was already in a tight place. There were delays. Then it was decided to take part of the cargo out and calk her topsides. This was done, the repairs finished, cargo reshipped; a new crew came on board, and we went out—for Bangkok. At the end of a week we were back again. The crew said they weren't going to Bangkok —a hundred and fifty days' passage —in a something hooker that wanted pumping eight hours out of the twenty-four; and the nautical papers inserted again the little paragraph: '*Judea*. Bark. Tyne to Bangkok; coals; put back to Falmouth leaky and with crew refusing duty.'

"There were more delays— more tinkering. The owner came down for a day, and said she was as right as a little fiddle. Poor old Captain Beard looked like the ghost of a Geordie skipper—through the worry and humiliation of it. Remember, he was sixty, and it was his first command. Mahon said it was a foolish business and would end badly. I loved the ship more than ever, and wanted awfully to get to Bangkok. To Bangkok! Magic name, blessed name. Mesopotamia wasn't a patch on it. Remember, I was twenty, and it was my first second-mate's billet, and the East was waiting for me.

"We went out and anchored in the outer roads with a fresh crew— the third. She leaked worse than ever. It was as if those confounded shipwrights had actually made a hole in her. This time we did not even go outside. The crew simply refused to man the windlass.

"They towed us back to the inner harbor, and we became a fixture, a feature, an institution of the place. People pointed us out to visitors as 'That 'ere bark that's going to Bangkok—has been here six months—put back three times.' On holidays the small boys pulling about in boats would hail, '*Judea*, ahoy!' and if a head showed above the rail shouted, 'Where you bound to?—Bangkok?' and jeered. We were only three on board. The poor old skipper mooned in the cabin. Mahon undertook the cooking, and unexpectedly developed all a Frenchman's genius for preparing nice little messes. I looked languidly after the rigging. We became citizens of Falmouth. Every shopkeeper knew us. At the barber's or tobacconist's they asked familiarly, 'Do you think you will ever get to Bangkok?' Meantime the owner, the underwriters, and the charterers squabbled amongst themselves in London, and our pay went on. . . . Pass the bottle.

"It was horrid. Morally it was worse than pumping for life. It seemed as though we had been forgotten by the world, belonged to nobody, would get nowhere; it seemed that, as if bewitched, we would have to live forever and ever in that inner harbor, a derision and a byword to generations of long-shore loafers and dishonest boatmen. I obtained three months' pay and a five days' leave, and made a rush for London. It took me a day to get there and pretty well another to come back—but three months' pay went all the same. I don't know what I did with it. I went to a music hall, I believe, lunched, dined, and supped in a swell place in Regent Street, and was back on time, with nothing but a complete set of Byron's works and a new railway rug to show for three months' work. The boatman who pulled me off to the ship said: 'Hallo! I thought you had left the old thing. *She* will never get to Bangkok.' 'That's all *you* know about it,' I said, scornfully—but I didn't like that prophecy at all.

"Suddenly a man, some kind of agent to somebody, appeared with full powers. He had grog-blossoms all over his face, an indomitable energy, and was a jolly soul. We leaped into life again. A hulk came alongside, took our cargo, and then we went into dry dock to get our copper stripped. No wonder she leaked. The poor thing, strained beyond endurance by the gale, had, as if in disgust, spat out all the oakum of her lower seams. She was recalked, new-coppered, and made as tight as a bottle. We went back to the hulk and reshipped our cargo.

"Then, on a fine moonlight night, all the rats left the ship.

"We had been infested with them. They had destroyed our sails, consumed more stores than the crew, affably shared our beds and our dangers, and now, when the ship was made seaworthy, concluded to clear out. I called Mahon to enjoy the spectacle. Rat after rat appeared on our rail, took a last look over his shoulder, and leaped with a hollow thud into the empty hulk. We tried to count them, but soon lost the tale. Mahon said: 'Well, well! don't talk to me about the intelligence of rats. They ought to have left before, when we had that narrow squeak from foundering. There you have the proof how silly is the superstition about them. They leave a good ship for an old rotten hulk, where there is nothing to eat, too, the fools! . . . I don't believe they know what is safe or what is good for them, any more than you or I.'

"And after some more talk we agreed that the wisdom of rats had been grossly overrated, being in fact no greater than that of men.

"The story of the ship was known, by this, all up the Channel from Land's End to the Forelands, and we could get no crew on the south coast. They sent us one all complete from Liverpool, and we left once more—for Bangkok.

"We had fair breezes, smooth water right into the tropics, and the old *Judea* lumbered along in the sunshine. When she went eight knots everything cracked aloft, and we tied our caps to our heads; but mostly she strolled on at the rate of three miles an hour. What could you expect? She was tired—that old ship. Her youth was where mine is— where yours is—you fellows who listen to this yarn; and what friend would throw your years and your weariness in your face? We didn't grumble at her. To us aft, at least, it seemed as though we had been born in her, reared in her, had lived in her for ages, had never known any other ship. I would just as soon have abused the old village church at home for not being a cathedral.

"And for me there was also my youth to make me patient. There was all the East before me, and all life, and the thought that I had been tried in that ship and had come out pretty well. And I thought of men of old who, centuries ago, went that road in ships that sailed no better, to the land of palms, and spices, and yellow sands, and of brown nations ruled by kings more cruel than Nero the Roman, and more splendid than Solomon the Jew. The old bark lumbered on, heavy with her age and the burden of her cargo, while I lived the life of youth in ignorance and hope. She lumbered on through an interminable procession of days; and the fresh gilding flashed back at the setting sun, seemed to cry out over the darkening sea the words painted on her stern, '*Judea*, London. Do or Die.'

"Then we entered the Indian Ocean and steered northerly for Java Head. The winds were light. Weeks slipped by. She crawled on, do or die, and people at home began to think of posting us as overdue.

"One Saturday evening, I being off duty, the men asked me to give them an extra bucket of water or so—for washing clothes. As I did not wish to screw on the fresh-water pump so late, I went forward whistling, and with a key in my hand to unlock the forepeak scuttle, intending to serve the water out of a spare tank we kept there.

"The smell down below was as unexpected as it was frightful. One would have thought hundreds of paraffin lamps had been flaring and smoking in that hole for days. I was glad to get out. The man with me coughed and said, 'Funny smell, sir.' I answered negligently, 'It's good for the health, they say,' and walked aft.

"The first thing I did was to put my head down the square of the midship ventilator. As I lifted the lid a visible breath, something like a thin fog, a puff of faint haze, rose from the opening. The ascending air was hot, and had a heavy, sooty, paraffiny smell. I gave one sniff, and put down the lid gently. It was no use choking myself. The cargo was on fire.

"Next day she began to smoke in earnest. You see, it was to be expected, for though the coal was of a safe kind, that cargo had been so handled, so broken up with handling, that it looked more like smithy coal than anything else. Then it had been wetted—more than once. It rained all the time we were taking it back from the hulk, and now with this long passage it got heated, and there was another case of spontaneous combustion.

"The captain called us into the cabin. He had a chart spread on the table, and looked unhappy. He said, 'The coast of West Australia is near, but I mean to proceed to our destination. It is the hurricane month, too; but we will just keep her head for Bangkok, and fight the fire. No more putting back anywhere, if we all get roasted. We will try first to stifle this 'ere damned combustion by want of air.'

"We tried. We battened down everything, and still she smoked. The smoke kept coming out through imperceptible crevices; it forced itself through bulkheads and covers; it oozed here and there and everywhere in slender threads, in an invisible film, in an incomprehensible manner. It made its way into the cabin, into the forecastle; it poisoned the sheltered places on the deck; it could be sniffed as high as the mainyard. It was clear that if the smoke came out the air came in. This was disheartening. This combustion refused to be stifled.

"We resolved to try water, and took the hatches off. Enormous volumes of smoke, whitish, yellowish, thick, greasy, misty, choking, ascended as high as the trucks. All hands cleared out aft. Then the poisonous cloud blew away, and we went back to work in a smoke that was no thicker now than that of an ordinary factory chimney.

"We rigged the force pump, got the hose along, and by and by it burst. Well, it was as old as the ship—a prehistoric hose, and past repair. Then we pumped with the feeble head pump, drew water with buckets, and in this way managed in time to pour lots of Indian Ocean into the main hatch. The bright stream flashed in sunshine, fell into a layer of white crawling smoke, and vanished on the black surface of coal. Steam ascended mingling with the smoke. We poured salt water as into a barrel without a bottom. It was our fate to pump in that ship, to pump out of her, to pump into her;

and after keeping water out of her to save ourselves from being drowned, we frantically poured water into her to save ourselves from being burnt.

"And she crawled on, do or die, in the serene weather. The sky was a miracle of purity, a miracle of azure. The sea was polished, was blue, was pellucid, was sparkling like a precious stone, extending on all sides, all round to the horizon—as if the whole terrestrial globe had been one jewel, one colossal sapphire, a single gem fashioned into a planet. And on the luster of the great calm waters the *Judea* glided imperceptibly, enveloped in languid and unclean vapors, in a lazy cloud that drifted to leeward, light and slow; a pestiferous cloud defiling the splendor of sea and sky.

"All this time of course we saw no fire. The cargo smoldered at the bottom somewhere. Once Mahon, as we were working side by side, said to me with a queer smile: 'Now, if she only would spring a tidy leak—like that time when we first left the Channel—it would put a stopper on this fire. Wouldn't it?' I remarked irrelevantly, 'Do you remember the rats?'

"We fought the fire and sailed the ship, too, as carefully as though nothing had been the matter. The steward cooked and attended on us. Of the other twelve men, eight worked while four rested. Everyone took his turn, captain included. There was equality, and if not exactly fraternity, then a deal of good feeling. Sometimes a man, as he dashed a bucketful of water down the hatchway, would yell out, 'Hurrah for Bangkok!' and the rest laughed. But generally we were taciturn and serious—and thirsty.

Oh! how thirsty! And we had to be careful with the water. Strict allowance. The ship smoked, the sun blazed. . . . Pass the bottle.

"We tried everything. We even made an attempt to dig down to the fire. No good, of course. No man could remain more than a minute below. Mahon, who went first, fainted there, and the man who went to fetch him out did likewise. We lugged them out on deck. Then I leaped down to show how easily it could be done. They had learned wisdom by that time, and contented themselves by fishing for me with a chainhook tied to a broom handle, I believe. I did not offer to go and fetch up my shovel, which was left down below.

"Things began to look bad. We put the longboat into the water. The second boat was ready to swing out. We had also another, a fourteen-foot thing, on davits aft, where it was quite safe.

"Then, behold, the smoke suddenly decreased. We redoubled our efforts to flood the bottom of the ship. In two days there was no smoke at all. Everybody was on the broad grin. This was on a Friday. On Saturday no work, but sailing the ship, of course, was done. The men washed their clothes and their faces for the first time in a fortnight, and had a special dinner given them. They spoke of spontaneous combustion with contempt, and implied *they* were the boys to put out combustions. Somehow we all felt as though we each had inherited a large fortune. But a beastly smell of burning hung about the ship. Captain Beard had hollow eyes and sunken cheeks. I had never noticed so much before how twisted and bowed he was. He and Mahon prowled soberly about

hatches and ventilators, sniffing. It struck me suddenly poor Mahon was a very, very old chap. As to me, I was pleased and proud as though I had helped to win a great naval battle. O youth!

"The night was fine. In the morning a homeward-bound ship passed us hull down—the first we had seen for months; but we were nearing the land at last, Java Head being about 190 miles off, and nearly due north.

"Next day it was my watch on deck from eight to twelve. At breakfast the captain observed, 'It's wonderful how that smell hangs about the cabin.' About ten, the mate being on the poop, I stepped down on the main deck for a moment. The carpenter's bench stood abaft the mainmast: I leaned against it sucking at my pipe, and the carpenter, a young chap, came to talk to me. He remarked, 'I think we have done very well, haven't we?' and then I perceived with annoyance the fool was trying to tilt the bench. I said curtly, 'Don't, Chips,' and immediately became aware of a queer sensation, of an absurd delusion—I seemed somehow to be in the air. I heard all round me like a pent-up breath released—as if a thousand giants simultaneously had said Phoo!—and felt a dull concussion which made my ribs ache suddenly. No doubt about it—I was in the air, and my body was describing a short parabola. But short as it was, I had the time to think several thoughts in, as far as I can remember, the following order: 'This can't be the carpenter—What is it?—Some accident—Submarine volcano?—Coals, gas!—By Jove! We are being blown up—Everybody's dead—I am falling into the afterhatch—I see fire in it.'

"The coaldust suspended in the air of the hold had glowed dull-red at the moment of the explosion. In the twinkling of an eye, in an infinitesimal fraction of a second since the first tilt of the bench, I was sprawling full length on the cargo. I picked myself up and scrambled out. It was quick like a rebound. The deck was a wilderness of smashed timber, lying crosswise like trees in a wood after a hurricane; an immense curtain of solid rags waved gently before me—it was the mainsail blown to strips. I thought: the masts will be toppling over directly; and to get out of the way bolted on all fours towards the poop ladder. The first person I saw was Mahon, with eyes like saucers, his mouth open, and the long white hair standing straight on end round his head like a silver halo. He was just about to go down when the sight of the main deck stirring, heaving up, and changing into splinters before his eyes, petrified him on the top step. I stared at him in unbelief, and he stared at me with a queer kind of shocked curiosity. I did not know that I had no hair, no eyebrows, no eyelashes, that my young mustache was burnt off, that my face was black, one cheek laid open, my nose cut, and my chin bleeding. I had lost my cap, one of my slippers, and my shirt was torn to rags. Of all this I was not aware. I was amazed to see the ship still afloat, the poop deck whole—and, most of all, to see anybody alive. Also the peace of the sky and the serenity of the sea were distinctly surprising. I suppose I expected to see them convulsed with horror. . . . Pass the bottle.

"There was a voice hailing the ship from somewhere—in the air, in the sky—I couldn't tell. Presently I saw the captain—and he was mad.

He asked me eagerly, 'Where's the cabin table?' and to hear such a question was a frightful shock. I had just been blown up, you understand, and vibrated with that experience—I wasn't quite sure whether I was alive. Mahon began to stamp with both feet and yelled at him, 'Good God! don't you see the deck's blown out of her?' I found my voice, and stammered out as if conscious of some gross neglect of duty, 'I don't know where the cabin table is.' It was like an absurd dream.

"Do you know what he wanted next? Well, he wanted to trim the yards. Very placidly, and as if lost in thought, he insisted on having the foreyard squared. 'I don't know if there's anybody alive,' said Mahon, almost tearfully. 'Surely,' he said, gently, 'there will be enough left to square the foreyard.'

"The old chap, it seems, was in his own berth winding up the chronometers, when the shock sent him spinning. Immediately it occurred to him—as he said afterwards—that the ship had struck something, and ran out into the cabin. There, he saw, the cabin table had vanished somewhere. The deck being blown up, it had fallen down into the lazarette of course. Where we had our breakfast that morning he saw only a great hole in the floor. This appeared to him so awfully mysterious, and impressed him so immensely, that what he saw and heard after he got on deck were mere trifles in comparison. And, mark, he noticed directly the wheel deserted and his bark off her course—and his only thought was to get that miserable, stripped, undecked, smoldering shell of a ship back again with her head pointing at her port of destination. Bangkok! That's what he was after. I tell you this quiet, bowed, bandy-legged, almost deformed little man was immense in the singleness of his idea and in his placid ignorance of our agitation. He motioned us forward with a commanding gesture, and went to take the wheel himself.

"Yes; that was the first thing we did—trim the yards of that wreck! No one was killed, or even disabled, but everyone was more or less hurt. You should have seen them! Some were in rags, with black faces, like coal heavers, like sweeps, and had bullet heads that seemed closely cropped, but were in fact singed to the skin. Others, of the watch below, awakened by being shot out from their collapsing bunks, shivered incessantly, and kept on groaning even as we went about our work. But they all worked. That crew of Liverpool hard cases had in them the right stuff. It's my experience they always have. It is the sea that gives it—the vastness, the loneliness surrounding their dark stolid souls. Ah! Well! We stumbled, we crept, we fell, we barked our shins on the wreckage, we hauled. The masts stood, but we did not know how much they might be charred down below. It was nearly calm, but a long swell ran from the west and made her roll. They might go at any moment. We looked at them with apprehension. One could not foresee which way they would fall.

"Then we retreated aft and looked about us. The deck was a tangle of planks on edge, of planks on end, of splinters, of ruined woodwork. The masts rose from that chaos like big trees above a matted undergrowth. The interstices of that mass of wreckage were full of something whitish, sluggish, stirring—of something that was like a greasy fog. The smoke of the invisi-ble fire was coming up again, was trailing, like a poisonous thick mist in some valley choked with dead wood. Already lazy wisps were beginning to curl upwards amongst the mass of splinters. Here and there a piece of timber, stuck upright, resembled a post. Half of a fife rail had been shot through the foresail, and the sky made a patch of glorious blue in the ignobly soiled canvas. A portion of several boards holding together had fallen across the rail, and one end protruded overboard, like a gangway leading upon nothing, like a gangway leading over the deep sea, leading to death—as if inviting us to walk the plank at once and be done with our ridiculous troubles. And still the air, the sky—a ghost, something invisible was hailing the ship.

"Someone had the sense to look over, and there was the helmsman, who had impulsively jumped overboard, anxious to come back. He yelled and swam lustily like a merman, keeping up with the ship. We threw him a rope, and presently he stood amongst us streaming with water and very crestfallen. The captain had surrendered the wheel, and apart, elbow on rail and chin in hand, gazed at the sea wistfully. We asked ourselves, What next? I thought, Now, this is something like. This is great. I wonder what will happen. O youth!

"Suddenly Mahon sighted a steamer far astern. Captain Beard said, 'We may do something with her yet.' We hoisted two flags, which said in the international language of the sea, 'On fire. Want immediate assistance.' The steamer grew bigger rapidly, and by and by spoke with two flags on her foremast, 'I am coming to your assistance.'

"In half an hour she was

abreast, to windward, within hail, and rolling slightly, with her engines stopped. We lost our composure, and yelled all together with excitement, 'We've been blown up.' A man in a white helmet, on the bridge, cried, 'Yes! All right! All right!' and he nodded his head, and smiled, and made soothing motions with his hand as though at a lot of frightened children. One of the boats dropped in the water, and walked towards us upon the sea with her long oars. Four Calashes pulled a swinging stroke. This was my first sight of Malay seamen. I've known them since, but what struck me then was their unconcern: they came alongside, and even the bowman standing up and holding to our main chains with the boathook did not deign to lift his head for a glance. I thought people who had been blown up deserved more attention.

"A little man, dry like a chip and agile like a monkey, clambered up. It was the mate of the steamer. He gave one look, and cried, 'O boys—you had better quit!'

"We were silent. He talked apart with the captain for a time—seemed to argue with him. Then they went away together to the steamer.

"When our skipper came back we learned that the steamer was the *Somerville*, Captain Nash, from West Australia to Singapore via Batavia with mails, and that the agreement was she should tow us to Anjer or Batavia, if possible, where we could extinguish the fire by scuttling, and then proceed on our voyage—to Bangkok! The old man seemed excited. 'We will do it yet,' he said to Mahon, fiercely. He shook his fist at the sky. Nobody else said a word.

"At noon the steamer began to tow. She went ahead slim and high, and what was left of the *Judea* followed at the end of seventy fathom of towrope—followed her swiftly like a cloud of smoke with mastheads protruding above. We went aloft to furl the sails. We coughed on the yards, and were careful about the bunts. Do you see the lot of us there, putting a neat furl on the sails of that ship doomed to arrive nowhere? There was not a man who didn't think that at any moment the masts would topple over. From aloft we could not see the ship for smoke, and they worked carefully, passing the gaskets with even turns. 'Harbor furl—aloft there!' cried Mahon from below.

"You understand this? I don't think one of those chaps expected to get down in the usual way. When we did I heard them saying to each other, 'Well, I thought we would come down overboard, in a lump—sticks and all—blame me if I didn't.' 'That's what I was thinking to myself,' would answer wearily another battered and bandaged scarecrow. And, mind, these were men without the drilled-in habit of obedience. To an onlooker they would be a lot of profane scalawags without a redeeming point. What made them do it—what made them obey me when I, thinking consciously how fine it was, made them drop the bunt of the foresail twice to try and do it better? What? They had no professional reputation—no examples, no praise. It wasn't a sense of duty; they all knew well enough how to shirk, and laze, and dodge —when they had a mind to it—and mostly they had. Was it the two pounds ten a month that sent them there? They didn't think their pay half good enough. No; it was something in them, something inborn and subtle and everlasting. I don't say positively that the crew of a French or German merchantman wouldn't have done it, but I doubt whether it would have been done in the same way. There was a completeness in it, something solid like a principle, and masterful like an instinct—a disclosure of something secret—of that hidden something, that gift of good or evil that makes racial difference, that shapes the fate of nations.

"It was that night at ten that, for the first time since we had been fighting it, we saw the fire. The speed of the towing had fanned the smoldering destruction. A blue gleam appeared forward, shining below the wreck of the deck. It wavered in patches, it seemed to stir and creep like the light of a glowworm. I saw it first, and told Mahon. 'Then the game's up,' he said. 'We had better stop this towing, or she will burst out suddenly fore and aft before we can clear out.' We set up a yell; rang bells to attract their attention; they towed on. At last Mahon and I had to crawl forward and cut the rope with an axe. There was no time to cast off the lashings. Red tongues could be seen licking the wilderness of splinters under our feet as we made our way back to the poop.

"Of course they very soon found out in the steamer that the rope was gone. She gave a loud blast of her whistle, her lights were seen sweeping in a wide circle, she came up ranging close alongside, and stopped. We were all in a tight group on the poop looking at her. Every man had saved a little bundle or a bag. Suddenly a conical flame with a twisted top shot up forward and threw upon the black sea a circle of light, with the two vessels side by side and heaving gently in its center. Captain Beard had been sitting on the gratings still and mute for hours, but now he rose slowly and advanced in front of us, to the mizzen-shrouds. Captain Nash hailed: 'Come along! Look sharp. I have mailbags on board. I will take you and your boats to Singapore.'

"'Thank you! No!' said our skipper. 'We must see the last of the ship.'

"'I can't stand by any longer,' shouted the other. 'Mails—you know.'

"'Ay! ay! We are all right.'

"'Very well! I'll report you in Singapore. . . . Good-by!'

"He waved his hand. Our men dropped their bundles quietly. The steamer moved ahead, and passing out of the circle of light, vanished at once from our sight, dazzled by the fire which burned fiercely. And then I knew that I would see the East first as commander of a small boat. I thought it fine; and the fidelity to the old ship was fine. We should see the last of her. Oh, the glamor of youth! Oh, the fire of it, more dazzling than the flames of the burning ship, throwing a magic light on the wide earth, leaping audaciously to the sky, presently to be quenched by time, more cruel, more pitiless, more bitter than the sea— and like the flames of the burning ship surrounded by an impenetrable night.

"The old man warned us in his gentle and inflexible way that it was part of our duty to save for the underwriters as much as we could of the ship's gear. Accordingly we went to work aft, while she blazed forward to give us plenty of light. We lugged out a lot of rubbish.

What didn't we save? An old barometer fixed with an absurd quantity of screws nearly cost me my life: a sudden rush of smoke came upon me, and I just got away in time. There were various stores, bolts of canvas, coils of rope; the poop looked like a marine bazaar, and the boats were lumbered to the gunwales. One would have thought the old man wanted to take as much as he could of his first command with him. He was very, very quiet, but off his balance evidently. Would you believe it? He wanted to take a length of old stream-cable and a kedge anchor with him in the longboat. We said, 'Ay, ay, sir,' deferentially, and on the quiet let the things slip overboard. The heavy medicine chest went that way, two bags of green coffee, tins of paint—fancy, paint!—a whole lot of things. Then I was ordered with two hands into the boats to make a stowage and get them ready against the time it would be proper for us to leave the ship.

"We put everything straight, stepped the longboat's mast for our skipper, who was to take charge of her, and I was not sorry to sit down for a moment. My face felt raw, every limb ached as if broken, I was aware of all my ribs, and would have sworn to a twist in the backbone. The boats, fast astern, lay in a deep shadow, and all around I could see the circle of the sea lighted by the fire. A gigantic flame arose forward straight and clear. It flared fierce, with noises like the whirr of wings, with rumbles as of thunder. There were cracks, detonations, and from the cone of flame the sparks flew upwards, as man is born to trouble, to leaky ships, and to ships that burn.

"What bothered me was that the ship, lying broadside to the swell and to such wind as there was—a mere breath—the boats would not keep astern where they were safe, but persisted, in a pigheaded way boats have, in getting under the counter and then swinging alongside. They were knocking about dangerously and coming near the flame, while the ship rolled on them, and, of course, there was always the danger of the masts going over the side at any moment. I and my two boatkeepers kept them off as best we could, with oars and boathooks; but to be constantly at it became exasperating, since there was no reason why we should not leave at once. We could not see those on board, nor could we imagine what caused the delay. The boatkeepers were swearing feebly, and I had not only my share of the work but also had to keep at it two men who showed a constant inclination to lay themselves down and let things slide.

"At last I hailed, 'On deck there,' and someone looked over. 'We're ready here,' I said. The head disappeared, and very soon popped up again. 'The captain says, All right, sir, and to keep the boats well clear of the ship.'

"Half an hour passed. Suddenly there was a frightful racket, rattle, clanking of chain, hiss of water, and millions of sparks flew up into the shivering column of smoke that stood leaning slightly above the ship. The catheads had burned away, and the two red-hot anchors had gone to the bottom, tearing out after them two hundred fathom of red-hot chain. The ship trembled, the mass of flame swayed as if ready to collapse, and the fore-topgallant mast fell. It darted down like an arrow of fire, shot under, and instantly leaping up within an oar's length of the boats, floated quietly, very black on the luminous sea. I hailed the deck again. After some time a man in an unexpectedly cheerful but also muffled tone, as though he had been trying to speak with his mouth shut, informed me, 'Coming directly, sir,' and vanished. For a long time I heard nothing but the whirr and roar of the fire. There were also whistling sounds. The boats jumped, tugged at the painters, ran at each other playfully, knocked their sides together, or, do what we would, swung in a bunch against the ship's side. I couldn't stand it any longer, and swarming up a rope, clambered aboard over the stern.

"It was as bright as day. Coming up like this, the sheet of fire facing me was a terrifying sight, and the heat seemed hardly bearable at first. On a settee cushion dragged out of the cabin Captain Beard, his legs drawn up and one arm under his head, slept with the light playing on him. Do you know what the rest were busy about? They were sitting on deck right aft, round an open case, eating bread and cheese and drinking bottled stout.

"On the background of flames twisting in fierce tongues above their heads they seemed at home like salamanders, and looked like a band of desperate pirates. The fire sparkled in the whites of their eyes, gleamed on patches of white skin seen through the torn shirts. Each had the marks as of a battle about him—bandaged heads, tied-up arms, a strip of dirty rag round a knee— and each man had a bottle between his legs and a chunk of cheese in his hand. Mahon got up. With his handsome and disreputable head, his hooked profile, his long white beard, and with an uncorked bottle in his hand, he resembled one of those reckless sea robbers of old making merry amidst violence and disaster. 'The last meal on board,' he explained solemnly. 'We had nothing to eat all day, and it was no use leaving all this.' He flourished the bottle and indicated the sleeping skipper. 'He said he couldn't swallow anything, so I got him to lie down,' he went on; and as I stared, 'I don't know whether you are aware, young fellow, the man had no sleep to speak of for days—and there will be dam' little sleep in the boats.' 'There will be no boats by and by if you fool about much longer,' I said, indignantly. I walked up to the skipper and shook him by the shoulder. At last he opened his eyes, but did not move. 'Time to leave her, sir,' I said quietly.

"He got up painfully, looked at the flames, at the sea sparkling round the ship, and black, black as ink farther away; he looked at the stars shining dim through a thin veil of smoke in a sky black, black as Erebus.

" 'Youngest first,' he said.

"And the ordinary seaman, wiping his mouth with the back of his hand, got up, clambered over the taffrail, and vanished. Others followed. One, on the point of going over, stopped short to drain his bottle, and with a great swing of his arm flung it at the fire. 'Take this!' he cried.

"The skipper lingered disconsolately, and we left him to commune alone for a while with his first command. Then I went up again and brought him away at last. It was time. The ironwork on the poop was hot to the touch.

"Then the painter of the longboat was cut, and the three boats, tied together, drifted clear of the ship. It was just sixteen hours after the explosion when we abandoned her. Mahon had charge of the second boat, and I had the smallest—the fourteen-foot thing. The longboat would have taken the lot of us; but the skipper said we must save as much property as we could—for the underwriters—and so I got my first command. I had two men with me, a bag of biscuits, a few tins of meat, and a breaker of water. I was ordered to keep close to the longboat, that in case of bad weather we might be taken into her.

"And do you know what I thought? I thought I would part company as soon as I could. I wanted to have my first command all to myself. I wasn't going to sail in a squadron if there were a chance for independent cruising. I would make land by myself. I would beat the other boats. Youth! Ah, youth! The silly, charming, beautiful youth.

"But we did not make a start at once. We must see the last of the ship. And so the boats drifted about that night, heaving and setting on the swell. The men dozed, waked, sighed, groaned. I looked at the burning ship.

"Between the darkness of earth and heaven she was burning fiercely upon a disc of purple sea shot by the blood-red play of gleams; upon a disc of water glittering and sinister. A high, clear flame, an immense and lonely flame, ascended from the ocean, and from its summit the black smoke poured continuously at the sky. She burned furiously; mournful and imposing like a funeral pile kindled in the night, surrounded by the sea, watched over by the stars. A magnificent death had come like a grace, like a gift, like a reward to that old ship at the end of her laborious days. The surrender of her weary ghost to the keeping of stars and sea was stirring like the sight of a glorious triumph. The masts fell just before daybreak, and for a moment there was a burst and turmoil of sparks that seemed to fill with flying fire the night patient and watchful, the vast night lying silent upon the sea. At daylight she was only a charred shell, floating still under a cloud of smoke and bearing a glowing mass of coal within.

"Then the oars were got out, and the boats forming in a line moved round her remains as if in procession—the longboat leading. As we pulled across her stern a slim dart of fire shot out viciously at us, and suddenly she went down, head first, in a great hiss of steam. The unconsumed stern was the last to sink; but the paint had gone, had cracked, had peeled off, and there were no letters, there was no word, no stubborn device that was like her soul, to flash at the rising sun her creed and her name.

"We made our way north. A breeze sprang up, and about noon all the boats came together for the last time. I had no mast or sail in mine, but I made a mast out of a spare oar and hoisted a boat-awning for a sail, with a boathook for a yard. She was certainly over-masted, but I had the satisfaction of knowing that with the wind aft I could beat the other two. I had to wait for them. Then we all had a look at the captain's chart, and, after a sociable meal of hard bread and water, got our last instructions. These were simple: steer north, and keep together as much as possible. 'Be careful with that jury-rig, Marlow,' said the captain; and Mahon, as I sailed proudly past his boat, wrinkled his curved nose and hailed, 'You will sail that ship of yours under water, if you don't look out, young fellow.' He was a malicious old man—and may the deep sea where he sleeps now rock him gently, rock him tenderly to the end of time!

"Before sunset a thick rain-squall passed over the two boats, which were far astern, and that was the last I saw of them for a time. Next day I sat steering my cockle-shell—my first command—with nothing but water and sky round me. I did sight in the afternoon the upper sails of a ship far away, but said nothing, and my men did not notice her. You see I was afraid she might be homeward bound, and I had no mind to turn back from the portals of the East. I was steering for Java—another blessed name—like Bangkok, you know. I steered many days.

"I need not tell you what it is to be knocking about in an open boat. I remember nights and days of calm, when we pulled, we pulled, and the boat seemed to stand still, as if bewitched within the circle of the sea horizon. I remember the heat, the deluge of rain-squalls that kept us bailing for dear life (but filled our water cask), and I remember sixteen hours on end with a mouth dry as a cinder and a steering oar over the stern to keep my first command head on to a breaking sea. I did not know how good a man I was till then. I remember the drawn faces, the dejected figures of my two men, and I remember my youth and the feeling that will never come back any more—the feeling that I could last forever, outlast the sea, the earth, and all men; the deceitful feeling that lures us on to joys, to perils, to love, to

vain effort—to death; the triumphant conviction of strength, the heat of life in the handful of dust, the glow in the heart that with every year grows dim, grows cold, grows small, and expires—and expires, too soon, too soon—before life itself.

"And this is how I see the East. I have seen its secret places and have looked into its very soul; but now I see it always from a small boat, a high outline of mountains, blue and afar in the morning; like faint mist at noon; a jagged wall of purple at sunset. I have the feel of the oar in my hand, the vision of a scorching blue sea in my eyes. And I see a bay, a wide bay, smooth as glass and polished like ice, shimmering in the dark. A red light burns far off upon the gloom of the land, and the night is soft and warm. We drag at the oars with aching arms, and suddenly a puff of wind, a puff faint and tepid and laden with strange odors of blossoms, of aromatic wood, comes out of the still night—the first sigh of the East on my face. That I can never forget. It was impalpable and enslaving, like a charm, like a whispered promise of mysterious delight.

"We had been pulling this finishing spell for eleven hours. Two pulled, and he whose turn it was to rest sat at the tiller. We had made out the red light in that bay and steered for it, guessing it must mark some small coasting port. We passed two vessels, outlandish and high-sterned, sleeping at anchor, and, approaching the light, now very dim, ran the boat's nose against the end of a jutting wharf. We were blind with fatigue. My men dropped the oars and fell off the thwarts as if dead. I made fast to a pile. A current rippled softly. The scented obscurity of the shore was grouped into vast masses, a density of colossal clumps of vegetation, probably —mute and fantastic shapes. And at their foot the semicircle of a beach gleamed faintly, like an illusion. There was not a light, not a stir, n⌃t a sound. The mysterious East faced me, perfumed like a flower, silent like death, dark like a grave.

"And I sat weary beyond expression, exulting like a conqueror, sleepless and entranced as if before a profound, a fateful enigma.

"A splashing of oars, a measured dip reverberating on the level of water, intensified by the silence of the shore into loud claps, made me jump up. A boat, a European boat, was coming in. I invoked the name of the dead; I hailed: 'Judea ahoy!' A thin shout answered.

"It was the captain. I had beaten the flagship by three hours, and I was glad to hear the old man's voice again, tremulous and tired. 'Is it you, Marlow?' 'Mind the end of that jetty, sir,' I cried.

"He approached cautiously, and brought up with the deep-sea lead line which we had saved—for the underwriters. I eased my painter and fell alongside. He sat, a broken figure at the stern, wet with dew, his hands clasped in his lap. His men were asleep already. 'I had a terrible time of it,' he murmured. 'Mahon is behind—not very far.' We conversed in whispers, in low whispers, as if afraid to wake up the land. Guns, thunder, earthquakes would not have awakened the men just then.

"Looking round as we talked, I saw away at sea a bright light traveling in the night. 'There's a steamer passing the bay,' I said. She was not passing, she was en-

tering, and she even came close and anchored. 'I wish,' said the old man, 'you would find out whether she is English. Perhaps they could give us a passage somewhere.' He seemed nervously anxious. So by dint of punching and kicking I started one of my men into a state of somnambulism, and giving him an oar, took another and pulled towards the lights of the steamer.

"There was a murmur of voices in her, metallic hollow clangs of the engine room, footsteps on the deck. Her ports shone, round like dilated eyes. Shapes moved about, and there was a shadowy man high up on the bridge. He heard my oars.

"And then, before I could open my lips, the East spoke to me, but it was in a Western voice. A torrent of words was poured into the enigmatical, the fateful silence; outlandish, angry words, mixed with words and even whole sentences of good English, less strange but even more surprising. The voice swore and cursed violently; it riddled the solemn peace of the bay by a volley of abuse. It began by calling me Pig, and from that went crescendo into unmentionable adjectives—in English. The man up there raged aloud in two languages, and with a sincerity in his fury that almost convinced me I had, in some way, sinned against the harmony of the universe. I could hardly see him but began to think he would work himself into a fit.

"Suddenly he ceased, and I could hear him snorting and blowing like a porpoise. I said:

" 'What steamer is this, pray?'

" 'Eh? What's this? And who are you?'

" 'Castaway crew of an English bark burnt at sea. We came here tonight. I am the second mate. The captain is in the longboat and wishes to know if you would give us a passage somewhere.'

" 'Oh, my goodness! I say. . . . This is the *Celestial* from Singapore on her return trip. I'll arrange with your captain in the morning, . . . and, . . . I say, . . . did you hear me just now?'

" 'I should think the whole bay heard you.'

" 'I thought you were a shore-boat. Now, look here—this infernal lazy scoundrel of a caretaker has gone to sleep again—curse him. The light is out, and I nearly ran foul of the end of this damned jetty. This is the third time he plays me this trick. Now, I ask you, can anybody stand this kind of thing? It's enough to drive a man out of his mind. I'll report him. . . . I'll get the Assistant Resident to give him the sack, by—! See—there's no light. It's out, isn't it? I take you to witness the light's out. There should be a light, you know. A red light on the—'

" 'There was a light,' I said, mildly.

" 'But it's out, man! What's the use of talking like this? You can see for yourself it's out—don't you? If you had to take a valuable steamer along this Godforsaken coast you would want a light, too. I'll kick him from end to end of his miserable wharf. You'll see if I don't. I will—'

" 'So I may tell my captain you'll take us?' I broke in.

" 'Yes, I'll take you. Good night,' he said, brusquely.

"I pulled back, made fast again to the jetty, and then went to sleep at last. I had faced the silence of the East. I had heard some of its language. But when I opened my eyes again the silence was as com-

plete as though it had never been broken. I was lying in a flood of light, and the sky had never looked so far, so high, before. I opened my eyes and lay without moving.

"And then I saw the men of the East—they were looking at me. The whole length of the jetty was full of people. I saw brown, bronze, yellow faces, the black eyes, the glitter, the color of an Eastern crowd. And all these beings stared without a murmur, without a sigh, without a movement. They stared down at the boats, at the sleeping men who at night had come to them from the sea. Nothing moved. The fronds of palms stood still against the sky. Not a branch stirred along the shore, and the brown roofs of hidden houses peeped through the green foliage, through the big leaves that hung shining and still like leaves forged of heavy metal. This was the East of the ancient navigators, so old, so mysterious, resplendent and somber, living and unchanged, full of danger and promise. And these were the men. I sat up suddenly. A wave of movement passed through the crowd from end to end, passed along the heads, swayed the bodies, ran along the jetty like a ripple on the water, like a breath of wind on a field— and all was still again. I see it now —the wide sweep of the bay, the glittering sands, the wealth of green infinite and varied, the sea blue like the sea of a dream, the crowd of attentive faces, the blaze of vivid color—the water reflecting it all, the curve of the shore, the jetty, the high-sterned outlandish craft floating still, and the three boats with the tired men from the West sleeping, unconscious of the land and the people and of the violence of sunshine. They slept thrown across the thwarts, curled on bottom-boards, in the careless attitudes of death. The head of the old skipper, leaning back in the stern of the longboat, had fallen on his breast, and he looked as though he would never wake. Farther out old Mahon's face was upturned to the sky, with the long white beard spread out on his breast, as though he had been shot where he sat at the tiller; and a man, all in a heap in the bows of the boat, slept with both arms embracing the stemhead and with his cheek laid on the gunwale. The East looked at them without a sound.

"I have known its fascination since; I have seen the mysterious shores, the still water, the lands of brown nations, where a stealthy Nemesis lies in wait, pursues, overtakes so many of the conquering race, who are proud of their wisdom, of their knowledge, of their strength. But for me all the East is contained in that vision of my youth. It is all in that moment when I opened my young eyes on it. I came upon it from a tussle with the sea—and I was young—and I saw it looking at me. And this is all that is left of it! Only a moment; a moment of strength, of romance, of glamor—of youth! . . . A flick of sunshine upon a strange shore, the time to remember, the time for a sigh, and—good-by!—Night—Good-by . . . !"

He drank.

"Ah! The good old time—the good old time. Youth and the sea. Glamor and the sea! The good, strong sea, the salt, bitter sea, that could whisper to you and roar at you and knock your breath out of you."

He drank again.

"By all that's wonderful it is the sea, I believe, the sea itself—or is it youth alone? Who can tell? But you here—you all had something out of life: money, love—whatever one gets on shore—and, tell me, wasn't that the best time, that time when we were young at sea; young and had nothing, on the sea that gives nothing, except hard knocks —and sometimes a chance to feel your strength—that only—that you all regret?"

And we all nodded at him: the man of finance, the man of accounts, the man of law, we all nodded at him over the polished table that like a still sheet of brown water reflected our faces, lined, wrinkled; our faces marked by toil, by deceptions, by success, by love; our weary eyes looking still, looking always, looking anxiously for something out of life, that while it is expected is already gone—has passed unseen, in a sigh, in a flash—together with the youth, with the strength, with the romance of illusions.

· QUESTIONS ·

1. State in not more than one sentence the theme of "Youth."
2. How does Conrad begin the story? How end it? What device does he use throughout the story to remind us of the setting for reciting this tale?
3. How old is Marlow at the time of the story? At the time of the retelling? What is gained for the story by the interval of years?
4. Do you consider the primary conflict of this story to be *physical*? If so, is it a story of man against the sea, in conflict with the elements? If it is more than this, what then is it?

5. The story is long. Too long? Or do you wish it could have been longer?
6. What is the point of view used in this story? Who is the focal character?
7. Can you trace on a map the journey(s) of the *Judea*?
8. Two of the most famous paragraphs in literature are those beginning "And she crawled on, do or die, in the serene weather" *and* "And this is how I see the East." Analyze the diction, tone, and sentence structure of each paragraph.

Theme Subjects: (1) The Real Meaning of "Youth"; (2) The Power of Illusions (a specific example or incident); (3) A Tiresome Tale Often Told by Grandpa; (4) What I Felt in the Presence of Death (an anecdote or incident); (5) Marlow: Then and Now; (6) "No Young Man Believes He Shall Ever Die."

A ROSE FOR EMILY

William Faulkner

WILLIAM FAULKNER (1897–1962) wrote from the background of his native Mississippi, where he lived most of his life. After service with the British Royal Air Force in 1918, he studied briefly at the University of Mississippi and then was postmaster of that college town (University, Mississippi) for two years. His more notable novels and collections of short stories are *The Sound and the Fury* (1929); *As I Lay Dying* (1930); *Sanctuary* (1931); *These Thirteen* (1931); *Light in August* (1932); *The Unvanquished* (1938); *The Wild Palms* (1939); *Go Down, Moses* (1942); *Intruder in the Dust* (1948); *Collected Stories* (1950); *Requiem for a Nun* (1951); *A Fable* (1954, Pulitzer Prize); *Dr. Martino and Other Stories* (1959); and *The Reivers* (1962, Pulitzer Prize). Mr. Faulkner was awarded the Nobel Prize for literature; see "Man Will Prevail."

I

When Miss Emily Grierson died, our whole town went to her funeral: the men through a sort of respectful affection for a fallen monument, the women mostly out of curiosity to see the inside of her house, which no one save an old man-servant—

a combined gardener and cook— had seen in at least ten years.

It was a big, squarish frame house that had once been white, decorated with cupolas and spires and scrolled balconies in the heavily lightsome style of the Seventies, set on what had once been our most select street. But garages and cotton gins had encroached and obliterated even the august names of that neighborhood; only Miss Emily's house was left, lifting its stubborn and coquettish decay above the cotton wagons and the gasoline pumps—an eyesore among eyesores. And now Miss Emily had gone to join the representatives of those august names where they lay in the cedar-bemused cemetery among the ranked and anonymous graves of Union and Confederate soldiers who fell at the battle of Jefferson.

Alive, Miss Emily had been a tradition, a duty, and a care; a sort of hereditary obligation upon the town, dating from that day in 1894 when Colonel Sartoris, the mayor —he who fathered the edict that no Negro woman should appear on the streets without an apron—remitted her taxes, the dispensation dating from the death of her father on into perpetuity. Not that Miss Emily would have accepted charity. Colonel Sartoris invented an involved tale to the effect that Miss Emily's father had loaned money to the town, which the town, as a matter of business, preferred this way of repaying. Only a man of Colonel Sartoris' generation and thought could have invented it, and only a woman could have believed it.

When the next generation, with its more modern ideas, became mayors and aldermen, this arrangement created some little dissatisfaction. On the first of the year they mailed her a tax notice. February came, and there was no reply. They wrote her a formal letter, asking her to call at the sheriff's office at her convenience. A week later the mayor wrote her himself, offering to call or to send his car for her, and received in reply a note on paper of an archaic shape, in a thin, flowing calligraphy in faded ink, to the effect that she no longer went out at all. The tax notice was also enclosed, without comment.

They called a special meeting of the Board of Aldermen. A deputation waited upon her, knocked at the door through which no visitor had passed since she ceased giving china-painting lessons eight or ten years earlier. They were admitted by the old Negro into a dim hall from which a stairway mounted into still more shadow. It smelled of dust and disuse—a close, dank smell. The Negro led them into the parlor. It was furnished in heavy, leather-covered furniture. When the Negro opened the blinds of one window, they could see that the leather was cracked; and when they sat down, a faint dust rose sluggishly about their thighs, spinning with slow motes in the single sun-ray. On a tarnished gilt easel before the fireplace stood a crayon portrait of Miss Emily's father.

They rose when she entered— a small, fat woman in black, with a thin gold chain descending to her waist and vanishing into her belt, leaning on an ebony cane with a tarnished gold head. Her skeleton was small and spare; perhaps that was why what would have been merely plumpness in another was obesity in her. She looked bloated, like a body long submerged in motionless water, and of that pallid hue. Her eyes, lost in the fatty ridges of her face, looked like two small pieces of coal pressed into a lump of dough as they moved from one face to another while the visitors stated their errand.

She did not ask them to sit. She just stood in the door and listened quietly until the spokesman came to a stumbling halt. Then they could hear the invisible watch ticking at the end of the gold chain.

Her voice was dry and cold. "I have no taxes in Jefferson. Colonel Sartoris explained it to me. Perhaps one of you can gain access to the city records and satisfy yourselves."

"But we have. We are the city authorities, Miss Emily. Didn't you get a notice from the sheriff, signed by him?"

"I received a paper, yes," Miss Emily said. "Perhaps he considers himself the sheriff . . . I have no taxes in Jefferson."

"But there is nothing on the books to show that, you see. We must go by the—"

"See Colonel Sartoris. I have no taxes in Jefferson."

"But, Miss Emily—"

"See Colonel Sartoris." (Colonel Sartoris had been dead almost ten years.) "I have no taxes in Jefferson. Tobe!" The Negro appeared. "Show these gentlemen out."

II

So she vanquished them, horse and foot, just as she had vanquished their fathers thirty years before about the smell. That was two years after her father's death and a short time after her sweetheart—the one we believed would marry her—had deserted her. After her father's death she went out very little; after her sweetheart went away, people

hardly saw her at all. A few of the ladies had the temerity to call but were not received, and the only sign of life about the place was the Negro man—a young man then—going in and out with a market basket.

"Just as if a man—any man —could keep a kitchen properly," the ladies said; so they were not surprised when the smell developed. It was another link between the gross, teeming world and the high and mighty Griersons.

A neighbor, a woman, complained to the mayor, Judge Stevens, eighty years old.

"But what will you have me do about it, madam?" he said.

"Why, send her word to stop it," the woman said. "Isn't there a law?"

"I'm sure that won't be necessary," Judge Stevens said. "It's probably just a snake or a rat that nigger of hers killed in the yard. I'll speak to him about it."

The next day he received two more complaints, one from a man who came in diffident deprecation. "We really must do something about it, Judge. I'd be the last one in the world to bother Miss Emily, but we've got to do something." That night the Board of Aldermen met —three graybeards and one younger man, a member of the rising generation.

"It's simple enough," he said. "Send her word to have her place cleaned up. Give her a certain time to do it in, and if she don't . . ."

"Dammit, sir," Judge Stevens said, "will you accuse a lady to her face of smelling bad?"

So the next night, after midnight, four men crossed Miss Emily's lawn and slunk about the house like burglars, sniffing along the base of the brickwork and at the cellar openings while one of them performed a regular sowing motion with his hand out of a sack slung from his shoulder. They broke open the cellar door and sprinkled lime there, and in all the outbuild-ings. As they recrossed the lawn, a window that had been dark was lighted and Miss Emily sat in it, the light behind her, and her up-right torso motionless as that of an idol. They crept quietly across the lawn and into the shadow of the locusts that lined the street. After a week or two the smell went away.

That was when people had be-gun to feel really sorry for her. Peo-ple in our town, remembering how Old Lady Wyatt, her great-aunt, had gone completely crazy at last, believed that the Griersons held themselves a little too high for what they really were. None of the young men were quite good enough for Miss Emily and such. We had long thought of them as a tableau: Miss Emily a slender figure in white in the background, her father a sprad-dled silhouette in the foreground, his back to her and clutching a horse-whip, the two of them framed by the back-flung front door. So when she got to be thirty and was still single, we were not pleased exactly, but vindicated; even with insanity in the family she wouldn't have turned down all of her chances if they had really materialized.

When her father died, it got about that the house was all that was left to her; and in a way, peo-ple were glad. At last they could pity Miss Emily. Being left alone, and a pauper, she had become hu-manized. Now she too would know the old thrill and the old despair of a penny more or less.

The day after his death all the ladies prepared to call at the house and offer condolence and aid, as is our custom. Miss Emily met them at the door, dressed as usual and with no trace of grief on her face. She told them that her father was not dead. She did that for three days, with the ministers calling on her, and the doctors, trying to per-suade her to let them dispose of the body. Just as they were about to resort to law and force, she broke down, and they buried her father quickly.

We did not say she was crazy then. We believed she had to do that. We remembered all the young men her father had driven away, and we knew that with nothing left, she would have to cling to that which had robbed her, as people will.

III

She was sick for a long time. When we saw her again, her hair was cut short, making her look like a girl, with a vague resemblance to those angels in colored church win-dows—sort of tragic and serene.

The town had just let the con-tracts for paving the sidewalks, and in the summer after her father's death they began the work. The construction company came with niggers and mules and machinery, and a foreman named Homer Bar-ron, a Yankee—a big, dark, ready man, with a big voice and eyes lighter than his face. The little boys would follow in groups to hear him cuss the niggers, and the niggers singing in time to the rise and fall of picks. Pretty soon he knew every-body in town. Whenever you heard a lot of laughing anywhere about the square, Homer Barron would be in the center of the group. Pres-ently we began to see him and Miss

Emily on Sunday afternoons driving in the yellow-wheeled buggy and the matched team of bays from the livery stable.

At first we were glad that Miss Emily would have an interest, because the ladies all said, "Of course a Grierson would not think seriously of a Northerner, a day laborer." But there were still others, older people, who said that even grief could not cause a real lady to forget *noblesse oblige*—without calling it *noblesse oblige*. They just said, "Poor Emily. Her kinsfolk should come to her." She had some kin in Alabama; but years ago her father had fallen out with them over the estate of Old Lady Wyatt, the crazy woman, and there was no communication between the two families. They had not even been represented at the funeral.

And as soon as the old people said, "Poor Emily," the whispering began. "Do you suppose it's really so?" they said to one another. "Of course it is. What else could . . ." This behind their hands; rustling of craned silk and satin behind jalousies closed upon the sun of Sunday afternoon as the thin, swift clop-clop-clop of the matched team passed: "Poor Emily."

She carried her head high enough—even when we believed that she was fallen. It was as if she demanded more than ever the recognition of her dignity as the last Grierson; as if it had wanted that touch of earthiness to reaffirm her imperviousness. Like when she bought the rat poison, the arsenic. That was over a year after they had begun to say "Poor Emily," and while the two female cousins were visiting her.

" I want some poison," she said to the druggist. She was over thirty then, still a slight woman, though thinner than usual, with cold, haughty black eyes in a face the flesh of which was strained across the temples and about the eye-sockets as you imagine a lighthouse-keeper's face ought to look. "I want some poison," she said.

"Yes, Miss Emily. What kind? For rats and such? I'd recom—"

"I want the best you have. I don't care what kind."

The druggist named several. "They'll kill anything up to an elephant. But what you want is—"

"Arsenic," Miss Emily said. "Is that a good one?"

"Is . . . arsenic? Yes, ma'am. But what you want—"

"I want arsenic."

The druggist looked down at her. She looked back at him, erect, her face like a strained flag. "Why, of course," the druggist said. "If that's what you want. But the law requires you to tell what you are going to use it for."

Miss Emily just stared at him, her head tilted back in order to look him eye for eye, until he looked away and went and got the arsenic and wrapped it up. The Negro delivery boy brought her the package; the druggist didn't come back. When she opened the package at home there was written on the box, under the skull and bones: "For rats."

IV

So the next day we all said, "She will kill herself"; and we said it would be the best thing. When she had first begun to be seen with Homer Barron, we had said, "She will marry him." Then we said, "She will persuade him yet," because Homer himself had remarked—he liked men, and it was known that he drank with the younger men in the

Elks' Club—that he was not a marrying man. Later we said "Poor Emily" behind the jalousies as they passed on Sunday afternoon in the glittering buggy, Miss Emily with her head high and Homer Barron with his hat cocked and a cigar in his teeth, reins and whip in a yellow glove.

Then some of the ladies began to say that it was a disgrace to the town and a bad example to the young people. The men did not want to interfere, but at last the ladies forced the Baptist minister— Miss Emily's people were Episcopal —to call upon her. He would never divulge what happened during that interview, but he refused to go back again. The next Sunday they again drove about the streets, and the following day the minister's wife wrote to Miss Emily's relations in Alabama.

So she had blood-kin under her roof again and we sat back to watch developments. At first nothing happened. Then we were sure that they were to be married. We learned that Miss Emily had been to the jeweler's and ordered a man's toilet set in silver, with the letters H.B. on each piece. Two days later we learned that she had bought a complete outfit of men's clothing, including a nightshirt, and we said, "They are married." We were really glad. We were glad because the two female cousins were even more Grierson than Miss Emily had ever been.

So we were not surprised when Homer Barron—the streets had been finished some time since—was gone. We were a little disappointed that there was not a public blowing-off, but we believed that he had gone on to prepare for Miss Emily's coming, or to give her a chance to get rid of the cousins. (By that time it was a cabal, and we were all Miss Emily's allies to help circumvent the cousins.) Sure enough, after another week they departed. And, as we had expected all along, within three days Homer Barron was back in town. A neighbor saw the Negro man admit him at the kitchen door at dusk one evening.

And that was the last we saw of Homer Barron. And of Miss Emily for some time. The Negro man went in and out with the market basket, but the front door remained closed. Now and then we would see her at a window for a moment, as the men did that night when they sprinkled the lime, but for almost six months she did not appear on the streets. Then we knew that this was to be expected too; as if that quality of her father which had thwarted her woman's life so many times had been too virulent and too furious to die.

When we next saw Miss Emily, she had grown fat and her hair was turning gray. During the next few years it grew grayer and grayer until it attained an even pepper-and-salt iron-gray, when it ceased turning. Up to the day of her death at seventy-four it was still that vigorous iron-gray, like the hair of an active man.

From that time on her front door remained closed, save for a period of six or seven years, when she was about forty, during which she gave lessons in china-painting. She fitted up a studio in one of the downstairs rooms, where the daughters and granddaughters of Colonel Sartoris' contemporaries were sent to her with the same regularity and in the same spirit that they were sent to church on Sundays with a twenty-five-cent piece for the collection plate. Meanwhile her taxes had been remitted.

Then the newer generation became the backbone and the spirit of the town, and the painting pupils grew up and fell away and did not send their children to her with boxes of color and tedious brushes and pictures cut from the ladies' magazines. The front door closed upon the last one and remained closed for good. When the town got free postal delivery, Miss Emily alone refused to let them fasten the metal numbers above her door and attach a mailbox to it. She would not listen to them.

Daily, monthly, yearly we watched the Negro grow grayer and more stooped, going in and out with the market basket. Each December we sent her a tax notice, which would be returned by the post office a week later, unclaimed. Now and then we would see her in one of the downstairs windows—she had evidently shut up the top floor of the house—like the carven torso of an idol in a niche, looking or not looking at us, we could never tell which. Thus she passed from generation to generation—dear, inescapable, impervious, tranquil, and perverse.

And so she died. Fell ill in the house filled with dust and shadows, with only a doddering Negro man to wait on her. We did not even know she was sick; we had long since given up trying to get any information from the Negro. He talked to no one, probably not even to her, for his voice had grown harsh and rusty, as if from disuse.

She died in one of the downstairs rooms, in a heavy walnut bed with a curtain, her gray head propped on a pillow yellow and moldy with age and lack of sunlight.

V

The Negro met the first of the ladies at the front door and let them in, with their hushed, sibilant voices and their quick, curious glances, and then he disappeared. He walked right through the house and out the back and was not seen again.

The two female cousins came at once. They held the funeral on the second day, with the town coming to look at Miss Emily beneath a mass of bought flowers, with the crayon face of her father musing profoundly above the bier and the ladies sibilant and macabre; and the very old men—some in their brushed Confederate uniforms—on the porch and the lawn, talking of Miss Emily as if she had been a contemporary of theirs, believing that they had danced with her and courted her perhaps, confusing time with its mathematical progression, as the old do, to whom all the past is not a diminishing road but, instead, a huge meadow which no winter ever quite touches, divided from them now by the narrow bottleneck of the most recent decade.

Already we knew that there was one room in that region above stairs which no one had seen in forty years, and which would have to be forced. They waited until Miss Emily was decently in the ground before they opened it.

The violence of breaking down the door seemed to fill this room with pervading dust. A thin, acrid pall as of the tomb seemed to lie everywhere upon this room decked and furnished as for a bridal: upon the valance curtains of faded rose color, upon the rose-shaded lights, upon the dressing table, upon the delicate array of crystal and the man's toilet things backed with tarnished silver, silver so tarnished that the monogram was obscured. Among them lay a collar and tie, as if they had just been removed, which, lifted, left upon the surface a pale crescent in the dust. Upon a chair hung the suit, carefully folded; beneath it the two mute shoes and the discarded socks.

The man himself lay in the bed.

For a long while we just stood there, looking down at the profound and fleshless grin. The body had apparently once lain in the attitude of an embrace, but now the long sleep that outlasts love, that conquers even the grimace of love, had cuckolded him. What was left of him, rotted beneath what was left of the nightshirt, had become inextricable from the bed in which he lay; and upon him and upon the pillow beside him lay that even coating of the patient and biding dust.

Then we noticed that in the second pillow was the indentation of a head. One of us lifted something from it, and leaning forward, that faint and invisible dust dry and acrid in the nostrils, we saw a long strand of iron-gray hair.

· QUESTIONS ·

1. State in approximately 100 words the plot of this story.
2. Why is the story broken up into five sections?
3. The handling of time is important in this story; can you clearly distinguish the different periods?
4. How important is setting in this story?
5. What examples of humor, grim and otherwise, does the narrative provide?
6. What are the intent and purpose of the final paragraph? Are both justified?
7. Aside from Miss Emily and Homer Barron, whom would you call the third and fourth most important characters? Is either of these latter two more important to the plot than Barron himself? Think carefully.
8. Faulkner has been described as America's finest novelist. Does this story, together with your knowledge of Faulkner's other work, justify such an opinion?

Theme Subjects: (1) An Unsolved Mystery in My Town; (2) I've Always Wondered About _____; (3) The Most Interesting Old Man (Woman) in My Town; (4) A Woman Scorned; (5) My Opinion of Faulkner's Work (read enough to form a sound judgment).

VANKA

Anton Chekhov

ANTON (PAVLOVICH) CHEKHOV (1860–1904) was born of peasant parents in southern Russia. He received a medical degree at the University of Moscow in 1884 but soon began to neglect the practice of medicine in order to write. His numerous stories and plays gave him a commanding position in literary Russia. Throughout much of the world today, he is considered a master writer because of his precision as a literary craftsman and the poignant illumination which he gives to such human experiences as loneliness, grief, hunger, and misery.

Nine-year-old Vanka Jukov, who had been apprentice to the shoemaker Aliakhine for three months, did not go to bed the night before Christmas. He waited till the master and mistress and the assistants had gone out to an early church-service, to procure from his employer's cupboard a small phial of ink and a penholder with a rusty nib; then, spreading a crumpled sheet of paper in front of him, began to write.

Before, however, deciding to make the first letter, he looked furtively at the door and at the window, glanced several times at the sombre ikon, on either side of which stretched shelves full of lasts, and heaved a heart-rending sigh. The sheet of paper was spread on a bench, and he himself was on his knees in front of it.

"Dear Grandfather Constantin Makaritch," he wrote, "I am writing you a letter. I wish you a Happy Christmas and all God's holy best. I have no father or mamenka, you are all I have."

Vanka gave a look toward the window in which shone the reflection of his candle and vividly pictured to himself his grandfather, Constantin Makaritch, who was night-watchman at Messrs. Jivarevev. He was a small, lean, unusually lively and active old man of sixty-five, always smiling and bleareyed. All day he slept in the servants' kitchen or trifled with the cooks. At night, enveloped in an ample sheepskin coat, he strayed round the domain, tapping with his cudgel. Behind him, each hanging its head, walked the old bitch Kashtanka, and Viune, so named because of his black coat and long body, and his resemblance to a loach. Viune was an unusually civil and friendly dog, looking as kindly at a stranger as at his masters, but he was not to be trusted. Beneath his deference and humbleness was hid the most inquisitorial maliciousness. No one better than he knew how to sneak up and take a bite at a leg, to slip into the larder or steal a moujik's chicken. More than once they had nearly broken his hindlegs, twice he had been hung up, every week he was nearly flogged to death, but he recovered from it all.

At this moment, for certain, his grandfather was standing at the gate, blinking his eyes at the bright red windows of the village church, stamping his feet in their high felt boots, and jesting with the people in the yard; his cudgel would be hanging from his belt, he would be hugging himself with cold, giving a little dry, old man's cough, and at times pinching a servant girl or a cook.

"Won't we take some snuff?" he asks, holding out his snuffbox to the women. The women take a pinch of snuff, and sneeze.

The old man goes into indescribable ecstasies, breaks into loud laughter, and cries:

"Off with it, it will freeze to your nose!"

He gives his snuff also to the dogs. Kashtanka sneezes, twitches her nose, and very offended walks away. Viune deferentially refuses to sniff and wags his tail. It is glorious weather, not a breath of wind, clear, and frosty; it is a dark night, but the whole village, its white roofs, and streaks of smoke from the chimneys, the trees silvered with hoarfrost, and the snowdrifts, you can see it all. The sky scintillates with bright twinkling stars, and the Milky Way stands out so clearly that it looks as if it had been polished and rubbed over with snow for the holidays. . . .

Vanka sighs, dips his pen in the ink, and continues to write:

"Last night I got a thrashing, the patron dragged me by my hair into the yard, belaboured me with a shoemaker's stirrup, because, while I was rocking their brat in its cradle, I unfortunately fell asleep. And during the week, my mistress told me to clean a herring, and I began by its tail, so she took the herring and thrust its phiz into my face. The assistants tease me, send me to the tavern for vodka, make me steal the patron's cucumbers, and the patron beats me with whatever is handy. Food there is none; in the morning it's bread, at dinner 'gruel,' and in the evening again bread; as for tea or sourcabbage soup, the patrons themselves guzzle that. They make me sleep in the vestibule, and when their brat cries I don't sleep at all but have to rock the cradle. Dear Grandpapa, for Heaven's sake take me away from here, home to our village, I can't bear this any more. . . . I bow to the ground to you, and will pray to God for ever and ever, take me from here or I shall die. . . ."

The corners of Vanka's mouth went down, he rubbed his eyes with his dirty fist, and sobbed.

"I'll grate your tobacco for you," he continued, "I pray to God for you, and if there is anything wrong, then flog me like the gray goat. And if you really think I shan't find work, then I'll ask the manager, for Christ's sake, to let me clean the boots, or I'll go instead of Fedia as underherdsman. Dear Grandpapa, I can't bear this any more, it'll kill me. . . . I wanted to run away to our village, but I have no boots, and I was afraid of the frost. And when I grow up I'll look after you, no one shall harm you, and when you die I'll pray for the repose of your soul, just like I do for mamma Pelagea.

"As for Moscow, it is a large town, there are all gentlemen's houses, lots of horses, no sheep, and the dogs are not vicious. The children don't come round at Christmas with a star, no one is allowed to sing in the choir, and once I saw in a shop window hooks on a line and fishing rods, all for sale, and for every kind of fish, awfully convenient. And there was one hook which would catch a sheatfish weighing a pound. And there are shops with guns, like the master's, and I am sure they must cost 100 roubles each. And in the meat-shops there are woodcocks, partridges, and hares, but who shot them or where they come from the shopman won't say.

"Dear Grandpapa, and when the masters give a Christmas tree, take a golden walnut and hide it in my green box. Ask the young lady, Olga Ignatievna, for it, say it's for Vanka."

Vanka sighed convulsively and again stared at the window. He remembered that his grandfather always went through the forest for the Christmas tree and took his grandson with him. What happy times! The frost crackled, his grandfather crackled, and as they both did, Vanka did the same. Then before cutting down the Christmas tree his grandfather smoked his pipe, took a long pinch of snuff, and made fun of poor frozen little Vanka. . . . The young fir trees, wrapt in hoar-frost, stand motion-less and wait; which of them will die? Suddenly a hare springing from somewhere darts over the snowdrift. . . . His grandfather could not help shouting:

"Catch it, catch it, catch it! Ah, short-tailed devil!"

When the tree was down, his grandfather dragged it to the master's house, and there they set about decorating it. The young lady, Olga Ignatievna, Vanka's great friend, busied herself most about it. When little Vanka's mother, Pelagea, was still alive, and was servant-woman in the house, Olga Ignatievna used to stuff him with sugar-candy, and, having nothing to do, taught him to read, write, count up to one hundred, and even to dance the quadrille. When Pelagea died, they placed the orphan Vanka in the kitchen with his grandfather, and from the kitchen he was sent to Moscow, to Aliakhine, the shoemaker.

"Come quick, dear Grandpapa," continued Vanka, "I beseech you for Christ's sake take me from here. Have pity on a poor orphan, for here they all beat me, and I am frightfully hungry, and so bored that I can't tell you, I cry all the time. The other day the patron hit me on the head with a last; I fell to the ground, and only just returned to life. My life is a disaster, worse than any dog's. . . . I send greetings to Aliona, to one-eyed Egor, and the coachman, and don't let anyone have my harmonium. I remain, your grandson, Ivan Jukov, dear Grandpapa, do come."

Vanka folded his sheet of paper in four and put it into an envelope, purchased the night before for a kopeck. He thought a little, dipped the pen into the ink, and wrote the address:

"The village, to my grandfather." He then scratched his head, thought again, and added: "Constantin Makaritch." Pleased at having been able to write without disturbance, he put on his cap, and, omitting his sheepskin coat, ran out in his shirt-sleeves into the street.

The shopman at the poulterer's, from whom he had inquired the night before, had told him that letters were to be put into post-boxes, and from thence they were conveyed over the whole earth in mail troikas by drunken post-boys and to the sound of bells. Vanka ran to the first post-box and slipped his precious letter into the slit.

An hour afterwards, lulled by hope, he was sleeping soundly. In his dreams he saw a stove, by the stove sat his grandfather with his legs dangling down, barefooted, and reading a letter to the cooks. . . . Around the stove walked Viune, wagging his tail. . . .

· QUESTIONS ·

1. What forces make up the central conflict of this story?
2. How is this conflict resolved? If it is not resolved, what prevents a resolution?
3. What part does setting play in this story?
4. What is the theme that underlies this story?
5. From what point of view is the story told?
6. Comment on the economy of this story.
7. Show how the author integrates the action and time elements of this story.
8. Is the tone of this story cynical and fatalistic or sympathetic and understanding?

Theme Subjects: (1) My First Homesick Week; (2) The Loneliness of Childhood; (3) A Cruel Boss I Once Had; (4) Six by Chekhov (a review of six other stories); (5) The Curse of Indifference; (6) The True Meaning of "Vanka."

THE OPEN WINDOW

"Saki" (*H. H. Munro*)

"SAKI" (HECTOR HUGH MUNRO, 1870–1916) was a British novelist, short-story writer, and political satirist who was killed in France during World War I. He was born in Burma but was largely educated in England and on tours with his father through continental Europe. His first, and most serious, book was *The Rise of the Russian Empire* (1900). He wrote many short stories, collections of which are variously entitled *Reginald* (1904); *Reginald in Russia* (1910); *The Chronicles of Clovis* (1911); and *Beasts and Super-Beasts* (1914). His novels are *The Unbearable Bassington* (1912) and *When William Came* (1913).

"My aunt will be down presently, Mr. Nuttel," said a very self-possessed young lady of fifteen; "in the meantime you must try to put up with me."

Framton Nuttel endeavoured to say the correct something which should duly flatter the niece of the moment without unduly discounting the aunt that was to come. Privately he doubted more than ever whether these formal visits on a succession of total strangers would do much toward helping the nerve cure which he was supposed to be undergoing.

"I know how it will be," his sister had said when he was preparing to migrate to this rural retreat; "you will bury yourself down there and not speak to a living soul, and your nerves will be worse than ever from moping. I shall just give you letters of introduction to all the people I know there. Some of them, as far as I can remember, were quite nice."

Framton wondered whether Mrs. Sappleton, the lady to whom he was presenting one of the letters of introduction, came into the nice division.

"Do you know many of the people round here?" asked the niece, when she judged that they had had sufficient silent communion.

"Hardly a soul," said Framton. "My sister was staying here, at the rectory, you know, some four years ago, and she gave me letters of introduction to some of the people here."

He made the last statement in a tone of distinct regret.

"Then you know practically nothing about my aunt?" pursued the self-possessed young lady.

"Only her name and address," admitted the caller. He was wondering whether Mrs. Sappleton was in the married or widowed state. An indefinable something about the room seemed to suggest masculine habitation.

"Her great tragedy happened just three years ago," said the child; "that would be since your sister's time."

"Her tragedy?" asked Framton; somehow, in this restful country spot, tragedies seemed out of place.

"You may wonder why we keep that window wide open on an October afternoon," said the niece, indicating a large French window that opened on to a lawn.

"It is quite warm for the time of the year," said Framton; "but has that window got anything to do with the tragedy?"

"Out through that window, three years ago to a day, her husband and her two young brothers went off for their day's shooting. They never came back. In crossing the moor to their favourite snipe-shooting ground they were all three engulfed in a treacherous piece of bog. It had been that dreadful wet summer, you know, and places that were safe in other years gave way suddenly without warning. Their bodies were never recovered. That was the dreadful part of it." Here the child's voice lost its self-possessed note and became falteringly

human. "Poor aunt always thinks that they will come back some day, they and the little brown spaniel that was lost with them, and walk in at that window just as they used to do. That is why the window is kept open every evening till it is quite dusk. Poor dear aunt, she has often told me how they went out, her husband with his white waterproof coat over his arm, and Ronnie, her youngest brother, singing 'Bertie, why do you bound?' as he always did to tease her, because she said it got on her nerves. Do you know, sometimes on still, quiet evenings like this, I almost get a creepy feeling that they will all walk in through that window—"

She broke off with a little shudder. It was a relief to Framton when the aunt bustled into the room with a whirl of apologies for being late in making her appearance.

"I hope Vera has been amusing you?" she said.

"She has been very interesting," said Framton.

"I hope you don't mind the open window," said Mrs. Sappleton briskly; "my husband and brothers will be home directly from shooting, and they always come in this way. They've been out for snipe in the marshes today, so they'll make a fine mess over my poor carpets. So like you men-folk, isn't it?"

She rattled on cheerfully about the shooting and the scarcity of birds and the prospects for duck in the winter. To Framton it was all purely horrible. He made a desperate but only partially successful effort to turn the talk on to a less ghastly topic; he was conscious that his hostess was giving him only a fragment of her attention, and her eyes were constantly straying past him to the open window and the lawn beyond. It was certainly an unfortunate coincidence that he should have paid his visit on this tragic anniversary.

"The doctors agree in ordering me complete rest, an absence of mental excitement, and avoidance of anything in the nature of violent physical exercise," announced Framton, who laboured under the tolerably wide-spread delusion that total strangers and chance acquaintances are hungry for the least detail of one's ailments and infirmities, their cause and cure. "On the matter of diet they are not so much in agreement," he continued.

"No?" said Mrs. Sappleton, in a voice which replaced a yawn only at the last moment. Then she suddenly brightened into alert attention—but not to what Framton was saying.

"Here they are at last!" she cried. "Just in time for tea, and don't they look as if they were muddy up to the eyes!"

Framton shivered slightly and turned toward the niece with a look intended to convey sympathetic comprehension. The child was staring out through the open window with dazed horror in her eyes. In a chill shock of nameless fear Framton swung round in his seat and looked in the same direction.

In the deepening twilight three figures were walking across the lawn toward the window; they all carried guns under their arms, and one of them was additionally burdened with a white coat hung over his shoulders. A tired brown spaniel kept close at their heels. Noiselessly they neared the house, and then a hoarse young voice chanted out of the dusk:. "I said, Bertie, why do you bound?"

Framton grabbed wildly at his stick and hat; the hall-door, the gravel-drive, and the front gate were dimly-noted stages in his headlong retreat. A cyclist coming along the road had to run into the hedge to avoid imminent collision.

"Here we are, my dear," said the bearer of the white mackintosh, coming in through the window; "fairly muddy, but most of it's dry. Who was that who bolted out as we came up?"

"A most extraordinary man, a Mr. Nuttel," said Mrs. Sappleton; "could only talk about his illness, and dashed off without a word of good-bye or apology when you arrived. One would think he had seen a ghost."

"I expect it was the spaniel," said the niece calmly; "he told me he had a horror of dogs. He was once hunted into a cemetery somewhere on the banks of the Ganges by a pack of pariah dogs and had to spend the night in a newly dug grave with the creatures snarling and grinning and foaming just above him. Enough to make anyone lose their nerve."

Romance at short notice was her specialty.

· QUESTIONS ·

1. Give a one-sentence description of each of the three central characters. What adjectives would best describe each?
2. What part does setting play in this story? What precise function has the open window? How are physical backgrounds inserted?

3. Comment on the names which "Saki" has given his characters.
4. Is the final sentence of the story necessary? Artistic?

Theme Subjects: (1) Romance at Short Notice Is _____ Specialty; (2) Highly Imaginative Children Should Be _____; (3) Why I Like (Dislike) Surprise Plots; (4) While I Was Waiting for My Date; (5) Nervous Men (Women) and Romancing Children.

THE SECRET LIFE OF
WALTER MITTY

James Thurber

JAMES THURBER (1894–1961) was born in Columbus, Ohio, and attended Ohio State University. He spent two years in diplomatic service in France, was a former staff member of *The New York Post,* and from 1926 until shortly before his death was a frequent contributor to *The New Yorker.* He wrote, among other books, *Is Sex Necessary?* (1929 and 1950, with E. B. White); *The Middle-Aged Man on the Flying Trapeze* (1935); *Let Your Mind Alone* (1937); *The Last Flower* (1939); *The Male Animal* (1940, a play, with Elliott Nugent); *Men, Women, and Dogs* (1943); *The Thurber Carnival* (1945); *The Thirteen Clocks* (1950); *The Years with Ross* (1959); and *Credos and Curios* (1962). He is best known for keenly nonsensical and absurd essays and sketches which are often accompanied by his own thin-line drawings; their amused detachment and their sense of frustration combine to make them significant examples of contemporary American humor and satire.

"We're going through!" The Commander's voice was like thin ice breaking. He wore his full-dress uniform, with the heavily braided white cap pulled down rakishly over one cold gray eye. "We can't make it, sir. It's spoiling for a hurricane, if you ask me." "I'm not asking you, Lieutenant Berg," said the Commander. "Throw on the power lights! Rev her up to 8500! We're going through!" The pounding of the cylinders increased: ta-pocketa-pocketa-pocketa-*pocketa-pocketa.* The Commander stared at the ice forming on the pilot window. He walked over and twisted a row of complicated dials. "Switch on No. 8 auxiliary!" he shouted. "Switch on No. 8 auxiliary!" repeated Lieutenant Berg. "Full strength in No. 3 turret!" shouted the Commander. "Full strength in No. 3 turret!" The crew, bending to their various tasks in the huge, hurtling eight-engined Navy hydroplane, looked at each other and grinned. "The Old Man'll get us through," they said to one another. "The Old Man ain't afraid of hell!"

"Not so fast! You're driving too fast!" said Mrs. Mitty. "What are you driving so fast for?"

"Hmm?" said Walter Mitty. He looked at his wife, in the seat beside him, with shocked astonishment. She seemed grossly unfamiliar, like a strange woman who had yelled at him in a crowd. "You were up to fifty-five," she said. "You know I don't like to go more than forty. You were up to fifty-five." Walter Mitty drove on toward Waterbury in silence, the roaring of the SN202 through the worst storm in twenty years of Navy flying fading in the remote, intimate airways of his mind. "You're tensed up again," said Mrs. Mitty. "It's one of your days. I wish you'd let Dr. Renshaw look you over."

Walter Mitty stopped the car in front of the building where his wife went to have her hair done. "Remember to get those overshoes while I'm having my hair done,"

she said. "I don't need overshoes," said Mitty. She put her mirror back into her bag. "We've been all through that," she said, getting out of the car. "You're not a young man any longer." He raced the engine a little. "Why don't you wear your gloves? Have you lost your gloves?" Walter Mitty reached in a pocket and brought out the gloves. He put them on, but after she had turned and gone into the building and he had driven on to a red light, he took them off again. "Pick it up, brother!" snapped a cop as the light changed, and Mitty hastily pulled on his gloves and lurched ahead. He drove around the streets aimlessly for a time, and then he drove past the hospital on his way to the parking lot.

. . . "It's the millionaire banker, Wellington McMillan," said the pretty nurse. "Yes?" said Walter Mitty, removing his gloves slowly. "Who has the case?" "Dr. Renshaw and Dr. Benbow, but there are two specialists here, Dr. Remington from New York and Dr. Pritchard-Mitford from London. He flew over." A door opened down a long, cool corridor and Dr. Renshaw came out. He looked distraught and haggard. "Hello, Mitty," he said. "We're having the devil's own time with McMillan, the millionaire banker and close personal friend of Roosevelt. Obstreosis of the ductal tract. Tertiary. Wish you'd take a look at him." "Glad to," said Mitty.

In the operating room there were whispered introductions: "Dr. Remington, Dr. Mitty. Dr. Pritchard-Mitford, Dr. Mitty." "I've read your book on streptothricosis," said Pritchard-Mitford, shaking hands. "A brilliant performance, sir." "Thank you," said Walter Mitty. "Didn't know you were in the States,

Mitty," grumbled Remington. "Coals to Newcastle, bringing Mitford and me up here for a tertiary." "You are very kind," said Mitty. A huge, complicated machine, connected to the operating table, with many tubes and wires, began at this moment to go pocketa-pocketa-pocketa. "The new anesthetizer is giving way!" shouted an intern. "There is no one in the East who knows how to fix it!" "Quiet, man!" said Mitty, in a low, cool voice. He sprang to the machine, which was now going pocketa-pocketa-queep-pocketa-queep. He began fingering delicately a row of glistening dials. "Give me a fountain pen!" he snapped. Someone handed him a fountain pen. He pulled a faulty piston out of the machine and inserted the pen in its place. "That will hold for ten minutes," he said. "Get on with the operation." A nurse hurried over and whispered to Renshaw, and Mitty saw the man turn pale. "Coreopsis has set in," said Renshaw nervously. "If you would take over, Mitty?" Mitty looked at him and at the craven figure of Benbow, who drank, and at the grave, uncertain faces of the two great specialists. "If you wish," he said. They slipped a white gown on him; he adjusted a mask and drew on thin gloves; nurses handed him shining . . .

"Back it up, Mac! Look out for that Buick!" Walter Mitty jammed on the brakes. "Wrong lane, Mac," said the parking-lot attendant, looking at Mitty closely. "Gee. Yeh," muttered Mitty. He began cautiously to back out of the lane marked "Exit Only." "Leave her sit there," said the attendant. "I'll put her away." Mitty got out of the car. "Hey, better leave the key." "Oh," said Mitty, handing the man the ignition key. The attendant vaulted into the car, backed it up with insolent skill, and put it where it belonged.

They're so damn cocky, thought Walter Mitty, walking along Main Street; they think they know everything. Once he had tried to take his chains off, outside New Milford, and he had got them wound around the axles. A man had to come out in a wrecking car and unwind them, a young, grinning garage-man. Since then Mrs. Mitty always made him drive to a garage to have the chains taken off. The next time, he thought, I'll wear my right arm in a sling; they won't grin at me then. I'll have my right arm in a sling and they'll see I couldn't possibly take the chains off myself. He kicked at the slush on the sidewalk. "Overshoes," he said to himself, and he began looking for a shoe store.

When he came out into the street again, with the overshoes in a box under his arm, Walter Mitty began to wonder what the other thing was his wife had told him to get. She had told him, twice, before they set out from their house for Waterbury. In a way he hated these weekly trips to town—he was always getting something wrong. Kleenex, he thought, Squibb's, razor blades? No. Tooth paste, toothbrush, bicarbonate, carborundum, initiative and referendum? He gave it up. But she would remember it. "Where's the what's-its-name?" she would ask. "Don't tell me you forgot the what's-its-name." A newsboy went by shouting something about the Waterbury trial.

. . . "Perhaps this will refresh your memory." The District Attorney suddenly thrust a heavy automatic at the quiet figure on the witness stand. "Have you ever seen this before?" Walter Mitty took the gun and examined it expertly. "This is my Webley-Vickers 50.80," he said calmly. An excited buzz ran around the courtroom. The Judge rapped for order. "You are a crack shot with any sort of firearms, I believe?" said the District Attorney, insinuatingly. "Objection!" shouted Mitty's attorney. "We have shown that the defendant could not have fired the shot. We have shown that he wore his right arm in a sling on the night of the fourteenth of July." Walter Mitty raised his hand briefly and the bickering attorneys were stilled. "With any known make of gun," he said evenly, "I could have killed Gregory Fitzhurst at three hundred feet *with my left hand*." Pandemonium broke loose in the courtroom. A woman's scream rose above the bedlam and suddenly a lovely, dark-haired girl was in Walter Mitty's arms. The District Attorney struck at her savagely. Without rising from his chair, Mitty let the man have it on the point of the chin. "You miserable cur!"

"Puppy biscuit," said Walter Mitty. He stopped walking and the buildings of Waterbury rose up out of the misty courtroom and surrounded him again. A woman who was passing laughed. "He said 'Puppy biscuit,'" she said to her companion. "That man said 'Puppy biscuit' to himself." Walter Mitty hurried on. He went into an A. & P., not the first one he came to but a smaller one farther up the street. "I want some biscuit for small, young dogs," he said to the clerk. "Any special brand, sir?" The greatest pistol shot in the world thought a moment. "It says, 'Puppies Bark for It' on the box," said Walter Mitty.

His wife would be through at the hairdresser's in fifteen minutes, Mitty saw in looking at his watch, unless they had trouble drying it; sometimes they had trouble drying it. She didn't like to get to the hotel first; she would want him to be there waiting for her as usual. He found a big leather chair in the lobby, facing a window, and he put the overshoes and the puppy biscuit on the floor beside it. He picked up an old copy of *Liberty* and sank down into the chair. "Can Germany Conquer the World Through the Air?" Walter Mitty looked at the pictures of bombing planes and of ruined streets.

. . . "The cannonading has got the wind up in young Raleigh, sir," said the sergeant. Captain Mitty looked up at him through tousled hair. "Get him to bed," he said wearily, "with the others. I'll fly alone." "But you can't, sir," said the sergeant anxiously. "It takes two men to handle that bomber and the Archies are pounding hell out of the air. Von Richtman's circus is between here and Saulier." "Somebody's got to get that ammunition dump," said Mitty. "I'm going over. Spot of brandy?" He poured a drink for the sergeant and one for himself. War thundered and whined around the dugout and battered at the door. There was a rending of wood, and splinters flew through the room. "A bit of a near thing," said Captain Mitty carelessly. "The box barrage is closing in," said the sergeant. "We only live once, Sergeant," said Mitty, with his faint, fleeting smile. "Or do we?" He poured another brandy and tossed it off. "I never see a man could hold his brandy like you, sir," said the sergeant. "Begging your pardon, sir." Captain Mitty stood up and strapped on his huge Webley-Vickers automatic. "It's forty kilometers through hell, sir," said the sergeant. Mitty finished one last brandy. "After all," he said softly, "what isn't?" The pounding of the cannon increased; there was the rat-tat-tatting of machine guns, and from somewhere came the menacing pocketa-pocketa-pocketa of the new flame-throwers. Walter Mitty walked to the door of the dugout humming "Auprès de Ma Blonde." He turned and waved to the sergeant. "Cheerio!" he said. . . .

Something struck his shoulder. "I've been looking all over this hotel for you," said Mrs. Mitty. "Why do you have to hide in this old chair? How did you expect me to find you?" "Things close in," said Walter Mitty vaguely. "What?" Mrs. Mitty said. "Did you get the what's-its-name? The puppy biscuit? What's in that box?" "Overshoes," said Mitty. "Couldn't you have put them on in the store?" "I was thinking," said Walter Mitty. "Does it ever occur to you that I am sometimes thinking?"

She looked at him. "I'm going to take your temperature when I get you home," she said.

They went out through the revolving doors that made a faintly derisive whistling sound when you pushed them. It was two blocks to the parking lot. At the drugstore on the corner she said, "Wait here for me. I forgot something. I won't be a minute." She was more than a minute. Walter Mitty lighted a cigarette. It began to rain, rain with sleet in it. He stood up against the wall of the drugstore, smoking. . . . He put his shoulders back and his heels together. "To hell with the handkerchief," said Walter Mitty scornfully. He took one last drag on his cigarette and snapped it away. Then, with that faint, fleeting smile playing about his lips, he faced the firing squad; erect and motionless, proud and disdainful, Walter Mitty the Undefeated, inscrutable to the last.

· QUESTIONS ·

1. How would you describe Walter Mitty's dominant character trait? Is it sufficiently developed by the author to make Mitty seem a plausible person? Is this trait shared by you? By most people?
2. What force (or forces) provides the central conflict of the story? Is this main conflict resolved? If not, what prevents a resolution?
3. What is the dominant theme, or idea, which underlies the story?
4. What part does setting play in the story? How much time elapses? Does Thurber economize by shortening actual elapsed time?
5. In what kind of thinking does Walter Mitty engage?
6. Is this story humorous or pathetic? Both? More one than the other? Which? Account for your answer.

Theme Subjects: (1) Timid, Depressed Men (Women); (2) The Secret Life of Mary Mitty (a feminine version); (3) My Favorite Daydream.

IN ANOTHER COUNTRY

Ernest Hemingway

ERNEST (MILLER) HEMINGWAY (1898–1961), "the fictional laureate of the 'lost generation,'" spent his early years in his native Oak Park, Illinois, became a reporter on *The Kansas City Star*, and began writing fiction after serving on the Italian front in World War I. Much of his writing emphasizes the somewhat studied disillusionment of the American expatriates among whom he lived in Paris during the postwar period. Typical of "lost generation" attitudinizing is preoccupation with the macabre, with suffering, death, and loss of values in his first two novels, *The Sun Also Rises* (1926) and *A Farewell to Arms* (1929). Later novels, *To Have and Have Not* (1937) and *For Whom the Bell Tolls* (1940), show a more positive faith in values and organized society. *A Moveable Feast* (1964) is an interesting series of autobiographical sketches which reveals much about the author's early writing and his formative years abroad. He received the 1954 Nobel Prize in literature.

In the fall the war was always there, but we did not go to it any more. It was cold in the fall in Milan and the dark came very early. Then the electric lights came on, and it was pleasant along the streets looking in the windows. There was much game hanging outside the shops, and the snow powdered in the fur of the foxes and the wind blew their tails. The deer hung stiff and heavy and empty, and small birds blew in the wind and the wind turned their feathers. It was a cold fall and the wind came down from the mountains.

We were all at the hospital every afternoon, and there were different ways of walking across the town through the dusk to the hospital. Two of the ways were alongside canals, but they were long. Always, though, you crossed a bridge across a canal to enter the hospital. There was a choice of three bridges. On one of them a woman sold roasted chestnuts. It was warm, standing in front of her charcoal fire, and the chestnuts were warm afterward in your pocket. The hospital was very old and very beautiful, and you entered through a gate and walked across a courtyard and out a gate on the other side. There were usually funerals starting from the courtyard. Beyond the old hospital were the new brick pavilions, and there we met every afternoon and were all very polite and interested in what was the matter, and sat in the machines that were to make so much difference.

The doctor came up to the machine where I was sitting and said: "What did you like best to do before the war? Did you practice a sport?"

I said: "Yes, football."

"Good," he said. "You will be able to play football again better than ever."

My knee did not bend and the leg dropped straight from the knee to the ankle without a calf, and the machine was to bend the knee and make it move as in riding a tricycle. But it did not bend yet, and instead the machine lurched when it came to the bending part. The doctor said: "That will all pass. You are a fortunate young man. You will play football again like a champion."

In the next machine was a major who had a little hand like a baby's. He winked at me when the doctor examined his hand, which was between two leather straps that bounced up and down and flapped the stiff fingers, and said: "And will I too play football, captain-doctor?" He had been a very great fencer, and before the war the greatest fencer in Italy.

The doctor went to his office in a back room and brought a photograph which showed a hand that had been withered almost as small as the major's, before it had taken a machine course, and after was a little larger. The major held the photograph with his good hand and looked at it very carefully. "A wound?" he asked.

"An industrial accident," the doctor said.

"Very interesting, very interesting," the major said, and handed it back to the doctor.

"You have confidence?"

"No," said the major.

There were three boys who came each day who were about the same age I was. They were all three from Milan, and one of them was to be a lawyer, and one was to be a painter, and one had intended to be a soldier, and after we were finished with the machines, sometimes we walked back together to the Café Cova, which was next door to the Scala. We walked the short way through the communist quarter because we were four together. The people hated us because we were officers, and from a wineshop someone would call out, "A basso gli ufficiali!"[1] as we passed. Another boy who walked with us sometimes and made us five wore a black silk handkerchief across his face because he had no nose then and his face was to be rebuilt. He had gone out to the front from the military academy and been wounded within an hour after he had gone into the front line for the first time. They rebuilt his face, but he came from a very old family and they could never get the nose exactly right. He went to South America and worked in a bank. But this was a long time ago, and then we did not any of us know how it was going to be afterward. We only

---

[1] Down with the officers!

knew then that there was always the war, but that we were not going to it any more.

We all had the same medals, except the boy with the black silk bandage across his face, and he had not been at the front long enough to get any medals. The tall boy with a very pale face who was to be a lawyer had been a lieutenant of Arditi and had three medals of the sort we each had only one of. He had lived a very long time with death and was a little detached. We were all a little detached, and there was nothing that held us together except that we met every afternoon at the hospital. Although, as we walked to the Cova through the tough part of town, walking in the dark, with light and singing coming out of the wineshops, and sometimes having to walk into the street when the men and women would crowd together on the sidewalk so that we would have had to jostle them to get by, we felt held together by there being something that had happened that they, the people who disliked us, did not understand.

We ourselves all understood the Cova, where it was rich and warm and not too brightly lighted, and noisy and smoky at certain hours, and there were always girls at the tables and the illustrated papers on a rack on the wall. The girls at the Cova were very patriotic, and I found that the most patriotic people in Italy were the café girls—and I believe they are still patriotic.

The boys at first were very polite about my medals and asked me what I had done to get them. I showed them the papers, which were written in very beautiful language and full of *fratellanza* and

abnegazione,[2] but which really said, with the adjectives removed, that I had been given the medals because I was an American. After that their manner changed a little toward me, although I was their friend against outsiders. I was a friend, but I was never really one of them after they had read the citations, because it had been different with them and they had done very different things to get their medals. I had been wounded, it was true; but we all knew that being wounded, after all, was really an accident. I was never ashamed of the ribbons, though, and sometimes, after the cocktail hour, I would imagine myself having done all the things they had done to get their medals; but walking home at night through the empty streets with the cold wind and all the shops closed, trying to keep near the street lights, I knew that I would never have done such things, and I was very much afraid to die, and often lay in bed at night by myself, afraid to die and wondering how I would be when I went back to the front again.

The three with the medals were like hunting-hawks; and I was not a hawk, although I might seem a hawk to those who had never hunted; they, the three, knew better and so we drifted apart. But I stayed good friends with the boy who had been wounded his first day at the front, because he would never know now how he would have turned out; so he could never be accepted either, and I liked him because I thought perhaps he would not have turned out to be a hawk either.

The major, who had been the great fencer, did not believe in bravery, and spent much time while

---

[2] "comradeship" and "self-sacrifice"

we sat in the machines correcting my grammar. He had complimented me on how I spoke Italian, and we talked together very easily. One day I had said that Italian seemed such an easy language to me that I could not take a great interest in it; everything was so easy to say. "Ah, yes," the major said. "Why, then, do you not take up the use of grammar?" So we took up the use of grammar, and soon Italian was such a difficult language that I was afraid to talk to him until I had the grammar straight in my mind.

The major came very regularly to the hospital. I do not think he ever missed a day, although I am sure he did not believe in the machines. There was a time when none of us believed in the machines, and one day the major said it was all nonsense. The machines were new then and it was we who were to prove them. It was an idiotic idea, he said, "a theory, like another." I had not learned my grammar, and he said I was a stupid, impossible disgrace, and he was a fool to have bothered with me. He was a small man and he sat straight up in his chair with his right hand thrust into the machine and looked straight ahead at the wall while the straps thumped up and down with his fingers in them.

"What will you do when the war is over if it is over?" he asked me. "Speak grammatically!"

"I will go to the States."

"Are you married?"

"No, but I hope to be."

"The more of a fool you are," he said. He seemed very angry. "A man must not marry."

"Why, Signor Maggiore?"

"Don't call me 'Signor Maggiore.'"

"Why must not a man marry?"

"He cannot marry. He cannot marry," he said angrily. "If he is to lose everything, he should not place himself in a position to lose that. He should not place himself in a position to lose. He should find things he cannot lose."

He spoke very angrily and bitterly, and looked straight ahead while he talked.

"But why should he necessarily lose it?"

"He'll lose it," the major said. He was looking at the wall. Then he looked down at the machine and jerked his little hand out from between the straps and slapped it hard against his thigh. "He'll lose it," he almost shouted. "Don't argue with me!" Then he called to the attendant who ran the machines. "Come and turn this damned thing off."

He went back into the other room for the light treatment and the massage. Then I heard him ask the doctor if he might use his telephone and he shut the door. When he came back into the room, I was sitting in another machine. He was wearing his cape and had his cap on, and he came directly toward my machine and put his arm on my shoulder.

"I am so sorry," he said, and patted me on the shoulder with his good hand. "I would not be rude. My wife has just died. You must forgive me."

"Oh—" I said, feeling sick for him. "I am so sorry."

He stood there biting his lower lip. "It is very difficult," he said. "I cannot resign myself."

He looked straight past me and out through the window. Then he began to cry. "I am utterly unable to resign myself," he said and choked. And then, crying, his head up looking at nothing, carrying himself straight and soldierly, with tears on both his cheeks and biting his lips, he walked past the machines and out the door.

The doctor told me that the major's wife, who was very young and whom he had not married until he was definitely invalided out of the war, had died of pneumonia. She had been sick only a few days. No one expected her to die. The major did not come to the hospital for three days. Then he came at the usual hour, wearing a black band on the sleeve of his uniform. When he came back, there were large framed photographs around the wall, of all sorts of wounds before and after they had been cured by the machines. In front of the machine the major used were three photographs of hands like his that were completely restored. I do not know where the doctor got them. I always understood we were the first to use the machines. The photographs did not make much difference to the major because he only looked out of the window.

· QUESTIONS ·

1. Comment on the style of this story. In particular, what do you think of the diction, rhythm, and imagery of the first paragraph? The last one?
2. In the first paragraph note such words as "fall," "cold," "dark." Rewrite the paragraph, introducing diction and effects to change the tone to one of cheerfulness.
3. Point out how many paragraphs contribute to the feeling that this is truly "another country."
4. What has the experience of living a "long time with death" done to each of the major characters in this story?
5. What elements in the story indicate that the major is truly a brave man? Is he more a tragic hero than anyone else in the story?

Theme Subjects: (1) My Definition of a Tragic Hero; (2) The Bravest Man I Know; (3) For My Friend _____, War Has Never Ended; (4) What the Narrator of This Story Really Feared; (5) The Famed Dialogue of Hemingway.

A TRIP TO CZARDIS

Edwin Granberry

EDWIN (PHILLIPS) GRANBERRY (1897–   ) was born in Meridian, Mississippi, and educated at the University of Florida, Columbia University (A.B.,
1920), and the 47 Workshop (drama) at Harvard (1922–1924). He taught
Romance languages at various colleges and engaged in free-lance newspaper work and creative writing before his appointment in 1933 to the staff
of Rollins College, where he is now Irving Bacheller Professor of Creative
Writing. Mr. Granberry is the author of several novels, among them *The
Ancient Hunger* (1927); *Strangers and Lovers* (1928); and *The Erl King*
(1930); he has contributed many articles and stories to various periodicals
here and abroad.

It was still dark in the pine woods when the two brothers awoke. But it was plain that day had come, and in a little while there would be no more stars. Day itself would be in the sky and they would be going along the road. Jim waked first, coming quickly out of sleep and sitting up in the bed to take fresh hold of the things in his head, starting them up again out of the corners of his mind where sleep had tucked them. Then he waked Daniel and they sat up together in the bed. Jim put his arm around his young brother, for the night had been dewy and cool with the swamp wind. Daniel shivered a little and whimpered, it being dark in the room and his baby concerns still on him somewhat, making sleep heavy on his mind and slow to give understanding its way.

"Hit's the day, Dan'l. This day that's right here now, we are goen. You'll recollect it all in a minute."

"I recollect. We are goen in the wagon to see papa—"

"Then hush and don't whine."

"I were dreamen, Jim."

"What dreamen did you have?"

"I can't tell. But it were fearful what I dreamt."

"All the way we are goen this time. We won't stop at any places, but we will go all the way to Czardis to see papa. I never see such a place as Czardis."

"I recollect the water tower—"

"Not in your own right, Dan'l.

From *Forum*, April, 1932. Reprinted by permission of the publishers.

Hit's by my tellen it you see it in your mind."

"And lemonade with ice in it I saw—"

"That too I seen and told to you."

"Then I never see it at all?"

"Hit's me were there, Dan'l. I let you play like, but hits me who went to Czardis. Yet I never till this day told half how much I see. There's sights I never told."

They stopped talking, listening for their mother's stir in the kitchen. But the night stillness was unlifted. Daniel began to shiver again.

"Hit's dark," he said.

"Hit's your eyes stuck," Jim said. "Would you want me to drip a little water on your eyes?"

"Oh!" cried the young one, pressing his face into his brother's side, "don't douse me, Jim, no more. The cold aches me."

The other soothed him, holding him around the body.

"You won't have e're chill or malarie ache to-day, Dan'l. Hit's a fair day—"

"I won't be cold?"

"Hit's a bright day. I hear mournen doves starten a'ready. The sun will bake you warm. . . . Uncle Holly might buy us somethen new to eat in Czardis."

"What would it be?"

"Hit ain't decided yet. . . . He hasn't spoke. Hit might be somethen sweet. Maybe a candy ball fixed on to a rubber string."

"A candy ball!" Daniel showed a stir of happiness. "Oh, Jim!" But it was a deceit of the imagination, making his eyes shine wistfully; the grain of his flesh was against it. He settled into a stillness by himself.

"My stomach would retch it up, Jim. . . . I guess I couldn't eat it."

"You might could keep a little down."

"No . . . I would bring it home and keep it. . . ."

Their mother when they went to bed had laid a clean pair of pants and a waist for each on the chair. Jim crept out of bed and put on his clothes, then aided his brother on with his. They could not hear any noise in the kitchen, but hickory firewood burning in the kitchen stove worked a smell through the house, and in the forest guinea fowls were sailing down from the trees and poking their way along the half-dark ground toward the kitchen steps, making it known the door was open and that within someone was stirring about at the getting of food.

Jim led his brother by the hand down the dark way of yellow-pine stairs that went narrowly and without banisters to the rooms below. The young brother went huddling in his clothes, ague-like, knowing warmth was near, hungering for his place by the stove, to sit in peace on the bricks in the floor by the stove's side and watch the eating, it being his nature to have a sickness against food.

They came in silence to the kitchen, Jim leading and holding his brother by the hand. The floor was lately strewn with fresh bright sand that would sparkle when the daybreak got above the forest, though now it lay dull as hoarfrost and cold to the unshod feet of the brothers. The door to the firebox of the stove was open, and in front of it their mother sat in a chair, speaking low as they entered, muttering under her breath. The two boys went near and stood still, thinking she was blessing the food, there being mush dipped up and steaming in two bowls. And they stood cast down until she lifted her eyes to them and spoke.

"Your clothes on already," she said. "You look right neat." She did not rise, but kept her chair, looking cold and stiff, with the cloth of her black dress sagging between her knees. The sons stood in front of her and she laid her hand on first one head and then the other and spoke a little about the day, charging them to be sober and of few words, as she had raised them.

Jim sat on the bench by the table and began to eat, mixing dark molasses sugar through his bowl of mush. But a nausea began in Daniel's stomach at sight of the sweet and he lagged by the stove, gazing at the food as it passed into his brother's mouth.

Suddenly a shadow filled the back doorway and Holly, their uncle, stood there looking in. He was lean and big and dark from wind and weather, working in the timber as their father had done. He had no wife and children and would roam far off with the timber gangs in the Everglades. This latter year he did not go far but stayed near them. Their mother stopped and looked at the man and he looked at her in silence. Then he looked at Jim and Daniel.

"You're goen to take them, after all?"

She waited a minute, seeming to get the words straight in her mind before bringing them out, making them say what was set there.

"He asked to see them. Nobody but God-Almighty ought to tell a soul hit can or can't have."

Having delivered her mind, she went out into the yard with the man and they spoke more words in an undertone, pausing in their speech.

In the silence of the kitchen, Daniel began to speak out and name what thing among his possessions he would take to Czardis to give his father. But the older boy belittled this and that and everything that was called up, saying one thing was of too little consequence for a man, and that another was of no account because it was food. But when the older boy had abolished the idea and silence had regained, he worked back to the thought, coming to it roundabout and making it new and as his own, letting it be decided that each of them would take their father a pomegranate from the tree in the yard.

They went to the kitchen door. The swamp fog had risen suddenly. They saw their mother standing in the lot while their uncle hitched the horse to the wagon. Leaving the steps, Jim climbed to the first crotch of the pomegranate tree. The reddest fruits were on the top branches. He worked his way up higher. The fog was now curling up out of the swamp, making gray mountains and rivers in the air and strange ghost shapes. Landmarks disappeared in the billows, or half-seen, they bewildered the sight and an eye could so little mark the known or strange that a befuddlement took hold of the mind, like the visitations sailors beheld in the fogs of Okeechobee. Jim could not find the ground. He seemed to have climbed into the mountains. The light was unnatural and dark and the pines were blue and dark over the mountains.

A voice cried out of the fog:

"Are worms gnawen you that you skin up a pomegranate tree at this hour? Don't I feed you enough?"

The boy worked his way down. At the foot of the tree he met his mother. She squatted and put her arm around him, her voice tight and quivering, and he felt tears on her face.

"We ain't come to the shame yet of you and Dan'l hunten your food off trees and grass. People seein' you gnawen on the road will say Jim Cameron's sons are starved, foragen like cattle of the field."

"I were getten the pomegranates for papa," said the boy, resigned to his mother's concern. She stood up when he said this, holding him in front of her skirts. In a while she said:

"I guess we won't take any, Jim. . . . But I'm proud it come to you to take your papa somethin."

And after a silence, the boy said:

"Hit were Dan'l it come to, Mamma."

Then she took his hand, not looking down, and in her throat, as if in her bosom, she repeated:

"Hit were a fine thought and I'm right proud . . . though today we won't take anything. . . ."

"I guess there's better pomegranates in Czardis where we are goen—"

"There's no better pomegranates in Czardis than right here over your head," she said grimly. "If pomegranates were needed, we would take him his own. . . . You are older'n Dan'l, Jim. When we get to the place we are goen, you won't know your papa after so long. He will be pale and he won't be as bright as you recollect. So don't labor him with questions . . . but speak when it behooves you and let him see you are upright."

When the horse was harnessed and all was ready for the departure, the sons were seated on a shallow bed of hay in the back of the wagon and the mother took the driver's seat alone. The uncle had argued for having the top up over the seat, but she refused the shelter, remarking that she had always driven under the sky and would do it still today. He gave in silently and got upon the seat of his own wagon, which took the road first, their wagon following. This was strange and the sons asked:

"Why don't we all ride in Uncle Holly's wagon?"

But their mother made no reply.

For several miles they traveled in silence through their own part of the woods, meeting no one. The boys whispered a little to themselves, but their mother and their uncle sat without speaking, nor did they turn their heads to look back. At last the narrow road they were following left the woods and came out to the highway, and it was seen that other wagons besides their own were going to Czardis. And as they got farther along, they began to meet many other people going to the town, and the boys asked their mother what day it was. It was Wednesday. And then they asked her why so many wagons were going along the road if it wasn't Saturday and a market day. When she told them to be quiet, they settled down to watching the people go by. Some of them were faces that were strange and some were neighbors who lived in other parts of the woods. Some who passed them stared in silence and some went by looking straight to the front. But there were none of them who spoke, for their mother turned her eyes neither right nor left, but drove the horses on like a woman in her sleep.

All was silent as the wagons passed, except the squeaking of the wheels and the thud of the horses' hoofs on the dry, packed sand.

At the edge of the town, the crowds increased and their wagon got lost in the press of people. All were moving in one direction.

Finally they were going along by a high brick wall on top of which ran a barbed-wire fence. Farther along the way in the middle of the wall was a tall, stone building with many people in front. There were trees along the outside of the wall and in the branches of one of the trees Daniel saw a man. He was looking over the brick wall down into the courtyard. All the wagons were stopping here and hitching through the grove in front of the building. But their Uncle Holly's wagon and their own drove on, making way slowly as through a crowd at a fair, for under the trees knots of men were gathered, talking in undertones. Daniel pulled at his mother's skirts and whispered:

"What made that man climb up that tree?"

Again she told him to be quiet.

"We're not to talk today," said Jim. "Papa is sick and we're not to make him worse." But his high, thin voice made his mother turn cold. She looked back and saw he had grown pale and still, staring at the iron-barred windows of the building. When he caught her gaze, his chin began to quiver and she turned back front to dodge the knowledge of his eyes.

For the two wagons had stopped now and the uncle gotten down and left them sitting alone while he went to the door of the building and talked with a man standing there. The crowd fell silent, staring at their mother.

"See, Jim, all the men up the trees!" Daniel whispered once more, leaning close in to his brother's side.

"Hush, Dan'l. Be still."

The young boy obeyed this time, falling into a bewildered stare at all the things about him he did not understand, for in all the trees along the brick wall men began to appear perched high in the branches, and on the roof of a building across the way stood other men, all gaping at something in the yard back of the wall.

Their uncle returned and hitched his horse to a ring in one of the trees. Then he hitched their mother's horse and all of them got out and stood on the ground in a huddle. The walls of the building rose before them. Strange faces at the barred windows laughed aloud and called down curses at the men below.

Now they were moving, with a wall of faces on either side of them, their uncle going first, followed by their mother who held to each of them by a hand. They went up the steps of the building. The door opened and their uncle stepped inside. He came back in a moment and all of them went in and followed a man down a corridor and into a bare room with two chairs and a wooden bench. A man in a black robe sat on one of the chairs, and in front of him on the bench, leaning forward looking down between his arms, sat their father. His face was lean and gray, which made him look very tall. But his hair was black, and his eyes were blue and mild and strange as he stood up and held the two sons against his body while he stooped to kiss their mother. The man in black left the room and walked up and down outside in the corridor. A second stranger stood in the doorway with his back to the room. The father picked up one of the sons and then the other in his arms and looked at them and leaned their faces on his own. Then he sat down on the bench and held them against him. Their mother sat down by them and they were all together.

A few low words were spoken and then a silence fell over them all. And in a while the parents spoke a little more and touched one another. But the bare stone floor and the stone walls and the unaccustomed arms of their father hushed the sons with the new and strange. And when the time had passed, the father took his watch from his pocket:

"I'm goen to give you my watch, Jim. You are the oldest. I want you to keep it till you are a grown man. . . . And I want you to always do what mamma tells you. . . . I'm goen to give you the chain, Dan'l. . . ."

The young brother took the chain, slipped out of his father's arms, and went to his mother with it. He spread it out on her knee and began to talk to her in a whisper. She bent over him, and again all of them in the room grew silent.

A sudden sound of marching was heard in the corridor. The man rose up and took his sons in his arms, holding them abruptly. But their uncle, who had been standing with the man in the doorway, came suddenly and took them and went out and down through the big doorway by which they had entered the building. As the doors opened to let them pass, the crowd gathered around the steps pressed forward to look inside. The older boy cringed in his uncle's arms. His uncle turned and stood with his back to the crowd. Their mother came through the doors. The crowd fell back. Again through a passageway of gazing eyes, they reached the wagons. This time they sat on the seat beside their mother. Leaving their uncle and his wagon behind, they started off on the road that led out of town.

"Is papa coming home with Uncle Holly?" Jim asked in a still voice.

His mother nodded her head.

Reaching the woods once more and the silence he knew, Daniel whispered to his brother:

"We got a watch and chain instead, Jim."

But Jim neither answered nor turned his eyes.

· QUESTIONS ·

1. Show how the details of the boys' awakening set the tone of the story, create atmosphere, and give a hint of the plot.
2. Mark the point at which you think you foresee the ending. After finishing the story, check your accuracy by marking the various pointers, guideposts, along the way.
3. Comment on the poetic rhythm of the dialogue. Does the speech (especially the dialect) seem unnatural or a genuine part of the details of characterization and setting?
4. The action is condensed. Show what parts could have been expanded. Would such expansion weaken the single effect of the story? Destroy unity? Shift the focus?
5. This has been called a "two-level" story—i.e., the reader sees more in the story than is apparent to the focal character or characters. How is this effect achieved

in this story? Does the reader perceive more of the implications of the situation than Jim? Does Jim see more of them than Dan'l does?

6. What details make the reader aware that the trip is to be of more than ordinary significance?

7. What effect does the author achieve in the final sentence of the story?

Theme Subjects: (1) Implication and Suggestion in "A Trip to Czardis"; (2) The Dialogue in "A Trip to Czardis"; (3) Granberry's Two-Level Story; (4) The Poised and Cadenced Language of Granberry's Story; (5) What You Don't Know Hurts You.

MIXED DOUBLES

Irwin Shaw

IRWIN SHAW (1913–   ) was born in New York City and educated at Brooklyn College. In the tradition of many writers he has had a varied career: tutor, clerk, truck driver, semiprofessional football player, factory worker. His experiences (and his keen observation and understanding) have provided material for such plays as *Bury the Dead* (1936); *The Gentle People* (1939); *The Assassin* (1945). Among his novels and collections of short stories are *Sailor Off the Bremen* (1940); *Welcome to the City* (1942); *Act of Faith* (1946); *The Young Lions* (1948); *Mixed Company* (1950); *Tip on a Dead Jockey* (1957); *In the Company of Dolphins* (1964). Mr. Shaw served overseas in the U. S. Signal Corps during World War II and has lived abroad much of the time since 1945. His home is now in Switzerland.

As Jane Collins walked out onto the court behind her husband, she felt once more the private, strong thrill of pride that had moved her again and again in the time she had known him. Jane and Stewart had been married six years, but even so, as she watched him stride before her in that curious upright, individual, half-proud, half-comic walk, like a Prussian drill sergeant on his Sunday off, Jane felt the same mix-

---

ture of amusement and delight in him that had touched her so strongly when they first met. Stewart was tall and broad and his face was moody and good-humored and original, and Jane felt that even at a distance of five hundred yards and surrounded by a crowd of people, she could pick him out unerringly. Now, in well-cut white trousers and a long-sleeved Oxford shirt, he seemed elegant and a little old-fashioned among the other players, and he looked graceful and debonair as he hit the first few shots in the preliminary rallying.

Jane was sensibly dressed, in shorts and tennis shirt, and her hair was imprisoned in a bandanna, so that it wouldn't get into her eyes. She knew that the shorts made her look a little dumpy and that the handkerchief around her head gave her a rather skinned and severe appearance, and she had a slight twinge of female regret when she looked across the net and saw Eleanor Burns soft and attractive in a prettily cut tennis dress and with a red ribbon in her hair, but she fought it down and concentrated on keeping her eye on the ball as Mr. Croker, Eleanor's partner, sliced it back methodically at her.

Mr. Croker, a vague, round, serious little man, was a neighbor of the Collinses' hosts. His shorts were too tight for him, and Jane knew, from having watched him on previous occasions, that his face would get more serious and more purple as the afternoon wore on, but he played a steady, dependable game and he was useful when other guests were too lazy or had drunk too much at lunch to play in the afternoon.

Two large oak trees shaded part of the court, and the balls flashed back and forth, in light and shadow, making guitar-like chords as they hit the rackets, and on the small terrace above the court, where the other guests were lounging, there was the watery music of ice in glasses and the bright flash of summer colors as people moved about.

How pleasant this was, Jane thought—to get away from the city on a weekend, to this cool, tree-shaded spot, to slip all the stiff bonds of business and city living and run swiftly on the springy surface of the court, feeling the country wind against her bare skin, feeling youth in her legs, feeling, for this short Sunday hour at least, free of desks and doors and weekday concrete.

Stewart hit a tremendous overhead smash, whipping all the strength of his long body into it, and the ball struck the ground at Eleanor's feet and slammed high in the air. He grinned. "I'm ready," he said.

"You're not going to do that to me in the game, are you?" Eleanor asked.

"I certainly am," Stewart said. "No mercy for women. The ancient motto of the Collins family."

They tossed for service, and Stewart won. He served and aced Eleanor with a twisting, ferocious shot that spun off at a sharp angle.

"Jane, darling," he said, grinning, as he walked to the other side, "we're going to be sensational today."

They won the first set with no trouble. Stewart played very well. He moved around the court swiftly and easily, hitting the ball hard in loose, well-coached strokes, with an almost exaggerated grace. Again and again, the people watching ap-

plauded or called out after one of
his shots, and he waved his racket,
smiling at them, and said, "Oh,
we're murderous today." He kept
humming between shots—a tune-
less, happy composition of his own
—like a little boy who is completely
satisfied with himself, and Jane
couldn't help smiling and adoring
him as he lightheartedly dominated
the game and the spectators and the
afternoon, brown and dashing and
handsome in his white clothes, with
the sun flooding around him like a
spotlight on an actor in the middle
of the stage.

Occasionally, when Stewart
missed a shot, he would stand,
betrayed and tragic, and stare up
at the sky and ask with mock despair, "Collins, why don't you just
go home?" And then he would turn
to Jane and say, "Janie, darling,
forgive me. Your husband's just no
good."

And even as she smiled at him
and said, "You're so right," she
could sense the other women, up
on the terrace, looking down at him,
their eyes speculative and veiled and
lit with invitation as they watched.

Jane played her usual game,
steady, unheroic, getting almost
everything back quite sharply, keeping the ball in play until Stewart
could get his racket on it and kill it.
They were a good team. Jane let
Stewart poach on her territory for
spectacular kills, and twice Stewart
patted her approvingly on the behind after she had made difficult
saves, and there were appreciative
chuckles from the spectators at the
small domestic vulgarity.

Stewart made the last point of
the set on a slamming deep backhand that passed Eleanor at the net.
Eleanor shook her head and said,
"Collins, you're an impossible man,"

and Croker said stolidly, "Splendid.
Splendid," and Stewart said, grinning, "Something I've been saving
for this point, old man."

They walked off and sat down
on a bench in the shade between
sets, and Croker and Jane had to
wipe their faces with towels and
Croker's alarming purple died a little
from his cheeks.

"That overhead!" Eleanor said
to Stewart. "It's absolutely frightening. When I see you winding up, I'm
just tempted to throw away my poor
little racket and run for my life."

Jane lifted her head and
glanced swiftly at Stewart to see
how he was taking it. He was taking
it badly, smiling a little too widely
at Eleanor, being boyish and charming. "It's nothing," he said. "Something I picked up on Omaha Beach."

That, too, Jane thought bitterly.
Foxhole time, too. She ducked her
head into her towel to keep from
saying something wifely. This is the
last time, she thought, feeling the
towel sticky against her sweaty forehead, the last time I am coming to
any of these weekend things, always
loaded with unattached or semi-
attached, man-hungry, half-naked,
honey-mouthed girls. She composed
her face, so that when she looked
up from the towel she would look
like a nice, serene woman who
merely was interested in the next
set of tennis.

Eleanor, who had wide green
eyes, was staring soberly and un-
ambiguously over the head of her
racket at Stewart, and Stewart, fascinated, as always, and a little
embarrassed, was staring back. Oh,
God, Jane thought, the long stare,
too.

"Well," she said briskly, "I'm
ready for one more set."

"What do you say," Stewart

asked, "we divide up differently this time? Might make it more even. Croker and you, Jane, and the young lady and me."

"Oh," said Eleanor, "I'd be a terrible drag to you, Stewart. And besides, I'm sure your wife loves playing on your side."

"Not at all," Jane said stiffly. The young lady! How obvious could a man be?

"No," said Croker surprisingly. "Let's stay the way we are." Jane wanted to kiss the round purple face, a bleak, thankful kiss. "I think we'll do better this time. I've been sort of figuring out what to do with you, Collins."

Stewart looked at him briefly and unpleasantly, then smiled charmingly. "Anything you say, old man. I just thought . . ."

"I'm sure we'll do better," Croker said firmly. He stood up. "Come on, Eleanor."

Eleanor stood up, lithe and graceful in her short dress, which whipped around her brown legs in the summer wind. Never again, Jane thought, will I wear shorts. Dresses like that, even if they cost fifty dollars apiece, and soft false bosoms to put in them, too, and no bandanna, even if I'm blinded on each shot.

Stewart watched Eleanor follow Croker onto the court, and Jane could have brained him for the buried, measuring glint in his eye.

"Let's go," Stewart said, and under his breath, as they walked to their positions on the base line, he added, "Let's really show the old idiot this time, Jane."

"Yes, dear," Jane said and pulled her bandanna straight and tight around her hair.

The first three games were ludicrously one-sided. Stewart stormed the net, made sizzling, malicious shots to Croker's feet, and purposely made him run, so that he panted pitifully and grew more purple than ever, and from time to time muttered to Jane, "Ridiculous old windbag," and "I thought he had me figured out," and "Don't let up, Janie, don't let up."

Jane played as usual, steady, undeviating, as predictably and sensibly as she always played. She was serving in the fourth game and was at 40–15 when Stewart dropped a shot just over the net, grinning as Croker galloped heavily in and barely got his racket on it. Croker's return wobbled over Stewart's head and landed three inches beyond the base line.

"Nice shot," she heard Stewart say. "Just in."

She looked at him in surprise. He was nodding his head emphatically at Croker.

Eleanor was at the net on the other side, looking at Stewart. "It looked out to me," she said.

"Not at all," Stewart said. "Beautiful shot. Serve them up, Janie."

Oh, Lord, Jane thought, now he's being sporting.

Jane made an error on the next point and Croker made a placement for advantage and Stewart hit into the net for the last point, and it was Croker's and Eleanor's game. Stewart came back to receive the service, not humming any more, his face irritable and dark.

Croker suddenly began to play very well, making sharp, sliding, slicing shots that again and again forced Stewart and Jane into errors. As they played, even as she swung at the ball, Jane kept remembering the shot that Stewart had called in, that had become the turning point of the set. He had not been able to resist the gallant gesture, especially when Eleanor had been standing so close, watching it all. It was just like Stewart. Jane shook her head determinedly, trying to concentrate on the game. This was no time to start dissecting her husband. They had had a lovely weekend till now and Stewart had been wonderful, gay and funny and loving, and criticism could at least be reserved for weekdays, when everything else was dreary, too. But it *was* just like Stewart. It was awful how everything he did was all of a piece. His whole life was crowded with gestures. Hitting his boss that time in the boss's own office with three secretaries watching, because the boss had bawled him out. Giving up his R.O.T.C. commission and going into the Army as a private, in 1942. Giving five thousand dollars, just about the last of their savings, to Harry Mather, for Mather's business, just because they had gone to school together, when everyone knew Mather had become a hopeless drunk and none of his other friends would chip in. To an outsider, all these might seem the acts of a generous and rather noble character, but to a wife, caught in the consequences . . .

"Damn these pants," Stewart was muttering after hitting a ball into the net. "I keep tripping over them all the time."

"You ought to wear shorts, like everyone else," Jane said.

"I will. Buy me some this week," Stewart said, taking time out and rolling his cuffs up slowly and obviously. Jane had bought him three pairs of shorts a month before, but he always pretended he couldn't find them and wore the long trousers. His legs are surprisingly skinny, Jane thought, hating herself for thinking it, and they're hairy, and his vanity won't let him. . . . She started to go for a ball, then stopped when she saw Stewart going for it.

He hit it out to the backstop. "Janie, darling," he said, "at least stay out of my way."

"Sorry," she said. Stewie, darling, she thought, Stewie, be careful. Don't lay it on. You're not really like this. I know you're not. Even for a moment, don't make it look as though you are.

Stewart ended the next rally by hitting the ball into the net. He stared unhappily at the ground. "The least they might do," he said in a low voice to Jane, "is roll the court if they invite people to play on it."

Please, Stewie, Jane begged within herself, don't do it. The alibis. The time he forgot to sign the lease for the apartment and they were put out and he blamed it on the lawyer, and the time he lost the job in Chicago and it was because he had gone to the wrong college, and the time . . . By a rigorous act of will, Jane froze her eyes on the ball, kept her mind blank as she hit it back methodically again and again.

Eleanor and Croker kept winning points. Croker had begun to chop every ball, spinning soft, deceptive shots that landed in midcourt and hardly bounced before they fell a second time. The only way that Jane could return them was to hit them carefully, softly, just getting them back. But Stewart kept going in on them furiously, taking his full, beautiful swing, sending the ball whistling into the net or over the court into the backstop. He looked as pretty and expert as ever as he played, but he lost point after point.

"What a way to play tennis," he grumbled, with his back to his opponents. "Why doesn't he play ping-pong or jacks?"

"You can't slam those dinky little shots like that," Janie said. "You have to get them back soft."

"You play your game," Stewart said, "and I'll play mine."

"Sorry," Jane said. Oh, Stewart, she mourned within her.

Stewart went after two more of Croker's soft chops, each time whipping his backhand around in his usual, slightly exaggerated, beautiful stroke, and each time knocking the ball into the net.

I can't help it, Jane thought. That *is* the way he is. Form above everything. If he were hanging over a cliff, he'd let himself fall to the rocks below rather than risk being ungraceful climbing to safety to save his life. He always has to pick up the check in bars and restaurants, no matter whom he is with or how many guests there are at the table, always with the same lordly, laughing, slightly derisive manner, even if we are down to our last fifty dollars. And when they had people in to dinner, there had to be two maids to wait on table, and French wines, and there always had to be those special bottles of brandy that cost as much as a vacation in the country. And he became so cold and remote when Jane argued with him about it, reminding him they were not rich and there was no sense in pretending they were. And his shoes. She blinked her eyes painfully, getting a sudden vision, there in the sun and shadow, of the long row of exquisite shoes, at seventy dollars a pair, that he insisted upon having

made to his order. How ridiculous, she thought, to allow yourself to be unnerved at your husband's taste in shoes, and she loyally reminded herself how much a part of his attraction it had been in the beginning that he was always so beautifully dressed and so easy and graceful and careless of money.

The score was 4–3 in favor of Eleanor and Croker. Stewart's shots suddenly began to work again, and he and Jane took the next game with ease. Stewart's grin came back then, and he cheerfully reassured Jane, "Now we're going to take them." But after winning the first two points of the next game he had a wild streak and missed the base line by a few inches three times in a row, and they eventually lost the game.

I will make no deductions from this, Jane told herself stonily as she went up to the net for Stewart's serve. Anybody is liable to miss a few shots like that—anybody. And yet, how like Stewart! Just when it was most important to be steady and dependable. . . . The time she'd been so sick and the maid had quit, and Jane lay, broken and miserable in bed for three weeks, with no one to take care of her except Stewart . . . He had been charming and thoughtful for the first week, fixing her meals, reading to her, sitting at her side for hours on end, cheerful and obliging, making her illness gently tolerable. And then he had suddenly grown nervous and abrupt, made vague excuses to leave her alone, and vanished for hours at a time, only to come back and hastily attend her for a few moments and vanish again, leaving her there in the rumpled bed, staring, lonely and shaken, at the ceiling as dusk faded into night and night into morning.

She had been sure there was another girl then and she had resolved that when she was well and able to move around again, she would come to some decision with him, but as unpredictably as his absences had begun, they stopped. Once more he was tender and helpful, once more he sat at her side and nursed her and cheered her, and out of gratitude and love she had remained quiet and pushed her doubts deep to the back of her mind. And here they were again, in the middle of a holiday afternoon, foolishly, in this most unlikely place, during this mild, pointless game, with half a dozen people lazily watching, laughing and friendly, over their drinks.

She looked at him a few moments later, handsome and dear and familiar at her side, and he grinned back at her, and she was ashamed of herself for the thoughts that had been flooding through her brain. It was that silly girl on the other side of the net who had started it all, she thought. That practiced, obvious, almost automatic technique of flattering the male sex. That meaningless, rather pitiful flirtatiousness. It was foolish to allow it to throw her into the bitter waters of reflection. Marriage, after all, was an up-and-down affair and in many ways a fragile and devious thing, and was not to be examined too closely. Marriage was not a bank statement or a foreign policy or an X-ray photograph in a doctor's hand. You took it and lived through it, and maybe, a long time later—perhaps the day before you died —you totalled up the accounts, if you were of that turn of mind, but not before. And if you were a reasonable, sensible, mature woman, you certainly didn't do your additions and subtractions on a tennis court every time your husband hit a ball into the net. Jane smiled at herself and shook her head.

"Nice shot," she said warmly to Stewart as he swept a forehand across court, past Croker, for a point.

But it was still set point. Croker placed himself to receive Stewart's service, tense and determined and a little funny-looking, with his purple face and his serious round body a little too tight under his clothes. The spectators had fallen silent, and the wind had died, and there was a sense of stillness and expectancy as Stewart reared up and served.

Jane was at the net and she heard the sharp twang of Stewart's racket hitting the ball behind her and the rifle-like report as it hit the tape and fell away. He had just missed his first service.

Jane didn't dare look around. She could feel Stewart walking into place, in that stiff-backed, pleasant way of his, and feel him shuffling around nervously, and she couldn't look back. Please, she thought, please get this one in. Helplessly, she thought of all the times when, just at the crucial moment, he had failed. Oh, God, this is silly, she thought. I mustn't do this. The time he had old man Sawyer's account practically in his hands and he got drunk. On the sporting pages, they called it coming through in the clutch. There were some players who did and some players who didn't, and after a while you got to know which was which. If you looked at it coldly, you had to admit that until now Stewart had been one of those who didn't. The time her father died, just after her sister had run off with the vocalist in that band, and if there had been a man around, taking hold of things, her father's partner wouldn't've been able to get away with most of the estate the way he did, and the vocalist could have been frightened off. One day's strength and determination, one day of making the right move at the right time. . . . But after the funeral, Stewart had pulled out and gone to Seattle on what he had said was absolutely imperative business, but that had never amounted to anything anyway, and Jane's mother and sister, and Jane, too, were still paying for that day of failure.

She could sense Stewart winding up for his service behind her back. Somewhere in her spine she felt a sense of disaster. It was going to be a double fault. She knew it. No, she thought, I mustn't. He isn't really like that. He's so intelligent and talented and good, he can go so far. She must not make this terrible judgment on her husband just because of the way he played tennis. And yet, his tennis was so much like his life. Gifted, graceful, powerful, showy, flawed, erratic . . .

Please, she thought, make this one good. Childishly, she felt, if this one is good it will be a turning point, a symbol, his whole life will be different. She hated herself for her thoughts and stared blankly at Eleanor, self-consciously alert and desirable in her pretty dress.

Why the hell did she have to come here this Sunday? Jane thought despairingly.

She heard the crack of the racket behind her. The ball whistled past her, hit the tape, rolled undecidedly on top of the net for a moment, then fell back at her feet for a double fault and the set.

"Too bad." She turned and smiled at Stewart, helplessly feeling herself beginning to wonder how she would manage to find the six weeks it would take in Reno. She shook her head, knowing that she wasn't going to Reno, but knowing, too, that the word would pass through her thoughts again and again, more and more frequently, with growing insistence, as the days went by.

She walked off the court with Stewart, holding his hand.

"The shadows," Stewart was saying. "Late in the afternoon, like this. It's impossible to see the service line."

"Yes, dear," Jane said.

· QUESTIONS ·

1. State the central theme (meaning) of this story.
2. This is a "he-she married couple" story. So is "The Secret Life of Walter Mitty." Compare and contrast the thematic detail of each.
3. What specific speech, images, and action contribute to the characterization of Stewart Collins? Of Jane? Of Mr. Croker?
4. What is the purpose of the last four words of the story?
5. Study carefully and then explain the smooth interpolation of Jane's "dissection" of Stewart. Does this analysis retard the action? Why? Why not?

Theme Subjects: (1) After All, It's Only a Game; (2) If You Really Want To Know a Person . . . ; (3) The Most Revealing Game I Ever Played; (4) When the Chips Are Down; (5) When My Best Friend Let Me Down.

THE SPOILER

Paul Brodeur

PAUL ADRIAN BRODEUR, JR. (1931–   ) was born in Boston and attended
Phillips Academy, Andover, and Harvard, where he was graduated in 1953.
A staff writer for *The New Yorker* since 1958, he is author of *The Sick Fox,*
published in 1963 by Atlantic-Little Brown. Mr. Brodeur lives in New York
City.

Stephen Drew saw the shaggy-haired
skiers when he was riding up the
chair lift for his first run of the day.
They came hurtling toward him
over the lip of a steep face—three
of them, strung out across the trail
that plunged down the mountain
beside the liftline. Hatless, wearing
tattered Levis and baggy sweaters,
and not deigning to make the slightest speed checks, they came straight
on, skiing powerfully and grace-
lessly, bounding high into the air
from the tops of moguls and landing heavily and often wavering off
balance until, exploding off other
moguls, they seemed miraculously
to regain their equilibrium in flight.
Stephen turned his attention to one
skier who was racing perilously
close to the steel towers that supported the chair-lift cable, and saw
the wind-burned face of a young
man in his early twenties—a blunt,
openmouthed face that was surrounded by a thick mane of red
hair, which, covering his ears and
most of his forehead, was kept out
of his eyes only because it was
streaming backward in the wake
of his tremendous speed. The red-
headed skier was past him in an instant, yet Stephen had the sensation
that he had not passed beneath him
but over him, like an avalanche or
a jet plane. Turning in the chair,
he watched the youth and his companions disappear over the lip of
another face, emerge again as
specks far down the mountain, and
finally pass from view behind a
screen of fir trees.

Stephen saw the shaggy-haired
skiers again half an hour later,
when he was halfway down the
mountain. He had stopped to rest
and was looking back to watch an
instructor—a model of skiing grace

—lead his class of students over a tortuous series of moguls when he heard a joyous shout from far above him and, glancing up the mountain, saw the red-headed skier silhouetted, arms outflung and skis apart, against the blue January sky as he came over the lip of another face. This time, however, the youth caught an edge when he landed and, teetering out of control, plunged into the midst of the skiing class, narrowly missing a girl in yellow stretch pants before he finally righted himself and came to a ragged stop a few yards below Stephen. Now, ignoring his two companions, who, whooping at his plight, swept past and disappeared, the red-headed skier leaned forward, thrust his weight against his poles, which bent in protest, and, shaking his head as if to clear it, spat into the snow between the tips of his skies. An instant later, Stephen's view of him was interrupted as the ski instructor passed between them with a straight downhill plunge and two quick finishing waggles. Placing himself directly in front of the red-headed youth, the instructor also leaned forward on his poles and, in a shrill German accent, began to scream slowly spaced words that seemed to ricochet off the hard-packed snow.

"If . . . I . . . effer . . . shall . . . see . . . such . . . foolishness . . . again . . . you . . . shall . . . be . . . taken . . . from . . . this . . . mount-a-a-ahn!" he shouted in a rising crescendo of outrage. "Haff . . . you . . . a-ahnderstood . . . me?"

For a moment, the two figures remained motionless, bent toward one another like a pair of stags locked in combat; then the shaggy-haired skier lifted his head and looked the ski instructor in the face.

For a long time, he simply stared at the instructor without the slightest expression, but just before he pushed off down the mountain he gave a faint grin that Stephen interpreted as a smirk of contempt.

With a surge of energy that seemed to be the residue of anger, the ski instructor began sidestepping briskly up the mountain to rejoin his class. When he drew abreast of Stephen, however, he paused for breath and, in a voice still full of rage, shouted, "They care not for any thing, this kind of people! They haff no idea what means responsibility! If he has fallen, that one, he can only haff badly hurt this girl in my class!"

Stephen nodded in agreement, but made no reply. There was something in the instructor's shrilly enunciated Teutonic anger that seemed improbable and out of place on this tree-covered mountain in Vermont. Besides, Stephen had been watching the shaggy-haired skier, who was plummeting down the mountainside with the same reckless abandon as before, and, remembering that he himself had skied with a certain abandon at the age of twenty, had been thinking with regret that the sensation of such speed was something he would never come close to experiencing again. He had, in fact, been in the process of acknowledging to himself that there were certain things he was past doing, because of fear. Not that he really wanted to ski beyond the brink of control, but to admit that he was past it and afraid to try was something else again, for, at thirty-five, Stephen considered himself a young man whose courage was still intact. Now, resuming his train of thought as the instructor resumed his climb, he realized that he envied the shaggy-haired youth who, envying no one and emulating nothing—not even the grace of ski instructors—skied only against himself, and in so doing conquered fear. Was it just a question of age? Stephen wondered. But once again the voice of the instructor intruded upon his reverie. It was a calm voice now, completely under control, and fading away as he called soothingly back to the students, who trailed him down the mountain.

"So remember, always in our linked turns we lock the knees together, and we dip up . . . and then down . . . and so-o-o-o . . ."

Stephen did not see the shaggy-haired skiers on the slopes again. At three o'clock, he took a final run down the mountain and found his wife, Marilyn, waiting for him outside the base lodge. She was sitting in the afternoon sun, looking very pretty in the new blue-and-white ski outfit he had bought her for the trip, and Stephen paused to admire her. Then, as he bent over to release his safety bindings, he realized that she had not brought the baby with her. "How's little Petey?" he asked.

"I left him with the sitter," Marilyn said proudly, as if she were announcing an achievement. "He's fine."

Stephen kicked his boots free of the bindings. Afterward, he strapped his skis together, placed them on his shoulder, and followed Marilyn through a parking lot to the place where she had left their car.

"Can we ski together tomorrow?" she asked, smiling.

"Of course!" he replied with a laugh. "Isn't that why we came up here—to ski?"

Marilyn nodded, but the smile had left her face. "The girl seems very good," she said sombrely. "Her name is Janice Pike. She's got funny bleached hair, but she's intelligent and competent, and Petey took to her right away. I spent the whole morning and most of the afternoon with them, and I've given her careful instructions about everything. I really don't think we have to worry."

"Then we won't worry," Stephen replied lightly. "Does the girl know we'll want her for the next few days?"

"Yes, and she's delighted about that. Evidently she needs the money."

They had reached the car, and after fastening his skis to the roof rack Stephen got inside, opened the door on Marilyn's side, and started up the engine. As they drove through the valley that led south, toward Worthington, Marilyn continued to tell him about the sitter.

"I've given Janice the telephone number at the base lodge so we could be paged if we were needed," she went on. "She, of course, knows all the doctors in the vicinity. Oh, and she's familiar with the house we're staying in, which makes me especially happy because of the stove and everything. It turns out the caretaker often hires her to clean up the place after weekends."

"I'd say we were lucky," Stephen said, glancing carefully at his wife. She has become more and more like me, he thought. She tries to think of all the awful possibilities.

"One thing worries me, though," Marilyn was saying.

"What's that?"

"Where the house is," she replied. "I mean it's so isolated. Not that I think anything would happen, but what if it did?"

Stephen reached across the seat and touched her arm. "Don't give in to that, baby," he said gently. But as they drove on through the valley, he realized that his words of admonition were a form of self-address. They had lost their first child—a boy of two—in an absurd accident, a year before. Little Peter had been born five months later, at the end of June, and except on rare occasions, when he had been safely tucked into his crib for the night and their neighbor, Mrs. Murphy, could come over to sit for them, they had never left him with anyone. Now, having been lent the use of a small chalet by friends in Boston, they had come skiing with the idea of spelling one another at the task of caring for the baby. (He would ski in the mornings and she in the afternoons —not an ideal solution, perhaps, but all they hoped for.) When they arrived in Worthington, the night before, they telephoned the caretaker, who came to open up the house. The caretaker was friendly and garrulous—a country handyman whose dealings with the winter sporting crowd had coated his native astuteness with a certain veneer of assurance.

"Your wife ski, too?" he asked, glancing at the baby.

"Yes," Stephen answered.

"Then you're goin' to need a sitter, ain't you?"

"Yes," Stephen replied, though he and Marilyn had scarcely bothered to discuss the possibility. "It would be nice if we could ski together," he added, glancing at her.

"I know just the girl," the caretaker said. "She's nineteen and real experienced. Lives in town. Why'nt I have her call you in the morning?"

"Fine," said Stephen. "I'd appreciate that."

After the caretaker left, he turned to Marilyn. "There's no harm in trying her out, is there?" he said.

Now, turning off the highway at a point midway between the mountain and the town, Stephen drove over a dirt road that wound up the side of the valley through thick stands of spruce and pine trees. The road was a washboard affair, bordered by high snowbanks that had been thrown up by plows, and the heavy growth had plunged it into premature shadow. There were half a dozen forks and turnoffs on the way to the house, and realizing for the first time that none of them was marked, Stephen suddenly found himself wondering how the girl could possibly give directions to summon help. He imagined her trying to remember all the twists and turns as precious minutes slipped away. "Don't give in to that," he had told Marilyn, sitting beside him. But he had merely been talking to himself.

The chalet, a prefabricated structure with two sides consisting of panel picture windows, was hidden from the road by a wooded knoll, and was reached by a narrow, rutted driveway that first passed before a similar dwelling, fifty yards away, which was unoccupied. The driveway ended in a cul-de-sac at the second house, where Stephen turned the car around and parked it. When he and Marilyn came through the door, they found the sitter watching television and Petey playing happily on the tile floor at her feet.

Ten minutes later, Stephen set out to drive Janice Pike home. As they descended over the washboard road toward the valley, the girl lit a cigarette, stubbed it out, and immediately lit another. To make conversation, Stephen asked her if she had always lived in Worthington.

Janice Pike shook her head, which tossed the bleached, teased mop of hair that crowned it, and blew out a cloud of smoke. "For a year after high school, I worked over to Brattleboro," she replied. "Waitressing."

"How did you like Brattleboro?"

"I liked it a lot. I have a boy friend there."

"What made you come back?"

"My family," she replied. "They want me to settle down, you know?"

"What about your boy friend?"

"Oh, he drives over to see me weekends. He's a plumber's apprentice and he got himself a car this year."

They had reached the valley highway and were driving past a series of ski lodges, restaurants, and roadhouses. "I suppose there's a lot doing here on weekends," Stephen said.

"Yeah, but we just seem to drive around," replied the girl morosely, and looked out the window. "Saturday night, we were driving around and I never saw so many cars parked out in front of these places," she went on. "I guess people must really be having a swell time in them. I mean little bitsy joints with just a guitar player or something and about twenty cars out front!"

Stephen glanced sidewise at Janice Pike, and decided that her hair was teased into its absurd pile as an antidote to boredom. Now he imagined her having worked over it for hours, only to drive around and look wistfully through the windshield of the apprentice plumber's car at lights in the windows of ski lodges. "You should get your boy friend to take you dancing in some of these places," he said.

"Yeah, but they're supposed to be kind of wild," she replied, with more yearning, however, than disapproval. "I mean a lot of the fellows who come skiing here are real maniacs, you know?"

"No kidding," Stephen said.

"Look, I wasn't going to say anything because your wife seems awful worried about leaving the baby and everything, but a whole carload of guys drove up to the house this afternoon. They sat out front awhile, honking and waving at me. Then they went over to the other house and left some skis and stuff inside and drove away. I'm pretty sure the caretaker doesn't know they're there, and I was a little worried 'cause they looked kind of wild, you know, but maybe they were just out for fun."

"Sure," Stephen said. "Probably a lark of some kind."

"Yeah, well, I kept the door locked anyway."

"That's a good idea," Stephen replied.

They had arrived in Worthington, a village built at the conjunction of two roads that crossed through the mountains, and packed with shabby frame houses. Following the girl's directions, Stephen drove to the lower end of town, where, next to a small stream and the gutted remnants of a factory that had once been used to manufacture wooden boxes, there stood a particularly ramshackle dwelling with a sagging roof, peeling shingles, and a veranda that was evolving into debris. For a moment, Stephen studied the house in silence; then, embarrassed, he took out his wallet and turned to the girl. "How much do we owe you, Janice?" he asked.

"Your wife picked me up at ten o'clock, so that would make about six hours I worked," she replied.

"And what do you charge by the hour?" Stephen asked.

"Fifty cents?"

Stephen looked again at the decrepit house, and winced. "Tell you what, Janice, let's call it eight hours," he said, handing her four one-dollar bills. "I'll come by for you tomorrow morning at nine."

"Oh, lovely!" she cried. "Thank you!" Now, jumping out of the car, she climbed the porch steps and, skirting a large hole where several rotten planks had fallen through, waved at Stephen and went into the house.

"Thank *you!*" Stephen called after her. A child of Appalachia, he thought as he turned the car around and headed back through town. He drove more quickly on the return trip, anxious to take a bath, have a drink, and play with Petey before his bedtime. He was happy with anticipation. For the first time in a year, he sensed that he and Marilyn were on the brink of resuming life. He told himself that it was a good thing they had decided to come skiing, and that they had been able to bring themselves to leave little Petey with the girl. They must not give in to the temptation to over-protect him. Yes, above all, they must not allow his life and theirs to be forever colored by tragedy. Entangled in these thoughts, Stephen was surprised when, fifteen minutes later, he came upon a black Volkswagen sitting in the driveway that led up to the house.

The Volkswagen was badly battered at the fenders and wore a bent Florida license plate, and it had been parked carelessly, in such a way that it half blocked the drive. Putting his car into second gear, Stephen drove slowly around it; then, glancing toward the porch of the other house, he saw that there were three young men sitting on it in deck chairs. The young men were drinking beer from cans, and, looking closer, Stephen saw that one of them was, unmistakably, the shaggy, red-headed youth he had seen on the mountain. None of the young men bothered to look at the passing car, but as Stephen drove by the redhead gave a flip of his wrist that sent his beer can over the porch railing and into a snowbank.

When he drew up before the house of his friends, Stephen parked the car, got out, and stood beside it for several minutes as he tried to decide what the three shaggy-haired skiers were doing in the other chalet. Perhaps the caretaker is allowing them to stay there in return for some chores, he thought. Or perhaps the caretaker is making money on the side with an illicit rental. But what if, as Janice Pike seemed to imply, the young men had simply broken into the place? Stephen thought of them catching sight of Janice's bleached hair through the picture window, and for a moment he toyed with the idea of telephoning the caretaker. Then he decided against it. Their honking at Janice was like their skiing, the parking of their car in the middle of the driveway, and the red-headed youth's disposal of his beer can. It was thoughtless, nothing more— just thoughtlessness. You're getting old, Stephen told himself. What's the point of spoiling other people's fun? But when he went into the house, he did not mention the presence of the shaggy-haired skiers to Marilyn.

In the morning, the sun was shining brilliantly in a cloudless sky. When Stephen left the house to pick up Janice Pike, the black Volkswagen was still parked before the other chalet. It was there when he returned with the girl, half an hour later, so he asked her if it was the same car that had honked at her the day before.

She took a deep drag on her cigarette, and nodded. "Yeah, that's the one," she replied. "I know from the dented fenders. They must be wild drivers, huh?"

Stephen looked quickly at Janice Pike. Had he detected a slight note of admiration in her voice, or was it his imagination? Everything was "wild" to this country girl, or was it simply that, out of sheer boredom, she hoped her life might become so? "Look, Janice," he said. "I don't want to mention anything about this to my wife, but on the other hand I don't want to spend my day worrying, either. So I'll speak frankly to you —O.K.?"

"Sure, but you don't have to worry, Mr. Drew. I'll keep the door locked—you can count on that."

"Fine," Stephen said, and glanced at her hair. "But maybe you'd better stay away from the window as much as possible. I mean, just don't be sitting too conspicuously next to it."

"Oh, sure," the girl replied. "O.K."

"And I'll phone you every couple of hours from the base lodge," Stephen said. "Just to make certain things are all right."

When they went into the house,

Marilyn went over a list of things she had made out for Janice to do. "Petey's lunch is on the stove," she said. "You'll just have to heat it up. If he balks at eating the beef mush, dip each spoonful into his banana-dessert mush. It sometimes works. He woke up at seven this morning, which means he'll be ready for his nap any time now. After lunch, of course, he'll take another nap. If it's still sunny when he wakes up from that one, bundle him into his snowsuit and take him outside for some air."

"No," Stephen said quickly. "Don't have him go out today."

"But if it's nice and sunny—"

Stephen shook his head, picked up an armload of jackets, poles, and ski boots, and started out the door. "A day or two won't matter," he said over his shoulder. "And I'll feel better if he stays inside."

When Stephen reached the car, he put the jackets, poles, and boots into the back and climbed in behind the wheel. He was about to start the engine when he heard the sharp crack of a rifle. The report sounded close by, but in the cold, dazzling brilliance of the morning light he could not be sure how close. Leaving the car door open, he listened intently, heard several more shots, and recognized the explicitly neat sound of a .22-calibre rifle. The shots seemed to be coming from the far side of the next house, but he could detect no movement there. When Marilyn climbed into the car, he started up the engine and drove slowly down the driveway.

"Really, Stephen, you shouldn't interfere that way," Marilyn said. "Why on earth shouldn't the girl take Petey out for some air?"

"There's a reason," Stephen

said absently, but they were drawing abreast of the other house, and he was not paying Marilyn any real attention, for at that moment the three young men, led by the shaggy red-headed youth, came around a corner from the back. The redhead was carrying a rifle, which, when he saw the car, he seemed to thrust out of sight between his body and the wall of the house. They must be there illegally, Stephen thought. He wondered if Marilyn had seen the weapon, but a moment later he realized that she had not.

"Goodness!" she exclaimed. "Who are *they*—beatniks?"

Stephen nodded his head, and turned to study the young men as he drove past. Unshaven and bleary-eyed, they seemed to have recently risen after a night of heavy drinking, and now they gave the car bold looks of appraisal that, because of their brazenness, also seemed to be defensive. Looking back, Stephen saw them duck quickly into the house. He was more certain than ever now that they had broken into it, but as he continued down the drive it was the rifle that stayed in his mind. He knew that it was against the law in almost every state to shoot a rifle so close to inhabited places. He wondered if he should not call the police.

"What's the matter?" Marilyn asked.

"Nothing," he told her.

His mind, however, was in ferment. The harsh vibrations of the washboard road that descended into the valley triggered his brain into conjuring up visions of catastrophe. Helplessly, he imagined the young men firing at a beer can, the bullet ricocheting off a rock, piercing the picture window behind which little Petey sat playing, or, perhaps, striking the girl and causing one of her interminable cigarettes to fall, smoldering, upon a scatter rug. . . . "They haff no idea what means responsibility," the outraged ski instructor had said. The sentence repeated itself within him endlessly.

"You're awfully silent," Marilyn remarked when they reached the highway.

"It's nothing," he told her again, and, stepping hard on the accelerator, drove quickly toward the mountain, already planning to telephone Janice Pike the moment they arrived. The miles seemed to pass slowly, however, and soon they found themselves behind a line of cars bearing other skiers to the slopes. When finally they reached the parking lot at the base lodge, he jumped from the car, unstrapped Marilyn's skis, and handed them to her. Then, as he reached inside the car for her boots and poles, he deliberately pushed his own boots out of sight beneath the seat.

"Damn!" he said, straightening up. "I've left my boots behind."

Marilyn made a grimace of sympathy and pain.

"Why don't you take a few runs on the beginner's slope," he told her. "It'll get you in the swing of things. I won't be more than half an hour—forty minutes at the most."

He scarcely waited to hear her assent, but, jumping into the car, started the engine, threw it into first gear, and tore away. There was no traffic on the road leading from the mountain, but the sun, rising higher in the sky, shed a brilliant light that, rebounding from the snow and glinting off the hood of the car, found its way into his eyes. The light—a sharp, metallic intrusion—cut into him, exposing his fear as a surgeon's scalpel lays open tissue to disclose a nerve, and now, as the valley broadened, so did the range of awful possibilities that haunted his mind.

When he swerved into the driveway, twenty minutes later, he jammed the car into second gear, topped the knoll with a roar, and swept past the first chalet and the Volkswagen, which was still parked, half blocking the road, before it. He was squinting through the windshield, hoping to get a glimpse of Janice Pike's massive blond coiffure in the picture window, when, dead ahead, walking toward him down the middle of the drive, he saw the shaggy red-headed youth. Stephen slammed on the brakes and brought the car to an abrupt halt; then, taking a deep breath, he was amazed to find himself filling with a curious kind of relief—the kind of relief that comes when the worst is apparent and no longer in the realm of fantasy—for the shaggy-haired youth, who was standing just ahead of the front bumper and looking at him without expression, was holding a rifle over his shoulder with one hand and the hind legs of a blood-spattered snowshoe hare with the other. Stephen's gaze travelled along the barrel of the rifle that, draped carelessly over the young man's shoulder, was pointing in the direction of the picture window, where he could see Janice Pike, holding little Peter. He got out of the car, walked toward the red-headed youth, and stopped directly in front of him.

"Is the rifle loaded?" he asked. He was looking into the young man's eyes, which were deep blue, and the sound of his voice came back to him as an alien presence— a cold breath that was still as the

icicles hanging perilously from the roof of the house.

The shaggy-haired youth made no reply, but gave the snowshoe hare a shake so that—as if gore were in itself sufficient answer— its bloody carcass was swung ever so slightly in Stephen's direction.

"Look where the rifle's pointing," Stephen said. Every instinct in him wanted to make a lunge for it, but fear of causing the weapon to discharge deterred him, and this terrible fear, plus the studied unconcern of the young man's face, unnerved him. He felt his control unravelling like a ball of twine. "Damn you," he said in a hoarse whisper. *"Look where it's pointing!"*

The shaggy-haired youth gave a quick sidewise glance toward the picture window; then he looked at Stephen again and shrugged. "Relax," he said. "The safety's on."

Cursing him, Stephen told him to take the rifle off his shoulder.

For a moment, the shaggy-haired youth looked at Stephen with the same detachment with which he had stared into the face of the angry ski instructor; then, with taunting slowness, he swung the rifle from his shoulder in a lazy arc and rested the tip of the barrel against the top of his shoe. "Man, you've gone and lost your cool," he told Stephen, and calmly pulled the trigger. Afterward, he gave an insolent grin and, to further affirm the fact that the safety was on, allowed the weight of the rifle to be suspended from his forefinger, which was still curled around the trigger.

Stephen looked at the unafraid, contemptuous face before him and, a second later, struck it. The blow —a roundhouse swing—landed just in front of the ear on the sideburn and knocked the shaggy-haired youth into a sitting position in the middle of the driveway. The rifle fell to the ground, and, stooping quickly, Stephen picked it up and pushed the safety button off.

The shaggy-haired youth had not uttered a sound, but when he saw Stephen pick up the rifle and push the safety button off, his mouth fell open, and the look of fear that Stephen hoped to see—desperately *wanted* to see—came over his face and filled his eyes. Sitting there, rubbing the side of his head with one hand and still clutching the bloody hare with the other, he suddenly looked like a small boy about to cry.

"Listen, man," he said in a voice that croaked. "Like we're low on funds, you know, and the rabbit's just for eating."

"Shut up!" Stephen replied. He wanted silence simply because he was trying to figure out what he should do next.

"So maybe it's out of season," the young man went on. "What d'you care? You're not a game warden."

"Shut up!" Stephen said again, but as he looked down at the youth he felt some of the anger and hatred draining out of him.

"Look, the house wasn't even locked! It was just sitting there, like waiting for us, and the rifle was standing in the corner behind the door."

"The rabbit and the house have nothing to do with it," Stephen told him. "It's my *child,* you fool! You were pointing the rifle at my *child!*"

"But nothing *happened!*" said the shaggy-haired youth, shaking his head in puzzlement and protest. "I mean, like, if nothing's happened—"

"Something's going to happen now," Stephen told him quietly. "Here's what's going to happen. You and your friends are going to pack up and be out of here in five minutes. You are only going to have five minutes—d'you understand?—and if you are not, the lot of you, out of here for good in five minutes, I am going to make damn sure you'll be here when the state police arrive. Now get on your feet and get moving."

The shaggy-haired youth did as he was told and, still clutching the snowshoe hare, stumbled off down the driveway to the other house. A moment later, Stephen saw a curtain being parted in the kitchen window and a pair of disembodied faces looking out at him. Suddenly he felt immensely weary. Glancing at his watch, he leaned against the fender of his car and waited.

Five minutes later, the young men had finished packing the Volkswagen. Stephen watched them in silence as, casting nervous glances in his direction like hired men anxious to please, they threw the last of their belongings into the back of the car. He was struck by the idea that they, who had skied without fear, were now dancing to the macabre tune of his own fear, but he derived no satisfaction from it. Presently the red-headed youth came out of the house, closed the door behind him, and, picking up the hare from the porch, walked around the front of the car to the driver's side. At this point, he hesitated, as if debating with himself; then he tossed the hare into some bushes and looked toward Stephen. For several moments, he stood there, gazing at Stephen with profound reproach, as if what had happened between them was caused by a gulf of misunderstanding that was far too deep to ever be bridged. Then, with a sad shake of his head, he got in behind the wheel, started the engine, and drove away.

Leaning against his car, Stephen listened as the Volkswagen growled toward the valley in second gear. He continued listening until the sound of its engine faded into silence; then he turned and walked toward the house where Janice Pike, still holding the baby at the picture window, was looking out at him with horror and awe. He was thinking that he would not return the rifle to the other house until he and Marilyn and little Peter left for good. He was trembling slightly as he reached the door, but he did not know whether it was with the aftermath of rage or with a mixture of relief and regret. He told himself, however, that even now the shaggy-haired skiers were probably heading for some other mountain, where, bounding high into the air with arms outflung and whoops of joy, they would continue to escape from care.

· QUESTIONS ·

1. What is the basic theme of this story?
2. To whom does the title of the story apply? Does your answer conform with the apparent intent of the author?
3. Write a one-sentence description of each of the following: Stephen Drew, the German ski instructor, Marilyn Drew, Janice Pike, the group of shaggy-haired skiers.
4. With whom do you most identify in this story? Most sympathize?
5. Comment on the dialogue and setting of this story.
6. Specifically, why do you like or dislike this story? Is your reaction dependent upon the contrasts involved, the suspense achieved, the human or "inhuman" behavior of Stephen, sympathy with one or another of the conflicting personalities?

Theme Subjects: (1) "Never Trust Anyone Over Thirty"; (2) An Experience I Had While Babysitting; (3) My Favorite Beatnik; (4) Youthful Spirits in "Youth" and "The Spoiler": A Contrast; (5) Why Stephen Drew Felt Immensely Weary.

COME DANCE WITH ME
IN IRELAND

Shirley Jackson

SHIRLEY JACKSON (1919–1965) was born in San Francisco. She was gradu-
ated from Syracuse University in 1940; here she met and married the critic
and staff writer for *The New Yorker*, Stanley Edgar Hyman. Among Miss
Jackson's books are *The Road Through the Wall* (1948); *The Lottery, or
The Adventures of James Harris* (1949); *Life Among the Savages* (1953);
Raising Demons (1957); *The Haunting of Hill House* (1959); and *We
Have Always Lived in the Castle* (1962).

Young Mrs. Archer was sitting on the bed with Kathy Valentine and Mrs. Corn, playing with the baby and gossiping, when the doorbell rang. Mrs. Archer, saying "Oh, dear!" went to push the buzzer that released the outside door of the apartment building. "We *had* to live on the ground floor," she called to Kathy and Mrs. Corn. "Everybody rings our bell for everything."

When the inner doorbell rang she opened the door of the apartment and saw an old man standing in the outer hall. He was wearing a long, shabby black overcoat and had a square white beard. He held out a handful of shoelaces.

"Oh," Mrs. Archer said. "Oh, I'm terribly sorry, but—" "Madam," the old man said, "if you would be so kind. A nickel apiece."

Mrs. Archer shook her head and backed away. "I'm afraid not," she said.

"Thank you anyway, Madam," he said, "for speaking courteously. The first person on this block who has been decently polite to a poor old man."

Mrs. Archer turned the doorknob back and forth nervously. "I'm awfully sorry," she said. Then, as he turned to go, she said, "Wait a minute," and hurried into the bedroom. "Old man selling shoelaces," she whispered. She pulled open the top dresser drawer, took out her pocketbook, and fumbled in the change purse. "Quarter," she said. "Think it's all right?"

"Sure," Kathy said. "Probably more than he's gotten all day." She was Mrs. Archer's age, and unmarried. Mrs. Corn was a stout woman in her middle fifties. They both lived in the building and spent a good deal of time at Mrs. Archer's, on account of the baby.

Mrs. Archer returned to the front door. "Here," she said, holding out the quarter. "I think it's a shame everyone was so rude."

The old man started to offer her some shoelaces, but his hand shook and the shoelaces dropped to the floor. He leaned heavily against the wall. Mrs. Archer watched, horrified. "Good Lord," she said, and put out her hand. As her fingers touched the dirty old overcoat she hesitated and then, tightening her lips, she put her arm firmly through his and tried to help him through the doorway. "Girls," she called, "come help me, quick!"

Kathy came running out of the bedroom, saying, "Did you call, Jean?" and then stopped dead, staring.

"What'll I do?" Mrs. Archer said, standing with her arm through the old man's. His eyes were closed and he seemed barely able, with her help, to stand on his feet. "For heaven's sake, grab him on the other side."

"Get him to a chair or something," Kathy said. The hall was too narrow for all three of them to go down side by side, so Kathy took the old man's other arm and half-led Mrs. Archer and him into the living-room. "Not in the good chair," Mrs. Archer exclaimed. "In the old leather one." They dropped the old man into the leather chair and stood back. "What on earth do we do now?" Mrs. Archer said.

"Do you have any whiskey?" Kathy asked.

Mrs. Archer shook her head. "A little wine," she said doubtfully.

Mrs. Corn came into the living-room, holding the baby. "Gracious!" she said. "He's drunk!"

"Nonsense," Kathy said. "I wouldn't have let Jean bring him in if he were."

"Watch out for the baby, Blanche," Mrs. Archer said.

"Naturally," Mrs. Corn said. "We're going back into the bedroom, honey," she said to the baby, "and then we're going to get into our lovely crib and go beddy-bye."

The old man stirred and opened his eyes. He tried to get up.

"Now you stay right where you are," Kathy ordered, "and Mrs. Archer here is going to bring you a little bit of wine. You'd like that, wouldn't you?"

The old man raised his eyes to Kathy. "Thank you," he said.

Mrs. Archer went into the kitchen. After a moment's thought she took the glass from over the sink, rinsed it out, and poured some sherry into it. She took the glass of sherry back into the living-room and handed it to Kathy.

"Shall I hold it for you or can you drink by yourself?" Kathy asked the old man.

"You are much too kind," he said, and reached for the glass. Kathy steadied it for him as he sipped from it, and then he pushed it away.

"That's enough, thank you," he said. "Enough to revive me." He tried to rise. "Thank you," he said to Mrs. Archer, "and thank *you*," to Kathy. "I had better be going along."

"Not until you're quite firm on your feet," Kathy said. "Can't afford to take chances, you know."

The old man smiled. "I can afford to take chances," he said.

Mrs. Corn came back into the living-room. "Baby's in his crib," she said, "and just about asleep already. Does *he* feel better now? I'll bet he was just drunk or hungry or something."

"Of course he was," Kathy said, fired by the idea. "He was hungry. That's what was wrong all the time, Jean. How silly we were. Poor old gentleman!" she said to the old man. "Mrs. Archer is certainly not going to let you leave here without a full meal inside of you."

Mrs. Archer looked doubtful. "I have some eggs," she said.

"Fine!" Kathy said. "Just the thing. They're easily digested," she said to the old man, "and especially good if you haven't eaten for"— she hesitated—"for a while."

"Black coffee," Mrs. Corn said, "if you ask me. Look at his hands shake."

"Nervous exhaustion," Kathy said firmly. "A nice hot cup of bouillon is all he needs to be good as ever, and he has to drink it very slowly until his stomach gets used to food again. The stomach," she told Mrs. Archer and Mrs. Corn, "shrinks when it remains empty for any great period of time."

"I would rather not trouble you," the old man said to Mrs. Archer.

"Nonsense," Kathy said. "We've got to see that you get a good hot meal to go on with." She took Mrs. Archer's arm and began to walk out to the kitchen. "Just some eggs," she said. "Fry four or five. I'll get you half a dozen later. I don't suppose you have any bacon. I'll tell you, fry up a few potatoes too. He won't care if they're half-raw. These people eat things like heaps of fried potatoes and eggs and—"

"There's some canned figs left over from lunch," Mrs. Archer said. "I was wondering what to do with them."

"I've got to run back and keep an eye on him," Kathy said. "He might faint again or something. You just fry up those eggs and potatoes. I'll send Blanche out if she'll come."

Mrs. Archer measured out enough coffee for two cups and set the pot on the stove. Then she took out her frying pan. "Kathy," she said, "I'm just a little worried. If he really is drunk, I mean, and if Jim should hear about it, with the baby here and everything. . . ."

"Why, Jean!" Kathy said. "You should live in the country for a while, I guess. Women always give out meals to starving men. And you don't need to *tell* Jim. Blanche and I certainly won't say anything."

"Well," said Mrs. Archer, "you're sure he isn't drunk?"

"I know a starving man when I see one," Kathy said. "When an old man like that can't stand up and his hands shake and he looks so funny, that means he's starving to death. Literally starving."

"Oh, my!" said Mrs. Archer. She hurried to the cupboard under the sink and took out two potatoes. "Two enough, do you think? I guess we're really doing a good deed."

Kathy giggled. "Just a bunch of Girl Scouts," she said. She started out of the kitchen, and then she stopped and turned around. "You have any pie? They always eat pie."

"It was for dinner, though," Mrs. Archer said.

"Oh, give it to him," Kathy said. "We can run out and get some more after he goes."

While the potatoes were frying, Mrs. Archer put a plate, a cup and saucer, and a knife and fork and spoon on the dinette table. Then, as an afterthought, she picked up the dishes and, taking a paper bag out of a cupboard, tore it in half and spread it smoothly on the table and put the dishes back. She got a glass and filled it with water from the bottle in the refrigerator, cut three slices of bread and put them on a plate, and then cut a small square of butter and put it on the plate with the bread. Then she got a paper napkin from the box in the cupboard and put it beside the plate, took it up after a minute to fold it into a triangular shape, and put it back. Finally she put the pepper and salt shakers on the table and got out a box of eggs. She went to the door and called, "Kathy! Ask him how does he want his eggs fried?"

There was a murmur of conversation in the living-room and Kathy called back, "Sunny side up!"

Mrs. Archer took out four eggs and then another and broke them one by one into the frying-pan. When they were done she called out, "All right, girls! Bring him in!"

Mrs. Corn came into the kitchen, inspected the plate of potatoes and eggs, and looked at Mrs. Archer without speaking. Then Kathy came, leading the old man by the arm. She escorted him to the table and sat him down in a chair. "There," she said. "Now, Mrs. Archer's fixed you a lovely hot meal."

The old man looked at Mrs. Archer. "I'm very grateful," he said.

"Isn't that nice!" Kathy said. She nodded approvingly at Mrs. Archer. The old man regarded the plate of eggs and potatoes. "Now pitch right in," Kathy said. "Sit down, girls. I'll get a chair from the bedroom."

The old man picked up the salt and shook it gently over the eggs. "This looks delicious," he said finally.

"You just go right ahead and eat," Kathy said, reappearing with a chair. "We want to see you get filled up. Pour him some coffee, Jean."

Mrs. Archer went to the stove and took up the coffeepot.

"Please don't bother," he said.

"That's all right," Mrs. Archer said, filling the old man's cup. She sat down at the table. The old man picked up the fork and then put it down again to take up the paper napkin and spread it carefully over his knees.

"What's your name?" Kathy asked.

"O'Flaherty, Madam. John O'Flaherty."

"Well, John," Kathy said, "I am Miss Valentine and this lady is Mrs. Archer and the other one is Mrs. Corn."

"How do you do?" the old man said.

"I gather you're from the old country," Kathy said.

"I beg your pardon?"

"Irish, aren't you?" Kathy said.

"I am, Madam." The old man plunged the fork into one of the eggs and watched the yolk run out onto the plate. "I knew Yeats," he said suddenly.

"Really?" Kathy said, leaning forward. "Let me see—he was the writer, wasn't he?"

"'Come out of charity, come dance with me in Ireland,'" the old man said. He rose and, holding on to the chair back, bowed solemnly to Mrs. Archer, "Thank you again, Madam, for your generosity." He turned and started for the front door. The three women got up and followed him.

"But you didn't finish," Mrs. Corn said.

"The stomach," the old man said, "as this lady has pointed out, shrinks. Yes, indeed," he went on reminiscently, "I knew Yeats."

At the front door he turned and said to Mrs. Archer, "Your kindness should not go unrewarded." He gestured to the shoelaces lying on the floor. "These," he said, "are for you. For your kindness. Divide them with the other ladies."

"But I wouldn't dream—" Mrs. Archer began.

"I insist," the old man said, opening the door. "A small return, but all that I have to offer. Pick them up yourself," he added abruptly. Then he turned and thumbed his nose at Mrs. Corn. "I hate old women," he said.

"Well!" said Mrs. Corn faintly.

"I may have imbibed somewhat freely," the old man said to Mrs. Archer, "but I never served bad sherry to my guests. We are of two different worlds, Madam."

"Didn't I tell you?" Mrs. Corn was saying. "Haven't I kept telling you all along?"

Mrs. Archer, her eyes on Kathy, made a tentative motion of pushing the old man through the door, but he forestalled her.

"'Come dance with me in Ireland,'" he said. Supporting himself against the wall, he reached the outer door and opened it. "And time runs on," he said.

· QUESTIONS ·

1. What foreshadowings of the ending do you detect upon a second reading of the story? Or did you note them on the first reading?
2. What adjectives best describe the focal character: vain, proud, conceited, obnoxious, besotted, courageous, self-respecting, senile, superior? Do you prefer others? If so, what are they?
3. What adjectives best describe each of the three women in the story: kind, thoughtful, charitable, discerning, condescending, spiteful, intolerant? If you prefer others, what are they?
4. Does the story have a symbolic meaning? What, for example, does the mention of Yeats contribute?

Theme Subjects: (1) A Good Deed That Backfired; (2) I Bit the Hand That Fed Me; (3) A Purse-Proud Relative; (4) Some Irishmen Are Different; (5) "Come Dance with Me in Ireland" and "The Lottery" (a comparison).

INFLEXIBLE LOGIC

Russell Maloney

RUSSELL MALONEY (1910–1948) was born in Brookline, Massachusetts, and was graduated from Harvard in 1932. After graduation he began tutoring Harvard undergraduates and sending in jokes and short articles to *The New Yorker*. Editors of the magazine were impressed by his contributions, offered him a job, and he was a staff member, 1934–1945. He turned out prodigious amounts of magazine material under varied pseudonyms. He published only two books before his early death: *It's Still Maloney* (1946); *Our Own Baedeker* (1947, with Eugene Kinkead).

When the six chimpanzees came into his life, Mr. Bainbridge was thirty-eight years old. He was a bachelor and lived comfortably in a remote part of Connecticut, in a large old house with a carriage drive, a conservatory, a tennis court, and a well-selected library. His income was derived from impeccably situated real estate in New York City, and he spent it soberly, in a manner which could give offense to nobody. Once a year, late in April, his tennis court was resurfaced, and after that anybody in the neighborhood was welcome to use it; his monthly statement from Brentano's seldom ran below seventy-five dollars; every third year, in November, he turned in his old Cadillac coupé for a new one; he ordered his cigars, which were mild and rather moderately priced, in shipments of one thousand, from a tobacconist in Havana; because of the international situation he had canceled arrangements to travel abroad, and after due thought had decided to spend his traveling allowance on wines, which seemed likely to get scarcer and more expensive if the war lasted. On the whole, Mr. Bainbridge's life was deliberately, and not too unsuccessfully, modeled after that of an English country gentleman of the late eighteenth century, a gentleman interested in the arts and in the expansion of science, and so sure of himself that he didn't care if some people thought him eccentric.

Mr. Bainbridge had many

friends in New York, and he spent several days of the month in the city, staying at his club and looking around. Sometimes he called up a girl and took her out to a theater and a night club. Sometimes he and a couple of classmates got a little tight and went to a prizefight. Mr. Bainbridge also looked in now and then at some of the conservative art galleries, and liked occasionally to go to a concert. And he liked cocktail parties, too, because of the fine footling conversation and the extraordinary number of pretty girls who had nothing else to do with the rest of their evening. It was at a New York cocktail party, however, that Mr. Bainbridge kept his preliminary appointment with doom. At one of the parties given by Hobie Packard, the stockbroker, he learned about the theory of the six chimpanzees.

It was almost six-forty. The people who had intended to have one drink and go had already gone, and the people who intended to stay were fortifying themselves with slightly dried canapés and talking animatedly. A group of stage and radio people had coagulated in one corner, near Packard's Capehart, and were wrangling about various methods of cheating the Collector of Internal Revenue. In another corner was a group of stockbrokers, talking about the greatest stockbroker of them all, Gauguin. Little Marcia Lupton was sitting with a young man, saying earnestly, "Do you really want to know what my greatest ambition is? I want to be myself," and Mr. Bainbridge smiled gently, thinking of the time Marcia had said that to him. Then he heard the voice of Bernard Weiss, the critic, saying, "Of course he wrote one good novel. It's not surprising.

After all, we know that if six chimpanzees were set to work pounding six typewriters at random, they would, in a million years, write all the books in the British Museum."

Mr. Bainbridge drifted over to Weiss and was introduced to Weiss's companion, a Mr. Noble. "What's this about a million chimpanzees, Weiss?" he asked.

"Six chimpanzees," Mr. Weiss said. "It's an old cliché of the mathematicians. I thought everybody was told about it in school. Law of averages, you know, or maybe it's permutation and combination. The six chimps, just pounding away at the typewriter keys, would be bound to copy out all the books ever written by man. There are only so many possible combinations of letters and numerals, and they'd produce all of them—see? Of course they'd also turn out a mountain of gibberish, but they'd work the books in, too. All the books in the British Museum."

Mr. Bainbridge was delighted; this was the sort of talk he liked to hear when he came to New York. "Well, but look here," he said, just to keep up his part in the foolish conversation, "what if one of the chimpanzees finally did duplicate a book, right down to the last period, but left that off? Would that count?"

"I suppose not. Probably the chimpanzee would get around to doing the book again, and put the period in."

"What nonsense!" Mr. Noble cried.

"It may be nonsense, but Sir James Jeans believes it," Mr. Weiss said, huffily. "Jeans or Lancelot Hogben. I know I ran across it quite recently."

Mr. Bainbridge was impressed. He read quite a bit of popular science, and both Jeans and Hogben were in his library. "Is that so?" he murmured, no longer feeling frivolous. "Wonder if it has ever actually been tried? I mean, has anybody ever put six chimpanzees in a room with six typewriters and a lot of paper?"

Mr. Weiss glanced at Mr. Bainbridge's empty cocktail glass and said dryly, "Probably not."

Nine weeks later, on a winter evening, Mr. Bainbridge was sitting in his study with his friend James Mallard, an assistant professor of mathematics at New Haven. He was plainly nervous as he poured himself a drink and said, "Mallard, I've asked you to come here— brandy? cigar?—for a particular reason. You remember that I wrote you some time ago, asking your opinion of . . . of a certain mathematical hypothesis, or supposition."

"Yes," Professor Mallard said, briskly. "I remember perfectly. About the six chimpanzees and the British Museum. And I told you it was a perfectly sound popularization of a principle known to every schoolboy who had studied the science of probabilities."

"Precisely," Mr. Bainbridge said. "Well, Mallard, I made up my mind. . . . It was not difficult for me, because I have, in spite of that fellow in the White House, been able to give something every year to the Museum of Natural History, and they were naturally glad to oblige me. . . . And after all, the only contribution a layman can make to the process of science is to assist with the drudgery of experiment. . . . In short, I—"

"I suppose you're trying to tell me that you have produced six

chimpanzees and set them to work at typewriters in order to see whether they will eventually write all the books in the British Museum. Is that it?"

"Yes, that's it," Mr. Bainbridge said. "What a mind you have, Mallard. Six fine young males, in perfect condition. I had a—I suppose you'd call it a dormitory—built out in back of the stable. The typewriters are in the conservatory. It's light and airy in there, and I moved most of the plants out. Mr. North, the man who owns the circus, very obligingly let me engage one of his best animal men. Really, it was no trouble at all."

Professor Mallard smiled indulgently. "After all, such a thing is not unheard of," he said. "I seem to remember that a man at some university put his graduate students to work flipping coins, to see if heads and tails came up an equal number of times. Of course they did."

Mr. Bainbridge looked at his friend very queerly. "Then you believe that any such principle of the science of probabilities will stand up under an actual test?"

"Certainly."

"You had better see for yourself." Mr. Bainbridge led Professor Mallard downstairs, along a corridor, through a disused music room, and into a large conservatory. The middle of the floor had been cleared of plants and was occupied by a row of six typewriter tables, each one supporting a hooded machine. At the left of each typewriter was a neat stack of yellow copy paper. Empty wastebaskets were under each table. The chairs were the unpadded, spring-backed kind favored by experienced stenographers. A large bunch of ripe bananas was hanging in one corner, and in another stood a Great Bear watercooler and a rack of Lily cups. Six piles of typescript, each about a foot high, were ranged along the wall on an improvised shelf. Mr. Bainbridge picked up one of the piles, which he could just conveniently lift, and set it on a table before Professor Mallard. "The output to date of Chimpanzee A, known as Bill," he said simply.

" '*Oliver Twist*, by Charles Dickens,' " Professor Mallard read out. He read the first and second pages of the manuscript, then feverishly leafed through to the end. "You mean to tell me," he said, "that this chimpanzee has written—"

"Word for word and comma for comma," said Mr. Bainbridge. "Young, my butler, and I took turns comparing it with the edition I own. Having finished *Oliver Twist*, Bill is, as you see, starting the sociological works of Vilfredo Pareto, in Italian. At the rate he has been going, it should keep him busy for the rest of the month."

"And all the chimpanzees—" Professor Mallard was pale, and enunciated with difficulty—"they aren't all—"

"Oh, yes, all writing books which I have every reason to believe are in the British Museum. The prose of John Donne, some Anatole France, Conan Doyle, Galen, the collected plays of Somerset Maugham, Marcel Proust, the memoirs of the late Marie of Rumania, and a monograph by a Dr. Wiley on the marsh grasses of Maine and Massachusetts. I can sum it up for you, Mallard, by telling you that since I started this experiment, four weeks and some days ago, none of the chimpanzees has spoiled a single sheet of paper."

Professor Mallard straightened up, passed his handkerchief across his brow, and took a deep breath. "I apologize for my weakness," he said. "It was simply the sudden shock. No, looking at the thing scientifically—and I hope I am at least as capable of that as the next man—there is nothing marvelous about the situation. These chimpanzees, or a succession of similar teams of chimpanzees, would in a million years write all the books in the British Museum. I told you some time ago that I believed that statement. Why should my belief be altered by the fact that they produced some of the books at the very outset? After all, I should not be very much surprised if I tossed a coin a hundred times and it came up heads every time. I know that if I kept at it long enough, the ratio would reduce itself to an exact fifty percent. Rest assured, these chimpanzees will begin to compose gibberish quite soon. It is bound to happen. Science tells us so. Meanwhile, I advise you to keep this experiment secret. Uninformed people might create a sensation if they knew."

"I will, indeed," Mr. Bainbridge said. "And I'm very grateful for your rational analysis. It reassures me. And now, before you go, you must hear the new Schnabel records that arrived today."

During the succeeding three months, Professor Mallard got into the habit of telephoning Mr. Bainbridge every Friday afternoon at five-thirty, immediately after leaving his seminar room. The Professor would say, "Well?" and Mr. Bainbridge would reply, "They're still at it, Mallard. Haven't spoiled a sheet of paper yet." If Mr. Bainbridge had to go out on Friday afternoon he would leave a written message with his butler, who would read it to Professor Mallard: "Mr. Bainbridge says we now have Trevelyan's *Life of Macaulay*, the *Confessions of St. Augustine, Vanity Fair,* part of Irving's *Life of George Washington,* the *Book of the Dead,* and some speeches delivered in Parliament in opposition to the Corn Laws, sir." Professor Mallard would reply, with a hint of a snarl in his voice, "Tell him to remember what I predicted," and hang up with a clash.

The eleventh Friday that Professor Mallard telephoned, Mr. Bainbridge said, "No change. I have had to store the bulk of the manuscript in the cellar. I would have burned it, except that it probably has some scientific value."

"How dare you talk of scientific value?" The voice from New Haven roared faintly in the receiver. "Scientific value! You—you—chimpanzee!" There were further inarticulate sputterings, and Mr. Bainbridge hung up with a disturbed expression. "I am afraid Mallard is overtaxing himself," he murmured.

Next day, however, he was pleasantly surprised. He was leafing through a manuscript that had been completed the previous day by Chimpanzee D, Corky. It was the complete diary of Samuel Pepys, and Mr. Bainbridge was chuckling over the naughty passages, which were omitted in his own edition, when Professor Mallard was shown into the room. "I have come to apologize for my outrageous conduct on the telephone yesterday," the Professor said.

"Please don't think of it any more. I know you have many things

on your mind," Mr. Bainbridge said. "Would you like a drink?"

"A large whisky, straight, please," Professor Mallard said. "I got rather cold driving down. No change, I presume?"

"No, none. Chimpanzee F, Dinty, is just finishing John Florio's translation of Montaigne's essays, but there is no other news of interest."

Professor Mallard squared his shoulders and tossed off his drink in one astonishing gulp. "I should like to see them at work," he said. "Would I disturb them, do you think?"

"Not at all. As a matter of fact, I usually look in on them around this time of day. Dinty may have finished his Montaigne by now, and it is always interesting to see them start a new work. I would have thought that they would continue on the same sheet of paper, but they don't, you know. Always a fresh sheet, and the title in capitals."

Professor Mallard, without apology, poured another drink and slugged it down. "Lead on," he said.

It was dusk in the conservatory, and the chimpanzees were typing by the light of student lamps clamped to their desks. The keeper lounged in a corner, eating a banana and reading *Billboard.* "You might as well take an hour or so off," Mr. Bainbridge said. The man left.

Professor Mallard, who had not taken off his overcoat, stood with his hands in his pockets, looking at the busy chimpanzees, "I wonder if you know, Bainbridge, that the science of probabilities takes everything into account," he said, in a queer, tight voice. "It is certainly almost beyond the bounds of credibility that these chimpanzees should write books without a single error, but that abnormality may be corrected by—*these!*" He took his hands from his pockets, and each one held a .38 revolver. "Stand back out of harm's way!" he shouted.

"Mallard! Stop it!" The revolvers barked, first the right hand, then the left, then the right. Two chimpanzees fell, and a third reeled into a corner. Mr. Bainbridge seized his friend's arm and wrested one of the weapons from him.

"Now I am armed, too, Mallard, and I advise you to stop!" he cried. Professor Mallard's answer was to draw a bead on Chimpanzee E and shoot him dead. Mr. Bainbridge made a rush, and Professor Mallard fired at him. Mr. Bainbridge, in his quick death agony, tightened his finger on the trigger of his revolver. It went off, and Professor Mallard went down. On his hands and knees he fired at the two chimpanzees which were still unhurt, and then collapsed.

There was nobody to hear his last words. "The human equation . . . always the enemy of science . . ." he panted. "This time . . . vice versa . . . I, a mere mortal, . . . savior of science . . . deserve a Nobel . . ."

When the old butler came running into the conservatory to investigate the noises, his eyes were met by a truly appalling sight. The student lamps were shattered, but a newly risen moon shone in through the conservatory windows on the corpses of the two gentlemen, each clutching a smoking revolver. Five of the chimpanzees were dead. The sixth was Chimpanzee F. His right arm disabled, obviously bleeding to death, he was slumped before his typewriter. Painfully, with his left hand, he took from the machine the completed last page of Florio's Montaigne. Groping for a fresh sheet, he inserted it, and typed with one finger, "*Uncle Tom's Cabin,* by Harriet Beecher Stowe. Chapte. . . ." Then he, too, was dead.

· QUESTIONS ·

1. This whimsical, "impossible" story has delighted hundreds of thousands of readers. What is your opinion of it? How would you correct Bernard Weiss' statement that, in a million years, six chimpanzees could write all the books in the British Museum?
2. How would you characterize Mallard? Does his dominant character trait account for the main conflict in this story?
3. How much time elapses in the story? Does the author shorten actual elapsed time?
4. From what point of view is the story told? Why?
5. How many of the authors and works mentioned can you identify?
6. What is the overall tone of this story?
7. In probability theory, is success as likely on the first trial as on any other? What bearing does Darrell Huff's "How To Look at a Statistic" have on the situation underlying "Inflexible Logic"?

Theme Subjects: (1) My Most Exciting Experiment; (2) Down with Mathematics! (3) The One Book I Most Wish I Had Written; (4) Murder Can Be Amusing When . . . ; (5) What I Think of the Human Equation.

A WORN PATH

Eudora Welty

EUDORA WELTY (1909–   ) was born in Jackson, Mississippi, studied at the Mississippi State College for Women, and secured a bachelor's degree from the University of Wisconsin in 1929. She is the author of *A Curtain of Green* (1941); *The Robber Bridegroom* (1942); *The Wide Net* (1943); *Delta Wedding* (1946); *The Golden Apples* (1949); *The Ponder Heart* (1954); *The Bride of the Innisfallen* (1955). She now lives in her birthplace. One of the most unusual and versatile short-story writers of our time, Miss Welty makes full use of her keen powers of observation of people in her native South. With psychological subtlety and genuine narrative skill she re-creates experiences and assays their impact upon those involved.

It was December—a bright frozen day in the early morning. Far out in the country there was an old Negro woman with her head tied in a red rag, coming along a path through the pinewoods. Her name was Phoenix Jackson. She was very old and small and she walked slowly in the dark pine shadows, moving a little from side to side in her steps, with the balanced heaviness and lightness of a pendulum in a grandfather clock. She carried a thin, small cane made from an umbrella, and with this she kept tapping the frozen earth in front of her. This made a grave and persistent noise in the still air, that seemed meditative like the chirping of a solitary little bird.

She wore a dark striped dress reaching down to her shoe tops, and an equally long apron of bleached sugar sacks, with a full pocket: all neat and tidy, but every time she took a step she might have fallen over her shoelaces, which dragged from her unlaced shoes. She looked straight ahead. Her eyes were blue with age. Her skin had a pattern all its own of numberless branching wrinkles and as though a whole little tree stood in the middle of her forehead, but a golden color ran underneath, and the two knobs of her cheeks were illumined by a yellow burning under the dark. Under the red rag her hair came down on her neck in the frailest of ringlets, still black, and with an odor like copper.

Now and then there was a quivering in the thicket. Old Phoenix said, "Out of my way, all you foxes, owls, beetles, jackrabbits, coons and wild animals! . . . Keep out from under these feet, little bobwhites. . . . Keep the big wild hogs out of my path. Don't let none of those come running my direction. I got a long way." Under her small black-freckled hand her cane, limber as a buggy whip, would switch at the brush as if to rouse up any hiding things.

On she went. The woods were deep and still. The sun made the pine needles almost too bright to look at, up where the wind rocked. The cones dropped as light as feathers. Down in the hollow was the mourning dove—it was not too late for him.

The path ran up a hill. "Seem like there is chains about my feet, time I get this far," she said, in the voice of argument old people keep to use with themselves. "Something always take a hold of me on this hill—pleads I should stay."

After she got to the top she turned and gave a full, severe look behind her where she had come. "Up through pines," she said at length. "Now down through oaks."

He eyes opened their widest, and she started down gently. But before she got to the bottom of the hill a bush caught her dress.

Her fingers were busy and intent, but her skirts were full and long, so that before she could pull them free in one place they were caught in another. It was not possible to allow the dress to tear. "I in the thorny bush," she said. "Thorns, you doing your appointed work. Never want to let folks pass, no sir. Old eyes thought you was a pretty little *green* bush."

Finally, trembling all over, she stood free, and after a moment dared to stoop for her cane.

"Sun so high!" she cried, leaning back and looking, while the thick tears went over her eyes. "The time getting all gone here."

At the foot of this hill was a place where a log was laid across the creek.

"Now comes the trial," said Phoenix.

Putting her right foot out, she mounted the log and shut her eyes. Lifting her skirt, leveling her cane fiercely before her, like a festival figure in some parade, she began to march across. Then she opened her eyes and she was safe on the other side.

"I wasn't as old as I thought," she said.

But she sat down to rest. She spread her skirts on the bank around her and folded her hands over her knees. Up above her was a tree in a pearly cloud of mistletoe. She did not dare to close her eyes, and when a little boy brought her a plate with a slice of marble-cake on it she spoke to him. "That would be acceptable," she said. But when she went to take it there was just her own hand in the air.

So she left that tree, and had to go through a barbed-wire fence. There she had to creep and crawl, spreading her knees and stretching her fingers like a baby trying to climb the steps. But she talked loudly to herself: she could not let her dress be torn now, so late in the day, and she could not pay for having her arms or her leg sawed off if she got caught fast where she was.

At last she was safe through the fence and risen up out in the clearing. Big dead trees, like black men with one arm, were standing in the purple stalks of the withered cotton field. There sat a buzzard.

"Who you watching?"

In the furrow she made her way along.

"Glad this not the season for bulls," she said, looking sideways, "and the good Lord made his snakes to curl up and sleep in the winter. A pleasure I don't see no two-headed snake coming around that tree, where it come once. It took a while to get by him, back in the summer."

She passed through the old cotton and went into a field of dead corn. It whispered and shook and was taller than her head. "Through the maze now," she said, for there was no path.

Then there was something tall, black, and skinny there, moving before her.

At first she took it for a man. It could have been a man dancing in the field. But she stood still and listened, and it did not make a sound. It was as silent as a ghost.

"Ghost," she said sharply, "who be you the ghost of? For I have heard of nary death close by."

But there was no answer—only the ragged dancing in the wind.

She shut her eyes, reached out her hand, and touched a sleeve. She found a coat and inside that an emptiness, cold as ice.

"You scarecrow," she said. Her face lighted. "I ought to be shut up for good," she said with laughter. "My senses is gone. I too old. I the

oldest people I ever know. Dance, old scarecrow," she said, "while I dancing with you."

She kicked her foot over the furrow, and with mouth drawn down, shook her head once or twice in a little strutting way. Some husks blew down and whirled in streamers about her skirts.

Then she went on, parting her way from side to side with the cane, through the whispering field. At last she came to the end, to a wagon track where the silver grass blew between the red ruts. The quail were walking around like pullets, seeming all dainty and unseen.

"Walk pretty," she said. "This the easy place. This the easy going."

She followed the track, swaying through the quiet bare fields, through the little strings of trees silver in their dead leaves, past cabins silver from weather, with the doors and windows boarded shut, all like old women under a spell sitting there. "I walking in their sleep," she said, nodding her head vigorously.

In a ravine she went where a spring was silently flowing through a hollow log. Old Phoenix bent and drank. "Sweet-gum makes the water sweet," she said, and drank more. "Nobody know who made this well, for it was here when I was born."

The track crossed a swampy part where the moss hung as white as lace from every limb. "Sleep on, alligators, and blow your bubbles." Then the track went into the road.

Deep, deep the road went down between the high green-colored banks. Overhead the live-oaks met, and it was as dark as a cave.

A black dog with a lolling tongue came up out of the weeds by the ditch. She was meditating, and not ready, and when he came at her she only hit him a little with her cane. Over she went in the ditch, like a little puff of milkweed.

Down there, her senses drifted away. A dream visited her, and she reached her hand up, but nothing reached down and gave her a pull. So she lay there and presently went to talking. "Old woman," she said to herself, "that black dog come up out of the weeds to stall you off, and now there he sitting on his fine tail, smiling at you."

A white man finally came along and found her—a hunter, a young man, with his dog on a chain.

"Well, Granny!" he laughed. "What are you doing there?"

"Lying on my back like a June-bug waiting to be turned over, mister," she said, reaching up her hand.

He lifted her up, gave her a swing in the air, and set her down. "Anything broken, Granny?"

"No sir, them old dead weeds is springy enough," said Phoenix, when she had got her breath. "I thank you for your trouble."

"Where do you live, Granny?" he asked, while the two dogs were growling at each other.

"Away back yonder, sir, behind the ridge. You can't even see it from here."

"On your way home?"

"No sir, I going to town."

"Why, that's too far! That's as far as I walk when I come out myself, and I get something for my trouble." He patted the stuffed bag he carried, and there hung down a little closed claw. It was one of the bob-whites, with its beak hooked bitterly to show it was dead. "Now you go on home, Granny!"

"I bound to go to town, mister," said Phoenix. "The time come around."

He gave another laugh, filling the whole landscape. "I know you old colored people! Wouldn't miss going to town to see Santa Claus!"

But something held old Phoenix very still. The deep lines in her face went into a fierce and different radiation. Without warning, she had seen with her own eyes a flashing nickel fall out of the man's pocket onto the ground.

"How old are you, Granny?" he was saying.

"There is no telling, mister," she said, "no telling."

Then she gave a little cry and clapped her hands and said, "Git on away from here, dog! Look! Look at that dog!" She laughed as if in admiration. "He ain't scared of nobody. He a big black dog." She whispered, "Sic him!"

"Watch me get rid of the cur," said the man. "Sic him, Pete! Sic him!"

Phoenix heard the dogs fighting, and heard the man running and throwing sticks. She even heard a gunshot. But she was slowly bending forward by that time, further and further forward, the lids stretched down over her eyes, as if she were doing this in her sleep. Her chin was lowered almost to her knees. The yellow palm of her hand came out from the fold of her apron. Her fingers slid down and along the ground under the piece of money with the grace and care they would have in lifting an egg from under a setting hen. Then she slowly straightened up, she stood erect, and the nickel was in her apron pocket. A bird flew by. Her lips moved. "God watching me the whole time. I come to stealing."

The man came back, and his own dog panted about them. "Well,

I scared him off that time," he said, and then he laughed and lifted his gun and pointed it at Phoenix.

She stood straight and faced him.

"Doesn't the gun scare you?" he said, still pointing it.

"No, sir, I seen plenty go off closer by, in my day, and for less than what I done," she said, holding utterly still.

He smiled, and shouldered the gun. "Well, Granny," he said, "you must be a hundred years old, and scared of nothing. I'd give you a dime if I had any money with me. But you take my advice and stay home, and nothing will happen to you."

"I bound to go on my way, mister," said Phoenix. She inclined her head in the red rag. Then they went in different directions, but she could hear the gun shooting again and again over the hill.

She walked on. The shadows hung from the oak trees to the road like curtains. Then she smelled wood-smoke, and smelled the river, and she saw a steeple and the cabins on their steep steps. Dozens of little black children whirled around her. There ahead was Natchez shining. Bells were ringing. She walked on.

In the paved city it was Christmas time. There were red and green electric lights strung and criss-crossed everywhere, and all turned on in the daytime. Old Phoenix would have been lost if she had not distrusted her eyesight and depended on her feet to know where to take her.

She paused quietly on the sidewalk where people were passing by. A lady came along in the crowd, carrying an armful of red-, green-and silver-wrapped presents; she gave off perfume like the red roses in hot summer, and Phoenix stopped her.

"Please, missy, will you lace up my shoe?" She held up her foot.

"What do you want, Grandma?"

"See my shoe," said Phoenix. "Do all right for out in the country, but wouldn't look right to go in a big building."

"Stand still then, Grandma," said the lady. She put her packages down on the sidewalk beside her and laced and tied both shoes tightly.

"Can't lace 'em with a cane," said Phoenix. "Thank you, missy. I doesn't mind asking a nice lady to tie up my shoe, when I gets out on the street."

Moving slowly and from side to side, she went into the big building, and into a tower of steps, where she walked up and around and around until her feet knew to stop.

She entered a door, and there she saw nailed up on the wall the document that had been stamped with the gold seal and framed in the gold frame, which matched the dream that was hung up in her head.

"Here I be," she said. There was a fixed and ceremonial stiffness over her body.

"A charity case, I suppose," said an attendant who sat at the desk before her.

But Phoenix only looked above her head. There was sweat on her face, the wrinkles in her skin shone like a bright net.

"Speak up, Grandma," the woman said. "What's your name? We must have your history, you know. Have you been here before? What seems to be the trouble with you?"

Old Phoenix only gave a twitch to her face as if a fly were bothering her.

"Are you deaf?" cried the attendant.

But then the nurse came in.

"Oh, that's just old Aunt Phoenix," she said. "She doesn't come for herself—she has a little grandson. She makes these trips just as regular as clockwork. She lives away back off the Old Natchez Trace." She bent down. "Well, Aunt Phoenix, why don't you just take a seat? We won't keep you standing after your long trip." She pointed.

The old woman sat down, bolt upright in the chair.

"Now, how is the boy?" asked the nurse.

Old Phoenix did not speak.

"I said, how is the boy?"

But Phoenix only waited and stared straight ahead, her face very solemn and withdrawn into rigidity.

"Is his throat any better?" asked the nurse. "Aunt Phoenix, don't you hear me? Is your grandson's throat any better since the last time you came for the medicine?"

With her hands on her knees, the old woman waited, silent, erect and motionless, just as if she were in armor.

"You mustn't take up our time this way, Aunt Phoenix," the nurse said. "Tell us quickly about your grandson, and get it over. He isn't dead, is he?"

At last there came a flicker and then a flame of comprehension across her face, and she spoke.

"My grandson. It was my memory had left me. There I sat and forgot why I made my long trip."

"Forgot?" The nurse frowned. "After you came so far?"

Then Phoenix was like an old woman begging a dignified forgiveness for waking up frightened in the night. "I never did go to school, I was too old at the Surrender," she said in a soft voice. "I'm an old woman without an education. It was my memory fail me. My little grandson, he is just the same, and I forgot it in the coming."

"Throat never heals, does it?" said the nurse, speaking in a loud, sure voice to old Phoenix. By now she had a card with something written on it, a little list. "Yes. Swallowed lye. When was it?—January —two-three years ago—"

Phoenix spoke unasked now. "No, missy, he not dead, he just the same. Every little while his throat begin to close up again, and he not able to swallow. He not get his breath. He not able to help himself. So the time come around, and I go on another trip for the soothing medicine."

"All right. The doctor said as long as you came to get it, you could have it," said the nurse. "But it's an obstinate case."

"My little grandson, he sit up there in the house all wrapped up, waiting by himself," Phoenix went on. "We is the only two left in the world. He suffer and it don't seem to put him back at all. He got a sweet look. He going to last. He wear a little patch quilt and peep out holding his mouth open like a little bird. I remembers so plain now. I not going to forget him again, no, the whole enduring time. I could tell him from all the others in creation."

"All right." The nurse was trying to hush her now. She brought her a bottle of medicine. "Charity," she said, making a check mark in a book.

Old Phoenix held the bottle close to her eyes, and then carefully put it into her pocket.

"I thank you," she said.

"It's Christmas time, Grandma," said the attendant. "Could I give you a few pennies out of my purse?"

"Five pennies is a nickel," said Phoenix stiffly.

"Here's a nickel," said the attendant.

Phoenix rose carefully and held out her hand. She received the nickel and then fished the other nickel out of her pocket and laid it beside the new one. She stared at her palm closely, with her head on one side.

Then she gave a tap with her cane on the floor.

"This is what come to me to do," she said. "I going to the store and buy my child a little windmill they sells, made out of paper. He going to find it hard to believe there such a thing in the world. I'll march myself back where he waiting, holding it straight up in this hand."

She lifted her free hand, gave a little nod, turned around, and walked out of the doctor's office. Then her slow step began on the stairs, going down.

· QUESTIONS ·

1. Miss Welty painted "quite earnestly" for some years. What specific details in this story lead you to believe that painting may have taught her something about writing, that she is still painting—with words?
2. What are the specific hazards (age, etc.) which Phoenix Jackson faces? How do they provide the conflict of this quietly dramatic narrative?
3. A less skilled writer might have overstressed the pathos of the situation and produced sentimentality. The tonal quality of the story is affected by Phoenix' lack of self-pity, the author's not revealing at the beginning the nature of Phoenix' errand, the humor displayed. Can you identify other elements of the story which affect its tone?
4. The story contains several superb figures of speech such as "like a little puff of milkweed." Can you find others?

Theme Subjects: (1) A Pathetic Sight; (2) The Courage of the Old; (3) My Oldest Relative (a sketch); (4) My Last Good Deed; (5) The Focal Characters in "A Worn Path" and "Come Dance with Me in Ireland" (a comparison).

THE DEVIL
AND DANIEL WEBSTER

Stephen Vincent Benét

STEPHEN VINCENT BENÉT (1898–1943) was born at Bethlehem, Pennsylvania, and educated at Yale (A.B., 1919; M.A., 1920). He later studied at the Sorbonne, on a scholarship, and while holding a Guggenheim Fellowship wrote *John Brown's Body* (1928), which received a Pulitzer Prize. Benét was only 17 when his first volume of poetry, *Five Men and Pompey*, was published. A large number of poems and four novels indicate his absorption in American tradition. Aside from *John Brown's Body*, his best-known works are *Ballads and Poems* (1931), *Thirteen O'Clock* (1937), *Tales Before Midnight* (1939), *Western Star* (1943, Pulitzer Prize) and *America* (1944).

It's a story they tell in the border country, where Massachusetts joins Vermont and New Hampshire.

Yes, Dan'l Webster's dead—or, at least, they buried him. But every time there's a thunderstorm around Marshfield, they say you can hear his rolling voice in the hollows of the sky. And they say that if you go to his grave and speak loud and clear, "Dan'l Webster—Dan'l Webster!" the ground'll begin to shiver and the trees to shake. And after a while you'll hear a deep voice saying, "Neighbor, how stands the Union?" Then you better answer the Union stands as she stood, rock-bottomed and copper-sheathed, one and indivisible, or he's liable to rear right out of the ground. At least that's what I was told when I was a youngster.

You see, for a while, he was the biggest man in the country. He never got to be President, but he was the biggest man. There were thousands that trusted in him right next to God Almighty, and they told stories about him that were like stories of patriarchs and such. They said, when he stood up to speak, stars and stripes came right out in the sky, and once he spoke against a river and made it sink into the ground. They said, when he walked the woods with his fishing rod, Killall, the trout would jump out of the streams right into his pockets, for they knew it was no use putting up a fight against him; and, when he argued a case, he could turn on the harps of the blessed and the shaking of the earth underground. That was the kind of man he was, and his big farm up at Marshfield was suitable to him. The chickens he raised were all white meat down to the drumsticks, the cows were tended like children, and the big ram he called Goliath had horns with a curl like a morning-glory vine and could butt through an iron door. But Dan'l wasn't one of your gentlemen farmers; he knew all the ways of the land, and he'd be up at candlelight to see that the chores got done. A man with a mouth like a mastiff, a brow like a mountain, and eyes like burning anthracite— that was Dan'l Webster in his prime. And the biggest case he argued never got written down in the books, for he argued it against the devil, nip and tuck and no holds barred. And this is the way I used to hear it told.

There was a man named Jabez Stone, lived at Cross Corners, New Hampshire. He wasn't a bad man to start with, but he was an unlucky man. If he planted corn, he got borers; if he planted potatoes, he got blight. He had good-enough land, but it didn't prosper him; he had a decent wife and children, but

the more children he had, the less there was to feed them. If stones cropped up in his neighbor's field, boulders boiled up in his; if he had a horse with the spavins, he'd trade it for one with the staggers and give something extra. There's some folks bound to be like that, apparently. But one day Jabez Stone got sick of the whole business.

He'd been plowing that morning and he'd just broke the plowshare on a rock that he could have sworn hadn't been there yesterday. And, as he stood looking at the plowshare, the off horse began to cough—that ropy kind of cough that means sickness and horse doctors. There were two children down with measles, his wife was ailing, and he had a whitlow on his thumb. It was about the last straw for Jabez Stone. "I vow," he said, and he looked around him kind of desperate—"I vow it's enough to make a man want to sell his soul to the devil! And I would, too, for two cents."

Then he felt a kind of queerness come over him at having said what he'd said; though naturally, being a New Hampshireman, he wouldn't take it back. But, all the same, when it got to be evening and, as far as he could see, no notice had been taken, he felt relieved in his mind, for he was a religious man. But notice is always taken, sooner or later, just like the Good Book says. And, sure enough, next day, about suppertime, a soft-spoken, dark-dressed stranger drove up in a handsome buggy and asked for Jabez Stone.

Well, Jabez told his family it was a lawyer, come to see him about a legacy. But he knew who it was. He didn't like the looks of the stranger, nor the way he smiled with his teeth. They were white teeth, and plentiful—some say they were filed to a point, but I wouldn't vouch for that. And he didn't like it when the dog took one look at the stranger and ran away howling, with his tail between his legs. But having passed his word, more or less, he stuck to it, and they went out behind the barn and made their bargain. Jabez Stone had to prick his finger to sign, and the stranger lent him a silver pin. The wound healed clean, but it left a little white scar.

After that, all of a sudden, things began to pick up and prosper for Jabez Stone. His cows got fat and his horses sleek, his crops were the envy of the neighborhood, and lightning might strike all over the valley, but it wouldn't strike his barn. Pretty soon, he was one of the prosperous people of the country; they asked him to stand for select-man, and he stood for it; there began to be talk of running him for the state senate. All in all, you might say the Stone family was as happy and contented as cats in a dairy. And so they were, except for Jabez Stone.

He'd been contented enough, the first few years. It's a great thing when bad luck turns; it drives most other things out of your head. True, every now and then, especially in rainy weather, the little white scar on his finger would give him a twinge. And once a year, punctual as clockwork, the stranger with the handsome buggy would come driving by. But the sixth year, the stranger lighted, and after that, his peace was over for Jabez Stone.

The stranger came through the lower field, switching his boots with a cane—they were handsome black boots, but Jabez Stone never liked the look of them, particularly the toes. And, after he'd passed the time of day, he said, "Well, Mr. Stone, you're a hummer! It's a very pretty property you've got here, Mr. Stone."

"Well, some might favor it and others might not," said Jabez Stone, for he was a New Hampshireman.

"Oh, no need to decry your industry!" said the stranger, very easy, showing his teeth in a smile. "After all, we know what's been done, and it's been according to contract and specifications. So when —ahem—the mortgage falls due next year, you shouldn't have any regrets."

"Speaking of that mortgage, mister," said Jabez Stone, and he looked around for help to the earth and the sky, "I'm beginning to have one or two doubts about it."

"Doubts?" said the stranger, not quite so pleasantly.

"Why, yes," said Jabez Stone. "This being the U.S.A. and me always having been a religious man." He cleared his throat and got bolder. "Yes, sir," he said, "I'm beginning to have considerable doubts as to that mortgage holding in court."

"There's courts and courts," said the stranger clicking his teeth. "Still, we might as well have a look at the original document." And he hauled out a big black pocketbook full of papers. "Sherwin, Slater, Stevens, Stone," he muttered. "I, Jabez Stone, for a term of seven years— Oh, it's quite in order, I think."

But Jabez Stone wasn't listening, for he saw something else flutter out of the black pocket-book. It was something that looked like a moth, but it wasn't a moth. And as Jabez Stone stared at it, it seemed to speak to him in a small sort of piping voice, terrible small and thin, but terrible human. "Neighbor Stone!" it squeaked. "Neighbor Stone! Help me! For God's sake, help me!"

But before Jabez Stone could stir hand or foot, the stranger whipped out a big bandanna handkerchief, caught the creature in it, just like a butterfly, and started tying up the ends of the bandanna.

"Sorry for the interruption," he said. "As I was saying—"

But Jabez Stone was shaking all over like a scared horse.

"That's Miser Stevens' voice!" he said, in a croak. "And you've got him in your handkerchief!"

The stranger looked a little embarrassed.

"Yes, I really should have transferred him to the collecting box," he said with a simper, "but there were some rather unusual specimens there and I didn't want them crowded. Well, well, these little contretemps will occur."

"I don't know what you mean by contertan," said Jabez Stone, "but that was Miser Stevens' voice! And he ain't dead! You can't tell me he is! He was just as spry and mean as a woodchuck, Tuesday!"

"In the midst of life—" said the stranger, kind of pious. "Listen!" Then a bell began to toll in the valley and Jabez Stone listened, with the sweat running down his face. For he knew it was tolled for Miser Stevens and that he was dead.

"These long-standing accounts," said the stranger with a sigh; "one really hates to close them. But business is business."

He still had the bandanna in his hand, and Jabez Stone felt sick as he saw the cloth struggle and flutter.

"Are they all as small as that?" he asked hoarsely.

"Small?" said the stranger. "Oh, I see what you mean. Why, they vary." He measured Jabez Stone with his eyes, and his teeth showed. "Don't worry, Mr. Stone," he said. "You'll go with a very good grade. I wouldn't trust you outside the collecting box. Now, a man like Dan'l Webster, of course—well, we'd have to build a special box for him, and even at that, I imagine the wing spread would astonish you. But, in your case, as I was saying—"

"Put that handkerchief away!" said Jabez Stone, and he began to beg and to pray. But the best he could get at the end was a three years' extension, with conditions.

But till you make a bargain like that, you've no idea how fast four years can run. By the last months of those years, Jabez Stone's known all over the state and there's talk of running him for governor—and it's dust and ashes in his mouth. For every day, when he gets up, he thinks, "There's one more night gone," and every night when he lies down, he thinks of the black pocketbook and the soul of Miser Stevens, and it makes him sick at heart. Till, finally, he can't bear it any longer, and in the last days of the last year, he hitches up his horse and drives off to seek Dan'l Webster. For Dan'l was born in New Hampshire, only a few miles from Cross Corners, and it's well known that he has a particular soft spot for old neighbors.

It was early in the morning when he got to Marshfield, but Dan'l was up already, talking Latin to the farm hands and wrestling with the ram, Goliath, and trying out a new trotter and working up speeches to make against John C. Calhoun. But when he heard a New Hampshire-man had come to see him, he dropped everything else he was doing, for that was Dan'l's way. He gave Jabez Stone a breakfast that five men couldn't eat, went into the history of every living man and woman in Cross Corners, and finally asked him how he could serve him.

Jabez Stone allowed that it was a kind of mortgage case.

"Well, I haven't pleaded a mortgage case in a long time, and I don't generally plead now, except before the Supreme Court," said Dan'l, "but if I can, I'll help you."

"Then I've got hope for the first time in ten years," said Jabez Stone, and told him the details.

Dan'l walked up and down as he listened, hands behind his back, now and then asking a question, now and then plunging his eyes at the floor, as if they'd bore through it like gimlets. When Jabez Stone had finished, Dan'l puffed out his cheeks and blew. Then he turned to Jabez Stone and a smile broke over his face like the sunrise over Monadnock.

"You'll take it?" said Jabez Stone, hardly daring to believe.

"Yes," said Dan'l Webster. "I've got about seventy-five other things to do and the Missouri Compromise to straighten out, but I'll take your case. For if two New Hampshiremen aren't a match for the devil, we might as well give the country back to the Indians."

Then he shook Jabez Stone by the hand and said, "Did you come down here in a hurry?"

"Well, I admit I made time," said Jabez Stone.

"You'll go back faster," said Dan'l Webster, and he told 'em to hitch up Constitution and Constellation to the carriage. They were matched grays with one white fore-foot, and they stepped like greased lightning.

Well, I won't describe how excited and pleased the whole Stone family was to have the great Dan'l Webster for a guest, when they finally got there. Jabez Stone had lost his hat on the way, blown off when they overtook a wind, but he didn't take much account of that. But after supper he sent the family off to bed, for he had most particular business with Mr. Webster. Mrs. Stone wanted them to sit in the front parlor, but Dan'l Webster knew front parlors and said he preferred the kitchen. So it was there they sat, waiting for the stranger, with a jug on the table between them and a bright fire on the hearth—the stranger being scheduled to show up on the stroke of midnight, according to specifications.

Well, most men wouldn't have asked for better company than Dan'l Webster and a jug. But with every tick of the clock Jabez Stone got sadder and sadder. His eyes roved around, and though he sampled the jug you could see he couldn't taste it. Finally, on the stroke of 11:30 he reached over and grabbed Dan'l Webster by the arm.

"Mr. Webster, Mr. Webster!" he said, and his voice was shaking with fear and a desperate courage. "For God's sake, Mr. Webster, harness your horses and get away from this place while you can!"

"You've brought me a long way, neighbor, to tell me you don't like my company," said Dan'l Webster, quite peaceable, pulling at the jug.

"Miserable wretch that I am!" groaned Jabez Stone. "I've brought you a devilish way, and now I see my folly. Let him take me if he wills. I don't hanker after it, I must say, but I can stand it. But you're the Union's stay and New Hampshire's pride! He mustn't get you!"

Dan'l Webster looked at the distracted man, all gray and shaking in the firelight, and laid a hand on his shoulder.

"I'm obliged to you, Neighbor Stone," he said gently. "It's kindly thought of. But there's a jug on the table and a case in hand. And I never left a jug or a case half finished in my life."

And just at that moment there was a sharp rap on the door.

"Ah," said Dan'l Webster, very coolly, "I thought your clock was a trifle slow, Neighbor Stone." He stepped to the door and opened it. "Come in!" he said.

The stranger came in—very dark and tall he looked in the firelight. He was carrying a box under his arm—a black, japanned box with little air holes in the lid. At the sight of the box Jabez Stone gave a low cry and shrank into a corner of the room.

"Mr. Webster, I presume," said the stranger, very polite, but with his eyes glowing like a fox's deep in the woods.

"Attorney of record for Jabez Stone," said Dan'l Webster, but his eyes were glowing too. "Might I ask your name?"

"I've gone by a good many," said the stranger carelessly. "Perhaps Scratch will do for the evening. I'm often called that in these regions."

Then he sat down at the table and poured himself a drink from the jug. The liquor was cold in the jug, but it came steaming into the glass.

"And now," said the stranger,

smiling and showing his teeth, "I shall call upon you, as a law-abiding citizen, to assist me in taking possession of my property."

Well, with that, argument began—and it went hot and heavy. At first, Jabez Stone had a flicker of hope, but when he saw Dan'l Webster being forced back at point after point, he just scrunched in his corner, with his eyes on that japanned box. For there wasn't any doubt as to the deed or the signature—that was the worst of it. Dan'l Webster twisted and turned and thumped his fist on the table, but he couldn't get away from that. He offered to compromise the case; the stranger wouldn't hear of it. He pointed out the property had increased in value, and state senators ought to be worth more; the stranger stuck to the letter of the law. He was a great lawyer, Dan'l Webster, but we know who's the King of Lawyers, as the Good Book tells us, and it seemed as if, for the first time, Dan'l Webster had met his match.

Finally, the stranger yawned a little. "Your spirited efforts on behalf of your client do you credit, Mr. Webster," he said, "but if you have no more arguments to adduce, I'm rather pressed for time"—and Jabez Stone shuddered.

Dan'l Webster's brow looked dark as a thundercloud.

"Pressed or not, you shall not have this man!" he thundered. "Mr. Stone is an American citizen, and no American citizen may be forced into the service of a foreign prince. We fought England for that in '12 and we'll fight all hell for it again!"

"Foreign?" said the stranger. "And who calls me a foreigner?"

"Well, I never yet heard of the dev—of your claiming American citizenship," said Dan'l Webster with surprise.

"And who with better right?" said the stranger, with one of his terrible smiles. "When the first wrong was done to the first Indian, I was there. When the first slaver put out for the Congo, I stood on her deck. Am I not in your books and stories and beliefs, from the first settlements on? Am I not spoken of, still, in every church in New England? 'Tis true the North claims me for a Southerner and the South for a Northerner, but I am neither. I am merely an honest American like yourself—and of the best descent—for, to tell the truth, Mr. Webster, though I don't like to boast of it, my name is older in this country than yours."

"Aha!" said Dan'l Webster, with the veins standing out in his forehead. "Then I stand on the Constitution! I demand a trial for my client!"

"The case is hardly one for an ordinary court," said the stranger, his eyes flickering. "And, indeed, the lateness of the hour—"

"Let it be any court you choose, so it is an American judge and an American jury!" said Dan'l Webster in his pride. "Let it be the quick or the dead; I'll abide the issue!"

"You have said it," said the stranger and pointed his finger at the door. And with that, and all of a sudden, there was a rushing of wind outside and a noise of footsteps. They came, clear and distinct, through the night. And yet, they were not like the footsteps of living men.

"In God's name, who comes by so late?" cried Jabez Stone, in an ague of fear.

"The jury Mr. Webster de-mands," said the stranger, sipping at his boiling glass. "You must pardon the rough appearance of one or two; they will have come a long way."

And with that the fire burned blue and the door blew open and twelve men entered, one by one.

If Jabez Stone had been sick with terror before, he was blind with terror now. For there was Walter Butler, the loyalist, who spread fire and horror through the Mohawk Valley in the times of the Revolution; and there was Simon Girty, the renegade, who saw white men burned at the stake and whooped with the Indians to see them burn. His eyes were green, like a catamount's, and the stains on his hunting shirt did not come from the blood of the deer. King Philip was there, wild and proud as he had been in life, with the great gash in his head that gave him his death wound; and cruel Governor Dale, who broke men on the wheel. There was Morton of Merry Mount, who so vexed the Plymouth Colony, with his flushed, loose, handsome face and his hate of the godly. There was Teach, the bloody pirate, with his black beard curling on his breast. The Reverend John Smeet, with his strangler's hand and his Geneva gown, walked as daintily as he had to the gallows. The red print of the rope was still around his neck, but he carried a perfumed handkerchief in one hand. One and all, they came into the room with the fires of hell still upon them, and the stranger named their names and their deeds as they came, till the tale of the twelve was told. Yet the stranger had told the truth—they had all played a part in America.

"Are you satisfied with the

jury, Mr. Webster?" said the stranger mockingly, when they had taken their places.

The sweat stood upon Dan'l Webster's brow, but his voice was clear.

"Quite satisfied," he said. "Though I miss General Arnold from the company."

"Benedict Arnold is engaged upon other business," said the stranger, with a glower. "Ah, you asked for justice, I believe."

He pointed his finger once more, and a tall man, soberly clad in Puritan garb, with the burning gaze of the fanatic, stalked into the room and took his judge's place.

"Justice Hathorne is a jurist of experience," said the stranger. "He presided at certain witch trials once held in Salem. There were others who repented of the business later, but not he."

"Repent of such notable wonders and undertakings?" said the stern old justice. "Nay, hang them —hang them all!" And he muttered to himself in a way that struck ice into the soul of Jabez Stone.

Then the trial began, and, as you might expect, it didn't look anyways good for the defense. And Jabez Stone didn't make much of a witness in his own behalf. He took one look at Simon Girty and screeched, and they had to put him back in his corner in a kind of swoon.

It didn't halt the trial, though; the trial went on, as trials do. Dan'l Webster had faced some hard juries and hanging judges in his time, but this was the hardest he'd ever faced, and he knew it. They sat there with a kind of glitter in their eyes, and the stranger's smooth voice went on and on. Every time

he'd raise an objection, it'd be "Objection sustained," but whenever Dan'l objected, it'd be "Objection denied." Well, you couldn't expect fair play from a fellow like this Mr. Scratch.

It got to Dan'l in the end, and he began to heat, like iron in the forge. When he got up to speak he was going to flay that stranger with every trick known to the law, and the judge and jury too. He didn't care if it was contempt of court or what would happen to him for it. He didn't care any more what happened to Jabez Stone. He just got madder and madder, thinking of what he'd say. And yet, curiously enough, the more he thought about it, the less he was able to arrange his speech in his mind.

Till, finally, it was time for him to get up on his feet, and he did so, all ready to bust out with lightnings and denunciations. But before he started he looked over the judge and jury for a moment, such being his custom. And he noticed the glitter in their eyes was twice as strong as before, and they all leaned forward. Like hounds just before they get the fox, they looked, and the blue mist of evil in the room thickened as he watched them. Then he saw what he'd been about to do, and wiped his forehead, as a man might who's just escaped falling into a pit in the dark.

For it was him they'd come for, not only Jabez Stone. He read it in the glitter of their eyes and in the way the stranger hid his mouth with one hand. And if he fought them with their own weapons, he'd fall into their power; he knew that, though he couldn't have told you how. It was his own anger and horror that burned in their eyes;

and he'd have to wipe that out or the case was lost. He stood there for a moment, his black eyes burning like anthracite. And then he began to speak.

He started off in a low voice, though you could hear every word. They say he could call on the harps of the blessed when he chose. And this was just as simple and easy as a man could talk. But he didn't start out by condemning or reviling. He was talking about things that make a country a country, and a man a man.

And he began with the simple things that everybody's known and felt—the freshness of a fine morning when you're young, and the taste of food when you're hungry, and the new day that's every day when you're a child. He took them up and he turned them in his hands. They were good things for any man. But without freedom, they sickened. And when he talked of those enslaved, and the sorrows of slavery, his voice got like a big bell. He talked of the early days of America and the men who had made those days. It wasn't a spread-eagle speech, but he made you see it. He admitted all the wrong that had ever been done. But he showed how, out of the wrong and the right, the suffering and the starvations, something new had come. And everybody had played a part in it, even the traitors.

Then he turned to Jabez Stone and showed him as he was—an ordinary man who'd had hard luck and wanted to change it. And because he'd wanted to change it, now he was going to be punished for all eternity. And yet there was good in Jabez Stone, and he showed that good. He was hard and mean,

in some ways, but he was a man. There was sadness in being a man, but it was a proud thing too. And he showed what the pride of it was till you couldn't help feeling it. Yes, even in hell, if a man was a man, you'd know it. And he wasn't pleading for any person any more, though his voice rang like an organ. He was telling the story and the failures and the endless journey of mankind. They got tricked and trapped and bamboozled, but it was a great journey. And no demon that was ever foaled could know the inwardness of it—it took a man to do that.

The fire began to die on the hearth and the wind before morning to blow. The light was getting gray in the room when Dan'l Webster finished. And his words came back at the end to New Hampshire ground, and the one spot of land that each man loves and clings to. He painted a picture of that, and to each one of that jury he spoke of things long forgotten. For his voice could search the heart, and that was his gift and his strength. And to one, his voice was like the forest and its secrecy, and to another like the sea and the storms of the sea; and one heard the cry of his lost nation in it, and another saw a little harmless scene he hadn't remembered for years. But each saw something. And when Dan'l Webster finished he didn't know whether or not he'd saved Jabez Stone. But he knew he'd done a miracle. For the glitter was gone from the eyes of judge and jury, and, for the moment, they were men again, and knew they were men.

"The defense rests," said Dan'l Webster, and stood there like a mountain. His ears were still ringing with his speech, and he didn't hear anything else till he heard Judge Hathorne say, "The jury will retire to consider its verdict."

Walter Butler rose in his place and his face had a dark, gay pride on it.

"The jury has considered its verdict," he said, and looked the stranger full in the eye. "We find for the defendant, Jabez Stone."

With that, the smile left the stranger's face, but Walter Butler did not flinch.

"Perhaps 'tis not strictly in accordance with the evidence," he said, "but even the damned may salute the eloquence of Mr. Webster."

With that, the long crow of a rooster split the gray morning sky, and judge and jury were gone from the room like a puff of smoke and as if they had never been there. The stranger turned to Dan'l Webster, smiling wryly.

"Major Butler was always a bold man," he said. "I had not thought him quite so bold. Nevertheless, my congratulations, as between two gentlemen."

"I'll have that paper first, if you please," said Dan'l Webster, and he took it and tore it into four pieces. It was queerly warm to the touch. "And now," he said, "I'll have you!" and his hand came down like a bear trap on the stranger's arm. For he knew that once you had bested anybody like Mr. Scratch in fair fight, his power on you was gone. And he could see that Mr. Scratch knew it too.

The stranger twisted and wriggled, but he couldn't get out of that grip. "Come, come, Mr. Webster," he said, smiling palely. "This sort of thing is ridic—ouch!—is ridiculous. If you're worried about the costs of the case, naturally, I'd be glad to pay—"

"And so you shall!" said Dan'l Webster, shaking him till his teeth rattled. "For you'll sit right down at that table and draw up a document, promising never to bother Jabez Stone nor his heirs or assigns nor any other New Hampshireman till doomsday! For any hades we want to raise in this state, we can raise ourselves, without assistance from strangers."

"Ouch!" said the stranger. "Ouch! Well, they never did run very big to the barrel, but—ouch!— I agree."

So he sat down and drew up the document. But Dan'l Webster kept his hand on his coat collar all the time.

"And now, may I go?" said the stranger, quite humble, when Dan'l'd seen the document was in proper and legal form.

"Go?" said Dan'l, giving him another shake. "I'm still trying to figure out what I'll do with you. For you've settled the costs of the case, but you haven't settled with me. I think I'll take you back to Marshfield," he said kind of reflective. "I've got a ram there named Goliath that can butt through an iron door. I'd kind of like to turn you loose in his field and see what he'd do."

Well, with that the stranger began to beg and to plead. And he begged and he pled so humbly that finally, Dan'l, who was naturally kindhearted, agreed to let him go. The stranger seemed terribly grateful for that and said, just to show they were friends, he'd tell Dan'l's fortune before leaving. So Dan'l agreed to that, though he didn't take much stock in fortune-tellers ordinarily. But, naturally, the stranger was a little different.

Well, he pried and peered at the lines in Dan'l's hands. And he told him one thing and another that was quite remarkable. But they were all in the past.

"Yes, all that's true, and it happened," said Dan'l Webster. "But what's to come in the future?"

The stranger grinned, kind of happily, and shook his head.

"The future's not as you think it," he said. "It's dark. You have a great ambition, Mr. Webster."

"I have," said Dan'l firmly, for everybody knew he wanted to be President.

"It seems almost within your grasp," said the stranger, "but you will not attain it. Lesser men will be made President and you will be passed over."

"And, if I am, I'll still be Dan'l Webster," said Dan'l. "Say on."

"You have two strong sons," said the stranger, shaking his head. "You look to found a line. But each will die in war and neither reach greatness."

"Live or die, they are still my sons," said Dan'l Webster. "Say on."

"You have made great speeches," said the stranger. "You will make more."

"Ah," said Dan'l Webster.

"But the last great speech you make will turn many of your own against you," said the stranger. "They will call you Ichabod; they will call you by other names. Even in New England, some will say you have turned your coat and sold your country, and their voices will be loud against you till you die."

"So it is an honest speech, it does not matter what men say," said Dan'l Webster. Then he looked at the stranger and their glances locked.

"One question," he said. "I have fought for the Union all my life. Will I see that fight won against those who would tear it apart?"

"Not while you live," said the stranger, grimly, "but it will be won. And after you are dead, there are thousands who will fight for your cause, because of words that you spoke."

"Why, then, you long-barreled, slab-sided, lantern-jawed, fortune-telling note shaver!" said Dan'l Webster, with a great roar of laughter, "be off with you to your own place before I put my mark on you! For, by the thirteen original colonies, I'd go to the Pit itself to save the Union!"

And with that he drew back his foot for a kick that would have stunned a horse. It was only the tip of his shoe that caught the stranger, but he went flying out of the door with his collection box under his arm.

"And now," said Dan'l Webster, seeing Jabez Stone beginning to rouse from his swoon, "let's see what's left in the jug, for it's dry work talking all night. I hope there's pie for breakfast, Neighbor Stone."

But they say that whenever the devil comes near Marshfield, even now, he gives it a wide berth. And he hasn't been seen in the state of New Hampshire from that day to this. I'm not talking about Massachusetts or Vermont.

· QUESTIONS ·

1. Compacts with the devil occur frequently in literature (Goethe's *Faust*, etc.). Can you give other examples?
2. In what sense is this story history? In what sense folklore? Do you understand the references made to history? Are the names of members of the jury familiar to you? Explain the reference to Ichabod.
3. How is the story representative of American culture?
4. What is the point of view? Who is the narrator? Is the focal character Mr. Scratch, Dan'l Webster, or Jabez Stone?
5. Point out the humorous reflections upon New Hampshire and its citizens.
6. Show how the style of the paragraphs reporting Webster's speech reflects his dignity and eloquence.
7. Compare the impression you gain of Webster in this story with that received from Kennedy's biographical portrait in this volume.

Theme Subjects: (1) A Popular Figure in American Folklore; (2) Orpheus and Daniel Webster; (3) Characteristic Traits of the New Englander; (4) A Tall Tale of My Home State; (5) A Legend That Is Real to Me; (6) A Review of *Stephen Vincent Benét: A Biography* by Charles A. Fenton (Yale University Press, 1960).

PLAYS

A NOTE ON READING

Our lives are surrounded by drama in some form or other—whether it be
the drama of the latest TV or movie thriller, a human-interest story in
yesterday's tabloid, or a scene in a park witnessed from a nearby apartment.
When people meet, talk, and move, new behavior patterns result. And
because people the world over are ruled by much the same passions, have
much the same frustrations, want alike to be appreciated, and hope for
illusory beauties and gains, they are naturally interested in other people's
successes and failures.

If these "other people" live far back in history, or if they are great
and powerful, or if they take great risks, or if they do murder in a castle
or a tenement—in short, if they somehow illuminate the universal pattern
—they provide alluring vicarious experience for the amusement, horror, or
education of their less-publicized fellow human beings. For out of people,
dialogue, and action set against a backdrop come many other components
of the drama-scheme of life: motives, morals, conflicts, causes, and so on.
Place all this in a building called a theater, add lighting effects, music
effects, costume, trained actors, and an intelligent version of some little
fable of human life, and you have drama in a technical, indeed in a magic,
sense.

Drama and fiction are alike in several respects. Both present a series of
related actions which form a plot (action). Both are deeply concerned with
characterization; both place emphasis upon setting, a play often more
deliberately and purposefully so than a short story or novel. Both types
develop a central theme.

The basic distinction between fiction and drama is that the former is
written to be read, the latter nearly always written to be acted. In a short
story we *read* what the characters say and do; in an acted play we *hear* what
characters say and *see* what they do.

A printed play is only an approximate sketch of what the author intended the acted play to be; he must depend on the skill of actors and direc-

tor, the adroitness of scene painters, the ingenuity of electricians. Drama on the printed page is so different from its effect on the stage that it imposes upon you a heavier responsibility than does fiction. When you read a play imaginatively you will serve as actor, director, scene designer, and electrician. The reader with a "spectator intelligence" should be able to "see" a play, although he will miss much of the visual detail. But you can compensate for this loss by an opportunity to reread lines and to study stage directions leisurely.

The good play and the good short story have the unmistakable unity of a living organism.

The modern student who thinks of a domestic tragedy in terms of a Broadway production would find many surprises if he went back via a Wellsian time-machine to ancient Greece. Early performances did not enjoy the luxury of a raised stage, although that did develop; audiences sat outdoors in a bowl-like structure. There was no scenery, almost nothing in the way of props. The chorus commented on the action. Deaths occurred offstage and were announced by messenger. When matters got hopelessly tangled, the *deus ex machina* (a god from a machine) was used. One or more of the unities of time, place, and action was observed. A well-made tragedy was expected to produce a catharsis (purification, purgation) in the audience. Masks were employed (a device revived by Eugene O'Neill). The story was familiar to onlookers. But unlike typical modern theatergoers, the Greeks did not go to a play for entertainment in the modern sense— the whole production was a serious undertaking for serious people who were moved by language and theme to intellectual and spiritual growth. The modern bystander would note many other differences, but these few will serve to create a superficial impression. Many Greek conventions were taken over by the Romans and eventually by Elizabethan playwrights, including Shakespeare. They have a long and honorable history which must be read elsewhere in full by any serious-minded student of the drama.

In analyzing a play, keep in mind the *values* implicit in every drama. These values have been isolated and commented upon by Professor Fred B. Millett in *Understanding Drama*. The editor acknowledges his indebtedness to Professor Millett for the skeletal remarks which follow.

1. *Factual Values*. Summarize the play in two or three sentences. What elements in the summary seem familiar? Unfamiliar? Does the factual value of the play depend on its familiarity or its unfamiliarity?

2. *Psychological Values*. The psychological values of a drama may be classified as sensory, emotional, empathetic, and analytical. The sensory values of a play involve experiencing a vivid and rich series of images. Try making a diagram representing the succession of feelings and emotions experienced by the major character(s) in the play. Do you find yourself following the line of the major characters' feelings and emotions? Do you find yourself identifying yourself with one character in the play, major or minor? If a major character is not analyzed by others in the play, are you challenged to make your own analysis?

3. *Technical Values*. The technical values of a play are those that belong to its formal aspects—giving to particular subject matter a form that will best express potential values. Divide the play into its parts; indicate the

time, place, and content of each part; indicate for each part whether the action is past, present, or to come. Are structure and plot well designed to bring out the theme of the drama? What are the basic traits of the major character(s)? What are the stylistic qualities of the dialogue? Does style constitute one of the major technical values of the play?

4. *Symbolical Values.* A play achieves added significance through the use of elements treated as symbols. In any play under discussion, can you detect the major symbols—persons, objects, actions? What theme or point do the symbols emphasize? Are the symbols and their significance clear to you?

5. *Ideational Values.* Every drama states or implies the ethical, philosophical, or religious attitudes of the playwright. What is the theme of the play? Is it explicit or implicit? What seems to be the author's attitude toward the theme? What ethical values are suggested by the play? What philosophical values? How important are these values in your final opinion of the play?

Your instructor may wish to expand the comments and questions given above, since they are adapted in brief and rudimentary form from *Understanding Drama.* As you read reviews of plays you will note that these values are frequently commented upon. You will also note that they are given attention in many of the reviews of plays and motion pictures which you hear on television and radio.

ANTIGONE

Sophocles

SOPHOCLES (c. 496 B.C.–c. 406) was born at Colonus in Attica, near Athens, and thus lived, of course, during the great Periclean Age of Athens. Little is authoritatively known of his life, but it is thought that he moved in the best society of his day and it is known that he was an important public and military figure. He certainly knew Herodotus, and he studied the art of writing tragedy with Aeschylus. It is reported that he was handsome, popular, and well versed in music and gymnastics.

It is generally agreed that *Antigone* was the first of his seven surviving plays to be produced. Probably written about 442 B.C., it is one of three dramas dealing with the Theban saga: *Oedipus the King* interprets the early part of the story; *Oedipus at Colonus* deals with the final hours and death of Oedipus; and *Antigone* treats of the last events of this famous legend.

According to the story, which Sophocles occasionally altered for dramatic purposes, Eteocles, son of Oedipus and now king of Thebes, had exiled his brother, Polyneices, who also coveted the vacated throne. Polyneices had secured aid and had led a host of warriors against the city of Thebes in order to seize the throne. In an ensuing battle, Eteocles and Polyneices had killed each other and thus fulfilled a curse which had been called down upon them by their now-dead father. The invaders were repulsed and Creon had become king. He issued a proclamation that the body of Eteocles should be given honorable burial but that Polyneices' corpse should lie unburied. The action of *Antigone* opens at this point on the day after the battle.

The translation given here is by Sir Richard C. Jebb (1841–1905), British scholar and the great authority of all time on Sophocles.

Principal Characters

ANTIGONE } *daughters of Oedipus*
ISMENE }
CREON   *king of Thebes, brother of Jocasta*
HAEMON   *son of Creon*
TEIRESIAS   *a blind prophet*
EURYDICE   *wife of Creon*
CHORUS OF THEBAN ELDERS

SCENE:

An open space before the royal palace, once that of Oedipus, at Thebes. The backscene represents the front of the palace, with three doors, of which the central and largest is the principal entrance into the house. The time is at daybreak on the morning after the fall of the two brothers, Eteocles and Polyneices, and the flight of the defeated Argives. ANTIGONE *calls* ISMENE *forth from the palace, in order to speak to her alone.*

ANTIGONE Ismene, sister, mine own dear sister, knowest thou what ill there is, of all bequeathed by Oedipus, that Zeus fulfils not for us twain while we live? Nothing painful is there, nothing fraught with ruin, no shame, no dishonour, that I have not seen in thy woes and mine.

And now what new edict is this of which they tell, that our Captain hath just published to all Thebes? Knowest thou aught? Hast thou heard? Or is it hidden from thee that our friends are threatened with the doom of our foes?[1]

ISMENE No word of friends, Antigone, gladsome or painful, hath come to me, since we two sisters were bereft of brothers twain, killed in one day by a twofold blow; and since in this last night the Argive host hath fled, I know no more, whether my fortune be brighter, or more grievous.

ANTIGONE I knew it well, and therefore sought to bring thee beyond the gates of the court, that thou mightest hear alone.

ISMENE What is it? 'Tis plain that thou art brooding on some dark tidings.

ANTIGONE What, hath not Creon destined our brothers, the one to honoured burial, the other to unburied shame? Eteocles, they say, with due observance of right and custom, he hath laid in the earth, for his honour among the dead below. But the hapless corpse of Polyneices—as rumour saith, it hath been published to the town that none shall entomb him or mourn, but leave unwept, unsepulchred, a welcome store for the birds, as they espy him, to feast on at will.

Such, 'tis said, is the edict

---

[1] The central conflict of this play depends, in part, upon the conventional Greek attitude toward the ritual of burial. The punishment which Creon had inflicted upon the dead Polyneices was looked upon with horror and terror not only by Antigone but by all others in Thebes at the time. What happens to a dead body may seem of comparatively little importance today, but to Thebans it was a matter of supreme importance. However, Sophocles has used this basic situation to explore the question of whether man-made and dictatorially enforced law should take precedence over an individual's concept of what he thinks is divine law. Thus, Creon seeks to impose his human law upon an Antigone who rebels and disobeys because of her respect for what she considers a higher law. This conflict is as modern as tomorrow's newspaper and plays a part in the daily lives of everyone now living in the twentieth century. The potentiality of men and women to be and to remain free spiritual beings is tested every day now just as it was in the days of legendary Thebes.

ANTIGONE

that the good Creon hath set forth for thee and for me,—yes, for *me*,—and is coming hither to proclaim it clearly to those who know it not; nor counts the matter light, but, whoso disobeys in aught, his doom is death by stoning before all the folk. Thou knowest it now; and thou wilt soon show whether thou art nobly bred, or the base daughter of a noble line.

ISMENE   Poor sister,—and if things stand thus, what could I help to do or undo?

ANTIGONE   Consider if thou wilt share the toil and the deed.

ISMENE   In what venture? What can be thy meaning?

ANTIGONE   Wilt thou aid this hand to lift the dead?

ISMENE   Thou wouldst bury him, —when 'tis forbidden to Thebes?

ANTIGONE   I will do my part,—and thine, if thou wilt not,—to a brother. False to him will I never be found.

ISMENE   Ah, over-bold! when Creon hath forbidden?

ANTIGONE   Nay, he hath no right to keep me from mine own.

ISMENE   Ah me! think, sister, how our father perished, amid hate and scorn, when sins bared by his own search had moved him to strike both eyes with self-blinding hand; then the mother wife, two names in one, with twisted noose did despite unto her life; and last, our two brothers in one day,—each shedding, hapless one, a kinsman's blood, —wrought out with mutual hands their common doom. And now *we* in turn—we two left all alone—think how we shall perish, more miserably than all the rest, if, in defiance of the law, we brave a king's decree or his powers. Nay, we must remember, first, that we were born women, as who should not strive with men; next, that we are ruled of the stronger, so that we must obey in these things, and in things yet sorer. I, therefore, asking the Spirits Infernal to pardon, seeing that force is put on me herein, will hearken to our rulers; for 'tis witless to be over busy.

ANTIGONE   I will not urge thee,— no, nor, if thou yet shouldst have the mind, wouldst thou be welcome as a worker with *me*. Nay, be what thou wilt; but I will bury him: well for me to die in doing that. I shall rest, a loved one with him whom I have loved, sinless in my crime; for I owe a longer allegiance to the dead than to the living: in that world I shall abide for ever. But if *thou* wilt, be guilty of dishonouring laws which the gods have stablished in honour.

ISMENE   I do them no dishonour; but to defy the State,—I have no strength for that.

ANTIGONE   Such be thy plea:—I, then, will go to heap the earth above the brother whom I love.

ISMENE   Alas, unhappy one! How I fear for thee!

ANTIGONE   Fear not for me: guide thine own fate aright.

ISMENE   At least, then, disclose this plan to none, but hide it closely,—and so, too, will I.

ANTIGONE   Oh, denounce it! Thou wilt be far more hateful for thy silence, if thou proclaim not these things to all.

ISMENE   Thou hast a hot heart for chilling deeds.

ANTIGONE   I know that I please

where I am most bound to please.

ISMENE Aye, if thou canst; but thou wouldst what thou canst not.

ANTIGONE Why, then, when my strength fails, I shall have done.

ISMENE A hopeless quest should not be made at all.

ANTIGONE If thus thou speakest, thou wilt have hatred from me, and will justly be subject to the lasting hatred of the dead. But leave me, and the folly that is mine alone, to suffer this dread thing; for I shall not suffer aught so dreadful as an ignoble death.

ISMENE Go, then, if thou must; and of this be sure,—that, though thine errand is foolish, to thy dear ones thou art truly dear.

(*Exit* ANTIGONE *on the spectators' left.* ISMENE *retires into the palace by one of the two side-doors. When they have departed, the* CHORUS OF THEBAN ELDERS *enters*)[2]

CHORUS (*singing*) (*strophe* 1) Beam of the sun, fairest light that ever dawned on Thebe of the seven gates, thou hast shone forth at last, eye of golden day, arisen above Dirce's streams! The warrior of the white shield, who came from Argos in his panoply, hath been stirred by thee to headlong flight, in swifter career;

LEADER OF THE CHORUS (*systema* 1) who set forth against our land by reason of the vexed claims of Polyneices; and, like shrill-screaming eagle, he flew over into our land, in snow-white pinion sheathed, with an armèd throng, and with plumage of helms.

CHORUS (*antistrophe* 1) He paused above our dwellings; he ravened around our sevenfold portals with spears athirst for blood; but he went hence, or ever his jaws were glutted with our gore, or the Fire-god's pine-fed flame had seized our crown of towers. So fierce was the noise of battle raised behind him, a thing too hard for him to conquer, as he wrestled with his dragon foe.

LEADER (*systema* 2) For Zeus utterly abhors the boasts of a proud tongue; and when he beheld them coming on in a great stream, in the haughty pride of clanging gold, he smote with

---

[2] In ancient Greece, the chorus was originally a group of men who performed at religious festivals; Greek drama may be said to have evolved from choral rites. At first, choral songs made up the bulk of a play, but later the chorus became somewhat subordinate. In this play, for example, the words and dancing of the chorus are intended largely to comment on the action rather than to develop it; Sophocles in *Antigone* primarily uses the chorus to comment upon the universality and paramount significance of the action and does not permit these masked, singing, and dancing characters to play an active role. The movement of a Greek chorus was highly stylized: as it sang the *strophe*, it moved from right to left; in singing the *antistrophe*, it retraced its steps and returned to the original position. The word *systema* is a Grecian term meaning "methodical in procedure and plan" and refers to a specific portion of the choral group's singing and dancing. The chorus here celebrates the victory over the Argive forces and Polyneices. ("Dirce" is a river on the Theban plain; the phrase "dragon foe" is a reference to the legend that Thebans sprang from dragon's teeth sown by Cadmus.)

brandished fire one who was now hasting to shout victory at his goal upon our ramparts.

CHORUS (*strophe* 2)   Swung down, he fell on the earth with a crash, torch in hand, he who so lately, in the frenzy of the mad onset, was raging against us with the blasts of his tempestuous hate. But those threats fared not as he hoped; and to other foes the mighty War-god dispensed their several dooms, dealing havoc around, a mighty helper at our need.

LEADER (*systema* 3)   For seven captains at seven gates, matched against seven, left the tribute of their panoplies to Zeus who turns the battle; save those two of cruel fate, who, born of one sire and one mother, set against each other their twain conquering spears, and are sharers in a common death.

CHORUS (*antistrophe* 2)   But since Victory of glorious name hath come to us, with joy responsive to the joy of Thebe whose chariots are many, let us enjoy forgetfulness after the late wars, and visit all the temples of the gods with night-long dance and song; and may Bacchus be our leader, whose dancing shakes the land of Thebe.

LEADER (*systema* 4)   But lo, the king of the land comes yonder, Creon, son of Menoeceus, our new ruler by the new fortunes that the gods have given; what counsel is he pondering, that he hath proposed this special conference of elders, summoned by his general mandate?

(*Enter* CREON, *from the central doors of the palace, in the garb of king, with two attendants*)

CREON   Sirs, the vessel of our State, after being tossed on wild waves, hath once more been safely steadied by the gods: and ye, out of all the folk, have been called apart by my summons, because I knew, first of all, how true and constant was your reverence for the royal power of Laïus; how, again, when Oedipus was ruler of our land, and when he had perished, your steadfast loyalty still upheld their children. Since, then, his sons have fallen in one day by a twofold doom,—each smitten by the other, each stained with a brother's blood,—I now possess the throne and all its powers, by nearness of kinship to the dead.

No man can be fully known, in soul and spirit and mind, until he hath been seen versed in rule and law-giving. For if any, being supreme guide of the State, cleaves not to the best counsels, but, through some fear, keeps his lips locked, I hold, and have ever held, him most base; and if any makes a friend of more account than his fatherland, that man hath no place in my regard. For I—be Zeus my witness, who sees all things always—would not be silent if I saw ruin, instead of safety, coming to the citizens; nor would I ever deem the country's foe a friend to myself; remembering this, that our country is the ship that bears us safe, and that only while she prospers in our voyage can we make true friends.

Such are the rules by which I guard this city's greatness. And in accord with them is the edict which I have now published to the folk touching the sons of Oedipus;—that Eteocles, who hath fallen fighting for our city, in all renown of arms, shall be entombed, and crowned with every rite that follows the noblest dead to their rest. But for his brother, Polyneices,—who came back from exile, and sought to consume utterly with fire the city of his fathers and the shrines of his fathers' gods, —sought to taste of kindred blood, and to lead the remnant into slavery;—touching this man, it hath been proclaimed to our people that none shall grace him with sepulture or lament, but leave him unburied, a corpse for birds and dogs to eat, a ghastly sight of shame.

Such the spirit of my dealing; and never, by deed of mine, shall the wicked stand in honour before the just; but whoso hath good will to Thebes, he shall be honoured of me, in his life and in his death.

LEADER OF THE CHORUS Such is thy pleasure, Creon, son of Menoeceus, touching this city's foe, and its friend; and thou hast power, I ween, to take what order thou wilt, both for the dead, and for all us who live.

CREON See, then, that ye be guardians of the mandate.

LEADER Lay the burden of this task on some younger man.

CREON Nay, watchers of the corpse have been found.

LEADER What, then, is this further charge that thou wouldst give?

CREON That ye side not with the breakers of these commands.

LEADER No man is so foolish that he is enamoured of death.

CREON In sooth, that is the meed; yet lucre hath oft ruined men through their hopes.

(*A* GUARD *enters from the spectators' left*)

GUARD My liege, I will not say that I come breathless from speed, or that I have plied a nimble foot; for often did my thoughts make me pause, and wheel round in my path, to return. My mind was holding large discourse with me; "Fool, why goest thou to thy certain doom?" "Wretch, tarrying again? And if Creon hears this from another, must not thou smart for it?" So debating, I went on my way with lagging steps, and thus a short road was made long. At last, however, it carried the day that I should come hither—to thee; and, though my tale be nought, yet will I tell it; for I come with a good grip on one hope,—that I can suffer nothing but what is my fate.

CREON And what is it that disquiets thee thus?

GUARD I wish to tell thee first about myself—I did not do the deed—I did not see the doer—it were not right that I should come to any harm.

CREON Thou hast a shrewd eye for thy mark; well dost thou fence thyself round against the blame; clearly thou hast some strange thing to tell.

GUARD Aye, truly; dread news makes one pause long.

CREON Then tell it, wilt thou, and so get thee gone?

GUARD Well, this is it.—The corpse—some one hath just given it burial, and gone away, —after sprinkling thirsty dust on the flesh, with such other rites as piety enjoins.

CREON What sayest thou? What living man hath dared this deed?

GUARD I know not; no stroke of pickaxe was seen there, no earth thrown up by mattock; the ground was hard and dry, unbroken, without track of wheels; the doer was one who had left no trace. And when the first day-watchman showed it to us, sore wonder fell on all. The dead man was veiled from us; not shut within a tomb, but lightly strewn with dust, as by the hand of one who shunned a curse. And no sign met the eye as though any beast of prey or any dog had come nigh to him, or torn him.

Then evil words flew fast and loud among us, guard accusing guard; and it would e'en have come to blows at last, nor was there any to hinder. Every man was the culprit, and no one was convicted, but all disclaimed knowledge of the deed. And we were ready to take redhot iron in our hands;—to walk through fire;—to make oath by the gods that we had not done the deed,—that we were not privy to the planning or the doing.

At last, when all our searching was fruitless, one spake, who made us all bend our faces on the earth in fear; for we saw not how we could gainsay him, or escape mischance if we obeyed. His counsel was that this deed must be reported to thee, and not hidden. And this seemed best; and the lot doomed my hapless self to win this prize. So here I stand, —as unwelcome as unwilling, well I wot; for no man delights in the bearer of bad news.

LEADER O king, my thoughts have long been whispering, can this deed, perchance, be e'en the work of gods?

CREON Cease, ere thy words fill me utterly with wrath, lest thou be found at once an old man and foolish. For thou sayest what is not to be borne, in saying that the gods have care for this corpse. Was it for high reward of trusty service that they sought to hide his nakedness, who came to burn their pillared shrines and sacred treasures, to burn their land, and scatter its laws to the winds? Or dost thou behold the gods honouring the wicked? It cannot be. No! From the first there were certain in the town that muttered against me, chafing at this edict, wagging their heads in secret; and kept not their necks duly under the yoke, like men contented with my sway.

'Tis by them, well I know, that these have been beguiled and bribed to do this deed. Nothing so evil as money ever grew to be current among men. This lays cities low, this drives men from their homes, this trains and warps honest souls till they set themselves to works of shame; this still teaches folk to practise villainies, and to know every godless deed.

But all the men who wrought this thing for hire have made it sure that, soon or late, they shall pay the price. Now, as Zeus still hath my reverence, know this—I tell it thee on my oath:—If ye find not the very author of this burial, and produce him before mine eyes, death alone shall not be enough for you, till first, hung up alive, ye have revealed this outrage, —that henceforth ye may thieve with better knowledge whence lucre should be won, and learn that it is not well to love gain from every source. For thou wilt find that ill-gotten pelf brings more men to ruin than to weal.

GUARD May I speak? Or shall I just turn and go?

CREON Knowest thou not that even now thy voice offends?

GUARD Is thy smart in the ears, or in the soul?

CREON And why wouldst thou define the seat of my pain?

GUARD The doer vexes thy mind, but I, thine ears.

CREON Ah, thou art a born babbler, 'tis well seen.

GUARD May be, but never the doer of this deed.

CREON Yea, and more,—the seller of thy life for silver.

GUARD Alas! 'Tis sad, truly, that he who judges should misjudge.

CREON Let thy fancy play with "judgment" as it will;—but, if ye show me not the doers of these things, ye shall avow that dastardly gains work sorrows.

(CREON *goes into the palace*)

GUARD Well, may he be found! so 'twere best. But, be he caught or be he not—fortune must settle that—truly thou wilt not see me here again. Saved, even now, beyond hope and thought, I owe the gods great thanks.

(*The* GUARD *goes out on the spectators' left*)

CHORUS (*singing*) (*strophe 1*) Wonders are many, and none is more wonderful than man; the power that crosses the white sea, driven by the stormy south-wind, making a path under surges that threaten to engulf him; and Earth, the eldest of the gods, the immortal, the unwearied, doth he wear, turning the soil with the offspring of horses, as the ploughs go to and fro from year to year.

(*antistrophe 1*) And the light-hearted race of birds, and the tribes of savage beasts, and the sea-brood of the deep, he snares in the meshes of his woven toils, he leads captive, man excellent in wit. And he masters by his arts the beast whose lair is in the wilds, who roams the hills; he tames the horse of shaggy mane, he puts the yoke upon its neck, he tames the tireless mountain bull.

(*strophe 2*) And speech, and wind-swift thought, and all the moods that mould a state, hath he taught himself; and how to flee the arrows of the frost, when 'tis hard lodging under the clear sky, and the arrows of the rushing rain; yea, he hath resource for all; without resource he meets nothing that must come: only against Death shall he call for aid in vain; but from baffling maladies he hath devised escapes.

(*antistrophe 2*) Cunning beyond fancy's dream is the fertile skill which brings him, now to evil, now to good. When he honours the laws of the land, and that justice which he hath sworn by the gods to uphold, proudly stands his city: no city hath he who, for his rashness, dwells with sin. Never may he share my hearth, never think my thoughts, who doth these things!

(*Enter the* GUARD *on the spectators' left, leading in* ANTIGONE)

LEADER OF THE CHORUS What portent from the gods is this?—my soul is amazed. I know her—how can I deny that yon maiden is Antigone?

O hapless, and child of hapless sire,—of Oedipus! What means this? Thou brought a prisoner?—thou, disloyal to the king's laws, and taken in folly?

GUARD Here she is, the doer of the deed:—we caught this girl burying him:—but where is Creon?

(CREON *enters hurriedly from the palace*)

LEADER Lo, he comes forth again from the house, at our need.

CREON What is it? What hath chanced, that makes my coming timely?

GUARD O king, against nothing should men pledge their word; for the afterthought belies the first intent. I could have vowed that I should not soon be here again,—scared by thy threats, with which I had just been lashed: but,—since the joy that surprises and transcends our hopes is like in fulness to no other pleasure,—I have come, though 'tis in breach of my sworn oath, bringing this maid; who was taken showing grace to the dead. This time there was no casting of lots; no, this luck hath fallen to me, and to none else. And now, sire, take her thyself, question her, examine her, as thou wilt; but I have a right to free and final quittance of this trouble.

CREON And thy prisoner here—how and whence hast thou taken her?

GUARD She was burying the man; thou knowest all.

CREON Dost thou mean what thou sayest? Dost thou speak aright?

GUARD I saw her burying the corpse that thou hadst forbidden to bury. Is that plain and clear?

CREON And how was she seen? how taken in the act?

GUARD It befell on this wise. When we had come to the place,—with those dread menaces of thine upon us,—we swept away all the dust that covered the corpse, and bared the dank body well; and then sat us down on the brow of the hill, to windward, heedful that the smell from him should not strike us; every man was wide awake, and kept his neighbour alert with torrents of threats, if anyone should be careless of this task.

So went it, until the sun's bright orb stood in mid heaven, and the heat began to burn: and then suddenly a whirlwind lifted from the earth a storm of dust, a trouble in the sky, and filled the plain, marring all the leafage of its woods; and the wide air was choked therewith: we closed our eyes, and bore the plague from the gods.

And when, after a long while, this storm had passed, the maid was seen; and she cried aloud with the sharp cry of a bird in its bitterness,—even as when, within the empty nest, it sees the bed stripped of its nestlings. So she also, when she saw the corpse bare, lifted up a voice of wailing, and called down curses on the doers of that deed. And straightway she brought thirsty dust in her hands; and from a shapely ewer of bronze, held high, with thrice-poured drink-offering she crowned the dead.

We rushed forward when we saw it, and at once closed upon our quarry, who was in no wise dismayed. Then we taxed her with her past and present doings; and she stood not on denial of aught,—at once to my joy and to my pain. To have escaped from ills one's self is a great joy; but 'tis painful to bring friends to ill. Howbeit, all such things are of less account to me than mine own safety.

CREON Thou—thou whose face is bent to earth—dost thou avow, or disavow, this deed?

ANTIGONE I avow it; I make no denial.

CREON (*to* GUARD) Thou canst betake thee whither thou wilt, free and clear of a grave charge.

(*Exit* GUARD)

(*to* ANTIGONE) Now, tell me thou—not in many words, but briefly—knewest thou that an edict had forbidden this?

ANTIGONE I knew it: could I help it? It was public.

CREON And thou didst indeed dare to transgress that law?

ANTIGONE Yes; for it was not Zeus that had published me that edict; not such are the laws set among men by the Justice who dwells with the gods below; nor deemed I that thy decrees were of such force, that a mortal could override the unwritten and unfailing statutes of heaven. For their life is not of to-day or yesterday, but from all time, and no man knows when they were first put forth.

Not through dread of any human pride could I answer to the gods for breaking *these*. Die I must,—I knew that well (how should I not?)—even without thy edicts. But if I am to die before my time, I count that a gain: for when any one lives, as I do, compassed about with evils, can such an one find aught but gain in death?

So for me to meet this doom is trifling grief; but if I had suffered my mother's son to lie in death an unburied corpse, that would have grieved me; for this, I am not grieved. And if my present deeds are foolish in thy sight, it may be that a foolish judge arraigns my folly.

LEADER OF THE CHORUS The maid shows herself passionate child of passionate sire, and knows not how to bend before troubles.

CREON Yet I would have thee know that o'er-stubborn spirits are most often humbled; 'tis the stiffest iron, baked to hardness in the fire, that thou shalt oftenest see snapped and shivered; and I have known horses that show temper brought to order by a little curb; there is no room for pride, when thou art thy neighbour's slave.—This girl was already versed in insolence when she transgressed the laws that had been set forth; and, that done, lo, a second insult,— to vaunt of this, and exult in her deed.

Now verily I am no man, she is the man, if this victory shall rest with her, and bring no penalty. No! be she sister's child, or nearer to me in blood than any that worships Zeus at the altar of our house,—she and her kinsfolk shall not avoid a doom most dire; for indeed I charge that other with a like share in the plotting of this burial.

And summon her—for I saw her e'en now within,—raving, and not mistress of her wits. So oft, before the deed, the mind stands self-convicted in its treason, when folks are plotting mischief in the dark. But verily this, too, is hateful,—when one who hath been caught in wickedness then seeks to make the crime a glory.

ANTIGONE   Wouldst thou do more than take and slay me?

CREON   No more, indeed; having that, I have all.

ANTIGONE   Why then dost thou delay? In thy discourse there is nought that pleases me,—never may there be!—and so my words must needs be unpleasing to thee. And yet, for glory—whence could I have won a nobler, than by giving burial to mine own brother? All here would own that they thought it well, were not their lips sealed by fear. But royalty, blest in so much besides, hath the power to do and say what it will.

CREON   Thou differest from all these Thebans in that view.

ANTIGONE   These also share it; but they curb their tongues for thee.

CREON   And art thou not ashamed to act apart from them?

ANTIGONE   No; there is nothing shameful in piety to a brother.

CREON   Was it not a brother, too, that died in the opposite cause?

ANTIGONE   Brother by the same mother and the same sire.

CREON   Why, then, dost thou render a grace that is impious in his sight?

ANTIGONE   The dead man will not say that he so deems it.

CREON   Yea, if thou makest him but equal in honour with the wicked.

ANTIGONE   It was his brother, not his slave, that perished.

CREON   Wasting this land; while *he* fell as its champion.

ANTIGONE   Nevertheless, Hades desires these rites.

CREON   But the good desires not a like portion with the evil.

ANTIGONE   Who knows but this seems blameless in the world below?

CREON   A foe is never a friend—not even in death.

ANTIGONE   'Tis not my nature to join in hating, but in loving.

CREON   Pass, then, to the world of the dead, and, if thou must needs love, love them. While I live, no woman shall rule me.

(*Enter* ISMENE *from the house, led in by two attendants*)

CHORUS (*chanting*)   Lo, yonder Ismene comes forth, shedding such tears as fond sisters weep; a cloud upon her brow casts its shadow over her darkly-flushing face, and breaks in rain on her fair cheek.

CREON   And thou, who, lurking like a viper in my house, wast secretly draining my life-blood, while I knew not that I was nurturing two pests, to rise against my throne—come, tell me now, wilt thou also confess thy part in this burial, or wilt thou forswear all knowledge of it?

ISMENE   I have done the deed,—if she allows my claim,—and share the burden of the charge.

ANTIGONE Nay, justice will not suffer thee to do that: thou didst not consent to the deed, nor did I give thee part in it.

ISMENE But, now that ills beset thee, I am not ashamed to sail the sea of trouble at thy side.

ANTIGONE Whose was the deed, Hades and the dead are witnesses: a friend in words is not the friend that I love.

ISMENE Nay, sister, reject me not, but let me die with thee, and duly honour the dead.

ANTIGONE Share not thou my death, nor claim deeds to which thou hast not put thy hand: my death will suffice.

ISMENE And what life is dear to me, bereft of thee?

ANTIGONE Ask Creon; all thy care is for him.

ISMENE Why vex me thus, when it avails thee nought?

ANTIGONE Indeed, if I mock, 'tis with pain that I mock thee.

ISMENE Tell me,—how can I serve thee, even now?

ANTIGONE Save thyself: I grudge not thy escape.

ISMENE Ah, woe is me! And shall I have no share in thy fate?

ANTIGONE Thy choice was to live; mine, to die.

ISMENE At least thy choice was not made without my protest.

ANTIGONE One world approved thy wisdom; another, mine.

ISMENE Howbeit, the offence is the same for both of us.

ANTIGONE Be of good cheer; thou livest; but my life hath long been given to death, that so I might serve the dead.

CREON Lo, one of these maidens hath newly shown herself foolish, as the other hath been since her life began.

ISMENE Yea, O king, such reason as nature may have given abides not with the unfortunate, but goes astray.

CREON Thine did, when thou chosest vile deeds with the vile.

ISMENE What life could I endure, without her presence?

CREON Nay, speak not of her "presence"; she lives no more.

ISMENE But wilt thou slay the betrothed of thine own son?

CREON Nay, there are other fields for him to plough.

ISMENE But there can never be such love as bound him to her.

CREON I like not an evil wife for my son.

ANTIGONE Haemon, beloved! How thy father wrongs thee!

CREON Enough, enough of thee and of thy marriage!

LEADER OF THE CHORUS Wilt thou indeed rob thy son of this maiden?

CREON 'Tis Death that shall stay these bridals for me.

LEADER 'Tis determined, it seems, that she shall die.

CREON Determined, yes, for thee and for me.—(*to the two attendants*) No more delay—servants, take them within! Henceforth they must be women, and not range at large; for verily even the bold seek to fly, when they see Death now closing on their life.

(*Exeunt attendants, guarding* ANTIGONE *and* ISMENE.—CREON *remains*)

CHORUS (*singing*) (*strophe 1*) Blest are they whose days have not tasted of evil. For when a house hath once been shaken from heaven, there the curse fails nevermore, passing from life to life of the race; even as, when the surge is driven over the darkness of the deep by the fierce breath of Thracian sea-winds, it rolls up the black sand from the depths, and there is a sullen roar from wind-vexed headlands that front the blows of the storm.

(*antistrophe 1*) I see that from olden time the sorrows in the house of the Labdacidae are heaped upon the sorrows of the dead; and generation is not freed by generation, but some god strikes them down, and the race hath no deliverance.

For now that hope of which the light had been spread above the last root of the house of Oedipus—that hope, in turn, is brought low—by the blood-stained dust due to the gods infernal, and by folly in speech, and frenzy at the heart.

(*strophe 2*) Thy power, O Zeus, what human trespass can limit? That power which neither Sleep, the all-ensnaring, nor the untiring months of the gods can master; but thou, a ruler to whom time brings not old age, dwellest in the dazzling splendour of Olympus.

And through the future, near and far, as through the past, shall this law hold good: Nothing that is vast enters into the life of mortals without a curse.

(*antistrophe 2*) For that hope whose wanderings are so wide is to many men a comfort, but to many a false lure of giddy desires; and the disappointment comes on one who knoweth nought till he burn his foot against the hot fire.

For with wisdom hath some one given forth the famous saying, that evil seems good, soon or late, to him whose mind the god draws to mischief; and but for the briefest space doth he fare free of woe.

LEADER OF THE CHORUS But lo, Haemon, the last of thy sons;—comes he grieving for the doom of his promised bride, Antigone, and bitter for the baffled hope of his marriage?

(*Enter* HAEMON)

CREON We shall know soon, better than seers could tell us.—My son, hearing the fixed doom of thy betrothed, art thou come in rage against thy father? Or have I thy good will, act how I may?

HAEMON Father, I am thine; and thou, in thy wisdom, tracest for me rules which I shall follow. No marriage shall be deemed by me a greater gain than thy good guidance.

CREON Yea, this, my son, should be thy heart's fixed law,—in all things to obey thy father's will. 'Tis for this that men pray to see dutiful children grow up around them in their homes,—that such may requite their father's foe with evil, and honour, as their father doth, his friend. But he who begets unprofitable children—what shall we say that he hath sown, but troubles for himself, and much triumph for his foes? Then do not thou, my son, at pleasure's beck, dethrone thy reason for a woman's sake; knowing that this is a joy that soon grows cold in clasping arms,—an evil woman to share thy bed and thy home. For what wound could strike deeper than a false friend? Nay, with loathing, and as if she were thine enemy, let this girl go to find a husband in the house of Hades. For since I have taken her, alone of all the city, in open disobedience, I will not make myself a liar to my people—I will slay her.

So let her appeal as she will to the majesty of kindred blood. If I am to nurture mine own kindred in naughtiness, needs must I bear with it in aliens. He who does his duty in his own household will be found righteous in the State also. But if any one transgresses, and does violence to the laws, or thinks to dictate to his rulers, such an one can win no praise from me. No, whomsoever the city may appoint, that man must be obeyed, in little things and great, in just things and unjust; and I should feel sure that one who thus obeys would be a good ruler no less than a good subject, and in the storm of spears would stand his ground where he was set, loyal and dauntless at his comrade's side.

But disobedience is the worst of evils. This it is that ruins cities; this makes homes desolate; by this, the ranks of allies are broken into headlong rout; but, of the lives whose course is fair, the greater part owes safety to obedience. Therefore we must support the cause of order, and in no wise suffer a woman to worst us. Better to fall from power, if we must, by a man's hand; then we should not be called weaker than a woman.

LEADER To us, unless our years have stolen our wit, thou seemest to say wisely what thou sayest.

HAEMON Father, the gods implant reason in men, the highest of all things that we call our own. Not mine the skill—far from me be the quest!—to say wherein thou speakest not aright; and yet another man, too, might have some useful thought. At least, it is my natural office to watch, on thy behalf, all that men say, or do, or find to blame. For the dread of thy frown forbids the citizen to speak such words as would offend thine ear; but I can hear these murmurs in the dark, these moanings of the city for this maiden; "no woman," they say, "ever merited her doom less,—none ever was to die so shamefully for deeds so glorious as hers; who, when her own brother had fallen in bloody strife, would not leave him unburied, to be devoured by carrion dogs, or by any bird:—deserves not *she* the meed of golden honour?"

Such is the darkling rumour that spreads in secret. For me, my father, no treasure is so precious as thy welfare. What, indeed, is a nobler ornament for children than a prospering sire's fair fame, or for sire than son's? Wear not, then, one mood only in thyself; think not that thy word, and thine alone, must be right. For if any man thinks that he alone is wise,—that in speech, or in mind, he hath no peer,—such a soul, when laid open, is ever found empty.

No, though a man be wise, 'tis no shame for him to learn many things, and to bend in season. Seest thou, beside the wintry torrent's course, how the trees that yield to it save every twig, while the stiff-necked perish root and branch? And even thus he who keeps the sheet of his sail taut, and never slackens it, upsets his boat, and finishes his voyage with keel uppermost.

Nay, forego thy wrath; permit thyself to change. For if I, a younger man, may offer my thought, it were far best, I ween, that men should be all-wise by nature; but, otherwise—and oft the scale inclines not so—'tis good also to learn from those who speak aright.

LEADER Sire, 'tis meet that thou shouldest profit by his words, if he speaks aught in season, and thou, Haemon, by thy father's; for on both parts there hath been wise speech.

CREON Men of my age—are we indeed to be schooled, then, by men of his?

HAEMON In nothing that is not right; but if I am young, thou shouldest look to my merits, not to my years.

CREON Is it a merit to honour the unruly?

HAEMON I could wish no one to show respect for evil-doers.

CREON Then is not she tainted with that malady?

HAEMON Our Theban folk, with one voice, denies it.

CREON Shall Thebes prescribe to me how I must rule?

HAEMON See, there thou hast spoken like a youth indeed.

CREON Am I to rule this land by other judgment than mine own?

HAEMON That is no city which belongs to one man.

CREON Is not the city held to be the ruler's?

HAEMON Thou wouldst make a good monarch of a desert.

CREON This boy, it seems, is the woman's champion.

HAEMON If thou art a woman; indeed, my care is for thee.

CREON Shameless, at open feud with thy father!

HAEMON Nay, I see thee offending against justice.

CREON Do I offend, when I respect mine own prerogatives?

HAEMON Thou dost not respect them, when thou tramplest on the gods' honours.

CREON O dastard nature, yielding place to woman!

HAEMON Thou wilt never find me yield to baseness.

CREON All thy words, at least, plead for that girl.

HAEMON And for thee, and for me, and for the gods below.

CREON Thou canst never marry her, on this side the grave.

HAEMON Then she must die, and in death destroy another.

CREON How! doth thy boldness run to open threats?

HAEMON What threat is it, to combat vain resolves?

CREON Thou shalt rue thy witless teaching of wisdom.

HAEMON Wert thou not my father, I would have called thee unwise.

CREON Thou woman's slave, use not wheedling speech with me.

HAEMON Thou wouldest speak, and then hear no reply?

CREON Sayest thou so? Now, by the heaven above us—be sure of it—thou shalt smart for taunting me in this opprobrious strain. Bring forth that hated thing, that she may die forthwith in his presence—before his eyes—at her bridegroom's side!

HAEMON No, not at my side—

never think it—shall she perish;
nor shalt thou ever set eyes
more upon my face:—rave,
then, with such friends as can
endure thee.

(*Exit* HAEMON)

LEADER   The man is gone, O king,
in angry haste; a youthful mind,
when stung, is fierce.

CREON   Let him do, or dream,
more than man—good speed to
him!—But he shall not save
these two girls from their doom.

LEADER   Dost thou indeed purpose
to slay both?

CREON   Not her whose hands are
pure: thou sayest well.

LEADER   And by what doom mean'st
thou to slay the other?

CREON   I will take her where the
path is loneliest, and hide her,
living, in a rocky vault, with so
much food set forth as piety
prescribes, that the city may
avoid a public stain. And there,
praying to Hades, the only god
whom she worships, perchance
she will obtain release from
death; or else will learn, at last,
though late, that it is lost labour
to revere the dead.

(CREON *goes into the palace*)

CHORUS (*singing*) (*strophe*) Love,
unconquered in the fight, Love,
who makest havoc of wealth,
who keepest thy vigil on the
soft cheek of a maiden; thou
roamest over the sea, and
among the homes of dwellers in
the wilds; no immortal can escape thee, nor any among men
whose life is for a day; and he
to whom thou hast come is mad.
(*antistrophe*) The just themselves have their minds warped
by thee to wrong, for their ruin:
'tis thou that hast stirred up this
present strife of kinsmen; victorious is the love-kindling light
from the eyes of the fair bride;
it is a power enthroned in sway
beside the eternal laws; for
there the goddess Aphrodite is
working her unconquerable will.

(ANTIGONE *is led out of
the palace by two of*
CREON'S *attendants who
are about to conduct her
to her doom*)

But now I also am carried
beyond the bounds of loyalty,
and can no more keep back the
streaming tears, when I see Antigone thus passing to the bridal
chamber where all are laid to
rest.

(*The following lines be-
tween* ANTIGONE *and the*
CHORUS *are chanted re-
sponsively*)

ANTIGONE   (*strophe* 1) See me,
citizens of my fatherland, setting forth on my last way, looking my last on the sunlight that
is for me no more; no, Hades
who gives sleep to all leads me
living to Acheron's shore; who
have had no portion in the chant
that brings the bride, nor hath
any song been mine for the
crowning of bridals; whom the
lord of the Dark Lake shall wed.

CHORUS   (*systema* 1) Glorious,
therefore, and with praise, thou
departest to that deep place of
the dead: wasting sickness hath
not smitten thee; thou hast not
found the wages of the sword;
no, mistress of thine own fate,
and still alive, thou shalt pass
to Hades, as no other of mortal
kind hath passed.

ANTIGONE (*antistrophe* 1) I have
heard in other days how dread
a doom befell our Phrygian
guest, the daughter of Tantalus,

on the Sipylian heights,[3] how, like clinging ivy, the growth of stone subdued her; and the rains fail not, as men tell, from her wasting form, nor fails the snow, while beneath her weeping lids the tears bedew her bosom; and most like to hers is the fate that brings me to my rest.

CHORUS (*systema* 2)   Yet she was a goddess, thou knowest, and born of gods; we are mortals, and of mortal race. But 'tis great renown for a woman who hath perished that she should have shared the doom of the godlike, in her life, and afterward in death.

ANTIGONE (*strophe* 2)   Ah, I am mocked! In the name of our fathers' gods, can ye not wait till I am gone,—must ye taunt me to my face, O my city, and ye, her wealthy sons? Ah, fount of Dirce, and thou holy ground of Thebe whose chariots are many; ye, at least, will bear me witness, in what sort, unwept of friends, and by what laws I pass to the rock-closed prison of my strange tomb, ah me unhappy! who have no home on the earth or in the shades, no home with the living or with the dead.

CHORUS (*strophe* 3)   Thou hast rushed forward to the utmost verge of daring; and against that throne where Justice sits on high thou hast fallen, my daughter, with a grievous fall. But in this ordeal thou art paying, haply, for thy father's sin.

ANTIGONE (*antistrophe* 2)   Thou hast touched on my bitterest thought,—awaking the ever-new lament for my sire and for all the doom given to us, the famed house of Labdacus. Alas for the horrors of the mother's bed! alas for the wretched mother's slumber at the side of her own son, —and my sire! From what manner of parents did I take my miserable being! And to them I go thus, accursed, unwed, to share their home. Alas, my brother, ill-starred in thy marriage, in thy death thou hast undone my life!

CHORUS (*antistrophe* 3)   Reverent action claims a certain praise for reverence; but an offence against power cannot be brooked by him who hath power in his keeping. Thy self-willed temper hath wrought thy ruin.

ANTIGONE   Unwept, unfriended, without marriage-song, I am led forth in my sorrow on this journey that can be delayed no more. No longer, hapless one, may I behold yon day-star's sacred eye; but for my fate no tear is shed, no friend makes moan.

     (CREON *enters from the palace*)

CREON   Know ye not that songs and wailings before death would never cease, if it profited to utter them? Away with her—away! And when ye have enclosed her, according to my word, in her vaulted grave, leave her alone, forlorn—whether she wishes to die, or to live a buried life in such a home. Our hands

---

[3] A Phrygian princess married to a Theban king boasted that she had had more children than Leto, mother of Apollo and Artemis. These latter two murdered her offspring, and the princess herself was turned into a rock on Mount Sipylus. Melted snow on the mountain caused "tears" to flow down the rock formation.

are clean as touching this maiden. But this is certain—she shall be deprived of her sojourn in the light.

ANTIGONE Tomb, bridal-chamber, eternal prison in the caverned rock, whither I go to find mine own, those many who have perished, and whom Persephone[4] hath received among the dead! Last of all shall I pass thither, and far most miserably of all, before the term of my life is spent. But I cherish good hope that my coming will be welcome to my father, and pleasant to thee, my mother, and welcome, brother, to thee; for, when ye died, with mine own hands I washed and dressed you, and poured drink-offerings at your graves; and now, Polyneices, 'tis for tending thy corpse that I win such recompense as this.

And what law of heaven have I transgressed? Why, hapless one, should I look to the gods any more,—what ally should I invoke,—when by piety I have earned the name of impious? Nay, then, if these things are pleasing to the gods, when I have suffered my doom, I shall come to know my sin; but if the sin is with my judges, I could wish them no fuller measure of evil than they, on their part, mete wrongfully to me.

CHORUS Still the same tempest of the soul vexes this maiden with the same fierce gusts.

CREON Then for this shall her guards have cause to rue their slowness.

ANTIGONE Ah me! that word hath come very near to death.

CREON I can cheer thee with no hope that this doom is not thus to be fulfilled.

ANTIGONE O city of my fathers in the land of Thebe! O ye gods, eldest of our race!—they lead me hence—now, now—they tarry not! Behold me, princes of Thebes, the last daughter of the house of your kings,—see what I suffer, and from whom, because I feared to cast away the fear of Heaven!

(ANTIGONE *is led away by the guards*)

CHORUS (*singing*) (*strophe 1*) Even thus endured Danae[5] in her beauty to change the light of day for brass-bound walls; and in that chamber, secret as the grave, she was held close prisoner; yet was she of a proud lineage, O my daughter, and charged with the keeping of the seed of Zeus, that fell in the golden rain.

But dreadful is the mysterious power of fate: there is no deliverance from it by wealth or by war, by fenced city, or dark, sea-beaten ships.

(*antistrophe 1*) And bonds tamed the son of Dryas,[6] swift to wrath, that king of the Edonians; so paid he for his frenzied taunts, when, by the will of Dionysus, he was pent in a rocky prison. There the fierce

---

[4] Persephone: the queen of the underworld

[5] Danae was the daughter of the king of Argos. It was prophesied that he would be slain by his daughter's sons; he shut up his daughter in a bronze tower. Zeus came to her "in the form of a shower" and she conceived a son, Perseus, who did indeed kill his grandfather.

[6] The son of Dryas was Lycurgus, a king who opposed introduction of the Dionysiac religion and was consequently imprisoned by the god.

exuberance of his madness slowly passed away. That man learned to know the god, whom in his frenzy he had provoked with mockeries; for he had sought to quell the god-possessed women, and the Bacchanalian fire; and he angered the Muses that love the flute.

(*strophe* 2) And by the waters of the Dark Rocks, the waters of the twofold sea, are the shores of Bosporus, and Thracian Salmydessus; where Ares, neighbour to the city, saw the accurst, blinding wound dealt to the two sons of Phineus by his fierce wife,—the wound that brought darkness to those vengeance-craving orbs, smitten with her bloody hands, smitten with her shuttle for a dagger.

(*antistrophe* 2) Pining in their misery, they bewailed their cruel doom, those sons of a mother hapless in her marriage; but she traced her descent from the ancient line of the Erechtheidae; and in far-distant caves she was nursed amid her father's storms, that child of Boreas, swift as a steed over the steep hills, a daughter of gods; yet upon her also the gray Fates bore hard, my daughter.[7]

(*Enter* TEIRESIAS, *led by a Boy, on the spectators' right*)

TEIRESIAS Princes of Thebes, we have come with linked steps, both served by the eyes of one; for thus, by a guide's help, the blind must walk.

CREON And what, aged Teiresias, are thy tidings?

TEIRESIAS I will tell thee; and do thou hearken to the seer.

CREON Indeed, it has not been my wont to slight thy counsel.

TEIRESIAS Therefore didst thou steer our city's course aright.

CREON I have felt, and can attest, thy benefits.

TEIRESIAS Mark that now, once more, thou standest on fate's fine edge.

CREON What means this? How I shudder at thy message!

TEIRESIAS Thou wilt learn, when thou hearest the warnings of mine art. As I took my place on mine old seat of augury, where all birds have been wont to gather within my ken, I heard a strange voice among them; they were screaming with dire, feverish rage, that drowned their language in a jargon; and I knew that they were rending each other with their talons, murderously; the whirr of wings told no doubtful tale.

Forthwith, in fear, I essayed burnt-sacrifice on a duly kindled altar: but from my offerings the Fire-god showed no flame; a dank moisture, oozing from the thigh-flesh, trickled forth upon the embers, and smoked, and sputtered; the gall was scattered to the air; and the streaming thighs lay bared of the fat that had been wrapped round them.

Such was the failure of the rites by which I vainly asked a sign, as from this boy I learned; for he is my guide, as I am guide to others. And 'tis thy counsel that hath brought

---

[7] This allusion is difficult to follow. A daughter of an Athenian princess was married to Phineus, the Thracian king, and bore him two sons. Phineus abandoned his wife and married another woman who, while Ares, the god of war, looked on, put out the eyes of her stepsons.

this sickness on our State. For the altars of our city and of our hearths have been tainted, one and all, by birds and dogs, with carrion from the hapless corpse, the son of Oedipus: and therefore the gods no more accept prayer and sacrifice at our hands, or the flame of meat-offering; nor doth any bird give a clear sign by its shrill cry, for they have tasted the fatness of a slain man's blood.

Think, then, on these things, my son. All men are liable to err; but when an error hath been made, that man is no longer witless or unblest who heals the ill into which he hath fallen, and remains not stubborn.

Self-will, we know, incurs the charge of folly. Nay, allow the claim of the dead; stab not the fallen; what prowess is it to slay the slain anew? I have sought thy good, and for thy good I speak: and never is it sweeter to learn from a good counsellor than when he counsels for thine own gain.

CREON   Old man, ye all shoot your shafts at me, as archers at the butts;—ye must needs practise on me with seer-craft also;—aye, the seer-tribe hath long trafficked in me, and made me their merchandise. Gain your gains, drive your trade, if ye list, in the silver-gold of Sardis and the gold of India; but ye shall not hide that man in the grave,—no, though the eagles of Zeus should bear the carrion morsels to their Master's throne —no, not for dread of that defilement will I suffer his burial: —for well I know that no mortal can defile the gods.—But, aged Teiresias, the wisest fall with a shameful fall, when they clothe shameful thoughts in fair words, for lucre's sake.

TEIRESIAS   Alas! Doth any man know, doth any consider . . .

CREON   Whereof? What general truth dost thou announce?

TEIRESIAS   How precious, above all wealth, is good counsel.

CREON   As folly, I think, is the worst mischief.

TEIRESIAS   Yet thou art tainted with that distemper.

CREON   I would not answer the seer with a taunt.

TEIRESIAS   But thou dost, in saying that I prophesy falsely.

CREON   Well, the prophet-tribe was ever fond of money.

TEIRESIAS   And the race bred of tyrants loves base gain.

CREON   Knowest thou that thy speech is spoken of thy king?

TEIRESIAS   I know it; for through me thou hast saved Thebes.

CREON   Thou art a wise seer; but thou lovest evil deeds.

TEIRESIAS   Thou wilt rouse me to utter the dread secret in my soul.

CREON   Out with it!—Only speak it not for gain.

TEIRESIAS   Indeed, methinks, I shall not,—as touching thee.

CREON   Know that thou shalt not trade on my resolve.

TEIRESIAS   Then know thou—aye, know it well—that thou shalt not live through many more courses of the sun's swift chariot, ere one begotten of thine own loins shall have been given by thee, a corpse for corpses; because thou hast thrust children of the sunlight to the shades, and ruthlessly lodged a living soul in the grave; but keepest in this world one who belongs to the gods infernal, a corpse unburied, unhonoured, all unhallowed. In such thou hast no part, nor have the gods above, but this is a violence done to them by thee. Therefore the avenging destroyers lie in wait for thee, the Furies of Hades and of the gods, that thou may-est be taken in these same ills.

And mark well if I speak these things as a hireling. A time not long to be delayed shall awaken the wailing of men and of women in thy house. And a tumult of hatred against thee stirs all the cities whose man-gled sons had the burial-rite from dogs, or from wild beasts, or from some winged bird that bore a polluting breath to each city that contains the hearths of the dead.[8]

Such arrows for thy heart —since thou provokest me— have I launched at thee, archer-like, in my anger,—sure arrows, of which thou shalt not escape the smart.—Boy, lead me home, that he may spend his rage on younger men, and learn to keep a tongue more temperate, and to bear within his breast a bet-ter mind than now he bears.

(*The Boy leads*
TEIRESIAS *out*)

LEADER OF THE CHORUS The man hath gone, O King, with dread prophecies. And, since the hair on this head, once dark, hath been white, I know that he hath never been a false prophet to our city.

CREON I, too, know it well, and am troubled in soul. 'Tis dire to yield; but, by resistance, to smite my pride with ruin—this, too, is a dire choice.

LEADER Son of Menoeceus, it be-hoves thee to take wise counsel.

CREON What should I do, then? Speak, and I will obey.

LEADER Go thou, and free the maiden from her rocky cham-ber, and make a tomb for the unburied dead.

CREON And this is thy counsel? Thou wouldst have me yield?

LEADER Yea, King, and with all speed; for swift harms from the gods cut short the folly of men.

CREON Ah me, 'tis hard, but I re-sign my cherished resolve,—I obey. We must not wage a vain war with destiny.

LEADER Go, thou, and do these things; leave them not to others.

CREON Even as I am I'll go:—on, on, my servants, each and all of you,—take axes in your hands, and hasten to the ground that ye see yonder! Since our judgment hath taken this turn, I will be present to un-loose her, as I myself bound her. My heart misgives me, 'tis best to keep the established laws, even to life's end.

(CREON *and his serv-ants hasten out on the spectators' left*)

CHORUS (*singing*)[9] (*strophe* 1) O thou of many names, glory of the Cadmeian bride, offspring

---

[8] Creon had exposed the bodies of all seven warriors, not just that of Poly-neices.

[9] This is a hymn to the god Dionysus (Bacchus), whose mother was a Theban princess, Semele. When pregnant by her lover, Zeus, Semele asked him to appear to her in his own shape. When he complied with her request, she was "blinded by his lightning."

of loud-thundering Zeus! thou who watchest over famed Italia, and reignest, where all guests are welcomed, in the sheltered plain of Eleusinian Deo! O Bacchus, dweller in Thebe, mother-city of Bacchants, by the softly-gliding stream of Ismenus, on the soil where the fierce dragon's teeth were sown!

(*antistrophe 1*) Thou hast been seen where torch-flames glare through smoke, above the crests of the twin peaks, where move the Corycian nymphs, thy votaries, hard by Castalia's stream.

Thou comest from the ivy-mantled slopes of Nysa's hills, and from the shore green with many-clustered vines, while thy name is lifted up on strains of more than mortal power, as thou visitest the ways of Thebe:

(*strophe 2*) Thebe, of all cities, thou holdest first in honour, thou, and thy mother whom the lightning smote; and now, when all our people is captive to a violent plague, come thou with healing feet over the Parnassian height, or over the moaning strait!

(*antistrophe 2*) O thou with whom the stars rejoice as they move, the stars whose breath is fire; O master of the voices of the night; son begotten of Zeus; appear, O king, with thine attendant Thyiads, who in night-long frenzy dance before thee, the giver of good gifts, Iacchus!

(*Enter* MESSENGER, *on the spectators' left*)

MESSENGER   Dwellers by the house of Cadmus and of Amphion, there is no estate of mortal life that I would ever praise or blame as settled. Fortune raises and Fortune humbles the lucky or unlucky from day to day, and no one can prophesy to men concerning those things which are established. For Creon was blest once, as I count bliss; he had saved this land of Cadmus from its foes; he was clothed with sole dominion in the land; he reigned, the glorious sire of princely children. And now all hath been lost. For when a man hath forfeited his pleasures, I count him not as living,—I hold him but a breathing corpse. Heap up riches in thy house, if thou wilt; live in kingly state; yet, if there be no gladness therewith, I would not give the shadow of a vapour for all the rest, compared with joy.

LEADER OF THE CHORUS   And what is this new grief that thou hast to tell for our princes?

MESSENGER   Death; and the living are guilty for the dead.

LEADER   And who is the slayer? Who the stricken? Speak.

MESSENGER   Haemon hath perished; his blood hath been shed by no stranger.

LEADER   By his father's hand, or by his own?

MESSENGER   By his own, in wrath with his sire for the murder.

LEADER   O prophet, how true, then, hast thou proved thy word!

MESSENGER   These things stand thus; ye must consider of the rest.

LEADER   Lo, I see the hapless Eurydice, Creon's wife, approaching; she comes from the house by chance, haply,—or because she knows the tidings of her son.

(*Enter* EURYDICE *from the palace*)

EURYDICE   People of Thebes, I

heard your words as I was going forth, to salute the goddess Pallas with my prayers. Even as I was loosing the fastenings of the gate, to open it, the message of a household woe smote on mine ear: I sank back, terror-stricken, into the arms of my handmaids, and my senses fled. But say again what the tidings were; I shall hear them as one who is no stranger to sorrow.

MESSENGER Dear lady, I will witness of what I saw, and will leave no word of the truth untold. Why, indeed, should I soothe thee with words in which I must presently be found false? Truth is ever best.—I attended thy lord as his guide to the furthest part of the plain, where the body of Polyneices, torn by dogs, still lay unpitied. We prayed the goddess of the roads, and Pluto,[10] in mercy to restrain their wrath; we washed the dead with holy washing; and with freshly-plucked boughs we solemnly burned such relics as there were. We raised a high mound of his native earth; and then we turned away to enter the maiden's nuptial chamber with rocky couch, the caverned mansion of the bride of Death. And, from afar off, one of us heard a voice of loud wailing at that bride's unhallowed bower; and came to tell our master Creon.

And as the king drew nearer, doubtful sounds of a bitter cry floated around him; he groaned, and said in accents of anguish, "Wretched that I am, can my foreboding be true? Am I going on the woefullest way that ever I went? My son's voice greets me.—Go, my servants,—haste ye nearer, and when ye have reached the tomb, pass through the gap, where the stones have been wrenched away, to the cell's very mouth,—and look, and see if 'tis Haemon's voice that I know, or if mine ear is cheated by the gods."

This search, at our despairing master's word, we went to make; and in the furthest part of the tomb we descried *her* hanging by the neck, slung by a thread-wrought halter of fine linen: while *he* was embracing her with arms thrown around her waist,—bewailing the loss of his bride who is with the dead, and his father's deeds, and his own ill-starred love.

But his father, when he saw him, cried aloud with a dread cry and went in, and called to him with a voice of wailing:—"Unhappy, what a deed hast thou done! What thought hath come to thee? What manner of mischance hath marred thy reason? Come forth, my child! I pray thee—I implore!" But the boy glared at him with fierce eyes, spat in his face, and, without a word of answer, drew his cross-hilted sword:—as his father rushed forth in flight, he missed his aim;—then, hapless one, wroth with himself, he straightway leaned with all his weight against his sword, and drove it, half its length, into his side; and, while sense lingered, he clasped the maiden to his faint

---

[10] The goddess of the roads (Hecate) and Pluto are divinities of the underworld.

embrace, and, as he gasped, sent forth on her pale cheek the swift stream of the oozing blood.

Corpse enfolding corpse he lies; he hath won his nuptial rites, poor youth, not here, yet in the halls of Death; and he hath witnessed to mankind that, of all curses which cleave to man, ill counsel is the sovereign curse.

> (EURYDICE *retires into the house*)

LEADER   What wouldst thou augur from this? The lady hath turned back, and is gone, without a word, good or evil.

MESSENGER   I, too, am startled; yet I nourish the hope that, at these sore tidings of her son, she cannot deign to give her sorrow public vent, but in the privacy of the house will set her handmaids to mourn the household grief. For she is not untaught of discretion, that she should err.

LEADER   I know not; but to me, at least, a strained silence seems to portend peril, no less than vain abundance of lament.

MESSENGER   Well, I will enter the house, and learn whether indeed she is not hiding some repressed purpose in the depths of a passionate heart. Yea, thou sayest well: excess of silence, too, may have a perilous meaning.

> (*The* MESSENGER *goes into the palace. Enter* CREON, *on the spectators' left, with attendants, carrying the shrouded body of* HAEMON *on a bier. The following lines between* CREON *and the* CHORUS *are chanted responsively*)

CHORUS   Lo, yonder the king himself draws near, bearing that which tells too clear a tale,—the work of no stranger's madness,—if we may say it,—but of his own misdeeds.

CREON (*strophe 1*)   Woe for the sins of a darkened soul, stubborn sins, fraught with death! Ah, ye behold us, the sire who hath slain, the son who hath perished! Woe is me, for the wretched blindness of my counsels! Alas, my son, thou hast died in thy youth, by a timeless doom, woe is me!—thy spirit hath fled,—not by thy folly, but by mine own!

CHORUS (*strophe 2*)   Ah me, how all too late thou seemest to see the right!

CREON   Ah me, I have learned the bitter lesson! But then, methinks, oh then, some god smote me from above with crushing weight, and hurled me into ways of cruelty, woe is me,—overthrowing and trampling on my joy! Woe, woe, for the troublous toils of men!

> (*Enter* MESSENGER *from the house*)

MESSENGER   Sire, thou hast come, methinks, as one whose hands are not empty, but who hath store laid up besides; thou bearest yonder burden with thee; and thou art soon to look upon the woes within thy house.

CREON   And what worse ill is yet to follow upon ills?

MESSENGER   Thy queen hath died, true mother of yon corpse—ah, hapless lady!—by blows newly dealt.

CREON (*antistrophe 1*)   Oh Hades, all-receiving, whom no sacrifice can appease! Hast thou, then, no mercy for me? O thou herald of evil, bitter tidings, what word dost thou utter? Alas, I was already as dead, and thou hast smitten me anew! What sayest thou, my son? What is this new message that thou bringest— woe, woe is me!—of a wife's doom,—of slaughter heaped on slaughter?

CHORUS   Thou canst behold: 'tis no longer hidden within.

(The doors of the palace are opened, and the corpse of EURYDICE *is disclosed)*

CREON *(antistrophe* 2*)*   Ah me,— yonder I behold a new, a second woe! What destiny, ah what, can yet await me? I have but now raised my son in my arms, —and there, again, I see a corpse before me! Alas, alas, un- happy mother! Alas, my child!

MESSENGER   There, at the altar, self-stabbed with a keen knife, she suffered her darkening eyes to close, when she had wailed for the noble fate of Megareus[11] who died before, and then for his fate who lies there,—and when, with her last breath, she had invoked evil fortunes upon thee, the slayer of thy sons.

CREON *(strophe* 3*)*   Woe, woe! I thrill with dread. Is there none to strike me to the heart with two-edged sword?—O miserable that I am, and steeped in miser- able anguish!

MESSENGER   Yea, both this son's doom, and that other's, were laid to thy charge by her whose corpse thou seest.

CREON   And what was the manner of the violent deed by which she passed away?

MESSENGER   Her own hand struck her to the heart, when she had learned her son's sorely la- mented fate.

CREON *(strophe* 4*)*   Ah me, this guilt can never be fixed on any other of mortal kind, for my acquittal! I, even I, was thy slayer, wretched that I am—I own the truth. Lead me away, O my servants, lead me hence with all speed, whose life is but as death!

CHORUS   Thy counsels are good, if there can be good with ills; briefest is best, when trouble is in our path.

CREON *(antistrophe* 3*)*   Oh, let it come, let it appear, that fairest of fates for me, that brings my last day,—aye, best fate of all! Oh, let it come, that I may never look upon to-morrow's light.

CHORUS   These things are in the future; present tasks claim our care: the ordering of the future rests where it should rest.

CREON   All my desires, at least, were summed in that prayer.

CHORUS   Pray thou no more; for mortals have no escape from destined woe.

CREON *(antistrophe* 4*)*   Lead me away, I pray you; a rash, fool- ish man; who have slain thee, ah my son, unwittingly, and thee, too, my wife—unhappy that I am! I know not which way I should bend my gaze, or where I should seek support; for all is amiss with that which is in my hands,—and yonder, again, a crushing fate hath leapt upon my head.

(As CREON *is being con- ducted into the palace, the* LEADER OF THE CHO- RUS *speaks the closing verses)*

LEADER   Wisdom is the supreme part of happiness; and rever-

---

[11] Megareus was killed during the siege of the city.

ence towards the gods must be inviolate. Great words of prideful men are ever punished with great blows, and, in old age, teach the chastened to be wise.[12]

---

[12] Now that you have read *Antigone,* consider this comment by Edith Hamilton, acknowledged authority on Greek and Roman life and literature and inspired writer on classical subjects: "In every way Sophocles is the embodiment of what we know as Greek, so much so that all definitions of the Greek spirit and Greek art are first of all definitions of his spirit and his art. He has imposed himself upon the world as the quintessential Greek . . . he is direct, lucid, simple, reasonable . . . a great tragedian, a supremely gifted poet, and yet a detached observer of life."

· QUESTIONS ·

It seems unwise and unnecessary to list specific questions. These would necessarily depend upon the amount of time devoted to reading *Antigone* and to discussing it in class.

But the comments given on reading drama which precede this play may prove a good starting point. In addition, you will enjoy reading *The Greek Way* by Edith Hamilton, a wise and even brilliant discussion of Grecian life and drama. Also recommended is *The Complete Greek Drama,* edited by Whitney J. Oates and Eugene O'Neill, Jr. This volume provides all the extant tragedies of Sophocles, Aeschylus, and Euripides and the comedies of Aristophanes and Menander. The general introduction to the book provides a helpful background for reading and understanding classical drama and the methods of its production. These titles will suggest many topics for papers you might write; your instructor may make additional suggestions.

THE TRAGEDY
OF MACBETH

William Shakespeare

WILLIAM SHAKESPEARE (1564–1616) was the "unchallenged chief of English letters and the English theater." Although the theater has changed beyond recognition during the last three and one-half centuries, his plays have survived all methods of presentation, styles of acting, and tastes in drama. Comparatively little is known of his life, but what is known is known so well that details here would be superfluous.

Shakespeare is not easy to read: he coins words freely, indulges in word-play, uses a large vocabulary, sometimes overcharges his rhetoric, and makes every word contribute to the total effect. But the effort spent in reading this supremely gifted playwright and poet is richly rewarding.

During your reading of the play, or after, you may wish to read De Quincey's famous essay on the knocking at the gate or Miss McCarthy's "General Macbeth" or the review by McCarten of a representative production of the play in modern times. If the Shakespearean diction occasionally and temporarily upsets you, turn to Armour's essay on *Macbeth* for some "comic relief."

Dramatis Personae

DUNCAN   *King of Scotland*

MALCOLM
DONALBAIN   } *his sons*

MACBETH
BANQUO   } *Generals of the Scottish Army*

MACDUFF
LENNOX
ROSS
MENTEITH   } *Noblemen of Scotland*
ANGUS
CAITHNESS

FLEANCE   *son to Banquo*
SIWARD   *Earl of Northumberland, General of the English forces*
YOUNG SIWARD   *his son*
SEYTON   *an Officer attending on Macbeth*
BOY   *son to Macduff*
A CAPTAIN
AN ENGLISH DOCTOR
A SCOTTISH DOCTOR
A PORTER
AN OLD MAN

LADY MACBETH
LADY MACDUFF
A GENTLEWOMAN   *attending on Lady Macbeth*

HECATE
THREE WITCHES
THE GHOST *of Banquo*
APPARITIONS
LORDS, GENTLEMEN, OFFICERS, SOLDIERS, MURDERERS,
MESSENGERS, ATTENDANTS

SCENE: *Scotland and England.*

ACT I

Scene I. Scotland. An open place.

(*Thunder and lightning.
Enter* THREE WITCHES)

1 WITCH   When shall we three meet again
In thunder, lightning, or in rain?
2 WITCH   When the hurlyburly's done,
When the battle's lost and won.
3 WITCH   That will be ere the set of sun.
1 WITCH   Where the place?
2 WITCH   Upon the heath.
3 WITCH   There to meet with Macbeth.
1 WITCH   I come, Graymalkin!
2 WITCH   Paddock calls.
3 WITCH   Anon!

ALL   Fair is foul, and foul is fair.
Hover through the fog and filthy air.

(*Exeunt*)

Scene II. A camp near Forres.

(*Alarum within. Enter*
KING [DUNCAN], MAL-
COLM, DONALBAIN, LEN-
NOX, *with* ATTENDANTS,
meeting a bleeding CAP-
TAIN)

KING   What bloody man is that?
He can report,
As seemeth by his plight, of the revolt
The newest state.
MALCOLM   This is the sergeant
Who like a good and hardy soldier fought

Graymalkin: gray cat   *Paddock:* toad; both terms are common names for witches' supernatural attendants   *Anon:* immediately, at once

'Gainst my captivity. Hail, brave
　　friend!
Say to the King the knowledge
　　of the broil
As thou didst leave it.
CAPT.　　　　　　　Doubtful it
　　stood,
As two spent swimmers that do
　　cling together
And choke their art. The merci-
　　less Macdonwald
(Worthy to be a rebel, for to that
The multiplying villainies of
　　nature
Do swarm upon him) from the
　　Western Isles
Of kerns and gallowglasses is
　　supplied;
And Fortune, on his damned
　　quarrel smiling,
Showed like a rebel's whore. But
　　all's too weak;
For brave Macbeth (well he de-
　　serves that name),
Disdaining Fortune, with his
　　brandished steel,
Which smoked with bloody exe-
　　cution
(Like valor's minion), carved out
　　his passage
Till he faced the slave;
Which ne'er shook hands nor
　　bade farewell to him
Till he unseamed him from the
　　nave to the chops
And fixed his head upon our
　　battlements.
KING　O valiant cousin! worthy
　　gentleman!
CAPT.　As whence the sun 'gins his
　　reflection

Shipwracking storms and dire-
　　ful thunders break,
So from that spring whence
　　comfort seemed to come
Discomfort swells. Mark, King
　　of Scotland, mark.
No sooner justice had, with
　　valor armed,
Compelled these skipping kerns
　　to trust their heels
But the Norweyan lord, survey-
　　ing vantage,
With furbished arms and new
　　supplies of men,
Began a fresh assault.
KING　　　　　　　　Dismayed
　　not this
Our captains, Macbeth and Ban-
　　quo?
CAPT.　　Yes,
As sparrows eagles, or the hare
　　the lion.
If I say sooth, I must report they
　　were
As cannons overcharged with
　　double cracks, so they
Doubly redoubled strokes upon
　　the foe.
Except they meant to bathe in
　　reeking wounds,
Or memorize another Golgotha,
I cannot tell—
But I am faint; my gashes cry
　　for help.
KING　So well thy words become
　　thee as thy wounds;
They smack of honor both. Go
　　get him surgeons.
　　　　(*Exit* CAPTAIN, *attended*)
　　　　(*Enter* ROSS *and* ANGUS)
Who comes here?

---

knowledge of the broil: what you knew about the battle　*kerns and gallowglasses:* Irish troops　*Showed like . . . :* was favorable for a brief time　*all's
too weak:* Macdonwald and Fortune together cannot withstand Macbeth　*minion:* favorite　*unseamed him . . . :* ripped him from navel to jaws　*'gins his
reflection:* begins to shine　*spring:* source　*surveying vantage:* seeing opportunity　*double cracks:* extra heavy charges　*memorize . . . Golgotha:* make
famous another place of skulls

MALCOLM The worthy Thane of Ross.

LENNOX What a haste looks through his eyes! So should he look
That seems to speak things strange.

ROSS God save the King!

KING Whence cam'st thou, worthy thane?

ROSS From Fife, great King,
Where the Norweyan banners flout the sky
And fan our people cold. Norway himself,
With terrible numbers,
Assisted by that most disloyal traitor
The Thane of Cawdor, began a dismal conflict,
Till that Bellona's bridegroom, lapped in proof,
Confronted him with self-comparisons,
Point against point, rebellious arm 'gainst arm,
Curbing his lavish spirit; and to conclude,
The victory fell on us.

KING Great happiness!

ROSS That now
Sweno, the Norways' king, craves composition;
Nor would we deign him burial of his men
Till he disbursed, at Saint Colme's Inch,
Ten thousand dollars to our general use.

KING No more that Thane of Cawdor shall deceive
Our bosom interest. Go pronounce his present death
And with his former title greet Macbeth.

ROSS I'll see it done.

KING What he hath lost noble Macbeth hath won.

(*Exeunt*)

Scene III. A heath near Forres.

(*Thunder. Enter* THREE WITCHES)

1 WITCH Where hast thou been, sister?

2 WITCH Killing swine.

3 WITCH Sister, where thou?

1 WITCH A sailor's wife had chestnuts in her lap
And mounched and mounched and mounched. "Give me," quoth I.
"Aroint thee, witch!" the rump-fed ronyon cries.
Her husband's to Aleppo gone, master 'o the *Tiger;*
But in a sieve I'll thither sail
And, like a rat without a tail,
I'll do, I'll do, and I'll do.

2 WITCH I'll give thee a wind.

1 WITCH Th' art kind.

3 WITCH And I another.

1 WITCH I myself have all the other,
And the very ports they blow,
All the quarters that they know
I' the shipman's card.
I'll drain him dry as hay.

---

seems to speak: appears ready to utter   *Fife:* county on the east coast of Ireland   *Where the Norweyan . . . .:* the Norwegian flags make the Scots cold with fear   *Bellona's bridegroom:* Macbeth is the bridegroom of this goddess of war   *lapped in proof:* wearing armor of tested strength   *lavish:* insolent   *craves composition:* desires peace terms   *Saint Colme's Inch:* St. Columba's Island, near Edinburgh   *dollars:* an Elizabethan anachronism   *bosom interest:* confidential business   *Aroint:* clear out   *rump-fed:* pampered   *ronyon:* mangy person   *shipman's card:* sailor's compass

Sleep shall neither night nor day
Hang upon his penthouse lid.
He shall live a man forbid.
Weary sev'nights, nine times nine,
Shall he dwindle, peak, and pine.
Though his bark cannot be lost,
Yet it shall be tempest-tost.
Look what I have.

2 WITCH   Show me! show me!

1 WITCH   Here I have a pilot's thumb,
Wracked as homeward he did come.

(*Drum within*)

3 WITCH   A drum, a drum!
Macbeth doth come.

ALL   The Weird Sisters, hand in hand,
Posters of the sea and land,
Thus do go about, about,
Thrice to thine, and thrice to mine,
And thrice again, to make up nine.
Peace! The charm's wound up.

(*Enter* MACBETH *and* BAN-QUO)

MACBETH   So foul and fair a day I have not seen.

BANQUO   How far is 't called to Forres? What are these,
So withered, and so wild in their attire,
That look not like the inhabitants o' the earth,
And yet are on 't? Live you? or are you aught
That man may question? You seem to understand me,
By each at once her choppy finger laying

Upon her skinny lips. You should be women,
And yet your beards forbid me to interpret
That you are so.

MACBETH   Speak, if you can. What are you?

1 WITCH   All hail, Macbeth! Hail to thee, Thane of Glamis!

2 WITCH   All hail, Macbeth! Hail to thee, Thane of Cawdor!

3 WITCH   All hail, Macbeth, that shalt be King hereafter!

BANQUO   Good sir, why do you start and seem to fear
Things that do sound so fair? I' the name of truth,
Are ye fantastical, or that indeed
Which outwardly ye show? My noble partner
You greet with present grace and great prediction
Of noble having and of royal hope,
That he seems rapt withal. To me you speak not.
If you can look into the seeds of time
And say which grain will grow and which will not,
Speak then to me, who neither beg nor fear
Your favors nor your hate.

1 WITCH   Hail!

2 WITCH   Hail!

3 WITCH   Hail!

1 WITCH   Lesser than Macbeth, and greater.

2 WITCH   Not so happy, yet much happier.

3 WITCH   Thou shalt get kings, though thou be none.

---

penthouse lid: a penthouse often had a roof with one slope; hence here compared with the eyelid   *forbid:* under a curse   *Posters:* rapid travelers   *question:* speak to   *choppy:* chapped   *fantastical:* imaginary   *noble having:* fortune or possession   *rapt:* entranced   *get:* beget, have

So all hail, Macbeth and Banquo!

1 WITCH Banquo and Macbeth,
all hail!

MACBETH Stay, you imperfect
speakers, tell me more!

By Sinel's death I know I am
Thane of Glamis,

But how of Cawdor? The Thane
of Cawdor lives,

A prosperous gentleman; and to
be King

Stands not within the prospect
of belief,

No more than to be Cawdor. Say
from whence

You owe this strange intelligence, or why

Upon this blasted heath you stop
our way

With such prophetic greeting.
Speak, I charge you.

(WITCHES *vanish*)

BANQUO The earth hath bubbles,
as the water has,

And these are of them. Whither
are they vanished?

MACBETH Into the air, and what
seemed corporal melted

As breath into the wind. Would
they had stayed!

BANQUO Were such things here as
we do speak about?

Or have we eaten on the insane
root

That takes the reason prisoner?

MACBETH Your children shall be
kings.

BANQUO You shall be King.

MACBETH And Thane of Cawdor
too. Went it not so?

BANQUO To the selfsame tune and
words. Who's here?

(*Enter* ROSS *and* ANGUS)

ROSS The King hath happily received, Macbeth,

The news of thy success; and
when he reads

Thy personal venture in the
rebels' fight,

His wonders and his praises do
contend

Which should be thine or his.
Silenced with that,

In viewing o'er the rest o' the
selfsame day,

He finds thee in the stout Norweyan ranks,

Nothing afeard of what thyself
didst make,

Strange images of death. As
thick as hail

Came post with post, and every
one did bear

Thy praises in his kingdom's
great defense

And poured them down before
him.

ANGUS We are sent

To give thee from our royal
master thanks;

Only to herald thee into his
sight,

Not pay thee.

ROSS And for an earnest of a
greater honor,

He bade me, from him, call thee
Thane of Cawdor;

In which addition, hail, most
worthy Thane!

For it is thine.

BANQUO What, can the devil speak
true?

MACBETH The Thane of Cawdor
lives. Why do you dress me
In borrowed robes?

Sinel's: Holinshed mentions Sinel as Macbeth's father   *corporal:* physical
or material   *insane root:* causing insanity   *His wonders . . . :* Duncan's astonishment at your achievements struggles with his desire to praise it   *earnest:*
advance payment to bind a contract   *addition:* title

ANGUS   Who was the
   Thane lives yet,
But under heavy judgment
   bears that life
Which he deserves to lose.
   Whether he was combined
With those of Norway, or did
   line the rebel
With hidden help and vantage,
   or that with both
He labored in his country's
   wrack, I know not;
But treasons capital, confessed
   and proved,
Have overthrown him.
MACBETH (*aside*)   Glamis, and
   Thane of Cawdor!
The greatest is behind.—(*to*
   ROSS *and* ANGUS) Thanks
   for your pains.
   (*aside to* BANQUO) Do you not
   hope your children shall be
   kings,
When those that gave the Thane
   of Cawdor to me
Promised no less to them?
BANQUO (*aside to* MACBETH)   That,
   trusted home,
Might yet enkindle you unto the
   crown,
Besides the Thane of Cawdor.
   But 'tis strange!
And oftentimes, to win us to
   our harm,
The instruments of darkness tell
   us truths,
Win us with honest trifles, to
   betray 's
In deepest consequence.—
Cousins, a word, I pray you.
MACBETH (*aside*)   Two
   truths are told,

As happy prologues to the swell-
   ing act
Of the imperial theme.—I thank
   you, gentlemen.—
(*aside*) This supernatural solic-
   iting
Cannot be ill; cannot be good.
   If ill,
Why hath it given me earnest
   of success,
Commencing in a truth? I am
   Thane of Cawdor.
If good, why do I yield to that
   suggestion
Whose horrid image doth unfix
   my hair
And make my seated heart
   knock at my ribs
Against the use of nature? Pres-
   ent fears
Are less than horrible imagin-
   ings.
My thought, whose murder yet
   is but fantastical,
Shakes so my single state of
   man that function
Is smothered in surmise and
   nothing is
But what is not.
BANQUO   Look how our partner's
   rapt.
MACBETH (*aside*)   If chance will
   have me King, why, chance
   may crown me,
Without my stir.
BANQUO   New honors come
   upon him,
Like our strange garments,
   cleave not to their mold
But with the aid of use.
MACBETH (*aside*)   Come
   what come may,

---

   line: support   . . . *is behind:* due to follow   *trusted home:* fully believed
betray 's . . . .: disappoint us in important matters   *soliciting:* urging   *sugges-*
tion . . . : Macbeth's preview of himself murdering Duncan   *single state of man:*
possibly a reference to the concept of the microcosm, a comparison of man's being
with that of the universe

Time and the hour runs through the roughest day.

BANQUO   Worthy Macbeth, we stay upon your leisure.

MACBETH   Give me your favor. My dull brain was wrought
With things forgotten. Kind gentlemen, your pains
Are registered where every day I turn
The leaf to read them. Let us toward the King.
(*aside to* BANQUO) Think upon what hath chanced, and, at more time,
The interim having weighed it, let us speak
Our free hearts each to other.

BANQUO (*aside to* MACBETH)   Very gladly.

MACBETH (*aside to* BANQUO)   Till then, enough.—Come, friends.

(*Exeunt*)

Scene IV. Forres. The Palace.

(*Flourish. Enter* KING [DUNCAN], LENNOX, MALCOLM, DONALBAIN, *and* ATTENDANTS)

KING   Is execution done on Cawdor? Are not
Those in commission yet returned?

MALCOLM   My liege,
They are not yet come back. But I have spoke
With one that saw him die; who did report
That very frankly he confessed his treasons,
Implored your Highness' pardon, and set forth
A deep repentance. Nothing in his life
Became him like the leaving it. He died
As one that had been studied in his death
To throw away the dearest thing he owed
As 'twere a careless trifle.

KING   There's no art
To find the mind's construction in the face.
He was a gentleman on whom I built
An absolute trust.

(*Enter* MACBETH, BANQUO, ROSS, *and* ANGUS)

O worthiest cousin,
The sin of my ingratitude even now
Was heavy on me! Thou art so far before
That swiftest wing of recompense is slow
To overtake thee. Would thou hadst less deserved,
That the proportion both of thanks and payment
Might have been mine! Only I have left to say,
More is thy due than more than all can pay.

MACBETH   The service and the loyalty I owe,
In doing it pays itself. Your Highness' part
Is to receive our duties; and our duties
Are to your throne and state children and servants,

---

at more time: when leisure permits   *free hearts:* open and free minds   *in commission:* charged with duty   *As one . . . :* like a person who knew how to die easily   *construction:* meaning or intent   *That the proportion . . . :* that I could have thanked and rewarded you generously and in proportion.

Which do but what they should
    by doing everything
Safe toward your love and
    honour.
KING   Welcome hither.
    I have begun to plant thee and
        will labor
    To make thee full of growing.
        Noble Banquo,
    That hast no less deserved, nor
        must be known
    No less to have done so, let me
        infold thee
    And hold thee to my heart.
BANQUO   There
    if I grow,
The harvest is your own.
KING   My
    plenteous joys,
    Wanton in fullness, seek to hide
        themselves
    In drops of sorrow. Sons, kins-
        men, thanes,
    And you whose places are the
        nearest, know
    We will establish our estate
        upon
    Our eldest, Malcolm, whom we
        name hereafter
    The Prince of Cumberland;
        which honour must
    Not unaccompanied invest him
        only,
    But signs of nobleness, like
        stars, shall shine
    On all deservers. From hence to
        Inverness,
    And bind us further to you.
MACBETH   The rest is labor, which
    is not used for you.
    I'll be myself the harbinger, and
        make joyful

The hearing of my wife with
    your approach;
So, humbly take my leave.
KING   My
    worthy Cawdor!
MACBETH (*aside*) The Prince of
    Cumberland! That is a step
    On which I must fall down, or
        else o'erleap,
    For in my way it lies. Stars, hide
        your fires!
    Let not light see my black and
        deep desires.
    The eye wink at the hand; yet
        let that be,
    Which the eye fears, when it is
        done, to see.   (*Exit*)
KING   True, worthy Banquo: he is
    full so valiant,
    And in his commendations I am
        fed;
    It is a banquet to me. Let's
        after him,
    Whose care is gone before to bid
        us welcome.
    It is a peerless kinsman.
        (*Flourish. Exeunt*)

Scene V. Inverness. Macbeth's Castle.

(*Enter* LADY MACBETH,
alone, with a letter)

LADY MACBETH (*reads*) "They met
me in the day of success; and
I have learned by the perfectest
report they have more in them
than mortal knowledge. When
I burned in desire to question
them further, they made themselves air, into which they vanished. Whiles I stood rapt in the

---

Which do: I do no more than I should   *Wanton:* abundant   *establish*
our estate: settle the succession of the throne   *wink at:* fail to see   *per-*
fectest: accurate

wonder of it, came missives from the King, who all-hailed me Thane of Cawdor, by which title, before, these Weird Sisters saluted me, and referred me to the coming on of time with 'Hail, King that shalt be!' This have I thought good to deliver thee, my dearest partner of greatness, that thou mightst not lose the dues of rejoicing by being ignorant of what greatness is promised thee. Lay it to thy heart, and farewell."

Glamis thou art, and Cawdor,
    and shalt be
What thou art promised. Yet do
    I fear thy nature.
It is too full o' the milk of hu-
    man kindness
To catch the nearest way. Thou
    wouldst be great;
Art not without ambition, but
    without
The illness should attend it.
    What thou wouldst highly,
That wouldst thou holily;
    wouldst not play false,
And yet wouldst wrongly win.
    Thou'dst have, great Glamis,
That which cries "Thus thou
    must do," if thou have it;
And that which rather thou dost
    fear to do
Than wishest should be undone.
    Hie thee hither,
That I may pour my spirits in
    thine ear
And chastise with the valor of
    my tongue

All that impedes thee from the
    golden round
Which fate and metaphysical
    aid doth seem
To have thee crowned withal.
    (*Enter* MESSENGER)
               What
    is your tidings?
MESS.   The King comes here to-
    night.
LADY MACBETH   Thou'rt mad to
    say it!
Is not thy master with him?
    who, were 't so,
Would have informed for prep-
    aration.
MESS.   So please you, it is true.
    Our Thane is coming.
One of my fellows had the speed
    of him,
Who, almost dead for breath,
    had scarcely more
Than would make up his mes-
    sage.
LADY MACBETH   Give him tending;
    He brings great news.
            (*Exit* MESSENGER)
               The raven
    himself is hoarse
That croaks the fatal entrance
    of Duncan
Under my battlements. Come,
    you spirits
That tend on mortal thoughts,
    unsex me here,
And fill me, from the crown to
    the toe, top-full
Of direst cruelty! Make thick my
    blood;
Stop up the access and pas-
    sage to remorse,

---

    missives: messengers   *milk . . . :* this figure of speech may mean "gentle nature" or "tender disposition" or possibly "weak sentimentality"   *illness:* evil or cruel nature   *metaphysical:* supernatural   *mortal thoughts:* homicidal intentions   *remorse:* pity

That no compunctious visitings of nature
Shake my fell purpose nor keep peace between
The effect and it! Come to my woman's breasts
And take my milk for gall, you murdering ministers,
Wherever in your sightless substances
You wait on nature's mischief! Come, thick night,
And pall thee in the dunnest smoke of hell,
That my keen knife see not the wound it makes,
Nor heaven peep through the blanket of the dark
To cry "Hold, hold!"
    (*Enter* MACBETH)
             Great Glamis!
worthy Cawdor!
Greater than both, by the all-hail hereafter!
Thy letters have transported me beyond
This ignorant present, and I feel now
The future in the instant.
MACBETH   My dearest love,
Duncan comes here tonight.
LADY MACBETH   And when goes hence?
MACBETH Tomorrow, as he purposes.
LADY MACBETH O, never
Shall sun that morrow see!
Your face, my Thane, is as a book where men
May read strange matters. To beguile the time,

Look like the time; bear welcome in your eye,
Your hand, your tongue; look like the innocent flower,
But be the serpent under 't. He that's coming
Must be provided for; and you shall put
This night's great business into my dispatch,
Which shall to all our nights and days to come
Give solely sovereign sway and masterdom.
MACBETH We will speak further.
LADY MACBETH   Only look up clear.
To alter favor ever is to fear.
Leave all the rest to me.
                (*Exeunt*)

Scene VI. The same. Before Macbeth's Castle.

    (*Hautboys and torches. Enter* KING [DUNCAN], MALCOLM, DONALBAIN, BANQUO, LENNOX, MAC-DUFF, ROSS, ANGUS, *and* ATTENDANTS)
KING This castle hath a pleasant seat. The air
Nimbly and sweetly recommends itself
Unto our gentle senses.
BANQUO   This guest of summer,
The temple-haunting martlet, does approve
By his loved mansionry that the heaven's breath
Smells wooingly here. No jutty, frieze,

That no compunctious . . . : that no merciful impulses come between my purpose and carrying it out   *take:* exchange   *sightless:* invisible   *mischief:* foul deeds   *beguile the time:* deceive everyone   *clear:* cheerfully   *To alter . . . :* to show concern may create suspicion   *martlet:* martin   *approve:* prove

Buttress, nor coign of vantage,
but this bird
Hath made his pendent bed and
procreant cradle.
Where they most breed and
haunt, I have observed
The air is delicate.
(*Enter* LADY MACBETH)
KING See, see, our
honored hostess!
The love that follows us some-
time is our trouble,
Which still we thank as love.
Herein I teach you
How you shall bid God 'ild us
for your pains
And thank us for your trouble.
LADY MACBETH All our service
In every point twice done, and
then done double,
Were poor and single business
to contend
Against those honors deep and
broad wherewith
Your Majesty loads our house.
For those of old,
And the late dignities heaped up
to them,
We rest your hermits.
KING Where's
the Thane of Cawdor?
We coursed him at the heels and
had a purpose
To be his purveyor; but he rides
well,
And his great love, sharp as his
spur, hath holp him
To his home before us. Fair and
noble hostess,
We are your guest tonight.
LADY MACBETH Your
servants ever

Have theirs, themselves, and
what is theirs, in compt,
To make their audit at your
Highness' pleasure,
Still to return your own.
KING Give me
your hand;
Conduct me to mine host. We
love him highly
And shall continue our graces
towards him.
By your leave, hostess.
(*Exeunt*)

Scene VII. The same. Macbeth's Castle.

(*Hautboys. Torches. En-
ter a* SEWER, *and divers*
SERVANTS *with dishes and
service over the stage.
Then enter* MACBETH)
MACBETH If it were done when
'tis done, then 'twere well
It were done quickly. If the as-
sassination
Could trammel up the conse-
quence, and catch,
With his surcease, success, that
but this blow
Might be the be-all and the end-
all here,
But here, upon this bank and
shoal of time,
We'd jump the life to come.
But in these cases
We still have judgment here,
that we but teach
Bloody instructions, which,
being taught, return
To plague the inventor. This
even-handed justice

---

coign of vantage: convenient corner   *'ild:* reward   *single:* weak, feeble
We rest your hermits: we shall continue to pray for you   *purveyor:* advance
agent   *holp:* helped   *in compt:* in trust   *Still:* always   *sewer:* butler, server
trammel up: entangle in a net   *surcease:* possibly "cessation" but more likely
"Duncan's death"   *jump:* risk   *the life to come:* eternity

Commends the ingredients of our poisoned chalice
To our own lips. He's here in double trust:
First, as I am his kinsman and his subject,
Strong both against the deed; then, as his host,
Who should against his murderer shut the door,
Not bear the knife myself. Besides, this Duncan
Hath borne his faculties so meek, hath been
So clear in his great office, that his virtues
Will plead like angels, trumpet-tongued, against
The deep damnation of his taking-off;
And pity, like a naked new-born babe,
Striding the blast, or heaven's cherubin, horsed
Upon the sightless couriers of the air,
Shall blow the horrid deed in every eye,
That tears shall drown the wind. I have no spur
To prick the sides of my intent, but only
Vaulting ambition, which o'erleaps itself
And falls on the other side.

(*Enter* LADY MACBETH)

How now? What news?

LADY MACBETH He has almost supped. Why have you left the chamber?

MACBETH Hath he asked for me?

LADY MACBETH Know you not he has?

MACBETH We will proceed no further in this business.
He hath honored me of late, and I have bought
Golden opinions from all sorts of people,
Which would be worn now in their newest gloss,
Not cast aside so soon.

LADY MACBETH Was the hope drunk
Wherein you dressed yourself? Hath it slept since?
And wakes it now to look so green and pale
At what it did so freely? From this time
Such I account thy love. Art thou afeard
To be the same in thine own act and valor
As thou art in desire? Wouldst thou have that
Which thou esteem'st the ornament of life,
And live a coward in thine own esteem,
Letting "I dare not" wait upon "I would,"
Like the poor cat i' the adage?

MACBETH Prithee peace!
I dare do all that may become a man.
Who dares do more is none.

LADY MACBETH What beast was 't then
That made you break this enterprise to me?
When you durst do it, then you were a man;
And to be more than what you were, you would
Be so much more the man. Nor time nor place

Commends . . . : offers or extends the contents   *faculties:* power   *clear:* without blame   *sightless couriers:* the winds   *ornament of life:* the crown   *poor cat . . . :* a saying about a cat that wanted fish but was unwilling to wet her feet   *break:* suggest, mention

Did then adhere, and yet you
would make both.
They have made themselves,
and that their fitness now
Does unmake you. I have given
suck, and know
How tender 'tis to love the babe
that milks me.
I would, while it was smiling in
my face,
Have plucked my nipple from
his boneless gums
And dashed the brains out, had
I so sworn as you
Have done to this.

MACBETH   If we should
fail?

LADY MACBETH   We fail?
But screw your courage to the
sticking place,
And we'll not fail. When Dun-
can is asleep
(Whereto the rather shall his
day's hard journey
Soundly invite him), his two
chamberlains
Will I with wine and wassail so
convince
That memory, the warder of the
brain,
Shall be a fume, and the receipt
of reason
A limbeck only. When in swin-
ish sleep
Their drenched natures lie as in
a death,
What cannot you and I perform
upon
The unguarded Duncan? what
not put upon
His spongy officers, who shall
bear the guilt
Of our great quell?

MACBETH   Bring forth
men-children only,
For thy undaunted mettle
should compose
Nothing but males. Will it not
be received,
When we have marked with
blood those sleepy two
Of his own chamber and used
their very daggers,
That they have done 't?

LADY MACBETH   Who dares
receive it other,
As we shall make our griefs and
clamor roar
Upon his death?

MACBETH   I am settled and
bend up
Each corporal agent to this terrible feat.
Away, and mock the time with
fairest show;
False face must hide what the
false heart doth know.
                    (*Exeunt*)

ACT II

Scene I. The same. Court of
Macbeth's Castle.

(*Enter* BANQUO *and* FLE-
ANCE, *with a torch before
them*)

BANQUO   How goes the night, boy?

FLEANCE   The moon is down; I
have not heard the clock.

BANQUO   And she goes down at
twelve.

FLEANCE   I take 't, 'tis later, sir.

BANQUO   Hold, take my sword.
There's husbandry in heaven;

---

convince: overpower   *limbeck:* an alembic, an instrument used in distillation   *spongy:* drunken   *quell:* murder   *mock the time:* deceive the whole
world   *husbandry:* thrift, frugality

Their candles are all out. Take
thee that too.
A heavy summons lies like lead
upon me,
And yet I would not sleep. Mer-
ciful powers,
Restrain in me the cursed
thoughts that nature
Gives way to in repose!
       (*Enter* MACBETH *and a*
SERVANT, *with a torch*)
                          Give me
my sword.
Who's there?
MACBETH   A friend.
BANQUO   What, sir, not yet at rest?
The King's abed.
He hath been in unusual pleas-
ure and
Sent forth great largess to your
offices.
This diamond he greets your
wife withal
By the name of most kind host-
ess, and shut up
In measureless content.
MACBETH   Being un-
prepared,
Our will became the servant to
defect,
Which else should free have
wrought.
BANQUO   All's well.
I dreamt last night of the three
Weird Sisters.
To you they have showed some
truth.
MACBETH   I think not of them.
Yet when we can entreat an
hour to serve,
We would spend it in some
words upon that business,
If you would grant the time.

BANQUO   At
your kind'st leisure.
MACBETH   If you shall cleave to
my consent, when 'tis,
It shall make honour for you.
BANQUO   So I
lose none
In seeking to augment it but
still keep
My bosom franchised and al-
legiance clear,
I shall be counseled.
MACBETH   Good repose
the while!
BANQUO   Thanks, sir. The like to
you!
           (*Exeunt* BANQUO *and*
                    FLEANCE)
MACBETH   Go bid thy mistress,
when my drink is ready,
She strike upon the bell. Get
thee to bed.
              (*Exit* SERVANT)
Is this a dagger which I see be-
fore me,
The handle toward my hand?
Come, let me clutch thee!
I have thee not, and yet I see
thee still.
Art thou not, fatal vision, sen-
sible
To feeling as to sight? or art
thou but
A dagger of the mind, a false
creation,
Proceeding from the heat-
oppressed brain?
I see thee yet, in form as pal-
pable
As this which now I draw.
Thou marshal'st me the way
that I was going,

---

that: probably a dagger   *heavy summons:* sleepiness   *largess:* gifts   *offices:*
servants' quarters   *shut up:* concluded his remarks   *Being unprepared . . . :*
had we been better prepared we could have entertained more hospitably   *franchised:* free from guilt   *sensible:* capable of being perceived by the senses, perceptible

And such an instrument I was
to use.
Mine eyes are made the fools o'
the other senses,
Or else worth all the rest. I see
thee still;
And on thy blade and dudgeon
gouts of blood,
Which was not so before.
There's no such thing.
It is the bloody business which
informs
Thus to mine eyes. Now o'er the
one half-world
Nature seems dead, and wicked
dreams abuse
The curtained sleep. Witchcraft
celebrates
Pale Hecate's offerings; and
withered murder,
Alarumed by his sentinel, the
wolf,
Whose howl's his watch, thus
with his stealthy pace,
With Tarquin's ravishing strides,
towards his design
Moves like a ghost. Thou sure
and firm-set earth,
Hear not my steps which way
they walk, for fear
Thy very stones prate of my
whereabout
And take the present horror
from the time,
Which now suits with it. Whiles
I threat, he lives;
Words to the heat of deeds too
cold breath gives.
                              (*A bell rings*)
I go, and it is done. The bell in-
vites me.

Hear it not, Duncan, for it is a
knell
That summons thee to heaven,
or to hell.
                                    (*Exit*)

Scene II. The same.

(*Enter* LADY MACBETH)

LADY MACBETH   That which hath
made them drunk hath made
me bold;
What hath quenched them hath
given me fire. Hark! Peace!
It was the owl that shrieked, the
fatal bellman
Which gives the stern'st goodnight. He is about it.
The doors are open, and the sur-
feited grooms
Do mock their charge with
snores. I have drugged their
possets,
That death and nature do con-
tend about them
Whether they live or die.
MACBETH (*within*)   Who's there?
What, ho?
LADY MACBETH   Alack, I am afraid
they have awaked,
And 'tis not done! The attempt,
and not the deed,
Confounds us. Hark! I laid their
daggers ready;
He could not miss 'em. Had he
not resembled
My father as he slept, I had
done 't.
                          (*Enter* MACBETH)
My husband!

Mine eyes: if the dagger is not real, my eyes have deceived me; if the dagger
is actually present, my sight is more reliable than my other sense   *dudgeon:*
handle   *informs:* takes shape, or speaks   *abuse . . . :* disturb sleep in a bed
with curtains   *Hecate:* goddess of witchcraft   *Tarquin:* a Roman who ravished
Lucrece   *fatal bellman:* the town crier who visited prisoners before their execution   *possets:* nightcaps, bedtime drinks   *Confounds:* ruins

MACBETH I have done the deed. Didst thou not hear a noise?

LADY MACBETH I heard the owl scream and the crickets cry. Did not you speak?

MACBETH When?

LADY MACBETH Now.

MACBETH As I descended?

LADY MACBETH Ay.

MACBETH Hark! Who lies i' the second chamber?

LADY MACBETH Donalbain.

MACBETH This is a sorry sight.

LADY MACBETH A foolish thought, to say a sorry sight.

MACBETH There's one did laugh in 's sleep, and one cried "Murder!" That they did wake each other. I stood and heard them. But they did say their prayers and addressed them Again to sleep.

LADY MACBETH There are two lodged together.

MACBETH One cried "God bless us!" and "Amen!" the other, As they had seen me with these hangman's hands, Listening their fear. I could not say "Amen!" When they did say "God bless us!"

LADY MACBETH Consider it not so deeply.

MACBETH But wherefore could not I pronounce "Amen"? I had most need of blessing, and "Amen" Stuck in my throat.

LADY MACBETH These deeds must not be thought After these ways. So, it will make us mad.

MACBETH Methought I heard a voice cry "Sleep no more! Macbeth does murder sleep"— the innocent sleep, Sleep that knits up the raveled sleave of care, The death of each day's life, sore labor's bath, Balm of hurt minds, great nature's second course, Chief nourisher in life's feast.

LADY MACBETH What do you mean?

MACBETH Still it cried "Sleep no more!" to all the house; "Glamis hath murdered sleep, and therefore Cawdor Shall sleep no more! Macbeth shall sleep no more!"

LADY MACBETH Who was it that thus cried? Why, worthy Thane, You do unbend your noble strength to think So brainsickly of things. Go get some water And wash this filthy witness from your hand. Why did you bring these daggers from the place? They must lie there. Go carry them and smear The sleepy grooms with blood.

MACBETH I'll go no more. I am afraid to think what I have done; Look on 't again I dare not.

LADY MACBETH Infirm of purpose! Give me the daggers. The sleeping and the dead Are but as pictures. 'Tis the eye of childhood That fears a painted devil. If he do bleed,

---

Sleep that knits . . . .: sleep that straightens out the tangled skeins of worry *witness:* evidence *painted:* depicted, represented

I'll gild the faces of the grooms
withal,

For it must seem their guilt.

(*Exit. Knocking within*)

MACBETH Whence is that knocking?

How is 't with me when every
noise appalls me?

What hands are here? Ha! they
pluck out mine eyes!

Will all great Neptune's ocean
wash this blood

Clean from my hand? No. This
my hand will rather

The multitudinous seas incarnadine,

Making the green one red.

(*Enter* LADY MACBETH)

LADY MACBETH My hands are of
your color, but I shame

To wear a heart so white.
(*knock*) I hear a knocking

At the south entry. Retire we to
our chamber.

A little water clears us of this
deed.

How easy is it then! Your constancy

Hath left you unattended.
(*knock*) Hark! more knocking.

Get on your nightgown, lest occasion call us

And show us to be watchers. Be
not lost

So poorly in your thoughts.

MACBETH To know my deed,
'twere best not know myself.

(*Knock*)

Wake Duncan with thy knocking! I would thou couldst!

(*Exeunt*)

Scene III. The same.

(*Enter a* PORTER. *Knocking within*)

PORTER Here's a knocking indeed!
If a man were porter of hell
gate, he should have old turning
the key. (*knock*) Knock, knock,
knock! Who's there, i' the name
of Beelzebub? Here's a farmer
that hanged himself on the expectation of plenty. Come in
time! Have napkins enow about
you; here you'll sweat for 't.
(*knock*) Knock, knock! Who's
there, in the other devil's name?
Faith, here's an equivocator,
that could swear in both the
scales against either scale; who
committed treason enough for
God's sake, yet could not equivocate to heaven. O, come in,
equivocator! (*knock*) Knock,
knock, knock! Who's there?
Faith, here's an English tailor
come hither for stealing out of
a French hose. Come in, tailor.
Here you may roast your goose.
(*knock*) Knock, knock! Never
at quiet! What are you? But
this place is too cold for hell.
I'll devil-porter it no further. I
had thought to have let in some
of all professions that go the
primrose way to the everlasting
bonfire. (*knock*) Anon, anon!
(*opens the gate*) I pray you remember the porter.

(*Enter* MACDUFF *and* LENNOX)

MACDUFF Was it so late, friend,
ere you went to bed,

---

gild: paint   green one red: uniformly and completely red   *Your constancy:* You have lost your firmness   *have old:* would have a gay old time or,
perhaps, have plenty of   *enow:* enough   *French hose:* tight-fitting hose
goose: smoothing iron   *remember the porter:* he expects a tip

That you do lie so late?

PORTER   Faith, sir, we were carousing till the second cock; and drink, sir, is a great provoker of three things.

MACDUFF   What three things does drink especially provoke?

PORTER   Marry, sir, nose-painting, sleep, and urine. Lechery, sir, it provokes, and unprovokes: it provokes the desire, but it takes away the performance. Therefore much drink may be said to be an equivocator with lechery: it makes him, and it mars him; it sets him on, and it takes him off; it persuades him, and disheartens him; makes him stand to, and not stand to; in conclusion, equivocates him in a sleep, and, giving him the lie, leaves him.

MACDUFF   I believe drink gave thee the lie last night.

PORTER   That it did, sir, i' the very throat on me; but I requited him for his lie; and, I think, being too strong for him, though he took up my legs sometime, yet I made a shift to cast him.

MACDUFF   Is thy master stirring?

(*Enter* MACBETH)

Our knocking has awaked him; here he comes.

LENNOX   Good morrow, noble sir.

MACBETH   Good morrow, both.

MACDUFF   Is the King stirring, worthy Thane?

MACBETH   Not yet.

MACDUFF   He did command me to call timely on him;
I have almost slipped the hour.

MACBETH   I'll bring you to him.

MACDUFF   I know this is a joyful trouble to you;
But yet 'tis one.

MACBETH   The labor we delight in physics pain.
This is the door.

MACDUFF   I'll make so bold to call,
For 'tis my limited service.

(*Exit*)

LENNOX   Goes the King hence today?

MACBETH   He does; he did appoint so.

LENNOX   The night has been unruly. Where we lay,
Our chimneys were blown down; and, as they say,
Lamentings heard i' the air, strange screams of death,
And prophesying, with accents terrible,
Of dire combustion and confused events
New hatched to the woeful time. The obscure bird
Clamored the livelong night. Some say the earth
Was feverous and did shake.

MACBETH   'Twas a rough night.

LENNOX   My young remembrance cannot parallel
A fellow to it.

(*Enter* MACDUFF)

MACDUFF   O horror, horror, horror! Tongue nor heart
Cannot conceive nor name thee!

MACBETH *and* LENNOX   What's the matter?

MACDUFF   Confusion now hath made his masterpiece!

---

second cock: 3 A.M.   Marry, sir, . . . : this speech, full of suggestive meanings, possibly plays up one of the themes of the play, the distinction between "desire" and "act"   cast him: throw him down, as in wrestling   timely: early   physics: treats or relieves   limited: appointed or designated   combustion: confusion, tumult   obscure bird: owl   Confusion: destruction

Most sacrilegious murder hath broke ope
The Lord's anointed temple and stole thence
The life o' the building!

MACBETH   What is 't you say? the life?

LENNOX   Mean you his Majesty?

MACDUFF   Approach the chamber, and destroy your sight
With a new Gorgon. Do not bid me speak.
See, and then speak yourselves.

(*Exeunt* MACBETH *and* LENNOX)

Awake, awake!
Ring the alarum bell. Murder and treason!
Banquo and Donalbain! Malcolm! awake!
Shake off this downy sleep, death's counterfeit,
And look on death itself! Up, up, and see
The great doom's image! Malcolm! Banquo!
As from your graves rise up and walk like sprites
To countenance this horror! Ring the bell!

(*Bell rings*)

(*Enter* LADY MACBETH)

LADY MACBETH   What's the business,
That such a hideous trumpet calls to parley
The sleepers of the house? Speak, speak!

MACDUFF   O gentle lady,
'Tis not for you to hear what I can speak!
The repetition in a woman's ear
Would murder as it fell.

(*Enter* BANQUO)

O Banquo, Banquo,
Our royal master's murdered!

LADY MACBETH   Woe, alas!
What, in our house?

BANQUO   Too cruel anywhere.
Dear Duff, I prithee contradict thyself
And say it is not so.

(*Enter* MACBETH, LENNOX, *and* ROSS)

MACBETH   Had I but died an hour before this chance,
I had lived a blessed time; for from this instant
There's nothing serious in mortality;
All is but toys; renown and grace is dead;
The wine of life is drawn, and the mere lees
Is left this vault to brag of.

(*Enter* MALCOLM *and* DONALBAIN)

DONALBAIN   What is amiss?

MACBETH   You are, and do not know 't.
The spring, the head, the fountain of your blood
Is stopped, the very source of it is stopped.

MACDUFF   Your royal father's murdered.

MALCOLM   O, by whom?

LENNOX   Those of his chamber, as it seemed, had done 't.
Their hands and faces were all badged with blood;
So were their daggers, which unwiped we found

Gorgon: a monster who, in Greek myth, turned its viewer to stone   *counterfeit:* imitation   *great doom's image:* likeness of doomsday, Judgment Day   *To countenance:* to accord with   *repetition:* report   *mortality:* human life   *toys:* trifles   *vault . . . :* a wine cellar, i.e., universe   *badged:* marked

Upon their pillows.
They stared and were distracted. No man's life
Was to be trusted with them.

MACBETH　O, yet I do repent me of my fury
That I did kill them.

MACDUFF　　　　　Wherefore did you so?

MACBETH　Who can be wise, amazed, temperate, and furious,
Loyal and neutral, in a moment? No man.
The expedition of my violent love
Outrun the pauser, reason. Here lay Duncan,
His silver skin laced with his golden blood,
And his gashed stabs looked like a breach in nature
For ruin's wasteful entrance; there, the murderers,
Steeped in the colors of their trade, their daggers
Unmannerly breeched with gore. Who could refrain
That had a heart to love and in that heart
Courage to make 's love known?

LADY MACBETH　Help me hence, ho!

MACDUFF　Look to the lady.

MALCOLM　(*aside to* DONALBAIN)
Why do we hold our tongues,
That most may claim this argument for ours?

DONALBAIN　(*aside to* MALCOLM)
What should be spoken here,
Where our fate, hid in an auger hole,
May rush and seize us? Let's away,

Our tears are not yet brewed.

MALCOLM　(*aside to* DONALBAIN)
Nor our strong sorrow
Upon the foot of motion.

BANQUO　　　　　　　　Look to the lady.

(LADY MACBETH
is carried out)

And when we have our naked frailties hid,
That suffer in exposure, let us meet
And question this most bloody piece of work,
To know it further. Fears and scruples shake us.
In the great hand of God I stand, and thence
Against the undivulged pretence I fight
Of treasonous malice.

MACDUFF　　　　　　　And so do I.

ALL　So all.

MACBETH　Let's briefly put on manly readiness
And meet i' the hall together.

ALL　　　　　　　　　　　Well contented.

(*Exeunt all but* MALCOLM
and DONALBAIN)

MALCOLM　What will you do? Let's not consort with them.
To show an unfelt sorrow is an office
Which the false man does easy. I'll to England.

DONALBAIN　To Ireland, I. Our separated fortune
Shall keep us both the safer. Where we are,
There's daggers in men's smiles; the near in blood,
The nearer bloody.

---

fury: frenzy　*amazed:* confused　*expedition:* haste　*golden:* red
breeched: covered or clothed　*argument:* subject　*auger hole:* a small place
foot of motion: time to act　*naked frailties hid:* poor bodies clothed　*scruples:*
suspicions　*pretence:* purpose　*briefly:* quickly　*readiness:* armor, battle
dress　*the near in blood . . . :* the nearer in relationship to the King, the more
likely to be killed

MALCOLM　　　　This murderous shaft that's shot
Hath not yet lighted, and our safest way
Is to avoid the aim. Therefore to horse!
And let us not be dainty of leave-taking
But shift away. There's warrant in that theft
Which steals itself when there's no mercy left.

(Exeunt)

Scene IV. The same. Outside Macbeth's Castle.

(Enter ROSS *with an* OLD MAN*)*

OLD MAN　　Threescore and ten I can remember well;
Within the volume of which time I have seen
Hours dreadful and things strange; but this sore night
Hath trifled former knowings.
ROSS　　　　　　　　　　Ah, good father,
Thou seest the heavens, as troubled with man's act,
Threaten his bloody stage. By the clock 'tis day,
And yet dark night strangles the traveling lamp.
Is 't night's predominance, or the day's shame,
That darkness does the face of earth entomb
When living light should kiss it?
OLD MAN　　'Tis unnatural,
Even like the deed that's done. On Tuesday last
A falcon, towering in her pride of place,
Was by a mousing owl hawked at and killed.
ROSS　　And Duncan's horses (a thing most strange and certain),
Beauteous and swift, the minions of their race,
Turned wild in nature, broke their stalls, flung out,
Contending 'gainst obedience, as they would make
War with mankind.
OLD MAN　　　　　　　'Tis said they eat each other.
ROSS　　They did so, to the amazement of mine eyes
That looked upon 't.
(Enter MACDUFF*)*
　　　　　　　　　　Here comes the good Macduff.
How goes the world, sir, now?
MACDUFF　　Why, see you not?
ROSS　　Is 't known who did this more than bloody deed?
MACDUFF　　Those that Macbeth hath slain.
ROSS　　　　　Alas, the day!
What good could they pretend?
MACDUFF　　They were suborned.
Malcolm and Donalbain, the King's two sons,
Are stol'n away and fled, which puts upon them
Suspicion of the deed.
ROSS　　　　　　　　'Gainst nature still!
Thriftless ambition, that will raven up
Thine own life's means! Then 'tis most like
The sovereignty will fall upon Macbeth.

---

dainty: particular, formal　　*shift:* slip　　*warrant:* justification　　*sore:* dreadful　　*hath trifled . . . :* made past experiences seem unimportant　　*traveling lamp:* the sun　　*minions of their race:* best of breed　　*pretend:* intend　　*suborned:* bribed　　*Thriftless:* wasteful　　*raven up:* greedily devour

MACDUFF He is already named, and gone to Scone
To be invested.

ROSS   Where is Duncan's body?

MACDUFF Carried to Colmekill,
The sacred storehouse of his predecessors
And guardian of their bones.

ROSS   Will
you to Scone?

MACDUFF No, cousin, I'll to Fife.

ROSS Well, I will thither.

MACDUFF Well, may you see things well done there. Adieu,
Lest our old robes sit easier than our new!

ROSS Farewell, father.

OLD MAN God's benison go with you, and with those
That would make good of bad, and friends of foes!

(Exeunt omnes)

ACT III

Scene I. Forres. The Palace.

(Enter BANQUO*)*

BANQUO Thou hast it now—King, Cawdor, Glamis, all,
As the Weird Women promised; and I fear
Thou play'dst most foully for 't. Yet it was said
It should not stand in thy posterity,
But that myself should be the root and father
Of many kings. If there come truth from them

(As upon thee, Macbeth, their speeches shine),
Why, by the verities on thee made good,
May they not be my oracles as well
And set me up in hope? But, hush, no more!

(Sennet sounded. Enter MACBETH, *as King;* LADY MACBETH, *as Queen;* LENNOX, ROSS, LORDS, *and* ATTENDANTS*)*

MACBETH Here's our chief guest.

LADY MACBETH If he had been forgotten,
It had been as a gap in our great feast,
And all-thing unbecoming.

MACBETH Tonight we hold a solemn supper, sir,
And I'll request your presence.

BANQUO Let your Highness
Command upon me, to the which my duties
Are with a most indissoluble tie
For ever knit.

MACBETH   Ride you this afternoon?

BANQUO Ay, my good lord.

MACBETH We should have else desired your good advice
(Which still hath been both grave and prosperous)
In this day's council; but we'll take tomorrow.
Is 't far you ride?

BANQUO As far, my lord, as will fill up the time
'Twixt this and supper. Go not my horse the better,
I must become a borrower of the night
For a dark hour or twain.

---

invested: installed as king   *benison:* blessing   *shine:* are clearly manifest
Sennet: flourish of trumpet sounds   *solemn supper:* official banquet   *still:* always   *prosperous:* useful   *Go . . . better:* unless my horse goes faster than expected

MACBETH   Fail
not our feast.

BANQUO   My lord, I will not.

MACBETH   We hear our bloody
cousins are bestowed

In England and in Ireland, not
confessing

Their cruel parricide, filling
their hearers

With strange invention. But of
that tomorrow,

When therewithal we shall have
cause of state

Craving us jointly. Hie you to
horse. Adieu,

Till you return at night. Goes
Fleance with you?

BANQUO   Ay, my good lord. Our
time does call upon 's.

MACBETH   I wish your horses swift
and sure of foot,

And so I do commend you to
their backs.
Farewell.

(*Exit* BANQUO)

Let every man be master of his
time

Till seven at night. To make society

The sweeter welcome, we will
keep ourself

Till supper time alone. While
then, God be with you!

(*Exeunt* LORDS *and
others, all but* MAC-
BETH *and a* SERVANT)

Sirrah, a word with you. Attend
those men

Our pleasure?

SERV.   They are, my lord, without
the palace gate.

MACBETH   Bring them before us.

(*Exit* SERVANT)

To be thus is nothing,

But to be safely thus. Our fears
in Banquo

Stick deep, and in his royalty of
nature

Reigns that which would be
feared. 'Tis much he dares,

And to that dauntless temper of
his mind

He hath a wisdom that doth
guide his valor

To act in safety. There is none
but he

Whose being I do fear; and under him

My genius is rebuked, as it is
said

Mark Antony's was by Caesar.
He chid the Sisters

When first they put the name of
King upon me,

And bade them speak to him.
Then, prophet-like,

They hailed him father to a line
of kings.

Upon my head they placed a
fruitless crown

And put a barren scepter in my
gripe,

Thence to be wrenched with an
unlineal hand,

No son of mine succeeding. If 't
be so,

For Banquo's issue have I filed
my mind;

For them the gracious Duncan
have I murdered;

Put rancors in the vessel of my
peace

---

cousins: Malcolm and Donalbain   *invention:* lies, falsehoods   *cause of
state . . . :* official business requiring attention of us   *While:* until   *Sirrah:*
form of greeting   *Attend:* await   *To be thus . . . :* to have the title of king is
nothing unless I can be safe   *in Banquo:* about Banquo   *under him . . . :* my
controlling spirit is daunted as was Antony's by Caesar   *gripe:* grasp   *filed:*
defiled   *rancors:* enmities

Only for them, and mine eternal
    jewel
Given to the common enemy of
    man
To make them kings, the seed
    of Banquo kings!
Rather than so, come, Fate, into
    the list,
And champion me to the utter-
    ance! Who's there?
        (*Enter* SERVANT *and two*
        MURDERERS)
Now go to the door and stay
    there till we call.
        (*Exit* SERVANT)
Was it not yesterday we spoke
    together?
MURDERERS It was, so please your
    Highness.
MACBETH   Well then, now
    Have you considered of my
        speeches? Know
    That it was he, in the times past,
        which held you
    So under fortune, which you
        thought had been
    Our innocent self. This I made
        good to you
    In our last conference, passed
        in probation with you
    How you were borne in hand,
        how crossed; the instru-
        ments;
    Who wrought with them; and
        all things else that might
    To half a soul and to a notion
        crazed
    Say "Thus did Banquo."
I MUR.   You
    made it known to us.

MACBETH I did so; and went fur-
    ther, which is now
    Our point of second meeting.
        Do you find
    Your patience so predominant
        in your nature
    That you can let this go? Are
        you so gospeled
    To pray for this good man and
        for his issue,
    Whose heavy hand hath bowed
        you to the grave
    And beggared yours for ever?
I MUR.   We
    are men, my liege.
MACBETH Ay, in the catalogue ye
    go for men,
    As hounds and greyhounds,
        mongrels, spaniels, curs,
    Shoughs, water-rugs, and demi-
        wolves are clept
    All by the name of dogs. The
        valued file
    Distinguishes the swift, the
        slow, the subtle,
    The housekeeper, the hunter,
        every one
    According to the gift which
        bounteous nature
    Hath in him closed; whereby he
        does receive
    Particular addition, from the
        bill
    That writes them all alike; and
        so of men.
    Now, if you have a station in
        the file,
    Not i' the worst rank of man-
        hood, say 't;

---

mine eternal jewel . . . : have given my soul to the devil   *list:* field of battle
champion me . . . : fight with me to the death   *under fortune:* out of favor
passed in probation: reviewed the evidence   *borne in hand:* deceived   *crossed:*
thwarted   *instruments:* agents   *half a soul:* halfwit   *notion:* mind   *gos-
peled:* conditioned   *catalogue:* list   *go:* pass   *Shoughs* . . . : shaggy dogs.
water dogs, half-breeds   *clept:* called   *valued file:* list of values   *housekeeper:* watchdog   *closed:* given, invested   *addition:* title   *bill:* list   *in the
file:* in the list *or* in the military rank

And I will put that business in
your bosoms
Whose execution takes your enemy off,
Grapples you to the heart and
love of us,
Who wear our health but sickly
in his life,
Which in his death were perfect.

2 MUR.   I am one, my liege,
Whom the vile blows and buffets
of the world
Have so incensed that I am reck-
less what
I do to spite the world.

1 MUR.   And I another,
So weary with disasters, tugged
with fortune,
That I would set my life on any
chance,
To mend it or be rid on 't.

MACBETH   Both of
you
Know Banquo was your enemy.

MURDERERS   True, my lord.

MACBETH   So is he mine, and in
such bloody distance
That every minute of his being
thrusts
Against my near'st of life; and
though I could
With barefaced power sweep
him from my sight
And bid my will avouch it, yet
I must not,
For certain friends that are both
his and mine,
Whose loves I may not drop, but
wail his fall
Who I myself struck down. And
thence it is

That I to your assistance do
make love,
Masking the business from the
common eye
For sundry weighty reasons.

2 MUR.   We
shall, my lord,
Perform what you command us.

1 MUR.   Though our lives—

MACBETH   Your spirits shine
through you. Within this
hour at most
I will advise you where to plant
yourselves,
Acquaint you with the perfect
spy o' the time,
The moment on 't; for 't must be
done tonight,
And something from the palace
(always thought
That I require a clearness), and
with him,
To leave no rubs nor botches in
the work,
Fleance his son, that keeps him
company,
Whose absence is no less material to me
Than is his father's, must embrace the fate
Of that dark hour. Resolve yourselves apart;
I'll come to you anon.

MURDERERS   We are
resolved, my lord.

MACBETH   I'll call upon you straight.
Abide within.
            (*Exeunt* MURDERERS)
It is concluded. Banquo, thy
soul's flight,
If it find heaven, must find it
out tonight.

                              (*Exit*)

---

bosoms: trust, hearts   *Who wear . . . :* who have a perilous life so long as
he (Banquo) lives   *tugged with:* pulled about by   *set:* risk   *distance:* enmity
near'st of life: vital part   *avouch:* justify   *wail:* I must wail   *perfect spy
. . . :* knowledge of the exact time *or* most suitable time   *thought:* carried in
mind   *clearness:* freedom from suspicion   *rubs:* defects

Scene II. The same.

(*Enter* LADY MACBETH *and a* SERVANT)

LADY MACBETH Is Banquo gone from court?

SERV. Ay, madam, but returns again tonight.

LADY MACBETH Say to the King I would attend his leisure
For a few words.

SERV.   Madam, I will.
                    (*Exit*)

LADY MACBETH Naught's had, all's spent,
Where our desire is got without content.
'Tis safer to be that which we destroy
Than by destruction dwell in doubtful joy.
          (*Enter* MACBETH)
How now, my lord? Why do you keep alone,
Of sorriest fancies your companions making,
Using those thoughts which should indeed have died
With them they think on?
Things without all remedy
Should be without regard.
What's done is done.

MACBETH We have scotched the snake, not killed it.
She'll close and be herself, whilst our poor malice
Remains in danger of her former tooth.
But let the frame of things disjoint, both the worlds suffer,
Ere we will eat our meal in fear and sleep
In the affliction of these terrible dreams
That shake us nightly. Better be with the dead,
Whom we, to gain our peace, have sent to peace,
Than on the torture of the mind to lie
In restless ecstasy. Duncan is in his grave;
After life's fitful fever he sleeps well.
Treason has done his worst: nor steel nor poison,
Malice domestic, foreign levy, nothing,
Can touch him further.

LADY MACBETH   Come on.
Gentle my lord, sleek o'er your rugged looks;
Be bright and jovial among your guests tonight.

MACBETH So shall I, love; and so, I pray, be you.
Let your remembrance apply to Banquo;
Present him eminence both with eye and tongue:
Unsafe the while, that we
Must lave our honours in these flattering streams
And make our faces vizards to our hearts,
Disguising what they are.

LADY MACBETH   You must leave this.

MACBETH O, full of scorpions is my mind, dear wife!
Thou know'st that Banquo, and his Fleance, lives.

---

sorriest: most contemptible   *Using:* consorting with   *scotched:* gashed, cut   *close:* heal   *poor malice:* feeble opposition   *let the frame . . . :* Macbeth would rather the universe fall apart than endure tormenting nightmares   *ecstasy:* strong emotion   *Malice domestic:* civil war   *eminence:* high rank   *lave:* dip   *vizards:* masks

LADY MACBETH But in them Nature's copy's not eterne.

MACBETH There's comfort yet; they are assailable.
Then be thou jocund. Ere the bat hath flown
His cloistered flight, ere to black Hecate's summons
The shard-borne beetle with his drowsy hums
Hath rung night's yawning peal, there shall be done
A deed of dreadful note.

LADY MACBETH What's to be done?

MACBETH Be innocent of the knowledge, dearest chuck,
Till thou applaud the deed. Come, seeling night,
Scarf up the tender eye of pitiful day,
And with thy bloody and invisible hand
Cancel and tear to pieces that great bond
Which keeps me pale! Light thickens, and the crow
Makes wing to the rooky wood.
Good things of day begin to droop and drowse,
Whiles night's black agents to their preys do rouse.
Thou marvell'st at my words; but hold thee still:
Things bad begun make strong themselves by ill.
So prithee go with me.

(*Exeunt*)

Scene III. The same. A park near the Palace.

(*Enter three* MURDERERS)

1 MUR. But who did bid thee join with us?

3 MUR. Macbeth.

2 MUR. He needs not our mistrust, since he delivers
Our offices, and what we have to do,
To the direction just.

1 MUR. Then stand with us.
The west yet glimmers with some streaks of day.
Now spurs the lated traveler apace
To gain the timely inn, and near approaches
The subject of our watch.

3 MUR. Hark!
I hear horses.

BANQUO (*within*) Give us a light there, ho!

2 MUR. Then 'tis he! The rest
That are within the note of expectation
Already are i' the court.

1 MUR. His horses go about.

3 MUR. Almost a mile; but he does usually,
So all men do, from hence to the palace gate
Make it their walk.

(*Enter* BANQUO *and* FLEANCE, *with a torch*)

2 MUR. A light, a light!

3 MUR. 'Tis he.

---

eterne: eternal   *shard-borne:* on hard or scaly wings   *chuck:* chick, an endearing term   *seeling:* eye-closing   *great bond:* Banquo's lease on life   *pale:* frightened   *rooky:* wood full of rooks (birds)   *go with me:* accompany me as we leave   *He needs not . . . :* we need not mistrust him   *delivers . . . :* reports our duties   *direction just:* precisely as Macbeth ordered   *timely:* in good time, early enough   *note of expectation:* list of those expected   *go about:* take a longer way

1 MUR.   Stand to 't.

BANQUO   It will be rain tonight.

1 MUR.   Let
it come down!
          (*They set upon* BANQUO)

BANQUO   O, treachery! Fly, good
Fleance, fly, fly, fly!
Thou mayst revenge. O slave!
          (*Dies.* FLEANCE *escapes*)

3 MUR.   Who did strike out the
light?

1 MUR.   Was 't not the way?

3 MUR.   There's but one down; the
son is fled.

2 MUR.   We have lost
Best half of our affair.

1 MUR.   Well, let's away, and say
how much is done.
                    (*Exeunt*)

Scene IV. The same. Hall in the
      Palace.

(*Banquet prepared. Enter*
MACBETH, LADY MACBETH,
ROSS, LENNOX, LORDS, *and*
ATTENDANTS)

MACBETH   You know your own degrees, sit down. At first
And last the hearty welcome.

LORDS   Thanks to your Majesty.

MACBETH   Ourself will mingle with
society
And play the humble host.
Our hostess keeps her state, but
in best time
We will require her welcome.

LADY MACBETH   Pronounce it for
me, sir, to all our friends,
For my heart speaks they are
welcome.

(FIRST MURDERER *appears
at the door*)

MACBETH   See, they encounter thee
with their hearts' thanks.
Both sides are even: here I'll
sit i' the midst.
Be large in mirth; anon we'll
drink a measure
The table round. (*Moves toward
MURDERER at door*) There's
blood upon thy face.

MUR.   'Tis Banquo's then.

MACBETH   'Tis better thee without
than he within.
Is he dispatched?

MUR.   My lord, his throat is cut.
That I did for him.

MACBETH   Thou art the best o' the
cutthroats! Yet he's good
That did the like for Fleance. If
thou didst it,
Thou art the nonpareil.

MUR.   Most royal
sir,
Fleance is 'scaped.

MACBETH (*aside*)   Then comes my
fit again. I had else been
perfect;
Whole as the marble, founded
as the rock,
As broad and general as the casing air.
But now I am cabined, cribbed,
confined, bound in
To saucy doubts and fears.—But
Banquo's safe?

MUR.   Ay, my good lord. Safe in a
ditch he bides,
With twenty trenched gashes on
his head,
The least a death to nature.

---

degrees: ranks   *At first . . . :* from beginning to end   *society:* the company gathered   *keeps her state:* remains seated in her chair of state   *require:*
request   *large:* generous   *'Tis better thee . . . :* It is better for Banquo's blood
to be on your face than in his veins   *perfect:* sound of health   *broad and general:* free and unconfined   *casing:* surrounding   *saucy:* insolent   *trenched:*
deep

MACBETH   Thanks
for that!
There the grown serpent lies;
the worm that's fled
Hath nature that in time will
venom breed,
No teeth for the present. Get
thee gone. Tomorrow
We'll hear ourselves again.
                              (*Exit* MURDERER)
LADY MACBETH   My royal lord,
You do not give the cheer. The
feast is sold
That is not often vouched, while
'tis a-making,
'Tis given with welcome. To
feed were best at home.
From thence, the sauce to meat
is ceremony;
Meeting were bare without it.
                        (*Enter* THE GHOST *of Ban-
                        quo, and sits in* MAC-
                        BETH'S *place*)
MACBETH   Sweet remembrancer!
Now good digestion wait on ap-
petite,
And health on both!
LENNOX   May 't please your High-
ness sit.
MACBETH   Here had we now our
country's honour, roofed,
Were the graced person of our
Banquo present;
Who may I rather challenge for
unkindness
Than pity for mischance!
ROSS   His ab-
sence, sir,
Lays blame upon his promise.
Please 't your Highness
To grace us with your royal
company?

MACBETH   The table's full.
LENNOX   Here is a
place reserved, sir.
MACBETH   Where?
LENNOX   Here, my good lord. What
is 't that moves your High-
ness?
MACBETH   Which of you have done
this?
LORDS   What, my good lord?
MACBETH   Thou canst not say I did
it. Never shake
Thy gory locks at me.
ROSS   Gentlemen, rise. His High-
ness is not well.
LADY MACBETH   Sit, worthy friends.
My lord is often thus,
And hath been from his youth.
Pray you keep seat.
The fit is momentary; upon a
thought
He will again be well. If much
you note him,
You shall offend him and extend
his passion.
Feed, and regard him not.—Are
you a man?
MACBETH   Ay, and a bold one, that
dare look on that
Which might appall the devil.
LADY MACBETH   O
proper stuff!
This is the very painting of your
fear.
This is the air-drawn dagger
which you said
Led you to Duncan. O, these
flaws and starts
(Impostors to true fear) would
well become
A woman's story at a winter's
fire,

---

worm: serpent   *hear ourselves:* confer   *give the cheer:* extend hospitality
The feast is sold . . . : Unless the host constantly welcomes his guests, hospitality is
like that bought at a public place   *remembrancer:* reminder   *roofed:* under
this roof   *challenge:* reprove   *upon a thought:* in a moment   *extend his passion:* prolong his attack   *air-drawn:* painted on air *or* unsheathed in the air
flaws: outbursts

Authorized by her grandam.
Shame itself!
Why do you make such faces?
When all's done,
You look but on a stool.

MACBETH Prithee see there! behold! look! lo! How say you?
Why, what care I? If thou canst nod, speak too.
If charnel houses and our graves must send
Those that we bury back, our monuments
Shall be the maws of kites.

(GHOST *vanishes*)

LADY MACBETH   What, quite unmanned in folly?

MACBETH If I stand here, I saw him.

LADY MACBETH Fie, for shame!

MACBETH Blood hath been shed ere now, i' the olden time,
Ere humane statute purged the gentle weal;
Ay, and since too, murders have been performed
Too terrible for the ear. The time has been
That, when the brains were out, the man would die,
And there an end! But now they rise again,
With twenty mortal murders on their crowns,
And push us from our stools. This is more strange
Than such a murder is.

LADY MACBETH   My worthy lord,
Your noble friends do lack you.

MACBETH I do forget.
Do not muse at me, my most worthy friends.
I have a strange infirmity, which is nothing
To those that know me. Come, love and health to all!
Then I'll sit down. Give me some wine, fill full.

(*Re-enter* GHOST)

I drink to the general joy o' the whole table,
And to our dear friend Banquo, whom we miss.
Would he were here! To all, and him, we thirst,
And all to all.

LORDS   Our duties, and the pledge.

MACBETH Avaunt, and quit my sight! Let the earth hide thee!
Thy bones are marrowless, thy blood is cold;
Thou hast no speculation in those eyes
Which thou dost glare with!

LADY MACBETH   Think of this, good peers,
But as a thing of custom. 'Tis no other.
Only it spoils the pleasure of the time.

MACBETH What man dare, I dare.
Approach thou like the rugged Russian bear,
The armed rhinoceros, or the Hyrcan tiger;
Take any shape but that, and my firm nerves

Authorized by: on the word of *our monuments . . . :* the best way to prevent ghosts from haunting us is to permit kites (birds) to devour their bodies *Ere humane statute . . . :* before law purified the state *murders on their crowns:* murderous gashes on their heads *lack:* miss *thirst:* are anxious to drink *speculation:* power of vision or of intelligence *Hyrcan:* of a province in ancient Persia, Hyrcania

Shall never tremble. Or be alive again
And dare me to the desert with thy sword.
If trembling I inhabit then, protest me
The baby of a girl. Hence, horrible shadow!
Unreal mockery, hence!

(*Exit* GHOST)

Why, so!
Being gone,
I am a man again. Pray you sit still.

LADY MACBETH   You have displaced the mirth, broke the good meeting
With most admired disorder.

MACBETH   Can such things be,
And overcome us like a summer's cloud
Without our special wonder? You make me strange
Even to the disposition that I owe,
When now I think you can behold such sights
And keep the natural ruby of your cheeks
When mine is blanched with fear.

ROSS   What sights, my lord?

LADY MACBETH   I pray you speak not. He grows worse and worse;
Question enrages him. At once, good night.
Stand not upon the order of your going,
But go at once.

LENNOX   Good night, and better health
Attend his Majesty!

LADY MACBETH   A kind good night to all!

(*Exeunt* LORDS *and* ATTENDANTS)

MACBETH   It will have blood, they say: blood will have blood.
Stones have been known to move and trees to speak;
Augurs and understood relations have
By maggot-pies and choughs and rooks brought forth
The secret'st man of blood. What is the night?

LADY MACBETH   Almost at odds with morning, which is which.

MACBETH   How say'st thou that Macduff denies his person
At our great bidding?

LADY MACBETH   Did you send to him, sir?

MACBETH   I hear it by the way; but I will send.
There's not a one of them but in his house
I keep a servant fee'd. I will tomorrow
(And betimes I will) to the Weird Sisters.
More shall they speak; for now I am bent to know
By the worst means the worst. For mine own good
All causes shall give way. I am in blood
Stepped in so far that, should I wade no more,

---

desert: solitary place   *If trembling . . . :* if I continue trembling   *protest:* proclaim   *baby of a girl:* infant   *admired:* amazing   *like a summer's cloud:* suddenly   *You make me . . . . :* you make me question the nature I thought was mine   *When mine is blanched:* when my cheek is made pale   *Augurs:* omens *understood relations:* utterances or rumors correctly understood   *maggot-pies and choughs:* magpies and crows   *by the way:* casually   *fee'd:* paid   *betimes:* speedily   *bent:* determined   *causes:* considerations

Returning were as tedious as go
o'er.
Strange things I have in head,
that will to hand,
Which must be acted ere they
may be scanned.

LADY MACBETH You lack the season of all natures, sleep.

MACBETH Come, we'll to sleep. My
strange and self-abuse
Is the initiate fear that wants
hard use.
We are yet but young in deed.
(*Exeunt*)

Scene V. A heath.

(*Thunder. Enter the*
WITCHES, *meeting* HECATE)

1 WITCH Why, how now, Hecate?
You look angerly.

HEC. Have I not reason, beldams
as you are,
Saucy and overbold? How did
you dare
To trade and traffic with Mac-
beth
In riddles and affairs of death;
And I, the mistress of your
charms,
The close contriver of all harms,
Was never called to bear my
part
Or show the glory of our art?
And, which is worse, all you
have done
Hath been but for a wayward
son,
Spiteful and wrathful, who, as
others do,
Loves for his own ends, not for
you.

But make amends now. Get you
gone
And at the pit of Acheron
Meet me i' the morning. Thither
he
Will come to know his destiny.
Your vessels and your spells pro-
vide,
Your charms and everything be-
side.
I am for the air. This night I'll
spend
Unto a dismal and a fatal end.
Great business must be wrought
ere noon.
Upon the corner of the moon
There hangs a vaporous drop
profound.
I'll catch it ere it come to
ground;
And that, distilled by magic
sleights,
Shall raise such artificial sprites
As by the strength of their illu-
sion
Shall draw him on to his con-
fusion.
He shall spurn fate, scorn death,
and bear
His hopes 'bove wisdom, grace,
and fear;
And you all know security
Is mortals' chiefest enemy.
(*Music and a song within.*
"Come away, come away,"
etc.)
Hark! I am called. My little
spirit, see,
Sits in a foggy cloud and stays
for me.
(*Exit*)

1 WITCH Come, let's make haste.

---

season: preservative, restorer　*self-abuse:* delusion　*initiate fear:* beginner's fear　*wants:* lacks　*beldams:* old crones　*close:* secret　*pit of Acheron:* the cavern where the Witches assemble in Act IV or, possibly, a reference to
the river in Hades　*dismal:* disastrous　*profound:* weighty　*sleights:* devices
confusion: ruin　*security:* over-confidence

She'll soon be back again.

(*Exeunt*)

Scene VI. Forres. The Palace.

(*Enter* LENNOX *and another* LORD)

LENNOX My former speeches have but hit your thoughts,
Which can interpret farther. Only I say
Things have been strangely borne. The gracious Duncan
Was pitied of Macbeth. Marry, he was dead!
And the right valiant Banquo walked too late;
Whom, you may say (if 't please you) Fleance killed,
For Fleance fled. Men must not walk too late.
Who cannot want the thought how monstrous
It was for Malcolm and for Donalbain
To kill their gracious father? Damned fact!
How it did grieve Macbeth! Did he not straight,
In pious rage, the two delinquents tear,
That were the slaves of drink and thralls of sleep?
Was not that nobly done? Ay, and wisely too!
For 'twould have angered any heart alive
To hear the men deny 't. So that I say
He has borne all things well; and I do think
That, had he Duncan's sons under his key

(As, an 't please heaven, he shall not), they should find
What 'twere to kill a father. So should Fleance.
But peace! for from broad words, and 'cause he failed
His presence at the tyrant's feast, I hear
Macduff lives in disgrace. Sir, can you tell
Where he bestows himself?

LORD   The son of Duncan,
From whom this tyrant holds the due of birth,
Lives in the English court, and is received
Of the most pious Edward with such grace
That the malevolence of fortune nothing
Takes from his high respect. Thither Macduff
Is gone to pray the holy King upon his aid
To wake Northumberland and warlike Siward;
That by the help of these (with Him above
To ratify the work) we may again
Give to our tables meat, sleep to our nights,
Free from our feasts and banquets bloody knives,
Do faithful homage and receive free honours—
All which we pine for now. And this report
Hath so exasperate the King that he
Prepares for some attempt of war.

---

hit: matched   *borne:* managed   *cannot want . . . :* who cannot help thinking   *fact:* evil deed   *pious:* loyal   *an't please:* if it please   *broad:* frank, plain   *tyrant's:* usurper's   *holds the due of birth:* withholds his birthright   *his high respect:* respect for him   *upon his aid:* for Edward's assistance   *wake:* arouse   *free honours:* earned or untainted honors

LENNOX   Sent he to Macduff?
LORD   He did; and with an abso-
    lute "Sir, not I!"
    The cloudy messenger turns me
        his back
    And hums, as who should say,
        "You'll rue the time
    That clogs me with this an-
        swer."
LENNOX   And that well might
    Advise him to a caution to hold
        what distance
    His wisdom can provide. Some
        holy angel
    Fly to the court of England and
        unfold
    His message ere he come, that
        a swift blessing
    May soon return to this our suf-
        fering country
    Under a hand accursed!
LORD   I'll send
    my prayers with him.
                            (*Exeunt*)

ACT IV

Scene I. A cavern. In the middle,
    a boiling cauldron.

(*Thunder. Enter the* THREE
    WITCHES)
1 WITCH   Thrice the brinded cat
    hath mewed.
2 WITCH   Thrice, and once the
    hedge-pig whined.
3 WITCH   Harpier cries; 'tis time,
    'tis time.
1 WITCH   Round about the caul-
    dron go;
    In the poisoned entrails throw.

Toad, that under cold stone
Days and nights has thirty-one
Sweltered venom sleeping got,
Boil thou first i' the charmed
    pot.
ALL   Double, double, toil and trou-
    ble;
    Fire burn, and cauldron bubble.
2 WITCH   Fillet of a fenny snake,
    In the cauldron boil and bake;
    Eye of newt, and toe of frog,
    Wool of bat, and tongue of dog,
    Adder's fork, and blindworm's
        sting,
    Lizard's leg, and howlet's wing;
    For a charm of powerful trouble
    Like a hell-broth boil and bub-
        ble.
ALL   Double, double, toil and trou-
    ble;
    Fire burn, and cauldron bubble.
3 WITCH   Scale of dragon, tooth
    of wolf,
    Witch's mummy, maw and gulf
    Of the ravined salt-sea shark,
    Root of hemlock, digged i' the
        dark;
    Liver of blaspheming Jew,
    Gall of goat, and slips of yew
    Slivered in the moon's eclipse;
    Nose of Turk and Tartar's lips;
    Finger of birth-strangled babe
    Ditch-delivered by a drab:
    Make the gruel thick and slab.
    Add thereto a tiger's chaudron
    For the ingredients of our caul-
        dron.
ALL   Double, double, toil and trou-
    ble;
    Fire burn, and cauldron bubble.
2 WITCH   Cool it with a baboon's
    blood,

---

cloudy: sullen, angry   *clogs:* encumbers   *Advise him . . . :* warn him to
keep at as safe a distance as he can contrive   *brinded cat:* Graymalkin
Harpier: the Witch's familiar   *Sweltered:* sweated   *Fillet:* slice   *fenny:* from
the fen (swamp)   *fork:* forked tongue   *mummy:* powder prepared from mum-
mies   *gulf:* gullet (throat)   *ravined:* ravenous   *slab:* sticky, thick   *chau-
dron:* entrails

Then the charm is firm and good.
(*Enter* HECATE *to the other* THREE WITCHES)

HEC. O, well done! I commend your pains,
And every one shall share i' the gains.
And now about the cauldron sing
Like elves and fairies in a ring,
Enchanting all that you put in.
(*Music and a song,* "Black spirit," *etc.*)

2 WITCH By the pricking of my thumbs,
Something wicked this way comes.
Open locks,
Whoever knocks!
(*Enter* MACBETH)

MACBETH How now, you secret, black, and midnight hags?
What is 't you do?

ALL A deed without a name.

MACBETH I conjure you by that which you profess
(Howe'er you come to know it), answer me.
Though you untie the winds and let them fight
Against the churches; though the yesty waves
Confound and swallow navigation up;
Though bladed corn be lodged and trees blown down;
Though castles topple on their warders' heads;
Though palaces and pyramids do slope
Their heads to their foundations; though the treasure
Of nature's germens tumble all together,
Even till destruction sicken— answer me
To what I ask you.

1 WITCH Speak.

2 WITCH Demand.

3 WITCH We'll answer.

1 WITCH Say, if th' hadst rather hear it from our mouths
Or from our masters.

MACBETH Call 'em!
Let me see 'em.

1 WITCH Pour in sow's blood, that hath eaten
Her nine farrow; grease that's sweaten
From the murderer's gibbet throw
Into the flame.

ALL Come, high or low;
Thyself and office deftly show!
(*Thunder. First* APPARITION, *an Armed Head*)

MACBETH Tell me, thou unknown power—

1 WITCH He knows thy thought.
Hear his speech, but say thou naught.

1 APPAR. Macbeth! Macbeth! Macbeth! Beware Macduff;
Beware the Thane of Fife. Dismiss me. Enough.
(*Descends*)

MACBETH Whate'er thou art, for thy good caution thanks!
Thou hast harped my fear aright. But one word more—

1 WITCH He will not be commanded. Here's another,
More potent than the first.
(*Thunder. Second* APPARITION, *a Bloody Child*)

---

by that which you . . . : by the power you claim to have   *yesty:* foamy
Confound: destroy   *lodged:* beaten down   *slope:* bend   *germens:* seeds
Armed Head: perhaps Macbeth's decapitated head which Macduff later presents
to Malcolm, perhaps merely a symbol of Macduff's rebellion   *harped:* guessed
or expressed   *Bloody Child:* Macduff

2 APPAR. Macbeth! Macbeth! Macbeth!

MACBETH Had I three ears, I'd hear thee.

2 APPAR. Be bloody, bold, and resolute; laugh to scorn
The power of man, for none of woman born
Shall harm Macbeth.
    (*Descends*)

MACBETH Then live, Macduff.
What need I fear of thee?
But yet I'll make assurance double sure
And take a bond of fate. Thou shalt not live!
That I may tell pale-hearted fear it lies
And sleep in spite of thunder.
    (*Thunder. Third* APPARITION, *a Child Crowned, with a tree in his hand*)
    What is this
That rises like the issue of a king
And wears upon his baby-brow the round
And top of sovereignty?

ALL   Listen, but speak not to 't.

3 APPAR. Be lion-mettled, proud, and take no care
Who chafes, who frets, or where conspirers are.
Macbeth shall never vanquished be until
Great Birnam Wood to high Dunsinane Hill
Shall come against him.
    (*Descends*)

MACBETH   That will never be.

Who can impress the forest, bid the tree
Unfix his earth-bound root?
Sweet bodements, good!
Rebellious dead rise never till the Wood
Of Birnam rise, and our high-placed Macbeth
Shall live the lease of nature, pay his breath
To time and mortal custom. Yet my heart
Throbs to know one thing. Tell me, if your art
Can tell so much—shall Banquo's issue ever
Reign in this kingdom?

ALL   Seek to know no more.

MACBETH I will be satisfied. Deny me this,
And an eternal curse fall on you!
Let me know.
Why sinks that cauldron? and what noise is this?
    (*Hautboys*)

1 WITCH Show!

2 WITCH Show!

3 WITCH Show!

ALL Show his eyes, and grieve his heart!
Come like shadows, so depart!
    (*A show of eight* KINGS, *the eighth with a glass in his hand, and* THE GHOST *of Banquo last*)

MACBETH Thou art too like the spirit of Banquo. Down!
Thy crown does sear mine eyeballs. And thy hair,
Thou other gold-bound brow, is like the first.

But yet I'll . . . : By killing Macduff, Macbeth will compel Fate to fulfill the promise that none born of woman will harm him, thus making "double sure" *Child Crowned:* Malcolm   *Birnam Wood:* a hill some 12 miles from Dunsinane *impress:* enlist   *Rebellious dead:* some editors believe that Shakespeare wrote "Rebellion's head," meaning an opposing armed force; "Rebellious dead" probably means Banquo   *lease of nature:* span of life   *mortal custom:* natural death *glass:* mirror

A third is like the former. Filthy hags!

Why do you show me this? A fourth? Start, eyes!

What, will the line stretch out to the crack of doom?

Another yet? A seventh? I'll see no more.

And yet the eighth appears, who bears a glass

Which shows me many more; and some I see

That twofold balls and treble scepters carry.

Horrible sight! Now I see 'tis true;

For the blood-boltered Banquo smiles upon me

And points at them for his. (APPARITIONS *descend*) What? Is this so?

1 WITCH   Ay, sir, all this is so. But why

Stands Macbeth thus amazedly?

Come, sisters, cheer we up his sprites

And show the best of our delights.

I'll charm the air to give a sound

While you perform your antic round,

That this great king may kindly say

Our duties did his welcome pay.
(*Music. The* WITCHES *dance, and vanish*)

MACBETH   Where are they? Gone? Let this pernicious hour

Stand aye accursed in the calendar!

Come in, without there!
(*Enter* LENNOX)

LENNOX   What's your Grace's will?

MACBETH   Saw you the Weird Sisters?

LENNOX   No, my lord.

MACBETH   Came they not by you?

LENNOX   No indeed, my lord.

MACBETH   Infected be the   air whereon they ride,

And damned all those that trust them! I did hear

The galloping of horse. Who was 't came by?

LENNOX   'Tis two or three, my lord, that bring you word

Macduff is fled to England.

MACBETH   Fled to England?

LENNOX   Ay, my good lord.

MACBETH (*aside*)   Time, thou anticipatest my dread exploits.

The flighty purpose never is o'ertook

Unless the deed go with it. From this moment

The very firstlings of my heart shall be

The firstlings of my hand. And even now,

To crown my thoughts with acts, be it thought and done!

The castle of Macduff I will surprise,

Seize upon Fife, give to the edge o' the sword

His wife, his babes, and all unfortunate souls

That trace him in his line. No boasting like a fool!

This deed I'll do before this purpose cool.

But no more sights!—Where are these gentlemen?

Come, bring me where they are.
(*Exeunt*)

---

blood-boltered: hair matted with blood   *amazedly:* in a trance   *antic round:* wild or fantastic dance   *flighty:* swift

Scene II. Fife. Macduff's Castle.

(Enter LADY MACDUFF, *her* SON, *and* ROSS*)*

LADY MACDUFF What had he done
    to make him fly the land?

ROSS You must have patience,
    madam.

LADY MACDUFF He had none.
    His flight was madness. When
      our actions do not,
    Our fears do make us traitors.

ROSS   You know not
    Whether it was his wisdom or
      his fear.

LADY MACDUFF Wisdom? To leave
    his wife, to leave his babes,
    His mansion, and his titles, in
      a place
    From whence himself does fly?
      He loves us not,
    He wants the natural touch. For
      the poor wren,
    (The most diminutive of birds)
      will fight,
    Her young ones in her nest,
      against the owl.
    All is the fear, and nothing is
      the love,
    As little is the wisdom, where
      the flight
    So runs against all reason.

ROSS   My
    dearest coz,
    I pray you school yourself. But
      for your husband,
    He is noble, wise, judicious, and
      best knows
    The fits o' the season. I dare not
      speak much further;
    But cruel are the times, when
      we are traitors

And do not know ourselves;
    when we hold rumor
From what we fear, yet know
    not what we fear,
But float upon a wild and vio-
    lent sea
Each way and none—I take my
    leave of you.
Shall not be long but I'll be here
    again.
Things at the worst will cease,
    or else climb upward
To what they were before.—My
    pretty cousin,
Blessing upon you!

LADY MACDUFF Fathered he is, and
    yet he's fatherless.

ROSS I am so much a fool, should
    I stay longer,
    It would be my disgrace and
      your discomfort.
    I take my leave at once.

                  (Exit)

LADY MACDUFF   Sirrah,
    your father's dead;
    And what will you do now? How
      will you live?

SON As birds do, mother.

LADY MACDUFF   What,
    with worms and flies?

SON With what I get, I mean; and
    so do they.

LADY MACDUFF Poor bird! thou'dst
    never fear the net nor lime,
    The pitfall nor the gin.

SON Why should I, mother? Poor
    birds they are not set for.
    My father is not dead, for all
      your saying.

LADY MACDUFF Yes, he is dead.
    How wilt thou do for a
    father?

---

    titles: possessions   *natural touch:* instinct to protect one's offspring   *fits o' the season:* violent events *or* emergencies which the future may produce   *And do not . . . :* without recognizing it   *when we hold rumor . . . :* we believe rumors because of fear   *lime:* a sticky substance used to catch birds   *gin:* snare

SON   Nay, how will you do for a husband?

LADY MACDUFF   Why, I can buy me twenty at any market.

SON   Then you'll buy 'em to sell again.

LADY MACDUFF   Thou speak'st with all thy wit; and yet, i' faith, With wit enough for thee.

SON   Was my father a traitor, mother?

LADY MACDUFF   Ay, that he was!

SON   What is a traitor?

LADY MACDUFF   Why, one that swears, and lies.

SON   And be all traitors that do so?

LADY MACDUFF   Every one that does so is a traitor and must be hanged.

SON   And must they all be hanged that swear and lie?

LADY MACDUFF   Every one.

SON   Who must hang them?

LADY MACDUFF   Why, the honest men.

SON   Then the liars and swearers are fools; for there are liars and swearers enow to beat the honest men and hang up them.

LADY MACDUFF   Now God help thee, poor monkey!
But how wilt thou do for a father?

SON   If he were dead, you'd weep for him. If you would not, it were a good sign that I should quickly have a new father.

LADY MACDUFF   Poor prattler, how thou talk'st!

(*Enter a* MESSENGER)

MESS.   Bless you, fair dame! I am not to you known,
Though in your state of honor I am perfect.
I doubt some danger does approach you nearly.
If you will take a homely man's advice,
Be not found here. Hence with your little ones!
To fright you thus methinks I am too savage;
To do worse to you were fell cruelty,
Which is too nigh your person. Heaven preserve you!
I dare abide no longer.

(*Exit*)

LADY MACDUFF   Whither should I fly?
I have done no harm. But I remember now
I am in this earthly world, where to do harm
Is often laudable, to do good sometime
Accounted dangerous folly. Why then, alas,
Do I put up that womanly defense
To say I have done no harm?—
What are these faces?

(*Enter* MURDERERS)

MUR.   Where is your husband?

LADY MACDUFF   I hope, in no place so unsanctified
Where such as thou mayst find him.

MUR.   He's a traitor.

SON   Thou liest, thou shag-eared villain!

MUR.   What, you egg!
(*Stabbing him*)
Young fry of treachery!

SON   He has killed me, mother.
Run away, I pray you!

---

swears, and lies: swears to tell the truth and then lies   *Though in your state . . . :* I know your rank well   *doubt:* fear   *shag-eared:* some editors change this to read "shag-haired"   *egg:* i.e., unhatched traitor

(Dies)

(Exit LADY MACDUFF, *crying* "Murder!" *followed by* MURDERERS)

Scene III. England. Before the King's Palace.

(Enter MALCOLM *and* MACDUFF)

MALCOLM   Let us seek out some desolate shade, and there
Weep our sad bosoms empty.

MACDUFF   Let us rather
Hold fast the mortal sword and, like good men,
Bestride our downfall'n birthdom. Each new morn
New widows howl, new orphans cry, new sorrows
Strike heaven on the face, that it resounds
As if it felt with Scotland and yelled out
Like syllable of dolor.

MALCOLM   What I believe, I'll wail;
What know, believe; and what I can redress,
As I shall find the time to friend, I will.
What you have spoke, it may be so perchance.
This tyrant, whose sole name blisters our tongues,
Was once thought honest; you have loved him well;
He hath not touched you yet. I am young; but something
You may discern of him through me, and wisdom

To offer up a weak, poor, innocent lamb
T' appease an angry god.

MACDUFF   I am not treacherous.

MALCOLM   But Macbeth is.
A good and virtuous nature may recoil
In an imperial charge. But I shall crave your pardon.
That which you are, my thoughts cannot transpose.
Angels are bright still, though the brightest fell.
Though all things foul would wear the brows of grace,
Yet grace must still look so.

MACDUFF   I have lost my hopes.

MALCOLM   Perchance even there where I did find my doubts.
Why in that rawness left you wife and child,
Those precious motives, those strong knots of love,
Without leave-taking? I pray you,
Let not my jealousies be your dishonours,
But mine own safeties. You may be rightly just,
Whatever I shall think.

MACDUFF   Bleed, bleed, poor country!
Great tyranny, lay thou thy basis sure,
For goodness dare not check thee! Wear thou thy wrongs;
The title is affeered! Fare thee well, lord.
I would not be the villain that thou think'st

---

birthdom: fatherland   *to friend:* friendly, favorable   *sole:* mere   *I am young . . . :* I am young and inexperienced and you may betray me to Macbeth so as to gain favor   *may recoil . . . :* yield to royal orders   *transpose:* change   *rawness:* unprotected condition   *jealousies:* suspicions   *wrongs:* ill-gotten benefits   *affeered:* confirmed

For the whole space that's in the tyrant's grasp
And the rich East to boot.

MALCOLM   Be not offended.
I speak not as in absolute fear of you.
I think our country sinks beneath the yoke;
It weeps, it bleeds, and each new day a gash
Is added to her wounds. I think withal
There would be hands uplifted in my right;
And here from gracious England have I offer
Of goodly thousands. But, for all this,
When I shall tread upon the tyrant's head
Or wear it on my sword, yet my poor country
Shall have more vices than it had before,
More suffer and more sundry ways than ever,
By him that shall succeed.

MACDUFF   What should he be?

MALCOLM   It is myself I mean; in whom I know
All the particulars of vice so grafted
That, when they shall be opened, black Macbeth
Will seem as pure as snow, and the poor state
Esteem him as a lamb, being compared
With my confineless harms.

MACDUFF   Not in the legions
Of horrid hell can come a devil more damned

In evils to top Macbeth.

MALCOLM   I grant him bloody,
Luxurious, avaricious, false, deceitful,
Sudden, malicious, smacking of every sin
That has a name. But there's no bottom, none,
In my voluptuousness. Your wives, your daughters,
Your matrons, and your maids could not fill up
The cistern of my lust; and my desire
All continent impediments would o'erbear
That did oppose my will. Better Macbeth
Than such an one to reign.

MACDUFF   Boundless intemperance
In nature is a tyranny. It hath been
The untimely emptying of the happy throne
And fall of many kings. But fear not yet
To take upon you what is yours. You may
Convey your pleasures in a spacious plenty,
And yet seem cold—the time you may so hoodwink.
We have willing dames enough. There cannot be
That vulture in you to devour so many
As will to greatness dedicate themselves,
Finding it so inclined.

MALCOLM   With this there grows
In my most ill-composed affection such

---

opened: exposed   *confineless:* limitless   *Luxurious:* lascivious   *Sudden:* violent   *continent:* restraining   *Convey:* plan (manage) secretly   *affection:* disposition

A stanchless avarice that, were
　　I King,
I should cut off the nobles for
　　their lands,
Desire his jewels, and this
　　other's house,
And my more-having would be
　　as a sauce
To make me hunger more, that
　　I should forge
Quarrels unjust against the
　　good and loyal,
Destroying them for wealth.

MACDUFF　　　　　　　　This
　　avarice
Sticks deeper, grows with more
　　pernicious root
Than summer-seeming lust; and
　　it hath been
The sword of our slain kings.
　　Yet do not fear.
Scotland hath foisons to fill up
　　your will
Of your mere own. All these are
　　portable,
With other graces weighed.

MALCOLM　But I have none. The
　　king-becoming graces,
As justice, verity, temperance,
　　stableness,
Bounty, perseverance, mercy,
　　lowliness,
Devotion, patience, courage, for-
　　titude,
I have no relish of them, but
　　abound
In the division of each several
　　crime,
Acting it many ways. Nay, had
　　I power, I should
Pour the sweet milk of concord
　　into hell,
Uproar the universal peace, con-
　　found
All unity on earth.

MACDUFF　　　　　　　O Scotland,
　　Scotland!

MALCOLM　If such a one be fit to
　　govern, speak.
I am as I have spoken.

MACDUFF　　　　　　　　Fit to
　　govern?
No, not to live. O nation miser-
　　able,
With an untitled tyrant bloody-
　　sceptered,
When shalt thou see thy whole-
　　some days again,
Since that the truest issue of
　　thy throne
By his own interdiction stands
　　accursed
And does blaspheme his breed?
　　Thy royal father
Was a most sainted king; the
　　queen that bore thee,
Oftener upon her knees than on
　　her feet,
Died every day she lived. Fare
　　thee well!
These evils thou repeat'st upon
　　thyself
Hath banished me from Scot-
　　land. O my breast,
Thy hope ends here!

MALCOLM　　　　　　Macduff, this
　　noble passion,
Child of integrity, hath from my
　　soul
Wiped the black scruples, rec-
　　onciled my thoughts
To thy good truth and honor.
　　Devilish Macbeth
By many of these trains hath
　　sought to win me
Into his power; and modest wis-
　　dom plucks me
From over-credulous haste; but
　　God above

---

　　　summer-seeming: temporary　　*foisons:* plenty　　*portable:* endurable　　*in-*
terdiction: ban *or* curse　　*blaspheme:* slander　　*Died:* did penance　　*trains:*
plots, devices

Deal between thee and me! for even now
I put myself to thy direction and
Unspeak mine own detraction, here abjure
The taints and blames I laid upon myself
For strangers to my nature. I am yet
Unknown to woman, never was forsworn,
Scarcely have coveted what was mine own,
At no time broke my faith, would not betray
The devil to his fellow, and delight
No less in truth than life. My first false speaking
Was this upon myself. What I am truly,
Is thine and my poor country's to command;
Whither indeed, before thy here-approach,
Old Siward with ten thousand warlike men
Already at a point was setting forth.
Now we'll together; and the chance of goodness
Be like our warranted quarrel! Why are you silent?

MACDUFF Such welcome and unwelcome things at once
'Tis hard to reconcile.

(*Enter a* DOCTOR)

MALCOLM Well, more anon. Comes the King forth, I pray you?

DOCT. Ay, sir. There are a crew of wretched souls
That stay his cure. Their malady convinces

The great assay of art; but at his touch,
Such sanctity hath heaven given his hand,
They presently amend.

MALCOLM   I thank you, doctor.

(*Exit* DOCTOR)

MACDUFF What's the disease he means?

MALCOLM   'Tis called the evil:
A most miraculous work in this good king,
Which often since my here-remain in England
I have seen him do. How he solicits heaven
Himself best knows; but strangely-visited people,
All swol'n and ulcerous, pitiful to the eye,
The mere despair of surgery, he cures,
Hanging a golden stamp about their necks,
Put on with holy prayers; and 'tis spoken,
To the succeeding royalty he leaves
The healing benediction. With this strange virtue,
He hath a heavenly gift of prophecy,
And sundry blessings hang about his throne
That speak him full of grace.

(*Enter* ROSS)

MACDUFF   See who comes here.

MALCOLM My countryman; but yet I know him not.

MACDUFF My ever gentle cousin, welcome hither.

---

at a point: prepared *goodness:* success *convinces . . . :* confuses medical science *presently:* immediately *the evil:* scrofula (enlarged lymphatic neck glands and, often, skin inflammations) *strangely-visited:* suffering from disease *mere:* complete *stamp:* coin *virtue:* power

MALCOLM   I know him now. Good
God betimes remove
The means that makes us stran-
gers!
ROSS   Sir, amen.
MACDUFF   Stands Scotland where
it did?
ROSS   Alas, poor country,
Almost afraid to know itself! It
cannot
Be called our mother, but our
grave; where nothing,
But who knows nothing, is once
seen to smile;
Where sighs and groans, and
shrieks that rent the air,
Are made, not marked; where
violent sorrow seems
A modern ecstasy. The dead
man's knell
Is there scarce asked for who;
and good men's lives
Expire before the flowers in their
caps,
Dying or ere they sicken.
MACDUFF   O, rela-
tion
Too nice, and yet too true!
MALCOLM   What's
the newest grief?
ROSS   That of an hour's age doth
hiss the speaker;
Each minute teems a new one.
MACDUFF   How does my wife?
ROSS   Why, well.
MACDUFF   And all my chil-
dren?
ROSS   Well too.
MACDUFF   The tyrant has not bat-
tered at their peace?
ROSS   No, they were well at peace
when I did leave 'em.
MACDUFF   Be not a niggard of your
speech. How goes 't?

ROSS   When I came hither to trans-
port the tidings
Which I have heavily borne,
there ran a rumor
Of many worthy fellows that
were out;
Which was to my belief wit-
nessed the rather
For that I saw the tyrant's power
afoot.
Now is the time of help. Your
eye in Scotland
Would create soldiers, make our
women fight
To doff their dire distresses.
MALCOLM   Be 't
their comfort
We are coming thither. Gracious
England hath
Lent us good Siward and ten
thousand men.
An older and a better soldier
none
That Christendom gives out.
ROSS   Would I could answer
This comfort with the like! But
I have words
That would be howled out in
the desert air,
Where hearing should not latch
them.
MACDUFF   What concern they?
The general cause? or is it a
fee-grief
Due to some single breast?
ROSS   No
mind that's honest
But in it shares some woe,
though the main part
Pertains to you alone.
MACDUFF   If it be
mine,
Keep it not from me, quickly
let me have it.

---

modern ecstasy: normal emotion   *teems:* produces   *were out:* in the field,
under arms   *Gracious England:* Edward the Confessor, King of England   *latch:*
catch   *fee-grief:* private sorrow

ROSS   Let not your ears despise my
      tongue for ever,
Which shall possess them with
      the heaviest sound
That ever yet they heard.
MACDUFF   Humh!
      I guess at it.
ROSS   Your castle is surprised; your
      wife and babes
Savagely slaughtered. To relate
      the manner
Were, on the quarry of these
      murdered deer,
To add the death of you.
MALCOLM   Merciful
      heaven!
What, man! Ne'er pull your hat
      upon your brows.
Give sorrow words. The grief
      that does not speak
Whispers the o'erfraught heart
      and bids it break.
MACDUFF   My children too?
ROSS   Wife,
      children, servants, all
That could be found.
MACDUFF   And I must
      be from thence?
My wife killed too?
ROSS   I have said.
MALCOLM   Be comforted.
Let's make us medicines of our
      great revenge
To cure this deadly grief.
MACDUFF   He has no children. All
      my pretty ones?
Did you say all? O hell-kite! All?
What, all my pretty chickens
      and their dam
At one fell swoop?
MALCOLM   Dispute it like a man.

MACDUFF   I shall do so;
But I must also feel it as a man.
I cannot but remember such
      things were
That were most precious to me.
      Did heaven look on
And would not take their part?
      Sinful Macduff,
They were all struck for thee!
      Naught that I am,
Not for their own demerits, but
      for mine,
Fell slaughter on their souls.
      Heaven rest them now!
MALCOLM   Be this the whetstone of
      your sword. Let grief
Convert to anger; blunt not the
      heart, enrage it.
MACDUFF   O, I could play the
      woman with mine eyes
And braggart with my tongue!
      But, gentle heavens,
Cut short all intermission. Front
      to front
Bring thou this fiend of Scot-
      land and myself.
Within my sword's length set
      him. If he 'scape,
Heaven forgive him too!
MALCOLM   This tune
      goes manly.
Come, go we to the King. Our
      power is ready;
Our lack is nothing but our
      leave. Macbeth
Is ripe for shaking, and the
      powers above
Put on their instruments. Re-
      ceive what cheer you may.
The night is long that never
      finds the day.
                        (*Exeunt*)

---

   quarry: heap (of slaughtered game)   *He has . . . :* Most editors agree that
the antecedent of "He" is Macbeth, not Malcolm   *Dispute:* fight   *Naught:* evil,
sinful   *intermission:* delay   *Front to front:* face to face   *power:* army   *Put
on . . . :* arm themselves

ACT V

Scene I. Dunsinane. Macbeth's
Castle.

(*Enter a* DOCTOR OF PHYSIC
and a WAITING GENTLE-
WOMAN)

DOCT. I have two nights watched
with you, but can perceive no
truth in your report. When was
it she last walked?

GENT. Since his Majesty went into
the field I have seen her rise
from her bed, throw her nightgown upon her, unlock her
closet, take forth paper, fold it,
write upon 't, read it, afterwards
seal it, and again return to bed;
yet all this while in a most fast
sleep.

DOCT. A great perturbation in nature, to receive at once the benefit of sleep and do the effects
of watching! In this slumbery
agitation, besides her walking
and other actual performances,
what (at any time) have you
heard her say?

GENT. That, sir, which I will not
report after her.

DOCT. You may to me, and 'tis
most meet you should.

GENT. Neither to you nor anyone,
having no witness to confirm my
speech.

(*Enter* LADY MACBETH,
with a taper)

Lo you, here she comes! This is
her very guise, and, upon my
life, fast asleep! Observe her;
stand close.

DOCT. How came she by that light?

GENT. Why, it stood by her. She
has light by her continually. 'Tis
her command.

DOCT. You see her eyes are open.

GENT. Ay, but their sense is shut.

DOCT. What is it she does now?
Look how she rubs her hands.

GENT. It is an accustomed action
with her, to seem thus washing
her hands. I have known her
continue in this a quarter of an
hour.

LADY MACBETH Yet here's a spot.

DOCT. Hark, she speaks! I will set
down what comes from her, to
satisfy my remembrance the
more strongly.

LADY MACBETH Out, damned spot!
out, I say! One; two. Why then
'tis time to do 't. Hell is murky.
Fie, my lord, fie! A soldier, and
afeard? What need we fear who
knows it, when none can call
our power to account? Yet who
would have thought the old
man to have had so much blood
in him?

DOCT. Do you mark that?

LADY MACBETH The Thane of Fife
had a wife. Where is she now?
What, will these hands ne'er
be clean? No more o' that, my
lord, no more o' that! You mar
all with this starting.

DOCT. Go to, go to! You have
known what you should not.

GENT. She has spoke what she
should not, I am sure of that.
Heaven knows what she has
known.

LADY MACBETH Here's the smell of
the blood still. All the perfumes
of Arabia will not sweeten this
little hand. Oh, oh, oh!

---

perturbation in nature: constitutional disorder *effects of watching:* actions of wakefulness *guise:* behavior *close:* concealed *satisfy:* support,
confirm

DOCT. What a sigh is there! The heart is sorely charged.

GENT. I would not have such a heart in my bosom for the dignity of the whole body.

DOCT. Well, well, well.

GENT. Pray God it be, sir.

DOCT. This disease is beyond my practice. Yet I have known those which have walked in their sleep who have died holily in their beds.

LADY MACBETH Wash your hands, put on your nightgown, look not so pale! I tell you yet again, Banquo's buried. He cannot come out on 's grave.

DOCT. Even so?

LADY MACBETH To bed, to bed! There's knocking at the gate. Come, come, come, come, give me your hand! What's done cannot be undone. To bed, to bed, to bed!

(*Exit*)

DOCT. Will she go now to bed?

GENT. Directly.

DOCT. Foul whisperings are abroad, Unnatural deeds
Do breed unnatural troubles. Infected minds
To their deaf pillows will discharge their secrets.
More needs she the divine than the physician.
God, God forgive us all! Look after her;
Remove from her the means of all annoyance,
And still keep eyes upon her. So good night.
My mind she has mated, and amazed my sight.
I think, but dare not speak.

GENT. Good night, good doctor.

(*Exeunt*)

Scene II. The country near Dunsinane.

(*Drum and Colors. Enter* MENTEITH, CAITHNESS, ANGUS, LENNOX, SOLDIERS)

MENTEITH The English power is near, led on by Malcolm,
His uncle Siward, and the good Macduff.
Revenges burn in them; for their dear causes
Would to the bleeding and the grim alarm
Excite the mortified man.

ANGUS Near Birnam Wood
Shall we well meet them; that way are they coming.

CAITHNESS Who knows if Donalbain be with his brother?

LENNOX For certain, sir, he is not. I have a file
Of all the gentry. There is Siward's son
And many unrough youths that even now
Protest their first of manhood.

MENTEITH What does the tyrant?

CAITHNESS Great Dunsinane he strongly fortifies.
Some say he's mad; others, that lesser hate him,
Do call it valiant fury; but for certain
He cannot buckle his distempered cause
Within the belt of rule.

ANGUS Now does he feel

---

charged: burdened *practice:* professional ability *annoyance:* injury (to herself) *mated:* bewildered *dear:* hearfelt *mortified:* dead *or* weakened *unrough:* beardless *Protest:* proclaim *He cannot buckle . . . :* he is unable to control his diseased passion

His secret murders sticking on his hands.
Now minutely revolts upbraid his faith-breach.
Those he commands move only in command,
Nothing in love. Now does he feel his title
Hang loose about him, like a giant's robe
Upon a dwarfish thief.

MENTEITH   Who then shall blame
His pestered senses to recoil and start,
When all that is within him does condemn
Itself for being there?

CAITHNESS   Well, march we on
To give obedience where 'tis truly owed.
Meet we the medicine of the sickly weal;
And with him pour we in our country's purge
Each drop of us.

LENNOX   Or so much as it needs
To dew the sovereign flower and drown the weeds.
Make we our march towards Birnam.

(Exeunt, marching)

Scene III. Dunsinane. A room in the Castle.

(Enter MACBETH, DOCTOR, *and* ATTENDANTS*)*

MACBETH   Bring me no more reports. Let them fly all!
Till Birnam Wood remove to Dunsinane,
I cannot taint with fear. What's the boy Malcolm?
Was he not born of woman? The spirits that know
All mortal consequences have pronounced me thus:
"Fear not, Macbeth. No man that's born of woman
Shall e'er have power upon thee." Then fly, false thanes,
And mingle with the English epicures.
The mind I sway by and the heart I bear
Shall never sag with doubt nor shake with fear.

(Enter SERVANT*)*
The devil damn thee black, thou cream-faced loon!
Where got'st thou that goose look?

SERV.   There is ten thousand—

MACBETH   Geese, villain?

SERV.   Soldiers, sir.

MACBETH   Go prick thy face and over-red thy fear,
Thou lily-livered boy. What soldiers, patch?
Death of thy soul! Those linen cheeks of thine
Are counselors to fear. What soldiers, whey-face?

SERV.   The English force, so please you.

MACBETH   Take thy face hence.
(Exit SERVANT*)*
Seyton!—I am sick at heart,
When I behold—Seyton, I say!
—This push
Will cheer me ever, or disseat me now.
I have lived long enough. My way of life

---

minutely: occurring every minute   *Let them . . . :* the thanes   *taint:* be infected   *epicures:* gluttons, i.e., no soldiers   *sway:* act, move   *lily-livered:* physiologists once held that the liver was the seat of courage   *patch:* fool   *counselors:* leaders, inducements   *push:* crisis, attack

Is fallen into the sere, the yellow
 leaf;
And that which should accompany old age,
As honour, love, obedience,
 troops of friends,
I must not look to have; but, in
 their stead,
Curses not loud but deep, mouth-
 honour, breath,
Which the poor heart would fain
 deny, and dare not.
Seyton!

(*Enter* SEYTON)

SEYTON What's your gracious pleasure?

MACBETH What news more?

SEYTON All is confirmed, my lord,
 which was reported.

MACBETH I'll fight, till from my
 bones my flesh be hacked.
 Give me my armor.

SEYTON   'Tis not needed
 yet.

MACBETH I'll put it on.
 Send out moe horses, skirr the
 country round;
 Hang those that talk of fear.
 Give me mine armor.
 How does your patient, doctor?

DOCT.   Not so sick, my lord,
 As she is troubled with thick-
 coming fancies
 That keep her from her rest.

MACBETH   Cure her of that!
 Canst thou not minister to a
 mind diseased,
 Pluck from the memory a rooted
 sorrow,
 Raze out the written troubles of
 the brain,
 And with some sweet oblivious
 antidote
 Cleanse the stuffed bosom of
 that perilous stuff
 Which weighs upon the heart?

DOCT.   Therein the patient
 Must minister to himself.

MACBETH Throw physic to the
 dogs, I'll none of it!—
 Come, put mine armor on. Give
 me my staff.
 Seyton, send out.—Doctor, the
 thanes fly from me.—
 Come, sir, dispatch.—If thou
 couldst, doctor, cast
 The water of my land, find her
 disease,
 And purge it to a sound and
 pristine health,
 I would applaud thee to the very
 echo,
 That should applaud again.—
 Pull 't off, I say.—
 What rhubarb, senna, or what
 purgative drug,
 Would scour these English
 hence? Hear'st thou of them?

DOCT. Ay, my good lord. Your
 royal preparation
 Makes us hear something.

MACBETH   Bring
 it after me!
 I will not be afraid of death and
 bane
 Till Birnam Forest come to Dunsinane.

DOCT. (*aside*) Were I from Dunsinane away and clear,
 Profit again should hardly draw
 me here.

(*Exeunt*)

Scene IV. Country near Birnam Wood.

(*Drum and Colors. Enter*
 MALCOLM, SIWARD, MAC-
 DUFF, SIWARD'S SON, MEN-
 TEITH, CAITHNESS, ANGUS,
 LENNOX, ROSS, *and* SOL-
 DIERS, *marching*)

---

sere: withered state   *moe:* more   *skirr:* scour   *Raze:* erase   *oblivious:*
causing forgetfulness   *cast / The water . . . :* make a urinalysis

MALCOLM   Cousins, I hope the days are near at hand
That chambers will be safe.

MENTEITH   We doubt it nothing.

SIWARD   What wood is this before us?

MENTEITH   The wood of Birnam.

MALCOLM   Let every soldier hew him down a bough
And bear 't before him. Thereby shall we shadow
The numbers of our host and make discovery
Err in report of us.

SOLDIERS   It shall be done.

SIWARD   We learn no other but the confident tyrant
Keeps still in Dunsinane and will endure
Our setting down before 't.

MALCOLM   'Tis his main hope;
For where there is advantage to be given,
Both more and less have given him the revolt;
And none serve with him but constrained things,
Whose hearts are absent too.

MACDUFF   Let our just censures
Attend the true event, and put we on
Industrious soldiership.

SIWARD   The time approaches
That will with due decision make us know
What we shall say we have, and what we owe.
Thoughts speculative their unsure hopes relate,
But certain issue strokes must arbitrate;
Towards which advance the war.
                    (*Exeunt, marching*)

Scene V. Dunsinane. Within the Castle.

(*Enter* MACBETH, SEYTON, *and* SOLDIERS, *with Drum and Colors*)

MACBETH   Hang out our banners on the outward walls.
The cry is still, "They come!" Our castle's strength
Will laugh a siege to scorn. Here let them lie
Till famine and the ague eat them up.
Were they not forced with those that should be ours,
We might have met them dareful, beard to beard,
And beat them backward home.
                    (*A cry within of women*)
                    What is that noise?

SEYTON   It is the cry of women, my good lord.
                    (*Exit*)

MACBETH   I have almost forgot the taste of fears.
The time has been, my senses would have cooled
To hear a night-shriek, and my fell of hair
Would at a dismal treatise rouse and stir
As life were in 't. I have supped full with horrors.
Direness, familiar to my slaughterous thoughts,
Cannot once start me.
                    (*Enter* SEYTON)

---

chambers: bedrooms (Malcolm is recalling his father's murder)   discovery: Macbeth's reconnaissance, or scouts   setting down: preparations for attack   forced: reinforced   dareful: boldly   fell of hair: hairy skin, scalp   treatise: story

Wherefore was that cry?

SEYTON The Queen, my lord, is dead.

MACBETH She should have died hereafter;
There would have been a time for such a word.
Tomorrow, and tomorrow, and tomorrow
Creeps in this petty pace from day to day
To the last syllable of recorded time;
And all our yesterdays have lighted fools
The way to dusty death. Out, out, brief candle!
Life's but a walking shadow, a poor player,
That struts and frets his hour upon the stage
And then is heard no more. It is a tale
Told by an idiot, full of sound and fury,
Signifying nothing.
(Enter a MESSENGER)
Thou com'st to use thy tongue. Thy story quickly!

MESS. Gracious my lord,
I should report that which I say I saw,
But know not how to do 't.

MACBETH   Well, say, sir!

MESS. As I did stand my watch upon the hill,
I looked toward Birnam, and anon methought
The wood began to move.

MACBETH   Liar and slave!

MESS. Let me endure your wrath if 't be not so.
Within this three mile may you see it coming;
I say, a moving grove.

MACBETH   If thou speak'st false,
Upon the next tree shalt thou hang alive,
Till famine cling thee. If thy speech be sooth,
I care not if thou dost for me as much.
I pull in resolution, and begin
To doubt the equivocation of the fiend,
That lies like truth. "Fear not, till Birnam Wood
Do come to Dunsinane!" and now a wood
Comes toward Dunsinane. Arm, arm, and out!
If this which he avouches does appear,
There is nor flying hence nor tarrying here.
I 'gin to be aweary of the sun,
And wish the estate o' the world were now undone.
Ring the alarum bell! Blow wind, come wrack,
At least we'll die with harness on our back!

(Exeunt)

Scene VI. Dunsinane. Before the Castle.

(Drum and Colors. Enter MALCOLM, SIWARD, MAC-DUFF, *and their* ARMY, *with boughs)*

MALCOLM Now near enough. Your leavy screens throw down
And show like those you are. You, worthy uncle,

She should have . . . : Possibly, her death ought to have been put off to a more convenient time   *word:* message, report   *cling thee:* shrivel you   *pull in:* check, rein   *harness:* armor   *leavy:* leafy

Shall with my cousin, your right noble son,
Lead our first battle. Worthy Macduff and we
Shall take upon 's what else remains to do,
According to our order.

SIWARD   Fare you well.
Do we but find the tyrant's power tonight,
Let us be beaten if we cannot fight.

MACDUFF   Make all our trumpets speak, give them all breath,
Those clamorous harbingers of blood and death.

(*Exeunt. Alarums continued*)

Scene VII. Another part of the field.

(*Enter* MACBETH)

MACBETH   They have tied me to a stake. I cannot fly,
But bearlike I must fight the course. What's he
That was not born of woman? Such a one
Am I to fear, or none.

(*Enter* YOUNG SIWARD)

Y. SIW.   What is thy name?

MACBETH   Thou'lt be afraid to hear it.

Y. SIW.   No; though thou call'st thyself a hotter name
Than any is in hell.

MACBETH   My name's Macbeth.

Y. SIW.   The devil himself could not pronounce a title
More hateful to mine ear.

MACBETH   No, nor more fearful.

Y. SIW.   Thou liest, abhorred tyrant! With my sword
I'll prove the lie thou speak'st.

(*Fight, and* YOUNG SIWARD *slain*)

MACBETH   Thou wast born of woman.
But swords I smile at, weapons laugh to scorn,
Brandished by man that's of a woman born.

(*Exit*)

(*Alarums. Enter* MACDUFF)

MACDUFF   That way the noise is. Tyrant, show thy face!
If thou beest slain and with no stroke of mine,
My wife and children's ghosts will haunt me still.
I cannot strike at wretched kerns, whose arms
Are hired to bear their staves. Either thou, Macbeth,
Or else my sword with an unbattered edge
I sheathe again undeeded. There thou shouldst be.
By this great clatter one of greatest note
Seems bruited. Let me find him, Fortune!
And more I beg not.

(*Exit. Alarums*)

(*Enter* MALCOLM *and* SIWARD)

SIWARD   This way, my lord. The castle's gently rendered:
The tyrant's people on both sides do fight;
The noble thanes do bravely in the war;
The day almost itself professes yours,
And little is to do.

---

battle: army of troops, division   *order:* battle plan   *bearlike:* bearbaiters chained bears to stakes in arenas and released dogs to attack them   *staves:* spears   *bruited:* announced   *rendered:* surrendered

MALCOLM We have met with foes
That strike beside us.

SIWARD Enter, sir, the castle.

(*Exeunt. Alarum*)

Scene VIII. Another part of the field.

(*Enter* MACBETH)

MACBETH Why should I play the Roman fool and die
On mine own sword? Whiles I see lives, the gashes
Do better upon them.

(*Enter* MACDUFF)

MACDUFF Turn, hell-hound, turn!

MACBETH Of all men else I have avoided thee.
But get thee back! My soul is too much charged
With blood of thine already.

MACDUFF I have no words;
My voice is in my sword, thou bloodier villain
Than terms can give thee out!

(*Fight. Alarum*)

MACBETH Thou losest labor.
As easy mayst thou the intrench-ant air
With thy keen sword impress as make me bleed.
Let fall thy blade on vulnerable crests.
I bear a charmed life, which must not yield
To one of woman born.

MACDUFF Despair thy charm!

And let the angel whom thou still hast served
Tell thee, Macduff was from his mother's womb
Untimely ripped.

MACBETH Accursed be that tongue that tells me so,
For it hath cowed my better part of man!
And be these juggling fiends no more believed,
That palter with us in a double sense,
That keep the word of promise to our ear
And break it to our hope! I'll not fight with thee!

MACDUFF Then yield thee, coward,
And live to be the show and gaze o' the time!
We'll have thee, as our rarer monsters are,
Painted upon a pole, and un-derwrit
"Here may you see the tyrant."

MACBETH I will not yield,
To kiss the ground before young Malcolm's feet
And to be baited with the rab-ble's curse.
Though Birnam Wood be come to Dunsinane,
And thou opposed, being of no woman born,
Yet I will try the last. Before my body
I throw my warlike shield. Lay on, Macduff,
And damned be him that first cries "Hold, enough!"

(*Exeunt fighting. Alarums*)

---

beside us: miss us   *Roman fool:* Roman officers often committed suicide to avoid dishonor; note Shakespeare's treatment of Brutus, Antony, Cassius   *terms can give:* words can describe   *intrenchant:* impenetrable   *angel:* demon   *still:* always   *cowed:* conquered (my spirit)   *Painted . . . :* i.e., on a placard stuck on a pole   *the last:* last resort, hope

(*Retreat and flourish. Enter, with Drum and Colors,* MALCOLM, *old* SIWARD, ROSS, THANES, *and* SOLDIERS)

MALCOLM   I would the friends we miss were safe arrived.

SIWARD   Some must go off; and yet, by these I see,
So great a day as this is cheaply bought.

MALCOLM   Macduff is missing, and your noble son.

ROSS   Your son, my lord, has paid a soldier's debt.
He only lived but till he was a man,
The which no sooner had his prowess confirmed
In the unshrinking station where he fought
But like a man he died.

SIWARD   Then he is dead?

ROSS   Ay, and brought off the field. Your cause of sorrow
Must not be measured by his worth, for then
It hath no end.

SIWARD   Had he his hurts before?

ROSS   Ay, on the front.

SIWARD   Why then, God's soldier be he!
Had I as many sons as I have hairs,
I would not wish them to a fairer death.
And so his knell is knolled.

MALCOLM   He's worth more sorrow,
And that I'll spend for him.

SIWARD   He's worth no more.
They say he parted well and paid his score,
And so, God be with him! Here comes newer comfort.

(*Enter* MACDUFF, *with* MACBETH'S *head*)

MACDUFF   Hail, King! for so thou art. Behold where stands
The usurper's cursed head. The time is free.
I see thee compassed with thy kingdom's pearl,
That speak my salutation in their minds;
Whose voices I desire aloud with mine—
Hail, King of Scotland!

ALL   Hail, King of Scotland!   (*Flourish*)

MALCOLM   We shall not spend a large expense of time
Before we reckon with your several loves
And make us even with you. My thanes and kinsmen,
Henceforth be earls, the first that ever Scotland
In such an honour named. What's more to do
Which would be planted newly with the time—
As calling home our exiled friends abroad
That fled the snares of watchful tyranny,
Producing forth the cruel ministers
Of this dead butcher and his fiendlike queen,
Who (as 'tis thought) by self and violent hands
Took off her life—this, and what needful else
That calls upon us, by the grace of Grace

---

go off: die   *unshrinking station:* position which he did not leave   *time:* (1) world; (2) nation   *pearl:* nobility   *reckon with:* reward   *self and . . . :* her own   *measure:* proper, suitable proportion

We will perform in measure,
time, and place.
So thanks to all at once and to
each one,

Whom we invite to see us
crowned at Scone.
(*Flourish. Exeunt omnes*)

· QUESTIONS ·

Your instructor will ask questions and provide suggestions for writing in accordance with the depth of your reading of *Macbeth* and the amount of time you have spent on the play. You might, however, review the suggestions for reading drama which precede this section. Also, if your interest in *Macbeth* has been aroused, you are urged to read *Macbeth: A Complete Guide to the Play* by Professor J. Wilson McCutchan (New York, 1963). This inexpensive paperback of only 128 pages will provide astoundingly rich comment to supplement your ideas about this great tragedy which, in the words of Marchette Chute, is "swift as night and dark as spilt blood, with death and battle and witchcraft bound together in wonderful poetry to tell the story of a man and woman who destroyed themselves."

PYGMALION

George Bernard Shaw

GEORGE BERNARD SHAW (1856–1950), Irish-born dramatist, critic, and tract writer, is considered by some the greatest English (British) dramatist since Shakespeare. Many scholars believe his best plays to be the greatest contribution to the English drama for more than a century. Certainly he was a master of razor-edged utterance which has provided audiences and readers keen intellectual satisfaction for many years. His career was too long and too brilliant for synopsis here, but you are urged to read something of his biography as an aid in studying *Pygmalion*. This play reveals and exploits Shaw's great interest in speech. His own speech was a model (at least in his own opinion); his ideas on scores of other subjects were keen and controversial, as are those exhibited in this drama.

ACT I

London at 11:15 P.M. *Torrents of heavy summer rain. Cab whistles blowing frantically in all directions. Pedestrians running for shelter into the portico of St. Paul's church (not Wren's cathedral but Inigo Jones's church in Covent Garden vegetable market), among them a lady and her daughter in evening dress. All are peering out gloomily at the rain, except one man with his back turned to the rest, wholly preoccupied with a notebook in which he is writing.*

 The church clock strikes the first quarter.

THE DAUGHTER (*in the space between the central pillars, close to the one on her left*) I'm getting chilled to the bone. What can Freddy be doing all this time? He's been gone twenty minutes.

THE MOTHER (*on her daughter's*

right) Not so long. But he ought to have got us a cab by this.

A BYSTANDER (*on the lady's right*) He wont[1] get no cab not until half-past eleven, missus, when they come back after dropping their theatre fares.

THE MOTHER   But we must have a cab. We cant stand here until half-past eleven. It's too bad.

THE BYSTANDER   Well, it ain't my fault, missus.

THE DAUGHTER   If Freddy had a bit of gumption, he would have got one at the theatre door.

THE MOTHER   What could he have done, poor boy?

THE DAUGHTER   Other people got cabs. Why couldnt he?

    (FREDDY *rushes in out of the rain from the South-ampton Street side, and comes between them clos-ing a dripping umbrella. He is a young man of twenty, in evening dress, very wet round the ankles*)

THE DAUGHTER   Well, havnt you got a cab?

FREDDY   Theres not one to be had for love or money.

THE MOTHER   Oh, Freddy, there must be one. You cant have tried.

THE DAUGHTER   It's too tiresome. Do you expect us to go and get one ourselves?

FREDDY   I tell you theyre all en-gaged. The rain was so sudden: nobody was prepared; and every-body had to take a cab. Ive been to Charing Cross one way and nearly to Ludgate Circus the other; and they were all en-gaged.

THE MOTHER   Did you try Trafal-gar Square?

FREDDY   There wasn't one at Tra-falgar Square.

THE DAUGHTER   Did you try?

FREDDY   I tried as far as Charing Cross Station. Did you expect me to walk to Hammersmith?

THE DAUGHTER   You havnt tried at all.

THE MOTHER   You really are very helpless, Freddy. Go again; and dont come back until you have found a cab.

FREDDY   I shall simply get soaked for nothing.

THE DAUGHTER   And what about us? Are we to stay here all night in this draught, with next to nothing on? You selfish pig—

FREDDY   Oh, very well: I'll go, I'll go.

    (*He opens his umbrella and dashes off Strand-wards, but comes into col-lision with a flower-girl who is hurrying in for shelter, knocking her bas-ket out of her hands. A blinding flash of light-ning, followed instantly by a rattling peal of thun-der, orchestrates the in-cident*)

THE FLOWER GIRL   Nah then, Freddy: look wh' y' gowin, deah.

FREDDY   Sorry. (*He rushes off*)

THE FLOWER GIRL (*picking up her scattered flowers and replacing them in the basket*) Theres

---

[1] Shaw was interested in phonetics, a reformed alphabet, and the omission of apostrophes in contractions. Normally, he retained this "useless" mark only when omission would be confusing (*I'll*, not *Ill*) or would affect pronunciation (*he's*, not *hes*).

menners f' yer! Tǝ-oo banches o voylets trod into the mad.[2]

(She sits down on the plinth of the column, sorting her flowers, on the lady's right. She is not at all a romantic figure. She is perhaps eighteen, perhaps twenty, hardly older. She wears a little sailor hat of black straw that has long been exposed to the dust and soot of London and has seldom if ever been brushed. Her hair needs washing rather badly: its mousy color can hardly be natural. She wears a shoddy black coat that reaches nearly to her knees and is shaped to her waist. She has a brown skirt with a coarse apron. Her boots are much the worse for wear. She is no doubt as clean as she can afford to be; but compared to the ladies she is very dirty. Her features are no worse than theirs; but their condition leaves something to be desired; and she needs the services of a dentist)

THE MOTHER   How do you know that my son's name is Freddy, pray?

THE FLOWER GIRL   Ow, eez yǝ-ooa san, ie e? Wal, fewd dan y' dǝ-ooty bawmz a mather should, eed now bettern to spawl a pore gel's flahrzn than ran awy athaht pyin. Will ye-oo py me f' them?

(Here, with apologies, this desperate attempt to represent her dialect without a phonetic alphabet must be abandoned as unintelligible outside London.)

THE DAUGHTER   Do nothing of the sort, mother. The idea!

THE MOTHER   Please allow me, Clara. Have you any pennies?

THE DAUGHTER   No. Ive nothing smaller than sixpence.

THE FLOWER GIRL   *(hopefully)*   I can give you change for a tanner, kind lady.

THE MOTHER   *(to CLARA)*   Give it to me. *(CLARA parts reluctantly)* Now. *(to the girl)* This is for your flowers.

THE FLOWER GIRL   Thank you kindly, lady.

THE DAUGHTER   Make her give you the change. These things are only a penny a bunch.

THE MOTHER   Do hold your tongue, Clara. *(to the girl)* You can keep the change.

THE FLOWER GIRL   Oh, thank you, lady.

THE MOTHER   Now tell me how you know that young gentleman's name.

THE FLOWER GIRL   I didnt.

THE MOTHER   I heard you call him by it. Dont try to deceive me.

THE FLOWER GIRL   *(protesting)* Who's trying to deceive you? I called him Freddy or Charlie same as you might yourself if you was talking to a stranger and wished to be pleasant.

THE DAUGHTER   Sixpence thrown away! Really, mamma, you might have spared Freddy that.

---

[2] "In the dialogue an e upside down [the schwa] indicates the indefinite vowel, sometimes called obscure or neutral, for which, though it is one of the commonest sounds in English speech, our wretched alphabet has no letter" (Shaw in his preface to the play).

(*She retreats in disgust behind the pillar*)

> (*An elderly gentleman of the amiable military type rushes into the shelter, and closes a dripping umbrella. He is in the same plight as* FREDDY, *very wet about the ankles. He is in evening dress, with a light overcoat. He takes the place left vacant by the* DAUGHTER)

THE GENTLEMAN Phew!

THE MOTHER (*to the* GENTLEMAN) Oh, sir, is there any sign of its stopping?

THE GENTLEMAN I'm afraid not. It started worse than ever about two minutes ago. (*He goes to the plinth beside the* FLOWER GIRL; *puts up his foot on it; and stoops to turn down his trouser ends*)

THE MOTHER Oh dear! (*She retires sadly and joins her daughter*)

THE FLOWER GIRL (*taking advantage of the military gentleman's proximity to establish friendly relations with him*) If it's worse, it's a sign it's nearly over. So cheer up, Captain; and buy a flower off a poor girl.

THE GENTLEMAN I'm sorry. I havnt any change.

THE FLOWER GIRL I can give you change, Captain.

THE GENTLEMAN For a sovereign? Ive nothing less.

THE FLOWER GIRL Garn! Oh do buy a flower off me, Captain. I can change half-a-crown. Take this for tuppence.

THE GENTLEMAN Now dont be troublesome: theres a good girl. (*trying his pockets*) I really havnt any change—Stop: heres three hapence, if thats any use

to you. (*He retreats to the other pillar*)

THE FLOWER GIRL (*disappointed, but thinking three halfpence better than nothing*) Thank you, sir.

THE BYSTANDER (*to the girl*) You be careful: give him a flower for it. Theres a bloke here behind taking down every blessed word youre saying.

> (*All turn to the man who is taking notes*)

THE FLOWER GIRL (*springing up terrified*) I aint done nothing wrong by speaking to the gentleman. Ive a right to sell flowers if I keep off the kerb. (*hysterically*) I'm a respectable girl: so help me, I never spoke to him except to ask him to buy a flower off me.

> (*General hubbub, mostly sympathetic to the* FLOWER GIRL, *but deprecating her excessive sensibility. Cries of* Dont start hollerin. Who's hurting you? Nobody's going to touch you. Whats the good of fussing? Steady on. Easy easy, *etc., come from the elderly staid spectators, who pat her comfortingly. Less patient ones bid her shut her head, or ask her roughly what is wrong with her. A remoter group, not knowing what the matter is, crowd in and increase the noise with question and answer:* Whats the row? What-she do? Where is he? A tec taking her down. What! him? Yes: him over there: Took money off the gentleman, *etc.*)

THE FLOWER GIRL (*breaking through them to the* GENTLEMAN, *crying wildly*) Oh, sir, dont let him charge me. You dunno what it means to me. Theyll take away my character and drive me on the streets for speaking to gentlemen. They—

THE NOTE TAKER (*coming forward on her right, the rest crowding after him*) There! there! there! there! who's hurting you, you silly girl? What do you take me for?

THE BYSTANDER It's aw rawt: e's a genleman: look at his bə-oots. (*explaining to the* NOTE TAKER) She thought you was a copper's nark, sir.

THE NOTE TAKER (*with quick interest*) Whats a copper's nark?

THE BYSTANDER (*inapt at definition*) It's a—well, it's a copper's nark, as you might say. What else would you call it? A sort of informer.

THE FLOWER GIRL (*still hysterical*) I take my Bible oath I never said a word—

THE NOTE TAKER (*overbearing but good-humored*) Oh, shut up, shut up. Do I look like a policeman?

THE FLOWER GIRL (*far from reassured*) Then what did you take down my words for? How do I know whether you took me down right? You just shew me what youve wrote about me. (*The* NOTE TAKER *opens his book and holds it steadily under her nose, though the pressure of the mob trying to read it over his shoulders would upset a weaker man*) Whats that? That aint proper writing. I cant read that.

THE NOTE TAKER I can (*reads, reproducing her pronunciation exactly*) "Cheer ap, Keptin; n' baw ya flahr orf a pore gel."

THE FLOWER GIRL (*much distressed*) It's because I called him Captain. I meant no harm. (*to the* GENTLEMAN) Oh, sir, dont let him lay a charge agen me for a word like that. You—

THE GENTLEMAN Charge! I make no charge. (*to the* NOTE TAKER) Really, sir, if you are a detective, you need not begin protecting me against molestation by young women until I ask you. Anybody could see that the girl meant no harm.

THE BYSTANDERS GENERALLY (*demonstrating against police espionage*) Course they could. What business is it of yours? You mind your own affairs. He wants promotion, he does. Taking down people's words! Girl never said a word to him. What harm if she did? Nice thing a girl cant shelter from the rain without being insulted, etc., etc., etc. (*She is conducted by the more sympathetic demonstrators back to her plinth, where she resumes her seat and struggles with her emotion*)

THE BYSTANDER He aint a tec. He's a blooming busybody: thats what he is. I tell you, look at his bə-oots.

THE NOTE TAKER (*turning on him genially*) And how are all your people down at Selsey?

THE BYSTANDER (*suspiciously*) Who told you my people come from Selsey?

THE NOTE TAKER Never you mind. They did. (*to the girl*) How do you come to be up so far east? You were born in Lisson Grove.

THE FLOWER GIRL (*appalled*) Oh, what harm is there in my leav-

ing Lisson Grove? It wasnt fit
for a pig to live in; and I had
to pay four-and-six a week. (*in
tears*) Oh, boo—hoo—oo—

THE NOTE TAKER   Live where you
like; but stop that noise.

THE GENTLEMAN (*to the girl*)
Come, come! he cant touch you:
you have a right to live where
you please.

A SARCASTIC BYSTANDER (*thrusting
himself between the* NOTE
TAKER *and the* GENTLEMAN)
Park Lane, for instance. I'd like
to go into the Housing Question
with you, I would.

THE FLOWER GIRL (*subsiding into
a brooding melancholy over her
basket, and talking very low-
spiritedly to herself*) I'm a
good girl, I am.

THE SARCASTIC BYSTANDER (*not attending to her*) Do you know
where *I* come from?

THE NOTE TAKER (*promptly*)   Hox-
ton.

(*Titterings. Popular interest in the* NOTE TAKER'S
performance increases)

THE SARCASTIC ONE (*amazed*) Well,
who said I didnt? Bly me! you
know everything, you do.

THE FLOWER GIRL (*still nursing her
sense of injury*) Aint no call
to meddle with me, he aint.

THE BYSTANDER (*to her*) Of course
he aint. Dont you stand it from
him. (*to the* NOTE TAKER) See
here: what call have you to
know about people what never
offered to meddle with you?

THE FLOWER GIRL Let him say
what he likes. I dont want to
have no truck with him.

THE BYSTANDER You take us for
dirt under your feet, dont you?
Catch you taking liberties with
a gentleman!

THE SARCASTIC BYSTANDER Yes:

tell him where he come from if
you want to go fortune-telling.

THE NOTE TAKER   Cheltenham, Harrow, Cambridge, and India.

THE GENTLEMAN   Quite right.

(*Great laughter. Reaction
in the* NOTE TAKER'S *favor.
Exclamations of* He knows
all about it. Told him
proper. Hear him tell the
toff where he come from?
etc.)

THE GENTLEMAN May I ask, sir,
do you do this for your living at
a music hall?

THE NOTE TAKER   I've thought of
that. Perhaps I shall some day.
(*The rain has stopped;
and the persons on the
outside of the crowd be-
gin to drop off*)

THE FLOWER GIRL (*resenting the
reaction*) He's no gentleman,
he aint, to interfere with a poor
girl.

THE DAUGHTER (*out of patience,
pushing her way rudely to the
front and displacing the* GEN-
TLEMAN, *who politely retires to
the other side of the pillar*)
What on earth is Freddy doing?
I shall get pneumownia if I stay
in this draught any longer.

THE NOTE TAKER (*to himself, hastily
making a note of her pronunciation of "monia"*) Earlscourt.

THE DAUGHTER (*violently*) Will
you please keep your impertinent remarks to yourself.

THE NOTE TAKER   Did I say that
out loud? I didnt mean to. I
beg your pardon. Your mother's
Epsom, unmistakably.

THE MOTHER (*advancing between
the* DAUGHTER *and the* NOTE
TAKER) How very curious! I
was brought up in Largelady
Park, near Epsom.

THE NOTE TAKER (*uproariously*

amused) Ha! ha! What a devil of a name! Excuse me. (*to the* DAUGHTER) You want a cab, do you?

THE DAUGHTER   Dont dare speak to me.

THE MOTHER   Oh please, please, Clara. (*Her daughter repudiates her with an angry shrug and retires haughtily*) We should be so grateful to you, sir, if you found us a cab. (*The* NOTE TAKER *produces a whistle*) Oh, thank you. (*She joins her daughter*)

> (*The* NOTE TAKER *blows a piercing blast*)

THE SARCASTIC BYSTANDER   There! I knowed he was a plain-clothes copper.

THE BYSTANDER   That aint a police whistle: thats a sporting whistle.

THE FLOWER GIRL (*still preoccupied with her wounded feelings*) He's no right to take away my character. My character is the same to me as any lady's.

THE NOTE TAKER   I dont know whether youve noticed it; but the rain stopped about two minutes ago.

THE BYSTANDER   So it has. Why didn't you say so before? and us losing our time listening to your silliness! (*He walks off towards the Strand*)

THE SARCASTIC BYSTANDER   I can tell where you come from. You come from Anwell. Go back there.

THE NOTE TAKER (*helpfully*) Hanwell.

THE SARCASTIC BYSTANDER (*affecting great distinction of speech*) Thenk you, teacher. Haw haw! So long. (*He touches his hat with mock respect and strolls off*)

THE FLOWER GIRL   Frightening people like that! How would he like it himself?

THE MOTHER   It's quite fine now, Clara. We can walk to a motor bus. Come. (*She gathers her skirts above her ankles and hurries off towards the Strand*)

THE DAUGHTER   But the cab—(*her mother is out of hearing*). Oh, how tiresome! (*She follows angrily*)

> (*All the rest have gone except the* NOTE TAKER, *the* GENTLEMAN, *and the* FLOWER GIRL, *who sits arranging her basket, and still pitying herself in murmurs*)

THE FLOWER GIRL   Poor girl! Hard enough for her to live without being worrited and chivied.

THE GENTLEMAN (*returning to his former place on the* NOTE TAKER'S *left*) How do you do it, if I may ask?

THE NOTE TAKER   Simply phonetics. The science of speech. Thats my profession: also my hobby. Happy is the man who can make a living by his hobby! You can spot an Irishman or a Yorkshireman by his brogue. *I* can place any man within six miles. I can place him within two miles in London. Sometimes within two streets.

THE FLOWER GIRL   Ought to be ashamed of himself, unmanly coward!

THE GENTLEMAN   But is there a living in that?

THE NOTE TAKER   Oh yes. Quite a fat one. This is an age of upstarts. Men begin in Kentish Town with £80 a year, and end in Park Lane with a hundred thousand. They want to drop Kentish Town; but they give themselves away every time they open their mouths. Now I can teach them—

THE FLOWER GIRL Let him mind his own business and leave a poor girl—

THE NOTE TAKER (*explosively*) Woman: cease this detestable boohooing instantly; or else seek the shelter of some other place of worship.

THE FLOWER GIRL (*with feeble defiance*) I've a right to be here if I like, same as you.

THE NOTE TAKER A woman who utters such depressing and disgusting sounds has no right to be anywhere—no right to live. Remember that you are a human being with a soul and the divine gift of articulate speech: that your native language is the language of Shakespeare and Milton and The Bible; and dont sit there crooning like a bilious pigeon.

THE FLOWER GIRL (*quite overwhelmed, looking up at him in mingled wonder and deprecation without daring to raise her head*) Ah-ah-ah-ow-ow-ow-oo!

THE NOTE TAKER (*whipping out his book*) Heavens! what a sound! (*He writes; then holds out the book and reads, reproducing her vowels exactly*) Ah-ah-ah-ow-ow-ow-oo!

THE FLOWER GIRL (*tickled by the performance, and laughing in spite of herself*) Garn!

THE NOTE TAKER You see this creature with her kerbstone English: the English that will keep her in the gutter to the end of her days. Well, sir, in three months I could pass that girl off as a duchess at an ambassador's garden party. I could even get her a place as lady's maid or shop assistant, which requires better English.

THE FLOWER GIRL What's that you say?

THE NOTE TAKER Yes, you squashed cabbage leaf, you disgrace to the noble architecture of these columns, you incarnate insult to the English language: I could pass you off as the Queen of Sheba. (*to the* GENTLEMAN) Can you believe that?

THE GENTLEMAN Of course I can. I am myself a student of Indian dialects; and—

THE NOTE TAKER (*eagerly*) Are you? Do you know Colonel Pickering, the author of *Spoken Sanscrit?*

THE GENTLEMAN I am Colonel Pickering. Who are you?

THE NOTE TAKER Henry Higgins, author of *Higgins's Universal Alphabet.*

PICKERING (*with enthusiasm*) I came from India to meet you.

HIGGINS I was going to India to meet you.

PICKERING Where do you live?

HIGGINS 27A Wimpole Street. Come and see me tomorrow.

PICKERING I'm at the Carlton. Come with me now and lets have a jaw over some supper.

HIGGINS Right you are.

THE FLOWER GIRL (*to* PICKERING, *as he passes her*) Buy a flower, kind gentleman. I'm short for my lodging.

PICKERING I really havnt any change. I'm sorry. (*He goes away*)

HIGGINS (*shocked at the girl's mendacity*) Liar. You said you could change half-a-crown.

THE FLOWER GIRL (*rising in desperation*) You ought to be stuffed with nails, you ought. (*flinging the basket at his feet*) Take the

whole blooming basket for sixpence.

> (*The church clock strikes
> the second quarter*)

HIGGINS (*hearing in it the voice of
God, rebuking him for his Phari-
saic want of charity to the poor
girl*) A reminder.

> (*He raises his hat sol-
> emnly; then throws a
> handful of money into
> the basket and follows
> PICKERING*)

THE FLOWER GIRL (*picking up a
half-crown*) Ah-ow-ooh! (*picking up a couple of florins*) Aaah-
ow-ooh! (*picking up several
coins*) Aaaaah-ow-ooh! (*picking
up a half-sovereign*) Aaaaaaaa-
aaaah-ow-ooh!!!

FREDDY (*springing out of a taxi-
cab*) Got one at last. Hallo!
(*to the girl*) Where are the two
ladies that were here?

THE FLOWER GIRL They walked to
the bus when the rain stopped.

FREDDY And left me with a cab on
my hands! Damnation!

THE FLOWER GIRL (*with grandeur*)
Never mind, young man. I'm
going home in a taxi. (*She sails
off to the cab. The driver puts
his hand behind him and holds
the door firmly shut against
her. Quite understanding his
mistrust, she shows him her
handful of money*) A taxi fare
aint no object to me, Charlie.
(*He grins and opens the door*)
Here. What about the basket?

THE TAXIMAN Give it here. Tuppence extra.

LIZA No: I dont want nobody to
see it. (*She crushes it into the
cab and gets in, continuing the
conversation through the window*) Goodbye, Freddy.

FREDDY (*dazedly raising his hat*)
Goodbye.

TAXIMAN Where to?

LIZA Bucknam Pellis [Buckingham
Palace].

TAXIMAN What d'ye mean—Bucknam Pellis?

LIZA Dont you know where it is?
In the Green Park, where the
King lives. Goodbye, Freddy.
Dont let me keep you standing
there. Goodbye.

FREDDY Goodbye. (*He goes*)

TAXIMAN Here? Whats this about
Bucknam Pellis? What business
have you at Bucknam Pellis?

LIZA Of course I havnt none. But
I wasn't going to let him know
that. You drive me home.

TAXIMAN And wheres home?

LIZA Angel Court, Drury Lane,
next Meiklejohn's oil shop.

TAXIMAN That sounds more like
it, Judy. (*He drives off*)

> (Let us follow the taxi to the en-
> trance to Angel Court, a nar-
> row little archway between two
> shops, one of them Meiklejohn's
> oil shop. When it stops there,
> Eliza gets out, dragging her bas-
> ket with her.)

LIZA How much?

TAXIMAN (*indicating the taximeter*)
Cant you read? A shilling.

LIZA A shilling for two minutes!!

TAXIMAN Two minutes or ten: it's
all the same.

LIZA Well, I dont call it right.

TAXIMAN Ever been in a taxi before?

LIZA (*with dignity*) Hundreds and
thousands of times, young man.

TAXIMAN (*laughing at her*) Good
for you, Judy. Keep the shilling,
darling, with best love from all
at home. Good luck! (*He drives
off*)

LIZA (*humiliated*) Impidence!

> (*She picks up the basket
> and trudges up the alley*

with it to her lodging: a small room with very old wall paper hanging loose in the damp places. A broken pane in the window is mended with paper. A portrait of a popular actor and a fashion plate of ladies' dresses, all wildly beyond poor Eliza's means, both torn from newspapers, are pinned up on the wall. A birdcage hangs in the window; but its tenant died long ago: it remains as a memorial only.

(These are the only visible luxuries: the rest is the irreducible minimum of poverty's needs: a wretched bed heaped with all sorts of coverings that have any warmth in them, a draped packing case with a basin and jug on it and a little looking glass over it, a chair and table, the refuse of some suburban kitchen, and an American alarum clock on the shelf above the unused fireplace: the whole lighted with a gas lamp with a penny in the slot meter. Rent: four shillings a week)

(Here Eliza, chronically weary, but too excited to go to bed, sits, counting her new riches and dreaming and planning what to do with them, until the gas goes out, when she enjoys for the first time the sensation of being able to put in another penny without grudging it. This prodigal mood does not extinguish her gnawing sense of the need for economy sufficiently to prevent her from calculating that she can dream and plan in bed more cheaply and warmly than sitting up without a fire. So she takes off her shawl and skirt and adds them to the miscellaneous bedclothes. Then she kicks off her shoes and gets into bed without any further change.)

ACT II

Next day at 11 A.M. HIGGINS's *laboratory in Wimpole Street. It is a room on the first floor, looking on the street, and was meant for the drawing room. The double doors are in the middle of the back wall; and persons entering find in the corner to their right two tall file cabinets at right angles to one another against the walls. In this corner stands a flat writing-table, on which are a phonograph, a laryngoscope, a row of tiny organ pipes with a bellows, a set of lamp chimneys for singeing flames with burners attached to a gas plug in the wall by an indiarubber tube, several tuning-forks of different sizes, a life-size image of half a human head, showing in section the vocal organs, and a box containing a supply of wax cylinders for the phonograph.*

Further down the room, on the same side, is a fireplace, with a comfortable leather-covered easy-chair at the side of the hearth nearest the door, and a coal-scuttle. There is a clock on the mantelpiece. Between the fireplace and the phonograph table is a stand for newspapers.

On the other side of the central door, to the left of the visitor, is a cabinet of shallow drawers. On it are a telephone and the telephone direc-

*tory. The corner beyond, and most of the side wall, is occupied by a grand
piano, with the keyboard at the end furthest from the door, and a bench for
the players extending the full length of the keyboard. On the piano is a
dessert dish heaped with fruit and sweets, mostly chocolates.*

*The middle of the room is clear. Besides the easy-chair, the piano
bench, and two chairs at the phonograph table, there is one stray chair.
It stands near the fireplace. On the walls, engravings: mostly Piranesis and
mezzotint portraits. No paintings.*

PICKERING *is seated at the table, putting down some cards and a tun-
ing-fork which he has been using.* HIGGINS *is standing up near him, closing
two or three file drawers which are hanging out. He appears in the morning
light as a robust, vital, appetizing sort of man of forty or thereabouts,
dressed in a professional-looking black frock-coat with a white linen collar
and black silk tie. He is of energetic, scientific type, heartily, even violently
interested in everything that can be studied as a scientific subject, and
careless about himself and other people, including their feelings. He is, in
fact, but for his years and size, rather like a very impetuous baby "taking
notice" eagerly and loudly, and requiring almost as much watching to keep
him out of unintended mischief. His manner varies from genial bullying
when he is in a good humor to stormy petulance when anything goes wrong;
but he is so entirely frank and void of malice that he remains likeable even
in his least reasonable moments.*

HIGGINS (*as he shuts the last drawer*) Well, I think thats the whole show.

PICKERING It's really amazing. I havnt taken half of it in, you know.

HIGGINS Would you like to go over any of it again?

PICKERING (*rising and coming to the fireplace, where he plants himself with his back to the fire*). No, thank you: not now. I'm quite done up for this morning.

HIGGINS (*following him, and standing beside him on his left*) Tired of listening to sounds?

PICKERING Yes. It's a fearful strain. I rather fancied myself because I can pronounce twenty-four distinct vowel sounds; but your hundred and thirty beat me. I cant hear a bit of difference between most of them.

HIGGINS (*chuckling, and going over to the piano to eat sweets*) Oh, that comes with practice. You hear no difference at first; but you keep on listening, and presently you find theyre all as different as A from B. (MRS PEARCE *looks in: she is* HIGGINS's *housekeeper*). Whats the matter?

MRS PEARCE (*hesitating, evidently perplexed*) A young woman asks to see you, sir.

HIGGINS A young woman! What does she want?

MRS PEARCE Well, sir, she says youll be glad to see her when you know what she's come about. She's quite a common girl, sir. Very common indeed. I should have sent her away, only I thought perhaps you wanted her to talk into your machines. I hope Ive not done wrong; but really you see such queer people sometimes—youll excuse me, I'm sure, sir—

HIGGINS Oh, thats all right, Mrs Pearce. Has she an interesting accent?

MRS PEARCE Oh, something dreadful, sir, really. I dont know how you can take an interest in it.

HIGGINS (*to* PICKERING) Lets have her up. Show her up, Mrs Pearce. (*He rushes across to his working table and picks out a cylinder to use on the phonograph*)

MRS PEARCE (*only half resigned to it*) Very well, sir. It's for you to say. (*She goes downstairs*)

HIGGINS This is rather a bit of luck. I'll show you how I make records. We'll set her talking; and I'll take it down first in Bell's Visible Speech; then in broad Romic; and then we'll get her on the phonograph so that you can turn her on as often as you like with the written transcript before you.

MRS PEARCE (*returning*) This is the young woman, sir.

(*The* FLOWER GIRL *enters in state. She has a hat with three ostrich feathers, orange, sky-blue, and red. She has a nearly clean apron, and the shoddy coat has been tidied a little. The pathos of this deplorable figure, with its innocent vanity and consequential air, touches* PICKERING, *who has already straightened himself in the presence of* MRS PEARCE. *But as to* HIGGINS, *the only distinction he makes between men and women is that when he is neither bullying nor exclaiming to the heavens against some feather-weight cross, he coaxes women as a child coaxes its nurse when it wants to get anything out of her*)

HIGGINS (*brusquely, recognizing her with unconcealed disappointment, and at once, babylike, making an intolerable grievance of it*) Why, this is the girl I jotted down last night. She's no use: I've got all the records I want of the Lisson Grove lingo; and I'm not going to waste another cylinder on it. (*to the girl*) Be off with you: I dont want you.

THE FLOWER GIRL Dont you be so saucy. You aint heard what I come for yet. (*to* MRS PEARCE, *who is waiting at the door for further instructions*) Did you tell him I come in a taxi?

MRS PEARCE Nonsense, girl! what do you think a gentleman like Mr Higgins cares what you came in?

THE FLOWER GIRL Oh, we are proud! He aint above giving lessons, not him: I heard him say so. Well, I aint come here to ask for any compliment; and if my money's not good enough I can go elsewhere.

HIGGINS Good enough for what?

THE FLOWER GIRL Good enough for yǝ-oo. Now you know, dont you? I've come to have lessons, I am. And to pay for em tǝ-oo: make no mistake.

HIGGINS (*stupent*[3]) Well!!! (*recovering his breath with a gasp*) What do you expect me to say to you?

THE FLOWER GIRL Well, if you was a gentleman, you might ask me to sit down, I think. Dont I tell you I'm bringing you business?

HIGGINS Pickering: shall we ask

---

[3] confused, bewildered, dumbfounded

this baggage to sit down, or shall we throw her out of the window?

THE FLOWER GIRL (*running away in terror to the piano, where she turns at bay*) Ah-ah-oh-ow-ow-ow-oo! (*wounded and whimpering*) I wont be called a baggage when Ive offered to pay like any lady.

(*Motionless, the two men stare at her from the other side of the room, amazed*)

PICKERING (*gently*) But what is it you want?

THE FLOWER GIRL I want to be a lady in a flower shop stead of sellin at the corner of Tottenham Court Road. But they wont take me unless I can talk more genteel. He said he could teach me. Well, here I am ready to pay him—not asking any favor—and he treats me zif I was dirt.

MRS PEARCE How can you be such a foolish ignorant girl as to think you could afford to pay Mr Higgins?

THE FLOWER GIRL Why shouldnt I? I know what lessons cost as well as you do; and I'm ready to pay.

HIGGINS How much?

THE FLOWER GIRL (*coming back to him, triumphant*) Now youre talking! I thought youd come off it when you saw a chance of getting back a bit of what you chucked at me last night. (*confidentially*) Youd had a drop in, hadnt you?

HIGGINS (*peremptorily*) Sit down.

THE FLOWER GIRL Oh, if youre going to make a compliment of it—

HIGGINS (*thundering at her*) Sit down.

MRS PEARCE (*severely*) Sit down, girl. Do as youre told.

THE FLOWER GIRL Ah-ah-ah-ow-ow-oo! (*She stands, half rebellious, half bewildered*)

PICKERING (*very courteous*) Wont you sit down? (*He places the stray chair near the hearthrug between himself and* HIGGINS)

LIZA (*coyly*) Dont mind if I do. (*She sits down.* PICKERING *returns to the hearthrug*)

HIGGINS Whats your name?

THE FLOWER GIRL Liza Doolittle.

HIGGINS (*declaiming gravely*) Eliza, Elizabeth, Betsy, and Bess, They went to the woods to get a bird's nes':

PICKERING They found a nest with four eggs in it:

HIGGINS They took one apiece, and left three in it.

(*They laugh heartily at their own fun*)

LIZA Oh, dont be silly.

MRS PEARCE (*placing herself behind* ELIZA's *chair*) You mustnt speak to the gentleman like that.

LIZA Well, why wont he speak sensible to me?

HIGGINS Come back to business. How much do you propose to pay me for the lessons?

LIZA Oh, I know whats right. A lady friend of mine gets French lessons for eighteenpence an hour from a real French gentleman. Well, you wouldnt have the face to ask me the same for teaching me my own language as you would for French; so I wont give more than a shilling. Take it or leave it.

HIGGINS (*walking up and down the room, rattling his keys and his cash in his pockets*) You know, Pickering, if you consider a shilling, not as a simple shilling, but as a percentage of this girl's income, it works out as fully equivalent to sixty or seventy guineas from a millionaire.

PICKERING How so?

HIGGINS Figure it out. A millionaire has about £150 a day. She earns about half-a-crown.

LIZA (*haughtily*) Who told you I only—

HIGGINS (*continuing*) She offers me two-fifths of her day's income for a lesson. Two-fifths of a millionaire's income for a day would be somewhere about £60. It's handsome. By George, it's enormous! It's the biggest offer I ever had.

LIZA (*rising, terrified*) Sixty pounds! What are you talking about? I never offered you sixty pounds. Where would I get—

HIGGINS Hold your tongue.

LIZA (*weeping*) But I aint got sixty pounds. Oh—

MRS PEARCE Dont cry, you silly girl. Sit down. Nobody is going to touch your money.

HIGGINS Somebody is going to touch you, with a broomstick, if you dont stop snivelling. Sit down.

LIZA (*obeying slowly*) Ah-ah-ah-ow-oo-o! One would think you was my father.

HIGGINS If I decide to teach you, I'll be worse than two fathers to you. Here! (*He offers her his silk handkerchief*)

LIZA Whats this for?

HIGGINS To wipe your eyes. To wipe any part of your face that feels moist. Remember: thats your handkerchief; and thats your sleeve. Dont mistake the one for the other if you wish to become a lady in a shop.

(LIZA, *utterly bewildered, stares helplessly at him*)

MRS PEARCE It's no use talking to her like that, Mr Higgins: she doesnt understand you. Besides, youre quite wrong: she doesnt do it that way at all. (*She takes the handkerchief*)

LIZA (*snatching it*) Here! You give me that handkerchief. He gev it to me, not to you.

PICKERING (*laughing*) He did. I think it must be regarded as her property, Mrs Pearce.

MRS PEARCE (*resigning herself*) Serve you right, Mr Higgins.

PICKERING Higgins: I'm interested. What about the ambassador's garden party? I'll say youre the greatest teacher alive if you make that good. I'll bet you all the expenses of the experiment you cant do it. And I'll pay for the lessons.

LIZA Oh, you are real good. Thank you, Captain.

HIGGINS (*tempted, looking at her*) It's almost irresistible. She's so deliciously low—so horribly dirty—

LIZA (*protesting extremely*) Ah-ah-ah-ah-ow-ow-oo-oo!!! I aint dirty: I washed my face and hands afore I come, I did.

PICKERING Youre certainly not going to turn her head with flattery, Higgins.

MRS PEARCE (*uneasy*) Oh, dont say that, sir: theres more ways than one of turning a girl's head; and nobody can do it better than Mr Higgins, though he may not always mean it. I do hope, sir, you wont encourage him to do anything foolish.

HIGGINS (*becoming excited as the idea grows on him*) What is life but a series of inspired follies? The difficulty is to find them to do. Never lose a chance: it doesnt come every day. I shall make a duchess of this draggle-tailed guttersnipe.

LIZA (*strongly deprecating this view of her*) Ah-ah-ah-ow-ow-oo!

HIGGINS (*carried away*) Yes, in six months—in three if she has a good ear and a quick tongue— I'll take her anywhere and pass her off as anything. We'll start today: now! this moment! Take her away and clean her, Mrs Pearce. Monkey Brand, if it wont come off any other way. Is there a good fire in the kitchen?

MRS PEARCE (*protesting*) Yes; but—

HIGGINS (*storming on*) Take all her clothes off and burn them. Ring up Whitely or somebody for new ones. Wrap her up in brown paper til they come.

LIZA Youre no gentleman, youre not, to talk of such things. I'm a good girl, I am; and I know what the like of you are, I do.

HIGGINS We want none of your Lisson Grove prudery here, young woman. Youve got to learn to behave like a duchess. Take her away, Mrs Pearce. If she gives you any trouble, wallop her.

LIZA (*springing up and running between* PICKERING *and* MRS PEARCE *for protection*) No! I'll call the police, I will.

MRS PEARCE But Ive no place to put her.

HIGGINS Put her in the dustbin.

LIZA Ah-ah-ah-ow-ow-oo!

PICKERING Oh come, Higgins! be reasonable.

MRS PEARCE (*resolutely*) You must be reasonable, Mr Higgins;

really you must. You cant walk over everybody like this.

(HIGGINS, *thus scolded, subsides. The hurricane is succeeded by a zephyr of amiable surprise*)

HIGGINS (*with professional exquisiteness of modulation*) I walk over everybody! My dear Mrs Pearce, my dear Pickering, I never had the slightest intention of walking over anyone. All I propose is that we should be kind to this poor girl. We must help her to prepare and fit herself for her new station in life. If I did not express myself clearly it was because I did not wish to hurt her delicacy, or yours.

(LIZA, *reassured, steals back to her chair*)

MRS PEARCE (*to* PICKERING) Well, did you ever hear anything like that, sir?

PICKERING (*laughing heartily*) Never, Mrs Pearce: never.

HIGGINS (*patiently*) Whats the matter?

MRS PEARCE Well, the matter is, sir, that you cant take a girl up like that as if you were picking up a pebble on the beach.

HIGGINS Why not?

MRS PEARCE Why not! But you dont know anything about her. What about her parents? She may be married.

LIZA Garn!

HIGGINS There! As the girl very properly says, Garn! Married indeed! Dont you know that a woman of that class looks a worn out drudge of fifty a year after she's married?

LIZA Whood marry me?

HIGGINS (*suddenly resorting to the most thrillingly beautiful low tones in his best elocutionary style*) By George, Eliza, the streets will be strewn with the bodies of men shooting themselves for your sake before Ive done with you.

MRS PEARCE Nonsense, sir. You mustnt talk like that to her.

LIZA (*rising and squaring herself determinedly*) I'm going away. He's off his chump, he is. I dont want no balmies teaching me.

HIGGINS (*wounded in his tenderest point by her insensibility to his elocution*) Oh, indeed! I'm mad, am I? Very well, Mrs Pearce: you neednt order the new clothes for her. Throw her out.

LIZA (*whimpering*) Nah-ow. You got no right to touch me.

MRS PEARCE You see now what comes of being saucy. (*indicating the door*) This way, please.

LIZA (*almost in tears*) I didnt want no clothes. I wouldnt have taken them. (*She throws away the handkerchief*) I can buy my own clothes.

HIGGINS (*deftly retrieving the handkerchief and intercepting her on her reluctant way to the door*) Youre an ungrateful wicked girl. This is my return for offering to take you out of the gutter and dress you beautifully and make a lady of you.

MRS PEARCE Stop, Mr Higgins. I wont allow it. It's you that are wicked. Go home to your parents, girl; and tell them to take better care of you.

LIZA I aint got no parents. They told me I was big enough to earn my own living and turned me out.

MRS PEARCE Wheres your mother?

LIZA I aint got no mother. Her that turned me out was my sixth stepmother. But I done without them. And I'm a good girl, I am.

HIGGINS Very well, then, what on earth is all this fuss about? The girl doesnt belong to anybody—is no use to anybody but me. (*He goes to* MRS PEARCE *and begins coaxing*) You can adopt her, Mrs Pearce: I'm sure a daughter would be a great amusement to you. Now dont make any more fuss. Take her downstairs; and—

MRS PEARCE But whats to become of her? Is she to be paid anything? Do be sensible, sir.

HIGGINS Oh, pay her whatever is necessary: put it down in the housekeeping book. (*impatiently*) What on earth will she want with money? She'll have her food and her clothes. She'll only drink if you give her money.

LIZA (*turning on him*) Oh you are a brute. It's a lie: nobody ever saw the sign of liquor on me. (*to* PICKERING) Oh, sir: youre a gentleman: dont let him speak to me like that.

PICKERING (*in good-humored remonstrance*) Does it occur to you, Higgins, that the girl has some feelings?

HIGGINS (*looking critically at her*) Oh no, I dont think so. Not any feelings that we need bother about. (*cheerily*) Have you, Eliza?

LIZA I got my feelings same as anyone else.

HIGGINS (*to* PICKERING, *reflectively*) You see the difficulty?

PICKERING Eh? What difficulty?

HIGGINS To get her to talk grammar. The mere pronunciation is easy enough.

LIZA I dont want to talk grammar. I want to talk like a lady in a flowershop.

MRS PEARCE Will you please keep to the point, Mr Higgins. I want to know on what terms the girl is to be here. Is she to have any wages? And what is to become of her when youve finished your teaching? You must look ahead a little.

HIGGINS (*impatiently*) Whats to become of her if I leave her in the gutter? Tell me that, Mrs Pearce.

MRS PEARCE Thats her own business, not yours, Mr Higgins.

HIGGINS Well, when Ive done with her, we can throw her back into the gutter; and then it will be her own business again; so thats all right.

LIZA Oh, youve no feeling heart in you: you dont care for nothing but yourself. (*She rises and takes the floor resolutely*) Here! Ive had enough of this. I'm going (*making for the door*). You ought to be ashamed of yourself, you ought.

HIGGINS (*snatching a chocolate cream from the piano, his eyes suddenly beginning to twinkle with mischief*) Have some chocolates, Eliza.

LIZA (*halting, tempted*) How do I know what might be in them? Ive heard of girls being drugged by the like of you.

　　　　(HIGGINS *whips out his penknife; cuts a chocolate in two; puts one half into his mouth and bolts it; and offers her the other half*)

HIGGINS Pledge of good faith, Eliza. I eat one half: you eat the other. (LIZA *opens her mouth to retort: he pops the half chocolate into it*) You shall have boxes of them, barrels of them, every day. You shall live on them. Eh?

LIZA (*who has disposed of the chocolate after being nearly choked by it*) I wouldnt have ate it, only I'm too ladylike to take it out of my mouth.

HIGGINS Listen, Eliza. I think you said you came in a taxi.

LIZA Well, what if I did? Ive as good a right to take a taxi as anyone else.

HIGGINS You have, Eliza; and in future you shall have as many taxis as you want. You shall go up and down and round the town in a taxi every day. Think of that, Eliza.

MRS PEARCE Mr Higgins: youre tempting the girl. It's not right. She should think of the future.

HIGGINS At her age! Nonsense! Time enough to think of the future when you havnt any future to think of. No, Eliza: do as this lady does: think of other people's futures; but never think of your own. Think of chocolates, and taxis, and gold, and diamonds.

LIZA No: I dont want no gold and no diamonds. I'm a good girl, I am. (*She sits down again, with an attempt at dignity*)

HIGGINS You shall remain so, Eliza, under the care of Mrs Pearce. And you shall marry an officer in the Guards, with a beautiful moustache: the son of a marquis, who will disinherit him for marrying you, but will relent when he sees your beauty and goodness—

PICKERING Excuse me, Higgins; but I really must interfere. Mrs

Pearce is quite right. If this girl is to put herself in your hands for six months for an experiment in teaching, she must understand thoroughly what she's doing.

HIGGINS How can she? She's incapable of understanding anything. Besides, do any of us understand what we are doing? If we did, would we ever do it?

PICKERING Very clever, Higgins; but not to the present point. (*to* ELIZA) Miss Doolittle—

LIZA (*overwhelmed*) Ah-ah-ow-oo!

HIGGINS There! Thats all youll get out of Eliza. Ah-ah-ow-oo! No use explaining. As a military man you ought to know that. Give her her orders: thats enough for her. Eliza: you are to live here for the next six months learning how to speak beautifully, like a lady in a florist's shop. If youre good and do whatever youre told, you shall sleep in a proper bedroom, and have lots to eat, and money to buy chocolates and take rides in taxis. If youre naughty and idle you will sleep in the back kitchen among the black beetles, and be walloped by Mrs Pearce with a broomstick. At the end of six months you shall go to Buckingham Palace in a carriage, beautifully dressed. If the King finds out youre not a lady, you will be taken by the police to the Tower of London, where your head will be cut off as a warning to other presumptuous flower girls. If you are not found out, you shall have a present of seven-and-sixpence to start life with as a lady in a shop. If you refuse this offer you will be a most ungrateful wicked girl; and the angels will weep for you. (*to* PICKERING) Now are you satisfied, Pickering? (*to* MRS PEARCE) Can I put it more plainly and fairly, Mrs Pearce?

MRS PEARCE (*patiently*) I think youd better let me speak to the girl properly in private. I dont know that I can take charge of her or consent to the arrangement at all. Of course I know you dont mean her any harm; but when you get what you called interested in people's accents, you never think or care what may happen to them or you. Come with me, Eliza.

HIGGINS Thats all right. Thank you, Mrs Pearce. Bundle her off to the bathroom.

LIZA (*rising reluctantly and suspiciously*) Youre a great bully, you are. I wont stay here if I dont like. I wont let nobody wallop me. I never asked to go to Bucknam Palace, I didnt. I was never in trouble with the police, not me. I'm a good girl—

MRS PEARCE Dont answer back, girl. You dont understand the gentleman. Come with me. (*She leads the way to the door, and holds it open for* ELIZA)

LIZA (*as she goes out*) Well, what I say is right. I wont go near the King, not if I'm going to have my head cut off. If I'd known what I was letting myself in for, I wouldnt have come here. I always been a good girl; and I never offered to say a word to him; and I dont owe him nothing; and I dont care; and I wont be put upon; and I have my feelings the same as anyone else—

(MRS PEARCE *shuts the*

door; and ELIZA's *plaints are no longer audible*)

(Eliza is taken upstairs to the third floor greatly to her surprise; for she expected to be taken down to the scullery. There Mrs Pearce opens a door and takes her into a spare bedroom.)

MRS PEARCE I will have to put you here. This will be your bedroom.

LIZA O-h, I couldnt sleep here, missus. It's too good for the likes of me. I should be afraid to touch anything. I aint a duchess yet, you know.

MRS PEARCE You have got to make yourself as clean as the room: then you wont be afraid of it. And you must call me Mrs Pearce, not missus. (*She throws open the door of the dressing-room, now modernized as a bathroom*)

LIZA Gawd! whats this? Is this where you wash clothes? Funny sort of copper I call it.

MRS PEARCE It is not a copper. This is where we wash ourselves, Eliza, and where I am going to wash you.

LIZA You expect me to get into that and wet myself all over! Not me. I should catch my death. I knew a woman did it every Saturday night; and she died of it.

MRS PEARCE Mr Higgins has the gentlemen's bathroom downstairs; and he has a bath every morning, in cold water.

LIZA Ugh! He's made of iron, that man.

MRS PEARCE If you are to sit with him and the Colonel and be taught you will have to do the same. They wont like the smell of you if you dont. But you can have the water as hot as you like. There are two taps: hot and cold.

LIZA (*weeping*) I couldnt. I dursnt. Its not natural: it would kill me. Ive never had a bath in my life: not what youd call a proper one.

MRS PEARCE Well, dont you want to be clean and sweet and decent, like a lady? You know you cant be a nice girl inside if youre a dirty slut outside.

LIZA Boohoo!!!!

MRS PEARCE Now stop crying and go back into your room and take off all your clothes. Then wrap yourself in this (*taking down a gown from its peg and handing it to her*) and come back to me. I will get the bath ready.

LIZA (*all tears*) I cant. I wont. I'm not used to it. Ive never took off all my clothes before. It's not right: it's not decent.

MRS PEARCE Nonsense, child. Dont you take off all your clothes every night when you go to bed?

LIZA (*amazed*) No. Why should I? I should catch my death. Of course I take off my skirt.

MRS PEARCE Do you mean that you sleep in the underclothes you wear in the daytime?

LIZA What else have I to sleep in?

MRS PEARCE You will never do that again as long as you live here. I will get you a proper nightdress.

LIZA Do you mean change into cold things and lie awake shivering half the night? You want to kill me, you do.

MRS PEARCE I want to change you from a frowzy slut to a clean respectable girl fit to sit with the gentlemen in the study. Are you going to trust me and do what I tell you or be thrown out and sent back to your flower basket?

LIZA But you dont know what the cold is to me. You dont know how I dread it.

MRS PEARCE Your bed won't be cold here: I will put a hot water bottle in it. (*pushing her into the bedroom*) Off with you and undress.

LIZA Oh, if only I'd known what a dreadful thing it is to be clean I'd never have come. I didn't know when I was well off. I— (MRS PEARCE *pushes her through the door, but leaves it partly open lest her prisoner should take to flight*)

(MRS PEARCE *puts on a pair of white rubber sleeves, and fills the bath, mixing hot and cold, and testing the result with the bath thermometer. She perfumes it with a handful of bath salts and adds a palmful of mustard. She then takes a formidable looking long handled scrubbing brush and soaps it profusely with a ball of scented soap.* ELIZA *comes back with nothing on but the bath gown huddled tightly round her, a piteous spectacle of abject terror*)

MRS PEARCE Now come along. Take that thing off.

LIZA Oh I couldnt, Mrs Pearce: I reely couldnt. I never done such a thing.

MRS PEARCE Nonsense. Here: step in and tell me whether it's hot enough for you.

LIZA Ah-oo! It's too hot.

MRS PEARCE (*deftly snatching the gown away and throwing* ELIZA down on her back) It wont hurt you. (*She sets to work with the scrubbing brush*)

(ELIZA'S *screams are heart-rending*)

(Meanwhile the Colonel has been having it out with Higgins about Eliza. Pickering has come from the hearth to the chair and seated himself astride of it with his arms on the back to cross-examine him.)

PICKERING Excuse the straight question, Higgins. Are you a man of good character where women are concerned?

HIGGINS (*moodily*) Have you ever met a man of good character where women are concerned?

PICKERING Yes: very frequently.

HIGGINS (*dogmatically, lifting himself on his hands to the level of the piano, and sitting on it with a bounce*) Well, I havnt. I find that the moment I let a woman make friends with me, she becomes jealous, exacting, suspicious, and a damned nuisance. I find that the moment I let myself make friends with a woman, I become selfish and tyrannical. Women upset everything. When you let them into your life, you find that the woman is driving at one thing and youre driving at another.

PICKERING At what, for example?

HIGGINS (*coming off the piano restlessly*) Oh, Lord knows! I suppose the woman wants to live her own life; and the man wants to live his; and each tries to drag the other on to the wrong track. One wants to go north and the other south; and the result is that both have to go east, though they both hate the east wind. (*He sits down on the bench at the keyboard*) So here I am, a confirmed old bachelor, and likely to remain so.

PICKERING (*rising and standing over him gravely*) Come, Higgins! You know what I mean. If I'm to be in this business I shall feel responsible for that girl. I hope it's understood that no advantage is to be taken of her position.

HIGGINS What! That thing! Sacred, I assure you. (*rising to explain*) You see, she'll be a pupil; and teaching would be impossible unless pupils were sacred. Ive taught scores of American millionairesses how to speak English; the best looking women in the world. I'm seasoned. They might as well be blocks of wood. *I* might as well be a block of wood. It's—

(MRS PEARCE *opens the door. She has* ELIZA's *hat in her hand.* PICKERING *retires to the easy-chair at the hearth and sits down*)

HIGGINS (*eagerly*) Well, Mrs Pearce: is it all right?

MRS PEARCE (*at the door*) I just wish to trouble you with a word, if I may, Mr Higgins.

HIGGINS Yes, certainly. Come in. (*She comes forward*) Dont burn that, Mrs Pearce. I'll keep it as a curiosity. (*He takes the hat*)

MRS PEARCE Handle it carefully, sir, please. I had to promise her not to burn it; but I had better put it in the oven for a while.

HIGGINS (*putting it down hastily on the piano*) Oh! thank you. Well, what have you to say to me?

PICKERING Am I in the way?

MRS PEARCE Not in the least, sir. Mr Higgins: will you please be very particular what you say before the girl?

HIGGINS (*sternly*) Of course. I'm always particular about what I say. Why do you say this to me?

MRS PEARCE (*unmoved*) No, sir: youre not at all particular when youve mislaid anything or when you get a little impatient. Now it doesnt matter before me: I'm used to it. But you really must not swear before the girl.

HIGGINS (*indignantly*) I swear! (*most emphatically*) I never swear. I detest the habit. What the devil do you mean?

MRS PEARCE (*stolidly*) Thats what I mean, sir. You swear a great deal too much. I dont mind your damning and blasting, and what the devil and where the devil and who the devil—

HIGGINS Mrs Pearce: this language from your lips! Really!

MRS PEARCE (*not to be put off*)— but there is a certain word I must ask you not to use. The girl used it herself when she began to enjoy the bath. It begins with the same letter as bath. She knows no better: she learnt it at her mother's knee. But she must not hear it from your lips.

HIGGINS (*loftily*) I cannot charge myself with having ever uttered it, Mrs Pearce. (*She looks at him steadfastly. He adds, hiding an uneasy conscience with a judicial air*) Except perhaps in a moment of extreme and justifiable excitement.

MRS PEARCE Only this morning, sir, you applied it to your boots, to the butter, and to the brown bread.

HIGGINS Oh, that! Mere alliteration, Mrs Pearce, natural to a poet.

MRS PEARCE Well, sir, whatever you choose to call it, I beg you not to let the girl hear you repeat it.

HIGGINS Oh, very well, very well. Is that all?

MRS PEARCE No, sir. We shall have to be very particular with this girl as to personal cleanliness.

HIGGINS Certainly. Quite right. Most important.

MRS PEARCE I mean not to be slovenly about her dress or untidy in leaving things about.

HIGGINS (*going to her solemnly*) Just so. I intended to call your attention to that. (*He passes on to* PICKERING, *who is enjoying the conversation immensely*) It is these little things that matter, Pickering. Take care of the pence and the pounds will take care of themselves is as true of personal habits as of money. (*He comes to anchor on the hearthrug, with the air of a man in an unassailable position*)

MRS PEARCE Yes, sir. Then might I ask you not to come down to breakfast in your dressing-gown, or at any rate not to use it as a napkin to the extent you do, sir. And if you would be so good as not to eat everything off the same plate, and to remember not to put the porridge saucepan out of your hand on the clean tablecloth, it would be a better example to the girl. You know you nearly choked yourself with a fishbone in a jam only last week.

HIGGINS (*routed from the hearthrug and drifting back to the piano*) I may do these things sometimes in absence of mind; but surely I dont do them habitually.

(*angrily*) By the way: my dressing-gown smells most damnably of benzine.

MRS PEARCE No doubt it does, Mr Higgins. But if you will wipe your fingers—

HIGGINS (*yelling*) Oh very well, very well: I'll wipe them in my hair in future.

MRS PEARCE I hope youre not offended, Mr Higgins.

HIGGINS (*shocked at finding himself thought capable of an unamiable sentiment*) Not at all, not at all. Youre quite right, Mrs Pearce: I shall be particularly careful before the girl. Is that all?

MRS PEARCE No, sir. Might she use some of those Japanese dresses you brought from abroad? I really cant put her back into her old things.

HIGGINS Certainly. Anything you like. Is that all?

MRS PEARCE Thank you, sir. Thats all. (*She goes out*)

HIGGINS You know, Pickering, that woman has the most extraordinary ideas about me. Here I am, a shy, diffident sort of man. Ive never been able to feel really grown-up and tremendous, like other chaps. And yet she's firmly persuaded that I'm an arbitrary overbearing bossing kind of person. I cant account for it.

(MRS PEARCE *returns*)

MRS PEARCE If you please, sir, the trouble's beginning already. Theres a dustman downstairs, Alfred Doolittle, wants to see you. He says you have his daughter here.

PICKERING (*rising*) Phew! I say!

HIGGINS (*promptly*) Send the blackguard up.

MRS PEARCE Oh, very well, sir. (*She goes out*)

PICKERING   He may not be a black-guard, Higgins.

HIGGINS   Nonsense. Of course he's a blackguard.

PICKERING   Whether he is or not, I'm afraid we shall have some trouble with him.

HIGGINS   (*confidently*)   Oh no: I think not. If theres any trouble he shall have it with me, not I with him. And we are sure to get something interesting out of him.

PICKERING   About the girl?

HIGGINS   No. I mean his dialect.

PICKERING   Oh!

MRS PEARCE   (*at the door*)   Doo-little, sir. (*She admits* DOOLIT-TLE *and retires*)

> (*Alfred is an elderly but vigorous dustman, clad in the costume of his pro-fession, including a hat with a back brim covering his neck and shoulders. He has well marked and rather interesting features, and seems equally free from fear and conscience. He has a remarkably ex-pressive voice, the result of a habit of giving vent to his feelings without reserve. His present pose is that of wounded honor and stern resolution*)

DOOLITTLE   (*at the door, uncertain which of the two gentlemen is his man*)   Professor Iggins?

HIGGINS   Here. Good morning. Sit down.

DOOLITTLE   Morning, Governor. (*He sits down magisterially*) I come about a very serious matter, Governor.

HIGGINS   (*to* PICKERING)   Brought up in Hounslow. Mother Welsh, I should think. (DOOLITTLE *opens his mouth, amazed.* HIGGINS

continues) What do you want, Doolittle?

DOOLITTLE   (*menacingly*)   I want my daughter: thats what I want. See?

HIGGINS   Of course you do. Youre her father, arnt you? You dont suppose anyone else wants her, do you? I'm glad to see you have some spark of family feel-ing left. She's upstairs. Take her away at once.

DOOLITTLE   (*rising, fearfully taken aback*)   What!

HIGGINS   Take her away. Do you suppose I'm going to keep your daughter for you?

DOOLITTLE   (*remonstrating*)   Now, now, look here, Governor. Is this reasonable? Is it fairity to take advantage of a man like this? The girl belongs to me. You got her. Where do I come in? (*He sits down again*)

HIGGINS   Your daughter had the audacity to come to my house and ask me to teach her how to speak properly so that she could get a place in a flowershop. This gentleman and my housekeeper have been here all the time. (*bullying him*) How dare you come here and attempt to black-mail me? You sent her here on purpose.

DOOLITTLE   (*protesting*)   No, Gov-ernor.

HIGGINS   You must have. How else could you possibly know that she is here?

DOOLITTLE   Dont take a man up like that, Governor.

HIGGINS   The police shall take you up. This is a plant—a plot to extort money by threats. I shall telephone for the police. (*He goes resolutely to the telephone and opens the directory*)

DOOLITTLE Have I asked you for a brass farthing? I leave it to the gentleman here: have I said a word about money?

HIGGINS (*throwing the book aside and marching down on* DOOLITTLE *with a poser*) What else did you come for?

DOOLITTLE (*sweetly*) Well, what would a man come for? Be human, Governor.

HIGGINS (*disarmed*) Alfred: did you put her up to it?

DOOLITTLE So help me, Governor, I never did. I take my Bible oath I aint seen the girl these two months past.

HIGGINS Then how did you know she was here?

DOOLITTLE (*"most musical, most melancholy"*) I'll tell you, Governor, if youll only let me get a word in. I'm willing to tell you. I'm wanting to tell you. I'm waiting to tell you.

HIGGINS Pickering: this chap has a certain natural gift of rhetoric. Observe the rhythm of his native woodnotes wild. "I'm willing to tell you: I'm wanting to tell you: I'm waiting to tell you." Sentimental rhetoric! thats the Welsh strain in him. It also accounts for his mendacity and dishonesty.

PICKERING Oh, please, Higgins: I'm west country myself. (*to* DOOLITTLE) How did you know the girl was here if you didnt send her?

DOOLITTLE It was like this, Governor. The girl took a boy in the taxi to give him a jaunt. Son of her landlady, he is. He hung about on the chance of her giving him another ride home. Well, she sent him back for her luggage when she heard you was willing for her to stop here. I met the boy at the corner of Long Acre and Endell Street.

HIGGINS Public house. Yes?

DOOLITTLE The poor man's club, Governor: why shouldnt I?

PICKERING Do let him tell his story, Higgins.

DOOLITTLE He told me what was up. And I ask you, what was my feelings and my duty as a father? I says to the boy, "You bring me the luggage," I says—

PICKERING Why didnt you go for it yourself?

DOOLITTLE Landlady wouldnt have trusted me with it, Governor. She's that kind of woman: you know. I had to give the boy a penny afore he trusted me with it, the little swine. I brought it to her just to oblige you like, and make myself agreeable. Thats all.

HIGGINS How much luggage?

DOOLITTLE Musical instrument, Governor. A few pictures, a trifle of jewelry, and a birdcage. She said she didnt want no clothes. What was I to think from that, Governor? I ask you as a parent, what was I to think?

HIGGINS So you came to rescue her from worse than death, eh?

DOOLITTLE (*appreciatively: relieved at being so well understood*) Just so, Governor. Thats right.

PICKERING But why did you bring her luggage if you intended to take her away?

DOOLITTLE Have I said a word about taking her away? Have I now?

HIGGINS (*determinedly*) Youre going to take her away, double quick. (*He crosses to the hearth and rings the bell*)

DOOLITTLE (*rising*) No, Governor. Dont say that. I'm not the man to stand in my girl's light. Heres a career opening for her, as you might say; and—

(MRS PEARCE *opens the door and awaits orders*)

HIGGINS Mrs Pearce: this is Eliza's father. He has come to take her away. Give her to him. (*He goes back to the piano, with an air of washing his hands of the whole affair*)

DOOLITTLE No. This is a misunderstanding. Listen here—

MRS PEARCE He cant take her away, Mr Higgins: how can he? You told me to burn her clothes.

DOOLITTLE Thats right. I cant carry the girl through the streets like a blooming monkey, can I? I put it to you.

HIGGINS You have put it to me that you want your daughter. Take your daughter. If she has no clothes, go out and buy her some.

DOOLITTLE (*desperate*) Wheres the clothes she come in? Did I burn them or did your missus here?

MRS PEARCE I am the housekeeper, if you please. I have sent for some clothes for your girl. When they come you can take her away. You can wait in the kitchen. This way, please.

(DOOLITTLE, *much troubled, accompanies her to the door; then hesitates; finally turns confidentially to* HIGGINS)

DOOLITTLE Listen here, Governor. You and me is men of the world, aint we?

HIGGINS Oh! Men of the world, are we? Youd better go, Mrs Pearce.

MRS PEARCE I think so, indeed, sir. (*She goes, with dignity*)

PICKERING The floor is yours, Mr Doolittle.

DOOLITTLE (*to* PICKERING) I thank you, Governor. (*to* HIGGINS, *who takes refuge on the piano bench, a little overwhelmed by the proximity of his visitor; for Doolittle has a professional flavour of dust about him*) Well, the truth is, I've taken a sort of fancy to you, Governor; and if you want the girl, I'm not so set on having her back home again but what I might be open to an arrangement. Regarded in the light of a young woman, she's a fine handsome girl. As a daughter she's not worth her keep; and so I tell you straight. All I ask is my rights as a father; and youre the last man alive to expect me to let her go for nothing; for I can see youre one of the straight sort, Governor. Well, whats a five-pound note to you? and whats Eliza to me? (*He turns to his chair and sits down judicially*)

PICKERING I think you ought to know, Doolittle, that Mr Higgins's intentions are entirely honorable.

DOOLITTLE Course they are, Governor. If I thought they wasn't I'd ask fifty.

HIGGINS (*revolted*) Do you mean to say that you would sell your daughter for £50?

DOOLITTLE Not in a general way I would; but to oblige a gentleman like you I'd do a good deal, I do assure you.

PICKERING Have you no morals, man?

DOOLITTLE (*unabashed*) Cant afford them, Governor. Neither could you if you was as poor as me. Not that I mean any harm, you know. But if Liza is going to have a bit out of this, why not me too?

HIGGINS (*troubled*) I dont know what to do, Pickering. There can be no question that as a matter of morals it's a positive crime to give this chap a farthing. And yet I feel a sort of rough justice in his claim.

DOOLITTLE Thats it, Governor. Thats all I say. A father's heart, as it were.

PICKERING Well, I know the feeling; but really it seems hardly right—

DOOLITTLE Dont say that, Governor. Dont look at it that way. What am I, Governors both? I ask you, what am I? I'm one of the undeserving poor: thats what I am. Think of what that means to a man. It means that he's up agen middle class morality all the time. If theres anything going, and I put in for a bit of it, it's always the same story: "Youre undeserving; so you cant have it." But my needs is as great as the most deserving widow's that ever got money out of six different charities in one week for the death of the same husband. I dont need less than a deserving man: I need more. I dont eat less hearty than him; and I drink a lot more. I want a bit of amusement, cause I'm a thinking man. I want cheerfulness and a song and a band when I feel low. Well, they charge me just the same for everything as they charge the deserving. What is middle class morality? Just an excuse for never giving me anything. Therefore, I ask you, as two gentlemen, not to play that game on me. I'm playing straight with you. I aint pretending to be deserving. I'm undeserving; and I mean to go on being undeserving. I like it; and thats the truth. Will you take advantage of a man's nature to do him out of the price of his own daughter what he's brought up and fed and clothed by the sweat of his brow until she's growed big enough to be interesting to you two gentlemen? Is five pounds unreasonable? I put it to you; and I leave it to you.

HIGGINS (*rising, and going over to* PICKERING) Pickering: if we were to take this man in hand for three months, he could choose between a seat in the Cabinet and a popular pulpit in Wales.

PICKERING What do you say to that, Doolittle?

DOOLITTLE Not me, Governor, thank you kindly. Ive heard all the preachers and all the prime ministers—for I'm a thinking man and game for politics or religion or social reform same as all the other amusements— and I tell you it's a dog's life any way you look at it. Undeserving poverty is my line. Taking one station in society with another, it's—it's—well, it's the only one that has any ginger in it, to my taste.

HIGGINS I suppose we must give him a fiver.

PICKERING He'll make a bad use of it, I'm afraid.

DOOLITTLE Not me, Governor, so help me I wont. Dont you be afraid that I'll save it and spare it and live idle on it. There wont be a penny of it left by Monday: I'll have to go to work same as if I'd never had it. It wont pauperize me, you bet. Just one good spree for myself and the missus, giving pleasure to ourselves and employment to others, and satisfaction to you to think it's not been throwed away. You couldnt spend it better.

HIGGINS (*taking out his pocket book and coming between* DOOLITTLE *and the piano*) This is irresistible. Lets give him ten. (*He offers two notes to the dustman*)

DOOLITTLE No, Governor. She wouldnt have the heart to spend ten; and perhaps I shouldnt neither. Ten pounds is a lot of money: it makes a man feel prudent like; and then goodbye to happiness. You give me what I ask you, Governor: not a penny more, and not a penny less.

PICKERING Why dont you marry that missus of yours? I rather draw the line at encouraging that sort of immorality.

DOOLITTLE Tell her so, Governor: tell her so. I'm willing. It's me that suffers by it. Ive no hold on her. I got to be agreeable to her. I got to give her presents. I got to buy her clothes something sinful. I'm a slave to that woman, Governor, just because I'm not her lawful husband. And she knows it too. Catch her marrying me! Take my advice, Governor: marry Eliza while she's young and dont know no better. If you dont you'll be sorry for it after. If you do, she'll be sorry for it after; but better her than you, because youre a man, and she's only a woman and dont know how to be happy anyhow.

HIGGINS Pickering: if we listen to this man another minute, we shall have no convictions left. (*to* DOOLITTLE) Five pounds I think you said.

DOOLITTLE Thank you kindly, Governor.

HIGGINS Youre sure you wont take ten?

DOOLITTLE Not now. Another time, Governor.

HIGGINS (*handing him a five-pound note*) Here you are.

DOOLITTLE Thank you, Governor. Good morning. (*He hurries to the door, anxious to get away with his booty. When he opens it he is confronted with a dainty and exquisitely clean young Japanese lady in a simple blue cotton kimono printed cunningly with small white jasmine blossoms.* MRS PEARCE *is with her. He gets out of her way deferentially and apologizes*) Beg pardon, miss.

THE JAPANESE LADY Garn! Dont you know your own daughter?

DOOLITTLE		Bly me! it's Eliza!
HIGGINS	*exclaiming simultaneously*	Whats that? This!
PICKERING		By Jove!

LIZA Dont I look silly?

HIGGINS Silly?

MRS PEARCE (*at the door*) Now, Mr Higgins, please dont say anything to make the girl conceited about herself.

HIGGINS (*conscientiously*) Oh! Quite right, Mrs Pearce. (*to* ELIZA) Yes: damned silly.

MRS PEARCE Please, sir.

HIGGINS (*correcting himself*) I mean extremely silly.

LIZA I should look all right with my hat on. (*She takes up her hat; puts it on; and walks across the room to the fireplace with a fashionable air*)

HIGGINS A new fashion, by George! And it ought to look horrible!

DOOLITTLE (*with fatherly pride*)

Well, I never thought she'd clean up as good looking as that, Governor. She's a credit to me, aint she?

LIZA I tell you, it's easy to clean up here. Hot and cold water on tap, just as much as you like, there is. Woolly towels, there is; and a towel horse so hot, it burns your fingers. Soft brushes to scrub yourself, and a wooden bowl of soap smelling like primroses. Now I know why ladies is so clean. Washing's a treat for them. Wish they could see what it is for the like of me!

HIGGINS I'm glad the bathroom met with your approval.

LIZA It didnt: not all of it; and I dont care who hears me say it. Mrs Pearce knows.

HIGGINS What was wrong, Mrs Pearce?

MRS PEARCE (*blandly*) Oh, nothing, sir. It doesnt matter.

LIZA I had a good mind to break it. I didnt know which way to look. But I hung a towel over it, I did.

HIGGINS Over what?

MRS PEARCE Over the looking-glass, sir.

HIGGINS Doolittle: you have brought your daughter up too strictly.

DOOLITTLE Me! I never brought her up at all, except to give her a lick of a strap now and again. Dont put it on me, Governor. She aint accustomed to it, you see: thats all. But she'll soon pick up your free-and-easy ways.

LIZA I'm a good girl, I am; and I wont pick up no free-and-easy ways.

HIGGINS Eliza: if you say again that youre a good girl, your father shall take you home.

LIZA Not him. You dont know my father. All he come here for was to touch you for some money to get drunk on.

DOOLITTLE Well, what else would I want money for? To put into the plate in church, I suppose. (*She puts out her tongue at him. He is so incensed by this that* PICKERING *presently finds it necessary to step between them*) Dont you give me none of your lip; and dont let me hear you giving this gentleman any of it neither, or youll hear from me about it. See?

HIGGINS Have you any further advice to give her before you go, Doolittle? Your blessing, for instance.

DOOLITTLE No, Governor: I aint such a mug as to put up my children to all I know myself. Hard enough to hold them in without that. If you want Eliza's mind improved, Governor, you do it yourself with a strap. So long, gentlemen. (*He turns to go*)

HIGGINS (*impressively*) Stop. Youll come regularly to see your daughter. It's your duty, you know. My brother is a clergyman; and he could help you in your talks with her.

DOOLITTLE (*evasively*) Certainly, I'll come, Governor. Not just this week, because I have a job at a distance. But later on you may depend on me. Afternoon, gentlemen. Afternoon, maam. (*He touches his hat to* MRS PEARCE, *who disdains the salutation and goes out. He winks at* HIGGINS, *thinking him probably a fellow-sufferer from* MRS PEARCE'S *difficult disposition, and follows her*)

LIZA Dont you believe the old liar. He'd as soon you set a bulldog on him as a clergyman. You wont see him again in a hurry.

HIGGINS   I dont want to, Eliza. Do you?

LIZA   Not me. I dont want never to see him again, I dont. He's a disgrace to me, he is, collecting dust, instead of working at his trade.

PICKERING   What is his trade, Eliza?

LIZA   Taking money out of other people's pockets into his own. His proper trade's a navvy; and he works at it sometimes too—for exercise—and earns good money at it. Aint you going to call me Miss Doolittle any more?

PICKERING   I beg your pardon, Miss Doolittle. It was a slip of the tongue.

LIZA   Oh, I dont mind; only it sounded so genteel. I should just like to take a taxi to the corner of Tottenham Court Road and get out there and tell it to wait for me, just to put the girls in their place a bit. I wouldnt speak to them, you know.

PICKERING   Better wait til we get you something really fashionable.

HIGGINS   Besides, you shouldnt cut your old friends now that you have risen in the world. Thats what we call snobbery.

LIZA   You dont call the like of them my friends now, I should hope. Theyve took it out of me often enough with their ridicule when they had the chance; and now I mean to get a bit of my own back. But if I'm to have fashionable clothes, I'll wait. I should like to have some. Mrs Pearce says youre going to give me some to wear in bed at night different to what I wear in the daytime; but it do seem a waste of money when you could get something to show. Besides, I never could fancy changing into cold things on a winter night.

MRS PEARCE (*coming back*)   Now, Eliza. The new things have come for you to try on.

LIZA   Ah-ow-oo-ooh! (*She rushes out*)

MRS PEARCE (*following her*)   Oh, dont rush about like that, girl. (*She shuts the door behind her*)

HIGGINS   Pickering: we have taken on a stiff job.

PICKERING (*with conviction*)   Higgins: we have.

(There seems to be some curiosity as to what Higgins's lessons to Eliza were like. Well, here is a sample: the first one.

(Picture Eliza, in her new clothes, and feeling her inside put out of step by a lunch, dinner, and breakfast of a kind to which it is unaccustomed, seated with Higgins and the Colonel in the study, feeling like a hospital outpatient at a first encounter with the doctors.

(Higgins, constitutionally unable to sit still, discomposes her still more by striding restlessly about. But for the reassuring presence and quietude of her friend the Colonel she would run for her life, even back to Drury Lane.)

HIGGINS   Say your alphabet.

LIZA   I know my alphabet. Do you think I know nothing? I dont need to be taught like a child.

HIGGINS (*thundering*)   Say your alphabet.

PICKERING   Say it, Miss Doolittle. You will understand presently. Do what he tells you; and let him teach you in his own way.

LIZA   Oh well, if you put it like that —ahyee, bəyee, cəyee, dəyee—

HIGGINS (*with the roar of a wounded lion*) Stop. Listen to this, Pickering. This is what we pay for as elementary education. This unfortunate animal has been locked up for nine years in school at our expense to teach her to speak and read the language of Shakespeare and Milton. And the result is ahyee, bəyee, cəyee, dəyee. (*to* ELIZA) Say A, B, C, D.

LIZA (*almost in tears*) But I'm sayin it. Ahyee, bəyee, cəyee—

HIGGINS Stop. Say a cup of tea.

LIZA A capətə-ee.

HIGGINS Put your tongue forward until it squeezes against the top of your lower teeth. Now say cup.

LIZA C-c-c—I cant. C-Cup.

PICKERING Good. Splendid, Miss Doolittle.

HIGGINS By Jupiter, she's done it the first shot. Pickering: we shall make a duchess of her. (*to* ELIZA) Now do you think you could possibly say tea? Not tə-yee, mind: if you ever say bə-yee cə-yee də-yee again you shall be dragged round the room three times by the hair of your head. (*Fortissimo*) T, T, T, T.

LIZA (*weeping*) I cant hear no difference cep that it sounds more genteel-like when you say it.

HIGGINS Well, if you can hear that difference, what the devil are you crying for? Pickering: give her a chocolate.

PICKERING No, no. Never mind crying a little, Miss Doolittle: you are doing very well; and the lessons wont hurt. I promise you I wont let him drag you round the room by your hair.

HIGGINS Be off with you to Mrs Pearce and tell her about it. Think about it. Try to do it by yourself: and keep your tongue well forward in your mouth instead of trying to roll it up and swallow it. Another lesson at half-past four this afternoon. Away with you.

(ELIZA, *still sobbing, rushes from the room*)

(And that is the sort of ordeal poor Eliza has to go through for months before we meet her again on her first appearance in London society of the professional class.)

ACT III

It is MRS HIGGINS's *at-home day. Nobody has yet arrived. Her drawing room, in a flat on Chelsea Embankment, has three windows looking on the river; and the ceiling is not so lofty as it would be in an older house of the same pretension. The windows are open, giving access to a balcony with flowers in pots. If you stand with your face to the windows, you have the fireplace on your left and the door in the right-hand wall close to the corner nearest the windows.*

MRS HIGGINS *was brought up on Morris and Burne Jones; and her room, which is very unlike her son's room in Wimpole Street, is not crowded with furniture and little tables and nicknacks. In the middle of the room there is a big ottoman; and this, with the carpet, the Morris wall-papers, and the Morris chintz window curtains and brocade covers of the ottoman and its cushions, supply all the ornament, and are much too handsome to be hidden by odds and ends of useless things. A few good oil-paintings from the exhibitions in the Grosvenor Gallery thirty years ago (the Burne Jones, not the Whistler side of them) are on the walls. The only landscape is a Cecil Lawson on the scale of a Rubens. There is a portrait of* MRS HIGGINS *as she was when she defied the fashion in her youth in one of the beautiful Rossettian costumes which, when caricatured by people who did not understand, led to the absurdities of popular estheticism in the eighteen-seventies.*

In the corner diagonally opposite the door MRS HIGGINS, *now over sixty and long past taking the trouble to dress out of the fashion, sits writing at an elegantly simple writing-table with a bell button within reach of her hand. There is a Chippendale chair further back in the room between her and the window nearest her side. At the other side of the room, further forward, is an Elizabethan chair roughly carved in the taste of Inigo Jones. On the same side a piano in a decorated case. The corner between the fireplace and the window is occupied by a divan cushioned in Morris chintz.*

It is between four and five in the afternoon.

The door is opened violently; and HIGGINS *enters with his hat on.*

MRS HIGGINS (*dismayed*) Henry! (*scolding him*) What are you doing here today? It is my at-home day: you promised not to come. (*As he bends to kiss her, she takes his hat off, and presents it to him*)

HIGGINS Oh bother! (*He throws the hat down on the table*)

MRS HIGGINS Go home at once.

HIGGINS (*kissing her*) I know, mother. I came on purpose.

MRS HIGGINS But you mustnt. I'm serious, Henry. You offend all my friends: they stop coming whenever they meet you.

HIGGINS Nonsense! I know I have no small talk; but people dont mind. (*He sits on the settee*)

MRS HIGGINS Oh! dont they? Small talk indeed! What about your large talk? Really, dear, you mustnt stay.

HIGGINS I must. Ive a job for you. A phonetic job.

MRS HIGGINS No use, dear. I'm sorry; but I cant get round your vowels; and though I like to get pretty postcards in your patent shorthand, I always have to read the copies in ordinary writing you so thoughtfully send me.

HIGGINS Well, this isnt a phonetic job.

MRS HIGGINS You said it was.

HIGGINS Not your part of it. Ive picked up a girl.

MRS HIGGINS Does that mean that some girl has picked you up?

HIGGINS Not at all. I dont mean a love affair.

MRS HIGGINS What a pity!

HIGGINS Why?

MRS HIGGINS Well, you never fall in love with anyone under forty-five. When will you discover that there are some rather nice-looking young women about?

HIGGINS Oh, I cant be bothered with young women. My idea of a lovable woman is somebody as like you as possible. I shall never get into the way of seriously liking young women: some habits lie too deep to be changed. (*rising abruptly and walking about, jingling his money and his keys in his trouser pockets*) Besides, theyre all idiots.

MRS HIGGINS Do you know what

you would do if you really loved me, Henry?

HIGGINS   Oh bother! What? Marry, I suppose.

MRS HIGGINS   No. Stop fidgeting and take your hands out of your pockets. (*With a gesture of despair, he obeys and sits down again*) That's a good boy. Now tell me about the girl.

HIGGINS   She's coming to see you.

MRS HIGGINS   I dont remember asking her.

HIGGINS   You didn't. *I* asked her. If youd known her you wouldnt have asked her.

MRS HIGGINS   Indeed! Why?

HIGGINS   Well, it's like this. She's a common flower girl. I picked her off the kerbstone.

MRS HIGGINS   And invited her to my at-home!

HIGGINS (*rising and coming to her to coax her*)   Oh, thatll be all right. Ive taught her to speak properly; and she has strict orders as to her behavior. She's to keep to two subjects: the weather and everybody's health —Fine day and How do you do, you know—and not to let herself go on things in general. That will be safe.

MRS HIGGINS   Safe! To talk about our health! about our insides! perhaps about our outsides! How could you be so silly, Henry?

HIGGINS (*impatiently*)   Well, she must talk about something. (*He controls himself and sits down again*) Oh, she'll be all right: dont you fuss. Pickering is in it with me. Ive a sort of bet on that I'll pass her off as a duchess in six months. I started on her some months ago; and she's getting on like a house on fire. I shall win my bet. She has a quick ear; and she's easier to teach than my middle-class pupils because she's had to learn a complete new language. She talks English almost as you talk French.

MRS HIGGINS   Thats satisfactory, at all events.

HIGGINS   Well, it is and it isnt.

MRS HIGGINS   What does that mean?

HIGGINS   You see, Ive got her pronunciation all right; but you have to consider not only how a girl pronounces, but what she pronounces; and that's where—

> (*They are interrupted by the parlor-maid, announcing guests*)

THE PARLOR-MAID   Mrs and Miss Eynsford Hill. (*She withdraws*)

HIGGINS   Oh Lord! (*He rises; snatches his hat from the table; and makes for the door; but before he reaches it his mother introduces him*)

> (*Mrs and Miss Eynsford Hill are the mother and daughter who sheltered from the rain in Covent Garden. The mother is well bred, quiet, and has the habitual anxiety of straitened means. The daughter has acquired a gay air of being very much at home in society: the bravado of genteel poverty*)

MRS EYNSFORD HILL (*to MRS HIGGINS*)   How do you do? (*They shake hands*)

MISS EYNSFORD HILL   How d'you do? (*She shakes*)

MRS HIGGINS (*introducing*)   My son Henry.

MRS EYNSFORD HILL   Your celebrated son! I have so longed to meet you, Professor Higgins.

HIGGINS (*glumly, making no move-*

ment in her direction) De-lighted. *(He backs against the piano and bows brusquely)*

MISS EYNSFORD HILL *(going to him with confident familiarity)* How do you do?

HIGGINS *(staring at her)* Ive seen you before somewhere. I havnt the ghost of a notion where; but Ive heard your voice. *(drearily)* It doesnt matter. Youd better sit down.

MRS HIGGINS I'm sorry to say that my celebrated son has no manners. You mustnt mind him.

MISS EYNSFORD HILL *(gaily)* I don't. *(She sits in the Elizabethan chair)*

MRS EYNSFORD HILL *(a little bewildered)* Not at all. *(She sits on the ottoman between her daughter and MRS HIGGINS, who has turned her chair away from the writing-table)*

HIGGINS Oh, have I been rude? I didnt mean to be.

> *(He goes to the central window, through which, with his back to the company, he contemplates the river and the flowers in Battersea Park on the opposite bank as if they were a frozen desert.*
> *(The parlor-maid returns, ushering in PICKERING)*

THE PARLOR-MAID Colonel Pickering. *(She withdraws)*

PICKERING How do you do, Mrs Higgins?

MRS HIGGINS So glad youve come. Do you know Mrs Eynsford Hill —Miss Eynsford Hill?

> *(Exchange of bows. The COLONEL brings the Chippendale chair a little forward between MRS HILL and MRS HIGGINS, and sits down)*

PICKERING Has Henry told you what weve come for?

HIGGINS *(over his shoulder)* We were interrupted: damn it!

MRS HIGGINS Oh Henry, Henry, really!

MRS EYNSFORD HILL *(half rising)* Are we in the way?

MRS HIGGINS *(rising and making her sit down again)* No, no. You couldnt have come more fortunately: we want you to meet a friend of ours.

HIGGINS *(turning hopefully)* Yes, by George! We want two or three people. You'll do as well as anybody else.

> *(The parlor-maid returns, ushering Freddy)*

THE PARLOR-MAID Mr Eynsford Hill.

HIGGINS *(almost audibly, past endurance)* God of Heaven! another of them.

FREDDY *(shaking hands with MRS HIGGINS)* Ahdedo?

MRS HIGGINS Very good of you to come. *(introducing)* Colonel Pickering.

FREDDY *(bowing)* Ahdedo?

MRS HIGGINS I dont think you know my son, Professor Higgins.

FREDDY *(going to HIGGINS)* Ahdedo?

HIGGINS *(looking at him much as if he were a pickpocket)* I'll take my oath Ive met you before somewhere. Where was it?

FREDDY I dont think so.

HIGGINS *(resignedly)* It dont matter, anyhow. Sit down.

> *(He shakes FREDDY'S hand, and almost slings him on to the ottoman with his face to the window; then comes round to the other side of it)*

HIGGINS Well, here we are, anyhow! *(He sits down on the otto-*

man next MRS EYNSFORD HILL, *on her left*) And now, what the devil are we going to talk about until Eliza comes?

MRS HIGGINS   Henry: you are the life and soul of the Royal Society's soirées; but really youre rather trying on more commonplace occasions.

HIGGINS   Am I? Very sorry. (*beaming suddenly*) I suppose I am, you know. (*uproariously*) Ha, ha!

MISS EYNSFORD HILL (*who considers* HIGGINS *quite eligible matrimonially*) I sympathize. I havnt any small talk. If people would only be frank and say what they really think!

HIGGINS   (*relapsing into gloom*) Lord forbid!

MRS EYNSFORD HILL (*taking up her daughter's cue*) But why?

HIGGINS   What they think they ought to think is bad enough, Lord knows; but what they really think would break up the whole show. Do you suppose it would be really agreeable if I were to come out now with what *I* really think?

MISS EYNSFORD HILL (*gaily*) Is it so very cynical?

HIGGINS   Cynical! Who the dickens said it was cynical? I mean it wouldnt be decent.

MRS EYNSFORD HILL (*seriously*) Oh! I'm sure you dont mean that, Mr Higgins.

HIGGINS   You see, we're all savages, more or less. We're supposed to be civilized and cultured—to know all about poetry and philosophy and art and science, and so on; but how many of us know even the meanings of these names? (*to* MISS HILL) What do you know of poetry? (*to* MRS HILL) What do you know of science? (*indicating* FREDDY) What does he know of art or science or anything else? What the devil do you imagine I know of philosophy?

MRS HIGGINS (*warningly*) Or of manners, Henry?

THE PARLOR-MAID (*opening the door*) Miss Doolittle. (*She withdraws*)

HIGGINS (*rising hastily and running to* MRS HIGGINS) Here she is, mother. (*He stands on tiptoe and makes signs over his mother's head to* ELIZA *to indicate to her which lady is her hostess*)

(ELIZA, *who is exquisitely dressed, produces an impression of such remarkable distinction and beauty as she enters that they all rise, quite fluttered. Guided by* HIGGINS's *signals, she comes to* MRS HIGGINS *with studied grace*)

LIZA (*speaking with pedantic correctness of pronunciation and great beauty of tone*) How do you do, Mrs Higgins? (*She gasps slightly in making sure of the H in Higgins, but is quite successful*) Mr Higgins told me I might come.

MRS HIGGINS (*cordially*) Quite right: I'm very glad indeed to see you.

PICKERING   How do you do, Miss Doolittle?

LIZA (*shaking hands with him*) Colonel Pickering, is it not?

MRS EYNSFORD HILL   I feel sure we have met before, Miss Doolittle. I remember your eyes.

LIZA   How do you do? (*She sits down on the ottoman gracefully in the place just left vacant by* HIGGINS)

MRS EYNSFORD HILL (*introducing*) My daughter Clara.

LIZA How do you do?

CLARA (*impulsively*) How do you do? (*She sits down on the ottoman beside* ELIZA, *devouring her with her eyes*)

FREDDY (*coming to their side of the ottoman*) Ive certainly had the pleasure.

MRS EYNSFORD HILL (*introducing*) My son Freddy.

LIZA How do you do?

   (FREDDY *bows and sits down in the Elizabethan chair, infatuated*)

HIGGINS (*suddenly*) By George, yes: it all comes back to me! (*They stare at him*) Covent Garden! (*lamentably*) What a damned thing!

MRS HIGGINS Henry, please! (*He is about to sit on the edge of the table*) Dont sit on my writing-table: youll break it.

HIGGINS (*sulkily*) Sorry.

   (*He goes to the divan, stumbling into the fender and over the fire-irons on his way; extricating himself with muttered imprecations; and finishing his disastrous journey by throwing himself so impatiently on the divan that he almost breaks it.* MRS HIGGINS *looks at him, but controls herself and says nothing. A long and painful pause ensues*)

MRS HIGGINS (*at last, conversationally*) Will it rain, do you think?

LIZA The shallow depression in the west of these islands is likely to move slowly in an easterly direction. There are no indications of any great change in the barometrical situation.

FREDDY Ha! ha! how awfully funny!

LIZA What is wrong with that, young man? I bet I got it right.

FREDDY Killing!

MRS EYNSFORD HILL I'm sure I hope it wont turn cold. Theres so much influenza about. It runs right through our whole family regularly every spring.

LIZA (*darkly*) My aunt died of influenza: so they said.

MRS EYNSFORD HILL (*clicks her tongue sympathetically*) ! ! !

LIZA (*in the same tragic tone*) But it's my belief they done the old woman in.

MRS HIGGINS (*puzzled*) Done her in?

LIZA Y-e-e-e-es, Lord love you! Why should she die of influenza? She come through diphtheria right enough the year before. I saw her with my own eyes. Fairly blue with it, she was. They all thought she was dead; but my father he kept ladling gin down her throat til she came to so sudden that she bit the bowl off the spoon.

MRS EYNSFORD HILL (*startled*) Dear me!

LIZA (*piling up the indictment*) What call would a woman with that strength in her have to die of influenza? What become of her new straw hat that should have come to me? Somebody pinched it; and what I say is, them as pinched it done her in.

MRS EYNSFORD HILL What does doing her in mean?

HIGGINS (*hastily*) Oh, thats the new small talk. To do a person in means to kill them.

MRS EYNSFORD HILL (*to* ELIZA, *horrified*) You surely dont believe that your aunt was killed?

LIZA Do I not! Them she lived with would have killed her for a hat-pin, let alone a hat.

MRS EYNSFORD HILL But it cant have been right for your father to pour spirits down her throat like that. It might have killed her.

LIZA Not her. Gin was mother's milk to her. Besides, he'd poured so much down his own throat that he knew the good of it.

MRS EYNSFORD HILL Do you mean that he drank?

LIZA Drank! My word! Something chronic.

MRS EYNSFORD HILL How dreadful for you!

LIZA Not a bit. It never did him no harm what I could see. But then he did not keep it up regular. (*cheerfully*) On the burst, as you might say, from time to time. And always more agreeable when he had a drop in. When he was out of work, my mother used to give him fourpence and tell him to go out and not come back until he'd drunk himself cheerful and lovinglike. Theres lots of women has to make their husbands drunk to make them fit to live with. (*now quite at her ease*) You see, it's like this. If a man has a bit of conscience, it always takes him when he's sober; and then it makes him low-spirited. A drop of booze just takes that off and makes him happy. (*to* FREDDY, *who is in convulsions of suppressed laughter*) Here! what are you sniggering at?

FREDDY The new small talk. You do it so awfully well.

LIZA If I was doing it proper, what was you laughing at? (*to* HIGGINS) Have I said anything I oughtnt?

MRS HIGGINS (*interposing*) Not at all, Miss Doolittle.

LIZA Well, thats a mercy, anyhow. (*expansively*) What I always say is—

HIGGINS (*rising and looking at his watch*) Ahem!

LIZA (*looking round at him; taking the hint; and rising*) Well: I must go. (*They all rise.* FREDDY *goes to the door*) So pleased to have met you. Goodbye. (*She shakes hands with* MRS HIGGINS)

MRS HIGGINS Goodbye.

LIZA Goodbye, Colonel Pickering.

PICKERING Goodbye, Miss Doolittle. (*They shake hands*)

LIZA (*nodding to the others*) Goodbye, all.

FREDDY (*opening the door for her*) Are you walking across the Park, Miss Doolittle? If so—

LIZA (*with perfectly elegant diction*) Walk! Not bloody likely. (*sensation*) I am going in a taxi. (*She goes out*)

(PICKERING *gasps and sits down.* FREDDY *goes out on the balcony to catch another glimpse of* ELIZA)

MRS EYNSFORD HILL (*suffering from shock*) Well, I really cant get used to the new ways.

CLARA (*throwing herself discontentedly into the Elizabethan chair*) Oh, it's all right, mamma, quite right. People will think we never go anywhere or see anybody if you are so old-fashioned.

MRS EYNSFORD HILL I daresay I am very old-fashioned; but I do hope you wont begin using that expression, Clara. I have got accustomed to hear you talking about men as rotters, and calling everything filthy and beastly: though I do think it horrible and unlady-like. But this last is really too much. Dont you think so, Colonel Pickering?

PICKERING Dont ask me. Ive been away in India for several years; and manners have changed so much that I sometimes dont know whether I'm at a respectable dinnertable or in a ship's forecastle.

CLARA It's all a matter of habit. Theres no right or wrong in it. Nobody means anything by it. And it's so quaint, and gives such a smart emphasis to things that are not in themselves very witty. I find the new small talk delightful and quite innocent.

MRS EYNSFORD HILL (*rising*) Well, after that, I think it's time for us to go.

> (PICKERING *and* HIGGINS *rise*)

CLARA (*rising*) Oh yes: we have three at-homes to go to still. Goodbye, Mrs Higgins. Goodbye, Colonel Pickering. Goodbye, Professor Higgins.

HIGGINS (*coming grimly at her from the divan, and accompanying her to the door*) Goodbye. Be sure you try on that small talk at the three at-homes. Dont be nervous about it. Pitch it in strong.

CLARA (*all smiles*) I will. Goodbye. Such nonsense, all this early Victorian prudery!

HIGGINS (*tempting her*) Such damned nonsense!

CLARA Such bloody nonsense!

MRS EYNSFORD HILL (*convulsively*) Clara!

CLARA Ha! ha! (*She goes out radiant, conscious of being thoroughly up to date, and is heard descending the stairs in a stream of silvery laughter*)

FREDDY (*to the heavens at large*) Well, I ask you—(*He gives it up, and comes to* MRS HIGGINS) Goodbye.

MRS HIGGINS (*shaking hands*) Goodbye. Would you like to meet Miss Doolittle again?

FREDDY (*eagerly*) Yes, I should, most awfully.

MRS HIGGINS Well, you know my days.

FREDDY Yes. Thanks awfully. Goodbye. (*He goes out*)

MRS EYNSFORD HILL Goodbye, Mr Higgins.

HIGGINS Goodbye. Goodbye.

MRS EYNSFORD HILL (*to* PICKERING) It's no use. I shall never be able to bring myself to use that word.

PICKERING Dont. It's not compulsory, you know. Youll get on quite well without it.

MRS EYNSFORD HILL Only, Clara is so down on me if I am not positively reeking with the latest slang. Goodbye.

PICKERING Goodbye (*They shake hands*)

MRS EYNSFORD HILL (*to* MRS HIGGINS) You mustnt mind Clara. (PICKERING, *catching from her lowered tone that this is not meant for him to hear, discreetly joins* HIGGINS *at the window*) We're so poor! and she gets so few parties, poor child! She doesnt quite know. (MRS HIGGINS, *seeing that her eyes are moist, takes her hand sympathetically and goes with her to the door*) But the boy is nice. Dont you think so?

MRS HIGGINS Oh, quite nice. I shall always be delighted to see him.

MRS EYNSFORD HILL Thank you, dear. Goodbye. (*She goes out*)

HIGGINS (*eagerly*) Well? Is Eliza

presentable? (*He swoops on his mother and drags her to the ottoman, where she sits down in* ELIZA'*s place with her son on her left*)

(PICKERING *returns to his chair on her right*)

MRS HIGGINS You silly boy, of course she's not presentable. She's a triumph of your art and of her dressmaker's; but if you suppose for a moment that she doesn't give herself away in every sentence she utters, you must be perfectly cracked about her.

PICKERING But dont you think something might be done? I mean something to eliminate the sanguinary element from her conversation.

MRS HIGGINS Not as long as she is in Henry's hands.

HIGGINS (*aggrieved*) Do you mean that my language is improper?

MRS HIGGINS No, dearest: it would be quite proper—say on a canal barge; but it would not be proper for her at a garden party.

HIGGINS (*deeply injured*) Well I must say—

PICKERING (*interrupting him*) Come, Higgins: you must learn to know yourself. I havent heard such language as yours since we used to review the volunteers in Hyde Park twenty years ago.

HIGGINS (*sulkily*) Oh, well, if you say so I suppose I dont always talk like a bishop.

MRS HIGGINS (*quieting* HENRY *with a touch*) Colonel Pickering: will you tell me what is the exact state of things in Wimpole Street?

PICKERING (*cheerfully: as if this completely changed the subject*) Well, I have come to live there with Henry. We work together at my Indian dialects; and we think it more convenient—

MRS HIGGINS Quite so. I know all about that: it's an excellent arrangement. But where does this girl live?

HIGGINS With us, of course. Where should she live?

MRS HIGGINS But on what terms? Is she a servant? If not, what is she?

PICKERING (*slowly*) I think I know what you mean, Mrs Higgins.

HIGGINS Well, dash me if *I* do! Ive had to work at the girl every day for months to get her to her present pitch. Besides, she's useful. She knows where my things are, and remembers my appointments and so forth.

MRS HIGGINS How does your housekeeper get on with her?

HIGGINS Mrs Pearce? Oh, she's jolly glad to get so much taken off her hands; for before Eliza came, she used to have to find things and remind me of my appointments. But she's got some silly bee in her bonnet about Eliza. She keeps saying "You dont think, sir": doesnt she, Pick?

PICKERING Yes: thats the formula. "You dont think, sir." Thats the end of every conversation about Eliza.

HIGGINS As if I ever stop thinking about the girl and her confounded vowels and consonants. I'm worn out, thinking about her, and watching her lips and her teeth and her tongue, not to mention her soul, which is the quaintest of the lot.

MRS HIGGINS You certainly are a pretty pair of babies, playing with your live doll.

HIGGINS Playing! The hardest job I ever tackled: make no mistake about that, mother. But you have no idea how frightfully interesting it is to take a human being and change her into a quite different human being by creating a new speech for her. It's filling up the deepest gulf that separates class from class and soul from soul.

PICKERING (*drawing his chair closer to* MRS HIGGINS *and bending over to her eagerly*) Yes: its enormously interesting. I assure you, Mrs Higgins, we take Eliza very seriously. Every week— every day almost—there is some new change. (*closer again*) We keep records of every stage— dozens of gramophone disks and photographs—

HIGGINS (*assailing her at the other ear*) Yes, by George: it's the most absorbing experiment I ever tackled. She regularly fills our lives up: doesnt she, Pick?

PICKERING We're always talking Eliza.

HIGGINS Teaching Eliza.

PICKERING Dressing Eliza.

MRS HIGGINS What!

HIGGINS Inventing new Elizas.

HIGGINS }
PICKERING } *speaking together*

HIGGINS You know, she has the most extraordinary quickness of ear:

PICKERING I assure you, my dear Mrs Higgins, that girl

HIGGINS just like a parrot. Ive tried her with every

PICKERING is a genius. She can play the piano quite beautifully.

HIGGINS }
PICKERING } *speaking together*

HIGGINS possible sort of sound that a human being can make—

PICKERING We have taken her to classical concerts and to music

HIGGINS Continental dialects, African dialects, Hottentot

PICKERING halls; and it's all the same to her: she plays everything

HIGGINS clicks, things it took me years to get hold of; and

PICKERING she hears right off when she comes home, whether it's

HIGGINS she picks them up like a shot, right away, as if she had

PICKERING Beethoven and Brahms or Lehar and Lionel Monckton;

HIGGINS been at it all her life.

PICKERING though six months ago, she'd never as much as touched a piano—

MRS HIGGINS (*putting her fingers in her ears, as they are by this time shouting one another down with an intolerable noise*) Sh- sh-sh—sh! (*They stop*)

PICKERING   I beg your pardon. (*He draws his chair back apologetically*)

HIGGINS   Sorry. When Pickering starts shouting nobody can get a word in edgeways.

MRS HIGGINS   Be quiet, Henry. Colonel Pickering: dont you realize that when Eliza walked in Wimpole Street, something walked in with her?

PICKERING   Her father did. But Henry soon got rid of him.

MRS HIGGINS   It would have been more to the point if her mother had. But as her mother didnt something else did.

PICKERING   But what?

MRS HIGGINS   (*unconsciously dating herself by the word*) A problem.

PICKERING   Oh, I see. The problem of how to pass her off as a lady.

HIGGINS   I'll solve that problem. Ive half solved it already.

MRS HIGGINS   No, you two infinitely stupid male creatures: the problem of what is to be done with her afterwards.

HIGGINS   I dont see anything in that. She can go her own way, with all the advantages I have given her.

MRS HIGGINS   The advantages of that poor woman who was here just now! The manners and habits that disqualify a fine lady from earning her own living without giving her a fine lady's income! Is that what you mean?

PICKERING   (*indulgently, being rather bored*) Oh, that will be all right, Mrs Higgins. (*He rises to go*)

HIGGINS   (*rising also*) We'll find her some light employment.

PICKERING   She's happy enough. Dont you worry about her. Goodbye. (*He shakes hands as if he were consoling a frightened child, and makes for the door*)

HIGGINS   Anyhow, theres no good bothering now. The thing's done. Goodbye, mother. (*He kisses her, and follows* PICKERING)

PICKERING   (*turning for a final consolation*) There are plenty of openings. We'll do whats right. Goodbye.

HIGGINS   (*to* PICKERING *as they go out together*) Lets take her to the Shakespeare exhibition at Earls Court.

PICKERING   Yes: lets. Her remarks will be delicious.

HIGGINS   She'll mimic all the people for us when we get home.

PICKERING   Ripping. (*Both are heard laughing as they go downstairs*)

MRS HIGGINS   (*rises with an impatient bounce, and returns to her work at the writing-table. She sweeps a litter of disarranged papers out of the way; snatches a sheet of paper from her stationery case; and tries resolutely to write. At the third time she gives it up; flings down her pen; grips the table angrily and exclaims*) Oh, men! men!! men!!!

(Clearly Eliza will not pass as a duchess yet; and Higgins's bet remains unwon. But the six months are not yet exhausted; and just in time Eliza does actually pass as a princess. For a glimpse of how she did it imagine an Embassy in London one summer evening after dark. The hall door has an awning and a carpet across the sidewalk to the kerb, because a grand reception is in progress. A small crowd is lined up to see the guests arrive.

(A Rolls-Royce car drives up.

Pickering in evening dress, with medals and orders, alights, and hands out Eliza, in opera cloak, evening dress, diamonds, fan, flowers, and all accessories. Higgins follows. The car drives off; and the three go up the steps and into the house, the door opening for them as they approach.

(Inside the house they find themselves in a spacious hall from which the grand staircase rises. On the left are the arrangements for the gentlemen's cloaks. The male guests are depositing their hats and wraps there.

(On the right is a door leading to the ladies' cloakroom. Ladies are going in cloaked and coming out in splendor. Pickering whispers to Eliza and points out the ladies' room. She goes into it. Higgins and Pickering take off their overcoats and take tickets for them from the attendant.

(One of the guests, occupied in the same way, has his back turned. Having taken his ticket, he turns round and reveals himself as an important looking young man with an astonishingly hairy face. He has an enormous moustache, flowing out into luxuriant whiskers. Waves of hair cluster on his brow. His hair is cropped closely at the back, and glows with oil. Otherwise he is very smart. He wears several worthless orders. He is evidently a foreigner, guessable as a whiskered Pandour from Hungary; but in spite of the ferocity of his moustache he is amiable and genially voluble.

(Recognizing Higgins, he flings his arms wide apart and approaches him enthusiastically.)

WHISKERS Maestro, maestro. (*He embraces* HIGGINS *and kisses him on both cheeks*) You remember me?

HIGGINS No I dont. Who the devil are you?

WHISKERS I am your pupil: your first pupil, your best and greatest pupil. I am little Nepommuck, the marvellous boy. I have made your name famous throughout Europe. You teach me phonetic. You cannot forget ME.

HIGGINS Why dont you shave?

NEPOMMUCK I have not your imposing appearance, your chin, your brow. Nobody notice me when I shave. Now I am famous: they call me Hairy Faced Dick.

HIGGINS And what are you doing here among all these swells?

NEPOMMUCK I am interpreter. I speak 32 languages. I am indispensable at these international parties. You are great cockney specialist: you place a man anywhere in London the moment he opens his mouth. I place any man in Europe.

(*A footman hurries down the grand staircase and comes to* NEPOMMUCK)

FOOTMAN You are wanted upstairs. Her Excellency cannot understand the Greek gentleman.

NEPOMMUCK Thank you, yes, immediately.

(*The footman goes and is lost in the crowd*)

NEPOMMUCK (*to* HIGGINS) This Greek diplomatist pretends he cannot speak nor understand English. He cannot deceive me. He is the son of a Clerkenwell watchmaker. He speaks English so villainously that he dare not utter a word of it without betraying his origin. I help him to pretend; but I make him pay through the nose. I make them all pay. Ha ha! (*He hurries upstairs*)

PICKERING Is this fellow really an expert? Can he find out Eliza and blackmail her?

HIGGINS We shall see. If he finds her out I lose my bet.

> (ELIZA *comes from the cloakroom and joins them*)

PICKERING Well, Eliza, now for it. Are you ready?

LIZA Are you nervous, Colonel?

PICKERING Frightfully. I feel exactly as I felt before my first battle. It's the first time that frightens.

LIZA It is not the first time for me, Colonel. I have done this fifty times—hundreds of times—in my little piggery in Angel Court in my day-dreams. I am in a dream now. Promise me not to let Professor Higgins wake me; for if he does I shall forget everything and talk as I used to in Drury Lane.

PICKERING Not a word, Higgins. (*to* ELIZA) Now, ready?

LIZA Ready.

PICKERING Go.

> (*They mount the stairs,* HIGGINS *last.* PICKERING *whispers to the footman on the first landing*)

FIRST LANDING FOOTMAN Miss Doolittle, Colonel Pickering, Professor Higgins.

SECOND LANDING FOOTMAN Miss Doolittle, Colonel Pickering, Professor Higgins.

> (*At the top of the staircase the Ambassador and his wife, with* NEPOMMUCK *at her elbow, are receiving*)

HOSTESS (*taking* ELIZA's *hand*) How d'ye do?

HOST (*same play*) How d'ye do? How d'ye do, Pickering?

LIZA (*with a beautiful gravity that awes her hostess*) How do you do? (*She passes on to the drawing room*)

HOSTESS Is that your adopted daughter, Colonel Pickering? She will make a sensation.

PICKERING Most kind of you to invite her for me. (*He passes on*)

HOSTESS (*to* NEPOMMUCK) Find out all about her.

NEPOMMUCK (*bowing*) Excellency— (*He goes into the crowd*)

HOST How d'ye do, Higgins? You have a rival here tonight. He introduced himself as your pupil. Is he any good?

HIGGINS He can learn a language in a fortnight—knows dozens of them. A sure mark of a fool. As a phonetician, no good whatever.

HOSTESS How d'ye do, Professor?

HIGGINS How do you do? Fearful bore for you, this sort of thing. Forgive my part in it. (*He passes on*)

(In the drawing room and its suite of salons the reception is in full swing. Eliza passes through. She is so intent on her ordeal that she walks like a somnambulist in a desert instead of a débutante in a fashionable crowd. They stop talking to look at her, admiring her dress, her jewels, and her strangely attractive self. Some of the younger ones at the back stand on their chairs to see.

(The Host and Hostess come in from the staircase and mingle with their guests. Higgins, gloomy and contemptuous of the whole business, comes into the group where they are chatting.)

HOSTESS Ah, here is Professor Higgins: he will tell us. Tell us all about the wonderful young lady, Professor.

HIGGINS (*almost morosely*) What wonderful young lady?

HOSTESS You know very well. They tell me there has been nothing like her in London since people stood on their chairs to look at Mrs. Langtry.

(NEPOMMUCK *joins the group, full of news*)

HOSTESS Ah, here you are at last, Nepommuck. Have you found out all about the Doolittle lady?

NEPOMMUCK I have found out all about her. She is a fraud.

HOSTESS A fraud! Oh, no.

NEPOMMUCK YES, yes. She cannot deceive me. Her name cannot be Doolittle.

HIGGINS Why?

NEPOMMUCK Because Doolittle is an English name. And she is not English.

HOSTESS Oh, nonsense! She speaks English perfectly.

NEPOMMUCK Too perfectly. Can you show me any English woman who speaks English as it should be spoken? Only foreigners who have been taught to speak it speak it well.

HOSTESS Certainly she terrified me by the way she said How d'ye do. I had a schoolmistress who talked like that; and I was mortally afraid of her. But if she is not English, what is she?

NEPOMMUCK Hungarian.

ALL THE REST Hungarian!

NEPOMMUCK Hungarian. And of royal blood. I am Hungarian. My blood is royal.

HIGGINS Did you speak to her in Hungarian?

NEPOMMUCK I did. She was very clever. She said "Please speak to me in English: I do not understand French." French! She pretended not to know the difference between Hungarian and French. Impossible: she knows both.

HIGGINS And the blood royal? How did you find that out?

NEPOMMUCK Instinct, maestro, instinct. Only the Magyar races can produce that air of the divine right, those resolute eyes. She is a princess.

HOST What do you say, Professor?

HIGGINS I say an ordinary London girl out of the gutter and taught to speak by an expert. I place her in Drury Lane.

NEPOMMUCK Ha ha ha! Oh, maestro, maestro, you are mad on the subject of cockney dialects. The London gutter is the whole world for you.

HIGGINS (*to the* HOSTESS) What does your Excellency say?

HOSTESS Oh, of course I agree with Nepommuck. She must be a princess at least.

HOST Not necessarily legitimate, of course. Morganatic perhaps. But that is undoubtedly her class.

HIGGINS I stick to my opinion.

HOSTESS Oh, you are incorrigible.

(*The group breaks up, leaving* HIGGINS *isolated.* PICKERING *joins him*)

PICKERING Where is Eliza? We must keep an eye on her.

(ELIZA *joins them*)

LIZA I dont think I can bear much more. The people all stare so at me. An old lady has just told me that I speak exactly like Queen Victoria. I am sorry if I have lost your bet. I have done my best; but nothing can make me the same as these people.

PICKERING You have not lost it, my dear. You have won it ten times over.

HIGGINS Let us get out of this. I have had enough of chattering to these fools.

PICKERING Eliza is tired; and I am hungry. Let us clear out and have supper somewhere.

ACT IV

The Wimpole Street laboratory. Midnight. Nobody in the room. The clock on the mantelpiece strikes twelve. The fire is not alight: it is a summer night. Presently HIGGINS *and* PICKERING *are heard on the stairs.*

HIGGINS (*calling down to* PICKER-ING) I say, Pick: lock up, will you? I shant be going out again.

PICKERING Right. Can Mrs Pearce go to bed? We dont want anything more, do we?

HIGGINS Lord, no!

(ELIZA *opens the door and is seen on the lighted landing in all the finery in which she has just won* HIGGINS's *bet for him. She comes to the hearth and switches on the electric lights there. She is tired: her pallor contrasts strongly with her dark eyes and hair; and her expression is almost tragic. She takes off her cloak; puts her fan and gloves on the piano; and sits down on the bench, brooding and silent.* HIGGINS, *in evening dress, with overcoat and hat, comes in, carrying a smoking jacket which he has picked up downstairs. He takes off the hat and overcoat; throws them carelessly on the newspaper stand; disposes of his coat in the same way; puts on the smoking jacket; and throws himself wearily into the easy-chair at the hearth.* PICKERING, *similarly attired, comes in. He also takes off his hat and overcoat, and is about to throw them on* HIGGINS's *when he hesitates*)

PICKERING I say: Mrs Pearce will row if we leave these things lying about in the drawing room.

HIGGINS Oh, chuck them over the bannisters into the hall. She'll find them there in the morning and put them away all right. She'll think we were drunk.

PICKERING We are, slightly. Are there any letters?

HIGGINS I didnt look. (PICKERING *takes the overcoats and hats and goes downstairs.* HIGGINS *begins half singing half yawning an air from* La Fanciulla del Golden West. *Suddenly he stops and exclaims*) I wonder where the devil my slippers are!

(ELIZA *looks at him darkly; then rises suddenly and leaves the room.*

(HIGGINS *yawns again, and resumes his song.*

(PICKERING *returns, with the contents of the letterbox in his hand*)

PICKERING. Only circulars, and

this coroneted billet-doux for you. (*He throws the circulars into the fender, and posts himself on the hearth-rug, with his back to the grate*)

HIGGINS (*glancing at the billet-doux*) Money-lender. (*He throws the letter after the circulars*)

(ELIZA *returns with a pair of large down-at-heel slippers. She places them on the carpet before* HIGGINS, *and sits as before without a word*)

HIGGINS (*yawning again*) Oh Lord! What an evening! What a crew! What a silly tomfoolery! (*He raises his shoe to unlace it and catches sight of the slippers. He stops unlacing and looks at them as if they had appeared there of their own accord*) Oh! theyre there, are they?

PICKERING (*stretches himself*) Well, I feel a bit tired. It's been a long day. The garden party, a dinner party, and the reception! Rather too much of a good thing. But youve won your bet, Higgins, Eliza did the trick, and something to spare, eh?

HIGGINS (*fervently*) Thank God it's over!

(ELIZA *flinches violently; but they take no notice of her; and she recovers herself and sits stonily as before*)

PICKERING Were you nervous at the garden party? *I* was. Eliza didnt seem a bit nervous.

HIGGINS Oh, she wasnt nervous. I knew she'd be all right. No: it's the strain of putting the job through all these months that has told on me. It was interesting enough at first, while we were at the phonetics; but after that I got deadly sick of it. If I

hadnt backed myself to do it I should have chucked the whole thing up two months ago. It was a silly notion: the whole thing has been a bore.

PICKERING Oh come! the garden party was frightfully exciting. My heart began beating like anything.

HIGGINS Yes, for the first three minutes. But when I saw we were going to win hands down, I felt like a bear in a cage, hanging about doing nothing. The dinner was worse: sitting gorging there for over an hour, with nobody but a damned fool of a fashionable woman to talk to! I tell you, Pickering, never again for me. No more artificial duchesses. The whole thing has been simple purgatory.

PICKERING Youve never been broken in properly to the social routine. (*strolling over to the piano*) I rather enjoy dipping into it occasionally myself: it makes me feel young again. Anyhow, it was a great success: an immense success. I was quite frightened once or twice because Eliza was doing it so well. You see, lots of the real people cant do it at all: theyre such fools that they think style comes by nature to people in their position; and so they never learn. Theres always something professional about doing a thing superlatively well.

HIGGINS Yes: thats what drives me mad: the silly people dont know their own silly business. (*rising*) However, it's over and done with; and now I can go to bed at last without dreading tomorrow.

(ELIZA'S *beauty becomes murderous*)

PICKERING   I think I shall turn in too. Still, it's been a great occasion: a triumph for you. Goodnight. (*He goes*)

HIGGINS (*following him*) Goodnight. (*over his shoulder, at the door*) Put out the lights, Eliza; and tell Mrs Pearce not to make coffee for me in the morning: I'll take tea. (*He goes out*)

(ELIZA *tries to control herself and feel indifferent as she rises and walks across to the hearth to switch off the lights. By the time she gets there she is on the point of screaming. She sits down in* HIGGINS's *chair and holds on hard to the arms. Finally she gives way and flings herself furiously on the floor, raging*)

HIGGINS (*in despairing wrath outside*) What the devil have I done with my slippers? (*He appears at the door*)

LIZA (*snatching up the slippers, and hurling them at him one after the other with all her force*) There are your slippers. And there. Take your slippers; and may you never have a day's luck with them!

HIGGINS (*astounded*) What on earth—! (*He comes to her*) Whats the matter? Get up. (*He pulls her up*) Anything wrong?

LIZA (*breathless*) Nothing wrong —with you. Ive won your bet for you, havnt I? Thats enough for you. *I* dont matter, I suppose.

HIGGINS   You won my bet! You! Presumptuous insect! *I* won it. What did you throw those slippers at me for?

LIZA   Because I wanted to smash your face. I'd like to kill you,

you selfish brute. Why didnt you leave me where you picked me out of—in the gutter? You thank God it's all over, and that now you can throw me back again there, do you? (*She crisps her fingers frantically*)

HIGGINS (*looking at her in cool wonder*) The creature is nervous, after all.

LIZA (*gives a suffocated scream of fury, and instinctively darts her nails at his face*) ! !

HIGGINS (*catching her wrists*) Ah! would you? Claws in, you cat. How dare you show your temper to me? Sit down and be quiet. (*He throws her roughly into the easy-chair*)

LIZA (*crushed by superior strength and weight*) Whats to become of me? Whats to become of me?

HIGGINS   How the devil do I know whats to become of you? What does it matter what becomes of you?

LIZA   You dont care. I know you dont care. You wouldnt care if I was dead. I'm nothing to you— not so much as them slippers.

HIGGINS (*thundering*) Those slippers.

LIZA (*with bitter submission*) Those slippers. I didnt think it made any difference now.

(*A pause.* ELIZA *hopeless and crushed.* HIGGINS *a little uneasy*)

HIGGINS (*in his loftiest manner*) Why have you begun going on like this? May I ask whether you complain of your treatment here?

LIZA   No.

HIGGINS   Has anybody behaved badly to you? Colonel Pickering? Mrs Pearce? Any of the servants?

LIZA   No.

HIGGINS I presume you dont pretend that *I* have treated you badly?

LIZA No.

HIGGINS I am glad to hear it. (*He moderates his tone*) Perhaps youre tired after the strain of the day. Will you have a glass of champagne? (*He moves towards the door*)

LIZA No. (*recollecting her manners*) Thank you.

HIGGINS (*good-humored again*) This has been coming on you for some days. I suppose it was natural for you to be anxious about the garden party. But thats all over now. (*He pats her kindly on the shoulder. She writhes*) Theres nothing more to worry about.

LIZA No. Nothing more for you to worry about. (*She suddenly rises and gets away from him by going to the piano bench, where she sits and hides her face*) Oh God! I wish I was dead.

HIGGINS (*staring after her in sincere surprise*) Why? In heaven's name, why? (*reasonably, going to her*) Listen to me, Eliza. All this irritation is purely subjective.

LIZA I dont understand. I'm too ignorant.

HIGGINS It's only imagination. Low spirits and nothing else. Nobody's hurting you. Nothing's wrong. You go to bed like a good girl and sleep it off. Have a little cry and say your prayers: that will make you comfortable.

LIZA I heard your prayers. "Thank God it's all over!"

HIGGINS (*impatiently*) Well, dont you thank God it's all over? Now you are free and can do what you like.

LIZA (*pulling herself together in desperation*) What am I fit for? What have you left me fit for? Where am I to go? What am I to do? Whats to become of me?

HIGGINS (*enlightened, but not at all impressed*) Oh, thats whats worrying you, is it? (*He thrusts his hands into his pockets and walks about in his usual manner, rattling the contents of his pockets, as if condescending to a trivial subject out of pure kindness*) I shouldnt bother about it if I were you. I should imagine you wont have much difficulty in settling yourself somewhere or other, though I hadnt quite realized that you were going away. (*She looks quickly at him: he does not look at her, but examines the dessert stand on the piano and decides that he will eat an apple*) You might marry, you know. (*He bites a large piece out of the apple and munches it noisily*) You see, Eliza, all men are not confirmed old bachelors like me and the Colonel. Most men are the marrying sort (poor devils!); and youre not bad-looking: it's quite a pleasure to look at you sometimes—not now, of course, because youre crying and looking as ugly as the very devil; but when youre all right and quite yourself, youre what I should call attractive. That is, to the people in the marrying line, you understand. You go to bed and have a good nice rest; and then get up and look at yourself in the glass; and you wont feel so cheap.

(ELIZA *again looks at him, speechless, and does not stir.*

(*The look is quite lost on*

him: he eats his apple with a dreamy expression of happiness, as it is quite a good one)

HIGGINS (*a genial afterthought occurring to him*) I daresay my mother could find some chap or other who would do very well.

LIZA We were above that at the corner of Tottenham Court Road.

HIGGINS (*waking up*) What do you mean?

LIZA I sold flowers. I didnt sell myself. Now youve made a lady of me I'm not fit to sell anything else. I wish youd left me where you found me.

HIGGINS (*slinging the core of the apple decisively into the grate*) Tosh, Eliza. Dont you insult human relations by dragging all this cant about buying and selling into it. You neednt marry the fellow if you dont like him.

LIZA What else am I to do?

HIGGINS Oh, lots of things. What about your old idea of a florist's shop? Pickering could set you up in one: he has lots of money. (*chuckling*) He'll have to pay for all those togs you have been wearing today; and that, with the hire of the jewellery, will make a big hole in two hundred pounds. Why, six months ago you would have thought it the millennium to have a flower shop of your own. Come! youll be all right. I must clear off to bed: I'm devilish sleepy. By the way, I came down for something: I forget what it was.

LIZA Your slippers.

HIGGINS Oh, yes, of course. You shied them at me. (*He picks them up, and is going out when she rises and speaks to him*)

LIZA Before you go, sir——

HIGGINS (*dropping the slippers in his surprise at her calling him Sir*) Eh?

LIZA Do my clothes belong to me or to Colonel Pickering?

HIGGINS (*coming back into the room as if her question were the very climax of unreason*) What the devil use would they be to Pickering?

LIZA He might want them for the next girl you pick up to experiment on.

HIGGINS (*shocked and hurt*) Is that the way you feel towards us?

LIZA I dont want to hear anything more about that. All I want to know is whether anything belongs to me. My own clothes were burnt.

HIGGINS But what does it matter? Why need you start bothering about that in the middle of the night?

LIZA I want to know what I may take away with me. I dont want to be accused of stealing.

HIGGINS (*now deeply wounded*) Stealing! You shouldnt have said that, Eliza. That shows a want of feeling.

LIZA I'm sorry. I'm only a common ignorant girl; and in my station I have to be careful. There cant be any feelings between the like of you and the like of me. Please will you tell me what belongs to me and what doesnt?

HIGGINS (*very sulky*) You may take the whole damned houseful if you like. Except the jewels. Theyre hired. Will that satisfy you? (*He turns on his heel and is about to go in extreme dudgeon*)

LIZA (*drinking in his emotion like nectar, and nagging him to provoke a further supply*) Stop, please. (*She takes off her jew-els*) Will you take these to your room and keep them safe? I dont want to run the risk of their being missing.

HIGGINS (*furious*) Hand them over. (*She puts them into his hands*) If these belonged to me instead of to the jeweller, I'd ram them down your ungrateful throat. (*He perfunctorily thrusts them into his pockets, uncon-sciously decorating himself with the protruding ends of the chains*)

LIZA (*taking a ring off*) This ring isnt the jeweller's: it's the one you bought me in Brighton. I dont want it now. (HIGGINS *dashes the ring violently into the fireplace and turns on her so threateningly that she crouches over the piano with her hands over her face, and exclaims*) Dont you hit me.

HIGGINS Hit you! You infamous creature, how dare you accuse me of such a thing? It is you who have hit me. You have wounded me to the heart.

LIZA (*thrilling with hidden joy*) I'm glad. Ive got a little of my own back, anyhow.

HIGGINS (*with dignity, in his finest professional style*) You have caused me to lose my temper: a thing that has hardly ever hap-pened to me before. I prefer to say nothing more tonight. I am going to bed.

LIZA (*pertly*) Youd better leave a note for Mrs Pearce about the coffee; for she wont be told by me.

HIGGINS (*formally*) Damn Mrs Pearce; and damn the coffee; and damn you; and (*wildly*) damn my own folly in having lavished my hard-earned knowl-edge and the treasure of my re-gard and intimacy on a heartless guttersnipe. (*He goes out with impressive decorum, and spoils it by slamming the door sav-agely*)

(ELIZA *goes down on her knees on the hearthrug to look for the ring. When she finds it she considers for a moment what to do with it. Finally she flings it down on the dessert stand and goes upstairs in a tearing rage*)

(The furniture of Eliza's room has been increased by a big wardrobe and a sumptuous dressing-table. She comes in and switches on the electric light. She goes to the wardrobe; opens it; and pulls out a walking dress, a hat, and a pair of shoes, which she throws on the bed. She takes off her evening dress and shoes; then takes a padded hanger from the wardrobe; adjusts it care-fully in the evening dress; and hangs it in the wardrobe, which she shuts with a slam. She puts on her walking shoes, her walk-ing dress, and hat. She takes her wrist watch from the dressing-table and fastens it on. She pulls on her gloves; takes her vanity bag; and looks into it to see that her purse is there before hang-ing it on her wrist. She makes for the door. Every movement expresses her furious resolution. (She takes a last look at herself in the glass.

(She suddenly puts out her tongue at herself; then leaves the room, switching off the elec-tric light at the door.

(Meanwhile, in the street out-side, Freddy Eynsford Hill, love-

lorn, is gazing up at the second floor, in which one of the windows is still lighted.
(*The light goes out.*)

FREDDY Goodnight, darling, darling, darling.
(*ELIZA comes out, giving the door a considerable bang behind her*)

LIZA Whatever are you doing here?

FREDDY Nothing. I spend most of my nights here. It's the only place where I'm happy. Dont laugh at me, Miss Doolittle.

LIZA Dont you call me Miss Doolittle, do you hear? Liza's good enough for me. (*She breaks down and grabs him by the shoulders*) Freddy: you dont think I'm a heartless guttersnipe, do you?

FREDDY Oh no, no, darling: how can you imagine such a thing? You are the loveliest, dearest—
(*He loses all self-control and smothers her with kisses. She, hungry for comfort, responds. They stand there in one another's arms.*
(*An elderly police constable arrives*)

CONSTABLE (*scandalized*) Now then! Now then!! Now then!!!
(*They release one another hastily*)

FREDDY Sorry, constable. Weve only just become engaged.
(*They run away*)

(*The constable shakes his head, reflecting on his own courtship and on the vanity of human hopes. He moves off in the opposite direction with slow professional steps.*
(*The flight of the lovers takes them to Cavendish Square.*

There they halt to consider their next move.)

LIZA (*out of breath*) He didnt half give me a fright, that copper. But you answered him proper.

FREDDY I hope I havent taken you out of your way. Where were you going?

LIZA To the river.

FREDDY What for?

LIZA To make a hole in it.

FREDDY (*horrified*) Eliza, darling. What do you mean? Whats the matter?

LIZA Never mind. It doesnt matter now. Theres nobody in the world now but you and me, is there?

FREDDY Not a soul.
(*They indulge in another embrace, and are again surprised by a much younger constable*)

SECOND CONSTABLE Now then, you two! Whats this? Where do you think you are? Move along here, double quick.

FREDDY As you say, sir, double quick.

(*They run away again, and are in Hanover Square before they stop for another conference.*)

FREDDY I had no idea the police were so devilishly prudish.

LIZA It's their business to hunt girls off the streets.

FREDDY We must go somewhere. We cant wander about the streets all night.

LIZA Cant we? I think it'd be lovely to wander about for ever.

FREDDY Oh, darling.
(*They embrace again, oblivious of the arrival of a crawling taxi. It stops*)

TAXIMAN Can I drive you and the lady anywhere, sir?
(*They start asunder*)

LIZA   Oh, Freddy, a taxi. The very thing.

FREDDY   But, damn it, I've no money.

LIZA   I have plenty. The Colonel thinks you should never go out without ten pounds in your pocket. Listen. We'll drive about all night; and in the morning I'll call on old Mrs Higgins and ask her what I ought to do. I'll tell you all about it in the cab. And the police wont touch us there.

FREDDY   Righto! Ripping. (*to the* TAXIMAN) Wimbledon Common. (*They drive off*)

ACT V

MRS HIGGINS's *drawing room. She is at her writing-table as before. The parlormaid comes in.*

THE PARLORMAID (*at the door*)   Mr Henry, maam, is downstairs with Colonel Pickering.

MRS HIGGINS   Well, show them up.

THE PARLORMAID   Theyre using the telephone, maam. Telephoning to the police, I think.

MRS HIGGINS   What!

THE PARLORMAID (*coming further in and lowering her voice*)   Mr Henry is in a state, maam. I thought I'd better tell you.

MRS HIGGINS   If you had told me that Mr Henry was not in a state it would have been more surprising. Tell them to come up when theyve finished with the police. I suppose he's lost something.

THE PARLORMAID   Yes, maam. (*going*)

MRS HIGGINS   Go upstairs and tell Miss Doolittle that Mr Henry and the Colonel are here. Ask her not to come down til I send for her.

THE PARLORMAID   Yes, maam.

(HIGGINS *bursts in. He is, as the* PARLORMAID *has said, in a state*)

HIGGINS   Look here, mother: heres a confounded thing!

MRS HIGGINS   Yes, dear. Good morning. (*He checks his impatience and kisses her, whilst the* PARLORMAID *goes out*) What is it?

HIGGINS   Eliza's bolted.

MRS HIGGINS (*calmly continuing her writing*)   You must have frightened her.

HIGGINS   Frightened her! nonsense! She was left last night, as usual, to turn out the lights and all that; and instead of going to bed she changed her clothes and went right off: her bed wasnt slept in. She came in a cab for her things before seven this morning; and that fool Mrs Pearce let her have them without telling me a word about it. What am I to do?

MRS HIGGINS   Do without, I'm afraid, Henry. The girl has a perfect right to leave if she chooses.

HIGGINS (*wandering distractedly across the room*)   But I cant find anything. I dont know what appointments Ive got. I'm— (PICKERING *comes in.* MRS HIGGINS *puts down her pen and turns away from the writing-table*)

PICKERING (*shaking hands*)   Good

morning, Mrs Higgins. Has Henry told you? (*He sits down on the ottoman*)

HIGGINS   What does that ass of an inspector say? Have you offered a reward?

MRS HIGGINS (*rising in indignant amazement*) You dont mean to say you have set the police after Eliza.

HIGGINS   Of course. What are the police for? What else could we do? (*He sits in the Elizabethan chair*)

PICKERING   The inspector made a lot of difficulties. I really think he suspected us of some improper purpose.

MRS HIGGINS   Well, of course he did. What right have you to go to the police and give the girl's name as if she were a thief, or a lost umbrella, or something? Really! (*She sits down again, deeply vexed*)

HIGGINS   But we want to find her.

PICKERING   We cant let her go like this, you know, Mrs Higgins. What were we to do?

MRS HIGGINS   You have no more sense, either of you, than two children. Why—

(*The* PARLORMAID *comes in and breaks off the conversation*)

THE PARLORMAID   Mr Henry: a gentleman wants to see you very particular. He's been sent on from Wimpole Street.

HIGGINS   Oh, bother! I cant see anyone now. Who is it?

THE PARLORMAID   A Mr Doolittle, sir.

PICKERING   Doolittle! Do you mean the dustman?

THE PARLORMAID   Dustman! Oh no, sir: a gentleman.

HIGGINS (*springing up excitedly*) By George, Pick, it's some relative of hers that she's gone to. Somebody we know nothing about. (*to the* PARLORMAID) Send him up, quick.

THE PARLORMAID   Yes, sir. (*She goes*)

HIGGINS (*eagerly, going to his mother*) Genteel relatives! now we shall hear something. (*He sits down in the Chippendale chair*)

MRS HIGGINS   Do you know any of her people?

PICKERING   Only her father: the fellow we told you about.

THE PARLORMAID (*announcing*) Mr Doolittle. (*She withdraws*)

(DOOLITTLE *enters. He is resplendently dressed as for a fashionable wedding, and might, in fact, be the bridegroom. A flower in his buttonhole, a dazzling silk hat, and patent leather shoes complete the effect. He is too concerned with the business he has come on to notice* MRS HIGGINS. *He walks straight to* HIGGINS *and accosts him with vehement reproach*)

DOOLITTLE (*indicating his own person*) See here! Do you see this? You done this.

HIGGINS   Done what, man?

DOOLITTLE   This, I tell you. Look at it. Look at this hat. Look at this coat.

PICKERING   Has Eliza been buying you clothes?

DOOLITTLE   Eliza! Not she. Why would she buy me clothes?

MRS HIGGINS   Good morning, Mr Doolittle. Wont you sit down?

DOOLITTLE (*taken aback as he becomes conscious that he has forgotten his hostess*) Asking your pardon, maam. (*He approaches her and shakes her proffered hand*) Thank you. (*He sits down on the ottoman, on* PICKERING'S *right*) I am that full of what has happened to me that I cant think of anything else.

HIGGINS What the dickens has happened to you?

DOOLITTLE I shouldnt mind if it had only happened to me: anything might happen to anybody and nobody to blame but Providence, as you might say. But this is something that you done to me: yes, you, Enry Iggins.

HIGGINS Have you found Eliza?

DOOLITTLE Have you lost her?

HIGGINS Yes.

DOOLITTLE You have all the luck, you have. I aint found her; but she'll find me quick enough now after what you done to me.

MRS HIGGINS But what has my son done to you, Mr Doolittle?

DOOLITTLE Done to me! Ruined me. Destroyed my happiness. Tied me up and delivered me into the hands of middle class morality.

HIGGINS (*rising intolerantly and standing over* DOOLITTLE) Youre raving. Youre drunk. Youre mad. I gave you five pounds. After that I had two conversations with you, at half-a-crown an hour. Ive never seen you since.

DOOLITTLE Oh! Drunk am I? Mad am I? Tell me this. Did you or did you not write a letter to an old blighter in America that was giving five millions to found Moral Reform Societies all over the world, and that wanted you to invent a universal language for him?

HIGGINS What! Ezra D. Wannafeller! He's dead. (*He sits down again carelessly*)

DOOLITTLE Yes: he's dead; and I'm done for. Now did you or did you not write a letter to him to say that the most original moralist at present in England, to the best of your knowledge, was Alfred Doolittle, a common dustman?

HIGGINS Oh, after your first visit I remember making some silly joke of the kind.

DOOLITTLE Ah! you may well call it a silly joke. It put the lid on me right enough. Just give him the chance he wanted to show that Americans is not like us; that they reckonize and respect merit in every class of life, however humble. Them words is in his blooming will, in which, Enry Iggins, thanks to your silly joking, he leaves me a share in his Pre-digested Cheese Trust worth four thousand a year on condition that I lecture for his Wannafeller Moral Reform World League as often as they ask me up to six times a year.

HIGGINS The devil he does! Whew! (*brightening suddenly*) What a lark!

PICKERING A safe thing for you, Doolittle. They wont ask you twice.

DOOLITTLE It aint the lecturing I mind. I'll lecture them blue in the face, I will, and not turn a hair. It's making a gentleman of me that I object to. Who asked him to make a gentleman of me? I was happy. I was free. I touched pretty nigh everybody for money when I wanted it, same as I touched you, Enry Iggins. Now I am worrited; tied neck and heels; and everybody touches me for money. It's a fine thing for you, says my solicitor. Is it? says I. You mean it's a good thing for you, I says. When I was a poor man and had a solicitor once when they found a pram in the dust cart, he got me off, and got shut of me and got me shut of him as quick as he could. Same with the doctors: used to shove me out of the hospital before I could hardly stand on my legs, and nothing to pay. Now they finds out that I'm not a healthy man and cant live unless they looks after me twice a day. In the house I'm not let do a hand's turn for myself: somebody else must do it and touch me for it. A year ago I hadnt a relative in the world except two or three that wouldnt speak to me. Now Ive fifty, and not a decent week's wages among the lot of them. I have to live for others and not for myself: that middle class morality. You talk of losing Eliza. Dont you be anxious: I bet she's on my doorstep by this: she that could support herself easy by selling flowers if I wasnt respectable. And the next one to touch me will be you, Enry Iggins. I'll have to learn to speak middle class language from you, instead of speaking proper English. Thats where youll come in; and I daresay thats what you done it for.

MRS HIGGINS   But, my dear Mr Doolittle, you need not suffer all this if you are really in earnest. Nobody can force you to accept this bequest. You can repudiate it. Isnt that so, Colonel Pickering?

PICKERING   I believe so.

DOOLITTLE (*softening his manner in deference to her sex*)   Thats the tragedy of it, maam. It's easy to say chuck it; but I havnt the nerve. Which of us has? We're all intimidated. Intimidated, maam: thats what we are. What is there for me if I chuck it but the workhouse in my old age? I have to dye my hair already to keep my job as a dustman. If I was one of the deserving poor, and had put by a bit, I could chuck it; but then why should I, acause the deserving poor might as well be millionaires for all the happiness they ever has. They dont know what happiness is. But I, as one of the undeserving poor, have nothing between me and the pauper's uniform but this here blasted four thousand a year that shoves me into the middle class. (*Excuse the expression, maam, youd use it yourself if you had my provocation.*) Theyve got you every way you turn: it's a choice between the Skilly of the workhouse and the Char Bydis of the middle class; and I havnt the nerve for the workhouse. Intimidated: thats what I am. Broke. Bought up. Happier men than me will call for my dust, and touch me for their tip; and I'll look on helpless, and envy them. And thats what your son has brought me to. (*He is overcome by emotion*)

MRS HIGGINS   Well, I'm very glad youre not going to do anything foolish, Mr Doolittle. For this solves the problem of Eliza's future. You can provide for her now.

DOOLITTLE (*with melancholy resignation*)   Yes, maam: I'm expected to provide for everyone now, out of four thousand a year.

HIGGINS (*jumping up*)   Nonsense! he cant provide for her. He shant provide for her. She doesnt belong to him. I paid him five pounds for her. Doolittle: either youre an honest man or a rogue.

DOOLITTLE (*tolerantly*) A little of both, Enry, like the rest of us: a little of both.

HIGGINS Well, you took that money for the girl; and you have no right to take her as well.

MRS HIGGINS Henry: dont be absurd. If you want to know where Eliza is, she is upstairs.

HIGGINS (*amazed*) Upstairs!!! Then I shall jolly soon fetch her downstairs. (*He makes resolutely for the door*)

MRS HIGGINS (*rising and following him*) Be quiet, Henry. Sit down.

HIGGINS I—

MRS HIGGINS Sit down, dear; and listen to me.

HIGGINS Oh very well, very well, very well. (*He throws himself ungraciously on the ottoman, with his face towards the windows*) But I think you might have told us this half an hour ago.

MRS HIGGINS Eliza came to me this morning. She told me of the brutal way you two treated her.

HIGGINS (*bounding up again*) What!

PICKERING (*rising also*) My dear Mrs Higgins, she's been telling you stories. We didnt treat her brutally. We hardly said a word to her; and we parted on particularly good terms. (*turning on* HIGGINS) Higgins: did you bully her after I went to bed?

HIGGINS Just the other way about. She threw my slippers in my face. She behaved in the most outrageous way. I never gave her the slightest provocation. The slippers came bang into my face the moment I entered the room—before I had uttered a word. And used perfectly awful language.

PICKERING (*astonished*) But why? What did we do to her?

MRS HIGGINS I think I know pretty well what you did. The girl is naturally rather affectionate, I think. Isnt she, Mr Doolittle?

DOOLITTLE Very tender-hearted, maam. Takes after me.

MRS HIGGINS Just so. She had become attached to you both. She worked very hard for you, Henry. I dont think you quite realize what anything in the nature of brain work means to a girl of her class. Well, it seems that when the great day of trial came, and she did this wonderful thing for you without making a single mistake, you two sat there and never said a word to her, but talked together of how glad you were that it was all over and how you had been bored with the whole thing. And then you were surprised because she threw your slippers at you! *I* should have thrown the fire-irons at you.

HIGGINS We said nothing except that we were tired and wanted to go to bed. Did we, Pick?

PICKERING (*shrugging his shoulders*) That was all.

MRS HIGGINS (*ironically*) Quite sure?

PICKERING Absolutely. Really, that was all.

MRS HIGGINS You didnt thank her, or pet her, or admire her, or tell her how splendid she'd been.

HIGGINS (*impatiently*) But she knew all about that. We didnt make speeches to her, if thats what you mean.

PICKERING (*conscience stricken*)

Perhaps we were a little inconsiderate. Is she very angry?

MRS HIGGINS (*returning to her place at the writing-table*) Well, I'm afraid she wont go back to Wimpole Street, especially now that Mr Doolittle is able to keep up the position you have thrust on her; but she says she is quite willing to meet you on friendly terms and to let bygones be bygones.

HIGGINS (*furious*) Is she, by George? Ho!

MRS HIGGINS If you promise to behave yourself, Henry, I'll ask her to come down. If not, go home; for you have taken up quite enough of my time.

HIGGINS Oh, all right. Very well. Pick: you behave yourself. Let us put on our best Sunday manners for this creature that we picked out of the mud. (*He flings himself sulkily into the Elizabethan chair*)

DOOLITTLE (*remonstrating*) Now, now, Enry Iggins! Have some consideration for my feelings as a middle class man.

MRS HIGGINS Remember your promise, Henry. (*She presses the bell-button on the writing-table*) Mr Doolittle: will you be so good as to step out on the balcony for a moment. I dont want Eliza to have the shock of your news until she has made it up with these two gentlemen. Would you mind?

DOOLITTLE As you wish, lady. Anything to help Enry to keep her off my hands. (*He disappears through the window*)

(*The PARLORMAID answers the bell. PICKERING sits down in DOOLITTLE'S place*)

MRS HIGGINS Ask Miss Doolittle to come down, please.

THE PARLORMAID Yes, maam. (*She goes out*)

MRS HIGGINS Now, Henry: be good.

HIGGINS I am behaving myself perfectly.

PICKERING He is doing his best, Mrs Higgins.

(*A pause. HIGGINS throws back his head; stretches out his legs; and begins to whistle*)

MRS HIGGINS Henry, dearest, you dont look at all nice in that attitude.

HIGGINS (*pulling himself together*) I was not trying to look nice, mother.

MRS HIGGINS It doesnt matter, dear. I only wanted to make you speak.

HIGGINS Why?

MRS HIGGINS Because you cant speak and whistle at the same time.

(*HIGGINS groans. Another very trying pause*)

HIGGINS (*springing up, out of patience*) Where the devil is that girl? Are we to wait here all day?

(*ELIZA enters, sunny, self-possessed, and giving a staggeringly convincing exhibition of ease of manner. She carries a little workbasket, and is very much at home. PICKERING is too much taken aback to rise*)

LIZA How do you do, Professor Higgins? Are you quite well?

HIGGINS (*choking*) Am I— (*He can say no more*)

LIZA But of course you are: you are never ill. So glad to see you again, Colonel Pickering. (*He rises hastily; and they shake hands*) Quite chilly this morning, isnt it? (*She sits down on his left. He sits beside her*)

HIGGINS Dont you dare try this game on me. I taught it to you; and it doesnt take me in. Get up and come home; and dont be a fool.

> (ELIZA *takes a piece of needlework from her basket, and begins to stitch at it, without taking the least notice of this outburst*)

MRS HIGGINS Very nicely put, indeed, Henry. No woman could resist such an invitation.

HIGGINS You let her alone, mother. Let her speak for herself. You will jolly soon see whether she has an idea that I havnt put into her head or a word that I havnt put into her mouth. I tell you I have created this thing out of the squashed cabbage leaves of Covent Garden; and now she pretends to play the fine lady with me.

MRS HIGGINS (*placidly*) Yes, dear; but youll sit down, wont you?

> (HIGGINS *sits down again, savagely*)

LIZA (*to* PICKERING, *taking no apparent notice of* HIGGINS, *and working away deftly*) Will you drop me altogether now that the experiment is over, Colonel Pickering?

PICKERING Oh dont. You mustnt think of it as an experiment. It shocks me, somehow.

LIZA Oh, I'm only a squashed cabbage leaf—

PICKERING (*impulsively*) No.

LIZA (*continuing quietly*) —but I owe so much to you that I should be very unhappy if you forgot me.

PICKERING It's very kind of you to say so, Miss Doolittle.

LIZA It's not because you paid for my dresses. I know you are generous to everybody with money. But it was from you that I learnt really nice manners; and that is what makes one a lady, isnt it? You see it was so very difficult for me with the example of Professor Higgins always before me. I was brought up to be just like him, unable to control myself, and using bad language on the slightest provocation. And I should never have known that ladies and gentlemen didnt behave like that if you hadnt been there.

HIGGINS Well!!

PICKERING Oh, thats only his way, you know. He doesnt mean it.

LIZA Oh, *I* didnt mean it either, when I was a flower girl. It was only my way. But you see I did it; and thats what makes the difference after all.

PICKERING No doubt. Still, he taught you to speak; and I couldnt have done that, you know.

LIZA (*trivially*) Of course: that is his profession.

HIGGINS Damnation!

LIZA (*continuing*) It was just like learning to dance in the fashionable way: there was nothing more than that in it. But do you know what began my real education?

PICKERING What?

LIZA (*stopping her work for a moment*) Your calling me Miss Doolittle that day when I first came to Wimpole Street. That was the beginning of self-respect for me. (*She resumes her stitching*) And there were a hundred little things you never noticed, because they came naturally to you. Things about standing up and taking off your hat and opening doors—

PICKERING   Oh, that was nothing.

LIZA   Yes: things that showed you thought and felt about me as if I were something better than a scullery-maid; though of course I know you would have been just the same to a scullery-maid if she had been let into the drawing room. You never took off your boots in the dining room when I was there.

PICKERING   You mustnt mind that. Higgins takes off his boots all over the place.

LIZA   I know. I am not blaming him. It is his way, isnt it? But it made such a difference to me that you didnt do it. You see, really and truly, apart from the things anyone can pick up (the dressing and the proper way of speaking, and so on), the difference between a lady and a flower girl is not how she behaves, but how she's treated. I shall always be a flower girl to Professor Higgins, because he always treats me as a flower girl, and always will; but I know I can be a lady to you, because you always treat me as a lady, and always will.

MRS HIGGINS   Please dont grind your teeth, Henry.

PICKERING   Well, this is really very nice of you, Miss Doolittle.

LIZA   I should like you to call me Eliza, now, if you would.

PICKERING   Thank you. Eliza, of course.

LIZA   And I should like Professor Higgins to call me Miss Doolittle.

HIGGINS   I'll see you damned first.

MRS HIGGINS   Henry! Henry!

PICKERING   (*laughing*)   Why dont you slang back at him? Dont stand it. It would do him a lot of good.

LIZA   I cant. I could have done it once; but now I cant go back to it. You told me, you know, that when a child is brought to a foreign country, it picks up the language in a few weeks, and forgets its own. Well, I am a child in your country. I have forgotten my own language, and can speak nothing but yours. Thats the real break-off with the corner of Tottenham Court Road. Leaving Wimpole Street finishes it.

PICKERING   (*much alarmed*)   Oh! but youre coming back to Wimpole Street, arnt you? Youll forgive Higgins?

HIGGINS   (*rising*)   Forgive! Will she, by George! Let her go. Let her find out how she can get on without us. She will relapse into the gutter in three weeks without me at her elbow.

(DOOLITTLE *appears at the centre window. With a look of dignified reproach at* HIGGINS, *he comes slowly and silently to his daughter, who, with her back to the window, is unconscious of his approach*)

PICKERING   He's incorrigible, Eliza. You wont relapse, will you?

LIZA   No: not now. Never again. I have learnt my lesson. I dont believe I could utter one of the old sounds if I tried. (DOOLITTLE *touches her on the left shoulder. She drops her work, losing her self-possession utterly at the spectacle of her father's splendor*) A-a-a-a-ah-ow-ooh!

HIGGINS   (*with a crow of triumph*)

Aha! Just so. A-a-a-a-ahowooh! A-a-a-a-ahowooh! A-a-a-a-ahow-ooh! Victory! Victory! (*He throws himself on the divan, folding his arms, and spraddling arrogantly*)

DOOLITTLE   Can you blame the girl? Dont look at me like that, Eliza. It aint my fault. Ive come into some money.

LIZA   You must have touched a millionaire this time, dad.

DOOLITTLE   I have. But I'm dressed something special today. I'm going to St. George's, Hanover Square. Your stepmother is going to marry me.

LIZA (*angrily*)   Youre going to let yourself down to marry that low common woman!

PICKERING (*quietly*)   He ought to, Eliza. (*to* DOOLITTLE) Why has she changed her mind?

DOOLITTLE (*sadly*)   Intimidated, Governor. Intimidated. Middle class morality claims its victim. Wont you put on your hat, Liza, and come and see me turned off?

LIZA   If the Colonel says I must, I—I'll— (*almost sobbing*) I'll demean myself. And get insulted for my pains, like enough.

DOOLITTLE   Dont be afraid: she never comes to words with anyone now, poor woman! Respectability has broke all the spirit out of her.

PICKERING (*squeezing* ELIZA'S *elbow gently*)   Be kind to them, Eliza. Make the best of it.

LIZA (*forcing a little smile for him through her vexation*)   Oh well, just to show theres no ill feeling. I'll be back in a moment. (*She goes out*)

DOOLITTLE (*sitting down beside* PICKERING)   I feel uncommon nervous about the ceremony, Colonel. I wish youd come and see me through it.

PICKERING   But youve been through it before, man. You were married to Eliza's mother.

DOOLITTLE   Who told you that, Colonel?

PICKERING   Well, nobody told me. But I concluded—naturally—

DOOLITTLE   No: that aint the natural way, Colonel: it's only the middle class way. My way was always the undeserving way. But dont say nothing to Eliza. She dont know: I always had a delicacy about telling her.

PICKERING   Quite right. We'll leave it so, if you dont mind.

DOOLITTLE   And youll come to the church, Colonel, and put me through straight?

PICKERING   With pleasure. As far as a bachelor can.

MRS HIGGINS   May I come, Mr Doolittle? I should be very sorry to miss your wedding.

DOOLITTLE   I should indeed be honored by your condescension, maam; and my poor old woman would take it as a tremenjous compliment. She's been very low, thinking of the happy days that are no more.

MRS HIGGINS (*rising*)   I'll order the carriage and get ready. (*The men rise, except* HIGGINS) I shant be more than fifteen minutes. (*As she goes to the door* ELIZA *comes in, hatted and buttoning her gloves*) I'm going to the church to see your father married, Eliza. You had better come in the brougham with me. Colonel Pickering can go on with the bridegroom.

> (MRS HIGGINS *goes out.* ELIZA *comes to the middle of the room between the centre window and the*

ottoman. PICKERING *joins her*)

DOOLITTLE   Bridegroom. What a word! It makes a man realize his position, somehow. (*He takes up his hat and goes towards the door*)

PICKERING   Before I go, Eliza, do forgive Higgins and come back to us.

LIZA   I dont think dad would allow me. Would you, dad?

DOOLITTLE (*sad but magnanimous*) They played you off very cunning, Eliza, them two sportsmen. If it had been only one of them, you could have nailed him. But you see, there was two; and one of them chaperoned the other, as you might say. (*To* PICKERING) It was artful of you, Colonel; but I bear no malice: I should have done the same myself. I been the victim of one woman after another all my life, and I dont grudge you two getting the better of Liza. I shant interfere. It's time for us to go, Colonel. So long, Enry. See you in St. George's, Eliza. (*He goes out*)

PICKERING (*coaxing*)   Do stay with us, Eliza. (*He follows* DOOLITTLE)

(ELIZA *goes out on the balcony to avoid being alone with* HIGGINS. *He rises and joins her there. She immediately comes back into the room and makes for the door; but he goes along the balcony and gets his back to the door before she reaches it*)

HIGGINS   Well, Eliza, youve had a bit of your own back, as you call it. Have you had enough? And are you going to be reasonable? Or do you want any more?

LIZA   You want me back only to pick up your slippers and put up with your tempers and fetch and carry for you.

HIGGINS   I havnt said I wanted you back at all.

LIZA   Oh, indeed. Then what are we talking about?

HIGGINS   About you, not about me. If you come back I shall treat you just as I have always treated you. I cant change my nature; and I dont intend to change my manners. My manners are exactly the same as Colonel Pickering's.

LIZA   Thats not true. He treats a flower girl as if she was a duchess.

HIGGINS   And I treat a duchess as if she was a flower girl.

LIZA   I see. (*She turns away composedly and sits on the ottoman, facing the window*) The same to everybody.

HIGGINS   Just so.

LIZA   Like father.

HIGGINS (*grinning, a little taken down*)   Without accepting the comparison at all points, Eliza, it's quite true that your father is not a snob, and that he will be quite at home in any station of life to which his eccentric destiny may call him. (*seriously*) The great secret, Eliza, is not having bad manners or good manners or any other particular sort of manners, but having the same manner for all human souls: in short, behaving as if you were in Heaven, where there are no third-class carriages, and one soul is as good as another.

LIZA   Amen. You are a born preacher.

HIGGINS (*irritated*)   The question is not whether I treat you rudely, but whether you ever heard me treat anyone else better.

LIZA (*with sudden sincerity*) I dont care how you treat me. I dont mind your swearing at me. I shouldnt mind a black eye: Ive had one before this. But (*standing up and facing him*) I wont be passed over.

HIGGINS Then get out of my way; for I wont stop for you. You talk about me as if I were a motor bus.

LIZA So you are a motor bus: all bounce and go, and no consideration for anyone. But I can do without you: dont think I cant.

HIGGINS I know you can. I told you you could.

LIZA (*wounded, getting away from him to the other side of the ottoman with her face to the hearth*) I know you did, you brute. You wanted to get rid of me.

HIGGINS Liar.

LIZA Thank you. (*She sits down with dignity*)

HIGGINS You never asked yourself, I suppose, whether *I* could do without you.

LIZA (*earnestly*) Dont you try to get round me. Youll have to do without me.

HIGGINS (*arrogant*) I can do without anybody. I have my own soul: my own spark of divine fire. But (*with sudden humility*) I shall miss you, Eliza. (*He sits down near her on the ottoman*) I have learnt something from your idiotic notions: I confess that, humbly and gratefully. And I have grown accustomed to your voice and appearance. I like them, rather.

LIZA Well, you have both of them on your gramophone and in your book of photographs. When you feel lonely without me, you can turn the machine on. It's got no feelings to hurt.

HIGGINS I cant turn your soul on. Leave me those feelings; and you can take away the voice and the face. They are not you.

LIZA Oh, you are a devil. You can twist the heart in a girl as easy as some could twist her arms to hurt her. Mrs Pearce warned me. Time and again she has wanted to leave you; and you always got round her at the last minute. And you dont care a bit for her. And you dont care a bit for me.

HIGGINS I care for life, for humanity; and you are a part of it that has come my way and been built into my house. What more can you or anyone ask?

LIZA I wont care for anybody that doesnt care for me.

HIGGINS Commercial principles, Eliza. Like (*reproducing her Covent Garden pronunciation with professional exactness*) s'yollin voylets [selling violets], isnt it?

LIZA Dont sneer at me. It's mean to sneer at me.

HIGGINS I have never sneered in my life. Sneering doesnt become either the human face or the human soul. I am expressing my righteous contempt for Commercialism. I dont and wont trade in affection. You call me a brute because you couldnt buy a claim on me by fetching my slippers and finding my spectacles. You were a fool: I think a woman fetching a man's slippers is a disgusting sight: did I ever fetch your slippers? I think a good deal more of you for throwing them in my face. No use slaving for me and then saying you want to be cared for:

who cares for a slave? If you come back, come back for the sake of good fellowship; for youll get nothing else. Youve had a thousand times as much out of me as I have out of you; and if you dare to set up your little dog's tricks of fetching and carrying slippers against my creation of a Duchess Eliza, I'll slam the door in your silly face.

LIZA What did you do it for if you didnt care for me?

HIGGINS (*heartily*) Why, because it was my job.

LIZA You never thought of the trouble it would make for me.

HIGGINS Would the world ever have been made if its maker had been afraid of making trouble? Making life means making trouble. Theres only one way of escaping trouble; and thats killing things. Cowards, you notice, are always shrieking to have troublesome people killed.

LIZA I'm no preacher: I dont notice things like that. I notice that you dont notice me.

HIGGINS (*jumping up and walking about intolerantly*) Eliza: youre an idiot. I waste the treasures of my Miltonic mind by spreading them before you. Once for all, understand that I go my way and do my work without caring twopence what happens to either of us. I am not intimidated, like your father and your step-mother. So you can come back or go to the devil: which you please.

LIZA What am I to come back for?

HIGGINS (*bouncing up on his knees on the ottoman and leaning over it to her*) For the fun of it. Thats why I took you on.

LIZA (*with averted face*) And you may throw me out tomorrow if I dont do everything you want me to?

HIGGINS Yes; and you may walk out tomorrow if I dont do everything you want me to.

LIZA And live with my step-mother?

HIGGINS Yes, or sell flowers.

LIZA Oh! if I only could go back to my flower basket! I should be independent of both you and father and all the world! Why did you take my independence from me? Why did I give it up? I'm a slave now, for all my fine clothes.

HIGGINS Not a bit. I'll adopt you as my daughter and settle money on you if you like. Or would you rather marry Pickering?

LIZA (*looking fiercely round at him*) I wouldnt marry you if you asked me; and youre nearer my age than what he is.

HIGGINS (*gently*) Than he is: not "than what he is."

LIZA (*losing her temper and rising*) I'll talk as I like. Youre not my teacher now.

HIGGINS (*reflectively*) I dont suppose Pickering would, though. He's as confirmed an old bachelor as I am.

LIZA Thats not what I want; and dont you think it. I've always had chaps enough wanting me that way. Freddy Hill writes to me twice and three times a day, sheets and sheets.

HIGGINS (*disagreeably surprised*) Damn his impudence! (*He recoils and finds himself sitting on his heels*)

LIZA He has a right to if he likes, poor lad. And he does love me.

HIGGINS (*getting off the ottoman*) You have no right to encourage him.

LIZA Every girl has a right to be loved.

HIGGINS What! By fools like that?

LIZA Freddy's not a fool. And if he's weak and poor and wants me, maybe he'd make me happier than my betters that bully me and dont want me.

HIGGINS Can he make anything of you? Thats the point.

LIZA Perhaps I could make something of him. But I never thought of us making anything of one another; and you never think of anything else. I only want to be natural.

HIGGINS In short, you want me to be as infatuated about you as Freddy? Is that it?

LIZA No I dont. Thats not the sort of feeling I want from you. And dont you be too sure of yourself or of me. I could have been a bad girl if I'd liked. Ive seen more of some things than you, for all your learning. Girls like me can drag gentlemen down to make love to them easy enough. And they wish each other dead the next minute.

HIGGINS Of course they do. Then what in thunder are we quarrelling about?

LIZA (*much troubled*) I want a little kindness. I know I'm a common ignorant girl, and you a book-learned gentleman; but I'm not dirt under your feet. What I done (*correcting herself*) what I did was not for the dresses and the taxis: I did it because we were pleasant together and I come—came—to care for you; not to want you to make love to me, and not forgetting the difference between us, but more friendly like.

HIGGINS Well, of course. Thats just how I feel. And how Pickering feels. Eliza: youre a fool.

LIZA Thats not a proper answer to give me. (*She sinks on the chair at the writing-table in tears*)

HIGGINS It's all youll get until you stop being a common idiot. If youre going to be a lady, youll have to give up feeling neglected if the men you know dont spend half their time snivelling over you and the other half giving you black eyes. If you cant stand the coldness of my sort of life, and the strain of it, go back to the gutter. Work til youre more a brute than a human being; and then cuddle and squabble and drink til you fall asleep. Oh, it's a fine life, the life of the gutter. It's real: it's warm: it's violent: you can feel it through the thickest skin: you can taste it and smell it without any training or any work. Not like Science and Literature and Classical Music and Philosophy and Art. You find me cold, unfeeling, selfish, dont you? Very well: be off with you to the sort of people you like. Marry some sentimental hog or other with lots of money, and a thick pair of lips to kiss you with and a thick pair of boots to kick you with. If you cant appreciate what youve got, youd better get what you can appreciate.

LIZA (*desperate*) Oh, you are a cruel tyrant. I cant talk to you: you turn everything against me: I'm always in the wrong. But you know very well all the time that youre nothing but a bully. You know I cant go back to the gutter, as you call it, and that I have no real friends in the world but you and the Colonel.

You know well I couldnt bear to live with a low common man after you two; and it's wicked and cruel of you to insult me by pretending I could. You think I must go back to Wimpole Street because I have nowhere else to go but father's. But dont you be too sure that you have me under your feet to be trampled on and talked down. I'll marry Freddy, I will, as soon as I'm able to support him.

HIGGINS (*thunderstruck*) Freddy!!! that young fool! That poor devil who couldnt get a job as an errand boy even if he had the guts to try for it! Woman: do you not understand that I have made you a consort for a king?

LIZA Freddy loves me: that makes him king enough for me. I dont want him to work: he wasnt brought up to it as I was. I'll go and be a teacher.

HIGGINS Whatll you teach, in heaven's name?

LIZA What you taught me. I'll teach phonetics.

HIGGINS Ha! ha! ha!

LIZA I'll offer myself as an assistant to that hairyfaced Hungarian.

HIGGINS (*rising in a fury*) What! That impostor! that humbug! that toadying ignoramus! Teach him my methods! my discoveries! You take one step in his direction and I'll wring your neck. (*He lays hands on her*) Do you hear?

LIZA (*defiantly non-resistant*) Wring away. What do I care? I knew youd strike me some day. (*He lets her go, stamping with rage at having forgotten himself, and recoils so hastily that he stumbles back into his seat on the ottoman*) Aha! Now I know how to deal with you. What a fool I was not to think of it before! You cant take away the knowledge you gave me. You said I had a finer ear than you. And I can be civil and kind to people, which is more than you can. Aha! (*purposely dropping her aitches to annoy him*) Thats done you, Enry Iggins, it az. Now I dont care that (*snapping her fingers*) for your bullying and your big talk. I'll advertize it in the papers that your duchess is only a flower girl that you taught, and that she'll teach anybody to be a duchess just the same in six months for a thousand guineas. Oh, when I think of myself crawling under your feet and being trampled on and called names, when all the time I had only to lift up my finger to be as good as you, I could just kick myself.

HIGGINS (*wondering at her*) You damned impudent slut, you! But it's better than snivelling; better than fetching slippers and finding spectacles, isn't it? (*rising*) By George, Eliza, I said I'd make a woman of you; and I have. I like you like this.

LIZA Yes: you turn round and make up to me now that I'm not afraid of you and can do without you.

HIGGINS Of course I do, you little fool. Five minutes ago you were like a millstone round my neck. Now youre a tower of strength: a consort battleship. You and I and Pickering will be three old bachelors instead of only two men and a silly girl.

(MRS HIGGINS *returns, dressed for the wedding.*

ELIZA *instantly becomes cool and elegant*)

MRS HIGGINS The carriage is waiting, Eliza. Are you ready?

LIZA Quite. Is the Professor coming?

MRS HIGGINS Certainly not. He cant behave himself in church. He makes remarks out loud all the time on the clergyman's pronunciation.

LIZA Then I shall not see you again, Professor. Goodbye. (*She goes to the door*)

MRS HIGGINS (*coming to* HIGGINS) Goodbye, dear.

HIGGINS Goodbye, mother. (*He is about to kiss her, when he recollects something*) Oh, by the way, Eliza, order a ham and a Stilton cheese, will you? And buy me a pair of reindeer gloves, number eights, and a tie to match that new suit of mine. You can choose the color. (*His cheerful, careless, vigorous voice shows that he is incorrigible*)

LIZA (*disdainfully*) Number eights are too small for you if you want them lined with lamb's wool. You have three new ties that you have forgotten in the drawer of your washstand. Colonel Pickering prefers double Gloucester to Stilton; and you dont notice the difference. I telephoned Mrs Pearce this morning not to forget the ham. What you are to do without me I cannot imagine. (*She sweeps out*)

MRS HIGGINS I'm afraid youve spoilt that girl, Henry. I should be uneasy about you and her if she were less fond of Colonel Pickering.

HIGGINS Pickering! Nonsense: she's going to marry Freddy. Ha ha! Freddy! Freddy!! Ha ha ha ha ha!!!!! (*He roars with laughter as the play ends*)

· QUESTIONS ·

As was suggested concerning *Macbeth* and *Antigone*, it seems unwise to try to list detailed questions here. Your instructor will make appropriate queries depending upon the vigor and depth of your study. He will also suggest "Theme Subjects" based upon similar considerations. Certainly you will wish to read the reviews in this volume by Henry Hewes, Bosley Crowther, and Brooks Atkinson.

POETRY

A NOTE ON READING

The reading of poems is rarely stressed in freshman classes, but poetry does offer certain advantages in learning to read well. Because good poets use language with unusual precision, making words serve their purposes exactly, careful reading of poetry helps you to see how language works. Such reading is not only useful as vocabulary study; it is also an excellent means of discovering how the meaning and effect of words are controlled by the contexts in which they appear. Good poets, moreover, use language with economy and compression for immediate and intense effects. Understanding poetry, where "each word must carry twenty other words upon its back," requires effort which will be repaid by an increase in reading skill.

Certain resources of language have a special importance in poetry. For instance, you should conceive of the rhythm of a poem as a means of communication, reinforcing and combining with the meaning of words, often suggesting or representing the attitude of a poem. But most of all, poetry calls for active contribution from you; the poet makes use of what you know and what you have felt. Good poetry blends sense and sound in ways which evoke images and extend your imagination, memory, and experience beyond the physical limits of your own life.

In this textbook, which deals with clear thinking and writing, examples of poetry are provided for further study of methods of communication. The editor hopes that these selections, by standards of clear expression and readability, will stimulate your reflection and curiosity and perhaps encourage the beginnings of an understanding of, and respect for, the power of expression latent in meter, rhyme, and other poetic devices.

A poem is to a piece of prose as an abstract painting is to a realistic portrait. From the same material the poet or artist intensifies by selecting parts or fragments of the idea or image, which he heightens (colors) by sound or pigments and rearranges in order to suggest a more sensitive, frequently more *accurate,* expression of the whole subject. Poetry is the quintessence of written feeling. The poet, departing from strict syntax and the literal sense of every word, discovers new powers of expression and often enriches our language with new words for concepts which we could not express or did not realize before.

Now let's get to some particulars. Six summary statements about poetry may be helpful:

1. Poetry is a language phenomenon—a way of saying things. Whether to teach, preach, or simply thrill, to paint, inform, or spellbind, this is not the language of over-the-counter existence, although many of the words are the same. A new blend of sound and sense is here, rich in connotation, imagery, impression, music, and offering new problems in semantics.

2. Poetry runs a wide gamut of subject matter and experience, familiar and unfamiliar. One age may sing of sea battle, another of a lady's eyes. Or in the same age one man may ponder the skylark while another weaves nightmarish dream-fantasies. The modern poet may use conventional topics, new topics, or apparently no topics at all, remaining content with patterns of sound and rhythm. In any period the gamut may be marked at one end by folk song and at the other by metaphysics.

3. Poetry has organization, purpose, style. Ideas and presentation vary from period to period.

4. Poetry, like music and other arts, has an evocative factor which varies with the experience and personality of the audience. A passage may jog your memory suddenly and help you re-enjoy a lost moment. It may startle you into action or a new belief. Poetry may help you escape reality for a moment's peace. It may offer you new illusions to replace the old. But it will not sledge-hammer a skeptic into belief. You must meet the poet halfway, then suspend disbelief for a time, "play along" sportingly. This is not to say that you should prostrate yourself as an ignoramus before genius. If, after reading and thinking, you honestly feel that your original poor impression of a poet, a poem, or poetry itself remains, maintain it stoutly; you will at least know by then why you feel the way you do—that knowledge itself is a step ahead.

5. Poetry comes in various shapes and forms, types and subtypes. Although matter is generally more important than form, the two are inextricably linked, and it is obvious that you should pick up at least a little information on ballads, odes, sonnets, and so on. Certain terms which you will need in studying poetry are briefly defined at the end of this introductory note. Do not memorize these rudimentary definitions, but do refer to them as your need or your instructor suggests.

6. Poetry has pronounced rhythms, generally resolvable into metrical patterns. It often has rhyme, and rhyme comes in varied patterns also. It often is musical. It relies heavily on figurative language and allusion. Quick study, as needed, of terms in the following glossary will provide what help you need in dealing with such matters, but perhaps a further word on rhyme and meter will be useful.

When two words rhyme (see definition of *rhyme* in the glossary), each is noted in what is called a *rhyme scheme* by use of the same letter of the alphabet. For example, if the first and third lines of a stanza rhyme, and the second and fourth do likewise, the scheme is referred to as *abab*. But be certain not to confuse true rhyme and *assonance* (see the glossary).

The term *meter* in English poetry refers to the pattern of stressed and unstressed syllables in a line, or verse, of a poem. The number of syllables in a line may be fixed and the number of stresses may vary, or the stresses may be fixed and the number of unstressed syllables may change. The number of stresses and syllables is fixed and definite in the most frequent forms of meter in English verse, although actually this basic pattern occasionally varies so as to avoid sounding like a metronome. In some modern poetry, regular meter is largely forsaken, and *cadences* (see the glossary) are employed to approximate the flow of speech. These are the meters most commonly used in English poetry: *iambic, trochaic, anapestic, dactylic,* and *spondaic.* Each is defined and illustrated in the glossary. Every such metrical unit, or group of syllables, is called a *foot;* the number of feet in a line of poetry determines its name as, for example, a verse of three feet is called *trimeter* and one of five feet is called *pentameter.*

With this information at hand in addition to that which is supplied in the glossary, what can you make of this part of Byron's "The Destruction of Sennacherib"?

> The Assyrian came down like a wolf on the fold,
> And his cohorts were gleaming in purple and gold;
> And the sheen of their spears was like stars on the sea,
> Where the blue wave rolls nightly on deep Galilee.

It is impossible to read this material without hearing its music and without realizing that it uses several figures of speech. Technically, the four lines, or verses, constitute a kind of stanza called a *quatrain;* the rhyme scheme is *aabb;* the meter is *anapestic tetrameter:*

> And the shéen/ of their spéars/ was like stárs/ on the séa

As has been mentioned, not every line of poetry is so definitely accented as this one, but your ear, properly attuned, and your mind, filled with basic knowledge about meter, should enable you to read other poetry with understanding allowance for subtly altered rhythmic effects.

Reading poetry requires the same skills and perceptions as reading prose. But since poetry may not be so familiar a form to you, these questions should suggest useful approaches:

1. Study the vocabulary of the poem. What passages are obscure? What key allusions must you check in a reference book? What ordinary words are employed in apparently unusual meanings? What other words must you look up and add to your reading vocabulary? Your writing vocabulary?

2. Who is speaking in the poem? To whom? What is the occasion? (A poem is often dramatic. Do not assume that "I" is the poet speaking in his own person.)

3. What is the attitude in the poem? (Answering this question is not primarily a matter of describing how the poet felt; it is a matter of describing the attitude that arises for you.)

4. What part of the effect of the poem is accounted for by its rhythm? Does the rhythm represent or suggest any sort of movement? Is the effect

of the rhythm consistent with, and does it reinforce, the emotion of the poem?

5. What words or expressions in the poem are so used that, beyond any function they may have in making a statement, they evoke in you images and feelings?

6. Does the poem have a theme which may be stated outside the terms of the poem itself? Is there a line or a short passage which states the theme? Is the theme implicit—suggested instead of being directly stated and left, therefore, for you to formulate?

Without answering these six questions in so many words, a discussion of some points raised by a reading of Robert Herrick's brief "Delight in Disorder" is given in the next paragraphs. This comment may seem too elaborate or too fanciful to you. Very well, then. Write your own commentary on this or some other poem. But remember: if you strive to meet a good poet halfway, your life will be richer for the effort.

The central thought of this poem is that a somewhat negligent dress in women is more exciting than meticulous good grooming. This is hardly a monumental thought. Yet the poem is memorable and affords pleasure by the way in which Herrick conveys the excitement of disorder in dress. After 12 lines in which the poet brings alive the gay bewitchingness of disorder he uses nine words to contrast the dullness and insipidity of superb grooming.

The animation of this poem is achieved in considerable part by the poet's diction. Do you ordinarily think of "disorder" as *sweet*? Of "distraction" as *fine* or of "civility" as *wild*? Herrick continues to transform passive objects into active agents: *erring* lace, *enthrals* the stomacher, *winning* wave, *tempestuous* petticoat, *careless* shoe-string, cuff *neglectful*. The various elements of dress *act* riotously, wantonly. A sense of activity permeates the poem; when "sweet disorder" *kindles* wantonness, the thought comes alive with unruliness.

This poem is a tribute to disorder and a contrast between artfulness and naturalness, a creation of a state of feeling that is unusual, to say the least. Even so, the description of clothing follows a definite order. Herrick proceeds to detail items of clothing from head to foot, much as would most men looking at most women. By the time we get to a "careless shoe-string" we are ready to accept the strange, even fantastic, idea of "wild civility." "Sweetness" and "disorder" might go together in an easy concept, but not "wildness" and "civility." What began as subdued whimsy has become a fantastic extravagance. Perhaps that is why the poet, realizing this, descends from Cloud Nine and gets back to ordered movement and language.

All words are born as sounds by which men attempt to convey ideas. This poem is an excellent illustration of how a good poet uses to the fullest, even exaggerates, the emotional content of words inherent in their sound. The way in which the sounds of this poem are manipulated and juggled by the poet greatly reinforces the overall idea. The presence of the clothes (line 2) is made apparent by the combined *l*, *s*, and *th* sounds, which seem to rustle. The pattern of consonants in "kindles in clothes" indicates that the garments are truly active and flaming. Note, too, the alliteration in "winning wave" and the similar sounds in "tem*pes*tuous petticoat." The word *tempestuous* actually sounds like rustling clothing. Notice also how in the last line the sharp syllables of *precise* and the punctuated effect of the percussive *p*'s in *precise* and *part* have a contrasting effect on our senses when set immediately following the poem's main body of sensuous sounds.

Even the meter of the poem conveys a sense of unruliness and disorder. The prevailing meter is iambic tetrameter—four feet, each consisting of an unaccented syllable followed by an accented one, eight syllables to the line. But the crucial word *kindles* reverses the accent and thus acquires special emphasis. In another example of unruliness, note that the last word in line 7, *thereby*, forces the reading on. This difference between a unit of verse and a unit of thought is not uncommon in poetry, but here it adds to the lack of order which fills the poem. If you will compare the first and the last lines of the poem by reading each aloud you will be able to feel rhythmically that, although the first line scans as perfectly as the last, it flows with soft consonants, unlike the staccato effect in the progression of quick, hard sounds composing the final measures of the poem.

More could be said of the technique and content of this little poem, but perhaps for your enjoyment too much has already been written. Yet the poem would not really be enjoyable unless it did employ exaggerated terms in a fanciful manner. The tone is playful and humorous, but this tone would not be so apparent had not the shaping hand of an accomplished poet used many devices of diction, meter, and even rhyme to convey his meaning.

GLOSSARY

Anapest. A metrical foot of two short syllables followed by one long (*to the end* or *to the end*).

Assonance. Similarity in sound between vowels; differs from rhyme in that final consonants involved are not the same (*wine–lime*). (See *Rhyme.*)

Ballad. Originally a song, then a narrative poem with popular and literary traditions, and today (a loose use of the term) a melodramatic or amatory song.

Ballad stanza. Commonly a four-line stanza with second and fourth lines rhyming and the meter running tetrameter, trimeter, tetrameter, trimeter in order. Many variations exist, however.

Blank verse. Unrhymed iambic pentameter used in dignified and lofty passages of epic poetry, drama, etc.

Cadence. Recognizable beat and rhythmic flow of phrase without formal stress pattern, in verse or prose.

Conceit. Term applied to a strained or involved comparison or idea.

Couplet. A pair of successive lines of verse, especially such as rhyme together and are of identical length.

Dactyl. A metrical foot consisting of an accented syllable followed by two unaccented ones (*murmuring*).

Dimeter. A line of poetry made up of two feet.

Dramatic monologue. A poem in which one character speaks to one or more mute listeners and incidentally reveals his own psychological

make-up. (See Tennyson's "Ulysses" and Browning's "My Last Duchess.")

Elegy.   A formal poem of mourning or brooding on the subject of death.

Epic.   A poetic type marked by its length, seriousness, noble characters,
central hero, etc.

Epitaph.   A subtype, a short poem suitable for a gravestone or valedictory.
Sometimes synonymous with an epigram on death. Sometimes wryly
humorous like Gay's, written for himself:

> Life is a jest, and all things show it;
> I thought so once, but now I know it.

Foot.   The basic rhythmic unit in a recognizable metric pattern. In English the commonest feet are iambic, trochaic, anapestic, and dactylic
(which see).

Free verse.   Verse which has no regular metrical pattern, but which does
have cadence, often set up irregularly as to length of line to "look like"
poetry; employs imagery and figures of conventional verse and definitely has some organization or over-all unity of effect. Not to be confused with *blank verse*. Often referred to as *vers libre*.

Heptameter.   A line of poetry having seven feet.

Heroic couplet.   A pair of rhyming lines in iambic pentameter; may be a
"closed" couplet with a unit organization of its own, or one unit with
other continuous "open" couplets, with run-on lines.

Hexameter.   A line of poetry having six feet.

Iambic.   Common type of foot with an unaccented syllable followed by
an accented one (ŏmīt).

Light verse.   Term (not to be confused with *blank verse* or *free verse*)
applied to those forms (limericks, triolets, certain songs) which are
light in touch but which require deftness and dexterity nevertheless.

Lyric.   Originally a poem to be sung to lyre accompaniment, hence
melodic; today, however, generally a short poem with strong emotional
basis and marked individual personality evident.

Metaphysical poetry.   Loosely, poetry dealing with reasoning processes
and philosophical complexities; in the seventeenth century, it was
marked by intellectual pyrotechnics, conceits, subtleties, unusual comparisons.

Meter.   A term used as a combining form to designate the number of
feet to a line (pentameter equals five-foot line, etc.). Not in combination, the word refers to any formal arrangement of rhythm.

Monometer.   Literally, a line of poetry having only one foot, obviously
seldom found.

Octameter.   A line of poetry having eight feet.

Ode.   A subtype of lyric poetry with serious tone, addressed in praise to
a person, object, or idea.

Pastoral.   A term, adjective or noun, applied to poetry or music or romance dealing with shepherds, flocks, fields, farms, etc. Classically it
is an artificial form with lofty language, set themes, and conventional
names.

Pentameter.   A line of poetry having five feet.

Petrarchan (Italian) sonnet. A 14-line love poem originally, introduced to England by Wyatt and Surrey. The first eight lines (octave) rhyme *abba, abba;* the last six (sestet) may take one of several patterns or be irregular, though strictly the last two lines should not rhyme.

Prosody. The study of metrical structure.

Quatrain. A four-line stanza or a unit group of four lines in a long composition.

Refrain. The repeated portion of a poem, ballad, song—used for choral effect, audience participation, etc.

Rhyme. Repetition of sound at the end of poetic lines (or at the middle and end of a line—"internal" rhyme). Stressed vowels and following consonants should be identical (*wine–mine*). (See *Assonance.*)

Scansion. The act of dividing a line of poetry into feet, placing accent marks, deciding meter, and perhaps reading aloud. The commonest lines in English are tetrameter, pentameter, and hexameter; the four familiar patterns are iambic, trochaic, anapestic, and dactylic.

Sestet. The last six lines of a Petrarchan or Italian sonnet (which see).

Shakespearean (English) sonnet. A form taking its name from the poet who handled it best, although Surrey introduced it. The 14 lines are divided into three quatrains and a couplet with an inflexible rhyme scheme: *abab, cdcd, efef, gg.*

Sonnet. A subtype of poetry identified as 14 lines in iambic pentameter with several possible rhyme schemes (see *Petrarchan, Spenserian,* and *Shakespearean sonnet*). In its long history it has been amatory, autobiographical, philosophical, topical.

Spenserian sonnet. A sonnet form with the following rhyme scheme: *abab, bcbc, cdcd, ee.* Superficially, it resembles the Shakespearean, but uses fewer rhymes, achieves coherence by the linking repetitions.

Spondee. A foot consisting of two accented syllables, used to prevent monotony in conjunction with commoner set patterns (*dāybrēak*).

Stanza. The equivalent in a poem to the paragraph in prose; a unit of verse marked by distinct rhyme, meter, or subject pattern. It is recognized by spacing or indentation.

Tetrameter. A line of poetry having four feet.

Trimeter. A line of poetry having three feet.

Trochee. A metrical foot consisting of an accented syllable followed by an unaccented one (*trĭp ĭt*).

Verse. Technically, a single line of poetry; also a synonym for poetry; in modern songs, another name for stanza.

NARRATIVE POEMS

Anonymous

THE TWA CORBIES

As I was walking all alane,
I herd twa corbies making a mane;[1]
The tane unto the t'other say,
"Where sall we gang and dine to-day?"

"In behint yon auld fail[2] dyke,
I wot there lies a new slain knight;
And naebody kens that he lies there,
But his hawk, his hound, and lady fair.

"His hound is to the hunting gane,
His hawk to fetch the wild-fowl hame,
His lady's ta'en another mate,
So we may mak our dinner sweet.

"Ye'll sit on his white hause-bane,[3]
And I'll pike out his bonny blue een;
Wi ae lock o his gowden hair
We'll theek[4] our nest when it grows
bare.

"Mony a one for him makes mane,
But nane sall ken where he is gane;

Oer his white banes when they are
bare,
The wind sall blaw for evermair."

BONNY BARBARA ALLAN

It was in and about the Martinmas
time,
When the green leaves were a fall-
ing,
That Sir John Graeme, in the West
Country,
Fell in love with Barbara Allan.

He sent his men down through the
town
To the place where she was dwell-
ing:
"O haste and come to my master dear,
Gin[5] ye be Barbara Allan."

O hooly,[6] hooly rose she up,
To the place where he was lying,
And when she drew the curtain by,
"Young man, I think you're dying."

---

1 two ravens (crows) complaining (talking)
2 turf
3 neck-bone
4 thatch
5 If
6 slowly

"O it's I'm sick, and very, very sick,
　And it's a' for Barbara Allan;
O the better for me ye's never be,
　Tho your heart's blood were a spill-
　　ing."

"O dinna ye mind, young man," said
　　she,
　"When ye was in the tavern a drink-
　　ing,
That ye made the healths gae round
　　and round,
　And slighted Barbara Allan?"

He turned his face unto the wall,
　And death was with him dealing;
"Adieu, adieu, my dear friends all,
　And be kind to Barbara Allan."

And slowly, slowly raise she up,
　And slowly, slowly left him,
And sighing said she could not stay,
　Since death of life had reft him.

She had not gane a mile but twa,
　When she heard the dead-bell ring-
　　ing,
And every jow that the dead-bell geid,
　It cry'd, Woe to Barbara Allan!

"O mother, mother, make my bed!
　O make it saft and narrow!
Since my love died for me today,
　I'll die for him tomorrow."

John Keats

LA BELLE DAME SANS

MERCI

O what can ail thee, Knight at arms,
　Alone and palely loitering?
The sedge has withered from the Lake,
　And no birds sing!

O what can ail thee, Knight at arms,
　So haggard and so woe-begone?

The Squirrel's granary is full,
　And the harvest's done.

I see a lily on thy brow,
　With anguish moist and fever dew;
And on thy cheeks a fading rose
　Fast withereth too.

I met a Lady in the Meads,
　Full beautiful, a faery's child;
Her hair was long, her foot was light,
　And her eyes were wild.

I made a Garland for her head,
　And bracelets, too, and fragrant
　　Zone,[7]
She look'd at me as she did love,
　And made sweet moan.

I set her on my pacing steed,
　And nothing else saw, all day long;
For sidelong would she bend, and sing
　A faery's song.

She found me roots of relish sweet,
　And honey wild, and manna dew;
And sure in language strange she said,
　"I love thee true."

She took me to her elfin grot,
　And there she wept and sigh'd full
　　sore;
And there I shut her wild, wild eyes
　With kisses four.

And there she lulled me asleep,
　And there I dreamed, ah woe betide!
The latest dream I ever dreamt,
　On the cold hill side.

I saw pale Kings, and Princes too,
　Pale warriors, death pale were they
　　all;
They cried, "La belle dame sans merci
　Thee hath in thrall!"

I saw their starv'd lips in the gloam
　With horrid warning gaped wide—
And I awoke, and found me here,
　On the cold hill's side.

And this is why I sojourn here,
　Alone and palely loitering;
Though the sedge is withered from the
　　Lake,
　And no birds sing.

---

[7] belt

Alfred, Lord Tennyson

ULYSSES

It little profits that an idle king,
By this still hearth, among these bar-
    ren crags,
Matched with an agèd wife, I mete
    and dole
Unequal laws unto a savage race,
That hoard, and sleep, and feed, and
    know not me.
I cannot rest from travel; I will drink
Life to the lees. All times I have en-
    joyed
Greatly, have suffered greatly, both
    with those
That loved me, and alone; on shore,
    and when
Through scudding drifts the rainy
    Hyades
Vexed the dim sea. I am become a
    name;
For always roaming with a hungry
    heart
Much have I seen and known—cities
    of men,
And manners, climates, councils, gov-
    ernments,
Myself not least, but honored of them
    all—
And drunk delight of battle with my
    peers,
Far on the ringing plains of windy
    Troy.
I am a part of all that I have met;
Yet all experience is an arch where-
    through
Gleams that untraveled world, whose
    margin fades
Forever and forever when I move.
How dull it is to pause, to make an
    end,
To rust unburnished, not to shine in
    use!
As though to breathe were life! Life
    piled on life
Were all too little, and of one to me

Little remains: but every hour is saved
From that eternal silence, something
    more,
A bringer of new things; and vile it
    were
For some three suns to store and hoard
    myself,
And this gray spirit yearning in desire
To follow knowledge like a sinking
    star,
Beyond the utmost bound of human
    thought.
    This is my son, my own Telemachus,
To whom I leave the scepter and the
    isle—
Well-loved of me, discerning to fulfill
This labor, by slow prudence to make
    mild
A rugged people, and through soft de-
    grees
Subdue them to the useful and the
    good.
Most blameless is he, centered in the
    sphere
Of common duties, decent not to fail
In offices of tenderness, and pay
Meet adoration to my household gods,
When I am gone. He works his work,
    I mine.
    There lies the port; the vessel puffs
        her sail;
There gloom the dark broad seas. My
    mariners,
Souls that have toiled, and wrought,
    and thought with me,—
That ever with a frolic welcome took
The thunder and the sunshine, and op-
    posed
Free hearts, free foreheads,—you and
    I are old;
Old age hath yet his honor and his toil.
Death closes all; but something ere the
    end,
Some work of noble note, may yet be
    done,
Not unbecoming men that strove with
    gods.
The lights begin to twinkle from the
    rocks;
The long day wanes; the slow moon
    climbs; the deep
Moans round with many voices. Come,
    my friends,
'Tis not too late to seek a newer world.

Push off, and sitting well in order
    smite
The sounding furrows; for my purpose
    holds
To sail beyond the sunset, and the
    baths
Of all the western stars, until I die.
It may be that the gulfs will wash us
    down;
It may be we shall touch the Happy
    Isles,
And see the great Achilles, whom we
    knew.
Though much is taken, much abides;
    and though
We are not now that strength which
    in old days
Moved earth and heaven; that which
    we are, we are;
One equal temper of heroic hearts,
Made weak by time and fate, but
    strong in will
To strive, to seek, to find, and not to
    yield.

TITHONUS[8]

The woods decay, the woods decay
    and fall,
The vapors weep their burthen to the
    ground,
Man comes and tills the field and lies
    beneath,
And after many a summer dies the
    swan.
Me only cruel immortality
Consumes; I wither slowly in thine
    arms,
Here at the quiet limit of the world,
A white-haired shadow roaming like a
    dream
The ever-silent spaces of the East,
Far-folded mists, and gleaming halls
    of morn.
    Alas! for this gray shadow, once a
    man—

So glorious in his beauty and thy
    choice,
Who madest him thy chosen, that he
    seemed
To his great heart none other than a
    God!
I asked thee, "Give me immortality."
Then didst thou grant mine asking
    with a smile,
Like wealthy men who care not how
    they give.
But thy strong Hours indignant worked
    their wills,
And beat me down and marred and
    wasted me,
And though they could not end me,
    left me maimed
To dwell in presence of immortal
    youth,
Immortal age beside immortal youth,
And all I was in ashes. Can thy love,
Thy beauty, make amends, though
    even now,
Close over us, the silver star, thy guide,
Shines in those tremulous eyes that
    fill with tears
To hear me? Let me go; take back thy
    gift.
Why should a man desire in any way
To vary from the kindly race of men,
Or pass beyond the goal of ordinance
Where all should pause, as is most
    meet for all?
    A soft air fans the cloud apart; there
    comes
A glimpse of that dark world where I
    was born.
Once more the old mysterious glimmer
    steals
From thy pure brows, and from thy
    shoulders pure,
And bosom beating with a heart re-
    newed.
Thy cheek begins to redden through
    the gloom,
Thy sweet eyes brighten slowly close
    to mine,

[8] Tithonus, a Trojan prince, was loved by the goddess of the dawn, Eos or Aurora, who obtained for him the gift of living forever but neglected to obtain for him the gift of everlasting youth. In the monologue, Tithonus appears as an aged man, dwelling still in the palace of the goddess, and cut off from the normal cycle of human life which ends in death. To him immortality, not death, is "cruel."

Ere yet they blind the stars, and the
　　wild team
Which love thee, yearning for thy
　　yoke, arise,
And shake the darkness from their
　　loosened manes,
And beat the twilight into flakes of
　　fire.
　Lo! ever thus thou growest beautiful
In silence, then before thine answer
　　given
Departest, and thy tears are on my
　　cheek.
　Why wilt thou ever scare me with
　　thy tears,
And make me tremble lest a saying
　　learnt,
In days far-off, on that dark earth, be
　　true?
"The Gods themselves cannot recall
　　their gifts."
　Ay me! ay me! with what another
　　heart
In days far-off, and with what other
　　eyes
I used to watch—if I be he that
　　watched—
The lucid outline forming round thee;
　　saw
The dim curls kindle into sunny rings;
Changed with thy mystic change, and
　　felt my blood
Glow with the glow that slowly crim-
　　soned all
Thy presence and thy portals, while I
　　lay,
Mouth, forehead, eyelids, growing
　　dewy-warm
With kisses balmier than half-opening
　　buds
Of April, and could hear the lips that
　　kissed
Whispering I knew not what of wild
　　and sweet,
Like that strange song I heard Apollo
　　sing,
While Ilion like a mist rose into tow-
　　ers.
　Yet hold me not forever in thine
　　East:
How can my nature longer mix with
　　thine?
Coldly thy rosy shadows bathe me, cold

Are all thy lights, and cold my wrin-
　　kled feet
Upon thy glimmering thresholds, when
　　the steam
Floats up from those dim fields about
　　the homes
Of happy men that have the power to
　　die,
And grassy barrows of the happier
　　dead.
Release me, and restore me to the
　　ground.
Thou seest all things, thou wilt see my
　　grave;
Thou wilt renew thy beauty morn by
　　morn,
I earth in earth forget these empty
　　courts,
And thee returning on thy silver
　　wheels.

Robert Browning

MY LAST DUCHESS

That's my last Duchess painted on
　　the wall,
Looking as if she were alive; I call
That piece a wonder, now: Fra Pan-
　　dolf's hands
Worked busily a day, and there she
　　stands.
Will't please you sit and look at her?
　　I said
"Fra Pandolf" by design, for never
　　read
Strangers like you that pictured coun-
　　tenance,
The depth and passion of its earnest
　　glance,
But to myself they turned (since none
　　puts by
The curtain I have drawn for you,
　　but I)
And seemed as they would ask me, if
　　they durst,
How such a glance came there; so, not
　　the first

Are you to turn and ask thus. Sir,
    'twas not
Her husband's presence only, called
    that spot
Of joy into the Duchess' cheek: per-
    haps
Fra Pandolf chanced to say, "Her man-
    tle laps
Over my Lady's wrist too much," or
    "Paint
Must never hope to reproduce the faint
Half-flush that dies along her throat";
    such stuff
Was courtesy, she thought, and cause
    enough
For calling up that spot of joy. She
    had
A heart . . . how shall I say? . . . too
    soon made glad,
Too easily impressed; she liked what-
    e'er
She looked on, and her looks went
    everywhere.
Sir, 'twas all one! My favor at her
    breast,
The dropping of the daylight in the
    West,
The bough of cherries some officious
    fool
Broke in the orchard for her, the white
    mule
She rode with round the terrace—all
    and each
Would draw from her alike the ap-
    proving speech,
Or blush, at least. She thanked men,
    —good; but thanked
Somehow . . . I know not how . . . as
    if she ranked
My gift of a nine-hundred-years-old
    name
With anybody's gift. Who'd stoop to
    blame
This sort of trifling? Even had you
    skill
In speech—(which I have not)—to
    make your will
Quite clear to such an one, and say,
    "Just this
Or that in you disgusts me; here you
    miss
Or there exceed the mark"—and if she
    let
Herself be lessoned so, nor plainly set

Her wits to yours, forsooth, and made
    excuse,
—E'en then would be some stooping,
    and I choose
Never to stoop. Oh, Sir, she smiled, no
    doubt,
Whene'er I passed her; but who passed
    without
Much the same smile? This grew; I
    gave commands,
Then all smiles stopped together.
    There she stands
As if alive. Will't please you rise? We'll
    meet
The company below, then. I repeat,
The Count your Master's known mu-
    nificence
Is ample warrant that no just pretence
Of mine for dowry will be disallowed;
Though his fair daughter's self, as I
    avowed
At starting, is my object. Nay, we'll go
Together down, Sir! Notice Neptune,
    though,
Taming a sea-horse, thought a rarity,
Which Claus of Innsbruck cast in
    bronze for me.

Lewis Carroll

JABBERWOCKY

'Twas brillig, and the slithy toves
    Did gyre and gimble in the wabe;
All mimsy were the borogoves,
    And the mome raths outgrabe.

"Beware the Jabberwock, my son!
    The jaws that bite, the claws that
    catch!
Beware the Jubjub bird, and shun
    The frumious Bandersnatch!"

He took his vorpal sword in hand;
    Long time the manxome foe he
    sought—
So rested he by the Tumtum tree,
    And stood awhile in thought.

And, as in uffish thought he stood,
  The Jabberwock, with eyes of flame,
Came whiffling through the tulgey
    wood,
  And burbled as it came!

One, two! One, two! And through and
    through
  The vorpal blade went snicker-
    snack!
He left it dead, and with its head
  He went galumphing back.

"And hast thou slain the Jabberwock?
  Come to my arms, my beamish boy!
O frabjous day! Callooh! Callay!"
  He chortled in his joy.

'Twas brillig, and the slithy toves
  Did gyre and gimble in the wabe;
All mimsy were the borogoves,
  And the mome raths outgrabe.

Edwin Arlington Robinson

RICHARD CORY

Whenever Richard Cory went down
    town,
  We people on the pavement looked
    at him:
He was a gentleman from sole to
    crown,
  Clean favored, and imperially slim.

And he was always quietly arrayed,
  And he was always human when he
    talked;
But still he fluttered pulses when he
    said,
  "Good-morning," and he glittered
    when he walked.

And he was rich—yes, richer than a
    king—
  And admirably schooled in every
    grace:
In fine, we thought that he was every-
    thing
  To make us wish that we were in
    his place.

So on we worked, and waited for the
    light,
  And went without the meat, and
    cursed the bread;
And Richard Cory, one calm summer
    night,
  Went home and put a bullet through
    his head.

Rudyard Kipling

DANNY DEEVER

"What are the bugles blowin' for?"
    said Files-on-Parade.
"To turn you out, to turn you out," the
    Color-Sergeant said.
"What makes you look so white, so
    white?" said Files-on-Parade.
"I'm dreadin' what I've got to watch,"
    the Color-Sergeant said.
  For they're hangin' Danny Deever,
    you can 'ear the Dead March play,
  The regiment's in 'ollow square—
    they're hangin' him today;
  They've taken of his buttons off an'
    cut his stripes away,
  An' they're hangin' Danny Deever
    in the mornin'.

"What makes the rear-rank breathe so
    'ard?" said Files-on-Parade.
"It's bitter cold, it's bitter cold," the
    Color-Sergeant said.
"What makes that front-rank man fall
    down?" says Files-on-Parade.
"A touch of sun, a touch of sun," the
    Color-Sergeant said.
  They are hangin' Danny Deever,
    they are marchin' of 'im round.
  They 'ave 'alted Danny Deever by 'is
    coffin on the ground:
  An 'e'll swing in 'arf a minute for a
    sneakin' shootin' hound—
  O they're hangin' Danny Deever in
    the mornin'!

" 'Is cot was right-'and cot to mine,"
  said Files-on-Parade.
" 'E's sleepin' out an' far tonight," the
  Color-Sergeant said.
"I've drunk 'is beer a score o' times,"
  said Files-on-Parade.
" 'E's drinkin' bitter beer alone," the
  Color-Sergeant said.
  They are hangin' Danny Deever, you
    must mark 'im to 'is place,
  For 'e shot a comrade sleepin'—
    you must look 'im in the face;
  Nine 'undred of 'is county an' the
    regiment's disgrace,
  While they're hangin' Danny Deever
    in the mornin'.

"What's that so black agin' the sun?"
  said Files-on-Parade.
"It's Danny fightin' 'ard for life," the
  Color-Sergeant said.
"What's that that whimpers over'ead?"
  said Files-on-Parade.
"It's Danny's soul that's passin' now,"
  the Color-Sergeant said.
  For they're done with Danny Dee-
    ver, you can 'ear the quickstep
    play,
  The regiment's in column, an'
    they're marchin' us away;
  Ho! the young recruits are shakin',
    an' they'll want their beer today,
  After hangin' Danny Deever in the
    mornin'.

W. H. Auden

BALLAD[9]

O what is that sound which so thrills
  the ear
  Down in the valley drumming,
    drumming?
Only the scarlet soldiers, dear,
  The soldiers coming.

O what is that light I see flashing so
  clear
  Over the distance brightly, brightly?
Only the sun on their weapons, dear,
  As they step lightly.

O what are they doing with all that
  gear;
  What are they doing this morning,
    this morning?
Only the usual maneuvers, dear,
  Or perhaps a warning.

O why have they left the road down
  there;
  Why are they suddenly wheeling,
    wheeling?
Perhaps a change in the orders, dear;
  Why are you kneeling?

O haven't they stopped for the doc-
  tor's care;
  Haven't they reined their horses,
    their horses?
Why, they are none of them wounded,
  dear,
  None of these forces.

O is it the parson they want, with
  white hair;
  Is it the parson, is it, is it?
No, they are passing his gateway, dear,
  Without a visit.

O it must be the farmer who lives so
  near;
  It must be the farmer, so cunning,
    cunning;
They have passed the farm already,
  dear,
  And now they are running.

O where are you going? stay with me
  here.
  Were the vows you swore me de-
    ceiving?
No, I promised to love you, my dear,
  But I must be leaving.

O it's broken the lock and splintered
  the door,
  O it's the gate where they're turn-
    ing, turning;
Their feet are heavy on the floor
  And their eyes are burning.

---

[9] From *On This Island*. Reprinted by permission of Random House, Inc. Copyright 1937 by Random House, Inc.

LYRIC POEMS

Sir Philip Sidney

WITH HOW SAD STEPS
(from "Astrophel and Stella")

31

With how sad steps, O Moon, thou
    climb'st the skies!
How silently, and with how wan a
    face!
What, may it be that even in heavenly
    place
That busy archer his sharp arrows
    tries?
Sure, if that long-with-love-acquainted
    eyes
Can judge of love, thou feel'st a lov-
    er's case.
I read it in thy looks; thy languished
    grace,
To me that feel the like, thy state de-
    scries.
Then, even of fellowship, O Moon, tell
    me,
Is constant love deemed there but
    want of wit?
Are beauties there as proud as here
    they be?
Do they above love to be loved, and yet
Those lovers scorn whom that love
    doth possess?
Do they call virtue there ungrateful-
    ness?

Christopher Marlowe

THE PASSIONATE
SHEPHERD TO HIS LOVE

Come live with me, and be my love;
And we will all the pleasures prove
That hills and valleys, dales and fields,
Woods, or steepy mountain yields.

And we will sit upon the rocks,
Seeing the shepherds feed their flocks
By shallow rivers, to whose falls
Melodious birds sing madrigals.

And I will make thee beds of roses,
And a thousand fragrant posies;
A cap of flowers, and a kirtle
Embroidered all with leaves of myrtle;

A gown made of the finest wool
Which from our pretty lambs we pull;
Fair-lined slippers for the cold,
With buckles of the purest gold;

A belt of straw and ivy-buds,
With coral clasps and amber studs;
And if these pleasures may thee move,
Come live with me, and be my love.

The shepherd-swains shall dance and
    sing
For thy delight each May morning;
If these delights thy mind may move,
Then live with me, and be my love.

Sir Walter Raleigh

THE NYMPH'S REPLY
TO THE SHEPHERD

If all the world and love were young,
And truth in every shepherd's tongue,
These pretty pleasures might me move,
To live with thee and be thy love.

But time drives flocks from field to
fold,
When rivers rage, and rocks grow cold;
And Philomel[10] becometh dumb;
The rest complains of cares to come.

The flowers do fade, and wanton fields
To wayward Winter reckoning yields;
A honey tongue, a heart of gall,
Is fancy's spring, but sorrow's fall.

Thy gowns, thy shoes, thy beds of
roses,
Thy cap, thy kirtle, and thy posies,
Soon break, soon wither, soon forgot-
ten,
In folly ripe, in reason rotten.

Thy belt of straw and ivy buds,
Thy coral clasps and amber studs,
All these in me no means can move,
To come to thee and be thy love.

But could youth last, and love still
breed,
Had joys no date, nor age no need,
Then these delights my mind might
move,
To live with thee and be thy love.

William Shakespeare

XV

When I consider every thing that
grows
Holds in perfection but a little mo-
ment,
That this huge stage presenteth naught
but shows
Whereon the stars in secret influence
comment;
When I perceive that men as plants
increase,
Cheered and checked even by the self-
same sky,
Vaunt in their youthful sap, at height
decrease,
And wear their brave state out of
memory;
Then the conceit[11] of this inconstant
stay
Sets you most rich in youth, before
my sight,
Where wasteful Time debateth with
Decay,
To change your day of youth to sullied
night;
   And, all in war with Time for love
of you,
   As he takes from you, I engraft[12]
your new.

XVIII

Shall I compare thee to a summer's
day?
Thou art more lovely and more temperate:
Rough winds do shake the darling
buds of May,

---

[10] Nightingale. This poem should be compared and contrasted with both
Marlowe's "The Passionate Shepherd to His Love" and John Donne's "The Bait."
   [11] idea
   [12] keep alive

And summer's lease hath all too short
a date:
Sometimes too hot the eye of heaven
shines,
And often is his gold complexion
dimmed;
And every fair from fair sometimes
declines,
By chance or nature's changing course
untrimmed;
But thy eternal summer shall not fade,
Nor lose possession of that fair thou
owest[13]
Nor shall Death brag thou wander'st
in his shade,
When in eternal lines to time thou
growest:
So long as men can breathe or eyes
can see,
So long lives this, and this gives life
to thee.

XXIX

When, in disgrace with fortune and
men's eyes,
I all alone beweep my outcast state,
And trouble deaf heaven with my boot-
less[14] cries,
And look upon myself and curse my
fate,
Wishing me like to one more rich in
hope,
Featured like him, like him with
friends possessed,
Desiring this man's art and that man's
scope,
With what I most enjoy contented
least;
Yet in these thoughts myself almost
despising,
Haply I think on thee,—and then my
state,
Like to the lark at break of day arising

From sullen earth, sings hymns at
heaven's gate;
For thy sweet love remembered such
wealth brings
That then I scorn to change my
state with kings.

CVI

When in the chronicle of wasted time
I see descriptions of the fairest
wights,[15]
And beauty making beautiful old
rhyme
In praise of ladies dead and lovely
knights,
Then, in the blazon of sweet beauty's
best,
Of hand, of foot, of lip, of eye, of brow,
I see their antique pen would have ex-
pressed
Even such a beauty as you master
now.
So all their praises are but prophecies
Of this our time, all you prefiguring;
And, for they looked but with divining
eyes,
They had not skill enough your worth
to sing:
For we, which now behold these
present days,
Have eyes to wonder, but lack
tongues to praise.

CXVI

Let me not to the marriage of true
minds
Admit impediments. Love is not love
Which alters when it alteration finds,
Or bends with the remover to remove:

---

[13] ownest
[14] useless
[15] creatures

O, no! it is an ever-fixèd mark
That looks on tempests and is never
    shaken;
It is the star to every wandering bark,
Whose worth's unknown, although his
    height be taken.
Love's not Time's fool, though rosy
    lips and cheeks
Within his bending sickle's compass
    come;
Love alters not with his brief hours
    and weeks,
But bears it out even to the edge of
    doom.
  If this be error and upon me proved,
  I never writ, nor no man ever loved.

Thomas Campion

NEVER LOVE UNLESS

YOU CAN

Never love unless you can
Bear with all the faults of man;
Men sometimes will jealous be,
Though but little cause they see,
And hang the head, as discontent,
And speak what straight they will re-
    pent.

Men that but one saint adore
Make a show of love to more;
Beauty must be scorned in none,
Though but truly served in one;
For what is courtship but disguise?
True hearts may have dissembling
    eyes.

Men when their affairs require
Must a while themselves retire,
Sometimes hunt, and sometimes hawk,
And not ever sit and talk.
If these and such like you can bear,
Then like, and love, and never fear.

John Donne

THE BAIT

Come live with me and be my love,
And we will some new pleasures prove,
Of golden sands and crystal brooks,
With silken lines and silver hooks.

There will the river whispering run,
Warmed by thy eyes more than the
    sun.
And there th' enamored fish will stay,
Begging themselves they may betray.

When thou wilt swim in that live bath,
Each fish, which every channel hath,
Will amorously to thee swim,
Gladder to catch thee, than thou him.

If thou, to be so seen, beest loath,
By sun or moon, thou darkenest both;
And if myself have leave to see,
I need not their light, having thee.

Let others freeze with angling reeds,
And cut their legs with shells and
    weeds,
Or treacherously poor fish beset
With strangling snare, or windowy net.

Let coarse bold hands from slimy nest
The bedded fish in banks out-wrest,
Or curious traitors, sleave-silk flies,
Bewitch poor fishes' wandering eyes.

For thee, thou needest no such deceit,
For thou thyself art thine own bait;
That fish that is not catched thereby,
Alas, is wiser far than I.

Robert Herrick

DELIGHT IN DISORDER

A sweet disorder in the dress
Kindles in clothes a wantonness;
A lawn about the shoulders thrown
Into a fine distractiòn;
An erring lace, which here and there
Enthrals the crimson stomacher;
A cuff neglectful, and thereby
Ribbons to flow confusèdly;
A winning wave (deserving note)
In the tempestuous petticoat;
A careless shoe-string, in whose tie
I see a wild civility:
Do more bewitch me, than when art
Is too precise in every part.

CHERRY-RIPE

Cherry-ripe, ripe, ripe, I cry,
Full and fair ones, come and buy;
If so be you ask me where
They do grow? I answer, There,
Where my Julia's lips do smile,
There's the land, or cherry isle,
Whose plantations fully show
All the year, where cherries grow.

UPON JULIA'S CLOTHES

Whenas in silks my Julia goes,
Then, then, methinks, how sweetly
    flows
The liquefaction of her clothes.

Next, when I cast mine eyes, and see
That brave vibration, each way free,
O, how that glittering taketh me!

TO THE VIRGINS, TO MAKE MUCH OF TIME

Gather ye rosebuds while ye may,
Old Time is still a-flying,
And this same flower that smiles to-
    day
Tomorrow will be dying.

The glorious lamp of heaven, the sun,
The higher he's a-getting,
The sooner will his race be run,
And nearer he's to setting.

That age is best which is the first,
When youth and blood are warmer;
But being spent, the worse, and worst
Times still succeed the former.

Then be not coy, but use your time,
And while ye may, go marry;
For having lost but once your prime,
You may forever tarry.

George Herbert

THE COLLAR

I struck the board and cried, No
    more!
            I will abroad.
What? Shall I ever sigh and pine?
My lines and life are free, free as the
    road,
    Loose as the wind, as large as store.
        Shall I be still in suit?
Have I no harvest but a thorn
To let me blood, and not restore
What I have lost with cordial fruit?
            Sure there was wine
    Before my sighs did dry it; there
        was corn
        Before my tears did drown it.
    Is the year only lost to me?
        Have I no bays to crown it?

No flowers, no garlands gay? All
    blasted
          All wasted?
Not so, my heart! But there is fruit,
       And thou hast hands.
      Recover all thy sigh-blown age
On double pleasures. Leave thy cold
    dispute
Of what is fit and not. Forsake thy
    cage,
       Thy rope of sands,
Which petty thoughts have made, and
    made to thee
Good cable, to enforce and draw,
       And be thy law,
While thou didst wink and wouldst
    not see.

      Away! Take heed!
      I will abroad.
Call in thy death's head there. Tie up
    thy fears.
      He that forbears
    To suit and serve his need
      Deserves his load.
But as I raved and grew more fierce
    and wild
      At every word,
  Methought I heard one calling,
    Child!
      And I replied, My Lord.

Edmund Waller

ON A GIRDLE

That which her slender waist con-
    fined,
Shall now my joyful temples bind;
No monarch but would give his crown,
His arms might do what this has done.

  It was my heaven's extremest
    sphere,
The pale which held that lovely deer;
My joy, my grief, my hope, my love,
Did all within this circle move!

A narrow compass! and yet there
Dwelt all that's good, and all that's
    fair;
Give me but what this ribband bound,
Take all the rest the sun goes round!

GO, LOVELY ROSE!

Go, lovely rose!
Tell her that wastes her time and me
    That now she knows,
When I resemble her to thee,
How sweet and fair she seems to be.

Tell her that's young,
And shuns to have her graces spied,
    That hadst thou sprung
In deserts, where no men abide,
Thou must have uncommended died.

Small is the worth
Of beauty from the light retired;
    Bid her come forth,
Suffer herself to be desired,
And not blush so to be admired.

Then die! that she
The common fate of all things rare
    May read in thee;
How small a part of time they share
That are so wondrous sweet and fair!

John Milton

ON HIS HAVING ARRIVED

AT THE AGE OF

TWENTY-THREE

How soon hath Time, the subtle thief
    of youth,
Stolen on his wing my three and twen-
    tieth year!

My hasting days fly on with full ca-
reer,
But my late spring no bud or blossom
shew'th.
Perhaps my semblance might deceive
the truth
That I to manhood am arrived so near;
And inward ripeness doth much less
appear,
That some more timely-happy spirits
endu'th.
Yet be it less or more, or soon or slow,
It shall be still in strictest measure
even
To that same lot, however mean or
high,
Toward which Time leads me, and the
will of Heaven;
All is, if I have grace to use it so,
As ever in my great Task-Master's eye.

ON HIS BLINDNESS

When I consider how my light is spent
Ere half my days, in this dark world
and wide,
And that one talent which is death to
hide
Lodged with me useless, though my
soul more bent
To serve therewith my Maker, and
present
My true account, lest he returning
chide;
"Doth God exact day-labor, light de-
nied?"
I fondly ask. But Patience, to prevent
That murmur, soon replies, "God doth
not need
Either man's work or his own gifts.
Who best
Bear his mild yoke, they serve him
best. His state
Is kingly: thousands at his bidding
speed,
And post o'er land and ocean without
rest;
They also serve who only stand and
wait."

Sir John Suckling

THE CONSTANT LOVER

Out upon it, I have loved
    Three whole days together!
And am like to love three more,
    If it prove fair weather.

Time shall moult away his wings,
    Ere he shall discover
In the whole wide world again
    Such a constant lover.

But the spite on't is, no praise
    Is due at all to me:
Love with me had made no stays,
    Had it any been but she.

Had it any been but she,
    And that very face,
There had been at least ere this
    A dozen dozen in her place.

Andrew Marvell

TO HIS COY MISTRESS

Had we but world enough, and time,
This coyness, Lady, were no crime.
We would sit down, and think which
    way
To walk, and pass our long love's day.
Thou by the Indian Ganges' side
Shouldst rubies find; I by the tide
Of Humber would complain. I would
Love you ten years before the Flood,
And you should, if you please, refuse
Till the conversion of the Jews.
My vegetable[16] love should grow
Vaster than empires and more slow;
An hundred years should go to praise

---

[16] active

Thine eyes, and on thy forehead gaze;
Two hundred to adore each breast,
But thirty thousand to the rest;
An age at least to every part,
And the last age should show your
  heart.
For, Lady, you deserve this state,
Nor would I love at lower rate.

  But at my back I always hear
Time's wingèd chariot hurrying near;
And yonder all before us lie
Deserts of vast eternity.
Thy beauty shall no more be found,
Nor, in thy marble vault, shall sound
My echoing song; then worms shall try
That long-preserved virginity,
And your quaint honor turn to dust,
And into ashes all my lust:
The grave's a fine and private place,
But none, I think, do there embrace.

  Now therefore, while the youthful
  hue
Sits on thy skin like morning dew,
And while thy willing soul transpires
At every pore with instant fires,
Now let us sport us while we may,
And now, like amorous birds of prey,
Rather at once our time devour
Than languish in his slow-chapped
  power.
Let us roll all our strength and all
Our sweetness up into one ball,
And tear our pleasures with rough
  strife
Thorough the iron gates of life;
Thus, though we cannot make our sun
Stand still, yet we will make him run.

William Blake

THE TIGER

Tiger! Tiger! burning bright
In the forests of the night,
What immortal hand or eye
Could frame thy fearful symmetry?

In what distant deeps or skies
Burnt the fire of thine eyes?
On what wings dare he aspire?
What the hand dare seize the fire?

And what shoulder, and what art,
Could twist the sinews of thy heart?
And when thy heart began to beat,
What dread hand and what dread
  feet?

What the hammer? what the chain?
In what furnace was thy brain?
What the anvil? what dread grasp
Dare its deadly terrors clasp?

When the stars threw down their
  spears,
And watered heaven with their tears,
Did He smile his work to see?
Did He who made the Lamb make
  thee?

Tiger! Tiger! burning bright
In the forests of the night,
What immortal hand or eye
Dare frame thy fearful symmetry?

William Wordsworth

COMPOSED UPON
WESTMINSTER BRIDGE,
SEPTEMBER 3, 1802

Earth has not anything to show more
  fair:
Dull would he be of soul who could
  pass by
A sight so touching in its majesty:
This City now doth like a garment
  wear
The beauty of the morning: silent,
  bare,
Ships, towers, domes, theatres, and
  temples lie
Open unto the fields, and to the sky,—
All bright and glittering in the smoke-
  less air.

Never did sun more beautifully steep
In his first splendor, valley, rock, or
    hill;
Ne'er saw I, never felt, a calm so deep!
The river glideth at his own sweet
    will:
Dear God! the very houses seem
    asleep;
And all that mighty heart is lying
    still!

THE WORLD IS TOO
MUCH WITH US

The world is too much with us: late
    and soon,
Getting and spending, we lay waste
    our powers.
Little we see in nature that is ours;
We have given our hearts away, a sor-
    did boon!
This sea that bares her bosom to the
    moon,
The winds that will be howling at all
    hours,
And are up-gathered now like sleeping
    flowers;
For this, for everything, we are out of
    tune;
It moves us not.—Great God! I'd rather
    be
A pagan suckled in a creed outworn;
So might I, standing on this pleasant
    lea,
Have glimpses that would make me
    less forlorn;
Have sight of Proteus rising from the
    sea;
Or hear old Triton blow his wreathèd
    horn.

LONDON, 1802

Milton! thou shouldst be living at this
    hour:
England hath need of thee; she is a
    fen

Of stagnant waters; altar, sword, and
    pen,
Fireside, the heroic wealth of hall and
    bower,
Have forfeited their ancient English
    dower
Of inward happiness. We are selfish
    men;
Oh! raise us up, return to us again;
And give us manners, virtue, freedom,
    power.
Thy Soul was like a Star, and dwelt
    apart;
Thou hadst a voice whose sound was
    like the sea;
Pure as the naked heavens, majestic,
    free,
So didst thou travel on life's common
    way,
In cheerful godliness; and yet thy
    heart
The lowliest duties on herself did lay.

Lord Byron

SHE WALKS IN BEAUTY

She walks in beauty, like the night
    Of cloudless climes and starry skies;
And all that's best of dark and bright
    Meet in her aspect and her eyes:
Thus mellowed to that tender light
    Which heaven to gaudy day denies.

One shade the more, one ray the less,
    Had half impaired the nameless
        grace
Which waves in every raven tress,
    Or softly lightens o'er her face;
Where thoughts serenely sweet express
    How pure, how dear their dwelling-
        place.

And on that cheek, and o'er that brow,
    So soft, so calm, yet eloquent,
The smiles that win, the tints that
    glow,
    But tell of days in goodness spent,
A mind at peace with all below,
    A heart whose love is innocent!

John Keats

WHEN I HAVE FEARS THAT

I MAY CEASE TO BE

When I have fears that I may cease
   to be
Before my pen has gleaned my teem-
   ing brain,
Before high-piled books, in charact'ry,
Hold like rich garners the full-ripened
   grain;
When I behold, upon the night's
   starred face,
Huge cloudy symbols of a high ro-
   mance,
And think that I may never live to
   trace
Their shadows, with the magic hand
   of chance;
And when I feel, fair creature of an
   hour,
That I shall never look upon thee
   more,
Never have relish in the faery power
Of unreflecting love—then on the
   shore
  Of the wide world I stand alone,
   and think,
  Till love and fame to nothingness
   do sink.

ODE ON A GRECIAN URN

1

Thou still unravished bride of quiet-
   ness,
  Thou foster-child of Silence and
   slow Time,
Sylvan historian, who canst thus express

A flowery tale more sweetly than
   our rhyme:
What leaf-fringed legend haunts about
   thy shape
Of dieties or mortals, or of both,
  In Tempe or the dales of Ar-
   cady?[17]
What men or gods are these? What
   maidens loth?
What mad pursuit? What struggle to
   escape?
  What pipes and timbrels? What
   wild ecstasy?

2

Heard melodies are sweet, but those
   unheard
  Are sweeter; therefore, ye soft pipes,
   play on;
Not to the sensual ear, but, more en-
   deared,
  Pipe to the spirit ditties of no tone:
Fair youth, beneath the trees, thou
   canst not leave
  Thy song, nor ever can those trees
   be bare;
   Bold Lover, never, never canst
   thou kiss,
Though winning near the goal—yet,
   do not grieve;
  She cannot fade, though thou
   hast not thy bliss,
  For ever wilt thou love, and she be
   fair!

3

Ah, happy, happy boughs! that cannot
   shed
  Your leaves, nor ever bid the Spring
   adieu;
And, happy melodist, unwearied,
  For ever piping songs for ever new.
More happy love! more happy, happy
   love!
  For ever warm and still to be en-
   joyed,
   For ever panting, and for ever
   young;

---

[17] regions in Greece suggesting a pastoral background

All breathing human passion far
above,
  That leaves a heart high-sorrowful
  and cloyed,
    A burning forehead, and a parch-
    ing tongue.

4

Who are these coming to the sacrifice?
  To what green altar, O mysterious
  priest,
Lead'st thou that heifer lowing at the
  skies,
  And all her silken flanks with gar-
  lands drest?
What little town by river or sea shore,
  Or mountain-built with peaceful
  citadel,
    Is emptied of this folk, this pious
    morn?
And, little town, thy streets for ever-
more
  Will silent be; and not a soul to tell
  Why thou art desolate, can e'er
  return.

5

O Attic shape! Fair attitude! with
  brede
  Of marble men and maidens over-
  wrought,
With forest branches and the trodden
  weed;
  Thou, silent form! dost tease us out
  of thought
As doth eternity: Cold Pastoral!
  When old age shall this generation
  waste,
    Thou shalt remain, in midst of
    other woe
Than ours, a friend to man, to
  whom thou say'st,
"Beauty is truth, truth beauty,"—that
  is all
  Ye know on earth, and all ye need
  to know.

Percy Bysshe Shelley

OZYMANDIAS

I met a traveler from an antique land
Who said: "Two vast and trunkless
  legs of stone
Stand in the desert. Near them, on the
  sand,
Half sunk, a shattered visage lies,
  whose frown,
And wrinkled lip, and sneer of cold
  command,
Tell that its sculptor well those pas-
  sions read
Which yet survive, stamped on these
  lifeless things,
The hand that mocked them, and the
  heart that fed:
And on the pedestal these words ap-
  pear:
'My name is Ozymandias, King of
  Kings:
Look on my works, ye Mighty, and
  despair!'
Nothing beside remains. Round the
  decay
Of that colossal wreck, boundless and
  bare
The lone and level sands stretch far
  away."

Elizabeth Barrett
Browning

HOW DO I LOVE THEE?

How do I love thee? Let me count the
  ways.
I love thee to the depth and breadth
  and height

My soul can reach, when feeling out
    of sight
For the ends of Being and ideal Grace.
I love thee to the level of everyday's
Most quiet need, by sun and candle
    light.
I love thee freely, as men strive for
    Right;
I love thee purely, as they turn from
    Praise.
I love thee with the passion put to use
In my old griefs, and with my child-
    hood's faith.
I love thee with a love I seemed to lose
With my lost saints—I love thee with
    the breath,
Smiles, tears, of all my life!—and, if
    God choose,
I shall but love thee better after death.

Henry Wadsworth Longfellow

DIVINA COMMEDIA

1

Oft have I seen at some cathedral door
A laborer, pausing in the dust and
    heat,
Lay down his burden, and with rever-
    ent feet
Enter, and cross himself, and on the
    floor
Kneel to repeat his paternoster o'er;
Far off the noises of the world retreat;
The loud vociferations of the street
Become an undistinguishable roar.
So, as I enter here from day to day,
And leave my burden at this minster
    gate,
Kneeling in prayer, and not ashamed
    to pray,
The tumult of the time disconsolate
To inarticulate murmurs dies away,
While the eternal ages watch and wait.

Walt Whitman

WHEN I HEARD THE LEARN'D ASTRONOMER

When I heard the learn'd astronomer,
When the proofs, the figures, were
    ranged in columns before me,
When I was shown the charts and dia-
    grams, to add, divide, and meas-
    ure them,
When I sitting heard the astronomer
    where he lectured with much ap-
    plause in the lecture-room,
How soon unaccountable I became
    tired and sick,
Till rising and gliding out I wander'd
    off by myself,
In the mystical moist night-air, and
    from time to time,
Look'd up in perfect silence at the
    stars.

I HEAR AMERICA SINGING

I hear America singing, the varied
    carols I hear,
Those of mechanics, each one singing
    his as it should be, blithe and
    strong,
The carpenter singing his as he meas-
    ures his plank or beam,
The mason singing his as he makes
    ready for work, or leaves off work,
The boatman singing what belongs to
    him in his boat, the deckhand
    singing on the steamboat deck,
The shoemaker singing as he sits on
    his bench, the hatter singing as
    he stands,
The woodcutter's song, the plowboy's
    on his way in the morning, or at
    noon intermission or at sundown,

The delicious singing of the mother, or
    of the young wife at work, or of
    the girl sewing or washing,
Each singing what belongs to him or
    her and to none else,
The day what belongs to the day—at
    night the party of young fellows,
    robust, friendly,
Singing with open mouths their strong
    melodious songs.

Matthew Arnold

DOVER BEACH

The sea is calm to-night,
The tide is full, the moon lies fair
Upon the Straits;—on the French
    coast, the light
Gleams and is gone; the cliffs of Eng-
    land stand,
Glimmering and vast, out in the tran-
    quil bay.
Come to the window, sweet is the
    night air!
Only, from the long line of spray
Where the sea meets the moon-
    blanch'd land,
Listen! you hear the grating roar
Of pebbles which the waves draw
    back, and fling,
At their return, up the high strand,
Begin, and cease, and then again be-
    gin,
With tremulous cadence slow, and
    bring
The eternal note of sadness in.

    Sophocles long ago
Heard it on the Aegean, and it brought
Into his mind the turbid ebb and flow
Of human misery; we
Find also in the sound a thought,
Hearing it by this distant northern sea.

    The sea of faith
Was once, too, at the full, and round
    earth's shore

Lay like the folds of a bright girdle
    furl'd;
But now I only hear
Its melancholy, long, withdrawing
    roar,
Retreating to the breath
Of the night-wind down the vast edges
    drear
And naked shingles of the world.

    Ah, love, let us be true
To one another! for the world, which
    seems
To lie before us like a land of dreams,
So various, so beautiful, so new,
Hath really neither joy, nor love, nor
    light,
Nor certitude, nor peace, nor help for
    pain;
And we are here as on a darkling plain
Swept with confused alarms of strug-
    gle and flight,
Where ignorant armies clash by night.

Emily Dickinson

I LIKE TO SEE IT

LAP THE MILES

I like to see it lap the miles,
And lick the valleys up,
And stop to feed itself at tanks;
And then, prodigious, step

Around a pile of mountains,
And, supercilious, peer
In shanties by the sides of roads;
And then a quarry pare

To fit its sides, and crawl between,
Complaining all the while
In horrid, hooting stanza;
Then chase itself down hill

And neigh like Boanerges;
Then, punctual as a star,
Stop—docile and omnipotent—
At its own stable door.

SUCCESS IS COUNTED
SWEETEST

Success is counted sweetest
By those who ne'er succeed.
To comprehend a nectar
Requires sorest need.

Not one of all the purple host
Who took the flag today
Can tell the definition,
So clear, of victory,

As he, defeated, dying,
On whose forbidden ear
The distant strains of triumph
Break, agonized and clear.

I DIED FOR BEAUTY

I died for beauty, but was scarce
Adjusted in the tomb,
When one who died for truth was lain
In an adjoining room.

He questioned softly why I failed?
"For beauty," I replied.
"And I for truth,—the two are one;
We brethren are," he said.

And so, as kinsmen met a night,
We talked between the rooms,
Until the moss had reached our lips
And covered up our names.

HE ATE AND DRANK THE
PRECIOUS WORDS

He ate and drank the precious words,
His spirit grew robust;
He knew no more that he was poor,
Nor that his frame was dust.

He danced along the dingy days,
And this bequest of wings
Was but a book. What liberty
A loosened spirit brings!

Gerard Manley
Hopkins

HURRAHING IN
HARVEST[18]

Summer ends now; now, barbarous in
    beauty, the stooks arise
    Around; up above, what wind-walks!
    what lovely behaviour
Of silk-sack clouds! has wilder, wil-
    ful-wavier
Meal-drift moulded ever and melted
    across skies?

I walk, I lift up, I lift up heart, eyes,
    Down all that glory in the heavens
    to glean our Saviour;
    And, éyes, heárt, what looks, what
    lips yet gave you a
Rapturous love's greeting of realer, of
    rounder replies?

And the azurous hung hills are his
    world-wielding shoulder
    Majestic—as a stallion stalwart,
    very-violet-sweet!—
These things, these things were here
    and but the beholder
    Wanting; which two when they once
    meet,
The heart réars wíngs bold and bolder
    And hurls for him, O half hurls earth
    for him off under his feet.

---

[18] From *Poems of Gerard Manley Hopkins*, Oxford University Press. Reprinted by permission of the publisher.

SPRING AND FALL:

TO A YOUNG CHILD

Margaret, are you grieving
Over Goldengrove unleaving?
Leaves, like the things of man, you
With your fresh thoughts care for, can
    you?
Ah! as the heart grows older
It will come to such sights colder
By and by, nor spare a sigh
Though worlds of wanwood leafmeal
    lie;
And yet you will weep and know why.
Now no matter, child, the name:
Sorrow's springs are the same.
Nor mouth had, no nor mind, ex-
    pressed
What heart heard of, ghost guessed:
It is the blight man was born for,
It is Margaret you mourn for.

GOD'S GRANDEUR

The world is charged with the gran-
    deur of God.
    It will flame out, like shining from
    shook foil;
    It gathers to a greatness, like the
    ooze of oil
Crushed. Why do men then now not
    reck his rod?
Generations have trod, have trod, have
    trod;
    And all is seared with trade; bleared,
    smeared with toil;
    And wears man's smudge and
    shares man's smell: the soil
Is bare now, nor can foot feel, being
    shod.

And for all this, nature is never spent;
There lives the dearest freshness
    deep down things;
And though the last lights off the black
    West went
    Oh, morning, at the brown brink
    eastward, springs—
Because the Holy Ghost over the bent
    World broods with warm breast and
    with ah! bright wings.

A. E. Housman

OH, WHEN I WAS IN

LOVE WITH YOU[19]

Oh, when I was in love with you,
    Then I was clean and brave,
And miles around the wonder grew
    How well did I behave.

And now the fancy passes by,
    And nothing will remain,
And miles around they'll say that I
    Am quite myself again.

WHEN I WAS

ONE-AND-TWENTY[20]

When I was one-and-twenty
I heard a wise man say,
"Give crowns and pounds and guineas
But not your heart away;
Give pearls away and rubies
But keep your fancy free."
But I was one-and-twenty—
No use to talk to me.

---

[19] From *A Shropshire Lad* by A. E. Housman. Reprinted by permission of
Henry Holt & Company, Inc.
    [20] From *A Shropshire Lad* by A. E. Housman. Reprinted by permission of
Henry Holt & Company, Inc.

When I was one-and-twenty
I heard him say again,
"The heart out of the bosom
Was never given in vain;
'Tis paid with sighs a plenty
And sold for endless rue."
And I am two-and-twenty,
And, oh, 'tis true, 'tis true.

WITH RUE MY HEART
IS LADEN[21]

With rue my heart is laden
    For golden friends I had,
For many a rose-lipt maiden
    And many a lightfoot lad.

By brooks too broad for leaping
    The lightfoot boys are laid;
The rose-lipt girls are sleeping
    In fields where roses fade.

"TERENCE, THIS IS
STUPID STUFF:"[22]

"Terence, this is stupid stuff:
You eat your victuals fast enough;
There can't be much amiss, 'tis clear,
To see the rate you drink your beer.
But oh, good Lord, the verse you make,
It gives a chap the belly-ache.
The cow, the old cow, she is dead;
It sleeps well, the hornèd head:
We poor lads, 'tis our turn now
To hear such tunes as killed the cow.
Pretty friendship 'tis to rhyme
Your friends to death before their time
Moping melancholy mad:
Come, pipe a tune to dance to, lad."

Why, if 'tis dancing you would be,
There's brisker pipes than poetry.
Say, for what were hop-yards meant,
Or why was Burton built on Trent?
Oh many a peer of England brews
Livelier liquor than the Muse,
And malt does more than Milton can
To justify God's ways to man.
Ale, man, ale's the stuff to drink
For fellows whom it hurts to think:
Look into the pewter pot
To see the world as the world's not.
And faith, 'tis pleasant till 'tis past:
The mischief is that 'twill not last.
Oh I have been to Ludlow fair
And left my necktie God knows where,
And carried half-way home, or near,
Pints and quarts of Ludlow beer:
Then the world seemed none so bad,
And I myself a sterling lad;
And down in lovely muck I've lain,
Happy till I woke again.
Then I saw the morning sky:
Heigho, the tale was all a lie;
The world, it was the old world yet,
I was I, my things were wet,
And nothing now remained to do
But begin the game anew.

Therefore, since the world has still
Much good, but much less good than
        ill,
And while the sun and moon endure
Luck's a chance, but trouble's sure,
I'd face it as a wise man would,
And train for ill and not for good.
'Tis true, the stuff I bring for sale
Is not so brisk a brew as ale:
Out of a stem that scored the hand
I wrung it in a weary land.
But take it: if the smack is sour,
The better for the embittered hour;
It should do good to heart and head
When your soul is in my soul's stead;
And I will friend you, if I may,
In the dark and cloudy day.

---

[21] From *A Shropshire Lad* by A. E. Housman. Reprinted by permission of Henry Holt & Company, Inc.
[22] From *A Shropshire Lad* by A. E. Housman. Reprinted by permission of Henry Holt & Company, Inc.

There was a king reigned in the
East:
There, when kings will sit to feast,
They get their fill before they think
With poisoned meat and poisoned
drink.
He gathered all that springs to birth
From the many-venomed earth;
First a little, thence to more,
He sampled all her killing store;
And easy, smiling, seasoned sound
Sate the king when healths went
round.
They put arsenic in his meat
And stared aghast to watch him eat;
They poured strychnine in his cup
And shook to see him drink it up:
They shook, they stared as white's
their shirt:
Them it was their poison hurt.
—I tell the tale that I heard told.
Mithridates, he died old.

William Butler Yeats

WHEN YOU ARE OLD[23]

When you are old and gray and full of
sleep,
And nodding by the fire, take down
this book,
And slowly read, and dream of the
soft look
Your eyes had once, and of their shadows deep;

How many loved your moments of glad
grace,
And loved your beauty with love false
or true;
But one man loved the pilgrim soul in
you,
And loved the sorrows of your changing face.

And bending down beside the glowing
bars
Murmur, a little sadly, how love fled
And paced upon the mountains overhead
And hid his face amid a crowd of
stars.

THE LAKE ISLE OF

INNISFREE[24]

I will arise and go now, and go to
Innisfree,
And a small cabin build there, of clay
and wattles made;
Nine bean rows will I have there, a
hive for the honey bee,
And live alone in the bee-loud glade.

And I shall have some peace there, for
peace comes dropping slow,
Dropping from the veils of the morning to where the cricket sings;
There midnight's all a glimmer, and
noon a purple glow,
And evening full of the linnet's wings.

I will arise and go now, for always
night and day
I hear lake water lapping with low
sounds by the shore;
While I stand on the roadway, or on
the pavements gray,
I hear it in the deep heart's core.

[23] William Butler Yeats, *Collected Poems*. Copyright 1956 by The Macmillan
Company and used with their permission.
[24] From *Collected Poems* by W. B. Yeats. Reprinted by permission of the publishers, The Macmillan Company.

Edgar Lee Masters

PETIT, THE POET[25]

Seeds in a dry pod, tick, tick, tick,
Tick, tick, tick, like mites in a
 quarrel—
Faint iambics that the full breeze wak-
 ens—
But the pine tree makes a symphony
 thereof.
Triolets, villanelles, rondels, rondeaus,
Ballades by the score with the same
 old thought:
The snows and roses of yesterday are
 vanished;
And what is love but a rose that fades?
Life all around me here in the village:
Tragedy, comedy, valor and truth,
Courage, constancy, heroism, failure—
All in the loom, and oh what patterns!
Woodlands, meadows, streams and
 rivers—
Blind to all of it all my life long.
Triolets, villanelles, rondels, rondeaus,
Seeds in a dry pod, tick, tick, tick,
Tick, tick, tick, what little iambics,
While Homer and Whitman roared in
 the pines?

LUCINDA MATLOCK[26]

I went to the dances at Chandlerville,
And played snap-out at Winchester.
One time we changed partners,
Driving home in the moonlight of mid-
 dle June,
And then I found Davis.

We were married and lived together
 for seventy years,
Enjoying, working, raising the twelve
 children,
Eight of whom we lost
Ere I had reached the age of sixty.
I spun, I wove, I kept the house, I
 nursed the sick,
I made the garden, and for holiday
Rambled over the fields where sang
 the larks,
And by Spoon River gathering many a
 shell,
And many a flower and medicinal
 weed—
Shouting to the wooded hills, singing
 to the green valleys.
At ninety-six I had lived enough, that
 is all,
And passed to a sweet repose.
What is this I hear of sorrow and
 weariness,
Anger, discontent and drooping hopes?
Degenerate sons and daughters,
Life is too strong for you—
It takes life to love Life.

Robert Frost

MENDING WALL[27]

Something there is that doesn't love a
 wall,
That sends the frozen-ground-swell under it,
And spills the upper boulders in the
 sun;
And makes gaps even two can pass
 abreast.

[25] From *Spoon River Anthology*, The Macmillan Company, 1915. Reprinted
by special permission of Mrs. Edgar Lee Masters.
[26] From *Spoon River Anthology*, The Macmillan Company, 1915. Reprinted
by special permission of Mrs. Edgar Lee Masters.
[27] From *Complete Poems of Robert Frost*. Copyright 1930, 1949 by Henry
Holt & Company, Inc. Reprinted by permission of the publishers.

The work of hunters is another thing:
I have come after them and made re-
    pair
Where they have left not one stone on
    a stone,
But they would have the rabbit out of
    hiding,
To please the yelping dogs. The gaps
    I mean,
No one has seen them made or heard
    them made,
But at spring mending-time we find
    them there.
I let my neighbor know beyond the
    hill;
And on a day we meet to walk the
    line
And set the wall between us once
    again.
We keep the wall between us as we
    go.
To each the boulders that have fallen
    to each.
And some are loaves and some so
    nearly balls
We have to use a spell to make them
    balance:
"Stay where you are until our backs
    are turned!"
We wear our fingers rough with han-
    dling them.
Oh, just another kind of out-door
    game,
One on a side. It comes to little more:
There where it is we do not need the
    wall:
He is all pine and I am apple orchard.
My apple trees will never get across
And eat the cones under his pines, I
    tell him.
He only says, "Good fences make good
    neighbors."
Spring is the mischief in me, and I
    wonder
If I could put a notion in his head:
"*Why* do they make good neighbors?
    Isn't it
Where there are cows? But here there
    are no cows.
Before I built a wall I'd ask to know
What I was walling in or walling out,

And to whom I was like to give of-
    fense.
Something there is that doesn't love a
    wall,
That wants it down." I could say
    "Elves" to him,
But it's not elves exactly, and I'd
    rather
He said it for himself. I see him there
Bringing a stone grasped firmly by the
    top
In each hand, like an old-stone savage
    armed.
He moves in darkness as it seems to
    me,
Not of woods only and the shade of
    trees.
He will not go behind his father's say-
    ing,
And he likes having thought of it so
    well
He says again, "Good fences make
    good neighbors."

BIRCHES[28]

When I see birches bend to left and
    right
Across the lines of straighter darker
    trees,
I like to think some boy's been swing-
    ing them.
But swinging doesn't bend them down
    to stay.
Ice-storms do that. Often you must
    have seen them
Loaded with ice a sunny winter morn-
    ing
After a rain. They click upon them-
    selves
As the breeze rises, and turn many-
    colored
As the stir cracks and crazes their
    enamel.
Soon the sun's warmth makes them
    shed crystal shells
Shattering and avalanching on the
    snow-crust—

Such heaps of broken glass to sweep
away
You'd think the inner dome of heaven
had fallen.
They are dragged to the withered
bracken by the load,
And they seem not to break; though
once they are bowed
So low for long, they never right themselves:
You may see their trunks arching in
the woods
Years afterwards, trailing their leaves
on the ground
Like girls on hands and knees that
throw their hair
Before them over their heads to dry in
the sun.
But I was going to say when Truth
broke in
With all her matter-of-fact about the
ice-storm
(Now am I free to be poetical?)
I should prefer to have some boy bend
them
As he went out and in to fetch the
cows—
Some boy too far from town to learn
baseball,
Whose only play was what he found
himself,
Summer or winter, and could play
alone.
One by one he subdued his father's
trees
By riding them down over and over
again
Until he took the stiffness out of them,
And not one but hung limp, not one
was left
For him to conquer. He learned all
there was
To learn about not launching out too
soon
And so not carrying the tree away
Clear to the ground. He always kept
his poise
To the top branches, climbing care-
fully
With the same pains you use to fill a
cup

Up to the brim, and even above the
brim.
Then he flung outward, feet first, with
a swish,
Kicking his way down through the air
to the ground.
So was I once myself a swinger of
birches.
And so I dream of going back to be.
It's when I'm weary of considerations,
And life is too much like a pathless
wood
Where your face burns and tickles
with the cobwebs
Broken across it, and one eye is weep-
ing
From a twig's having lashed across it
open.
I'd like to get away from earth awhile
And then come back to it and begin
over.
May no fate willfully misunderstand
me
And half grant what I wish and
snatch me away
Not to return. Earth's the right place
for love:
I don't know where it's likely to go
better.
I'd like to go by climbing a birch tree,
And climb black branches up a snow-
white trunk
Toward heaven, till the tree could bear
no more,
But dipped its top and set me down
again.
That would be good both going and
coming back.
One could do worse than be a swinger
of birches.

THE ROAD NOT TAKEN[29]

Two roads diverged in a yellow wood,
And sorry I could not travel both
And be one traveler, long I stood
And looked down one as far as I could
To where it bent in the undergrowth;

---

[29] From *Complete Poems of Robert Frost.* Copyright 1930, 1949 by Henry
Holt & Company, Inc. Reprinted by permission of the publishers.

Then took the other, as just as fair,
And having perhaps the better claim,
Because it was grassy and wanted
    wear;
Though as for that the passing there
Had worn them really about the same,

And both that morning equally lay
In leaves no step had trodden black.
Oh, I kept the first for another day!
Yet knowing how way leads on to way,
I doubted if I should ever come back.
I shall be telling this with a sigh
Somewhere ages and ages hence:
Two roads diverged in a wood, and I—
I took the one less traveled by,
And that has made all the difference.

MY OBJECTION TO

BEING STEPPED ON[30]

At the end of the row
I stepped on the toe
Of an unemployed hoe.
It rose in offence
And struck me a blow
In the seat of my sense.
It wasn't to blame
But I called it a name.
And I must say it dealt
Me a blow that I felt
Like malice prepense.
You may call me a fool,
But *was* there a rule
The weapon should be
Turned into a tool?
And what do we see?
The first tool I step on
Turned into a weapon.

Carl Sandburg

COOL TOMBS[31]

When Abraham Lincoln was shovelled
    into the tombs, he forgot the cop-
    perheads and the assassin . . . in
    the dust, in the cool tombs.

And Ulysses Grant lost all thought of
    con men and Wall Street, cash
    and collateral turned ashes . . . in
    the dust, in the cool tombs.

Pocahontas' body, lovely as a poplar,
    sweet as a red haw in November
    or a pawpaw in May, did she
    wonder? does she remember? . . .
    in the dust, in the cool tombs?

Take any streetful of people buying
    clothes and groceries, cheering a
    hero or throwing confetti and
    blowing tin horns . . . tell me if
    the lovers are losers . . . tell me
    if any get more than the lovers
    . . . in the dust . . . in the cool
    tombs.

CHICAGO[32]

Hog Butcher for the World,
Tool Maker, Stacker of Wheat,
Player with Railroads and the Na-
    tion's Freight Handler;
Stormy, husky, brawling,
City of the Big Shoulders:
They tell me you are wicked, and I
    believe them; for I have seen your
    painted women under the gas
    lamps luring the farm boys.

And they tell me you are crooked, and
    I answer: Yes, it is true I have
    seen the gunman kill and go free
    to kill again.
And they tell me you are brutal, and
    my reply is: On the faces of
    women and children I have seen
    the marks of wanton hunger.
And having answered so I turn once
    more to those who sneer at this
    my city, and I give them back the
    sneer and say to them:
Come and show me another city with
    lifted head singing so proud to
    be alive and coarse and strong
    and cunning.
Flinging magnetic curses amid the
    toil of piling job on job, here is a
    tall bold slugger set vivid against
    the little soft cities;
Fierce as a dog with tongue lapping
    for action, cunning as a savage
    pitted against the wilderness,
      Bareheaded,
      Shovelling,
      Wrecking,
      Planning,
      Building, breaking, rebuilding,
Under the smoke, dust all over his
    mouth, laughing with white teeth,
Under the terrible burden of destiny
    laughing as a young man laughs,
Laughing even as an ignorant fighter
    laughs who has never lost a bat-
    tle,
Bragging and laughing that under his
    wrist is the pulse, and under his
    ribs the heart of the people,
      Laughing!
Laughing the stormy, husky, brawling
    laughter of Youth, half-naked,
    sweating, proud to be Hog
    Butcher, Tool Maker, Stacker of
    Wheat, Player with Railroads and
    Freight Handler to the Nation.

Marianne Moore

SILENCE[33]

My father used to say,
"Superior people never make long
    visits,
have to be shown Longfellow's grave
or the glass flowers at Harvard.
Self-reliant like the cat—
that takes its prey to privacy,
the mouse's limp tail hanging like a
    shoelace from its mouth—
they sometimes enjoy solitude,
and can be robbed of speech
by speech which has delighted them.
The deepest feeling always shows it-
    self in silence;
not in silence, but restraint."
Nor was he insincere in saying, "Make
    my house your inn."
Inns are not residences.

HE "DIGESTETH
HARDE YRON"

Although the aepyornis
    or roc that lived in Madagascar, and
the moa are extinct,
the camel-sparrow, linked
    with them in size—the large spar-
      row
Xenophon saw walking by a stream—
    was and is
a symbol of justice.

This bird watches his chicks with
    a maternal concentration—and he's
been mothering the eggs
at night six weeks—his legs
    their only weapon of defence.
He is swifter than a horse; he has a
    foot hard
as a hoof; the leopard

---

[33] This poem and the one that follows are from *Collected Poems*. Copyright 1951 by Marianne Moore. Reprinted by permission of the publishers, The Macmillan Company.

is not more suspicious. How
  could he, prized for plumes and eggs
    and young, used
even as a riding-
beast, respect men hiding
  actor-like in ostrich-skins, with
the right hand making the neck move
    as if alive and
from a bag the left hand

  strewing grain, that ostriches
    might be decoyed and killed! Yes
    this is he
whose plume was anciently
the plume of justice; he
  whose comic duckling head on its
great neck revolves with compass-
    needle nervousness
when he stands guard, in S-

  like foraging as he is
  preening the down on his leaden-
    skinned back.
The egg piously shown
as Leda's very own
  from which Castor and Pollux
    hatched,
was an ostrich-egg. And what could
    have been more fit
for the Chinese lawn it

  grazed on as a gift to an
  emperor who admired strange birds,
    than this
one who builds his mud-made
nest in dust yet will wade
  in lake or sea till only the head
    shows.

  .   .   .   .

  Six hundred ostrich-brains served
    at one banquet, the ostrich-plume-
    tipped tent
and desert spear, jewel-
gorgeous ugly egg-shell
  goblets, eight pairs of ostriches
in harness, dramatize a meaning al-
    ways missed
by the externalist.

The power of the visible
is the invisible; as even where
no tree of freedom grows,
so-called brute courage knows.
  Heroism is exhausting, yet
it contradicts a greed that did not
    wisely spare
the harmless solitaire

  or great auk in its grandeur;
  unsolicitude having swallowed up
all giant birds but an
alert gargantuan
  little-winged, magnificently speedy
    running-bird. This one
remaining rebel
is the sparrow-camel.

T. S. Eliot

JOURNEY OF THE MAGI[34]

"A cold coming we had of it,
Just the worst time of the year
For a journey, and such a long jour-
  ney:
The ways deep and the weather sharp,
The very dead of winter."
And the camels galled, sore-footed, re-
  fractory,
Lying down in the melting snow.
There were times we regretted
The summer palaces on slopes, the
  terraces,
And the silken girls bringing sherbet.
Then the camel men cursing and
  grumbling
And running away, and wanting their
  liquor and women,
And the night-fires going out, and the
  lack of shelters,

And the cities hostile and the towns
    unfriendly
And the villages dirty and charging
    high prices:
A hard time we had of it.
At the end we preferred to travel all
    night,
Sleeping in snatches,
With the voices singing in our ears,
    saying
That this was all folly.

Then at dawn we came down to a
    temperate valley,
Wet, below the snow line, smelling of
    vegetation;
With a running stream and a water
    mill beating the darkness,
And three trees on the low sky,
And an old white horse galloped away
    in the meadow.
Then we came to a tavern with vine-
    leaves over the lintel,
Six hands at an open door dicing for
    pieces of silver,
And feet kicking the empty wineskins.
But there was no information, and so
    we continued
And arrived at evening, not a moment
    too soon
Finding the place; it was (you may
    say) satisfactory.

All this was a long time ago, I remem-
    ber,
And I would do it again, but set down
This set down
This: were we lead all that way for
Birth or Death? There was a Birth,
    certainly,
We had evidence and no doubt. I had
    seen birth and death,
But had thought they were different;
    this Birth was
Hard and bitter agony for us, like
    Death, our death.
We returned to our places, these King-
    doms,
But no longer at ease here, in the old
    dispensation,
With an alien people clutching their
    gods.
I should be glad of another death.

Agnes Rogers Allen

LINES TO A DAUGHTER—
ANY DAUGHTER[35]

One of the things that you really
    should know
Is when to say "yes," and when to say
    "no."
It's terribly, terribly risky to guess
At when to say "no" and when to say
    "yes."
Girls who are slaving for Woolworth
    and Kress
Lament for the day when they might
    have said "yes,"
Others are crying at night apropos
Of moments when clearly they should
    have said "no."

There aren't any textbooks, there
    aren't many rules,
The subject's neglected in orthodox
    schools.
Experience helps, but you seldom re-
    member
Your April mistakes by the first of
    November.
You can't be consistent; there's often
    a reason
For changing your mind with a change
    in the season.
You may be quite right in accepting
    at seven
Suggestions you'd better refuse at
    eleven.

Perhaps you'll consider these tentative
    hints:
"No" to a dirndl of highly glazed
    chintz,
"Yes" to the bashful young man at the
    dance,
"No" to the man who's been living in
    France,
"Yes" to a walk in the park in the rain,
"Yes" if he asks for a chance to explain,
"No" to all slacks unless you're too
    thin,
"No" to that impulse to telephone him,

---

[35] From *Harper's Magazine*, February, 1947. Reprinted by permission.

"Yes" to a baby, and "no" to a bore,
"No" if you're asked if you've heard it
before,
"Yes" to the friend when she says,
"Don't you think
Rabbit is just as becoming as mink?"
"Yes" to a Saturday, "no" to a Monday,
"Yes" to a salad and "no" to a sundae,
"No" to a wastrel and "yes" to a ranger,
"No" to a toady, and "yes" to a stranger

(That is, providing you use some dis-
cretion),
"No" to three cocktails in rapid suc-
cession,
"No" to magenta and chocolate brown,
"Yes" to a whisper and "no" to a
frown,
"No" if he's misunderstood by his wife,
"Yes" if you want it the rest of your
life.
Remember, my darling, careers and
caresses
Depend on our choices of "noes" and
of "yesses."

Countee Cullen

YET DO I MARVEL[36]

I doubt not that God is good, well-
meaning, kind,
And did He stoop to quibble could tell
why
The little buried mole continues blind.
Why flesh that mirrors Him must some
day die;
Make plain the reason tortured Tan-
talus
Is baited by the fickle fruit, declare
If merely brute caprice dooms Sisy-
phus
To struggle up a never-ending stair.

Inscrutable His ways are, and im-
mune
To catechism by a mind too strewn
With petty cares to slightly under-
stand
What awful brain compels His awful
hand.
Yet do I marvel at this curious thing:
To make a poet black and bid him
sing.

W. H. Auden

MUSÉE DES BEAUX ARTS[37]

About suffering they were never
wrong,
The Old Masters: how well they un-
derstood
Its human position; how it takes place
While someone else is eating or open-
ing a window or just walking
dully along;
How, when the aged are reverently,
passionately waiting
For the miraculous birth, there always
must be
Children who did not specially want
it to happen, skating
On a pond at the edge of the wood:
They never forgot
That even the dreadful martyrdom
must run its course
Anyhow in a corner, some untidy spot
Where the dogs go on with their doggy
life and the torturer's horse
Scratches its innocent behind on a
tree.

In Breughel's *Icarus,* for instance: how
everything turns away
Quite leisurely from the disaster; the
ploughman may
Have heard the splash, the forsaken
cry,
But for him it was not an important
failure; the sun shone
As it had to on the white legs disappearing into the green
Water; and the expensive delicate ship
that must have seen
Something amazing, a boy falling out
of the sky,
Had somewhere to get to and sailed
calmly on.

But waking sees
Bird-flocks nameless to him, through
doorway voices
Of new men making another love.

Save him from hostile capture
From sudden tiger's spring at corner:
Protect his house,
His anxious house where days are
counted
From thunderbolt protect,
From gradual ruin spreading like a
stain:
Converting number from vague to cer-
tain
Bring joy, bring day of his returning,
Lucky with day approaching, with
leaning dawn.

CHORUS FROM A PLAY[38]

Doom is dark and deeper than any
sea-dingle:
Upon what man it fall
In spring, day-wishing flowers appear-
ing,
Avalanche sliding, white snow from
rock-face,
That he should leave his house;
No cloud-soft hands can hold him, re-
straint by women,
But ever that man goes
By place-keepers, by forest trees,
A stranger to strangers over undried
sea,
Houses for fishes, suffocating water;
Or lonely on fell as chat,
By pot-holed becks
A bird stone-haunting, an unquiet
bird.

There head falls forward, fatigued at
evening,
And dreams of home:
Waving from window, spread of wel-
come,
Kissing of wife under single sheet;

CHORUS
(*from "Paid on Both Sides"*)[39]

To throw away the key and walk away
Not abrupt exile, the neighbors asking
why,
But following a line with left and right
An altered gradient at another rate
Learns more than maps upon the
white-washed wall
The hand put up to ask; and makes us
well
Without confession of the ill. All pasts
Are single old past now, although some
posts
Are forwarded, held looking on a new
view;
The future shall fulfill a surer vow
Not smiling at queen over the glass
rim
Nor making gunpowder in the top
room,
Not swooping at the surface still like
gulls
But with prolonged drowning shall de-
velop gills.

---

[38] From *Collected Poetry of W. H. Auden.* Reprinted by permission of Random
House, Inc. Copyright 1945 by W. H. Auden.
[39] From *Collected Poetry of W. H. Auden.* Reprinted by permission of Random
House, Inc. Copyright 1945 by W. H. Auden.

But there are still to tempt; areas not
  seen
Because of blizzards or an erring sign
Whose guessed-at wonders would be
  worth alleging,
And lies about the cost of a night's
  lodging.
Travelers may sleep at inns but not
  attach,
They sleep one night together, not
  asked to touch;
Receive no normal welcome, not the
  pressed lip,
Children to lift, not the assuaging lap.
Crossing the pass descend the growing
  stream
Too tired to hear except the pulses'
  strum,
Reach villages to ask for a bed in
Rock shutting out the sky, the old life
  done.

Stephen Spender

DAYBREAK[40]

At dawn she lay with her profile at
  that angle
Which, sleeping, seems the stone face
  of an angel;
Her hair a harp the hand of a breeze
  follows
To play, against the white cloud of the
  pillows.
Then in a flush of rose she woke, and
  her eyes were open
Swimming with blue through the rose
  flesh of dawn.
From her dew of lips, the drop of one
  word
Fell, from a dawn of fountains, when
  she murmured

"Darling"—upon my heart the song of
  the first bird.
"My dream glides in my dream," she
  said, "come true.
I waken from you to my dream of
  you."
O, then my waking dream dared to
  assume
The audacity of her sleep. Our dreams
Flowed into each other's arms, like
  streams.

OH YOUNG MEN

OH YOUNG COMRADES[41]

Oh young men oh young comrades
  it is too late now to stay in those
  houses
your fathers built where they built you
  to build to breed
money on money it is too late
to make or even to count what has
  been made
Count rather those fabulous possessions
which begin with your body and your
  fiery soul:—
the hairs on your head the muscles extending
in ranges with their lakes across your
  limbs
Count your eyes as jewels and your
  valued sex
then count the sun and the innumerable coined light
sparkling on waves and spangled under trees
It is too late to stay in great houses
  where the ghosts are prisoned
—those ladies like flies perfect in amber
those financiers like fossils of bones in
  coal.

Oh comrades, step beautifully from
    the solid wall
advance to rebuild and sleep with
    friend on hill
advance to rebel and remember what
    you have
no ghost ever had, immured in his hall.

Wallace Stevens

THE EMPEROR OF
ICE-CREAM[42]

Call the roller of big cigars,
The muscular one, and bid him whip
In kitchen cups concupiscent curds.
Let the wenches dawdle in such dress
As they are used to wear, and let the
    boys
Bring flowers in last month's news-
    papers.
Let be be finale of seem.
The only emperor is the emperor of
    ice-cream.

Take from the dresser of deal,
Lacking the three glass knobs, that
    sheet
On which she embroidered fantails
    once
And spread it so as to cover her face.
If her horny feet protrude, they come
To show how cold she is, and dumb.
Let the lamp affix its beam.
The only emperor is the emperor of
    ice-cream.

Karl Shapiro

BUICK[43]

As a sloop with a sweep of immaculate
    wing on her delicate spine
And a keel as steel as a root that holds
    in the sea as she leans,
Leaning and laughing, my warm-
    hearted beauty, you ride, you ride,
You tack on the curves with parabola
    speed and a kiss of goodbye,
Like a thoroughbred sloop, my new
    high-spirited spirit, my kiss.

As my foot suggests that you leap in
    the air with your hips of a girl,
My finger that praises your wheel and
    announces your voices of song,
Flouncing your skirts, you blueness of
    joy, you flirt of politeness,
You leap, you intelligence, essence of
    wheelness with silvery nose,
And your platinum clocks of excite-
    ment stir like the hairs of a fern.

But how alien you are from the boom-
    ing belts of your birth and the
    smoke
Where you turned on the stinging
    lathes of Detroit and Lansing at
    night
And shrieked at the torch in your se-
    cret parts and the amorous tests,
But now with your eyes that enter the
    future of roads you forget;
You are all instinct with your phos-
    phorous glow and your streaking
    hair.

And now when we stop it is not as the
    bird from the shell that I leave
Or the leathery pilot who steps from
    his bird with a sneer of delight,
And not as the ignorant beast do you
    squat and watch me depart,

---

[42] Reprinted from *Harmonium* by Wallace Stevens, by permission of Alfred
A. Knopf, Inc. Copyright 1923, 1931 by Alfred A. Knopf, Inc.
[43] From *Person, Place and Thing* by Karl Shapiro. Copyright 1941 by Karl
Shapiro. Reprinted by permission of Random House, Inc.

But with exquisite breathing you
    smile, with satisfaction of love,
And I touch you again as you tick in
    the silence and settle in sleep.

Richard Eberhart

1934[44]

Caught upon a thousand thorns, I
    sing,
Like a rag in the wind,
Caught in the blares of the automobile
    horns
And on the falling airplane's wing.
Caught napping in my study
Among a thousand books of poetry.

Doing the same thing over and over
    again
Brings about an obliteration of pain.
Each day dies in a paper litter
As the heart becomes less like a rapier.
In complexity, feeling myself absurd
Dictating an arbitrary word,

My self my own worst enemy,
Hunting the past through all its fears,
That on the brain that glory burst
Bombing a ragged future's story,
Caught in iron individuality
As in the backwash of a sea

Knowing not whether to fight out,
Or keep silent; to talk about the
    weather,
Or rage again through wrong and
    right,
Knowing knowledge is a norm of noth-
    ing,
And I have been to the Eastern seas
And walked on all the Hebrides.

Ashamed of loving a long-practised
    selfhood,
Lost in a luxury of speculation,

At the straight grain of a pipe I stare
And spit upon all worlds of Spain;
Time like a certain sedative
Quelling the growth of the purpose
    tree.

Aware of the futility of action,
Of the futility of prayer aware,
Trying to pry from the vest of poetry
The golden heart of mankind's deep
    despair,
Unworthy of a simple love
In august, elected worlds to move

Stern, pliant in the modern world, I
    sing,
Afraid of nothing and afraid of every-
    thing,
Curtailing joy, withholding irony,
Pleased to condemn contemporaneity
Seeking the reality, skirting
The dangerous absolutes of fear and
    hope,

And I have eased reality and fiction
Into a kind of intellectual fruition
Strength in solitude, life in death,
Compassion by suffering, love in strife,
And ever and still the weight of mys-
    tery
Arrows a way between my words and
    me.

Dylan Thomas

ESPECIALLY WHEN THE
OCTOBER WIND[45]

Especially when the October wind
With frosty fingers punishes my hair,
Caught by the crabbing sun I walk on
    fire
And cast a shadow crab upon the land,
By sea's side, hearing the noise of
    birds,

Hearing the raven cough in winter
  sticks,
My busy heart who shudders as she
  talks
Sheds the syllabic blood and drains
  her words.

Shut, too, in a tower of words, I mark
On the horizon walking like the trees
The wordy shapes of women, and the
  rows
Of the star-gestured children in the
  park.
Some let me make you of the vowelled
  beeches,
Some of the oaken voices, from the
  roots
Of many a thorny shire tell you notes,
Some let me make you of the water's
  speeches.

Behind a pot of ferns the wagging
  clock
Tells me the hour's word, the neural
  meaning
Flies on the shafted disc, declaims the
  morning
And tells the windy weather in the
  cock.
Some let me make you of the meadow's
  signs;
The signal grass that tells me all I
  know
Breaks with the wormy winter through
  the eye.
Some let me tell you of the raven's
  sins.

Especially when the October wind
(Some let me make you of autumnal
  spells,
The spider-tongued, and the loud hill
  of Wales)
With fist of turnips punishes the land,
Some let me make you of the heartless
  words.
The heart is drained that, spelling in
  the scurry
Of chemic blood, warned of the com-
  ing fury.
By the sea's side hear the dark-
  vowelled birds.

AND DEATH SHALL
HAVE NO DOMINION[46]

And death shall have no dominion.
Dead men naked they shall be one
With the man in the wind and the west
  moon;
When their bones are picked clean and
  the clean bones gone,
They shall have stars at elbow and
  foot;
Though they go mad they shall be
  sane,
Though they sink through the sea they
  shall rise again;
Though lovers be lost love shall not;
And death shall have no dominion.

And death shall have no dominion.
Under the windings of the sea
They lying long shall not die windily;
Twisting on racks when sinews give
  way,
Strapped to a wheel, yet they shall not
  break;
Faith in their hands shall snap in two,
And the unicorn evils run them
  through;
Split all ends up they shan't crack;
And death shall have no dominion.

And death shall have no dominion.
No more may gulls cry at their ears
Or waves break loud on the seashores;
Where blew a flower may a flower no
  more
Lift its head to the blows of the rain;
Though they be mad and dead as
  nails,
Heads of the characters hammer
  through daisies;
Break in the sun till the sun breaks
  down,
And death shall have no dominion.

Theodore Roethke

HER LONGING[47]

Before this longing,
I lived serene as a fish,
At one with the plants in the pond,
The mare's tail, the floating frogbit,
Among my eight-legged friends,
Open like a pool, a lesser parsnip,
Like a leech, looping myself along,
A bug-eyed edible one,
A mouth like a stickleback,—
A thing quiescent!

But now—
The wild stream, the sea itself cannot
    contain me:
I dive with the black hag, the cor-
    morant,
Or walk the pebbly shore with the
    humpbacked heron,
Shaking out my catch in the morning
    sunlight,
Or rise with the gar-eagle, the great-
    winged condor,
Floating over the mountains,
Pitting my breast against the rushing
    air,
A phoenix, sure of my body,
Perpetually rising out of myself,
My wings hovering over the shorebirds,
Or beating against the black clouds of
    the storm,
Protecting the sea-cliffs.

I WAITED

I waited for the wind to move the dust;
But no wind came.
I seemed to eat the air;
The meadow insects made a level
    noise.
I rose, a heavy bulk, above the field.

It was as if I tried to walk in hay,
Deep in the mow, and each step deeper
    down,
Or floated on the surface of a pond,
The slow long ripples winking in my
    eyes.
I saw all things through water, mag-
    nified,
And shimmering. The sun burned
    through a haze,
And I became all that I looked upon.
I dazzled in the dazzle of a stone.

And then a jackass brayed. A lizard
    leaped my foot.
Slowly I came back to the dusty road;
And when I walked, my feet seemed
    deep in sand.
I moved like some heat-weary animal.
I went, not looking back. I was afraid.

The way grew steeper between stony
    walls,
Then lost itself down through a rocky
    gorge.
A donkey path led to a small plateau.
Below, the bright sea was, the level
    waves,
And all the winds came toward me. I
    was glad.

INDEX OF AUTHORS

NOTES

NOTES

NOTES

Format by MARGARET F. PLYMPTON

Set in Linotype Primer
Composed by The Haddon Craftsmen, Inc.
Printed by Copifyer Lithograph Corporation
Bound by The Haddon Craftsmen, Inc.
HARPER & ROW, PUBLISHERS, INCORPORATED

THEME RECORD

(With Number of Serious Errors)

Figures in parentheses refer to Handbook sections, pages 179–336.

NUMBER OF THEME	1	2	3	4	5	6	7	8	9	10	11	12	13	14	15
GRADE ON THEME															
Adjective and adverb (69)															
Comma splice (2)															
Comma misuse (47)															
Parallelism, coordination, subordination (7, 8, 9)															
Dangling modifiers (5)															
Diction (17–30)															
Fused sentences (3)															
Pronouns, case (64)															
Pronouns—antecedents, agreement, reference (12, 63)															
Punctuation and mechanics other than comma (46, 48–60)															
Sentence fragment— incompleteness (1)															
Spelling (16)															
Subject, predicate (62)															
Verb forms—tense, voice, etc. (65–68)															

In the blank spaces at the bottom of this chart add names of other errors you need to guard against. Make a copy of the chart for additional records.